S0-BYO-437

CRIMINAL LAW

Cases and Materials

EDITORIAL ADVISORY BOARD

Little, Brown and Company
Law Book Division

CRIMINAL LAW

Cases and Materials

JOHN KAPLAN
Jackson Eli Reynolds Professor of Law
Stanford University

ROBERT WEISBERG
Associate Professor of Law
Stanford University

Little, Brown and Company
Boston Toronto

Library of Congress Catalog Card No. 85-50141

ISBN 0-316-48280-3

Fourth Printing

HAL

Published simultaneously in Canada
by Little, Brown & Company (Canada) Limited

Printed in the United States of America

To Jürgen Habermas and Susan Weisberg

SUMMARY OF CONTENTS

TABLE OF CONTENTS

10

COMPLICITY 577

11

CONSPIRACY 665

VII

ADDITIONAL CRIMES 1009

PREFACE

The authors of yet another criminal law casebook should have a good excuse before adding to what most people would regard as a surplus. Certainly, if we had not produced such a book we would have argued just that. But we have produced a new book and are confident in our justification. It is that we think this work will help our teaching and, what is the same thing, help to engage students' interest and broaden their understanding by extending and enriching the criminal law curriculum with new material on the most fertile issues.

This book differs from virtually all of the others in that it is entirely a book on substantive criminal law. We do not deny the importance of procedure in the everyday practice of criminal law, or even the influence of procedure on the development of the substantive law. It seems to us, however, that there is more than enough substantive law to be covered in the traditional first year courses, and that substantive law has so much to say about the values of the society that shapes it, that it is properly the subject of a first year course all to itself. After all, most schools offer, and most students take later courses in criminal procedure. In addition, Appendix A takes advantage of the Encyclopedia of Crime and Justice to reprint what we believe to be, in short compass, the most sophisticated introduction to the institutions of the criminal law.

Indeed, this is the first casebook to make use of two quite recent developments in criminal law thinking—the Encyclopedia of Crime and Justice, edited and with contributions by the most distinguished authorities in academic criminal law, and the 1985 edition of the Commentaries to the Model Penal Code. Both of these works have permitted us to select commentary that is generally an improvement over what has formerly been available. We predict, in fact, that new editions of other casebooks will be using this commentary in the coming years.

In addition, we have tried to go somewhat more deeply into the issues of white collar and corporate crimes. We were able to find materials on the *Pinto* case that not only fit in well with our discussion of manslaughter but that revealed the complexities of attributing criminality to a large organization. By that point in the course, when students will have assimilated a reasonable amount of tort doctrine, we expect criminal law students to consider the proper relation between the tort law and the criminal law with respect to large and solvent organizations. Later in the course, we take up the other major issues of corporate and white collar criminality—the criminal liability of the corporation for clearly criminal acts of individuals associated with it, as well as the liability of individuals for those acts that are held to be crimes of the corporation.

We have also included a uniquely detailed treatment of capital punishment law. Many casebooks briefly treat this issue as a somewhat disconcerting tangent into constitutional abstraction or general political arguments. We recognize that the post-*Furman* death penalty laws have settled into a pattern that permits us to view them as extensions of the established state substantive law of homicide. The new doctrinal structure of aggravating circumstances thus becomes a fascinating test of the intellectual and moral coherence of traditional criminal law doctrine.

Finally, at all times we attempt to show the law in action, not only through appellate decisions and what we regard as hard—if sometimes tendentious—questions, but through a number of other interesting materials, such as examination questions and a sizeable number of newspaper stories. It is our experience that—far out of proportion to the space they take—these items pique the students' interest not only in the materials themselves but in the cases that proceed and follow them. In addition, they are a constant reminder to the students that the cases we discuss really do happen, and that though in some ways Criminal Law is an unusually theoretical course for many students, it can come to life with at least the vividness of any other part of their nonclinical legal education.

In short, this is what we have done. We hope it "works" for other teachers and their students as it has for us and ours.

John Kaplan
Robert Weisberg

September 1985

ACKNOWLEDGMENTS

We would like to thank many people for their help and advice. Those who contributed ideas should consider themselves thanked. Those who contributed real work deserve particular mention. They are students: Jay Alexander, Stephanie Glennon, Laurence Goldman, David Hollander, Wilbur Martin, Robert Minion, and John Whitelaw, and secretaries: Mary Tye, Marion Holys, Roberta Pottorff, and Beth Drufva.

We would also like to thank the following authors and copyright holders for permission to use their materials:

Allen, F., Criminal Justice, Legal Values and the Rehabilitative Ideal, 50 J. Crim L. and Criminology 266 (1959). Copyright © 1959 by Northwestern University School of Law. Reprinted by special permission of the Journal of Criminal Law and Criminology.

A man who unwittingly married . . . , Boston Globe, Sept. 12, 1984. Reprinted by permission of Associated Press.

American Bar Association, Criminal Justice Mental Health Standards (1st draft) 271 (1983). Reprinted with permission of the American Bar Association.

American Law Institute, Model Penal Code §§1.02, 1.04, 1.05, 1.07, 1.12, 1.13, 2.01-2.13, 3.01-3.11, 4.01-4.10, 5.01-5.07, 6.01, 6.03-6.09, 210.0-210.6, 211.0-211.3, 212.0-212.5, 213.0-213.6, 220.1-220.3, 221.0-221.2, 222.1, 223.0-223.9, 224.0-224.14, 230.1, 230.2, 230.4, 230.5, 250.1-250.8, 251.1-251.3. Copyright © 1985 by The American Law Institute. Reprinted with permission of The American Law Institute.

Article on Bernard Hugo Goetz, New York Times, Jan. 6, 1985. Copyright © 1985 by The New York Times Co. Reprinted by permission.

A 27-year-old former Livermore resident . . . , San Jose Mercury News, May 23, 1984. Reprinted by permission of the San Jose Mercury News.

A young policeman . . . , San Jose Mercury News, May 3, 1984. Reprinted by permission of The Associated Press.

Boyce, Justification: Law Enforcement. Reprinted with permission of The Free Press, a Division of Macmillan, Inc. from 3 Encyclopedia of Crime and Justice 953-957. Sanford H. Kadish, Editor in Chief. Copyright © 1983 by The Free Press, a Division of Macmillan, Inc.

Bowen, Trudie, Letter to San Francisco Chronicle, Aug. 8, 1984.

Brahams, Premenstrual Syndrome: A Disease of the Mind? 11 The Lancet 1238-1240 (1981).

Burke and Kadish, Conspiracy. Reprinted with permission of The Free Press, a Division of Macmillan, Inc. from 1 Encyclopedia of Crime and Justice 253. Sanford H. Kadish, Editor in Chief. Copyright © 1983 by The Free Press, a Division of Macmillan, Inc.

Burkhardt, Bjorn, Is There a Rational Justification for Punishing an Accomplished Crime More Severely Than an Attempted Crime? Paper presented to the German-Anglo-American Workshop, July 19, 1984.

Cabarga, Ted, Letter to San Francisco Chronicle, Aug. 5, 1984.

Campane, Chains, Wheels and Single Conspiracy, FBI Law Enforcement Bulletin 24, 26-31 (Aug. 1981), 24-30 (Sept. 1981). Reprinted by permission of FBI Law Enforcement Bulletin.

Chakravarty, Tunnel Vision, Forbes 214, 218 (May 21, 1984). Copyright © 1984 Forbes, Inc.

Chicago Plant Where Worker Died Described as Huge Gas Chamber, Peninsula Times Tribune, Oct. 20, 1983. Reprinted by permission of The Associated Press.

Couple Arraigned in Youth's Slaying, San Francisco Chronicle, June 20, 1980. Copyright © 1984 by San Francisco Chronicle. Reprinted by permission.

Developments—Conspiracy, 75 Harv. L. Rev. 933-935, 945-948 (1959). Copyright © 1959 by the Harvard Law Review Association.

Dix, Justification: Self Defense. Reprinted with permission of The Free Press, a Division of Macmillan, Inc. from 3 Encyclopedia of Crime and Justice 948-950. Sanford H. Kadish, Editor in Chief. Copyright © 1983 by The Free Press, a Division of Macmillan, Inc.

Doherty, Man Accused of Arson, Boston Globe, Nov. 15, 1984.

Field, Rape: Legal Aspects. Reprinted with permission of The Free Press, a Division of Macmillan, Inc. from 4 Encyclopedia of Crime and Justice 1359-1362. Sanford H. Kadish, Editor in Chief. Copyright © 1983 by The Free Press, a Division of Macmillan, Inc.

Filvaroff, Conspiracy and the First Amendment, 121 U. Pa. L. Rev. 189, 198-200 (1972). Copyright © 1972 by University of Pennsylvania Law Review.

Fisse, Reconstructing Corporate Criminal Law: Deterrence, Retribution, Fault, and Sanctions, 56 S. Cal. L. Rev. 1141, 1191-1192, 1197-1200 (1983). Reprinted by permission of Southern California Law Review.

Fletcher, G., Rethinking Criminal Law 837-843 (1978). Copyright © 1978 by George Fletcher. Reprinted by permission of Little, Brown and Company.

Giovannetti, The Principle of Analogy in Sino-Soviet Laws, 8 Dal. L.J. 321-382, 399-400 (1984).

Goodhart, Possession of Drugs and Absolute Liability, 84 L.Q. Rev. 385 (1968).

Gordon, W., Crime and Criminal Law: The California Experience 7-8, 10-14, 52-53 (1981). Copyright © by Associated Faculty Press.

Hart, H. L. A., Essays in Jurisprudence and Philosophy 194-196, 388-390 (1983). Copyright © 1983 by Oxford University Press. Reprinted by permission of Oxford University Press.

Hart, H. L. A., Punishment and Responsibility 10, 11-13, 18-20 (1968). Copyright © 1968 by Oxford University Press. Reprinted by permission of Oxford University Press.

Hart, H. L. A. and Honore, A. M., Causation and the Law 341 (1959). Copyright © 1959 by Oxford University Press. Reprinted by permission of Oxford University Press

Hart, H. M., The Aims of Criminal Law, 23 Law and Contemp. Probs. 401, 402 (1958).

Hawkins, G. and Morris, N., The Honest Politician's Guide to Crime Control 178-185 (1970). Reprinted by permission of University of Chicago Press.

Hazard, Criminal Justice System: Overview. Reprinted with permission of The Free Press, a Division of Macmillan, Inc. from 2 Encyclopedia of Crime and Justice 450-469. Sanford H. Kadish, Editor in Chief. Copyright © 1983 by The Free Press, a Division of Macmillan, Inc.

Hazle, Obscure Law against For Sale Signs Nearly Hits S. J. Woman for $50, San Jose Mercury News, Sept. 29, 1983. Reprinted by permission of the San Jose Mercury News.

Hoppe, Is Anyone Ever Guilty? San Francisco Chronicle, Aug. 5, 1984.

Howe, M., Holmes-Laski Letters 806 (1953). Reprinted by permission of Harvard University Press.

Hughes, Criminal Omissions, 67 Yale L.J. 600, 624 (1958). Reprinted by permission of The Yale Law Journal Company and Fred B. Rothman & Company.

Johnson, Strict Liability. Reprinted with permission of The Free Press, a Division of Macmillan, Inc. from 4 Encyclopedia of Crime and Justice 1519. Sanford H. Kadish, Editor in Chief. Copyright © 1983 by The Free Press, a Division of Macmillan, Inc.

Judge Upholds Woman's Right to Nurse Her Baby, San Jose Mercury, May 31, 1984. Reprinted with permission of United Press International, Inc.

Jury Acquits Vt. Protestors of Trespass, Boston Globe, Nov. 17, 1984. Reprinted by permission of Associated Press.

Kadish, Sanford, Causation: Preliminary Draft (1966).

Kaplan, Foreword in Inverarity, Lauderdale and Feld, Law and Society xxiii-xvi (1983). Copyright © 1983 by James M. Inverarity, Pat Lauderdale, and Barry C. Feld. Reprinted by permission of Little, Brown and Company.

Kaplan, J., The Problem of Capital Punishment 565-570 (1983). Copyright © 1983 by the Board of Trustees of the University of Illinois.

Kaplan, J. and Skolnick, J., Criminal Justice: Cases and Materials 79 (1982). Reprinted by permission of Foundation Press.

Kelman, Interpretive Construction, 33 Stan. L. Rev. 591, 605-611, 637-640, 649-650 (1981). Copyright © 1981 by the Board of Trustees of the Leland Stanford Junior University.

Kelman, Strict Liability. Reprinted with permission of The Free Press, a Division of Macmillan, Inc. from 4 Encyclopedia of Crime and Justice 1516-1518. Sanford H. Kadish, Editor in Chief. Copyright © 1983 by The Free Press, a Division of Macmillan, Inc.

Law Women find Sexism in 1L CB, The Commentator, Mar. 19, 1984.

McClain, Criminal Law Reform: Historical Development in the United States. Reprinted with permission of The Free Press, a Division of Macmillan, Inc. from 2 Encyclopedia of Crime and Justice 510-512. Sanford H. Kadish, Editor in Chief. Copyright © 1983 by The Free Press, a Division of Macmillan, Inc.

Marquis, D., Spider and the Fly, from Archie and Mehitabel. Copyright © 1927 by Doubleday & Co., Inc. Reprinted by permission of Doubleday & Co., Inc.

Marston, Contemporaneity of Act and Intention in Crime, 86 L.Q.R. 215-219 (1970).

Mercy Killer Gets Probation, $10,000 Fine, San Francisco Chronicle, June 20, 1984. Reprinted by permission of Associated Press.

Meyers, An Alternative Approach to Writing Forensic Mental Health Reports, 13 J. Psychiatry and L.—(1985). Reprinted by permission of Federal Legal Publications.

Morris, Somnambulistic Homicide, 5 Res Judicatae 29-32 (1951).

Morse, Undiminished Confusion, Diminished Capacity, 75 J. of Crim. Law and Criminology (1984). Copyright © 1984 by Northwestern University School of Law. Reprinted by permission of the Journal of Criminal Law and Criminology.

Mother Said That She Was Told to Sit on Child, Who Died. The National Law Journal, Mar. 14, 1983. Copyright © 1983 by The National Law Journal. Reprinted with permission.

Mueller, Mens Rea and the Corporation, 19 U. Pitt. L. Rev. 21, 40-41 (1957). Copyright © 1957 by University of Pittsburgh Law Review.

Murphy, Marxism and Retribution, 2 Phil. and Pub. Aff. 217 (1973). Reprinted by permission of Princeton University Press.

Note, 8 Univ. Chi. L. Rev. 338-340 (1940).

Note: Conspiracy, 75 Col. L. Rev. 1122, 1129-1132, 1149-1153, 1182-1183 (1985). Copyright © 1985 by the Directors of the Columbia Law Review Association, Inc. All rights reserved. Reprinted by permission.

Note, Corporate Homicide, 8 Pepperdine L. Rev. 367, 367-370, 372-374 (1981). Reprinted by permission of the Pepperdine Law Review.

Note: Developments in the Law—Corporate Crime, 92 Harv. L. Rev. 1227, 1247-1251 (1979). Copyright © 1979 by the Harvard Law Review Association.

Packer, H., Limits of Criminal Sanction 37-39, 53-55, 65-69, 73-77, 130-131, 261 (1968). Reprinted by permission of Stanford University Press.

Pokorny, N.H. Death Raises Tricky Legal Issues, Boston Globe, Dec. 30, 1984.

Reason, The Psychopathology of Everyday Slips, The Sciences 15 (Sept./Oct. 1984) Copyright © 1984 by the New York Academy of Sciences.

Robinson, Causing the Conditions of One's Own Defense: A Study in the Limits of Theory in Criminal Law Doctrine, 71 Va. L. Rev. 1, 27-29 (1985).

Robinson, P., 1 Criminal Law Defenses 93 (1984).

Robinson, P., 2 Criminal Law Defenses 69-73 (1984).

Robinson and Grall, Element Analysis in Defining Criminal Liability, 35 Stan. L. Rev. 682-690, 694-699 (1983). Copyright © 1983 by the Board of Trustees of the Leland Stanford Junior University.

Ruling to Take Movie Makers to Trial Is Praised, Criticized, Peninsula Times Tribune, Apr. 24, 1984. Reprinted by permission of The Associated Press.

Sabbag, R., Snowblind: A Brief Career in the Cocaine Trade 149-152, 154-155, 171-174, 204-206 (1976). Copyright © 1976 by Robert Sabbag. Reprinted by permission of Dorothy Pittman Literary Agent.

Schwartz, Theft. Reprinted with permission of The Free Press, a Division of Macmillan, Inc. from 4 Encyclopedia of Crime and Justice 1537-1551. Sanford H. Kadish, Editor in Chief. Copyright © 1983 by The Free Press, a Division of Macmillan, Inc.

Shoplifting Suspect's Excuse Is Convincing, San Jose Mercury News, Apr. 20, 1984. Reprinted by permission of United Press International, Inc.

Smith, J. C., Liability for Omissions in the Criminal Law, 4 Legal Stud. 88, 98-100 (1984). Reprinted by permission of the Society of Public Teachers of Law.

Smith, K. M. J., Withdrawal from Criminal Liability, 12 Anglo-Am. L. Rev. 200, 205. (1983).

Stone, Alan, paper presented to St. Elizabeth's Hospital, Aug. 1982. Reprinted by permission of Hospital and Community Psychiatry.

Thomson, Judith, Self Defense and Rights, from V. Lindley Lectures 1976.

Walker, N., Punishment, Danger and Stigma 24-42 (1980). Reprinted by permission of Barnes & Noble.

Walker, N., Sentencing in a Rational Society 56-59 (1969). Copyright © 1969 by Nigel Walker. Reprinted by permission of Basic Books, Inc.

Weinreb, Homicide: Legal Aspects. Reprinted with permission of The Free Press, a Division of Macmillan, Inc. from 2 Encyclopedia of Crime and

Justice 858, 859-861. Sanford H. Kadish, Editor in Chief. Copyright © 1983 by The Free Press, a Division of Macmillan, Inc.

Wexler, An Offense-Victim Approach to Insanity Defense Reform, 26 Ariz. L. Rev. 17 (1984). Copyright © 1984 by the Arizona Board of Regents.

Wheeler, Product Liability, Civil or Criminal, 17 Forum 250-251 (1981). Reprinted by permission of American Bar Association.

Wheeler, The Use of Criminal Statutes to Regulate Product Safety, 13 J. of Legal Stud. 593-618 (1984).

Williams, G., Textbook of Criminal Law 35, 70, 157-158, 378-382, 397-399, 408-409 (2d ed. 1983).

Wilson, James Q., Thinking About Crime 41-57, 59, 61-62, 65-66 (1983). Copyright © by Basic Books, Inc. Reprinted by permission.

Witness's Fatal Heart Attack in Court Is Ruled Homicide, San Jose Mercury News, May 25, 1984. Reprinted by permission of the Associated Press.

Woman Says She Bombed Abortion Clinics Out of Guilt, Boston Globe, Dec. 28, 1984. Reprinted by permission of United Press International, Inc.

Wootton, Lady Barbara, Crime and the Criminal Law 51-53 (1963).

Zimring, The Medium is the Message: Firearm Caliber, 1 J. Legal Stud. 97, 117, 121-122 (1972).

Zimring and Zuehl, Victim in Urban Robbery: A Chicago Study,—J. of Legal Stud.—(Jan. 1986). Copyright © by the University of Chicago. All rights reserved.

SPECIAL NOTICE

Some citations have been edited from the cases for the sake of smoother reading. Footnotes in cases and other quoted materials have generally been eliminated without indication. Those that were not edited have been renumbered.

References to the Model Penal Code, unless otherwise indicated, are to American Law Institute, Model Penal Code and Commentaries (1985).

CRIMINAL LAW

Cases and Materials

I

THE PRINCIPLES OF CRIMINAL PUNISHMENT

1

THE REASONS FOR AND THE LIMITING PRINCIPLES OF CRIMINAL PUNISHMENT

A. INTRODUCTION

Case 1. Edward Jones has been arrested and charged with murder for killing his father.

Jones is a 22-year-old community college graduate working as a computer programmer. He was born into a family of considerable emotional and, occasionally, physical violence. His father was an alcoholic who was prone to abuse his family during drinking bouts. Jones himself was often struck harshly by his father as a young child, and throughout his life saw his father strike and loudly berate his mother. When he was seven years old, his mother sought psychological counseling for him as he alternated between periods of brooding and withdrawal and fits of "acting out" at school.

Jones's father was influenced by fantasies of his wife's sexual infidelity, and on many occasions Jones had seen his father denounce her as a whore. Over the years, the mother suffered several minor bruises at the hands of her husband, though she never suffered broken bones or other serious injuries. Jones's father had once been a successful salesman and had provided well for the family, but his income fluctuated wildly with his drinking, and in recent years he has been frequently unemployed. Jones himself gives part of his salary to his mother, but because of the father's alcoholism and unemployment, his mother, who suffers from arthritis, has had to work full-time as a store clerk to help support the younger children. The pressure of work, worry about finances, and the toll of her husband's frequent denunciations have left Jones's mother in a state of constant emotional strain.

Jones came home one evening to see his mother in tears. She recounted that Jones's father had had another alcoholic fit and had screamed at her wildly and shoved her to the couch, though he had inflicted no injuries on her. The father had then stalked off to a bar. Jones had been brooding angrily over his father lately, frustrated and furious over the miserable life his father had imposed on his mother. This incident brought his anger to a fever. Shortly after his father returned that evening and skulked sullenly into his room, Jones took his father's pistol from a drawer and shot his father to death. He immediately turned himself in to the police.

A psychiatrist examining Jones for the court said that he was an extremely neurotic and high-strung young man; that he had accumulated anguished hatred for his father; that he could no longer bear his mother's suffering; that he was prone to bouts of depression; but that he was perfectly sane.

Jones was charged with second-degree murder, defined by state law as "the intentional killing of another, not in immediate self-defense or in defense of another to save the other from imminent grievous bodily harm." The penalty for second-degree murder is from 10 to 20 years in prison. Because of the sentencing discretion afforded trial judges, the average sentence handed down for this crime is 13 years; because most prisoners are paroled before their sentences expire, the average time actually served for this crime is 8 years plus a period of supervision in the community on parole.

Case 2. Charles Green has been arrested for breaking into a house and stealing about $100 in jewelry and a small television set. No one was home at the time.

Green is 23 years old. His father died when he was seven, and his mother supported him and three other children through welfare and unskilled jobs. Because his mother was usually working, Green was unsupervised as a child and from the age of ten on was involved with gangs in various forms of petty delinquency. When he was 13, he spent six months in a youth detention center for petty theft. He later completed high school, where he displayed above average intelligence and got good grades when he tried. Since high school, he has worked off and on in clerical jobs, but has been arrested and convicted three times for breaking and entering and for theft. He has served a total of seven months in the county jail. On one occasion he was arrested for a robbery-mugging, but the charge was dismissed when the complainant refused to testify. Green often uses heroin and cocaine, but his criminal activity preceded his use of these drugs. The police suspect that he has committed a large number of larcenies and burglaries and perhaps a few street robberies. But his latest burglary presents them with the clearest case they have been able to make against him. The probation report shows that Green has "antisocial tendencies," but that he suffers from no clinical mental illness, and has rejected employment opportunities simply because he does not like to work regularly.

Green has been charged with second-degree burglary, which the state defines as "entering a dwelling without permission with intent to commit therein a larceny." The statutory penalty for this crime is between one and five years in prison or up to a year in the county jail. The average sentence for this crime in the state is eleven months in the county jail.

Notes and Questions

1. Why should Jones be punished? Why should Green?
2. What punishment is appropriate for Jones? For Green?
3. Do you find the criminal statutes under which Jones and Green were charged, and the sentencing ranges they provide, adequate to determine the appropriate punishment?
4. Would it be preferable if the state had only a single criminal law that stated as follows?

> It shall be a crime for any person to commit any act that causes or threatens harm to society, unless the person can present a plausible excuse or justification for the act. The court [or jury] shall determine the proper punishment for the offender upon consideration of all relevant factors.

Return to these questions after you have read the following material.

B. REASONS FOR PUNISHMENT

1. Deterrence

DEUTERONOMY 19:16-22
The New English Bible (1970)

When a malicious witness comes forward to give false evidence against a man, and the two disputants stand before the Lord, before the priests and the judges then in office, if, after careful examination by the judges, he be proved to be a false witness giving false evidence against his fellow, you shall treat him as he intended to treat his fellow, and thus rid yourselves of this wickedness. The rest of the people when they hear of it will be afraid: never again will anything as wicked as this be done among you. You shall show no mercy . . . .

JAMES Q. WILSON, THINKING ABOUT CRIME
117-121 (rev. ed. 1983)

The average citizen hardly needs to be persuaded of the view that crime will be more frequently committed if, other things being equal, crime becomes more profitable compared to other ways of spending one's time. Accordingly, the average citizen thinks it obvious that one major reason why crime has gone up is that people have discovered it is easier to get away with it; by the same token, the average citizen thinks a good way to reduce crime is to make the consequences of crime to the would-be offender more costly (by making penalties swifter, more certain, or more severe), or to make the value of alternatives to crime more attractive (by increasing the availability and pay of legitimate jobs), or both. Such opinions spring naturally to mind among persons who notice, as a fact of everyday life, that people take their hands off hot stoves, shop around to find the best buy, smack their children to teach them not to run out into a busy street, and change jobs when the opportunity arises to earn more money for the same amount of effort.

These citizens may be surprised to learn that social scientists who study crime are deeply divided over the correctness of such views. To some scholars, especially economists, the popular view is also the scientifically correct one—becoming a criminal can be explained in much the same way we explain becoming a carpenter or buying a car. To other scholars, especially sociologists, the popular view is wrong—crime rates do not go up because people discover they can get away with it and will not come down just because society decides to get tough on criminals.

The debate over the effect on crime rates of changing the costs and benefits of crime is usually referred to as a debate over deterrence—a debate, that is, over the efficacy (and perhaps even the propriety) of trying to prevent crime by making would-be offenders more fearful of committing crime. But that is something of a misnomer, because the theory of human nature on which is erected the idea of deterrence (the theory that people respond to the penalties associated with crime) is also the theory of human nature that supports the idea that people will take jobs in preference to crime if the jobs are more attractive. In both cases, we are saying that would-be offenders are reasonably rational and respond to their perception of the costs and benefits attached to alternative courses of action. When we use the word "deterrence," we are calling attention only to the cost side of the equation. There is no word in common scientific usage to call attention to the benefit side of the equation; perhaps "inducement" might serve. To a psychologist, deterring persons from committing crimes or inducing persons to engage in noncriminal activities are but special cases of using "reinforcements" (or rewards) to alter behavior.

The reason there is a debate among scholars about deterrence is that the socially imposed consequences of committing a crime, unlike the market consequences of shopping around for the best price, are characterized by delay, uncertainty, and ignorance. In addition, some scholars contend that a large fraction of crime is committed by persons who are so impulsive, irrational, or abnormal that even if there were no delay, uncertainty, or ignorance attached to the consequences of criminality, we would still have a lot of crime.

Imagine a young man walking down the street at night with nothing on his mind but a desire for good times and high living. Suddenly he sees a little old lady standing alone on a dark corner stuffing the proceeds of her recently cashed social security check into her purse. There is nobody else in view. If the boy steals the purse, he gets the money immediately. That is a powerful incentive, and it is available immediately and without doubt. The costs of taking it are uncertain; the odds are at least fourteen to one that the police will not catch a given robber, and even if he is caught the odds are very good that he will not go to prison, unless he has a long record. On the average, no more than three felonies out of one hundred result in the imprisonment of the offender. In addition to this uncertainty, whatever penalty may come his way will come only after a long delay; in some jurisdictions, it might take a year or more to complete the court disposition of the offender, assuming he is caught in the first place. Moreover, this young man may, in his ignorance of how the world works, think the odds in his favor are even greater and that the delay will be even longer.

Compounding the problems of delay and uncertainty is the fact that society cannot feasibly reduce the uncertainty attached to the chances of being arrested by more than a modest amount, and though it can to some degree increase the probability and severity of a prison sentence for those who are caught, it cannot do so drastically by, for example, summarily executing all convicted robbers or even by sending all robbers to twenty-year prison terms. Some scholars add a further complication: the young man may be incapable of assessing the risks of crime. How, they ask, is he to know his chances of being caught and punished? And even if he does know, is he perhaps "driven" by uncontrollable impulses to snatch purses whatever the risks?

As if all this were not bad enough, the principal method by which scholars have attempted to measure the effect on crime of differences in the probability and severity of punishment has involved using data about aggregates of people (entire cities, counties, states, and even nations) rather than about individuals. In a typical study, of which there have been several dozen, the rate at which, say, robbery is committed in each state is "explained" by means of a statistical procedure in which the analyst takes into account both the socioeconomic features of each state that might affect the supply of robbers (for example, the percentage of persons with low incomes, the unemployment rate, or the population density of the big cities) and the operation of the criminal justice system of each state as it attempts to cope with robbery (for example, the probability of being caught and imprisoned for a given robbery and the length of the average prison term for robbery). Most such studies find, after controlling for socioeconomic differences among the states, that the higher the probability of being imprisoned, the lower the robbery rate. Isaac Ehrlich, an economist, produced the best known of such analyses using data on crime in the United States in 1940, 1950, and 1960. To simplify a complex analysis, he found, after controlling for such factors as the income level and age distribution of the population, that the higher the probability of imprisonment for those convicted of robbery, the lower the robbery rate. Thus, differences in the certainty of punishment seem to make a difference in the level of crime. At the same time, Ehrlich did not find that the severity of punishment (the average time served in prison for robbery) had, independently of certainty, an effect on robbery rates in two of the three time periods (1940 and 1960).

But there are some problems associated with studying the effect of sanctions on crime rates using aggregate data of this sort. One is that many of the most important factors are not known with any accuracy. For example, we are dependent on police reports for our measure of the robbery rate, and these undoubtedly vary in accuracy from place to place. If all police departments were inaccurate to the same degree, this would not be important; unfortunately, some departments are probably much less accurate than others, and this variable error can introduce a serious bias into the statistical estimates of the effect of the criminal justice system.

Moreover, if one omits from the equation some factor that affects the crime rate, then the estimated effect of the factors that are in the equation may be in error because some of the causal power belonging to the omitted factor will be falsely attributed to the included factors. For example, suppose we want to find out whether differences in the number of policemen on patrol among American cities are associated with differences in the rate at which robberies take place in those cities. If we fail to include in our equation a measure of the population density of the city, we may wrongly conclude that the more police there are on the streets, the *higher* the robbery rate and thus give support to the absurd policy proposition that the way to reduce robberies is to fire police officers. Since robberies are more likely to occur in larger, densely settled cities (which also tend to have a higher proportion of police), it would be a grave error to omit such measures of population from the equation. Since we are not certain what causes crime, we always run the risk of inadvertently omitting a key factor from our efforts to see if deterrence works.

Even if we manage to overcome these problems, a final difficulty lies in wait. The observed fact (and it has been observed many times) that states in which the probability of going to prison for robbery is low are also states which have high rates of robbery can be interpreted in one of two ways. It can mean *either* that the higher robbery rates are the results of the lower imprisonment rates (and thus evidence that deterrence works) *or* that the lower imprisonment rates are caused by the higher robbery rates. To see how the latter might be true, imagine a state that is experiencing, for some reason, a rapidly rising robbery rate. It arrests, convicts, and imprisons more and more robbers as more and more robberies are committed, but it cannot quite keep up. The robberies are increasing so fast that they "swamp" the criminal justice system; prosecutors and judges respond by letting more robbers off without a prison sentence, or perhaps without even a trial, in order to keep the system from becoming hopelessly clogged. As a result, the proportion of arrested robbers who go to prison goes down while the robbery rate goes up. In this case, we ought to conclude, not that prison deters robbers, but that high robbery rates "deter" prosecutors and judges.

The best analysis of these problems in statistical studies of deterrence is to be found in a report of the Panel on Research on Deterrent and Incapacitative Effects, set up by the National Research Council (an arm of the National Academy of Sciences). That panel, chaired by Alfred Blumstein of Carnegie-Mellon University, concluded that the available statistical evidence (as of 1978) did not warrant reaching any strong conclusions about the deterrent effect of existing differences among states or cities in the probability of punishment. The panel (of which I was a member) noted that "the evidence certainly favors a proposition supporting deterrence more than it favors one asserting that deterrence is absent" but urged "scientific caution" in interpreting this evidence. . . .

Some commentators believe that these criticisms have proved that "deterrence doesn't work" and thus the decks have now been cleared to get on with the task of investing in those programs, such as job creation and income maintenance, that *will* have an effect on crime. Such a conclusion is, to put it mildly, a bit premature. . . .

People are governed in their daily lives by rewards and penalties of every sort. We shop for bargain prices, praise our children for good behavior and scold them for bad, expect lower interest rates to stimulate home building and fear that higher ones will depress it, and conduct ourselves in public in ways that lead our friends and neighbors to form good opinions of us. To assert that "deterrence doesn't work" is tantamount to either denying the plainest facts of everyday life or claiming that would-be criminals are utterly different from the rest of us. They may well be different to some degree—they most likely have a weaker conscience, worry less about their reputation in polite society, and find it harder to postpone gratifying their urges—but these differences of degree do not make them indifferent to the risks and gains of crime. If they were truly indifferent, they would scarcely be able to function at all, for their willingness to take risks would be offset by their indifference to loot. Their lives would consist of little more than the erratic display of animal instincts and fleeting impulses.

The question before us is whether feasible changes in the deferred and uncertain penalties of crime (and, as we shall see, in the deferred and uncertain opportunities for employment) will affect crime rates in ways that can be detected by the data and statistical methods at our disposal.

NIGEL WALKER, SENTENCING IN A RATIONAL SOCIETY

56-59 (1969)

Deterrence has become a dirty word in penological discussion, partly because it has so often been the battle-cry of those who support capital or corporal punishment, partly because of a fashionable assumption that it is more enlightened and scientific to talk about social hygiene and reformation. Even penologists who think more logically than this are apt to succumb to a pseudo-scientific assumption. Because the statistical evidence for the effectiveness of deterrents is scarce and of limited applicability they regard it as irrational to act on the expectation that *any* deterrent will be effective.

It is true that the very nature of the process of deterrence makes its operation very hard to study objectively. While a deterrent is in operation it is very difficult, if not altogether impracticable, to devise a satisfactory way of finding out the number of occasions on which it has been the decisive consideration in the mind of a person who rejected an opportunity for law-breaking.

Moreover, we are seldom, if ever, in a position to measure what can be called the "absolute efficacy" of a deterrent: that is, to compare a situation in which there is *no* deterrent with a situation in which there is *only that* deterrent. This is sometimes forgotten in discussions of the effect of abolishing or reimposing a type of penalty, such as capital or corporal punishment; and the fact that "abolition" really means "replacement with long sentences of imprisonment" is overlooked. For this reason, the most that we can usually hope to measure is "comparative efficacy": that is, the extent to which a given deterrent is more effective than the alternatives to it.

Even when we are fortunate enough to find a situation in which some type of conduct has recently been made criminal, and punishable with a more or less specific penalty, such as a fine, we are seldom in a position to answer the question "How frequent was it before it became punishable?" since it is not until conduct becomes a crime that police begin to keep statistical records of it.

Only in rather special conditions is it possible to make even cautious inferences from official statistics. The necessary conditions are

(a) that statistics of the frequency with which a given type of offence is reported are kept in a uniform way over a period;

(b) that during this period the penalties for the offence are changed, whether by statute or by an alteration in sentencing policy. The sharper the change the better from the scientist's point of view;

(c) that this change is publicized;

(d) that it does not coincide with any other development that is likely to affect the frequency of the offence in question (such as an increase or decrease in opportunities, or in police activity);

(e) that the probability of incurring the usual penalty for the commission of the offence is fairly high.

The relevance of most of these conditions seems obvious, but they are easily overlooked. For example, a recent report to the California legislature cites a study of the bad cheque problem in Nebraska and other states (Beutel, 1957) in support of the statement that regional variations in the severity of penalties have no effect on crime rates. The study had certainly demonstrated that in Colorado—and other states—where penalties for bad cheques were more lenient prosecutions for this type of offence were relatively *less* common. It had also disclosed, however, how few bad cheques were ever brought to the notice of the law: the percentage in the Nebraska sample was about 2 per cent! If the chance of actually incurring the penalty was as low as this, it is hardly surprising that the difference between a short and a medium term of imprisonment seemed to have no effect in reducing the frequency of the offence.

The importance of ensuring that publicity is given to any changes in the penalty is illustrated by a Finnish experiment (Tornudd, 1968). This is one of the very few instances in which social scientists have been able to persuade agencies of law enforcement to alter their policy as a deliberate test of penological hypothesis. The ethical reactions to proposals of this kind are usually so adverse that it is only when the offence in question is not regarded as serious and the penalties are not considered drastic that this sort of experiment seems practicable.

This one was concerned with the offence of public drunkenness. Drunks are notoriously apt to reappear in court again and again for this offence, a fact which casts doubt on the effectiveness of fining and imprisonment as deterrents in their case. In Finland, where police not only make the arrests but also decide in the first place whether the drunk should be fined (subject to confirmation by the court), the police forces in three medium-sized towns were persuaded to reduce the percentages which were fined in the three years 1962-1964. In one of the towns the percentage of arrests for drunkenness which led to fines was reduced from more than 50 to less than 20 per cent, and the reductions in the other two, though less spectacular, were very marked. Three similar towns were used as controls, and in them the fining percentages remained fairly stable, between 50 and 60 per cent.

In the first year of the experiment the rate of arrests for drunkenness remained much the same as [it] had been in the experimental towns. In the second year there was a sharp rise in one of the towns, almost certainly the result of a new highway project which brought many migrant workers—always heavy drinkers—to the area; the rates in the other two towns did not increase, and were if anything a little below average. Two of the control towns showed slight increases, one showed a marked decrease!

In short, there were no changes in the rates—in an upward or downward direction—which could be attributed to the experimental reduction in the percentage of arrests leading to fines. Unfortunately, it had been deliberately decided not to publicize the reduction, and investigators who mixed with the chronic drunks in the experimental towns found that in fact they had not guessed that there had been a change of policy; those who were released by the police without a fine simply explained their good luck by saying "I suppose I wasn't so drunk after all." All that the experiment demonstrated, therefore, was that even a marked change in sentencing policy, lasting for at least three years, did not seem to have been noticed by the offenders directly affected. . . .

The nearest approach to a sound and successful experiment in testing a deterrent is probably that achieved by Professor Richard Schwartz and Miss Sonya Orleans, with the help of the United States Internal Revenue Service. Nearly 400 taxpayers were divided into four matched groups. Members of the "sanction" group were interviewed, and asked questions designed to remind them indirectly of the penalties which they might suffer if they tried to evade taxes. Members of the "conscience" group were interviewed with questions designed to arouse their civic sense and feelings of duty. The third, or "placebo" group were asked only neutral questions, which avoided both sorts of stimulus. The fourth group were not interviewed at all, in order to test the possibility that even a "placebo" interview produced some effect (which on the whole it did not seem to do). The interviews took place in the month before the taxpayers were due to file their returns for 1962. Without disclosing information about individuals, the Internal Revenue Service compared the returns of the four groups for the year before the experiment and the year 1962. The reported gross incomes of both the "sanction" and the "conscience" groups showed an increase, compared with small decreases in the "placebo" and uninterviewed groups. In other words the attempts to stimulate both fear of penalties and civic conscience seemed to have had effect.

HOLMES-LASKI LETTERS
806 (M. Howe ed. 1963)

If I were having a philosophical talk with a man I was going to have hanged (or electrocuted), I should say, "I don't doubt that your act was inevitable for you but to make it more avoidable by others we propose to sacrifice you to the common good. You may regard yourself as a soldier dying for your country if you like. But the law must keep its promises." I fear that the touch of sentiment that I notice in your political writing will be revolted at this, but personally I feel neither doubt nor scruple.

H. L. A. HART, PUNISHMENT AND RESPONSIBILITY
18-20 (1968)

Bentham's argument was a reply to Blackstone who, in expounding the main excusing conditions recognized in the criminal law of his day, claimed that "all the several pleas and excuses which protect the committer of a forbidden act from punishment which is otherwise annexed thereto may be reduced to this single consideration: the want or defect of *will*" [and to the principle] "that to constitute a crime . . . there must be first, a vicious will." In his Introduction to the Principles of Morals and Legislation, under the heading, "Cases unmeet for punishment" Bentham sets out a list of the main excusing conditions similar to Blackstone's; he then undertakes to show that the infliction of punishment on those who have done, while in any of these conditions, what the law forbids "must be inefficacious: it cannot act so as to prevent the mischief." All the common talk about want or defect of will or lack of a "vicious" will is, he says, "nothing to the purpose," except so far as it implies the reason (inefficacy of punishment) which he himself gives for recognizing these excuses.

Bentham's argument is in fact a spectacular non sequitur. He sets out to prove that to *punish* the mad, the infant child or those who break the law unintentionally or under duress or even under "necessity" must be inefficacious; but all that he proves (at the most) is the quite different proposition that the *threat* of punishment will be ineffective so far as the class of persons who suffer from these conditions is concerned. Plainly it is possible that though (as Bentham says) the *threat* of punishment could not have operated on them, the actual *infliction* of punishment on those persons, may secure a higher measure of conformity to law on the part of normal persons than is secured by the admission of excusing conditions. If this is so and if Utilitarian principles only were at stake, we should, without any sense that we were sacrificing any principle of value or were choosing the lesser of two evils, drop from the law the restriction on punishment entailed by the admission of excuses: unless, of course, we believed that the terror or insecurity or misery produced by the operation of laws so Draconic was worse than the lower measure of obedience to law secured by the law which admits excuses.

This objection to Bentham's rationale of excuses is not merely a fanciful one. Any increase in the number of conditions required to establish criminal liability increases the opportunity for deceiving courts or juries by the pretence that some condition is not satisfied. When the condition is a psychological factor the chances of such pretence succeeding are considerable. Quite apart from the provision made for mental disease, the cases where an accused person pleads that he killed in his sleep or accidentally or in some temporary abnormal state of unconsciousness show that deception is certainly feasible. From the Utilitarian point of view this may lead to two sorts of "losses." The belief that such deception is feasible may embolden persons who would not otherwise risk punishment to take their chance of deceiving a jury in this way. Secondly, a criminal who actually succeeds in this deception will be left at large, though belonging to the class which the law is concerned to incapacitate.

2. Incapacitation

JAMES Q. WILSON, THINKING ABOUT CRIME
145-158 (rev. ed. 1983)

When criminals are deprived of their liberty, as by imprisonment (or banishment, or very tight control in the community), their ability to commit offenses against citizens is ended. We say these persons have been "incapacitated," and we try to estimate the amount by which crime is reduced by this incapacitation.

Incapacitation cannot be the sole purpose of the criminal justice system; if it were, we would put everybody who has committed one or two offenses in prison until they were too old to commit another. And if we thought prison too costly, we would simply cut off their hands or their heads. Justice, humanity, and proportionality, among other goals, must also be served by the courts.

But there is one great advantage to incapacitation as a crime control strategy—namely, it does not require us to make any assumptions about human nature. By contrast, deterrence works only if people take into account the costs and benefits of alternative courses of action and choose that which confers the largest net benefit (or the smallest net cost). Though people almost surely do take such matters into account, it is difficult to be certain by how much such considerations affect their behavior and what change, if any, in crime rates will result from a given change in either the costs of crime or the benefits of not committing a crime. Rehabilitation works only if the values, preferences, or time-horizon of criminals can be altered by plan. There is not much evidence that we can make these alterations for large numbers of persons, though there is some evidence that it can be done for a few under certain circumstances.

Incapacitation, on the other hand, works by definition: Its effects result from the physical restraint of the offender and not from his subjective state. More accurately, it works provided at least three conditions are met: Some offenders must be repeaters; offenders taken off the streets must not be immediately and completely replaced by new recruits; and prison must not sufficiently increase the post-release criminal activity of those who have been incarcerated sufficiently to offset the crimes prevented by their stay in prison.

The first condition is surely true. Every study of prison inmates shows that a large fraction (recently, about two-thirds) of them had prior criminal records before their current incarceration; every study of ex-convicts shows that a significant fraction (estimates vary from a quarter to a half) are rearrested for new offenses within a relatively brief period. In short, the great majority of persons in prison are repeat offenders, and thus prison, whatever else it may do, protects society from the offenses these persons would commit if they were free.

The second condition—that incarcerating one robber does not lead automatically to the recruitment of a new robber to replace him—seems plausible. Although some persons, such as Ernest van den Haag, have argued that new offenders will step forward to take the place vacated by the imprisoned offenders, they have presented no evidence that this is the case, except, perhaps, for certain crimes (such as narcotics trafficking or prostitution), which are organized along business lines. For the kinds of predatory street crimes with which we are concerned—robbery, burglary, auto theft, larceny—there are no barriers to entry and no scarcity of criminal opportunities. No one need wait for a "vacancy" to appear before he can find an opportunity to become a criminal. The supply of robbers is not affected by the number of robbers practicing, because existing robbers have no way of excluding new robbers and because the opportunity for robbing (if you wish, the "demand" for robbery) is much larger than the existing number of robberies. In general, the earnings of street criminals are not affected by how many "competitors" they have.

The third condition that must be met if incapacitation is to work is that prisons must not be such successful "schools for crime" that the crimes prevented by incarceration are outnumbered by the increased crimes committed after release attributable to what was learned in prison. It is doubtless the case that for some offenders prison is a school; it is also doubtless that for other offenders prison is a deterrent. The former group will commit more, or more skillful, crimes after release; the latter will commit fewer crimes after release. The question, therefore, is whether the net effect of these two offsetting tendencies is positive or negative. The evidence presented in chapter 9 bears directly on this issue. All studies of the extent to which prisons reform offenders are also, in effect, studies of whether they *de*form them. In other words, when we compare the post-release crime rates of persons who have gone to prison with the crime rates of similar persons who have not, we can ask whether prison has made them better off (that is, rehabilitated them) or made them worse off (that is, served as a "school for crime"). In general, there is no evidence that the prison experience makes offenders as a whole more criminal, and there is some evidence that certain kinds of offenders (especially certain younger ones) may be deterred by a prison experience. Moreover, interviews with prisoners reveal no relationship between the number of crimes committed and whether the offenders had served a prior prison term. . . .

To determine the amount of crime that is prevented by incarcerating a given number of offenders for a given length of time, the key estimate we must make is the number of offenses a criminal commits per year free on the street. If a community experiences one thousand robberies a year, it obviously makes a great deal of difference whether these robberies are the work of ten robbers, each of whom commits one hundred robberies per year, or the work of one thousand robbers, each of whom commits only one robbery per year. In the first case, locking up only five robbers will cut the number of robberies in half; in the second case, locking up one hundred robbers will only reduce the number of robberies by 10 percent.

In the first edition of this book, I reported, in the concluding chapter, on the work that had just been completed by Shlomo and Reuel Shinnar in which they produced an elegant mathematical formula for estimating the crime-reduction potential of incapacitation under various assumptions. Their key assumption was that the average rate of offending—that is, the number of crimes committed by the average criminal per year free—was ten. On the basis of this assumption and others, they estimated that the street robbery rate in New York State would be only one-fifth what it was in 1970 if every person convicted of such a crime spent five years in prison. . . .

. . . Working with individual adult criminal records of all those persons arrested in Washington, D.C., during 1973 for any one of six major crimes (over five thousand persons in all), Alfred Blumstein and Jacqueline Cohen suggested that the individual offense rate varied significantly for different kinds of offenders. For example, it was highest for larceny and lowest for aggravated assault. But they also found, as had other scholars before them, that there was not a great deal of specialization among criminals—a person arrested today for robbery might be arrested next time for burglary. The major contribution of their study was the ingenious method they developed for converting the number of times persons were arrested into an estimate of the number of crimes they actually committed, a method that took into account the fact that many crimes are not reported to the police, that most crimes known to the police do not result in an arrest, and that some crimes are likely to be committed by groups of persons rather than by single offenders. Combining all the individual crime rates, the offenders in this study (a group of adults who had been arrested at least twice in Washington, D.C.) committed between nine and seventeen serious offenses per year free.

This number was strikingly similar to the original estimates used by the Shinnars that had provoked so much criticism. And confidence in the Blumstein-Cohen estimates was increased when the results of a major study at the Rand Corporation became known. Researchers there had been interviewing prisoners (first in California, then in other states) to find out directly from known offenders how much crime they were committing while free. No one can be certain, of course, that the reports of the convicts constitute an accurate record of their crimes, undetected as well as detected, but the Rand researchers cross-checked the information against arrest records and looked for evidence of internal consistency in the self-reports. Moreover, the inmates volunteered information about crimes they had committed but for which they had not been arrested. Still, it is quite possible that the self-reports were somewhat inaccurate. However, it is reasonable to assume that inmates would be more likely to conceal crimes they did commit rather than admit to crimes they did not commit. Thus, any errors in these self-reports probably lead to an underestimate of the true rate of criminality of these persons.

The Rand group found that the average California prisoner had committed about fourteen serious crimes per year during each of the three years he was free. This number falls squarely within the range estimated, using very different methods, by Blumstein and Cohen and, again, is comparable to the original estimate of the Shinnars. To state the California findings in slightly different terms, if no one was confined in state prison, the number of armed robberies in California would be about 22 percent higher than it now is. . . .

But the Rand group learned something else which would turn out to be even more important. The "average" individual offense rate was virtually a meaningless term because the inmates they interviewed differed so sharply in how many crimes they committed. A large number of offenders committed a small number of offenses while free and a small number of offenders committed a very large number of offenses. In statistical language, the distribution of offenses was highly skewed. For example, the median number of burglaries committed by the inmates in the three states was about 5 a year, but the 10 percent of the inmates who were the highest-rate offenders committed an average of 232 burglaries a year. The median number of robberies was also about 5 a year, but the top 10 percent of offenders committed an average of 87 a year. As Peter W. Greenwood, one of the members of the Rand group, put it, incarcerating one robber who was among the top 10 percent in offense rates would prevent more robberies than incarcerating eighteen offenders who were at or below the median. . . .

Joan Petersilia and Peter Greenwood, both members of the Rand group, also came to the conclusion that reducing crime by a significant amount through longer prison terms would be very costly. They analyzed the arrest records of 625 persons convicted in Denver, Colorado, of serious crimes between 1968 and 1970. Instead of estimating the effect of differing sentencing policies on a large group of offenders whose individual behavior was unknown, they looked at the actual arrest record of each person individually and asked whether a particular sentencing policy (say, a three-year mandatory minimum) would have led to the imprisonment of the offender for his last offense and thereby have prevented the offense from being committed. Knowing this, they could then calculate how many additional persons would have to be sent to prison. Their analysis suggested that incapacitation works, but at a price. If every person convicted of a felony received a five-year prison term, the number of felonies committed would drop by 45 percent but the size of the prison population would increase by 450 percent. If the mandatory five-year term were reserved for repeat offenders, such as convicted felons who had previously been convicted of a felony, then the crime rate would drop by 18 percent and the prison population would increase by 190 percent. . . .

[A]ll the evidence we have implies that, for crime-reduction purposes, the most rational way to use the incapacitative powers of our prisons would be to do so selectively. Instead of longer sentences for everyone, or for persons who have prior records, or for persons whose present crime is especially grave, longer sentences would be given primarily to those who, when free, commit the most crimes. . . .

But how do we know who these high-rate, repeat criminals are? Knowing the nature of the present offense is not a good clue. The reason for this is quite simple—most street criminals do not specialize. Today's robber can be tomorrow's burglar and the next day's car thief. When the police happen to arrest him, the crime for which he is arrested is determined by a kind of lottery—he happened to be caught red-handed, or as the result of a tip, committing a particular crime that may or may not be the same as either his previous crime or his next one. If judges give sentences based entirely on the gravity of the present offense, then a high-rate offender may get off lightly because on this occasion he happened to be caught snatching a purse. The low-rate offender may get a long sentence because he was unlucky enough to be caught robbing a liquor store with a gun.

Prosecutors have an understandable tendency to throw the book at persons caught committing a serious crime, especially if they have been caught before. To a certain extent, we want to encourage that tendency. After all, we not only want to reduce crime, we want to see criminals get their just deserts. Society would not, and should not, tolerate a system in which a prosecutor throws the book at purse snatchers and lets armed robbers off with a suspended sentence. But while society's legitimate desire for retribution must set the outer bounds of any sentencing policy, there is still room for flexibility within those bounds. We can, for example, act so that all robbers are punished with prison terms, but give, within certain relatively narrow ranges, longer sentences to those robbers who commit the most crimes.

If knowing the nature of the present offense and even knowing the prior record of the offender are not accurate guides to identifying high-rate offenders, what is? Obviously, we cannot ask the offenders. They may cooperate with researchers once in jail, but they have little incentive to cooperate with prosecutors before they go to jail, especially if the price of cooperation is to get a tougher sentence. But we can see what legally admissible, objective attributes, of the offenders best predict who is and who is not a high-rate offender. In the Rand study, Greenwood and his colleagues discovered, by trial and error, that the following seven factors, taken together, were highly predictive of a convicted person being a high-rate offender: he (1) was convicted of a crime while a juvenile (that is, before age sixteen), (2) used illegal drugs as a juvenile, (3) used illegal drugs during the previous two years, (4) was employed less than 50 percent of the time during the previous two years, (5) served time in a juvenile facility, (6) was incarcerated in prison more than 50 percent of the previous two years, and (7) was previously convicted for the present offense.

Using this scale, Greenwood found that 82 percent of those predicted to be low-rate offenders in fact were, and 82 percent of those predicted to be medium- or high-rate offenders also were. To understand how big these differences are, the median California prison inmate who is predicted to be a low-rate offender will in fact commit slightly more than one burglary and slightly less than one robbery per year free. By contrast, the median California inmate who is predicted to be a high-rate offender will commit ninety-three burglaries and thirteen robberies per year free. In other states, this prediction scale may be more or less accurate. . . .

[But is] it fair for a low-rate offender who is caught committing a serious crime to serve a shorter sentence (because he is not much of a threat to society) than a high-rate offender who gets caught committing a relatively minor offense? Probably not. Sentences would have to have legal boundaries set so that the use of selective incapacitation could not lead to perverse sentences—armed robbers getting one year, purse-snatchers getting five. Since, to the best of my knowledge, selective incapacitation has never been made the explicit basis of a state sentencing policy, we cannot be certain how manageable this problem of reconciling justice and crime control will be.

Finally, there is bound to be a debate about the legal and even ethical propriety of using certain facts as the basis for making predictions. Everyone would agree that race should not be a factor; everyone would probably agree that prior record should be a factor. I certainly believe that it is proper to take into account an offender's juvenile as well as his adult record, but I am aware that some people disagree. But can one take into account alcohol or drug use? Suppose the person claims to be cured of his drinking or his drug problem; do we believe him? And if we do, do we wipe the slate clean of information about these matters? And should we penalize more heavily persons who are chronically unemployed, even if unemployment is a good predictor of recidivism? Some people will argue that this is tantamount to making unemployment a crime, though I think that overstates the matter. After all, advocates of pretrial release of arrested persons, lenient bail policies, and diverting offenders away from jail do not hesitate to claim that having a good employment record should be counted in the accused's favor. If employment counts in favor of some, then obviously unemployment may be counted against others. Since advocates of "bail reform" are also frequent opponents of incapacitation, selective or collective, it is incumbent on them to straighten out their own thinking on how we make use of employment records. Nonetheless, this important issue deserves thoughtful attention.

3. Rehabilitation

HERBERT PACKER, THE LIMITS OF THE CRIMINAL SANCTION
50 (1968)

The most immediately appealing justification for punishment is the claim that it may be used to prevent crime by so changing the personality of the offender that he will conform to the dictates of law; in a word, by reforming him. . . .

[W]hat we do to the offender in the name of reform is being done to him by compulsion and for *our* sake, not for his. Rehabilitation may be the most humane goal of punishment, but it is a goal of *punishment* so long as its invocation depends upon finding that an offense has been committed, and so long as its object is to prevent commission of [other] offenses. . . .

If rehabilitation is the goal, the nature of the offense is relevant only for what it tells us about what is needed to rehabilitate the offender. . . . The rehabilitative ideal teaches us that we must treat each offender as an individual whose special needs and problems must be known as fully as possible in order to enable us to deal effectively with him. Punishment, in this view, must be forward-looking. The gravity of the offense, however measured, may give us a clue to the intensity and duration of the measures needed to rehabilitate; but it is only a clue, not a prescription. There is, then, no generally postulated equivalence between the offense and the punishment, as there would be in the case of the retributive or even the deterrent theory of punishment.

It follows from this offender-oriented aspect of the rehabilitative ideal that the intensity and duration of punishment are to be measured by what is thought to be required in order to change the offender's personality. Unlike the related goal of incapacitation, the inquiry is not into how dangerous the offender is but rather into how amenable to treatment he is. If a writer of bad checks can be cured of his underlying disorder only by five years of intensive psychotherapy, then that is what he is to receive. And of course, no one knows at the outset how much of what kind of therapy will be needed in his or anyone else's case, so it cannot be said in advance what the duration of his punishment will be. It ends whenever those in authority decide that he has been rehabilitated. Of course, if he does not yield to treatment and is thought to present a danger, he will not be released.

[There is a] major objection to making rehabilitation the primary justification for punishment [which] probably comes very close to settling the matter for present purposes. It is, very simply, that we do not know how to rehabilitate offenders, at least within the limit of the resources that are now or might reasonably be expected to be devoted to the task. The more we learn about the roots of crime, the clearer it is that they are nonspecific, that the social and psychic springs lie deep within the human condition. To create on a large scale the essentials of a society that produced no crime would be to remake society itself. . . .

FRANCIS A. ALLEN, CRIMINAL JUSTICE, LEGAL VALUES, AND THE REHABILITATIVE IDEAL

Justice Punishment Treatment: The Correctional Process
193-196 (L. Orland ed. 1973)

The rehabilitative ideal is itself a complex of ideas which, perhaps, defies completely precise statement. The essential points, however, can be articulated. It is assumed, first, that human behavior is the product of antecedent causes. These causes can be identified as part of the physical universe, and it is the obligation of the scientist to discover and to describe them with all possible exactitude. Knowledge of the antecedents of human behavior makes possible an approach to the scientific control of human behavior. Finally, and of primary significance for the purposes at hand, it is assumed that measures employed to treat the convicted offender should serve a therapeutic function, that such measures should be designed to effect changes in the behavior of the convicted person in the interests of his own happiness, health, and satisfactions and in the interest of social defense.

Although these ideas are capable of rather simple statement, they have provided the arena for some of the modern world's most acrimonious controversy. And the disagreements among those who adhere in general to these propositions have been hardly less intense than those prompted by the dissenters. This is true, in part, because these ideas possess a delusive simplicity. No idea is more pervaded with ambiguity than the notion of reform or rehabilitation. Assuming, for example, that we have techniques to accomplish our ends of rehabilitation, are we striving to produce in the convicted offender something called "adjustment" to his social environment or is our objective something different from or more than this? By what scale of values do we determine the ends of therapy?

There is, of course, nothing new in the notion of reform or rehabilitation of the offender as one objective of the penal process. This idea is given important emphasis, for example, in the thought of the medieval churchmen. The church's position, as described by Sir Francis Palgrave, was that punishment was not to be "thundered in vengeance for the satisfaction of the state, but imposed for the good of the offender: in order to afford the means of amendment and to lead the transgressor to repentance, and to mercy." Even Jeremy Bentham, whose views modern criminology has often scorned and more often ignored, is found saying: "It is great merit in a punishment to contribute to the *reformation of the offender,* not only through fear of being punished again, but by a change in his character and habits." But this is far from saying that the modern expression of the rehabilitative ideal is not to be sharply distinguished from earlier expressions. The most important differences, I believe, are two. First, the modern statement of the rehabilitative ideal is accompanied by, and largely stems from, the development of scientific disciplines concerned with human behavior, a development not remotely approximated in earlier periods when notions of reform of the offender were advanced. Second, and of equal importance for the purposes at hand, in no other period has the rehabilitative ideal been so completely dominated by theoretical and scholarly inquiry, to such an extent that in some quarters it is almost assumed that matters of treatment and reform of the offender are the only questions worthy of serious attention in the whole field of criminal justice and corrections.

. . . This narrowing of interests prompted by the rise of the rehabilitative ideal during the past half-century should put us on our guard. No social institutions as complex as those involved in the administration of criminal justice serve a single function or purpose. Social institutions are multi-valued and multi-purposed. Values and purposes are likely on occasion to prove inconsistent and to produce internal conflict and tension. A theoretical orientation that evinces concern for only one or a limited number of purposes served by the institution must inevitably prove partial and unsatisfactory. In certain situations it may prove positively dangerous. This stress on the unfortunate consequences of the rise of the rehabilitative ideal need not involve failure to recognize the substantial benefits that have also accompanied its emergence. Its emphasis on the fundamental problems of human behavior, its numerous contributions to the decency of the criminal-law processes are of vital importance. But the limitations and dangers of modern trends of thought need clearly to be identified in the interest, among others, of the rehabilitative ideal, itself.

My first proposition is that the rise of the rehabilitative ideal has dictated what questions are to be investigated, with the result that many matters of equal or even greater importance have been ignored or cursorily examined. This tendency can be abundantly illustrated. Thus, the concentration of interest on the nature and needs of the criminal has resulted in a remarkable absence of interest in the nature of crime. This is, indeed, surprising, for on reflection it must be apparent that the question of what is a crime is logically the prior issue: how crime is defined determines in large measure who the criminal is who becomes eligible for treatment and therapy. . . .

. . . [U]nder the dominance of the rehabilitative ideal, the language of therapy is frequently employed, wittingly or unwittingly, to disguise the true state of affairs that prevails in our custodial institutions and at other points in the correctional process. Certain measures, like the sexual psychopath laws, have been advanced and supported as therapeutic in nature when, in fact, such a characterization seems highly dubious. Too often the vocabulary of therapy has been exploited to serve a public-relations function. Recently, I visited an institution devoted to the diagnosis and treatment of disturbed children. The institution had been established with high hopes and, for once, with the enthusiastic support of the state legislature. Nevertheless, fifty minutes of an hour's lecture, delivered by a supervising psychiatrist before we toured the building, were devoted to custodial problems. This fixation on problems of custody was reflected in the institutional arrangements which included, under a properly euphemistic label, a cell for solitary confinement. Even more disturbing was the tendency of the staff to justify these custodial measures in therapeutic terms. Perhaps on occasion the requirements of institutional security and treatment coincide. But the inducements to self-deception in such situations are strong and all too apparent. In short, the language of therapy has frequently provided a formidable obstacle to a realistic analysis of the conditions that confront us. And realism in considering these problems is the one quality that we require above all others.

There is a second sort of unintended consequence that has resulted from the application of the rehabilitative ideal to the practical administration of criminal justice. Surprisingly enough, the rehabilitative ideal has often led to increased severity of penal measures. This tendency may be seen in the operations of the juvenile court. Although frequently condemned by the popular press as a device of leniency, the juvenile court is authorized to intervene punitively in many situations in which the conduct, were it committed by an adult, would be wholly ignored by the law or would subject the adult to the mildest of sanctions. The tendency of proposals for wholly indeterminate sentences, a clearly identifiable fruit of the rehabilitative ideal, is unmistakably in the direction of lengthened periods of imprisonment. A large variety of statutes authorizing what is called "civil" commitment of persons, but which except for the reduced protections afforded the parties proceeded against, are essentially criminal in nature, provide for absolutely indeterminate periods of confinement. Experience has demonstrated that, in practice, there is a strong tendency for the rehabilitative ideal to serve purposes that are essentially incapacitative rather than therapeutic in character.

. . . The reference to the tendency of the rehabilitative ideal to encourage increasingly long periods of incarceration brings me to my final proposition. It is that the rise of the rehabilitative ideal has often been accompanied by attitudes and measures that conflict, sometimes seriously, with the values of individual liberty and volition. . . . We are concerned here with the perennial issue of political authority: Under what circumstances is the state justified in bringing its force to bear on the individual human being? These issues, of course, are not confined to the criminal law, but it is in the area of penal regulation that they are most dramatically manifested. The criminal law, then, is located somewhere near the center of the political problem, as the history of the twentieth century abundantly reveals. It is no accident, after all, that the agencies of criminal justice and law enforcement are those first seized by an emerging totalitarian regime. In short, a study of criminal justice is most fundamentally a study in the exercise of political power. No such study can properly avoid the problem of the abuse of power.

4. Retribution

LEVITICUS 24:17-22
The New English Bible

When one man strikes another and kills him, he shall be put to death. Whoever strikes a beast and kills it shall make restitution, life for life. When one man injures and disfigures his fellow-countryman, it shall be done to him as he has done; fracture for fracture, eye for eye, tooth for tooth; the injury and disfigurement that he has inflicted upon another shall in turn be inflicted upon him.

HERBERT PACKER, THE LIMITS OF THE CRIMINAL SANCTION
37-39 (1968)

The retributive view rests on the idea that it is right for the wicked to be punished: because man is responsible for his actions, he ought to receive his just deserts. The view can take either of two main versions: the revenge theory or the expiation theory. Revenge as a justification for punishment is deeply ingrained in human experience, and goes back at least as far as the *lex talionis:* an eye for an eye, a tooth for a tooth, and, we might add, a life for a life. Its marks on the criminal process are similarly deep, the most conspicuous example today being the death penalty for murder. If, as F. H. Bradley has observed, the revenge morality represents the view of the man in the street, then punishment can be seen as a way of satisfying what is essentially a community blood lust. Thus it is an important sociological question whether this view is as widely held today as it was in Victorian England.

. . . [A] distinguished Victorian judge and historian of criminal law, Sir James Fitzjames Stephen . . . is known as the most eloquent exponent of the revenge theory, but curiously enough his views have utilitarian underpinnings. To him the punishment of criminals was simply a desirable expression of the hatred and fear aroused in the community by criminal acts. In [a] famous passage . . . Stephen observed that punishment bears the same relation to the appetite for revenge as marriage bears to the sexual appetite. The figure is an arresting one, but it does not express a pure revenge theory. Instead, it conveys a disguised utilitarian position: punishment is justifiable because it provides an orderly outlet for emotions that, denied it, would express themselves in socially less acceptable ways.

This is but one example of the ways in which an ostensibly retributionist theory may have an implicit utilitarian connotation. We are somehow not content to say that criminals should be punished because *we* hate them and want to hurt them. It has to be because others hate them and would, were it not for our prudence in providing them with this spectacle, stage a far worse one of their own. This kind of hypocrisy is endemic in arguments about the death penalty, but it does not seem to be empirically verified. Lynchings do not, as this theory would lead us to conclude, seem to increase in places that have abolished capital punishment.

The other principal version of the retributive view is that only through suffering punishment can the criminal expiate his sin. Atonement through suffering has been a major theme in religious thought through the ages, and it doubtless plays a role in thought about secular punishment as well. In this view the emphasis is shifted from our demands on the criminal and becomes a question of demands that the criminal does or should make on himself to reconcile himself to the social order. In the absence of assurance that his sense of guilt is equal to the demands made upon it, we help to reinforce it by providing an external expression of guilt.

It hardly matters which aspect of the theory is espoused. The result is the same. The criminal is to be punished simply because he has committed a crime. It makes little difference whether we do this because we think we owe it to him or because we think he owes it to us. Each theory rests on a figure of speech. Revenge means that the criminal is paid back; expiation means that he pays back. The revenge theory treats all crimes as if they were certain crimes of physical violence: you hurt *X;* we will hurt you. The expiation theory treats all crimes as if they were financial transactions: you got something from *X;* you must give equivalent value. Underlying both figures of speech and rendering irrelevant a choice [of which figure is] to be employed is the thought that it is right for punishment to be inflicted on persons who commit crimes. This familiar version of the retributive position, which I shall call the affirmative version, has no useful place in a theory of justification for punishment, because what it expresses is nothing more than dogma, unverifiable and on its face implausible. The usefulness of the retributive position resides, as we shall see later, in what it denies rather than in what it affirms.

NIGEL WALKER, PUNISHMENT, DANGER, AND STIGMA: THE MORALITY OF CRIMINAL JUSTICE

24, 25, 37-42 (1980)

> Certain things are simply wrong and ought to be punished. And this we do believe (Doing Justice, Report for the Committee for the Study of Incarceration).

[This quotation illustrates] the revival of interest in the retributive [justification] for punishment. This revival is a reaction against the utilitarian approach, which is becoming unpopular partly because of the excessive prison terms imposed in the United States in the name of rehabilitation or public protection, and partly because of discouraging evidence about the efficacy of sentences designed to reform or deter. Like other revivalists, however, latter-day preachers of these doctrines are slightly confused about what they are selling. . . .

The authors of Doing Justice seem unaware of most of the difficulties of retributivism. . . .

[The retributivist] holds that the justification for inflicting a penalty is that the offender *deserves* it because of his offence. The pure retributivist also believes that the severity of the penalty should match the offender's culpability. Culpability varies according to the gravity of the harm done, intended or consciously risked, the offender's motives, and any circumstances relevant enough to mitigate or aggravate it. . . .

. . . Some objections to [retributivism] are rational, some emotional. The emotional objections treat it as nothing more than a dignified form of vindictiveness. It is true that in practice it is sometimes difficult to be sure whether a sentencer is being genuinely retributive or giving vent to his sympathy with the victim. In theory, however, there is a clear distinction between reacting to injury or outrage and punishing *for the breach of a rule.* Only when the latter is the reason is the penalty genuine retributive punishment.

A more serious criticism is the difficulty which retributive sentencers feel, or ought to feel in deciding what kind and amount of punishment corresponds to the culpability of this or that offender. The decision involves two difficult feats of estimation: the assessment of his culpability and the prediction of the amount of suffering which different punishments will impose on him. It is much easier to say whether a man is or is not culpable than to say exactly how culpable: even his intimates can only guess at the strengths of the impulses temptations or pressures to which he was subject. As for how much he will suffer from six months' or 12 months' imprisonment, or from a £100 fine; this is equally incalculable. It is not surprising that some modern retributivists have given up the hope of matching the quantum of punishment to the culpability of the offender, and argue that their objective is not commensurability but mere proportionality . . . together with the avoidance of obvious inconsistencies (such as imprisoning one accomplice and fining the other).

The most difficult question for the retributivist, however, is "Why *should* breaches of laws (or rules) be penalised?" Many moral philosophers have wrestled with this question, and offered a variety of answers. Most of the answers fall into one of three groups:

(a) that punishment *purges* the offender's guilt by making him suffer. Undoubtedly this is sometimes true as a psychological statement. Some people feel guilty about some of the things they do; and some of those who feel guilty feel less guilty if they undergo suffering (voluntarily, accidentally or compulsorily) which they can in some way link to the offence. Moreover, there are also people who feel less censorious towards an offender who has been made to suffer for an offence. These, however, are mere psychological truths, and are not even true about all offenders or all their condemners. They do not alter the fact that an offender has acted culpably, and they do not therefore satisfy those who want a nonpsychological reason for retributive punishment, as distinct from a mere explanation.

(b) that punishment induces repentance and other moral improvements in the offender. This should not be confused with the reductive aim of reform: it relies on moral improvement, not better behaviour. No doubt as a psychological statement it is sometimes true, just as it is sometimes true that suffering a penalty *lessens* feelings of guilt. One awkward question is whether it is true often enough to make it reasonable to hope for an induced repentance. But if it is granted that a reducer[1] can be discredited only by showing that he *never* achieves his aims, the same concession must be made to this kind of punisher. A much more awkward question is whether he would regard as punishment a penalty inflicted on an offender who is known to be incapable of moral improvement (supposing such certainty to be possible). . . . On the whole such a view does not seem to correspond with what is usually meant by retribution.

(c) that punishment is an effort to *cancel* the offence: to bring about a state of affairs in which it is as if it had not been committed. This is sometimes possible. A thief who has stolen money can sometimes be made to return it; and unless the owner was beggared by the theft he is no worse off. A vandal can be made to pay for the restoration of what he has damaged; and if it is not an irreparable work of art nobody else suffers. Such situations, however, are rare. Even if the loss or damage is of a kind which is capable of being put right, the offender usually lacks the means to do so. (State compensation is a more effective way of restoring the *status quo ante* where this is at all possible: but that is not punishing the offender.) In fact, we tend to *distinguish* between penalty and restitution. This being so, in what sense does a fine or a prison sentence *cancel* the offence? Only in some non-literal sense. For example, a society might regard the doing of wrong to a wrongdoer as a *symbol* of the cancellation which they would have liked to achieve in reality. If this is what is being argued, it belongs to the expressive justification rather than the retributive; for the symbolic function would be adequately performed if people believed that the offender had been punished, whether he had in fact been or not.

(d) that punishment is *deserved* by the offender. Philosophers, however, do not find it easy to explain what is meant by "deserving." It has even been suggested that a desert is "a right"; but a right is something that one claims or not, as one wishes, and it is only in special circumstances that offenders claim the right to be punished. More plausible is the suggestion that offenders have *forfeited* a right, variously defined as the right not to be deliberately made to suffer, or the right to one's liberty and property. It does not much matter how the right is defined; for the notion of a forfeited right cannot provide the positive justification for punishing which the retributivist needs. The notion of desert seems to involve the belief that a person who has acted culpably should suffer for his action, and that unpunished wrong-doing is somehow a greater evil than punished wrong-doing.

1. One who advocates criminal punishment as a means of reducing crime in the future, as by deterrence, incapacitation or rehabilitation.—EDS.

A satisfactory retributive answer to the question, "Why should offences be punished?" has to meet a number of requirements:

(i) it must make retribution clearly distinguishable from mere vengeance or denunciation;

(ii) it must allow penalties to be proportional to rather than commensurate with culpability;

(iii) it must account psychologically for the retributivist's feeling that unpunished wrongdoing is a greater evil than punished wrongdoing (without implying that it is *sufficient* to explain it psychologically);

(iv) it must make punishment not permissible but obligatory (in the absence of excuses). If it made it merely permissible some other positive justification for it would have to be found; and if the retributive answer did not supply this it would follow that the answer must be non-retributive.

Some people would also argue that:

(v) the answer must also make it clear why the natural or accidental consequences of wrongdoing are not punishment. If, for example, a burglar is injured by barbed wire or by an outraged householder, is his injury distinguishable from punishment? If so, is this reconcilable with the fact that even a retributively minded sentencer might well lighten his sentence because of the injury he had suffered? Some people feel that guilt is partially—or even wholly—purged by suffering which is the natural or accidental result of the wrongdoing. . . .

Only one answer seems to meet all these points: that *retributive punishment is a penalty imposed in fulfilment of a requirement in a rule that it should be imposed on those who have infringed a rule.* As has already been said, this is what distinguishes it from mere vengeance, which is inflicted for emotional reasons. It also distinguishes it from denunciation, which requires only the belief that the offender will suffer the penalty. It allows the penalty to be proportional rather than commensurate to culpability; for the rule need not insist on commensurability. It provides a psychological explanation of the feeling that an unpunished infringement is worse than a punished one. Man is a rule-making, rule-following animal, and most of his activities—linguistic, social, recreational and sexual—are governed by rules or conventions. There is nothing like conforming with a rule for inducing a feeling of propriety or even righteousness. An unpunished infraction means two infractions.

KAPLAN, THE PROBLEM OF CAPITAL PUNISHMENT

1983 U. Ill. L. Rev. 565-570

Let us now move on to a very different kind of argument—the argument for retribution. This must be carefully distinguished from the pragmatic arguments, for it is in essence a moral argument. Insofar as an argument insists that the use of capital punishment will have an effect, direct or indirect, upon the murder rate, it becomes pragmatic and is exposed to the possibility, however slim, of empirical refutation. A moral argument is different. We can reason about it, but not prove it with statistics, though often it will prove to have some kind of factual predicate on which its force depends.

The view that we should impose capital punishment because it is morally right is often phrased as an assertion that the person who would commit murder—or, more likely, some especially aggravated form of murder—should properly forfeit his own life. One problem with this argument is that it is usually supported simply by its assertion as a moral principle, rather than by any reasoning.

Often this kind of argument is phrased in terms of the victim and draws its emotional force from a feeling that somehow, by placing the defendant in the position that his victim now occupies, we will right some moral balance. Of course this is not a pragmatic argument; obviously nothing that we do to the defendant will do the victim any good. Nor is the condition of the victim, no matter how horrible, enough in itself to invoke this type of reasoning. Some view as to the moral responsibility of the defendant must differentiate the proper subject of capital punishment, for those who argue for the death penalty do not intend that those executed should suffer the same kinds of agonizing deaths themselves. Rather, they often argue for one means or another of inflicting a death penalty that is painless.

It is probable that the great majority of those who are sentenced to capital punishment have committed horrible crimes of the kind that the majority of us would agree deserved capital punishment, based simply on reading about them in the newspapers. Prototypically, this justification for capital punishment has in mind the "hit man"; the cold, calculating killer who performs his job of murder just the way the majority of the population work at their own law-abiding occupations. Typically, this killer is felt to be a fully and morally responsible agent who has chosen his career for its rewards, with full knowledge of the harm he is inflicting on others. In practice, however, such a hit man is almost never sentenced to death.[2] Being a professional, he is rarely caught, and, when he is, he frequently is given leniency from the prosecutor in exchange for his testimony against those who have hired him and are felt to be even more morally guilty.

In general, the people who commit those especially vicious, baffling, senseless crimes which do result in death sentences, fall into one of three categories. First of all there are those in whom the cultural connection between male sexuality and aggression and the need to dominate becomes unbalanced. This type of personality unfortunately exists throughout our society in more or less attenuated form. In extreme cases, sexuality becomes so unbalanced—indeed it can only be described as "perverted"—that the individual has a kind

2. Florida executed one in 1984.—Eds.

of sexual need to kill. Whether one defines this as a kind of mental illness, the perpetrators are far from normal. The next major kind of aggravated murderer is the person who is infused with a hatred which surfaces either almost continuously or else explosively on random occasions in a way that is virtually inexplicable. Finally, there is the person whose values can only be called feral. He looks upon the world as we envision a wild animal would look from the jungle. He feels no moral reason not to injure anyone, just as he feels that those around him have no moral reason not to injure him.

The interesting thing about all three of these kinds of people is that the more closely one examines their backgrounds and what has happened to them as they were growing up, the less one feels that it is morally necessary to kill them, any more than one would feel it was morally necessary to kill an escaped leopard from the zoo. They may be very, very dangerous people, but when one sees the kinds of backgrounds that the overwhelming majority of them have come from, the moral argument for executing them grows weaker. Though we certainly do not want anything to do with them, there appears to be no moral requirement that we injure further those whose humanity has been so diluted over the years by past injuries.

For instance, consider the background of one Robert Harris, presently on Death Row in California for the wanton and remorseless killing of two young men during the theft of their car for use in a bank robbery.[3]

> Harris was born January 15, 1953, several hours after his mother was kicked in the stomach. She was 6½ months pregnant and her husband, an insanely jealous man . . . came home drunk and accused her of infidelity. He claimed that the child was not his, threw her down and kicked her. She began hemorrhaging, and he took her to the hospital. . . .
>
> His father was an alcoholic who was twice convicted of sexually molesting his daughters. He frequently beat his children, Barbara Harris [his sister] said, and often caused serious injury. Their mother also became an alcoholic and was arrested several times, once for bank robbery.
>
> All of the children had monstrous childhoods. But even in the Harris family, Barbara said, the abuse Robert was subjected to was unusual. . . .
>
> When Robert's father visited his wife in the hospital and saw his son for the first time . . . the first thing he said was, "Who is the father of that bastard?" When his mother picked him up from the hospital, after four months in an incubator, she said it was like taking a stranger's baby home.
>
> The pain and permanent injury Robert's mother suffered as a result of the birth . . . and the constant abuse she was subjected to by her husband, turned her against her son. Money was tight, she was overworked and he was her fifth child in just a few years. She began to blame all of her problems on Robert, and she grew to hate the child.
>
> "I remember one time we were in the car and Mother was in the back seat with Robbie in her arms. He was crying and my father threw a glass bottle at him, but hit my mother in the face, the glass shattered and Robbie started

3. Corwin, Icy Killer's Life Steeped in Violence, L.A. Times, May 16, 1982, at 1, col. 1.

screaming. I'll never forget it," Barbara Harris said, closing her eyes and slowly shaking her head.

"Her face was all pink, from the mixture of blood and milk. She ended up blaming Robbie for all the hurt, all the things like that. She felt helpless and he was someone to vent her anger on."

Their father was a warrant officer in the Army, and Robert Harris spent his first eight years near Ft. Jackson, S.C. Harris had a learning disability and a speech problem, but there was no money for therapy. When he was at school he felt stupid and classmates teased him, his sister said, and when he was at home he was abused.

"He was the most beautiful of all my mother's children; he was an angel," she said. "He would just break your heart. He wanted love so bad he would beg for any kind of physical contact.

"He'd come up to my mother and just try to rub his little hands on her leg or her arm. He just never got touched at all. She'd just push him away or kick him. One time she bloodied his nose when he was trying to get close to her."

Barbara Harris put her head in her hands and cried softly. "One killer out of nine kids. . . . The sad thing is that he was the most sensitive of all of us. When he was [ten] and we all saw 'Bambi,' he cried and cried when Bambi's mother was shot. Everything was pretty to him as a child; he loved animals. But all that changed; it all changed so much."

When their father left the Army, the family moved to a farm labor camp near Bakersfield, Calif. The children worked in the fields, Barbara said, and their father stayed drunk.

When Harris was 9, his father was convicted of molesting a daughter and was sent to Atascadero State Hospital. The family survived on welfare. Several years later, their father returned home, Barbara said, and was convicted again for the same offense.

When Barbara Harris was 13, she put a .45-caliber pistol to her father's temple when he was sleeping but could not pull the trigger. She has regretted that decision many times.

All nine children are psychologically crippled as a result of their father, she said, but most have been able to lead useful lives. But Robert was too young, and the abuse lasted too long, she said, for him ever to have had a chance to recover.

Barbara Harris, 34, who has two children and two grandchildren, married at 15 to get out of the house. She asked that the name of the city where she lives not be published, so that her father will not learn her whereabouts.

Harris continued to have difficulty in school and was ignored at home. He began getting into trouble and was arrested several times for minor offenses. He left home at 14, lived with a brother for a few months, then hitchhiked to Oklahoma and moved in with Barbara Harris and her husband.

A few months later, he and two other youths stole a car. They were arrested in Florida and Harris was sentenced to a federal youth detention center in Kentucky. He was one of the youngest inmates there, Barbara Harris said, and he grew up "hard and fast."

Robert Harris was raped several times, his sister said, and he slashed his wrists twice in suicide attempts. He spent more than four years behind bars as a result of an escape, an attempted escape and a parole violation.

The centers were "gladiator schools," Barbara Harris said, and Harris

> learned to fight and to be mean. By the time he was released from federal prison at 19, all his problems were accentuated. Everyone in the family knew that he needed psychiatric help.
>
> He was paroled to Visalia, where his mother and several brothers and sisters were living. There Daniel, several years younger, spent time with his older brother for the first time.
>
> "Every encounter I ever had with Robert was an insane encounter," Daniel said in a telephone interview from federal prison in Florida. "Whether it was toward animals, property or whatever, he always had the crazy instinct to destroy."
>
> The child who had cried at the movies when Bambi's mother died had evolved into a man who was arrested several times for abusing animals. "He killed cats and dogs," Daniel said, "and laughed while torturing them with mop handles, darts and pellet guns. Once he stabbed a prize pig more than 1000 times."
>
> "The only way he could vent his feelings was to break or kill something," Barbara Harris said. "He took out all the frustrations of his life on animals. He had no feeling for life, no sense of remorse. He reached the point where there wasn't that much left in him."

One does not have to go so far as to say, with the French, "To understand all is to forgive all" in order to recognize that a great part of the moral imperative behind executing someone like Robert Harris disappears when we know about the conditions in which he was raised and the forces that shaped him. Such people may be as dangerous as escaped leopards, but there is no moral imperative to executing such an animal if the danger can be handled in other ways.

This moral issue requires more examination. If we believe that everyone is responsible for his own acts, it is harder to regard those who perpetrate the most vicious killings as an exception to this. But the fact is we do not regard everyone as responsible for his acts. The huge edifice of *mens rea* in criminal law[4], which requires that for all serious crimes some blameworthy state of mind exist, is testament to that.

People who do not know the harm they are doing are not as guilty as those who do. And people who had no reason to know are probably not guilty at all. Similarly, though, the insanity defense is under challenge; it has been attacked primarily on pragmatic grounds—that those acquitted on the grounds of insanity are too often returned to society while they are still dangerous, and few have argued that it does not state a correct moral principle—that those who are mentally ill are not fully responsible for a wide range of their actions.

More important, we recognize that many different conditions which do not prevent some responsibility for one's actions may nonetheless lessen that responsibility. Negligent homicide is virtually always treated as a lesser crime than intentional killing and even among those intentional homicides, those

4. See pages 131-179.

committed in hot blood or some kind of passion are less severely punished than more calculated killings. Under some circumstances, even though by no means an excuse, youth, drunkenness, mental retardation, previous blameless life, or extreme emotion all can lessen what would otherwise be seen as the proper punishment. If all these things are properly seen as mitigating factors, does not the history of Robert Harris lessen the moral imperative of executing him?

THIS WORLD

San Francisco Chronicle, Aug. 5, 1984, at 9.

On February 6, 1982, 2½-year-old Tara Burke was abducted from her parents' car at a Concord shopping center. An 11-year old Vietnamese boy, Mac Lin Nguyen, was reported missing in San Francisco on April 21.

On December 19, Mac Lin appeared at the door of a friend in the Mission district; a second friend called the police. Mac Lin led the police to a battered bread van parked near China Basin, its windows covered with cardboard. The police broke into the van and arrested Luis Reynaldo (Tree Frog) Johnson, 33, who leapt from the rear of the van shouting obscenities, and Alex Cabarga, 18, who was lying in the van under a blanket with Tara Burke. Both Alex and Tara were naked below the waist.

Mac Lin told the police that for eight months he and Tara were held prisoner in the van. Tara was kept undressed so she would not try to get away. They were both sexually molested, and Mac Lin was often beaten with a rubber hose. Tara was not beaten, but she was continually forced to perform sex acts in exchange for food.

Police found in the van videotapes and photos of the children engaged in sexual acts with the men. They also found sexual paraphernalia, sex magazines and a copy of the book Summerhill—A Radical Approach to Child Raising.

Johnson was charged with 121 counts of kidnapping, false imprisonment, lewd conduct, sodomy, rape, oral copulation and assault. Cabarga was charged with 93 similar counts.

Cabarga had turned 18 the day before he was arrested. One of his lawyers, James Collins, sought to have him tried as a juvenile, claiming that Alex, who had been virtually raised by Johnson, was himself a victim—molested, brainwashed and beaten by the older man since the age of 9. Collins maintained that Alex, after his long subjugation to Johnson, had lost all will of his own, and that for years Alex had been isolated from any person who could have taught him the difference between right and wrong.

Juvenile Court Judge Daniel Hanlon ruled that Alex must be tried as an adult. "I realize the tragedy of this case as far as Alex Cabarga is concerned, and realize the position of vulnerability he also was in," the judge said. But he added that Alex's abuse of Tara had gone far "beyond innocent sexual exploration found among adolescents," and that Alex had failed to report what he must have known was a terrible crime.

The trial dragged through nine weeks of sickening details. In her closing argument to the jury, prosecutor Judith Whitmer said, "These two men committed slow murder on the souls of these two children. They stripped them of their human decency, they stripped them of their trust . . . and taught them they were worthless except as sexual objects. For that, they deserve the utmost condemnation of the law." Collins repeated his plea that his client was a "third victim" of Tree Frog Johnson, who for more than 10 years had been Cabarga's "parent, teacher and lover."

Johnson and Cabarga were found guilty of the nearly 200 charges against them. Johnson was sentenced to 527 years in prison, Cabarga to 208 years.

Alex's lawyers asked that he be turned over to the California Youth Authority rather than sent to state prison. San Francisco Superior Court Judge Robert Dossee refused, saying, "He is a pedophile. If he is sent to the Youth Authority, he may be a danger to younger inmates." Steve Scherr, a second attorney for Alex, said Dossee's ruling will be appealed.

On July 6, The Chronicle's Art Hoppe wrote a column about Alex, reprinted below. Soon afterward Hoppe received two letters, printed on the following pages.

Art Hoppe, *Is Anyone Ever Guilty?*

The picture of Alex Cabarga on the front page of The Chronicle was that of a handsome, soft-featured youth of 19 with a sullen, sensuous mouth. His almost-feminine eyes were downcast and he was scratching his cheek reflectively. The caption said: "A 208-year term."

Alex Cabarga had been convicted of kidnaping and performing despicable sexual acts with two young children. There was no question of his guilt, and the sympathy of a warm-hearted public was, of course, overwhelmingly for the victims.

A jury had found him mentally disturbed but legally sane. A judge, to the plaudits of most, had imposed the draconian sentence after rejecting defense pleas for rehabilitation.

It all seemed cut and dried. I hadn't been following the daily stories closely. The details were too sordid. I knew that young Cabarga was a protege of Luis "Tree Frog" Johnson, who, at 34, sounded like a thoroughly evil man. Johnson had been sentenced to 527 years. Now it was Cabarga's turn. He will be eligible for parole when he is 165.

This time, I read the story through to the end. Why had this young man done what he had done? Then I came across the sentence: "Testimony showed his parents allowed him to move in with Johnson at the age of 9, and he was sexually and physically abused by him until the arrests."

So Cabarga was a victim, too. Here was a boy, who, long before the age of puberty, had been beaten and molested almost daily. He had, said the psychiatrists at the trial, understandably developed "a pathological dependence" on his mentor, and at Johnson's behest he had done unto others what had been done unto him. And now, after this incredibly unfair life, society will lock him up and throw away the key.

I was angry. Where was the public sympathy for this victim? "Mr. Cabarga led a very tragic and disturbed life," agreed the prosecutor. "But we can't excuse him. The parents can't be convicted of the sexual assault." And someone must be found guilty.

Yet who is guilty? Is the boy guilty of being warped by abuse? Are the parents guilty of turning him over to a child molester? Or is the molester guilty of warping the child? And what made each of them do what he did? There must be reasons.

So I came, in the end, to that uneasy question that has bothered me for years: Is anyone ever guilty of anything?

There can be no guilt without free will. If we have no choice in making a decision, we cannot be held responsible for the choice we make. And I have long worried that there is no free will.

The argument against it has always seemed to me hopelessly irrefutable: We are solely the end products of our heredity and our environment—what we began with and what we have learned. Each decision we make is based on those two factors. At the moment of birth we have absolutely no control over either. Thus the first decision we make—whether to reach for the pretty flower, perhaps—is predetermined by whether we have inherited a love of, or an aversion to, pretty flowers. This decision affects our next decision and so on. We may slowly change our environment, then, but only through predetermined decisions. Therefore, we never make a choice that is free.

I hate this argument. I much prefer to think of us as blithe spirits controlling our own destinies under the sleepy eye of a benevolent and tolerant Deity. For it is the fear of guilt that makes most of us behave. And without guilt, our present social order would collapse.

If there is no free will, then Alex Cabarga isn't guilty. I can't believe he's guilty. When I think about his case, I think the day must come—probably not in my lifetime—when society attacks not those who commit antisocial acts, but rather the environmental conditions that caused their aberrations.

I realize that this is a traditional bleeding-heart liberal position. I subscribe to it thoroughly.

Letter from a Juror, July 9, 1984

To Art Hoppe and the editor of the Chronicle:

My name is Trudie Bowen. I was a member of the jury on the Tara Burke trial, and Art Hoppe's column moved me to tears. Where indeed is the sympathy for Alex Cabarga?

Very little was evident during the deliberation, when I heard frequent statements like these: "Alex and Johnson were like a married couple." (So who gets married at 9 years of age?) "Oh, those scars on Alex's back aren't so bad" (Even though they were inflicted with the same hose we convicted Johnson for using on Mac Lin!) "So what if Alex goes to prison? He'll probably enjoy getting gang-raped." (From a gay man!)

Especially frustrating was dealing with the gross double-standard shared by too many jurors: Whereas Mac Lin and Tara were horribly abused victims, when evidence showed that Alex endured worse and for a much longer time, Alex "chose" that lifestyle and "enjoyed" being physically, mentally and sexually abused.

Statements made outside of deliberation were as bad. Many people suggested that Tara would have been better off dead. Better murdered than sexually abused. That poor child's suffering has just begun if society has deemed her life so worthless that 10 months of sexual abuse can completely wipe out any of its value.

Unfortunately for Alex, we were asked only to decide what crimes were committed and whether he was legally insane. We had no idea of the possible length of the prison sentence, and we were never asked if we felt Alex was or was not a victim. We were, however, instructed frequently to put "mere sympathy" aside.

I feel very used by our legal system and angry at having been a part in putting that boy in prison. His entire life has been a series of people not wanting to accept responsibility for him—starting with his parents and ending with Judge Robert Dossee.

I, for one, accept responsibility for my role in his life, and I am ashamed. Had I known the outcome of that trial I would have been less honest in my "civic duty" and listened more to "mere sympathy."

Trudie Bowen
San Francisco

cc:Judge Robert Dossee

Letter From Alex's Father

Dear Mr. Hoppe:

I'd like to explain a few things to you, I suppose because I know that you, having been cut from the very same piece of bleeding-heart liberal cloth as I, will understand that your instincts about Alex Cabarga are right.

First, a little family background. Basically, we were New Yorkers. That is, we lived in New Jersey because New Yorkers with large families cannot afford to live in New York. But we were doing all right—we lived in a big new house, and on the surface we seemed the same as everyone else.

Alex and his four older siblings were raised by one of the most conscientious mothers who ever lived. Diane's sole purpose in those years was to raise her children. She had immense energy for them, and the ability to immerse herself in them. She could talk to them and play with them. She personified the words *love* and *nurture.* Above all, she believed in freedom, respect and equality for children.

I agreed with much of Diane's philosophy, but I was less well suited as a parent. I was impatient and preoccupied. I did a lot of escaping into television and whatnot. I was too emotionally deprived myself to be able to give very much to my children, although I did provide physical support and the image of stability.

By the time I was 20, I believed everything you, Art Hoppe, believe. (I have read you enough to know that our positions on almost any issue are as close as any two bleeding-heart liberals can get.)

Both Diane and I, in our own ways, had trouble with authority. I had been raised by a cruel, insensitive loudmouth of a father who always treated me as some sort of curiosity. I determined never to be like him in any way. Diane spent the first years of our married life discovering for herself what I had learned as a teenager—that the system stinks. Her teachers were the cold, imperiously smug doctors and nurses in hospitals where she gave birth, and later the public schools that attempted to run roughshod over the delicate psyches of our children.

Diane first became a crusader for natural childbirth and rooming-in [leaving the newborn in the room with mother, as opposed to placing him in the nursery]; later, she became a group leader for La Leche League, an organization that pioneered the swing back to breast-feeding; and finally, after several years of pitched battles with the public school system, Diane founded her own school based on the ideal of freedom for kids, as espoused by A.S. Neill in *Summerhill.* At every step we taught our kids to question everything.

By 1970 we were fed up with the wasteland of central New Jersey. We sold our house and most of our possessions and migrated to San Francisco.

We were determined to discover, to invent, a new way of living that would relieve the neurotic, bickering tendencies of our larger nuclear family. As parents, we were too "hip" to sit around watching our children rebel against us as they grew up, and we were too "hip" for them to rebel against, in the traditional sense.

We joined a newly forming warehouse community on Mariposa Street, on Potrero Hill. We were among a group of about 25 people who wanted to build a "community." It was an experiment in living—in the same spirit, no doubt, as many previous utopias. For us, in particular, it offered an extended family situation in which our children would have the opportunity to associate closely with adults from whom they could learn crafts, trades and ideas.

Luis "Tree Frog" Johnson came to the community just a few weeks after our family was settled in. I disliked him from the beginning. He just wasn't "my kind of people." But we were into experimentation, into learning about people and situations other than what our middle-class background had exposed us to.

The kids took to Tree Frog immediately. He was a Pied Piper. He became very close with the family. The kids—primarily Alex's two older brothers—spent more and more time with Tree Frog, and he went on trips with us and joined in other family activities. Tree Frog's involvement with the family continued at that level over the next two years.

Meanwhile, long-festering problems between Diane and me came to a head, and we separated after 20 years of marriage. During the next several years the various family members moved from place to place. By the time of our breakup, Alex, at age 9, had received two strong messages: One, that we, as a family, were "different" and unconventional, and that society's rules didn't necessarily apply to us; and two, that his family "security base" was not stable. He knew that Diane and I loved him. He did not feel abandoned by us. But he was, by now, being seduced by Johnson.

Johnson came after Alex the way a normal man goes for a woman. He besieged him with "love" and attention, treated him like a little prince. He also sexually abused him and started him on the syndrome of sexual abuse, a phenomenon that, since Alex's arrest, has become well known to us. Alex was overwhelmed and saw in Johnson a source of support that was not available from his confused parents at that time. And in keeping with the syndrome, Alex never said a word to us about his "special" relationship with Johnson.

Sexually abused children, we later found out, never tell. They are constrained by guilt and fear. They feel guilt because their abuser pays them a type and a degree of attention that they are not emotionally prepared to deal with. Then he requires that they reciprocate. When they are unable to do so, as is invariably the case, they are made to feel guilty and inadequate. They are constrained by fear, either because they have been exhorted and threatened by the abuser, and/or because they are afraid of their parent's reaction, should they find out.

Johnson's custodianship of Alex was a slow, subtle, evolutionary process. We never did, and never intended to, "give" Alex over to Johnson. In the earlier stages of the relationship, Alex's older brothers were involved. We found ourselves in a situation where three of our sons were hanging out with Johnson much of the time. This happened in the warehouse, so that the kids were always about, and so we thought we were monitoring their activities. Later, Alex's two older brothers lived with Tree Frog in an old school bus parked on a country property in Mendocino, while Alex lived with Diane in a trailer on the same site. As the older boys grew up, they finally became disenchanted with Tree Frog and broke away from him and his influence.

It seems Tree Frog was himself in the process of becoming a full-fledged pedophile. The oldest of our three children made a clean break, and had had little if any sexual contact with Johnson. The next oldest was sexually and physically abused by Tree Frog, but he also managed to break away. Tree Frog was less inclined to control the older boys because they were too old for his sexual tastes. Alex, the youngest and most vulnerable, was Tree Frog's special victim. Only the police were eventually able to free him.

Alex's older brothers failed to tell us what was going on for two reasons: They were victims of the same conspiracy of silence as Alex, and the activities had not reached anything like the proportions of degradation that Alex later experienced.

There are many reasons why we "allowed" Alex to be with Johnson, but much had to do with concern for Alex's rights. Our philosophy about children constrained us not to interfere with their desires unless it was an extreme matter of their physical or psychological well-being. Alex always expressed the desire to be with Johnson, while they both effectively concealed from us the nature of their relationship. We had little objective reason to be suspicious.

Toward the end we sensed the unhealthiness of the relationship, but we suffered two particular disadvantages: First, our unconventional lifestyle, which included explorations into the unknown to learn about people and their habits, and our commitment to be "open" and tolerant about these new types of people we met; and second, our utter ignorance about pedophilia and child abuse. With regard to the former, we were in the process of rejecting the conventional wisdom and tradition of family and child-rearing. We had seen our parents' failures. We wanted to be better. We had rejected the authoritarian public school system. We had found much of society to be grievously lacking in morality, to be ethically bankrupt. We were re-examining everything we had learned from our corrupt society.

Johnson was beyond our limited experience. He appeared to be a free-spirited young man with radical ideas similar to our own. He appeared to be high-minded and idealistic. He was into freedom for children, health foods and more humane politics, as we were. We wanted to believe that this young black man was a decent sort who had been victimized by a prejudiced society. We were not vulnerable to insurance salesmen or Jehovah's Witnesses, but Tree Frog was a different breed of con man.

I tell you these things not in self-justification—I am way beyond any need for that—but because I know you'll be able to understand what happened as I explain it to you.

As for Alex, the simple fact is that by any reasonable definition of the word, he is innocent. What happened to him could have happened to any child because of the ignorance we shared with the general public in regard to the syndrome of sexual child abuse. But Alex's experience is unusual. Hitler is alleged to have said, "Give me their first five years. . . ." But Johnson didn't get Alex's first five years. Alex was treated only with love and respect for his first 9 years, which I believe has made a big difference. The difference is that Alex was not as deeply traumatized as a child who was exposed to abuse at a more tender age.

Alex's behavior is not so much that of an abused child who then becomes an abuser as it is that of a brainwashed person. Alex Cabarga, like Patty Hearst, committed his crimes while under a "forcibly imposed belief system," as described by Dr. Donald Lunde, a brainwashing expert. In an article on the subject Lunde states,

> There is little justification for isolation of defendants convicted of crime under the influence of forcibly imposed belief systems. Those convicted to the extent they are dangerous at all, have been proved to be dangerous only while under the influence of the alternate belief system.

He also said, "The defendant usually begins an immediate recovery spontaneously upon return from the captivity environment. His behavior returns to normal." During the year and a half that Alex has been in jail, we have watched him rapidly mature and emerge from under Johnson's forcibly imposed belief system.

Alex is innocent for a second reason: He was almost completely unaware that he was doing anything wrong. He was vaguely aware that he was doing things that society wouldn't approve of, but his life was full of that!

Alex was physically beaten by Johnson and sexually abused. Johnson is a pedophile whose sexual preference is for little boys. He is also, like most pedophiles, a pornographer. He taught Alex that sex between adults and children was good and right, and necessary for a child's healthy sexual development.

By the manipulative process I described earlier, he had Alex at his mercy. He conceived the depraved idea that they should kidnap a little girl that Johnson could raise to be a "perfect" mother for a child that Johnson would father with her—preferably as soon as possible. Johnson had read accounts of very young girls getting pregnant and hoped that the girl they acquired would be able to conceive by the time she was 8 years old. I think he believed that their offspring would be his own sexual plaything, since it would be his "own" child. (Incestuous fathers often think of their own children that way.)

Alex had long since stopped trying to think for himself. Tree Frog had him so bamboozled that he distrusted his own thoughts. He looked to Tree Frog for all guidance and ideas. Bitter experience had taught him that his own mental processes would lead him to thoughts and ideas that Tree Frog would punish him for. Any idea Alex himself would author, Johnson would characterize as treasonous, unloving and ungrateful. Alex felt bewildered and worthless. Failure to please Johnson or conform to his dictates resulted in physical and emotional punishment. Taking the initiative in one instance would incur Johnson's wrath, while his failure to do so in another instance would have the same result. It was Catch-22.

Alex has said that he perceived himself as in a perpetual mental fog. He had shut down his own mental processes in self-defense. When the kidnapping idea arose, Alex did the only thing he could do—obey Johnson. To question or criticize or resist was totally beyond him by then. Alex recently described to us how he felt as he carried Tara Burke to Tree Frog's car. He said that he felt a tremendous sense of relief because he had done what Tree Frog wanted. He was oblivious to all the other implications of the act.

During the 10 months that they held Tara captive, Alex was required to perform, for Tree Frog's sexual gratification, and for his camera, many sexual acts with Tara and with the 11-year-old boy, Mac Lin. Alex was beaten for noncompliance. Mac was also beaten, but Tara was not. At no time has Alex ever been violent. He did not force himself sexually on the children—Mac testified to that at the trial. The nature of the relationship is, of course, that the children were psychically coerced, as was Alex, into performing these sex acts. For Alex sex with children was a poor substitute for what he knew he really preferred—a girlfriend his own age.

Ironically, the photographs and films Tree Frog took were used as evidence against Alex. Their real significance, which the court entirely overlooked, was that they were evidence of Alex being abused—every bit as much as they were evidence of Mac and Tara being abused. Alex was being subjected to the extreme humiliation of performing sexually under Tree Frog's direction. But because Alex was so much older than the other children, he appeared to be the perpetrator.

From all we have learned about child sexual abuse, we know that Alex is not a pedophile and would never again commit sex crimes. Diane and I, and his therapist, know this in our hearts and heads. We are dedicated to vindicating him, and we deeply appreciate your sympathetic observations. Your bleeding-heart liberal instinct that the punishment meted out to Alex Cabarga is cruel, inhuman and outlandish is totally correct.

Ted Cabarga
San Francisco

MURPHY, MARXISM AND RETRIBUTION
2 Phil. & Pub. Aff. 217, 239-240, 242 (1973)

The retributive theory claims to be grounded on justice; but is it just to punish people who act out of those very motives that society encourages and reinforces? . . . [M]uch criminality is motivated by greed, selfishness, and indifference to one's fellows; but does not the whole society encourage motives of greed and selfishness ("making it," "getting ahead"), and does not the competitive nature of the society alienate men from each other and thereby encourage indifference—even, perhaps, what psychiatrists call psychopathy? . . . There is something perverse in applying principles that presuppose a sense of community in a society which is structured to destroy genuine community.

Related to this is the whole allocation of benefits in contemporary society. The retributive theory really presupposes what might be called a "gentlemen's club" picture of the relation between man and society—i.e., men are viewed as being a part of a community of shared values and rules. The rules benefit all concerned and, as a kind of debt for the benefits derived, each man owes obedience to the rules. In the absence of such obedience, he deserves punishment in the sense that he owes payment for the benefits. For, as a rational man, he can see that the rules benefit everyone (himself included) and that he would have selected them in the original position of choice. . . .

. . . But to think that [this picture] applies to the typical criminal, from the poorer classes, is to live in a world of social and political fantasy. . . . [T]hey certainly would be hard-pressed to name the benefits for which they are supposed to owe obedience. If justice, as both Kant and Rawls suggest, is based on reciprocity, it is hard to see what these persons are supposed to reciprocate for. . . .

Consider one example: a man has been convicted of armed robbery. On investigation, we learn that he is an impoverished black whose whole life has been one of frustrating alienation from the prevailing socio-economic structure—no job, no transportation if he could get a job, substandard education for his children, terrible housing and inadequate health care for his whole family, condescending-tardy-inadequate welfare payments, harassment by the police but no real protection by them against the dangers in his community, and near total exclusion from the political process. Learning all this, would we still want to talk—as many do—of his suffering punishment under the rubric of "paying a debt to society"? Surely not. Debt for what? I do not, of course, pretend that all criminals can be so described. But I do think that this is a closer picture of the typical criminal than the picture that is presupposed in the retributive theory—i.e., the picture of an evil person who, of his own free will, intentionally acts against those just rules of society which he knows, as a rational man, benefit everyone, including himself.

But what practical help does all this offer, one may ask. How should we design our punitive practices in the society in which we now live? This is the question we want to ask, and it does not seem to help simply to say that our society is built on deception and inequity. How can Marx help us with our real problem? The answer, I think, is that he cannot and obviously does not desire to do so. For Marx would say that we have not focused (as all piecemeal reform fails to focus) on what is the real problem. And this is changing the basic social relations. Marx is the last person from whom we can expect advice on how to make our intellectual and moral peace with bourgeois society. And this is surely his attraction and his value.

5. Denunciation

NIGEL WALKER, PUNISHMENT, DANGER, AND STIGMA: THE MORALITY OF CRIMINAL JUSTICE
22-42 (1980)

Organising the future . . . is not the major function of the criminal law. Even if we cannot control the future, this does not mean we must ignore the present and the past. We still need to do something about wrongful acts: to register our social disapproval, to publicly denounce them and to reaffirm the values violated by them. (Our Criminal Law, Law Reform Commission of Canada.)

[The expressive (denunciatory) view] holds that the justification for penalising an offender is that doing so expresses an important statement about the offence. A penalty declares, in effect, that in the society in question the offence is not tolerated. On the expressive view this statement is not sufficiently declared by laws which merely prohibit certain conduct: penalties must be provided and people must be sentenced.

It is important to be clear whether a "denouncer" (as I shall call someone who holds this view) is really a "reducer," or something else. If he believes that the point of declaring society's non-toleration of this or that sort of law-breaking is to strengthen people's disapproval of it, and so reduce its frequency, he is simply a reducer who believes in a particular technique. . . .

If, on the other hand, the denouncer denies that he is a mere reducer, he must tell us what it is that makes the expression of non-toleration a good thing. Sociologically-minded denouncers usually give Durkheim's answer to this question: that denunciation promotes social cohesion. If this is offered as a justification (and not as a mere description) it is implied that social cohesion is a good thing, and the answer is again a utilitarian one, although rather vaguer and harder to test than the reductive version.

It is possible, however, to be a less utilitarian denouncer, and justify penalties by talking not of any future benefit but simply of the immediate satisfaction which they give to people who know and disapprove of the offence, in much the same way as funerals and other ceremonials give satisfaction to most, if not all participants. This is probably the version of the expressive justification which comes nearest to being both non-utilitarian and non-retributive: I call it "ceremonial denunciation."

It should be easy to distinguish any version of the denunciatory justification from retributivism, although it is possible to confuse the two:

> I will start with retribution. The Old Testament concept of an eye for an eye and a tooth for a tooth no longer plays any part in our criminal law. There is, however, another aspect of retribution . . . it is that society, through the courts, must show its abhorrence of particular types of crime. . . . The courts do not have to reflect public opinion. On the other hand the courts must not disregard it. Perhaps the main duty of the court is to *lead* public opinion. [Regina v. Sargeant, (1974) 60 CR. App. R. 74.]

But that is by the way. In either form the expressive view is clearly distinguishable from the retributive. For if denunciation is to be achieved the penalty must be publicly announced, whereas retribution can be achieved by secret punishment.

Paradoxically, however, denouncers could not exist without retributivists. For the penalty could not have any of the effects in which denouncers believe (whether the giving of immediate satisfaction or the promotion of disapproval or social cohesion) unless the people upon whom it is meant to have this effect regarded it as just, in the retributive sense. This paradox, however, does not imply that the expressive view is really retributivism after all; for the latter demands that the penalty be genuinely appropriate to the offender's culpability, or actually inflicted on a culpable offender, whereas all the denouncer can demand is that those at whom he aims his effect should *believe* it to be retributively appropriate. Moreover, he cannot logically demand that the penalty should actually be inflicted: merely that it should (i) be publicly ordered and (ii) be thought to have been inflicted.

A few denouncers, however, have a more limited aim than influencing public opinion or giving satisfaction to those who are outraged by an individual offence. They see the penalty as a symbolic way of telling the offender something. That something may be either society's disapproval or the inherent wickedness of his act. This view does not require that the penalty be publicized; but it seems to require that the offender himself believe that it is going to be inflicted, in order to make him take its symbolism seriously.

JOHN KAPLAN, FOREWORD TO LAW AND SOCIETY

xiii-xvi (Inverarity, Lauderdale, and Feld, eds., 1983)

[A]cceptance of Durkheim's social theory into the sociology of law has been handicapped by several factors. First is its deceptive appearance of simplicity. His view—that a major purpose of criminal punishment is to draw formally the line between acceptable and unacceptable conduct and thereby reinforce both the solidarity of the group and the norms which have been violated—runs counter to the usual utilitarian view that the purpose of criminal punishment is to repress crime by deterrence, isolation, and so on. In addition, two specific criticisms have been leveled at the Durkheimian view. First of all, it seems to be inapplicable to the crimes we worry about most. One might argue that so far as homicide and mugging are concerned, we do not require the reinforcement of any moral boundary where everyone knows that the conduct is wrong. A second and quite different objection is that Durkheim's views of organic solidarity may be inapplicable to a modern, highly differentiated and complex society with many subgroups, all with differing norms.

The first of these criticisms is easier to answer. Although what we think of as homicide may always be regarded as wrong, the killing of a human being does not always violate our norms. We slay in war, administer capital punishment (though rarely), take life in defense of ourselves or our property, or kill accidentally in pursuit of our business (as in traffic accidents). Similarly, there are many occasions when we recognize the right to deprive someone of his property. Denunciation and punishment reinforce our views as to which of many types of functionally similar conduct violate our norms.

The second of the objections is harder to grapple with (and therefore more interesting and provocative as well). First of all, while many social scientists seem aware of the noncontractual bases of the social contract, they have, in a sense, too often taken for granted the moral underpinnings of our social life. Even Durkheim thought this mostly missing in complex societies. In fact, concepts of majority rule, fairness, and allegiance to the group can be noted even in the complex American society of today. Moreover, though Durkheimian processes are more clearly visible in relatively non-differentiated societies than in a complex one such as ours, there are enclaves within our society that do function like tribal villages. To most of us, the most familiar of these is the university.

I observed one remarkable episode myself at Stanford, the explanation of which is strikingly and surprisingly Durkheimian. The events on the Stanford campus took place during what are now referred to as "the troubles," so long ago that it will seem incomprehensible to today's students—about 1972. At that time, some students who were displeased with the state of the world had developed a pattern of disrupting classes—marching, yelling, chanting—to vent their anger with the university and the Vietnam War. Often, they were charged before the university disciplinary system, and convicted. The disciplinary system in essence said, "This is bad behavior; you shouldn't do this." However, the [students'] punishment was a term or two on probation or a suspension for the summer quarter; when they would not be attending school anyway. These punishments were hardly draconian; indeed they were seen as extremely light. The students and faculty on the disciplinary board, however, did say as clearly as they could, "Look, this is a university! Its essence is that people are coming here trying to learn. Those who disrupt classes are striking at the very heart of the educational process."

Finally, after several years of class disruption, the disciplinary system took real action. A group of students disrupted a class, as had happened many times before, but this time the board imposed a real punishment. Writing a long opinion in the name of the community and saying what the previous boards had said, it suspended them indefinitely and told them to reapply in two years so that it could be determined whether they were "ready to live in a civilized community." This banishment surprised many students because, although the university had said again and again that disrupting classes was a very serious offense, it had never before acted that way.

Knowing about deterrence, one would have expected that there would be a drop in the number of classes disrupted, and that, of course, happened; it did not take a Durkheim to predict that. Jeremy Bentham would have done the job perfectly well. What was interesting to me, however, and what changed my views as to the relevance of Durkheim's theory, was something else.

For a long time members of the faculty had wondered why the great majority of students, who disapproved of the disruptions, nonetheless stood idly by while their classes were being disrupted. On simple deterrence principles one really wouldn't expect the increase in the severity of the punishments to change the behavior of these onlookers. They, after all, were not being threatened with anything. One would have expected merely a deterrent effect on the disrupters. In any event, to protest against the punishing of the original disrupters, another group of students disrupted another class. To their—and the faculty's—enormous surprise, the students in the class stood up and hooted and yelled at them, "Get the hell out of here! You don't belong here!" The disrupters left, literally in tears.

What happened? Throwing people out of school for misbehavior actually did what Durkheim said it would do: it reaffirmed the university's value that the classroom as a place for education was not to be interfered with. Moreover, what may be more remarkable, it influenced the group's conduct as well as its values.

Since then I have looked for other examples of this Durkheimian phenomenon in the university setting and have found a few. In one law school, somewhat more recently, there had been a problem with the library. Students had been taking out books that were on reserve and returning them very casually: a three-hour book would be returned a week later. Finally, after warnings of dire punishments seemed to do no good, the judicial system there suspended for a year the student who had been the most flagrant offender. It was a very harsh punishment as nobody had ever been punished at all before—even though everyone knew such behavior was against the rules.

What happened then was very interesting. Not only did people start returning their books, which one would have expected on deterrence grounds, but in all other ways, people began to treat the library with more respect. For instance, the noise level in the library dropped, as did the number of abandoned coffee cups and other litter—and usage of the library went up. By punishing somebody for violating the library in one way, the community had reaffirmed to everybody that the library was an essential resource which everyone had to depend on, and that to make it work they had to pull together and observe certain ideas of right and wrong. It caught on, not only in terms of values, but in behavior as well.

Admittedly Durkheim's ideals apply much better to a tribal university community than to the larger society. Nonetheless, every once in a while, we can see this phenomenon writ large. The Watergate case provided an example of this. There were two positions the press and the courts as community institutions could have taken. They could have said, "Oh, well, a lot of politicians do this. So what!" Many people did say this; Ronald Reagan was widely quoted as saying that Watergate offenders weren't "real criminals." Alternatively they could have treated it as an outrage, increasing the likelihood that such political behavior would be stamped as unacceptable.

Judge Sirica, more than any other person, had the decision whether these should be regarded as serious wrongs or as trivial misconduct. By sending some people off to very stiff jail terms and acting with considerable vigor, he did his part to see that the matter was seriously regarded. Had he given the Watergate buggers (if you will pardon the expression), and those who covered up, a fifty-dollar fine each, that would have made it a very different kind of business. True, the judge apparently was also trying to get defendants to talk, but even that fact is an assertion of the importance of the matter. It is in general true that the only way to get things taken seriously is to treat them as if they were serious.

In any event, the outcome of Watergate is clear. We were deluged with political breastbeating; clean political campaign laws were passed; and Spiro Agnew, in resigning, referred to the fact that what he had done might have been wrong under the "post-Watergate morality"—as if somehow before then it was all right to take bribes.

C. THE LIMITING PRINCIPLES OF PUNISHMENT

1. In General

H. L. A. HART, ESSAYS IN JURISPRUDENCE AND PHILOSOPHY
194-196 (1983)

[O]nly in our own time has a direct frontal attack been made on the central maximizing principle of utilitarianism. This modern critique has been developed largely in the United States in the last twenty years, most notably in John Rawls's A Theory of Justice, which is the most important work of political philosophy written in English since John Stuart Mills. Rawls's work is already profoundly influential, though both its critique of utilitarianism and its positive theory of basic rights are controversial and incomplete. A similar critique of utilitarianism is now to be found among many other modern writers, American and English.

The thrust of this modern critique consists of a claim that utilitarianism "does not take seriously the distinction between persons," since it licenses the imposition of sacrifices in individual cases whenever this can be shown to advance aggregate welfare. Persons on this view are of no intrinsic value, but are merely the receptacles for the experiences which will increase or diminish the sole intrinsic value, namely aggregate welfare.

These considerations show why utilitarianism, once regarded as the great inspiration of progressive social thought, also possesses a darker, sinister side permitting the sacrifice of one individual to secure the greater happiness of others.

Accordingly, the contemporary modern philosophers of whom I have spoken, and pre-eminently Rawls in his Theory of Justice, have argued that any morally adequate political philosophy must recognize that there must be, in any morally tolerable form of social life, certain protections for the freedom and basic interests of individuals, which constitute an essential framework of individual rights. Though the pursuit of the general welfare is a legitimate and indeed necessary concern of governments, it is something to be pursued only within certain constraints imposed by recognition of such rights.

The modern philosophical defense put forward for the recognition of basic human rights does not wear the same metaphysical or conceptual dress as the earlier doctrines of the seventeenth- and eighteenth-century rights of man, which men were said to have in a state of nature or to be endowed with by their creator. Nonetheless, the most complete and articulate version of this modern critique of utilitarianism has many affinities with the theories of social contract which in the seventeenth and eighteenth centuries accompanied the doctrine of natural rights. Thus Rawls has argued in A Theory of Justice that though any rational person must know that in order to live even a minimally tolerable life he must live within a political society with an ordered government, no rational person bargaining with others on a footing of equality could agree to regard himself as bound to obey the laws of any government if his freedom and basic interests, what Mill called "the groundwork of human existence," were not given protection and treated as having priority over mere increases in aggregate welfare, even if the protection cannot be absolute.

Both the philosophical foundations of this new critique of utilitarianism and the detailed application of its doctrine of basic rights to contemporary constitutional, social and economic problems of society are still highly controversial. It cannot be said that we have had, either from the European or from American political theorists who have now become acutely conscious of the defects of an undiluted maximizing utilitarianism, a sufficiently detailed or adequately articulate theory showing the foundation for such rights and how they are related to other values which are pursued through government. Nothing is yet available of this kind comparable in clarity and detailed articulation to Bentham's elaborate exposition and application of utilitarianism. Indeed the revived doctrines of basic rights, as currently presented, are in spite of much brilliance still unconvincing. In fact, I think this is due to their authors seeking to design their point of view too exclusively in terms of the ways in which utilitarianism has ignored certain values taken to be uncontroversial, whereas what is first needed is some more radical and detailed consideration of the ways in which rights relate to other values pursued in society. Among such writers examples could now be found in both the Conservative Right and the Liberal Left of the political spectrum. The work of these writers certainly demands careful assessment, but that is a task for another time.

Yet it is plain that a theory of rights is urgently called for. During the last half century man's inhumanity to man has been such that the most basic and elementary freedoms and protections have been denied to innumerable men and women guilty, if of anything, only of claiming such freedoms and protections for themselves and others, and sometimes these have been denied to them on the specious pretense that this denial is demanded by the general welfare of a society. So the protection of a doctrine of basic human rights limiting what a state may do to its citizens seems to be precisely what the political problems of our own age most urgently require, or at any rate they require this more urgently than a call to maximise general utility. And in fact the philosophical developments which I have sketched have been accompanied by a growth, recently accelerated, of an international human rights movement.

2. Retribution as a Limiting Principle

H. L. A. HART, PUNISHMENT AND RESPONSIBILITY
10-13 (1968)

[I]n relation to any social institution, after stating what general aim or value its maintenance fosters we should enquire whether there are any and if so what principles limiting the unqualified pursuit of that aim or value. Just because the pursuit of any single social aim always has its restrictive qualifier, our main social institutions always possess a plurality of features which can only be understood as a compromise between partly discrepant principles. . . .

. . . [T]hough we may be clear as to what values the practice of punishment is to promote, we have still to answer as a question of Distribution "Who may be punished?" Secondly, if in answer to this question we say "only an offender for an offence" this admission of retribution in Distribution is not a principle from which anything follows as to the severity or amount of punishment; in particular it neither licenses nor requires, as Retribution in General Aim does, more severe punishments than deterrence or other utilitarian criteria would require.

The root question to be considered is, however, why we attach the moral importance which we do to retribution in Distribution. Here I shall consider the efforts made to show that restriction of punishment to offenders is a simple consequence of whatever principles (Retributive or Utilitarian) constitute the Justifying Aim of punishment.

The standard example used by philosophers to bring out the importance of retribution in Distribution is that of a wholly innocent person who has not even unintentionally done anything which the law punishes if done intentionally. It is supposed that in order to avert some social catastrophe officials of the system fabricate evidence on which he is charged, tried, and convicted and sent to prison or death. Or it is supposed that without resort to any fraud more persons may be deterred from crime if wives and children of offenders were punished vicariously for their crimes. In some forms this kind of thing may be ruled out by a consistent, sufficiently comprehensive utilitarianism. Certainly expedients involving fraud or faked charges might be very difficult to justify on utilitarian grounds. . . . Certainly vicarious punishment of an offender's family might [avert some evils,] and legal systems have occasionally though exceptionally resorted to this. An example . . . is the Roman *Lex Quisquis,* providing for the punishment of the children of those guilty of *majestas.* In extreme cases many might still think it right to resort to these expedients but we should do so with the sense of sacrificing an important principle. We should be conscious of choosing the lesser of two evils, and this would be inexplicable if the principle sacrificed to utility were itself only a requirement of utility.

Similarly, the moral importance of the restriction of punishment to the offender cannot be explained as merely a consequence of the principle that the General Justifying Aim is Retribution for immorality involved in breaking the law. Retribution in the Distribution of punishment has a value quite independent of Retribution as Justifying Aim. This is shown by the fact that we attach importance to the restrictive principle that only offenders may be punished, even where breach of this law might not be thought immoral. Indeed even where the laws themselves are hideously immoral as in Nazi Germany, e.g. forbidding activities (helping the sick or destitute of some racial group) which might be thought morally obligatory, the absence of the principle restricting punishment to the offender would be a further *special* iniquity; whereas admission of this principle would represent some residual respect for justice shown in the administration of morally bad laws.

NIGEL WALKER, PUNISHMENT, DANGER, AND STIGMA: THE MORALITY OF CRIMINAL JUSTICE

25-26 (1980)

The "limiting" retributivist does not insist that severity of the penalty should match the offender's culpability; only that it should not exceed what would match it. In other words, the penalty could be the minimum necessary to achieve other aims (e.g., deterrence) so long as it was not excessively severe by retributive standards.

The other important version of the retributive point of view can be called "distributive." It insists merely that a penalty should not be inflicted on a person who has not culpably broken a rule. It does not insist that the severity of the penalty should either match or be limited by culpability. The principle "no penalty without culpability" is observed, in theory at least, by all civilised penal codes, although many of them allow exceptions (as in the case of offences of "strict liability").

Most penal codes are also constructed on lines consistent with limiting retributivism, providing *maximum* sentences which set the upper limit to severity without obliging the court to impose the maximum. (Many such systems, however, have obligatory penalties for a few offences, such as death or "life" for murder, which are more consistent with the pure form of the retributive theory.) A few systems, such as the Scots', set no upper limit to the length of a prison sentence or the amount of a fine when imposed by the highest court, but even they honour the principle of "no penalty without culpability."

Limiting and distributive retributivists are able to compromise with holders of non-retributive points of view. Indeed, their views *imply* some other, non-retributive justification of penalties, since all they offer [are] principles for restricting punishment, not reasons for imposing it.

retributive justification of penalties, since all they offer [are] principles for restricting punishment, not reasons for imposing it.

HERBERT L. PACKER, THE LIMITS OF THE CRIMINAL SANCTION
65-66, 67-69 (1968)

If all that is at stake is the propensity of punishment to scare people, if our image of man is exclusively that of the rational hedonist who will do anything that promises to enhance his well-being if he thinks he can get away with it, then it is hard to answer the argument that permitting excuses weakens the deterrent efficacy of the criminal law. But if deterrence (or prevention) is more broadly conceived as a complex psychological phenomenon meant primarily to create and reinforce the conscious morality and the unconscious habitual controls of the law-abiding, then the flank of the old argument may be turned. Punishment of the morally innocent does not reinforce one's sense of identification as a law-abider, but rather undermines it. A society in which excuses were not allowed would be a society in which virtue would indeed have to be its own reward. What could be more certain to undermine one's sense that it is important to avoid the intentional or reckless or negligent infliction of harm upon others than the knowledge that, if one inflicts harm, he may be punished even though he cannot be blamed for having done so? If we are to be held liable for what we cannot help doing, there is little incentive to avoid what we can help doing. One may as well be hanged for a sheep as a lamb. . . .

Law, including the criminal law, must in a free society be judged ultimately on the basis of its success in promoting human autonomy and the capacity for individual human growth and development. The prevention of crime is an essential aspect of the environmental protection required if autonomy is to flourish. It is, however, a negative aspect and one which, pursued with single-minded zeal, may end up creating an environment in which all are safe but none is free. The limitations included in the concept of culpability are justified not by an appeal to the Kantian dogma of "just deserts" but by their usefulness in keeping the state's powers of protection at a decent remove from the lives of its citizens. . . .

. . . [S]ingle-minded pursuit of the goal of crime prevention will slight and in the end defeat the ultimate goal of law in a free society, which is to liberate rather than to restrain. Human autonomy is an illusion if we make it conditional on human perfection. . . . I see an important limiting principle in the criminal law's traditional emphasis on blameworthiness as a prerequisite to the imposition of punishment. But it is a *limiting* principle, not a justification for action. It is wrong to say that we should punish persons simply because they commit offenses under circumstances that we can call blameworthy. It is right to say that we should not punish those who commit offenses unless we can say that their conduct is blameworthy. . . .

The view I take of the role of culpability in the justification for punishment is an instrumental one. I see this limitation on the utilitarian position as desirable not for any inherent quality that it possesses but because it serves ends that I think require attention in a criminal system. It does so in several different ways. First, it establishes a firm basis for resisting the attenuation of the offense as a component in the definition of punishment. Without an offense—a more or less specifically defined species of conduct—there can be no basis for imputing blame. A man may be a danger to others, or in need of help, or any other equivalent in the current cant that denotes an inconvenient human being whom we would like to get out of the way; but unless he has committed an offense, unless he has done something rather than merely been something, we cannot say that he has been culpable. And, it follows from the view taken of culpability as a necessary condition, that he cannot be found guilty through the criminal process and subjected to criminal punishment. . . .

Another aspect of this instrumental case for culpability is that there is a rough correspondence between the dictates of the culpability limitation and aspects of the desirable operation of the criminal sanction. People ought in general to be able to plan their conduct with some assurance that they can avoid entanglement with the criminal law; by the same token the enforcers and appliers of the law should not waste their time lurking in the bushes ready to trap the offender who is unaware that he is offending. It is precisely the fact that in its normal and characteristic operation the criminal law provides this opportunity and this protection to people in their everyday lives that makes it a tolerable institution in a free society. Take this away, and the criminal law ceases to be a guide to the well-intentioned and a restriction on the restraining power of the state. Take it away is precisely what you do, however, when you abandon culpability as the basis for imposing punishment. While it may often serve the state's purposes not to interfere with its citizens unless they have acted with foresight, on many occasions their foresight or lack of it may seem immaterial. If we leave to a purely utilitarian calculus the decision whether a man's innocence or ignorance shall count for him, the answer on any given occasion will be uncertain. Only by providing the shield of a culpability requirement can this desirable aspect of the criminal law be preserved.

Finally, the singular power of the criminal law resides, as I have argued, not in its coercive effect on those caught in its toils but rather in its effect on the rest of us. That effect, I have tried to show, is a highly complex one. It includes elements of coercion and of terror: if I do as he did, I too shall suffer for it. But it also includes conscious and unconscious moralizing and habit-forming effects that go far beyond the crassness of a narrowly conceived deterrence. If it is not thought enough of a justification that the law *be* fair, the argument may seem appealing that a criminal law system cannot attract and retain the respect of its most important constituents—the habitually law-abiding—unless it *is seen to be* fair. And whatever fairness may be thought to mean on the procedural side, its simplest (if most neglected) meaning is that no one should be subjected to punishment without having an opportunity to litigate the issue of his culpability. Even imagining a system in which, once forbidden physical conduct has taken place, no excuses are listened to is enough to show the importance of making culpability a necessary condition of liability to punishment.

SAMUEL BUTLER, EREWHON
112-118 (1872) (Penguin ed. 1970)

In Erewhon as in other countries there are some courts of justice that deal with special subjects. Misfortune generally, as I have above explained, is considered more or less criminal, but it admits of classification, and a court is assigned to each of the main heads under which it can be supposed to fall. Not very long after I had reached the capital I strolled into the Personal Bereavement Court, and was both much interested and pained by listening to the trial of a man who was accused of having just lost a wife to whom he had been tenderly attached, and who had left him with three little children, of whom the eldest was only three years old.

The defense which the prisoner's counsel endeavoured to establish was, that the prisoner had never really loved his wife; but it broke down completely, for the public prosecutor called witness after witness who deposed to the fact that the couple had been devoted to one another, and the prisoner repeatedly wept as incidents were put in evidence that reminded him of the irreparable nature of the loss he had sustained. The jury returned a verdict of guilty after very little deliberation, but recommended the prisoner to mercy on the ground that he had but recently insured his wife's life for a considerable sum, and might be deemed lucky inasmuch as he had received the money without demur from the insurance company, though he had only paid two premiums.

I have just said that jury found the prisoner guilty. When the judge passed sentence, I was struck by the way in which the prisoner's counsel was rebuked for having referred to a work in which the guilt of such misfortunes as the prisoner's was extenuated to a degree that roused the indignation of the court.

"We shall have," said the judge, "these crude and subversary books from time to time until it is recognized as an axiom of morality that luck is the only fit object of human veneration. How far a man has any right to be more lucky and hence more venerable than his neighbours, is a point that always has been, and always will be settled proximately by a kind of higgling and haggling of the market, and ultimately by brute force; but however this may be, it stands to reason that no man should be allowed to be unlucky to more than a very moderate extent."

Then, turning to the prisoner, the judge continued:—"You have suffered a great loss. Nature attaches a severe penalty to such offenses, and human law must emphasize the decrees of nature. But for the recommendation of the jury

I should have given you six months' hard labour. I will, however, commute your sentence to one of three months, with the option of a fine of twenty-five percent of the money you have received from the insurance company."

The prisoner thanked the judge, and said that as he had no one to look after his children if he was sent to prison, he would embrace the option mercifully permitted him by his lordship, and pay the sum he had named. He was then removed from the dock.

The next case was that of a youth barely arrived at man's estate, who was charged with having been swindled out of large property during his minority by his guardian, who was also one of his nearest relations. His father had been long dead, and it was for this reason that this offense came on for trial in the Personal Bereavement Court. The lad, who was undefended, pleaded that he was young, inexperienced, greatly in awe of his guardian and without independent professional advice. "Young man," said the judge sternly, "do not talk nonsense. People have no right to be young, inexperienced, greatly in awe of their guardians, and without independent professional advice. In such indiscretions they outrage the moral sense of their friends, and they must expect to suffer accordingly." He then ordered the prisoner to apologize to his guardian, and to receive twelve strokes with a cat-of-nine-tails.

But I shall perhaps best convey to the reader an idea of the entire perversion of thought which exists among this extraordinary people, by describing the public trial of a man who was accused of pulmonary consumption—an offense which was punished with death until quite recently. It did not occur till I had been some months in the country, and I am deviating from chronological order in giving it here; but I had perhaps better do so in order that I may exhaust this subject before proceeding to others. Moreover, I should never come to an end were I to keep to a strictly narrative form, and detail the infinite absurdities with which I daily came in contact.

The prisoner was placed in the dock and the jury were sworn much as in Europe; almost all our own modes of procedure were reproduced, even to the requiring the prisoner to plead guilty or not guilty. He pleaded not guilty, and the case proceeded. The evidence for the prosecution was very strong; but I must do the court justice to observe that the trial was absolutely impartial. Counsel for the prisoner was allowed to urge everything that could be said in his defense: The line taken was that the prisoner was simulating consumption in order to defraud an insurance company, from which he was about to buy an annuity, and that he hoped thus to obtain it on more advantageous terms. If this could have been shown to be the case he would have escaped a criminal prosecution, and been sent to a hospital as for a moral ailment. The view, however, was one which could not be reasonably sustained, in spite of all the ingenuity and eloquence of one of the most celebrated advocates of the country. The case was only too clear, for the prisoner was almost at the point of death, and it was astonishing that he had not been tried and convicted long previously. His coughing was incessant during the whole trial, and it was all that the two jailors in charge of him could do to keep him on his legs until it was over.

The summing up of the judge was admirable. He dwelt upon every point that could be construed in favour of the prisoner, but as he proceeded it became clear that the evidence was too convincing to admit of doubt, and there was but one opinion in the court as to the impending verdict when the jury retired from the box. They were absent for about ten minutes, and on their return the foreman pronounced the prisoner guilty. There was a faint murmur of applause, but it was instantly repressed. The judge then proceeded to pronounce sentence in words which I can never forget, and which I copied out into a notebook the next day from the report that was published in the leading newspaper. I must condense it somewhat, and nothing which I could say would give more than a faint idea of the solemn, not to say majestic, severity with which it was delivered. The sentence was as follows:—

> Prisoner at the bar, you have been accused of the great crime of labouring under pulmonary consumption, and after an impartial trial before a jury of your countrymen, you have been found guilty. Against the justice of the verdict I can say nothing: the evidence against you was conclusive, and it only remains for me to pass such a sentence upon you as shall satisfy the ends of the law. That sentence must be a very severe one. It pains me much to see one who is yet so young, and whose prospects in life were otherwise so excellent, brought to this distressing condition by a constitution which I can only regard as radically vicious; but yours is no case for compassion: this is not your first offense: you have led a career of crime, and have only profited by the leniency shown you upon past occasions, to offend yet more seriously against the laws and institutions of your country. You were convicted of aggravated bronchitis last year: and I find that though you are now only twenty-three years old, you have been imprisoned on no less than fourteen occasions for illnesses of a more or less hateful character; in fact, it is not too much to say that you have spent the greater part of your life in jail.
>
> It is all very well for you to say that you came of unhealthy parents, and had a severe accident in your childhood which permanently undermined your constitution; excuses such as these are the ordinary refuge of the criminal; but they cannot for one moment be listened to by the ear of justice. I am not here to enter upon curious metaphysical questions as to the origin of this or that—questions to which there would be no end were their introduction once tolerated, and which would result in throwing the only guilt on the tissues of the primordial cell, or on the elementary gases. There is no question of how you came to be wicked, but only this—namely, are you wicked or not? This has been decided in the affirmative, neither can I hesitate for a single moment to say that it has been decided justly. You are a bad and dangerous person, and stand branded in the eyes of your fellow-countrymen with one of the most heinous known offenses.
>
> It is not my business to justify the law: the law may in some cases have its inevitable hardships, and I may feel regret at times that I have not the option of passing a less severe sentence than I am compelled to do. But yours is no such case; on the contrary, had not the capital punishment for consumption been abolished, I should certainly inflict it now.
>
> It is intolerable that an example of such terrible enormity should be allowed to go at large unpunished. Your presence in the society of respectable people would lead the less able-bodied to think more lightly of all forms of illness;

neither can it be permitted that you should have the chance of corrupting unborn beings who might hereafter pester you. The unborn must not be allowed to come near you: and this not so much for their protection (for they are our natural enemies), as for our own; for since they will not be utterly gainsaid, it must be seen to that they shall be quartered upon those who are least likely to corrupt them.

But independently of this consideration, and independently of the physical guilt which attaches itself to a crime so great as yours, there is yet another reason why we should be unable to show you mercy, even if we were inclined to do so. I refer to the existence of a class of men who lie hidden among us, and who are called physicians. Were the severity of the law or the current feeling of the country to be relaxed ever so slightly, these abandoned persons, who are now compelled to practise secretly and who can be consulted only at the greatest risk, would become frequent visitors in every household; their organization and their intimate acquaintance with all family secrets would give them a power, both social and political, which nothing could resist. The head of the household would become subordinate to the family doctor, who would interfere between man and wife, between master and servant, until the doctors should be the only depositaries of power in the nation, and have all that we hold precious at their mercy. A time of universal dephysicalization would ensue; medicine-vendors of all kinds would abound in our streets and advertise in all our newspapers. There is one remedy for this, and one only. It is that which the laws of this country have long received and acted upon, and consists in the sternest repression of all diseases whatsoever, as soon as their existence is made manifest to the eye of the law. Would that that eye were far more piercing than it is.

But I will enlarge no further upon things that are themselves so obvious. You may say that it is not your fault. The answer is ready enough at hand, and it amounts to this—that if you had been born of healthy and well-to-do parents, and been well taken care of when you were a child, you would never have offended against the laws of your country, nor found yourself in your present disgraceful position. If you tell me that you had no hand in your parentage and education, and that it is therefore unjust to lay these things to your charge, I answer that whether your being in a consumption is your fault or no, it is a fault in you and it is my duty to see that against such faults as this the commonwealth shall be protected. You may say that it is your misfortune to be criminal; I answer that it is your crime to be unfortunate.

Lastly, I should point out that even if the jury had acquitted—a supposition that I cannot seriously entertain—I should have felt it my duty to inflict a sentence hardly less severe than that which I must pass at present; for the more you had been found guiltless of the crime imputed to you, the more you would have been found guilty of one hardly less heinous—I mean the crime of having been maligned unjustly.

I do not hesitate, therefore, to sentence you to imprisonment, with hard labour, for the rest of your miserable existence. During that period I would earnestly entreat you to repent of the wrongs you have done already, and to entirely reform the constitution of your whole body. I entertain but little hope that you will pay attention to my advice; you are already far too abandoned. Did it rest with myself, I should add nothing in mitigation of the sentence which I have passed, but it is the merciful provision of the law that even the most hardened criminal shall be allowed some one of the three official remedies, which is to be prescribed at the time of his conviction. I shall therefore order that you receive two tablespoonfuls of castor oil daily, until the pleasure of the court be further known.

When the sentence was concluded the prisoner acknowledged in a few scarcely audible words that he was justly punished, and that he had had a fair trial. He was then removed to the prison from which he was never to return. There was a second attempt at applause when the judge had finished speaking, but as before it was at once repressed; and though the feeling of the court was strongly against the prisoner, there was no show of any violence against him, if one may except a little hooting from the bystanders when he was being removed in the prisoners' van. Indeed, nothing struck me more during my whole sojourn in the country, than the general respect for law and order.

JOHN KAPLAN AND JEROME SKOLNICK, CRIMINAL JUSTICE: CASES AND MATERIALS
79 (1982)

Even if the state decided that deterrence, incapacitation, rehabilitation or any one of a number of other reasons would justify intervention by the state in an individual's life, the limiting principle requiring that retribution be appropriate would protect the individual, unless his conduct in a sense was blameworthy. This can be seen as a protection to the individual against the power of the state and a guarantee of security from punishment, including rehabilitation, for those who are not morally culpable.

Fathers shall not be put to death for their children, nor children for their fathers; a man shall be put to death only for his own sin.[5]

Certainly, we would increase deterrence by punishing a son for the sins of his father. Indeed, Soviet law until relatively recently provided serious punishment for the family of a Soviet citizen who unlawfully defected. In the United States, parents are sometimes civilly liable to pay for damage done by their children up to a given amount—often $300. Is it possible that in both these cases the point is not so much to deter the wrongdoer by threatening to punish his loved ones, but rather to make those close to an individual exercise proper supervision?[6]

5. Deuteronomy 24:16, The New English Bible (1970).
6. For further discussion involving the limitations upon criminal punishment see Chapters 16-18.

II

CULPABILITY

2

THE REQUIREMENT OF AN ACT

PROCTOR v. STATE

Criminal Court of Appeals of Oklahoma
176 P. 771 (1918)

GALBRAITH, Special Judge. The plaintiff in error was convicted of "keeping a place, to wit, a two-story building, with the intent and for the purpose of unlawfully selling, bartering, and giving away spirituous, vinous, fermented and malt liquors," etc.

To the information a demurrer was interposed upon the ground that the information fails to charge a public offense . . . that section 4 of chapter 26, Session Laws of Oklahoma 1913, on which said information is based, is unconstitutional and void.

The statute under which the charge was laid (section 4 of chapter 26, Session Laws 1913) reads as follows:

> Sec. 4. It shall be unlawful for any person to rent to another or keep a place with the intention of, or for the purpose of manufacturing, selling, bartering, giving away, or otherwise furnishing, any spirituous, vinous, fermented or malt liquors. Any person violating any provision of this section shall be punished by a fine of not less than fifty ($50.00) dollars, nor more than two thousand ($2,000.00) dollars, and by imprisonment of not less than thirty (30) days in the county jail, nor more than five (5) years in the state penitentiary.

It is alleged upon this appeal that the demurrer to the information was improperly overruled.

It is argued that the above statute is in excess of the power vested in the Legislature, in this, that it makes a mere intention, unexecuted, and not connected with any overt act, a crime, and that this is an impossible thing in organized society under a constitutional government. It is further argued that the ownership of property, namely, "the keeping of a place," is an entirely lawful act and that, when this lawful act is accompanied with an unlawful intent to violate the law at some future and indefinite time, that cannot be declared by statute to be a crime, so long as the unlawful intent is not connected with some overt act, to place the unlawful intent into operation by possession of intoxicating liquors only actual "sale or barter"; that this statute runs counter to the first and fundamental principles of law and is absolutely inoperative and void.

It is admitted on behalf of the state that ownership of property, that is, "the keeping of a place," is an innocent and lawful act, but it is contended that this statute was enacted in the exercise of the police power, and that, if the Legislature determined that "the keeping of a place" with the purpose and intent of selling, bartering, and giving away of intoxicating liquors was detrimental to the good morals and public welfare, or was essential in the enforcement of the prohibitory law, it was within the legislative power to declare such use of property to be criminal, and an offense against the law; that the statute itself does not run counter to the fundamental principles of the law; and that it does not condemn the ownership or use of property, a mere "keeping of a place," but, when property is kept or used with the unlawful intent to violate the law, it is within the condemnation of the statute and is properly denominated a crime; that the keeping a place connected with an intent to violate the law constitutes an overt act and may properly be declared to be an offense against the law. The following excerpt from the Attorney General's brief will render his position clear:

> Can it be said that the Legislature intended to make that punishable which is absolutely incapable of proof? An "unexecuted intent" to do a thing amounts merely to a thought, and thoughts without action cannot be punished and were never intended to be punished. But it may be said that, if a person shall establish a building or place without having possession of liquor, and thereafter should say to several of his friends that some time in the future he intended to sell liquors in that particular building or place, what is to prevent his punishment under the laws?
>
> Here we have the keeping of the place and his voluntary statements that he intends to use such place unlawfully in the future. Our answer is that there must exist a present keeping and a present intent, and this keeping and intent, coupled, constitute the overt act. The intent is a question of fact, not of law. No intent, however felonious, unless coupled with some overt act, is criminal.

It will be observed that here is a clear admission on the part of the state that the information in the instant case was insufficient, inasmuch as the unlawful intent was not connected directly with some overt act and therefore that the demurrer thereto was well taken. It cannot be true that "the keeping of a place," coupled with the present intent to violate the law, constitutes an overt act. It is admitted that "the keeping of a place" is an innocent thing, and that an unexecuted criminal intent is not punishable as a crime, and therefore that no crime is charged.

The possession or ownership of liquors is not alleged in the information, nor is it alleged that the liquors were manufactured, bartered, or given away in the place kept. The information does not attempt to charge an overt act or any attempt to place the unlawful intention into execution. As it stands, the information upon its face charges: First, the keeping of a place, an admittedly lawful act; and, second, the possession of an unexecuted unlawful intent to barter, sell, or give away liquor. And it is admitted that this unlawful intent, so long as unexecuted, amounts merely to a thought, and is not subject to punishment. In the language of Mr. Justice Sherwood, of the Supreme Court of Missouri: "With a mere guilty intent unconnected with an overt act, or outward manifestation, the law has no concern." Ex parte Smith, 135 Mo. 223, 36 S.W. 628, 33 L.R.A. 606, 53 Am. St. Rep. 576.

So in the instant case the information merely charges an innocent act, "the keeping of a place," and the possession of an unlawful, unexecuted intent, and attempts to make that a crime. There is no overt act charged in the information in connection with the unlawful intent. It is true the charging part of the information is in the language of the statute, and would be sufficient if the statute defined a crime, but the statute itself fails to define a crime, inasmuch as it attempts to make an innocent act, namely "keeping a place," accompanied with an unlawful and unexecuted intent to violate the law, a crime. This the Legislature had no power to do, whatever may have been its intention in enacting the statute under consideration. To constitute a crime there must be some omission or commission.

An intent to commit a crime is not indictable, and, although the intent, is in general, of the very essence of a crime, some overt act is the only sufficient evidence of the criminal intent. Kelley's Crim. Law & Prac. par. 5; 4 Blackstone Comm. 21, Howell v. Stewart, 54 Mo. 400; State v. Painter, 67 Mo. 84. The essential elements necessary to constitute a crime under the law are enumerated in Blackstone Comm. book 4, p.20, as follows:

> An involuntary act, as it has no claim to merit, so neither can it induce any guilt; the concurrence of the will, when it has its choice either to do or to avoid the fact in question being the only thing that renders human action either praiseworthy or culpable. Indeed, to make a complete crime cognizable by human laws, there must be both a will and an act. For, though, in foro conscientiae, a fixed design or will to do an unlawful act is almost as heinous as the commission of it, yet as no temporal tribunal can search the heart, or fathom the intention of the mind, otherwise than as they are demonstrated by outward actions, it therefore cannot punish for what it cannot know. For which reason, in all temporal jurisdictions, an overt act, or some open evidence of an intended crime, is necessary in order to demonstrate the depravity of the will, before the man is liable to punishment. And, as a vicious will without a vicious act is no civil crime, so, on the other hand, an unwarrantable act without a vicious will is no crime at all. So that to constitute a crime against human laws there must be, first, a vicious will; and, secondly, an unlawful act consequent upon such vicious will.

To the same effect Mr. Bishop, in his work on Criminal Law, vol. 1, announces the rule applicable to the question under consideration as follows, in section 204:

> Now the state that complains in criminal causes, does not suffer from the mere imaginings of men. To entitle her to complain, therefore, some act must have followed the unlawful thought. This doctrine is fundamental, and, in a general way, universal; but slight differences in its common law applications appear in the books, and now and then a statute is enacted departing from judicial precedent.

In section 206:

> Sec. 206. From the foregoing views results the rule established in the legal authorities that an act and evil intent must combine to constitute in law a crime.

And in section 207:

> Sec. 207. And generally, perhaps always, the act and intent must, to constitute an offense, concur in point of time.

We quite agree with Justice Sherwood that:

> Human laws and human agencies have not yet arrived at such a degree of perfection as to be able without some overt act done, to discern and to determine by what intent or purpose the human heart is actuated.

We conclude that "the keeping of a place" with the unlawful purpose and intent to sell, barter, or give away intoxicating liquors cannot be declared to be a crime, for the reason that such an act, although connected with an unlawful intent, still lacks an essential element necessary to constitute a crime under the law, in this, that the statute fails to connect such unlawful intent with any overt act, as a result or consequence, and further fails to charge the possession of the liquors, the very means essential to the consummation of the unlawful purpose to violate the prohibitory law, and therefore the statute under consideration does not define a crime, and that the information in the instant case did not charge an offense, and the demurrer thereto was well taken, and should have been sustained.

It is therefore ordered that the judgment of conviction be vacated, and the cause remanded, with direction to the trial court to discharge the accused.

Notes and Questions

1. Courts and scholars often describe the requirement of an act as a fundamental necessity of criminal punishment in a civilized state. Why? Is it

that we do not want to punish people merely for their thoughts or for their evil dispositions? If so, why not? Or is it the difficulty of proving evil intent, unless the person has committed some act manifesting it? Or is it that we feel that the state should allow individuals to know precisely at what point they will be crossing the line beyond which they will incur punishment?

One commentator[1] has explained the requirement of an act:

> It may hardly seem a startling notion that the criminal law, or law in general for that matter, is concerned with conduct—people's actions (including their verbal and other expressive actions) and their failures to act. Yet there is nothing in the nature of things that compels this focus. The criminal law could be concerned with people's thoughts and emotions, with their personality patterns and character structures. It is true that if this rather than conduct was the focus, it would still be expedient in most cases to ascertain these essentially internal characteristics through inquiry into conduct. But if these internal characteristics were the focus, conduct would simply be evidence of what we are interested in rather than the thing itself; and we would not hesitate to use other evidence to the extent that it became available. If, for example, we could determine through projective tests like the Rorschach or through other and more sophisticated forms of psychological testing that a given individual was likely to inflict serious physical injury on someone, someday, somewhere, and if we viewed conduct as a prerequisite rather than as merely evidentiary, we would presumably not hesitate to inflict punishment on that person for his propensities, or, as the old cliché has it, for thinking evil thoughts. We might rationalize this simply by saying that we were punishing him for the offense of having flunked his Rorschach test, but we would then be acting on a somewhat Pickwickian definition of "conduct."
>
> Why do we not do so? The obvious historical answer is that, aside from a few antiquarian anomalies such as the offense of imagining the King's death, we have not been sufficiently stirred by the danger presented or sufficiently confident of our ability to discern propensities in the absence of conduct to use the instruments of the criminal law in this fashion. For some it may be enough to rejoice that historically this was so and to rest on that historical accident for the present and the future, but I think that a further answer is required. This answer turns, in my view, on the idea of culpability, that necessary but insufficient condition of criminal liability that is an important part of our integrated theory of criminal punishment.
>
> Among the notions associated with the concept of "culpability" are those of free will and human autonomy. I do not mean this in any deep philosophical sense but in a contingent and practical social sense. It is important, especially in a society that likes to describe itself as "free" and "open," that a government should be empowered to coerce people only for what they do and not for what they are.
>
> If this is important for law generally, it is a fortiori important for that most coercive of legal instruments, the criminal law. Now, this self-denying ordinance can be and often is attacked as being inconsistent with the facts of human nature. People may in fact have little if any greater capacity to control their conduct

1. Herbert Packer, The Limits of the Criminal Sanction 73-75, 76 (1968).

(some say in part, some say in whole) than their emotions or their thoughts. It is therefore either unrealistic or hypocritical, so the argument runs, to deal with conduct as willed or to treat it differently from personality or character.

This attack is, however, misconceived. Neither philosophic concepts nor psychological realities are actually at issue in the criminal law. The idea of free will in relation to conduct is not, in the legal system, a statement of fact, but rather a value preference having very little to do with the metaphysics of determinism and free will. The fallacy that legal values describe physical reality is a very common one. . . . But we need to dispose of it here, because it is such a major impediment to rational thought about the criminal law. Very simply, the law treats man's conduct as autonomous and willed, not because it is, but because it is desirable to proceed as if it were. It is desirable because the capacity of the individual human being to live his life in reasonable freedom from socially imposed external constraints (the only kind with which the law is concerned) would be fatally impaired unless the law provided a *locus poenitentiae,* a point of no return beyond which external constraints may be imposed but before which the individual is free—not free of whatever compulsions determinists tell us he labors under but free of the very specific social compulsions of the law. . . .

It may seem anomalous, particularly to those with some training in the conventional doctrines of the criminal law, that we should fasten here on conduct as limitation on culpability. The orthodox view is that culpability is primarily a matter of the actor's mental state, rather than of the conduct in which he engages. . . . And yet, the paradoxical fact is that the limitation of criminal punishment to conduct constitutes the first and most important line of defense against erosion of the idea of culpability, for it keeps the criminal law from becoming purely the servant of the utilitarian ideal of prevention.

2. Note that not all moral systems require an act as a prerequisite to sinning. The Baltimore Catechism teaches:

64. What is Actual Sin?

Actual sin is any willful thought, desire, word, action, or omission forbidden by the law of God.[2]

The Sermon on the Mount in two places indicates that such a rule applies in the realm of heavenly judgment.

You have learned that our forefathers were told, "Do not commit murder; anyone who commits murder must be brought to judgment." But what I tell you is this: Anyone who nurses anger against his brother must be brought to judgment.

You have learned that they were told, "Do not commit adultery." But what I tell you is this: If a man looks on a woman with a lustful eye, he has already committed adultery with her in his heart.[3]

2. This We Believe: By This We Live, Revised Edition of the Baltimore Catechism No. 3, pp. 49-50.

3. Matthew 5 (21-22, 27-28) New English Bible (1970).

Is there a reason why we might wish to apply a different rule in earthly courts?

3. Is the *Proctor* court concerned that the conduct proscribed by the express terms of the statute has caused no one any harm? Should that matter when the legislature has forbidden the conduct?

4. The principle that the criminal law punishes only a person who has committed an act needs considerable qualification. According to the court, the prosecutor here failed to charge Proctor with an act in connection with the alleged culpable intent. Is it true that Proctor never committed such an act? How did the prosecutor prove that Proctor had the requisite evil intent?

5. The *Proctor* court suggests that it would have been a different case had the defendant been charged with possessing liquor. Why? Is possession of something an act? Specifically, should possession of certain types of material that the legislature has deemed dangerous be regarded as an act? Statutes often do make such possession criminal. An example is section 5851 of Title 26 U.S.C., which provides:

> It shall be unlawful for any person to possess any firearm which has not been registered as required by Section 5841. Whenever on trial for a violation of this section the defendant is shown to have or to have had possession of such firearm, such possession shall be deemed sufficient evidence to authorize conviction, unless the defendant explains such possession to the satisfaction of the jury.

Under this statute, how would you decide the following case? The appellant's brief in United States v. P__________, No. 17399 (9th Cir. Oct. 2, 1961), stated the facts and argued as follows:

> Appellant graduated in June 1960 from Jackson Union High School, with, among others, one Larry B__________ (hereinafter referred to as Larry), also 18 years of age. One night during the following Christmas season appellant, while visiting Larry (at the Globe Hotel in Jackson, where Larry resided), saw a sawed-off shotgun on the bureau in Larry's room. Appellant did not handle or touch the gun. Later, on Slav Christmas, about January 5, 1961, appellant saw Larry shoot the gun into the air in the alley behind the Globe Hotel. This was in accordance with a Slavic custom. Again, appellant did not handle or touch the gun. Later, and on January 23, 1961, Larry wanted to go to Richmond to pay a traffic citation, and thereafter visit his father, stepmother and brother, Ronald, at Rodeo, California. Appellant agreed to drive Larry down. When appellant went to pick up Larry on the evening of January 23, Larry had the gun in his hand, got into the front seat and deposited it beside him. Because appellant was afraid of the gun, either he or Larry put it under the seat. After arriving in Rodeo, the following morning, at the invitation of Larry's stepmother, they had breakfast at the __________ home. After breakfast, appellant drove Larry, his brother Ronald, and Ronald's fiancee, Dorothy, to Richmond, where Larry paid his traffic ticket. On returning to Rodeo, at the request of the __________ boys, appellant stopped in front of a store and while he and

Dorothy sat in the car, the __________ boys entered the store and bought a carton of shells. They drove to the __________ home in Rodeo and from there went to a field which faces on the water (the San Francisco Bay) and there the __________ boys engaged in some target shooting. They passed the gun over to appellant and permitted him to fire it twice. These two brief moments (actually seconds) constitute the only physical handling of the gun by appellant (unless we include a possible physical handling for seconds when either appellant or Larry put the gun under the seat of the car). Later, the __________ boys took the gun into the house and put it on the top of the sewing machine. While appellant was watching television, Dorothy attempted to hand the gun over to Ronald, it went off, and she was mortally wounded. . . .

The law is clear. The possession required in these cases (absent a satisfactory explanation, and it must be remembered that a satisfactory explanation was given in this case) is as prescribed in the following language from the cases. . . .

In Rodella v. United States, Ninth Circuit, decided December 31, 1960, the Court of Appeals, through Judge Barnes, said:

> Possession means having something in one's power. Cf: 33 Words & Phrases, Perm. Edition 75, and cases cited. Actual possession exists when the thing is in the immediate possession or control of the party. Mullaney v. United States, 9 Cir., 1936, 82 F.2d 638, 642. Constructive possession is that which exists without actual personal occupation of land or without actual personal present dominion over a chattel, but with an intent and capability to maintain control and dominion. Possession may, but need not, imply title. It is not limited to manual touch or personal custody. Hawaii v. Awai, 1899, 12 Haw. 174. It is not necessary that possession be immediate or exclusive. Borgfeldt v. United States, 9 Cir., 1933, 67 F.2d 967.
>
> The Restatement of Torts, Section 216, defines "Possession of chattel" as being where a person has physical control of a chattel with intent to exercise such control in his own behalf, or, one who has had such physical control with such intent to exercise control although he is no longer in physical control, if he has not abandoned it and no other person has obtained possession.
>
> This factor of dominion and control over an object so as to give power of disposal to one who so dominates and controls, has been held applicable in "liquor possession" cases. Toney v. United States, D.C. Cir., 1933, 67 F.2d 573. And we think it clearly applicable to narcotic cases.

Here there was never a "factor of dominion and control over an object so as to give power of disposal to one who so dominates and controls." Here the so-called possession was not such as would have been held applicable in "liquor possession cases." The same rule should apply in the "firearms cases."

The brief for the prosecution replied:

Appellant's argument is basically that the possession he had of the illegal firearm was so limited that it was not possession within the meaning of Title 26, United States Code. There seems to be no doubt, however, that appellant held the gun long enough to fire it twice, passing it to a co-defendant to reload between the shots. The appellee submits that even under the cases cited by the appellant, possession is clearly shown.

Though appellant argues that the possession was too limited in time and extent to violate the provisions of Title 26, United States Code, the examination of his entire brief indicates that the real point was not that there was no posses-

> sion, but rather that the possession was—or should have been—explained to the satisfaction of the jury (here the court). It is doubtful whether this question is reviewable in any way on appeal. Moreover, on the facts of this case the decision is more than defensible. The District Judge obviously believed the defendant had violated the statute by possession even for a brief time of the illegal firearm. Moreover, the District Judge did not regard as sufficient explanation the fact that appellant had had no previous record and that the appellant did not compound the illegal possession by using or attempting to use the firearm for an illegal purpose. That the District Judge, however, was not blind to these factors is shown by the relatively light sentence given to the appellant.

The Court of Appeals reversed the conviction without opinion.

Why did the prosecution prosecute this case? (The defendant had no previous record, nor was he suspected of any other crimes.) Why did the appellate court reverse the conviction? Why did it do so without opinion? Of course, you cannot know the answers to these questions. Can you make plausible guesses?

6. In People v. Valot, 33 Mich. App. 49, 189 N.W.2d 873 (1971), the defendant was charged with violating a state law making it a crime for a person to "possess" or to "have under his or her control any narcotic drug." Valot had rented a motel room for himself and several friends. The room was registered in Valot's name, and he paid the first day's rent, but a friend had paid for the second day's rent, and the third day's rent was still due. The motel manager complained to the police that "hippie-type" people had been using the room for three days. The police searched the room and discovered five people, including the defendant, asleep or in beds, and observed marijuana and drug paraphernalia in the room. Valot said he knew one of his friends had used marijuana, but denied any knowledge of marijuana in the motel room. The Michigan Court of Appeals held that the trial judge could have reasonably found that Valot had "control" of the marijuana, regardless of who had brought the drug into the room.

Judge Levin strongly dissented. He conceded that Valot had been in control of the room and had probably been aware that his friends had marijuana in the room. But he argued that there was no evidence that Valot had brought the marijuana into the room or had ever used marijuana, on this or any other occasion.

Assuming Valot merely invited or allowed his friends to smoke marijuana in the room or failed to evict them for doing so, did he violate the statute?

7. In State v. Bugger, 25 Utah 404, 483 P.2d 442 (1971), the defendant was convicted of violating a state law making it a crime "for any person who is under the influence of intoxicating liquor to drive or be in actual physical control of any vehicle." An officer found Bugger asleep in his car. The car was on the side of the road, completely away from the traveled portion, and the motor was off. The officer aroused Bugger and established he was drunk. The court reversed Bugger's conviction, holding that he was not exercising any physical control or dominion over the car at the time of his arrest.

Why do you think the Utah legislature made it a crime to be "in control" of a car while drunk as well as to drive it while drunk? Is the court correct in holding that Bugger was not in control of the car? Can you think of sound reasons why the legislature would have wanted to punish Bugger? How much difference would it have made if Bugger had left the engine running?

A. VOLUNTARY ACTS

PEOPLE v. NEWTON

Supreme Court, Appellate Division of New York
72 Misc. 2d 646, 340 N.Y.S.2d 77 (1973)

Moses M. WEINSTEIN, Justice.

Petitioner (defendant) comes before this Court to enforce his civil right to liberty. He resorts to the great writ of habeas corpus which has for centuries been the only real and sufficient bastion of personal freedom and dignity. He inquires not into the offense charged to him but into the esteemed right to liberty which is the matrix of our judicial system. The instant writ tests the legality of petitioner's detention, notwithstanding the criminal act he is alleged to have committed.

A hearing was held before this Court on January 19, 1973 and January 22, 1973 and the Court has examined the minutes of a hearing held in the New York City Criminal Court, Queens County, on December 14, 1972. The following findings of fact and conclusions of law are made in the absence of any testimony offered before the Court by any person aboard flight #101 from the Bahamas to Luxembourg:

On December 7, 1972 petitioner boarded Air International Bahamas' flight #101 bound from the Bahamas to Luxembourg. While on board, the petitioner had concealed on his person a loaded .38 caliber revolver and a quantity of ammunition. At some time during the flight, the captain became aware of the fact that petitioner might possibly be carrying a firearm. There is some indication that the petitioner, severely handicapped and ambulatory only with the aid of prosthetic devices, caused himself to be unruly. The extent to which petitioner was unruly on board the plane, if in fact he was, cannot be ascertained from the evidence before the Court. Suffice it to say that the captain of flight #101, for reasons best known to himself, saw fit to interrupt the course of the plane which was flying over international waters and effected a landing in the County of Queens at the John F. Kennedy International Airport. The landing was made at approximately 12:35 A.M. on December 8, 1972. Officers from the Port Authority Police Department, in response to a radio transmission, went to the runway where the plane, with petitioner on board, was waiting. One of the officers boarded the plane, approached the defendant-petitioner, and inquired of him as to whether or not he had a weapon. The petitioner answered that he did have a weapon which he allowed to be removed from his person. He was then arrested and charged with a violation of section 265.05(2) of the Penal Law of the State of New York after his admission that he had no license to possess or carry the weapon in question. Section 265.05(2) of the Penal Law is as follows:

> Any person who has in his possession any firearm which is loaded with ammunition, or who has in his possession any firearm and, at the same time, has in his possession a quantity of ammunition which may be used to discharge such firearm is guilty of a class D felony.

The Court finds that the petitioner, William Jesse Newton, Jr. did not subject himself to criminal liability by virtue of a voluntary act. Flight #101 was not scheduled to terminate in or pass through the territorial jurisdiction of the United States. The landing at John F. Kennedy International Airport on December 8, 1972 was merely an interruption of flight not attributable to a voluntary action by the petitioner. It is therefore, the opinion of this Court that the Writ of Habeas Corpus be sustained and the petitioner be discharged from custody forthwith.

Notes and Questions

1. Why shouldn't Newton be guilty of an offense under New York law?
2. What act did Newton perform in New York? What could he have done to avoid criminal liability?
3. Does *Newton* raise the same question about criminal liability as did *Proctor?*
4. Should it matter if it is a crime to possess a loaded firearm in either the Bahamas or Luxembourg? Does it matter whether Air International is an American airline? Should it matter whether it is a federal offense to carry a loaded firearm on an American airline?

MARTIN v. STATE

Court of Appeals of Alabama
17 So. 2d 427 (1944)

SIMPSON, Judge.

Appellant was convicted of being drunk on a public highway, and appeals. Officers of the law arrested him at his home and took him onto the highway, where he allegedly committed the proscribed acts, viz., manifested a drunken condition by using loud and profane language.

The pertinent provisions of our statute are: "Any person who, while intoxicated or drunk, appears in any public place where one or more persons are present . . . and manifests a drunken condition by boisterous or indecent conduct, or loud and profane discourse, shall, on conviction, be fined," etc., Code 1940, Title 14, Section 120.

Under the plain terms of this statute, a voluntary appearance is presupposed. The rule has been declared, and we think it sound, that an accusation of drunkenness in a designated public place cannot be established by proof that the accused, while in an intoxicated condition, was involuntarily and forcibly carried to that place by the arresting officer.

Conviction of appellant was contrary to this announced principle and, in our view, erroneous. . . .

Reversed and rendered.

Notes and Questions

1. Should it matter that it was the police who brought Martin into the street on the way to the police car? Would it matter if instead Martin was thrown out onto the street from a private party for drunken misbehavior? Because of his political beliefs? What if he had gotten drunk in his room but came into the street because his house had caught fire?

2. Should it matter what Martin was originally arrested for? Should it matter whether the arrest was legal? Should it matter if he were innocent of the charges for which he was arrested?

3. What if Martin had been arrested while sober but, while being driven to the police station, discovered a bottle of whiskey in the back of the patrol car and drank it, causing him to be intoxicated upon arrival at the police station (assuming it to be a public place within the meaning of the statute)?

4. The statute Martin was accused of violating can be read to require three acts: getting drunk, being in a public place, and engaging in boisterous conduct. Is the point of the court that only the last of the elements to take place must be a voluntary act? If so, wasn't Martin boisterous after he was carried into a public place?

5. Why should the law preclude criminal liability in the absence of a voluntary act? Is the point that the criminal law cannot hope to deter involuntary behavior, and thus cannot deter any crime by making an individual liable for actions he or she could not control? Is this true? The drafters of the Model Penal Code[4] give a different reason:

> [T]he sense of personal security would be undermined in a society where such movement or inactivity could lead to formal social condemnation of the sort that a conviction necessarily entails. [The American Law Institute Model Penal Code and commentaries, Part I (1985) p.251.]

4. For a discussion of the origin and significance of the Model Penal Code see Appendix B, p.1113.

The Model Penal Code itself provides:

Section 2.01. Requirement of Voluntary Act. . . .

(1) A person is not guilty of an offense unless his liability is based on conduct that includes a voluntary act. . . .

(4) Possession is an act, within the meaning of this Section, if the possessor knowingly procured or received the thing possessed or was aware of his control thereof for a sufficient period to have been able to terminate his possession.

Can the requirement of voluntariness be understood as the legal response to the basic intuition that it would be grossly unfair to punish a person who lacked the capacity to conform to the law?

How narrowly are we to construe the voluntary/involuntary distinction? Are intuitive conceptions of "fairness" helpful?

6. One commentator[5] has written:

> Situational offences are committed by those who find themselves in a specified situation not involving any relevant conduct on their part. The most important illustrations turn on attributed (vicarious) liability. Situational liability does not offend our sense of justice in "ticket" cases, when the penalty is light and imposed without court proceedings, or when it requires fault by the defendant, but grave doubts arise when the liability is both situational and strict. Offences of this kind strike one as being particularly tyrannical. The criminal code of Stalin's Russia provided a scandalous example in the offence of being a "relative of an enemy of the people." In our law these offences arise partly because of the wording of some legislation and partly because of the failure of the courts to develop a liberal principle of interpretation.
>
> A case that is generally regarded as marking the extreme of severity in this country is *Larsonneur,* where a Frenchwoman who went from England to Ireland was arrested by the Irish police and delivered by them in custody back to the Welsh police at Holyhead. The police charged her with the offence under the Aliens Order of being an alien who was "found" in the United Kingdom without permission; they had, of course, "found" her in their own custody when they received delivery of her protesting body from the Irish police. The London Sessions sentenced her to imprisonment for 3 days with a recommendation for deportation, and the conviction and sentence were upheld by the Court of Criminal Appeal. . . .
>
> It is difficult to understand why the unfortunate woman was prosecuted, since she could simply have been sent back to her native country without prosecution. Nor was there any exegetical necessity for the court to read the Aliens Order as creating an offence in the absence of a culpable act or omission: the word "found" might well have been interpreted as meaning "found at liberty"— not "found" in police custody. Alternatively, the court might have extended the defence of duress to include compulsion by law, or compulsion of circumstances. . . .
>
> The proper mode of construing such legislation was exemplified by the Supreme Court of Alabama in a case where the police came to the defendant

5. Glanville Williams, Textbook of Criminal Law 157-158 (2d ed. 1983).

when he was sitting drunk in his house, carried him out on the street, and then arrested him for being drunk and disorderly in a public place. The statute under which the defendant was charged referred to "any person who, while intoxicated or drunk, appears in any public place . . . and manifests a drunken condition by boisterous or indecent conduct," etc. Literally the defendant had "appeared" on the street, but the court declared that "under the plain terms of this statute a voluntary appearance is presupposed."

It was remarked . . . that there is no objection on principle to convicting a person of a situational offence if he was negligent in bringing about the situation. So a man who creeps into someone else's house, drinks himself silly, is found by the owner and is ejected on to the street, could properly be convicted of being drunk in a public place because he might reasonably have foreseen that he would end up drunk in a public place. The conviction of Mlle. Larsonneur, likewise, has been supported on the ground that she had been ordered to leave the United Kingdom and did so by going to the Irish Free State; she should have foreseen that she might be expelled from Ireland back to the United Kingdom. But this would be expecting great prescience of her. It was surely quite reasonable for her to think that even if she should prove to be as unwelcome to the Irish as she was to the English, she would be allowed to make her own way from Ireland back to France. Although situational offences may be unobjectionable if some kind of culpability is required, it would be strained to find any culpability in *Larsonneur,* and no such finding was in fact made.

PEOPLE v. GRANT

Appellate Court of Illinois, Fourth District
46 Ill. App. 3d 125, 360 N.E.2d 809 (1977)

REARDON, Justice.

The defendant, Seth Grant, was sentenced to 3 to 9 years in the penitentiary after a Logan County jury found him guilty of aggravated battery and obstructing a police officer. The court entered judgment on both verdicts, but only sentenced the defendant for the offense of aggravated battery.

On December 13, 1974, the defendant was a patron at a tavern known as the "Watering Place" in the City of Lincoln where he consumed four drinks consisting of whisky and cola during a 2½ hour period. The defendant then witnessed an altercation between another patron and the tavern owner. The Lincoln police were called to the scene and they forcibly escorted the other patron outside where he continued to resist arrest. A hostile crowd of approximately forty persons accompanied the police and patron as they exited from the tavern and approached the officers' automobile. The crowd was cheering for the patron. Suddenly, the defendant burst through the crowd, and, using a parking meter for leverage, he leaped into the air, striking Officer Raymond Vonderahe twice in the face.

Thereafter, Officer Michael Yarcho placed the defendant under arrest and forcibly led him to the officers' automobile. Yarcho testified that the defendant was very upset and that great force was required to place the defendant in the automobile. Another officer, David Morrow, testified that the defendant was excited, agitated and upset. Morrow also stated that the defendant had not been involved in the altercation prior to his attack on Vonderahe.

The defendant was transported to the Logan County jail and placed in a cell. Approximately one hour after being arrested, one of the jailers discovered the defendant lying on his cot gasping for breath. Defendant's eyes were fixed and his back formed a rigid reversed arch, typical symptoms of a grand mal convulsive seizure. The defendant was immediately transported to a Lincoln hospital by the Lincoln fire department, and then to a Springfield hospital where the defendant remained until December 23, 1974.

The record on appeal reflects that the defendant has a complicated legal and medical history. The defendant suffers from an illness known as psychomotor epilepsy. This history includes a number of violent attacks on other persons which have varied in severity. In some, physical assistance from others was required to subdue the defendant. One, a knife assault in a hospital, was of such violence that a police officer seeking to restrain the defendant was forced to use a weapon. The affray ended only when the defendant was shot in the pelvis and kidney. His past history is replete with emotional outbursts and he has been convicted on separate occasions of involuntary manslaughter and aggravated assault. . . .

Defendant relies on his testimony that his mind went blank at the "Watering Place" and that he remembered nothing until he awoke three days later. He stated that he has had previous blackouts and that he takes medicine for epilepsy. Defendant also relies on Dr. Albert Ludin's testimony that defendant has temporal lobe epilepsy with symptoms described as psychomotor and grand mal seizures. Dr. Ludin expressed his opinion that, at the time the offenses were committed, defendant was suffering from a psychomotor seizure which prevented his conscious mind from controlling his actions.

The jury is not required to accept the conclusions of a psychiatrist . . . and the weight of the psychiatrist's opinion is to be measured by the reasons given for the conclusion and the factual details supporting it. . . .

Here, Dr. Ludin stated that his opinion would be different if the defendant was not telling the truth. Analysis of the record on appeal discloses facts on which the jury could base their opinion that the defendant was being untruthful.

First, defendant alleges that he cannot remember anything that occurred during the three-day period following his arrest. The doctor, however, testified that on December 14, 1974, defendant was alert, awake and in contact with reality. Officer Yarcho also stated that the defendant was alert and not confused when he was arrested. The defendant also responded in an appropriate manner when questioned about his personal history. Next, is Officer Yarcho's troubling testimony that defendant's arrest required a great deal of force. Such testimony coincides with Dr. Ludin's statement that a person having a psychomotor seizure exhibits a great deal of strength. This testimony, however, as the

State points out, must be contrasted with Officer Yarcho's later testimony that it took four men to place the defendant in an ambulance at the jail, while he initially took the defendant into custody by himself. Furthermore, Officer Yarcho testified that defendant was much stronger during the jail incident than he was during the arrest. Finally, Officer Yarcho stated that in his opinion the defendant was in possession of his "complete faculties" and "normal" at the time of his arrest. The evidence showing that the defendant had a grand mal seizure at the jail does not necessarily reflect that the defendant also had a psychomotor seizure a short time before. While Dr. Ludin did say that sometimes a grand mal seizure is preceded by a psychomotor seizure, he did not say that this always occurs. . . .

The trial court instructed the jury on the question of the defendant's sanity by giving the following instruction which is taken from the Illinois Pattern Jury Instructions, Criminal, No. 24.01 (1968):

> A person is insane and not criminally responsible for his conduct if at the time of the conduct, as a result of mental disease or mental defect, he lacks substantial capacity either to appreciate the criminality of his conduct or to conform his conduct to the requirements of law.

. . . This instruction, however, fails to distinguish behavior by a person lacking ". . . substantial capacity either to appreciate the criminality of his conduct or to conform his conduct to the requirements of law . . ." from automatic behavior by an individual who possesses the requisite capacity.

We note that this is a case of first impression in Illinois since no Illinois court has determined that a person's actions during a psychomotor epileptic seizure are the actions of an insane person or merely the involuntary or automatic actions of a sane person.

The term automatism is defined as the state of a person who, though capable of action, is not conscious of what he is doing. Automatism is not insanity. . . . [I]t is manifested by the performance of involuntary acts that can be of a simple or complex nature. Clinically, automatism has been identified in a wide variety of physical conditions including: epilepsy, organic brain disease, concussional states following head injuries, drug abuse, hypoglycemia and, less commonly, in some types of schizophrenia and acute emotional disturbance. . . . Psychomotor epileptics not only engage in automatic or fugue-like activity, but they may also suffer convulsive seizures.

Section 4-1 of our Criminal Code provides:

> A material element of every offense is a voluntary act, which includes an omission to perform a duty which the law imposes on the offender and which he is physically capable of performing.

While the Illinois Pattern Jury Instructions contain an instruction relating to this statute . . . that instruction was neither requested by the defendant nor read to the jury in this case. . . .

Ordinarily, a defendant cannot complain on appeal that an instruction was not given if he failed to tender that instruction at trial. . . . [However,] "substantial defects [in jury instructions] are not waived by failure to make timely objections thereto if the interests of justice require." Accordingly, we hold that the interests of justice require reversal of the defendant's convictions because the jury instructions are substantially defective in that they do not contain an instruction on the defense of involuntary conduct. We note that courts in other jurisdictions have held that the defendant who introduces evidence of abnormal mental condition, bearing upon the state of mind required for the crime with which he is charged, is entitled to an instruction drawing the jury's attention to that evidence.

We distinguish People v. Espenscheid (1969), 109 Ill. App. 2d 107, 249 N.E.2d 866, which held that the trial court properly refused to give such an instruction because there was no evidence tending to prove that the defendant performed an involuntary act. The entire record on appeal here, especially the testimony of Dr. Ludin, reflects that the defendant suffers from psychomotor epilepsy, which is not insanity. The record reflects that the defendant may have been acting in a state of automatism when he attacked Officer Vonderahe on December 13, 1974. We therefore leave the factual resolution of this question to a jury that is properly instructed.

Although a voluntary act is an absolute requirement for criminal liability under section 4-1 of our Code . . . there is no requirement that every act preceding the actual commission of the offense be voluntary. Thus, the jury may, on remand, determine that the defendant attacked Officer Vonderahe while in a state of automatism, but that he nevertheless committed an offense for which he is criminally responsible if he had prior notice of his susceptibility to engage in violent involuntary conduct brought on by drinking alcoholic beverages or by some other conscious causal behavior. . . .

In Illinois, we have a generally well-reasoned and modern Criminal Code. This Code provides for the affirmative defense of insanity and requires that every offense be the result of a voluntary act. Our legislature has provided that a person found not guilty of an offense by reason of insanity can be committed to a mental health facility for treatment, although no such provision applies to an alleged offender who commits an involuntary act. These provisions are rational and constitute policy responses to a compelling need by a legislature empowered to act.

On remand, the defendant will again run the risk of being convicted for the offenses of aggravated battery or obstructing a police officer if the jury finds that he was not insane when he attacked Officer Vonderahe and that he either consciously committed the offense or recklessly brought about his alleged psychomotor epileptic seizure and its accompanying state of automatism. As some commentators have suggested, the jury plays an important role when the defense is raised:

> [A]utomatism as a result of psychomotor seizures should be [a] valid criminal defense. The dearth of cases employing this defense suggests that the problem is one of proof. If one is sane immediately prior to and after the unlawful act is

committed it is difficult to establish that a particular violent act occurred as a result of a psychomotor seizure. (Barrow & Fabing, Epilepsy and the Law 92-93 (1956).)

If the jury finds that the defendant was sane but not responsible for the attack on Officer Vonderahe, then he cannot be committed for the offenses. We find this course to be mandated by our legislature, which only provided for the commitment of persons who are criminally insane. . . .

In view of the fact that we are remanding this case for a new trial, we do not address the question of whether the 3 to 9 year sentence of imprisonment imposed by the trial court is excessive.

For the reasons stated herein, we reverse the defendant's convictions for aggravated battery and obstructing a police officer, and we remand the case to the Circuit Court of Logan County for a new trial. . . .

Reversed and remanded with directions.

Notes and Questions

1. The Model Penal Code excludes the following from the definition of a voluntary act:

Section 2.01.

(1) The following are not voluntary acts within the meaning of this Section:

(a) a reflex or convulsion;
(b) a bodily movement during unconsciousness or sleep;
(c) conduct during hypnosis or resulting from hypnotic suggestion;
(d) a bodily movement that otherwise is not a product of the effort or determination of the actor, either conscious or habitual.

Note that the Model Penal Code definition of a voluntary act not only requires a muscular movement or contraction—which occurred in *Grant* but arguably did not take place when Proctor "kept" his building, when Newton entered New York holding the gun, and when Martin appeared in the street—but also requires that there be an element of conscious control over the act. One commentator[6] has explained the reason for this rule as follows:

> [T]he universally recognized doctrine [is] that conduct that occurs while the actor is in an unconscious state—sleepwalking, epileptic seizures, automatism—may not be dealt with criminally. Conduct must be, as the law's confusing term has it, "voluntary." The term is one that will immediately raise the hackles of the determinist, of whatever persuasion. But, once again, the law's language should

6. Herbert Packer, The Limits of the Criminal Sanction 76-77 (1968).

> not be read as plunging into the deep waters of free will vs. determinism, Cartesian duality, or any of a half-dozen other philosophic controversies that might appear to be invoked by the use of the term "voluntary" in relation to conduct. The law is not affirming volition; it is excluding, in a crude kind of way, conduct that in any view is not. And it does so primarily in response to the simple intuition that nothing would more surely undermine the individual's sense of autonomy and security than to hold him to account for conduct that *he* does not think he can control. He may be deluded, if the determinists are right, in his belief that such conduct differs significantly from any other conduct in which he engages. But that is beside the point. *He* thinks there is a difference, and that is what the law acts upon.

2. Consider Lord Denning's comments in Bratty v. Attorney General [1963] A.C. 386, 409 (H.L. 1961):

> No act is punishable if it is done involuntarily: and an involuntary act in this context—some people nowadays prefer to speak of it as "automatism"—means an act which is done by the muscles without any control by the mind such as a spasm, a reflex action or a convulsion; or an act done by a person who is not conscious of what he is doing such as an act done whilst suffering from concussion or whilst sleep-walking. The point was well put by Stephen, J., in 1889: "Can anyone doubt that a man who, though he might be perfectly sane, committed what would otherwise be a crime in a state of somnambulism, would be entitled to be acquitted? And why is this? Simply because he would not know what he was doing."

3. The Model Penal Code asserts that acts performed while under hypnotic trance are involuntary:

> The case of hypnotic suggestion also seems to warrant explicit treatment. Hypnosis differs from both sleep and fugue, but as it is characterized by the subject's dependence on the hypnotist, it does not seem politic to treat conduct resulting from hypnotic suggestion as voluntary, despite the state of consciousness involved. The widely held view that the hypnotized subject will not follow suggestions that are repugnant to him was deemed insufficient to warrant treating his conduct while hypnotized as voluntary; his dependency and helplessness are too pronounced.

4. In People v. (Huey) Newton, 8 Cal. App. 3d 359, 87 Cal. Rptr. 394 (1970), the court held that the defendant had a right to a jury instruction on the defense of involuntary action due to automatism. Newton, a political activist and leader of the Black Panthers, had been stopped by two police officers and ordered out of his car. Though the evidence was unclear, Newton and one of the officers apparently struggled over a gun, and the gun went off, wounding the officer. The wounded officer then shot Newton in the abdomen from close range and as the fight continued, Newton fired shots, killing the second officer. A medical expert testified for the defense that:

> a gunshot wound which penetrates in a body cavity, the abdominal cavity or the thoracic cavity is very likely to produce a profound reflex shock reaction, that is quite different than [sic] a gunshot wound which penetrates only skin and muscle and it is not at all uncommon for a person shot in the abdomen to lose consciousness and go into this reflex shock condition for short periods of time up to half an hour or so.

The court rejected the state's argument that such "reflex shock condition" could not constitute involuntary action and remanded the case to let the jury consider Newton's claim that he committed no voluntary act.

5. The United States Supreme Court briefly entertained the notion that the Constitution contained an *actus reus* requirement that forbade criminal liability where the defendant suffered from drug or alcohol addiction. In Robinson v. California, 370 U.S. 660 (1962), the court struck down a California statute which made addiction to the use of narcotics a criminal offense. The court reasoned that drug addiction is an illness which may be contracted innocently or involuntarily, similar to epilepsy and mental illness, and that punishing the addict was therefore cruel and unusual punishment in violation of the Eighth and Fourteenth Amendments. Justice Stewart, writing for the majority, stated:

> It is unlikely that any State at this moment in history would attempt to make it a criminal offense for a person to be mentally ill, or a leper, or to be afflicted with a venereal disease. A state might determine that the general health and welfare require that the victims of these and other human afflictions be dealt with by compulsory treatment, involving quarantine, confinement, or sequestration. But, in the light of contemporary human knowledge, a law which made a criminal offense of such a disease would doubtless be universally thought to be an infliction of cruel and unusual punishment in violation of the Eighth and Fourteenth Amendments.
>
> We cannot but consider the statute before us as of the same category. In this Court counsel for the State recognized that narcotic addiction is an illness. Indeed, it is apparently an illness which may be contracted innocently or involuntarily. We hold that a state law which imprisons a person thus afflicted as a criminal, even though he has never touched any narcotic drug within the State or been guilty of any irregular behavior there, inflicts a cruel and unusual punishment in violation of the Fourteenth Amendment. To be sure, imprisonment for ninety days is not, in the abstract, a punishment which is either cruel or unusual. But the question cannot be considered in the abstract. Even one day in prison would be a cruel and unusual punishment for the "crime" of having a common cold.

In his concurrence, Justice Douglas noted,

> Today we have our differences over the legal definition of insanity. But however insanity is defined, it is in effect treated as a disease. While afflicted people may be confined either for treatment or for the protection of society, they are not branded as criminals . . . We would forget the teachings of the Eighth

> Amendment if we allowed sickness to be made a crime and permitted sick people to be punished for being sick. The age of enlightenment cannot tolerate such barbarous action.

Six years later in Powell v. Texas, 392 U.S. 514 (1968), the court substantially recanted. The facts of *Powell* were as follows:

> [The defendant] was arrested and charged with being found in a state of intoxication in a public place, in violation of Texas Penal Code, Art. 477 (1952) which reads as follows: "Whoever shall get drunk or be found in a state of intoxication in any public place, or at any private house except his own, shall be fined not exceeding one hundred dollars."
>
> Appellant was tried . . . found guilty, and fined $20. . . . His counsel urged that appellant was "afflicted with the disease of chronic alcoholism," that "his appearance in public while drunk was . . . not of his own volition," and therefore that to punish him criminally for such conduct would be cruel and unusual, in violation of the . . . U.S. Constitution.

The Supreme Court rejected the claim, stating:

> Appellant . . . seeks to come within the application of the Cruel and Unusual Punishment Clause announced in Robinson v. California, 370 U.S. 660 (1962), which involved a state statute making it a crime to "be addicted to the use of narcotics." This Court held there that a "state statute which imprisons a person thus afflicted (with narcotic addiction) as a criminal, even though he has never touched any narcotic drug within the State or been guilty of any irregular behavior there, inflicts a cruel and unusual punishment. . . .
>
> On its face the present case does not fall within that holding, since appellant was convicted, not for being a chronic alcoholic, but for being in public while drunk on a particular occasion. The State of Texas thus has not sought to punish a mere status, as California did in *Robinson;* nor has it attempted to regulate appellant's behavior in the privacy of his own home. Rather, it has imposed upon appellant a criminal sanction for public behavior which may create substantial health and safety hazards, both for appellant and for members of the general public, and which offends the moral and esthetic sensibilities of a large segment of the community. This seems a far cry from convicting one for being an addict, being a chronic alcoholic, being "mentally ill or a leper. . . ."
>
> . . . If Leroy Powell cannot be convicted of public intoxication, it is difficult to see how a State can convict an individual for murder, if that individual, while exhibiting normal behavior in all other respects, suffers from a "compulsion" to kill.

How did the court distinguish *Powell* from *Robinson?* Does *Powell* overrule *Robinson?* If so, can you see why the court chose to do so?

What if a defendant could prove that his criminal behavior was a result of his being abused as a child? Would a claim of involuntariness be successful?

6. Acts performed while sleepwalking also preclude liability as voluntary behavior. See M.P.C. 2.01(2)(b). Consider Morris, Somnambulistic Homicide: Ghosts, Spiders, and North Koreans, 5 Res Judicatae 29, 29-30, 31-32 (1951):

The unreported case of The King v. Cogdon, heard in the Supreme Court of Victoria before Mr. Justice Smith in December, 1950, though clear as to its facts and unchallengeable in law, compels reconsideration of some of our basic premises of responsibility for criminal actions.

Mrs. Cogdon was charged with the murder of her only child, a daughter called Pat, aged nineteen. Pat had for some time been receiving psychiatric treatment for a relatively minor neurotic condition of which, in her psychiatrist's opinion, she was now cured. Despite this, Mrs. Cogdon continued to worry unduly about her. Describing the relationship betwen Pat and her mother, Mr. Cogdon testified: "I don't think a mother could have thought any more of her daughter. I think she absolutely adored her." On the conscious level, at least, there was no reason to doubt Mrs. Cogdon's deep attachment to her daughter.

To the charge of murdering Pat, Mrs. Cogdon pleaded not guilty. Her story, though somewhat bizarre, was not seriously challenged by the Crown, and led to her acquittal. She told how, on the night before her daughter's death, she had dreamt that their house was full of spiders and that these spiders were crawling all over Pat. In her sleep, Mrs. Cogdon left the bed she shared with her husband, went into Pat's room, and awakened to find herself violently brushing at Pat's face, presumably to remove the spiders. This woke Pat. Mrs. Cogdon told her she was just tucking her in. At the trial, she testified that she still believed, as she had been told, that the occupants of a nearby house bred spiders as a hobby, preparing nests for them behind pictures on their walls. It was these spiders which in her dreams had invaded their home and attacked Pat. There had also been a previous dream in which ghosts had sat at the end of Mrs. Cogdon's bed and she had said to them, "Well, you have come to take Pattie." It does not seem fanciful to accept the psychological explanation of these spiders and ghosts as the projections of Mrs. Cogdon's subconscious hostility towards her daughter; a hostility which was itself rooted in Mrs. Cogdon's own early life and marital relationship.

The morning after the spider dream she told her doctor of it. He gave her a sedative and, because of the dream and certain previous difficulties she had reported, discussed the possibility of psychiatric treatment. That evening Mrs. Cogdon suggested to her husband that he attend his lodge meeting, and asked Pat to come with her to the cinema. After he had gone Pat looked through the paper, not unusually found no tolerable programme, and said that as she was going out the next evening she thought she would rather go to bed early. Later, while Pat was having a bath preparatory to retiring, Mrs. Cogdon went into her room, put a hot water bottle in the bed, turned back the bedclothes, and placed a glass of hot milk beside the bed ready for Pat. She then went to bed herself. There was some desultory conversation between them about the war in Korea, and just before she put out her light Pat called out to her mother, "Mum, don't be so silly worrying there about the war, it's not on our front door step yet."

Mrs. Cogdon went to sleep. She dreamt that "the war was all around the house," that soldiers were in Pat's room, and that one soldier was on the bed attacking Pat. This was all of the dream she could later recapture. Her first "waking" memory was of running from Pat's room, out of the house to the home of her sister who lived next door. When her sister opened the front door Mrs. Cogdon fell into her, crying, "I think I've hurt Pattie."

In fact Mrs. Cogdon had, in her somnambulistic state, left her bed, fetched an axe from the woodheap, entered Pat's room, and struck her two accurate forceful blows on the head with the blade of the axe, thus killing her.

Mrs. Cogdon's story was supported by the evidence of her physician, a psychiatrist, and a psychologist. The burden of the evidence of all three, which was not contested by the prosecution, was that Mrs. Cogdon was suffering from a form of hysteria with an overlay of depression, and that she was of a personality in which such dissociated states as fugues, amnesias, and somnambulistic acts are to be expected. They agreed that she was not psychotic. . . . They hazarded no statement as to her motives, the idea of defence of the daughter being transparently insufficient. However, the psychologist and the psychiatrist concurred in hinting that the emotional motivation lay in an acute conflict situation in her relations with her parents; that during marital life she suffered very great sexual frustration; and that she over-compensated for her own frustration by over-protection of her daughter. Her exaggerated solicitude for her daughter was a conscious expression of her subconscious emotional hostility to her, and the dream ghosts, spiders, and Korean soldiers were projections of that aggression. How manifold can be the possible motives for a "motiveless" killing!

At all events the jury believed Mrs. Cogdon's story, and regarded the presumption that the natural consequences of her acts were intended as being completely rebutted by her account of her mental state at the time of the killing, and by the unanimous support given to it by the medical and psychological evidence. She was acquitted. It must be stressed that insanity was not pleaded as a defence—she was acquitted because the act of killing itself was not, in law, regarded as her act at all.

The case illustrates the impossibility of . . . satisfactorily . . . sever[ing] "act" from "intention." . . .

Thus, Mrs. Cogdon's action not being "voluntary," no question of criminal liability arose. . . . Mrs. Cogdon escapes basically because of the state of her consciousness; not because she had no conscious intention or rational motive to kill, a state she shares with many convicted murderers. She was "asleep": had she been "awake" her only defence would have been one of insanity. . . .

But the difference between being "asleep" and "awake" is not absolute. Consciousness is not like a light, either off or on; it is a finely graded scale ranging from death to the extreme awareness of the artist. Indeed, with the electroencephalograph we can even chart certain variations of consciousness between people, and in one person at different times. Had Mrs. Cogdon been "awake," that is, just a little more conscious, a little more aware of her actions, then her act may have had to be regarded as "voluntary." The line is an extremely fine one, as is shown by the fact that in and during her dream Mrs. Cogdon was "aware" of the axe, her daughter and the soldiers. Not unexpectedly, she could not remember this part of the dream, for within us we struggle to repress such profoundly disturbing and shocking memory traces. Thus we all dream, but some, for various reasons, remember more than others. Nor would Mrs. Cogdon's position have been legally different even if she could have then recalled all the dream, including the killing. Her exculpation lay not in the state of her memory but in her inability to bring into consciousness her emotional motivations, and consequently her diminished awareness of the deed. . . .

7. What if Mrs. Cogdon had been hospitalized for the very sort of episode that led to the killing, but, on the day of the killing, had escaped from the hospital because she preferred to sleep at home? Compare this case to People v. Grant, above, and to People v. Decina, 2 N.Y.2d 133, 139-140, 138 N.E.2d 799, 803-804 (1956). Decina had an epileptic seizure while driving and his car struck and killed four people on a sidewalk. The court held that, although the defendant's epileptic seizure was involuntary, he nonetheless was criminally liable.

> Assuming the truth of the indictment, as we must on demurrer, this defendant knew he was subject to epileptic attacks and seizures that might strike *at any time.*
>
> He also knew that a moving motor vehicle uncontrolled on a public highway is a highly dangerous instrumentality capable of unrestrained destruction. With this *knowledge,* and without anyone accompanying him, he deliberately took a chance by making a conscious choice of a course of action, in disregard of the consequences which he knew might follow from his conscious act, and which in this case did ensue.
>
> To hold otherwise would be to say that a man may freely indulge himself in liquor in the same hope that it will not affect his driving, and if it later develops that ensuing intoxication causes dangerous and reckless driving resulting in death, his unconsciousness or involuntariness at that time would relieve him from a prosecution under the statute. His awareness of a condition which he knows may produce such consequences as here, and his disregard of the consequences, renders him liable for culpable negligence, as the courts below have properly held. . . . To have a sudden sleeping spell, an unexpected heart or other disabling attack, without any prior knowledge or warning thereof, is an altogether different situation.

Did Decina commit a punishable act? When? Did Grant?

How is society to protect itself against Grant if it cannot use the criminal law?

B. OMISSIONS

JONES v. UNITED STATES

United States Court of Appeals, District of Columbia Circuit
308 F.2d 307 (1962)

Wright, Circuit Judge.

Appellant was tried . . . for involuntary manslaughter through failure to perform [her] legal duty of care for Anthony Lee Green, which failure resulted in his death. . . . [A]ppellant was convicted of involuntary manslaughter. . . .

Appellant urges several grounds for reversal. We need consider but two. First, appellant argues that there was insufficient evidence as a matter of law to warrant a jury finding of breach of duty in the care she rendered Anthony

Lee. Alternatively, appellant argues that the trial court committed plain error in failing to instruct the jury that it must first find that appellant was under a legal obligation to provide food and necessities to Anthony Lee before finding her guilty of manslaughter in failing to provide them. The first argument is without merit. Upon the latter we reverse.

A summary of the evidence, which is in conflict upon almost every significant issue, is necessary for the disposition of both arguments. In late 1957, Shirley Green became pregnant, out of wedlock, with a child, Robert Lee, subsequently born August 17, 1958. Apparently to avoid the embarrassment of the presence of the child in the Green home, it was arranged that appellant, a family friend, would take the child to her home after birth. Appellant did so, and the child remained there continuously until removed by the police on August 5, 1960. Initially appellant made some motions toward the adoption of Robert Lee, but these came to nought, and shortly thereafter it was agreed that Shirley Green was to pay appellant $72 a month for his care. According to appellant, these payments were made for only five months. According to Shirley Green, they were made up to July, 1960.

Early in 1959 Shirley Green again became pregnant, this time with the child Anthony Lee, whose death is the basis of appellant's conviction. This child was born October 21, 1959. Soon after birth, Anthony Lee developed a mild jaundice condition, attributed to a blood incompatibility with his mother. The jaundice resulted in his retention in the hospital for three days beyond the usual time, or until October 26, 1959, when, on authorization signed by Shirley Green, Anthony Lee was released by the hospital to appellant's custody. Shirley Green, after a two or three day stay in the hospital, also lived with appellant for three weeks, after which she returned to her parents' home, leaving the children with appellant. She testified she did not see them again, except for one visit in March, until August 5, 1960. Consequently, though there does not seem to have been any specific monetary agreement with Shirley Green covering Anthony Lee's support,[7] appellant had complete custody of both children until they were rescued by the police.

With regard to medical care, the evidence is undisputed. In March, 1960, appellant called a Dr. Turner to her home to treat Anthony Lee for a bronchial condition. Appellant also telephoned the doctor at various times to consult with him concerning Anthony Lee's diet and health. In early July, 1960, appellant took Anthony Lee to Dr. Turner's office where he was treated for "simple diarrhea." At this time the doctor noted the "wizened" appearance of the child and told appellant to tell the mother of the child that he should be taken to a hospital. This was not done. . . .

On August 5, 1960, officers removed the children to the D.C. General Hospital where Anthony Lee was diagnosed as suffering from severe malnutrition and lesions over large portions of his body, apparently caused by severe diaper rash. Following admission, he was fed repeatedly, apparently with no

7. It was uncontested that during the entire period the children were in appellant's home, appellant had ample means to provide food and medical care.

difficulty, and was described as being very hungry. His death, 34 hours after admission, was attributed without dispute to malnutrition. At birth Anthony Lee weighed six pounds, fifteen ounces—at death at age ten months, he weighed seven pounds, thirteen ounces. Normal weight at this age would have been approximately 14 pounds.

Appellant argues that nothing in the evidence establishes that she failed to provide food to Anthony Lee. She cites her own testimony and the testimony of a lodger, Mr. Wills, that she did in fact feed the baby regularly. At trial, the defense made repeated attempts to extract from the medical witnesses opinions that the jaundice, or the condition which caused it, might have prevented the baby from assimilating food. The doctors conceded this was possible but not probable since the autopsy revealed no condition which would support the defense theory. It was also shown by the disinterested medical witnesses that the child had no difficulty in ingesting food immediately after birth, and that Anthony Lee, in the last hours before his death, was able to take several bottles, apparently without difficulty, and seemed very hungry. This evidence, combined with the absence of any physical cause for nonassimilation, taken in the context of the condition in which these children were kept, presents a jury question on the feeding issue.

Moreover, there is substantial evidence from which the jury could have found that appellant failed to obtain proper medical care for the child.

Appellant also takes exception to the failure of the trial court to charge that the jury must find beyond a reasonable doubt, as an element of the crime, that appellant was under a legal duty to supply food and necessities to Anthony Lee. . . .

The problem of establishing the duty to take action which would preserve the life of another has not often arisen in the case law of this country. The most commonly cited statement of the rule is found in People v. Beardsley, 150 Mich. 206, 113 N.W. 1128, 1129, 13 L.R.A., N.S., 1020:

> The law recognizes that under some circumstances the omission of a duty owed by one individual to another, where such omission results in the death of the one to whom the duty is owing, will make the other chargeable with manslaughter. . . . This rule of law is always based upon the proposition that the duty neglected must be a legal duty, and not a mere moral obligation. It must be a duty imposed by law or by contract, and the omission to perform the duty must be the immediate and direct cause of death.

There are at least four situations in which the failure to act may constitute breach of a legal duty. One can be held criminally liable: first, where a statute imposes a duty to care for another; second, where one stands in a certain status relationship to another;[8] third, where one has assumed a contractual duty to

8. [10 A.L.R. Annot. 1137 (1921)] (parent to child); Territory v. Manton, 8 Mont. 95, 19 P. 387 (husband to wife); Regina v. Smith, 8 Carr. & P. 153 (Eng. 1837) (master to apprentice); United States v. Knowles, 26 Fed. Cas. 800 (No. 15,540) (ship's master to crew and passengers); cf. State v. Reitze, 86 N.J.L. 407, 92 A. 576 (innkeeper to inebriated customers).

care for another; and fourth, where one has voluntarily assumed the care of another and so secluded the helpless person as to prevent others from rendering aid.

It is the contention of the Government that either the third or the fourth ground is applicable here. However, it is obvious that in any of the four situations, there are critical issues of fact which must be passed on by the jury—specifically in this case, whether appellant had entered into a contract with the mother for the care of Anthony Lee or, alternatively, whether she assumed the care of the child and secluded him from the care of his mother, his natural protector. On both of these issues, the evidence is in direct conflict, appellant insisting that the mother was actually living with appellant and Anthony Lee, and hence should have been taking care of the child herself, while Shirley Green testified she was living with her parents and was paying appellant to care for both children.

In spite of this conflict, the instructions given in the case failed even to suggest the necessity for finding a legal duty of care. The only reference to duty in the instructions was the reading of the indictment which charged, inter alia, that the defendants "failed to perform their legal duty." A finding of legal duty is the critical element of the crime charged and failure to instruct the jury concerning it was plain error. . . .

Reversed and remanded.

Notes and Questions

1. Though the defendant was successful on appeal in *Jones,* the case makes clear that the state may sometimes punish people for omissions. Does this violate the principle of *Proctor?* Is it not obvious that all citizens face potential criminal liability for such omissions as failure to file income tax returns?

2. Model Penal Code Section 2.01(3):

> Liability for the comission of an offense may not be based on an omission unaccompanied by action unless:
>
> (a) the omission is expressly made sufficient by the law defining the offense; or
>
> (b) a duty to perform the omitted act is otherwise imposed by law.

3. Since different rules apply depending on whether the defendant has performed some voluntary act or has been guilty of an omission, a common issue is whether the defendant has committed some act or simply failed to act. One commentator[9] has argued as follows:

9. Kelman, Interpretive Construction in the Substantive Criminal Law, 33 Stan. L. Rev. 637-640 (1981).

> Unless the defendant has a duty to act, an omission is not culpable. Of course, the line between omissions and commissions is blurry. There is considerable circularity in claiming that a defendant can be culpable only if he has committed an act, when we often describe an event in active conduct terms rather than passively if we have already (somehow) determined that the party is culpable. For instance, a parent who *does not feed* a child may readily be said to *starve* the child—to commit an act—while a stranger would be said to *fail to feed*—a passive nonact.

Is this correct? Is "starving" someone an act?

4. What of the physician who discontinues the life support systems of a terminally ill patient? Is that an act or an omission? Would the distinction matter in such a case?

In a celebrated New Jersey case, a young woman had fallen into a comatose, insentient state, and her father sought court permission to discontinue all extraordinary medical procedures for sustaining her vital functions. The court held that the father could do so without any liability if the hospital ethics committee determined that there was no chance the woman would ever emerge from her vegetative condition. See In the Matter of Quinlan, 70 N.J. 10, 355 A.2d 647 (1976).

5. Why should we hesitate to impose criminal punishment for a failure to act? Consider the following hypothetical:

> A small child is drowning in a public swimming pool as twenty adults look on. The spectators include: various bystanders, the lifeguard, the child's babysitter, a municipal official, the child's cousin, a close friend of the child's parents, and a stranger who had stumbled, accidentally pushing the child into the pool.

Do they all have a duty to save him? Does any one? Does only the adult closest to the child have a duty? The best swimmer?

6. The court in *Jones* sets out four situations in which the failure to act may constitute a breach of a legal duty. What do these situations have in common? Are they broad enough to ensure the punishment for all blameworthy omissions? To what extent do you think courts and juries rely on moral repugnance, and not law, in finding legal duties?

What of the wealthy individual who ignores or refuses a beggar's plea for a few pennies for food, when the beggar subsequently starves to death? Consider T. B. Macaulay, Notes on the Indian Penal Code (1837), India Law Commission note M, 53-56 (1888):

> It is true that the man who, having abundance of wealth, suffers a fellow creature to die of hunger at his feet, is a bad man—a worse man, probably, than many of those for whom we have provided very severe punishment. But we are unable to see where, if we make such a man punishable, we can draw the line. If the rich man who refuses to save a beggar's life at the cost of a little copper is a murderer, is the poor man just one degree above beggary also to be a murderer if he omits to invite the beggar to partake his hard-earned rice?

Again: If the rich man is a murderer for refusing to save the beggar's life at the cost of a little copper, is he also to be a murderer if he refuses to save the beggar's life at the cost of a thousand rupees?

7. What of a person driving along an empty highway across the Nevada desert with no signs of civilization anywhere in sight? The driver sees an obviously injured person lying near the road. If the injured person dies, but would have survived if the driver had taken her to a hospital, should the driver face criminal punishment?

PEOPLE v. BEARDSLEY

Supreme Court of Michigan
150 Mich. 205, 113 N.W. 1128 (1907)

McAlvay, C.J. Respondent was convicted of manslaughter before the circuit court for Oakland county, and was sentenced to the state prison at Jackson for a minimum term of one year and a maximum term not to exceed five years.

He was a married man living at Pontiac, and at the time the facts herein narrated occurred he was working as a bartender and clerk at the Columbia Hotel. He lived with his wife in Pontiac, occupying two rooms on the ground floor of a house. Other rooms were rented to tenants, as was also one living room in the basement. His wife being temporarily absent from the city, respondent arranged with a woman named Blanche Burns, who at the time was working at another hotel, to go to his apartments with him. He had been acquainted with her for some time. They knew each other's habits and character. They had drunk liquor together, and had on two occasions been in Detroit and spent the night together in houses of assignation. On the evening of Saturday, March 18, 1905, he met her at the place where she worked, and they went together to his place of residence. They at once began to drink, and continued to drink steadily, and remained together, day and night, from that time until the afternoon of the Monday following, except when respondent went to his work on Sunday afternoon. There was liquor at these rooms, and when it was all used they were served with bottles of whisky and beer by a young man who worked at the Columbia Hotel, and who also attended respondent's fires at the house. He was the only person who saw them in the house during the time they were there together. Respondent gave orders for liquor by telephone. On Monday afternoon, about 1 o'clock, the young man went to the house to see if anything was wanted. At this time he heard respondent say they must fix up the rooms, and the woman must not be found there by his wife, who was likely to return at any time. During this visit to the house the woman sent the young man to a drug store to purchase, with money she gave him, camphor and morphine tablets. He procured both articles. There were six grains of morphine in quarter-grain tablets. She concealed the morphine from respondent's notice, and was discovered putting something into her mouth by him and the young man as they were returning from the other room after taking a drink of beer. She in fact was taking morphine. Respondent struck the box from her hand. Some of the tablets fell on the floor, and of these respondent crushed several with his foot. She picked up and swallowed two of them, and the young man put two of them in the spittoon. Althogether it is probable she took from three to four grains of morphine. The young man went away soon after this. Respondent called him by telephone about an hour later, and after he came to the house requested him to take the woman into the room in the basement which was occupied by a Mr. Skoba. She was in a stupor, and did not rouse when spoken to. The young man proceeded to take her downstairs. While doing this, Skoba arrived, and together they put her in his room on the bed. Respondent requested Skoba to look after her, and let her out the back way when she waked up. Between 9 and 10 o'clock in the evening, Skoba became alarmed at her condition. He at once called the city marshal and a doctor. An examination by them disclosed that she was dead.

Many errors are assigned by respondent, who asks to have his conviction set aside. The principal assignments of error are based upon the charge of the court and refusal to give certain requests to charge, and are upon the theory that under the undisputed evidence in the case, as claimed by the people and detailed by the people's witnesses, the respondent should have been acquitted and discharged. In the brief of the prosecutor, his position is stated as follows:

> It is the theory of the prosecution that the facts and circumstances attending the death of Blanche Burns in the house of respondent were such as to lay upon him a duty to care for her, and the duty to take steps for her protection, the failure to take which was sufficient to constitute such an omission as would render him legally responsible for her death. . . . There is no claim on the part of the people that the respondent was in any way an active agent in bringing about the death of Blanche Burns, but simply that he owed her a duty which he failed to perform, and that in consequence of such failure on his part she came to her death.

Upon this theory a conviction was asked and secured.

The law recognizes that under some circumstances the omission of a duty owed by one individual to another, where such omission results in the death of the one to whom the duty is owing, will make the other chargeable with manslaughter. . . . This rule of law is always based upon the proposition that the duty neglected must be a legal duty, and not a mere moral obligation. It must be a duty imposed by law or by contract, and the omission to perform the duty must be the immediate and direct cause of death. Although the literature upon the subject is quite meager and the cases few, nevertheless the authorities are in harmony as to the relationship which must exist between the parties to create the duty, the omission of which establishes legal responsibility. One authority has briefly and correctly stated the rule, which the prosecution claims should be applied to the case at bar, as follows:

> If a person who sustains to another the legal relation of protector, as husband to wife, parent to child, master to seaman, etc., knowing such person to be in peril, willfully and negligently fails to make such reasonable and proper efforts to rescue him as he might have done, without jeopardizing his own life, or the lives of others, he is guilty of manslaughter at least, if by reason of his omission of duty the dependent person dies. . . . So one who from domestic relationship, public duty, voluntary choice, or otherwise, has the custody and care of a human being, helpless either from imprisonment, infancy, sickness, age, imbecility, or other incapacity of mind or body is bound to execute the charge with proper diligence, and will be held guilty of manslaughter, if by culpable negligence he lets the helpless creature die.

. . . Seeking for a proper determination of the case at bar by the application of the legal principles involved, we must eliminate from the case all consideration of mere moral obligation, and discover whether respondent was under a legal duty towards Blanche Burns at the time of her death, knowing her to be in peril of her life, which required him to make all reasonable and proper effort to save her, the omission to perform which duty would make him responsible for her death. This is the important and determining question in this case. If we hold that such legal duty rested upon respondent, it must arise by implication from the facts and circumstances already recited. The record in this case discloses that the deceased was a woman past 30 years of age. She had been twice married. She was accustomed to visiting saloons and to the use of intoxicants. She previously had made assignations with this man in Detroit at least twice. There is no evidence or claim from this record that any duress, fraud, or deceit had been practiced upon her. On the contrary, it appears that she went upon this carouse with respondent voluntarily, and so continued to remain with him. Her entire conduct indicates that she had ample experience in such affairs.

It is urged by the prosecutor that the respondent "stood towards this woman for the time being in the place of her natural guardian and protector, and as such owed her a clear legal duty which he completely failed to perform." The cases establish that no such legal duty is created based upon a mere moral obligation. The fact that this woman was in his house created no such legal duty as exists in law and is due from a husband towards his wife, as seems to be intimated by the prosecutor's brief. Such an inference would be very repugnant to our moral sense. Respondent had assumed either in fact or by implication no care or control over his companion. Had this been a case where two men under like circumstances had voluntarily gone on a debauch together, and one had attempted suicide, no one would claim that this doctrine of legal duty could be invoked to hold the other criminally responsible for omitting to make effort to rescue his companion. How can the fact that in this case one of the parties was a woman change the principle of law applicable to it? Deriving and applying the law in this case from the principle of decided cases, we do not find that such legal duty as is contended for existed in fact or by implication on the part of respondent towards the deceased, the omission of which involved criminal liability. We find no more apt words to apply to this case than those used by Mr. Justice Field, . . . "In the absence of such obligations, it is undoubtedly the moral duty of every person to extend to others assistance when in danger . . . and, if such efforts should be omitted by any one when they could be made without imperiling his own life, he would by his conduct draw upon himself the just censure and reproach of good men; but this is the only punishment to which he would be subjected by society."

Other questions discussed in the briefs need not be considered.

The conviction is set aside, and respondent is ordered discharged.

Notes and Questions

1. Assume that a major problem in all omission cases is our difficulty in answering the hypothetical defendant's question "Why me?" Does this problem exist in *Beardsley?* Is the problem that the court is unwilling to equate the victim's status to that of the defendant's wife—to whom the defendant would concededly owe a duty? Or is the problem that the court thought that the deceased had brought her need for help upon herself by abusing a drug?

2. Hughes, Criminal Omissions, 67 Yale L.J. 590, 600, 624 (1958), calls for a generalized duty requirement, asserting that:

> [I]n the immense complexity and interdependency of modern life, those who elect to pursue certain activities or calling must, for the welfare of their fellow citizens, submit to a host of regulations, some of which will naturally and properly impose positive duties to act. . . .
>
> . . . In a civilized society, a man who finds himself with a helplessly ill person who has no other source of aid should be under a duty to summon help, whether the person is his wife, his mistress, a prostitute, or a Chief Justice. The *Beardsley* decision deserves emphatic repudiation by the jurisdiction which was responsible.

Can you see any problems with Hughes's theory?

COMMONWEALTH v. CALI

Supreme Judicial Court of Massachusetts
141 N.E. 510 (1923)

BRALEY, J. The defendant having been indicted, tried and convicted under G.L. c. 266, §10, of burning a building in Leominster belonging to Maria Cali, which at the time was insured against loss or damage by fire, with intent to injure the insurer, the case is here on his exceptions to the denial of his motion for a directed verdict, and to rulings at the trial. . . .

The only evidence as to the origin, extent and progress of the fire were the statements of the defendant to the police inspector, and as a witness. The jury who were to determine his credibility and the weight to be given his testimony could find notwithstanding his explanations of its origin as being purely accidental, that when all the circumstances were reviewed he either set it, or after the fire was under way purposely refrained from any attempt to extinguish it in order to obtain the benefit of the proceeds of the policy, which when recovered, would be applied by the mortgagee on his indebtedness. If they so found, a specific intent to injure the insurer had been proved. The motion and the defendant's requests insofar as not given were denied rightly. . . . The instructions to the jury that:

> If a man does start an accidental fire what is his conduct in regard to it? A question—as if after the fire has started accidentally, and he then has it within his power and ability to extinguish the fire and he realizes and knows that he can, and then he forms and entertains an intent to injure an insurance company, he can be guilty of this offense. It is not necessary that the intent be formed before the fire is started,"

—also show no error of law.

Exceptions overruled.

Notes and Questions

1. Can we answer the "Why me?" question in *Cali?* How?

2. Does Cali not have a right to claim that he is in fact being punished for accidently and without fault starting a fire? If not, where does his blameworthiness come from?

3. Consider Jones v. State, 220 Ind. 384, 43 N.E.2d 1017 (1942), in which the defendant raped a child of twelve, who, "distraught by pain and grief," jumped or fell into a creek where she drowned. Defendant made no attempt to rescue her although he easily could have done so without any risk to himself. The court affirmed a conviction of murder.

4. Can we hold in certain cases that even though our policy views on omissions could permit liability, the words of the criminal statute in question so strongly imply action that liability predicated on omission would be improper. Consider the following:[10]

> The assumption that "assault" requires an act should not go unchallenged. Is there some special magic in the word which distinguishes it from "kill," "slay," etc.? If *D* digs a pit with the intention that *P* should fall into it, and he does, that

10. Smith, Liability for Omissions in the Criminal Law, Legal Stud.: J. Socy. Pub. Tchrs. of L. 88, 98-100 (1984).

is said to be an assault. If *D* is sitting in a corridor and, hearing *P* running towards him, he puts out his foot with the intention that *P* shall fall over it, and he does, that is plainly an assault. Should it not equally be an assault if *D*, having dug the pit with no criminal intention, decides to leave it uncovered so that *P* will fall into it—which he does? Of if *D*'s legs are already extended and he decides not to draw them back, so that P will fall over them? These seem to be cases where there might properly be held to be a duty to act . . . *D*'s act has created the peril and he knows it. . . .

There seems in fact, to be no actual decision that assault cannot be committed by omission. The matter was considered by the English divisional Court in Fagan v. Metropolitan Police Commissioner,[11] the case of "parking on a copper's foot." . . . The defendant, having been directed by a policeman to pull in to the side of the road, did so with his mini-car coming to rest on the officer's foot. When told, "Get off, you are on my foot," Fagan replied in abusive terms, switched off the ignition and remained in the car. Only after several requests from the officer did he drive the car off the officer's foot. The trial court thought that driving on to the officer's foot may have been accidental but they were satisfied that he "knowingly, unnecessarily and provocatively" allowed the car to remain there. The majority of the Divisional Court held that the defendant was guilty of an act constituting an assault. They reasoned as follows:

> Knowing that the wheel was on the officer's foot the appellant (1) remained seated in the car so that his body through the medium of the car was in contact with the officer, (2) switched off the ignition of the car, (3) maintained the wheel of the car on the foot and (4) used words indicating the intention of keeping the wheel in that position. For our part we cannot regard such conduct as mere omission or inactivity.

[Glanville] Williams criticises this reasoning as unconvincing:

> Suppose that the defendant had got out of the car, saying nothing, leaving the engine running and leaving the officer helplessly imprisoned; would the court then have called it a mere omission and not an assault? The outcome would seem to depend on whether an assault can be committed by omission. James LJ, speaking for the majority in *Fagan,* said that it was unnecessary to formulate any concluded views on this point. Bridge LJ, dissenting, however, stated firmly "No mere omission to act can amount to an assault." Since, as he found, the defendant had done precisely nothing after the car came to rest on the constable's foot, it followed that there was no assault. . . .

Fagan, . . . seems to be an appropriate case for conviction. . . . The only valid reason for not convicting of assault would be that the word "assault" excludes omission.

5. Certain convictions for possession may be based on an omissions theory according to Professor Williams. Glanville Williams, Textbook of Criminal Law, 153 (2d ed. 1983):

> The *acquisition* of possession usually involves an act (an act of grasping an object, for example), in which case there is no difficulty. Even when another

11. [1969] 1 Q.B. 439.

person delivers goods to my premises without my touching them, I shall usually have ordered him to do so. However, one can instance cases where there is no relevant act. Take the statutory offence of "knowingly possessing explosives." A man is in possession of a package which, when he first received it, he did not realise contained explosives, but he has later come to know that it does. There is no "act" on his part after he acquires the knowledge. The courts hold that he commits an offence if he retains the explosives, unless he does so only in order to inform the police. . . . The offence is one of omission in breach of duty.

3

STRICT LIABILITY

In the previous chapter, we examined the view that the criminal law, in accord with our basic moral intuition, should punish only those actions which are voluntary. In this chapter, we examine the legal implications of another fundamental moral intuition: that the state should punish only those actions that are morally blameworthy. We first address the question of when, if ever, a person who acts with no culpable state of mind may nonetheless suffer criminal punishment for causing harm. In the next chapter, assuming that the criminal law does normally require a blameworthy state of mind, we address the complex questions of how to identify and distinguish among the various culpable mental states.

UNITED STATES v. BALINT

United States Supreme Court
258 U.S. 250 (1922)

Mr. Chief Justice Taft delivered the opinion of the court.

. . . Defendants in error were indicted for a violation of the Narcotic Act. The indictment charged them with unlawfully selling to another a certain amount of a derivative of opium and a certain amount of a derivative of coca leaves, not in pursuance of any written order on a form issued in blank for that purpose by the Commissioner of Internal Revenue, contrary to the provisions of §2 of the [Narcotic] Act. The defendants demurred to the indictment on the ground that it failed to charge that they had sold the inhibited drugs knowing them to be such. The statute does not make such knowledge an element of the offense. The District Court sustained the demurrer and quashed the indictment. The correctness of this ruling is the question before us.

While the general rule at common law was that the *scienter* was a necessary element in the indictment and proof of every crime, and this was followed in regard to statutory crimes even where the statutory definition did not in terms include it there has been a modification of this view in respect to prosecutions under statutes the purpose of which would be obstructed by such a requirement. It is a question of legislative intent to be construed by the court. It has been objected that punishment of a person for an act in violation of law when ignorant of the facts making it so, is an absence of due process of law. But that objection is considered and overruled in Shevlin-Carpenter Co. v. Minnesota, 218 U.S. 57, 69, 70, in which it was held that in the prohibition or punishment of particular acts, the State may in the maintenance of a public policy provide "that he who shall do them shall do them at his peril and will not be heard to plead in defense good faith or ignorance." Many instances of this are to be found in regulatory measures in the exercise of what is called the police power where the emphasis of the statute is evidently upon achievement of some social betterment rather than the punishment of the crimes as in cases of *mala in se.* So, too, in the collection of taxes, the importance to the public of their collection leads the legislature to impose on the taxpayer the burden of finding out the facts upon which his liability to pay depends and meeting it at the peril of punishment. Again where one deals with others and his mere negligence may be dangerous to them, as in selling diseased food or poison, the policy of the law may, in order to stimulate proper care, require the punishment of the negligent person though he be ignorant of the noxious character of what he sells.

The question before us, therefore, is one of the construction of the statute and of inference of the intent of Congress. . . .

. . . It is very evident from a reading of it that the emphasis of [§2 of the Narcotic Act] is in securing a close supervision of the business of dealing in these dangerous drugs by the taxing officers of the Government and that it merely uses a criminal penalty to secure recorded evidence of the disposition of such drugs as a means of taxing and restraining the traffic. Its manifest purpose is to require every person dealing in drugs to ascertain at his peril whether that which he sells comes within the inhibition of the statute, and if he sells the inhibited drug in ignorance of its character, to penalize him. Congress weighed the possible injustice of subjecting an innocent seller to penalty against the evil of exposing innocent purchasers to danger from the drug, and concluded that the latter was the result preferably to be avoided. Doubtless considerations as to the opportunity of the seller to find out the fact and the difficulty of proof of knowledge contributed to this conclusion. We think the demurrer to indictment should have been overruled.

Judgement reversed.

Notes and Questions

1. Since the *Balint* case came to the Supreme Court on objections to an indictment, we do not know the facts of the case. Let us imagine for the moment that the facts were these:

> Balint was a retired pharmacist. To clear out his attic he sold an old desk that had been gathering dust for many years, together with its contents. The desk had been willed to Balint by his uncle. After the used-furniture dealer transported the desk back to his store, he looked through the desk drawers. He found a packet of illegal drugs taped to the back of one drawer. The drugs, apparently still potent, had been in the desk since before Balint received it.

Should Balint be guilty of selling illegal drugs? Does the language of the statute suggest that Congress intended that Balint's type of conduct be punished?

2. Consider this excerpt from Gilbert and Sullivan's The Mikado (1885):

Mik. (*To* Ko-Ko.) My poor fellow, in your anxiety to carry out my wishes you have beheaded the heir to the throne of Japan!

Ko. I beg to offer an unqualified apology.

Pooh. I desire to associate myself with that expression of regret.

Pitti. We really hadn't the least notion—

Mik. Of course you hadn't. How could you? Come, come, my good fellow, don't distress yourself—it was no fault of yours. If a man of exalted rank chooses to disguise himself as a Second Trombone, he must take the consequences. It really distresses me to see you take on so. I've no doubt he thoroughly deserved all he got. (*They rise.*)

Ko. We are infinitely obliged to your Majesty—

Pitti. Much obliged, your Majesty.

Pooh. Very much obliged, your Majesty.

Mik. Obliged? Not a bit. Don't mention it. How *could* you tell?

Pooh. No, of course we couldn't tell who the gentleman really was.

Pitti. It wasn't written on his forehead, you know.

Ko. It might have been on his pocket-handkerchief, but Japanese don't use pocket handkerchiefs! Ha! ha! ha!

Mik. Ha! ha! ha! (*To* Katisha.) I forget the punishment for compassing the death of the Heir Apparent.

Ko., Pooh., Pitti. Punishment? (*They drop down on their knees again.*)

Mik. Yes. Something lingering, with boiling oil in it, I fancy. Something of that sort. I think boiling oil occurs in it, but I'm not sure. I know it's something humorous, but lingering, with either boiling oil or melted lead. Come, come, don't fret—I'm not a bit angry.

Ko. (in abject terror). If your Majesty will accept our assurance, we had no idea—

Mik. Of course—

Pitti. I knew nothing about it.

Mik. That's the pathetic part of it. Unfortunately, the fool of an Act says "compassing the death of the Heir Apparent." There's not a word about a mistake—

Ko., Pitti., and Pooh. No!.

Mik. Or not knowing—

Ko. No!
Mik. Or having no notion—
Pitti. No!
Mik. There should be, of course—
Ko., Pitti., and Pooh. Yes!
Mik. But there isn't.
Ko., Pitti., and Pooh. Oh!
Mik. That's the slovenly way in which these Acts are always drawn. However, cheer up, it'll be all right. I'll have it altered next session. Now, let's see about your execution—will after luncheon suit you? Can you wait till then?
Ko., Pitti., and Pooh. Oh yes—we can wait till then!
Mik. Then we'll make it after luncheon.
Pooh. I don't want any lunch.
Mik. I'm really very sorry for you all, but it's an unjust world, and virtue is triumphant only in theatrical performances.

Notice how W. S. Gilbert, who had been a barrister in London, comments on the problem of strict liability. Is it true that "virtue is triumphant only in theatrical performances"? Should we construct a legal system on that basis?

3. In tort law, liability without fault is quite common. "Strict" or "absolute" liability is a consequence of the courts' view that under some conditions, as between an "innocent" plaintiff and an "innocent" defendant, the defendant should have to bear the loss. The argument often runs, in economic terms as follows: If a defendant bears all the costs of his activity, he will engage in the "optimal" level of the activity. He can spread the risks among all his customers and can more efficiently purchase insurance against the loss.

Do these principles apply in criminal cases? Recall the materials in Chapter I about the limitations upon criminal punishment. Do they suggest that the tort arguments should not apply, and that the criminal law should punish someone only for conduct that may be regarded as his or her fault?

4. According to the Model Penal Code, Section 2.05, when the state imposes liability without fault, the criminal offense may be punished only as a violation. Section 1.04(5) distinguishes a violation from a crime, by defining the former as an offense punishable only by "a fine, or fine and forfeiture, or other civil penalty [which] shall not give rise to any disability or legal disadvantage based on conviction of a criminal offense."

Consider the Model Penal Code's explanation of this decision:

> This [section] makes a frontal attack on absolute or strict liability in the penal law, whenever the offense carries the possibility of criminal conviction, for which a sentence of probation or imprisonment may be imposed. The method used is not to abrogate strict liability completely, but to provide that when conviction rests upon that basis the grade of the offense is reduced to a violation. . . .

This position is affirmed not only with respect to offenses defined by the penal code; it is superimposed on the entire corpus of the law, so far as penal sanctions are involved. Since most strict liability offenses involve special regulatory legislation, . . . this superimposition is essential if the principle of no criminality . . . for strict liability offenses is to be made effective.

. . . The liabilities involved are indefensible unless reduced to terms that insulate conviction from the type of moral condemnation that is and ought to be implicit when a sentence of imprisonment may be imposed. It has been argued, and the argument undoubtedly will be repeated, that strict liability is necessary for enforcement in a number of areas where it obtains. But if practical enforcement precludes litigation of the culpability of alleged deviation from legal requirements, the enforcers cannot rightly demand the use of penal sanctions for the purpose. Crime does and should mean condemnation and no court should have to pass that judgment unless it can declare that the defendant's act was culpable. This is too fundamental to be compromised. The law goes far enough if it permits the imposition of a monetary penalty in cases where strict liability has been imposed.

5. Roman Catholic Doctrine clearly sets its face against strict liability for sin. According to the Baltimore Catechism:[1]

69. What Three Things Are Necessary to Make a Sin Mortal?

To make a sin mortal these three things are necessary: *first,* the thought, desire, word, action, or omission must be seriously wrong or considered seriously wrong; *second,* the sinner must be mindful of the serious wrong; *third,* the sinner must fully consent to it. . . .

(b) The sinner is mindful of the serious wrong if at the time he commits the sin or places a cause from which he foresees the sin will follow, he either is clearly aware or at least thinks that the action is grievously sinful.

(c) A sinner fully consents to the wrong when he freely chooses to do evil, although he is entirely free not to do it. . . .

(e) When a person does wrong but is in no way mindful of it, he is said to commit a *material* sin; for example, a person who misses Mass, unmindful that it Sunday, commits a material sin. God does not hold us accountable for material sins and they do not deprive us of sanctifying grace.

Scripture

Before man is life and death, good and evil: that which he shall choose shall be given him. [Ecclesiasticus 15:18.]

Can one argue, however, that an earthly court might find strict liability necessary to compensate for the difficulty of proving the defendant's state of mind?

6. If an accused murderer argued that the horrendous child abuse she

1. This We Believe: By This We Live, Revised Edition of the Baltimore Catechism No. 3, 49-50.

herself had suffered had doomed her to a life of violent impulse, would the arguments against strict liability lend her support?

One commentator[2] has argued that the debate over strict liability has been so vigorous primarily because we wish to be able to punish such a person:

> The uniformity of commentators' hostility results less from reasoned consideration of the actual issues than from a misleading rhetorical ploy which implies that the strictly liable defendant was unable to avoid criminality, and from a failure to take account of perfectly standard liberal legalist arguments against ad hoc standards. The root of this blindness to the case for strict liability is most likely the desire to reassure oneself that only the blameworthy are punished; obviously, the most significant attack on the claim that society is punishing only the wicked comes from general determinists who see criminality as grounded in adverse socioeconomic conditions. One way of blocking out the degree to which we are all more or less drawn to the determinists' position is to show how ultrasensitive we are to punishing the blameless without paying much heed to how blamelessness is defined. The ritual attack on strict-liability crime, then, is largely an exercise in mutual flattery of our moral solemnity and deflects attention from the serious charges of moral inadequacy.

UNITED STATES v. DOTTERWEICH

United States Supreme Court
320 U.S. 277 (1943)

Mr. Justice FRANKFURTER delivered the opinion of the Court.

This was a prosecution begun by two informations, consolidated for trial, charging Buffalo Pharmacal Company, Inc., and Dotterweich, its president and general manager, with violations of the Federal Food, Drug, and Cosmetic Act. The Company, a jobber in drugs, purchased them from their manufacturers and shipped them, repacked under its own label, in interstate commerce. . . . The informations were based on §301 of that Act which prohibits "The introduction or delivery for introduction into interstate commerce of any . . . drug . . . that is adulterated or misbranded." "Any person" violating this provision is, by paragraph (a) of §303 made "guilty of a misdemeanor." Three counts went to the jury—two for shipping misbranded drugs in interstate commerce, and a third, for so shipping an adulterated drug. The jury disagreed as to the corporation and found Dotterweich guilty on all three counts. We start with the finding of the Circuit Court of Appeals that the evidence was adequate to support the verdict of adulteration and misbranding. . . .

. . . The Circuit Court of Appeals, one judge dissenting, reversed the conviction. . . . We then brought the case here, on the Government's petition for certiorari, 318 U.S. 753, because [the Court of Appeals'] construction raised questions of importance in the enforcement of the Food, Drug, and Cosmetic Act. . . .

2. Kelman, Strict Liability, 14 Encyclopedia of Crime and Justice 1516, 1518 (1983).

. . . The prosecution to which Dotterweich was subjected is based on a now familiar type of legislation whereby penalties serve as effective means of regulation. Such legislation dispenses with the conventional requirement for criminal conduct—awareness of some wrongdoing. In the interest of the larger good it puts the burden of acting at hazard upon a person otherwise innocent but standing in responsible relation to a public danger. United States v. Balint, 258 U.S. 250. And so it is clear that shipments like those now in issue are "punished by the statute if the article is misbranded (or adulterated), and that the article may be misbranded (or adulterated) without any conscious fraud at all. It was natural enough to throw this risk on shippers with regard to the identity of their wares. . . ." . . .

The Act is concerned not with the proprietory relation to a misbranded or an adulterated drug but with its distribution. In the case of a corporation such distribution must be accomplished, and may be furthered, by persons standing in various relations to the incorporeal proprietor. . . .

. . . Hardship there doubtless may be under a statute which thus penalizes the transactions though consciousness of wrongdoing be totally wanting. Balancing relative hardships, Congress has preferred to place [the burden] upon those who have at least the opportunity of informing themselves of the existence of conditions imposed for the protection of consumers before sharing in illicit commerce, rather than to throw the hazard on the innocent public who are wholly helpless.

It would be too treacherous to define or even to indicate by way of illustration the class of employees which stands in such responsible relation. To attempt a formula embracing the variety of conduct whereby persons may responsibly contribute in furthering a transaction forbidden by an Act of Congress, to wit, to send illicit goods across state lines, would be mischievous futility. In such matters the good sense of prosecutors, the wise guidance of trial judges, and the ultimate judgment of juries must be trusted. Our system of criminal justice necessarily depends on "conscience and circumspection in prosecuting officers," Nash v. United States, 229 U.S. 373, 378, even when the consequences are far more drastic than they are under the provision of law before us. See United States v. Balint, supra (involving the maximum sentence of five years). For present purpose it suffices to say that in what the defense characterized as "a very fair charge" the District Court properly left the question of the responsibility of Dotterweich for the shipment to the jury, and there was sufficient evidence to support its verdict.

Reversed.

Mr. Justice MURPHY, dissenting:

Our prime concern in this case is whether the criminal sanctions of the Federal Food, Drug, and Cosmetic Act of 1938 plainly and unmistakably apply to the respondent in his capacity as a corporate officer. He is charged with violating §301(a) of the Act, which prohibits the introduction or delivery for introduction into interstate commerce of any adulterated or misbranded drug. There is no evidence in this case of any personal guilt on the part of the respondent. There is no proof or claim that he ever knew of the introduction into commerce of the adulterated drugs in question, much less that he actively participated in their introduction. Guilt is imputed to the respondent solely on the basis of his authority and responsibility as president and general manager of the corporation.

It is a fundamental principle of Anglo-Saxon jurisprudence that guilt is personal and that it ought not lightly to be imputed to a citizen who, like the respondent, has no evil intention or consciousness of wrongdoing. It may be proper to charge him with responsibility to the corporation and the stockholders for negligence and mismanagement. But in the absence of clear statutory authorization it is inconsistent with established canons of criminal law to rest liability on an act in which the accused did not participate and of which he had no personal knowledge. Before we place the stigma of a criminal conviction upon any such citizen the legislative mandate must be clear and unambiguous. Accordingly that which Chief Justice Marshall has called "the tenderness of the law for the rights of individuals" entitles each person, regardless of economic or social status, to an unequivocal warning from the legislature as to whether he is within the class of persons subject to vicarious liability. Congress cannot be deemed to have intended to punish anyone who is not "plainly and unmistakably" within the confines of the statute. . . .

The dangers inherent in any attempt to create liability without express Congressional intention or authorization are illustrated by this case. Without any legislative guides, we are confronted with the problem of determining precisely which officers, employees and agents of a corporation are to be subject to this Act by our fiat. To erect standards of responsibility is a difficult legislative task and the opinion of this Court admits that it is "too treacherous" and a "mischievous futility" for us to engage in such pursuits. But the only alternative is a blind resort to "the good sense of prosecutors, the wise guidance of trial judges, and the ultimate judgment of juries." Yet that situation is precisely what our constitutional system sought to avoid. Reliance on the legislature to define crimes and criminals distinguishes our form of jurisprudence from certain less desirable ones. The legislative power to restrain the liberty and to imperil the good reputation of citizens must not rest upon the variable attitudes and opinions of those charged with the duties of interpreting and enforcing the mandates of the law. I therefore cannot approve the decision of the Court in this case.

Mr. Justice Roberts, Mr. Justice Reed and Mr. Justice Rutledge join in this dissent.

Notes and Questions

1. Note that in *Dotterweich* the Court asserts that the government need not prove "awareness of some wrongdoing." Rather, the jury must find only that the defendant had "a responsible relation to the violative transaction or condi-

tion." Do the facts suggest that Dotterweich was careless in the way he ran the company, and so might have deserved punishment on that ground? Is it fair to say that a company president is necessarily careless if some social harm results from the company's actions?

2. In United States v. Park, 421 U.S. 658 (1975), the defendant, the President of Acme Markets, was charged with allowing food that was being stored for shipment in interstate commerce to be contaminated, in violation of 21 U.S.C. §342 and 21 U.S.C. §331. The court found Park criminally liable for the adulterated shipments, stating that:

> [In *Dotterweich,*] this Court looked to the purposes of the Act and noted that they "touch phases of the lives and health of people, which, in the circumstances of modern industrialism, are largely beyond self-protection." It observed that the Act is of "a now familiar type" which "dispenses with the conventional requirement for criminal conduct—awareness of some wrongdoing. In the interest of the larger good it puts the burden of acting at hazard upon a person otherwise innocent, but who stands in responsible relation to a public danger." . . . [This Court] has reaffirmed the proposition that "the public interest in the purity of its food is so great as to warrant the imposition of the highest standard of care on distributors." Smith v. California, 361 U.S. 147, 152 (1959). In order to make "distributors of food the strictest censors of their merchandise," ibid., the Act punishes "neglect where the law requires care, or inaction where it imposes a duty." Morissette v. United States [342 U.S.] at 255. "The accused, if he does not will the violation, usually is in a position to prevent it with no more care than society might reasonably expect and no more exertion than it might reasonably exact from one who assumed his responsibilities." Id. at 256. . . .
>
> . . . *Dotterweich* and the cases which have followed reveal that in providing sanctions which reach and touch the individuals who execute the corporate mission—and this is by no means necessarily confined to a single corporate agent or employee—the Act imposes not only a positive duty to seek out and remedy violations when they occur but also, and primarily, a duty to implement measures that will ensure that violations will not occur. The requirements of foresight and vigilance imposed on responsible corporate agents are beyond question demanding, and perhaps onerous, but they are no more stringent than the public has a right to expect of those who voluntarily assume positions of authority in business enterprises whose services and products affect the health and well-being of the public that supports them. . . .
>
> . . . The duty imposed by Congress on responsible corporate agents is, we emphasize, one that requires the highest standard of foresight and vigilance, but the Act, in its criminal aspect, does not require that which is objectively impossible. The theory upon which responsible corporate agents are held criminally accountable for "causing" violations of the Act permits a claim that a defendant was "powerless" to prevent or correct the violation. . . .

The *Park* Court says that the statute does not require people to do the "impossible." What if some of Acme's food had suffered contamination which could not be prevented by any technology currently available to Acme or any other company, but which could have been prevented if Acme had invested in research and development of more advanced technology? If the law announces that it punishes a person with a "responsible relation" to the social harm, does it state a tautology?

3. In Morissette v. United States, 342 U.S. 246 (1952), the defendant, a junk dealer, openly entered an Air Force practice bombing range and appropriated spent bomb casings that had been lying about for years, exposed to the weather and rusting away. He flattened them out and sold them at a city junk market at a profit of $84. He was indicted and convicted of violating 19 U.S.C. §641, which made it a crime "knowingly to convert" government property. There was no question that the defendant knew that what he took and sold were Air Force bomb casings. His defense was that he honestly believed that they had been abandoned by the Air Force and that he was therefore violating no one's rights by taking them.

The Court reversed Morissette's conviction in an often-cited opinion by Justice Robert Jackson, stating:

> The contention that an injury can amount to a crime only when inflicted by intention is no provincial or transient notion. It is as universal and persistent in mature systems of law as belief in freedom of the human will and a consequent ability and duty of the normal individual to choose between good and evil. A relation between some mental element and punishment for a harmful act is almost as instinctive as the child's familiar exculpatory "But I didn't mean to," and has afforded the rational basis for a tardy and unfinished substitution of deterrence and reformation in place of retaliation and vengeance as the motivation for public prosecution. . . .
>
> Crime, as a compound concept, generally constituted only from concurrence of an evil-meaning mind with an evil-doing hand, was congenial to an intense individualism and took deep and early root in American soil. As the states codified the common law of crimes, even if their enactments were silent on the subject, their courts assumed that the omission did not signify disapproval of the principle but merely recognized that intent was so inherent in the idea of the offense that it required no statutory affirmation.
>
> However, the [*Balint* offense belongs] to a category of another character, with very different antecedents and origins. The crimes there involved depend on no mental element but consist only of forbidden acts or omissions. This, while not expressed by the Court, is made clear from examination of a century-old but accelerating tendency, discernible both here and in England, to call into existence new duties and crimes which disregard any ingredient of intent. The industrial revolution multiplied the number of workmen exposed to injury from increasingly powerful and complex mechanisms, driven by freshly discovered sources of energy, requiring higher precautions by employers. Traffic of velocities, volumes and varieties unheard of came to subject the wayfarer to intolerable casualty risks if owners and drivers were not to observe new cares and uniformities of conduct. Congestion of cities and crowding of quarters called for health and welfare regulations undreamed of in simpler times. Wide distribution of goods became an instrument of wide distribution of harm when those who

dispersed food, drink, drugs, and even securities, did not comply with reasonable standards of quality, integrity, disclosure and care. Such dangers have engendered increasingly numerous and detailed regulations which heighten the duties of those in control of particular industries, trades, properties or activities that affect public health, safety or welfare.

While many of these duties are sanctioned by a more strict civil liability, lawmakers, whether wisely or not, have sought to make such regulations more effective by invoking criminal sanctions to be applied by the familiar technique of criminal prosecutions and convictions. This has confronted the courts with a multitude of prosecutions, based on statutes or administrative regulations, for what have been aptly called "public welfare offenses." These cases do not fit neatly into any of such accepted classifications of common-law offenses, such as those against the state, the person, property, or public morals. Many of these offenses are not in the nature of positive aggressions or invasions, with which the common law so often dealt, but are in the nature of neglect where the law requires care, or inaction where it imposes a duty. Many violations of such regulations result in no direct or immediate injury to person or property but merely create the danger or probability of injury which the law seeks to minimize. . . .

Neither this court nor, so far as we are aware, any other has undertaken to delineate a precise line or set forth comprehensive criteria for distinguishing between crimes that require a mental element and crimes that do not. We attempt no closed definition, for the law on the subject is neither settled nor static. The conclusion reached in [*Balint*] has our approval and adherence for the circumstances to which it was there applied. A quite different question here is whether we will expand the doctrine of crimes without intent to include those charged here.

Stealing, larceny, and its variants and equivalents, were among the earliest offenses known to the law that existed before legislation. . . . State courts of last resort, on whom fall the heaviest burden of interpreting criminal law in this country, have consistently retained the requirement of intent in larceny-type offenses. If any state has deviated, the exception has neither been called to our attention nor disclosed by our research.

Congress, therefore, omitted any express prescription of criminal intent from the enactment before us in the light of an unbroken course of judicial decision in all constituent states of the Union holding intent inherent in this class of offense, even when not expressed in statutes. Congressional silence as to mental elements in an Act merely adopting into federal statutory law a concept of crime already so well defined in common law and statutory interpretation by the states may warrant quite contrary inferences than the same silence in creating an offense new to general law, for whose definition the courts have no guidance except the Act. Because the offenses before this Court in [*Balint*] were of this latter class, we cannot accept them as authority for eliminating intent from offenses incorporated from the common law. . . .

The Government asks us by a feat of construction radically to change the weights and balances in the scales of justice. The purpose and obvious effect of doing away with the requirement of a guilty intent is to ease the prosecution's path to conviction, to strip the defendant of such benefit as he derived at common law from innocence of evil purpose, and to circumscribe the freedom here-

> tofore allowed juries. Such a manifest impairment of the immunities of the individual should not be extended to common-law crimes on judicial initiative. . . .
>
> We hold that the mere omission from §641 of any mention of intent will not be construed as eliminating that element from the crimes denounced.

In The Aims of the Criminal Law, 23 Law & Contemp. Prob. 401, 432 n.70 (1958), Professor Henry M. Hart criticizes the court's reasoning in *Morissette:*

> In the area of regulatory crimes, . . . the moral quality of the act is often neutral; and on occasion, the offense may consist not of any act at all, but simply of an intrinsically innocent omission, so that there is no basis for moral condemnation whatever. Thus, in *Dotterweich,* the court upheld a conviction of the president and general manager of a corporation doing a reputable business merely because the corporation had happened to ship an adulterated and misbranded drug in interstate commerce and Dotterweich happened to be its responsible executive. . . . [T]he court is right in holding that Morissette should have been allowed to go to the jury on the question of his consciousness of wrongdoing. But it will take something more than the lucubrations of the present opinion to convince me that Morissette had a better title to do so than Dotterweich.

What distinctions can be drawn between *Morissette* and *Balint?* Is the difference simply that narcotics are more dangerous than spent bomb casings? Was the defendant in *Balint* more blameworthy than the defendant in *Morissette?* Was the defendant in *Dotterweich* more blameworthy? After *Morissette,* are *Balint* and *Dotterweich* still good law?

4. What of the individual who is driving carefully, but unfortunately hits and kills a child who has run out in front of his car? What kind of society would hold the driver guilty? Yet, isn't the physical capacity to kill a child at least as dangerous as the possession of narcotics?

5. In People v. Dillard, 154 Cal. App. 3d 261, 201 Cal. Rptr. 136 (1984), the defendant was charged with violating a statute which stated that "every person who carries a loaded firearm on his or her person while in any public place or any public street . . . is guilty of a misdemeanor." Dillard was riding a bicycle and carrying a rifle case when a policeman stopped him. The rifle in the case turned out to be loaded, but Dillard claimed that he had just picked it up from his stepfather and had not realized that it was loaded. Dillard argued that the statute should be construed to require proof that he knew the rifle was loaded. The court rejected his argument. The court held that the statute belonged to the category of "public safety" or "regulatory" offenses for which the legislature could impose strict liability. It noted the difficulty the state would face in proving the defendant's knowledge, and added:

> The potential danger to the public safety from the prohibited conduct is dramatically illustrated by the facts of the instant case. Officer Torres, an expert

> in the operation and use of rifles, testified that the 30.30 Winchester is a "very high-powered rifle" that is primarily used for bear and deer hunting. As examples of the rifle's extraordinary force, he stated that one round fired would penetrate not only a police vest, "[i]t would go through the window, through the vest, through (the officer) and through the car" [and that] "If you were to line up six jurors and fire at the first one, the last one would be fatally wounded." The weapon had no safety latch and the chances of its going off if it were dropped from appellant's bicycle were about 75 percent. Without question, society has a legitimate interest in placing on the possessor of such a weapon the burden of ascertaining at his peril that it is unloaded before he ventures forth with it in public. Moreover, one who carries such a weapon in ignorance of the fact that it is loaded could in some circumstances pose a greater threat to the public safety than one who wilfully violates the law by carrying the weapon with knowledge that it is loaded. The latter, at least, presumably would handle the weapon with the greater care its potential danger dictates, whereas the former would be unaware of the need for caution. Thus, if appellant, as he contends, were truly unaware that the rifle was loaded, the public safety was endangered by that very fact as he rode with it on his bicycle and when he placed it on the ground at Officer Torres' direction.

Wasn't the defendant at fault for carrying the rifle on his bicycle without checking to see whether it was loaded? What if his stepfather had assured him that the rifle was not loaded?

6. Strict liability is often seen as a dilution of the impact of the criminal sanction. Consider Herbert Packer, Limits of the Criminal Sanction 261 (1968):

> [T]he rationale of criminal punishment requires that no one should be treated as criminal unless his conduct can be regarded as culpable. The flouting of this requirement that takes place when offenses are interpreted as being of "strict liability" contributes to the dilution of the criminal law's moral impact. The ends of the criminal sanction are disserved if the notion becomes widespread that being convicted of a crime is no worse than coming down with a bad cold.

Is Professor Packer correct in asserting that the stigma associated with the criminal sanction will be reduced by the widespread adoption of strict liability? If so, why use the criminal sanction at all for strict liability violations, such as public welfare offenses? Why not simply invoke civil penalties?

Consider Professor Henry M. Hart's opposition to the use of strict liability to impose criminal sanction upon morally blameless individuals:[3]

> Moral, rather than crassly utilitarian, considerations re-enter the picture when the claim is made, as it sometimes is, that strict liability operates, in fact, only against people who are really blameworthy, because prosecutors only pick out the really guilty ones for criminal prosecution. This argument reasserts the

3. H. M. Hart, The Aims of the Criminal Law, 23 L. and Contemp. Probs. 401, 424 (1958).

traditional position that a criminal conviction imports moral condemnation. To this, it adds the arrogant assertion that it is proper to visit the moral condemnation of the community upon one of its members on the basis solely of the private judgement of his prosecutors. Such a circumvention of the safeguards with which the law surrounds other determinations of criminality seems not only irrational, but immoral as well.

But moral considerations in a still larger dimension are the ultimately controlling ones. In its conventional and traditional applications, a criminal conviction carries with it an ineradicable connotation of moral condemnation and personal guilt. Society makes an essentially parasitic, and hence illegitimate, use of this instrument when it uses it as a means of deterrence (or compulsion) of conduct which is morally neutral. This would be true even if a statute were to be enacted proclaiming that no criminal conviction hereafter should ever be understood as casting any reflection on anybody. For statutes cannot change the meaning of words and make people stop thinking what they do think when they hear the words spoken. But it is doubly true—it is ten-fold, a hundred-fold, a thousand-fold true—when society continues to insist that some crimes *are* morally blameworthy and then tries to use the same epithet to describe conduct which is not.

7. From Glanville Williams, Textbook of Criminal Law 70 (1983):

Do you mean that Oedipus did not commit incest, merely because he did not know Jocasta was his mother? What he knew made no difference to what he did. Surely he committed incest.

The union was incestuous (it was subject to the genetic risks attaching to incest), but Oedipus did not commit incest morally or (under English law) legally. . . . If a driver accidentally kills a pedestrian, would you say that he commits murder "in fact"? He commits an act that would be murder if he had the necessary intent, which is however lacking. In lawyer's language, Oedipus and the driver commit the *actus reus* of a crime, without committing the crime. This bit of legal jargon comes from [a] Latin maxim . . . which also gives us the corresponding term *mens rea*. . . .

[*Mens rea*] means a guilty mind, but in legal use it denotes the mental state (subjective element) required for the particular crime in question. Or it can refer to the mental states commonly required for serious crimes. . . . *Actus reus* denotes the external situation forbidden by law—the external elements of the offence.

Should Danny Bass be criminally liable in the following circumstances?[4]

Charlotte, Tenn.—A man who unwittingly married his mother pleaded repeatedly for a divorce after he discovered the relationship, but she vowed "to make up some wild criminal charge" if he left her, the son's attorney said yesterday.

Danny James Bass, 26, ran away and joined the Army when, a few months after they wed on Jan. 21, 1978, "his suspicions were confirmed" that his wife was actually his mother, said the attorney, Doug Jackson.

4. Boston Globe, Sept. 12, 1984, at 5.

Mary Ann Bass, 43, was in seclusion at her home yesterday after pleading innocent Monday of felonious criminal incest. She is free on $5000 bond pending an Oct. 5 court date and faces 5 to 21 years in prison if convicted.

Authorities said Bass is the son of the woman's first husband and that she gave him up for adoption when he was 3 to Horace Sullivan, the brother of one of her other former husbands, authorities said.

Bass lived with the uncle until he was 18, when he asked who his natural mother was.

Jackson said the uncle gave Bass an address, where he went in late 1977, and met the woman, who used the name of a former husband and "denied being his mother."[5]

8. Professor Mark Kelman has taken a skeptical view of the hostility traditional liberal scholarship has exhibited toward strict liability crimes:[6]

> Commentators who attack the use of strict liability in criminal law invariably use narrow time-framing. They imply that the defendant deemed guilty of an offense which allows no mental state excuses as to some element of the crime is treated unjustly because he could somehow not avoid criminality. Look, for instance, at H. L. A. Hart's comments on criminal responsibility:
>
>> The reason why, according to modern ideas, strict liability is odious, and appears as a sacrifice of valued principle . . . is that those whom we punish should have had, when they acted, the normal capacities . . . for doing what the law requires and abstaining from what it forbids. . . . [T]he moral protest is that it is morally wrong to punish [a lawbreaker] because "he could not have helped it" or "he could not have done otherwise" or "he had no real choice." [Punishment and Responsibility (1968), p.152.]
>
> But this implication is not valid. Often, the actor could readily avoid liability—so that all metaphors of "unobeyable laws," or "helpless victims" are inappropriate—if we simply broaden the time frame. Chief Justice Burger did precisely this in United States v. Park. *Park* sustained the conviction of a responsible corporate official for shipping adulterated food, though the official had not been "aware of wrongdoing." The Chief Justice argued that future violations will not occur when responsible corporate officials take on managerial responsibility. . . .
>
> In terms of "explaining" the narrow time-framed interpretation that suppresses the policy complexities of the strict liability issue, one could conceivably see the construction in either result-oriented or ideological terms. One can view this attack on strict liability as a simple class-biased, result-oriented defense of corporate managers, those persons most likely to "unintentionally" harm others through routine business operations. Certainly, the bulk of strict liability crimes are regulatory crimes which, unlike the traditional common law incidental

5. Unfortunately, like many an interesting hypothetical, the above story has been mugged by the facts. Danny Bass later pleaded "no contest" to perjury charges and admitted that he had known the identity of his mother before the marriage ceremony.—Eds.

6. Interpretive Construction in the Substantive Criminal Law, 33 Stan. L. Rev. 591, 605-611 (1981).

harms, are most likely to be committed by those who control the means of production. Of course, the *defense* of strict liability crimes is likewise grounded in a political agenda—in an attempt to "get" harm-causing managers—rather than in abstract "legal" thought. But since [punishments for] strict liability crimes have rarely been imposed in ways that threaten corporate managers, the narrow-time-frame-based dismissal of strict liability more likely serves ideological needs.

What does Professor Kelman mean by "often, the actor could readily avoid criminal liability"? If the actor knew? Is "often" enough? According to Professor Kelman, what did Dotterweich do wrong? What should he have done?

9. One commentator, Walter L. Gordon, has gone further and traced criticism of strict liability offenses to support for large business enterprises:[7]

At the core of the traditional criminal law were the common law felonies such as murder, assault, robbery, burglary, rape and larceny. Experience taught that these crimes were present in both industrial and agricultural societies. These crimes were defined in Anglo-American law at a time when religion had a strong impact on legal concepts. The traditional criminal law stipulated that criminal liability required two elements—a forbidden act and a guilty mind. This last element, the guilty mind, appeared in the English criminal law in the twelfth century and was derived from the religious law. In substance the concept of *mens rea* holds that moral blameworthiness is the foundation of legal culpability. Frances B. Sayre, in his classic analysis of the concept, noted:

> Under the pervasive influence of the Church, the teaching of the penitential books, that punishment should be dependent upon moral guilt gave powerful impetus to this growth for the very essence of moral guilt is a mental element. Henceforth, the criminal law of England, developing in the general direction of moral blameworthiness, begins to insist upon a *mens rea* as an essential of criminality.

The concept of *mens rea,* or moral blameworthiness, was incorporated into American criminal law and became one of its central organizing concepts.

During the last half of the nineteenth century, the pace of industrialization quickened in the United States as the foundation of the current capitalistic system was laid. These changes in the economic base created an impersonal market where the small producer was replaced by large industrial organizations that distributed huge quantities of products. In reaction to the changed economic situation, in order to protect the public, legislatures began to pass criminal statutes that did not require *mens rea,* or moral guilt, for criminal conviction. The new doctrine rejected the requirement that a criminal act was comprised of union of a forbidden act and a guilty mind. This new doctrine, often called "strict liability," meant that penal punishment (including prison) could be imposed for a forbidden act alone, and it was not necessary for the prosecutor to prove that the criminal had a guilty mind, intent, or *mens rea.* In other words, it was irrelevant whether or not the accused person was morally blameworthy

7. Crime and Criminal Law: The California Experience: 1960-1975, 7-12 (1976).

when doing the forbidden act. In practice, the strict liability offense was aimed at the businessman operating in the impersonal national market. . . . The proliferation of strict liability offenses posed a distinct threat to businessmen since they could go to jail or be branded as criminal for acts for which they had no moral or personal culpability. It is natural that such statutes were not favored by them. . . .

In the language of sociology, "strict penal liability" is reflected in the idea of white collar crime. There are no criminal statistics collected on the nature and extent of business crime in the United States. However, the observance of such data does not mean that such crime does not exist. In fact, the available evidence indicates that there is widespread criminality among the large corporations and those who run them. Earlier studies conducted in the 1930s and 1940s detected such criminality. Edwin H. Sutherland found in his empirical study of corporate criminality that [officers of] 60 percent of the seventy larger corporations in this country had criminal convictions and most were habitual offenders. There is no reason to believe that criminal behavior by the large corporations has stopped. Ferdinand Lundberg notes:

> The United States, the plain unvarnished facts show, is a very criminal society, led in its criminality by its upper socio-economic classes. Has the ominous outlook altered since Sutherland terminated analysis as of 1944? It has not changed in the slightest. In the two decades since 1945 the acts cited by Sutherland continued—in many cases with redoubled force; for the penalties imposed by law are obviously not of sufficient weight to deter.

Business crimes cost the public far more than the street crimes [the public] fear[s] so much. One recent estimate places the 1977 cost of street crime at $3 to $4 billion, while [during the same year] white collar criminals cost the public $40 billion. The most common white collar crimes involved frauds, price fixing, monopolistic practices, tax evasion, adulterated products, bribery and like practices. "Violations of the law by businessmen," notes Conklin, "not only cost money; they may also lead to physical harm or even death."

Moreover, business crimes destroy trust and confidence in the political and economic institutions in the nation. Silk collar criminals occupy high social positions, often of trust, in the social system. The President's Commission on Law Enforcement and Administration of Justice noted in its report:

> [A]s serious as the physical and financial costs of corporate crime may be, it is probable that they are less serious than the damage [corporate crime] does to the Nation's social, economic, and political institutions. Restraint of trade tends to undermine the principles of free enterprise that the anti-trust laws are intended to protect. . . . Serious erosion of morals accompanies violations of this nature. It is reasonable to assume that prestigious companies that flout the law set an example for other businesses and influence individuals, particularly young people, to commit other kinds of crime on the ground that everyone is taking what he can get.

Due to the power and status of silk collar criminals, they are not treated or perceived as sharing the same stigma as street criminals. Moreover, powerful interests are at work to remove many business crimes from the ambit of the criminal law. This was certainly the case with the MPC and this attitude was shared by its drafters. Paul Tappan was the most outspoken critic of the concept of white collar crime as formulated by Sutherland. Tappan argued that the concept was vague and ideological. In 1947, he published an article on the subject in the American Sociological Review in which he argued:

> A special hazard exists in the employment of the term, "white collar criminal," in that it invites individual systems of private values to run riot in an area (economic ethics) where gross variation exists among criminologists as well as others. The rebel may enjoy a veritable orgy of delight in damning as criminal most anyone he pleases; one imagines that some experts would thus consign to the criminal classes any successful capitalistic business man [or woman]; the reactionary or conservative, complacently viewing the occupational practices of the business world might find all in perfect order in this best of all possible worlds. The result may be fine indoctrination or catharsis achieved through blustering broadsides against the "existing system." It is not criminology. It is not social science.

Herbert Wechsler was the person in charge of the drafters of the MPC. He became head of the ALI in 1962, after the official draft of the MPC was published. In his articles Wechsler did not attack the concept of white collar crime directly but instead focused his arguments against strict penal liability which was one of its manifestations in the criminal law. Wechsler argued that to label a person criminal was the harshest condemnation that society could make about an individual or entity. The criminal sanction, he argued, should not be used unless there was evidence that the accused was morally blameworthy. To condemn on less, he maintained, was "barbaric" and the "badge of tyranny." This was the case because there were less onerous methods to control the behavior outlawed by strict liability statutes, such as the wide range of civil sanctions used by administrative agencies like the Security and Exchange Commission (SEC) or the Federal Trade Commission (FTC).

10. Is it better to convict one innocent man of violating a public welfare offense than to allow ten guilty others to escape punishment? Consider Goodhart, Possession of Drugs and Absolute Liability, 84 L.Q. Rev. 382, 385-386 (1968):

> [The] function of absolute liability is in certain circumstances a procedural and not a penal one. Thus there are certain offences that have . . . serious effect[s] on the public interest but which [are] difficult to prove under the usual procedure. It is then necessary to take other and more stringent steps to wipe out the evil, even at a minimal risk that an innocent man may be convicted. Lord Reid cites, although he does not entirely agree with . . . the long-established saying that "it is better that ten guilty men should escape than that one innocent man should be convicted." . . . On the other hand it may be necessary in certain circumstances to alter the strict rules where[by] an act, such as tempting young persons to buy drugs, is peculiarly harmful.
>
> The point here is that the future harm that the ten guilty men who have been acquitted may do, either by repeating their own offenses or by encouraging others by showing how easy it is to avoid conviction, far exceeds any injury that the innocent man can suffer by his conviction.

Do you agree? Do the benefits of strict liability in reducing behavior that is harmful to the public interest outweigh the risks of convicting morally innocent individuals? Does your answer depend upon the margin of error—that is, how many innocent people are convicted for every individual convicted under a rule of absolute liability? Or is that the wrong question? Is Professor Goodhart assuming that we have no way, apart from the criminal law, of coping with public welfare offenses? Is this assumption correct?

11. Our rules of criminal blameworthiness have their costs. Consider how they are manipulated by Zachary Swan, a clever cocaine smuggler, in the following three excerpts from Robert Sabbag's Snowblind—A Brief Career in the Cocaine Trade 149-152, 154-155, 171-174, 204-206 (1978):

I

Brown Gold Coffee, imported and packaged by the Andes Coffee Corporation of Palisades Park, New Jersey, is, as its label points out, "100% Colombian." A unique blend of the Medellin Excelso and the Armenia Excelso coffee beans, the label adds, it is "worth its *taste* in gold." Cocaine, on the other hand, a blend of coca leaf alkaloids and neutral crystals, very often 100% Colombian, is worth approximately its exact *weight* in gold—and that is before it crosses the border. The mathematics of this coincidence appealed to Zachary Swan, who over his morning coffee was scanning the travel page of The New York Times.

"Perfect," he said.

"Find what you were looking for?" Alice asked.

"Avianca Airlines is offering a ten-day excursion. Santa Marta, Barranquilla and Cartagena. Leaves from New York. It even names the hotels."

"Lucky you."

Alice, at this point, was the only person in whom Swan had confided. But to assure the success of this, his most Byzantine move, Swan would need the help of at least two others. He would use Davis on the New York end and Canadian Jack in Cartagena. He would contact them later. What he needed now was an office. He needed an office, a telephone number, a few jars of coffee, a handful of printed material, and a lot of luck. He moved fast.

The office was a small one near Lüchow's restaurant on 14th Street. He rented it on a month-to-month basis. Into it he moved an old desk, a new filing cabinet, a swivel chair and a coffee percolator. While he waited for a telephone, he worked on getting the printed material he needed. This was not hard. As a former packaging executive (in essence a printing salesman) he had very little trouble coming by the necessary four-color work and stationery. Most of it he ordered from the Andes Coffee people himself—labels, poster ads, and packaging paper, all stamped with the Andes logo and address: ANDES COFFEE CORP., S.A. Schonbrunn & Co., Inc., Palisades Park, N.J. 07650. What he did not get directly from Andes, he got from business associates who had access to the Andes printing buyer, and what he did not get from them, he had printed on his own. The most important piece of original printing was a miniature folded brochure stamped with his new office number.

He decorated the office in appropriate bad taste with all the trappings he had accumulated—posters on the wall, coffee cans adorning the desk, subway ads, supermarket art, labels glued to everything—bought the coffee and moved in to work. It was difficult work, but after a while and several containers of coffee, he finally managed to remove the vacuum seal from a four-ounce jar of freeze-dried instant without tearing it. He inserted his brochure, replaced the seal with rubber cement, capped the jar and drove to Queens to put the jar in a grocery store.

Mrs. Vagelatos called about 4:30 in the afternoon.

"Brown Gold Company."

"Hello."

"Hello."

"I am Mrs. Vagelatos."

"Yes, Mrs. Vagelatos."

"I am number 21-27-37-31-32."

"Are you calling about the contest, Mrs. Vagelatos?"

"Yes. The contest. Yes, I am."

"And what is your number again, Mrs. Vagelatos?"

"Number 21-27-37-31-32."

"Did I hear you correctly, Mrs. Vagelatos? Will you repeat that number?"

She did. (Swan's filing system was quite simple: there was only one number—it was printed into the brochure, it came with the order. There was only one number, and only one of the brochures was in circulation. If Mrs. Vagelatos had not called, Swan would have waited and tried again—he did not want too many copies of the brochure floating around.)

"Mrs. Vagelatos. Mrs. Vagelatos, you are a winner. You have won a prize. You have won *first prize.* You have won a free ten-day trip to Colombia."

Mrs. Vagelatos said she was old and that her husband was retired. He was old too, she said. She spoke English poorly. Mrs. Vagelatos had, however, lived in America for some time.

"Can I have the money, instead?" she asked.

Swan explained the rules of the contest to her—essentially, "It doesn't work that way, lady." Mrs. Vagelatos said she would think it over. She called back the next day, having talked it over with her husband, and told Swan that she and Mr. Vagelatos would take the trip.

"You will enjoy it, Mrs. Vagelatos. Yes. What? Of course. And in addition to the vacation, there will be many gifts and souvenirs."

Of course.

Swan opened a checking account in the name of S.A. Schonbrunn & Co., Inc., and bought tickets for the Avianca tour in the Vagelatoses' name. He enclosed the tickets in a Brown Gold envelope, added a letter of congratulations and an itinerary typewritten on Brown Gold stationery, and mailed them to the couple in Queens.

The itinerary: Santa Marta, Baranquilla and Cartagena. Swan knew where the Vagelatoses would be, and when they would be there, all the time they were in Colombia. In his letter of congratulations he had informed them that a representative of the company would meet them in Cartagena to present them with their gifts. He called Armando from New York and told him he would be down in a week.

Two weeks later he took $22,000 cash from a safe deposit box on the East Side and flew to Bogotá.

Armando delivered. He charged Swan six thousand a kilo for the three keys, a five dollar increase per gram, partly for holding the load and partly because at the time the price of cocaine was going up all around the world. Angel and Rudolpho made the fill.

Swan and Canadian Jack took [a] midweek, morning flight from Bogotá to Cartagena and checked into the Hotel Caribe. Shortly after he arrived, Swan called the Vagelatoses' room and asked the couple to meet him at the pool to receive their gifts. While Swan, sporting a full beard and dark glasses, awarded the Vagelatoses their prizes and made a big show of certifying with the waiter that the coffee they were drinking was 100 percent Colombian, laughing all the way, Canadian Jack dashed around with the camera.

Swan loaded the Vagelatoses down with rolling pins, statues, wall hangings, hammocks, blankets, *ruanas,* straw hats, leather bags—about forty pounds of paraphernalia that cost him close to $150 and which would retail in the United States for over $500, all of it dragged out of two great, overflowing plastic bags. In his room, Swan had a duplicate of every one of the souvenirs. He asked the Vagelatoses to sign an agreement by which they were bound to be photographed again with their presents in the New York office. He made an offhand joke, unacknowledged, about Greeks bearing gifts, gave them a copy of the agreement to keep, and wished them a safe trip home.

The Vagelatoses were due back in New York two days later. Swan left a day early and made a dry run with his duplicates. They were not examined. The Vagelatoses were supposed to call Swan's office as soon as they returned. They did not. Swan waited. He worried. He had to call them. They were tired, it turned out—they had arrived on schedule. Swan groaned out loud over the phone. He dispatched a limousine, which he paid for in cash, to pick them up at their home in Queens.

Davis took the New York photos. And while Swan bought the Vagelatoses lunch at Lüchow's, Davis made the switch. The Vagelatoses returned to the office, picked up their gifts, Swan wished them health, wealth and happiness, escorted them to the limousine, and sent them home. He closed down the office the next day and never saw the couple from Queens again.

Quidquid id est, timeo Danaos et dona ferentes.

The Customs man, obviously, had never read Virgil.

II

And Swan gave Canadian Jack the Duplicate Bag Switch. Like all of Swan's flim-flams, the Duplicate Bag Switch is designed not to protect the goods, but to protect the carrier. . . .

Given the odds on the coke (and when you mule it, no matter where you put it, those odds conform to nothing more profound than the law of averages) and taking for granted that *there's no way you can deny it's yours, man, if it's strapped to your back,* then the Duplicate Bag Switch is the perfect scam.

". . . you have to buy two suitcases, and they have to be exactly alike in every way," Swan said.

"Right," said Jack.

"Have Angel and Rudolpho pack the load for you—a statue, a rolling pin, anything. It should look like a souvenir."

Jack nodded.

"Now the suitcases have to open like this"—he drew his arms inward—"at a right angle. No zippers. And it's got to stand up—she has to be able to open it away from her—so that when it is open and the inspector is going through it, she can't see what he's doing, the top's between them. O.K.? I'm talking about a standard suitcase, very simple, nothing fancy.

"O.K. Now, in one of the suitcases, she puts everything she owns, all her clothes, her shoes, anything that fits, and a few things that will identify her. And *she* packs it. O.K.?

"Got it."

"Now, the other suitcase, the duplicate, is where the load goes. And *you* have to pack it. Her fingerprints can't be anywhere near the duplicate bag. *You* pack it, and you pack it with a lot of women's clothes, all size ten . . . what size are you, Susan, about a six?"

"Six," she said.

"Good. So all the clothes in with the load are size ten. Shoes to match. Cosmetics, everything. Just as if it were a woman's suitcase like any other. Everything two sizes too big, all of it clean, no prints, and none of it hers. She never touches this particular bag. Understand?" he said to Susan.

"I understand."

"O.K. You take the same plane and you don't sit together. Both bags are checked aboard and they are exactly alike except for a scuff mark on one of them. That's the loaded one. When you get off the plane, Susan, you pick up the loaded bag—this is the first time you've touched it—and you carry it through Customs. Jack, you're delayed. Susan opens the loaded bag—away from you, Susan, you undo the clasps and pull the top up toward you—and she can't see what the Customs man is doing. The lid of the suitcase is between them. She's short, so that helps; the counters are usually high at Customs. And, while the agent is examining the contents of the bag, she's fiddling with the rest of her stuff—whatever else she's carrying. She's not looking at what he's doing. If that bag goes through, Jack, you just pick up her real bag and carry it through yourself.

"*If* the man cracks the statue, Susan, *if* they nail you, you've never seen that bag before in your life. 'This isn't my bag. That must be mine running around all alone on the conveyor belt over there.' And it is. Jack has left it there. Everything fits. You got I.D. in it. No way the loaded bag is yours, nothing in it fits. No way they can put anything in it with you, no fingerprints, no belongings, no nothing, you got the wrong bag, you moved in on somebody else's hustle, no record, no nothing, out. You walk away."

"It can't fail."

(And it did not fail. They got the load through. If they had not, they could have tried it again and again until the money ran out. The Duplicate Bag Switch, if handled correctly, is arrest proof wherever the rules of evidence apply.)

III

Angel had compressed the coke, and now Trude stuffed the [toy] rabbit, sewing it carefully back together along its original seams when she was done. Charlie took the rabbit back to the Tequendama, where he kept it on top of the dresser in his room, innocent and evident to anyone who might enter. He, Swan, and Trude made separate reservations on a midweek, off-peak flight to New York. They arrived at the airport separately.

On uncrowded Avianca flights, passengers may sit where they want. Their seating assignments are simply a formality. Charlie Kendricks, carrying the rabbit in a shopping bag, boarded first, choosing a window seat over the wing in the coach compartment. He removed the rabbit from the bag and stuffed it under the seat, careful that it was not visible to anyone who might sit across the aisle from Kendricks. She and Kendricks did not speak. Swan followed close behind Trude and chose a seat behind Charlie on the aisle. A stranger, whose name and address Charlie managed to get, in writing, in the course of the flight—he was good that way—sat directly in front of Swan, in the aisle seat between Kendricks and Trude. He was a free witness.

The jet was not in the air five minutes when Charlie Kendricks, making sure the stewardess was nowhere around, "found" the bunny.

"Oh, look what I found."

He held up the bunny and called for the stewardess. The stranger shrugged. Before Kendricks could call a second time, the silver-haired gentleman in the seat behind the stranger tapped Kendricks on the shoulder.

"Why don't you give it to the baby?"

The gentleman pointed to Elaine. The stranger nodded his agreement. Charlie smiled. He handed it over.

"Oh, thank you," said Trude.

Kendricks, Trude and Swan walked through Customs in New York in the order they had boarded the plane. Trude preceded her witness.

When he laid out the plan, Swan had asked Trude:

"Who are they going to arrest?"

He was unable to find anyone to answer the question.

A criminal justice system that requires proof of blameworthiness would not convict Susan or Trude, both smugglers whom the omniscient reader knows to be guilty. Conversely, a system that does not consider moral culpability to be relevant—a strict liability system—would convict even the innocent and trusting Mr. and Mrs. Vagelatos.

What system could you devise that would convict Susan and Trude but not the Vagelatoses?

STATE v. ARIZONA MINES SUPPLY CO.

Supreme Court of Arizona
484 P.2d 619 (1971)

UDALL, Justice.

This is a special action, filed by the State of Arizona ex rel Moise Berger, Maricopa County Attorney, on December 10, 1970, seeking relief from a ruling by a Superior Court judge requiring that the State prove criminal intent as a pre-requisite to a conviction for violation of this state's Air Pollution Act. On December 15, 1970, we accepted jurisdiction of the state's petition for special action, allowing time for both parties to submit additional briefs.

The facts out of which this controversy arose are as follows: On September 23, 1970, an information was filed by the County Attorney's office in the

Superior Court of Maricopa County, charging defendant-respondent, Arizona Mines Supply Co., with two counts of "air pollution," a misdemeanor. The information charged specifically that the defendant-respondent on or about June 19, 1970 (Count I), and June 29, 1970 (Count II),

> did charge, suffer, allow or permit the discharge into the atmosphere from a single source of emission, air contaminants for a period or periods aggregating more than three minutes in one hour as dark as or darker in shade than that designated as No. 2 on the Ringelmann Chart as published by the U.S. Bureau of Mines, or of opacity equal to or greater than air contaminants designated as No. 2 on the Ringelmann Chart, all in violation of [regulations.] . . .

Prior to the verdict of the jury, the State filed a "Motion in Limine," in which it sought to exclude certain anticipated evidence, requesting that the court exclude: (1) any evidence as to the amount of money expended by Arizona Mines Supply Co. for air pollution equipment; and (2) any testimony which defendant might seek to introduce with regard to its lack of criminal intent to violate the statute and regulations. The court ruled in favor of the defendant on both points, ordering that the motion in limine be denied. From the denial the State filed this petition for special action. . . .

Section IV, Regulation 1, Maricopa County Air Pollution Regulations, provides that:

> No person shall cause, suffer, allow or permit the discharge into the atmosphere from any single source of emission whatsoever any air contaminants for a period or periods aggregating more than three minutes in any one hour which is:
>
> a. As dark as or darker in shade than that designated as No. 2 on the Ringelmann Chart as published by the U.S. Bureau of Mines, or;
>
> b. Of an opacity equal to or greater than an air contaminant designated as No. 2 on the Ringelmann Chart."

Nowhere does this regulation (or the Air Pollution Act, for that matter) provide, either expressly or impliedly, that before the state may convict someone of "air pollution" it must first prove that the air contaminant was discharged knowingly or intentionally. Defendant argues that some degree of knowledge or intent is pre-requisite to conviction. The State, on the other hand, contends that it need not prove intent or knowledge since this offense is more in the nature of "malum prohibitum."

After having carefully considered the apparent intent of the legislature, arguments advanced by opposing counsel, the circumstances surrounding this case and the consequences of unabated air pollution to public health; we find that the state need not prove intent or knowledge on the part of the accused as a pre-requisite to conviction. That the legislature may make the doing of an act or the neglect to do something a crime without requiring criminal intent is well-settled. The intent of the legislature, therefore, is the controlling factor.

> Whether a criminal intent or guilty knowledge is a necessary element of a statutory offense is a matter of construction to be determined from the language of the statute, *in view of its manifest purpose and design.* There are many instances in recent times where the legislature in the exercise of the police power has prohibited, under penalty, the performance of a specified act. *The doing of the inhibited act constitutes the crime,* and the moral turpitude or *purity of the motive* by which it was prompted *and knowledge or ignorance* of its criminal character *are immaterial circumstances* on the question of guilt. The only fact to be determined in these cases is whether the defendant did the act. [Emphasis added.] 17 Ariz. 506 at 508, 154 P. 1048, at 1049.

With regard to the introduction by a defendant of evidence of expenditures made in installing pollution control equipment and precautions taken to avoid pollution, such will not constitute a defense to prosecution and conviction, and are, therefore, inadmissible at trial. Evidence of "extenuating circumstances" may, however, be presented to the court after [a] verdict in [order to mitigate] the penalty to be imposed. . . .

The basic premise of the concept of "strict liability" or "malum prohibitum" offenses is that the mere doing of the act constitutes the offense and the fact that the act was done without intent or in "happy ignorance" will not exonerate the party, nor does this make the prohibited act any less harmful to society. . . .

In accordance with the foregoing, we hold that the state need not prove criminal intent as a pre-requisite to conviction. It is therefore ordered that the petitioner's "Motion in Limine" be granted without prejudice to defendant-respondent's right to introduce evidence *after verdict* of extenuating circumstances, in mitigation of the penalty to be imposed.

Notes and Questions

1. The court in *Arizona Mines* asserts that moral culpability is not necessary for a finding of liability. It notes, however, that the defendant may present "extenuating circumstances" to the court *after a verdict,* in order to mitigate the penalty to be imposed. Would you agree with adopting this view toward all crimes? One authority has advocated strict liability for all offenses. Lady Barbara Wootton, in Crime and the Criminal Law 51-53 (1963) wrote:

> If the primary function of the courts is conceived as the prevention of forbidden acts, there is little cause to be disturbed by the multiplication of offences of strict liability. If the law says that certain things are not to be done, it is illogical to [distinguish] the reasons for prohibiting them, whether they are the result of sinister or malicious plotting, of negligence, or of sheer accident. A man is equally dead and his relatives equally bereaved whether he was stabbed or run over by a drunken motorist or by an incompetent one.
>
> [Under a strict liability system there] would be two separate stages of deter-

minations made in the case of a person accused of a crime. At the first stage there would be decided only whether the defendant committed the act prohibited by the criminal law, without regard to whether he acted intentionally, knowingly, recklessly, and even negligently, or whether he had the capacity to conform to the law under the circumstances. His mental state would be altogether irrelevant. The second stage would arise if it were found that he committed the prohibited act. Now the issue would be to decide what ought to be done with the defendant considering all we know and can find out about him—from psychiatrists, from social workers or from any other source—including, but not limited to, his mental and emotional state at the time he acted. The choice of the disposition would be governed by whatever is desirable to protect the public from his further criminality, whether what is required be medical or psychiatric treatment, training, a permissive or rigorous environment, punishment or incarceration. Presumably if the offender did not pose a danger he would be released immediately. If he did, he would be held whether he was a villain or a helpless victim of his own incapacities, and for as long as he continued to pose the danger.

Lady Wootton's "behavorial position" focuses upon sentencing policy. In comparing the retributive position to her behaviorist proposal, Herbert Packer, in The Limits of the Criminal Sanction 14 (1968), notes:

The retributive position holds that punishment must be proportioned to the offense. The graver the offense (on some kind of scale of moral outrage), the more severe the punishment. Nonsense, say the proponents of the behavioral view. Punishment (or treatment, as they usually prefer to call it) should be suited to the needs of the offender and of the rest of the community rather than to the nature of his offense. That is the only way [punishment] can look forward to those needs rather than backward to the expiation of [the offender's] crime. Legislatures can decide in advance on the range of punishment that should be allowable for a given offense, e.g., a minimum of one year of imprisonment and a maximum of ten for, say, burglary. (Even that much in the way of a priori limitation would offend hard-core adherents to the behavioral view, who would want to see the correctional authorities left entirely free). But legislatures have no way of determining how much punishment should be allowable for a given offender. If punishment (or treatment) is to be individualized, there should be large if not complete discretion in the sentencing authority to decide the kind and length of treatment for each offender. In the allocation of sentencing authority, then, the judge should simply turn the offender over to the correctional experts for a completely indeterminate sentence, as opposed to the conventional and traditional procedure by which the judge says to the defendant "Five years" (or whatever), or as opposed to any modification of this procedure whereby limits are placed on the discretion of correctional authorities. To proponents of the behavioral position, any sentence that invokes the nature of the offense rather than the situation of the offender is a throwback to retributive ideas or, at best, to classic utilitarian ideas of deterrence, which these proponents see simply as retribution thinly disguised.

Is the "behavioral" argument persuasive? Should liability depend upon an intuitive sense of moral culpability? Is the debate over Lady Wootton's position really about a question of procedure, or about the relative competence of state institutions to decide whether to incarcerate or otherwise deal with individuals? Is it a question of which organ of the state—the court, the jury, the legislature, or some administrative body of experts—should set the punishment for an offender? Or is there a much larger principle at stake?

2. Another commentator[8] espouses a different view of cases such as *Arizona Mines:*

> As a "policy" matter, the legislative decision whether to condemn a defendant only where [fault] is shown, or to condemn wherever harm is caused, is nothing more than the outcome of a perfectly traditional balance of interests between strict, easily applied rules and vaguer, ad hoc standards.
>
> If the legislature enacts a negligence standard so that, for example, a manufacturer is liable for shipping adulterated food only if he acted unreasonably, or a liquor license holder is liable for selling to underage customers only if he screened customers unreasonably, two rather poor, although different, sets of bad consequences can result. If the negligence standard is defined vaguely, so that each jury is simply instructed to determine whether the particular defendant was reasonable, jury verdicts will be inconsistent, unpredictable, and biased. Moreover, if the particular jury equates reasonable behavior with ordinary behavior, an entire industry may free itself of responsibility by uniformly acting less carefully than the legislature would like.
>
> 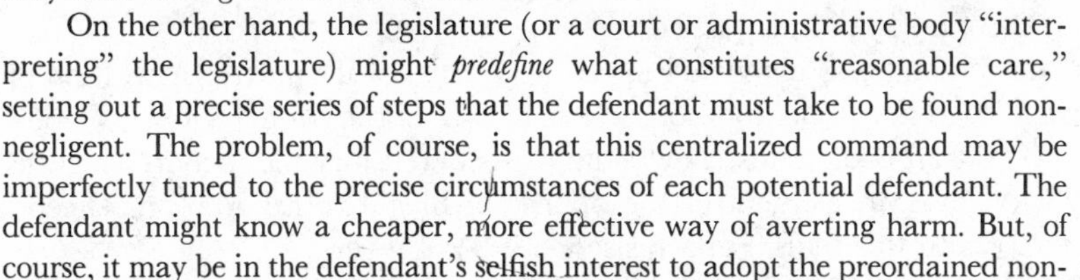
>
> On the other hand, the legislature (or a court or administrative body "interpreting" the legislature) might *predefine* what constitutes "reasonable care," setting out a precise series of steps that the defendant must take to be found non-negligent. The problem, of course, is that this centralized command may be imperfectly tuned to the precise circumstances of each potential defendant. The defendant might know a cheaper, more effective way of averting harm. But, of course, it may be in the defendant's selfish interest to adopt the preordained non-negligent technique, even if it will cause more harm.
>
> For example, if a liquor license holder faces a $100 fine for each violation of the sale-to-minors proscription, under strict liability he would adopt the system best suited to his particular circumstances (System A), which costs $400 to implement and which would result in five violations. (The net private *and* social cost is $900.) In a regime of negligence, however, he might adopt instead the system the legislature has preordained as non-negligent (System B), although it costs $600 to implement and will result in ten violations. If it is assumed that he is certain he will be found non-negligent using System B and that he is fairly certain that his System A (although in fact better in his circumstances at avoiding the socially feared result) will be judged negligent by juries, given a preordained description of reasonable care, then he will adopt B. Although B's social cost is $1,600 rather than $900, B's private cost will be only $600, whereas System A will cost him $900. (Nothing here turns on the cost being one of fines: for example, if a person were jailed whenever he had violated the "no sales" act more than five times, the defendant in a negligence system would adopt the high-harm but no-violation preordained non-negligent system, although it was both more costly and harmful.)

8. M. Kelman, Strict Liability, Encyclopedia of Crime and Justice 1517 (1983).

Switching to strict liability—essentially making a conclusive presumption that causing harm is blameworthy—has its costs, too, which "policy" analysts would readily note. Like all conclusive presumptions, it is bound to be inaccurate in particular situations: there will doubtless be cases where someone is blamed who, on closer analysis, society would not have wanted to blame. But that is true in the "rule-like" form of negligence too, where society demands that actors take predefined steps even though others who take different steps may have behaved at least as carefully.

It is possible that someone might be condemned simply because he failed to take the steps he had been ordered to take. But it is to be suspected that few would feel comfortable in condemning someone who could honestly claim that he so strongly shared the legislative goal of minimizing the incidence of some proscribed harm, such as sales of liquor to minors, that he had taken steps which were designed to, and in fact did, lower the incidence of that harm. Not only will the "rule-like" form of negligence be unjust when it occasionally condemns these especially good citizens, but even worse, it may frequently induce socially irrational behavior.

PEOPLE v. HUTCHISON

Appellate Court of Illinois, Fourth District
361 N.E.2d 328 (1977)

CRAVEN, Presiding Justice.

Defendant was convicted upon the verdict of illegal transportation of an alcoholic liquor in violation of section 11-502 of the Motor Vehicle Code. . . .

The trial court refused defendant's tendered jury instruction which listed knowledge as an element of the offense of illegal transportation. Defendant appeals both this refusal and his sentence. We reverse.

Without reciting at length the evidence, it appears that defendant was involved in an accident in the city of Champaign. During the police investigation of the accident, a paper bag containing a half-empty bottle of whiskey was found on the transmission hump separating the driver and passenger seats. The bottle belonged to defendant's passenger and defendant had no knowledge it was in the car.

Most crimes require proof of some knowledge or intent on the part of the defendant to support a conviction. . . . [I]n misdemeanor offenses where there is no possibility of imprisonment and no fine greater than $500 may be imposed no mental state need be proven. Such offenses create an absolute statutory liability. Motor vehicle regulations for the protection of the public safety are generally such offenses.

In these cases however, absolute liability was established for acts the very nature of which requires some conceptualized requirement of knowledge or intent. One cannot, for instance, be arrested for driving without a valid driver's license unless he is knowingly engaged in the act of driving. That is not the case here, as the operator of a motor vehicle, including the defendant here, can never know for certain the possessions of his passenger. To establish absolute liability for such transgressions would be tantamount to punishing a defendant for the sins of his neighbor—sins that he had no knowledge of nor reason to have knowledge of. In this light, "absolute liability" for this offense is contrary to the very basis of our criminal law which requires some knowing omission or commission. We therefore are of the opinion that it was error for the trial court here to refuse defendant's tendered instruction requiring knowledge as an element of the offense and reverse defendant's conviction and remand the case for a new trial.

Reversed and remanded. . . .

MILLS, Justice dissenting.

The somewhat offhand and cavalier dismissal of this issue by the majority is disturbing.

But what is more important, I believe my brothers are wrong.

The majority recognizes the statutory absolute liability provisions of Section 4-9 of the Criminal Code and that motor vehicle regulations generally fall under its purview. But, they say, the charge at bar of illegal transportation of alcoholic liquor is distinguishable from such cases in that scienter, or "knowledge" of the presence of the intoxicant, is an essential element. Such distinction with controlling precedents and Illinois case law escapes me.

In the exercise of police power for the protection of the public at large, the legislation may create offenses malum prohibitum—wrong only because they are *prohibited,* not because they are wrong in themselves or are inherently evil. And historically, motor vehicle violations in Illinois have long been considered in this category.

The taproot case is People v. Fernow (1919), 286 Ill. 627, 122 N.E. 155. It was put to us this way:

> At common law a crime consisted of an unlawful act with evil intent, and in crimes created by statute a specific intent may be required so that the intent and act may constitute the crime, and in such cases the intent must be alleged and proved. Where a specific intent is not an element of the crime it is not always necessary that a criminal intent should exist. In the exercise of the police power for the protection of the public the performance of a specific act may constitute the crime regardless of either knowledge or intent, both of which are immaterial on the question of guilt. For the effective protection of the public the burden is placed upon the individual of ascertaining at his peril whether his act is prohibited by criminal statute. The law in that regard has most frequently arisen in police regulations of the liquor traffic, but it has been applied in precisely the same way in other cases coming within the same rule and reason, such as a sale of imitation butter, the sale of milk below a prescribed quality, the obstruction of a public highway by a railroad corporation for longer than a specified time, the admission of a minor to a pool room, driving an unregistered automobile, killing for sale an animal under a designated age, carriage by an express company for transportation beyond the state line of fish or game, and in prosecutions for bigamy. (286 Ill. 630-31, 122 N.E. 157). . . .

Professor Bowman's thorough and comprehensive committee comments to Section 4-9 of the Criminal Code traces the legal history in this area, and with considerable clarity digests the pertinent pre-Code opinions. Several sections of the Motor Vehicle Code, interpreted prior to the enactment of the Criminal Code in 1961, interpreted as "absolute liability"—malum prohibitum—offenses. Following 1961, these sections were consistently interpreted as not requiring any particular scienter (either intent or knowledge).

To my view the charge of illegal transportation of liquor is essentially no different from the other Motor Vehicle Code offenses heretofore found by Illinois courts to be malum prohibitum and where knowledge or intent are not required. The police power is the legislature's and violates no constitutional injunction. The purpose is the public good, and therefore, laudable—"the greatest good to the greatest number," as Johnson put it.

The statute here—like all absolute liability, malum prohibitum offenses—casts a wide net. It drags in the "hotrodder" with five buddies, a couple of opened cold sixpacks, a tank full of gas and time on their hands. It *may* also snare the unsuspecting and kind old gentleman who gives a lift from church to the little old lady with the flask of communion wine in her handbag. Well, the kind old gentleman is simply going to have to be more careful in choosing his passengers unless, indeed, he wishes to be punished for the "sins of his neighbors." There are few of us, I wager, who have not had an uneasy moment or two somewhere along the pathway of life. But when you run with the pack and the shotgun is fired, a stray pellet now and then finds an innocent target—or, at least, one without scienter!

As phrased in *Fernow,* "For the effective protection of the public the burden is placed upon the individual of ascertaining at his peril whether his act is prohibited by criminal statute." Such is not, to my view, too high a price to pay for public safety and a legitimate legislative purpose.

I would affirm.

Notes and Questions

1. After reading the dissent in *Hutchison,* do you find W. S. Gilbert's depiction of strict liability in The Mikado so far-fetched? What is the difference?

2. Consider Herbert Packer, The Limits of the Criminal Sanction 130-131 (1967):

> Despite the enormous body of judge-made law that affirms dispensing with the mental element in violations of food and drug regulations, liquor regulations, traffic rules, and the like, . . . few courts have explicitly considered and avowed the propriety of applying distinctively "criminal" sanctions to minor infractions. On the contrary, these offenses have been treated as something different from traditional criminal law, as a kind of hybrid category to which the odium and hence the safeguards of the criminal process do not attach. . . .

> [T]he criminal sanction should not be applied to trivial infractions such as minor traffic offenses, to cite perhaps the most conspicuous example of current misuse. The culpability issue highlights this point. Treating every kind of conduct that the legislature unthinkingly labels as criminal with the full doctrinal apparatus of culpability would place an intolerable burden on the courts. . . . A line must be drawn that does not depend simply upon the fortuitous use of the label "criminal." Labels aside, the combination of stigma and loss of liberty involved in a conditional or absolute sentence of imprisonment sets that sanction apart from anything else the law imposes. When the law permits that degree of severity, the defendant should be entitled to litigate the issue of culpability.

How can courts determine what is or is not a public welfare offense? Are not all violations of the law, regardless of strict liability, contrary to the public interest?

3. Consider United States v. Freed, 401 U.S. 601 (1971). Appellees were indicted under the National Firearms Act for possessing unregistered hand grenades. The district court dismissed the case because the indictment failed to allege scienter, that is, knowledge that the hand grenades were not registered. The Supreme Court reversed, stating that:

> The Act requires no specific intent or knowledge that the hand grenades were unregistered. It makes it unlawful for any person to "receive or possess a firearm which is not registered to him."

Is the possession of an unregistered hand grenade a violation of a public welfare statute? Does the answer to that question depend upon the reasons why the defendants possessed the grenades? Should it? How does *Freed* differ from *Morissette*? Some courts draw a distinction between malum in se (inherently evil) and malum prohibitum (evil because prohibited by law) offenses. Does such a distinction help here?

REGINA v. PRINCE

Court for Crown Cases Reserved
L.R. 2 Crim. Cas. Res. 154 (1875)

Case stated by DENMAN, J.

At the assizes for Surrey, held at Kingston-upon-Thames, on the 24th of March last, Henry Prince was tried upon the charge of having unlawfully taken one Annie Phillips, an unmarried girl, being under the age of sixteen years, out of the possession and against the will of her father. The indictment was framed under s.55 of 24 & 25 Vict. c. 100.[9]

9. By 24 & 25 Vict. c. 100, s.55, "Whosoever shall unlawfully take or cause to be taken any unmarried girl, being under the age of sixteen years, out of the possession and against the will of her father or mother, or of any other person having the lawful care or charge of her, shall be guilty of a misdemeanor, and being convicted thereof shall be liable, at the discretion of the Court, to be imprisoned for any term not exceeding two years, with or without hard labour."

He was found guilty.

All the facts necessary to support a conviction existed, unless the following facts constituted a defence. The girl Annie Phillips, though proved by her father to be fourteen years old on the 6th of April following, looked very much older than sixteen, and the jury found upon reasonable evidence that before the defendant took her away she had told him that she was eighteen, and that the defendant bona fide believed that statement, and that such belief was reasonable.

If the Court should be of the opinion that under these circumstances a conviction was right, the defendant was to appear for judgment at the next assizes for Surrey; otherwise the conviction was to be quashed. . . .

June 26. The following judgments were delivered:—

Brett, J. . . . [I]f the facts had been as the prisoner, according to the findings of the jury, believed them to be, and had reasonable ground for believing them to be, he would have done no act which has ever been a criminal offence in England; he would have done no act in respect of which any civil action could have ever been maintained against him; he would have done no act for which, if done in the absence of the father, and done with the continuing consent of the girl, the father could have had any legal remedy. . . .

Upon all the cases I think it is proved that there can be no conviction for crime in England in the absence of a criminal mind or *mens rea.*

Then comes the question, what is the true meaning of the phrase. I do not doubt that it exists where the prisoner knowingly does acts which would constitute a crime if the result were as he anticipated, but in which the result may not improbably end by bringing the offence within a more serious class of crime. As if a man strikes with a dangerous weapon, with intent to do grievous bodily harm, and kills, the result makes the crime murder. The prisoner has run the risk. So, if a prisoner [does] the prohibited acts, without caring to consider what the truth is as to facts—as if a prisoner were to abduct a girl under sixteen without caring to consider whether she was in truth under sixteen—he runs the risk. So if he without abduction defiles a girl who is in fact under ten years old, with a belief that she is between ten and twelve. If the facts were as he believed he would be committing the lesser crime. Then he runs the risk of his crime resulting in the greater crime. It is clear that ignorance of the law does not excuse. It seems to me to follow that the maxim as to *mens rea* applies whenever the facts which are present to the prisoner's mind, and which he has reasonable ground to believe, and does believe to be the facts, would, if true, make his acts no criminal offence at all. . . .

The following judgment (in which Cockburn, C.J., Mellor, Lush, Quain, Denman, Archibald, Field, and Lindley, JJ., and Pollock, B., concurred) was delivered by Blackburn, J. . . .

The question, therefore, is reduced to this, whether the words in 24 & 25 Vict. c. 100, s.55, that whosoever shall take "any unmarried girl, being under the age of sixteen, out of the possession of her father," are to be read as if they were "being under the age of sixteen, and he knowing she was under that age." No such words are contained in the statute, nor is there the word "maliciously," "knowingly" or any other word used that can be said to involve a similar meaning.

The argument in favour of the prisoner must therefore entirely proceed on the ground that, in general, a guilty mind is an essential ingredient in a crime, and that where a statute creates a crime, the intention of the legislature should be presumed to be to include "knowingly" in the definition of the crime, and the statute should be read as if that word were inserted, unless the contrary intention appears. We need not inquire at present whether the canon of construction goes quite so far as above stated, for we are of opinion that the intention of the legislature sufficiently appears to have been to punish the abduction, unless the girl, in fact, was of such an age as to make her consent an excuse, irrespective of whether he knew her to be too young to give an effectual consent and to fix that age at sixteen. The section in question is one of a series of enactments beginning with s.48, and ending with s.55, forming a code for the protection of women, and the guardians of young women. These enactments are taken with scarcely any alteration from the repealed statute, 9 Geo. 4, c.31, which had collected them into a code from a variety of old statutes all repealed by it.

Section 50 enacts, that whosoever shall "unlawfully and carnally know and abuse any girl under the age of ten years," shall be guilty of felony. Section 51, whoever shall "unlawfully and carnally know and abuse any girl being above the age of ten years, and under the age of twelve years," shall be guilty of a misdemeanor.

It seems impossible to suppose that the intention of the legislature in those two sections could have been to make the crime depend upon the knowledge of the prisoner of the girl's actual age. It would produce the monstrous result that a man who had carnal connection with a girl, in reality not quite ten years old, but whom he on reasonable grounds believed to be a little more than ten, was to escape altogether. He could not, in that view of the statute, be convicted of the felony, for he did not know her to be under ten. He could not be convicted of the misdemeanor, because she was in fact not above the age of ten. It seems to us that the intention of the legislature was to punish those who had connection with young girls, though with their consent, unless the girl was in fact old enough to give valid consent. The man who has connection with a child, relying on her consent, does it at his peril, if she is below the statutable age. . . .

The following judgment (in which Kelly, C.B., Cleasby, Pollock, and Amphlett, B.B., and Grove, Quain, and Denman, JJ., concurred) was delivered by Bramwell, B.

. . . [T]he question is whether he is guilty where he knows, as he thinks, that she is over sixteen. This introduces the necessity for reading the statute with some strange words introduced; as thus: "Whosoever shall take any unmarried girl, being under the age of sixteen, and not believing her to be over the age of sixteen, out of the possession," etc. Those words are not there, and the question is, whether we are bound to construe the statute as though they were, on account of the rule that the *mens rea* is necessary to make an act a crime. I am of opinion that we are not, nor as though the word "knowingly" was there, and for the following reasons: The act forbidden is wrong in itself, if without lawful cause; I do not say illegal, but wrong. I have not lost sight of this, that though the statute probably principally aims at seduction for carnal purposes, the taking may be by a female with a good motive. Nevertheless, though there may be such cases, which are not immoral in one sense, I say that the act forbidden is wrong.

Let us remember what is the case supposed by the statute. It supposes that there is a *girl*—it does not say a woman, but a girl—something between a child and a woman; it supposes she is in the *possession* of her father or mother, or other person having lawful *care or charge* of her; and it supposes there is a *taking,* and that that taking is *against the will* of the person in whose possession she is. It is, then, a *taking of a girl,* in the *possession* of someone, *against his will.* I say that done without lawful cause is wrong, and that the legislature meant it should be at the risk of the taker whether or not she was under sixteen. I do not say that taking a woman of fifty from her brother's or even father's house is wrong. She is at an age when she has a right to choose for herself; she is not a *girl,* nor of such tender age that she can be said to be in the *possession* of or under the *care or charge* of anyone. I am asked where I draw the line; I answer at when the female is no longer a girl in anyone's possession.

But what the statute contemplates, and what I say is wrong, is the taking of a female of such tender years that she is properly called a *girl,* can be said to be in another's *possession,* and in that other's *care or charge.* No argument is necessary to prove this; it is enough to state the case. The legislature has enacted that if anyone does this wrong act, he does it at the risk of her turning out to be under sixteen. This opinion gives full scope to the doctrine of *mens rea.* If the taker believed he had the father's consent, though wrongly, he would have no *mens rea;* so if he did not know she was in anyone's possession, nor in the care or charge of anyone. In those cases he would not know he was doing the *act* forbidden by the statute—an act which, if he knew she was in possession and in care or charge of anyone, he would know was a crime or not, according as she was under sixteen or not. He would not know he was doing an act wrong in itself, whatever was his intention, if done without lawful cause . . . .

DENMAN, J. . . .

. . . Bearing in mind the previous enactments relating to the abduction of girls under sixteen, and the general course of the decisions upon those enactments, and upon the present statute, and looking at the mischief intended to be guarded against, it appears to me reasonably clear that the word "unlawfully," in the true sense in which it was used, is fully satisfied by holding that it is equivalent to the words "without lawful excuse," using those words as equivalent to "without such an excuse as being proved would be a complete legal justification for the act, even where all the facts constituting the offence exist."

Cases may easily be suggested where such a defence might be made out, as, for instance, if it were proved that he had the authority of a Court of competent jurisdiction, or of some legal warrant, or that he acted to prevent some illegal violence not justified by the relation of parent and child, or school-mistress, or other custodian, and requiring forcible interference by way of protection.

In the present case the jury find that the defendant believed the girl to be eighteen years of age; even if she had been of that age, she would have been in the lawful care and charge of her father, as her guardian by nature. Her father had a right to her personal custody up to the age of twenty-one, and to appoint a guardian by deed or will, whose right to her personal custody would have extended up to the same age. The belief that she was eighteen would be no justification to the defendant for taking her out of his possession, and against his will. By taking her, even with her own consent, he must at least have been guilty of aiding and abetting her in doing an unlawful act, viz. in escaping against the will of her natural guardian from his lawful care and charge. This, in my opinion, leaves him wholly without lawful excuse or justification for the act he did, even though he believed that the girl was eighteen, and therefore unable to allege that what he has done was not unlawfully done, within the meaning of the clause. In other words, having knowingly done a wrongful act, viz. in taking the girl away from the unlawful possession of her father against his will, and in violation of his rights as guardian by nature, he cannot be heard to say that he thought the girl was of an age beyond that limited by the statute for the offence charge against him. He had wrongfully done the very thing contemplated by the legislature: He had wrongfully and knowingly violated the father's rights against the father's will. And he cannot set up a legal defence by merely proving that he thought he was committing a different kind of wrong from that which in fact he was committing.

Conviction affirmed.

Notes and Questions

1. Does the statute in *Prince* give us any help in deciding what, if any, mental culpability the law requires? Do the four opinions have differing views as to what is necessary for Prince's conviction? Which of the justices would hold Prince guilty regardless of his moral blameworthiness? As for those who would not, how would they determine whether Prince was blameworthy? Does blameworthiness mean any more or less than exhibiting the culpable state of mind implicitly required by the statute? Which opinion is most persuasive?

2. What if the girl in question, though under 16, had suffered from a rare disease that made her look 30? 70? Would it make any difference if Prince had taken her to work in a brothel?

3. What if Prince had driven off from the Phillips' house and had not

realized that the girl had secreted herself in the trunk of his carriage? Would he still be guilty? What if Prince had reasonably thought the girl he took away was an 18-year-old orphan who had no guardian? Would he still be guilty? Would it make any difference if Prince had taken her to work in a brothel? What if he had been planning to drive her away at a speed over the speed limit? What if the carriage had, to his knowledge, been stolen? What if, upon mounting his carriage, Prince had seen a piece of a girl's dress hanging out from the trunk but had driven off and had not thought further about the matter, even though he knew that the fabric did not belong there?

4. Examination Question in Criminal Law, Stanford Law School:

> Driver was out for a leisurely drive through his neighborhood. He passed over a bridge and happened to look down to see a figure struggling in the water. Although he heard a shout for help, he decided that the day was simply too beautiful for him to stop, even though he could have done so with perfect safety, and indeed, even though he had a long rope in his car, which he could easily have thrown to rescue the drowning individual. It was only later that Driver found out that the drowned boy, whose cries for help he had ignored, was his own son. Is Driver liable for his son's death?

Is the refusal to aid someone obviously in distress blameworthy? If so, why should one have to know of a particular duty? Or do we require a particular kind of blameworthiness for criminal guilt?

4

CULPABILITY AND THE GUILTY MIND

A. CATEGORIES OF CULPABILITY

REGINA v. FAULKNER

Court of Crown Cases Reserved
Ireland, 13 Cox C.C. 550 (1877)

. . . The indictment was as follows: "That Robert Faulkner, on the 26th day of June, 1876, on board a certain ship called the *Zemindar,* the property of Sandback, Tenne, and Co., on a certain voyage on the high seas, then being on the high seas, feloniously, unlawfully, and maliciously, did set fire to the said ship. . . ."

It was proved that the *Zemindar,* was on her voyage home with a cargo of rum, sugar, and cotton, worth 50,000 [pounds]. That the prisoner was a seaman on board, that he went into the forecastle hold, opened the sliding door in the bulk head, and so got into the hold where the rum was stored; he had no business there, and no authority to go there, and went for the purpose of stealing some rum, that he bored a hole in the cask with a gimlet, that the rum ran out, that when trying to put a spile in the hole out of which the rum was running, he had a lighted match in his hand; that the rum caught fire; that the prisoner himself was burned on the arms and neck; and that the ship caught fire and was completely destroyed. At the close of the case for the Crown, counsel for the prisoner asked for a direction of an acquittal on the ground that on the facts proved the indictment was not sustained, nor the allegation that the prisoner had unlawfully and maliciously set fire to the ship proved. The Crown contended that inasmuch as the prisoner was at the time engaged in the commission of a felony, the indictment was sustained, and the allegation of the intent was immaterial.

At the second hearing of the case before the Court for Crown Cases

Reserved, the learned judge made the addition of the following paragraph to the case stated by him for the court.

> It was conceded that the prisoner had no actual intention of burning the vessel, and I was not asked to leave any question to the jury as to the prisoner's knowing the probable consequences of his act, or as to his reckless conduct.

The learned judge told the jury that although the prisoner had no actual intention of burning the vessel, still if they found he was engaged in stealing the rum, and that the fire took place in the manner above stated, they ought to find him guilty. The jury found the prisoner guilty on both counts, and he was sentenced to seven years penal servitude. The question for the court was whether the direction of the learned judge was right, if not, the conviction should be quashed. . . .

Dowse, B., gave judgment to the effect that the conviction should be quashed.

Barry, J.—A very broad proposition has been contended for by the Crown, namely, that if, while a person is engaged in committing a felony, or, having committed it, is endeavouring to conceal his act, or prevent or spoil waste consequent on that act, he accidently does some collateral act, which if done wilfully would be another felony either at common law or by statute, he is guilty of the latter felony. I am by no means anxious to throw any doubt upon, or limit in any way, the legal responsibility of those who engage in the commission of felony, or acts mala in se; but I am not prepared without more consideration to give my assent to so wide a proposition. No express authority either by way of decision or dictum from judge or text writer has been cited in support of it. . . .

Fitzgerald, J.—I concur in opinion with my brother Barry, that the direction of the learned judge cannot be sustained in law, and that therefore the conviction should be quashed. I am further of opinion that in order to establish the charge . . . the intention of the accused forms an element in the crime to the extent that it should appear that the defendant intended to do the very act with which he is charged, or that it was the necessary consequence of some other felonious or criminal act in which he was engaged, or that having a probable result which the defendant foresaw, or ought to have foreseen, he, nevertheless, persevered in such other felonious or criminal act. The prisoner did not intend to set fire to the ship—the fire was not the necessary result of the felony he was attempting; and if it was a probable result, which he ought to have foreseen, of the felonious transaction on which he was engaged, and from which a malicious design to commit the injurious act with which he is charged might have been fairly imputed to him, that view of the case was not submitted to the jury. On the contrary, it was excluded from their consideration on the requisition of the counsel for the prosecution. Counsel for the prosecution in effect insisted that the defendant, being engaged in the commission of, or in an attempt to commit a felony, was criminally responsible for every result that was occasioned thereby, even though it was not a probable consequence of his act or such as he could have reasonably foreseen or intended. No authority has been cited for a proposition so extensive and I am of opinion that it is not warranted by law. . . .

O'Brien, J.—I am also of opinion that the conviction should be quashed, and I was of that opinion before the case for our consideration was amended by my brother Lawson. I had inferred from the original case that his direction to the jury was to the effect now expressly stated by amendment, and that, at the trial, the Crown's counsel conceded that the prisoner had no intention of burning the vessel, or of igniting the rum; and raised no questions as to prisoner's imagining or having any ground for supposing that the fire would be the result or consequence of his act in stealing the rum. With respect to Reg. v. Pembliton (12 Cox C.C. 607), it appears to me there were much stronger grounds in that case for upholding the conviction than exist in the case before us. In that case the breaking of the window was the act of the prisoner. He threw the stone that broke it; he threw it with the unlawful intent of striking some one of the crowd about, and the breaking of the window, was the direct and immediate result of his act. And yet the Court unanimously quashed the conviction upon the ground that, although the prisoner threw the stone intending to strike some one or more persons, he did not intend to break the window. The courts above have intimated their opinion that if the jury (upon a question to that effect being left to them) had found that the prisoner, knowing the window was there, might have reasonably expected that the result of his act would be the breaking of the window, that then the conviction should be upheld. During the argument of this case the Crown counsel required us to assume that the jury found their verdict upon the ground that in their opinion the prisoner may have expected that the fire would be the consequence of his act in stealing the rum, but nevertheless did the act recklessly, not caring whether the fire took place or not. But at the trial there was not even a suggestion of any such ground, and we cannot assume that the jury formed an opinion which there was no evidence to sustain, and which would be altogether inconsistent with the circumstances under which the fire took place. The reasonable inference from the evidence is that the prisoner lighted the match for the purpose of putting the spile in the hole to stop the further running of the rum, and that while he was attempting to do so the rum came in contact with the lighted match and took fire. . . .

Keogh, J.—I have the misfortune to differ from the other members of the Court. I think it very fortunate for the prisoner that this case has lasted so long, and has received such elaborate consideration, for I cannot be considered as violating judicial confidence when I state that if the case were decided when the arguments closed the conviction would stand. . . . I am . . . of opinion, that the conviction should stand, as I consider all questions of intention and malice are closed by the finding of the jury, that the prisoner committed the act with which he was charged whilst engaged in the commission of a substantive felony. On this broad ground, irrespective of all refinements as to "recklessness" and "wilfulness," I think the conviction is sustained. . . .

Notes and Questions

1. Faulkner obviously did not intend to burn the ship. But was he nevertheless properly blameworthy for the ship's loss? Is it not necessarily blameworthy to burn a ship? Or is Faulkner blameworthy for burning the ship because he burned it while he was stealing rum? Would he be less blameworthy if he had been in the cargo area on legitimate business and had, equally carelessly, lit a match that set the rum afire?

2. How would *Faulkner* have been decided under the holding in *Prince*?

3. The Malicious Damage Act, the statute under which Faulkner was prosecuted, made it a crime "feloniously, unlawfully, and maliciously" to set fire to the ship. Does the legislature's choice of adverbs help us determine what state of mind should be necessary for punishment under the statute?

MODEL PENAL CODE

American Law Institute, Model Penal Code and Commentaries (1985)

SECTION 2.02. GENERAL REQUIREMENTS OF CULPABILITY.

(1) *Minimum Requirements of Culpability.* Except as provided in Section 2.05, a person is not guilty of an offense unless he acted purposely, knowingly, recklessly or negligently, as the law may require, with respect to each material element[1] of the offense.

1. The Model Penal Code provides in §1.12:

(9) "element of an offense" means (i) such conduct or (ii) such attendant circumstances or (iii) such a result of conduct as
- (a) is included in the description of the forbidden conduct in the definition of the offense; or
- (b) establishes the required kind of culpability; or
- (c) negatives an excuse or justification for such conduct; or
- (d) negatives a defense under the statute of limitations; or
- (e) establishes jurisdiction or venue;

(10) "material element of an offense" means an element that does not relate exclusively to the statute of limitations, jurisdiction, venue or to any other matter similarly unconnected with (i) the harm or evil, incident to conduct, sought to be prevented by the law defining the offense, or (ii) the existence of a justification or excuse for such conduct. . . .—EDS.

(2) *Kinds of Culpability Defined.*

(a) *Purposely.*

A person acts purposely with respect to a material element of an offense when:

(i) if the element involves the nature of his conduct or a result thereof, it is his conscious object to engage in conduct of that nature or to cause such a result; and

(ii) if the element involves the attendant circumstances, he is aware of the existence of such circumstances or he believes or hopes that they exist.

(b) *Knowingly.*

A person acts knowingly with respect to a material element of an offense when:

(i) if the element involves the nature of his conduct or the attendant circumstances, he is aware that his conduct is of that nature or that such circumstances exist; and

(ii) if the element involves a result of his conduct, he is aware that it is practically certain that his conduct will cause such a result.

(c) *Recklessly.*

A person acts recklessly with respect to a material element of an offense when he consciously disregards a substantial and unjustifiable risk that the material element exists or will result from his conduct. The risk must be of such a nature and degree that, considering the nature and purpose of the actor's conduct and the circumstances known to him, its disregard involves a gross deviation from the standard of conduct that a law-abiding person would observe in the actor's situation.

(d) *Negligently.*

A person acts negligently with respect to a material element of an offense when he should be aware of a substantial and unjustifiable risk that the material element exists or will result from his conduct. The risk must be of such a nature and degree that the actor's failure to perceive it, considering the nature and purpose of his conduct and the circumstances known to him, involves a gross deviation from the standard of care that a reasonable person would observe in the actor's situation.

Notes and Questions

1. Note that the language of the Model Penal Code is quite complicated. Can you categorize any of these blameworthy states of mind in more readily understandable terms without sacrificing the Code's precision of meaning?

2. Why do we need such precision at all? Consider Robinson & Grall, Element Analysis in Defining Criminal Liability: The Model Penal Code and Beyond, 35 Stan. L. Rev. 681, 682-690 (1983):

> Because penal law protects the most important societal interests and authorizes the most serious sanctions the government may impose—the stigma of conviction, imprisonment, and even death—a criminal code, more than any other body of law, should be rational, clear, and internally consistent. Only a precise, principled code that sufficiently defines forbidden conduct can achieve its goals of condemnation and deterrence. Such a code gives citizens fair warning of what will constitute a crime, limits governmental discretion in determining whether a particular individual has violated the criminal law, and provides the distinctions among degrees of harm and degrees of culpability that create the foundation of a fair sentencing system.
>
> American criminal law has advanced significantly towards providing such precision, clarity, and rationality, owing in large part to the Model Penal Code. The common law and older codes defined an offense to require only a single mental state. . . . The general culpability provisions of The Model Penal Code, in contrast, recognize that a single offense definition may require a different culpable state of mind for each objective element of the offense. . . .
>
> The majority of American jurisdictions have adopted criminal codes that incorporate the Model Penal Code innovation by requiring courts to apply an element analysis to each offense and theory of liability. . . .
>
> . . . [I]n early law, *mens rea* doubtless meant little more than a general immorality of motive and was described as "a general notion of moral blameworthiness," an "evil-meaning mind," and a "vicious will." In Regina v. Prince, for example, the defendant's reasonable belief that the girl was over sixteen did not provide a defense to the crime of taking a girl under sixteen from the possession of her father. The defendant had the necessary *mens rea,* the court reasoned, because even if the girl had been over sixteen, the defendant's conduct would have been "wrong." . . .
>
> [This common law vague notion of wickedness gradually gave way to a requirement of a specific state of mind for criminal liability. But even more profound was the Model Penal Code innovation of recognizing that different objective elements of an offense could have different accompanying culpable state of mind requirements.]
>
> . . . Under the Code, a culpable state of mind requirement may exist for "*each* material *element*" of an offense. Further, the culpability requirement may be different for different elements of the same offense. . . .
>
> For many offenses, one particular element may be of central concern. Some murder statutes require that an actor intend to kill another human being, and some manslaughter statutes require that an actor be reckless as to causing the death of another human being. Thus, murder is commonly described as an "intentional" or "knowing" offense, and manslaughter as a "reckless" offense. But even with murder, where a single culpability—culpability as to causing death—is of central concern, other culpability issues exist. An independent culpability element of homicide concerns the deceased's status as a "human being." A homicide case may hinge, for example, upon a doctor's state of mind as to

whether an aborted fetus had matured into a "human being." While intention may be the proper mental state to require for the objective element of "causing death," it may not be the appropriate mental state to require for the objective element of status as a "human being."

3. If we agree that, in general, some blameworthy state of mind must attach to a voluntary act in order to justify the condemnation of the law, the issue does not end here. We can, in various ways, specify different kinds of blameworthy states of mind. As we will see, the modern trend in American jurisdictions is to use the categories of blameworthiness adopted and refined by the Model Penal Code. Though these are not the only ways one could slice the concept of a blameworthy state of mind, they do accord with certain of our basic intuitions.

Imagine for instance a mother who has come into a room and found that her child has just smashed a valuable vase:

Mother. You smashed that vase deliberately! (This is her most serious charge—that the child's conscious object was to break the valuable vase; in other words, that the child had "purpose.")

Child. No, that is not what I wanted to do at all. I didn't want to break the vase.

Mother (presumably trained as a lawyer). Even if that is true, you knew that when you let the vase hit the ground it would break, even though you might only have wanted to make a loud noise.

Child. No, I did not know that it would break at all, especially since my friend dropped a vase at his house and it didn't break, but I realize now that his is made of unbreakable plastic.

Mother. Even so, You knew that the vase *might* break. You recognized the risk when you dropped it or threw it to the ground, and despite this recognition you acted anyway. You took the chance. In other words, you were reckless.

Child. No, I didn't. It never occurred to me that the vase might break. I was sure it wouldn't.

Mother. In that case, *you should have known* that the vase would break. You are six years old and we expect a six-year-old to have knowledge that such a result would occur. In other words, you were negligent.

Child. From now on you can expect me to have this knowledge, but it is too much to ask of a six-year-old, who has had no previous experience dropping vases, that they might break.

Mother (adopting a kind of mental state that the Model Penal Code did not use but certainly is now familiar to you from the reasoning of Baron Bramwell in Regina v. Prince (p.127 supra)). You should not have been playing with the vase to begin with. You should have been in your room resting at the time.

Child. In that case, I should be punished only for not resting in my room or for playing with the vase, but not for the more serious offense of breaking it.

Mother (impressed with her child's argument for his lack of a blameworthy state of mind with respect to the vase, but nonetheless eager to punish). It does not matter; I will punish you for breaking the vase because you are *strictly liable.*

Child. That is fundamentally unjust.

4. The comments to the Model Penal Code give a more detailed exposition of the culpable states of mind it has classified in Section 2.02 General Requirements of Culpability:

> This section expresses the Code's basic requirement that unless some element of mental culpability is proved with respect to each material element of the offense, no valid criminal conviction may be obtained [except as provided in Section 2.05]. . . .
>
> . . . The Code provision on rape will afford an illustration [of the Model Code's approach]. Under Section 213.1(1), a purpose to effect the sexual relation is clearly required. But other circumstances are also made relevant by the definition of the offense. The victim must not have been married to the defendant and her consent to sexual relations would, of course, preclude the crime. Must the defendant's purpose have encompassed the facts that he was not the husband of the victim and that she opposed his will? These are certainly entirely different questions. Recklessness may be sufficient for these circumstances of the offense, although purpose is required with respect to the sexual result that is an element of the offense. . . .[2] [The Code] delineates four levels of culpability: purpose, knowledge, recklessness and negligence. It requires that one of these levels of culpability must be proved with respect to each "material element" of the offense, which may involve (1) the nature of the forbidden conduct or (2) the attendant circumstances, or (3) the result of conduct. The question of which level of culpability suffices to establish liability must be addressed separately with respect to each material element, and will be resolved either by the particular definition of the offense or the general provisions of this section.
>
> The purpose of articulating these distinctions in detail is to advance the clarity of draftsmanship in the delineation of the definitions of specific crimes . . . and to dispel the obscurity with which the culpability requirement is often treated when such concepts as "general criminal intent," "mens rea," "presumed intent," "malice," "wilfulness," "scienter" and the like have been employed. What Justice Jackson called "the variety, disparity and confusion" of judicial definitions of "the requisite but elusive mental element" in crime [Morissette v. United States, 342 U.S. 246, 252 (1952)] should, insofar as possible, be rationalized by a criminal code." . . .
>
> . . . In defining the kinds of culpability, the Code draws a narrow distinction between acting purposely and knowingly, one of the elements of ambiguity in legal usage of the term "intent." Knowledge that the requisite external circumstances exist is a common element in both conceptions. But action is not purpos-

ive with respect to the nature or the result of the actor's conduct unless it was his conscious object to perform an action of that nature or to cause such a result. . . .

. . . [T]here are areas where the discrimination is required and is made under traditional law, which uses the awkward concept of "specific intent." This is true in treason, for example, insofar as purpose to aid the enemy is an ingredient of the offense, and in attempts, complicity and conspiracy, where a true purpose to effect the criminal result is requisite for liability. . . .

. . . An important discrimination is drawn between acting either purposely or knowingly and acting recklessly. As the Code uses the term, recklessness involves conscious risk creation. It resembles acting knowingly in that a state of awareness is involved, but the awareness is of risk, that is of a probability less than substantial certainty; the matter is contingent from the actor's point of view. Whether the risk relates to the nature of the actor's conduct or to the existence of the requisite attendant circumstances, or to the result that may ensue, is immaterial; the concept is the same. . . .

[The Code requires, however, that the risk thus consciously disregarded by the actor be "substantial" and "unjustifiable" to be considered reckless.] Even substantial risks . . . may be created without recklessness when the actor is seeking to serve a proper purpose, as when a surgeon performs an operation that he knows is very likely to be fatal but reasonably thinks to be necessary because the patient has no other, safer chance. Some principle must, therefore, be articulated to indicate the nature of the final judgment to be made after everything has been weighed. . . . There is no way to state this value judgment that does not beg the question in the last analysis; the point is that the jury must evaluate the actor's conduct and determine whether it should be condemned. The Code proposes . . . that this difficulty be accepted frankly, and that the jury be asked to measure the substantiality and justifiability of the risk by asking whether its disregard, given the actor's perceptions involved a gross deviation from the standard of conduct that a law-abiding person in the actor's situation would observe. . . .

. . .The fourth kind of culpability is negligence. It is distinguished from [acting purposely, knowingly or recklessly] in that it does not involve a state of awareness. A person acts negligently . . . when he inadvertently creates a substantial and unjustifiable risk of which he ought to be aware . . . [considering its nature and degree, the nature and the purpose of his conduct and the care that would be exercised by a reasonable person in his situation.] [A]gain it is quite impossible to avoid tautological articulation of the final question. The tribunal must evaluate the actor's failure of perception and determine whether, under all the circumstances, it was serious enough to be condemned. The jury must find fault, and must find that it was substantial and unjustified; that is the heart of what can be said in legislative terms. . . .

. . . [S]ome critics have opposed any penal consequences for negligent behavior. Since the actor is inadvertent by hypothesis, it has been argued that the "threat of punishment for negligence must pass him by, because he does not realise that it is addressed to him." So too, it has been urged that education or corrective treatment, not punishment, is the proper social method for dealing with persons with inadequate awareness, since what is implied is not a moral defect. This analysis, however, oversimplifies the issue. . . . [K]nowledge that conviction and sentence, not to speak of punishment, may follow conduct that inadvertently creates improper risk [supplies people] with an additional motive to take care before acting, to use their faculties and draw on their experience in gauging the potentialities of contemplated conduct. To some extent, at least, this motive may promote awareness and thus be effective as a measure of control. . . . [L]egislators act on these assumptions in a host of situations, and it would be dogmatic to assert that they are wholly wrong. Accordingly, negligence, as here defined, should not be wholly rejected as a ground of culpability that may suffice for purposes of penal law, though it should not generally be deemed sufficient in the definition of specific crimes and it should often be differentiated from conduct involving higher culpability.

5. For another effort to clarify the Model Penal Code definitions, see Robinson and Grall, Element Analysis in Defining Criminal Liability: The Model Penal Code and Beyond, 35 Stan. L. Rev. 681, 694-699 (1983):

A. Culpability Terms Defined in Relation to Each Objective Element

The Model Penal Code distinguishes between culpability terms as follows: A person acts "purposely" with respect to a result if his conscious objective is to cause such a result. A person acts "knowingly" with respect to a result if it is not his conscious objective, yet he is practically certain that his conduct will cause that result. The essence of the narrow distinction between these two culpability levels is the presence or absence of a *positive desire* to cause the result; purpose requires a culpability beyond the knowledge of a result's near certainty. In the broader sense, this distinction divides the vague notions of "maliciousness" or "viciousness" from "callousness." The former may simply be an aggressively ruthless form of the latter, which is perhaps the very quality that distinguishes the two levels of culpability.

A person acts "knowingly" with respect to a result if he is nearly certain that his conduct will cause the result. If he is aware only of a substantial risk, he acts "recklessly" with respect to the result. The narrow distinction between knowledge and recklessness lies in the *degree of risk*—"highly probable" versus "substantial"—of which the actor is aware. The important distinction between recklessness (and lower levels of culpability) and both higher levels of culpability is that we condemn purposeful and knowing conduct for being "wilful," while we merely scold reckless conduct for being at most "careless." An offender whose conduct falls within the first category is often condemned for "intentional" conduct; one in the latter is scolded for "taking risks."

A person acts "recklessly" with respect to a result if he consciously disregards a substantial risk and acts only "negligently" if he is unaware of a substantial risk he should have perceived. The narrow distinction lies in the actor's *awareness of risk.* The distinction, one of the most critical to criminal law, between negligence and all three higher levels of culpability, reflects that a defendant acting purposely, knowingly, or recklessly is aware of the harmful consequences that may result and is therefore both blameworthy and deterrable, but a defendant acting negligently is unaware of harmful consequences and therefore is arguably neither blameworthy nor deterrable. While most reject this view of

CHART I
Model Penal Code §2.02(2) Culpability Definitions

A person acts [culpability level] with respect to [type of objective element] when:

	Type of Objective Element		
	Circumstance	*Result*	*Conduct*
Purposely	he is aware of such circumstances or hopes that exist	it is his conscious object . . . to cause such a result	it is his conscious object to engage in conduct of that nature
Knowingly	he is aware . . . that such circumstances exist	he is aware that it is practically certain that his conduct will cause such a result	he is aware that his conduct is of that nature
Recklessly	he consciously disregards a substantial and unjustifiable risk that the material element exists	he consciously disregards a substantial and unjustifiable risk that the material element . . . will result from his conduct	
Negligently	he should be aware of a substantial and unjustifiable risk that the material element exists	he should be aware of a substantial and unjustifiable risk that the material element . . . will result from his conduct	

negligent culpability, all nonetheless recognize that negligence represents a lower level of culpability, qualitatively different from recklessness because the negligent actor fails to recognize, rather than consciously disregards, a risk. For this reason, recklessness is considered the norm for criminal culpability, and negligence is punished only in the exceptional case.

A person who fails to appreciate the risk that his conduct will cause a specific result is "negligent" only if that failure "involves a gross deviation from the standard of care that a reasonable person would observe in the actor's situation." Thus, unless he grossly deviates from the standard of care that a reasonable person would observe, an actor is not negligent and, at least in the eyes of criminal law, is without recognizable fault. Liability imposed for faultless conduct is termed "absolute" or "strict" liability. The narrow distinction between negligence and strict liability focuses on whether the defendant's awareness of the risk is a *failure to meet the objective standard of the reasonable person.* The broader distinction between the four categories of culpability and faultlessness is between conduct that grossly deviates from that of the reasonable, law-abiding person and conduct that does not and is therefore not blameworthy. Theoretical objections to strict liability understandably stem from a reluctance to punish conduct that is not unreasonable.

Model Penal Code section 2.02(2) defines each culpability term with respect to each of the three kinds of objective elements: conduct, circumstance, and result. Chart I gives the section 2.02(2) definition for each variation.

The Code's definition of each culpability term with respect to each kind of objective element of an offense reflects a fundamental and critical principle of the Code's culpability scheme: *Different degrees of culpability may be required with respect to different elements of the same offense.* [Thus Model Penal Code §241.5 defines the crime of "Falsely Incriminating Another" as:

> A person who knowingly gives false information to any law enforcement officer with purpose to implicate another commits a misdemeanor.]

Why would the drafters of the Model Penal Code want to require different states of mind for different elements of the same offense?

6. Sometimes situations arise in which the meaning of the *mens rea* construct is not as clear as we might desire. In United States v. Jewell, 532 F.2d 697 (9th Cir. 1976), the court was faced with a situation where the defendant claimed that, though he knew of a secret compartment in the automobile that he drove into the United States and knew of facts indicating that marijuana had been placed there, "he deliberately avoided positive knowledge . . . to avoid responsibility in the event of discovery." The court, over a strong dissent, held that this "willful blindness" was equivalent to knowledge, and hence that the defendant "knowingly brought marijuana into the United States" in violation of the law.

7. Review the facts of Regina v. Faulkner, and assume that Faulkner was prosecuted under the Model Penal Code. Section 220.1(1)(a) of the Code provides that a person is guilty of arson "if he starts a fire or causes an explosion with the purpose of . . . destroying" an occupied building or vehicle. Is Faulkner guilty of arson? If not, is he guilty of one of the following Model Penal Code offenses?

§220.2. Causing or Risking Catastrophe.

(1) *Causing Catastrophe.* A person who causes a catastrophe by explosion, fire, flood . . . or other harmful or destructive force or substance . . . commits a felony of the second degree if he does so purposely or knowingly, or a felony of the third degree if he does so recklessly.

§220.3. Criminal Mischief.

(1) *Offense Defined.* A person is guilty of criminal mischief if he:

(a) damages tangible property of another purposely, recklessly, or by negligence in the employment of fire, explosives, or other dangerous means. . . .

(b) purposely or recklessly tampers with tangible property of another so as to endanger person or property. . . .

(2) *Grading.* Criminal mischief is a felony of the third degree if the actor purposely causes pecuniary loss in excess of $5,000, or a substantial interruption or impairment of public communication, transportation . . . or other public service. It is a misdemeanor if the actor causes pecuniary loss in excess of $100, or a petty misdemeanor if he purposely or recklessly causes pecuniary loss in excess of $25. Otherwise criminal mischief is a violation.

B. *MENS REA* AND MISTAKE

STATE v. GUEST
Supreme Court of Alaska
583 P.2d 836 (1978)

MATTHEWS, Justice.

The question presented in the State's petition for review is whether an honest and reasonable mistake of fact regarding a victim's age may serve as a defense to a charge of statutory rape.

On April 7, 1977, the respondents, Moses Guest and Jacob Evan, were charged with the statutory rape of T.D.G., age fifteen. . . .[2]

. . . The parties entered into a stipulation that "the evidence expected to be presented at trial will support a reasonable belief on the part of each defendant that the alleged victim, age 15, was sixteen years of age or older at the time of the alleged act of sexual intercourse." In light of that stipulation, the court ordered that it would instruct the jurors as follows:

> It is a defense to a charge of statutory rape that the defendant reasonably and in good faith believed that the female person was of the age of sixteen years or older even though, in fact, she was under the age of sixteen years. If from all the evidence you have a reasonable doubt as to the question whether defendant reasonably and in good faith believed that she was sixteen years of age or older, you must give the defendant the benefit of that doubt and find him not guilty.

The state brings a petition for review from that order.

2. AS 11.15.120 provides in relevant part:

> Rape. (a) a person who . . . being 16 years of age or older, carnally knows and abuses a person under 16 years of age, is guilty of rape.

Respondents concede that in most jurisdictions a reasonable mistake of age is not a defense to a charge of statutory rape.[3] Although the validity of this defense to a statutory rape charge has not been decided in Alaska, we were presented with a similar issue in Anderson v. State, 384 P.2d 669 (Alaska 1963) where the charge was contributing to the delinquency of a minor by a consensual act of sexual intercourse. We said that "[a]ppellant's belief that prosecutrix was over the age of eighteen, even though it may have some support, is no excuse" and "[p]ersons having illegal relations with children do so at their [own] peril." Id. at 671.

We recognized in Speidel v. State, 460 P.2d 77 (Alaska 1969), that consciousness of wrongdoing is an essential element of penal liability. "It is said to be a universal rule that an injury can amount to a crime only when inflicted by intention—that conduct cannot be criminal unless it is shown that one charged with criminal conduct had an awareness or consciousness of some wrongdoing." . . .

Our opinion in *Speidel* stated that there are exceptions to the general requirement of criminal intent which are categorized as "public welfare" offenses. These exceptions are a rather narrow class of regulation, "caused primarily by the industrial revolution, out of which grew the necessity of imposing more stringent duties on those connected with particular industries, trades, properties, or activities that affect public health, safety or welfare." The penalties for the infraction of these strict liability offenses are usually relatively small and conviction of them carries no great opprobrium.

Statutory rape may not appropriately be categorized as a public welfare offense. It is a serious felony. If the offender is less than nineteen years of age, he may be imprisoned for up to twenty years. If he is nineteen years of age or older, he may be punished by imprisonment for any term of years.

We believe that the charge of statutory rape is legally unsupportable under the principles of *Speidel,* unless a defense of reasonable mistake of age is allowed. To refuse such a defense would be to impose criminal liability without any criminal mental element. The defense of reasonable mistake of fact is generally allowed in criminal cases to permit the defendant to show that he lacked criminal intent.[4] When that opportunity is foreclosed the result is strict criminal liability.

3. . . . This point of view has also been [rejected] by the 1978 revisors of the Alaska Criminal Code. Alaska Criminal Code revision (effective 1980) provides:

> 11.41.445. . . . whenever a provision of law defining an offense depends upon a victim's being under a certain age, it is an affirmative defense that, at the time of the alleged offense, the defendant reasonably believed the victim to be that age or older, unless the victim was under 13 years of age at the time of the alleged offense.

4. The defense of mistake has been generally explained as follows:

> Instead of speaking of ignorance or mistake of fact or law as a defense, it would be just as easy to note simply that the defendant cannot be convicted when it is shown that he does not have the mental state required by law for commission of that particular offense. For

Although AS 11.15.120 is silent as to any requirement of intent, this is true of many felony statutes. The requirement of criminal intent is then commonly inferred. In fact, in such cases, where the particular statute is not a public welfare type of offense, either a requirement of criminal intent must be read into the statute or it must be found unconstitutional.

Since statutes should be construed where possible to avoid unconstitutionality, it is necessary here to infer a requirement of criminal intent.

It has been urged in other jurisdictions that where an offender is aware he is committing an act of fornication he therefore has sufficient criminal intent to justify a conviction for statutory rape because what was done would have been unlawful under the facts as he thought them to be. We reject this view. While it is true that under such circumstances a mistake of fact does not serve as a complete defense, we believe that it should serve to reduce the offense to that which the offender would have been guilty of had he not been mistaken. See Model Penal Code §2.04(2) (Proposed Official Draft 1962).[5] Thus, if an accused had a reasonable belief that the person with whom he had sexual intercourse was sixteen years of age or older, he may not be convicted of statutory rape. If, however, he did not have a reasonable belief that the victim was eighteen years of age or older, he may still be criminally liable for contribution to the delinquency of a minor.[6] It is significant that the Alaska Statutes do not proscribe fornication, and therefore, it may not be considered an offense of a lesser degree.

For the foregoing reasons, we hold that a charge of statutory rape is defensible where an honest and reasonable mistake of fact as to the victim's age is shown. Anderson v. State, supra, is overruled to the extent that its holding is inconsistent with the views expressed herein. The order of the superior court is affirmed.

Affirmed.

---

example, to take the classic case of the man who takes another's umbrella out of a restaurant because he mistakenly believes that the umbrella is his, it is not really necessary to say that the man, if charged with larceny, has a valid defense of mistake of fact; it would be more direct and to the point to assert that the man is not guilty because he does not have the mental state (intent to steal the property of another) required for the crime of larceny. Yet, the practice has developed of dealing with such mistakes as a matter of defense, perhaps because the facts showing their existence are usually brought out by the defendant. . . . LaFave & Scott, Criminal Law, §47 at 356-357 (1972).

5. Section 2.04(2) of the Model Penal Code provides:

> . . . Although ignorance or mistake would otherwise afford a defense to the offense charged, the defense is not available if the defendant would be guilty of another offense had the situation been as he supposed. In such a case, however, the ignorance or mistake of the defendant shall reduce the grade and degree of the offense of which he may be convicted to those of the offense of which he would be guilty had the situation been as he supposed.

6. AS 11.40.130 provides:

> **Contributing to Delinquency of Child**
>
> (a) A person who commits an act, or omits the performance of a duty, which causes or tends to cause, encourage or contribute to the delinquency of a child under the age of 18 years, is guilty of a misdemeanor.

Notes and Questions

1. According to the court's interpretation of the Alaska statutory rape statute in *Guest,* what *mens rea* attaches to the element of the age of the girl?

2. If that same Alaska statutory rape law were part of the Model Penal Code, what *mens rea* would attach to the element of the age of the girl?

In this regard, consider Model Penal Code §2.02(3):

> *Culpability Required Unless Otherwise Provided.* When the culpability sufficient to establish a material element of an offense is not prescribed by law, such element is established if a person acts purposely, knowingly or recklessly with respect thereto.

What is the principle behind this provision? According to the Comments to §2.02(3) of the Model Penal Code:

> Subsection (3) provides that unless the kind of culpability sufficient to establish a material element of an offense has been prescribed by law, it is established if a person acted purposely, knowingly or recklessly with respect thereto. This accepts as the basic norm what usually is regarded as the common law position. More importantly, it represents the most convenient norm for drafting purposes. When purpose or knowledge is to be required, it is conventional to be explicit. And since negligence is an exceptional basis of liability, it should be excluded . . . unless explicitly prescribed.

3. The actual substantive provisions of the Model Penal Code addressing the statutory rape situation are as follows:

Section 213.3. Corruption of Minors and Seduction.

(1) *Offense Defined.* A male who has sexual intercourse with a female not his wife, or any person who engages in deviate sexual intercourse or causes another to engage in deviate sexual intercourse, is guilty of an offense if:

(a) the other person is less than [sixteen] years old and the actor is at least [four] years older than the other person; or

(b) the other person is less than [twenty-one] years old and the actor is his guardian or otherwise responsible for general supervision of his welfare. . . .

Section 213.6. Provisions Generally Applicable to Article 213.

(1) *Mistake as to Age.* Whenever in this Article the criminality of conduct depends on a child's being below the age of [ten,] it is no defense that the actor did not know the child's age, or reasonably believed the child to be older than [ten]. When criminality depends on the child's being below a critical age other than [ten], it is a defense for the actor to prove by a preponderance of the evidence that he reasonably believed the child to be above the critical age.

Is §213.6 a departure from the general requirements of a culpable mental state? If so, how can it be defended?

4. Consider Guest's probable liability under the court's holding and under the Model Penal Code in the following hypothetical situations.

a. The girl had a very mature physical appearance, and most people would have assumed she was close to twenty. Moreover, Guest asked to see her driver's license, and she showed him her (perfectly forged) license, which indicated she was of age.

b. The girl looked and acted like an average junior high school student. Indeed, Guest knew that the girl was in the eighth grade. But the girl told him that she had missed several years of schooling because of a mysterious illness from which she had now recovered, and that she had fallen behind in school.

5. The *Guest* case is an exception to the traditional rule in many jurisdictions that neither knowledge, recklessness, or negligence with regard to the age of a girl is an element of statutory rape—in short, that a girl's age is a "strict liability" element.

Consider this defense of the Model Penal Code provisions which reject the traditional rule:[7]

> The justification for employing strict liability in such cases is that it is much easier to prove the victim's age than the defendant's state of mind concerning it, and it is thought not unfair to punish a person who has done something which would be "immoral" even if done with a person of legal age. This justification seems absurd when applied to such anachronistic offenses as statutory rape of a female under eighteen, because so many teenagers today are sexually active. On the other hand, it is rarely questioned when applied to cases involving children under the age of puberty. No one is upset that a man may be convicted on a charge of having sexual relations with a child under the age of ten, even though he may have thought that the child was ten years old or even eleven. The law cannot avoid drawing an arbitrary line, and it is not troubling that defendants who want to be safe must keep a good distance from this particular borderline.

For a criticism of the modern trend represented by *Guest* and the Model Penal Code, consider the following:[8]

> It is significant to note that only by constructing the underlying material in the strict-liability situations with a very narrow time frame that the distinction between liability predicated on negligence, and strict liability, maintains its practical import in many critical situations.
>
> An example is the familiar problem of "reasonable" (non-negligent) mistakes as to the victim's age in the statutory rape setting. Is one's view of a "reasonable" belief to be ascertained solely by reference to perceptions available

7. Johnson, Strict Liability: The Prevalent View, 4 Encyclopedia of Crime and Justice 1519 (1983).

8. Kelman, Strict Liability: An Unorthodox View, Encyclopedia of Crime and Justice 1516-1517 (1983).

to the defendant during the purportedly illegal seduction (she "*looked* sixteen or "she told me she was sixteen"), or does one require that some checks prior to seduction be taken, such as checking birth certificates or asking parents? Of course, if one is hostile to statutory rape laws in general, it is perfectly reasonable to negate them by defining negligent perceptions in terms of the girl's physical appearance—that is, in terms of judgments which can be made at the narrow time-framed moment of the allegedly criminal incident. But it is hardly conceivable that a defendant ought to attract serious sympathy as someone unable to avoid crime when he has certainly had the opportunity to check on the legal appropriateness of his companion as an object of sexual desire.

If one really cared about using statutory rape laws to protect the chastity of the young, one would have to insist that people take steps to avoid mistakes of age, not simply that they refrain from sexual relations once they believe or know that the girl is underage. It is difficult to imagine that a strict-liability interpretation ensnares many defendants who have taken extensive steps to avoid mistakes: for example, in People v. Hernandez, 61 Cal. 2d 529, 393 P.2d 673 (1964), the much-heralded California case overturning the imposition of strict liability as to the victim's age in the statutory rape context, the defendant had known the prosecutrix for several months before they had sexual relations, but the court chose to focus instead on how mature the prosecutrix appeared.

Once one dissipates the opponent's rhetorical move—the image of the hopelessly ensnared, powerless victim of state power—one can come to see the proper debate in the area rather differently than it has been seen. As a "policy" matter, the legislative decision whether to condemn a defendant only where negligence is shown, or to condemn wherever harm is caused, is nothing more than the outcome of a perfectly traditional balance of interests between strict, easily applied rules and vaguer, ad hoc standards.

6. Courts and commentators examining issues of *mens rea* such as the one in *Guest* often describe the issue as one of "mistake of fact." Thus, Guest argued that his impression about the girl's age was a mistake of fact and that this mistake exculpated him of the crime. In this respect, examine Model Penal Code §2.04(1).

Section 2.04. Ignorance or Mistake.

(1) Ignorance or mistake as to a matter of fact or law is a defense if:

(a) the ignorance or mistake negatives the purpose, knowledge, belief, recklessness or negligence required to establish a material element of the offense; or

(b) the law provides that the state of mind established by such ignorance or mistake constitutes a defense.

Do these provisions do anything more than affirm the §2.02 rule that a person has not committed a particular crime unless he acted with the specific *mens rea* designated by the statute?

7. Consider the following story from the San Jose Mercury News, April 20, 1984:

San Antonio, Texas (UPI)—A Russian immigrant who thought a shopping mall was a single large store has been acquitted of shoplifting charges. [As the woman told the jurors,] she had never been shopping in America before the [incident]. She selected [a $50 dress] and then carried it out the door to continue shopping at other stores.

She testified that she thought the entire mall was a single store and that she intended to pay for the dress before leaving.

Is she guilty under Texas Penal Code §31.03?

Theft

(a) A person commits an offense if he unlawfully appropriates property with intent to deprive the owner of property.

(b) Appropriation of property is unlawful if:

(1) it is without the owner's effective consent. . . .

Would she be guilty under the following Illinois statute?

A person commits the offense of retail theft when he knowingly takes possession of, carries away, or transfers any merchandise displayed, held, stored, or offered for sale in a retail mercantile establishment with the intention of retaining such merchandise or with intention of depriving the merchant permanently of the possession, use, or benefit of such merchandise without paying the full retail value of such merchandise. . . . Ill. Ann. Stat. ch. 38 §16A-3(a).

Is someone who takes goods from the clothing to the hardware department of a store guilty of retail theft? What if the hardware department is run by an independent businessman?

8. The Model Penal Code defines burglary as follows in §221.1:

(1) *Burglary Defined.* A person is guilty of burglary if he enters a building or occupied structure . . . with purpose to commit a crime therein . . . unless the actor is . . . privileged to enter.

(2) *Grading.* Burglary is a felony of the second degree if it is perpetrated in the dwelling of another at night. . . . Otherwise, burglary is a felony of the third degree.

Of what offenses, if any, are the following people guilty under this section, and under §§2.02 and 2.04?

a. Susan agreed to feed the cat in her friend Betty's townhouse while Betty was away. Susan misremembered the number of Betty's house and went to the house next door. She found the door unlocked, entered, and then realized she was in the wrong house. But she spotted some expensive pieces of jewelry and left with them.

b. Brad saw a small brick building and decided to break in and look for something valuable he could fence for narcotics money. It was night time, and the building appeared to be a small warehouse with no one in it. He broke in and was surprised to find Fred, who was actually renting it for sleeping quarters.

Notice that the burglary statute mentions "purpose." Does "purpose" apply to all elements of the crime? Examine §2.02(4) of the Code:

> *Prescribed Culpability Requirement Applies to All Material Elements.* When the law defining an offense prescribes the kind of culpability that is sufficient for the commission of an offense, without distinguishing among the material elements thereof, such provision shall apply to all the material elements of the offense, unless a contrary purpose plainly appears.

Does it apply here? If it does not, does §2.02(3) help?

9. In Liparota v. United States, 53 U.S.L.W. 4530 (S. Ct., May 14, 1985), the Supreme Court resolved a conflict in the lower courts over the required *mens rea* for the federal statute governing illegal transfers of food stamps. Under 7 U.S.C. §2024(b)(1):

> [W]hoever *knowingly* . . . acquires [food stamp] coupons . . . in any manner not authorized by this chapter or the regulations issued pursuant to this chapter shall, if such coupons . . . are of a value of $100 or more, be guilty of a felony. . . .

Frank Liparota owned a sandwich shop in Chicago. Under federal law, food stamps may only be used to buy food in retail stores. A restaurant may, under special circumstances, receive food stamps as payment for meals if it receives permission from the Department of Agriculture. Liparota had received no such permission.

The government proved at trial that on three occasions Liparota bought food stamps from an undercover Department of Agriculture agent for roughly two-thirds of their face value. Liparota claimed that he had no idea that his purchase was "not authorized" under the statute. The trial judge, however, refused to instruct the jury that the government had to prove that Liparota knew that the exchange was unauthorized. The jury convicted Liparota, and the court of appeals affirmed, but the Supreme Court reversed the conviction. It held that the language and legislative history of the statute were ambiguous on this key issue, and so invoked the principle that ambiguous criminal statutes must be construed in favor of the accused. Does the Court's holding make sense under the principles of *mens rea* discussed in this chapter?

Under this decision, would the government have any chance of a conviction on retrial? According to the Court, in addition to evidence of the substantial discount Liparota received for the food stamps, the government had offered evidence that he had conducted part of the transaction in a back room of his restaurant, and that the stamps themselves were stamped "nontransferable."

Would the result be different if the trial court were to follow Model Penal Code §2.02(4)? Does "knowingly" apply to all elements of the crime?

Keeping *Liparota* in mind, consider the following cases.

PEOPLE v. BRAY

California Court of Appeal
52 Cal. App. 3d 494, 124 Cal. Rptr. 913 (1975)

Gerald Brown, Presiding Justice.

James Eugene Bray appeals the judgment following his jury conviction on two counts of being a felon in possession of a concealable firearm.

Bray's meritorious contention is the trial court should have instructed the jury that ignorance or mistake of fact is a defense to the crime.[9]

In 1969 Bray pled guilty in Kansas to being an accessory after the fact. At sentencing, the Kansas prosecutor recommended Bray be granted probation because he had no previous criminal record, he had been unwilling to participate in the crime but had gotten involved by driving a friend away from the scene and he had cooperated fully with the district attorney's office. Bray was placed on two years summary probation which he successfully completed before moving to California in 1971. While in California Bray first worked at Convair Aircraft and later was employed by the County of San Diego in the Department of Public Health. Near the end of 1973 he transferred to the district attorney's office.

In January 1972, Bray filled out an application to vote in the State of California. He discussed the problems he had had in Kansas with the Deputy of the Registrar of Voters and asked if he would be allowed to vote. The Deputy could not answer the question and suggested he say on the registration form he had been convicted of a felony and fill out a supplementary explanatory form to find out if he, in fact, had committed a felony. This Bray did; he was allowed to vote.

In early July of 1973, Bray applied for a part-time job as a guard with ADT Sterling Security Company. On the application he answered that he had been arrested or charged with a crime but had not been convicted of a felony. At the bottom of the page Bray explained the circumstances surrounding his

9. Bray requested jury instructions from CALJIC [The book of California Jury Instructions] reading:

CALJIC 4.35—Ignorance or Mistake of Fact

An act committed or an omission made under an ignorance or mistake of fact which disproves any criminal intent is not a crime.

Thus a person is not guilty of a crime if he commits an act or omits to act under an honest and reasonable belief in the existence of certain facts and circumstances which, if true, would make such an act or omission lawful.

CALJIC 1.21—Knowingly—Defined

The word "knowingly" as used in my instructions, imports only a knowledge of the existence of the facts in question, when those facts are such as bring the act or omission within the provision of the law. The word does not require in its meaning any knowledge of the unlawfulness of such act or omission.

Here the instruction would have required the jury to find Bray knew he was a felon and knew he had possession of a concealable firearm.

arrest and period of probation. In September he received a notice from the Bureau of Collection and Investigative Services that he had been registered as a guard or patrolman.

Later in July of 1973 Bray bought a .38 caliber revolver from a pawn shop, Western Jewelry and Loan Company, to use in guard assignments requiring an armed patrolman. On one of the required forms he said he had not been convicted of a felony; on another he said he had not been convicted of a crime with a punishment of more than one year. After the statutory five-day waiting period, the gun was delivered to him.

On September 14, 1973 Bray filled out an application for a job as a contract compliance investigator. In response to the question asking whether he had been convicted of a felony or misdemeanor, Bray answered with a "?". He again explained the circumstances surrounding his arrest and the sentence he received.

On November 16, 1973 and April 12, 1974 Bray filled out job applications for positions as an audio-visual technician and as an eligibility worker I. In each instance he answered that he had been convicted of a "felony or misdemeanor"; in each instance he explained his Kansas arrest and sentence.

In July of 1974, two investigators from the district attorney's office conducted a search with a warrant of Bray's house and car. Bray voluntarily led the investigators to a closet where he kept the .38 and a .22 pistol.

In order to gain a conviction under the relevant statute, the prosecutor must prove (1) conviction of a felony and (2) ownership, possession, custody or control of a firearm capable of being concealed on the person. There was no question here that Bray had been in possession of a concealable firearm; there was no question he had been convicted of the crime of being an "accessory after the fact" in Kansas. Bray says there must be proof he knew he was a felon. Or, in the alternative, he says mistake of fact is a defense and the court erred in denying this requested instruction.

It appears to be a question of first impression whether Penal Code §12021 [the statute in question] requires proof of the defendant's knowledge of his or her felony status, and whether such a prosecution may be defended by showing the defendant lacked knowledge he was a felon. The prevailing trend of decisions is to avoid constructions of penal statutes which would impose strict liability. The Attorney General agrees the statute should not be one of strict liability but then says it is not necessary for the People to prove the defendant had knowledge.

In considering the role of knowledge, whether the defendant knew he had committed an offense is irrelevant. The question here is whether the defendant must know of the existence of those facts which bring him within the statute's proscription. Even though §12021 does not explicitly require knowledge, the defendant must know he has possession of a concealable weapon (People v. Burch, 196 Cal. App. 2d 754, 771, 17 Cal. Rptr. 102). In addition, as to whether a defendant must know he is an alien under §12021, this court, in dictum, has said:

> Knowledge that one is in the State of California might conceivably be relevant in the case of a person who unwittingly had overstepped the boundary of a neighboring state, who might have been carried into the state against his will, or as the result of mistake in taking some vehicle of public transportation.
>
> In the present case, defendant knew he was no longer in Mexico. (People v. Mendoza, 251 Cal. App. 2d 835, 843, 60 Cal. Rptr. 5, 10.)

Likewise, knowledge that one is a felon becomes relevant where there is doubt the defendant knew he had committed a felony. Here, even the prosecution had substantial difficulty in determining whether the offense was considered a felony in Kansas. In arguing to the court the necessity of a Kansas attorney's expert testimony, the district attorney said, ". . . in even our own jurisdiction, let alone a foreign jurisdiction such as the State of Kansas, it's extremely difficult to determine whether a sentence was a felony or a misdemeanor." Although the district attorney had great difficulty in determining whether the Kansas offense was a felony or a misdemeanor, he expects the layman Bray to know its status easily. There was no doubt Bray knew he had committed an offense: there was, however, evidence to the effect he did not know the offense was a felony. Without this knowledge Bray would be ignorant of the facts necessary for him to come within the proscription of section 12021. Under these circumstances the requested instructions on mistakes or ignorance of fact and knowledge of the facts which make the act unlawful should have been given.

Notes and Questions

1. In *Bray,* what is the *mens rea* attached to the fact that the possessor of the gun had formerly been convicted of a felony? What was the defendant's *mens rea?* Note here that the mistake made by the defendant was about a law rather than the usual mistake of fact. If a defendant makes a mistake of law that deprives him of the *mens rea* necessary for being found guilty of a crime, should we nonetheless treat him as if he had that *mens rea?* Why would we do that?

In most cases where a defendant's objective conduct falls within the terms of a criminal statute but he or she is nonetheless not blameworthy, the reason is that because of a mistake of fact the defendant lacks the *mens rea* required for the crime. This, however, is not always the case. Let us assume that a statute provides that it is a crime for someone with a living wife to go through a marriage ceremony with someone else, attaching the *mens rea* of recklessness, let us say, to the issue of whether one has a living wife. In such a case it should not matter whether the defendant was wrongly convinced that his wife had perished in an airplane crash or was equally convinced that his divorce from her was valid. It is true that the former error could be categorized as a mistake of fact and the latter a mistake of law, but since either would deprive the accused of the *mens rea* attached to his having a living wife, which the statute makes necessary for guilt, the distinction is not significant.

This is just as well because, although we may be convinced that we know the difference between a question of fact and of law, any question which can be phrased as a question of fact can also be phrased as one of law (though the reverse does not appear to be true). Thus, while we usually think of the question whether a person is dead as being one of fact (Did he perish in the airplane accident? We have not heard from him for a long time and he would be very old now, so he is probably dead), the question of whether a person is dead could also be one of law and might arise where we are completely familiar with all the facts. (She is lying in a hospital, having fluids pumped in and out of her with her heart beating only because of electrical stimulation, and having a flat electro-encephalograph, which has shown no sign of brain activity for two months.) In this case, whether or not she was dead would be a question of law. We are also familiar with the same issue with respect to the ownership of property and various other issues. Sometimes the distinction is drawn here between errors of civil law, which are exculpating, and errors of criminal law, which are not. In fact, even an error of criminal law can exculpate if it negates the *mens rea* required by the criminal statute. Note that in *Bray* the error was one of criminal law.

2. Consider Regina v. Smith (David) 2 Q.B. 354, 58 Cr. App. 320 (1974).

> [A]ppellant [and his brother] became tenants of a ground floor flat . . . and installed some electric wiring for use with stereo equipment. Also, with the landlord's permission, they put up roofing material, wall panels, and laid floor boards. There is no dispute that the roofing, wall panels, and floor boards became part of the house, and, in law, property of the landlord. . . . Then in 1972, appellant gave notice to quit and asked the landlord to allow the appellant's brother to remain as tenant of the flat. . . . [T]he landlord informed the appellant that his brother could not remain. On the next day, the appellant damaged the roofing, wall panels, and floorboards he had installed in order . . . to gain access and remove the wiring. . . . When interviewed by the police, appellant said,
>
> "Look, how can I be done for smashing my own property, I put the flooring and that in, so if I want to pull it down it's a matter for me."
>
> The appellant's defence was that he honestly believed that the damage he did was to his own property, that he believed that he was entitled to damage his own property, and therefore he had a lawful excuse for his actions causing the damage.
>
> The court found Smith not guilty:
>
>> [I]n our judgment no offense is committed under this section if a person destroys or causes damage to property belonging to another if he does so in the honest though mistaken belief that the property is his own, and provided that the belief is honestly held it is irrelevant to consider whether or not such it is a justifiable belief.

The court viewed it as being a matter of property law that any fixtures (items of personal property attached to real estate) that a tenant installs in a rented apartment become part of the landlord's real estate and cease to be the property of the tenant. What was Smith's *mens rea* on the issue of the ownership of the damaged property? What was the *mens rea* for the crime? Should his error as to the law of fixtures negate his *mens rea* for the crime? What does the court say?

3. Refer again to the Model Penal Code bigamy statute.

Section 230.1. Bigamy and Polygamy.

(1) *Bigamy.* A married person is guilty of bigamy, a misdemeanor, if he contracts or purports to contract another marriage, unless at the time of the subsequent marriage:

(a) the actor believes that the prior spouse is dead; or
(b) the actor and the prior spouse have been living apart for five consecutive years throughout which the prior spouse was not known by the actor to be alive. . . .

Consider the following hypotheticals.

a. Joan Jones last saw her husband in 1981 when he went to South America to serve as a mercenary. In 1983 she read in the newspaper that several mercenaries fighting for the same movement her husband had joined had been killed. Having heard nothing from Fred, she assumed he was dead, and married another man. Fred later reappeared.

b. Larry Long, a New Hampshire resident, went to Mexico to obtain a divorce from his wife. Under Mexican law, a person can obtain a divorce in an "ex parte" proceeding—that is, without the other spouse present—so long as the absent spouse receives some notice of the divorce hearing. When Larry returned to New Hampshire, he remarried. He later learned to his dismay that New Hampshire did not recognize ex parte divorces made in other jurisdictions.

Are Joan and Larry guilty of bigamy? Is either?

RICHARDSON v. UNITED STATES

United States Court of Appeals, District of Columbia Circuit
403 F.2d 574 (1968)

EDGERTON, Senior Circuit Judge.

Appellant was charged with robbery (count one), assault with a dangerous weapon (count two), and carrying a dangerous weapon (count three). A jury found him guilty as charged on count one, guilty of simple assault on count two and not guilty on count three.

The complaining witness Snowden testified that appellant and another held him up at gunpoint and took $98 from his wallet. Appellant testified that Snowden, who had recently been convicted of a gambling offense, owed him a

$270 gambling debt which he had several times unsuccessfully tried to collect. He admitted reaching into Snowden's wallet and removing $138 without his consent, but denied having a gun. His mother corroborated his story of the gambling debt and testified that Snowden was a known gambler.

The chief ground of this appeal is the trial court's denial of appellant's request for the following standard instruction:

> Evidence has been introduced that the defendant believed that he had a right to take the property he is alleged to have stolen.
>
> If a person takes the property of another, but does so in the good faith belief that he has a right to take the property, the specific intent essential to the crime of robbery is lacking.
>
> The Government must prove beyond a reasonable doubt that the defendant acted with the specific intent to steal. If you have a reasonable doubt whether or not the defendant acted with a specific intent to steal, you must find him not guilty.

I

A defendant is not guilty of robbery unless he has a specific intent to take the property of another. Viewing the evidence most favorably to the defendant, as we must where he appeals from the denial of a favorable instruction, he believed in good faith that he was entitled to the money. If so, he did not have that specific intent. We therefore find that the requested instruction should have been given.

The government's position seems to be that no instruction on a claim of right is necessary unless the defendant had a legally enforceable right to the property he took. But specific intent depends upon a state of mind, not upon a legal fact. If the jury finds that the defendant believed himself entitled to the money, it cannot properly find that he had the requisite specific intent for robbery. Cf. Morissette v. United States, 342 U.S. 246, 72 S. Ct. 240, 96 L. Ed. 288 (1952) (an unfounded but genuine belief that the property taken had been abandoned negatives specific intent).

The government urges affirmance for policy reasons, claiming that a reversal of this robbery conviction would encourage violent takings and would frustrate the policy of the law that a successful gambler may not recover his winnings from the loser. But "the taking and carrying away of the property of another in the District of Columbia without right to do so" is a misdemeanor. D.C. Code (1967 ed.) §22-1211. Since this section can be violated without specific intent, it provides a deterrent to self-help by a winning gambler without rejecting the principle that specific intent turns on the actor's state of mind and not upon an objective fact.

Reversed.

TAMM, Circuit Judge [dissented].

Notes and Questions

1. The District of Columbia Code's definition of "robbery" (a definition that is very typical in substance, if not in style) reads as follows, in §22-2901:

> Whoever by force or violence, whether against resistance or by sudden or stealthy seizure, or by putting in fear, shall take from the person of immediate actual possession of another anything of value, is guilty of robbery. . . .

In the crime of robbery, what *mens rea* attaches to the element of the money's belonging to another and not oneself? In what sense was Richardson mistaken about being entitled to take the money? Even if a jurisdiction treats gambling debts as enforceable like other contracts (so that Richardson would have a legal claim against Snowden for the amount of the debt), under the common law of personal property and contractual remedies, Richardson normally would not have had the right to exercise "self-help" to seize specific property of Snowden's in order to satisfy the debt. Should Richardson have known of this rule of law? If he did not have the *mens rea* for the crime because he made an error of law, should he nonetheless be treated as if he had the necessary *mens rea?*

The court decides that in the parallel misdemeanor section of the District of Columbia Code, a different *mens rea* attaches to the fact that the property belongs to another. Why?

2. Examine the following "urban legend":[10]

> Her true story was about a jogger in Central Park in New York City. He had been running along early one morning at his customary pace and surrounded by streams of others out getting their prework exercise, when suddenly another jogger passed by him on the path and bumped him rather hard. Checking quickly, the jogger discovered that his billfold was missing from his pocket, and he thought, "This can't happen to me; I'm not going to let it happen." He upped his speed a bit, caught up to the other jogger, and confronted him. "Give me that billfold," he snarled, trying to sound as menacing as possible, and hoping for the best. The other jogger quickly handed it over, and our hero turned back toward his apartment for a shower and a quick change of clothes. But when he got home, there was his own billfold on the dresser, and the one he had in his pocket belonged to someone else.

Can one argue that the subject was negligent? Should he be guilty of robbery? Of any crime?

3. If one cannot be a robber through negligence, can one be a rapist with no higher degree of *mens rea?* Examine the facts of Regina v. Morgan, House of Lords, [1976] A.C. 182:

10. Jan Harold Brunvand, The Choking Doberman and Other "New" Urban Legends 188-189 (1984).

> The appellant Morgan and his three co-appellants, who were all members of the RAF, spent the evening of August 15, 1973 in one another's company. The appellant Morgan was significantly older than the other three, and considerably senior to them in rank. He was . . . married to the alleged victim, but not, it seems, at the time habitually sleeping in the same bed. . . . [B]y the time the appellants arrived at Morgan's house, Mrs. Morgan was already in bed and asleep, until she was awoken by their presence.
>
> According to the version of the facts which she gave in evidence, and which was evidently accepted by the jury, she was aroused from her sleep . . . held by each of her limbs . . . while each of the three young appellants in turn had intercourse with her in the presence of the others. . . .
>
> According to Mrs. Morgan she consented to none of this and made her opposition to what was being done very plain indeed. . . .
>
> All four defendants explained in the witness box that they had spent the evening together in Wolverhampton, and by the time of the alleged offences had had a good deal to drink. Their original intention had been to find some women in the town but, when this failed, Morgan made the surprising suggestion to the others that they should all return to his home and have sexual intercourse with his wife. According to the three younger appellants (but not according to Morgan who described this part of their story as "lying") Morgan told them that they must not be surprised if his wife struggled a bit, since she was "kinky" and this was the only way in which she could get "turned on." However this may be, it is clear that Morgan did invite his three companions home in order that they might have sexual intercourse with his wife and, no doubt, he may well have led them in one way or another to believe that she would consent to their doing so.

All the defendants were convicted. The Court of Appeals affirmed all the convictions but certified the following question to the House of Lords:

> Whether in rape the defendant can properly be convicted notwithstanding that he in fact believed that the woman consented, if such belief was not based on reasonable grounds.

According to Lord Hailsham, for the majority of the Law-Lords:

> Once one has accepted, what seems to me abundantly clear, that the prohibited act in rape is non-consensual sexual intercourse, and that the guilty state of mind is an intention to commit it, it seems to me to follow as a matter of inexorable logic that there is no room either for a "defence" of honest belief or mistake, or of a defence of honest and reasonable belief and mistake. Either the prosecution proves that the accused had the requisite intent, or it does not. In the former case it succeeds, and in the latter it fails. Since honest belief clearly negatives intent, the reasonableness or otherwise of that belief can only be evidence for or against the view that the belief and therefore the intent was actually held. . . .
>
> For the above reasons I would answer the question certified in the negative. . . .

The House of Lords, however, affirmed the conviction on the ground that no miscarriage of justice had occurred since, under the facts of the case, no reasonable jury could have believed that the defendants really thought that the victim had consented.

Can one make an argument that a negligent robber should not be held guilty of robbery while a negligent rapist should be held criminally liable? Are negligent robbers a social problem? Are those who unreasonably believe women consent to their sexual advances? Perhaps a reasonable solution of the *Morgan* problem would be to make "negligent rape" an offense, but a less serious one than rape itself. What about the man who wrongly but reasonably concludes that a woman has consented?

C. CAPACITY FOR *MENS REA*

PEOPLE v. WETMORE
Supreme Court of California
149 Cal. Rptr. 265, 583 P.2d 1308 (1978)

TOBRINER, Justice.

Charged with burglary, defendant argued that psychiatric reports showed that as a result of mental illness he lacked the specific intent required for conviction of that crime.

The only evidence submitted to the trial court in this case was the testimony of Joseph Cacciatore, the victim of the burglary, at the preliminary hearing, and three psychiatric reports. Cacciatore testified that he left his apartment on March 7, 1975. When he returned three days later, he discovered defendant in his apartment. Defendant was wearing Cacciatore's clothes and cooking his food. The lock on the front door had been broken; the apartment lay in a shambles. Cacciatore called the police, who arrested defendant for burglary. Later Cacciatore discovered that a ring, a watch, a credit card, and items of clothing were missing.[11]

The psychiatric reports submitted to the court explain defendant's long history of psychotic illness, including at least 10 occasions of hospital confinement for treatment. According to the reports, defendant, shortly after his last release from Brentwood Veteran's Hospital, found himself with no place to go. He began to believe that he "owned" property, and was "directed" to Cacciatore's apartment. When he found the door unlocked he was sure he owned the apartment. He entered, rearranged the apartment, destroyed some advertising he felt was inappropriate, and put on Cacciatore's clothes. When the police

11. At the preliminary hearing defendant appeared wearing one of Cacciatore's shirts. The magistrate directed the sheriff to provide defendant with a county shirt, and admitted Cacciatore's shirt into evidence as an exhibit.

arrived, defendant was shocked and embarrassed, and only then understood that he did not own the apartment.

Defendant pled not guilty to a charge of burglary and requested court appointment of a psychiatrist to advise him whether to enter a plea based on insanity. After receiving the report from Dr. John Woodward, defendant entered a plea of not guilty by reason of insanity. The court then appointed Drs. Michael Colburn and Marshall Cherkas to examine defendant.

When the matter was called for trial defendant personally and all counsel waived trial by jury and stipulated that the cause be submitted on the transcript of the preliminary hearing, which contained only the testimony of Cacciatore, and the reports of Drs. Colburn and Cherkas. Defense counsel pointed out that burglary requires an entry with specific intent to commit larceny or felony. The reports of Drs. Colburn and Cherkas, counsel argued, indicate that defendant entered the apartment under the delusion that he owned the apartment and its contents; he thus had no intent to commit theft or any felony.

In response to counsel's argument, the court acknowledged that defendant might lack the specific intent required to commit the crime of burglary. It stated, however, that under the controlling cases, "if a defendant's mental capacity which would preclude the forming of a specific intent is that of insanity," that mental condition is "not admissible to establish the question of lack of specific intent due to diminished capacity." The court thereupon found defendant guilty of second degree burglary.

[The] distinction between evidence that defendant did not entertain the requisite intent, which is admissible, and evidence that he could not entertain that intent, which is inadmissible, cannot be supported. "[A]s a matter of logic, any proof tending to show that a certain mental condition could not exist is relevant and should be admissible to show that it did not exist. And, of course, proof that something could not exist is the best possible evidence that it did not exist." Moreover . . . evidence which tends to prove that a defendant could not entertain a certain intent may, when subject to cross-examination, convince the trier of fact that defendant was able to entertain the intent but did not do so on the occasion of the crime. Thus, . . . the trial court cannot refuse to admit such evidence when offered to prove diminished capacity. [The] distinction between evidence which tends to prove insanity and evidence probative of diminished capacity cannot stand. . . . Although the cases occasionally reiterate the dictum that evidence of insanity cannot be admitted to prove diminished capacity, the appellate courts nevertheless consistently rely upon such evidence to resolve issues of diminished capacity, to hold that the trial courts err in refusing to consider such evidence at the guilt phase, and to rule that counsel who fail to offer such evidence at the guilt phase are incompetent. . . .

We therefore hold that evidence of diminished capacity is admissible at the guilt phase whether or not that evidence may also be probative of insanity. . . .

Amicus Los Angeles City Attorney urges that we sustain the trial court's ruling on a different ground. He contends that a defendant should be permitted to assert the defense of diminished capacity caused by mental disease or defect only to reduce a specific crime to a lesser included offense. Claiming that there is no lesser included offense in burglary, amicus argues that the trial court correctly refused to consider evidence of defendant Wetmore's diminished mental capacity.

No decisions support amicus' contention that diminished capacity does not apply to crimes lacking lesser included offenses. Clearly, if a crime requires specific intent, a defendant who because of mental disease or defect lacks that intent, cannot commit that crime. The presence or absence of a lesser included offense within the charged crime cannot affect the result. The prosecution must prove all elements of the crime beyond a reasonable doubt; we do not perceive how a defendant who has in his possession evidence which rebuts an element of the crime can logically be denied the right to present that evidence merely because it will result in his acquittal.

Amicus' argument, although legally flawed, addresses a matter of real concern. A defendant whose criminal activity arises from mental disease or defect usually requires confinement and special treatment. . . .

The solution to this problem thus does not lie in barring the defense of diminished capacity when the charged crime lacks a lesser included offense, but in providing for the confinement and treatment of defendants with diminished capacity arising from mental disease or defect.

The Lanterman-Petris-Short Act provides for the civil commitment of any person who, "as a result of mental disorder, is a danger to others, or to himself, or gravely disabled."

Recognizing that evidence of such mental disorder may arise at trial, the Legislature provided that a judge of the county where a prisoner is confined may institute evaluation and treatment procedures under the Lanterman-Petris-Short Act. Thus if evidence adduced in support of a successful diminished capacity defense indicates to the trial judge that the defendant is dangerous, the court is not compelled to foist the defendant upon the public; it may, instead, initiate procedures for civil commitment.

The Attorney General points out that a person who commits a crime against property, such as defendant Wetmore, might not be commitable under the Lanterman-Petris-Short Act unless he were "gravely disabled." A more serious omission lies in the act's failure to provide for long term commitment of persons dangerous to others; unless found "gravely disabled," a "person who, as a result of mental disorder, presents an imminent threat of substantial physical harm to others" cannot be confined beyond the initial 90-day post-certification treatment period unless "he has threatened, attempted, or actually inflicted physical harm to another during his period of postcertification treatment." If the Lanterman-Petris-Short Act does not adequately protect the public against crimes committed by persons with diminished mental capacity, the answer lies either in amendment to that act or in the enactment of legislation that would provide for commitment of persons acquitted by virtue of a successful diminished capacity defense in the same manner as persons acquitted by reason of insanity are presently committed. It does not lie in judicial creation of an illogical—and possibly unconstitutional—rule denying the defense of diminished capacity to persons charged with crimes lacking a lesser included offense.

Bird, C.J., and Mosk, Clark, Richardson, Manuel and Newman, JJ., concur.

Notes and Questions

1. That the house in question must belong to someone else obviously must be an element of the crime of burglary. What is the *mens rea* attached to this element?

2. Is not "diminished capacity" simply an inability, caused by a mental disease or defect, to possess a required *mens rea*? If a defendant did not have the *mens rea* for a crime because of a psychiatric disability, should he nonetheless be treated as if he did have the *mens rea* required? Do *mens rea* principles adequately address the issue in this case? What argument does the prosecution make against admission of Wetmore's "diminished capacity" evidence?

3. Section 4.02(1) of the Model Penal Code states:

> Evidence that the defendant suffered from a mental disease or defect is admissible whenever it is relevant to prove that the defendant did or did not have a state of mind which is an element of the offense.

How rigorous a standard of "mental disease or defect" must a court apply in admitting psychological evidence offered to negate an element of the offense? In United States v. Bright, 517 F.2d 584 (C.A. 2 1975), the defendant was charged with unlawful possession of stolen checks "knowing the same to have been stolen." 18 U.S.C. §1708. Bright admitted that she had possessed welfare checks stolen from the mail. She said that she had cashed them for a man named Scott, who was an acquaintance of her "boyfriend," after Scott told her he had received the checks in payment of debts owed him but that he had no bank account of his own. She claimed that out of naivete she believed everything Scott told her was true. The defense sought to introduce the testimony of a psychiatrist that though Bright suffered no clinically defined mental illness, she had a "dependent, childlike character" and that she "unconsciously 'needed' to believe" that she could trust the word of men. In effect, her "passive dependent personality" required her to deny the possibility that her male friends would deceive her, and thus she did not truly believe or "know" that the checks were stolen. The appellate court upheld the trial judge's refusal to admit this evidence.

Did the court unfairly exclude logically relevant evidence? What would be the implications of a rule that allowed the admission of the psychiatric testimony excluded in *Bright*?

PEOPLE v. GUILLETT

Supreme Court of Michigan
69 N.W.2d 140 (1955)

BUTZEL, Justice. Lawrence Guillett was informed against for assault with intent to commit rape. He pleaded not guilty and was tried in circuit court where a jury found him guilty of the crime charged. Appellant *in propria persona* has appealed from his conviction on various grounds. The complainant had agreed to spend an evening with him. He, with two other friends, called for her and they visited a tavern where each of them consumed three glasses of beer. She and appellant then went to the home of the latter's parents, and later purchased a bottle of wine out of which she took one glass which she only partially consumed while he apparently finished the bottle. They sat together on a davenport and he made indecent advances which she repulsed. After she arose he then struck her, [and] knocked her down. . . . During a struggle she grabbed a telephone receiver and struck him so many blows on the head that he required hospitalization. She then escaped, ran across the road and the police and an ambulance were summoned. Appellant's mother testified that he had been drinking for several days and that he had come home drunk earlier that day, but she left him to go to work shortly after 3 P.M. His father said that he appeared "dozy."

In view of the testimony the trial judge in his charge to the jury stated:

> Now, there has been injected here to a great extent, the question of intoxication. I will give you an instruction on that.
>
> It is a well settled law in this state that voluntary drunkenness is not a defense to crime. A man who puts himself in a position to have no control over his actions must be held to intend the consequences. The safety of the community requires this rule. Intoxication is so easily counterfeited, and, when real, is so often resorted to as a means of nerving a person up to the commission of some deliberate act, and withal is so inexcusable in itself, that the law has never recognized it as an excuse for crime.
>
> In the case of an offense such as the one charged, committed during a period of intoxication, the law presumes the defendant to have intended the obscuration and perversion of his faculties which followed his voluntary intoxication. He must be held to have purposely blinded his moral perception and set his will free from the control of reason—to have suppressed the guards and invited the mutiny; and should therefore be held responsible as well for the vicious excesses of the will thus set free as for the acts done by its prompting.

Defendant has assigned error on the ground that the charge as given was incomplete and therefore misleading because it failed to state that intoxication may serve to negate the existence of the intent required for conviction of the crime charged. . . .

We must conclude that the charge was erroneous. In Roberts v. People, 19 Mich. 401, 418, 420, the defendant was convicted of assault with intent to commit murder. On appeal, after considering the necessity for finding intent in fact, or specific intent, Justice Christiancy discussed the issue of whether drunkenness might negative the existence of that intent. He concluded:

> In determining the question whether the assault was committed with the intent charged, it was therefore material to inquire whether the defendant's mental faculties were so far overcome by the effect of intoxication, as to render him incapable of entertaining the intent. And for this purpose, it was the right and the duty of the jury—as upon the question of intent of which this forms a part—to take into consideration the nature and the circumstances of the assault, the actions, conduct and demeanor of the defendant, and his declaration, before, at the time, and after the assault; and especially to consider the nature of the intent, and what degree of mental capacity was necessary to enable him to entertain the simple intent to kill, under the circumstances of this case—or, which is the same thing, how far the mental faculties must be obscured by intoxication to render him incapable of entertaining that particular intent. . . .
>
> But the Circuit Court held, in effect that no extent of intoxication could have the effect to disprove the intent; treating the intent as an inference of law for the Court, rather than a question of fact for the jury. In this we think there was error.

A consideration of later Michigan authority reveals that Roberts v. People, supra, remains as the most eloquent and correct statement of law on the subject. Thus, in People v. Walker, 38 Mich. 156, Judge Cooley wrote an opinion reversing a conviction of larceny stating:

> While it is true that drunkenness cannot excuse crime, it is equally true that when a certain intent is a necessary element in a crime, the crime cannot have been committed when the intent did not exist. In larceny the crime does not consist in the wrongful taking of the property, for that might be a mere trespass; but it consists in the wrongful taking with felonious intent, [without which] the crime cannot have been committed. This was fully explained by Mr. Justice Christiancy in Roberts v. People, 19 Mich. 401, and is familiar law.

It is to be noted that we are here concerned with intoxication insofar as it might negative the requisite intent, as distinguished from insanity or delirium tremens brought on by intoxication, the latter, if present, being a complete excuse rather than a partial one, as here. . . .

Because of the error in the charge . . . the verdict and judgment are set aside and the case remanded for a new trial.

Notes and Questions

1. Guillett was charged with assault with intent to commit rape. Assume that the Michigan statute defined this crime as "using or threatening the use of force to have sexual intercourse with a woman against her will." What is the required *mens rea* for this crime? Could a reasonable jury, hearing evidence of

Guillett's intoxication, conclude that he lacked the requisite *mens rea*? How can the prosecutor rebut this evidence? If the defendant can show that he lacked the required *mens rea,* is there any legal ground for nevertheless convicting him, where it is undisputed that he had voluntarily worked himself up to a drunken state? What other facts about the defendant would you want to know to answer this question?

2. The difficulties of proof mentioned in *Guillett,* moral concerns about allowing drunkenness to mitigate responsibility, and the perceived need to protect the public have led many jurisdictions to bar a claim of voluntary intoxication to disprove *mens rea.* Some states wholly bar proof of intoxication to negate the required *mens rea,* e.g., McDaniel v. State, 356 So. 2d 1151 (Miss. 1978) (intoxication may be offered only to show defendant was an automaton); State v. Vaughn, 268 S.C. 119, 232 S.E.2d 328 (1977) (intoxication can only serve to prove permanent insanity). Can these rules be squared with the fundamental principle of blameworthiness?

3. Model Penal Code:

Section 2.08. Intoxication.

(1) [Voluntary] intoxication of the actor is not a defense unless it negatives an element of the offense.

(2) When recklessness establishes an element of the offense, if the actor, due to self-induced intoxication, is unaware of a risk of which he would have been aware had he been sober, such unawareness is immaterial.

How do you explain subsection (2)? Does it say that anyone who voluntarily becomes intoxicated is reckless as to the consequences, or is it an exception to subsection (1)?

D. MISTAKE OF GOVERNING LAW

STATE v. HATCH

Supreme Court of New Jersey
64 N.J. 179, 313 A.2d 797 (1973)

JACOBS, J. The defendant Leonard E. Hatch, a resident of Erving, Massachusetts, was driving in New Jersey on his way to Philadelphia, Pennsylvania. He was stopped for a traffic violation on Route 22 in the Bound Brook area. The police officer saw a rifle and shotgun under some clothing in the rear seat of the defendant's car. The defendant told the officer that he was traveling from Massachusetts to Pennsylvania in the hope of finding employment in the heavy construction field and that he had taken the guns with him for hunting and related sporting use. He had a Massachusetts hunting license, was a member of a Massachusetts gun club, and had been issued a firearm identification card in accordance with Massachusetts law. He had no New Jersey "firearms purchaser identification card" (N.J.S.A. 2A:151-41(b)) and his firearms were not "in a closed and fastened case, gunbox, securely tied package, or locked in the trunk of the automobile" (N.J.S.A. 2A:151-42(c)). He testified that his mode of carrying the firearms complied with Massachusetts law and that he was unaware of any further legal requirement on his part in passing through New Jersey.

The defendant was indicted for unlawful possession of the rifle and shotgun in violation of N.J.S.A. 2A:151-41 and, after trial, the jury returned a verdict of guilty. However, during the trial the judge had reserved decision on a motion for acquittal and thereafter he entered an order setting aside the jury's verdict and acquitting the defendant in accordance with the provisions of R.3:18-2. In his reported opinion the trial judge seemed to take the broad position that in the absence of notice or knowledge of further requirement by New Jersey, a nonresident passing through New Jersey may possess a handgun or other firearm so long as his possession is not violative of the law of his own home state. . . .

While there is much to be said in favor of the wide recognition of lack of scienter as a defense, there are fields in which the dangers are so high and the regulations so prevalent that, on balance, the legislative branch may as a  matter of sound public policy and without impairing any constitutional guarantees, declare the act itself unlawful without any further requirement of *mens rea* or its equivalent. See United States v. Freed, 401 U.S. 601. Gun control is clearly such a field and consequently New Jersey's regulations may, to the extent that the Legislature so intended, properly be applied to nonresidents as well as residents, without regard to notice or knowledge on their part. . . .

We assume that the defendant Hatch had fulfilled the licensing and other requirements of his home state when he placed the guns in his car and set out for Pennsylvania to obtain employment and do some hunting. When he came into New Jersey, however, he subjected himself to New Jersey's gun control regulations. While we doubt that the Legislature ever contemplated that one in his situation as aforedescribed would be called upon to hold a New Jersey purchaser identification card for the rifle and shotgun, he was at least obliged to fulfill its pertinent requirement with respect to their proper encasing as set forth in N.J.S.A. 2A:151-42(c). That requirement was entirely reasonable and did not unduly or unfairly burden interstate travel. The Law Division, in acquitting the defendant, stressed that he could not "be expected to know, or to ascertain" the New Jersey requirement. The New Jersey administrative authorities might well have taken suitable precautions to publicize the requirement so that licensed hunters who planned to travel through with firearms in their cars would presumably have had actual notice or knowledge; but as we have already indicated, there is no constitutional infirmity in applying New Jersey's statutory requirement even in the absence of notice or knowledge.

Both the Law Division and the Appellate Division were evidently satisfied that the guns were intended for hunting and related sporting use as the defendant had testified and that he had acted in good faith and without notice or knowledge of New Jersey's requirement. Though they were in error in concluding that his lack of notice or knowledge was a legal defense, there had been no controlling judicial pronouncement and the Law Division's acquittal of the defendant was understandable. As was indicated in the opening paragraph of this opinion, we did not certify with the view of interfering with the acquittal which we shall now let stand. Prospectively, however, the principles set forth herein shall, in the absence of legislative clarification or modification, fully control the possession and transportation of firearms not only by residents but also by nonresidents within or passing through New Jersey.

Affirmed.

Notes and Questions

1. Hatch clearly knew that he was in possession of an unencased shotgun. Did he therefore have the required *mens rea* for the crime? Was he blameworthy because he had failed to learn the relevant law of New Jersey, the jurisdiction in which he committed the act? If not, and if we hold him guilty, have we not departed from our requirement of blameworthiness?

2. The Court cites United States v. Freed (p.125, supra) in support of its holding. What is the difference between *Freed* and *Hatch*?

3. If Hatch merits punishment under the New Jersey statute, why does the appellate court let stand the lower court ruling in his favor?

4. Consider Rex v. Esop, 6 Will. IV, 456 (1836):

> The prisoner was indicted for an unnatural offence, committed on board of an East India ship, lying in St. Katherine's Docks. It appeared that he was a native of Bagdad.
>
> CHAMBERS, for the prisoner.—In the country from which the prisoner comes, it is not considered an offence; and a person who comes into this country and does an act, believing that it is a perfectly innocent one, cannot be convicted according to the law of England. A party must know that what he does is a crime. This is the principle upon which infants, idiots, and lunatics are held not be answerable. If a person is unconscious that he is doing a wrong act, or believes that it is a right or innocent act, he is exonerated. Where one man kills another under the persuasion that he is doing a good action, he is not liable for punishment, for he knows not the distinction between right and wrong, and upon that point is insane.
>
> BOSANQUET, J.—I am clearly of opinion that this is no legal defence.
>
> VAUGHAN, J.—Where is the evidence that it is not a crime in the prisoner's own country? But if it is not a crime there, that does not amount to a defence here. Numbers have been most improperly executed if it is a defence.

Should it be a defense that Esop did not know his act was illegal? What does the court say?

5. Consider Model Penal Code §2.02(9):

> *Culpability as to Illegality of Conduct.* Neither knowledge nor recklessness or negligence as to whether conduct constitutes an offense or as to the existence, meaning or application of the law determining the elements of an offense is an element of such offense, unless the definition of the offense or the Code so provides.

Is this section necessary?

6. What is the difference between *Bray,* page 151, supra, and *Smith,* page 154, supra, on the one hand, and *Hatch* and *Esop* on the other?

7. Consider the following newspaper story from the San Jose Mercury, Sept. 29, 1983 at 6B:

Obscure Law Against For-Sale Signs
Nearly Hits S.J. Woman for $50

Marilyn Neves took her twin 2-year-old girls to the park Sunday morning, an outing that almost cost her $50.

Her crime was parking a car with a for-sale sign in the window on a San Jose street. The usual fine for first offenders is $50, officials said.

"I don't even jaywalk," she said, fuming, "And I'd never park my car in a red zone or under a no-parking sign. The fine for those things is $10 or $20. Now this, for a section of the San Jose Municipal Code that is unknown, is going to cost me $50."

Neves lives on Manitoba Drive, a few blocks away from San Tomas Park. She found a parking space at Fenian and Valerie drives Sunday morning. The misdemeanor citation was under the windshield wiper when she and the girls returned about an hour later.

So, first thing Monday morning Neves called San Jose's code compliance office and talked to code compliance officer Basil Brunner.

"He told me it was a law, all right," she said. "He didn't even have to look it up because he just got a ticket for the same thing a few weeks ago."

Neves also talked to police officer Margaret Edillo, who issued the ticket.

"I asked her if, while she was writing the ticket, she had looked over in the park and seen the lady with the babies. I was pushing the kids in the swings," Neves said.

"It's not like I just parked it there and left it."

Fran McVey, a city planner in the code compliance division, said the city council enacted the law more than 20 years ago after a series of complaints about used-car dealers who parked their wares on city streets.

"You're not supposed to sell anything on the public right of way," McVey said. "We (code compliance) take care of the private property. Every day we chase vendors off of vacant lots and the parking lots of other businesses.

"The police department takes care of the streets and I hear they've been pretty tight about the law lately."

Police say they issue about 20 citations a month for violations of the ordinance.

Sgt. Bill Mitchell in the police traffic enforcement unit, though, said he believes the law would be more fair if warnings preceded citations.

"That's really a sore point with me. If you were parking in a red zone or something, those things you know are illegal. These other things you don't know about and I don't think it's fair at all. I'm 100 percent in sympathy with her," he said of Neves.

Other officers said they usually don't issue a citation under the ordinance unless there has been a complaint.

Neves asked the citing officer, Edillo, if there has been a complaint about her car.

"She said no. She just saw it there and wrote the ticket. She said, 'Well, see you in court,' " Neves said.

Court was exactly where Neves intended to take her case until a telephone call Tuesday from Lt. Ken Hawkes.

Hawkes told her that her complaint prompted a check with the city attorney's office, which ruled that the ticket was unprosecutable and would be dropped, Neves said.

"It's a matter of following the intent of the law, not the letter of the law, as he explained it," Neves said.

"I'm very pleased. He was extremely courteous. This has really done something to restore my faith in police."

Hawkes could not be reached for comment.

8. One commentator[12] has written:

Imagine a small town in the United States which, to prevent people from defrauding motel owners by leaving early, has passed an ordinance requiring that, before departing, one must ring the door bell of the motel keeper and personally turn in the key to him. Such a law is very unusual and most people have never heard of it. Let us say that the defendant, having paid in advance because he knew that he was leaving quite early, did not wish to awake the motel owner and simply left, leaving his key in his room. On his arrest as he departed, he would, under the law of virtually all American jurisdictions, have no defence—even though no notice of the law was posted in the motel or otherwise brought home to him. It would seem that a conviction in such circumstances would be a shocking violation of our moral sense. Even where such a notice was put up in the motel room so that he could read it, our moral sense might still be violated by a conviction, unless, for some reason, we could expect a person to read all the notices on his wall. . . .

Liability for the defendant in the United States might be somewhat less offensive to our moral sense than it would be in [Germany or England] simply because the American prosecutor would have a complete discretion not to prosecute; though cases of course would arise where he did not use his discretion, it is safe to say that most cases of this type, in fact, would not be prosecuted in the

12. Kaplan, unpublished paper for presentation to the German-Anglo-American Workshop on Basic Problems in Criminal Theory, Freiburg, July 19, 1984.

United States. In Germany, where, we are told, the prosecutor has no such discretion, it might well be that a law exempting the defendant from criminality in such circumstances might be more necessary. Britain might lie between the two extremes; where the institution of private prosecution exists, the reliance on the public prosecutor's discretion might simply not be enough, since someone else—perhaps the motel owners association—might bring its own prosecution.

9. Now consider this newspaper story from the San Francisco Chronicle, June 19, 1980, at 1, Col. 1:

> Marvin Keola was 14 years old and in love for the first time. Sometimes at night he would sneak out of his house to the home of his girlfriend, Nurah Yahya, a pretty 15-year-old of Arab descent. Nurah would open the ground floor bedroom window as Marvin climbed in. They would spend precious hours alone together, exploring the sweetness of teenage infatuation, then Marvin would slip out the window and return home undetected.
>
> "They were like Romeo and Juliet," Marvin's sister said, "They thought they'd never get caught." Marvin did not come home one morning from a rendezvous with Nurah. Police found his bullet-ridden body under Nurah's bed. Investigators said he was shot to death after his girlfriend's parents found him hiding in her bedroom at 2:30 A.M. Police said that the parents entered the bedroom and began searching the room. Nurah ran, later stating that if she didn't run, her father was going to kill her too.
>
> The Yahyas were a very religious Moslem family. Investigators believe that the boy was killed because he and the girl defied Islamic codes prohibiting mixing of the sexes without marriage, prompting a violent reaction in her father. The Yahya's attorney, a prominent civil rights lawyer, said, "It would be lynching if the community decides to convict the father because his religion is different from ours."

What mistake did the Yahyas make? Let us assume that in Yemen it is simply understood that parents who discover an unwanted male alone with their young daughter have the legal right to execute him and that the Yahyas simply thought the same was the case in California. Let us further assume that in Yemen they would in fact have had the moral duty to execute him and perhaps even a legal duty. Would this make them less blameworthy in this country? Less guilty? Does the concept of "moral negligence" make sense here?

HOPKINS v. STATE

Court of Appeals of Maryland
69 A.2d 456 (1950)

DELAPLAINE, Judge.

This appeal was taken by the Rev. William F. Hopkins, of Elkton, from the judgment of conviction entered upon the verdict of a jury in the Circuit

Court for Cecil County for violation of the statute making it unlawful to erect or maintain any sign intended to aid in the solicitation or performance of marriages.

The State charged that on September 1, 1947, defendant maintained a sign at the entrance to his home at 148 East Main Street in Elkton, and also a sign along a highway leading into the town, to aid in the solicitation and performance of marriages. Four photographs were admitted in evidence. One photograph, taken on an afternoon in September, 1947, shows the sign in Elkton containing the name "Rev. W.F. Hopkins." Another, taken at night, shows the same sign illuminated at night by electricity. The third shows the other sign along the highway containing the words, "W.F. Hopkins, Notary Public, Information." The fourth shows this sign illuminated at night.

The State showed that during the month of August, 1947, thirty ministers performed 1,267 marriages in Cecil Country, and of this number defendant performed 286, only three of which were ceremonies in which the parties were residents of Cecil County.

The Act of 1943, now under consideration, was passed by the Legislature of Maryland to curb the thriving business which unethical ministers had built up as a result of the tremendous increase in the numbers of couples coming into the State to be married following the passage of stringent marriage laws in nearby States. . . .

Defendant contended that the judge erred in excluding testimony offered to show that the State's Attorney advised him in 1944 before he erected the signs, that they would not violate the law. It is generally held that the advice of counsel, even though followed in good faith, furnishes no excuse to a person for violating the law and cannot be relied upon as a defense in a criminal action. Moreover, advice given by a public official, even a State's Attorney, that a contemplated act is not criminal will not excuse an offender if, as a matter of law, the act performed did amount to a violation of the law. These rules are founded upon the maxim that ignorance of the law will not excuse its violation. If an accused could be exempted from punishment for crime by reason of the advice of counsel, such advice would become paramount to the law.

While ignorance of fact may sometimes be admitted as evidence of lack of criminal intent, ignorance of the law ordinarily does not give immunity from punishment for crime, for every man is presumed to intend the necessary and legitimate consequences of what he knowingly does. In the case at bar defendant did not claim that the State's Attorney misled him regarding any facts of the case, but only that the State's Attorney advised him as to the law based upon the facts. Defendant was aware of the penal statute enacted by the Legislature. He knew what he wanted to do, and he did the thing he intended to do. He claims merely that he was given advice regarding his legal rights. If there was any mistake, it was a mistake of law and not of fact. If the right of a person to erect a sign of a certain type and size depends upon the construction and application of a penal statute, and the right is somewhat doubtful, he erects the sign at his peril. In other words, a person who commits an act which the law declares to be criminal cannot be excused from punishment upon the theory that he misconstrued or misapplied the law. For these reasons the exclusion of the testimony offered to show that defendant had sought and received advice from the State's Attorney was not prejudicial error. . . .

Judgment affirmed, with costs.

Notes and Questions

1. What were the elements of Hopkins's crime? What *mens rea* attached to each element? Did Hopkins have the required *mens rea*? Precisely what mistake did Hopkins make? Was Hopkins blameworthy?

2. Assuming that the principle of *Hatch* and *Esop* would prevent Hopkins's mistake from exculpating him, does he not have another argument available? Examine Model Penal Code §2.04(3):

> A belief that conduct does not legally constitute an offense is a defense to a prosecution for that offense based upon such conduct when:
>
> (a) the statute or other enactment defining the offense is not known to the actor and has not been published or otherwise reasonably made available prior to the conduct alleged; or
>
> (b) he acts in reasonable reliance upon official statement of the law, afterward determined to be invalid or erroneous, contained in (i) a statute or other enactment; (ii) a judicial decision, opinion or judgment; (iii) an administrative order or grant of permission; or (iv) an official interpretation of the public officer or body charged by law with responsibility for the interpretation, administration or enforcement of the law defining the offense.

Would this section have excused Hopkins?

3. Does M.P.C. §2.04(3)(b) protect the person who in good faith reasonably relies on advice given by a private attorney? Should it? Do you see any differences between allowing public officials to give legal advice which, if followed, will immunize conduct from the criminal law, and giving the same power to private attorneys?

4. The law professor reporters to the California Joint Legislative Committee for Revision of the Penal Code could not agree as to whether a person like Hopkins or Hatch should be exculpated if:

> . . . he otherwise diligently pursues all means available to ascertain the meaning and application of the crime to his conduct and honestly and in good faith concludes his conduct is not a crime in circumstances in which a law-abiding and prudent person would also so conclude.

Their commentary discussed the advantages and disadvantages of the provision:

[I]t generalizes the essential quality of the unfairness in holding defendants who are misled by official reliance; i.e., they did all that could be done to learn the nature of the prohibition and in concluding that it was lawful reacted no differently than would any law-abiding and prudent person. . . .

The central point is that it is plainly unjust to hold a defendant criminally liable where a jury is prepared to conclude that the conditions of this subsection are met.

It cannot be said to "encourage ignorance" of the law where the defense requires a showing of diligent and exhaustive effort to comprehend the law. And difficulties of proof are not here substantial since the defendant is required to show affirmative acts of inquiry addressed to an objective standard. It is difficult to conceive what more could be reasonably expected of a "model citizen" than that he guide his conduct by "the law" ascertained in good faith, not merely by efforts which might seem adequate to a person in his situation, but by efforts as well designed to accomplish ascertainment as available under our system. [U]nder the proposed draft the defense is not available simply on the ground that an attorney advised the defendant of the noncriminality of the proposed conduct. Still such advice would normally figure in any defense made under this subdivision. But where the defendant's conduct constitutes a diligent pursuit of all means available to comprehend the law and his conclusion that his conduct is not criminal is one which he reaches honestly and in good faith, as opposed to a pretext, and that conclusion is found by the jury to be one which a law-abiding and prudent person would reach, the fact that the evidence leading to this conclusion rested in part on private legal advice should not dissolve the defense. The risk of disingenuous legal advice, which presumably is the main concern in this area, is substantially reduced by the additional requirements stated in the draft.

On the other hand some feel that this provision is subject to abuse. It opens up a new and potentially time-consuming defense in many cases. Further, the defense can be too easily fabricated out of disingenuous advice obtained from lawyers ready to lend themselves to a scheme of evasion through venality or partisanship in their client's cause. Finally, it is believed that the potential injustice is adequately guarded against by the use of the prosecutor's discretion not to prosecute in cases in which the accused acted in good faith, and his conduct was not harmful.[13]

5. One commentator[14] has written:

One could argue that we do not wish to give any commercial advantage to the lawyer who does not inform his clients of statutes which restrict them, and hence allows his or her clients a freer hand than would be given to the clients of those more diligent lawyers—who in fact are always correct. It is admittedly conceivable that under a rule which excused non-negligent errors of the governing law, some situations might arise where a lawyer who did not properly inform

13. Project Director's Note: Recognition of the defense of mistake or ignorance of law as defined in the draft, if limited to non-violent offenses or to offenses not involving damage, injury or disturbances of public order, may afford a solution to the problem.

14. Kaplan, unpublished paper for presentation to the German-Anglo-American Workshop on Basic Problems in Criminal Theory, Freiburg, July 19, 1984.

a client of the criminal liability inherent in a course of action, could protect them from criminal liability and place the clients (and the lawyer) at a competitive advantage. . . . In the great majority of cases, however, it would seem that the lawyer who ignored a criminal statute would not be gaining any reputation for such a clever means of protecting the client from the criminal law, even if the client's failure to know the law was exculpating. Rather, such a lawyer would be more likely to be thought of as a bungler, to be avoided by all. This is especially the case where civil penalties or some other adverse consequences would follow upon the client who took the legal advice. . . .

The second argument in favour of regarding mistake of governing law as no excuse is the "thin-ice" theory. This, however, is an argument which cuts both ways. There are, to be sure, some cases where the law lays out a specific prohibition and a court might take the view that the legislature has enacted a penumbra around it. Such a view is not a popular one where the issue is *mens rea.* In that case we are unsympathetic to the argument that the legislature wished people to stay out of an area even though it did not make the matter criminal. An example of this perhaps might be the age of consent in statutory rape cases. As a factual matter, it might be that the legislature had felt that young girls of 17 should not be held meaningfully to consent to sexual intercourse but that, to make absolutely sure, it fixed the age at 16. Someone who made a mistake of fact in that kind of situation would nonetheless be exculpated (the *Prince* case to the contrary) even though there is apparently no social interest in his being able to come right up to the line. The case for a penumbra does not seem much stronger where a mistake of law as to the age of consent is concerned, though the law seems to adopt it with gusto. Moreover, in areas trenching upon free speech, for instance, if one takes the "marketplace of ideas" seriously, there is a strong societal interest in having the defendant free to come as close as possible to the specific legislative line drawn. Moreover, even where no other interest exists, autonomy may be enough of a reason for not erecting the dangerous penumbra.

Take the case which occurred in a nonspeech context, when a company wished to sell an electron microscope to the Soviet Union. It was a scientific instrument and its sale was not forbidden by any government regulation. However, the heart of this microscope was a computer of the kind whose export to the Soviet Union was prohibited. The manufacturer pointed out that in order to get the computer out of the microscope, the Soviet Union would have to destroy and make useless an instrument worth far more than it would cost to get an identical computer from other countries. The manufacturer's attorney therefore argued that the sale of the microscope, even though it contained the computer, would not be held within the statute. The question of law was a difficult and rather subtle one. The "thin-ice" theory would say that it is no business of the law to tell people in advance where they might fall through when they skate on thin ice. On the other hand, there were, at the time, numerous policies of the United States in favour of scientific exchange and cooperation with the Soviet Union. In other words, there were encouragements to skate and it would seem that a court, once having determined that the electron microscope was within the list of forbidden items of export, would then wish to determine how strong the policies were in favour of ice skating before it decided to use a thin-ice theory. Obviously, the proper way to handle this kind of question is to provide some forum for the authoritative determination of the legal question.

With respect to the private individual who accepts an attorney's advice as to a question of the meaning of a law, several of the policies that we have discussed with respect to the businessman arise in a different context. The typical case one might envision here is an assembly where the authorities have "read the riot act" and demanded that the assembly disband. The attorney for the group, who is typically a committed activist himself, sharing the values and objects of the movement, then announces that the sheriff's order is an unconstitutional interference with free speech. It is possible that the courts might apply a thin-ice theory if the activist turns out to be wrong even though the area involves free speech, since it also involves the danger of injury and riot. Courts might also worry about exculpating the members of the group because of their mistake of law when the effect of this would be to give more power and prestige to the people who took the most extreme view—or at least announced that they took it—of the law.

In addition, in this situation there is an institutional factor which, in the United States, would militate against granting a mistake of law defence more than would be the case in England or Germany. In the United States, assuming that mistake of law in the situation were regarded as a defence, the trial judge would instruct the jury that the assembly was illegal but that, if the jury found the defendants, because of their legal advice, to have reasonably believed that the law did not apply to them, it should acquit them. Assume now a repetition of the exact same event the next month. Again the sheriff orders the group to disperse and again the attorney gets up. This time he says:

> You remember the last time you listened to my advice you were acquitted. Secondly, for those of you who know that the acquittal might have come about because of our lenient rule as to mistake of law, you should also know that it was no mistake. Although the judge who charged the jury disagreed with me and agreed with the sheriff, that is precisely what you have to expect from such lower court judges who basically know nothing or care nothing about the Constitution. I am a constitutional lawyer and in every case where we have received vindication we have been vindicated by the Appellate Courts and the Supreme Court of the United States. I am even more confident that my original statement to you a month ago was correct.

A legal system which permits appellate review of the legal questions arising in a case terminated by an acquittal might have more reason to grant a mistake of law defence in this kind of situation. It is much easier to grant an excuse once than to have to grant it over and over again.

LAMBERT v. CALIFORNIA

United States Supreme Court
355 U.S. 225 (1957)

Mr. Justice Douglas delivered the opinion of the Court.

Section 52.38(a) of the Los Angeles Municipal Code defines "convicted person" as follows:

> Any person who, subsequent to January 1, 1921, has been or hereafter is convicted of an offense punishable as a felony in the State of California, or who has been or who is hereafter convicted of any offense in any place other than the

State of California, which offenses, if committed in the State of California, would have been punishable as a felony.

Section 52.39 provides that it shall be unlawful for "any convicted person" to be or remain in Los Angeles for a period of more than five days without registering; it requires any person having a place of abode outside the city to register if he comes into the city on five occasions or more during a 30-day period; and it prescribes the information to be furnished the Chief of Police on registering.

Section 52.43(b) makes the failure to register a continuing offense, each day's failure constituting a separate offense.

Appellant, arrested on suspicion of another offense was charged with a violation of this registration law. The evidence showed that she had been at the time of her arrest a resident of Los Angeles for over seven years. Within that period she had been convicted in Los Angeles of the crime of forgery, an offense which California punishes as a felony. Though convicted of a crime punishable as a felony, she had not at the time of her arrest registered under the Municipal Code. At the trial, appellant asserted that §52.39 of the Code denies her due process of law and other rights under the Federal Constitution. . . . The trial court denied this objection. The case was tried to a jury which found appellant guilty. The court fined her $250 and placed her on probation for three years. . . . The case having been argued and reargued, we now hold that the registration provisions of the Code as sought to be applied here violate the Due Process requirement of the Fourteenth Amendment.

The registration provision, carrying criminal penalties, applies if a person has been convicted "of an offense punishable as a felony in the State of California" or, in case [he or she] has been convicted in another State, if the offense "would have been punishable as a felony" had it been committed in California. No element of willfulness is by terms included in the ordinance nor read into it by the California court as a condition necessary for a conviction.

We must assume that appellant had no actual knowledge of the requirement that she register under this ordinance, as she offered proof of this defense which was refused. The question is whether a registration act of this character violates due process where it is applied to a person who has no actual knowledge of his duty to register, and where no showing is made of the probability of such knowledge.

We do not go with Blackstone in saying that a "vicious will" is necessary to constitute a crime, for conduct alone without regard to the intent of the doer is often sufficient. There is wide latitude in the lawmakers to declare an offense and to exclude elements of knowledge and diligence from its definition. But we deal here with conduct that is wholly passive—mere failure to register. It is unlike the commission of acts, or the failure to act under circumstances that should alert the doer to the consequences of his deed. United States v. Balint, 258 U.S. 250; United States v. Dotterweich, 320 U.S. 277, 284. The rule that "ignorance of the law will not excuse" is deep in our law, as is the principle that of all the powers of local government, the police power is "one of the least limitable." On the other hand, due process places some limits on its exercise. Engrained in our concept of due process is the requirement of notice. . . .

. . . Registration laws are common and their range is wide. Many such laws are akin to . . . the regulation of business activities. But the present ordinance is entirely different. Violation of its provisions is unaccompanied by any activity whatever, mere presence in the city being the test. Moreover, circumstances which might move one to inquire as to the necessity of registration are completely lacking. At most the ordinance is but a law enforcement technique designed for the convenience of law enforcement agencies through which a list of the names and addresses of felons then residing in a given community is compiled. The disclosure is merely a compilation of former convictions already publicly recorded in the jurisdiction where obtained. Nevertheless, this appellant on first becoming aware of her duty to register was given no opportunity to comply with the law and avoid its penalty, even though her default was entirely innocent. She could but suffer the consequences of the ordinance, namely, conviction with the imposition of heavy criminal penalties thereunder. We believe that actual knowledge of the duty to register or proof of the probability of such knowledge and subsequent failure to comply are necessary before a conviction under the ordinance can stand. As Holmes wrote in The Common Law, "A law which punished conduct which would not be blameworthy in the average member of the community would be too severe for that community to bear." Its severity lies in the absence of an opportunity either to avoid the consequences of the law or to defend any prosecution brought under it. Where a person did not know of the duty to register and where there was no proof of the probability of such knowledge, he may not be convicted consistently with due process. Were it otherwise, the evil would be as great as it is when the law is written in print too fine to read or in a language foreign to the community.

Reversed.

Mr. Justice BURTON dissents because he believes that, as applied to this appellant, the ordinance does not violate her constitutional rights.

Mr. Justice FRANKFURTER, whom Mr. Justice HARLAN and Mr. Justice WHITTAKER join, dissenting.

The present laws of the United States and of the forty-eight States are thick with provisions that command that some things not be done and others be done, although persons convicted under such provisions may have had no awareness of what the law required or that what they did was wrongdoing. The body of decisions sustaining such legislation, including innumerable registration laws, is almost as voluminous as the legislation itself. The matter is summarized in United States v. Balint, 258 U.S. 250, 252: "Many instances . . . are to be found in regulatory measures in the exercise of what is called the police power where the emphasis of the statute is evidently upon achievement of some social betterment rather than the punishment of the crimes as in cases of *mala in se*."

Surely there can hardly be a difference as a matter of fairness, of hardship, or of justice . . . between the case of a person wholly innocent of wrongdoing, in the sense that he was not remotely conscious of violating any law, who is imprisoned for five years for conduct relating to narcotics, and the case of another person who is placed on probation for three years on condition that she pay $250, for failure, as a local resident, convicted under local law of a felony, to register under a law passed as an exercise of the State's "police power." Considerations of hardship often lead courts, naturally enough, to attribute to a statute the requirement of a certain mental element—some consciousness of wrongdoing and knowledge of the law's command—as a matter of statutory construction. Then, too, a cruelly disproportionate relation between what the law requires and the sanction for its disobedience may constitute a violation of the Eighth Amendment as a cruel and unusual punishment, and, in respect to the States, even offend the Due Process Clause of the Fourteenth Amendment.

But what the Court here does is to draw a constitutional line between a State's requirement of doing and not doing. What is this but a return to Year Book distinctions between feasance and nonfeasance—a distinction that may have significance in the evolution of common-law notions of liability, but is inadmissible as a line between constitutionality and unconstitutionality. One can be confident that Mr. Justice Holmes would have been the last to draw such a line. What he wrote about "blameworthiness" is worth quoting in its context:

> It is not intended to deny that criminal liability, as well as civil, is founded on blameworthiness. Such a denial would shock the moral sense of any civilized community; or, to put it another way, a law which punished conduct which would not be blameworthy in the average member of the community would be too severe for that community to bear. (This passage must be read in the setting of the broader discussion of which it is an essential part. Holmes, The Common Law, at 49-50.)

If the generalization that underlies, and alone can justify, this decision were to be given its relevant scope, a whole volume of the United States Reports would be required to document in detail the legislation in this country that would fall or be impaired. I abstain from entering upon a consideration of such legislation, and adjudications upon it, because I feel confident that the present decision will turn out to be an isolated deviation from the strong current of precedents—a derelict on the waters of the law. Accordingly, I content myself with dissenting.

Notes and Questions

1. According to Justice Douglas in *Lambert,* the fact that Mrs. Lambert was guilty of an omission rather than an act is crucial. Why?

2. In *Lambert,* what was the defendant's mistake? Was it a mistake that showed she lacked the *mens rea* required for the crime, which the law generally regards as exculpatory, or was it a mistake of the governing law, which, as in *Hatch* and *Hopkins,* the law generally regards as no excuse?

3. What does Justice Frankfurter mean when he says,

> If the generalization that underlies, and alone can justify, this decision were to be given its relevant scope, a whole volume of United States Reports would be required to document in detail the legislation in this country that would fall or be impaired?

What generalization is he talking about? Is he correct?

4. The New Jersey court in *Hatch,* supra, distinguished *Lambert* as follows:

> [I]n *Lambert,* the crime was one of omission rather than commission, the situation was one in which inquiry as to the applicable law was unlikely, and the purpose of the ordinance was simply to compile a list which might ultimately assist law enforcement agencies. On contrast, statutes dealing with gun control are concerned with acts of commission, in situations where regulations abound and inquiries are likely, and where the purposes are to insure the public safety and protect against current acts and threats of violence. [313 A.2d at 799]

Does the court persuade you that Hatch deserved punishment more than did Lambert?

5. Consider the case of an Italian "guestworker" who, on his third day in West Germany, went to shoot thrushes. In Italy, shooting songbirds is common and legally permissible, while in most European countries, including West Germany, it is criminal. The German court held him not liable, on the ground that his ignorance of the law was "invincible." See Arzt, Ignorance or Mistake of Law, 24 Am. J. of Comp. Law 675 (1976).

III

HOMICIDE

This Part examines how the criminal law identifies, classifies, and punishes unlawful killings according to their degree of culpability. The grading of homicide generally depends upon the *mens rea* of the accused; indeed the law of homicide provides the ideal case study in the general principles of *mens rea* we have already studied. In addition, it provides a setting for other fundamental doctrines—such as attempt, causation, complicity, and justification and excuse—which we will examine in later parts. Among the major crimes, homicide is uniquely suited to this role because of the richness of its appellate literature and the complexity of its gradations. In this Part, we examine the law of criminal homicide by moving progressively from the lowest degree to the highest.

5

MANSLAUGHTER

A. INVOLUNTARY MANSLAUGHTER

1. Sample Statutes

KAN. STAT. ANN.
(Rev. Stat. 1979)

§21-3404. Involuntary Manslaughter.

(a) Involuntary manslaughter is the unlawful killing of a human being, without malice, which is done unintentionally in the wanton commission of an unlawful act not amounting to felony, or in the commission of a lawful act in an unlawful or wanton manner.

(b) As used in this section, an "unlawful act" is any act which is prohibited by a statute of the United States or the state of Kansas or an ordinance of any city within the state, which statute or ordinance is enacted for the protection of human life or safety.

(c) Involuntary manslaughter is a class D felony [punishable by 1-5 years in prison].

PA. CONS. STAT. ANN.
(1983)

§2504. Involuntary Manslaughter.

(a) General Rule.—A person is guilty of involuntary manslaughter when as a direct result of the doing of an unlawful act in a reckless or grossly negligent manner, or the doing of a lawful act in a reckless or grossly negligent manner, he causes the death of another person.

(b) *Grading.*—Involuntary manslaughter is a misdemeanor of the first degree [punishable by a maximum of 5 years in prison].

ILLINOIS ANN. STAT.
(1983)

CH. 38 ¶9-3. INVOLUNTARY MANSLAUGHTER AND RECKLESS HOMICIDE.

(a) A person who unintentionally kills an individual without lawful justification commits involuntary manslaughter if his acts whether lawful or unlawful which cause the death are such as are likely to cause death or great bodily harm to some individual, and he performs them recklessly, except in cases in which the cause of the death consists of the driving of a motor vehicle, in which case the person commits reckless homicide.

(b) Sentence.

(1) Involuntary manslaughter is a Class 3 felony [punishable by 2-5 years in prison].

(2) Reckless homicide is a Class 4 felony [punishable by 1-3 years in prison].

MINN. STAT. ANN.
(1982)

§609.205. MANSLAUGHTER IN THE SECOND DEGREE

Whoever causes the death of another by any of the following means is guilty of manslaughter in the second degree and may be sentenced to imprisonment of not more than seven years or to payment of a fine of not more than $7,000, or both:

(1) By his culpable negligence whereby he creates an unreasonable risk, and consciously takes chances of causing death or great bodily harm to another; or

(2) By shooting another with a firearm or other dangerous weapon as a result of negligently believing him to be a deer or other animal; or

(3) By setting a spring gun, pit fall, deadfall, snare, or other like dangerous weapon or device; or

(4) By negligently or unintentionally permitting any animal, known by him to have vicious propensities, to go at large, . . .

WIS. STAT. ANN.
(1982)

§940.06. Homicide by Reckless Conduct.

(1) Whoever causes the death of another human being by reckless conduct is guilty of a Class C felony.

(2) Reckless conduct consists of an act which creates a situation of unreasonable risk and high probability of death or great bodily harm to another and which demonstrates a conscious disregard for the safety of another and a willingness to take known chances of perpetrating an injury. It is intended that this definition embraces all of the elements of what was heretofore known as gross negligence in the criminal law of Wisconsin [punishable by up to 10 years in prison].

CAL. PENAL CODE
(1970)

§192. Manslaughter; Voluntary, Involuntary, and in Driving a Vehicle Defined; Construction of Section.

Manslaughter is the unlawful killing of a human being, without malice. It is of three kinds: . . .

2. Involuntary—in the commission of an unlawful act, not amounting to felony; or in the commission of a lawful act which might produce death, in an unlawful manner, or without due caution and circumspection; provided that this subdivision shall not apply to acts committed in the driving of a vehicle [punishable by 2-4 years in prison].

2. Negligent and Reckless Homicide

STATE v. O'BRIEN
Supreme Court of New Jersey
32 N.J.L. 169 (1867)

Dalrimple, J.

On the fifteenth day of November, 1865, the defendant was a switchtender, in the employ of the New Jersey Railroad and Transportation Company. His duty was, to adjust, and keep adjusted, the switches of the road at a certain point in the city of Newark, so that passenger trains running over the road would continue on the main track thereof, and pass thence to the city of

Elizabeth. He failed to perform such duty, whereby a passenger train of cars, drawn by a locomotive engine, was unavoidably diverted from the main track to a side track, and thence thrown upon the ground. The cars were thrown upon each other with great force and violence, by means whereof one Henry Gardner, a passenger upon the train, was so injured that he died. The defendant was indicted for manslaughter, and convicted upon trial in the Essex Oyer and Terminer. He insisted, and in different forms, asked the court to charge the jury, that he could not legally be convicted, unless his will concurred in his omission of duty; the court refused so to charge. A rule to show cause why the verdict should not be set aside was granted, and the case certified into this court for its advisory opinion, as to whether there was any error in the charge of the court below, or in the refusal to charge, as requested.

The indictment was for the crime of manslaughter. If the defendant's omission of duty was wilful . . . he was guilty of murder. Intent to take life, whether by an act of omission or commission, distinguishes murder from manslaughter. In order to make out against the defendant the lesser offense of manslaughter, it was not necessary that it should appear that the act of omission was wilful or of purpose. The court was right in its refusal to charge, as requested.

The only other question is, whether there is error in the charge delivered. The error complained of is, that the jury were instructed that a mere act of omission might be so criminal or culpable as to be the subject of an indictment for manslaughter. Such, we believe, is the prevailing current of authority. Professor Greenleaf, in the third volume of his work on evidence, §129, in treating of homicide, says:

> It may be laid down, that where one, by his negligence, has contributed to the death of another, he is responsible. The caution which the law requires in all these cases, is not the utmost degree which can possibly be used, but such reasonable care as is used in the like cases, and has been found, by long experience, to answer the end.

Wharton, in his Treatise on Criminal Law, p.382, says:

> There are many cases in which death is the result of an occurrence, in itself unexpected, but which arose from negligence or inattention. How far in such cases the agent of such misfortune is to be held responsible, depends upon the inquiry, whether he was guilty of gross negligence at the time. Inferences of guilt are not to be drawn from remote causes, and the degree of caution requisite to bring the case within the limits of misadventure, must be proportioned to the probability of danger of attending the act immediately conducive to the death.

The propositions so well stated by the eminent writers referred to, we believe to be entirely sound, and are applicable to the case before us. The charge, in the respect complained of, was in accordance with them. It expressly states, that is was a question of fact for the jury to settle, whether the defendant was, or was not guilty of negligence; whether his conduct evinced under the circumstances such care and diligence as were proportionate to the danger of life impending. The very definition of crime is an act omitted or committed in violation of public law. The defendant in this case omitted his duty under such circumstances, as amounted to gross or culpable or criminal negligence. The court charged the jury, that if the defendant, at the time of the accident was intending to do his duty, but in a moment of forgetfulness omitted something which any one of reasonable care would be likely to omit, he was not guilty. The verdict of guilty finds the question, in fact, involved in this proposition against the defendant, and convicts him of gross negligence. He owed a personal duty not only to his employers, but to the public. He was found to have been grossly negligent in the performance of that duty, whereby human life was sacrificed. His conviction was right, and the court below should be so advised.

Notes and Questions

1. What precisely did the defendant do here that was negligent? Is he accused of committing an act? Does it matter whether his "conduct" was an act or an omission?

2. What is the standard used in *O'Brien* to measure "gross negligence"? How gross does the negligence have to be? Granted that O'Brien may be liable in tort, does that mean he should be punished by the criminal law? What should be the difference in the quantum of negligence sufficient to allow recovery in tort law and the quantum of negligence justifying criminal punishment?

3. Should the defendant have been guilty of a crime if people had been injured in the train crash but no one had died? Under the law of most states he would be guilty of no crime.

4. Often criminal negligence consists in making a catastrophic blunder. In many cases we associate this negligence with colossal stupidity. One psychologist[1] who has studied the issue argues that this is not the case:

> Two years ago, during NATO training exercises over West Germany, the pilot of a Royal Air Force Phantom jet accidentally fired a live Sidewinder missile at a Royal Air Force Jaguar. The Jaguar pilot parachuted safely to earth, but his twelve-million-dollar aircraft was destroyed. Earlier that same year, the top deck of a double-decker bus traveling on a country road in south Wales was sheared off when the driver tried to pass under a low bridge. Six passengers died in the accident. And in 1977, the pilot of a Boeing 747 jumbo jet, about to make the short hop from Santa Cruz, on the island of Tenerife, to Las Palmas, on the island of Gran Canaria, off the coast of northwest Africa, failed to wait for

1. Reason, The Psychopathology of Everyday Slips, The Sciences 45, 45, 48, 49 (Sept./Oct. 1984).

takeoff clearance from the control tower. Roaring down the tarmac at a speed of 150 miles an hour, the plane crashed into another 747 still taxiing on the runway. Of the 637 passengers and crew aboard the two craft, 577 were killed.

There is a natural tendency to suppose that disasters such as these are the product of some rare species of monumental blunder, but the evidence suggests otherwise. In fact, the mental errors that lead to horrendous accidents are indistinguishable in nature from the trivial, absentminded slips and lapses of everyday life. The true hallmark of absentminded errors, whatever their consequences, is not inexperience or ineptitude but misapplied competence—habit gone wrong, in a sense.

All of us can probably remember times when our words or actions were no longer running according to plan. We may have struggled to open a friend's front door with our own latchkey, forgotten the name of someone we've known for many years, tried to drive away from the curb without switching on the ignition, or said thank you to a vending machine. Our lives are strewn with such inconsequential lapses—what Freud called "the refuse of the phenomenal world," or, in a more daunting phrase, "the psychopathology of everyday life. . . ."

It seems clear from our close examination of slips and lapses that whenever thoughts, words, or actions depart from their planned course, they tend to go in the direction of something familiar, expected, and in keeping with existing knowledge structures. Or, more briefly: errors tend to be more conservative than intentions—and the more frequently a particular routine is set in motion and achieves the desired outcome, the more likely it is to recur unbidden at the wrong time, as a slip of habit. William James likened habits to flywheels: once set in motion, they require little additional effort to keep them going. But habits are hard to control.

These findings underscore a crucial point about absentminded errors: they are characteristic of highly skilled activities—a problem of the expert, not the beginner. That seems to run contrary to common sense, since people expend a great deal of effort to acquire skills so that they will not make mistakes. Yet, paradoxically, the probability of making an absentminded error increases with proficiency at a particular task. The more skilled we become at an activity, the fewer demands it makes upon consciousness. To quote James again, "Habit diminishes the conscious attention with which our acts are performed. . . ."

The Royal Air Force pilot who absentmindedly dispatched a live Sidewinder missile into another plane testified at his court martial that at the moment when he fired he had completely forgotten about the missiles and believed himself to be on the kind of routine training mission he had been flying for the previous eight years. In the pilot's defense, a senior officer argued that combat procedures were dinned so intensively into pilots that the men reacted automatically. At the inquest into the double-decker bus accident, the driver explained that he normally drove a single-decker on that route and that on the fatal trip he forgot he was driving a two-tiered vehicle. As for the horrific runway crash on Tenerife, the American Airline Pilots Association made a number of significant observations about the Dutch captain who did not wait for his takeoff instructions. His principal job was as head of KLM's flight-training department. During the preceding six years he had spent some fifteen hundred hours in a flight-training simulator, and he had not actually flown for twelve weeks before the catastrophe. In the simulator, the instructor always issued airways (the designated route along which the plane would fly to reach its destination) and takeoff clearance at the same time; to reduce operating costs, simulator pilots were never required to hold position while awaiting takeoff clearance. Instead of reacting to the real circumstances of a real takeoff, the captain may have reverted to a preprogrammed mode of action derived from long experience in the predictable world of the simulator.

From these cases it is apparent that habit intrusions are not confined to minor errors. The central figure in each of the three disasters was a competent, experienced professional. On the fatal day, none of the three behaved in any extraordinary or bizarre fashion; on the contrary, they all carried out habitual actions with practiced skill. Unfortunately, the circumstances in each instance demanded not the automatic repetition of familiar actions but behavior specially tailored to a special situation. Clearly, the attention of the three unfortunate men somehow lapsed, and old habit-schemata took over. Ordinarily, that would not have mattered much, but in these cases circumstances were unforgiving. Indeed, the differences between catastrophic and trivial errors are nearly always environmental rather than psychological. Horrendous consequences arise only when errors are made in punishing situations. And even then, errors usually have to occur in diabolical combinations before an unfriendly environment exacts its worst penalty.

5. The Model Penal Code requires recklessness for manslaughter but provides a lesser homicide crime for which negligence will suffice:

Model Penal Code §210.3.

(1) Criminal homicide constitutes manslaughter when:
(a) it is committed recklessly; . . .
(2) Manslaughter is a felony of the second degree.

Model Penal Code §210.4.

(1) Criminal homicide constitutes negligent homicide when it is committed negligently.
(2) Negligent homicide is a felony of the third degree.

The Model Penal Code comments explain the purpose of the drafters:

4. *Reckless Homicide.* It is a fair summary of common-law homicide that three levels of risk-creation were recognized: that which was sufficient for a conviction of murder, that which was sufficient for a conviction of manslaughter, and that which was sufficient only for civil liability. The lines between these three categories were at best unclear . . .

Sections 210.3(1)(a) and 2.02(2)(c) resolve these issues under the Model Code with respect to the offense of manslaughter. Section 210.3(1)(a) treats reckless homicide as manslaughter. Under Section 2.02(2)(c), a person acts recklessly with respect to the death of another when he consciously disregards a substantial and unjustifiable risk that his conduct will cause that result. Additionally, the nature and degree of risk must be such that, considering all the circumstances, its disregard "involves a gross deviation from the standard of conduct that a law-abiding person would observe in the actor's situation." . . .

Under the Model Code, liability for manslaughter cannot be premised on negligence. Statutes derived from the common law classify unintentional homicide as involuntary manslaughter without any attempt to distinguish conscious disregard of homicidal risk from inadvertent risk creation. This failure to differentiate across a broad spectrum of culpability raises serious grading difficulties. On the one hand, involuntary manslaughter may be graded as is its voluntary counterpart, in which case disproportionately severe sanctions are assigned to conduct that is merely negligent. On the other hand, reduced penalties may be authorized for involuntary manslaughter, in which case persons guilty of serious wrongdoing benefit from formal categorization with less culpable homicides. Section 210.3(1)(a) refines the traditional definition of manslaughter by demanding proof of conscious disregard of perceived homicidal risk. In such instances, punishment as a felony of the second degree is warranted. Negligent homicide is relegated to a separate provision carrying lesser sanctions. . . .

. . . The essence of the difference between recklessness and negligence as those terms are defined in Section 2.02 of the Model Code is that the reckless actor must "consciously disregard" a substantial and unjustifiable homicidal risk created by his conduct, whereas the negligent actor need only disregard a risk of which he "should be aware." Inadvertence to risk is thus the basis upon which condemnation for negligence proceeds, coupled with the judgment that the actor's failure to perceive the risk involves a "gross deviation from the standard of care that a reasonable person would observe in the actor's situation." . . .

In summary, therefore, the Model Penal Code was drafted against a background of inconsistency and imprecision in determining the content of negligence for purposes of criminal homicide. There was also a general failure to focus upon the need for a grading differential between conduct involving conscious risk creation and conduct involving inadvertence. The most common situation was that negligent homicide was treated as a species of involuntary manslaughter, with judicial formulation of the appropriate standard expressed in a jumble of language that obscured the essential character of the inquiry.

. . . Conscious risk creation is adequately covered by the Model Code in the crime of manslaughter and, in some instances of especially grievous conduct, in the crime of murder. Whether there is need to include the inadvertent risk creator within the penal prohibition presents an issue of principle that deserves explicit consideration.

It has been urged that inadvertent negligence is not a sufficient basis for criminal conviction, both on the utilitarian ground that threatened sanctions cannot influence the inadvertent actor and on the moral ground that criminal punishment should be reserved for cases involving conscious fault. The utilitarian argument is that the inadvertent actor by definition does not perceive the risks of his conduct, and thus cannot be deterred from risk creation. The moral argument is that the legitimacy of criminal condemnation is premised upon personal accountability of the sort that is usually and properly measured by an estimate of the actor's willingness consciously to violate clearly established societal norms. Those who hold this view argue that the actor who does not perceive the risks associated with his conduct presents a moral situation different in kind from that of the actor who knows exactly what he is doing and what risks he is running and who nevertheless makes a conscious choice condemned by the penal law.

These arguments are canvassed in more detail in the commentary to Section 2.02, [see pp.138-140] as is the basis of the Model Code response to them. Suffice it to say here that neither contention was regarded by the Institute as persuasive. Criminal punishment of negligent homicide is not impotent to stimulate care that might otherwise not be taken, nor is a person's failure to use his faculties for the protection of others an improper basis for condemnation. The Model Code definition of negligence insists on proof of substantial fault and limits penal sanctions to cases where "the significance of the circumstances of fact would be apparent to one who shares the community's general sense of right and wrong." Justice is safeguarded by insisting upon that gross deviation from ordinary standards of conduct which is contemplated by the Model Code definition of negligence. Liability for inadvertent risk creation is thus properly limited to cases where the actor is grossly insensitive to the interests and claims of other persons in society.

On the other hand, the distinction between conscious and inadvertent risk creation is important both for assessing the dangerousness of the actor's conduct and for evaluating the gravity of his moral fault. For that reason, the Model Code punishes negligent homicide as an offense of lesser grade than manslaughter. The range of sanctions authorized for negligent homicide under Section 210.4 falls considerably short of that prevailing at the time the Code was drafted in states where manslaughter was a single category. The penalties provided, however, are somewhat higher than the norm for involuntary manslaughter in states where voluntary and involuntary manslaughter were distinguished for purposes of sentence. Given the ameliorative powers vested in the courts by the Model Code, these sanctions do not seem excessive.

Although the majority rule is probably to the contrary, some states, like the Code, require recklessness for involuntary manslaughter, rather than gross negligence. Examine the following case.

COMMONWEALTH v. WELANSKY

Supreme Judicial Court of Massachusetts
316 Mass. 383, 55 N.E.2d 902 (1944)

Lummus, Justice. On November 28, 1942, and for about nine years before that day, a corporation named New Cocoanut Grove, Inc., maintained and operated a "night club" in Boston, having an entrance at 17 Piedmont Street, for the furnishing to the public for compensation of food, drink and entertainment, consisting of orchestra and band music, singing and dancing. It employed about eighty persons. The corporation, its officers and employees, and its business, were completely dominated by the defendant Barnett Welansky, who is called in this opinion simply the defendant, since his codefendants were acquitted by the jury. He owned, and held in his own name or in the names of others, all the capital stock. . . .

The defendant was accustomed to spend his evenings at the night club, inspecting the premises and superintending the business. On November 16, 1942, he became suddenly ill, and was carried to a hospital, where he was in bed for three weeks and remained until discharged on December 11, 1942. During his stay at the hospital, although employees visited him there, he did not concern himself with the night club, because as he testified, he "knew it would be all right" and that "the same system . . . [he] had would continue" during his absence. There is no evidence of any act, omission or condition at the night club on November 28, 1942 (apart from the lighting of a match hereinafter described), that was not within the usual and regular practice during the time before the defendant was taken ill when he was at the night club nearly every evening. While the defendant was at the hospital, his brother James Welansky and an employee named Jacob Goldfine, who were made codefendants, assumed some of the defendant's duties at the night club, but made no change in methods. Under these circumstances the defendant was not entitled to a verdict of not guilty on the ground that any acts or omissions on the evening of November 28, 1942, were the transitory and unauthorized acts or omissions of servants or other persons, for which the defendant could not be held criminally responsible.

The physical arrangement of the night club on November 28, 1942, as well as on November 16, 1942, when the defendant last had personal knowledge of it, was as follows. The total area of the first or street floor was nine thousand seven hundred sixty-three square feet. Entering the night club through a single revolving door at 17 Piedmont Street, one found himself in a foyer or hall having an area of six hundred six square feet. . . . In the front corner of the foyer, to the left, beyond the office, was a passageway leading to a stairway about four feet wide, with fifteen risers. The stairway led down to the Melody Lounge in the basement, which was the only room in the basement open to the public. There were to be found a bar, tables, and chairs.

The extreme dimensions of the Melody Lounge were about thirty-six feet by fifty-five feet, and its area was one thousand eight hundred ninety-five square feet. It was separated from a narrow corridor leading to the kitchen (which was located under the main dining room) by a wooden partition. In that partition was a wooden door, two feet and two inches wide, which could have been found to be unmarked. Passing from the Melody Lounge through that door, and thus entering the narrow corridor, one could turn to the left and go to a door which swung inward and could be opened only to a width of eighteen inches, at the top of three steps. That door was barred by a wooden bar that had to be lifted off before the door could be opened at all. On opening that door, one could pass into an outdoor alley about three and one-half feet wide. That alley led to a yard, from which egress could be had through inswinging doors into another passageway and thence to Shawmut Street.

If, instead, one passing from the Melody Lounge into the narrow corridor should turn to the right, he might pass, as employees were accustomed to do, through a door two and one half feet wide swinging into the corridor from the kitchen. Once in the kitchen, he could traverse that room with all its equipment to the other end of it near Shawmut Street, and then go upstairs and through swinging doors into a corner of the main dining room.

It is evident that in an emergency escape from the Melody Lounge by either of these courses would be difficult for a patron not thoroughly familiar with parts of the premises not ordinarily open to him.

Returning to the foyer, and standing as though one had just entered it by the revolving door, to the right, in the front of the building on Piedmont Street, was a room called the Caricature Bar, with an area of one thousand three hundred ninety-nine square feet, containing two bars, stools and chairs. Toward Shawmut Street, and separated from the Caricature Bar by a railing, was the main dining room, with an area of three thousand seven hundred sixty-five square feet. The foyer opened into both the Caricature Bar and the main dining room. In the main dining room was a dance floor with an area of six hundred sixty square feet, and behind it, in the direction of Broadway, was a stage with an area of four hundred thirty-six square feet.

From the Caricature Bar and from the main dining room one could pass into a corridor near the stage, about four feet wide, up some steps and through a passageway about seven feet wide into the new Cocktail Lounge, which was first opened on November 17, 1942, and which had an area of seven hundred eighty-one square feet. There one found a bar, stools, tables and seats, and also a check room and toilets. In the farther corner of the Cocktail Lounge was a door three feet wide, swinging inward, through which one could enter a small vestibule from which he could go through a pair of doors to Broadway at 59 Broadway.

That pair of doors, and the revolving door at 17 Piedmont Street, were the only entrances and exits intended for the ordinary use of patrons. Besides these doors, and the exit through the wooden partition from the Melody Lounge, already described, there were five possible emergency exits from the night club, all on the first or street floor. These will now be listed and described.

(1) A door, opening outward to Piedmont Street, two and one-half feet wide, at the head of the stairway leading to and from the basement Melody Lounge. That door apparently was not visible from the greater part of the foyer, for it was in a passageway that ran from one end of the foyer past the office to the stairway. That door was marked "Exit" by an electric sign. It was equipped with a "panic" or "crash" bar, intended to unbolt and open the door upon pressure from within the building. But on the evidence it could have been found that the device just mentioned was regularly made ineffective by having the door locked by a separate lock operated by a key that was kept in a desk in the office. . . .

(2) A door two and one-third feet wide leading from the foyer, near the revolving door, into the small vestibule adjoining the office, already described.

From that vestibule another similar door, swinging inward, gave egress to Piedmont Street, near the revolving door. The door to Piedmont Street could not be opened fully, because of a wall shelf. And that door was commonly barred in the evening, as it was on November 28, 1942, by a removable board with clothing hooks on it, and by clothing, for in the evening the office and vestibule were used for checking clothing.

(3) A door, opening outward, from the middle of the wall of the main dining room to Shawmut Street, and marked "Exit" by an electric sign. The opening was about three and two-thirds feet wide. The defendant testified that this was the principal exit provided for emergencies. From the sides of the opening hung double doors, equipped with "panic" bars intended to unbolt and open the doors upon pressure from within. But on the evening of November 28, 1942, one of the two doors did not open upon pressure, and had to be hammered with a table before it would open. Besides the "panic" doors were hidden from the view of the diners by a pair of "Venetian" wooden doors, swinging inward, and fastened by a hook, which had to be opened before one could operate the "panic" doors. In addition, dining tables were regularly placed near the Venetian doors, one of them within two feet, and these had to be moved away in order to get access to the doors. That condition prevailed on the evening of November 28, 1942.

(4) The service door, two and one-half feet wide, swinging inward, leading to Shawmut Street at 8 Shawmut Street. This door was near the stage, at the foot of a stairway leading to dressing rooms on the second floor, and was in a part of the premises to which patrons were not admitted and which they could not see. This door was known to employees, but doubtless not to patrons. It was kept locked by direction of the defendant, and the key was kept in a desk in the office.

(5) The door, two and three-fourths feet wide, swinging inward, leading from a corridor into which patrons had no occasion to go, to Shawmut Street at 6 Shawmut Street. No patron was likely to know of this door. It was kept locked by direction of the defendant, but he ordered the key placed in the lock at seven every evening.

We now come to the story of the fire. A little after ten o'clock on the evening of Saturday, November 28, 1942, the night club was well filled with a crowd of patrons. It was during the busiest season of the year. An important football game in the afternoon had attracted many visitors to Boston. Witnesses were rightly permitted to testify that the dance floor had from eighty to one hundred persons on it, and that it was "very crowded." Witnesses were rightly permitted to give their estimates, derived from their observations, of the number of patrons in various parts of the night club. Upon the evidence it could have been found that at that time there were from two hundred fifty to four hundred persons in the Melody Lounge, from four hundred to five hundred in the main dining room and the Caricature Bar, and two hundred fifty in the Cocktail Lounge. Yet it could have been found that the crowd was no larger than it had been on other Saturday evenings before the defendant was taken ill, and that there had been larger crowds at earlier times. There were about seventy tables in the dining room, each seating from two to eight persons. There was testimony that all but two were taken. Many persons were standing in various rooms. The defendant testified that the reasonable capacity of the night club, exclusive of the new Cocktail Lounge, was six hundred fifty patrons. He never saw the new Cocktail Lounge with the furniture installed, but it was planned to accommodate from one hundred to one hundred twenty-five patrons.

A bartender in the Melody Lounge noticed that an electric light bulb which was in or near the cocoanut husks of an artificial palm tree in the corner had been turned off and that the corner was dark. He directed a sixteen-year-old bar boy who was waiting on customers at the tables to cause the bulb to be lighted. A soldier sitting with other persons near the light told the bar boy to leave it unlighted. But the bar boy got a stool, lighted a match in order to see the bulb, turned the bulb in its socket, and thus lighted it. The bar boy blew the match out, and started to walk away. Apparently the flame of the match had ignited the palm tree and that had speedily ignited the low cloth ceiling near it, for both flamed up almost instantly. The fire spread with great rapidity across the upper part of the room, causing much heat. The crowd in the Melody Lounge rushed up the stairs, but the fire preceded them. People got on fire while on the stairway. The fire spread with great speed across the foyer and into the Caricature Bar and the main dining room, and thence into the Cocktail Lounge. Soon after the fire started the lights in the night club went out. The smoke had a peculiar odor. The crowd were panic stricken, and rushed and pushed in every direction through the night club, screaming, and overturning tables and chairs in their attempts to escape.

The door at the head of the Melody Lounge stairway was not opened until firemen broke it down from outside with an axe and found it locked by a key lock, so that the panic bar could not operate. Two dead bodies were found close to it, and a pile of bodies about seven feet from it. The door in the vestibule of the office did not become open, and was barred by the clothing rack. The revolving door soon jammed, but was burst out by the pressure of the crowd. The head waiter and another waiter tried to get open the panic doors from the main dining room to Shawmut Street, and succeeded after some difficulty. The other two doors to Shawmut Street were locked, and were opened by force from outside by firemen and others. Some patrons escaped through them, but many dead bodies were piled up inside them. A considerable number of patrons escaped through the Broadway door, but many died just inside that door. Some employees, and a great number of patrons, died in the fire. Others were taken out of the building with fatal burns and injuries from smoke, and died within a few days. . . .

The defendant, his brother James Welansky, and Jacob Goldfine, were indicted for manslaughter. . . .

Each of the counts numbered from 7 to 12, inclusive, as amended alleged in substance that the New Cocoanut Grove, Inc., a corporation, did for a period of time prior to and including November 28, 1942, maintain and operate a night club, to which it invited members of the general public; that it was under a legal duty to its invitees to use reasonable care to keep its premises safe for their use; that the three persons indicted were authorized by the corporation to maintain, control, operate, construct, alter, supervise, and manage its premises in its behalf; that said three persons accepted the responsibility for such acts, and were therefore under a duty to its invitees to use such reasonable care; that in reckless disregard of such duty to one (naming the victim) who was lawfully upon said premises pursuant to such invitation to the general public, and of the probable harmful consequences to him of their failure to perform said duty, they and each of them did "wilfully, wantonly and recklessly neglect and fail to fulfill their said legal duty and obligation to the said" victim, by reason whereof he on November 28, 1942, received a mortal injury, as a result of which on that day he died. . . .

The defendant was found guilty. . . . He was sentenced to imprisonment in the State prison upon each count for a term of not less than twelve years and not more than fifteen years, the first day of said term to be in solitary confinement and the residue at hard labor, the sentences to run concurrently. . . .

The Commonwealth disclaimed any contention that the defendant intentionally killed or injured the persons named in the indictments as victims. It based its case on involuntary manslaughter through wanton or reckless conduct.

To convict the defendant of manslaughter, the Commonwealth was not required to prove that he caused the fire by some wanton or reckless conduct. Fire in a place of public resort is an ever present danger. It was enough to prove that death resulted from his wanton or reckless disregard of the safety of patrons in the event of fire from any cause. . . .

Usually wanton or reckless conduct consists of an affirmative act, like driving an automobile or discharging a firearm, in disregard of probable harmful consequences to another. But whereas in the present case there is a duty of care for the safety of business visitors invited to premises which the defendant controls, wanton or reckless conduct may consist of intentional failure to take such care in disregard of the probable harmful consequences to them or of their right to care.

To define wanton or reckless conduct so as to distinguish it clearly from negligence and gross negligence is not easy. Sometimes the word "wilful" is prefaced to the words "wanton" and "reckless" in expressing the concept. That only blurs it. Wilful means intentional. In the phrase "wilful, wanton or reckless conduct," if "wilful" modifies "conduct" it introduces something different from wanton or reckless conduct, even though the legal result is the same. Wilfully causing harm is a wrong, but a different wrong from wantonly or recklessly causing harm. If "wilful" modifies "wanton or reckless conduct" its use is accurate. What must be intended is the conduct, not the resulting harm. The words "wanton" and "reckless" are practically synonymous in this connection, although the word "wanton" may contain a suggestion of arrogance or insolence or heartlessness that is lacking in the word "reckless." But intentional conduct to which either word applies is followed by the same legal consequences as though both words applied.

The standard of wanton or reckless conduct is at once subjective and objective. Knowing facts that would cause a reasonable man to know the danger is equivalent to knowing the danger. The judge charged the jury correctly when he said,

> To constitute wanton or reckless conduct, as distinguished from mere negligence, grave danger to others must have been apparent and the defendant must have chosen to run the risk rather than alter his conduct so as to avoid the act or omission which caused the harm. If the grave danger was in fact realized by the defendant, his subsequent voluntary act or omission which caused the harm amounts to wanton or reckless conduct, no matter whether the ordinary man would have realized the gravity of the danger or not. But even if a particular defendant is so stupid [or] so heedless . . . that in fact he did not realize the grave danger, he cannot escape the imputation of wanton or reckless conduct in his dangerous act or omission, if an ordinary normal man under the same circumstances would have realized the gravity or the danger. A man may be reckless within the meaning of the law although he himself thought he was careful.

The essence of wanton or reckless conduct is intentional conduct, by way of either commission or of omission where there is a duty to act, which conduct involves a high degree of likelihood that substantial harm will result to another. Wanton or reckless conduct amounts to what has been variously described as indifference to or disregard of probable consequences to that other. But we are not prepared to give unqualified approval to a further statement found in some of our reported decisions, that to constitute wanton or reckless conduct, disregard of the rights of another must be as complete or utter as though such rights did not exist. If taken literally, that statement would permit a trifling regard for the rights of another to exonerate a defendant from the criminal consequences of flagrant wrongdoing.

The words "wanton" and "reckless" are thus not merely rhetorical or vituperative expressions used instead of negligent or grossly negligent. They express a difference in the degree of risk and in the voluntary taking of risk so marked as compared with negligence, as to amount substantially and in the eyes of the law to a difference in kind. For many years this court has been careful to preserve the distinction between negligence and gross negligence, on the one hand, and wanton or reckless conduct on the other. In pleading as well as in statutes the rule is that "negligence and willful and wanton conduct are so different in kind that words properly descriptive of the one commonly exclude the other."

Notwithstanding language used commonly in earlier cases, and occasionally in later ones, it is now clear in the Commonwealth that at common law conduct does not become criminal until it passes the borders of negligence and gross negligence and enters into the domain of wanton or reckless conduct. There is in Massachusetts at common law no such thing as "criminal negligence."

The Commonwealth was properly allowed to show that an exit from the Cocktail Lounge to Shawmut Street and fire doors in the Cocktail Lounge and between that and the older part of the premises, called for by the plans that were approved by the building department of the city of Boston under St. 1907, c.550, §12, as amended, had not been provided when the defendant last had knowledge of the premises on November 16, 1942, although he planned to open the Cocktail Lounge the next day; that the mode of construction of the Cocktail Lounge indicated that he did not intend to provide either; and that they had not been provided at the time of the fire. As planned, the fire doors were to be held open by fusible plugs that would melt and allow the door to close automatically in case of fire. They and the exits might have afforded some protection to persons in the Cocktail Lounge. The violation of such statute is not negligence per se but sometimes is evidence of negligence. Standing by itself, it would not warrant a finding of wanton or reckless conduct. But it might be considered with other evidence. There was no error in its admission. . . .

Judgments affirmed.

Notes and Questions

1. What "wanton and reckless" acts did Welansky perform? What risks did he advert to?

2. What relevant "intentional" acts did he perform? Why does the court reject negligence as the basis for manslaughter?

3. Reread the trial court's charge to the jury. Does the instruction permit conviction for negligence?

4. What statements in the appellate court's opinion support the view that, despite its many assertions to the contrary, recklessness is not necessary for conviction for manslaughter—or is it merely not necessary for this defendant's conviction? Why would a court possibly feel that way about the case?

PEOPLE v. STRONG

Court of Appeals of New York

37 N.Y.2d 568, 338 N.E.2d 602 (1975)

Jasen, Judge.

Defendant was charged, in a one-count indictment, with manslaughter in the second degree for causing the death of Kenneth Goings. At the trial, the defense requested that the court submit to the jury, in addition to the crime charged, the crime of criminally negligent homicide. The court refused, and the jury found defendant guilty as charged.

The sole issue upon this appeal is whether the trial court erred in refusing to submit to the jury the lesser crime of criminally negligent homicide. . . .

"The essential distinction between the crimes of manslaughter, second degree, and criminally negligent homicide . . . is the mental state of the defendant at the time the crime was committed. In one, the actor perceives the risk, but consciously disregards it. In the other, he negligently fails to perceive the risk. The result and the underlying conduct, exclusive of the mental element, are the same. . . ." [People v. Stanfield, 36 N.Y.2d 467, 369 N.Y.S.2d 118, 330 N.E.2d 75.]

In determining whether the defendant in the case was entitled to the charge of the lesser crime, the focus must be on the evidence in the record relating to the mental state of the defendant at the time of the crime. The record discloses that the defendant, 57 years old at the time of trial, had left his native Arabia at the age of 19, emigrating first to China and then coming to the United States three years later. . . . He testified that he had been of the Sudan Muslim religious faith since birth, and had become one of the sect's leaders, claiming a sizable following. Defendant articulated the three central beliefs of this religion as "cosmetic consciousness, mind over matter and psysiomatic psychomatic consciousness." He stated that the second of these beliefs, "mind over matter," empowered a "master," or leader, to lie on a bed of nails without bleeding, to walk through fire or on hot coals, to perform surgical operations without anesthesia, to raise people up off the ground, and to suspend a person's heartbeat, pulse, and breathing while that person remained conscious. In one particular type of ceremony, defendant, purportedly exercising his powers of "mind over matter," claimed he could stop a follower's heartbeat and breathing and plunge knives into his chest without any injury to the person. There was testimony from at least one of defendant's followers that he had successfully performed this ceremony on previous occasions. Defendant himself claimed to have performed this ceremony countless times over the previous 40 years without once causing an injury. Unfortunately, on January 28, 1972, when defendant performed this ceremony on Kenneth Goings, a recent recruit, the wounds from the hatchet and three knives which defendant had inserted into him proved fatal.

We view the record as warranting the submission of the lesser charge of criminally negligent homicide since there is a reasonable basis upon which the jury could have found that the defendant failed to perceive the risk inherent in his actions. The defendant's conduct and claimed lack of perception, together with the belief of the victim and defendant's followers, if accepted by the jury, would justify a verdict of guilty of criminally negligent homicide. There was testimony, both from defendant and from one of his followers, that the victim himself perceived no danger, but in fact volunteered to participate. Additionally, at least one of the defendant's followers testified that the defendant had previously performed this ritual without causing injury. Assuming that a jury would not believe that the defendant was capable of performing the acts in question without harm to the victim, it still could determine that this belief held by the defendant and his followers was indeed sincere and that defendant did not in fact perceive any risk of harm to the victim.

That is not to say that the court should in every case where there is some subjective evidence of lack of perception of danger submit the lesser crime of criminally negligent homicide. Rather, the court should look to other objective indications of a defendant's state of mind to corroborate, in a sense, the defendant's own subjective articulation. . . .

Therefore, on the particular facts of this case, we conclude that there is a reasonable view of the evidence which, if believed by the jury, would support a finding that the defendant was guilty only of the crime of criminally negligent homicide, and that the trial court erred in not submitting, as requested, this lesser offense to the jury.

Accordingly, we would reverse and order a new trial.

GABRIELLI, Judge (dissenting).

. . . [T]he evidence established defendant's awareness and conscious disregard of the risk his ceremony created and is entirely inconsistent with a negligent failure to perceive that risk. Testimony was adduced that just prior to being stabbed, Goings, a voluntary participant up to that point, objected to continuance of the ceremony saying, "No, father" and that defendant, obviously envincing an awareness of the possible result of his actions, answered, "It will be all right, son." Defendant testified that after the ceremony, he noticed blood seeping from the victim's wounds and that he attempted to stop the flow by bandaging the mortally wounded Goings. Defendant further stated that when he later learned that Goings had been removed to another location and had been given something to ease the pain, he became "uptight," indicating, of course, that defendant appreciated the risks involved and the possible consequences of his acts.

Examination of the two homicide sections of the Penal Law, here involved, is important.

> A person is guilty of manslaughter in the second degree when: 1. He recklessly causes the death of another person" (Penal Law, §125.15, subd. 1); and subdivision 3 of section 15.05 provides that a person acts "recklessly" with respect to a result when he is aware of and disregards a substantial and unjustifiable risk that such result will occur.
>
> A person is guilty of criminally negligent homicide when, with criminal negligence, he causes the death of another person" (Penal Law, §125.10); and a person acts with "criminal negligence" with respect to a result when he fails to perceive a substantial and unjustifiable risk that such result will occur (Penal Law, §15.05, subd. 4).

Simply stated, a reckless offender (manslaughter) is aware of the risk and consciously disregards it; whereas, on the other hand, the "criminally negligent" offender is not aware of the risk created and cannot thus be guilty of disregarding it.

Can it be reasonably claimed or argued that, when the defendant inflicted the several stab wounds, one of which penetrated the victim's heart and was four and three quarter inches deep, the defendant failed to perceive the risk? The only and obvious answer is simply "no."

Moreover, the record is devoid of evidence pointing toward a *negligent* lack of perception on defendant's part. The majority concludes otherwise by apparently crediting the testimony of defendant, and one of his followers, that at the time defendant was plunging knives into the victim, the defendant thought "there was no danger to it." However, it is readily apparent that the quoted statement does not mean, as the majority assert, that defendant saw no risk of harm in the ceremony, but, rather, that he thought his powers so extraordinary that resultant injury was impossible. Thus, the testimony does not establish defendant's negligent perception for even a grossly negligent individual would perceive the patent risk of injury that would result from plunging a knife into a human being; instead, the testimony demonstrates defendant's conscious disregard of the possible consequences that would naturally flow from his acts.

This case might profitably be analogized to one where an individual believing himself to be possessed of extraordinary skill as an archer attempts to duplicate William Tell's feat and split an apple on the head of another individual from some distance. However, assume that rather than hitting the apple, the archer kills the victim. Certainly, his obtuse subjective belief in his extraordinary skill would not render his actions criminally negligent. Both, in the context of ordinary understanding and Penal Law definition, the archer was unquestionably reckless and would, therefore, be guilty of manslaughter in the second degree. The present case is indistinguishable.

Notes and Questions

1. Do you believe that the defendant actually thought he would cause no harm to the victim by thrusting three knives and an ax into his chest? Could anyone be that stupid? If not, why reverse the case?

2. Examine this case from the National Law Journal, Mar. 14, 1983, at 4:

Mother Said That She Was Told to Sit on Child, Who Died

San Jose, Calif.—A jury trial began last week over whether a 200-pound woman was grossly negligent or reckless in following a counselor's alleged advice to discipline her 8-year-old son by sitting on him.

Betty Mentry, 45, an electronics worker here, was charged with involuntary manslaughter after her son, Stephen, died last May 31 when she sat on him for the fourth time. People v. Mentry, 84637 (Santa Clara County Superior Court).

Meantime, Ms. Mentry is suing the Alum Rock Communications Center, a San Jose counseling service funded by the county with state money, for allegedly advising her to sit on her son. Her malpractice suit seeks $2.5 million. Mentry v. Alum Rock Communications, Inc., 517164 (Santa Clara County Superior Court).

Police had suggested to Ms. Mentry to take her son to Alum Rock to break him of a stealing habit, said local lawyer Cyril R. Ash, Jr., who represents her in both the civil and the criminal cases.

Mr. Ash claims that center counselor Jorge Sousa "insisted" that Ms. Mentry use a technique developed in the 1960s by Dr. Milton H. Erickson of New York. Mr. Sousa, the attorney said, threatened to advise the courts to remove Stephen from her custody if she refused to follow his advice.

The technique consisted, literally, of sitting on the child to make him understand who was in charge. Mr. Ash said Dr. Erickson detailed the case of a 27-year-old woman with an 8-year-old son who "refused to respond to punishment" until, as advised, his mother "threw him quickly to the floor on his stomach and sat her full weight upon him."

"I was to eat in front of him and I was to talk on the telephone [while sitting on Stephen]," Ms. Mentry testified at a preliminary examination in the criminal case last August. "I was supposed to act like I was having a gay old time. [Mr. Sousa] assured me that Stephen would yell, scream and cuss and carry on, and I was to ignore him. And when it was over, he said he was positive that Stephen would have the message that I was in charge."

The woman said she sat her "full weight" on her son for eight hours the first time she used the technique. On the next two occasions, she said, she sat on him for a half hour and for 1½ hours. The last time, she sat on him for two hours before she noticed he had stopped breathing. He died nine days later.

Mr. Ash claims the counselor failed in his duty to warn her of any danger. In fact, he said, "the counselor assured her no harm would come to the boy." And Ms. Mentry, he said, is "the type of individual who tends to follow such instructions explicitly."

The counselor's threat to strip her of custody, he said, also is enough to absolve her of any crime.

But a person is responsible for exercising a certain amount of common sense, said John F. Marshall, a Santa Clara County deputy district attorney.

"Even somebody who's less intelligent than normal, when a kid says, 'I can't breathe,' you do something about it," he said. "And if you don't, that's gross negligence."

Ms. Mentry's 11-year-old daughter, Sherry, testified at the preliminary hearing that she walked into the room and heard her brother say he couldn't breathe. Lawyers were expected to use her preliminary hearing testimony rather than bring her back to the stand at trial.

Alum Rock's director, George Doub, denied Ms. Mentry's allegations, saying his counselors never advised her to sit on her son. He called her claim a "unique shift of blame."

Mr. Sousa has been unavailable for comment.

Was Ms. Mentry grossly negligent? Were the counselors? What standard should be used to determine this question? That of a reasonable person or that of a person with the common sense or intelligence of the defendant?

3. Examine the facts of Gian-Cursio v. State, 180 So. 2d 396 (Fla. Dist. Ct. App. 1965).

> The record discloses that one Roger Mozian died of pulmonary tuberculosis in May of 1963. His disease had been diagnosed in 1951 by Dr. Matis, a New York medical doctor in whose charge he remained for some ten years, during which his tuberculosis continued dormant or arrested. An X-ray examination of Mozian by Dr. Matis in January of 1962 showed his disease had become active. Dr. Matis recommended hospitalization and drug treatment, which Mozian refused. Mozian went under the care of Dr. Gian-Cursio, a licensed chiropractic physician in the State of New York, who practiced Natural Hygiene. Dr. Gian-Cursio was advised that Mozian was suffering from tuberculosis. His treatment of the patient was without drugs and by a vegetarian diet, interspersed with fasting periods. Evidence was in conflict as to length of fasting. There was testimony that on occasion the fasting continued 14 days. Dr. Epstein was a licensed chiropractic physician of Florida. Acting with Dr. Gian-Cursio and under his direction, Dr. Epstein operated a home or establishment for patients in Dade County, Florida. Beginning in the winter of 1962, on the advice of Dr. Gian-Cursio, Mozian went there and was treated by the appellant doctors, in the manner stated above. Eventually, in May of 1963 he was hospitalized, where through other doctors he was given drugs and other approved treatment for the disease but within a matter of days he died, on May 16, 1963. There was testimony that the treatment given Mozian was not approved medical treatment for one with active tuberculosis, and that had he been treated by approved medical methods and given available drugs his disease could have been arrested or controlled.

The court went on to discuss the criminal negligence standard:

> [C]riminal negligence exists where the physician or surgeon, or person assuming to act as such, exhibits gross lack of competency, or gross inattention, or criminal indifference to the patient's safety, and that this may arise from his gross ignorance of the science of medicine or surgery and of the effect of the remedies employed, through his gross negligence in the application and selection of remedies and his lack of proper skill in the use of instruments, or through his failure to give proper instructions to the patient as to the use of the medicines; that where the person treating the case does nothing that a skillful person might not do, and death results merely from an error of judgment on his part, or an inadvertent mistake, he is not criminally liable.

Were Gian-Cursio and/or Epstein criminally negligent? Is it significant that they were licensed chiropractors? Does it matter that Mozian chose of his own free will the treatment he wanted?

STATE v. WILLIAMS

Court of Appeals of Washington
4 Wash. App. 908, 484 P.2d 1167 (1971)

HOROWITZ, Chief Judge.

Defendants, husband and wife, were charged by information filed October 3, 1968, with the crime of manslaughter for negligently failing to supply their 17-month child with necessary medical attention, as a result of which he died on September 12, 1968. Upon entry of findings, conclusions and judgment of guilty, sentences were imposed on April 22, 1969. Defendants appeal.

The defendant husband, Walter Williams, is a 24-year-old full-blooded Sheshont Indian with a sixth-grade education. His sole occupation is that of laborer. The defendant wife, Bernice Williams, is a 20-year-old part Indian with an eleventh-grade education. At the time of the marriage, the wife had two children, the younger of whom was a 14-month-old son. Both parents worked and the children were cared for by the 85-year-old mother of the defendant husband. The defendant husband assumed parental responsibility with the defendant wife to provide clothing, care and medical attention for the child. Both defendants possessed a great deal of love and affection for the defendant wife's young son.

The court expressly found:

> That both defendants were aware that William Joseph Tabafunda was ill during the period September 1, 1968 to September 12, 1968. The defendants were ignorant. They did not realize how sick the baby was. They thought that the baby had a toothache and no layman regards a toothache as dangerous to life. They loved the baby and gave him aspirin in hopes of improving its condition. They did not take the baby to a doctor because of fear that the Welfare Department would take the baby away from them. They knew that medical help was available because of previous experience. They had no excuse for not taking the baby to a doctor.
>
> The defendants Walter L. Williams and Bernice J. Williams were negligent in not seeking medical attention for William Joseph Tabafunda.
>
> That as a proximate result of this negligence, William Joseph Tabafunda died. . . .

Defendants take no exception to findings but contend that the findings do not support the conclusions that the defendants are guilty of manslaughter as charged. . . .

. . . On the question of the quality or seriousness of breach of the duty, at common law, in the case of involuntary manslaughter, the breach had to amount to more than mere ordinary or simple negligence—gross negligence was essential. In Washington, however, RCW 9.48.060 . . . and RCW 9.48.150 supersede both voluntary and involuntary manslaughter as those crimes were defined at common law. Under these statutes the crime is deemed committed even though the death of the victim is the proximate result of only simple or ordinary negligence.

The concept of simple or ordinary negligence describes a failure to exercise the "ordinary caution" necessary to make out the defense of excusable homicide. Ordinary caution is the kind of caution that a man of reasonable prudence would exercise under the same or similar conditions. If, therefore, the conduct of a defendant, regardless of his ignorance, good intentions and good faith, fails to measure up to the conduct required of a man of reasonable prudence, he is guilty of ordinary negligence because of his failure to use "ordinary caution." If such negligence proximately causes the death of the victim, the defendant, as pointed out above, is guilty of statutory manslaughter. . . .

. . . The law does not mandatorily require that a doctor be called for a child at the first sign of any indisposition or illness. The indisposition or illness may appear to be of a minor or very temporary kind, such as a toothache or cold. If one in the exercise of ordinary caution fails to recognize that his child's symptoms require medical attention, it cannot be said that the failure to obtain such medical attention is a breach of the duty owed. In our opinion, the duty as formulated in People v. Pierson, 176 N.Y. 201, 68 N.E. 243 (1903) . . . properly defines the duty contemplated by our manslaughter statutes RCW 9.48.060 and RCW 9.48.150. The court there said:

> We quite agree that the Code does not contemplate the necessity of calling a physician for every trifling complaint with which the child may be afflicted, which in most instances may be overcome by the ordinary household nursing by members of the family; that a reasonable amount of discretion is vested in parents, charged with the duty of maintaining and bringing up infant children; and that the standard is at what time would an ordinarily prudent person, solicitous for the welfare of his child and anxious to promote its recovery, deem it necessary to call in the services of a physician.

It remains to apply the law discussed to the facts of the instant case.

Because of the serious nature of the charge against the parent and stepparent of a well-loved child, and out of our concern for the protection of the constitutional rights of the defendants, we have made an independent examination of the evidence to determine whether it substantially supports the court's express finding on proximate cause and its implied finding that the duty to furnish medical care became activated in time to prevent death of the child.

Dr. Gale Wilson, the autopsy surgeon and chief pathologist for the King County Coroner, testified that the child died because an abscessed tooth had been allowed to develop into an infection of the mouth and cheeks, eventually becoming gangrenous. This condition, accompanied by the child's inability to eat, brought about malnutrition, lowering the child's resistance and eventually producing pneumonia, causing the death. Dr. Wilson testified that in his opinion the infection had lasted for approximately 2 weeks, and that the odor generally associated with gangrene would have been present for approximately 10 days before death. He also expressed the opinion that had medical care been first obtained in the last week before the baby's death, such care would have been obtained too late to have saved the baby's life. Accordingly, the baby's apparent condition between September 1 and September 5, 1968 became the critical period for the purpose of determining whether in the exercise of ordinary caution defendants should have provided medical care for the minor child.

The testimony concerning the child's apparent condition during the critical period is not crystal clear, but is sufficient to warrant the following statement of the matter. The defendant husband testified that he noticed the baby was sick about 2 weeks before the baby died. The defendant wife testified that she noticed the baby was ill about a week and a half or 2 weeks before the baby died. The evidence showed that in the critical period the baby was fussy; that he could not keep his food down; and that a cheek started swelling up. The swelling went up and down, but did not disappear. In that same period, the cheek turned "a bluish color like." The defendants, not realizing that the baby was as ill as it was or that the baby was in danger of dying, attempted to provide some relief to the baby by giving the baby aspirin during the critical period and continued to do so until the night before the baby died. The defendants thought the swelling would go down and were waiting for it to do so; and defendant husband testified, that from what he had heard, neither doctors nor dentists pull out a tooth "when it's all swollen up like that." There was an additional explanation for not calling a doctor given by each defendant. Defendant husband testified that "the way the cheek looked . . . and that stuff on his hair, they would think we were neglecting him and take him away from us and not give him back." Defendant wife testified that the defendants were "waiting for the swelling to go down," and also that they were afraid to take the child to a doctor for fear that the doctor would report them to the welfare department, who, in turn, would take the child away. "It's just that I was so scared of losing him." They testified that they had heard that the defendant husband's cousin lost a child that way. The evidence showed that the defendants did not understand the significance or seriousness of the baby's symptoms. However, there is no evidence that the defendants were physically or financially unable to obtain a doctor, or that they did not know an available doctor, or that the symptoms did not continue to be a matter of concern during the critical period. Indeed, the evidence shows that in April 1968, defendant husband had taken the child to a doctor for medical attention.

In our opinion, there is sufficient evidence from which the court could find, as it necessarily did, that applying the standard of ordinary caution, i.e., the caution exercisable by a man of reasonable prudence under the same or similar conditions, defendants were sufficiently put on notice concerning the symptoms of the baby's illness and lack of improvement in the baby's apparent condition in the period from September 1 to September 5, 1968 to have required them to have obtained medical care for the child. The failure so to do in this case is ordinary or simple negligence, and such negligence is sufficient to support a conviction of statutory manslaughter.

The judgment is affirmed.

UTTER and WILLIAMS, JJ., concur.

Notes and Questions

1. What is the legal standard the court applies here? Would the defendants be guilty of manslaughter under the Model Penal Code? Would they be guilty of anything else?

2. What is the relevance of the fact that the defendants belonged to an insular minority that has suffered discrimination in the United States? Should they be held to the same standard of care that we require of someone in the dominant mainstream of America? If not, what would be the consequences of such a ruling?

In the words of a recent article in The Commentator (N.Y.U. Law School Newspaper), March 9, 1984, describing one well-known casebook (not this one!):

> Given the drastic editing of these cases, what values or policies are served by the inclusion of certain seemingly immaterial facts? For example, in State v. Williams . . . , the fact that the defendants were Shoshone Indians was left in the text of the case. The case is about the application of the reasonably prudent person standard. The defendant parents were convicted of manslaughter after their baby died from pneumonia resulting from an infected abscessed tooth. The parents hadn't taken the child to a doctor because they didn't realize how sick he was and because they were afraid that the doctor would report them to the welfare department who would take the baby away. They had heard of another Shoshone family who had lost their child that way. The state applied the standard of a reasonable white middle class parent, rather than determining the reasonableness of the defendants' conduct in context of their situation.
>
> In the note following the case, the editors acknowledge that many readers will find the decision to convict the parents of manslaughter unjust but fail to admit that part of this feeling may stem from a reader's recognition of the inequitable application of the reasonable person standard. Isn't it important to address the fact that racism probably played a role in the court's decision? [Law Women Find Sexism in 1L Casebook, at 7]

Is the author's criticism valid?

3. Would defendants have been charged and/or convicted if they had been Christian Scientists? Do religious beliefs have special immunity, where plain ignorance does not? Or should it depend on what the judges think of the

tenets of the religion? If so, does this help explain the result in People v. Strong, supra?

4. Under what conditions should we make allowance for the ignorance of one who causes a death? Should we say there is no criminal liability for negligence if someone did as well as he or she could? Is it fair to demand more of someone than he or she can deliver? Where a 17-year-old is charged with involuntary manslaughter, should we ask whether he or she fell below the standard to be expected of an ordinary American adult or of a 17-year-old? What about people who are stupid—or rash? Can we expect them to be otherwise? One criminal law authority[2] has analyzed the relation between subjective and objective components of negligence as follows:

> At least four different ideas interweave in the contrast expressed by the terms "objective" and "subjective." Note the following contrasts:
>
> 1. "Objective" standards are "standards of general application." "Subjective" standards by implication take "account of the infinite varieties of temperament, intellect and education which make the internal character of a given act so different."
>
> 2. "Objective standards" are external; they apply regardless of whether the actor thinks he is doing the right thing; "subjective" standards focus on the actor's state of mind.
>
> 3. The question of wrongdoing is an objective standard, for it focuses on the act in abstraction from the actor; the issue of attribution is subjective in the sense that it focuses on the actor's personal accountability for wrongdoing.
>
> 4. Standards are objective if they are factual; subjective, if they require a value judgment.
>
> The first two contrasts between "objective" and "subjective" liability find their genesis in Holmes' influential work and therefore we shall focus on these two in refuting Holmes' thesis that objective standards entail a utilitarian theory of law. Both of the first two contrasts are designed to establish that objective standards in the law are logically inescapable. The way Holmes sets up the contrast, he is unquestionably right. Standards must possess some generality; a standard hewn to the unique attributes of each person would be no standard at all.
>
> . . . [A]s used in Holmes' first contrast, the term "objective" is redundant. All standards are, to varying degrees, general. And there is nothing in the process of judging or the application of standards that supports a utilitarian theory of law.
>
> Holmes' case for a utilitarian theory of law finds critical support in the second dichotomy between objective or external standards and those that are rooted in the actor's state of mind. As indicated by Holmes' opinion in the leading case of Commonwealth v. Pierce [138 Mass. 165 (1884)] the alternative precluded by an objective standard would be one that took the defendant's own view of his conduct as controlling. In *Pierce,* the defendant, who was practicing publicly as a physician, had caused the death of a patient by applying kerosene-soaked flannels to her skin. Concluding that the standard of liability was "external," Justice Holmes wrote that the question was whether the treatment would

2. G. Fletcher, Rethinking Criminal Law 506-510 (1978).

have been "reckless in a man of reasonable prudence." In the context of the case, however, it is clear that all Holmes was concerned about was whether the defendant's view of the treatment would constitute a good defense. The point of saying that the standard was "external" was to stress that good faith was not a defense and that the defendant might be guilty even though he thought he was doing the prudent thing. . . .

Holmes' implicit strategy is to adopt the psychological or descriptive theory of guilt by equating the latter with the "condition of a man's heart or conscience." With this theory as his target, Holmes then rejects the requirement of guilt and blameworthiness in particular cases. There is no doubt that the psychological theory of guilt ought to be rejected, but Holmes' mistake consists in not considering alternative theories for properly holding individuals accountable for their wrongdoing. If he had considered these alternatives, he might have tempered his commitment to the calculus of utility as the only rational account of the criminal law.

The argument of this book is precisely that there is an alternative mode for assessing individual culpability and accountability for wrongdoing. That alternative mode is expressed in the claim that the analysis of liability consists of both an objective and a subjective dimension. The objective dimension focuses on the act and, in some cases, on the harm that actor causes. The subjective dimension focuses on the actor and the question whether the particular actor is accountable for the act of wrongdoing. The assessment of attribution and accountability obviously requires the application of standards to the particular situation of the actor. As worked out more elaborately in the theory of excuses, the standard has a variety of forms, but it always recurs to the same normative question: could the actor have been fairly expected to avoid the act of wrongdoing? Did he or she have fair opportunity to perceive the risk, to avoid the mistake, to resist the external pressure, or to counteract the effects of mental illness? This is the critical question that renders the assessment of liability just. And when sanctions are justly imposed, there is no need to assume, as does Holmes, that the determination of liability sacrifices innocent individuals.

3. Misdemeanor Manslaughter

UNITED STATES v. WALKER

Court of Appeals of District of Columbia
380 A.2d 1388 (1977)

Before KELLY, KERN and YEAGLEY, Associate Judges.

KERN, Associate Judge.

Appellee was charged with two counts of involuntary manslaughter and one count of carrying a pistol without a license (D.C. Code 1973, §22-3204). The government appeals from the trial court's dismissal of the count in the indictment which charged that appellee

> feloniously, in perpetrating and attempting to perpetrate the crime of carrying a pistol without a license, involving danger of injury, did shoot Ernestine Curry

> with a pistol, thereby causing injuries from which the said Ernestine Curry died. . . .[3]

At the hearing on appellee's motion to dismiss this count of the indictment, the government's proffer of evidence was that appellee, while carrying a pistol without a license, dropped it in the stairwell of an apartment building, and that the gun went off, fatally wounding a bystander. Appellee's proffer was that a firearms expert had determined that when the hammer of the pistol was not cocked, it would fire on impact only if dropped at a particular angle. These proffers constitute the only explanation in the record of the incident underlying the indictment.

There is no statutory definition of manslaughter in this jurisdiction;[4] this court had occasion in United States v. Bradford, D.C. App. 344, A.2d 208 (1975), however, to review at length the law of manslaughter in the District of Columbia. In respect to involuntary manslaughter, we said:

> Involuntary manslaughter is an unlawful killing which is unintentionally committed. By unintentionally it is meant that there is no intent to kill or to do bodily injury. The crime may occur as the result of an unlawful act which is a *misdemeanor involving danger of injury*. . . . The requisite intent in involuntary manslaughter is supplied by the intent to commit the misdemeanor, or by gross or criminal negligence. . . .
>
> The state of mind in involuntary manslaughter is characterized, on the one hand, by a lack of intent to cause death or injury and, on the other, by a lack of awareness of the consequences of the act amounting to an unreasonable failure of perception [criminal negligence] or *the intention to do an act which is a misdemeanor and is in some way dangerous.*

We defined the elements of involuntary manslaughter as: "(1) an unlawful killing of a human being (2) with either (a) *the intent to commit a misdemeanor dangerous in itself* or (b) an unreasonable failure to perceive the risk of harm to others." Id. at 216, emphasis added.

This appeal therefore presents for our determination the question whether the unlawful act of carrying a pistol without a license is also a dangerous act. The pertinent statute provides:

> No person shall within the District of Columbia carry either openly or concealed on or about his person, except in his dwelling house or place of business or on other land possessed by him, a pistol, without a license therefor issued as hereinafter provided. . . . [D.C. Code 1973, §22-3204.]

Appellee . . . argues that the plain intent of Section 3204 is to stop the prohibited conduct *before* danger of injury arises, and that such danger is not a

3. Another count of the indictment charged appellee with involuntary manslaughter in shooting Curry "unlawfully, feloniously, and with gross negligence" thereby fatally injuring her.
4. The Code specifies only the punishment for manslaughter. D.C. Code 1973, §22-2405.

necessary concomitant of the offense. Appellee proceeds to illustrate what he deems to be the "essence" of the offense of carrying a pistol without a license by the following hypothetical:

> [T]wo persons [are] walking peaceably on a public street carrying holstered pistols. One . . . has a license to carry a pistol, but the other has no license. The second person is violating section 3204, and the first is not. Yet there is no difference between them in terms of the danger presented to others. . . .

Appellee's hypothetical and argument notwithstanding, we conclude that carrying a pistol without a license exposes the community to such inherent risk of harm that when death results, even though an unintended consequence, the defendant may be nonetheless charged with involuntary manslaughter. Appellee in the instant case was carrying a loaded handgun, which, so far as the record shows, had no purpose other than its use as a weapon. . . .

Additionally, we think it significant in assessing the dangerousness vel non of the unlawful act of carrying a pistol without a license that Congress has expressly required one who seeks the license to be "a suitable person to be so licensed." Issuance of these licenses is the responsibility of the Chief of the Metropolitan Police Department, and is subject to restrictive regulations which, among other things, require the applicant to be of sound mind, to be without prior criminal record, not be an alcoholic or user of narcotics, to "be trained and experienced in the use, functioning and safe operation of the pistol," and finally, "to be free from physical defects which would impair his safe use of the weapon."

Thus, taking up appellee's hypothetical of the two persons carrying pistols on a public street, one of whom is licensed and the other of whom is not, we conclude that Congress intended to preclude the non-licensee from being on the street with his weapon because of the danger he posed to the community as a result (1) of the inherent dangerousness of the weapon he carried, and (2) of the absence of any evidence of his capability to carry safely such a dangerous instrumentality. . . .

. . . We now hold that a charge of violation of Section 3204 resulting in the shooting and death of another validly charges involuntary manslaughter because the misdemanor of carrying a pistol without a license is dangerous in and of itself. Accordingly, the trial court's order must be reversed and the count at issue restored to the indictment.

So ordered.

Notes and Questions

1. Was Walker guilty of negligence in his handling of the pistol? Was his conviction based on such a finding?

2. Note that the court does not seem interested in the *mens rea* of the defendant with respect to the death. Rather, the court merely asks whether the

death resulted from the commission of a misdemeanor. What moral theory allows this kind of increase in criminal liability where the result of committing a relatively minor crime is the death of a human being? Isn't this precisely the view that the court rejected in *Faulkner?* Isn't the element analysis of the Model Penal Code designed to prevent just this?

3. The Model Penal Code rejected the misdemeanor-manslaughter rule. The commentary to §210.3 of the recent edition of the Code explains why:

> The common law recognized a manslaughter version of the felony-murder doctrine. Commonly called the misdemeanor-manslaughter rule, it too imposed strict liability for homicide. Baldly stated, the rule punished as involuntary manslaughter any homicide caused in the commission or attempted commission of an unlawful act. The unlawful act was usually a misdemeanor, though the rule was not so limited in every jurisdiction. Indeed, some statutes still bring within their sweep homicide caused by conduct violative of a civil ordinance. Additionally, the rule applies in some jurisdictions to felonies that are excluded by statute or decision from operation of the felony-murder doctrine. . . .
>
> However explained and confined, the misdemeanor-manslaughter rule is objectionable. . . . It dispenses with proof of culpability and imposes liability for a serious crime without reference to the actor's state of mind. This result is not only morally unjustified, but it also operates quite inequitably among individuals. Application of the rule in the context of traffic offenses illustrates the point. Speed limits are in part set to prevent accidents dangerous to life. Occasionally, speeding causes the death of another in circumstances in which the actor was unaware of the risk of death and indeed cannot even be judged negligent with respect thereto. Subjecting such a driver, who is engaged in behavior so like many others, to a severe prison term introduces an unfair haphazardness to criminal punishment. For reasons explained more fully in connection with the felony-murder rule, the Model Code rejects any form of strict liability in the law of homicide.
>
> Most modern codifications and proposals follow the Model Penal Code in abolishing the misdemeanor-manslaughter rule. There are, however, at least 12 reform efforts that continue the rule in some form. There are in addition a number of jurisdictions which have not recently revised their codes and in which the common-law rule is substantially retained.

PEOPLE v. GOODMAN

Court of Appeals of New York
44 N.Y.S.2d 715 (1943)

BERGAN, Justice.

Defendant has been indicted by the grand jury of Sullivan County for manslaughter, first degree. Having inspected the minutes, he moves for a dismissal of the indictment upon the ground that the proof before the grand jury is insufficient to sustain the charge.

The proof upon which the indictment is founded is that on October 2, 1943, about noon, the defendant was driving an automobile on Route 17, a main highway, easterly between Livingston Manor and Liberty. Anna Husch, a girl eighteen years old, was walking along the highway in the same direction. Defendant stopped his car and asked the girl if she wanted a ride. She said she was going only a short distance, but the defendant persuaded her to get in the car.

The car was started, and almost immediately thereafter, when it had reached a rate of speed of about 25 miles an hour, the defendant said to the girl that he would pay her one dollar to have sexual intercourse. She immediately opened the door of the car, hesitated a moment on the running board, and jumped. Her skull was fractured in the fall and she died. The proof of the occurrences prior to the opening of the door of the car rests upon admissions of defendant. The opening of the door, the momentary hesitation, and the jump from the car were independently established by the testimony of a witness in a car following that of defendant. The defendant did not stop his car, but continued on and drove home. Defendant is a man about 28 years old and is apparently one of limited intelligence. There was no proof before the jury that he made any physical move toward the deceased or did anything except to make the proposal which has been described.

Upon these facts, I think, a jury could find felonious homicide. The proposal made to the deceased was itself a felony. Any person who shall induce or entice any woman or girl for the purpose of prostitution "or for any other immoral purpose" or attempt to do so "shall be deemed guilty of a felony." Penal Law, §2460, subd. 3. The proposal established before the jury was therefore at least an attempt within the statute. . . . From the close proximation in time between the invitation to the girl to get into the car and the crime, a jury might find the entire course of events was in furtherance of the crime, and upon this question could consider defendant's failure to stop his car after the deceased had jumped from it.

Where one person, by the felonious or wrongful act of another, has reasonable ground to believe himself in danger, his act in escaping that danger and a consequent injury or death are deemed to arise from the original wrongful act. And I do not perceive the difference in principle in the rule to be applied between the apprehension of danger from assault by a burglar who breaks into a house at night, or the apprehension of one who believes his life in danger at the hands of another bent on doing him injury, and the reasonable fear by a young girl of attack or assault at the hands of one who suddenly and feloniously proposes an act of prostitution. The difference is not one of degree, but of factual detail, and a jury could find from these facts that she acted reasonably for her own safety under the force of substantial apprehension of immediate danger suggested by an outrageous proposal. Thus, under general principles of law, the death is to be deemed the natural consequence of the wrongful act, if a jury so find.

The bullet or the blow are not the sole means of homicide. It is not always to be dependent upon direct physical force, or even upon an agency such as poison. . . .

. . . That one who, by unlawful means, creates a well-grounded fear of danger in another prompting an attempt at self-protective escape resulting in injury or death is criminally answerable for such a consequence is almost universally recognized. . . .

Somewhat similar to the facts in this case were those considered in 1915 by the Court of Kings Bench of Quebec on appeal in Rex v. Valade, 26 Canadian Crim. Cases 233. Defendant took a girl under age of consent to a secluded apartment and had sexual intercourse. She apparently went freely to the apartment. Afterward she jumped out of the window to get away from him and was killed by the fall. Lacking legal consent, the court felt she was in the apartment "by constructive force," and since defendant had charge of her by such constructive force he was responsible for her act of escaping. Trenholme, J., remarked: "If he threw her out at the window, or drove her by fright to jump out of the window, it would have been murder."

A jury might say that deceased was placed in substantial apprehension of danger by defendant's criminal act in the circumstances then surrounding her. Her apprehension would necessarily be examined from her viewpoint at the time and considered in the light of her action. The jury, therefore, could find that her escape was induced by the wrong and that defendant is responsible for its consequences. The facts may possibly fall within a higher degree of felonious homicide than that charge in the indictment, but with this, I suppose, the defendant cannot complain.

Motion denied.

Notes and Questions

1. Does the result in People v. Goodman strike you as a sound one? Can one argue that once a person undertakes to violate the law, he or she should be responsible for all the consequences, regardless of how far-fetched?

2. The modern trend is to deny such responsibility, and numerous limitations have been engrafted upon the misdemeanor manslaughter rule to narrow the kinds of underlying offenses which can provide the foundation for a misdemeanor manslaughter conviction.

The Model Penal Code commentary to §210.3 discusses some of these limitations:

> Recently, courts and legislatures have acted to limit the misdemeanor-manslaughter rule in a variety of ways that in general parallel limitations developed on the felony-murder rule. It has been held to apply generally to misdemeanors mala in se rather than mala prohibita. The authorities are divided on the question whether the misdemeanor-manslaughter rule can be based on an underlying crime that is itself one of strict liability, and there is substantial unanimity in limiting the rule's scope by confining notions of causation. At a minimum, death of another must result from the course of conduct constituting

an unlawful act. Some courts go farther and require that the homicide must be caused by that aspect of the defendant's conduct that renders it unlawful.[5] Thus, for example, a death caused while speeding would not fall within the rule if driving at the posted speed would not have avoided the occurrence. . . .

Mere coincidence of time and place of the unlawful act and a homicide is insufficient; there must be a direct causal connection between the unlawful act and the homicide. E.g., Commonwealth v. Williams, 133 Pa. Super. 104, 1 A.2d 812 (1938), where the defendant, a good driver who had failed to renew his driver's license, was forced off the road into a telephone pole by another vehicle, resulting in the death of his passenger. The court reversed a conviction of manslaughter because the unlawful act of driving without a license did not cause the death.

PEOPLE v. STUART

Supreme Court of California
302 P.2d 5 (1956)

TRAYNOR, Justice.

Defendant was charged by information with manslaughter, Pen. Code, §192. . . . He was convicted . . . by the court sitting without a jury. . . . He appeals from the judgment of conviction and the order denying his motion for a new trial.

Defendant was licensed as a pharmacist by this state in 1946 and has practiced here since that time. He holds a B.S. degree in chemistry from Long Island University and a B.S. degree in pharmacy from Columbia University. In April, 1954, he was employed as a pharmacist by the Ethical Drug Company in Los Angeles.

On July 16, 1954, he filled a prescription for Irvin Sills. It had been written by Dr. D.M. Goldstein for Sills' eight-day-old child. It called for "Sodium phenobarbital grains eight. Sodium citrate, drams three. Simple Syrup, ounces two. Aqua peppermint, ounces one. Aqua distilate QS, ounces four." Defendant assembled the necessary drugs to fill the prescription. He believed that the simple syrup called for was unavailable and therefore used syrup of orange. The ingredients were incompatible, and the syrup of orange precipitated out the phenobarbital. Defendant then telephoned Dr. Goldstein to ask if he could use some other flavoring. Dr. Goldstein told him that since it was midnight, if he could not find any simple syrup "it would be just as well to use another substance, elixir, mesopine, P.B." Defendant spoke to a clerk and learned that there was simple syrup behind the counter. He mixed the prescription with this syrup, put a label on the bottle according to the prescrip-

5. Commonwealth v. Samson, 130 Pa. Super. 65, 196 A. 564 (1938). Defendant operated an apartment house without a license in violation of a criminal statute. He argued that the fire which resulted in the death of several of his tenants would have occurred even if he had the license. The court upheld the manslaughter conviction on the grounds that he never would have received a license if he had applied, due to the condition of the apartment.

tion, and gave it to Sills. Sills returned home, put a teaspoonful of the prescription in the baby's milk and gave it to the baby. The baby died a few hours later.

Defendant stipulated that there was nitrite in the prescription bottle and that "the cause of death was methemoglobinemia caused by the ingestion of nitrite." When he compounded the prescription, there was a bottle containing sodium nitrite on the shelf near a bottle labeled sodium citrate. He testified that at no time during his employment at the Ethical Drug Company had he filled any prescription calling for sodium nitrite and that he had taken the prescribed three drams of sodium citrate from the bottle so labeled. [Apparently the sodium citrate bottle had contained sodium nitrite.]

There is nothing in the record to indicate that the contents of the bottle labeled sodium citrate could have been identified as containing sodium nitrite without laboratory analysis. There was testimony that at first glance sodium citrate and sodium nitrite are identical in appearance, that in form either may consist of small colorless crystals or white crystalline powder, that the granulation of the crystals may vary with the manufacturer, and that there may be a slight difference in color between the two. The substance from the bottle labeled sodium citrate was exhibited to the court, but no attempt was made to compare it with unadulterated sodium citrate or sodium nitrite. A chemist with Biochemical Procedures, Incorporated, testified that the mixture did not appear to be homogenous but that from visual observation alone he could not identify the crystals as one substance or the other. Defendant testified that he had no occasion before July 16th to examine or fill any prescription from the sodium citrate bottle.

No evidence whatever was introduced that would justify an inference that defendant knew or should have known that the bottle labeled sodium citrate contained sodium nitrite. On the contrary, the undisputed evidence shows conclusively that defendant was morally entirely innocent and that only because of a reasonable mistake or unavoidable accident was the prescription filled with a substance containing sodium nitrite. Section 20 of the Penal Code[6] makes the union of act and intent or criminal negligence an invariable element of every crime unless it is excluded expressly or by necessary implication. Moreover, section 26 of the Penal Code lists among the persons incapable of committing crimes "[p]ersons who committed the act or made the omission charge under an ignorance or mistake of fact, which disproves any criminal intent," subd. 4, and "[p]ersons who committed the act or made the omission charged through misfortune or by accident, when it appears that there was no evil design, intention, or culpable negligence." The question is thus presented whether a person can be convicted of manslaughter[7] . . . in the absence of any evidence of criminal intent or criminal negligence.

6. "In every crime or public offense there must exist a union, or joint operation of act and intent, or criminal negligence."

7. California Penal Code §192: "Manslaughter is the unlawful killing of a human being without malice. It is of three kinds:

The answer to this question as it relates to the conviction of manslaughter depends on whether or not defendant committed an "unlawful act" within the meaning of section 192 of the Penal Code when he filled the prescription. The Attorney General contends that even if he had no criminal intent and was not criminally negligent, defendant violated section 26280 of the Health and Safety Code and therefore committed an unlawful act within the meaning of section 192 of the Penal Code.

Section 26280 of the Health and Safety Code provides: "The manufacture, production, selling, offering for sale, advertising or keeping for sale within the State of California . . . of any drug or device which is adulterated or misbranded is prohibited."[8] In view of the analyses of the contents of the prescription bottle and the bottle labeled sodium citrate and defendant's stipulation, there can be no doubt that he prepared, compounded, and sold an adulterated and misbranded drug.

Because of the great danger to the public health and safety that the preparation, compounding, or sale of adulterated or misbranded drugs entails, the public interest in demanding that those who prepare, compound, or sell drugs make certain that they are not adulterated or misbranded and the belief that although an occasional nonculpable offender may be punished, it is necessary to incur that risk by imposing strict liability to prevent the escape of great numbers of culpable offenders, public welfare statutes like section 26280 are not ordinarily governed by section 20 of the Penal Code and therefore call for the sanctions imposed even though the prohibited acts are committed without criminal intent or criminal negligence.

It does not follow, however, that such acts, committed without criminal intent or criminal negligence, are unlawful acts within the meaning of section 192 of the Penal Code, for it is settled that this section is governed by section 20 of the Penal Code. Thus, in People v. Penny, 44 Cal. 2d 861, 877-880, 285 P.2d 926, 936, we held that "there was nothing to show that the Legislature intended to except section 192 of the Penal Code from the operation of section 20 of the same code" and that the phrase "without due caution and circumspection" in section 192 was therefore the equivalent of criminal negligence. Since section 20 also applies to the phrase "unlawful act," the act in question must be committed with criminal intent or criminal negligence to be an un-

---

1. Voluntary—upon a sudden quarrel or heat of passion.

2. Involuntary—in the commission of an unlawful act, not amounting to felony; or in the commission of a lawful act which might produce death, in an unlawful manner, or without due caution and circumspection; provided that this subdivision shall not apply to acts committed in the driving of a vehicle. . . . Penal Code §192.

8. "A drug shall be deemed to be adulterated . . . (4) if any substance has been (a) mixed or packed therewith so as to reduce its quality or strength; or (b) substituted wholly or in part therefor." Health and Safety Code, §26235.

"The term 'misbranded' shall apply to all drugs or devices, the package or label of which bears any statement, design, or emblem regarding such article or the ingredients or substances contained therein which shall be false or misleading in any particular. . . ." Health and Safety Code §26240.

lawful act within the meaning of section 192. By virtue of its application to both phrases, section 20 precludes the incongruity of imposing on the morally innocent the same penalty, appropriate only for the culpable. Words such as "unlawful act, not amounting to a felony" have been included in most definitions of manslaughter since the time of Blackstone and even since the time of Lord Hale, "unlawful act" as it pertains to manslaughter has been interpreted as meaning an act that aside from its unlawfulness was of such a dangerous nature as to justify a conviction of manslaughter if done intentionally or without due caution. To be an unlawful act within the meaning of section 192, therefore, the act in question must be dangerous to human life or safety and meet the conditions of section 20.

It follows, therefore, that only if defendant had intentionally or through criminal negligence prepared, compounded, or sold an adulterated or misbranded drug, would his violation of section 26280 of the Health and Safety Code be an unlawful act within the meaning of §192 of the Penal Code. . . . When, as in this case, however, the defendant did not know and could not reasonably be expected to know, that the sodium citrate bottle contained nitrite, those conditions are not met and there is therefore lacking the culpability necessary to make the act an unlawful act within the meaning of section 192. . . .

The judgment and order are reversed.

GIBSON, C.J., and SHENK, CARTER, SCHAUER, SPENCE, and MCCOMB, JJ., concur.

Notes and Questions

1. Does the court in *Stuart* renounce absolute liability as a basis for criminal punishment? Does it say that a misdemeanor-manslaughter conviction can never be founded upon a violation of §26280 of the Health and Safety Code? What does it say?

2. People v. Penny, cited by the court, involved a prosecution for involuntary manslaughter of a defendant who was practicing cosmetology without a license and who apparently applied too strong a solution to the face of his customer, with fatal results. The state had two theories: first that defendant was guilty of misdemeanor manslaughter and, second, that the defendant was guilty on a negligence theory. The court rejected the prosecution's misdemeanor manslaughter argument on the ground that no causation was shown between the lack of a cosmetology license and the death. It rejected the "without due caution and circumspection" argument on the ground that the trial judge had instructed the jury that civil negligence was enough. The court held that, at least in non-automobile cases, criminal negligence was required under

§192(2). One of its reasons was that §20 required for "every crime . . . a union or joint operation of act and intent or criminal negligence."

Does *Penny* really help the defendant in *Stuart*?

3. In People v. Nelson, 309 N.Y. 231, 128 N.E.2d 391 (1955) the defendant was convicted of manslaughter for the deaths of several of his tenants in an apartment building fire. The condition of the building violated certain fire regulations but the defendant argued that he did not know of the violations. The majority, in upholding the conviction, stated:

> In the case at bar the conviction must also be upheld. From the time of the appellant's acquisition of title to the date of the fire, a period of about one and one-half years, the lack of a secondary means of egress or a sprinkler system constituted a continuing misdemeanor "affecting the person . . . killed." . . . It is undeniable that a tremendous duty is placed upon the owners and those in charge of property under the applicable section of the Multiple Dwelling Law; however, it is quite apparent that the Legislature intended the burden to be onerous so that owners would be impressed with the consequences flowing from violation of the statute, which violations could so readily endanger human life in the congested conditions under which people must live in the city of New York.

Judge Van Voorhis, dissenting, argued:

> Appellant's defense was chiefly based upon his lack of knowledge or notice of the existence of these violations, but the trial court excluded such testimony upon the ground that the misdemeanors with which appellant was charged were mala prohibita, that he could be guilty of these violations of the Multiple Dwelling Law without having created or even knowing the condition of the building, and that, if the deaths of the persons named in the indictment resulted therefrom, he is automatically guilty of manslaughter regardless of culpable negligence and irrespective of any criminal intent. If the last conclusion is correct, it seems to me that the law has retreated a long distance into a stage of primitive formalism.
>
> Appellant had himself been a tenant in these premises for a number of years. He is . . . seventy-one years old whose education ended with the first grade in elementary school. His defense was that he had recently bought this real property; that he did so for a cash consideration of $1,000 and a purchase-money mortgage of $7,500, under threat of eviction by the former owner unless he became the owner; that these violations had been filed against the former owner without having been caused to be removed by the city department of housing and buildings, and were deliberately concealed from him by his vendor in order to induce him to purchase the property and to relieve the former owner of responsibility; that although there is a general recital in the deed that the conveyance is subject to building violations, he did not read it personally or know its full contents, and that the deed was recorded by the vendor's agent who procured it back from the register's office and kept it in his possession in order to prevent these matters from coming to appellant's attention. Appellant contends that he was in complete ignorance of these circumstances until he found himself confronted with a charge of manslaughter, but that the trial court withheld this

defense from the jury on the ground that criminal intent is unrelated to his guilt or innocence. . . .

The surest reply to the distorted view that criminal liability depends upon chance is to insist wherever possible upon moral guilt in felony convictions. Although the common-law crime of involuntary manslaughter has been superseded by statute, the Legislature should not readily be deemed to have required manslaughter convictions without criminal intent. Death caused by a person "engaged in committing a misdemeanor" was designed to mean by a person consciously engaged in committing a misdemeanor. Criminal intent is not a necessary factor in some misdemeanors, and may not be required in case of violations of these sections of the Multiple Dwelling Law. But under the doctrine of transferred intent, which is as applicable to manslaughter growing out of misdemeanor under section 1050, subd. 1 of the Penal Law as it is in felony murder under section 1044, subd. 2, it by no means follows that the Legislature intended to create constructive criminal liability to the felony charge. "Outside of a narrow class of exceptions, punishment is meted out by the law of crimes for specific unlawful intent." Such crimes as are merely mala prohibita are of lesser magnitude and, even in such instances, are strictly construed. The general minor character of such offenses is thus described in People v. D'Antonio, "There is no doubt about the general rule that one cannot be convicted of a crime without proving a criminal intent; but this rule has its exceptions. Statutes which are in their nature police regulations, as the one here under consideration is, impose criminal penalties, irrespective of any intent and obviously for the purpose of requiring a degree of diligence for the protection of the public against violations." Manslaughter is not a police regulation, and is not lightly to be regarded as having been intended by the Legislature to be capable of being sustained without evidence of criminal intent in the commission of the underlying misdemeanor. . . .

Knowingly to neglect to provide proper means of egress in case of fire would constitute malum in se in the form of culpable negligence. That charge is not before us. Elimination of knowledge of the existence of a statutory violation as a factor in misdemeanors consisting in violations of the Multiple Dwelling Law, renders such misdemeanors mala prohibita. No one questions that an owner is guilty of misdemeanor even though he is ignorant of the building violation. But to have been found guilty of misdemeanor manslaughter, a defendant should have known at least of the existence of the underlying offense, yet the trial court ruled and instructed the jury on this count in the indictment, that not only was this defendant held to strict compliance with this statute (which was correct so far as being guilty of the misdemeanor went), but that neither ignorance of the condition of the building nor of the Multiple Dwelling Law was a defense to first degree manslaughter. This was almost equivalent to charging the jury that he was guilty under the first count as matter of law. Defendant's counsel duly excepted to these portions of the charge and to the rulings excluding evidence of that character. . . .

The conviction should be reversed and a new trial granted.

Judge Van Voorhis's dissent suggests that the majority holding would rest criminal liability "upon chance." Is that true here? Is this case like People v. Stuart?

4. Vehicular Homicide

The automobile is so common in our society today that many states have defined a category of criminal homicide less severe than involuntary manslaughter, or even less severe than negligent homicide, for those who kill accidentally while operating an automobile. Some have argued that these laws reflect legislators' belief that invoking the general manslaughter principle would expose too large a percentage of the population to the risk of prosecution for a very serious crime. Alternatively, such statutes are often defended on the ground that, right or wrong, juries are not prepared to convict the ordinary motorist of a very serious crime—even when they find gross negligence in the operation of an automobile.

Yet another defense of such a statute is that, unlike many other kinds of negligent conduct which do not result in a death, negligent driving of an automobile is punishable if no one is killed or injured. Thus, the entire burden of deterring grossly negligent conduct does not have to fall on those whose negligence in fact causes a death.

Typical vehicle homicide statutes follow:

KANSAS STAT. ANN.
(Rev. Stat. 1979)

§21-3405. Vehicular Homicide.

(1) Vehicular homicide is the killing of a human being by the operation of automobile, airplane, motor boat or other motor vehicle in a manner which creates an unreasonable risk of injury to the person or property of another and which constitutes a material deviation from the standard of care which a reasonable person would observe under the same circumstances.

(2) This section shall be applicable only when the death of the injured person ensues within one (1) year as the proximate result of the operation of a vehicle in the manner described in subsection (1) of this section.

(3) Vehicular homicide is a class A misdemeanor [punishable by one year in jail].

CALIFORNIA PENAL CODE

Penal Code §192. Manslaughter; Voluntary, Involuntary, and Vehicular, Construction of Section . . .

3. *Vehicular—*
   (a) Driving a vehicle, not involving drugs or alcohol and in the commission of an unlawful act, not amounting to a felony, and with gross negligence; or driving a vehicle, not involving drugs

or alcohol, and in the commission of a lawful act which might produce death, in an unlawful manner, and with gross negligence.

(b) Driving a vehicle in violation of Section 23152 (driving under the influence of alcohol) or 23153 of the Vehicle Code and in the commission of an unlawful act, not amounting to felony, but without gross negligence; or driving a vehicle in violation of Section 23152 or 23153 of the Vehicle Code and in the commission of a lawful act which might produce death, in an unlawful manner, and with gross negligence.

(c) Driving a vehicle in violation of Section 23152 or 23153 of the Vehicle Code and in the commission of an unlawful act, not amounting to felony, but without gross negligence; or driving a vehicle in violation of Section 23152 or 23153 of the Vehicle Code and in the commission of a lawful act which might produce death, in an unlawful manner, but without gross negligence.

(d) Driving a vehicle in violation of Section 23152 or 23153 of the Vehicle Code and in the commission of an unlawful act, not amounting to felony, but without gross negligence; or driving a vehicle in violation of Section 23152 or 23153 of the Vehicle Code and in the commission of a lawful act which might produce death, in an unlawful manner, but without gross negligence.

This section shall not be construed as making any homicide in the driving of a vehicle punishable which is not a proximate result of the commission of an unlawful act, not amounting to a felony, or of the commission of a lawful act which might produce death, in an unlawful manner.

[Vehicular homicides carry punishments ranging from 1-8 years in prison.]

COLORADO REV. STAT.

§18-3-106. Vehicular Homicide.

(1)(a) If a person operates or drives a motor vehicle in a reckless manner, and such conduct is the proximate cause of the death of another, he commits vehicular homicide. . . .

(1)(b)(I) If a person operates or drives a motor vehicle while under the influence of any drug or intoxicant and such conduct is the proximate cause of the death of another, he commits vehicular homicide. This is a strict liability crime. (II) For the purposes of this paragraph (b), being under the influence of any drug shall include the use of glue-sniffing, aerosol inhalation, or the inhalation of any other toxic vapor. . . .

(c) Vehicular homicide is a class 4 felony [punishable by up to 10 years in prison].

Vehicular homicide falls under the negligent homicide section of the Model Penal Code. Comment 4 to section 210.4 defends the decision not to have a separate vehicular homicide section:

> The structure of the Model Code homicide offenses obviates any necessity for special treatment of vehicular homicide. The case for such legislation arose in the first instance from the indiscriminate punishment of both reckless and negligent homicide as the serious crime of manslaughter. Under Section 210.4, this problem is solved by punishing all forms of negligent homicide as an offense of lesser grade. Furthermore, as is explained in the commentary to Section 2.02, the Model Code is opposed in principle to the imposition of criminal sanctions for ordinary negligence. If the evidence does not make out a case of negligent homicide, as defined in the Model Code, liability for the homicide, as distinct from the traffic offense, is unwarranted.

PORTER v. STATE

Supreme Court of Florida
88 So. 2d 924 (1956)

Roberts, Justice.

Appellant was convicted of manslaughter for causing the death of a human being by culpable negligence in the operation of his automobile, and has appealed from the judgment of conviction. The point for determination on this appeal is the sufficiency of the evidence to support the conviction.

The accident resulting in the death of the decedent occurred at 9:30 AM on a Saturday morning at a street intersection on the outskirts of the city of Bradenton, but apparently outside the city limits. The appellant was proceeding north on a street which was well marked with "stop" signs prior to its intersection with the street upon which the decedent was travelling in a westerly direction, and which was marked only with a "slow" sign. The right front of appellant's car collided with the left front and side of decedent's car. There was ample evidence from which the jury could find that the appellant was driving at the rate of 60 or 65 miles per hour and did not stop before entering the intersection.

"Culpable negligence," within the meaning of our manslaughter statute, Section 782.07, Fla. Stat. 1953, F.A.A., means negligence of "a gross and flagrant character, evincing reckless disregard of human life or of the safety of persons exposed to its dangerous effects; or that entire want of care which would raise the presumption of indifference to consequences; or such wantonness or recklessness or grossly careless disregard of the safety and welfare of the public, or that reckless indifference to the rights of others, which is equivalent to an intentional violation of them."

While excessive speed alone is not sufficient to support a conviction of manslaughter by culpable negligence, we think that appellant's action in "running" a stop sign at high rate of speed was, in the circumstances shown by this record, negligence of a "gross and flagrant character" within the definition of culpable negligence, quoted above.

Accordingly, the verdict and judgment of manslaughter should be and it is hereby

Affirmed.

DREW, Chief Justice (dissenting).

I cannot agree that the evidence in this cause sustains the verdict of manslaughter.

The accident occurred outside the city limits on a county road in the daylight. There is no evidence in the record establishing the speed limit in this area so we must presume that it was sixty miles per hour. The evidence in the light most favorable to the State establishes the speed of the car at about sixty miles per hour. The driver was perfectly sober and there is no suggestion to the contrary. The sole evidence of reckless driving is that he failed to stop or slow down at a stop street which crossed the highway on which he was travelling. The record shows there was a stop sign on the right side of the road 112 feet from the intersection but there is no evidence in the record that the defendant had ever traversed this road before or was familiar with the locality.

To sustain the conviction of the defendant in this case is tantamount to holding that if a person is killed because of the failure of a driver of an automobile to stop at a stop sign, such conduct constitutes in itself negligence of such gross and flagrant character that it evinces a reckless disregard of human life.

There are few, if any, of us who have not through momentary lapse of attention—particularly on strange roads—been guilty of traversing stop streets without slowing down. Such, no doubt, constitutes such negligence as to support a damage action, but I do not think it was ever intended that negligence of that kind was sufficient to support a verdict of manslaughter. It is exceedingly doubtful that such negligence would be sufficient to support an action for punitive damages. I think the case should be reversed. . . .

HOBSON and THORNAL, JJ. concur.

On rehearing granted.

O'CONNELL, Justice.

This cause is before us now on petition for rehearing of our opinion affirming the verdict and judgment of guilty of manslaughter.

Appellant, who will hereafter be referred to as defendant, was convicted of manslaughter for causing the death of a human being by culpable negligence in the operation of an automobile. The facts are set forth in the opinion and dissenting opinion rendered by the Court and filed on April 18, 1956 and will not be repeated herein.

From the evidence in this cause it appears that the only evidence of culpable negligence is that the appellant failed to stop at an intersection which was marked by (1) a perpendicular "stop" sign on the side of the road defendant was traveling and by (2) the word "stop" painted on the road. There is no evidence of heavy traffic, weather conditions or other unusual circumstances surrounding the accident or its locale, which was not in the corporate limits of any municipality. There is no evidence of or suggestion that the defendant was drinking or intoxicated. The accident happened in broad daylight. The speed limit we assume to be 60 miles per hour, and the evidence shows that the jury could have found the defendant to have been going between 60-65 miles per hour.

We feel that to sustain the conviction of the defendant under the facts in this cause will be tantamount to a holding that the death of a human being caused by the failure of the driver to stop at an intersection marked by stop sign constitutes, in and of itself, negligence of such a gross and flagrant character that it evinces a reckless disregard of human life. We do not believe that such was the intent of the legislature in enacting the statute in question.

There are few, if any, persons who drive automobiles who have not, through momentary lapse of attention, error of judgment, failing to see what they should have seen, particularly on roads not in municipalities, been guilty of running a stop sign at an intersection without slowing down. Such, no doubt, constitutes negligence sufficient to support a damage suit based on simple negligence. We doubt that it would support a verdict under our guest statute. Nor do we believe that it is sufficient to support a verdict of manslaughter.

True the jury was entitled to consider as evidence, all inferences which would logically flow from the proven facts. It does not follow logically, that one who runs a "stop" sign on a country road while travelling at a speed at or near the limit prescribed by law has exercised the entire want of care which would raise the presumption of a conscious indifference to consequences. Defendant was required to be proved guilty of culpable negligence beyond and to the exclusion of a reasonable doubt.

We feel that the evidence before the jury, taken with all inferences to be logically drawn therefrom, was insufficient to meet the required proof and to overcome the presumption of innocence of the defendant.

The verdict and judgment appealed from is—reversed, on rehearing granted, and we recede from the majority opinion on April 18, 1956.

Drew, C.J., and Terrell, Hobson and Thornal, JJ., concur.
Thomas and Roberts, JJ., dissent.

Notes and Questions

1. Was Porter reckless? Civilly negligent? Grossly negligent? Should a driver who ignores a stop sign at over 60 miles per hour escape criminal liability for a death caused by his driving?

2. Would a manslaughter charge have been more appropriate if Porter had been drunk? If the accident had happened at night? If Porter had been in his own neighborhood? Why?

3. What argument can you make for overturning the jury verdict here? Does the fact that the jury found Porter guilty refute Justice O'Connell's views on the driving habits of "ordinary" people?

4. Should the misdemeanor-manslaughter rule apply here? Is this case like *Stuart*?

5. In at least one state, the rule that ordinary negligence suffices to establish involuntary manslaughter if the accused causes the death through an "inherently dangerous instrumentality" (such as firearms) applies to motor vehicles. State v. Barnett, 218 S.C. 415, 63 S.E.2d 57 (1951). Does this rule make sense as applied to the automobile? Does it make sense as applied to firearms—or to anything else?

6. As we will see in the next chapter, some courts have begun developing a doctrine of vehicular *murder* for egregious, unintentional vehicular killings.

5. Corporate Homicide

COMMONWEALTH v. McILWAIN SCHOOL BUS LINES

Superior Court of Pennsylvania
423 A.2d 413 (1980)

SPAETH, Judge.

This is an appeal by the Commonwealth from an order quashing an information. The principal issue is whether a private corporation may be held criminally liable for homicide by vehicle. On April 3, 1978, a school bus owned by the McIlwain School Bus Lines, Inc. (hereinafter, the corporation) and operated by one of its employees, ran over and killed 6-year-old Lori Sharp; she had just gotten off the bus and was walking in front of it when she was run over. On May 26, 1978, the corporation was charged with homicide by vehicle. The corporation waived its right to a preliminary hearing, but subsequently filed a motion to quash the information against it. One ground of the motion was that by definition, the offense could only be committed by a natural person, not by a corporation. . . .

. . . The statute provides:

> Any person who unintentionally causes the death of another person while engaged in the *violation of any law of the Commonwealth or municipal ordinance* applying to *the operation or use of a vehicle or to the regulation of traffic* is guilty of homicide by vehicle, a misdemeanor of the first degree, when the violation is *the cause of death.* 75 P.S. §3732. (Emphasis added.)

[T]he corporation filed a request for a bill of particulars, asking that the Commonwealth "[p]lease specify the law of this Commonwealth or municipal ordinance which the Defendant was violating which caused the death of Lori Sharp." The Commonwealth answered as follows:

> Sections 4551, 4552 of the Pennsylvania Vehicle Code require the Department of Transportation to promulgate rules and regulations pertaining to the equipment required on school buses.
>
> Specifically the rules and regulations require that a mirror be placed on the front of the bus which will permit the operator to see any pedestrian in front of the bus. This mirror was missing.
>
> Also the bus is required to be equipped with a rear view mirror to provide the operator with a proper view to the rear and side of the bus.
>
> The rear view mirror was not properly positioned to afford the operator proper view of the area.[9]

The criminal law has not always regarded a corporation as subject to criminal liability. Indeed, it was once widely accepted that a corporation was incapable of committing a criminal offense:

> This doctrine of nonliability for crime arose from the theory that a corporation, being an intangible entity, could neither commit a crime nor be subjected to punishment, because any illegal act of a corporate agent was done without authority of the corporation and ultra vires.

Today, however, it is generally recognized that a corporation may be held criminally liable for criminal acts performed by its agents on its behalf.

9. 75 Pa. C.S.A. §4551 provides:

> (a) General rule.—All school buses and all other vehicles used in the transportation of school children, owned by or under contract with any school district or parochial or private school, shall conform to standards prescribed by the department. Regulations shall be promulgated by the department governing the safe design, construction, equipment and operation of vehicles engaged in the transportation of school children.
>
> (b) Violation and penalty.—No person shall operate or permit the operation of a vehicle of a type specified in this subchapter which is not in compliance with the requirements of this subchapter or applicable regulations issued under this subchapter. Violation of this section constitutes a summary offense punishable by a fine not less than $50 nor more than $100.

Act of June 17, 1976, P.L. 162, No. 81 §1, eff. July 1, 1977, 75 Pa. C.S.A. §4551.

75 Pa. C.S.A. §4552(e) provides:

Visibility.—Every school bus shall be designed and equipped so as to provide the driver with an unobstructed view of any pedestrian in proximity to the vehicle.

See, e.g., United States v. Wise, 370 U.S. 405, 82 S. Ct. 1354, 8 L. Ed. 2d 590 (1962) (conspiracy, violation of Sherman Act); United States v. Johns-Manville Corporation, 231 F. Supp. 690 (E.D. Pa. 1964) (antitrust, conspiracy); People v. Schomig, 74 Cal. App. 109, 239 P. 413 (1925) (violation of legislation regulating real estate brokerages); West Valley Estates, Inc. v. Florida, Fla. App., 286 So. 2d 208 (1973) (violation of statute proscribing dredging of lands); Southern Ry. Co. v. State, 125 Ga. 287, 54 S.E. 160 (1906) (violation of state penal code re: operation of passenger cars); State v. Adjustment Dept. Credit Bureau, Inc., 94 Idaho 156, 483 P.2d 687 (1971) (extortion); People v. Duncan, 363 Ill. 495, 2 N.E.2d 705 (1936) (violation of Motor Fuel Tax Act); Golden Guernsey Farms v. State, 223 Ind. 606, 63 N.E.2d 699 (1945) (violation of Uniform Food, Drug & Cosmetic Act); G. & H. Cattle Co. v. Commonwealth, 312 Ky. 315, 227 S.W.2d 420 (1950) (nuisance, pollution); Telegram Newspaper Co. v. Commonwealth, 172 Mass. 294, 52 N.E. 445 (1898) (criminal contempt); State v. Worker's Socialist Pub. Co., 150 Minn. 406, 185 N.W. 931 (1921) (criminal syndicalism); Department of Health of State of New Jersey v. Borough of Fort Lee, 108 N.J. Eq. 139, 154 A. 319 (1931) (criminal contempt); People v. Canadian Fur Trappers' Corp., 248 N.Y. 159, 161 N.E. 455 (1928) (larceny); Hardeman King Co. v. State, 29 Okl. Cr. 319, 233 P. 792 (1925) (violation of laws re: selling agricultural seeds); Commonwealth v. American Baseball Club of Philadelphia, 290 Pa. 136, 138 A. 497 (1927) (violation of Sunday laws); Love v. Nashville Agricultural & Normal Institute, 146 Tenn. 550, 243 S.W. 304 (1922) (nuisance); Postal Tel. Cable Co. v. City of Charlottesville, 126 Va. 800, 101 S.E. 357 (1919) (violation of intrastate telegraph laws); Vulcan Last Co. v. State, 194 Wis. 636, 217 N.W. 412 (1928) (attempt to influence votes of employees in referendum election).

It is true that Section 3732 does not use the word "corporation." However, given the definition of the word "person," there is no need for it to do so. It is also true—at least so far as we know—that no court in Pennsylvania has applied Section 3732 to a corporation; the present case appears to be of first impression. However, given the fact that the section did not become effective until July 1, 1977, the fact that no case other than this one has been brought against a corporation for homicide by vehicle is hardly conclusive proof that the section may not be so applied. Neither are we persuaded by the next two reasons of the lower court—that since a corporation cannot be put in jail or have its license revoked, Section 3732 does not apply to corporations.

The offense of homicide by vehicle is a misdemeanor of the first degree. 75 Pa. C.S.A. §3732. It is true that one of the punishments that may be imposed for committing a misdemeanor of the first degree is a term of imprisonment:

> A person who has been convicted of a misdemeanor may be sentenced to imprisonment for a definite term which shall be fixed by the court and shall be not more than:

(1) Five years in the case of a misdemeanor of the first degree. 18 Pa. C.S.A. §1104.

It is also true that another possible punishment for homicide by vehicle is the revocation of one's driver license:

> The department shall revoke the operating privilege of any driver for one year upon receiving a certified record of the driver's conviction of any of the following offenses:
>
> . . . Section 3732 (relating to homicide by vehicle). Pa. C.S. §1532(a)(3).

However, a third possible punishment is the imposition of a fine:

> A person who has been convicted of any offense may be sentenced to pay a fine not exceeding:
>
> . . . (3) $10,000, when the conviction is of a misdemeanor of the first degree. 18 Pa. C.S.A. §1101.

Where alternate punishments are provided for a crime, the court may in appropriate circumstances impose the fine only:

> *Fine only.*—The court may, as authorized by law, sentence the defendant only to pay a fine, when, having regard to the nature and circumstances of the crime and to the history and character of the defendant, it is of the opinion that the fine alone suffices. 18 Pa. C.S. §1326(a).

In United States v. Houghland Barge Line, Inc., 387 F. Supp. 1110 (W.D. Pa. 1974), the court held that a statute requiring any "person in charge" of a vessel to notify the United States Coast Guard of oil discharges from the vessel applied to corporations as well as individuals, and that when applied to a corporation, only a fine may be imposed:

> The defendant also argues that as a corporation it cannot be imprisoned, and therefore, this would indicate that it [the statute in question] was not intended to apply to corporations. Innumerable federal penal statutes prohibit certain activities, including business entities, and provide penalties for violation of such prohibited acts. Both individuals and corporations are penalized even though a corporation may not be imprisoned. Thus, as illustrated by antitrust cases and Internal Revenue cases, where a statute calls for imprisonment, when imposed against a defendant corporation, only the fine portion of the penalty may be imposed.

Courts in other jurisdictions have similarly applied this principle, recognizing that to do otherwise would in effect confer upon the corporation immunity for its criminal acts. . . .

. . . [W]e are unable to accept the lower court's conclusion that §3732 "is strictly natural person solely operational driver oriented." For the reasons we have given, it appears to us equally to include corporations.

Reversed.

VAN DER VOORT, J., notes his dissent.

Notes and Questions

1. If a corporation can be guilty of homicide, does that mean that some individual working for the corporation must also be guilty? How should we handle the situation where a corporation releases a toxic chemical that causes a death under the following conditions:

> Engineer *A* knows that the chemical is toxic, but does not know that it is being released. Engineer *B* knows that he is releasing the chemical by twisting a valve, but is under the impression that the chemical is harmless.

If neither *A* nor *B* is negligent, who should be criminally liable? Or is civil liability enough? Might it be that no individual agent of the corporation knows both that the material is toxic and that it is being released? Can you conceive of circumstances under which no individual would even be negligent in lacking such knowledge? In such a case should no individual be criminally liable? What about the person who designed the system under which this could happen? Could the corporation nonetheless be criminally liable anyway? Why?

2. Why restrict the criminal liability of organizations to those organized as corporations? What about partnerships—such as law firms? If a partner, moving her typewriter, happens to rest it on a window sill from which it falls into the street and kills a passer-by, should the firm be guilty of involuntary manslaughter?

What about other organizations, such as the Boy Scouts or churches? A case like *McIlwain* could easily arise where the bus line was owned by a school district. Should a governmental entity be liable for homicide?

3. Note that we do not here grapple with the problem of how high a position a corporate official must hold in order for his or her authorization of the criminal violation to make the corporation criminally liable. We address this problem in Chapter 10, infra p.636-663.

4. Under what conditions should those working for this corporation be themselves liable as a consequence of the corporation's criminal liability? Is this not an easy question?

5. Should anyone be criminally liable in the following case?[10]

10. Chakravarty, Tunnel Vision, Forbes 214, 218 (May 21, 1984).

In the late 1960s, the hot technology was birth control. Companies like Syntex, Eli Lilly, and Johnson & Johnson were commanding multiples of about 35, as leaders in the manufacture of birth control pills. But there was another means of birth control becoming available, the intrauterine device, or IUD. Although nobody knew how it worked, work it did, preventing women from conceiving when they didn't want to, with an effectiveness approaching 100 percent. The first IUD, the Lippes loop, was already widely used when A. H. Robins Co. decided to jump into the business and market an IUD.

The problem was, Robins didn't have an IUD. A small ($133 million sales) Richmond, Va.-based manufacturer of pharmaceuticals and other food products, Robins was best known for its nonprescription products, Sergeant's Flea and Tick collars, Robitussin cough medicine, and Chap Stick lip balm. When Robins first decided to enter the IUD market, it did not have a single obstetrician or gynecologist on its staff. After Robins acquired the rights to an IUD, the Dalkon Shield, from inventor Irwin S. Lerner and Lerner's company, the Dalkon Corp., in June 1970, it assigned assembly of the Shield to its Chap Stick division.

Without the requisite knowledge or experience, Robins appears to have handled the Shield improperly, almost from the beginning. In good science, for example, research should be categorically confirmed by an outside disinterested party. For sales literature on the Shield's effectiveness, however, Robins relied on a report by Dr. Hugh J. Davis of Johns Hopkins University. Robins knew, but others did not, that Davis was one of the co-owners of Dalkon Corp. Robins ignored an internal company memo, written within days of the Shield's acquisition, that cited evidence from inventor Lerner himself that pregnancy rates with the Dalkon Shield were considerably higher than Dr. Davis had reported, and emphasized that more research was needed. Eager to get to the market before competitors piled in, Robins was selling Dalkon Shields nationally six months after the rights were acquired.

That the Shield was not as effective as touted was no problem, but when the device failed, severe infections developed in scores of cases, leading to miscarriages midway during the unwanted pregnancies. A Robins internal memo of October 1975 cites 248 cases among Shield users in the U.S. of infection-caused miscarriages; compared with only 55 for users of all other IUDs. Even more serious, some Shield users developed pelvic inflammatory disease (PID), which can lead to sterility, removal of a woman's reproductive organs or even death. At least 20 women have died in the U.S. from Shield-related complications.

What did Robins do about the problem? The company insisted, and continues to insist to this day, that it was not responsible. Dr. Thad J. Earl, another investor in the Dalkon Corp., wrote Robins in 1972 warning that women who did not have their Shields removed if pregnancy resulted might develop infections that would lead to miscarriage. But not until almost two years later did Robins finally send a letter to doctors recommending removal of the Shield if pregnancy occurred.

But pelvic inflammatory disease proved to be a far more significant problem associated with the Shield. What caused it? The answer may lie in one unique design feature of the Dalkon Shield. All IUDs have an attached string, or "tail," that runs from the IUD in the uterus, through the cervix and into the vagina. The tail has two purposes: to allow the user to check that the IUD is in place, and to facilitate removal. All other IUDs use a single impervious strand, usually of nylon, while the Shield used a multifilament tail—many strands, encased in a nylon sheath to protect against bacteria. But the sheath was cut at both ends and, therefore, did not sufficiently protect the strands. In fact, the effect of the Dalkon Shield's tail was to create a "wick," which could draw bacteria-laden body fluids up from the vagina into the uterus.

When confronted with this problem, the logical thing might have been for Robins to recall the Shields. Procter & Gamble for example, took its Rely tampons off the shelves in 1980, as soon as there was an indication they might be linked to toxic shock syndrome, another disease caused by vaginal infection.

But to take the Dalkon Shield off the market would be to kill an extremely promising—and profitable—new product. Shields generated operating margins of over 40 percent in the U.S. and over 70 percent overseas. Perhaps Robins was blinded by the probability that it could make millions. From January 1971 until sales were suspended in the U.S. in June 1974, at the request of the Food & Drug Administration, and overseas in April 1975, Robins sold some 4.6 million Shields worldwide, making them the largest-selling IUDs in the world.

Robins then, and even now, contends that "medical evidence continues to support the view that the Dalkon Shield had no greater risks when properly used than do other IUDs."

But authoritative studies show otherwise. For example, a study conducted between 1976 and 1978 by doctors at the federal government's prestigious Center for Disease Control in Atlanta showed that the risk of PID was 5 to 10 times greater for the Shield than for other IUDs, depending on length of use. The problems with the tail may well be the reason for that enormously increased risk, the CDC study said.

Was Robins aware of the danger of wicking while it continued to insist that there was nothing wrong with its product? In an internal memo dated June 29, 1970, less than a month after acquiring the Shield, and five months before nationwide marketing began, a Robins executive said the inventor Lerner had reported the wicking tendency. Court documents show that no one from Robins' medical department contacted Lerner on the subject or conducted a wicking test. A year later Wayne Crowder, a quality control supervisor in the Chap Stick division, conducted a simple wicking test and sent his superior a memo about it. Crowder was rebuffed and the position he held was subsequently eliminated. Neither memo was provided to the FDA when it investigated the Shield's problems in 1974.

What happened when all these complaints surfaced is exactly what you would expect. A. H. Robins Co. has been sued all over the lot, by women who claim to have suffered Shield-related miscarriages, PID and loss of their reproductive function, and by families of women who have died. In fact, since 1974 more than 10,000 product liability claims have been filed against Robins. So far, 36 cases have gone to judgment, with the company winning 19 and losing 17. But another 6,500 cases have been settled out of court at a cost to Robins and its insurance company, Aetna Life & Casualty, of $179 million.

The remaining 3,700 cases may be a great deal more expensive. When Shield suits were being settled back in 1976, the average settlement was just $8,000. By 1983, it was $35,000. Five cases settled in Minneapolis earlier this year averaged $400,000. And still not settled are claims totaling nearly $12 billion, as well as more than 2,000 cases in which damages have not yet been specified. Included in the overall total are 1,350 cases for which, the insurance company contends, Robins is totally uninsured.

The company's executives have even been publicly chastised. In February, Robins' President and CEO E. Claiborne Robins Jr., William A. Forest Jr., the company's general counsel, and Dr. Carl D. Lunsford, Robins' director of research, were forced to endure an extraordinary public rebuke at the hands of Miles Lord, chief judge for the Federal District Court of Minnesota. Following the Minneapolis settlements, Judge Lord excoriated the three in a 14-page statement that said in part: "You have taken the bottom line as your guiding beacon and the low road as your route."[11]

But Judge Lord's words, angry as they are, do not put the suits into their final proper perspective. The clearest warning on the dangers of lightly entering into a new technology come from Roger Tuttle, the company's former general attorney, who managed Robins' defense from 1971 to 1975. In a recent article in the Oklahoma Bar Journal, Tuttle wrote:

> Robins entered a therapeutic area with no prior experience, no trained personnel, and reliance on statistics from an admittedly biased source. Although the device was based on sound scientific principles, Robins over-promoted it without doing sufficient clinical testing in an effort to ride the crest of a marketing wave for financial gain.

Should A. H. Robins Company be criminally liable? Should the company be charged with manslaughter for the deaths of the 20 women? Should the company's executives be criminally liable? If so, which ones? Is not the company's civil liability enough?

5. Should the corporation employing the individual defendants also be held criminally liable in the following case?

Ruling to Take Movie Makers to Trial Is Praised, Criticized

Los Angeles (AP)—A judge's decision that three film makers should stand trial in the deaths of three actors on the set of the movie "Twilight Zone" could

11. The trial judge was subsequently reprimanded by the court of appeals for these remarks. According to US Law Week:

> The judge's comments from the bench during the proceeding sufficiently implicated the constitutionally-protected liberty interests of the three officers, and property interests of the defendant company, such that they were entitled to notice and an opportunity to be heard by an impartial tribunal. Additionally, the officers' personal liberty interests were infringed when the judge directed each officer to appear in his court and to remain and read his speeches, even though the officers were not parties to the litigation pending before the judge. Such intimidation of private citizens who are not parties to proceedings before the district court is antithetical to notions of fundamental fairness and the proper function of the judicial system.
>
> The record is clear that at the time he issued the reprimand the judge had decided the merits of the underlying dispute even though there had been no trial. The judge stated that he believed the truth of the plaintiff's allegations, adding that he had become an advocate for the plaintiffs and that he was, in fact, prejudiced.—Lay, Ch.J.—C.A. 8; Gardiner v. A. H. Robins Co., Inc., No. 84-5061, 11/2/84. [53 L.W. 2271 (12/4/84)].—Eds.

set a dangerous precedent that would send "thousands of innocent people" to jail, a defense attorney says.

But Municipal Court Judge Brian Crahan's ruling Monday in the deaths of Vic Morrow and two children, killed when a helicopter crashed amid special-effects explosions, won praise from a lawyer for the family of one of the victims.

"There are certain limits beyond which none of us have the right to go for reality and authenticity. Just because we are portraying the war doesn't mean we have to kill anybody," said attorney Jerome Berchin, who has sued the film makers and Warner Bros. for $200 million in the death of Renee Chen, 6.

Crahan ordered director John Landis, special-effects coordinator Paul Stewart and helicopter pilot Dorcey Wingo to stand trial on charges of involuntary manslaughter in the deaths of Morrow, 53, Chen and Myca Dinh Le, 7. However, Crahan dismissed charges against two other film makers—associate producer George Folsey and unit production chief Dan Allingham.

The deaths occurred July 23, 1982, when the copter crashed on the three actors during filming of a Vietnam War scene about 40 miles north of here. The scene was being filmed for the first of four segments, each with a different director, that made up "Twilight Zone: The Movie," which was released last summer.

Landis' attorney, Harland Braun, maintained that the accident was caused by misfiring of special-effects explosions by a worker who was not charged. He said Crahan's reasoning means that "if someone under you does something wrong . . . you are responsible for that."

Braun said he will ask a Superior Court judge to set aside Crahan's decision, which followed a lengthy preliminary hearing that ended April 9. Any trial would be held in Superior Court.

Crahan said evidence indicated that Landis, Stewart and Wingo were criminally responsible for the circumstances leading to the fatal crash.

"Each one of these three acting on his own and in consort with each other, created an unreasonable exposure of harm to the persons who ultimately died as a result of the helicopter crash," Crahan said.

He said Stewart was responsible as "ultimate arbiter of the special effects," and Wingo "knowingly hovered his helicopter" so close to the explosions "as to create a known risk of harm to anyone within the danger zone of the crash."

Landis' "attempt to obtain visual truth" caused "the combination of circumstances that in the final second of filming caused death and destruction," Crahan added.

The National Transportation Safety Board ruled in March that the crash's probable cause was the copter's proximity to special-effects explosions, which threw debris into the craft's tail rotor and caused it to fall off. The board also cited a lack of communications between Wingo and Landis. [Peninsula Times Tribune, April 24, 1984 at A-3.]

What precedent is the defense attorney worried about? Is there a question of absolute liability here? Will this decision have a "chilling effect" on the movie industry? Should there be criminal liability here? Would the decision be different if the three were not acting "in concert with each other"?

6. The Ford Motor Company in 1978 became the first automaker to face criminal homicide liability. See Note, Corporate Homicide: The Stark Realities of Artificial Beings and Legal Fictions, 8 Pepperdine L. Rev. 367, 367-370, 372-374, 404-408 (1981).

> [The] Ford Motor Company proceeded to sell some one and a half million Pintos, vintage 1971-1976, *knowing* that its gas tank posed a dangerous risk of fuel leakage and explosion. The company made no attempt to fix or redesign the gas tank, nor warn its customers of the hazards until forced to do so by the federal government. The results were tragic.
>
> . . . [A] van smashed into the back of a 1973 Ford Pinto traveling on U.S. 33 toward Goshen, Indiana. The gas tank impacted against the differential, ripping it open on four protruding bolts; gasoline splashed into the passenger compartment, igniting and engulfing the interior of the car in flames. The two girls trapped inside the Pinto were incinerated; a third girl partially thrown from the vehicle, received burns over ninety percent of her body and died six hours later.
>
> Elkhart County prosecutor Michael Cosentino brought Ford Motor Company to trial on three reckless homicide charges; he claimed the three girls died as a result of a high-level corporate decision to risk human life for greater company profit. . . . [T]he county prosecutor was forced to bring the case on a new and unchallenged Indiana statute permitting criminal prosecution of a corporation, and in doing so, he took a pioneering step in products liability. Previously, corporations faced criminal sanctions in antitrust, environmental, and securities laws, but never before have manufacturers been criminally indicted for the reckless design of their products.
>
> Indiana's Pinto Case raised for the first time in a legal setting the fascinating issue of whether or not a corporation is capable of committing homicide through the reckless design of its products. It was Ford's contention that the legislature did not intend to charge reckless homicide to a corporation. Instead, they argued the statutes were intended only to prevent *people* from killing other *people*. The prosecutor found fault with Ford's analysis, stating that it "patently exploits the corporate fiction." The state also noted that while it "does not desire to chill manufacturing generally, it does desire to deter outrageous decisions to sacrifice human life for private profit."
>
> Although one of the most bitter and highly publicized trials in product liability history, its ultimate precedential value remains in conflict—the victim of a judicial stalemate. For the first time, a court of law has ruled that a corporation can be indicted for the reckless design of a product, opening the door to new theories of corporate liability. Whether this fact is construed as achievement or legal extremism, it is counteracted by the additional fact that Ford Motor Company today stands acquitted of all criminal charges—hence the stalemate.
>
> This is not to say that the same marketing decision by Ford that resulted in acquittal on *criminal* charges in Indiana was not found to be culpable under *civil* liability theories elsewhere. Indeed, the factual allegations in Indiana were hauntingly similar to those raised in Grimshaw v. Ford Motor Co., where the jury found Ford's disregard of human life so blatant as to justify the original $125 million punitive damage award. . . .

A. The Pinto Cases

Ford Motor Company made a decision to place on the market a car whose gas tank design was fully expected to injure and kill a substantial number of people. The charge is supported by evidence, much of which comes from Ford's own company documents. One of those documents, the Grush-Saunby Report, was prepared for the company in its efforts to lobby the federal government to reduce its fuel tank standards. The heart of that document reveals a typical cost-benefit analysis, which resulted in a company decision not to redesign the Pinto gas tank, despite having the technology to do so. On June 11, 1978, 60 Minutes was televised with an interview between Mike Wallace and one of the plaintiff's attorneys from the case of Grimshaw v. Ford Motor Company, Arthur Hews:

Wallace. Table three is the heart of this document.
Hews. That's right.
Wallace. And it says, "Benefits: savings of 180 burn deaths, 180 serious burn injuries, and 2100 burned vehicles—at a total cost of $49.5 million." What does this mean, "savings," "benefit"?
Hews. All right. The first thing that they are measuring is the value of human lives. They are taking 180 lives and they figure that a human being's life is worth $200,000. So they multiply that out. They then—they—they take 180 serious burns, such as Richard Grimshaw, and they figure that's only worth $67,000—and they multiply that out. And they come out and they say that—that that's worth $49.5 million. They're using numbers to place value on life and burn.
Wallace. All right.
Hews. They then turn around and say it's going to cost us eleven dollars a car to save these 180 lives and to save these 180 burns.
Wallace. And they would come to a total cost of $137 million?
Hews. Yes.
Wallace. And what you're saying is that the Ford Motor Company said they did not want to spend $137 million in order to get a mere $50 million benefit?
Hews. That's correct.

Another internal company report, dated April 1971, discussed the added design costs of installing a protective shield between the gas tank and the rear axle. Noting a four dollar per vehicle design cost, the report recommended deferring installation of the protective shield or "flak suit" for two years to reduce overall design costs. "Defer adoption of the 'flak' suit or bladder on all affected cars until 1976 to realize a design cost savings of $20.9 million. . . . Continue with engineering testing and development to assure that final design approaches can be continued *with minimum financial impact.*"

Complementing the numerous written documents were films of crash tests conducted by Ford on the Pinto showing that fuel escaped in collisions of low to moderate speeds. The car was tested on five separate occasions by running it into a stationary barrier at speeds of around nineteen and a half miles per hour. The Pinto leaked gas on all five occasions. Ford put the car into production, knowing that it had never passed a fuel tank test. . . .

Opponents of corporate criminal liability advance several justifications for retaining the limited scope of this liability. One reason is the resulting inequity to innocent parties. Shareholders, are one such group, who in the final analysis feel the sting of any verdict against a corporation. Yet they are most likely innocent of personal wrongdoing and incapable of exerting any effective control over actions of the corporate agents.

While innocent shareholders are similarly "stung" by civil damage awards, it is critical to understand that corporate liability is achieved by the concept of vicarious liability which arose in the civil arena. As such, a criminal liability theory that penalizes innocent shareholders is a "substantial departure from the ordinary rule that a principal is not answerable *criminally* for the acts of his agent without the principal's authorization, consent or knowledge."

In addition to the basic unfairness theory was the idea of an "historical quid pro quo." Since the investor already had to deal with the inherent economic risk, the courts did not choose to impose an additional legal risk as well, in fear that capital investments would be curtailed.

In actual practice, however, criminal liability may not be the substantial departure that was originally presumed. If it is true that decisions to market "defective products in flagrant disregard of excessive dangers spring from the intensity of the profit motive rather than from animus toward consumers," then such behavior could be impliedly consented to and authorized by the shareholder who seeks a high return on his investment. Moreover, any impact upon the shareholder is minimized in at least two ways. First, shareholder losses are limited only to the amount of individual capital investment. Secondly, it is believed by some that corporations often transfer the costs of fines to the consumer in the form of higher product prices.

Another concern is the impact of placing criminal liability on unknowing corporate directors, on the theory that the wrongful activity occurred as a result of the principal's failure to exercise due care and attention to corporate affairs. Directors who are primarily concerned about long term planning and company goal setting, may never become aware that the product they recently marketed had failed all its safety tests or for some other reason is dangerously defective. Given the complexity of many corporate bureaucracies, a director cannot possibly know of the day to day details which surround the marketing of the company's products. This expanded liability of directors has stopped many able businessmen from accepting directorships in large companies. "[S]cores of men are politely declining offers they once would have jumped at to serve on prestigious boards. . . . There now is a real shortage of competent men willing and able to serve as directors. . . ."

Yet the fact remains that corporations do not commit crimes—people do, and thus it would seem to be more appropriate to proceed directly against the individual perpetrator than the corporation as a whole. While holding the entire corporate body criminally liable for acts of reckless disregard for human life would be a dramatic improvement over present liability schemes, punishment of the particular individual offenders by means of frequently imposed jail sentences, would provide a better mechanism for deterrence. As compared to monetary fines assessed upon the corporation as a whole, even where the fine is correlated to the amount of economic wrongdoing, corporations will eventually pass the costs on to consumers, thereby minimizing any deterrent impact there would have been otherwise. Additionally, concerns for the "innocent" shareholders would be removed.

Of major concern with the individual liability approach is the difficulty in identifying the guilty party. At common law, this was not such a problem given the corporation's limited size and complexity, and hence, courts found no reason to subject the corporation to liability. Today the corporate diversity and complexity has necessitated the expansion of corporate liability to the point where a court has held a corporation guilty of manslaughter. There is even scholarly support for the concept of corporate murder.

Yet even when the particular wrongdoers cannot be ascertained, there remains justification for criminal corporate liability as opposed to individual liability, which stems from the effects of the organization on individual behavior. Consider the following:

> What prevents most of us from committing murder is not a calculation based upon the threat of what the law will do, but mechanisms—guilt, shame, anxiety, conscience, superego—internalized within us through the forces of family, school, church, and peer group. When individuals are placed in an organizational structure, some of the ordinary internalized restraints seem to lose their hold.

The economic pressures which ferment within the corporate structure are sometimes strong enough to cause employees to risk their own liability for the sake of corporate gain. "[I]f the penalty for corporate wrongdoing were punishment of the corporation the punishment would ipso facto fall upon the true logical wrongdoer."

What does it mean to say, as does this excerpt, that the corporation *knew* that its gas tank posed a dangerous risk of explosion? Could one design an automobile which posed virtually no risk of danger to those inside? What would such a car look like? Why do we not require all our automobiles to be built this way?

At its trial, Ford was able to cite figures of the National Transportation Safety Administration which showed that, overall, passengers in a Pinto stood less risk of death or serious injury in a crash than did occupants of any of the other automobiles in the Pinto's price and size class. Should this make a difference?

Consider the Pinto case from the perspective of the Harvard Business school:

Managing Product Safety: The Ford Pinto[12]

On Tuesday August 9, 1977, Herbert L. Misch, vice president of environmental and safety engineering at Ford Motor Company, picked up a copy of the magazine *Mother Jones* featuring an article entitled "Pinto Madness." This exclu-

12. Copyright © 1984 by the President and Fellows of Harvard College. This case was prepared by Dekkers Davidson under the supervision of Kenneth Goodpaster as the basis for class discussion rather than to illustrate either effective or ineffective handling of an administrative situation. Reprinted by permission of the Harvard Business School.

sive story would surely stir up a public controversy over the safety of the company's successful subcompact car, the Ford Pinto.

This self-styled radical magazine had cited Ford "secret documents" which, according to the author, proved the company had known for eight years that the Pinto was a "firetrap." The article claimed that preproduction rear-end crash tests had revealed the dangerous nature of the design and placement of the car's fuel tank. According to the author's investigation, Ford was so anxious to get the car on the market that it decided design changes would not be made—they would "take too much time and cost too much money." The article went on to charge that Ford had used "some blatant lies" to delay enactment of a government safety standard that would have forced the company to change the Pinto's "fire-prone" gas tank. The article concluded: "By conservative estimates, Pinto crashes have caused 500 burn deaths to people who would not have been seriously injured if the car had not burst into flames."[13]

Nothing in Ford's records supported the contentions made in the article. Nevertheless, Misch knew that the overall effect of this *Mother Jones* article—one that relied heavily on the testimony of a former Ford engineer—could be highly damaging to the company. It would sharpen consumer criticism of the U.S. auto industry in general and Ford in particular. Misch and his associates at Ford were angered by the allegations and were ready to denounce the article as "unfair and distorted." They knew, however, that it would not be an easy task to counter such sensational charges with their own statistical analyses of accident reports.

Ford's management believed that the source of this trouble, like so much of the criticism leveled at the auto industry, was external to its operation. The development of a large consumer movement, along with the enactment of the National Traffic and Motor Vehicle Safety Act of 1966, had revolutionized the car business. In the view of *Mother Jones,* the industry had been considered the "last great unregulated business" in the United States. The industry now had to answer to many more people than just auto buyers. The multitude of often conflicting regulations had, according to auto executives, placed unreasonable burdens on domestic automakers. An exasperated company chairman, Henry Ford, II, lamented, "It's the mess in which we live."

Competitive Environment

The American automobile industry's fortune had historically been tied to the pattern of the nation's economic cycle. Three or four good years were inexorably followed by one or two poor years. There had been a shakeout of the weakest companies over the years, leaving four major U.S. automakers. In 1977 General Motors (46.4 percent market share), Ford (22.3 percent), Chrysler (11.1 percent), and American Motors (1.8 percent) shared the $100-plus billion U.S. auto market. Imports, consisting mostly of subcompact cars, had captured 18.4 percent of this market. Car sales were made primarily through manufacturers' franchised dealers located across the country.

Competition among the four U.S. firms was intense: Pricing, performance features, consumer financing, and advertising had always been important competitive weapons. With the arrival of stiffer foreign competition, however, pricing became an even more critical selling feature. Moreover, in the aftermath of the

13. Mark Dowie, Pinto Madness, Mother Jones 10 (Sept.-Oct. 1977).

Arab oil embargo, good fuel economy became especially important, a trend that had favored foreign producers because they had adapted to high fuel costs in their home markets.

For domestic car companies profit margins on all vehicles had declined in the early 1970s, mostly reflecting poor recovery from inflation-related cost increases. Pricing was limited first by price controls, then by the 1974-1975 recession. According to industry experts, domestic labor costs had served significantly to disadvantage American automakers. Small-car margins continued to decline after the recession as a result of reduced demand for small cars in general, heightened competition from imports, and cost increases to achieve safety, dam-ageability, and emission requirements. Large cars, still in demand, fared much better.

Though auto companies were very secretive about new car designs and technologies, there were otherwise very few secrets in the car business. Auto company engineers could, and often would, tear apart a competitor's new car to glean details about a new design or production technique. If one firm changed its price structure or its financing rate, the competition would be able to adjust its strategy quickly. Because of its dominance in the American market, General Motors was considered the market leader and usually dictated the sales strategies for its smaller rivals.

Much like its principal competitor, GM, Ford produced a complete range of cars and trucks. The company had scored some notable successes, however, in cultivating market segments ill-served by General Motors. Ford gained an early edge on its rival by producing the first American-made compact car, the Falcon, in 1960. Its luxury cars, the Thunderbird and Cougar, were also considered attractive by the American car buyer. The Mustang, designed and introduced in 1964 by Lee Iacocca (who later became Ford's [and then Chrysler's] president), gained wide favor as the "sports car for the masses."

Despite the successes of these specialty cars, Ford did not gain any ground on General Motors during the 1960s. Furthermore, some Ford executives believed that imports were posing a threat to Ford's traditionally strong position in the small-car market. Though the company was ready with new compact cars (the Maverick was introduced in 1969), it still did not have a subcompact to counter effectively the import challenge.

In June 1967 Ford management became embroiled in a protracted internal debate over the company's position on subcompacts. When it was over, Lee Iacocca had become Ford's president and the Pinto was born. Iacocca directed that the Pinto was to be in showrooms with 1971 models. Formal planning started immediately and the journey to production took less time than the prevailing industry average. In September 1970 the Pinto was introduced as a "carefree little American car," and it gained quick acceptance by the market. After six years of production over 2 million Pintos had been sold, making it one of the company's all-time best-selling automobiles. . . .

Product Safety Controversy, 1970-1977

To meet the competition from imported subcompacts, Ford accelerated the Pinto planning process. In June 1967 Ford commenced the design and development process; production of the Pinto began on August 10, 1970. Ford achieved this 38-month development time, 5 months under the average time of 43 months, by assembling a special team of engineers who directed their efforts entirely to the Pinto. Unlike the development cycles of most new car lines, Pinto start-up planning was simplified and included only a two-door sedan (hatchbacks and station wagons were added in later years). Pinto engineers were constrained by Iacocca's goal, known as "the limits of 2000"—the Pinto was not to weigh an ounce over 2,000 pounds and not to cost a cent over $2,000. These limits, according to former Ford engineers, were strictly enforced. Even at this price and weight, the Pinto would still cost and weigh more than some imported subcompacts.

An early question during the car's design stage was where to safely put the gas tank. Although engineers were familiar with ways to move the gas tank away from the rear of the car—Ford had a patent for a saddle-type tank that could fit above and mostly forward of the car's rear axle—they opted for a strap-on tank arrangement located under the rear floorpan and behind the rear axle. At that time almost every American-made car had the fuel tank located in the same place. Late in the design process, however, an engineering study determined that "the safest place for a fuel tank is directly above the rear axle." It was later determined by senior company engineers that such a design, while moving the tank farther away from a rear-end collision, actually increased the threat of ignition in the passenger compartment. The over-the-axle location of the fuel tank would also require a circuitous filler pipe more likely to be dislodged in an accident. Raising the height of the fuel tank by putting it above the axle would also raise the car's center of gravity, thereby diminishing its handling capabilities. In the opinion of Ford's senior engineers, this would undermine the car's general safety. Practical considerations also dictated the traditional location. The fuel tank could not be placed over the axle, for example, if a station wagon or a hatchback option was going to be offered. The over-axle location would also greatly reduce storage space and would make servicing more difficult.

When the Pinto was in the blueprint stage, the federal government had no standards concerning how safe a car must be from gas leakage in rear-end crashes. In January 1969, NHTSA proposed its first rear-end fuel system integrity standard, called Standard 301. The original standard required that a stationary vehicle should leak less than one ounce of fuel per minute after being hit by a 4,000 pound barrier moving at 20 mph. Ford supported such a standard in writing and voluntarily adopted the 20-mph standard as an internal design objective for its entire line of cars. In mid-1969 the company began a series of crash tests with preproduction Pinto prototypes, as well as with other car lines, in an attempt to meet this objective. Four tests were conducted on vehicles modified to simulate the Pinto's rear-end design. In three of these tests, the leakage slightly exceeded the one-ounce-per-minute standard. In the other test, massive fuel leakage occurred because an improperly welded fuel tank split at the seams. After these tests Ford altered the Pinto's fuel tank design and was able to incorporate these changes before production began. The first Pinto rolled off the assembly line on August 10, 1970. A month later the subcompact was introduced to the American consumer, boasting a price tag of $1,919—about $170 less than GM's subcompact and within $80 of the best-selling Volkswagen Beetle.

The 20-mph *moving-barrier* standard proposed by the government was never adopted. Just days after the manufacture of the first Pinto, NHTSA announced a proposal requiring all vehicles to meet a 20-mph *fixed-barrier* standard within

18 months. In a fixed-barrier test, the vehicle is towed backwards into a fixed barrier at the specified speed. The wall does not absorb any momentum and hence the automobile bears the full force of the impact. NHTSA also indicated that its long-term objective for rear-end crashes included a 30-mph fixed-barrier standard. This new proposal caught automakers by surprise and provoked universal industry opposition. Ford estimated that a 20-mph fixed-barrier test could, because of the laws of kinetic energy, be nearly twice as severe as a 20-mph moving-barrier test. In a moving-barrier test, a large wooden rectangular block, approximately 6 feet by 6 feet and weighing 4,000 pounds, is propelled on a track at the specified speed into the rear of a stationary automobile that is in neutral gear with no brakes on. The forward movement of the automobile absorbs some of the momentum of the crash. Many auto engineers were quick to point out the unrealistic nature of fixed-barrier tests: in the real world, vehicles are not driven backwards into walls. Moreover, data available to Ford indicated that 85 percent of rear-end collisions occurred at speeds equivalent to or less than a 20-mph moving-barrier standard. In addition, the available information indicated that only .45 percent of injury-producing accidents involved fire. Preventing injuries from fires caused by rear-end impacts at very high speeds was beyond practical technology, according to many auto executives. Protection against fire at such high speeds would be of little benefit, it was argued, since the force of impact alone was likely to be fatal.

Ford considered it unlikely that the government would adopt fixed-barrier standards. Nevertheless, the company began to test its vehicles against this proposed requirement to determine what would have to be done to meet NHTSA's proposals. Subsequent fixed-barrier tests conducted with standard Pintos at 20 and 30 mph resulted in excessive leakage. To meet the more stringent fixed-barrier standards, a major tear-up of all cars would be required to modify vehicle design. Because of the significant costs involved and doubts about the viability of the fixed-barrier standard, Ford management decided to continue with its own internal 20-mph moving-barrier standard. Engineering work on developing ways to meet a 30-mph moving-barrier standard—which Ford believed NHTSA would eventually adopt—continued.

In early 1971 a junior company engineer began to explore various ways to make the company's smaller cars capable of meeting the 30-mph moving-barrier standard. A 30-page study, called the "Pricor Report," listed several specific recommendations for how to make the car substantially safer from fuel leakage and fire in rear-end crashes. An over-the-axle gas tank, a repositioned spare tire, installation of body rails, a redesigned filler pipe, and an "innertank" rubber bladder were among major options for improving the Pinto's overall performance. The first four suggestions were ruled out on the grounds that they would require extensive vehicle design changes. The rubber bladder—a tank liner with an estimated variable cost of $5.80—was seriously considered. On the basis of a crash test in which a bladder was hand placed inside a Pinto tank, a company engineer concluded that the bladder tank "provided a substantial improvement in crash-worthiness." In cold weather, however, the bladders became stiff, making gas filling very difficult. And in very hot climates, the bladders failed under test conditions.

In August 1973, NHTSA announced a proposal for a 30-mph *moving-barrier*, rear-end fuel system integrity standard, effective September 1976 for all 1977 models. A prolonged debate ensued between government officials and industry executives over the appropriate test technique. NHTSA was a proponent of car-to-car testing, arguing that this was a closer approximation to actual accident situations. In car-to-car testing, another automobile is driven at the specified speed into the rear of the automobile to be tested, while the latter automobile remains in neutral gear with no brakes on. As in the moving-barrier test, the automobile to be tested absorbs some of the forward momentum of the crash by moving forward. In addition the car striking it absorbs additional amounts of the energy by being deformed itself. As a result, this kind of testing, at any given speed, is less rigorous than a moving-barrier test, and much less rigorous than a fixed-barrier one. On the other hand, for various reasons, car-to-car testing produces a much less reproducible series of effects than does either moving- or fixed-barrier testing. Auto representatives maintained that a standard moving barrier (which was towed along a track to the point of impact) was much more appropriate because it was repeatable and, therefore, a more reliable measurement of crashworthiness.

At the same time that NHTSA proposed the rear-end crash standard, it also adopted a fuel system integrity standard applicable to rollover accidents. Although Ford did not oppose the rear-end standard, it vigorously fought the rollover standard. Under provisions of the rollover test, minimal gasoline leakage would be permitted when a car was turned upside down in an accident. This presented automakers with obvious problems, since leakage would occur from the carburetor, fuel vents, and the gas cap air hole when a car was upside down; yet, each of these openings was necessary for the normal functioning of the fuel intake. After extensive study Ford determined that the rollover requirement might be met by installing an $11 valve on each of its 12.5 million cars and trucks then on the road. Among the materials submitted was a cost-benefit analysis prepared according to NHTSA criteria and using government figures ($200,000 per death, $67,000 per injury). The values reflected only the economic loss to society resulting from injuries and deaths, because the government had no estimate to place on human pain and suffering. The analysis, done by Ford personnel with no design responsibilities, presented the case that the $137 million in cost far outweighed the dollar values assigned for the 180 burn deaths, 180 serious burn injuries, and 2,100 burned vehicles. The rollover standard was eventually adopted with some minor modifications. The cost-benefit analysis on rollover accidents became the basis for countless media claims that Ford delayed *rear-end* fuel system integrity standards because "its internal cost-benefit analysis, which places a dollar value on human life, said it wasn't profitable to make the changes sooner."

The first notable public criticism of the Pinto's fuel tank design came in late 1973. Byron Bloch, an independent consultant in automobile safety design, warned a Department of Transportation conference that the Pinto's fuel system design was "very vulnerable . . . to even minor damage." On a national television program, Bloch held up a model of a Pinto and pointed out what he saw as its fuel system hazards. When Ford announced it was recalling the Pinto for minor repairs, Bloch urged the government to require a recall that would improved the car's resistance to fire in rear-end crashes. Early in 1974 the Center for Auto Safety pressed NHTSA to investigate the fuel system integrity of the Ford Pinto and the Chevrolet Vega. The center cited concerns expressed by attorneys engaged in liability lawsuits, as well as its own research findings, in calling for a defect investigation. NHTSA reviewed these complaints and determined that there was no demonstrable safety problem.

NHTSA, still a relatively new federal agency in the mid-1970s, was seriously hampered in most of its investigatory work by a lack of relevant and meaningful statistical information. In early 1975 a study commissioned by the Insurance Institute for Highway Safety concluded that the number of fire-related incidents involving vehicles was growing more rapidly than the number of other incidents of fire. The study noted a striking difference between Ford's 20 percent national representation among domestic passenger cars and its 35 percent frequency in surveyed collision-ruptured fuel tanks. The study's author cautioned, however, that it was not possible to draw definitive conclusions about causal relationships; nor was it possible to identify differences between car models. This study, and others like it, came at a time of growing public concern over motor vehicle fires. Between 1974 and 1976 consumer groups and Congress exerted considerable political pressure on NHTSA to finally implement all provisions of the fuel system integrity standard. In 1977 Standard 301 was fully enacted.

On August 10, 1977, the allegations contained in the Mother Jones article were first made public at a news conference in Washington, D.C. The charges against Ford appeared to have been based on quotes attributed to either past or present company engineers, along with a digest of confidential company memoranda. Ford executives took a dim view of the magazine, but they knew its editors had obtained some key sensitive documents that could easily be misinterpreted by the public. As far as the company knew, no government investigation was being conducted that concerned the Pinto's fuel system.

Postscript

On September 26, 1977, Ford officials publicly responded to the Mother Jones article—which had appeared seven weeks earlier—by issuing a news release aimed at refuting the magazine's allegations. The news release claimed: "There is no serious fire hazard in the fuel system of the Ford Pinto, nor are any Pinto models exceptionally vulnerable to rear-impact collision fires. [NHTSA] statistics established that Ford Pinto is involved in fewer fire-associated collisions than might be expected considering the total number of Pintos in operation." Ford cited government figures for the period 1975-1976 for which comprehensive information was available. These figures showed that Pintos were involved in about 1.9 percent of fire-accompanied passenger car fatalities in 1975-1976, years in which Pintos made up an average of about 1.9 percent of passenger cars. Ford explained that early experiments with its rubber bladder gas tank were conducted to see if the company could meet its own ambitious performance requirements. "The truth is that in every model year the Pinto has been tested and met or surpassed the federal fuel system integrity standards applicable to it."

The company acknowledged that the later-model Pintos had an improved fuel system design, but argued that "it simply is unreasonable and unfair to contend that a car is somehow unsafe if it does not meet standards proposed for future years or embody the technological improvements that are introduced in later model years." The company denied that it had purposely delayed Standard 301 and said it had only "opposed . . . certain excessive testing requirements."

In September 1977, NHTSA opened an investigation into the Pinto's fuel tank system and ran an engineering analysis of the pre-1977 Pinto. As reported by the Wall Street Journal, the agency found that "the fuel tank's location and the structural parts around it permitted easy crushing or puncturing of the tank in a crash. Officials also found that the short fuel tank filler pipe could easily pull away from the tank." There was "a real potential for trouble," said one government official.

Ford's management was angered by NHTSA's inquiry and believed the basis for its examination to be unfounded. In a 1974 investigation of complaints, NHTSA had determined that no action concerning Pinto fuel system integrity was necessary. Indeed, by NHTSA's own admission, its action was in response to the enormous flood of mail demanding that it do something about the Pinto. Company management was further incensed when the agency acknowledged that its accident statistics were "notoriously incomplete." NHTSA had only begun to develop a comprehensive accident reporting system.

By early 1978 the Pinto controversy began to attract national attention. The Center for Auto Safety had called for a national campaign to force Ford to recall the country's 2-million-odd Pintos and retrofit a safety bladder into the gas tank of *all* Pintos. The car's image was further tarnished by recalls due to piston scuffing and steering failures.

In February 1978 a California jury handed down a verdict that assessed $125 million in punitive damages against Ford in a case involving the rupture and explosion of the fuel tank on a 1972 Pinto. One person had died in the fiery Pinto crash, and the surviving passenger had undergone 60 different operations in the six years since the accident. It was testimony by Harley Copp, a former Ford senior engineer, that apparently convinced the court the Pinto was, in the words of one juror, "a lousy and unsafe product." The massive amount of money awarded by the jury, easily the highest for such a suit in American history, led to heightened media interest in the Pinto issue. A judge later reduced punitive damages to $3.5 million.

During the same month as the California verdict, NHTSA conducted experimental crash tests of the Pinto as part of its ongoing investigation. A total of 11 rear-end crash tests of 1971-1976 Pintos were staged at speeds between 30 and 35 mph. Two cars tested at 35 mph caught fire, and the other tests at 30 mph resulted in "significant leakage." When NHTSA similarly tested GM's Chevrolet Vega, a larger and slightly heavier vehicle than the Pinto, minimal gasoline leakage was reported. Ford management believed these tests were unfair and inappropriate. Some of the tests more severe than the government required even for later-model vehicles, and this was apparently the first time the agency had ever used car-to-car crash tests to determine if there was a safety defect.

In March 1978 Pinto owners in Alabama and California filed class action suits, demanding that Ford recall all Pintos built from 1971 through 1976 and modify their fuel systems. The California civil complaint alleged that Ford "persistently and willfully failed and refused to remedy the design defect in the fuel tank." Around this time the head of the American Trial Lawyers Association, in an unprecedented step, had appealed to the company to "recall all of the cars in question." Later that same month, NHTSA notified Ford that its 1976 Pintos had not passed a 30-mph *front-end* barrier test. This test result, which revealed occasional fuel leakage in the engine compartment, led to a recall of 300,000 Pintos.

On May 9, 1978, NHTSA announced that it had made an "initial determination" that a safety defect existed in the fuel systems of Ford Pintos for the 1971 through 1976 model years. This finding had been reached after eight months of analysis, testing, and review of pertinent company records. The government claimed that it was aware of 38 cases in which rear-end collisions of Pintos had resulted in fuel tank damage, leakage, and/or ensuing fires. Of those 38 cases, it said, there were 27 fatalities among occupants and 24 instances in which individuals suffered nonfatal burns. In its four-paragraph letter to Ford's President Iacocca, NHTSA informed the company that it could respond to the initial findings at a public hearing scheduled for mid-June. During late May and early June, Ford officials met with NHTSA to discuss privately the government's findings and to consider possible remedies. A few days before the hearing date, the decision was made to recall the cars.

On June 9, 1978, after years of vigorously defending the safety of the Pinto's fuel system, Ford management announced the recall of 1.5 million of its subcompacts. In a press release issued on the day of the recall announcement, Ford management insisted "that it does not agree with the agency's initial determination . . . that an unreasonable risk to safety is involved in the design of [the Pinto], and that it believed it can be demonstrated that the actual performance of the vehicles is comparable to that of other subcompact and compact cars manufactured during the same periods." The company did concede that "NHTSA had identified areas in which the risk of fuel leakage could be reduced significantly on a practical basis." Accordingly, Ford decided to offer the modifications to "end public concern that had resulted from criticism of the fuel system in these vehicles." The company agreed to notify all Pinto owners that it was ready to replace the fuel filler pipe and install a polyethylene shield across the front of the fuel tank. Ford estimated this offer could cost the company as much as $20 million after taxes. During the previous year Ford had earned a total of $1.5 billion after taxes.

NHTSA administrator Joan Claybrook said the government wanted to work out a voluntary agreement with Ford to avoid a long drawn-out court battle. In response to Ford's recall, the government closed its investigation without making a final determination.

In Detroit, Michigan, Ford Chairman Henry Ford, II, said: "The lawyers would shoot me for saying this, but I think there's some cause for concern about the [Pinto]. I don't even listen to the cost figures—we've got to fix it."

According to some authorities, the precise problem with the Pinto was that in rear-end collisions the gas tank would come loose and move forward. This, though serious, was not as dangerous as might be thought, since gas tanks are designed to be quite rugged. In the Pinto of the years in question, however, there was a rough bolt on the rear differential, into which the gas tank moved, that could puncture and then split the gas tank. This could have been easily corrected by putting a smooth piece of plastic on top of the bolt; it is not clear, however, when the problem and this solution were discovered. It is also not clear as to how long it took after the information was discovered by lower echelon engineers for it to filter up to the top, nor how convincing the evidence was, at various times, both of the existence of the problem and the solution.

Under what conditions should the corporation be held to be criminally negligent for not knowing about and fixing the problem? What about an engineer who knew and did not "go public"? What about an omission theory—that once Ford finally did know about the problem and the solution, it had a duty to recall and fix all the Pintos in circulation?

One commentator[14] has argued that on utilitarian grounds it is wrong to subject corporations to criminal penalties for defective products:

To achieve the benefits of deterrence, society must incur some combination of enforcement costs and punishment costs. Enforcement costs are the costs of detecting, apprehending, convicting, and sentencing criminals—including the costs that criminal defendants incur in defending themselves and that the government incurs in providing defense assistance to indigents. The punishment costs that society incurs in imposing fines—the only criminal sanction generally applicable to corporate manufacturers—include the cost of collecting the fines and the unintended harm that befalls innocent persons, such as innocent employees and shareholders, who, solely because of their relationship with the punished defendant, suffer damage to their pocketbooks, their reputations, the marketability of their services, or their general well-being.

It is not desirable to try to induce manufacturers to produce products that totally eliminate the risk of harm. Here, as elsewhere, absolute safety is impossible to obtain. Manufacturers cannot predict the infinite variety of ways in which their products can be misused, altered, or affected by events in nature. More important, long before absolute safety is approached, the marginal cost of further precautions will far exceed the social value of that risk reduction, both in design cases and in warning cases.

An economically efficient use of society's manufacturing resources requires manufacturers to employ risk-reducing design, manufacturing, and warning measures whose marginal cost does not exceed the value of the expected marginal risk reduction those measures will provide. Products that do not satisfy this criterion are unsafe, or defective, products. Manufacturers are induced to refrain from making defective products if, through the use of deterrent forces, they internalize—that is, take into account in their own cost-benefit analyses—all of the social costs that their products impose. Optimal deterrence thus anticipates that some defective products will continue to be produced, but also recognizes that the social cost of eliminating those products would exceed the costs imposed by those products. *Over*deterrence generates social losses every bit as great as underdeterrence.

II. An Analysis of the Marginal Deterrent Benefit That Criminal Sanctions Might Provide If Used to Regulate Product Safety

To decide whether criminal sanctions are needed to increase deterrence of the manufacture of defective products to the optimal level, we must first analyze both existing noncriminal deterrent forces and their possible improvement.

14. Wheeler, The Use of Criminal Statutes to Regulate Product Safety, Journal of Legal Studies 600-617 (August 1984).

A. Elements That Contribute to Deterrence in the Absence of Criminal Sanctions

In the absence of criminal sanctions, one element that deters manufacturers from producing defective products is the civil lawsuit. Plaintiffs injured by products may sue in strict liability, negligence, breach of express warranty, breach of implied warranty, or fraud.

The threat of civil litigation forces the manufacturer to consider two expected costs of a direct monetary nature: (1) the cost (including defense attorney's fees and value of employee-witness time) of defending the suit and (2) the cost of paying an adverse judgment or settlement. The first of these two costs must be considered even by a manufacturer that makes only nondefective products and believes that no jury asked to examine its products would find them defective, because manufacturers who successfully defend product liability suits cannot recover their attorneys' fees or any other significant litigation cost. In short, even a manufacturer that believes to a certainty that it never should and never will lose a product liability action must nevertheless internalize the expected cost of defending meritless lawsuits.

Recent common-law and statutory developments have greatly expanded the types of injuries for which private plaintiffs can recover compensatory damages, thereby forcing manufacturers to internalize more of the social costs imposed by defective products. Plaintiffs injured by products can now recover for medical expenses and other out-of-pocket costs associated with physical injuries and deaths; loss of earnings and impairment of earning capacity; lost profits; damage to property; and pain, suffering, embarrassment, and similar intangible harms.

In addition, many individuals who suffer harm from products and who historically would have been unable to sue because of a legal impediment or because of a practical impediment can now successfully sue. Unmarried cohabitants can sue for loss of consortium. Children whose parents are injured or killed can sue for loss of parental society and companionship. Persons who have not themselves suffered direct injury can sue for emotional harm they suffered upon viewing an accident injuring a close relative. Class actions can be brought on behalf of injured persons with claims too small to warrant the cost of individual lawsuits.

A few social losses caused by unsafe products remain noncompensable in tort actions and therefore do not have to be internalized by manufacturers. The principal one is the successful plaintiff's attorney's fees and other significant litigation costs, such as experts' fees, deposition reporters' fees, and exhibits. Indeed, the absence of compensation for plaintiffs' litigation costs not only creates a social cost not internalized by manufacturers but also tends to deter plaintiffs from suing. This in turn lessens the probability that a manufacturer of a defective product will be civilly "apprehended," which in turn further reduces manufacturers' expected costs of making defective products.

The overall significance of this factor should not be overemphasized, however. A typical plaintiff's litigation costs pale in comparison with a typical manufacturer's litigation costs, because interparty discovery is generally a one-way affair favoring the plaintiff. Only the manufacturer has thousands of documents that must be culled by its employees from still larger document collections. Only the manufacturer has numerous employees who designed, tested, produced, and marketed the product and can therefore be deposed.

Other noncompensable social losses, considerably more speculative and difficult to evaluate, are intangible losses such as the emotional suffering of the victim's friends and the community's loss of the victim's charitable services in religious and benevolent organizations.

On the other hand, at least some of the noncognizable social losses inflicted by unsafe products are offset by noncognizable social benefits produced by the same products. For example, if a malicious bully dies as a result of his use of a defective product, the law does not allow anyone to sue for the social loss of the deceased's occasional good deeds for friends, but that noncognizable loss may be partially offset by the elimination of the harm he would have inflicted by hectoring others and by engaging in tortious or criminal conduct and other socially undesirable activities. Given the highly speculative nature of all such intangible losses and benefits, and given their small size relative to the costs and benefits that are legally cognizable, it seems unlikely that manufacturers' failure to internalize the noncognizable losses can justify the use of criminal sanctions.

Another factor that increases the magnitude of manufacturer's expected costs from private civil actions factor is punitive damages. These can be awarded in substantial multiples of the allowable compensatory damages, because most jurisdictions place no specific limit on the size of punitive damages awards relative to the size of compensatory damages awards.

In deciding whether to adopt additional risk-reducing measures with their products, manufacturers also must consider that the closer their products are to being legally defective (even if not defective in fact), the more likely it is that product liability suits will be filed and will have to be defended. The social costs and benefits of any specific design are difficult to quantify and are likely to be evaluated differently by the manufacturer before production has begun and by plaintiffs' attorneys long after the product has been produced and sold. The closer the manufacturer perceives the benefits and the costs of the design to be, the more likely it is that injured persons' lawyers will, with hindsight, find the costs to outweigh the benefits or at least conclude that a jury would so find. This problem is exacerbated by erroneously broad legal standards that may permit recovery where it should be denied. The threat of these suits and judgments against manufacturers of nondefective products means manufacturers must internalize substantial expected costs that are not social costs of defective products, but social costs of a defective legal system. Overdeterrence is never without its own costs.

Additional deterrent force in the form of private civil actions arises from actions for rescission or money damages on a breach of contract or fraud theory. These do not even require the plaintiffs to have suffered physical injury or property damage; rather, the disappointed purchaser need show only that he did not obtain that which was promised.

The government contributes to the noncriminal deterrent force by adding to the costs manufacturers can expect to incur if they sell defective products. Various federal and state administrative agencies regulating thousands of products have the power to require recalls and warnings and to impose civil penalties. In addition, by requiring specific safety features on products they buy, government purchasing agencies may cause some manufacturers to modify their products to avoid a loss of government contracts.

Manufacturers must also consider costs they might incur other than in judicial and regulatory proceedings if they sell defective products. For example, derogatory publicized evaluations of products by government agencies, by private testing entities such as Consumers' Union and the Center for Automotive Safety, and by discontented users may cause potential buyers to shun the products. The effect may be even greater if potential buyers are also persuaded to shun the manufacturer's other products. Adverse publicity about injuries caused by the manufacturer's products, about lawsuits brought against the manufacturer, or about regulatory proceedings against the manufacturer may cause even more potential buyers to shun the manufacturer's products.

B. *Factors Affecting the Probability That a Manufacturer Who Sells Defective Products Will Incur Noncriminal Costs as a Result*

The probability that a manufacturer of defective products will incur the noncriminal costs described in the preceding subsection is a function of the probability that the defect will be detected; that the manufacturer will be identified as the maker of the product; that injured persons will have sufficient incentive to sue and to persist in litigating; that those plaintiffs will win; that the plaintiffs' verdicts will accurately reflect the size of the social costs compensable by law; that the verdicts will withstand appeals; that government agencies will investigate, institute proceedings, and require recalls or warnings or impose civil penalties; that any such agency action will be upheld by the judiciary; that independent private entities will criticize the manufacturer's products; and that adverse publicity and lost sales will result from private lawsuits, from government proceedings, from criticisms by independent private entities, or from accidents in which physical harm, death, or property damage occurs.

Several factors suggest a substantial probability that the manufacturer of defective products will in fact incur some of the noncriminal costs described in the preceding subsection. First, the probability that the defect will be detected once it causes a social loss is great. The fact that an injury has occurred will almost always be obvious to the individual whose person or property has been harmed. This distinguishes product-related harm from much of the harm caused by violations of the antitrust laws, securities laws, and tax laws, and even from some amount of harm caused by fraud, misappropriation of trade secrets, and other tortious or criminal conduct by corporations. In these latter forms of wrongdoing, the resulting harm often is monetary and caused by clandestine conduct; the person who suffers a monetary loss because of the wrongdoing may never realize that he has been injured or may realize that fact only after the statute of limitations has run.

Second, the probability that the injured person will perceive some causal relationship between his injury and the defective product is also substantial for most, but not all, products. This is especially apparent with respect to most machines (but not, for example, X-ray machines and microwave equipment) and similar products that generally cause injuries by mechanical force or by causing visible changes in a person's appearance, rather than by chemically interacting with internal bodily tissue. For example, when a defective punch press crushes a worker's hand, the existence of some causal connection between the product and the injury is obvious.[15] The existence of a causal relationship

15. The National Safety Council has estimated that in 1978, 77.2 percent of all injuries to persons hospitalized for accidents, poisonings, or violence were fractures, internal organ injuries, sprains, open wounds, contusions, superficial injuries, dislocations, burns, or foreign body injuries.

may not be as readily apparent when the product is a pharmaceutical drug or other chemical product, because the injury may not become observable until long after the injured person used the product, so that other, intervening events may seem to have caused the injury.[16]

Third, the probability that the injured person will be able to identify the wrongdoer—the manufacturer of the product—is likewise substantial. The vast majority of products have a trademark, a design feature, or some other characteristic that associates the product with its maker. Even products that do not, or that are used by being totally consumed, can often be traced to a particular manufacturer. The druggist who dispensed a pharmaceutical drug may have an identifying record; the prescribing doctor may have specified a particular brand and may have a record of that fact; the injured person may not have consumed every capsule, and the remaining capsules or packaging may contain an identifying mark; the marketing history, geographic and temporal, of the various manufacturers of the generic product may be such that only one of them could have sold the injury-producing item in the particular place at the particular time in question; or there may be only one manufacturer of the patented product. Moreover, through developing doctrines such as alternative liability, enterprise liability, concert of action, and market-share liability, plaintiffs are now more likely than before to be able to recover, even if they cannot produce any evidence of which manufacturer made the particular injury-causing item.

The ease of identification of manufacturers of defective products markedly distinguishes those wrongdoers from many others. Burglars and arsonists, for example, generally seek to commit their crimes without being seen. Robbers and rapists often wear masks or other disguising devices. Murderers and manslaughterers eliminate the persons otherwise most likely to identify them. . . .

Fourth, the probability that the manufacturer of defective products will, once identified, be "apprehended" by private plaintiffs or by regulatory officials appears greater than the probability that many other types of wrongdoers once identified, will be apprehended. Corporate manufacturers are easily amenable to service of process, while individual wrongdoers such as murderers, arsonists, burglars, and robbers can flee the vicinity of their wrongful acts and make service of civil process less feasible, more costly, and therefore less likely.

Fifth, the probability that civil sanctions can be imposed on a manufacturer of defective products who is found liable in a civil suit or in a regulatory proceeding appears greater than the probability that civil sanctions can be imposed on many other types of wrongdoers. Corporations typically have substantial assets that individual wrongdoers as natural persons lack.

Sixth, twentieth-century developments in the procedural and substantive law have greatly increased the probability that plaintiffs in product cases will obtain favorable settlements or verdicts and that regulatory agencies will require

---

See National Safety Council, Accident Facts—1982 Edition at 20. Approximately 75 percent of all accidental deaths were caused by motor vehicles, falls, drownings, or burns. Id. at 9. In virtually all of those cases, the fact of injury and the likely cause of the injury were undoubtedly apparent.

16. See, for example, Borel v. Fibreboard Paper Products Corp., 493 F.2d 1076 (5th Cir. 1973), cert. denied, 419 U.S. 869 (1974) (asbestosis, alleged to have been caused by prolonged exposure to asbestos dust, not observable until several years after first internal injury occurred); Mizell v. Eli Lilly & Co., 526 F. Supp. 589 (D.S.C. 1981) (plaintiff's cancer alleged to have been caused by ingestion by plaintiff's mother of diethylstilbestrol).

warnings or initiate recalls or impose civil penalties. There has been, for example, a vast increase in the number of statutory product-safety requirements, regulatory product-safety standards, published industry product-safety standards, and product-safety standards set by independent testing organizations such as Underwriters Laboratories and American National Standards Institute. Violations of the governmental standards may constitute negligence per se. Violations of any of the other standards are admissible as evidence of negligence and of a product defect; as a practical matter, that evidence can be dispositive for the plaintiff. In addition, modern regulatory standards and their related certification requirements have increased the amount of testing that manufacturers must perform and document, thereby providing private and governmental plaintiffs with more evidence of the products' design, development, testing, and performance, as well as evidence of the manufacturers' knowledge of risks attending the products.

Many of the agencies regulating product safety have large budgets and, using independent testing facilities, conduct their own tests of products. Some also compile accident statistics and technical libraries. Moreover, most have imposed on manufacturers a variety of reporting requirements, and much of this information, as well as information obtained informally and through subpoenae in defect investigations and proceedings, is available to private plaintiffs, for whom it eases the cost of suit.

Some of the procedural developments that have assisted private and governmental plaintiffs in product actions are not unique to those actions, but apply to all civil tort actions. The broad scope of civil discovery contained in the Federal Rules of Civil Procedure and in similar state discovery provisions provides easy access to manufacturers' documents; to design, testing, and manufacturing facilities; and to the testimony of employees, officers, and directors. The expanded use of offensive collateral estoppel makes it far easier for some plaintiffs to establish a product defect by enabling them to rely on a prior determination of product defect by a different plaintiff against the same defendant manufacturer, in an unrelated action alleging the same defect, to establish the existence of a defect. The broad provision in Rule 20 of the Federal Rules of Civil Procedure facilitates the joinder of parties, which may reduce plaintiffs' litigation costs and increase their sharing of information.

The substantive developments in the same direction have, if anything, been more dramatic than their procedural counterparts. The doctrine of strict product liability has been steadily expanded since its birth in Greenman v. Yuba Power Products and its subsequent endorsement in Section 402A of the Second Restatement of Torts. One critical movement has been the steadily increasing willingness of courts to impute to a product manufacturer time-of-trial knowledge of a product's risk in design-defect cases and in failure-to-warn cases, even though it is stipulated or proved that the risk was neither known nor reasonably discoverable when the manufacturer designed, manufactured, and sold the product. Similarly, in a manufacturing-defect case, strict liability generally precludes the admission of evidence that the manufacturer's quality-control procedures were reasonable, or even extraordinarily good, to prove that he should not be held liable for harm caused by a single unit that failed to conform to his design specifications. Nor can a manufacturer adduce evidence that its own internal design standards were superior to reasonable, or nonnegligent, standards. If the unit as manufactured met or exceeded the standard of reasonableness, it may still be found defective because it did not meet the manufacturer's voluntarily adopted, more stringent standards. . . .

In an area closer to criminal sanctions, the law of punitive damages has expanded to allow recovery not only for intentional harm, but also for reckless harm. A typical common-law doctrine now requires the plaintiff to prove only that the manufacturer acted "in wanton and reckless disregard for the rights of others," with "flagrant indifference" to the rights of others, or in an "outrageous" manner.

Some courts have aided the plaintiff's cause in products cases by altering the rules of evidence in their favor. One traditional rule of evidence in negligence cases held that evidence of postaccident repairs, improvements, or remedial measures was inadmissable to establish the negligence or culpability of the defendants. Yet in strict liability products actions, some courts have eliminated this ban, so that this evidence may be used, often with great power, to prove a defect in the defendant's product. Some courts have also held that the manufacturer cannot introduce evidence that its products complied with industry custom to show that they were not defective, even though such evidence is admissible in negligence actions to prove the absence of negligence.

Wholly apart from these doctrinal developments, many features of the manufacturing environment work to the plaintiff's advantage in product litigation. The wealth of information about the designing, testing, and development of products demands the coordinated efforts of many employees. Testimony supporting the plaintiff is therefore easier to obtain; rapid mobility of workers reduces their loyalty to employers; and "whistle-blowing" becomes both more protected and more common. Also, an abundance of documentary evidence must be preserved, for both business and legal reasons. Furthermore, the presence of many competitors in most markets gives the plaintiff the opportunity to identify superior products (even those at higher prices) against which to measure the defendant's products for defectiveness. Likewise, the information that competitors supply to regulatory bodies can often be used advantageously in products liability actions.

There also has been continuing development of testing technology, analytical technology, biomechanical technology, statistical data gathering, and other technological and informational disciplines that assist private plaintiffs and regulatory agencies in reconstructing the manner in which accidents have occurred, in determining the causes of harm, and in determining and comparing the costs and benefits of particular product designs. A related but somewhat different factor is the growth in communications and copying technology, and cooperation among plaintiffs' lawyers through organizations such as the American Trial Lawyers Association, all of which enable persons who have suffered injuries from the same type of product to benefit from each other's evidence, to reduce their litigation costs, to avoid each other's tactical errors, to benefit from each other's tactical successes, and, in sum, to recover from manufacturers.

The foregoing discussion suggests that there is no compelling reason why criminal sanctions are needed to achieve a desirable level of deterrence against the manufacture of defective products. The gap, if any, between manufacturers' internalized expected costs of producing defective products and society's expected costs from that conduct appears, for the several reasons described above, to be much narrower than the gap between most other wrongdoers' internalized expected costs and their attendant social costs.

Moreover, because most manufacturers are corporations, the problem of what Stigler has labeled "illicit" utility seems much less likely to arise in the context of the manufacture of defective products than in the context of many other forms of wrongdoing. While many murderers, rapists, and arsonists gain substantial satisfaction from the harm they inflict, it seems unlikely that corporate decision makers gain similar satisfaction from a belief that products sold by their corporate employers will injure or kill innocent strangers.

Criminal sanctions against manufacturers of defective products also cannot be justified on the ground, advanced by Posner and Landes as the rationale for criminal sanctions against other types of wrongdoers, that manufacturers tend to be judgment proof and therefore undeterrable by the threat of civil actions for damages. There is no evidence that manufacturers as a group tend to be judgment proof, especially not for awards of compensatory damages based on proof of culpability.[17] Moreover, because corporations cannot be imprisoned, the only criminal sanction against most manufacturers is a fine; but if the reason for imposing the criminal sanction is the manufacturer's lack of financial resources sufficient to pay civil judgments, the addition of another monetary penalty alone cannot increase the level of deterrence.[18]

Perhaps the strongest argument, then, that can be given in support of the use of criminal sanctions to regulate product safety is a rhetorical question: Why should manufacturers of defective products be exempt from the general criminal laws governing murder, manslaughter, negligent homicide, mayhem, assault, battery, criminal recklessness, criminal negligence, and reckless endangerment? One answer is that, as suggested above, criminal sanctions are not needed to deter the manufacture of defective products, even though they are needed to deter other forms of wrongdoing in those categories of general crimes. An additional answer may be discoverable in an analysis of the social costs of using criminal sanctions to deter the manufacture of defective products; if those costs demonstrably exceed the costs of using criminal sanctions to deter most other forms of wrongdoing, society should, ceteris paribus, be more hesitant to use criminal sanctions to regulate product safety than to deter other socially undesirable conduct.

III. The Cost of Adding Criminal Sanctions to the Means Used to Regulate Product Safety

The addition of criminal sanctions against manufacturers to the host of

The addition of criminal sanctions against manufacturers to the host of other forces that tend to deter the manufacture of defective products entails a variety of social costs. The most significant of these can be divided conveniently into seven general categories:

1. government expenditures for detecting, investigating, prosecuting, and sentencing manufacturers of defective products;
2. costs incurred by manufacturers to prevent detection of evidence of reck-

17. On the other hand, claiming that the adverse judgments for compensatory and punitive damages in some 17,000 pending suits arising out of asbestos-related injuries could force it into bankruptcy, Johns-Manville Corp. and several of its affiliates have filed for reorganization in bankruptcy court. See 10 Prod. Safety & Liability Rep. (BNA) 573 (Aug. 27, 1982); N.Y. Times, August 27, 1982, at A1, col. 6.

18. Of course, the deterrent effect of the stigma attending a criminal fine must also be considered. . . .

less or knowing manufacture of defective products (for example, destruction of otherwise useful documents);

3. costs incurred by manufacturers to reduce the risk that design decisions made in a good-faith attempt to provide optimal safety will subsequently be found to have been knowingly or recklessly improper (for example, by creating otherwise unnecessary documents explaining the full basis of design decisions, by holding training sessions for employees on how to avoid using language in internal documents that can be misconstrued as evidence of an improper concern for safety, and by implementing a document-retention program based on a fear of prosecutorial abuse rather than on a concern for operational efficiency);

4. the cost of any overdeterrence—manufacturers' selecting suboptimal, but safer, designs—that might result;

5. various indirect costs (for example, the cost of relocating, retraining, or subsidizing employees of manufacturers who retrench or go out of business as a result of the direct and indirect consequences of a criminal conviction; employee embarrassment and unhappiness resulting from being affiliated with a company stigmatized as criminally heedless of the public safety; consumers' loss of confidence in, and refusal to buy, the defendant's products, even though superior to competitive products; loss of morale, security, and general happiness if manufacturing employees believe that undercover operatives might be used to detect wrongful decision making);

6. the cost of employees' invoking, even in ordinary depositions, the fifth amendment's self-incrimination privilege to protect themselves against being prosecuted for design decisions they made in the past; and

7. costs incurred by manufacturers and employees to defend themselves in criminal investigations and prosecutions.

The nature of most of these cost categories is plain, but a few warrant additional comment.

A. Government Expenditures for Detecting, Investigating, Prosecuting, and Sentencing

The magnitude of the costs incurred by society under this heading will depend on, among other factors, the number and nature of agencies given the authority to perform those functions. At one extreme, a single federal agency could be given sole investigative and prosecutorial authority in this area. At the other extreme, every state prosecutor and United States Attorney could have the authority to investigate or prosecute.

To the extent that general criminal statutes—those, for example, defining murder, manslaughter, and reckless homicide—are used to regulate product safety, the latter extreme is likely to obtain. In the Pinto prosecution, for example, the prosecuting attorney of Elkhart County, Indiana, prosecuted Ford Motor Company for reckless homicide and criminal recklessness. If not barred by [the] double jeopardy clause, additional prosecutions for reckless homicide could be commenced in any other jurisdiction where a similar Pinto-related death occurs, while further prosecution for criminal recklessness could be commenced in any jurisdiction where a Pinto is being driven. This risk of multiple uncoordinated prosecutions exists, moreover, for all products that are used and marketed on a national scale. The probability that the errors in individual cases would cancel out on some grand scale is so obviously small that it can be safely disregarded.

In addition, substantial expenditures will be required for each prosecution of a manufacturer under a general criminal statute. In the Pinto prosecution, for example, the Indiana prosecutor used the state's laboratories, airplane, automobiles, and other facilities and property; obtained the services of automobile and accident-reconstruction experts from California and Arizona; obtained assistance from federal regulatory agencies, the local coroner's office, the local fire department, the highway patrol, and the local sheriff's office; assembled a litigating team consisting of himself, his deputy, two private attorneys, two law professors, several law students, and the prosecutor in the county to which the case was moved for trial; and received assistance from nationally known expert witnesses, including an Illinois pathologist, several automotive experts, and a statistician from Washington, D.C.

The Pinto prosecution suggests that the criminal prosecution of a manufacturer for having produced a defective product requires an especially substantial diversion of investigative and prosecutorial resources from other uses when the prosecution proceeds under a general criminal statute, rather than under a regulatory scheme prescribing a precise safety standard for the product in issue. It also suggests, by the Elkhart County prosecutor's reliance on private attorneys with product liability expertise, that the use of prosecutorial resources normally devoted to the investigation and prosecution of markedly different types of criminal conduct is inefficient.

This inefficiency is especially apparent at an early stage in a criminal investigation, when the prosecutor decides whether the government's case is strong enough to warrant the expenditures needed to prosecute it. Generally, prosecutors have had no training in risk analysis and no experience in manufacturing, product design, or product liability litigation. Their preliminary judgments about whether a product's design is so defective as to suggest that its producer must have acted recklessly or knowingly are likely to be relatively unsophisticated and, therefore, erroneous.

Moreover, when it prosecutes a manufacturer for having sold a defective product, the government confronts several barriers that are not confronted either by a private plaintiff or by a government plaintiff seeking civil remedies. These barriers have been discussed in detail elsewhere but warrant a brief listing here. The criminal prosecution must prove its case, including each element of the offense, beyond a reasonable doubt. It cannot rely upon the simple preponderance-of-evidence test used in civil cases, much less on the burden-shifting rules adopted by the California court in Barker v. Lull Engineering Co. The ordinary civil presumption that, if a warning had been given, it would have been read and heeded is also likely to be unavailable to the prosecution.

The government in criminal cases must also overcome the panoply of constitutional safeguards applicable to criminal defendants. These include the fourth amendment's prohibition against unreasonable searches and seizures and the exclusionary rule used to implement it; the fifth amendment's prohibition against double jeopardy; the fifth and fourteenth amendments' due process safeguards applicable in criminal cases; and various sixth amendment safeguards.

Finally, the rules of criminal discovery do not give prosecutors the same freedom to probe that the rules of civil discovery give to plaintiffs in civil actions. This, however, is somewhat balanced by the availability in criminal cases of grand juries and of grand jury subpoenae, which enable prosecutors to conduct sweeping discovery before the prosecution has commenced.

Do these arguments convince you? What precisely does the above excerpt argue—that corporations should never be criminally prosecuted? What about retribution? Isn't that a reason for punishing corporations? Mr. Wheeler says no:

> Retributive theory posits that punishment can and must be imposed upon persons who, as moral agents, have acted immorally and therefore deserve to be punished. The theory demands mens rea, a guilty mind. It precludes punishing an infant or an insane person incapable of distinguishing right from wrong. It also precludes punishing a corporation, which, even more clearly than infants and insane persons, is incapable of distinguishing right from wrong. A corporation as such lacks a mind and cannot know anything, including the nature or consequences of its "acts." Indeed, a corporation cannot actually act at all. It can be *said* to act, and it can be *said* to know the nature of its acts, but this terminological ploy obscures the critical difference between abstract entities and true moral agents. The retributive theory cannot justify, and does not even permit, the imposition of criminal sanctions on corporate manufacturers.
>
> Nor does retributive theory permit criminal sanctions to be imposed on a corporation in the hope that the punishment will filter down to the individual corporate agents morally responsible for the criminal conduct. The state may not, for example, fine a corporation to induce the board of directors to seek out and fire the morally responsible agents, because that practice punishes morally innocent shareholders to make them do what the state has failed to do directly. Retribution does not permit such an instrumentalist use of one group of moral agents to make another group suffer its just deserts.[19] [Wheeler, supra, at 598.]

The author above attempts to rebut the justifications for criminal punishment in product liability cases. Does he consider the denunciatory justification (see p.39)? What would we be denouncing?

B. VOLUNTARY MANSLAUGHTER

1. Sample Statutes

KAN. STAT. ANN.
(Rev. Stat. 1979)

§21-3403. Voluntary Manslaughter.

Voluntary manslaughter is the unlawful killing of a human being, without malice, which is done intentionally upon a sudden quarrel or in the heat of passion.

19. Immanuel Kant, Philosophy of Law ("punishment can never be administered merely as a means for promoting another Good . . . but must in all cases be imposed only because the individual on whom it is inflicted *has committed a Crime*").

Voluntary manslaughter is a class C felony [punishable by 1-20 years in prison].

PA. CONS. STAT. ANN.
(1983)

§2503. VOLUNTARY MANSLAUGHTER.

(a) *General Rule.*—A person who kills an individual without lawful justification commits voluntary manslaughter if at the time of the killing he is acting under a sudden and intense passion resulting from serious provocation by:

(1) the individual killed; or
(2) another whom the actor endeavors to kill, but he negligently or accidentally causes the death of the individual killed. . . .

(c) Grading—Voluntary manslaughter is a felony of the second degree

[punishable by up to 10 years in prison].

CAL. PENAL CODE
(1970)

§192. MANSLAUGHTER; VOLUNTARY, INVOLUNTARY, AND VEHICULAR, CONSTRUCTION OF SECTION.

Manslaughter is the unlawful killing of a human being without malice. It is of three kinds.

1. Voluntary—upon a sudden quarrel or heat of passion [punishable by 3-11 years in prison].

2. THE NATURE OF PROVOCATION

STATE v. YANZ
Supreme Court of Errors of Connecticut
50 A. 37 (1901)

George Yanz was convicted of murder in the second degree, and he appeals. Reversed.

The defendant upon the trial introduced evidence, mainly for himself as a witness in his own behalf, that on the day in question he discovered his wife in a piece of woods near his house, with a man, whom he did not recognize; that they were partially reclining on the ground, and that the man had his arms around her; that, thinking the man might be armed, he ran home, and got his rifle; that he returned, loading it as he ran, and found her in the man's arms, lying on her back, with her clothes up, and the man in a position justifying the belief that they were in the act of adultery; that he rushed upon them through the bushes, and in so doing the rifle was accidentally discharged, killing the man. The state claimed and offered evidence tending to prove that he had previously made statements materially different as to the circumstances of the homicide; that the man killed, George Goering, had been on friendly and familiar terms with Yanz, and was well acquainted with Mrs. Yanz; that he had occasionally called upon the defendant at his house; that on this occasion the defendant found him standing in the wood, in conversation with Mrs. Yanz, and, having got his rifle and loaded it, deliberately shot him as he (Goering) was walking away. . . . The defendant, through his counsel, claimed that, if the jury should not believe his story that the shooting was accidental or involuntary, then, at the very most, he could only be convicted of manslaughter.

BALDWIN, J. (after stating the facts). . . .

The trial court, in its charge to the jury, used this language:

> If the accused saw his wife in any such situation as he has described, he had at least a legal right to interfere and separate them, and to carry with him a weapon for defense against any possible attack. And, further, if in pushing his way through the bushes, and under the excitement naturally and ordinarily to be expected under the circumstances, the rifle was accidentally discharged, and the man thus met his death, then the homicide was by misadventure, and the verdict should be "Not Guilty." . . . There is one kind of provocation, gentlemen, which is of such a grievous nature that the law concludes it cannot be borne in the first transport of passion. This is where or when a man finds another in the act of adultery with his wife; when, if he kills him in the first transport of passion thereby aroused, he is only guilty of manslaughter. The law does not hold him altogether guiltless of the crime. To kill, even in the first transport of passion, when under that highest and strongest provocation, is in law criminal. It is manslaughter, the lowest form of criminal homicide; not murder. The adulterer, under our law, has a right to live; and the injured husband has no legal right to kill him, even in the first transport of passion aroused by finding him in the act. To have the effect of reducing the homicide from murder to manslaughter, the husband must find the adulterer in the act of adultery. The finding may be by any such observation of the circumstances and of the situation of the guilty parties as justifies the belief that adultery is being committed. Knowledge that the adultery is at the time being committed is sufficient; but if the husband, merely hearing that the adultery had already been accomplished, or merely observing the situation which leads to the belief that adultery has been accomplished, pursues and kills, the offender, it will be murder. The witnessing of a passing fact is regarded as having a greater tendency to excite a transport of passion than the mere hearing or the mere belief that it has been accomplished.

> If, in fact, no adultery was going on, and the husband is mistaken as to the fact, though the circumstances were such as to justify a belief, even, of adultery, the offense would not be reduced to manslaughter. The husband must judge at his peril that the jury may find that he was mistaken, and so find him guilty of murder instead of manslaughter.

There are inconsistent expressions in these instructions, but it is to be presumed that those used last were accepted by the jury as controlling, and they were the least favorable to the accused. In case, then, they believed so much of the defendant's testimony as described the circumstances in which he found his wife and Goering together, and the effect which they produced, and were reasonably calculated to produce, upon his mind, but disbelieved his statement that the gun was accidentally discharged, the charge gave them to understand that, if the act of adultery was not in fact committed, the killing was murder. The law justifies a jury in calling it manslaughter when, on finding his wife in the act of adultery, a man, in the first transport of passion, kills her paramour. This is because from a sudden act of this kind, committed under the natural excitement of feeling induced by so gross an outrage, malice, which is a necessary ingredient of the crime of murder, cannot fairly be implied. The excitement is the effect of a belief, from ocular evidence, of the actual commission of adultery. It is the belief, so reasonably formed, that excites the uncontrollable passion. Such a belief, though a mistaken one, is calculated to induce the same emotions as would be felt were the wrongful act in fact committed.

The crime of murder in the second degree, under our statute, rests upon implied malice. It is not sufficient to establish merely a criminal intent followed by a homicide. Malice is not to be implied if the fatal act were the sudden result of what the law deems either a sufficient provocation, or an uncontrollable passion naturally excited by the circumstances of the occasion. The law deems a husband's passion, excited by surprising his wife in the act of adultery, so far uncontrollable, from the frailty of human nature, that, if he kill her paramour on the impulse of the moment, and no actual malice is disclosed, none ought to be implied. He is not justified; but he is not a murderer. The reason of this rule of law being the existence of an uncontrollable passion, naturally induced, it must logically follow that it suffices if such a passion has been naturally induced in the mind of the slayer by the sight of his wife in the embrace of the man whom he killed, and a reasonable belief of her guilt, formed under circumstances such as those to which the accused testified in the present case. If the jury believed this testimony, or so much of it as showed a state of facts which, in their opinion, justified and produced a reasonable belief on the part of the accused that adultery was being committed when the shot was fired, then, there having been no proof of actual malice, although they may also have believed that it was fired intentionally, the natural excitement of passion and want of premeditation make the offense manslaughter. The judgment is set aside, and a new trial is ordered.

Torrance and Hall, JJ., concurred. Andrews, C.J., and Hamersley, J., dissented.

Hamersley, J. (dissenting). The particular passage of the charge claimed to be erroneous is this: "If in fact no adultery was going on, and the husband is mistaken as to the fact, though the circumstances were such as to justify a belief, even, of adultery, the offense would not be reduced to manslaughter." The statement is correct. . . . To make the offense manslaughter, the injury must have been done. Intentional unlawful killing in a rage is murder, and not manslaughter. Anger thirsting for the blood of an enemy is in itself an earmark of murder, no less than revenge or brutal ferocity; but when it is provoked by the wrongful act of the person slain, who thus brings upon himself the fatal blow, given in the first outbreak of rage, caused by himself, the offense is manslaughter; not only because the voluntary act is, in a way, compelled by an ungovernable rage but also because the victim is the aggressor; and his wrong, although it cannot justify, may modify, the nature of the homicide thus induced. The court therefore correctly told the jury that, to make the offense manslaughter, the injury claimed as a provocation must have in fact been done. Our law of homicide recognizes no provocation as legally competent to so modify the cruelty of intentional, unlawful killing as to reduce the offense to manslaughter, except the provocation involved in an actual and adequate injury and insult. A different rule of provocation applies when the killing is not intentional; as where it results from the use of force, not intended, and not naturally adapted, to cause death. But where the killing is both intentional and unlawful, the only legal provocation is that given by an actual injury and insult.

The decision of the majority of the court is based on the assertion that the intentional unlawful killing of an innocent person who had done the slayer no wrong may be manslaughter; or, in other words, an actual injury done to the slayer is not essential in order to reduce such killing from murder to manslaughter. I find no authority in our law for this assertion. During the three centuries in which the distinction between the crime of murder and that of manslaughter has been developed and established, there is, so far as I have been able to discover, no dictum, or jurist, or decision of court which has failed to recognize the necessity of an actual injury and insult given by the killed and suffered by the killer as necessary to the reduction of intentional unlawful killing from murder to manslaughter. It seems to me unquestionable that the decision involves a clean-cut and radical change of existing law. I think such a change would be unwise, and inconsistent with the considerations of public policy that underlie our law of homicide. . . . If there is any mistake in the particular passage of the charge, it is the statement of a general rule not material in the state of evidence before the jury. The only question in respect to the alleged injury claimed as a provocation was the truth or falsity of the testimony describing the positions of the defendant's wife and the deceased just prior to the firing of the fatal shot. The defendant testified that he discovered his wife upon the ground, lying on her back, with her clothes up, and the man in the position detailed, and which the finding says justified the belief that they were engaged in the act of adultery. There was no qualifying evidence. If the testimony was credible, adultery had been committed, and the injury alleged had been given. There was, therefore, no occasion to state the rule of law applicable to a state of facts which might justify a reasonable belief that adultery had been committed, and also show that in fact it had not been. The court might properly have omitted reference to a rule not applicable to the state of fact as claimed; or, possibly, if the reference were made, might properly have added that, if the conduct of the deceased with the prisoner's wife did not satisfy the jury that adultery had been committed, yet the conduct detailed was in itself a grievous injury and insult and legal provocation. That such conduct is a legal provocation seems to me demonstrable, but such question is not now involved, and no claim in respect to it is made. If it were a mistake to state the rule of law governing a case where there was a reasonable belief in adultery which was in fact unfounded, the mistake was harmless, and would not be less harmless if the qualification suggested had been made. The record shows with certainty that the only question before the jury as to this part of the case was the credibility of the defendant's testimony as to the fact of adultery. If credible, adultery had been committed, and the offense was manslaughter. Upon this question the charge of the court is clear, full, and impartial. It could not have been misunderstood, and could not have been affected by the statement in the general definition of legal provocation as to the necessity of proving the fact of adultery. Neither court nor counsel contemplated the contingency of the jury finding as a fact the circumstances under which the parties were claimed to have been discovered, and also finding that no adultery had been committed. There was no such contingency. It involved an absurdity approaching grotesqueness, and yet a new trial cannot be lawfully granted without gravely assuming the probability of the verdict having been influenced by such an absurdity. A mistake, or even an error, in the passage of the charge objected to, would relate to a state of facts not before the jury, was rendered harmless by those portions of the charge directly dealing with the evidence, and could not have affected the conclusion of the jury. The defendant has had a fair trial. The charge of the court is correct in law, full and impartial in its review of the evidence and presentation of all claims made by the parties; and, even if the passage objected to might properly have been omitted or qualified, there is no ground for a new trial. I think there is no error, and that a new trial should be denied.

Notes and Questions

1. What is the dispute between the majority and the dissent?
2. Manslaughter encompasses two very different kinds of killings. Volun-

tary manslaughter differs from involuntary manslaughter, the kind of homicide previously discussed, in that it is intentional; the defendant has with knowledge or purpose killed another human being rather than having done so with gross negligence or recklessness or merely with the intent to commit some other crime.

As we will see subsequently, however, an intentional killing is generally murder. The criminal law reduces the murder to voluntary manslaughter where there has been "provocation" that has caused the defendant to act in "the heat of passion."

At common law, the provocation that would mitigate an intentional killing from murder to voluntary manslaughter fell into one of two categories. One was a physical, assaultive blow, which the common law viewed as such an affront as to arouse a reasonable person to passion. The other was the sight of one's spouse in an act of adultery. Appellate cases involving a blow are extremely rare, perhaps because juries tend to find defendants innocent on the grounds of self-defense or because the law is so clear in this area that it raises few legal issues. As a result, some commentators[20] have argued that the unifying theme of voluntary manslaughter cases is male sexual insecurity:

> The common thread running through the majority of the cases in this section involves men defending their virility with violence.
>
> What are we to conclude from this? If the principal legally sufficient provocation is physical battery, why aren't the majority of the cases about battery? Conversely, if the provocation rule is used primarily as a defense by men who resort to violence when they feel their masculinity has been threatened, what values are being reflected and perpetuated by the provocation rule? Are they the same as those underlying self-defense? Or is the provocation rule merely a rationalization for male aggression?

3. Does the law as to voluntary manslaughter imply that the provocation must be such that a reasonable person would kill? If that is the case, why are we convicting a reasonable person of a serious crime? If this is not the case, why does the law mitigate the grade of homicide? How does the issue of "provocative temptation" square with the goal of general deterrence? Should the criminal law *reduce* the accused's punishment where his temptation to kill is greater, or is deterrence even more necessary here?

4. In some jurisdictions, provocation is not the only reason to reduce an unlawful intentional killing from murder to voluntary manslaughter. For example, a person who kills in the unreasonable and mistaken belief that he or she must do so in self-defense or who kills in the face of an actual threat of death or serious injury but who provoked the attack may in some jurisdictions be guilty of voluntary manslaughter. We address these situations in the later chapters on justification and excuse.

20. Law Women Find Sexism in 1L Casebook, The Commentator, New York University Law School, Mar. 19, 1984 at 7).

5. The Model Penal Code Commentaries to §210.3 discuss the provocation doctrine as it existed at common law.

> At most provocation affects the quality of the actor's state of mind as an indicator of moral blameworthiness. Provocation is thus properly regarded as a recognition by the law that inquiry into the reasons for the actor's formulation of an intent to kill will sometimes reveal factors that should have significance in grading. It is a concession to human weakness and perhaps to non-deterrability, a recognition of the fact that one who kills in response to certain provoking events should be regarded as demonstrating a significantly different character deficiency than one who kills in their absence.
>
> Although statements of the rule vary slightly, common law provocation has two essential requirements. The first is objective in character. The provocation must be "adequate," and adequacy is measured by reference to the objective standard of the reasonable man. . . . The second requirement is subjective in nature. The defendant must in fact have been provoked; he must have acted in response to the provocation. . . . He also must not have acted from any previously settled intention to kill. These requirements necessitate a subjective assessment of the particular individual's state of mind at the time of the killing. These elements of the rule of provocation will each be examined in turn.
>
> Provocation is said to be "adequate" if it would cause a reasonable person to lose his self-control. Of course, a reasonable person does not kill even when provoked, but events may so move a person to violence that a homicidal reaction, albeit unreasonable in some sense, merits neither the extreme condemnation nor the extreme sanctions of a conviction of murder. The underlying judgment is thus that some instances of intentional homicide may be as much attributable to the extraordinary nature of the situation as to the moral depravity of the actor. This observation supplies the essential rationale for the law of provocation: "The more strongly most persons would be moved to kill by circumstances of the sort that provoked the actor to the homicidal act, and the more difficulty they would experience in resisting the impulse to which he yielded, the less does his succumbing serve to differentiate his character from theirs." This rationale explains the rule's secure grounding in an objective view of what constitutes sufficient provocation. The lighter the provocation, when understood in terms of the way ordinary people would react, "the more basis there is for ascribing the actor's act to an extraordinary susceptibility to intense passion, to an unusual deficiency in those other desires which counteract in most men the desires which impel them to homicidal acts, or to an extraordinary weakness of reason and consequent inability to bring such desires into play." Yet it is also clear that some characteristics of the individual actor must be considered. A taunting attack that would seem trivial to the ordinary citizen may be extremely threatening to the blind man. And a person experiencing an adverse reaction to chemotherapy cannot be expected to maintain the same judgment and restraint that he would otherwise possess. The common law viewed such concessions grudgingly, however, and the courts took a firm stance against individualization of the standard for determining adequacy of provocation.
>
> Traditionally, the courts have also limited the circumstances of adequate provocation by casting generalizations about reasonable human behavior into rules of law that structured and confined the operation of the doctrine. Thus, the decisions usually required that the provocation arise from some action of the

deceased or at least that the defendant reasonably so believe. Further, there emerged a series of categories defining conduct that a jury might deem adequate provocation. First and foremost, physical attack might constitute provocation, though not every technical battery could suffice. Of course, even a violent blow would be inadequate if the deceased were entitled to use force, as for example in self-defense. Mutual combat became another established category of provocation. Less clearly, a threat of physical attack might constitute provocation, at least in extreme cases. Unlawful arrest would sometimes suffice, and the law frequently recognized witnessing adultery as provocation for intentional homicide of either the unfaithful spouse or the paramour. Certain other acts—chiefly violent or sexual assault on a close relative—might also constitute adequate provocation. Most importantly, the courts excluded some situations from the jury's consideration altogether. Thus, it became an established rule at common law that words alone, no matter how insulting, could not amount to adequate provocation. The only apparent exception concerned informational words disclosing a fact that would have been adequate provocation had the actor observed it himself.

The second branch of the common-law rule of provocation is subjective rather than objective in character. Circumstances sufficient to rob a reasonable man of self control will not mitigate a resulting homicide unless the defendant in fact acted in a sudden heat of passion. Passion usually means rage, but it also includes fear or any violent and intense emotion sufficient to dethrone reason. Thus, a person of exceptional restraint or maturity of judgment is held to a higher standard than is his more susceptible counterpart. The same rule applies to cooling time. One who kills after adequate provocation and before a reasonable man would regain self-control is nonetheless guilty of murder if he recovered from the affront with unusual quickness. The underlying rationale is that the individual whose passions are not aroused by provocation merits the same condemnation and punishment as one who kills without provocation of any sort.

subjective

6. As noted above, the common law limited "adequate provocation" to legally defined categories, and one of the core situations in which the common law found legally adequate provocation was where the accused actually discovered his spouse in the act of adultery and killed either his spouse or her "paramour." (Although we know of no reports in the appellate literature of this situation with the genders reversed, let us charitably assume that the same result would hold.) With that legal principle as a foundation, assume you are in a precedent-based common law state, and consider whether the following variants present legally adequate provocation, where Brown kills Smith:

a. Smith brags to Brown that Smith has just committed adultery with Brown's wife.

b. Smith brags to Brown that Smith long ago had an intense affair with Brown's wife:

i. after the Browns were married.
ii. before the Browns were married.

c. Green tells Brown that Smith has just committed adultery with Brown's wife.

d. Smith approaches Brown and calls Brown's wife an adulteress.

7. If somebody is provoked under conditions that would provoke a reasonable person, should he or she be denied the mitigation to voluntary manslaughter if it turns out that his or her judgment as to the underlying facts was incorrect? What if his or her judgment was unreasonable? Is that the issue in *Yanz?* Refer back to the state voluntary manslaughter statutes at pages 257 to 258. How should we interpret these statutes in light of the principles of *mens rea* discussed in Chapter 4?

EX PARTE FRALEY

Oklahoma Criminal Court of Appeals
109 P. 295 (1910)

RICHARDSON, J. This is an original application in this court by M. F. Fraley for a writ of habeas corpus, by which he seeks to be let to bail pending the final hearing and determination of a charge of murder filed against him in Osage county. . . .

Petitioner contends that he should be let to bail . . . because the proof of his guilt of a capital offense is not evident or the presumption thereof great. . . .

Petitioner did not testify in the examining trial, nor were any witnesses introduced in his behalf. The testimony taken, which is uncontradicted in this court, shows: That the deceased, Dan Parker, on April 11, 1910, was sitting upon or leaning against a railing in front of a drug store in the city of Pawhuska. That he had been in that position for some 10 or 15 minutes engaged in conversation with some gentlemen beside him in regard to the sale of certain walnut timber. That the petitioner came around the corner, walked up in front of the deceased, said, "Hello, Dan," and without further warning immediately fired two shots into the deceased in quick succession. That the deceased jumped up, threw up his hands, staggered, and fell off the sidewalk. The petitioner thereupon walked around an obstruction and fired four more shots into the deceased. That the petitioner then walked off, and, after going some distance, turned and came back, and putting his pistol close to the head of the deceased, snapped it a time or two, and said: "You damned son of a bitch! I told you I'd kill you. You killed my boy." The substance of the foregoing facts are testified to positively by seven eyewitnesses, and they stand in the record undisputed. It is further shown that after the deceased fell off the sidewalk his pistol fell out of his pocket; but the evidence nowhere tends to show that the deceased ever at any time had his pistol in his hand, or that he ever made any effort or demonstration to draw it. No previous conversation or difficulty of any kind or character between the petitioner and the deceased was shown or intimated.

The testimony does not show it, but it was stated by counsel for the petitioner in presenting this case, that the deceased, some 9 or 10 months previously, had shot and killed the son of the petitioner, and that the deceased had been acquitted; and it is urged here that, when the petitioner saw the deceased on this occasion, the recollection of that event must have engendered in him a passion which overcame him, that the killing was committed in the heat of such passion, was without premeditation, and therefore not murder. To this we cannot assent. . . . In Ragland v. State, 125 Ala. 19, 27 So. 983, four hours intervening between the provocation and the killing was held as a matter of law to be sufficient cooling time to preclude the reduction of a homicide to manslaughter. Perry v. State, 102 Ga. 365, 30 S.E. 903, and Rockmore v. State, 93 Ga. 123, 19 S.E. 32, each hold three days as a matter of law sufficient. Commonwealth v. Aiello, 180 Pa. 597, 36 A. 1079, holds from 1 to 2 hours sufficient, and State v. Williams, 141 N.C. 827, 53 S.E. 823, holds 15 minutes sufficient. And the authorities are all agreed that the question is not alone whether the defendant's passion in fact cooled, but also was there sufficient time in which the passion of a reasonable man would cool? If in fact the defendant's passion did cool, which may be shown by circumstances, such as the transaction of other business in the meantime, rational conversations upon other subjects, evidence of preparation for the killing, etc., then the length of time intervening is immaterial. But if in fact it did not cool, yet if such time intervened between the provocation and the killing that the passion of the average man would have cooled, and his reason have resumed its sway, then still there is no reduction of the homicide to manslaughter. If the fatal wound be inflicted immediately following a sufficient provocation given, then the question as to whether the defendant's passion thereby aroused had in fact cooled, or as to whether or not such time had elapsed that the passion of a reasonable man would have cooled, is a question of fact to be determined upon a consideration of all the facts and circumstances in evidence; but, when an unreasonable period of time has elapsed between the provocation and the killing, then the court is authorized to say as a matter of law that the cooling time was sufficient.

Ordinarily one day, or even half a day, is in law much more than a sufficient time for one's passion to cool; and a killing committed upon a provocation given some 9 or 10 months before, is not, on account of that provocation or any passion engendered thereby, reduced to manslaughter. A deliberate killing committed in revenge for an injury inflicted in the past, however near or remote, is "murder."

The uncontradicted testimony in this case convinces us that the proof of the petitioner's guilt of a capital offense is evident, and that he is not therefore entitled to bail as a matter of right. . . .

Notes and Questions

1. According to the Model Penal Code Commentaries to §210.3:

> The courts supplemented their rules about adequate provocation by requiring that there not elapse between provocation and resulting homicide sufficient time

for a reasonable man to cool off. For the reasonable man, at least, passion subsides and reason reasserts its sway as the provoking event grows stale. The courts refused to allow mitigation of intentional homicide where the actor had enjoyed a reasonable opportunity for his passion to cool. Generally, this rule obtained even where the defendant in fact did not cool off but was still enraged at the time he killed. This view is consistent with the application of an objective, reasonable-person test to the cooling period as well as to the existence of provocation. If a reasonable person would have cooled off before the killing occurred, the passion was held to have subsided, and the provocation was not longer effective to reduce the homicide from murder to manslaughter. Although some courts allowed a subsequent event to revive prior provocation, others applied the cooling-time limitation with surprising strictness. In the famous case of State v. Gounagias [153 P. 9 (Wash. 1915)], the deceased committed sodomy on the unconscious defendant and subsequently spread the news of his accomplishment. Those who learned of the event taunted and ridiculed the defendant until he finally lost control and killed his assailant some two weeks after the sodomy. The court rejected the defendant's theory that the cumulative effect of reminders of former wrongs could support a sudden passion and allow mitigation and held that the passage of time precluded the original act of sodomy from being a basis for mitigation. In other instances of cumulative provocation, however, courts have held that the cooling time began with the occurrence of the last provocative event preceding the homicide.

2. If the killing of Fraley's son was legally adequate provocation, why does Fraley lose?

3. The court seems to assume that by killing Fraley's son, Parker "provoked" Fraley within the meaning of the law. Is that necessarily true? How do we square this assumption with Parker's acquittal? Can you imagine facts supporting Parker's acquittal that would either support or undermine the court's assumption?

4. Why should the law mitigate a killing if it is done rashly on the spur of the moment, but not where the killing is the result of a long process of anguished brooding? In State v. Gounagias, discussed in the Model Penal Code excerpt above, 153 P. 9 (Wash. 1915), the Washington Supreme Court discussed the criteria of adequate provocation and reasonable cooling time, where the deceased had humiliated the accused by sodomizing him, and then, over a course of two weeks, had bragged about his sexual triumph over the accused to other men in their town:

> The doctrine of mitigation is briefly this: That if the act of killing, though intentional, be committed under the influence of sudden, intense anger, or heat of blood, obscuring the reason, produced by an adequate or reasonable provocation, and before sufficient time has elapsed for the blood to cool and reason to reassert itself, so that the killing is the result of temporary excitement rather than of wickedness of heart or innate recklessness of disposition, then the law, recognizing the standard of human conduct as that of the ordinary or average man, regards the offense so committed as of less heinous character than premeditated or deliberate murder. Measured as it must be by the conduct of the average man, what constitutes adequate cause is incapable of exact definition. . . .

By this it is not meant that the reason should be so entirely obscured as to destroy intelligent volition; otherwise, there could never be any mitigation short of actual insanity. . . .

Though many courts have held to the contrary, we are convinced that, for the very reason that it cannot be measured by any Procrustean standard or reduced to any fixed rule, the question of adequate or reasonable cause is essentially a question of fact, to be submitted to the jury under proper instructions whenever it can be said that the alleged provocation would have any reasonable tendency to produce sudden and uncontrollable anger and heat of blood in the ordinary man. The question of such reasonable *tendency* is of necessity a question for the court arising upon the admission of testimony. . . .

What is a reasonable cooling time is also, we think, generally a question for the jury. While there are many authorities which hold that it is always a question of law for the court, that view seems to us clearly invasive of the constitutional guaranty of jury trial. All courts agree that the time necessary for cooling is a reasonable time. The question of reasonable time is always a conclusion to be drawn from all of the facts and circumstances of the particular case. This is true where reasonable time is the ultimate issue, even in civil cases, when what is a reasonable time is not defined by statute. . . .

. . . As stated in 2 Bishop's New Criminal Law (8th Ed.) §712:

> We have no rule for determining how much time is necessary for cooling; in the nature of things, it must depend much on what is special to the particular case. Commonly the time in which an ordinary man under like circumstances would cool is deemed reasonable.

We apprehend that the true rule is precisely the same as that in other cases where reasonableness of human conduct is necessarily measured by the conduct of the ordinary or average man in like situation, so frequently announced and applied in cases where the ultimate question is one of negligence. It is only where it can be said that, giving to the evidence every reasonable inference that can be drawn from it favorable to the defendant, the minds of reasonable men could not differ in the conclusion that a reasonable cooling time had elapsed, the question is one for the court. Wanting this inevitable conclusion both from the evidence and inference therefrom, the question is always one for the jury upon proper instructions. . . .

Measured by these principles, in which we have adopted the most liberal views expressed by any court, did the court err in refusing to admit the offered evidence of provocation? For the purpose of this discussion we must, of course, assume that the offered evidence was true. There can be no doubt that the original outrage committed by the deceased would have been a sufficient provocation to take the case to the jury, if the appellant, immediately upon realizing its perpetration, had sought out and slain the deceased. There can be little doubt that, had the appellant slain the deceased when, on meeting him the next day, the deceased impudently treated the outrage as inconsequential, the question of provocation would have been for the jury. No court would be warranted in saying that such callous conduct, while the original wrong was but a day old, would have no reasonable tendency to produce immediate, uncontrollable anger, destroying the capacity for cool reflection in the average man. In such a case evidence of both the previous conduct and the insolent behavior of deceased on the subsequent meeting would have been admissible.

The court then concluded:

> The offered evidence makes it clear that the appellant knew and appreciated for days before the killing the full meaning of the words, signs, and vulgar gestures of his countrymen, which, as the offer shows, he had encountered from day to day for about three weeks following the original outrage, wherever he went. The final demonstration in the coffeehouse was nothing new. It was exactly what the appellant, from his experience for the prior three weeks, must have anticipated. To say that it alone tended to create the sudden passion and heat of blood essential to mitigation is to ignore the admitted fact that the same thing had created no such condition on its repeated occurrence during the prior three weeks. To say that these repeated demonstrations, coupled with the original outrage, *culminated* in a sudden passion and heat of blood when he encountered the same character of demonstration in the coffeehouse on the night of the killing, is to say that sudden passion and heat of blood in the mitigative sense may be a cumulative result of repeated reminders of a single act of provocation occurring weeks before, and this, whether that provocation be regarded as the original outrage or the spreading of the story among appellant's associates, both of which he knew and fully realized for three weeks before the fatal night. This theory of the cumulative effect of reminders of former wrongs, not of new acts of provocation by the deceased, is contrary to the idea of sudden anger as understood in the doctrine of mitigation. In the nature of the thing *sudden* anger cannot be cumulative. A provocation which does not cause instant resentment, but which is only resented after being thought upon and brooded over, is not a provocation sufficient in law to reduce intentional killing from murder to manslaughter, or under our statute to second degree murder, which includes every inexcusable, unjustifiable, unpremeditated, intentional killing. . . .
>
> The evidence offered had no tendency to prove sudden anger and resentment. On the contrary, it did tend to prove brooding thought, resulting in the design to kill. It was therefore properly excluded.

5. What if the distraught father in Ex Parte Fraley had, without a "cooling off" period, mistakenly shot the brother of the man who had killed his son? Should that fact affect his claim of mitigation, assuming that he would be punished for no less than voluntary manslaughter anyway? What if Fraley made the error because he was drunk?

6. Why should we insist that the defendant who concededly is not reasonable in killing be reasonable in apprehending the facts that will mitigate her killing to manslaughter?

PEOPLE v. BERRY

Supreme Court of California

18 Cal. 3d 509, 134 Cal. Rptr. 415, 556 P.2d 777 (1976)

SULLIVAN, Justice.

Defendant Albert Joseph Berry was charged by indictment with one count of murder (Pen. Code §187). . . . A jury found defendant guilty as charged. . . . Defendant was sentenced to state prison for the term prescribed by law. He appeals from the judgment of conviction.

Defendant contends that there is sufficient evidence in the record to show that he committed the homicide while in a state of uncontrollable rage caused by provocation and . . . therefore that it was error for the trial court to fail to instruct the jury on voluntary manslaughter as indeed he had requested. He claims . . . that he was entitled to an instruction on voluntary manslaughter as defined by statute (§192) since the killing was done upon a sudden quarrel or heat of passion. . . .

Defendant, a cook, 46 years old, and Rachel Pessah, a 20-year-old girl from Israel, were married on May 27, 1974. Three days later Rachel went to Israel by herself, returning on July 13, 1974. On July 23, 1974, defendant choked Rachel into unconsciousness. She was treated at a hospital where she reported her strangulation by defendant to an officer of the San Francisco Police Department. On July 25, Inspector Sammon, who had been assigned to the case, met with Rachel and as a result of the interview a warrant was issued for defendant's arrest.

While Rachel was at the hospital, defendant removed his clothes from their apartment and stored them in a Greyhound Bus Depot locker. He stayed overnight at the home of a friend, Mrs. Jean Berk, admitting to her that he had choked his wife. On July 26, he telephoned Mrs. Berk and informed her that he had killed Rachel with a telephone cord on that morning at their apartment. The next day Mrs. Berk and two others telephoned the police to report a possible homicide and met Officer Kelleher at defendant's apartment. They gained entry and found Rachel on the bathroom floor. A pathologist from the coroner's office concluded that the cause of Rachel's death was strangulation. Defendant was arrested on August 1, 1974, and confessed to the killing.

At trial defendant did not deny strangling his wife, but claimed through his own testimony and the testimony of a psychiatrist, Dr. Martin Blinder, that he was provoked into killing her because of a sudden and uncontrollable rage so as to reduce the offense to one of voluntary manslaughter. He testified that upon her return from Israel, Rachel announced to him that while there she had fallen in love with another man, one Yako, and had enjoyed his sexual favors, that he was coming to this country to claim her and that she wished a divorce. Thus commenced a tormenting two weeks in which Rachel alternately taunted defendant with her involvement with Yako and at the same time sexually excited defendant, indicating her desire to remain with him. Defendant's detailed testimony, summarized below, chronicles this strange course of events.

After their marriage, Rachel lived with defendant for only three days and then left for Israel. Immediately upon her return to San Francisco she told defendant about her relationship with and love for Yako. This brought about further argument and a brawl that evening in which defendant choked Rachel and she responded by scratching him deeply many times. Nonetheless they continued to live together. Rachel kept taunting defendant with Yako and demanding a divorce. She claimed she thought she might be pregnant by Yako. She showed defendant pictures of herself with Yako. Nevertheless, during a return trip from Santa Rosa, Rachel demanded immediate sexual intercourse with defendant in the car, which was achieved; however upon reaching their apartment, she again stated that she loved Yako and that she would not have intercourse with the defendant in the future.

On the evening of July 22d defendant and Rachel went to a movie where they engaged in heavy petting. When they returned home and got into bed, Rachel announced that she had intended to make love with defendant, "But I am saving myself for this man Yako, so I don't think I will." Defendant got out of bed and prepared to leave the apartment whereupon Rachel screamed and yelled at him. Defendant choked her into unconsciousness.

Two hours later defendant called a taxi for his wife to take her to the hospital. He put his clothes in the Greyhound bus station and went to the home of his friend Mrs. Berk for the night. The next day he went to Reno and returned the day after. Rachel informed him by telephone that there was a warrant for his arrest as a result of her report to the police about the choking incident. On July 25th defendant returned to the apartment to talk to Rachel, but she was out. He slept there overnight. Rachel returned around 11 A.M. the next day. Upon seeing defendant there, she said, "I suppose you have come here to kill me." Defendant responded, "yes," changed his response to "no," and then again to "yes," and finally stated "I have really come to talk to you." Rachel began screaming. Defendant grabbed her by the shoulder and tried to stop her screaming. She continued. They struggled and finally defendant strangled her with a telephone cord.

Dr. Martin Blinder, a physician and psychiatrist, called by the defense, testified that Rachel was a depressed, suicidally inclined girl and that this suicidal impulse led her to involve herself ever more deeply in a dangerous situation with defendant. She did this by sexually arousing him and taunting him into jealous rages in an unconscious desire to provoke him into killing her and thus consummating her desire for suicide. Throughout the period commencing with her return from Israel until her death, that is from July 13 to July 26, Rachel continually provoked defendant with sexual taunts and incitements, alternating acceptance and rejection of him. This conduct was accompanied by repeated references to her involvement with another man; it led defendant to choke her on two occasions, until finally she achieved her unconscious desire and was strangled. Dr. Blinder testified that as a result of this cumulative series of provocations, defendant at the time he fatally strangled Rachel, was in a state of uncontrollable rage, completely under the sway of passion.

We first take up defendant's claim that on the basis of the foregoing evidence he was entitled to an instruction on voluntary manslaughter as defined by statute which is "the unlawful killing of a human being, without malice . . . upon a sudden quarrel or heat of passion." (§192.) In People v. Valentine (1946) 28 Cal. 2d 121, 169 P.2d 1, this court, in an extensive review of the law of manslaughter, specifically approved the following quotation from People v. Logan (1917) 175 Cal. 45, 48-49, 164 P. 1121 as a correct statement of the law:

> In the present condition of our law *it is left to the jurors* to say whether or not the facts and circumstances in evidence are sufficient to lead them to believe that the defendant did, or to create a reasonable doubt in their minds as to whether or not he did, commit his offense under a heat of passion. The jury is further to be admonished and advised by the court that this heat of passion must be such a passion as would naturally be aroused in the mind of an ordinarily reasonable person under the given facts and circumstances, and that, consequently, no defendant may set up his own standard of conduct and justify or excuse himself because in fact his passions were aroused, unless further the jury believe that the facts and circumstances were sufficient to arouse the passions of the ordinarily reasonable man. . . . For the fundamental of the inquiry is whether or not the defendant's reason was, at the time of his act, so disturbed or obscured by some passion—not necessarily fear and never, of course, the passion for revenge—to such an extent as would render ordinary men of average disposition liable to act rashly or without due deliberation and reflection, and from this passion rather than from judgment.

We further held in *Valentine* that there is no specific type of provocation required by section 192 and that verbal provocation may be sufficient. In People v. Borchers (1958) 50 Cal. 2d 321, 329, 325 P.2d 97 in the course of explaining the phrase "heat and passion" used in the statute defining manslaughter we pointed out that " 'passion' need not mean 'rage' or 'anger' " but may be any "[v]iolent, intense, high-wrought or enthusiastic emotion" and concluded there "that defendant was aroused to a heat of 'passion' by a series of events over a considerable period of time. . . ." Accordingly we there declared that evidence of admissions of infidelity by the defendant's paramour, taunts directed to him and other conduct, "supports a finding that defendant killed in wild desperation induced by long continued provocatory conduct." We find this reasoning persuasive in the case now before us. Defendant's testimony chronicles a two-week period of provocatory conduct by his wife Rachel that could arouse a passion of jealousy, pain and sexual rage in an ordinary man of average disposition such as to cause him to act rashly from this passion. It is significant that both defendant and Dr. Blinder testified that the former was in the heat of passion under an uncontrollable rage when he killed Rachel.

The Attorney General contends that the killing could not have been done in the heat of passion because there was a cooling period, defendant having waited in the apartment for 20 hours. However, the long course of provocatory conduct, which had resulted in intermittent outbreaks of rage under specific provocation in the past, reached its final culmination in the apartment when Rachel began screaming. Both defendant and Dr. Blinder testified that defendant killed in a state of uncontrollable rage, of passion, and there is ample evidence in the record to support the conclusion that this passion was the result of the long course of provocatory conduct by Rachel, just as the killing emerged from such conduct in *Borchers.* The Attorney General relies principally on People v. Bufarale (1961) 193 Cal. App. 2d 551, 559-563, 14 Cal. Rptr. 381 but the reliance is misplaced. *Bufarale* merely held that the defendant's killing of a married woman with whom he had been living was not, as a matter of law, upon the heat of passion since the defendant's act was one of vengeance, preceded by neither a quarrel with, nor by adequate provocatory conduct on the part of, the victim, who had decided to return to her husband.

As to Count One, charging a violation of Section 187, the judgment is reversed.

Notes and Questions

1. Did Pessah "provoke" Berry within the conventional meaning of the concept of legally adequate provocation?

2. How exactly was Dr. Blinder's testimony relevant in this case? Did the jury need the expert testimony of a psychiatrist to determine whether Berry had acted in the heat of passion? Did his testimony bear in any way on the question of whether a reasonable person would have been provoked into the heat of passion in these circumstances? What are the implications of Dr. Blinder's testimony for our assumptions about volition and determinism?

3. After *Berry,* how would you state California's definition of legally adequate provocation?

4. The trend among states, as reflected in *Berry,* is to trust juries with a relatively broad provocation standard, rather than to permit or require the trial judge to screen provocation claims by means of fixed legal categories. Consider the Model Penal Code provision for voluntary manslaughter:

§210.3. Manslaughter.

(1) Criminal homicide constitutes manslaughter when . . .

(b) a homicide which would otherwise be murder is committed under the influence of extreme mental or emotional disturbance for which there is reasonable explanation or excuse. The reasonableness of such explanation or excuse shall be determined from the viewpoint of a person in the actor's situation under the circumstances as he believes them to be.

(2) Manslaughter is a felony of the second degree [punishable by 1 to 10 years in prison].

What changes does the Model Code make from the common law? The Model Penal Code Commentaries explain in Comment 5:

Section 210.3 of the Model Code continues a modified and substantially enlarged version of the rule of provocation. Subsection (1)(b) punishes as manslaughter "homicide which would otherwise be murder [if it] is committed under the influence of extreme mental or emotional disturbance for which there is reasonable explanation or excuse." This formulation effects substantial changes in the traditional notion of provocation. For one thing, the Code does not require that the actor's emotional distress arise from some injury, affront, or other provocative act perpetrated upon him by the deceased. Under the Code, mitigation may be appropriate where the actor believes that the deceased is responsible for some injustice to another or even where he strikes out in a blinding rage and kills an innocent bystander. In some such cases, the cause and intensity of the actor's emotion may be less indicative of moral depravity than would be a homicidal response to a blow to one's person. By eliminating any reference to provocation in the ordinary sense of improper conduct by the deceased, the Model Code avoids arbitrary exclusion of some circumstances that may justify reducing murder to manslaughter.

Section 210.3 also sweeps away the rigid rules that limited provocation to certain defined circumstances. Instead, it casts the issue in phrases that have no common-law antecedents and hence no accumulated doctrinal content. Where there is evidence of extreme mental or emotional disturbance, it is for the trier of fact to decide, in light of all the circumstances of the case, whether there exists a reasonable explanation or excuse for the actor's mental condition. This issue cannot be resolved successfully by categorization of conduct. It must be confronted directly on the facts of each case. By restating the ultimate inquiry, Subsection (1)(b) avoids the strictures of early precedents and puts the issue in the terms in which it should be considered. This development reflects the trend of many modern decisions to abandon preconceived notions of what constitutes adequate provocation and to submit that question to the jury's deliberation.

5. Appellate cases addressing the provocation issue normally arise when the accused appeals a conviction of murder. Most often, the defendant claims that the trial judge wrongly refused to give the jury a voluntary manslaughter instruction where the trial judge believed as matter of law that the asserted provocation could not constitute legally adequate provocation. Thus, the defendant complains that he never got to the jury on the provocation issue, while the state argues that the judge's ruling accords with appellate precedent, and that, in any event, no reasonable jury could have found adequate provocation.

Would it be better if the trial judge simply left all provocation claims to the jury? Imagine a rule that provides that automatically on request of the defendant, the judge must instruct the jury that it can mitigate the murder charge to manslaughter if it finds that "the defendant acted in the heat of passion due to a provocation that would have caused a reasonable person to lose his self-control."

How should the power to decide on the provocation issue be allocated between judge and jury? Assume that in each of the hypotheticals on page 265, the judge did grant the defendant this general instruction, and in each case the jury nevertheless convicted the defendant of murder. Would the defendant have any ground for an appeal?

6. Can you imagine a situation where the prosecution would ask the trial

judge to give the jury a provocation instruction, but the defense would resist the instruction?

7. Could misbehavior of a child be adequate provocation? In People v. Crews, 38 Ill. 2d 331 (1967), the evidence showed that after a 2-year-old child turned on the hot water tap while in the bathtub, her soon-to-be adoptive mother beat her to death. The autopsy showed the child had bruises and wounds over 60 percent of her body and a broken right shoulder bone. The court, upholding defendant's murder conviction said, "The doctrine of provocation is a compassionate one, based on a recognition of human frailty. It is ludicrous, however, to suggest that a 'reasonable person' could have been provoked by the actions of a 2-year-old child."

8. Could a reasonable jury find legally adequate provocation where Lee kills Sandy because:

a. Sandy defrauded Lee in a scheme that ruined Lee's business and left Lee bankrupt?

b. Sandy, a racially bigoted employer, fired Lee upon discovering that Lee, a black, was married to a white?

c. Sandy, a viciously insensitive slum owner, evicted Lee and Lee's family and left them homeless?

DIRECTOR OF PUBLIC PROSECUTIONS v. CAMPLIN

House of Lords

[1978] 2 All E.R. 168

The respondent, who was aged 15, went to the house of one *K*, a man in his fifties. Whilst the respondent was there *K* buggered him. The respondent hit *K* over his head with a pan and killed him. He was charged with murder. At his trial he put forward the defence of provocation, pursuant to §3 of the Homicide Act 1957, and gave evidence (i) that the act of buggery had been forcibly committed on him by *K* against his will, (ii) that afterwards he had become overwhelmed by shame and (iii) that when he had heard *K* laughing at his sexual triumph, he had lost his self-control and hit *K* with the pan. The jury were directed that the criterion to apply where the defence of provocation was put forward was whether a reasonable man of full age would in like circumstances have acted as the respondent had done. The respondent was convicted of murder, but the Court of Appeal substituted a verdict of manslaughter, holding that, where a person accused of murder raised the defence of provocation, the "reasonable man" test was designed to exclude from consideration to the accused's advantage mental or physical abnormalities which might make him exceptionally deficient in self-control, but youth, and the immaturity which accompanied youth, were not abnormalities; accordingly where the accused was of tender years, the proper direction to the jury was to invite them to consider whether the provocation was enough to have made a reasonable man of the same age as the appellant act, in the same circumstances, as he had done. The Crown appealed to the House of Lords. . . .

Lord DIPLOCK. . . .

In his address to the jury on the defence of provocation, counsel for Camplin had suggested to them that when they addressed their minds to the question whether the provocation relied on was enough to make a reasonable man do as Camplin had done, what they ought to consider was not the reaction of a reasonable adult but the reaction of a reasonable boy of Camplin's age. The judge thought that this was wrong in law. So in this summing-up he took pains to instruct the jury that they must consider whether—

> the provocation was sufficient to make a reasonable man in like circumstances act as the defendant did. Not a reasonable boy, as [counsel for Camplin] would have it, or a reasonable lad; it is an objective test—a reasonable man.

The jury found Camplin guilty of murder. On appeal the Court of Appeal, Criminal Division, allowed the appeal and substituted a conviction for manslaughter on the ground that the passage I have cited from the summing-up was a misdirection. The court held that—

> the proper direction to the jury is to invite the jury to consider whether the provocation was enough to have made a reasonable person of the same age as the appellant in the same circumstances do as he did.

The point of law of general public importance involved in the case has been certified as being:

> Whether, on the prosecution for murder of a boy of 15, where the issue of provocation arises, the jury should be directed to consider the question, under §3 of the Homicide Act 1957, whether the provocation was enough to make a reasonable man do as he did by reference to a "reasonable adult" or by reference to a "reasonable boy of 15."

My Lords, the doctrine of provocation in crimes of homicide has always represented an anomaly in English law. In crimes of violence which result in injury short of death, the fact that the act of violence was committed under provocation, which has caused the accused to lose his self-control, does not affect the nature of the offence of which he is guilty; it is merely a matter to be taken into consideration in determining the penalty which it is appropriate to impose: whereas in homicide provocation effects a change in the offence itself from murder, for which the penalty is fixed by law (formerly death and now imprisonment for life), to the lesser offence of manslaughter, for which the penalty is in the discretion of the judge. . . .

For my part I find it instructive to approach this question by a brief survey of the historical development of the doctrine of provocation at common law. Its origin at a period when the penalty for murder was death is to be found as Tindal C.J., echoing Sir Michael Foster, put it in R. v. Hayward, in "the law's compassion to human infirmity." The human infirmity on which the law first took compassion in a violent age when men bore weapons for their own protection when going about their business appears to have been chance medley or a sudden falling out at which both parties had recourse to their weapons and fought on equal terms. Chance medley as a ground of provocation was extended to assault and battery committed by the deceased on the accused in circumstances other than a sudden falling out. But with two exceptions actual violence offered by the deceased to the accused remained the badge of provocation right up to the passing of the 1957 Act. The two exceptions were the discovery by a husband of his wife in the act of committing adultery and the discovery by a father of someone committing sodomy on his son; but these apart, insulting words or gestures unaccompanied by physical attack did not in law amount to provocation.

The "reasonable man" was a comparatively late arrival in the law of provocation. As the law of negligence emerged in the first half of the 19th century he became the anthropomorphic embodiment of the standard of care required by the law. It would appear that Keating J. in R. v. Welsh was the first to make use of the reasonable man as the embodiment of the standard of self-control required by the criminal law of persons exposed to provocation, and not merely as a criterion by which to check the credibility of a claim to have been provoked to lose his self-control made by an accused who at that time was not permitted to give evidence himself. . . .

The reasonable man referred to by Keating J. was not then a term of legal art nor has it since become one in criminal law. He (or she) has established his (or her) role in the law of provocation under a variety of different sobriquets in which the noun "man" is frequently replaced by "person" and the adjective "reasonable" by "ordinary," "average" or "normal." At least from as early as 1914 the test of whether the defence of provocation is entitled to succeed has been a dual one: the conduct of the deceased to the accused must be such as (1) might cause in any reasonable or ordinary person and (2) actually causes in the accused a sudden and temporary loss of self-control as the result of which he commits the unlawful act that kills the deceased. But until the 1957 Act was passed there was a condition precedent which had to be satisfied before any question of applying this dual test could arise. The conduct of the deceased had to be of such a kind as was capable in law of constituting provocation; and whether it was or was not was a question for the judge, not for the jury. This House so held in *Mancini* where it also laid down a rule of law that the mode of resentment, as for instance the weapon used in the act that caused the death, must bear a reasonable relation to the kind of violence that constituted the provocation.

It is necessary for the purposes of the present appeal to spend time on a detailed account of what conduct was or was not capable in law of giving rise to a defence of provocation immediately before the passing of the 1957 Act. It had remained much the same as when Stephen was writing in the last quarter of the 19th century. What, however, is important to note is that this House had recently confirmed that words alone, save perhaps in circumstances of a most extreme and exceptional nature, were incapable in law of constituting provocation.

My Lords, this was the state of law when *Bedder* fell to be considered by this House. The accused had killed a prostitute. He was sexually impotent. According to his evidence he had tried to have sexual intercourse with her and failed. She taunted him with his failure and tried to get away from his grasp. In the course of her attempts to do so she slapped him in the face, punched him in the stomach and kicked him in the groin, whereupon he took a knife out of his pocket and stabbed her twice and caused her death. The struggle that led to her death thus started because the deceased taunted the accused with his physical infirmity; but in the state of the law as it then was, taunts unaccompanied by any physical violence did not constitute provocation. The taunts were followed by violence on the part of the deceased in the course of her attempt to get away from the accused, and it may be that this subsequent violence would have a greater effect on the self-control of an impotent man already enraged by the taunts than it would have had on a person conscious of possessing normal physical attributes. So there might be some justification for the judge to instruct the jury to ignore the fact that the accused was impotent when they were considering whether the deceased's conduct amounted to such provocation as would cause a reasonable or ordinary person to lose his self-control. This indeed appears to have been the ground on which the Court of Criminal Appeal had approved the summing-up when they said:

> . . . no distinction is to be made in the case of a person who, though it may not be a matter of temperament is physically impotent, is conscious of that impotence, and therefore mentally liable to be more excited unduly if he is "twitted" or attacked on the subject of that particular infirmity.

This statement . . . was approved by Lord Simonds L.C. speaking on behalf of all the members of this House who sat on the appeal; but he also went on to lay down the broader proposition that:

> It would be plainly illogical not to recognise an unusually excitable or pugnacious temperament in the accused as a matter to be taken into account but yet to recognise for that purpose some unusual physical characteristic, be it impotence or another.

Section 3 of the 1957 Act is in the following terms:

> Where on a charge of murder there is evidence on which the jury can find that the person charged was provoked (whether by things done or by things said or

> by both together) to lose his self-control, the question whether the provocation was enough to make a reasonable man do as he did shall be left to be determined by the jury; and in determining that question the jury shall take into account everything both done and said according to the effect which, in their opinion, it would have on a reasonable man.

My Lords, this section was intended to mitigate in some degree the harshness of the common law of provocation as it had been developed by recent decisions in this House. It recognises and retains the dual test: the provocation must not only have caused the accused to lose his self-control but also be such as might cause a reasonable man to react to it as the accused did. Nevertheless it brings about two important changes in the law. The first is it abolishes all previous rules of law as to what can or cannot amount to provocation and in particular the rule of law that, save in the two exceptional cases I have mentioned, words unaccompanied by violence could not do so. Secondly it makes it clear that if there was any evidence that the accused himself at the time of the act which caused the death in fact lost his self-control in consequence of some provocation however slight it might appear to the judge, he was bound to leave to the jury the question, which is one of opinion not of law, whether a reasonable man might have reacted to that provocation as the accused did. . . .

The public policy that underlay the adoption of the "reasonable man" test in the common law doctrine of provocation was to reduce the incidence of fatal violence by preventing a person relying on his own exceptional pugnacity or excitability as an excuse for loss of self-control. The rationale of the test may not be easy to reconcile in logic with more universal propositions as to the mental element in crime. Nevertheless it has been preserved by the 1957 Act but falls to be applied now in the context of a law of provocation that is significantly different from what it was before the Act was passed . . . .

. . . [F]or the purposes of the law of provocation the "reasonable man" has never been confined to the adult male. It means an ordinary person of either sex, not exceptionally excitable or pugnacious, but possessed of such powers of self-control as everyone is entitled to expect that his fellow citizens will exercise in society as it is today. A crucial factor in the defence of provocation from earliest times has been the relationship between the gravity of provocation and the way in which the accused retaliated, both being judged by the social standards of the day. When Hale was writing in the 17th century pulling a man's nose was thought to justify retaliation with a sword; when *Mancini* was decided by this House, a blow with a fist would not justify retaliation with a deadly weapon. But so long as words unaccompanied by violence could not in common law amount to provocation the relevant proportionality between provocation and retaliation was primarily one of degrees of violence. Words spoken to the accused before the violence started were not normally to be included in the proportion sum. But now that the law has been changed so as to permit of words being treated as provocation, even though unaccompanied by any other acts, the gravity of verbal provocation may well depend on the particular characteristics or circumstances of the person to whom a taunt or insult is addressed. To taunt a person because of his race, his physical infirmities or some shameful incident in his past may well be considered by the jury to be more offensive to the person addressed, however equable his temperament, if the facts on which the taunt is founded are true than it would be if they were not. It would stultify much of the mitigation of the previous harshness of the common law in ruling out verbal provocation as capable of reducing murder to manslaughter if the jury could not take into consideration all those factors which in their opinion would affect the gravity of taunts and insults when applied to the person to whom they are addressed. So to this extent at any rate the unqualified proposition accepted by this House in *Bedder* that for the purposes of the "reasonable man" test any unusual physical characteristics of the accused must be ignored requires revision as a result of the passing of the 1957 Act.

That he was only 15 years of age at the time of the killing is the relevant characteristic of the accused in the instant case. It is a characteristic which may have its effects on temperament as well as physique. If the jury think that the same power of self-control is not to be expected in an ordinary, average or normal boy of 15 as in an older person, are they to treat the lesser powers of self-control possessed by an ordinary, average or normal boy of 15 as the standard of self-control with which the conduct of the accused is to be compared?

It may be conceded that in strict logic there is a transition between treating age as a characteristic that may be taken into account in assessing the gravity of the provocation addressed to the accused and treating it as a characteristic to be taken into account in determining what is the degree of self-control to be expected of the ordinary person with whom the accused's conduct is to be compared. But to require old heads on young shoulders is inconsistent with the law's compassion of human infirmity to which Sir Michael Foster ascribed the doctrine of provocation more than two centuries ago. The distinction as to the purpose for which it is legitimate to take the age of the accused into account involves considerations of too great nicety to warrant a place in deciding a matter of opinion, which is no longer one to be decided by a judge trained in logical reasoning but by a jury drawing on their experience of how ordinary human beings behave in real life. . . .

In my opinion a proper direction to a jury on the question left to their exclusive determination by §3 of the 1957 Act would be on the following lines. The judge should state what the question is, using the very terms of the section. He should then explain to them that the reasonable man referred to in the question is a person having the power of self-control to be expected of an ordinary person of the sex and age of the accused, but in other respects sharing such of the accused's characteristics as they think would affect the gravity of the provocation to him, and that the question is not merely whether such a person would in like circumstances be provoked to lose his self-control but also would react to the provocation as the accused did. . . .

Lord MORRIS of Borth-y-Gest. . . .

Before the time when Bedder v. Director of Public Prosecutions came under consideration, the courts seemed to have created the conception of "the reasonable man" as a mythical person seemingly not only detached from but also rather remote from the accused person and having certain attributes as laid down by the court as the courts directed juries to accept.

Who then or what then was the "reasonable man"? If a reasonable man is a man who normally acts reasonably, it becomes important to consider the mind of the accused person when considering his reactions to some provocation. To consider the mind of some different person, and to consider what his reactions would have been if comparably provoked, could involve an unreal test. In the argument in *Bedder's* case the question was raised as to the position of a dwarf. If at the date of that case things said could have amounted to provocation and if grossly offensive things in relation to his stature had been said to a dwarf, had the jury to consider not whether the dwarf only acted as a reasonable dwarf might have acted in being subject to passion and in doing what he did, or must the jury consider what would have been the reactions of a man of normal physique if the things said had been said to him?

These questions in regard to the reasonable man must now be reviewed in the light of the provisions of the 1957 Act. Those contained in §2 in reference to persons suffering from diminished responsibility may merely be noted in passing. Those contained in §3 are of supreme importance. That section provides as follows:

> Where on a charge of murder there is evidence on which the jury can find that the person charged was provoked (whether by things done or by things said or by both together) to lose his self-control, the question whether the provocation was enough to make a reasonable man do as he did shall be left to be determined by the jury; and in determining that question the jury shall take into account everything both done and said according to the effect which, in their opinion, it would have on a reasonable man.

. . . Who then or what then is the "reasonable man" who is referred to in the section? It seems to me that the courts are no longer entitled to tell juries that a reasonable man has certain stated and defined features. It is for the jury to consider all that the accused did; it is for them to say whether the provocation was enough to make "a reasonable man" do as the accused did. The jury must take into account "everything both done and said." What do they think would have been the effect on a reasonable man? They must bring their "collective good sense" to bear. As Lord Goddard, C.J. said in R. v. McCarthy:

> No court has ever given, nor do we think ever can give, a definition of what constitutes a reasonable or average man. That must be left to the collective good sense of the jury, and what, no doubt, would govern their opinion would be the nature of the retaliation used by the provoked person.

So in relation to the facts in *Bedder's* case apart from the painful physical kick, a jury would now have to consider the effect of the things said on a reasonable man. If an impotent man was taunted about his impotence the jury would not today be told that an impotent man could not be a reasonable man as contemplated by the law. The jury would be entitled to decide that the accused man acted as "a reasonable man" in being provoked as he was and in doing "as he did.". . .

In my view it would now be unreal to tell the jury that the notional "reasonable man" is someone without the characteristics of the accused: it would be to intrude into their province. A few examples may be given. If the accused is of particular colour or particular ethnic origin and things are said which to him are grossly insulting it would be utterly unreal if the jury had to consider whether the words would have provoked a man of different colour or ethnic origin, or to consider how such a man would have acted or reacted. The question would be whether the accused if he was provoked only reacted as even any reasonable man in his sitution would or might have reacted. If the accused was ordinarily and usually a very unreasonable person, the view that on a particular occasion he acted just as a reasonable person would or might have acted would not be impossible of acceptance. . . .

In the instant case the considerations to which I have been referring have application to a question of age. The accused was a young man. Sometimes in the summing-up he was called a boy or a lad. He was at the time of the events described at the trial under 16 years of age: he was accountable in law for the charge perferred against him. More generally in the summing-up he was referred to as a young man; that would appear to me to have been appropriate. In his summing-up, however, the learned judge in referring to a reasonable man seemed to emphasize to the jury that the reasonable man with whom they must compare the accused could not be a young man of the age of the accused but had to be someone older and indeed had to be someone of full age and maturity. In my view that was not correct. The jury had to consider whether a young man of about the same age as the accused but placed in the same situation as that which befell the accused could, had he been a reasonable young man, have reacted as did the accused and could have done what the accused did. For the reasons which I have outlined the question so to be considered by the jury would be whether they considered that the accused, placed as he was, and having regard to all the things that they find were said, and all the things that they find were done, only acted as a reasonable young man might have acted, so that, in compassion, and having regard to human frailty, he could to some extent be excused even though he had caused death.

I consider that the Court of Appeal came to the correct conclusion and agreeing with what my noble and learned friend, Lord Diplock, has said as to the direction to a jury, I would dismiss the appeal. . . .

Notes and Questions

1. When we talk of provocation sufficient to put a reasonable person in a heat of passion, why should we not consider the fact that the defendant may himself not have been a "reasonable person" to begin with?

2. In *Camplin,* the court held that the defendant should be held to the standard of a young person his age rather than to that of the objective standard of a reasonable person. Should a defendant who is deformed or handicapped be judged according to the insult that a reasonable person would feel at the same remarks if he were similarly deformed or handicapped? See Rex v. Raney, 29 C.A. 14 (1942) (murder conviction of defendant, a one-legged man, reduced to manslaughter because the knocking away of one of defendant's crutches was provocation). What if the defendant is simply bad-tempered? Should she be judged by the standard applicable to a bad-tempered person? What if the defendant were drunk?

3. How does the Model Penal Code divide the cases in which the law will take consideration of a defendant's abnormality from those of which it will not? Is the distinction between a physical and a mental abnormality a satisfactory one? The Model Penal Code drafters have defended their approach as follows in the Commentaries to Section 210.3:

> The critical element in the Model Code formulation is the clause requiring that reasonableness be assessed "from the viewpoint of a person in the actor's situation." The word "situation" is designedly ambiguous. On the one hand, it is clear that personal handicaps and some external circumstances must be taken into account. Thus, blindness, shock from traumatic injury, and extreme grief are all easily read into the term "situation." This result is sound, for it would be morally obtuse to appraise a crime for mitigation of punishment without reference to these factors. On the other hand, it is equally plain that idiosyncratic moral values are not part of the actor's situation. An assassin who kills a political leader because he believes it is right to do so cannot ask that he be judged by the standard of a reasonable extremist. Any other result would undermine the normative message of the criminal law. In between these two extremes, however, there are matters neither as clearly distinct from individual blameworthiness as blindness or handicap nor as integral a part of moral depravity as a belief in the rightness of killing. Perhaps the classic illustration is the unusual sensitivity to the epithet "bastard" of a person born illegitimate. An exceptionally punctilious sense of personal honor or an abnormally fearful temperament may also serve to differentiate an individual actor from the hypothetical reasonable man, yet none of these factors is wholly irrelevant to the ultimate issue of culpability. The proper role of such factors cannot be resolved satisfactorily by abstract definition

of what may constitute adequate provocation. The Model Code endorses a formulation that affords sufficient flexibility to differentiate in particular cases between those special aspects of the actor's situation that should be deemed material for purpose of grading and those that should be ignored. There thus will be room for interpretation of the word "situation," and that is precisely the flexibility desired. There will be opportunity for argument about the reasonableness of explanation or excuse, and that too is a ground on which argument is required. In the end, the question is whether the actor's loss of self-control can be understood in terms that arouse sympathy in the ordinary citizen. Section 210.3 faces this issue squarely and leaves the ultimate judgment to the ordinary citizen in the function of a juror assigned to resolve the specific case.

4. In People v. Washington, 58 Cal. App. 3d 620, 130 Cal. Rptr. 96 (1976) defendant, a homosexual, was convicted for the murder of his homosexual partner. "The killing resulted from a lover's quarrel, claimed to have been provoked by unfaithfulness on the part of the victim and his expressed desire to terminate the relationship." The defendant contended that provocation should not have been measured by the "ordinary reasonable person of average disposition" standard but "by a standard applicable to . . . the average servient homosexual." Should the defendant's standard be used? What does the Model Penal Code say?

5. Consider this view in Kelman, Interpretive Construction in the Substantive Criminal Law, 33 Stan. L. Rev. 591, 636-637, 646 (1981):

Courts include or exclude certain traits of the defendant in the profile of the typical individual to whom the defendant's conduct is to be compared. For instance, a court may say that it is irrelevant that a particular defendant is generally impotent in assessing whether a prostitute's taunts on the subject are reasonable provoking; commentators respond that the defendant's reaction ought to be compared to the reasonable impotent man's. Presumably, everyone tries to exclude from his vision of the typical man to whom the defendant is to be compared all the narrow-focused traits the defendant has that the criminal law is designed to alter—hotheadedness, hypersensitivity, proclivity to violence—but this line ultimately collapses. Of course the criminal code is not trying to deter or to blame impotence itself. But if the impotent as a group pose a menace because impotence is associated with hypersensitivity, if they are prone to violence when confronted by situations that routinely confront people, it is not clear why we would want to exculpate them. Ultimately, the real battle here is between our asserted determinist (excusing) notions of impotence and our intentionalist (inculpatory) models of hotheadedness. Unconscious interpretive construction avoids this more openly political battle. As we take a broader, more categorical view of the typical provoked defendant, fewer and fewer defendants appear to have acted reasonably.

If we hypothesize that people have "true" characters outside the fortuitous circumstances in which they live, we should at least search for a full determinist account. The behavior of the former battered child tells us nothing of the defendant's "true character," just as the behavior of the coerced, threatened thief tells us nothing of his "real nature." And, if character is nothing but a summary of *actual* behavior given *actual* life circumstances, then it is part of a defendant's character" that he "is" a killer if he has, given the pressures he has faced, killed.

6. What would be the effect of taking the subjective approach to voluntary manslaughter to its logical extreme? What if the law mitigated an intentional killing to manslaughter whenever the killer at the time of the crime was in an irrational passion or frenzy similar to what we observe in "legally provoked" killers, but where no legal provocation occurred. This situation would arise when a person, though not legally insane, suffers from an unstable personality that makes him or her overreact to stressful experiences.

7. One commentator[21] has attacked head-on the concept of mitigation to voluntary manslaughter, regardless of whether a subjective or an objective standard is used:

> [So far as] the provocation/passion formula for reducing murder to voluntary manslaughter [is concerned] I would abolish this hoary distinction and convict all intentional killers of murder.[22] Reasonable people do not kill no matter how much they are provoked, and even enraged people generally retain the capacity to control homicidal or any other kind of aggressive or antisocial desires. We cheapen both life and our conception of responsibility by maintaining the provocation/passion mitigation. This may seem harsh and contrary to the supposedly humanitarian reforms of the evolving criminal law. But this "whig" interpretation of criminal law history is morally mistaken.[23] It is humanitarian only if one focuses sympathetically on perpetrators and not on their victims, and views the former as mostly helpless objects of their overwhelming emotions and irrationality. This sympathy is misplaced, however, and is disrespectful to the perpetrator. As virtually every human being knows because we all have been enraged, it is easy not to kill, even when one is enraged.
>
> One may object at this point that there are provocation/passion cases that compel the need for such a formula. Imagine the following case. A parent returns home to fine that his child has been brutally attacked by a perpetrator who is now running away. There is no further immediate danger to the child, the parent, or anyone else. Nevertheless, the understandably enraged parent shoots and kills the fleeing criminal. In jurisdictions that do not allow the use of deadly force for the purpose of civilian law enforcement under such conditions, it is a case of second degree murder unless the provocation/passion formula exists.[24]

21. Morse, Undiminished Confusion in Diminished Capacity, 75 J. of Crim. L. and Criminology, 33-34 (1984).

22. The conviction would simply be for murder where there are no degrees of murder, and, because of the absence of premeditation in most cases of provocation and passion, it would be for second degree murder where there are degrees.

23. In its most general form, a "whig" interpretation interprets the past in terms of the present and ratifies present arrangements as the inevitable result of beneficent progress in human affairs. The classic essay on this type of historical understanding is H. Butterfield, The Whig Interpretation of History (1931). By contrast, I believe the development is a case of unjustified sympathy. I also assume that abolition of the provocation/passion formula would be a constitutional exercise of a state's power to make substantive criminal law.

24. This assumes, too, that the State would prosecute under such circumstances.

The better solution, I believe, is to provide a total defense based on irrationality or lack of self-control where the provocation and consequent lack of rationality were both so great that it would be unjust to punish the defendant at all. The hypothetical may be just such a case. These cases, like all those where a complete defense is possible, will be extreme.[25] This is as it should be. Most intentional killers deserve little sympathy.

25. Although passion produced by provocation usually compromises rationality or self-control, almost all impassioned persons nevertheless can and should be expected to control themselves. It is a matter of degree, however. In those cases where the loss of rationality or self-control is both extreme and nonculpable, there is ground for a complete excuse. The provocation/passion formula would then operate like the insanity or duress defenses.

6

MURDER

A. INTRODUCTION

Murder is, in a sense, the basic homicide crime against which all degrees of homicide are measured. We have already seen, in discussing manslaughter, that an unlawful, unintentional homicide is usually treated as involuntary manslaughter—that is, a crime less culpable than murder; and that an intentional killing, which would otherwise be murder, might, in the presence of "provocation," be mitigated to voluntary manslaughter.

Alternatively, as we will see in the next chapter, the offense of murder may, in many jurisdictions, be aggravated to first-degree or capital murder. All other unaggravated murders—if one can speak of an unaggravated variant of such a serious crime—are, in most jurisdictions, denominated second-degree murder.

Merely naming something, however, does not define it. The fact is that second-degree murder consists of a variety of distinguishable kinds of killing.

The traditional definition of *murder* is that it is a homicide committed with "malice aforethought." Whatever its dictionary meaning, that phrase, as it developed in English law, was a technical term referring to the mental state of the actor, or to what were regarded as equivalent circumstances, that qualified a homicide as murder. It did not invariably require either malice in the ordinary sense or forethought. While it is still common to use the phrase in connection with murder, "malice aforethought" has no independent descriptive significance.

Under the common law, the defendant manifested malice aforethought if the homicide was accomplished by (1) an intention to kill; (2) an intention to cause serious bodily harm; (3) extreme recklessness or disregard of a very substantial risk of causing death; (4) the commission, or attempted commission, of a felony; or (5) according to some authorities, resistance to a lawful arrest. Although modern definitions have sometimes clarified and limited these requisites of the crime of murder, in general the distinguishing feature of the crime remains an intent to kill, or a disregard of risk of death so blatant that it should be treated as the equivalent of an intent to kill.

Sample Statutes[1]

CAL. PENAL CODE
(1979)

§187. MURDER DEFINED. . . .

(a) Murder is the unlawful killing of a human being . . . with malice aforethought.

§188. MALICE, EXPRESS MALICE, AND IMPLIED MALICE DEFINED.

Such malice may be express or implied. It is express when there is manifested a deliberate intention unlawfully to take away the life of a fellow creature. It is implied, when no considerable provocation appears, or when the circumstances attending the killing show an abandoned and malignant heart.

When it is shown that the killing resulted from the intentional doing of an act with express or implied malice as defined above, no other mental state need be shown to establish the mental state of malice aforethought. Neither an awareness of the obligation to act within the general body of laws regulating society nor acting despite such awareness is included within the definition of malice. [The minimum punishment for murder is 25 years to life in prison.]

ILL. REV. STAT.
(1983)

CH. 38 ¶9-1.

(a) A person who kills an individual without lawful justification commits murder if, in performing the acts which cause the death:

(1) He either intends to kill or do great bodily harm to that indi-

1. The aggravated murder sections are set out in Chapter 7.

vidual or another, or knows that such acts will cause death to that individual or another; or

(2) He knows that such acts create a strong probability of death or great bodily harm to that individual or another; or

(3) He is attempting or committing a forcible felony other than voluntary manslaughter. [Minimum punishment is 20-40 years in prison.]

CONN. GEN. STAT.
(1983)

§53A-54A.

(a) A person is guilty of murder when, with intent to cause the death of another person, he causes the death of such person or of a third person or causes a suicide by force, duress or deception; except that in any prosecution under this subsection, it shall be an affirmative defense that the defendant committed the proscribed act or acts under the influence of extreme emotional disturbance for which there was a reasonable explanation or excuse, the reasonableness of which is to be determined from the viewpoint of a person in the defendant's situation under the circumstances as the defendant believed them to be, provided nothing contained in this subsection shall constitute a defense to a prosecution for, or preclude a conviction of, manslaughter in the first degree or any other crime.

(b) Evidence that the defendant suffered from a mental disease, mental defect or other mental abnormality is admissible, in a prosecution under subsection (a), on the question of whether the defendant acted with intent to cause the death of another person.

(c) Murder is punishable as a class A felony [minimum punishment 25 years to life] . . . unless it is a capital felony.

KAN. STAT. ANN.
(Rev. Stat. 1981)

§21-3402. Murder in the Second Degree.

Murder in the second degree is the malicious killing of a human being, committed without deliberation or premeditation and not in the perpetration or attempt to perpetrate a felony.

Murder in the second degree is a class B felony [punishable by minimum of 5-15 years in prison].

WIS. STAT.
(1982)

§940.02. Second-degree Murder.

Whoever causes the death of another human being under either of the following circumstances is guilty of a Class B felony:

(1) By conduct imminently dangerous to another and evincing a depraved mind, regardless of human life; or

(2) As a natural and probable consequence of the commission of or attempt to commit a felony. [Punishable by up to 20 years in prison.]

PENN. CONS. STAT.
(1983)

Tit. 18, §2502. Murder. . . .

(b) *Murder of the second degree.*—A criminal homicide constitutes murder of the second degree when it is committed while defendant was engaged as a principal or an accomplice in the perpetration of a felony [punishable by life in prison].

(c) *Murder of the third degree.*—All other kinds of murder shall be murder of the third degree. Murder of the third degree is a felony of the first degree [punishable by up to 20 years in prison].

(d) *Definitions.*—As used in this section the following words and phrases shall have the meanings given to them in this subsection. . . .

"Perpetration of a felony." The act of the defendant in engaging in or being an accomplice in the commission of, or an attempt to commit, or flight after committing, or attempting to commit robbery, rape, or deviate sexual intercourse by force or threat of force, arson, burglary or kidnapping.

MINN. STAT.
(1982)

§609.19. Murder in the Second Degree.

Whoever does either of the following is guilty of murder in the second degree and may be sentenced to imprisonment for not more than 40 years:

(1) Causes the death of a human being with intent to effect the death of that person or another, but without premeditation, or

(2) Causes the death of a human being, without intent to effect the death of any person, while committing or attempting to commit a felony offense other than criminal sexual conduct in the first or second degree with force or violence.

§609.195. Murder in the Third Degree.

Whoever, without intent to effect the death of any person, causes the death of another by perpetrating an act eminently dangerous to others and evincing a depraved mind, without regard for human life, is guilty of murder in the third degree and may be sentenced to imprisonment for not more than 25 years.

N.Y. PEN. LAW
(1984)

§125.25. Murder in the Second Degree.

A person is guilty of murder in the second degree [punishable by minimum of 15-25 years in prison] when:

1. With intent to cause the death of another person, he causes the death of such person or of a third person; except that in any prosecution under this subdivision, it is an affirmative defense that:
   (a) The defendant acted under the influence of extreme emotional disturbance for which there was a reasonable explanation or excuse, the reasonableness of which is to be determined from the viewpoint of a person in the defendant's situation under the circumstances as the defendant believed them to be. Nothing contained in this paragraph shall constitute a defense to a prosecution for, or preclude a conviction of, manslaughter in the first degree or any other crime; or
   (b) The defendant's conduct consisted of causing or aiding, without the use of duress or deception, another person to commit suicide. Nothing contained in this paragraph shall constitute a defense to a prosecution for, or preclude a conviction of, manslaughter in the second degree or any other crime; or
2. Under circumstances evincing a depraved indifference to human life, he recklessly engages in conduct which creates a grave risk of death to another person, and thereby causes the death of another person; or
3. Acting either alone or with one or more other persons, he commits or attempts to commit robbery, burglary, kidnapping, arson, rape in the first degree, sodomy in the first degree, sexual abuse in the first degree, aggravated sexual abuse, escape in the first degree, or escape in the second degree, and, in the course of and in furtherance of such

crime or of immediate flight therefrom, he, or another participant, if there be any, causes the death of a person other than one of the participants; except that in any prosecution under this subdivision, in which the defendant was not the only participant in the underlying crime, it is an affirmative defense that the defendant:

(a) Did not commit the homicidal act or in any way solicit, request, command, importune, cause or aid the commission thereof; and

(b) Was not armed with a deadly weapon, or any instrument, article or substance readily capable of causing death or serious physical injury and of a sort not ordinarily carried in public places by law-abiding persons; and

(c) Had no reasonable ground to believe that any other participant was armed with such a weapon, instrument, article or substance; and

(d) Had no reasonable ground to believe that any other participant intended to engage in conduct likely to result in death or serious physical injury.

MODEL PENAL CODE

§210.2 MURDER.

(1) Except as provided in Section 210.3(1)(b), criminal homicide constitutes murder when:

(a) it is committed purposely or knowingly; or

(b) it is committed recklessly under circumstances manifesting extreme indifference to the value of human life. Such recklessness and indifference are presumed if the actor is engaged or is an accomplice in the commission of, or an attempt to commit, or flight after committing or attempting to commit robbery, rape or deviate sexual intercourse by force or threat of force, arson, burglary, kidnapping or felonious escape.

(2) Murder is a felony of the first degree [punishable by imprisonment or capital punishment].

B. INTENT TO KILL

Intent to kill would seem to be an easy concept to understand. But as with *mens rea* in a criminal case, it is often difficult to prove, especially where the prosecution has no eyewitnesses and where the defendant, on ambiguous circumstantial evidence, claims he caused death accidentally.

Consider this case:

> On March 10, 1980, Jean Struen Harris, headmistress of the exclusive Madeira School for girls in Northern Virginia, shot and killed Doctor Herman Tarnower, author of the best seller, The Complete Scarsdale Medical Diet. Accused of second degree murder, she claimed his death was a tragic accident which happened while he was trying to stop her from killing herself. The prosecution's theory was that Harris, enraged over Tarnower's alleged plan to marry his medical assistant, killed him out of jealousy.
>
> On the night he died, the 69-year-old Tarnower had given one of his many small dinner parties at his $500,000 estate near Purchase, in Westchester County, New York. A wealthy hunter, fisherman and traveler, Tarnower was also known as a "womanizer." He had known Jean Harris, the defendant, for more than 14 years; they had once been lovers and he had even proposed marriage. She had accepted his proposal, but he later called it off.
>
> Over the years, the 57-year-old Harris had been a frequent guest at the Tarnower estate. She also owned a small house 24 miles away in Mahopac. A 1945 graduate of Smith College, divorced with two children, Harris became headmistress of the Madeira School in 1977. There she was known as "Integrity Jean" for her strict discipline and strong opposition to drugs and alcohol. Less than a week prior to the death of Tarnower, she had expelled four popular girls from the school for possessing drug paraphernalia. Harris' relationship with Tarnower, however, had deteriorated in the months before his death. He was spending increasing amounts of time with his 37-year-old medical assistant, Lynn Tryforus. They had been seen in public together and had taken a vacation to the Bahamas. Tryforus was also a guest at Tarnower's dinner party the night he died.
>
> Jean Harris' "proper" public image masked a deeply disturbed woman. According to her testimony she had originally planned to kill herself at a pond on Tarnower's estate, and had even fired a practice round of her .32 caliber pistol, what she had called "a security blanket." Having called earlier in the day, pleading to see him, she drove five hours from Virginia to New York, arriving at Tarnower's estate sometime after the dinner guests had left. Unable to wake him at first, she testified, "I felt hurt and frustration . . . the script wasn't going the way I expected it to . . . I simply wanted to get the dying over with." Rummaging around in Tarnower's room she found another woman's negligee and hair curlers, which she threw through a window. Tarnower woke up and hit her. In response she begged, "Hit me again, make it hard enough to kill me." She then took the gun out of her bag and Tarnower grabbed it. In the struggle he was shot in the hand. While he went to the bathroom to clean up, she picked up the gun again. He returned and knocked it away. She implored him, "Hy, please give me the gun or shoot me yourself." Another struggle ensued and Harris claimed when she felt the muzzle in her stomach she pulled the trigger. Instead of shooting herself, however, she shot and wounded Tarnower.
>
> At that point Harris "put the gun to my head, took two deep breaths, but it just clicked." Aiming the gun away, she pulled the trigger and another shot rang

out. Then, "I put it to my head and I shot and I shot and I shot and it just clicked." Eventually the gun slipped out of her hands and the cylinder fell out.

According to the testimony of Tarnower's housekeeper-cook, Suzanne Van der Ureken, she heard the intercom in his room shortly before 11:00 P.M. There was "a lot of yelling" and a shot. After the police arrived, in response to Van der Ureken's call, Harris knelt beside the dying Tarnower saying, "Why didn't you kill me?" In her initial statement to the police, Harris had admitted, "I shot him. I did it. . . . I've been through so much hell with him. He slept with every woman he could."

The prosecution brought out several inconsistencies in Harris' testimony. She could account for only three shots on the day of the killing, but the gun had been fired five times, and Tarnower had been hit four times in the hand, chest, arm and back. Despite the alleged struggle with Tarnower after he had been wounded in the hand, Harris had no blood on her clothes. Harris could also not explain why, if Tarnower had been expecting her, he was asleep in bed when she arrived.

On the day of the killing, Harris had also mailed a bitter, ten-page letter in red ink to Tarnower. The letter contained little to suggest that Harris intended to commit suicide. In it she revealed the extent of her jealousy toward Tryforus, calling her "your psychotic whore" and "a thieving slut." She demanded to accompany Tarnower to an important medical society dinner "even if the slut comes." She also admitted phoning Tryforus every night for a month and taking money from Tarnower's wallet to pay for clothes allegedly ruined by Tryforus. The letter clearly revealed the lengths Harris had been willing to go in a futile attempt to keep Tarnower for herself. She had even considered plastic surgery to make herself more attractive to Tarnower, but balked out of fear that it would turn out badly. At one point she referred bitterly to the engagement ring Tarnower had given to her, which she returned after he had called off the wedding:

> I desperately needed money all these years . . . [but] I couldn't have sold that ring. It was tangible proof of your love and it meant more to me than life itself. That you sold it the summer your adulterous slut finally got her divorce and needed money is a kind of sick, cynical act that left me old and bitter and sick.

Another section of the letter read:

> I have indeed grown poor loving you, while a self-serving ignorant slut has grown very rich. . . . It didn't matter all that much, really—all I ever asked for was to be with you—and when I left you, to know when we would see each other again. . . . Now you are taking that away from me too, and I am unable to cope—I can hear you saying "Look, Jean—it's your problem. I don't want to hear about it."

After a three-month trial, the eight woman, four man jury took eight days to reach a verdict. During this period they requested all 400 pieces of evidence and attempted to reenact the death scene in the jury room. Swayed finally by the inconsistencies in Harris' testimony, they returned a guilty verdict to the charge of second degree murder. As a final irony, the guilty verdict prevented Harris from receiving the $220,000 Tarnower had left her in his will, because of a New York law prohibiting convicted murderers from receiving bequests from their victims. Harris was sentenced to fifteen years to life in prison.

If you were the jury and heard all the facts above, would you find beyond a reasonable doubt that Harris intended to kill Tarnower, and hence merited a conviction for intentional murder? If you were the prosecutor, what sort of jury instruction would you request to enhance your chances of winning a conviction? Consider the following case.

FRANCIS v. FRANKLIN
United States Supreme Court
105 S. Ct. 1965 (1985)

Justice BRENNAN delivered the opinion of the Court. . . .

Respondent Raymond Lee Franklin, then 21 years old and imprisoned for offenses unrelated to this case, sought to escape custody on January 17, 1979, while he and three other prisoners were receiving dental care at a local dentist's office. The four prisoners were secured by handcuffs to the same 8-foot length of chain as they sat in the dentist's waiting room. At some point Franklin was released from the chain, taken into the dentist's office and given preliminary treatment, and then escorted back to the waiting room. As another prisoner was being released, Franklin, who had not been reshackled, seized a pistol from one of the two officers and managed to escape. He forced the dentist's assistant to accompany him as a hostage.

In the parking lot Franklin found the dentist's automobile, the keys to which he had taken before escaping, but was unable to unlock the door. He then fled with the dental assistant after refusing her request to be set free. The two set out across an open clearing and came upon a local resident. Franklin demanded this resident's car. When the resident responded that he did not own one, Franklin made no effort to harm him but continued with the dental assistant until they came to the home of the victim, one Collie. Franklin pounded on the heavy wooden front door of the home and Collie, a retired 72-year-old carpenter, answered. Franklin was pointing the stolen pistol at the door when Collie arrived. As Franklin demanded his car keys, Collie slammed the door. At this moment Franklin's gun went off. The bullet traveled through the wooden door and into Collie's chest killing him. Seconds later the gun fired again. The second bullet traveled upward through the door and into the ceiling of the residence.

Hearing the shots, the victim's wife entered the front room. In the confusion accompanying the shooting, the dental assistant fled and Franklin did not attempt to stop her. Franklin entered the house, demanded the car keys from the victim's wife, and added the threat "I might as well kill you." When she did not provide the keys, however, he made no effort to thwart her escape. Franklin then stepped outside and encountered the victim's adult daughter. He repeated his demand for car keys but made no effort to stop the daughter when she refused the demand and fled. Failing to obtain a car, Franklin left and remained at large until nightfall.

Shortly after being captured, Franklin made a formal statement to the authorities in which he admitted that he had shot the victim but emphatically denied that he did so voluntarily or intentionally. He claimed that the shots were fired in accidental response to the slamming of the door. He was tried in the Superior Court of Bibb County, Georgia, on charges of malice murder[2] . . . and kidnaping. His sole defense to the malice murder charge was a lack of the requisite intent to kill. To support his version of the events Franklin offered substantial circumstantial evidence tending to show a lack of intent. He claimed that the circumstances surrounding the firing of the gun, particularly the slamming of the door and the trajectory of the second bullet, supported the hypothesis of accident, and that his immediate confession to that effect buttressed the assertion. He also argued that his treatment of every other person encountered during the escape indicated a lack of disposition to use force.

On the dispositive issue of intent, the trial judge instructed the jury as follows:

> A crime is a violation of a statute of this State in which there shall be a union of joint operation of act or omission to act, and intention or criminal negligence. A person shall not be found guilty of any crime committed by misfortune or accident where it satisfactorily appears there was no criminal scheme or undertaking or intention or criminal negligence. The acts of a person of sound mind and discretion are presumed to be the product of the person's will, but the presumption may be rebutted. A person of sound mind and discretion is presumed to intend the natural and probable consequences of his acts, but the presumption may be rebutted. A person will not be presumed to act with criminal intention but the trier of facts, that is, the Jury, may find criminal intention upon a consideration of the words, conduct, demeanor, motive and all other circumstances connected with the act for which the accused is prosecuted.

Approximately one hour after the jury had received the charge and retired for deliberation, it returned to the courtroom and requested reinstruction on the element of intent and the definition of accident. Upon receiving the requested reinstruction, the jury deliberated 10 more minutes and returned a verdict of guilty. . . .

Franklin levels his constitutional attack at the following two sentences in the jury charge: "The acts of a person of sound mind and discretion are presumed to be the product of a person's will, but the presumption may be rebutted. A person of sound mind and discretion is presumed to intend the

2. The malice murder statute at the time in question provided:

> A person commits murder when he unlawfully and with malice aforethought, either express or implied, causes the death of another human being. . . . Malice shall be implied where no considerable provocation appears and where all the circumstances of the killing show an abandoned and malignant heart. Ga. Code Ann. §26-1101(a)(1978).

natural and probable consequences of his acts, but the presumption may be rebutted."[3] The Georgia Supreme Court has interpreted this language as creating no more than a permissive inference. . . . The question, however, is not what the State Supreme Court declares the meaning of the charge to be, but rather what a reasonable juror could have understood the charge as meaning. The federal constitutional question is whether a reasonable juror could have understood the two sentences as a mandatory presumption that shifted to the defendant the burden of persuasion on the element of intent once the State had proved the predicate acts.

"The challenged sentences are cast in the language of command. They instruct the jury that "acts of a person of sound mind and discretion *are presumed* to be the product of the person's will," and that a person "*is presumed* to intend the natural and probable consequences of his acts," (emphasis added). These words carry precisely the message of the language condemned in [Sandstrom v. Montana, 442 U.S. 510 (1979)] (" '[t]he law presumes that a person intends the ordinary consequences of his voluntary acts' "). The jurors "were not told that they had a choice, or that they *might* infer that conclusion; they were told only that the law presumed it. It is clear that a reasonable juror could easily have viewed such an instruction as mandatory." 442 U.S., at 515 (emphasis added). The portion of the jury charge challenged in this case directs the jury to presume an essential element of the offense—intent to kill—upon proof of other elements of the offense—the act of slaying another. In this way the instructions "undermine the factfinder's responsibility at trial, based on evidence adduced by the State, to *find* the ultimate facts beyond a reasonable doubt."

The language challenged here differs from *Sandstrom,* of course, in that the jury in this case was explicitly informed that the presumptions "may be rebutted." The State makes much of this additional aspect of the instruction in seeking to differentiate the present case from *Sandstrom.* This distinction does not suffice, however, to cure the infirmity in the charge. Though the Court in *Sandstrom* acknowledged that the instructions there challenged could have been reasonably understood as creating an irrebuttable presumption, it was not on this basis alone that the instructions were invalidated. Had the jury reasonably understood the instructions as creating a mandatory *rebuttable* presumption the instructions would have been no less constitutionally infirm.

An irrebuttable or conclusive presumption relieves the State of its burden of persuasion by removing the presumed element from the case entirely if the State proves the predicate facts. A mandatory rebuttable presumption does not remove the presumed element from the case if the State proves the predicate facts, but it nonetheless relieves the State of the affirmative burden of persuasion on the presumed element by instructing the jury that it must find the presumed element unless the defendant persuades the jury not to make such a finding. A mandatory rebuttable presumption is perhaps less onerous

3. Intent to kill is an element of the offense of malice murder in Georgia.

from the defendant's perspective, but it is no less unconstitutional. Our cases make clear that "[s]uch shifting of the burden of persuasion with respect to a fact which the State deems so important that it must be either proved or presumed is impermissible under the Due Process Clause." . . .

When combined with the immediately preceding mandatory language, the instruction that the presumptions "may be rebutted" could reasonably be read as telling the jury that it was required to infer intent to kill as the natural and probable consequence of the act of firing the gun unless the defendant persuaded the jury that such an inference was unwarranted. The very statement that the presumption "may be rebutted" could have indicated to a reasonable juror that the defendant bore an affirmative burden of persuasion once the State proved the underlying act giving rise to the presumption. Standing alone, the challenged language undeniably created an unconstitutional burden-shifting presumption with respect to the element of intent. . . .

The jury, of course, did not hear only the two challenged sentences. The jury charge taken as a whole might have explained the proper allocation of burdens with sufficient clarity that any ambiguity in the particular language challenged could not have been understood by a reasonable juror as shifting the burden of persuasion. The State argues that sufficient clarifying language exists in this case. In particular, the State relies on an earlier portion of the charge instructing the jurors that the defendant was presumed innocent and that the State was required to prove every element of the offense beyond a reasonable doubt. The State also points to the sentence immediately following the challenged portion of the charge, which reads: "[a] person will not be presumed to act with criminal intention. . . ."

As we explained in *Sandstrom,* general instructions on the State's burden of persuasion and the defendant's presumption of innocence are not "rhetorically inconsistent with a conclusive or burden-shifting presumption," because "[t]he jury could have interpreted the two sets of instructions as indicating that the presumption was a means by which proof beyond a reasonable doubt as to intent could be satisfied." In light of the instructions on intent given in this case, a reasonable juror could thus have thought that, although intent must be proved beyond a reasonable doubt, proof of the firing of the gun and its ordinary consequences constituted proof of intent beyond a reasonable doubt unless the defendant persuaded the jury otherwise. These general instructions as to the prosecution's burden and the defendant's presumption of innocence do not dissipate the error in challenged portion of the instructions. . . .

Sandstrom v. Montana made clear that the Due Process Clause of the Fourteenth Amendment prohibits the State from making use of jury instructions that have the effect of relieving the State of the burden of proof on the critical question of intent in a criminal prosecution. Today we reaffirm the rule of *Sandstrom* and the wellspring due process principle from which it was drawn. . . .

Justice POWELL, dissenting.

In *Sandstrom* v. *Montana,* 442 U.S. 510 (1979), we held that instructing the jury that "the law presumes that a person intends the ordinary consequences of his voluntary acts" violates due process. We invalidated this instruction because a reasonable juror could interpret it either as "an irrebuttable direction by the court to find intent once convinced of the facts triggering the presumption" or "as a direction to find intent upon proof of the defendant's voluntary actions . . . unless *the defendant* proved the contrary by some quantum of proof which may well have been considerably greater than 'some' evidence—thus effectively shifting the burden of persuasion on the element of intent." Id., at 517 (original emphasis). Either interpretation, we held, would have relieved the State of its burden of proving every element of the crime beyond a reasonable doubt.

Unlike the charge in *Sandstrom,* the charge in the present case is not susceptible of either interpretation. It creates no "irrebuttable direction" and a reasonable juror could not conclude that it relieves the State of its burden of persuasion. The Court, however, believes that two sentences make the charge infirm:

> The acts of a person of sound mind and discretion are presumed to be the product of the person's will, but the presumption may be rebutted. A person of sound mind and discretion is presumed to intend the natural and probable consequences of his acts but the presumption may be rebutted.

I agree with the Court that *"[s]tanding alone,"* the challenged language could be viewed as "an unconstitutional burden-shifting presumption with respect to the element of intent." The fact is, however, that this language did *not* stand alone. It is but a small part of a lengthy charge, other parts of which clarify its meaning. . . .

Together, I believe that the instructions on reasonable doubt and the presumption of innocence, the instruction that "criminal intention" cannot be presumed, and the instructions governing the interpretation of circumstantial evidence removed any danger that a reasonable juror could have believed that the two suspect sentences placed on the defendant the burden of persuasion on intent. When viewed as a whole, the jury instructions did not violate due process. I accordingly dissent.

Justice REHNQUIST, with whom THE CHIEF JUSTICE and JUSTICE O'CONNOR join, dissenting. . . .

Today the Court sets aside Franklin's murder conviction, but not because either the trial judge or the trial jury found that his guilt had not been proven beyond a reasonable doubt. The conviction is set aside because this Court concludes that one or two sentences out of several pages of instructions given by the judge to jury could be read as allowing the jury to return a guilty verdict in the absence of proof establishing every statutory element of the crime beyond a reasonable doubt. The Court reaches this result even though the judge admonished the jury at least four separate times that they could convict only if they found guilt beyond a reasonable doubt. The Court, instead of examining the charge to the jury as a whole, seems bent on piling syllogism on syllogism to prove that someone *might* understand a few sentences in the charge to allow conviction on less than proof beyond a reasonable doubt. Such fine parsing of the jury instructions given in a state court trial is not required by anything in the United States Constitution.

Notes and Questions

1. How should the Court have instructed the jury on the issue of intent to kill?

2. Would the jury instructions rejected by Justice Brennan have significantly benefited the prosecution in the *Franklin* case? In the *Harris* case?

3. One authority[4] has commented:

> All jurisdictions place the intentional killing of another without justification, excuse, or mitigating circumstances within the category of murder. . . . While intentional killings may be classified further into subcategories of greater or lesser gravity, there is no controversy about their general classification as murder. Intent to kill has nothing to do with motive as such. While the circumstances that give rise to the intent may mitigate culpability, the law makes no differentiation between a killing with a benevolent motive, like euthanasia, and any other intentional killing.
>
> Ambiguities in the general use of the concept of "intention" to describe conduct have caused trouble in its use to define murder. If the actor's very purpose is to kill, there is no difficulty. It may be, however, that the death of another is an apparently necessary means to the accomplishment of his purpose but that he would be just as satisfied if it were achieved otherwise. Or, he may be aware that a death is a substantially certain consequence of his conduct, without wanting or trying to bring it about. Courts have wrestled with the distinctions among such states of mind and sometimes offer elaborate analyses of them in the context of particular facts. While such efforts may help to explain the result based on those facts, they do not yield generalizations beyond the ordinary open use of the concept of intention. In general, if the actor is aware that the likelihood of a death resulting from his conduct goes beyond the level of risk to the level of certainty or near-certainty, the element of intent is satisfied. . . .
>
> Since persons who intend to kill unlawfully are not likely to proclaim their intention, murder must often be established without explicit proof of intent to kill. The use of a deadly weapon is ordinarily sufficient to establish that element of the crime. While this result may be based on a "presumption" arising from use of a deadly weapon, the presumption amounts only to the usual inference that a person intends the ordinary and probable consequences of his actions.

4. Consider the commentary to Model Penal Code, Section 210.2:

> *Purposeful or Knowing Homicide.* Under Section 210.2(1)(a), both purposeful and knowing homicides are classified as murder, assuming the absence of justifi-

4. Weinreb, Homicide: Legal Aspects, 2 Encyclopedia of Crime and Justice 858, 859-861 (1983).

cation or excuse under Articles 2 and 3 of the Code and the absence of mitigation based on mental or emotional disturbance under Section 210.3(1)(b). This result reflects the judgments that purpose and knowledge should be assimilated for grading purposes, as was generally the case with prevailing law, and that no further grading distinctions, save for the possibility of provocation or similar mitigating circumstances, can usefully be made with respect to sentences to imprisonment. . . .

As defined in Section 2.02, "purposely" and "knowingly" refer to the actor's subjective state of mind. It is, therefore, misleading to speak, as some courts are prone to do, of a "presumption" that a person intends the natural or probable consequences of his acts. Liability under Section 210.2(1)(a) may not rest merely on a finding that the defendant purposely or knowingly did something which had death of another as its natural and probable consequence. Rather, the prosecution must establish that the defendant engaged in conduct with the conscious objective of causing death of another or at least with awareness the death of another was practically certain to result from his act. Of course, the required state of mind may be proved circumstantially, and a finding of purpose or knowledge may be a permissible inference from the character of the defendant's conduct and the circumstances under which it took place.

5. Consider the following case:

> Defendant, through nagging, threats of violence, and actual physical violence weakened her husband mentally and physically. Defendant knew her husband had a serious heart ailment (of which he was unaware) and that any exertion could kill him. The husband, after being coerced by defendant to walk with her through deep snow on a cold and windy day, died from exertion and exposure after travelling two blocks. Defendant's apparent motive was to get her husband's money. [Vesey v. Vesey, 54 N.W.2d 385 (Minn. 1952).]

Although this case was a civil case, the court implied that the evidence could be sufficient to support a murder conviction on the theory that defendant intended to kill her husband.

6. What if Gray purposely shoots to kill Smith, but misses Smith and kills Johnson? Is Gray guilty of the intentional killing of Johnson? The virtually universal rule is that he is guilty, thanks to the hoary legal fiction that his intent to kill Smith is "transferred" to his unintended killing of Johnson. Can we reach this result without the notion of "transferred intent"?

B. EXTREME RECKLESSNESS

PEOPLE v. JERNATOWSKI

Court of Appeals of New York
238 N.Y. 188, 144 N.E. 497 (1924)

Hiscock, C.J. . . .

The background of this alleged crime was a railroad strike in Buffalo.

The decedent's husband was a foreman in the employ of the railroad company and stayed at his post when the strike occurred. It does not appear whether the defendant was a striker, but apparently he had a vicious animosity toward those who continued in or entered into the employ of the railroad company at the time of the strike. As standing out against this background the jury were entitled to find the following facts, amongst others:

On the night of the homicide defendant and several other young men, after spending the evening on the streets and in various resorts, at a late hour passed a house where lived the decedent, her husband, and a son with his wife and young child. After the defendant and one or two others had gone a short distance beyond this house one of the number said that he had seen a man or men in the Hanover yard, and, the defendant saying something about strike-breakers or scabs, and one of the gang making a vile threat, the defendant and his brother started on a run toward the Hanover house, stopping in front thereof. There were lights in the house which could be seen from the outside, and the deceased, who was standing close to the window, called out, "Get away from there!," "What do you fellows want here?," "What are you doing there?" or something like that, and immediately defendant and his brother fired several shots into the house and one of these shots fired by defendant killed the decedent. . . .

The substantial complaint made by appellant's counsel, and the only one which requires any consideration, is that, in order to constitute the crime of which defendant has been convicted, there must have been present in his mind at the time he fired the shot which killed the decedent a specific and well-defined intention to kill some one, and that there was no evidence of such intention. That is the only question which we find it necessary to discuss even briefly, whether an intent to kill is made a necessary element by the statute under which the defendant has been convicted. We do not think that it is.

It is certain that neither principles of fundamental justice nor the more technical rules of criminal law demand that such intent should be made a necessary ingredient of this class of murders. Where a person, as the jury found this defendant did, aware that there are human beings in a house, fires several shots into it, knowing that someone may be killed, and with reckless indifference whether he is or not, he ought not to be relieved from the natural consequences of his act because at the time he fired he did not say or think, "I am going to kill." . . .

So in this case, when the defendant fired two or more shots into the house where he knew there were human beings, he committed an act which the jury certainly could say was imminently dangerous, and which evinced a wicked and depraved mind, regardless of human life, and which amply supplied the evidence of malice and felonious intent which were charged in the indictment. . . . [A]n act such as this supplied all of [the] requirements [of the statute under consideration], and furnished all of the elements of murder as defined by it, although there was no specific intent to kill, but only a reckless indifference whether some one was killed as a natural consequence of the act performed. . . .

Notes and Questions

1. Consider the following, from L. Weinreb, Homicide: Legal Aspects, 2 Encyclopedia of Crime and Justice 858, 859 (1983):

> *Extreme recklessness.* The common law recognized as the equivalent of an intent to kill an attitude of extreme recklessness toward the life of others. One whose conduct displayed plain disregard for a substantial, unjustified risk to human life was guilty of murder if his conduct caused a death. Various formulas have been used to describe this category of malice aforethought, including phrases such as "a depraved mind regardless of human life," "an abandoned and malignant heart," and "a heart regardless of social duty and fatally bent on mischief." Whatever formula is used, the key elements are that the actor's conduct perceptibly creates a very large risk that someone will be killed, which he ignores without adequate justification. The risk must be large, and it must be evident; there must also not be circumstances that make it reasonable to impose such risk on others. It is not necessary that the actor be aware of the identity of the person or persons whose life he endangers or that he have any desire that they be killed. The Model Penal Code sums this up in a requirement of recklessness "under circumstances manifesting extreme indifference to the value of human life" (§210.2(1)(b)).
>
> The scope of this category of murder evidently depends considerably on how "extreme" the actor's conduct has to be. Properly limited, the category includes only conduct about which it might fairly be said that the actor "as good as" intended to kill his victim and displayed the same unwillingness to prefer the life of another person to his own objectives. Examples of such conduct, which have been the basis of convictions for murder, are firing a gun into a moving vehicle or an occupied house, firing in the direction of a group of persons, and failing to feed an infant while knowing that it was starving to death. Expanded much beyond cases of this kind, the category might include conduct involving a high degree of carelessness or recklessness that is nevertheless distinct from an intent to kill and more properly included within some lesser category of homicide.
>
> The question is occasionally raised whether the actor must be aware of the risk he creates, if it would be plain to an ordinary reasonable person. Unless the actor is subject to some personal disability that accounts for his lack of awareness, it is most unlikely that he will be unaware of, rather than simply indifferent to, a plain risk so extreme that murder is in issue. In such a case, the resolution will probably depend on the jurisdiction's treatment of that kind of disability generally. If the disability is accepted as a defense or mitigation generally, then it will avoid the charge of murder; otherwise, the actor's lack of awareness will not help him. Thus, for example, while the Model Penal Code's formulation requires conscious disregard of the risk of death, one who was unaware of the risk because he was drunk could nevertheless be found guilty of murder, because the Code elsewhere provides that self-induced intoxication does not avoid a charge of recklessness as an element of an offense. Aside from special cases of this kind, it is probably safe to conclude that the extreme recklessness which characterizes this category of murder includes a realization of the risk. A lesser degree of risk, of which the actor might be unaware, would suffice for manslaughter but not murder.

2. The Model Penal Code Commentary to Section 210.2 explains:

Reckless Homicide Manifesting Extreme Indifference. Section 210.2(1)(b) also provides that criminal homicide constitutes murder when it is "committed recklessly under circumstances manifesting extreme indifference to the value of human life." This provision reflects the judgment that there is a kind of reckless homicide that cannot fairly be distinguished in grading terms from homicides committed purposely or knowingly.

Recklessness, as defined in Section 2.02(2)(c), presupposes an awareness of the creation of substantial homicidal risk, a risk too great to be deemed justifiable by any valid purpose that the actor's conduct serves. Since risk, however, is a matter of degree and the motives for risk creation may be infinite in variation, some formula is needed to identify the case where recklessness may be found and where it should be assimilated to purpose or knowledge for purposes of grading. Under the Model Code, this judgment must be made in terms of whether the actor's conscious disregard of the risk, given the circumstances of the case, so far departs from acceptable behavior that it constitutes a "gross deviation from the standard of conduct that a law-abiding person would observe in the actor's situation." Ordinary recklessness in this sense is made sufficient for a conviction of manslaughter under Section 210.3(1)(a). In a prosecution for murder, however, the Code calls for the further judgment whether the actor's conscious disregard of the risk, under the circumstances, manifests extreme indifference to the value of human life. The significance of purpose or knowledge as a standard of culpability is that, cases of provocation or other mitigation apart, purposeful or knowing homicide demonstrates precisely such indifference to the value of human life. Whether recklessness is so extreme that it demonstrates similar indifference is not a question, it is submitted, that can be further clarified. It must be left directly to the trier of fact under instructions which make it clear that recklessness that can fairly be assimilated to purpose or knowledge should be treated as murder and that less extreme recklessness should be punished as manslaughter.

Insofar as Subsection (1)(b) includes within the murder category cases of homicide caused by extreme recklessness, though without purpose to kill, it reflects both the common law and much pre-existing statutory treatment usually cast in terms of conduct evidencing a "depraved heart regardless of human life" or some similar words. Examples usually given include shooting into a crowd or into an occupied house or automobile, though they are not, of course, exhaustive.

Some indication of the content of this concept as a means of differentiating murder and manslaughter may be afforded by prior decisional law. One case involved a game of Russian roulette, where the defendant pointed a revolver loaded with a single cartridge at his friend. The weapon fired on the third try, and the fatal wound resulted. The court affirmed the conviction for murder, despite ample evidence that the defendant had not desired to kill his friend, with the statement that "malice in the sense of a wicked disposition is evidenced by the intentional doing of an uncalled-for act in callous disregard of its likely harmful effects on others." In another case, the defendant's claimed intention was to shoot over his victim's head in order to scare him. The court held that, even crediting this assertion, the jury could find the defendant guilty of murder on the ground that his act showed "such a reckless disregard for human life as was the equivalent of a specific intent to kill." A third illustration involved a defendant who fired several shots into a house which he knew to be occupied by several persons. The court affirmed his conviction of murder because the defendant's conduct was "imminently dangerous" and "evinced a wicked and depraved mind regardless of human life." Other acts held to show sufficient recklessness to justify a conviction of murder include shooting into a moving automobile and throwing a heavy beer glass at a woman carrying a lighted oil lamp.[5]

The Model Code formulation would permit a jury to reach the same conclusion in each of these cases. . . .

Given the Model Code definition of recklessness, the point involved is put adequately and succinctly by asking whether the recklessness rises to the level of "extreme indifference to the value of human life." As has been observed, it seems undesirable to suggest a more specific formulation. The variations referred to above retain in some instances greater fidelity to the common-law phrasing but they do so at great cost in clarity. Equally obscure are the several attempts to depart from the common law to which reference has been made. The result of these formulations is that the method of defining reckless murder is impaired in its primary purpose of communicating to jurors in ordinary language the task expected of them. The virtue of the Model Penal Code language is that it is a simpler and more direct method by which this function can be performed.

3. In Commonwealth v. Malone, 47 A.2d 445 (Pa. 1946), the defendant appealed from a second degree murder conviction for the killing of 13-year-old William Long. Defendant and Long were friends at the time of the shooting. The court set out the facts as follow:

On the evening of February 26th, 1945, when the defendant went to a moving picture theater, he carried in the pocket of his raincoat a revolver which he had obtained at the home of his uncle on the preceding day. In the afternoon preceding the shooting, the decedent procured a cartridge from his father's room and he and the defendant placed it in the revolver.

After leaving the theater, the defendant went to a dairy store and there met the decedent. Both youths sat in the rear of the store ten minutes, during which period the defendant took the gun out of his pocket and loaded the chamber to the right of the firing pin and then closed the gun. A few minutes later, both youths sat on stools in front of the lunch counter and ate some food. The defendant suggested to the decedent that they play "Russian Poker." Long replied: "I don't care; go ahead." The defendant then placed the revolver against the right side of Long and pulled the trigger three times. The third pull resulted in a fatal wound to Long. The latter jumped off the stool and cried: "Oh! Oh! Oh!" and Malone said: "Did I hit you, Billy? Gee, Kid, I'm sorry." Long died from the wounds two days later.

The defendant testified that the gun chamber he loaded was the first one to the right of the firing chamber and that when he pulled the trigger he did not "expect to have the gun go off." He declared he had no intention of harming Long, who was his friend and companion.

5. Mayes v. People, 106 Ill. 306, 46 Am. Rep. 698 (1883) (held to be murder whether the glass was intended to hit the woman, someone else, or whether it was thrown with "general malicious recklessness, disregarding any and all consequences").

The court then held that the facts justified a conviction of second degree murder:

> A specific intent to take life is, under our law, an essential ingredient of murder in the first degree. At common law, the "grand criterion" which "distinguished murder from other killing" was malice on the part of the killer and this malice was not necessarily "malevolent to the deceased particularly" but "any evil design in general; the dictate of a wicked, depraved and malignant heart"; 4 Blackstone 199. . . .
>
> When an individual commits an act of gross recklessness for which he must reasonably anticipate that death to another is likely to result, he exhibits that "wickedness of disposition, hardness of heart, cruelty, recklessness of consequences, and a mind regardless of social duty" which proved that there was at that time in him "the state or frame of mind termed malice." . . .
>
> The killing of William H. Long by this defendant resulted from an act intentionally done by the latter, in reckless and wanton disregard of the consequences which were at least sixty percent certain from his thrice attempted discharge of a gun known to contain one bullet and aimed at a vital part of Long's body. This killing was, therefore, murder, for malice in the sense of a wicked disposition is evidenced by the intentional doing of an uncalled-for act in callous disregard of its likely harmful effects on others.

Was Malone reckless or merely negligent?

The court stated that there was a 60 percent chance of the gun's going off. Where did the court get that figure?

Assume that the defendant's testimony that the bullet was in the chamber to the right of the firing pin was true. If the defendant told the truth, how could the gun have gone off? If the defendant had honestly forgotten that the gun was loaded, would he still be guilty of murder?

4. From the Peninsula Times-Tribune, Oct. 20, 1983, at A-7, Col. 1:

> **Chicago Plant Where Worker Died Described as "Huge Gas Chamber"**
>
> Chicago (AP)—Dense cyanide fumes and deliberately obscured skull-and-crossbones labels were among the "shocking" conditions in a plant where a worker died, according to a prosecutor who charged five company officers with murder.
>
> Cook County State's Attorney Richard Daley on Wednesday described the Film Recovery Systems Inc.[6] facility, where silver was extracted from discarded X-ray film, as a "huge gas chamber."
>
> He said the company recruited and hired undocumented workers who did not understand English and couldn't complain about lethal working conditions. . . .
>
> Daley said he believed it was the first time officials of a company had ever been charged with murder for the work-related death of an employee. Film Recovery's officers also face 21 counts of reckless conduct, he said.

6. The company had filed for bankruptcy the month before.—Eds.

> "The plant conditions are the most shocking I've seen in my career," Daley said at a news conference after arrest warrants were issued for the five officers.
>
> Two of the officers surrendered to authorities Wednesday and were free on bond. A lawyer for the company, meanwhile, called the charges excessive.
>
> The indictments resulted from the cyanide poisoning death of Stefan Golab, 45, a Polish immigrant who worked at Film Recovery System's now-defunct plant in the Chicago suburb of Elk Grove Village.
>
> Golab was dead on arrival at a hospital in February after complaining of dizziness and nausea at the plant, where he worked [for two years] among tanks that bubbled with cyanide gas . . . Daley said.
>
> "But he was not the only employee who came to work daily in what can only be described as a huge gas chamber," Daley said.
>
> According to the indictments, warning labels on drums of lethal chemicals were defaced by burning or obscuring the skull and crossbones.

Did the officers manifest "abandoned and malignant hearts"? Should the company itself be charged with murder under the principle of Commonwealth v. McIlwain in Chapter 5?

PEARS v. STATE

Court of Appeals of Alaska
672 P.2d 903 (1983)

COATS, Judge.

While driving while intoxicated, Richard Pears caused an automobile accident in which two people died and one was injured. The state charged Pears with two counts of murder in the second degree. . . . A jury convicted Pears. . . . Judge Jay Hodges sentenced Pears to twenty years for the murder convictions. . . . We affirm Pears' conviction and sentence.

Pears first argues that Judge Hodges should have dismissed the grand jury indictment for second degree murder. The second degree murder statute under which Pears was charged, AS 11.41.110(a)(2), provides:

> A person commits the crime of murder in the second degree if . . .
>
> (2) he intentionally performs an act that results in the death of another person under circumstances manifesting an extreme indifference to the value of human life.

Pears argues that the legislature did not intend to have a motor vehicle homicide prosecuted as murder and that his offense should only have been charged as manslaughter. Manslaughter is defined in AS 11.41.120(a) and provides:

> A person commits the crime of manslaughter if he
>
> (1) intentionally, knowingly, or recklessly causes the death of another person under circumstances not amounting to murder in the first or second degree.

We find unpersuasive Pears' argument that the legislature did not intend for any motor vehicle homicide which was caused by an intoxicated driver to be charged as murder. This court discussed the relationship between second-degree murder and manslaughter in Neitzel v. State, 655 P.2d 325, 335-338 (Alaska App. 1982). In that case we indicated that the difference between second-degree murder and manslaughter was one of degree which was a question for the jury under proper instructions:

> Under the Revised Code, negligent homicide and reckless manslaughter are satisfied by conduct creating a significant risk of death absent justification or excuse. They differ only in the actor's knowledge of the risk. In differentiating reckless murder from reckless manslaughter, the jury is asked to determine whether the recklessness manifests an extreme indifference to human life. . . .
>
> . . . [T]he jury must consider the nature and gravity of the risk, including the harm to be foreseen and the likelihood that it will occur. For both murder and manslaughter, the harm to be foreseen is a death. Therefore, the significant distinction is in the likelihood that a death will result from the defendant's act. Where the defendant's act has limited social utility, a very slight though significant and avoidable risk of death may make him guilty of manslaughter if his act causes death. Driving an automobile has some social utility although substantially reduced when the driver is intoxicated. The odds that a legally intoxicated person driving home after the bars close will hit and kill or seriously injure someone may be as low as one chance in a thousand and still qualify for manslaughter. Where murder is charged, however, an act must create a much greater risk that death or serious physical injury will result.

Id. at 337.

The legislature has not indicated that no motor vehicle homicide could be charged as second degree murder. It is certainly clear that an automobile can be as dangerous a weapon as a gun or a knife and the results of its misuse just as deadly. It seems clear to us from the Revised Criminal Code that where a driver's recklessness manifests an extreme indifference to human life he can be charged with murder even though the instrument by which he causes death is an automobile. We conclude Judge Hodges did not err in refusing to dismiss the indictment charging Pears with murder in the second degree.[7] . . .

Pears . . . contends that Judge Hodges erred in not granting his motion for judgment of acquittal for murder in the second degree. "In determining whether to grant a motion for a judgment of acquittal, the trial court must view the evidence and the inferences therefrom in the light most favorable to the state and decide whether reasonable minds could conclude that guilt had been established beyond a reasonable doubt." Siggelkow v. State, 648 P.2d 611, 613 (Alaska App. 1982). When we look at the evidence in the light most favorable to the state, we conclude that a jury could find that Pears committed

7. We emphasize that a charge of second-degree murder should only rarely be appropriate in a motor vehicle homicide. The murder charge in this case is supported by the extreme facts which are set out more fully later in the opinion.

second-degree murder. The evidence produced at trial indicated that Pears voluntarily drank in a bar to the point of intoxication. After becoming intoxicated he drove recklessly, speeding, running through stop signs and stop lights and failing to slow for yield signs. His passenger at the time, Kathy Hill, told him that his driving scared her. Pears and Kathy Hill then went to another bar and had more drinks. Pears and Hill then left the bar and while they were approaching his truck on foot, Pears was stopped by two uniformed police officers in a patrol car. One of the officers told Pears not to drive because he was too intoxicated. Pears and Hill walked back toward the bar until the officers were out of sight. They then returned to his truck and drove away. Once again, with Hill protesting, Pears drove over the speed limit and ran red lights and stop signs. Pears then dropped Kathy Hill off and continued to drive around. Shortly before the fatal collision Pears was seen by Steve Call, who was turning his car onto the four-lane Steese Highway. According to Call, Pears' car ran a red light on the highway, going through the light at a high rate of speed and passing two cars which were stopped at the light. Call said he was going about forty-five miles per hour, the speed limit, but Pears was going faster. As they approached the next intersection Call could clearly see the red light against them and the cars stopping. Pears got around the cars which were stopping by passing them in the right turn lane, going into the intersection without braking or slowing down. Pears collided with one of the cars entering the intersection on the green light, an orange Datsun. The impact of the collision knocked the Datsun 146 feet, killing two of the three people in the car and seriously injuring the third.

We believe that a jury could have found that Pears' driving constituted circumstances manifesting an extreme indifference to human life. He was made abundantly aware of the dangerous nature of his driving by both his passenger, Kathy Hill, and the police officers who warned him not to drive. The fact that Pears drove recklessly and ran stop signs and red lights several times before the fatal collision supports the theory that he did not inadvertently run the red light when the collision occurred but that he was intentionally running the red light at high speed without regard for the fact that other cars were crossing the intersection.[8] We believe this evidence would support a second degree murder conviction and conclude that Judge Hodges did not err in refusing to grant Pears' motion for judgment of acquittal. . . .

8. Pears claims that he was passed out when he entered the intersection. Under the instructions given by the court the jury apparently rejected this contention and concluded that Pears intended to drive while intoxicated in a manner constituting extreme indifference to human life. The court charged:

> Our law provides that voluntary intoxication is generally not a defense to a prosecution for an offense.
>
> However, in the crime of murder in the second degree for which the defendant is charged in Counts I and II, the necessary element is the existence in the mind of the defendant of the intent to drive a motor vehicle while intoxicated in a manner constituting extreme indifference for the value of human life.
>
> If the evidence shows that the defendant was intoxicated at the time of the alleged

Pears also contends that his sentence of twenty years' imprisonment is excessive. There is little question from the extreme recklessness which resulted in the collision that Pears' offense was particularly serious and that Judge Hodges did not err in imposing a substantial sentence of imprisonment. On the other hand, Pears' sentence appears to be substantially greater than other sentences that courts have imposed in this state for homicides caused by intoxicated drivers. For instance, in Sandvik v. State, 564 P.2d 20, 26 (Alaska 1977), the supreme court upheld a sentence of twenty years with eight years suspended for the offense of negligent homicide. The defendant in that case had six prior convictions for operating a motor vehicle while under the influence of alcohol and had a twenty-year alcohol problem. In Rosendahl v. State, 591 P.2d 538, 539-540 (Alaska 1979), the supreme court upheld ten-year concurrent sentences for negligent homicide and failure to render assistance to an injured person. The court noted that the defendant had a "significant driving offense record which includes both alcohol and non-alcohol related offenses." In Layland v. State, 549 P.2d 1182, 1184 (Alaska 1976), the supreme court upheld an eight-year sentence. Layland had two convictions for operating a motor vehicle under the influence of alcohol, one of which arose out of an incident that occurred after the motor vehicle homicide. In Godwin v. State, 554 P.2d 453, 455 (Alaska 1976), the supreme court upheld a sentence of ten years with five suspended on a manslaughter charge which arose from operating a motor vehicle while under the influence of alcohol. The defendant in that case had prior convictions for several driving offenses including negligent driving and reckless driving. He was also on probation for breaking and entering at the time of the accident. In Gullard v. State, 497 P.2d 93, 94 (Alaska 1972), the supreme court upheld a ten-year sentence for manslaughter, although the court disapproved any restriction on parole. Gullard killed four people. Gullard also was convicted twice of operating a motor vehicle under the influence of alcohol after the fatal accident but before sentencing. These appear to be some of the more severe sentences for intoxicated drivers who committed motor vehicle homicides. There are also many cases where much more lenient sentences have been imposed.

We note that in the former cases where courts have sentenced drivers who were convicted of a motor vehicle homicide to sentences in the range of ten years, a significant factor in justifying that sentence appears to be the existence of convictions for operating a motor vehicle under the influence of alcohol (now driving while intoxicated) or similar offenses. Frequently these offenses occurred after the fatal accident. Although Pears has several driving offenses, he has not been convicted of driving while intoxicated, reckless driving or negligent driving.

---

offense, the jury should consider the state of intoxication in determining if defendant had such intent.

If from all the evidence you have a reasonable doubt whether the defendant was capable of forming such intent, you must find that he did not have such intent.

"Intoxication" includes intoxication from the use of a drug or alcohol.

Of course, one problem with relying on these former cases in deciding whether Pears' sentence is appropriate is that the former sentences were imposed for either negligent homicide or manslaughter. Pears is the first person in this state to be convicted of murder for a motor vehicle homicide. The jury found that Pears' conduct was extreme; it manifested an extreme indifference to human life. In addition, Pears' conduct resulted in two deaths and severe injury to a third person.

The question of whether the sentence imposed in this case is excessive is a close one. Balanced on one side is Pears' conduct and the result of that conduct. Balanced on the other side is the fact that Pears' sentence appears to be the most severe ever imposed for a vehicular homicide in the State of Alaska. Pears was only nineteen at the time of this offense and had no prior record of alcohol related driving offense. We conclude that the former Alaska cases which involved sentences for motor vehicle homicide can and should be distinguished because those sentences were imposed for negligent homicide and manslaughter. The instant case involves a charge of murder. If Pears' sentence is looked at as a sentence for murder, we do not believe that we can find that it was clearly mistaken. In Page v. State, 657 P.2d 850, 855 (Alaska App. 1983) we said:

> A review of the sentences for second-degree murder considered by the supreme court and this court since [1980] indicate that the typical sentence is twenty to twenty-five years. It is possible that the reported cases overstate sentences, since someone receiving less than twenty years may not be strongly motivated to appeal. Twenty years is therefore a proper benchmark to measure sentences for this crime. Any sentence substantially exceeding that amount should appear at least provisionally suspect. It would appear appropriate, therefore, in light of AS 12.55.-125(b) and experience in sentencing second-degree murderers, both before and after enacting the revised code, that one convicted of that offense should receive a sentence of from twenty to thirty years. Naturally, mitigating circumstances could reduce the sentence down to the five-year minimum and aggravating circumstances could enhance it up to the ninety-nine year maximum. [footnote omitted]

Thus Pears' twenty-year sentence does not appear to be out of line with other sentences which have been imposed for murder. We conclude that although Pears' sentence is severe and certainly appears to be significantly greater than any sentence which has formerly been imposed in a case in this state involving a motor vehicle homicide, the sentence is not clearly mistaken.

The conviction and sentence are affirmed.

Notes and Questions

1. In 1981, the California Supreme Court held that a drunk driver who causes a fatal car accident can be charged with second-degree murder. People v. Watson, 30 Cal. 3d 290, 179 Cal. Rptr. 43 (1981). The facts of the case are as follows:

> In the late night and early morning hours of January 2 and 3, 1979, defendant Robert Watson consumed large quantities of beer in a Redding bar. Approximately an hour and a half after leaving the bar, defendant drove through a red light on a Redding street and avoided a collision with another car only by skidding to a halt in the middle of the intersection. After this near collision, defendant drove away at high speed, approached another intersection and, although he again applied his brakes, struck a Toyota sedan. Three passengers in the Toyota were ejected from the vehicle and the driver and her six-year-old daughter were killed. Defendant left 112 feet of skid marks prior to impact, and another 180 feet of skid marks to the vehicle's point of rest.
>
> The applicable speed limit at the accident scene was 35 miles per hour. Expert testimony based on the skid marks and other physical evidence estimated defendant's speed immediately prior to applying his brakes at 84 miles per hour. At point of impact, the experts concluded that defendant's speed was approximately 70 miles per hour. Eyewitness Henke testified that defendant's car passed him "real fast" (estimated by Henke at 50 to 60 miles per hour) shortly before the collision. According to Henke, defendant swerved from the slow lane into the fast lane, suddenly braked and skidded into the intersection, and thereupon struck the other vehicle. Henke believed that the traffic light was green when defendant entered the intersection.
>
> Defendant's blood alcohol content one-half hour after the collision was .23 percent, more than twice the percentage necessary to support a finding that he was legally intoxicated.

The court rejected defendant's claim that the state's vehicular manslaughter statute precluded a murder charge.

> Rather, we conclude that if the facts surrounding the offense support a finding of "implied malice," second degree murder may be charged; if the facts demonstrate only "gross negligence," a vehicular manslaughter charge may be sustained. Although the terms "gross negligence" and "implied malice" are similar in requiring an awareness of a risk of harm, the degrees of awareness differ. Because of that fact, the more specific vehicular manslaughter statute does not preclude application of the more general murder statute.

Finally, the court held that the evidence would support a finding of "implied malice," stating:

> The facts upon which we base this conclusion are as follows: Defendant had consumed enough alcohol to raise his blood alcohol content to a level which would support a finding that he was legally intoxicated. He had driven his car to the establishment where he had been drinking, and he must have known that he would have to drive it later. It also may be presumed that defendant was aware of the hazards of driving while intoxicated. As we stated in Taylor v. Superior Court (1979) 24 Cal. 3d 890, 897, 157 Cal. Rptr. 693, 598 P.2d 854:
>
> > One who wilfully consumes alcoholic beverages to the point of intoxication, knowing that he thereafter must operate a motor vehicle, thereby combining sharply impaired physical and mental faculties with a vehicle capable of great force and

> speed, reasonably may be held to exhibit a conscious disregard of the safety of others.

> Defendant drove at highly excessive speeds through city streets, an act presenting a great risk of harm or death. Defendant nearly collided with a vehicle after running a red light; he avoided the accident only by skidding to a stop. He thereafter resumed his excessive speed before colliding with the victims' car, and then belatedly again attempted to brake his car before the collision (as evidenced by the extensive skid marks before and after impact) suggesting an actual awareness of the great risk of harm which he had created. In combination, these facts reasonably and readily support a conclusion that defendant acted wantonly and with a conscious disregard for human life.

Chief Justice Bird dissented, arguing that the majority distorted the evidence and rewrote the law of implied malice. She stated:

> The majority opinion fails to take into account the following evidence which was presented at the preliminary hearing. The prosecutor called Paul Henke as an adverse witness. Henke testified that he was driving along Cypress Avenue when respondent sped by at 55 or 60 miles per hour. As respondent approached the intersection of Cypress and Athens, where the fatal accident occurred, the light was green. At the scene, Henke spoke to some officers, whom he later identified at the trial. No one asked him to make a statement, and the officers merely told him to get out of the way. The next day Henke called the police because he had heard a news report requesting that witnesses identify themselves. He informed them that he had been a witness. Henke did not know respondent before the accident and had not had any contact with him since.

Chief Justice Bird then argued:

> Given Henke's testimony, it cannot be found that respondent committed an act likely to kill. The act of speeding through a green light at 55 or 60 miles per hour in a 35-mile-per-hour zone was dangerous, but was not an act likely to result in the death of another. It was 1 o'clock in the morning. The person whose car respondent nearly collided with testified that he saw no other cars around. . . .

> The fact that respondent was under the influence of alcohol made his driving more dangerous. A high percentage of accidents is caused by such drivers. No one holds a brief for this type of activity. However, a rule should not be promulgated by this court that driving while under the influence of alcohol is sufficient to establish an act "likely to kill." Death or injury is not the probable result of driving while under the influence of alcohol. Thousands, perhaps hundreds of thousands, of Californians each week reach home without accident despite their driving intoxicated.

> The majority also fail to demonstrate that it is reasonable to infer that respondent had a conscious disregard for life. Can a conscious disregard for life be established by the fact that several hours *before* the accident respondent drove his car to a bar? The majority hold as a matter of law that he "must have

known" he would have to drive his car later and that he wilfully drank alcohol until he was under its influence.

How does respondent's state of mind at the time he drove to the bar and began drinking justify an inference that he had a reckless state of mind at the time of the accident? This meager evidence does not justify the inference that by drinking alcohol he harbored a conscious disregard for life when he later drove his car! I submit that the majority's reasoning that such an inference may be drawn to support a finding of implied malice will be used to establish second degree murder in every case in which a person drives a car to a bar, a friend's home, or a party, drinks alcohol so that he is under its influence, drives away and is involved in a fatal accident. Moreover, newly enacted legislation will make it easier than ever to establish implied malice. Under a bill recently signed by the Governor, the rebuttable presumption that a person is under the influence of alcohol if his blood alcohol content is 0.10 percent or more has been eliminated. Instead, the new statute makes it a crime to drive with a blood alcohol content of 0.10 percent or more. In effect, it creates a *conclusive* presumption that the driver is under the influence of alcohol. Under this conclusive presumption and the majority's erroneous expansion of the concept of implied malice, a person who had only a few drinks could readily find himself charged with and convicted of second degree murder.

The majority's reasoning also perpetuates the fiction that when a person drinks socially, he wilfully drinks to come under the influence of alcohol and with this knowledge drives home at a later time. This unfounded conclusion ignores social reality. "[T]ypically [a person] sets out to drink without becoming intoxicated, and because alcohol distorts judgment, he overrates his capacity, and misjudges his driving ability after drinking too much." (*Taylor,* supra.)

Clearly, evidence regarding respondent's drinking earlier in the evening bears little relevance to his state of mind at the time of the accident. The majority's reliance on evidence of respondent's presumed state of mind before he began driving violates the basic principle that a crime cannot be committed unless there is unity of act and intent. (Pen. Code, §20.)

The majority's errors are compounded by the fact that they improperly *presume* that respondent harbored a conscious disregard for life. Thus, they state that respondent "must have known" he would drive after drinking and that it "may be presumed that [he] was aware of the hazards of driving while intoxicated." These presumptions improperly dilute the requirement that the prosecution must *prove* the accused's intent to commit an act likely to kill with conscious disregard for life.

The majority point to respondent's drinking as evidence of the implied-malice element that he committed an act likely to kill. However, they ignore the fact that driving while under the influence may also show lack of a conscious appreciation of the risk of harm presented to others. (See Pen. Code, §22.) . . .[9]

9. Section 22 provides:

No act committed by a person while in a state of voluntary intoxication is less criminal by reason of his having been in such condition. *But whenever the actual existence of any particular purpose, motive, or intent is a necessary element to constitute any particular species or degree of crime, the jury may take into consideration the fact that the accused was intoxicated at the time, in determining the purpose, motive, or intent with which he committed the act.* (Emphasis added.)

Is the Chief Justice correct when she says the majority opinion will support a finding of implied malice to establish second-degree murder whenever a drunk driver is involved in a fatal accident?

Is not the Chief Justice correct when she says driving under the influence may "show lack of a conscious appreciation of the risk presented to others"? Why does the majority seem to say the more drunk you are the more reckless? Can this conflict be resolved?

What does Chief Justice Bird think are the facts of the case? What is the majority's view? Compare the *Watson* facts to those in *Pears.* In both cases the defendant had some form of prior warning to make him aware of the risk. Is the fact that Pears did not brake but Watson did significant? Does Chief Justice Bird think so?

In 1983, California amended its vehicular manslaughter statute to read:

> Gross negligence, as used in this section, shall not be construed as prohibiting or precluding a charge of murder under Section 188 upon facts exhibiting wantonness and a conscious disregard for life to support a finding of implied malice, or upon facts showing malice, consistent with the holding of the California Supreme Court in People v. Watson (1981) 30 Cal. 3d 290.

2. Consider this article from the San Jose Mercury News, May 23, 1984, at 4B:

> A 27-year-old former Livermore resident on Tuesday became the first person ever convicted of murder in a drunken-driving case in Alameda County.
>
> After three days of deliberation, a Superior Court jury found Ronald Albright guilty of second-degree murder in a 1982 accident that killed a Pleasanton teen-ager.
>
> Depressed over losing his job, prosecutors said, Albright got drunk and then climbed into his 1964 Ford station wagon for a high-speed suicide attempt.
>
> But instead of ending his own life, Albright rammed into a car driven by 17-year-old Daniel Rueda. Rueda's car burst into flames, and he was killed instantly.
>
> Albright now faces 15 years to life in prison when Superior Court Judge Martin Pulich sentences him on July 3.
>
> To agree on a murder verdict, the jury had to find that Albright killed Rueda because of his "willful, wanton and reckless disregard for human life" and that he had "malicious intent," according to state law.
>
> The jury also found Albright guilty of driving under the influence of alcohol. Tests showed that Albright had a blood-alcohol level of .17, more than the legal limit of .10.
>
> Albright became the seventh person in California to be convicted of murder in a drunken-driving case, according to JoAnne Sanzeri, a spokeswoman for Mothers Against Drunk Drivers. Two of those convictions have been returned in Santa Clara County.
>
> Calling the verdict "a fantastic judgment," deputy district attorney Russ Giuntini said it will be tougher for other drunken drivers to escape harsh penalties in Alameda County.

"I hope it sends out a message to other people that if you drive drunk and kill someone, you can be convicted of murder," he said. "In this case, that's exactly what happened. It was a clear case of murder."

Albright's attorney, Tim Rien, contended that his client was innocent of murder because he did not intend to injure anyone else at the time of the accident and was not aware of the consequences of driving at such a high speed.

Rien said he will ask Pulich for a new trial because "the facts don't support the findings in this case." If that motion is not granted, Rien said, he will appeal.

C. INTENT TO DO SERIOUS BODILY INJURY

COMMONWEALTH v. DORAZIO

Supreme Court of Pennsylvania
365 Pa. 291, 74 A.2d 125 (1950)

Allen M. STEARNE, Justice.

The appellant, Gustav Dorazio appeals from the judgment and sentence entered against him on a verdict of guilty of murder in the second degree.

On Friday, January 7, 1949, the appellant and Albert Blomeyer, the deceased, were both employees of C. Schmidt & Sons Brewing Company of Philadelphia, employed in different departments. They were members of rival unions, each of which sought to represent the brewery workers. The deceased and two other employees had for some time been circulating a petition seeking an election supervised by the National Labor Relations Board to determine union representation.

At about 9:30 A.M. on the day of the killing the defendant complained to the vice-president of the company that a petition was being circulated by a man named Hornung, that if Hornung were not stopped he (defendant) "was going to let [him] have it." At about 10 A.M. the defendant approached Hornung and threatened him "to lay off taking up this petition, to stop taking it around, and if [he] didn't [defendant] was going to send [him] home in an ambulance." Defendant also spoke to another employee, Keehfus, at about 10 A.M., saying, "I just told Hornung I am going to send him to the hospital. You better watch out, I am going to send you home in an undertaker's wagon."

From the Commonwealth's evidence the jury could have found the following facts: shortly after 3 P.M. the victim and several other men went to the Sternewirt, a brewery tap room, where beer is gratuitously served to employees and guests of the brewery. The victim had several beers. He also was securing signatures to a union petition. Morton L. Smith, the business agent for the union to which defendant belonged, was also in the Sternewirt at this time. At about 4 P.M. the victim left the plant in the company of two men, Witt and Amberg, employed in the same department, (the fermenting room of the brewhouse) and he was walking between them. As the victim and his companions were walking on a street adjacent to the brewery the defendant was standing alone behind a pillar near the brewery plant. The defendant came from behind the pillar and followed behind the three men. He overtook them and "started swinging" at the victim and struck him. The victim turned, apparently recognized the defendant, and said, "It's Gus Dorazio." In turn the victim started to run down Edward Street back towards the brewery. The defendant followed in close pursuit. As the victim ran up the street he passed Smith, the rival union's agent, who put his hand out, whether or not to stop the victim is not clear. The victim ran into a brewery building known as the brewhouse; he ran up a flight of steps and passed through a door into a corridor. The Commonwealth's witness stated that neither Blomeyer nor defendant fell as they went up the steps and passed through the door immediately fronting on these steps. Immediately thereafter eye-witnesses observed the victim on the floor of the corridor either "in a crouched position" or lying on his left side; the defendant was standing over Blomeyer punching him repeatedly in and about the head and body. Witt, one of the men who had been walking with the deceased had followed the flight and sought to pull defendant away from the victim. The defendant beat Witt, knocked him down several times and struck him until and after he said he had enough. The assistant brew master ran up to stop the defendant and the defendant struck him in the stomach and knocked him across the corridor, down on one knee, momentarily helpless and breathless. Two witnesses testified that defendant struck the victim, while he lay prostrate, at least ten to fifteen times. After this incident the defendant ran or was pursued a short distance by an increasing crowd of brewery employees to a delicatessen store on Second street, where he was apprehended and taken into custody by the police.

The victim washed, was taken to a neighborhood hospital and was discharged after a brief course of treatment. The victim became ill a short time later that day, passed into semi-conscious state, and was removed from his home to a hospital where he died about 9 P.M. that evening.

The coroner's physician testified that death was "a result of hemorrhage with pressure against the brain resulting from a fracture of the skull"; that there was "a widespread comminuted fracture throughout the right temporal and parietal bones" with massive epidural hemorrhage pressing in and distorting the right anterior lateral surface of the brain. Under cross-examination the doctor testified that there were various lines of fracture as though the head either hit or was hit by a hard object. He stated "it is seldom that a fist—a blow of a fist can cause a comminuted fracture like that, but I would not exclude the possibility." The doctor after looking at the defendant's hands testified he could have caused the injuries; he further stated that he did not believe that the kind of fracture deceased sustained could result from tripping and striking his head on a door, *that it was a smash fracture.* The doctor stated that it was his opinion that the injuries were the result of *one powerful blow.*

The defendant's version of this occurrence was that unnamed persons had been threatening him and calling him names; that on the night before the incident he received an anonymous threatening phone call. The defendant denied having made threats against anyone. He testified that he knew the three men were connected with the CIO because he had seen them around the plant; that he had stopped the three men to ask them about the phone call; that he merely touched the victim on the shoulder to start a conversation and the victim punched him and ran. He stated that he did chase the victim into the corridor but what took place there was only a general fight in which he was only defending himself. The defendant contends that the victim's head injury resulted not from any alleged beating but from a fall either at the top of the steps or in the corridor. Defendant testified, "as he was starting to go up the steps, he was stumbling up the steps, climbing up the steps and he squashed his head in the door, and as he squashed his head against one door, the other door opened." After the fall, defendant said he was picking the victim up when the victim and Witt started to punch him and he fought back.

The defendant had been a professional heavyweight prize fighter for about 8 years prior to 1944; he fought a "great many" times and had been a contender for the heavyweight championship of the world in 1941, being defeated by the then champion, Joe Louis. Defendant was about five feet nine inches tall and weighed about 190 pounds.

In reviewing a record of conviction for murder . . . it is our duty to determine wheither the degree or elements of murder in the specified degree are present; whether there is sufficient evidence from which the jury could find beyond a reasonable doubt that the degree of murder was committed by the accused. . . . In the determination of such question we ordinarily confine ourselves to the Commonwealth's evidence; however, where the complaint is directed to the judge's charge we must assume the facts in their most beneficial aspect to the accused and determine how the charge may have governed those findings of fact by the jury.

The appellant contends that since he had no weapon of any kind in his possession the essential element of intent to kill or to do great bodily harm cannot be inferred "from the making of a mere assault, without a battery," with bare fists. . . .

Murder in this Commonwealth, though divided by statute into degrees, is still determined by the common law . . . . The division of murder into degrees was for the purpose of fixing punishment in relation to the heinousness of the offense, not to change the common law principles. The distinguishing criterion between murder and other homicide is malice.

The appellant argues that the malice necessary to support a conviction for murder cannot be imported from the use of the fists in the circumstances of this case; that such malice could only be shown by evidence that there was an intent to inflict great bodily harm.

Ordinarily where an assault is made with bare fists only, without a deadly weapon, and death results there would only be manslaughter. This follows naturally from the requirement that there appear an intent to inflict great bodily harm. In Wellar v. People, 30 Mich. 16, this principle was well stated as follows:

> It is not necessary in all cases that one held for murder must have intended to take the life of the person he slays by his wrongful act. . . . But it is necessary that the intent with which he acted shall be equivalent in legal character to a criminal purpose aimed against life. . . . And if the intent be directly to produce a bodily injury, it must be such an injury as may be expected to involve serious consequences, either perilling life or leading to great bodily harm. There is no rule recognized as authority which will allow a conviction of murder where a fatal result was not intended, unless the injury intended was one of a very serious character which might naturally and commonly involve loss of life or grievous mischief. Every assault involves bodily harm. But any doctrine which would hold every assailant as a murderer where death follows his act, would be barbarous and unreasonable . . . . In general, it has been held that where the assault is not committed with a deadly weapon, the intent must be clearly felonious, or the death will be subject only to the charge of manslaughter. The presumption arising from the character of the instrument of violence, is not conclusive in either way, but where such weapons are used as do not usually kill, the deadly intent ought to be left in no doubt. There are cases on record where death by beating and kicking has been held to warrant a verdict of murder, the murderous intent being found. But where there was no such intent the ruling has been otherwise. . . . The willful use of a deadly weapon, without excuse or provocation, in such a manner as to imperil life, is almost universally recognized as showing a felonious intent. . . . But where the weapon or implement used is not one likely to kill or to maim, the killing is held to be manslaughter, unless there is an actual intent which shows a felonious purpose.

Whether the malice necessary to constitute murder may be implied from the use of fists alone must depend on the particular circumstances. The size of the assailant, the manner in which the fists are used, the ferocity of the attack and its duration and the provocation are all relevant to the question of malice. . . . [F]ists though not ordinarily a deadly weapon may become deadly by repeated and continued blows applied to vital and delicate parts of the body of a defenseless, unresisting victim. The appellant refers to an illustrative footnote in Commonwealth v. Malone, 354 Pa. 180, 186, 47 A.2d 445, footnote 3, as requiring an intent to inflict "enormous" bodily harm to satisfy the requirement of malice in second degree murder. That illustration does not establish a minimum test of what is required to constitute "serious bodily harm." It is unnecessary to now detail what constitutes such harm. We agree, however, that it is not necessary that the injury be intended to be permanent or dangerous to life, it is malicious to intend injury such as to seriously interfere with health and comfort. . . .

The defendant indulged himself in an unjustified, unprovoked, brutal and persistent attack upon the deceased. He received a fair trial and the judge properly instructed the jury on the evidence.

The judgment is affirmed and the record is remitted to the court below so that the sentence imposed may be carried out.

Notes and Questions

1. Does the court suggest that if the defendant had not been a former heavyweight boxer he would not be guilty of murder?

2. From Weinreb, Homicide: Legal Aspects, 2 Encyclopedia of Crime and Justice 858, 858-859 (1983):

> *Intention to injure seriously.* The intention to injure that constituted one of the common law's categories of malice aforethought was an intention to cause serious physical injury, stopping short of death itself. Provided that the intended injury is truly serious, so that an accidental death from an ordinary assault is not included, few homicides that fall within this category would not also fall within one of the other categories of murder. Death having in fact been the result, in most cases in which a jury is able to find the necessary intent to injure it will be able to find either an intent to kill or extreme disregard of a risk to life. One of the functions of this category of malice aforethought may indeed have been to relieve somewhat the burden of finding an intent specifically to kill rather than to inflict a serious injury.
>
> The Model Penal Code eliminates intent to injure as a separate basis of liability for murder. The drafters concluded that proper cases for liability of this type will be included without it. The only clear case of murder under the common law that is excluded under the Code is one in which the actor inflicts serious injury while taking express precautions not to kill his victim, and the victim dies anyway. Such a case would in any event fall within some category of criminal homicide—manslaughter, if not murder. On the other hand, retention of the common-law classification leaves the possibility that unless the degree of seriousness of the intended injury is emphasized, an unintentional killing not accompanied by the same culpability as an intentional killing will be treated in the same way. Some jurisdictions follow the lead of the Model Penal Code; many others retain this category of murder.

3. Treating an intent to cause grievous bodily harm as a substitute for an intent to kill is quite important in practice. One researcher[10] writes:

> . . . [O]ne conclusion that can be drawn from the sequence of studies here reported is that the intention to wound with an extremely deadly weapon is, in the United States, a more serious problem than unambiguously lethal attacks. . . .
>
> . . . No area of the criminal law is more notorious for fine and often artificial distinctions between mental states accompanying acts than the law of homicide. . . . Distinguishing between killings "with malice" and killings "without malice," if that distinction rests on anything other than the simple intention to kill, is also

10. Zimring, The Medium is the Message: Firearm Caliber as a Determinant of Death from Assault, Law & Socy. Rev. 97, 117, 121-122 (1972).

a task best left to word-magicians or judges and juries trying to conform results in homicide cases to personal instincts about rough justice. . . .

. . . The distinction is an important one. . . .

But to say that this distinction is important does not mean that it is viable in all cases. There were several hundred cases in one four-month period in Chicago in which an individual wounded another with a firearm in an area where such a wound could prove fatal and three out of four times he only wounded his victim once. Are all of these attacks committed, at the time of the first firing of the weapon, with "intent to kill"? What further data can discriminate attacks intended to kill in this category from other attacks? If we could crawl inside the minds of particular offenders, and if their own emotions were something other than ambiguous about what results were desired, we might obtain some more precise answers and some more precise distinctions. But the combination of the limitations of modern science and those imposed by modern criminal procedure makes this further step into the offender's mind unlikely, and in the circumstances it is not entirely unfortunate. In judging these serious attacks one either operates with a set of almost conclusive presumptions about intent, or one leaves the question of intention to kill . . . to the discretion of the trier of fact. . . .

D. FELONY MURDER

Felony murders are usually associated with killings that take place during the commission of a classic violent felony against the person, such as robbery or rape. The next chapter deals with these crimes in the context of aggravated murder. It is helpful first, however, to examine the doctrinal structure of and justifications for the felony-murder rule as applied to those killings resulting from the commission of other, usually nonviolent, felonies. Here the homicide is generally classified as second-degree, or unaggravated murder.

PEOPLE v. BURROUGHS

Supreme Court of California

35 Cal. 3d 824, 201 Cal. Rptr. 319, 678 P.2d 894 (1984)

GRODIN, Justice.

Defendant Burroughs, a 77-year-old self-styled "healer," appeals from a judgment convicting him of unlawfully selling drugs, compounds, or devices for alleviation or cure of cancer (Health & Saf. Code, §1707.1); felony practicing medicine without a license (Bus. & Prof. Code, §2141.5, now §2053); and second degree felony murder (Pen. Code, §187) in the treatment and death of Lee Swatsenbarg.

Burroughs challenges his second degree murder conviction by contending the felonious unlicensed practice of medicine is not an "inherently dangerous" felony, as that term has been used in our previous decisions to describe and limit the kinds of offenses which will support application of the felony-murder rule. We conclude that while the felonious unlicensed practice of medicine can, in many circumstances, pose a threat to the health of the individual being treated, commission of that crime as defined by statute does not inevitably pose danger to human life. Under well-established principles it cannot, therefore, be made the predicate for a finding of murder, absent proof of malice. As a consequence, we must reverse defendant's second degree felony-murder conviction.

The trial court did properly instruct the jury with respect to the unlawful selling of drugs, compounds, or devices for alleviation or cure of cancer, and felony practicing medicine without a license. There was substantial evidence presented from which the jury could have convicted defendant of these crimes. We affirm these convictions.

Lee Swatsenbarg had been diagnosed by the family physician as suffering from terminal leukemia. Unable to accept impending death, the 24-year-old Swatsenbarg unsuccessfully sought treatment from a variety of traditional medical sources. He and his wife then began to participate in Bible study, hoping that through faith Lee might be cured. Finally, on the advice of a mutual acquaintance who had heard of defendant's ostensible successes in healing others, Lee turned to defendant for treatment.

During the first meeting between Lee and defendant, the latter described his method of curing cancer. This method included consumption of a unique "lemonade," exposure to colored lights, and a brand of vigorous massage administered by defendant. Defendant remarked that he had successfully treated "thousands" of people, including a number of physicians. He suggested the Swatsenbargs purchase a copy of his book, Healing for the Age of Enlightenment. If after reading the book Lee wished to begin defendant's unorthodox treatment, defendant would commence caring for Lee immediately. During the 30 days designated for the treatment, Lee would have to avoid contact with his physician.

Lee read the book, submitted to the conditions delineated by defendant, and placed himself under defendant's care. Defendant instructed Lee to drink the lemonade, salt water, and herb tea, but consume nothing more for the ensuing 30 days. At defendant's behest, the Swatsenbargs bought a lamp equipped with some colored plastic sheets, to bathe Lee in various tints of light. Defendant also agreed to massage Lee from time to time, for an additional fee per session.

Rather than improve, within two weeks Lee's condition began rapidly to deteriorate. He developed a fever, and was growing progressively weaker. Defendant counseled Lee that all was proceeding according to plan, and convinced the young man to postpone a bone marrow test urged by his doctor.

During the next week Lee became increasingly ill. He was experiencing severe pain in several areas, including his abdomen, and vomiting frequently. Defendant administered "deep" abdominal massages on two successive days, each time telling Lee he would soon recuperate.

Lee did not recover as defendant expected, however, and the patient began to suffer from convulsions and excruciating pain. He vomited with increasing frequency. Despite defendant's constant attempts at reassurance, the Swatsenbargs began to panic when Lee convulsed for a third time after the latest abdominal massage. Three and a half weeks into the treatment, the couple spent the night at defendant's house, where Lee died of a massive hemorrhage of the mesentery in the abdomen. The evidence presented at trial strongly suggested the hemorrhage was the direct result of the massages performed by defendant.

I

Defendant's conviction of second degree felony murder arose out of the jury's determination that Lee Swatsenbarg's death was a homicide committed by defendant while he was engaged in the felonious unlicensed practice of medicine. The trial court ruled that an underlying felony of unlicensed practice of medicine could support a felony-murder conviction because such practice was a felony "inherently dangerous to human life."[11]

Consequently, the trial judge instructed the jury that if the homicide resulted directly from the commission of this felony, the homicide was felony murder of the second degree.[12] This instruction was erroneous as a matter of law.

When an individual causes the death of another in furtherance of the perpetration of a felony, the resulting offense may be felony murder. This court has long held the felony-murder rule in disfavor. "We have repeatedly

11. Felony practicing medicine without a license violates section 2053 of the Business and Professions Code (formerly §2141.5) which states:

> Any person who willfully, under circumstances or conditions which cause or create a risk of great bodily harm, serious physical or mental illness, or death, practices or attempts to practice, or advertises or holds himself or herself out as practicing, any system or mode of treating the sick or afflicted in this state, or diagnoses, treats, operates for, or prescribes for any ailment, blemish, deformity, disease, disfigurement, disorder, injury, or other physical or mental condition of any person, without having at the time of so doing a valid, unrevoked or suspended certificate as provided in this chapter, or without being authorized to perform such act pursuant to a certificate obtained in accordance with some other provision of law, is punishable by imprisonment in the county jail for not exceeding one year or in the state prison.

12. Second degree felony murder was defined for the jury as,

> The unlawful killing of a human being, whether intentional, unintentional or accidental, which occurs as a direct causal result of the commission of or attempt to commit a felony inherently dangerous to human life, namely, the crime of practicing medicine without a license under circumstances or conditions which cause or create risk of great bodily harm, serious mental or physical illness, or death, and where there was in the mind of the perpetrator the specific intent to commit such crime, is murder of the second degree.
>
> The specific intent to commit such felony, i.e., practicing medicine without a license under circumstances or conditions which cause or create risk of great bodily harm, serious mental or physical illness, or death, and the commission of or attempt to commit such crime must be proved beyond any doubt.

stated that felony murder is a 'highly artificial concept' which 'deserves no extension beyond its required application.' " (People v. Dillon (1983) 34 Cal. 3d 441, 462-463.) For the reasons stated below, we hold that to apply the felony-murder rule to the facts of the instant case would be an unwarranted extension of this highly "anachronistic"[13] notion. . . .

At the outset we must determine whether the underlying felony is "inherently dangerous to human life." (People v. Ford (1964) 60 Cal. 2d 772, 795, 36 Cal. Rptr. 620, 388 P.2d 892.) We formulated this standard because "[i]f the felony is not inherently dangerous, it is highly improbable that the potential felon will be deterred; he will not anticipate that injury or death might arise solely from the fact that he will commit the felony." (People v. Williams (1965) 63 Cal. 2d 452, 458, fn.4, 47 Cal. Rptr. 7, 406 P.2d 647.)

In assessing whether the felony is inherently dangerous to human life, "we look to the elements of the felony in the abstract, not the particular 'facts' of the case." This form of analysis is compelled because there is a killing in every case where the rule might potentially be applied. If in such circumstances a court were to examine the particular facts of the case prior to establishing whether the underlying felony is inherently dangerous, the court might well be led to conclude the rule applicable despite any unfairness which might redound to the defendant by so broad an application: the existence of the dead victim might appear to lead inexorably to the conclusion that the underlying felony is exceptionally hazardous. We continue to resist such unjustifiable bootstrapping.

In our application of the second degree felony-murder analysis we are guided by the bipartite standard articulated by this court in People v. Henderson, 19 Cal. 3d 86, 137 Cal. Rptr. 1, 560 P.2d 1180. In *Henderson,* we stated a reviewing court should look first to the primary element of the offense at issue, then to the "factors elevating the offense to a felony," to determine whether the felony, taken in the abstract, is inherently dangerous to human life or whether it possibly could be committed without creating such peril. In this examination we are required to view the statutory definition of the offense as a whole, taking into account even nonhazardous ways of violating the provisions of the law which do not necessarily pose a threat to human life.

The primary element of the offense in question here is the practice of medicine without a license. The statute defines such practice as "treating the sick or afflicted." One can certainly conceive of treatment of the sick or af-

13. People v. Phillips, 64 Cal. 2d 574, 583, n.6, 51 Cal. Rptr. 225, 414 P.2d 353 (1966). "The felony-murder doctrine has been censured not only because it artificially imposes malice as to one crime because of defendant's commission of another but because it anachronistically resurrects from a bygone age a 'barbaric' concept that has been discarded in the place of its origin."

In People v. Dillon, 34 Cal. 3d 441, 462-472, 194 Cal. Rptr. 390, 668 P.2d 697 (1983) we reaffirmed the first degree felony-murder rule despite serious reservations as to its rationality and moral vitality, because we regarded ourselves bound by the explicit statutory provision (Pen. Code §189) from which that rule derived. The second degree felony-murder rule, by contrast, is a creature of judicial invention, and as the Chief Justice's concurring opinion suggests the time may be ripe to reconsider its continued vitality. We decline to do so here, however, since that issue has not been raised, briefed, or argued.

flicted which has quite innocuous results—the affliction at stake could be a common cold, or a sprained finger, and the form of treatment an admonition to rest in bed and drink fluids or the application of ice to mild swelling. Thus, we do not find inherent dangerousness at this stage of our investigation.

The next level of analysis takes us to consideration of the factors which elevate the unlicensed practice of medicine to a felony: "circumstances or conditions which cause or create a risk of great bodily harm, serious mental or physical illness, *or death.*" That the Legislature referred to "death" as a separate risk, and in the disjunctive, strongly suggests the Legislature perceived that one may violate the proscription against the felonious practice of medicine without a license and yet not necessarily endanger human life. Our analysis of the other two categories of risk delineated in Business and Professions Code §2053 further supports this conclusion.

"Great bodily harm" is not defined in §2053, but the closely analogous term "serious bodily injury" is defined in Penal Code §243—which establishes appropriate punishments for the crime of battery when committed under various circumstances—as "[a] serious impairment of physical condition, including, but not limited to the following: loss of consciousness; concussion; bone fracture; protracted loss or impairment of function of any bodily member or organ; a wound requiring extensive suturing; and serious disfigurement." Pursuant to this definition, a broken arm or leg would constitute serious bodily injury—and by implication, great bodily harm as well. While painful and debilitating, such bone fractures clearly do not, by their nature, jeopardize the life of the victim.

In addition, we acknowledge that " '[s]erious bodily injury' and 'great bodily injury' are essentially equivalent elements." (People v. Corning (1983) 146 Cal. App. 3d 83, 90-91.) The term "great bodily injury," defined for purposes of enhancement in Penal Code section 12022.7 as "significant or substantial physical injury," has been held to include a broken jaw and a broken hand. Obviously these injuries do not rise to the level of being inherently life-threatening.

There is no indication the Legislature intended to ascribe a different meaning to "great bodily harm," as that term is used in §2053, than is signified by "great bodily injury," or, for that matter, "serious bodily injury," in the Penal Code sections we have discussed. Thus, we must conclude that the risk of great bodily harm under §2053 is likewise not [equivalent to conduct that is] inherently dangerous to human life.

The statute at issue can also be violated by administering to an individual in a manner which threatens risk of serious mental or physical illness. Whether risk of serious physical illness is inherently dangerous to life is a question we do not reach; however, we believe the existence of the category of risk of serious mental illness also renders a breach of the statute's prohibitions potentially less than a breach that is inherently dangerous to life.

As with the term "great bodily harm," "mental illness" is not defined in §2053. We have found no case in which a court of this state has made an attempt at such definition in the context of an adjudication pursuant to that statutory provision. Based on the meaning of "mental illness" in other contexts under California law, however, we are convinced this term encompasses a range of conditions, some of which are not inherently threatening to human life. . . .

. . . It is not difficult, for example, to envision one who suffers from delusions of grandeur, believing himself to be the President of the United States. An individual who purports without the proper license to be able to treat such a person need not be placing the patient's life in jeopardy, though such treatment, if conducted, for example, without expertise, may lead to the need for more serious psychiatric attention.

Consequently, we are disinclined to rule today that the risks set forth in §2053 are so critical as to render commission of this felony of necessity inherently dangerous to human life. Indeed, were we to interpret either the risk of great bodily harm or serious mental illness as being synonymous with the risk of death for purposes of the felony-murder rule, we would be according those terms a more restrictive meaning than that which the Legislature obviously meant them to have in the definition of the felony itself. Such a reading would require that an unlicensed practitioner of medicine actually perform treatment under circumstances or conditions which necessarily place the very life of the patient in jeopardy before such a practitioner could be susceptible to a conviction for *felonious* unlicensed practice. We possess grave doubts that the Legislature intended such a result.

Moreover, our analysis of precedent in this area reveals that the few times we have found an underlying felony inherently dangerous (so that it would support a conviction of felony murder), the offense has been tinged with malevolence totally absent from the facts of this case. In People v. Mattison (1971) 4 Cal. 3d 177, 93 Cal. Rptr. 185, 481 P.2d 193, we held that poisoning food, drink, or medicine with intent to injure was inherently dangerous. The wilful and malicious burning of an automobile (located in a garage beneath an occupied home) was ruled inherently dangerous in People v. Nichols (1970) 3 Cal. 3d 150, 162-163, 89 Cal. Rptr. 721, 474 P.2d 673. Finally, we held kidnapping to be such an offense in People v. Ford, supra, 60 Cal. 2d 772, 795, 36 Cal. Rptr. 620, 388 P.2d 892. . . .

To hold, as we do today, that a violation of §2053 is not inherently so dangerous that by its very nature, it cannot be committed without creating a substantial risk that someone will be killed, is consistent with our previous decisions in which the underlying felony has been held not inherently hazardous. We have so held where the underlying felony was felony false imprisonment (People v. Henderson, supra, 19 Cal. 3d 86, 137 Cal. Rptr. 1, 560 P.2d 1180), possession of a concealable firearm by an ex-felon (People v. Satchell, supra, 6 Cal. 3d 28, 98 Cal. Rptr. 33, 489 P.2d 1361), escape from a city or county penal facility (People v. Lopez, supra, 6 Cal. 3d 45, 98 Cal. Rptr. 44, 489 P.2d 1372), and in other, less potentially threatening circumstances.[14]

14. Including where the underlying felonies were grand theft by false pretenses and conspiracy to possess methedrine illegally.

Finally, the underlying purpose of the felony-murder rule, to encourage felons to commit their offenses without perpetrating unnecessary violence which might result in a homicide, would not be served by applying the rule to the facts of this case. Defendant was or should have been aware he was committing a crime by treating Swatsenbarg in the first place.[15] Yet, it is unlikely he would have been deterred from administering to Lee in the manner in which he did for fear of a prosecution for murder, given his published beliefs on the efficacy of massage in the curing of cancer. Indeed, nowhere is it claimed that defendant attempted to perform any action with respect to Swatsenbarg other than to heal him—and earn a fee for doing so.

This clearly is a case in which conviction of felony murder is contrary to our settled law, as well as inappropriate as a matter of sound judicial policy. The instruction regarding felony murder was erroneous.

Accordingly, defendant's second degree murder conviction is reversed.

II

In addition to asserting the felonious unlicensed practice of medicine will not provide the predicate for a felony-murder conviction because felonious unlicensed medical practice is not inherently dangerous to human life, Burroughs claims the trial court erroneously refused to give an instruction, requested by defendant, on the purportedly lesser included offense of involuntary manslaughter. Our conclusion the felony of practicing medicine without a license is not inherently dangerous, of course, obviates the necessity of reaching this alternative basis for purposes of reversal. To provide guidance to the trial court should Burroughs be retried for the death of Lee Swatsenbarg, however, we now consider whether, on the facts alleged, Burroughs could properly be charged and convicted of involuntary manslaughter. We will conclude that while there was no evidence to suggest Swatsenbarg's demise was the intended consequence of Burroughs' treatment of the decedent, there was substantial evidence that this treatment, the administering of "deep abdominal massages" in particular, was performed "without due caution and circumspection," and was the proximate cause of Lee Swatsenbarg's death. Thus, on the evidence presented, Burroughs was susceptible to a possible conviction of involuntary manslaughter, and the jury should have been so instructed.

MOSK, KAUS, BROUSSARD, and REYNOSO, JJ., concur.

BIRD, Chief Justice, concurring.

The majority reverse appellant's second degree felony-murder conviction on the ground that practicing medicine without a license is not an inherently dangerous felony. I agree with that conclusion, as well as with the directions

15. He had been convicted of practicing medicine without a license in 1960.

that on retrial appellant may be prosecuted for involuntary manslaughter. However, I would rest the reversal on a broader ground. The time has come for this court to discard the artificial and court-created offense of second degree felony murder.

As Justice Mosk noted for the court in People v. Dillon (1983) 34 Cal. 3d 441, 462, 194 Cal. Rptr. 390, 668 P.2d 697, this court "hold[s] no brief for the felony-murder rule." Felony murder has been described as "a highly artificial concept that deserves no extension beyond its required application." (People v. Phillips (1966) 64 Cal. 2d 574, 582, 51 Cal. Rptr. 225, 414 P.2d 353, fn. omitted.) "[T]he rule is much censured 'because it anachronistically resurrects from a bygone age a "barbaric" concept that has been discarded in the place of its origin.' . . . and because 'in almost all cases in which it is applied it is unnecessary' and 'it erodes the relation between criminal liability and moral culpability.' " (People v. Dillon, supra, 34 Cal. 3d at p.463, 194 Cal. Rptr. 390, 668 P.2d 697).

This court is responsible for the legal doctrines which it creates. The second degree felony-murder rule is, "as it has been since 1872, a judge-made doctrine without any express basis in the Penal Code. Therefore, the power to do away "with . . . the 'barbaric' anachronism which we are responsible for creating" lies with this court. Such long overdue judicial surgery would not intrude upon the prerogatives of the other two branches of government.

Accordingly, this court should take the long-overdue step and eliminate the second degree felony-murder rule.[16]

I

Many writers and commentators[17] have concluded that the common law doctrine of felony murder is of questionable origin. In an attempt to understand the development of the doctrine and the numerous restrictions and limi-

16. This court would not be the first to take such a step. In People v. Aaron (1980) 409 Mich. 672, 299 N.W.2d 304, the Michigan Supreme Court, interpreting a statute similar to Penal Code section 189, concluded after an exhaustive and scholarly analysis that the statute did not codify the common law felony-murder rule but merely elevated any murder otherwise proven to murder of the first degree when committed during the perpetration of one of the named felonies. This interpretive step was not a radical one. Several other state courts had so interpreted similar statutes. The Michigan court went further, however. It reviewed the *common law* doctrine of felony murder and concluded that "it violates the basic premise of individual moral culpability upon which our criminal law is based." As a result, the court abolished the felony-murder rule in Michigan.

In *Dillon,* a majority of the court declined to follow the *Aaron* court's lead with respect to the first degree felony-murder rule since the rule had been codified by the Legislature. Thus, "[h]owever much [the court] agree[d] with the reasoning of *Aaron,* [it could not] duplicate its solution to the problem. . . ." (34 Cal. 3d at p. 463, 194 Cal. Rptr. 390, 668 P.2d 697.) However, no statutory bar appears with respect to the second degree felony-murder rule so this court may in that context follow the lead of the Michigan Supreme Court.

17. The author owes a great debt to the late Justice Mathew O. Tobriner for his work in this area. He more than anyone is responsible for any clarity this opinion may bring to this intractable area of the law.

tations which have been imposed by both courts and legislatures, it is necessary to briefly review the common law concept of homicide and its relationship to the felony-murder rule.

At early common law, all homicides were criminal[18] without regard to the mental state of the actor. As with every other felony,[19] homicide was punishable by death.[20]

The law soon recognized the need to distinguish between intentional and accidental killings. By the thirteenth century, it was clear that an accidental killing or killing "by misadventure," while not subject to acquittal, would entitle the person convicted to a royal pardon.

The influence of the Church and canon law also resulted in the addition of certain distinctions to the law of homicide. Ecclesiastic courts had always retained jurisdiction to try clerics accused of felonies. Because the Church refused to impose capital punishment, submission of a case to Church jurisdiction resulted in leniency of the most important sort. "Benefit of clergy," as this practice was known, thus became a means of mitigating the harshness of the common law's meat-axe approach to all homicides, regardless of mental state. The punishment for those felons eligible for benefit of clergy was limited to the branding of a thumb and one year's imprisonment. Focusing on the character of the offender rather than the nature of the offense, the practice was gradually expanded by the use of a presumption that any person who could read and write was a cleric, and thus ineligible for the death penalty.[21]

As a greater proportion of the society became literate, the injustice of the system became apparent. Moreover, the principle of benefit of clergy conflicted with the fundamental philosophy of canon law, which had always emphasized the importance of subjective moral blameworthiness in assessing the degree of criminal culpability. These factors led to a series of statutes in the fifteenth and sixteenth centuries which abolished the benefit of clergy for certain of the more culpable homicides. These more culpable homicides, denominated murder,[22] were distinguished as having been committed with "malice

18. The law at this point recognized no distinction between a crime and a tort. Liability for a homicide included both punishment of the offender and payment to the surviving relatives of the deceased.

19. The common law concept of a felony is, of course, considerably different from the felony as it appears in modern statutory codes. At common law, the term was limited to a few very serious crimes, nearly all involving assaultive conduct or the danger of physical harm. (See Perkins & Boyce, Criminal Law (1982) pp. 14-15.)

20. There is some evidence to believe that while the punishment of death was theoretically possible in the case of all felonies, it was far from uniformly applied, varying principally with the seriousness of the offense. (See 2 Pollack and Maitland, The History of English Law (2d ed. 1909) p.488.)

21. Medieval England was, perhaps, more candid than twentieth century America. Compare Furman v. Georgia (1972) 408 U.S. 238, 365-366, 92 S. Ct. 2726, 2790-2791, 33 L. Ed. 2d 346 (conc. opn. of Marshall, J.): "It also is evident that the burden of capital punishment falls upon the poor, the ignorant, and the underprivileged members of society."

22. "Murder" derives from the term *murdrum* which originally referred to a heavy amercement which was levied against an English village whenever a Norman lord was killed in ambush. By the mid-fourteenth century, there were no longer any foreign-born Norman

aforethought" or "malice prepensed." All other homicides, for which benefit of clergy was still available, developed into the crime of manslaughter.

It is within this framework that the felony-murder rule was born. The exact origins of the rule, however, are far from clear. The most oft-cited early statement of the rule appears in Lord Coke's Third Institute (6th ed. 1680) page 56. Coke did not propose a rationale but rather illustrated by example:

> If the act be unlawful it is murder. As if A. meaning to steal a deer in the park of B., shooteth at the deer, and by the glance of the arrow killeth a boy that is hidden in a bush: this is murder, for that the act was unlawful, although A. had no intent to hurt the boy, nor knew not of him. But if B. the owner of the park had shot at his own deer, and without any ill intent had killed the boy by the glance of his arrow, this had been homicide by misadventure, and no felony.
>
> So, if one shoot at any wild fowle upon a tree, and the arrow killeth any reasonable creature afar off, without any evil intent in him, this is *per infortunium* [misadventure]: for it was not unlawful to shoot at the wilde fowle: but if he had shot at a cock or hen, or any tame fowle of another mans, and the arrow by mischance had killed a man, this had been murder, for the act was unlawfull.

This statement of the rule was refined by Hale and Foster, who limited the murder designation to any killing in the course of a felony.

The basis for Lord Coke's statement, which went unquestioned for several hundred years, appears dubious. Two sixteenth century English cases have been suggested as support, but courts and commentators have concluded that each was, in reality, based on an entirely different proposition.[23] Professors Moreland and Perkins, in their respective treatises, analyze in a historical

---

England and the requirement for an amercement was statutorily abolished. *Murdrum,* however, remained a part of the language as a way of referring to the most serious kind of homicide.

23. In People vs. Aaron, supra, 229 N.W.2d at pages 307-308, the Michigan Supreme Court discussed these two cases as follows:

> The first formal statement of the doctrine is often said to be *Lord Dacres'* case, Moore 86; 72 Eng. Rep. 458 (KB, 1535). Lord Dacres and some companions agreed to enter a park without permission to hunt, an unlawful act, *and to kill anyone who might resist them.* While Lord Dacres was a quarter of a mile away, one member of his group killed a gamekeeper who confronted him in the park. Although Lord Dacres was not present when the killing occurred, he, along with the rest of his companions, was convicted of murder and was hanged. Contrary to the construction placed on this case by those who see it as a source of the felony-murder rule, the holding was not that Lord Dacres and his companions were guilty of murder because they had joined in an unlawful hunt in the course of which a person was killed, but rather that those not present physically at the killing were held liable as principals on the theory of constructive presence. Moreover, because they had agreed previously to kill anyone who might resist them, all the members of the group shared in the *mens rea* of the crime. Thus, because *Lord Dacres'* case involved express malice, no doctrine finding malice from the intention to commit an unlawful act was necessary or in fact utilized.
>
> Another early case which has been cited for the origin of the felony-murder doctrine was decided after *Lord Dacres'* case. In *Mansell & Herbert's* case, 2 Dyer 128b; 73 Eng. Rep. 279 (KB 1558), Herbert and a group of more than 40 followers had gone to Sir Richard Mansfield's house "with force to seize goods under pretence of lawful authority." One of Herbert's servants threw a stone at a person in the gateway which instead hit and killed an unarmed woman coming out of Mansfield's house. The question was agreed to be whether

sense the genesis of the rule, but neither theory provides much support for the rationality of the doctrine.[24]

Regardless of whether Coke's statement may properly be termed the first formal expression of the felony-murder rule, it nonetheless has served as the focal point of analysis and criticism of the doctrine. As has been noted, Hale and Foster saw fit to substantially limit Coke's version of the rule by confining its application to felonies, rather than to all unlawful acts. Writing in the seventeenth century Hobbes commented that the rule "is not distinguished by any statute but is the *common law* only of Sir Edward Coke."

In 1883, Judge Sir James Fitzjames Stephen embarked on an extensive criticism of Coke's conclusion. Stephen termed the felony-murder rule "astonishing" and "monstrous." He further stated that the Coke passage is "entirely unwarranted by the authorities which he quotes." Modern writers have reached the similar conclusion that Coke's "creation" of the felony-murder rule was totally without legal or rational foundation.[25]

---

the accused were guilty of murder or manslaughter. Since misadventure was not considered, it can be assumed that the throwing of the stone was not a careless act but that the servant who threw the stone intended at least to hit, if not kill, some person on Mansfield's side. Although the court divided, the majority held that if one deliberately performed an act of violence to third parties, and a person not intended died, it was murder regardless of any mistake or misapplication of force. The minority would have held it to be manslaughter because the violent act was not directed against the woman who died. Thus, *Herbert's* case involved a deliberate act of *violence* against a person, which resulted in an unintended person being the recipient of the violent act.

24. Quoting again from People v. Aaron, supra, 299 N.W.2d at page 309, footnote 24:

Moreland sees the felony-murder rule as an extension of the doctrine of malice aforethought. For this proposition he cites Lambard, who states:

And therefore if a thief do kill a man whom he never saw before and whom he intended to rob only, it is murder in the judgment of law, which implyeth a former malicious disposition in him rather to kill the man than not to have his money from him." 3 Stephen [op. cit] supra, pp. 50-51. Moreland observes that this was an attempt to justify the rule as an inference of fact in order to satisfy the definition of malice aforethought prevailing at that time. But, in Moreland's opinion, it does not carry conviction as such. Moreland, Law of Homicide (Indianapolis: Bobbs-Merrill, 1952), p.14.

Stephen, commenting on the above passage from Lambard, states:

"The law can hardly be justified in 'presupposing' that a thief 'carryeth that malicious mind that he will achieve his purpose though it be with the death of him against whom it is directed,' from the fact that he trips a man up in order to rob him and happens to kill him." 3 Stephen . . . supra, p.51.

Perkins contends that the primary purpose of the felony-murder rule was to deal with homicides committed during unsuccessful attempted felonies. An attempt to commit a felony was only a misdemeanor at common law. The felony-murder rule placed the defendant in the position he would have been in had the felony been successful without the homicide, for in either case it would be a capital crime.

25. See Recent Developments, op. cit, supra, 65 Colum. L. Rev. at page 1496, footnote 2: "A telling historical comment on the essential non-logic of the rule is made by those who see its genesis as a blunder by Coke in the translation and interpretation of a passage from Bracton." The passage from Bracton referred to suggests only that a killing which results from an unlawful act is also unlawful, not that such a killing is *murder*. In addition, the example of an unlawful act used by Bracton (throwing a stone toward a commonly used walkway) arguably suggests what would today be considered equivalent to a reckless state of mind independently sufficient to establish the actual malice necessary for murder.

II

The history of the felony-murder rule is in reality a history of limitation. The path of limitation, as well as the result, has differed depending on the jurisdiction.

As early as 1834, an English governmental commission described the felony-murder rule as being "totally incongruous with the general principles of our jurisprudence." (First Rep. of His Majesty's Commissioners on Crim. Law (1834) at p. 29, quoted in Recent Developments, op. cit, supra, 65 Colum. L. Rev. at p. 1496.) The statement merely made explicit what was an ongoing process in English common law to limit application of the felony-murder doctrine.

A series of cases in the nineteenth century culminating with Regina v. Serne (1887), 16 Cox Crim. Cas. 311, virtually abolished the common law felony-murder rule in England. In *Serne,* Judge Stephen, whose pointed criticism of Coke was noted earlier, stated the law as follows: "[I]nstead of saying that any act done with intent to commit a felony and which causes death amounts to murder, it would be reasonable to say that any act known to be dangerous to life, and likely in itself to cause death done for the purpose of committing a felony which caused death, should be murder."

Stephen's characterization of the law strongly suggests that a reckless *mens rea* is required to prove murder. The actor must *know* that his act is "likely in itself to cause death." Professor Perkins concluded that Stephen was "inclined to require for murder . . . the same degree of wanton and wilful disregard for human life which would constitute malice aforethought if no felony were being attempted."[26]

Yet Judge Stephen's enlightened view was not long-lived. A series of cases beginning in 1898[27] and culminating with the House of Lords decision in Director of Public Prosecutions v. Beard (1920) App. Cas. 479 re-established the felony-murder rule, albeit with some restrictions.[28] Notwithstanding its renewed existence, the rule was rarely invoked in the twentieth century. It was applied, if at all, in cases in which there was ample independent evidence that the defendant possessed at least a reckless mental state. (Prevezer, [The Eng-

26. See CALJIC No. 8.31 (4th ed. 1982 pocket pt.) page 64:

> Murder of the second degree is [also] the unlawful killing of a human being as the direct causal result of an act involving a high degree of probability that it will result in death, which act is done for a base, antisocial purpose and with wanton disregard for human life.
>
> When the killing is the direct result of such an act, it is not necessary to establish that the defendant intended that his act would result in the death of a human being.

(Compare Model Pen. Code (Proposed Official Draft 1962) §2.02, subd. (2)(c), p.26.)

27. See generally Moreland, The Law of Homicide, supra, at page 45 and cases cited therein.

28. In *Beard,* the defendant was charged with murder when he accidentally suffocated his rape victim while trying to quiet her screams. The House of Lords held that if the defendant, in the course of a violent felony, commits a violent act which results in death, he is guilty of murder

lish Homicide Act: A New Attempt to Revise the Law of Murder (1957) 57 Colum. L. Rev. 624, 635.])

The death knell for the felony-murder rule in England was sounded by the Homicide Act of 1957. Section 1 of the act provided in relevant part: "Where a person kills another in the course or furtherance of some other offence, the killing shall not amount to murder unless done with the same malice aforethought (express or implied) as is required for a killing to amount to murder when not done in the course or furtherance of another offence." Thus by statute, Parliament vindicated the view expressed by Judge Stephen some 60 years earlier that a killing in the course of a felony is not murder unless the essential element of malice is independently proved.[29]

In the United States, the rule has followed a somewhat similar path. Since the state of English common law in 1776 served as the basis for the development of American jurisprudence, Blackstone's version of the felony-murder rule[30] became an integral part of the common law of the first 13 states. Not surprisingly, the Atlantic separation did nothing to reduce the amount of criticism to which the doctrine has been subjected. As early as 1845, this criticism appears to have resulted in the statutory abolition of the felony-murder rule in Ohio.

Oliver Wendell Holmes questioned the rule's deterrent effect in 1881. "[I]f a man does an act with intent to commit a felony, and thereby accidentally kills another. . . . [t]he fact that the shooting is felonious does not make it any more likely to kill people. If the object of the rule is to prevent such accident, it should make accidental killing with firearms murder, not accidental killing in the effort to steal; while, if its object is to prevent stealing, it would do better to hang one thief in every thousand by lot." (Holmes, The Common Law (1881) pp.57-58.)

Two states, Hawaii and Kentucky, have followed Ohio in abolishing the felony-murder rule by statute. (Hawaii Rev. Stat., §707-701 (1976); Ky. Rev. Stat., §507.020 (1975).) The comment to the Hawaii statute is instructive.

> Even in its limited formulation the felony-murder rule is still objectionable. It is not sound principle to convert an accidental, negligent, or reckless homicide into a murder simply because, without more, the killing was in furtherance of a criminal objective of some defined class. Engaging in certain penally-prohibited behavior may, of course, evidence a recklessness sufficient to establish manslaughter, or a practical certainty or intent, with respect to causing death, suffi-

---

regardless of how unintended the resulting death was. The attempt to quiet the girl's screams was held in *Beard* to be a sufficiently violent act. . . .

29. Criticism of the felony-murder rule and the concept of presumed or constructive malice appears in virtually every country whose legal system, based on the tradition of English common law, is "blessed" with this relic of our medieval heritage. None of the nations of continental Europe has a concept of criminal law analogous to the felony-murder rule. (Ibid.)

30. "[W]hen an involuntary killing happens in consequence of an unlawful act, it will be either murder or manslaughter according to the nature of the act which occasioned it. If it be in prosecution of a felonious intent, or in it's [sic] consequences naturally tended to bloodshed, it will be murder; but if no more was intended than a mere civil trespass, it will only amount to manslaughter." (4 Blackstone's Commentaries (Tucker ed. 1803) 192-193, fn. omitted.)

> cient to establish murder, but such a finding is an independent determination which must rest on the facts of each case. . . .
>
> In recognition of the trend toward, and the substantial body of criticism supporting, the abolition of the felony-murder rule, and because of the extremely questionable results which the rule has worked in other jurisdictions, the Code has eliminated from our law the felony-murder rule. (Hawaii Rev. Stat., §707-701 (1976) commentary, p.347.)

The drafters of the Model Penal Code concluded that the felony-murder rule should be abandoned. (Model Pen. Code, §201.2, Com. 4 (Tent. Draft No. 9, 1959) p.33. However, concern over possible political opposition to the idea led them to insert a provision in section 201.2(b)'s definition of reckless murder, to the effect that "recklessness and [extreme] indifference [to the value of human life] are [rebuttably] presumed if the actor is engaged or is an accomplice in the commission of, or an attempt to commit or flight after committing or attempting to commit [one of seven enumerated felonies]." . . .

While New Hampshire is the only state to have adopted the Model Penal Code formulation,[31] several other states require that the accused exhibit a *mens rea* above and beyond the mere intent to commit a felony. Arkansas requires that the defendant cause death "under circumstances manifesting extreme indifference to the value of human life." (Ark. Stat. Ann., §41.1502; compare CALJIC No. 8.31, cited at fn. [26] ante.) The Texas Penal Code provides that the act causing death must be "clearly dangerous to human life." (Tex. Pen. Code Ann., §19.02(a)(3) (Vernon 1974).) The Delaware first degree murder statute mandates that the accused at least have acted with criminal negligence in the course of committing certain enumerated felonies or recklessly in the course of committing non-enumerated felonies. (Del. Code, tit. 11, §636(a)(2), (6) (1979).)

Numerous other states have passed legislation modifying the rule or restricting its application. In at least six states, a conviction based on a felony-murder theory can only be punished as second degree murder. Wisconsin treats felony murder as a class B felony,[32] while Maine distinguishes it from any other degree of murder. . . .[33]

While some state legislatures have been active in modifying the felony-murder rule, most of the limitations on the doctrine have been imposed by the courts as part of their role in the continuing development of the common law.[34] In 1959 the drafters of the Model Penal Code listed seven major limita-

31. If the presumption of recklessness and extreme indifference is not rebutted, the defendant is guilty of second degree murder. (N.H. Rev. Stat. Ann., §630.1-b(I)(b) (1974).)

32. Wisconsin requires that the killing be a "natural and probable consequence of the commission or attempt to commit a felony." (Wis. Stat. Ann., §940.02(2) (West 1982).) A class B felony in Wisconsin is punishable by a term of imprisonment not to exceed 20 years. (§939.50(3)(b).)

33. Felony murder in Maine can result in a maximum imprisonment of 20 years. (Me. Rev. Stat. Ann., tit. 17A §§202, 1252(2)(A) . . . .)

34. It was on this basis that the *Aaron* court abolished the common law felony-murder rule in Michigan.

tions which had been imposed by various state courts.[35] The intervening 25 years have done little to reduce the need for or number of limitations on the rule. The most important of these include requirements that the underlying felony be inherently dangerous (Wade v. State (Okl. Cr. 1978) 581 P.2d 914; Commonwealth v. Bowden (1973), 456 Pa. 278, 309 A.2d 714 (conc. opn. of Nix, J.); see also Annot. (1973) 50 A.L.R.3d 397;[36] that the killing be committed by one of the felons (State v. Canola (1977) 73 N.J. 206, 374 A.2d 20; Commonwealth ex rel. Smith v. Myers, supra, 438 Pa. 218, 261 A.2d 550; Commonwealth v. Balliro (1965) 349 Mass. 505, 209 N.E.2d 308; see also Annot. (1974) 56 A.L.R.3d 239); that the duration of the felony be strictly construed (e.g., People v. Smith (1974) 55 Mich. App. 184, 222 N.W.2d 172, 175; State v. Golladay (1970) 78 Wash. 2d 121, 470 P.2d 191, 197-198; People v. Jackson (1967) 20 N.Y.2d 440, 285 N.Y.S.2d 8, 231 N.E.2d 722, 732; see also Annot. (1974) 58 A.L.R.3d 851); and that the purpose of the underlying felony be independent of the killing. (E.g., Garrett v. State (Tex. Cr. App. 1978) 573 S.W.2d 543; State v. Branch (1966) 244 Or. 97, 415 P.2d 766; see also Annot. (1971) 40 A.L.R.3d 1341.)

California's approach to the rule mirrors these developments. This court has consistently reiterated that the " 'highly artifical concept' . . . of strict criminal liablity" (People v. Satchell (1971) 6 Cal. 3d 28, 34, 98 Cal. Rptr. 33, 489 P.2d 1361) embodied in the felony-murder rule " 'should not be extended beyond any rational function that it is designed to serve.' " (People v. Smith (1984) 35 Cal. 3d 798, 803, . . . , quoting People v. Washington, supra, 62 Cal.

35. See Model Penal Code section 201.2, Comment 4 (Tent. Draft No. 9, 1959) at page 37:

> Some American courts have responded to the plea for limitation by imposing one or more of the following requirements:
>
> (1) The felonious act must be dangerous to life. See, e.g., People v. Pavlic, 227 Mich. 562, 199 N.W. 373 (1924); State v. Diebold, 152 Wash. 68, 277 P. 394, 395-396 (1929); cf. People v. Goldvarg, 346 Ill. 398, 178 N.E. 892 (1931).
>
> (2) The homicide must be a natural and probable consequence of the felonious act. See, e.g., Powers v. Commonwealth, 110 Ky. 386, 61 S.W. 735 (1901).
>
> (3) Death must be "proximately" caused. See, e.g., Burton v. State, 122 Tex. Cr. 363, 55 S.W.2d 813 (1933).
>
> (4) The felony must be malum in se. See, e.g., People v. Pavlic, supra.
>
> (5) The act must be a common law felony. See, e.g., Commonwealth v. Exler, 243 Pa. 155, 89 A. 968 (1914); State v. Burrell, 120 N.J.L. 277, 199 A. 18 (1938).
>
> (6) The period during which the felony is in the process of commission must be narrowly construed. See, e.g., State v. Diebold, 152 Wash. 68, 277 P. 394 (1929); People v. Smith, 232 N.Y. 239, 133 N.E. 574 (1921); Huggins v. State, 149 Miss. 280, 115 So. 213 (1928); State v. Taylor, 173 La. 1010, 139 So. 463 (1931); People v. Marwig, 227 N.Y. 382, 125 N.E. 535 (1919).
>
> (7) The underlying felony must be "independent" of the homicide. People v. Moran, 246 N.Y. 100, 158 N.E. 35 (1927); People v. Huther, 184 N.Y. 237, 77 N.E. 6 (1906); State v. Fisher, 120 Kan. 226, 243 P. 291 (1926); State v. Severns, 158 Kan. 453, 148 P.2d 488 (1941); State v. Shock, 68 Mo. 552 (1878).

36. One of the earliest expressions of this limitation appears in Powers v. Commonwealth (1901) 110 Ky. 386, 61 S.W. 735, 742: "Under our statute the removal of a corner stone is punishable by a short term in the penitentiary, and is therefore a felony. If, in attempting this offense, death were to result to one conspirator by his fellows accidentally dropping the stone upon him, no Christian court would hesitate to apply this ['inherently dangerous'] limitation."

2d at p.783, 44 Cal. Rptr. 442, 402 P.2d 130.) Accordingly, in deciding whether to apply the rule in various factual settings, this court has "sought to insure that the . . . doctrine be given the narrowest possible application consistent with its ostensible purpose—which is to deter those engaged in felonies from killing negligently or accidentally. . . ." (People v. Satchell, supra, 6 Cal. 3d at p.34, 98 Cal. Rptr. 33, 489 P.2d 1361, citations omitted.)

The reasons for limiting the rule were well summarized over a decade ago in People v. Satchell, supra, 6 Cal. 3d 28, 98 Cal. Rptr. 33, 489 P.2d 1361. This court observed that the felony-murder rule is "usually unnecessary for conviction. . . ." (Id., at p. 33, 98 Cal. Rptr. 33, 489 P.2d 1361.) In almost all cases in which the rule is applied, conviction " 'can be predicated on the normal rules as to murder and as to accomplice liability. . . .' "

" 'If the defendant commits the felony in a highly reckless manner, he can be convicted of second degree murder independently of the shortcut of the felony-murder rule. Under California's interpretation of the implied malice provision of the Penal Code [§188], proof of conduct evidencing extreme or wanton recklessness establishes the element of malice aforethought required for a second degree murder conviction. . . . [In cases where the facts suggested such a theory], the prosecutions would be free to prove the extreme recklessness of the conduct. The jury would decide whether the evidence, including the defendant's conduct and inferences arising from it, established the requisite malice aforethought. . . .' " (Id., at pp.33-34, fn.11, 98 Cal. Rptr. 33, 489 P.2d 1361.) In the "small residuum" of cases where the "normal rules" of murder would not apply, " 'there may be a substantial question whether the rule reaches a rational result or does not at least distract attention from more relevant criteria.' "

In keeping with this view of the rule, the limitations on its application have been extensive. This court has "refused to apply the doctrine in cases wherein the killing is committed by persons other than the defendant or an accomplice acting in furtherance of a common felonious design . . . in cases wherein the operation of the doctrine depends upon 'a felony which is an integral part of the homicide and which the evidence produced by the prosecution shows to be an offense included *in fact* within the offense charged' . . . and in cases wherein the underlying felony is not one of the six enumerated in section 189 of the Penal Code and is not inherently dangerous to human life. . . ." (People v. Satchell, supra, 6 Cal. 3d at p. 34, 98 Cal. Rptr. 33, 489 P.2d 1361, citations omitted.)[37] . . .

37. The Courts of Appeal have also found ways in which to limit the harsh application of the rule.

Consider People v. Carlson (1974) 37 Cal. App. 3d 349, 112 Cal. Rptr. 321. There, the court reversed a second degree felony-murder conviction where the underlying felony, manslaughter of the accused's wife, furnished the basis for the second degree felony-murder conviction of an unborn fetus carried by the wife. The court found it "unnecessary to resort to the felony-murder rule where the homicide of two persons by the same act constitutes separate offenses for which separate prosecutions and conviction may be had independent of the short cut of the felony-murder rule." (Id., at p. 354, 112 Cal. Rptr. 321.) Such a finding was compelled by the conclusion "that a man

As the list of limitations and modifications grows longer, the California second degree felony-murder rule bears less and less resemblance to Blackstone's simple statement that "when an involuntary killing happens . . . in prosecution of a felonious intent . . . it will be murder."[38] (4 Blackstone's Commentaries, supra, at pp. 192-193.) As the *Aaron* court noted, "[t]o the extent that these modifications reduce the scope and significance of the common-law doctrine, they also call into question the continued existence of the doctrine itself." (299 N.W.2d at p. 316). In sum—and particularly in light of the fact that this court has sole responsibility for the creation of the rule—the viability of it is a question that can no longer be ignored.

III

The second degree felony-murder rule erodes the important relationship between criminal liability and an accused's mental state. That relationship has been described as "the most basic principle of the criminal law."[39] (Gegan, Criminal Homicide in the Revised New York Penal Law (1966) 12 N.Y.L. Forum 565, 586; see also Sayre, [Mens Rea (1932)], 45 Harv. L. Rev. 974; Perkins, Some Weak Points in the Model Penal Code (1965) 17 Hastings L.J. 3, 12-14.) "It is as universal and persistent in mature systems of law as belief in freedom of the human will and a consequent ability and duty of the normal individual to choose between good and evil." (Morissette v. United States (1952) 342 U.S. 245, 250, 72 S. Ct. 240, 243, 96 L. Ed. 288, fn. omitted.)

The second degree felony-murder rule, as a strict liability concept, violates this most important principle.[40] (See People v. Henderson, supra, 19 Cal. 3d at pp.92-93, 137 Cal. Rptr. 1, 560 P.2d 1180.) Not only does it obliterate

---

assaulting two persons at the same time and by the same act would not be deterred by the felony-murder rule since the assault was an integral part of the resulting homicide of the two victims." (Ibid.)

38. On the other hand, certain felonies have been found to be inherently dangerous to human life. (People v. Mattison (1971) 4 Cal. 3d 177, 184, 93 Cal. Rptr. 185, 481 P.2d 193 [poisoning food, drink, or medicine with intent to injure]; People v. Nichols (1970) 3 Cal. 3d 150, 163, 89 Cal. Rptr. 721, 474 P.2d 673 [wilful and malicious burning of a motor vehicle]; People v. Kelso (1976) 64 Cal. App. 3d 538, 541, 134 Cal. Rptr. 364; People v. Romo (1975) 47 Cal. App. 3d 976, 989, 121 Cal. Rptr. 684 [simple kidnaping]; People v. Calzada (1970) 13 Cal. App. 3d 603, 605, 91 Cal. Rptr. 912 [driving a vehicle under the influence of narcotics]; People v. Taylor (1970) 11 Cal. App. 3d 57, 59, 89 Cal. Rptr. 697; People v. Cline (1969) 270 Cal. App. 2d 328, 333, 75 Cal. Rptr. 459 [furnishing or administering dangerous drugs]; Brooks v. Superior Court (1966) 239 Cal. App. 2d 538, 541, 48 Cal. Rptr. 762 [forcibly preventing a police officer from performing his duty].) In these few cases, as today's majority observe, the felony at issue "has been tinged with malevolence. . . ."

39. Our modern-day notion of *mens rea* as an essential criminal element is derived from Blackstone's concept of a "vicious will": "[A]n unwarrantable act without a vi[c]ious will is no crime at all." (4 Blackstone's Commentaries (Tucker ed. 1803) 21.)

40. Mr. Justice Marshall has criticized the felony-murder rule on this ground: "Whether a death results in the course of a felony (thus giving rise to felony-murder liability) turns on fortuitous events that do not distinguish the intention or moral culpability of the defendants." (Lockett v. Ohio (1978) 438 U.S. 586, 620, 98 S. Ct. 2954, 2972, 57 L. Ed. 2d 973 (conc. opn.).)

the distinction between intended and unintended homicides, but it seeks to apply the same ponderous sanction to any participant in the criminal conspiracy or enterprise from which a death results. . . .

Legal commentators have been virtually unanimous in their condemnation of the felony-murder rule because it ignores the significance of the actor's mental state in determining his criminal liability. As the drafters of the Model Penal Code concluded in 1959, "principled argument in . . . defense [of the felony murder rule] is hard to find." (Model Pen. Code, §201.2, Com. 4 (Tent. Draft No. 9, 1959) at p.37. . . .)

As noted earlier, the rule is perhaps the last vestige of an archaic and indiscriminate philosophy still present in our modern system of criminal law.[41] "The rationale of the doctrine is that one who commits a felony is a bad person with a bad state of mind, and he has caused a bad result, so that we should not worry too much about the fact that the fatal result he accomplished was quite different and a good deal worse than the bad result he intended. Yet it is a general principle of criminal law that one is not ordinarily criminally liable for bad results which differ greatly from intended results." (LaFave & Scott, Criminal Law (1972) p.560.) Thus, it is difficult to take issue with one commentator's conclusion that "the felony-murder rule, as a hold-over from the days of our barbarian Anglo-Saxon ancestors . . . has very little right to existence in modern society." (Mueller, Criminal Law and Administration 34 N.Y.U.L. Rev. 83, 98.)

Of course, recognition of the irrationality of the felony-murder doctrine is not novel. This court's pronouncements on the disfavored status that the rule holds in California jurisprudence are numerous. Indeed, this court's decisions over the past 20 years may probably best be characterized as an attempt to avoid rather than to apply the rule. Given the court's repeated conclusion that application of the second degree felony-murder rule is not mandated by any California statute, a decision to abrogate that rule would be merely a natural extension of our prior holdings.

This court could, of course, leave the decision of whether to apply the second degree felony-murder rule in a given instance to the trier of fact. It is well established that the jury has the power to disregard the law and/or the facts in returning a verdict which is contrary to the evidence, as long as such verdict does not prejudice the accused.

However, the harshness of the rule, which leads some juries to disregard the law and others to follow it only with great reluctance, results in haphazard application of the criminal sanction. As the Ohio Supreme Court concluded more than a century ago in deciding to abandon the felony-murder rule, "crime is more effectually prevented by the *certainty* than by any unreasonable

41. As Professor Hall has noted, "[t]he underlying rationale of the felony-murder doctrine—that the offender has shown himself to be a 'bad actor,' and that this is enough to exclude the niceties bearing on the gravity of the harm actually committed—might have been defensible in early law. The survival of the felony-murder doctrine is a tribute to the tenacity of legal conceptions rooted in simple moral attitudes." (Hall, General Principles of Criminal Law (1947) p.455, quoted in People v. Aaron, supra, 299 N.W.2d at p.318.)

severity of punishment disproportionate to the turpitude and danger of the offense." In my view, it is far preferable to do away with an irrational doctrine than to permit it to be applied in an irrational manner.

IV

The abrogation of the common law second degree felony-murder rule would not change the result in the majority of homicide cases. (Cf. People v. Aaron, supra, 299 N.W.2d at p.327.) In cases other than first degree felony-murders, malice would remain the essential distinguishing element of murder. As in the past, malice would be established in one of two ways: (1) when the accused "manifest[s] a deliberate intention unlawfully to take away the life of a fellow creature" (Pen. Code, §188), or (2) when he (a) commits an act which is likely to cause death, and (b) consciously and unjustifiably disregards the substantial probability that death will result. (People v. Washington, supra, 62 Cal. 2d at p.780, 44 Cal. Rptr. 442, 402 P.2d 130; People v. Poddar (1974) 10 Cal. 3d 750 p. 759.) In order to establish conscious disregard in this context, the state would still have to show that the accused understood "the duty imposed upon him not to commit [such] acts" and that he acted despite this understanding. (Id., at p.760.)

If the trier of fact found malice by one of these two theories, section 187 would, as in the past, classify the killing as murder. In such a situation, a killing which occurs in the course of any inherently dangerous felony not enumerated in Penal Code section 189 would be murder in the second degree.

No longer would a killing which occurs during the commission of an inherently dangerous felony, standing alone, constitute second degree murder. However, one should not conclude that when death ensues in such a situation, the commission of a dangerous felony is an irrelevant factor in determining whether or not the defendant acted with malice. To the contrary, the circumstances of the crime including the commission of the felony may provide strong circumstantial evidence that the defendant intended to kill the victim or that he committed an act in conscious disregard of the substantial probability that death would result. (See Pen. Code, §21.)

The jury would be given the opportunity to make an independent determination of each defendant's individual culpability, a determination which would not be reversed on appeal unless unsupported by substantial evidence. Therefore, abolishing the second degree felony-murder rule would not significantly reduce the number of murder convictions.

This conclusion is supported by the experience of jurisdictions which have abolished the felony-murder rule. Additionally, even if a jury were to find that a killing was without malice, the accused is still liable for the underlying felony as well as any lesser degree of homicide which the evidence may support.[42]

42. There may well be few, if any, cases involving a killing in the course of an inherently dangerous felony in which the evidence would not support an involuntary manslaughter conviction based on a defendant's criminal negligence. (See Pen. Code, §§192 and 193.)

There will be times when a jury is convinced that the accused's mental state does not justify a murder conviction. In the first degree felony-murder context, this court's powers are circumscribed because the rule is a creature of statute. However, where no statutory bar appears, this court should not mandate a murder conviction in the absence of a finding of malice. To do so violates very basic concepts of rationality and proportionality.

As Holmes so eloquently stated, "It is revolting to have no better reason for a rule of law than that so it was laid down in the time of Henry IV. It is still more revolting if the grounds upon which it was laid down have vanished long since, and the rule simply persists from blind imitation of the past." (Holmes, Collected Legal Papers (1920) p.187.) It is time this court laid this ill-conceived rule to rest.

RICHARDSON, Justice, dissenting.

I respectfully dissent. In my view, the unauthorized practice of medicine "under circumstances or conditions which cause or create a risk of great bodily harm, serious physical or mental illness, or death" (Bus. & Prof. Code, §2053) fully supports application of the second degree felony-murder rule.

Relying on hypertechnical and irrelevant distinctions between great bodily harm, serious physical and mental injury, and the risk of death, the majority ignores the "rational function that [the felony-murder rule] is designed to serve." . . . As we have frequently reiterated, that purpose "is to deter those engaged in felonies from killing negligently or accidentally." . . .

In those cases in which we have found the felony-murder doctrine not to apply, the felony, properly viewed in the abstract, contained by definition elements which did not usually entail any risk of harm to the victim. Thus the possibility of negligent or accidental death did not flow logically from each possible element of the crime. . . .

In contrast, the statute at issue here explicitly *requires* a risk of actual harm or "injury" to a person. (See People v. Mattison (1971) 4 Cal. 3d 177, 186, 93 Cal. Rptr. 185, 481 P.2d 193.) In *Mattison,* we considered the application of the felony-murder doctrine where the underlying felony was the wilful administration of poison "with intent that the same shall be taken by any human being *to his injury*. . . ." (Former Pen. Code, §347, [emphasis added].) We noted that, "Absent section 347, a defendant who administered poison to another not with conscious disregard for life, but only for the purpose of making the other mildly ill or intoxicated, could at most be found guilty only of involuntary manslaughter if an unexpected death resulted. (Pen. Code, §192, subd. 2.) By making it a felony to administer poison with the intent to cause *any injury,* the Legislature has evidenced its concern for the dangers involved in such conduct, and the invocation of the second degree felony-murder rule in such cases when unforeseen death results serves further to deter such dangerous conduct." (p. 186, [emphasis added].) Accordingly, we held that even though the felony was not sufficient to sustain a first degree felony-murder conviction because there was no requirement of a "conscious disregard for life," instructions on second degree felony murder were indeed appropriate. (Ibid.)

In so holding, we relied in part on People v. Taylor (1970) 11 Cal. App. 3d 57, 89 Cal. Rptr. 697, where the Court of Appeal upheld a second degree murder conviction under the felony-murder rule when the underlying felony was furnishing of heroin to the victim. As we enunciated in *Mattison,* "In other words the felony was not done with the intent to commit injury which would cause death. Giving a felony-murder instruction in such a situation serves rather than subverts the purpose of the rule. 'While the felony-murder rule can hardly be much of a deterrent to a defendant who has decided to assault his victim with a deadly weapon, it seems obvious that in the situation presented in the case at bar, it does serve a rational purpose: knowledge that the death of a person to whom heroin is furnished may result in a conviction for murder should have some effect on the defendant's readiness to do the furnishing.' (People v. Taylor, supra, 11 Cal. App. 3d 57, 63 [89 Cal. Rptr. 697].)" (People v. Mattison, supra, 4 Cal. 3d at p.185, 93 Cal. Rptr. 185, 481 P.2d 193.) Similarly, here, knowledge that the death of a "sick or afflicted" person whom the unauthorized practitioner treats, "willfuly, under circumstances or conditions which cause or create a risk of great bodily harm, serious mental or physical illness, or death," may have an effect on such person's willingness to so practice.

The majority's fine distinctions become even more dubious when one considers the holding in People v. Nichols (1970) 3 Cal. 3d 150, 89 Cal. Rptr. 721, 474 P.2d 673, approving a second degree murder conviction premised on the burning of an automobile. While we have questioned that holding to the extent that the underlying felony had not been considered in the abstract and it contained a "proscription against a variety of burnings of personal property not all of which are dangerous to human life" (People v. Henderson, supra, 19 Cal. 3d at p.96, 137 Cal. Rptr. 1, 560 P.2d 1180), we did not imply that if the crime of arson of a motor vehicle were contained in a separate discrete section it would not serve as a sufficient basis for invocation of the felony-murder rule. In *Nichols,* we declared that "the burning of a motor vehicle, which usually contains gasoline and which is usually found in close proximity to people, is inherently dangerous to human life. We therefore conclude that the wilful and malicious burning of a motor vehicle calls into play the second degree felony-murder rule." (3 Cal. 3d at p. 163, 89 Cal. Rptr. 721, 474 P.2d 673.) How can the underlying felony at issue here be less "inherently dangerous to human life" than the burning of an automobile?

In enacting Business and Professions Code section 2053, the Legislature clearly sought to impose a greater penalty in those cases where the unauthorized practice of medicine causes significant risks that may lead to death. The use of the felony-murder rule in this context clearly furthers the goal of deterring such conduct. The underlying conduct proscribed by section 2053 is manifestly "inherently dangerous to life." Viewed in the abstract, improper treatment of the "sick and afflicted" under the dangerous circumstances and conditions specified in that section is almost synonymous with inherently dangerous conduct.

I would affirm the judgment of conviction.

Notes and Questions

1. Could Burroughs have been convicted of murder without the felony-murder rule?

2. Would the majority have regarded the felony as inherently dangerous if the statute had made no mention of "mental illness"? Why does the majority go out of its way to assert that the defendant could be convicted of manslaughter on a gross negligence theory? Couldn't he be convicted under a "misdemeanor"-manslaughter theory even more easily?

3. If a defendant, like Burroughs, commits a felony in an obviously dangerous manner, why should it matter that the felony is not "inherently dangerous"?

4. Is the purpose of the felony-murder rule to deter inherently dangerous felonies, or to induce felons to commit their felonies carefully?

5. Chief Justice Bird says that the felony-murder rule is a dangerous anachronism. Is the rule any less valid now than it was in England centuries ago? What do you think would be the legislature's reaction if the court abandoned the judge-made felony murder rule? In view of the majority's footnote on p.330, is there any reason why the California legislature should wait?

6. If, as the court and Chief Justice Bird agree, the prosecutor rarely needs the felony-murder rule anyway, is the mild overbreadth of the rule so high a price to pay for slightly lessening the prosecution's burden of proof?

7. The opinions in *Burroughs* usefully review the cases that have distinguished "inherently dangerous" felonies from those that are not inherently dangerous. How does one tell the difference?

In People v. Satchell, 6 Cal. 3d 28, 98 Cal. Rptr. 33, 489 P.2d 1361 (1971), the court emphasized that in answering this question, one must ignore the facts of each specific case, and contemplate the nature of the felony "in the abstract." If that is the test, was the *Satchell* court correct in excluding from the felony-murder rule the crime of possession of a concealed weapon by an ex-felon? To follow the test, must one ignore the fact that Satchell accidentally killed a man with a sawed-off shotgun during a street fight?

8. The difficulty of the *Satchell* "abstractness" test is evident in the Missouri case of State v. Chambers, 524 S.W.2d 826 (1975), where the court upheld a felony-murder conviction on the following facts:

> On September 4, 1973, defendant and Ray Collins were together from about 9:00 P.M. until sometime after 1:00 A.M., September 5, 1973. They had been drinking, and defendant announced his intention "to go get a pickup at Hi Dollar Joe Burtrum's" at 4800 Range Line south of Joplin in Newton County,

> Missouri. When they arrived at Burtrum Brothers Motor Company, defendant "busted a window out of the pickup, hooked a chain onto it" and "started pulling the pickup down the road . . . real fast and all over the road." Collins was in the pickup to steer it and defendant was towing the pickup with his Ford Torino. During the asportation, the pickup collided with an oncoming automobile. Defendant and Collins were observed in the theft of the pickup truck, a 1969, 1/2-ton, 6-cylinder Chevrolet equipped with a camper body, by Joe Burtrum. He heard the sound of glass breaking, after which he observed the Ford Torino pulling the pickup camper north on Range Line (U.S. Highway 71). It was dark; there were no lights on either of the vehicles; and, as they proceeded down Range Line, "they were accelerating rather rapidly, weaving from side to side of the road." They crossed the center line several times. He tried unsuccessfully to stop the thieves by firing two or three shots from his pistol. He followed in a car, heard a crash, and saw that the pickup truck had crossed into the southbound lane and hit a Valiant automobile head on about a quarter of a mile from the car lot at 44th and Range Line. There were four persons in the Valiant, all of whom died in or as a result of the collision.

Was the underlying felony in *Chambers*—auto theft—inherently dangerous?

9. From Weinreb, Homicide: Legal Aspects, 2 Encyclopedia of Crime and Justice 858, 859-861 (1983):

> *Felony Murder.* The common-law crime of murder included a homicide committed by a person in the course of committing (or attempting to commit) a felony. The felon—and, according to the rules of accomplice liability, his accomplices—was guilty of murder even if he had no intent to kill or injure anyone and committed no act manifesting extreme recklessness toward human life. The origin of this doctrine may reflect the difficulty of proving specifically an intent to kill, in circumstances in which the intent to commit a felony may suggest a willingness to kill if necessary and other proof either way is lacking. Felonies under early English law were mostly violent crimes and were in any case punishable by death. An attempt to commit a felony was only a misdemeanor, however; the felony-murder doctrine, which also applied to uncompleted felonies, did change the outcome if a homicide was committed during an unsuccessful attempt.
>
> The number of felonies has increased dramatically under modern law. Statutory felonies include a large number of offenses that, however serious on other grounds, do not ordinarily pose great danger to life. Application of the felony-murder doctrine to them distorts the concept of murder as a crime involving a serious direct attack on the value of human life. The explanation that the intent to commit the felony "supplies" the malice aforethought merely states the conclusion. So also, stretched to its logical limits, the felony-murder doctrine would make a felon guilty of murder even if the victim were killed by someone else trying to prevent the felony, provided it were found that the commission of the felony caused the death. . . .
>
> Far as such a death is from the intentional killing that is the paradigm of murder, one can perhaps understand the attitude which leads to the conclusion that the felon should be liable. If not for the felon's conduct—the commission of

the felony—the victim would not be dead, accidentally or not. Since in that sense the commission of the felony is the cause of death and the felon has in any case engaged in criminal conduct, it is easy to hold him responsible for the death as well. Even so, it is not appropriate to describe his conduct as murder if he has not engaged in conduct that seriously endangers life. Murder is not simply homicide, but homicide of a particularly culpable nature because it is accompanied by defined mental states; although willingness to commit a felony is itself culpable, it is not the same as, or equivalent to, the culpability that qualifies a homicide as murder.

While the doctrine of felony murder has sometimes been extended to cases very remote from an intentional killing, the courts and legislatures have quite generally adopted rules to restrict its scope. One restriction that responds to the large number of nonviolent statutory felonies is that the doctrine is applicable only if the underlying felony involves violence or danger to life. Sometimes it is required that the *type* of the underlying felony meet this requirement; or it may be enough if the commission of the felony in the particular circumstances is violent or dangerous. The first approach retains the felony-murder doctrine on its own terms but confines it to a more limited group of felonies; to the same general effect are requirements that the felony have been a felony at common law or that it be malum in se. The second approach may create liability in a case not covered by the first; it looks in the direction of a displacement of felony murder by a different rationale based directly on the dangerousness of the actor's conduct. . . .

Another way of restricting felony murder places strong weight on the element of causation. Mere temporal conjunction of the felony and death has never been sufficient for felony murder; it is necessary at least that the death would not have occurred but for the felony. Some courts have explicitly required more than "but for" causation; the death must be a reasonably foreseeable, or natural and probable, consequence of the felony and must not be attributable primarily to a separable, intervening cause. Various ad hoc rules rejecting felony murder when someone other than the felon or an accomplice actually commits the homicide or when an accomplice is killed take a similar approach, although they refer to the party who kills or is killed rather than to causation as such. . . .

A more general attack on felony murder rejects it entirely and subsumes appropriate cases of homicide in the course of a felony under another category of murder. If a felon acting either with intent to kill or with extreme recklessness commits a homicide, then he is guilty of murder on that basis; the fact that the acts were committed in furtherance of a felony obviously does not count against liability. Reflecting the conclusion that if no element of that kind is present, then the felon's liability for murder is gratuitous, the Model Penal Code and the statutes of a few states have eliminated the felony-murder doctrine. Elsewhere, there has been a partial displacement of the strict liability doctrine by allowance of an affirmative defense if the felon's own conduct was not intended to and did not in any way endanger life. Of course, if the commission of a felony is itself deemed sufficient to satisfy the requirement of extreme recklessness (on the ground that a felony of that nature is always extremely dangerous to life), the concept of felony murder is reintroduced with the pretense of a different rationale. The Model Penal Code, for example, notwithstanding its strong criticism of the felony-murder doctrine, provides that recklessness and extreme indifference to the value of human life, which support liability for murder, are presumed if the actor is committing, or is in flight after committing, one of half a dozen named violent felonies (§210.2(1)(b)). Some courts occasionally criticize the doctrine but preserve its force in particular cases by tenuous application of an alternative basis of liability to the specific facts. England, where the doctrine originated, abolished it by statute in 1957 (Homicide Act of 1957, 5 & 6 Eliz. 2, c.11, §1).

The uneven record of legislative and judicial efforts to limit or eliminate the felony-murder doctrine suggests strongly the central themes of the law of criminal homicide. When a death occurs and its occurrence can be attributed to the conduct of an identifiable person who is not blameless, there is a strong impulse to hold that person liable for the death, even if, from his point of view, the death should be viewed as accidental. The law not only reflects considered judgments about culpability; it also reflects an unconsidered effort to find an explanation and assign responsibility for an occurrence as disturbing to our sense of order as an unnatural death.

Resistance to a lawful arrest. Some of the older accounts of murder under the common law include resistance to a lawful arrest as a category of malice aforethought. Such a rule would impose strict liability for murder on a person whose resistance to a lawful arrest caused a death, even if it were accidental. It is now generally agreed that there is no such independent category of murder, although a statutory provision reflecting the traditional rule survives in a few states. A lawful arrest does not mitigate or excuse conduct in opposition to it, as might an unlawful application of similar physical force. Otherwise, homicide resulting from resistance to a lawful arrest is not treated differently from other homicide. Even in those states that have a special statutory provision, it is doubtful whether a wholly accidental death would be treated as murder if it did not also satisfy some other category of the crime. (England explicitly abolished this category of murder along with felony murder by means of the Homicide Act of 1957.)

10. Is not the felony-murder rule based on precisely the same reasoning that was abandoned in the cases after Regina v. Faulkner, supra, at page 131?

STATE v. THOMPSON

Supreme Court of Washington
88 Wash. 2d 13, 558 P.2d 202 (1977)

DOLLIVER, Associate Justice.

This is an appeal from a conviction for murder in the second degree. The victim was defendant's husband, Wayland D. Thompson. On the day of the killing, the defendant's husband had consumed considerable amounts of alcohol and used drugs excessively. During the evening, he had been driving recklessly with defendant and two other passengers in the car and had struck defendant and threatened to kill her. The car reached the Thompson residence and the two passengers got out and went into the house. Shortly thereafter, shots were heard. Defendant called the sheriff and reported she had shot her husband. At the trial she claimed she had shot him in self-defense.

Defendant was charged by an amended information with causing the death of Wayland Thompson while engaged in the commission of a felony, assault in the second degree. In the trial before a jury, defendant was found guilty of murder in the second degree. We affirm. . . .

The state produced evidence that the defendant reported she shot her husband. There was additional evidence that there were three shots fired with a .38 caliber pistol. Testimony of the state's witnesses revealed that the defendant and her husband had been drinking on the evening of the shooting, that they had argued violently and that he had struck her. While the defendant claims that the shooting was done in self-defense, she apparently was disbelieved by the jury. In reviewing the record, we are satisfied that there was sufficient evidence to send the case to the jury and to support the verdict.

Finally, appellant urges that we overrule State v. Harris, 69 Wash. 2d 928, 421 P.2d 662 (1966). The relevant statutes considered in *Harris* are, in part: . . .

> The killing of a human being, unless it is excusable or justifiable, is murder in the second degree when—
>
> (2) . . . perpetrated by a person engaged in the commission of, or in an attempt to commit, or in withdrawing from the scene of, a felony other than those enumerated in RCW 9.48.030.
>
> RCW 9.48.040.

In *Harris,* we held that, where the precedent felony in a felony murder is an assault and inherent in the homicide, the assault does not merge into the resulting homicide. Most states which have considered the question have adopted the merger rule, resulting in a holding that only felonies independent of the homicide can support a felony murder conviction. Washington and Maine appear to be the only jurisdictions which have considered and rejected the merger rule. Both appellant and the courts of other jurisdictions consider this to be a matter of statutory interpretation rather than one of constitutional rights.

In State v. Mosley, supra, we granted a petition to review the *Harris* rule. Before the day set for hearing, the petitioner escaped from custody. Consequently, the petition was dismissed.

While it may be that the felony murder statute is harsh, and does relieve the prosecution from the burden of proving intent to commit murder, it is the law of this state. The legislature recently modified some parts of our criminal code, effective July 1, 1976. However, the statutory context in question here was left unchanged.

The rejection by this court of the merger rule has not been challenged by the legislature during the nearly 10 years since *Harris,* nor have any circumstances or compelling reasons been presented as to why we should overrule the views we expressed therein.

The judgment is affirmed.

STAFFORD, C.J., HAMILTON and BRACHTENBACH, JJ., and HALE, J. Pro tem., concur.

UTTER, Associate Justice (dissenting).

At the time the [felony-murder] rule developed all felonies were punishable by death; thus, the use of the felony-murder rule was generally not of serious consequence to the defendant. As the number and nature of activities constituting felonies increased, and the penalties for the convictions thereof began to vary, the rule came to have a progressively greater impact upon the criminal law. The result of this greater impact has been an almost universal effort to restrict the harsh and often logically unsupportable consequences of the rule. The doctrine of felony murder was abolished in its entirety by Great Britain almost 20 years ago. See English Homicide Act, 5 and 6 Eliz. 2, c.11, §1 (1957). It continues to survive in various forms in the United States. However, American jurisdictions have limited the operation of the rule in a number of ways, including: limiting its application only to specific felonies or categories of felonies; introducing a strict proximate cause requirement; narrowing the scope of the time during which a felony is said to be in the process of commission; and finally, by requiring that the underlying felony be independent of the homicide.

The only act of the appellant relied upon to establish the felony necessary for conviction of murder in the second degree under RCW 9.48.040(2) was the shooting itself, which standing alone, constitutes the crime of second-degree assault. RCW 9.11.020(4).[43] The application of the felony-murder rule thus eliminated the necessity for proof by the state of the element of specific intent, which is the distinguishing aspect, in our statutory scheme, of murder in the second degree. Absent the proof of acts constituting an assault, the appellant could not have been found guilty of murder. In this situation it is apparent that the single act of shooting the victim can constitute one crime and one crime only. There exists no general malicious intent based upon proof of the commission of a separate felony which may be "transferred" from that crime to an independent homicide committed in the course thereof. The existence of such a separate intent is an analytical necessity to an inference of intent to kill. For this reason the felony-murder rule should not apply where the underlying felony sought to be used as a basis for the operation of the rule is an offense

43. "9.11.020 . . . Every person who, under circumstances not amounting to assault in the first degree—

"(4) Shall wilfully assault another with a weapon or other instrument or thing likely to produce bodily harm. . . .

"Shall be guilty of assault in the second degree. . . ."

included in fact in the homicide itself. To hold otherwise constitutes, as Chief Justice Cardozo observed, "a futile attempt to split into unrelated parts an indivisible transaction." People v. Moran, 246 N.Y. 100, 104, 158 N.E. 35, 36 (1937).

This conclusion has been reached by every jurisdiction in this country, with the exception of the state of Washington, required to directly face the issue.[44] The states have formulated their conclusions in slightly different ways. See, e.g., People v. Huther, 184 N.Y. 237, 77 N.E. 6 (1906) (where the only felony committed apart from the homicide itself is the assault upon the victim, the assault "merges" with the killing and does not provide a basis for operation of the felony-murder rule); State v. Fisher, 120 Kan. 226, 243 P.291 (1926) (the felony must be so distinct as to not be an ingredient of the homicide). . . . [T]he California Supreme Court [has stated]:

> We have concluded that the utilization of the felony-murder rule in circumstances such as those before us extends the operation of that rule "beyond any rational function that it is designed to serve." . . . To allow such use of the felony-murder rule would effectively preclude the jury from considering the issue of malice aforethought in all cases wherein homicide has been committed as a result of a felonious assault—a category which includes the great majority of all homicides. This kind of bootstrapping finds support neither in logic nor in law.

People v. Ireland, supra, 70 Cal. 2d at 539, 75 Cal. Rptr. at 198, 450 P.2d at 590.

In State v. Harris, 69 Wash. 2d 928, 421 P.2d 662 (1966), a majority of this court declined to adopt this position, taking the view that the legislature had, by establishing degrees of murder and limiting the first degree felony-murder rule to only specific crimes, effectively eliminated the compelling need for the merger rule which had been found to exist under New York's statutory scheme. In so doing the majority overlooked the fact that the merger rule has been expressly adopted in the state of Oregon. That state's homicide statutes are virtually identical to our own.

The dissenters in *Harris* pointed out that the use of the rule approved by the majority would effectively convert into second-degree murder any crime properly viewed as manslaughter, because manslaughter itself is a felony, and

44. . . . The majority suggests that our position is shared by the state of Maine. However, the Maine Supreme Court has not clearly enunciated its position. In State v. Trott, 289 A.2d 414 (Me. 1972), that court suggested in a footnote that the act of carrying a man to a wharf and then casting him unconscious into the sea would constitute an aggravated assault sufficient to support a conviction of felony murder. The statement cannot be said to have precedential value for two distinct reasons. First, proper objection to the felony-murder instruction had not been made at trial. The court therefore expressly held that the issue had not been preserved for appeal. Second, the court noted in the same footnote that the defendant had also committed two other felonies against the victim (assault with intent to rob and robbery) prior to the "assault" which occurred on the wharf, neither of which constituted an act directly responsible for the victim's death and both of which supported a finding of felony murder.

that prevention of precisely such a result was the purpose of the New York court in adopting the felony-murder merger rule.

I believe it clear that the underpinnings of the *Harris* dissent and the decisions of those courts adopting a merger rule, or its functional equivalent, are far more substantial than those recognized by the majority in *Harris*. Implicit in these holdings is a recognition that any statutory definition of murder, as a crime malum in se, must include an element of specific intent. A statutory formulation which eliminates the requirement of establishing this essential element is fundamentally defective and therefore violative of the defendant's right to substantive due process. State v. Turner, 78 Wash. 2d 276, 474 P.2d 91 (1970); Seattle v. Gordon, 54 Wash. 2d 516, 342 P.2d 604 (1959). Where, as here, there can fairly be said to have been but one culpable act committed by the appellant, the use of the felony-murder rule effectively obviates the necessity to establish any element of intent in support of the conviction because the defendant has committed no distinct felony which provides a basis for transfer of felonious intent. The result is that Mrs. Thompson was convicted of murder in the second degree without the establishment of any distinct felonious intent, a requirement for the operation of the conclusive presumption of intent to kill established by the felony-murder rule. . . .

State v. Harris, supra, should be overruled and Washington should join the other states of this nation which have rejected this doctrine.

HOROWITZ, HAMILTON and ROSSELLINI, JJ., concur.

Notes and Questions

1. Jones intentionally kills Brown in the heat of passion due to legally adequate provocation. Isn't voluntary manslaughter an "inherently dangerous" felony? Therefore, didn't Jones kill Brown in the act of committing an inherently dangerous felony? If so, is Jones guilty of murder? Could we accept that result?

2. Why did the state need the felony-murder rule in *Thompson*? How can you support the majority holding? (Note that it is by far a minority holding among the states.) Is it relevant that Washington does not follow the common law rule and mitigate murder to manslaughter where the defendant acts under "provocation"?

3. How much room is there for the felony-murder rule between the *Burroughs* (supra, page 323) principle and the merger rule?

In People v. Northrop, 182 Cal. Rptr. 197 (1982), the defendant unintentionally caused the death of a child as a result of felony child abuse, in violation of Cal. Pen. Code §273a(1), which provides:

> Any person who, under circumstances or conditions likely to produce great bodily harm or death, willfully causes or permits any child to suffer, or inflicts

> thereon unjustifiable physical pain or mental suffering, or having the care or custody of any child, willfully causes or permits the person or health of such child to be injured, or willfully causes or permits such child to be placed in such situation that its person or health is endangered, is punishable by imprisonment in the county jail not exceeding one year, or in the state prison for 2, 3 or 4 years.

Assuming this felony is inherently dangerous, the defendant argued that it was *so* inherently dangerous that the merger rule should apply. The court rejected his argument. Was the argument so fanciful, once we accept the premises of the felony murder and the merger rules?

4. The New York Court of Appeals, in People v. Miller, 32 N.Y.2d 157, 344 N.Y.S.2d 342, 297 N.E.2d 85 (1973), has explained its adoption of the merger doctrine as follows:

> We developed this doctrine to remedy a fundamental defect in the old felony-murder statute (Penal Law of 1909, §1044). Under that statute, any felony, including assault, could be the predicate for a felony murder. Since, a fortiori, every homicide, not excusable or justifiable, occurs during the commission of an assault, every homicide would constitute a felony murder.

Nevertheless, the court in *Miller* refused to extend the merger doctrine to a burglary committed with intent to assault. The facts of the case were as follows:

> On the morning of October 25, 1970, the defendant knocked on the door of an apartment directly below his own apartment. When Robert Fennell, one of the occupants, opened the door, the defendant, armed with a butcher knife and a spray can, sprayed at Fennell's face and then stabbed him in the arm. As Fennell backed away, the defendant followed him into the apartment, continuing to spray and stab him. As Fennell tripped and fell to the floor, he shouted to his roommate, Rasul Aleem, to help him. When Aleem responded to Fennell's call and attempted to aid him, the defendant turned and stabbed Aleem in the chest, killing him. . . .

The court, after noting that burglary was one of the enumerated felonies in New York's felony murder statute went on to say:

> We deem this evidence to be legally sufficient for the jury to find that the defendant committed the crime of burglary by knowingly entering unlawfully Fennell's apartment with the intent to assault Fennell. Clearly, had there been no homicide, but merely an unlawful entry by defendant into Fennell's apartment with the intent to assault Fennell, the crime of burglary would have been committed. Thus, since the defendant killed Aleem in the course of and in furtherance of his commission of burglary, the requirements of the felony-murder statute are satisfied. . . .
>
> . . .[T]he Legislature in 1965 . . . includ[ed] in the revised Penal Law a list of specified felonies—all involving violence or substantial risk of physical in-

jury—as the only felonies forming a basis for felony murder. The legislative purpose for this limitation was "to exclude from felony murder, cases of accidental or not reasonably foreseeable fatality occurring in an unlikely manner in the course of a non-violent felony.". . .

It should be apparent that the Legislature, in including burglary as one of the enumerated felonies as a basis for felony murder, recognized that persons within domiciles are in greater peril from those entering the domicile with criminal intent, than persons on the street who are being subjected to the same criminal intent. Thus, the burglary statutes prescribe greater punishment for a criminal act committed within the domicile than for the same act committed on the street. Where, as here, the criminal act underlying the burglary is an assault with a dangerous weapon, the likelihood that the assault will culminate in a homicide is significantly increased by the situs of the assault. When the assault takes place within the domicile, the victim may be more likely to resist the assault; the victim is also less likely to be able to avoid the consequences of the assault, since his paths of retreat and escape may be barred or severely restricted by furniture, walls and other obstructions incidental to buildings. Further, it is also more likely that when the assault occurs in the victim's domicile, there will be present family or close friends who will come to the victim's aid and be killed. Since the purpose of the felony-murder statute is to reduce the disproportionate number of accidental homicides which occur during the commission of the enumerated predicate felonies by punishing the party responsible for the homicide not merely for manslaughter, but for murder, the Legislature, in enacting the burglary and felony-murder statutes, did not exclude from the definition of burglary, a burglary based upon the intent to assault, but intended that the definition be "satisfied if the intruder's intent, existing at the time of the unlawful entry or remaining, is to commit *any* crime."

The California Supreme Court, in People v. Wilson, 1 Cal. 3d 431, 82 Cal. Rptr. 494 (1970) reached a result precisely the opposite to that in *Miller:*

Here the prosecution sought to apply the felony-murder rule on the theory that the homicide occurred in the course of a burglary, but the only basis for finding a felonious entry is the intent to commit an assault with a deadly weapon. When, as here, the entry would be nonfelonious but for the intent to commit the assault, and the assault is an integral part of the homicide and is included in fact in the offense charged, utilization of the felony-murder rule extends that doctrine "beyond any rational function that it is designed to serve.". . .

"The purpose of the felony-murder rule is to deter felons from killing negligently or accidentally by holding them strictly responsible for killings they commit." [People v. Washington (1965) 402 P.2d 130, 133.] Where a person enters a building with an intent to assault his victim with a deadly weapon, he is not deterred by the felony-murder rule. That doctrine can serve its purpose only when applied to a felony independent of the homicide. In [the case of assault], we reasoned that a man assaulting another with a deadly weapon could not be deterred by the second degree felony-murder rule, since the assault was an integral part of the homicide. Here, the only distinction is that the assault and homicide occurred inside a dwelling so that the underlying felony is burglary based on an intention to assault with a deadly weapon, rather than simply assault with a deadly weapon.

We do not suggest that no relevant differences exist between crimes committed inside and outside dwellings. We have often recognized that persons within dwellings are in greater peril from intruders bent on stealing or engaging in other felonious conduct. Persons within dwellings are more likely to resist and less likely to be able to avoid the consequences of crimes committed inside their homes. However, this rationale does not justify application of the felony-murder rule to the case at bar. Where the intended felony of the burglar is an assault with a deadly weapon, the likelihood of homicide from the lethal weapon is not significantly increased by the site of the assault. Furthermore, the burglary statute in this state includes within its definition numerous structures other than dwellings as to which there can be no conceivable basis for distinguishing between an assault with a deadly weapon outdoors and a burglary in which the felonious intent is solely to assault with a deadly weapon.

[In the case of assault], we rejected the bootstrap reasoning involved in taking an element of a homicide and using it as the underlying felony in a second degree felony-murder instruction. We conclude that the same bootstrapping is involved in instructing a jury that the intent to assault makes the entry burglary, and that the burglary raises the homicide resulting from the assault to first degree murder without proof of malice aforethought. . . .

Which court's reasoning is more persuasive, that of New York's or that of California's? Does your answer depend entirely on how you feel about the felony murder rule? If you are in favor of the rule, don't you side with New York, while if you are against it, don't you side with California? Is there any other way to decide the cases?

7

AGGRAVATED MURDER

In this chapter, we explore the factors that so enhance the culpability of a murder that the murderer merits first-degree punishment—normally life imprisonment or the death penalty.

A. FIRST-DEGREE MURDER

1. Sample Statutes

CAL. PENAL CODE
(1982)

§189. MURDER; DEGREES.

All murder which is perpetrated by means of a destructive device or explosive, knowing use of ammunition designed primarily to penetrate metal or armor, poison, lying in wait, torture, or by any other kind of willful, deliberate, and premeditated killing, or which is committed in the perpetration of, or attempt to perpetrate, arson, rape, robbery, burglary, mayhem, or any act punishable under Section 288, is murder of the first degree; and all other kinds of murders are of the second degree.

As used in this section, "destructive device" shall mean any destructive device as defined in section 12301, and "explosive" shall mean any explosive as defined in Section 12000 of the Health and Safety Code.

To prove the killing was "deliberate and premeditated," it shall not be necessary to prove the defendant maturely and meaningfully reflected upon the gravity of his or her act.

KAN. STAT. ANN.
(Rev. Stat. 1972)

§21-3201. Murder in the First Degree.

Murder in the first degree is the killing of a human being committed maliciously, willfully, deliberately and with premeditation or committed in the perpetration of or attempt to perpetrate any felony.

Murder in the first degree is a class A felony.

MINN. STAT.
(1982)

609.185. Murder in the First Degree.

Whoever does any of the following is guilty of murder in the first degree and shall be sentenced to imprisonment for life:

(1) Causes the death of a human being with premeditation and with intent to effect the death of the person or of another;

(2) Causes the death of a human being while committing or attempting to commit criminal sexual conduct in the first or second degree with force or violence, either upon or affecting the person or another,

(3) Causes the death of a human being with intent to effect the death of the person or another, while committing or attempting to commit burglary, aggravated robbery, kidnapping, arson in the first or second degree, tampering with a witness in the first degree, or escape from custody; or

(4) Causes the death of a peace officer or a guard employed at a Minnesota state correctional facility, with intent to effect the death of that person or another, while the peace officer or guard is engaged in the performance of his official duties.

2. Premeditation

AUSTIN v. UNITED STATES
United States Court of Appeals, District of Columbia Circuit
382 F.2d 129 (1967)

Leventhal, Circuit Judge.

Appellant Bernard Austin was indicted for murdering Nettie Scott with premeditation, deliberation, and malice aforethought. There was no felony-murder count. Appellant was convicted of first-degree murder. The prosecutor did not request the death penalty. The jury recommended life imprisonment and appellant was sentenced accordingly. On this appeal he challenges various portions of the trial court's charge to the jury and contends that the evidence at the close of the Government's case in chief was insufficient to withstand a motion for acquittal of first degree murder. . . .

I

The Government's evidence was as follows: Appellant was seen in the company of the deceased, Nettie Scott, for some period of time on the night in question. They were drinking together at an after-hours establishment called Will's Place, where appellant bought deceased a sandwich. During this period appellant was seen using a sharp pocket knife to repair the broken thumb nail of another female patron sitting at his table. At about 4:00 A.M. appellant left Will's Place together with the deceased and her acquaintance, Mabel Proctor, and went to an all-night carry-out shop. The sandwiches bought there were eaten in appellant's truck. Appellant then drove Mabel Proctor home, dropping her off about 4:30 A.M., and drove off in his truck with deceased. The Government produced no witness as to what happened thereafter. However, at approximately 5:00 A.M. that morning, two policemen, cruising in an unmarked car, saw appellant's truck stopped in a parking bay off the Anacostia Parkway. As they approached to investigate they noticed some clothing lying on the grass near the truck. At that point appellant came up the bank from the river, got in his truck and drove away. Further investigation revealed bloody clothing and a pool of blood in the grassy area near the parking bay. The officers retrieved from the river the mutilated and nearly lifeless body of the deceased, nude except for a piece of clothing around her neck. She died almost immediately. Appellant was apprehended later that morning. Expert testimony revealed that deceased had suffered approximately 26 major stab wounds, culminating in a stab wound to the head, penetrating the brain, and lodging the broken blade in the skull. The body had suffered at least the same number of superficial lacerations. The expert concluded that the death had been caused by hemorrhage and shock from the multiple knife wounds.

The Government also produced evidence showing that the body of the deceased had been dragged from the grassy area where the bloody clothes were found to the sea wall, and that on the slope leading down to the river had been found a man's torn and bloody shirt, similar to one owned by appellant. There was no testimony as to any fights, quarrels, animosity, or threats between appellant and deceased.

Defense counsel moved for acquittal only of first degree murder at the close of the prosecution's case and again when defense rested. Although the District Court's denial of those motions was without opinion, its underlying views of the concepts of premeditation and deliberation are reflected in its rulings and actions on instructions. The court's charge on premeditation and deliberation[1] instructed the jury that premeditation is the formation of an intention to kill, and deliberation means a further thought upon the plan to kill. The judge charged the jury that "although some time" is required for deliberation, deliberation may be sufficient "though it be of an exceedingly brief duration," and that the time "may be in the nature of hours, minutes or seconds."

Appellant requested that the time required for deliberation be stated as "some appreciable period of time," rather than "some period of time" as originally proposed by the judge. The court not only declined this request but changed the instruction submitted to counsel ("it does not require the lapse of days or hours or even minutes") to include the reference to "seconds.". . .

II

1. It may be helpful to approach the issues presented by this appeal with the perspective of history.

At common law, unlawful homicides were divided into two classes, murder and manslaughter, depending on whether the killing was with or without malice aforethought. Although the term malice aforethought was most probably intended to be applied literally when it was first introduced into the law of homicide, the courts soon converted it into a term of art. To the popular understanding of subjective malice was added an objective standard, by which negligence tantamount to recklessness might make a culpable homicide murder. The objective standard persists in the law, but what we are primarily concerned with here is not so much the extension of "malice" as the elimination of the literal significance of the word "aforethought." The courts held it sufficient to establish common law murder, subject to capital punishment, if the homicide was accompanied by the intention to cause death or grievous bodily harm, whether the slaying was calculated or only impulsive.

The nineteenth century ushered in a new approach. Beginning in 1794 with Pennsylvania, state legislatures began to separate murder into two degrees, reserving the death penalty for the first degree. These statutes typically

1. "Now as to the fourth element of first degree murder, that the defendant acted with premeditation and with deliberation. Now premeditation is the formation of the intent or plan to kill; the formation of a positive design to kill. Deliberation means further, or to put it another way—I am speaking now of deliberation—that deliberation means a further thought upon the plan or design to kill. It must have been considered by the defendant Bernard Austin.

"It is your duty to determine from all of the facts and the circumstances which have been presented to you in this case that you may find surrounding the killing on April 24, some time between four-forty and five o'clock, whether there was any reflection and consideration amounting to deliberation by the defendant Bernard Austin. Now if there was such deliberation, even though it be of an exceedingly brief duration, that is in itself, so far as the deliberation is concerned, is sufficient. Because it is the fact of deliberation rather than the length of time it required that is important. Although some time, that is there must be some time to deliberate and to create in the mind of the defendant Austin the premeditation and the deliberation. As I have told you before, the time itself may be in the nature of hours, minutes, or seconds. But there must be the deliberation and the premeditation."

defined murder in the first degree as an intended killing, accompanied by premeditation and deliberation (as well as malice aforethought); murder in the second degree was defined residually to include all other unlawful homicides with malice aforethought. In 1901 Congress passed such a statute for the District of Columbia. D.C. Code §§22-2401, 22-2403 (1961).

As we have noted:

> Statutes like ours, which distinguish deliberate and premeditated murder from other murder, reflect a belief that one who meditates an intent to kill and then deliberately executes it is more dangerous, more culpable or less capable of reformation than one who kills on sudden impulse; or that the prospect of the death penalty is more likely to deter men from deliberate than from impulsive murder. The deliberate killer is guilty of first degree murder; the impulsive killer is not. [Bullock v. United States, 74 App. D.C. 220, 221, 122 F.2d 213, 214 (1941)].

The reports reflect the effort of some courts to carry out the legislative conception, by interpreting "deliberation" to call for elements which the word normally signifies—that the determination to kill was reached calmly and in cold blood rather than under impulse or the heat of passion[2] and was reached some appreciable time prior to the homicide. The more widespread judicial tendency was marked by a restrictive reading of the statutory terms. "The statutory scheme was apparently intended to limit administrative discretion in the selection of capital cases. As so frequently occurs, the discretion which the legislature threw out the door was let in the window by the courts."

Judge, later Justice, Cardozo, in a memorable 1928 address,[3] voiced his concern over the judicial attenuation of premeditation and deliberation. He spoke against the background of the New York experience, where, although the courts had abandoned their early statement that it sufficed if intention preceded the act though the act followed instantly, they held that the time for deliberation need not be long, and seconds might suffice, provided there was time for a choice to kill or not to kill. Judge Cardozo said:

> There can be no intent unless there is a choice, yet . . . the choice without more is enough to justify the inference that the intent was deliberate and premeditated. The presence of a sudden impulse is said to mark the dividing line, but how can an impulse be anything but sudden when the time for its formation is measured by the lapse of seconds? Yet the decisions are to the effect that seconds may be enough. . . . The present distinction is so obscure that no jury hearing it for the

2. See, e.g., State v. Kotosky, 74 Mo. 247, 249-250 (1881):

> Deliberation is also premeditation, but is something more. It is not only to think of beforehand, which may be but for an instant, but the inclination to do the act is considered, weighed, pondered upon, for such a length of time after a provocation is given, as the jury may find was sufficient for the blood to cool. One in "a heat of passion" may premeditate without deliberating. Deliberation is only exercised in a "cool state of the blood.". . .

3. What Medicine Can Do for Law, reprinted in Law and Literature 70, 96-101 (1931).

> first time can fairly be expected to assimilate and understand it. I am not at all sure that I understand it myself after trying to apply it for many years and after diligent study of what has been written in the books. Upon the basis of this fine distinction with its obscure and mystifying phraseology, scores of men have gone to their death.

In 1937 we abandoned an earlier conception that deliberation and premeditation may be instantaneous, and held, in Bostic v. United States, "that some appreciable time must elapse in order that reflection and consideration amounting to deliberation may occur."

This change in rule was reiterated in Bullock v. United States, already quoted, where the court, holding the evidence insufficient to support a conviction of first degree murder, stated, 74 App. D.C. at 221, 122 F.2d at 214: "There is nothing deliberate and premeditated about a killing which is done within a second or two after the accused first thinks of doing it. . . ."

In Fisher v. United States, 328 U.S. 463, 469-470 n.3, (1946), the Supreme Court quoted with approval the trial court's general instructions[4] wherein premeditation and deliberation were defined carefully, so as to include an instruction that deliberation requires "that an appreciable time elapse between formation of the design and the fatal act within which there is, in fact, deliberation." The Supreme Court commented, 328 U.S. at 470, 66 S. Ct. at 1322: "The necessary time element was emphasized and the jury was told that premeditation required a preconceived design to kill, a 'second thought.' "

. . . Serious students of the problem have suggested that the legislatures change this approach and eliminate degrees of murder in classifying the offense,[5] but we must apply the statute as it stands. The need for careful attention to the requirement of premeditation and deliberation, and for clear distinction between the first and second degrees of murder, remains a cardinal tenet of our jurisprudence.

4. "Then, there is the element of premeditation. That is, giving thought, before acting, to the idea of taking a human life and reaching a definite decision to kill. In short, premeditation is the formation of a specific intent to kill.

"Deliberation, that term of which you have heard much in the arguments and one of the elements of murder in the first degree, is consideration and reflection upon the preconceived design to kill; turning it over in the mind; giving it second thought.

"Although formation of a design to kill may be instantaneous, as quick as thought itself, the mental process of deliberating upon such a design does require that appreciable time elapse between formation of the design and the fatal act within which there is, in fact, deliberation.

"The law prescribes no particular period of time. It necessarily varies according to the peculiar circumstances of each case. Consideration of a matter may continue over a prolonged period—hours, days, or even longer. Then again, it may cover but a brief span of minutes. If one forming an intent to kill does not act instantly, but pauses and actually gives second thought and consideration to the intended act, he has, in fact deliberated. It is the fact of deliberation that is important, rather than the length of time it may have continued."

5. The draftsmen of the Model Penal Code recommend abandoning the degree device. They comment that it was developed to avoid the mandatory imposition of the death penalty in all cases of undifferentiated "murder," and that now capital punishment is not automatic even for "first degree" murders. They propose that "degrees" should be taken into account in sentencing,

2. This historical review underscores our concern over three aspects of the court's instruction on first degree murder. The rulings of this court and the Supreme Court (in *Fisher*) establish the propriety of the defense request for a charge that the design of the accused to kill must have preceded his actions by an "appreciable" period of time before deliberation can be found. The Government contends that this error was not prejudicial because, as is clearly established by the cases,[6] the crux of the issue of premeditation and deliberation is not the time involved but whether defendant did engage in the process of reflection and meditation.[7] Certainly the charge should focus primarily on the defendant's actual thought processes in terms of meditation and conscious weighing of alternatives. The "appreciable time" element is subordinate, necessary for but not sufficient to establish deliberation. Yet the "appreciable time" charge is a meaningful way to convey to the jury the core meaning of premeditation and deliberation and for that reason should be given, at least where specifically requested by the defense. Moreover, the court's refusal so to instruct was compounded here by the charge that the time to deliberate "may be in the nature of hours, minutes *or seconds*." As *Bostic* and *Bullock, Fisher* and *Frady,* all make clear, no particular length of time is necessary for deliberation, and the time required need not be longer than a span of minutes. But none of our post-*Bostic* opinions sanctions the reference to "or seconds" injected by the trial judge. The obvious problem with such a reference is that it tends to blur, rather than clarify, the critical difference between impulsive and deliberate killings.

Finally, we note that after giving this misleading first degree instruction, the court offered only a skimpy explanation of second degree murder.[8] Our

---

and point out that there are cases where extreme depravity is revealed by a murder on impulse, without extenuating circumstances. The Code also suggests reducing even some premeditated homicides from murder to manslaughter if they are the product of deep emotional disturbance:

> . . . we think it plain that the case for a mitigated sentence does not depend on a distinction between impulse and deliberation; the very fact of long internal struggle may be evidence that the actor's homicidal impulse was deeply aberrational, far more the product of extraordinary circumstances than a true reflection of the actor's normal character, as, for example, in the case of mercy killings, suicide pacts, many infanticides and cases where a provocation gains in its explosive power as the actor broods about his injury. Model Penal Code §201.6, comment at 70 (Tent. Draft No. 9, 1959).

6. This court has consistently pointed out that no particular length of time is necessary for deliberation, and it is not the lapse of time itself which constitutes deliberation but the reflection and turning over in the mind of the accused concerning his existing design and purpose to kill.

7. The Government argues that the instruction as given "implicitly includes the concept of an appreciable time lapse." No reason is advanced why the judge might properly have refused the requested instruction. The judge did not even use the phrase "turning over in the mind," discussed in Wenkley v. United States, 91 U.S. App. D.C. 8, 198 F.2d 940 (1952). His phrase "a further thought upon the plan or design to kill" would also apply to an additional but virtually simultaneous thought.

8. On second degree murder the court charged in essence: "Now if you find that the killing was one with malice but without premeditation and deliberation, you will then have for consideration the lesser included offense of murder in the second degree. . . .

"In other words, murder in the second degree is the unlawful killing of another, with malice aforethought. Murder in the second degree may be committed either with or without any purpose

concern is that there was no straightforward explanation to the jury of the difference between the two degrees of murder—that first degree murder, with its requirement of premeditation and deliberation, covers calculated and planned killings, while homicides that are unplanned or impulsive, even though they are intentional and with malice aforethought, are murder in the second degree.

In homespun terminology, intentional murder is in the first degree if committed in cold blood, and is murder in the second degree if committed on impulse or in the sudden heat of passion . These are the archetypes, that clarify by contrast. The real facts may be hard to classify and may lie between the poles. A sudden passion, like lust, rage, or jealousy, may spawn an impulsive intent yet persist long enough and in such a way as to permit that intent to become the subject of a further reflection and weighing of consequences and hence to take on the character of a murder executed without compunction and "in cold blood." The term "in cold blood" does not necessarily mean the assassin lying in wait, or the kind of murder brilliantly depicted by Truman Capote in In Cold Blood (1965). Thus the common understanding might find both passion and cold blood in the husband who surprises his wife in adultery, leaves the house to buy a gun at a sporting goods store, and returns for a deadly sequel. The analysis of the jury would be illuminated, however, if it is first advised that a typical case of first degree is the murder in cold blood; that murder committed on impulse or in sudden passion is murder in the second degree; and then instructed that a homicide conceived in passion constitutes murder in the first degree only if the jury is convinced beyond a reasonable doubt that there was an appreciable time after the design was conceived and that in this interval there was a further thought, and a turning over in the mind—and not a mere persistence of the initial impulse of passion.

The court did not give an instruction on manslaughter, but none was requested. An unlawful killing in the sudden heat of passion—whether produced by rage, resentment, anger, terror or fear—is reduced from murder to manslaughter only if there was adequate provocation, such as might naturally induce a reasonable man in the passion of the moment to lose self-control and commit the act on impulse and without reflection. There is no contention before us of adequate provocation, and so appellant's crime is murder. The issue is, what degree of murder. . . .

In our opinion the Government's evidence was insufficient to warrant submission to the jury of the issue of premeditation and deliberation. The police produced and the prosecutor presented ample evidence of intent to kill

---

or intent ot kill, if it is accompanied by malice, as I have previously defined malice to you." (Tr. 1730).

The trial judge did not make the mistake of indicating that second degree murder meant an absence of intent to kill, as was done in Weakley v. United States, 91 U.S. App. D.C. 8, 198 F.2d 940 (1952). But we do think the cold blood—hot blood distinction discussed in the text provides an instruction more understandable to the jury as to the kind of intentional killing that constitutes second degree as contrasted with first degree murder.

and malice aforethought—putting to one side appellant's claim of insanity. Indeed there was evidence of a particularly frightful and horrible murder, of a crime that was murder at common law and is murder under our statute. . . .

The facts of a savage murder generate a powerful drive, almost a juggernaut for jurors, and indeed for judges, to crush the crime with the utmost condemnation available, to seize whatever words or terms reflect maximum denunciation, to cry out murder "in the first degree." But it is the task and conscience of a judge to transcend emotional momentum with reflective analysis. The judge is aware that many murders most brutish and bestial are committed in a consuming frenzy or heat of passion, and that these are in law only murder in the second degree. The Government's evidence sufficed to establish an intentional and horrible murder—the kind that could be committed in a frenzy or heat of passion. However the core responsibility of the court requires it to reflect on the sufficiency of the Government's case. We conclude that, making all due allowance for the trial court's function, but applying proper criteria as to the elements of murder in the first degree, the Government's evidence in this case did not establish a basis for a reasoned finding, surpassing speculation, that beyond all reasonable doubt this was not murder committed in an orgy of frenzied activity, possibly heightened by drink, but the act of "one who meditates an intent to kill and then deliberately executes it." (See Bullock v. United States, supra, 74 App. D.C. at 221, 122 F.2d at 214).

That appellant used a knife to accomplish the murder is not probative of premeditation and deliberation because he did not procure it specifically for that purpose but rather carried it about with him as a matter of course. The violence and multiple wounds, while more than ample to show an intent to kill, cannot standing alone support an inference of a calmly calculated plan to kill requisite for premeditation and deliberation, as contrasted with an impulsive and senseless, albeit sustained, frenzy. That there was a half-hour period (4:30 A.M. until 5:00 A.M.) during which appellant had ample time to premeditate and deliberate is not evidence that appellant actually did cogitate and mull over the intent to kill. Finally the Government was not able to show any motive for the crime or any prior threats or quarrels between appellant and deceased which might support an inference of premeditation and deliberation. Thus the jury could only speculate and surmise, without any basis in the testimony or evidence, that appellant acted with premeditation and deliberation. The office of the motion for acquittal is precisely to avoid such improper and unfounded conjecture.

The claim that appellant acted not merely intentionally but with deliberation when he stabbed the unfortunate woman to death is manifestly not established beyond a reasonable doubt by evidence showing that he acted with deliberation afterward, in an effort to avoid detection and punishment—dragging the victim on the point of death down to the river; then fleeing; then feigning lack of any knowledge when the officer arrived. These facts may intensify emotional recoil against appellant. But they do not provide a reasoned basis for concluding beyond a reasonable doubt that the crime appellant sought to wash away, and run away from, was a crime he had committed not merely intentionally, in sustained frenzy or heat of passion, but beyond that with premeditation and deliberation! . . .

Notes and Questions

1. Precisely what did the court find wrong with the trial judge's instructions in this case? Was it crucial that the judge said that the time to deliberate could be a matter of mere seconds?

2. Judge Leventhal suggests that an "appreciable" amount of time is necessary, but not sufficient, for premeditation, but that the reference to "seconds" in the instruction "tends to blur, rather than clarify, the critical difference between impulsive and deliberate killings." What is that critical difference? What is the quality of contemplation which Judge Leventhal is trying to capture? What theory of the purposes of criminal punishment does Judge Leventhal rely on in distinguishing "calculated and planned" killings from "unplanned or impulsive killings?"

3. See Stephen, 3 A History of the Criminal Law in England 94 (1883):

> As much cruelty, as much indifference to the life of others, a disposition at least as dangerous to society, probably even more dangerous, is shown by sudden as by premeditated murders. The following cases appear to me to set this in a clear light. A man passing along the road, sees a boy sitting on a bridge over a deep river and, out of mere wanton barbarity, pushes him into it and so drowns him. A man makes advances to a girl who repels him. He deliberately but instantly cuts her throat. A man civilly asked to pay a just debt pretends to get the money, loads a rifle and blows out his creditor's brains. In none of these cases is there premeditation unless the word is used in a sense as unnatural as "aforethought" in "malice aforethought," but each represents even more diabolical cruelty and ferocity than that which is involved in murders premeditated in the natural sense of the word.

Does Stephen reflect a retributivist view of the criminal law? Does his criticism of the premeditation formula take account of the deterrent or incapacitative functions of the criminal law?

4. From The San Francisco Chronicle, June 20, 1984 at 4:

> **Mercy Killer Gets Probation, $10,000 Fine**
>
> San Diego—A 71-year-old woman who admitted strangling her bedridden husband with a nylon stocking was placed on probation yesterday by a judge who said, "She wanted to release him and free him of his pain." Dorothy Healy of La Jolla had pleaded guilty earlier to voluntary manslaughter in the slaying of her 92-year-old husband, Walter, and could have been jailed for up to 11 years. But Municipal Judge Frederic Link said he saw moral and ethical reasons why Mrs. Healy committed the homicide. He ordered her to serve five years'

> probation, pay a $10,000 fine and perform 1000 hours of community-service work.
>
> "Mr. Healy was in severely declining health," the judge said. He suffered loss of hearing. He had had a series of strokes since 1973 and was in constant pain and almost totally bedridden.
>
> "But for the valiant efforts of Dorothy Healy, Mr. Healy probably would not have lived as long as he did. Walter Healy had often said he didn't want to go to a hospital or a rest home. Mrs. Healy believed in what she was doing. She had said: 'Walter would thank me. Walter would appreciate what I did.' " Healy suffered from emphysema, arteriosclerosis and other illnesses. Mrs. Healy first told authorities that her husband of 48 years had died in his sleep on March 20. She was arrested when an autopsy revealed he had been strangled. She told police she used a nylon stocking to kill him.
>
> "I didn't want to believe that this sweet little old thing could possibly have anything to do with killing her husband," San Diego County Deputy Coroner Chuck Bolton said after her arrest.

How would you defend Mrs. Healy under *Austin*?

5. Some states, contrary to *Austin,* have refused to read any express duration requirement into the definition of premeditation, or to guide the jury with any detailed refinement of the concept of premeditation. For example, examine Commonwealth v. Scott, 284 Pa. 159, 130 A. 317 (1925). According to the opinion by Justice Walling:

> . . . This appeal by defendant is from sentence on conviction of murder of the first degree. George Rea, the chief of police of the borough of West Newton, Westmoreland county, and its only police officer, while on duty as such at about 3 o'clock on the morning of September 16, 1924, met the defendant, James Scott, and another young . . . man named Evans and two . . . girls. Attracted by their conversation, he stopped them to ascertain if they had any "moonshine." Satisfying himself that Evans had not, the officer turned to Scott, and asked him, inter alia, if he had any "moonshine," at which the latter drew a .38 caliber revolver, and saying, "This is what I have for you," shot him through the abdomen, inflicting a mortal wound. Defendant fled, but was apprehended eight days later in West Virginia, where he was known by another name, and at first denied his identity. Defendant set up self-defense to the effect that before he shot, the officer reached for his gun and said, "I will fix you," but this defense was supported only by his own testimony, and was disproved by that of his three companions and by other witnesses . . .
>
> . . . [A]lthough there was no evidence that defendant bore the officer any ill will prior to the meeting that night, it was for the jury to say, under the instructions of the trial judge, whether during that brief conversation, defendant formed in his mind the conscious purpose of taking life and selected the instrument of death, and, as they so found, we cannot disturb the verdict. We have often sustained capital convictions where the time for deliberation was equally brief. It is the fully formed purpose, not the time, which constitutes the higher degree, and of the fact that it was so formed the jury must be well satisfied. The responsibility, however, rests upon them and upon the trial court; the most we can do is to see that the defendant was accorded all his legal rights. . . .

In *Scott,* the Court readily concluded that the defendant intended to kill the police officer, and that he did not act under the influence of any legally adequate provocation. He should thus be guilty of at least second-degree murder. But what were the aggravating aspects of the killing that explain the first-degree conviction? For how long a time did Scott think about the killing? Would he have been any more culpable if he had been hoping all along to encounter a policeman so he could kill one? What is a "fully formed" purpose to kill, as opposed to a mere intent to kill?

In Commonwealth v. Carroll, 412 Pa. 525, 526, 194 A.2d 911, 915 (1963), the Supreme Court of Pennsylvania made it clear that its view had not changed in the intervening 38 years:

> Whether the intention to kill and the killing, that is, the premeditation and the fatal act, were within a brief space of time or a long space of time is immaterial if the killing was in fact intentional, wilful, deliberate and premeditated.

6. On the other hand, the California Supreme Court has tried to guide trial courts and juries with specific criteria to evaluate the evidence offered on the premeditation issue. It said in People v. Anderson, 70 Cal. 2d 15, 73 Cal. Rptr. 550, 557, 447 P.2d 942 (1968):

> The type of evidence which this court has found sufficient to sustain a finding of premeditation and deliberation falls into three basic categories: (1) facts about how and what defendant did *prior* to the actual killing which show that the defendant was engaged in activity directed toward, and explicable as intended to result in, the killing—what may be characterized as "planning" activity; (2) facts about the defendant's *prior* relationship and/or conduct with the victim from which the jury could reasonably infer a "motive" to kill the victim, which inference of motive, together with facts of type (1) or (3), would in turn support an inference that the killing was the result of "a pre-existing reflection" and "careful thought and weighing of considerations" rather than "mere unconsidered or rash impulse hastily executed" (People v. Thomas, supra, 25 Cal. 2d 880, at pp. 898, 900, 901, 156 P.2d 7, at p. 14); (3) facts about the nature of the killing from which the jury could infer that the *manner* of killing was so particular and exacting that the defendant must have intentionally killed according to a "preconceived design" to take his victim's life in a particular way for a "reason" which the jury can reasonably infer from facts of type (1) or (2).
>
> Analysis of the cases will show that this court sustains verdicts of first degree murder typically when there is evidence of all three types and otherwise requires at least extremely strong evidence of (1) or evidence of (2) in conjunction with either (1) or (3).

7. As noted in *Austin,* the Model Penal Code rejects the traditional premeditation formula and treats all murder as being of a single degree, leaving a quite different scheme to differentiate capital from noncapital murder (See pages 294, 429).

COMMONWEALTH v. GOULD

Supreme Judicial Court of Massachusetts
405 N.E.2d 927 (1980)

ABRAMS, Justice.

On July 17, 1978, the defendant fatally stabbed his former girlfriend. After a witness to the attack intervened and told the defendant to stop, he mumbled, "I attacked her. She was impure . . . [i]mpure, impure." For more than five years preceding the fatal stabbing the defendant had suffered from constant, fixed delusions in which he believed that he had a divine mission on earth and that he was required to kill his girlfriend because she was "impure." After a trial at which criminal responsibility was the sole issue, the jury convicted the defendant of murder in the first degree. The defendant appeals.

Initially, the defendant argues that it was error for the judge to have denied his motion for a verdict of not guilty on so much of the indictment as alleged murder in the first degree. Alternatively, the defendant asks that we order a new trial or reduce the verdict to murder in the second degree.

Although we find no error at trial . . . we think the defendant is entitled to a new trial at which he may produce expert testimony on the issue of whether or not the impairment of his mental processes precluded him from being able to deliberately premeditate. At a new trial the jury may also consider the defendant's mental impairment on the issue of whether he committed the murder with extreme atrocity or cruelty.

We summarize the evidence. At approximately 7 A.M. on July 17, 1978, the defendant was seen in a restaurant near the nursing home where the victim worked. Shortly afterwards witnesses observed him keeping the nursing home under surveillance from a covert position. James McPherson drove into the parking lot of the nursing home at approximately 8:30 A.M., and observed the defendant leaning on the back of a van. The victim walked down a ramp from the parking lot to the building. McPherson saw the defendant go "right down after [the victim]," and then saw the defendant on top of the victim, apparently beating her. McPherson ran down the ramp and yelled at the defendant to stop. The defendant straightened up, dropped his knife, and permitted McPherson to seat him on a wall abutting the ramp. McPherson left the defendant to get help for the victim. When he returned, the defendant was again stabbing the victim. Once more, McPherson told the defendant to sit down on the wall; after one final lunge at the victim, the defendant did so, and remained there until the police came. McPherson testified that the defendant was bleary-eyed and "excited," and that he repeatedly stated that she was "impure."

Quincy policeman Kevin Murphy arrived at the nursing home at approximately 9 A.M., and observed the victim lying at the foot of the ramp, covered with blood, and gasping for breath. A knife protruded from underneath her left breast.[9] Officer Murphy placed the defendant under arrest and recited the *Miranda* warnings. In response to a question, the defendant told the officer, "There was nobody with me. I did it myself." Officer Murphy testified that the defendant's shirt and arm were covered with blood when he first saw him; otherwise, he appeared "natural."

The defendant was interrogated at the Quincy police station at approximately 11 A.M., and a transcription of a tape recording of that interview was read in evidence. During this interview, the defendant, appearing somewhat nervous, described his acquaintance with the victim,[10] and his history of hospitalization at various mental institutions since approximately 1973. He admitted that he had intentionally caused his right arm to be amputated by falling on a train track. The defendant started to describe the earlier events of that morning, but claimed not to remember anything between the time he got out of his car and the time he found himself sitting on the wall (for what the evidence indicated was the second time). After the tape recorder was turned off, the defendant said, "I know why I did it," but refused to explain.

At one point all but one police officer left the room, and the defendant made several spontaneous statements. The defendant stated that he was commanded to commit the murder: "The rabbi looked at me from his pulpit and told me 'thou shalt kill her.'" He said that he probably would not go to jail or to a hospital, but that he would instead be taken to Israel and tortured or nailed to a cross. He asked the officer what "they" would do to him if they found out he was Jesus Christ. Finally, the officer testified, the defendant said "that she was impure, that all Jewish woman were impure, 'including [his] mother . . . ,'" and that he though what he did was "right." The officer added that the defendant appeared normal throughout this conversation.

It was uncontradicted that the defendant had a long-standing, constant delusional belief system. The defendant's delusions were religious in nature. He believed that he was the Messiah; he believed that he was the Saviour of the Jewish people; he believed that he was required by God to kill the victim because of his divine mission and because she was "impure."

From 1973 until 1978, the defendant was in and out of various institutions for the mentally ill.[11] The defendant was treated with drugs and psycho-

9. The victim died that day as a result of multiple stab wounds with massive hemorrhage. The pathologist testified that there were thirty-one stab wounds, including wounds to her head, chest, abdomen, left arm, and left leg.

10. The defendant had met the victim in early 1973 and dated her regularly until the summer of 1973 when she terminated the relationship after the defendant became delusional and threatened her with a knife. There was testimony that the defendant made frequent threats against the victim. Six months before the homicide the defendant had again threatened the victim. The defendant was placed on probation for two years, and was under court order not to contact the victim or go near her house.

11. According to testimony by the psychiatrist who treated the defendant, the defendant was twice admitted to Worcester State Hospital in 1973. He was hospitalized for approximately fifteen months. In April 1975, the defendant was admitted to Massachusetts General Hospital after he

therapy; as a result he was better able to think and perceive reality, although he never gave up his delusional ideas.

The Commonwealth's expert diagnosed the defendant's mental illness as paranoid psychosis.[12] The expert said that during the course of his interviews with the defendant, the defendant took responsibility for the killing. The defendant told the doctor that he could not "justify a killing," that he (the defendant) could not "say whether it was wrong or it was right" and that he could "only sanctify it" (i.e., the killing).

The expert testified that the defendant also stated "that he knew at the time of the stabbing that his actions were illegal in the Commonwealth of Massachusetts and were considered to be wrong by society, that he could have stopped himself from stabbing the victim and that he was responsible for what he had done." The defendant later told the expert that he sometimes thought he might "get off through insanity."

The expert concluded that, despite the defendant's mental illness, the defendant appreciated, at the moment of the homicide, that his act was "immoral, wrong and a criminal and illegal thing to do," and that "he was capable of controlling his behavior to such an extent that he could have stopped himself from doing it." In essence, the expert admitted that the defendant's mental powers were impaired, but could not "quantify" the degree of the impairment except to say it was not "substantial."

The defense in this case consisted solely of the testimony of psychiatrists on the issue of criminal responsibility. Dr. Larry Strasburger and Dr. John Snell both testified that the defendant had suffered from a severe and long-standing mental illness, namely, paranoid schizophrenia, and that this was a "clear-cut" and "straightforward" case of lack of criminal responsibility.

Dr. Strasburger testified that the defendant's chronic disease had led to a functional impairment which made him unable to appreciate the consequences of his actions in a normal, rational way,[13] and to "widespread diffi-

---

had intentionally placed his right arm under the path of a trolley car so that it would be amputated. He was transferred from Massachusetts General Hospital's psychiatric unit to Worcester State Hospital, and then to McLean Hospital in Belmont. He was released from McLean in October 1975, but continued as an outpatient until the homicide, with the exception of a brief period of hospitalization in August 1976.

12. Every other doctor who had examined the defendant both before and after the crime had diagnosed him as a paranoid schizophrenic. On cross-examination, the Commonwealth's expert acknowledged that the defendant's mental illness "may even be schizophrenia," but stated he would need further evidence as to auditory and visual hallucinations before he would change his diagnosis.

13. The defendant's statements to Dr. Strasburger were used to illustrate the quality of the defendant's irrational thinking. When asked about the incident, the defendant said, "I didn't want her to die. It was something I had to do. Like in war, when you kill someone, you're not doing the right thing. It's like war. You have to, even though it's not the right thing." When asked directly whether he knew that killing the victim was against the law, the defendant replied, "I wrote the law, the Ten Commandments. That's the law." When asked what he thought about the whole thing in retrospect, he said, "When you're at war, captured, sometimes you escape. I plan to

culty checking hostile impulses." Although massive drug treatment improved the defendant's thought disorder, his underlying delusional system remained unchanged. Thus, he might appear to function normally for some period of time, but stress or anxiety would cause his delusional thinking to predominate. Dr. Snell's testimony focused on the causal relationship between the homicide and the defendant's delusions. Dr. Snell testified that the defendant's crime was a direct outgrowth of his delusions and that the defendant could not view his conduct in a rational way, but only viewed his actions as divine. . . .

The defendant argues, on the basis of two distinct theories, that the Commonwealth's evidence was insufficient as a matter of law to support a conviction of murder in the first degree. Therefore, he claims the judge should have directed a verdict of not guilty of murder in the first degree, thus making murder in the second degree the most severe verdict that could be returned. Initially, the defendant claims that as a result of his mental abnormality he could not form the specific intent required for murder in the first degree. Alternatively the defendant argues that because of the unanimity of psychiatric opinion that there was a causal connection between his long-standing mental illness and the crime, the judge was required to direct a verdict on the charge of murder in the first degree.[14]

The same short answer applies to each of these arguments. The defendant concedes that the evidence, considered without regard to the defendant's mental disease, was sufficient to support a conviction of murder in the first degree. Directing a verdict in these circumstances would constitute an unwarranted invasion of the province of the jury. See G.L. c. 265, §1 (the jury determine the degree of murder). Moreover, jurors find the facts, including those facts or issues on which they hear psychiatric testimony. "The law should not, and does not, give the opinions of experts . . . the benefit of conclusiveness, even if there are no contrary opinions introduced at the trial." [Commonwealth v. Smith, 258 N.E.2d 1320 (1970).] Thus, there was no error in the denial of the defendant's motion for a directed verdict of not guilty of murder in the first degree. . . .

The defendant also argues, however, that we should exercise our supervisory power, and either grant him a new trial or reduce his conviction to murder in the second degree. Our duty under G.L. c. 278, §33E, is to consider broadly the whole case on the law and the facts to determine whether the verdict is "consonant with justice." [Commonwealth v. Seit, 364 N.E.2d 1243 (1977).] "General Law c. 278, §33E, 'operates as a type of "safety valve" by ensuring review as to all aspects of cases regardless of the absence of claim of error.' Commonwealth v. Brown, 380 N.E.2d 113 (1978). See Commonwealth v. Hall, 369 Mass. 715, 736, 343 N.E.2d 388 (1976) ('The broad scope of the

---

escape, not from here but from everywhere. Let everyone escape. Open the doors so the blind can see and the deaf can hear."

14. There was, however, no unanimity of opinion regarding the issue of criminal responsibility. . . .

review which this court is required to make under G.L. c. 278, §33E, in a capital case is not limited to questions based on exceptions saved during the course of the trial'). In short, while recognizing that the power of this court under §33E is to be exercised with restraint, we have not hesitated to act under §33E in appropriate cases. . . ." [Commonwealth v. Cole, 402 N.E.2d 55, 61 (1980).] We conclude that this is an appropriate case for the exercise of our power under §33E. Although the trial judge was scrupulous in his concern for the problems raised by the defendant's mental illness and indeed went to considerable lengths throughout the trial to safeguard the defendant's rights, for the reasons set out, infra, we think a new trial is required.

. . . The record raises a substantial issue as to deliberate premeditation; namely, should a judge instruct the jury that they may consider a defendant's long-standing mental illness in ascertaining whether the defendant had sufficient mental capacity to deliberately premeditate the acts charged? We have previously held that a jury may consider a defendant's voluntary use of liquor (i.e., drunkenness) or a defendant's voluntary use of narcotics or harmful drugs on the issue of deliberate premeditation. If a defendant who has voluntarily used alcohol or drugs is found by the jury to be incapable of deliberately premeditating the acts charged, he may not be found guilty of murder in the first degree but may be found guilty of murder in the second degree. . . . This rule "is merely an application of the ordinary rules of law pertaining to the requisite mental state for conviction of a particular crime charged." Commonwealth v. Mazza, 366 Mass. 30, 34, 313 N.E.2d 875, 878 (1974).

We think there is no justifiable reason to treat the effect of the defendant's involuntary mental illness on his capacity for deliberate premeditation in a manner different from the effect of the voluntary use of liquor or drugs. "Neither logic nor justice can tolerate a jurisprudence that defines the elements of an offense as requiring a mental state such that one defendant can properly argue that his voluntary drunkenness removed his capacity to form the specific intent but another defendant is inhibited from a submission of his contention that an abnormal mental condition, for which he was in no way responsible, negated his capacity to form a particular specific intent, even though the condition did not exonerate him from all criminal responsibility." United States v. Brawner, 471 F.2d 969, 999 (D.C. Cir. 1972).

Permitting a jury to consider whether a defendant's mental illness affected his capacity to deliberately premeditate is not tantamount to adopting a doctrine of diminished responsibility. This change merely broadens our present practice by allowing jury consideration of mental impairment as well as voluntary intoxication on the issue of deliberate premeditation. Our rule "contemplates full responsibility, not partial, but only for the crime actually committed." State v. Padilla, 66 N.M. 289, 292, 347 P.2d 312, 314 (1959). Evidence of the defendant's mental disease, like voluntary intoxication, bears on the specific intent required for murder in the first degree based on deliberate premeditation.

The Commonwealth suggests that . . . [e]vidence of the defendant's mental illness is relevant only to the issue of criminal responsibility. We disagree. "It would be a legal as well as a logical incongruity to hold that the crime of murder in the first degree could only be committed after deliberate thought or premeditated malice, and yet that it might be committed by one who was without mental capacity to think deliberately or determine rationally." [Aszman v. State, 24 N.E. 123 (1889).] To the extent that [our previous] cases are inconsistent with this result, we no longer follow them.

We conclude that psychiatric testimony may properly be offered to distinguish "between 'intent' in the sense of a conscious desire, 'planning' in the sense of considering the mechanical feasibility of effectuating that desire, and 'premeditation' in the sense of critically evaluating the pros and cons of proceeding to effectuate the desire [thereby explaining] in understandable terms how a person could logically entertain an intent, plan the effectuation of that intent, but not [deliberately] premeditate regarding the objective of that intent." Dix, Psychological Abnormality as a Factor in Grading Criminal Liability: Diminished Capacity, Diminished Responsibility, and the Like, 62 J. Crim. L., Criminology & Police Sci. 313, 325. If expert testimony to this effect is elicited, then the judge should instruct the jury that the defendant's mental illness may be considered on the issue of deliberate premeditation. . . .

Pursuant to our power under G.L. c. 278, §33E, the judgment is reversed, the verdict is set aside, and a new trial is ordered.

So ordered.

Notes and Questions

1. Though all the examining psychiatrists believed that Gould was a paranoid psychotic or schizophrenic, he was not insane at the time of the killing under Massachusetts law because he appreciated that his act was wrong, and he was capable of self-restraint. If so, what bearing did the psychiatric evidence have on the issue of premeditation? In the court's view, what precisely was the trial court's error? Didn't the jury hear all the relevant evidence?

2. If, despite his psychosis, the defendant had the intent to kill required to establish second degree murder, how could the psychiatric evidence disprove premeditation? Once we assume the defendant was sane enough to intend to kill, would the Commonwealth have a strong case for premeditation under *Austin* or *Anderson,* supra? *Gould* creates a kind of "diminished capacity" defense to a premeditation charge. The term "diminished capacity," however, is variable and often misleading. If a defendant can show that mental illness or some other impairment prevented him from premeditating the killing within the meaning of the statute, an independent concept or defense of "diminished capacity" seems unnecessary, since the defendant is simply offering relevant evidence to rebut the state's proof of evidence of an element of the crime.

The California Supreme Court, however, experimented with a somewhat more elusive concept of diminished capacity for first-degree murder. In People v. Wolff, 61 Cal. 2d 795, 40 Cal. Rptr. 271, 394 P.2d 959 (1964) the 15-year-old defendant calmly and carefully killed his mother under circumstances clearly establishing premeditation under People v. Anderson, supra. Wolff, however, though legally sane, exhibited a form of schizophrenia involving a "complete disassociation between intellect and emotion." The Court held that the premeditation formula required, beyond the conventional evidence of deliberation, a qualitative element of "personal depravity" or "turpitude." Specifically, the state had to prove that the defendant was psychologically and emotionally capable of "maturely and meaningfully" reflecting upon the killing. The court reduced Wolff's liability to second-degree murder. In *Wolff,* the Court may simply have been trying to circumvent the narrow California insanity rule, see Chapter 15, and the then-narrow death penalty law, which did not formally permit evidence of mental impairment to mitigate punishment. In any event, the *Wolff* decision was not followed in other jurisdictions, and the California legislature expressly overruled it in 1981. (See page 355.) Nevertheless, *Wolff* illustrates that courts sometimes are unwilling to rely wholly on sentencing discretion to adjust the penalty according to the subtleties of the moral culpability of the defendant, preferring to incorporate some mitigating factor into the statutory definition of the crime.

3. One commentator[15] has criticized both the *Gould* and *Wolff* cases:

> Note well what the *Gould* court has and has not done. . . . [T]he court is allowing the jury to consider mental abnormality in order to determine if the lower verdict of second degree murder is more consonant with justice. This is partial responsibility language, much akin to the language of the *Wolff* case in California (and to the cognitive branch of insanity defense tests), but it is adopted in the guise of interpreting the elements. The court has adopted true partial responsibility, but has limited its application to a theory of first degree murder. If the ability to appreciate the consequences of one's choices is relevant to one's responsibility for a killing committed in an objectively brutal manner, why is it not relevant to responsibility for any crime? If the law will consider partial responsibility at all, is not the ability to appreciate the consequences of choices a factor in one's moral capacities that should bear on accountability for all actions? As the California experience demonstrated and *Gould* confirms, it is difficult to avoid illogical limitations on partial responsibility if one adopts this partial defense in the guise of interpreting the elements of specific crimes.

4. The *Gould* court notes earlier holdings that a defendant who voluntarily consumes alcohol or other drugs before a killing can claim that he was therefore incapable of premeditating. Why? Does that rule invoke Stephen's criticism of the premeditation formula, supra page 364 ?

15. Morse, Undiminished Confusion in Diminished Capacity, 75 J. Crim. L. and Criminology, 1, 33-34 (1984).

PEOPLE v. ROBERTS

Supreme Court of Michigan
178 N.W. 690 (1920)

BIRD, J. Defendant was adjudged guilty of murder in the first degree in the Isabella circuit court. . . . Several errors are now assigned on the proceedings in behalf of respondent.

[The key testimony was as follows.]

Dr. Michael Bronstetter was . . . called by the people, and testified as follows:

I am coroner of Isabella county. I presided at the inquest upon the body of Katie Roberts, whom I knew in her life. The body over which I held the inquest was her body. I knew her as the wife of Frank Roberts. I was the surgeon who opened up the body, and I examined her stomach, and other intestinal organs. . . .

Q. From the condition of the body, as you found it, and the amount of paris green so found in the stomach, what would you say as to what was the cause of death?

A. Aceto-arsenical poison. . . .

Examined by Dusenberry [defense attorney]:

Q. You had reference to a time you had seen Mrs. Roberts as a patient?

A. Yes, sir.

Q. When was that, Doctor?

A. I could not say just when, . . . about three or four months before her death. I saw her at her home where they lived. . . . She was in bed, and I believe she said she was unable to do any kind of work. Whether she could get up and around or not I don't know. Her body was considerably wasted. She showed evidence of a long drawn out sickness. She showed symptoms of a multiple sclerosis.

Q. What is that?

A. It is a disease of the central nervous system, affecting both the brain and cord. The causes of these patches in the brain and cord is unknown. This condition I found with this patient. She had the outward signs of multiple sclerosis, the rapid pulse, hesitating, singsong speech. And from these signs you diagnose the multiple sclerosis.

Q. Was she practically helpless?

A. I should say practically. Just how specifically I could not say.

Q. Basing your answer upon your observation at that time, did you consider her a hopeless patient, or did you consider she might possibly recover?

A. I considered her case as incurable. . . .

Defendant, Roberts, then took the stand, and was interrogated by counsel as follows:

Examined by Mr. Dusenberry:

Q. Your wife was sent to the hospital at Ann Arbor?
A. I took her myself. She was there 30 days, I think. I did not stay there at Ann Arbor while she was there. I took her myself, and made three trips down to see her while she was there, and I brought her back myself. I paid the expenses incident to her going to the hospital and staying there 30 days. It wasn't paid by the county. I paid it out of my own pocket.

Examined by Mr. McClintic:

Q. On May 23, 1919, Mr. Roberts, I understand, you told me that you had mixed a quantity of paris green in a cup?
A. Yes, sir.
Q. At your wife's request, and placed that on a chair near her side?
A. Yes, sir.
Q. Is that right?
A. Yes, sir.
Q. You did that?
A. Yes, sir.
Q. And that she had requested you to do that, so she could drink it. Is that right?
A. Yes, sir.
Q. And that she subsequently did take that?
A. Yes, sir.
Q. And a few hours after that she died. Is that right?
A. Yes, sir.

Examined by Mr. Dusenberry:

Q. Had she ever tried to commit suicide before?
A. Yes, sir.
Q. When was that?
A. Last summer.
Q. What means did she try to use?
A. Carbolic acid.
Q. So that by her previous actions you knew that she was desirous of dying?
A. Yes, sir.

The court, after having a private conference with defendant, proceeded to sentence him in the following language:

> After hearing your plea of guilty as charged in the information in this case to killing, and murdering your wife, Mr. Roberts, and after hearing testimony and evidence introduced in court bearing upon the degree of the crime charged, the court hereby determines that you have committed murder in the first degree, . . . and the punishment shall be confinement in the state's prison.
>
> It is beyond my comprehension how a human being of normal conditions at least, or apparent normal conditions, can commit such a crime as you have in this case, by placing poison within reach of your wife or giving it to your wife with the intention as you claim. It doesn't make any difference whether she had that intention or not of committing suicide. You are a principal, under the law of the state, to committing the crime of murder. It was, indeed, an inhuman and dastardly act. The sentence of the court is that you be confined to the state's prison, located at Marquette, for the period of your natural life, at hard labor, and in solitary confinement, in accordance with section 15192 of the Compiled Laws of 1915. . . .

[Defendant] is charged with murder, and the theory of the people was that he committed the crime by means of poison. He has come into court and confessed that he mixed poison with water and placed it within her reach, but at her request. The important question, therefore, arises as to whether what defendant did constitutes murder by means of poison.

"All murder which shall be perpetrated by means of poison, or lying in wait, or any other kind of willful, deliberate and premeditated killing, or shall be committed in the perpetration, or attempt to perpetrate in arson, rape, robbery or burglary, shall be deemed murder of the first degree, and shall be punished by solitary confinement at hard labor in the state prison for life." C.L. 1915, §15192. . . .

In [Blackburn v. State, 23 Ohio St. 146], the facts and questions raised bear a close analogy to the case we are considering. . . .

Whether the act of mixing the strychnine with wine and giving it to the deceased to drink was administering poison within the meaning of the statute, the opinion says:

> We think also that the court was right in instructing the jury, as in substance and effect it did, that it is immaterial whether the party taking the poison took it willingly, intending thereby to commit suicide, or was overcome by force, or overreached by fraud. True, the atrocity of the crime, in a moral sense, would be greatly diminished by the fact that suicide was intended; yet the law, as we understand it, makes no discrimination on that account. The lives of all are equally under the protection of the law, and under that protection to their last moment. The life of those to whom life has become a burden—of those who are hopelessly diseased or fatally wounded—nay, even the lives of criminals condemned to death, are under the protection of the law, equally as the lives of those who are in the full tide of life's enjoyment, and anxious to continue to live. If discriminations are to be made in such cases as to the amount of punishment due to offenders, they must be made by the exercise of executive clemency or legisla-

> tive provision. Purposely and maliciously to kill a human being, by administering to him or her poison, is declared by the law to be murder, irrespective of the wishes or the condition of the party to whom the poison is administered, or the manner in which, or the means by which, it is administered. The fact that the guilty party intends also to take his own life, and that the administration of the poison is in pursuance of an agreement that both will commit suicide, does not, in the legal sense, vary the case. If the prisoner furnished the poison to the deceased for the purpose and with the intent that she should with it commit suicide, and she accordingly took and used it for that purpose, or if he did not furnish the poison, but was present at the taking thereof by the deceased, participating by persuasion, force, threats, or otherwise, in the taking thereof, or the introduction of it into her stomach or body, then, in either of the cases supposed, he administered the poison to her within the meaning of the statute.

We are of the opinion that, when defendant mixed the paris green with water and placed it within reach of his wife to enable her to put an end to her suffering by putting an end to her life, he was guilty of murder by means of poison within the meaning of the statute, even though she requested him to do so. By this act he deliberately placed within her reach the means of taking her own life, which she could have obtained in no other way by reason of her helpless condition.

Notes and Questions

1. Consider what level of homicide Roberts would be guilty of if Michigan had not included "perpetration by means of poison" in the first-degree murder statute. Could Roberts by guilty of first-degree murder anyway? How does the use of poison add to one's culpability?

2. What if a father negligently gave poison to his sick child, thinking it was medicine? In virtually all jurisdictions with first-degree murder laws like §189, the father's use of poison cannot make him guilty of first-degree murder if without the first-degree provision he would at most be guilty of involuntary manslaughter, not second-degree murder. But what if his administration of the poison was grossly reckless?

In State v. Wells, 61 Iowa 629, 17 N.W. 90 (1883), the defendants, trying to escape from prison, administered chloroform to a guard. The defendants had no intention of killing the guard, but the dosage nevertheless proved fatal. The court held that by unlawfully administering poison to the guard, the defendants committed murder, and that the "perpetration by means of poison provision aggravated the crime to first-degree murder." The court noted that if "they had beaten the deceased and effected their escape, they might not have been guilty of [first-degree] murder, because no such consequence is by the statute attached to the beating as there is to the administration of poison." Id. at 94.

Is such a distinction between intended killing by beating and intended killing by poison defensible? Is the "poison" provision a species of strict or formal liability, analogous to the felony-murder doctrine?

PEOPLE v. BENJAMIN

California Court of Appeal

42 Cal. App. 3d 69, 124 Cal. Rptr. 799 (1975)

Franson, Acting Presiding Justice.

In the early morning hours of December 23, 1973, appellant and Bobby Lee Gibson were in an after-hours bar-restaurant called Henry VIII—The Dungeon in Bakersfield. Delbert Adams, the victim, was also in the bar. Appellant was wearing a wide-brimmed, leather or suede hat, a sleeveless shirt, and had a coat draped over one arm. Gibson wore a tight fitting navy watch-cap.

An argument developed between Adams and appellant. Some foul language was exchanged but no blows occurred. Appellant and Gibson left the bar after the argument subsided.

Adams remained in the Dungeon, was introduced to Marlene Reel, and danced until about 5:30 A.M. Mrs. Reel then declined an invitation to have breakfast with Adams, so Adams walked Mrs. Reel to her car in the parking lot as she had decided to go home. . . .

James Irwin worked as a parking lot guard at The Dungeon. Irwin's shift was from 10 P.M. to 6 A.M. At approximately 5 to 5:15 A.M. on December 23, Mr. Irwin observed a Volkswagen with a white top, dark body and missing front bumper make two or three passes through The Dungeon parking lot. The Volkswagen contained two occupants. The passenger wore a wide-brimmed hat and was bent over looking toward the exit door of The Dungeon.

Mrs. Reel testified that as she and Adams exited The Dungeon at approximately 5:30 A.M. someone called the name John or Johnny. The couple walked to Mrs. Reel's car and entered the vehicle. Mrs. Reel sat in the center of the front seat, and Adams sat behind the steering wheel with his left leg protruding out the open driver's door. A Volkswagen with a light top and dark bottom approached the rear of Mrs. Reel's car, paused and continued away. The driver of the Volkswagen had a very white face and was wearing a tight, knit cap. Shortly thereafter a man approached Mrs. Reel's car and inquired, "Are you the one who wanted a piece of us?" The man, identified as appellant by Mrs. Reel, then shot Adams once. Mrs. Reel leaped from the car and ran inside The Dungeon. While running Mrs. Reel heard three more shots.

From a distance of 50 yards, Irwin saw a man pull the door of Mrs. Reel's parked car open, step back and fire several shots into the car. The man wore a wide-brimmed hat and a windbreaker. After firing the shots the man turned and ran.

The police arrived at The Dungeon parking lot at 5:50 A.M. Adams' body was still in Mrs. Reel's car. An APB was issued for the two-toned Volkswagen with the missing front bumper.

Adams suffered four .22 caliber bullet wounds—two in the upper back area and two in the lower pelvic area. Adams died as a result of the multiple gunshot wounds.

The two-toned Volkswagen with the missing front bumper was located at 6:30 P.M. on December 23, 1973, at the Bakersfield residence of Mr. Reil Hunt. Inside the car was a brown felt hat, a plaid carcoat and a nylon windbreaker.

Mr. Reil Hunt was Bobby Lee Gibson's grandfather and he owned a Volkswagen with a white top, blue body and a missing front bumper. Bobby Lee Gibson lived in the Hunt residence during December 1973 and used the Volkswagen. . . .

One of the prosecution's principal theories in the case was that it was murder by means of lying in wait which is by statute declared to be murder in the first degree. (Pen. Code, §189.) Over appellant's objection the jury was instructed on murder by means of lying in wait in terms of CALJIC No. 8.25:

> Murder which is immediately preceded by lying in wait is murder of the first degree.
>
> The term "lying in wait" is defined as a waiting and watching for an opportune time to act, together with a concealment by ambush or some other secret design to take the other person by surprise. The lying in wait need not continue for any particular period of time provided that its duration is such as to show a state of mind equivalent to premeditation or deliberation.
>
> To constitute murder by means of lying in wait there must be, in addition to the aforesaid conduct by the defendant, an intentional infliction upon the person killed of bodily harm involving a high degree of probability that it will result in death and which shows a wanton disregard for human life.

Appellant contends that (1) murder by means of lying in wait is inapplicable to the facts of this case, and (2) CALJIC No. 8.25 is inaccurate because it erroneously implies that specific intent to kill is unnecessary in this crime.

There was evidence that appellant and Gibson left the bar after the argument with the victim, that they were later seen several times driving through the bar parking lot watching the bar door, that after the victim and Mrs. Reel left the bar and entered her car, appellant and Gibson drove by once more, and that appellant then appeared at the door of the parked car and spoke before the victim was aware of his presence. He immediately thereafter shot the victim.

Lying in wait is sufficiently shown by proof of concealment and watchful waiting. The element of concealment may manifest itself by either an ambush or by the creation of a situation where the victim is taken unawares even though he sees his murderer. There was evidence here from which the jury could have concluded that appellant was waiting for the victim "with the intention of killing or inflicting injury upon [him], and that the killing was accomplished by the means of his watching and waiting in concealment." Therefore, it was not error to instruct on the theory of murder by means of lying in wait.

Appellant also contends that the instruction erroneously implies that intent to kill is not a necessary element of this type of first degree murder. Appellant argues that the fact of lying in wait merely dispenses with the necessity of finding premeditation and deliberation but that the other elements of murder, intent and malice, must be found. Specifically, appellant contends that the last paragraph of CALJIC No. 8.25 supra dispenses with intent to kill. The instruction states that lying in wait for a sufficient time shows a state of mind equivalent to premeditation and deliberation, and it goes on to say that there must also be an intentional infliction upon the person killed of bodily harm involving a high degree of probability that it will result in death and which shows a wanton disregard for human life. The latter statement is essentially a definition of implied malice.

Penal Code section 189 provides in pertinent part:

> All murder which is perpetrated by means of a destructive device or explosive, poison, lying in wait, torture, or by any other kind of willful, deliberate, and premeditated killing, or which is committed in the perpetration of, or attempt to perpetrate, arson, rape, robbery, burglary, mayhem, or any act punishable under Section 288, is murder of the first degree; and all other kinds of murders are of the second degree.

In People v. Thomas, 41 Cal. 2d 470, 261 P.2d 1, Justice Traynor, in a concurring opinion, explains:

> By the use of the phrase "or any *other* kind of willful, deliberate, and premeditated killing" (emphasis added) following the phrase "All murder which is perpetrated by means of poison, or lying in wait, torture," the Legislature identified murder committed by any of the enumerated means as a "kind of" willful, deliberate, and premeditated killing. Ordinarily, to prove that a killing was deliberate, and premeditated, evidence must be introduced from which the trier of fact can determine the state of mind of the defendant before he committed the act that resulted in his victim's death, that is, whether the killing resulted from a deliberate intention to take human life.
>
> [However], if the killing is murder within the meaning of Penal Code, sections 187 and 188, and is by one of the means enumerated in section 189, the use of such means makes the killing as a matter of law the equivalent of a "willful, deliberate, and premeditated killing." Since any question as to the defendant's

> willfulness, deliberation, and premeditation is taken from the trier of fact by force of the statute, it bears emphasis that a "killing" by one of the three means enumerated in the statute is not the equivalent of a "willful, deliberate, and premeditated killing" unless it is first established that it is murder. (People v. Thomas, 41 Cal. 2d 470, 477-478, 261 P.2d 1, 5.)

In People v. Dickerson, 23 Cal. App. 3d 721, 727, 100 Cal. Rptr. 533, the defendant argued that a specific intent to kill must be independently shown for murder by lying in wait to be first degree murder. He urged that a distinction be drawn between murder by poison and torture, specified in Penal Code section 189, [and murder by lying in wait] because the use of poison or torture in itself is extremely likely to produce death, while lying in wait is not, unless accompanied by an intent to kill. The court disagreed, stating:

> Even if we were to agree with defendant in his subjective classification, the obvious answer must be that the Legislature clearly does not. If the murder was perpetrated by means of lying in wait, it need not be independently determined to have been "willful, deliberate, and premeditated." [Citations.] The crime of which defendant was convicted was not lying in wait, but murder. If it was perpetrated by means of lying in wait it is, by definition, first degree murder. Defendant has offered no reason why such a definiton is contrary to law, and none is apparent. (23 Cal. App. 3d at p.727, 100 Cal. Rptr. at p.537.)

CALJIC No. 8.25 is a correct statement of the law. It first states that *murder* which is immediately preceded by lying in wait is murder of the first degree. This means that the jury must find that the killing was with malice aforethought. (Pen. Code, §187.) The instruction then defines implied malice which informs the jury that there must be an intentional infliction upon the person killed of bodily harm involving a high degree of probability that it will result in death, and which shows a wanton disregard for human life. Thus, there was no error in not instructing that murder by lying in wait must be accompanied by a specific intent to kill in order to be first degree murder.

Notes and Questions

1. Assume that Benjamin shot at Adams only with the intent to frighten or wound him. Is he nevertheless guilty of murder on a ground independent of §189? What ground? Even if he is guilty of murder, why should the fact that he waited for Adams in his car aggravate the murder to first-degree?

2. Do you agree with the court's interpretation of §189? Can you read that section to require proof of intent to kill where the state seeks a first-degree conviction on the ground that defendant was lying in wait?

3. In People v. Thomas, quoted in *Benjamin,* the defendant had a perversely plausible argument that he had not intended to kill the victim.

Thomas was a sexual sadist who gratified himself by shooting and wounding women. Before the killing, he had shot and wounded, but not killed, three other women. In the fourth incident, he shot at a woman, Mrs. Bice, at a lunch counter, intending to terrify her by shooting her coffee cup out of her hand. But Thomas was a poor shot, and the bullet killed her. The court had no trouble concluding that Thomas was at least guilty of "abandoned and malignant heart murder." In justifying the first-degree conviction under §189, Justice Traynor explained the lying-in-wait provision:

> Lying in wait requires the elements of waiting, watching, and concealment for the purpose of taking a victim unawares. It does not mean that the defendant's body must be in a lying position; it is immaterial whether he is lying, sitting, standing, or moving about, so long as the elements of waiting, watching, and concealment are all present for the purpose of taking the victim unawares. The defendant may either wait for his victim to come to his place of hiding or he may go to a hiding place near his victim and wait for a favorable moment to murder him.
>
> The duration of the waiting, watching, and concealment necessary to constitute lying in wait cannot be arbitrarily fixed in units of time, just as the time necessary for the ordinary willful, deliberate, and premeditated killing cannot be so fixed. There must, however, be substantial evidence of a long enough period of waiting and watching in concealment to show a state of mind equivalent to premeditation and deliberation before the court can properly give an instruction on lying in wait. It is now settled that a mere specific intent to kill is not enough to constitute first degree murder under the classification of "any other kind of willful, deliberate, and premeditated killing," and that there must be substantial evidence that the intent to kill was arrived at as a result of premeditation and deliberation. If it is claimed that the murder was by one of the means enumerated in section 189, there must also be substantial evidence of the use of such means. Thus in the case of murder by lying in wait it is not enough that the victim be unaware of the presence of his assailant until the fatal wound is inflicted. It is also necessary that there be substantial evidence of the elements of waiting and watching. Otherwise a killing that was the result of a rash impulse would be converted into first degree murder.
>
> In my opinion if the only evidence in this case was that with respect to the murder of Mrs. Bice, it would not be sufficient to sustain a finding of murder by means of lying in wait. Defendant saw deceased, a stranger to him, as he drove by in his automobile. He then drove around the block and parked in an alley in a position from which he could shoot at her. Standing alone, this evidence supplies no clue as to whether defendant was waiting and watching for an opportunity to shoot only after the opportunity presented itself. Moreover, the fact that after seeing his victim, he drove round the block and parked in a position from which he could shoot, is not, when considered by itself, evidence of lying in wait. His victim was then at hand. He did not drive round the block into the alley to watch and wait for her but only to enable him to shoot her. Any delay in doing so after he had located his victim in an exposed position would not contribute to his success in executing his crime, but only increase the possibility that his victim

might escape by moving from the area of danger. Thus unless defendant was watching and waiting for his victim before he came upon her, the murder was not committed by means of lying in wait.

The shooting of Mrs. Bice was not an isolated incident. On six other occasions defendant shot at women under similar circumstances. He carried his rifle with him in his automobile. His only motive for the shootings was sexual gratification. From this evidence the jury could reasonably infer that defendant drove about the city waiting and watching for whatever victims might present themselves. They could infer that he was waiting and watching for a victim on the night when he murdered decedent. Since in addition the murder was committed from a position of concealment, all of the elements necessary to constitute murder committed by means of lying in wait were present, and it was not error to present that theory to the jury.

3. First-Degree Felony Murder

PEOPLE v. STAMP
California Court of Appeal
2 Cal. App. 2d 203, 82 Cal. Rptr. 598 (1969)

Cobey, Associate Justice.

These are appeals by Jonathan Earl Stamp, Michael John Koory and Billy Dean Lehman, following jury verdicts of guilty of robbery and murder, both in the first degree. Each man was given a life sentence on the murder charge together with the time prescribed by law on the robbery count.

Defendants appeal their conviction of the murder of Carl Honeyman who, suffering from a heart disease, died between 15 and 20 minutes after Koory and Stamp held up his business, the General Amusement Company, on October 26, 1965, at 10:45 A.M. Lehman, the driver of the getaway car, was apprehended a few minutes after the robbery; several weeks later Stamp was arrested in Ohio and Koory in Nebraska. . . .

On this appeal appellants primarily rely upon their position that the felony-murder doctrine should not have been applied in this case due to the unforeseeability of Honeyman's death.

The Facts

Defendants Koory and Stamp, armed with a gun and a blackjack, entered the rear of the building housing the offices of General Amusement Company, [and] ordered the employees they found there to go to the front of the premises, where the two secretaries were working. Stamp, the one with the gun, then went into the office of Carl Honeyman, the owner and manager.

Thereupon Honeyman, looking very frightened and pale, emerged from the office in a "kind of hurry." He was apparently propelled by Stamp who had hold of him by an elbow.

The robbery victims were required to lie down on the floor while the robbers took the money and fled out the back door. As the robbers, who had been on the premises 10 to 15 minutes, were leaving, they told the victims to remain on the floor for five minutes so that no one would "get hurt."

Honeyman, who had been lying next to the counter, had to use it to steady himself in getting up off the floor. Still pale, he was short of breath, sucking air, and pounding and rubbing his chest. As he walked down the hall, in an unsteady manner, still breathing hard and rubbing his chest, he said he was having trouble "keeping the pounding down inside" and that his heart was "pumping too fast for him." A few minutes later, although still looking very upset, shaking, wiping his forehead and rubbing his chest, he was able to walk in a steady manner into an employee's office. When the police arrived, almost immediately thereafter, he told them he was not feeling very well and that he had a pain in his chest. About two minutes later, which was 15 to 20 minutes after the robbery had occurred, he collapsed on the floor. At 11:25 he was pronounced dead on arrival at the hospital. The coroner's report listed the immediate cause of death as heart attack.

The employees noted that during the hours before the robbery Honeyman had appeared to be in normal health and good spirits. The victim was an obese, sixty-year-old man, with a history of heart disease, who was under a great deal of pressure due to the intensely competitive nature of his business. Additionally, he did not take good care of his heart.

Three doctors, including the autopsy surgeon, Honeyman's physician, and a professor of cardiology from UCLA, testified that although Honeyman had an advanced case of atherosclerosis, a progressive and ultimately fatal disease, there must have been some immediate upset to his system which precipitated the attack. It was their conclusion in response to a hypothetical question that but for the robbery there would have been no fatal seizure at that time. The fright induced by the robbery was too much of a shock to Honeyman's system. There was opposing expert testimony to the effect that it  could not be said with reasonable medical certainty that fright could ever be fatal. . . .

Application of the Felony-Murder Rule

Appellants' contention that the felony-murder rule is inapplicable to the facts of this case is . . . without merit. Under the felony-murder rule of section 189 of the Penal Code, a killing committed in either the perpetration of or an attempt to perpetrate robbery is murder of the first degree. This is true whether the killing is willful, deliberate and premeditated, or merely accidental or unintentional, and whether or not the killing is planned as a part of the commission of the robbery. . . .

The doctrine presumes malice aforethought on the basis of the commission of a felony inherently dangerous to human life.[16] This rule is a rule of substantive law in California and not merely an evidentiary shortcut to finding malice as it withdraws from the jury the requirement that they find either express malice or the implied malice which is manifested in an intent to kill. Under this rule no intentional act is necessary other than the attempt to or the actual commission of the robbery itself. When a robber enters a place with a deadly weapon with the intent to commit robbery, malice is shown by the nature of the crime.

There is no requirement that the killing occur, "while committing" or "while engaged in" the felony, or that the killing be "a part of" the felony, other than that the few acts be a part of one continuous transaction. Thus the homicide need not have been committed "to perpetrate" the felony. There need be no technical inquiry as to whether there has been a completion or abandonment of or desistence from the robbery before the homicide itself was completed. . . .

The doctrine is not limited to those deaths which are foreseeable. Rather a felon is held strictly liable for *all* killings committed by him or his accomplices in the course of the felony. . . .

Appellants contend that the trial court erred in refusing their proffered instruction on proximate cause, reading as follows: "Where the defendant's criminal act is not the proximate cause of the death and the sole proximate cause was the negligent or reckless conduct of the victim, a conviction is unwarranted." They assert that Article VI, Section 13 of the California Constitution guarantees the right of a defendant to have the jury determine every material issue presented by the evidence.

It can be argued that the refusal of the trial court to give the instruction was justified. The evidence before the jury was not such that the jury could have reasonably assumed that negligent or reckless conduct by Honeyman was the *sole* cause of his death. (See People v. Bronson, 263 Cal. App. 2d 831, 842-843, 70 Cal. Rptr. 162, hear. den.) But, in any event, the three instructions given on the issue of the proximate causation of Honeyman's death were much more complete and accurate than appellants' quoted instruction.[17] Any error in this respect was harmless.

The judgment is affirmed.

SCHWEITZER and ALLPORT, JJ., concur.

16. In view of the fact that the Legislature has not seen fit to change the language of Penal Code section 189 since the decisions holding that the requisite malice aforethought is to be implied from the commission of those felonies inherently dangerous to human life, it must be presumed that these cases accurately state the law.

17. "If the death of the victim occurred by natural causes and was not a proximate result of the defendants' unlawful activity, you must find the defendant not guilty of murder.

Notes and Questions

1. What type of homicide, if any, would the defendants in *Stamp* be guilty of if there were no felony-murder rule? Does felony murder make sense in this case? Review the purposes for having a felony-murder rule listed in *Burroughs* in Chapter 6.

2. What about defendant Lehman? He had no contact with Honeyman, but was in the getaway car the entire time. Should he still be liable for felony murder? (We offer some guidance on this problem on page 402.)

3. To appreciate the reach of the felony-murder rule, one must understand that the reach of the underlying felonies has been greatly expanded since their common law origins. For example, consider the California burglary statute, Penal Code §487:

> Every person who enters any house, room, apartment, tenement, shop, warehouse, store, mill, barn, stable, outhouse or other building, tent, vessel, railroad, car, trailer, coach, as defined in Section 635 of the Vehicle Code, any house, car, as defined in Section 243 of the Vehicle Code, vehicle as defined by the Vehicle Code when the doors of such vehicle are locked, aircraft as defined by the Harbors and Navigation Code, mine or any underground portion thereof, with intent to commit grand or petit larceny or any felony is guilty of burglary.

burglary case

Carolyn Cautious coveted a tennis bag owned by Tom, a healthy young man. She spotted it in Tom's car, which was parked downtown while Tom was having a haircut. Carolyn used her illegal master key to open the car door, and, just as she did, Tom, whose appointment took less time than usual, turned the corner and saw her. As he shouted "Stop thief!" he carelessly entered the street, where he was fatally struck by a car. Is Carolyn guilty of first-degree murder? Under *Stamp,* are there limiting principles in the felony-murder rule which can save her?

4. The most common felonies enumerated by first degree felony-murder statutes are arson, rape, robbery, burglary, deviate sexual intercourse by force

---

"To constitute a felonious homicide there must be, in addition to the death of a human being, an unlawful act which proximately caused that death.

"The proximate cause of death is that cause which, in natural and continuous sequence, unbroken by any efficient intervening cause, produces the death, and without which the result would not have occurred. It is the efficient cause—the one that necessarily sets in operation the factors that accomplish the death." (CALJIC No. 312, modified.)

"If a person unlawfully does an act or unlawfully sets in operation factors which are a proximate cause of another person's death, such conduct of the former constitutes an unlawful homicide even though the unlawful act or the factors set in operation were not the only cause of the death, and although the person killed had been already enfeebled by disease, injury, physical condition or other cause and although it is probable that a person in sound physical condition would not have died as a result of the act or the factors set in operation, and although it is probable that the act or the factors set in operation only hastened the death of the deceased person and that he would have died soon thereafter anyhow from another cause or other causes." (CALJIC No. 313-B, modified.)

or threat of force, and kidnapping. Statistics measuring the relation of total felonies to homicides occurring during the felony for robbery, rape, burglary, and auto theft are given below in the Commentary to Section 210.2 of the Model Penal Code:

In fact, the number of all homicides which occur in the commission of such crimes as robbery, burglary, or rape is lower than might be expected. For example, comparison of the figures for solved and unsolved homicides from M. Wolfgang, Criminal Homicide (1958), with statistics on basic felonies taken from the FBI Uniform Crime Reports reveals the following for Philadelphia from 1948-1952:

Relation of Total Felonies to Homicides Occuring During the Felony Philadelphia 1948-1952

Offense	*No. of crimes reported*	*No. accompanied by homicide*	*%*	*No. per 1000*
Robbery	6,432	38	0.59	5.9
Rape	1,133	4	0.35	3.5
Burglary	27,669	1	0.0036	.036
Auto Theft	10,315	2	0.019	.19

Similar figures are found in Cook County, Illinois, robbery statistics from 1926-1930. There were 71 murders committed during robberies in Cook County during 1926 and 1927. Illinois Crime Survey 610 (1929). Although robbery statistics for those years are not available, 7,196 robberies were committed in the county in 1930. Assuming this number of robberies in 1926 and 1927, it appears that only .49 per cent of the robberies in those two years resulted in homicide. More recent statistics derived from N.J. State Police, Crime in New Jersey: Uniform Crime Reports 42-45 (1975) reveal strikingly similar percentages. In 1975, there were 1,382 forcible rapes and 111,264 forcible breaking-and-enterings in New Jersey in addition to the 16,273 robberies. These crimes resulted in 136 deaths. Thus only .10 percent of these serious felonies resulted in homicide.

Recall that one of the purposes of the felony-murder rule is to deter people from committing felonies. Do the above statistics refute this purpose? With probabilities so low, would the felony-murder rule deter anybody from committing a felony?

5. The authors of a detailed study[18] of a sample of robberies in Chicago note another aspect of the robbery murder rule:

In most American jurisdictions, what is popularly called the felony murder rule is really two rules. The first is the "malice rule," which holds that the

18. F. Zimring and J. Zuehl, Victim Injury and Death in Urban Robbery: A Chicago Study. To be published in the January 1986 issue of The Journal of Legal Studies.

intention to commit a forcible felony is a substitute for, or equivalent, to the mental state of malice usually required to hold an offender accountable for murder when causing another's death. In the array of knife, gun, bottle, baseball bat, and beating deaths that we observed in this study, the principal effect of bypassing a requirement of the mental state of malice is the generation of murder liability for accomplices in robbery for the lethal acts of their confederates.

The second felony-murder rule, usually provided by statute, is the automatic upgrading of any murder involving a robbery to the status of first degree, as well as the automatic inclusion of the robbery as a circumstance that generates eligibility for the death penalty in those state criminal codes that include capital punishment.

Malice

On the malice question the relevance of our data depend on the reason for the rule. The most powerful arguments both in favor of and against the so-called malice rule have little to do with the structure of robbery in the ordinary course of events. They are questions, instead, of how to balance ease of prosecution of co-felons against the injustices of implicating pacific accomplices in unanticipated lethal events. This trade-off turns out to be an extraordinarily difficult question to investigate empirically. In most robbery killings, malice on the part of the lethal actor in a robbery scenario is anything but difficult to infer. The culpability of co-defendants is more difficult to determine. Difficulty of proof is the reason why the malice rule is both supported as necessary and attacked as unjust. The defenders of the rule note that the conclusive presumption is the only way to secure convictions of the accomplices in robbery offenses. Yet using difficulty of proof to reach that result increases the risk of possible injustice of a murder liability based solely upon involvement in a robbery.

The low base probabilities of death associated with any combination of weapon and situation may seem to some readers to fall well below the malice standard. But here, too, the numbers do not compel a policy conclusion. It is our view, consistent with critical criminal law scholarship on this issue over a number of years, that a malice rule imputed to accomplices without evidence of complicity in the lethal act is incorrect, overbroad and inappropriate. But this value preference is not derived from the present data, which add little to what is already known.

If, however, the malice rule is intended to save the lives of robbery victims, as prominent cases have recently stated, then our data suggest that the rule would better serve its ends if it were restricted to more lethal weapons. If the weapon specific death rate is a good measure of the rate of accidental and negligent dangerous behavior, restricting the scope of the malice rule to robberies with guns, knives, and other equally dangerous instruments might be expected to produce offsetting effects, with life-saving benefits outweighing costs. Some potential offenders, presently afraid of the wider malice rule, might take up robbery with personal force once the rule was cut back. Other personal force robbers could be more careless in the conduct of robbery without lethal weapons. However, some robbers who might otherwise use lethal weapons might be channeled into robbery attempts without such weapons if the scope of the malice rule were so restricted.

How much such channeling behavior might take place is a matter of conjecture. In our view, the likelihood that the malice rule itself or any variation in it would have a measurable or significant influence on robbery behavior is very small. But that may be beside the point. If the saving of life is regarded as the primary purpose of the malice rule, the large differences noted in death rates make restricting its operation to deadly weapons a good bet. If such a restriction generated eight new personal force robberies for every gun robbery converted into a personal force crime, it would still save lives. Any smaller ratio would increase the benefits. A sense of justice and statistics on relative death risk convergently argue for narrowing the rule.

Automatic Upgrading

We also believe that the information about robbery killings reported above undermines the basis for the automatic liability for first degree murder based on the existence of a predicate robbery. The many borderline cases between robbery and non-robbery killing have been important both in the estimates of robbery homicide and in its implications for criminological theory. For the cases on the borderline, we felt that the ultimate classification made little difference. The conclusion seemed appropriate for penal treatment as well.

Note that the punishment difference between second and first degree murder is enormous in most jurisdictions. If legislative trends toward huge minimum prison terms as the minimum sanction for first degree murder continue, the importance of defining the border between first and second degree murder in a morally acceptable way becomes greater. A lethal drug ripoff is a terrible thing, but how much more so than a shooting generated by a fight for territorial rights to sell drugs? The old man purposefully and violently mugged but accidentally killed by a group of teen-aged boys may call for serious punishment. But the same punishment should not necessarily be meted out to the adolescent who used the lead pipe and to his accomplice who stripped the wallet and stood by.

All three elements of the common modern equation that produces these results are individually problematic: the malice felony murder rule, the automatic treatment of robbery murders as first degree, and the mandatory minimum punishment for all first degree murders. They interact to produce an unprincipled rigidity which is even more troublesome.

The conceptual problems associated with the treatment of felony killings in the criminal law of homicide can, of course, be addressed without the benefit of empirical studies of robbery and robbery killing. The Chicago data add three dimensions to these theoretical concerns. First, the present study suggests that it is frequently quite difficult to determine whether a criminal homicide involves robbery. Adding another element of guesswork in the fact finding process, and then making momentous differences in outcome hinge on the characterization is a recurrent problem according to our data.

The present study helps illuminate a second problem associated with rigid regimes and special treatment for classified robbery cases. The homicide so treated will frequently depart from the paradigm cases that inspired the legislation creating special treatment. In Chicago, difficult-to-characterize residential cases occur almost as often as commercial robbery and street robbery deaths combined. The important minority of non-stranger and drug cases are as frequent as commercial robbery killings. Some of these non-paradigm cases may be more hideous, and more worthy of extreme penal sanctions than the archetypal robbery death. But these are not the classes of cases that inspired the special legislation.

Finally, to illustrate what we see as the problem of the penological relevance of the robbery category being associated with sharp differences in minimum prison terms, consider the following three case summaries:

1. The body of the victim, Jimmy Ray Christian, was found in the front seat of his parked car. Christian, who was twenty-nine years old, white and married had been shot once in the chest, probably two days earlier, while he was in the car. His wallet, its contents, and car keys were not found by the police, but they did find several packets of a white powdery substance under the front seat. The doors of the car were locked when the police arrived. A neighbor saw the car pull over and park around 6:00 A.M. two days earlier. The victim had left his home around 5:00 A.M. that morning according to his wife. He worked in Skokie and although he was not due to begin working until 7:30 A.M., he usually left home quite early. His wife reported knowing nothing about any illegal behavior or problems her husband might have had.

2. The victim, Irene Factor, was strangled to death in the living room of her home by Phillip Ramirez, a tenant, who she thought had come to pay her $50 in back due rent. After killing the victim, Ramirez, a twenty year old, married Hispanic took $60 from the victim's purse along with some rent receipts and then fled. Factor was a seventy-five year old, white woman who lived alone. Instead of bringing the money he owed her, Ramirez brought a length of clothesline, he later confessed to police. After the victim berated him for failing to produce the money, he strangled her with the rope.

The police reports do not indicate clearly the offender's intentions when he arrived at the victim's home. The presence of the clothesline suggests that from the start he may have intended to kill the victim. The fact that he killed her at a time when he was expected to visit her house suggests that he planned poorly or than he acted somewhat spontaneously.

The motive for the killing is also not clear. Ramirez had reason to be angry with his landlady: the day before she had announced that he would have to vacate the apartment. His minimal effort to obtain valuables after the killing is inconsistent with a planned robbery. The question of whether the $60 was taken after and independent of the fatal attack would seem crucial to the legal classification of the murder as felony related.

3. Charles Mundock was stabbed to death in the bedroom of his home by one or more offenders who remain unknown to the police. When the police arrived at the scene they found that the victim's automobile was missing and they suspected that items from his wallet had been taken. The car was later recovered on the other side of town. The victim, a 42 year old, black college teacher, was a homosexual who also sold drugs. No drugs were found at the scene by police. The evening before the incident, the victim attended several

parties. His naked body was found with as many as fifteen stab wounds. The bedroom was in disarray, apparently the result of a struggle.

The unclothed condition of the victim's body, the absence of any indication of forced entry, and the brutal nature of the killing suggest to the police that the offender and victim had some prior relationship. The motive for the killing and its relation to the taking of property remain unclear.

Two of the cases (1 and 3) are taken from the "motive unknown" killings nominated as possible robberies in the re-rating process. The third (#2) is a police classified robbery in a residential setting. We cannot claim the cases represent typical cases in the categories from which they are drawn. But they are not atypical of a substantial number of cases in each category.

Is case #2 a robbery killing? When the defendant formed the intent to take the money must be inferred from events. Arming himself is consistent both with an attempt to steal and to attack without theft. A sharp difference in punishment tied to the robbery label makes guesswork more fateful. But the deeper point is that the intent to take property prior to the attack does not seem an important element in determining a just penalty in this case. The Ramirez crime might be an admirable candidate for the highest grade of murder, but the theft element seems low on the list of reasons why.

Is case #3 robbery murder or murder followed by theft? Should it make a great deal of difference? Our hunch is that the same prior relationship, motive for attack, and offender characteristics were present in either event. The same might well be true for case #1. Further, none of these cases apparently fit the image of robbery killing that motivated an automatic first degree classification.

These cases are not infrequent. Any law professor worth his critical salt can draft a clever hypothetical to show the presence or absence of theft by force as a morally trivial element in a homicide that leads to widely different degrees of penal liability. What these data go a long way toward showing is that this has become a major problem in the administration of the criminal law of homicide, a problem not unrelated to concerns about plea bargaining, sentencing equity, equality of punishment, and the incoherence of the substantive criminal law here invoking its largest sanctions.

6. One author[19] has attributed the persistence of the felony-murder rule to class and race bias:

Although the drafters of the MPC were outraged by strict liability penal offenses they did retain a form of strict liability with respect to the felony-murder rule. Felony-murder is usually a crime of the lower classes in the United States. In any given year over two-thirds of the willful homicides are committed by a friend, acquaintance, relative, or some other person who has some contact with the victim. That is why willful homicide has the highest arrest rate of any major felony. Moreover, murder is primarily an intra-racial crime, that is, whites kill whites and blacks kill blacks and so on.

19. W. Gordon, Crime and Criminal Law: The California Experience 1960-75 at 13-14, 52-53 (1981).

But felony-murder is an exception to this rule. A felony-murder involves a situation in which a killing takes place while a person is committing or attempting to commit a robbery, burglary, rape, or other dangerous felony. FBI data for 1974 indicate that twenty-eight percent of the homicides committed in the United States during that year were felony-murders, sixty percent of which occurred during the commission of robbery. Felony-murder often is an interracial killing, with blacks killing whites the most common pattern. In 1974, sixty-three percent of the victims of felony-murder were white.

The felony-murder rule provides that if a death takes place during the commission of an enumerated dangerous felony, the defendant is strictly liable for the deaths that result. It makes no difference if the defendant did not have the *mens rea* for murder; that is, if the defendant had no intent to kill and the killing in fact took place accidently he still is strictly liable for the deaths that ensue. The United States is the only major industrial nation that retains the felony-murder rule. England abolished the rule in 1957 and it is unknown in Continental Europe. The felony-murder rule is made more significant by the fact that the death penalty is imposed in felony-murders more frequently than in the other homicides, which usually are crimes of passion.

The MPC retained a modified version of the felony-murder rule. In effect it sought to mitigate the harshness of the rule by allowing the defendant to present evidence that the killing was unintentional or accidental. This was a compromise that the drafters of the MPC made in order to get the support of the prosecutorial lobby within the ALI. The drafters were aware that it was a compromise of their principled position against strict liability to accept a modified form of strict liability. This compromise reveals the class bias of the drafters of the MPC. They expressed outrage about strict liability; they eliminated the adverse consequences of a conviction of such an offense for the upper classes through the concept of the "violation." However, they retained a form of strict liability for the lower classes through the felony-murder rule; a conviction of violation of this rule often results in the death penalty.

Nor, according to the author, did the draftsmen of California's proposed Penal Code do any better:

Rex Collings, a professor at Boalt Hall and a member of the university staff, was a special consultant to the ALI and one of the drafters of the MPC sections on violent crime, particularly homicide. He drafted the proposals on homicide, creating one crime of murder which required a culpability level of intent, knowledge or recklessness "manifesting extreme indifference to the value of human life." The professors made no recommendation on the retention of the death penalty. However, they recommended that if it was retained it should apply in only three situations: (1) murder of a peace officer or a person assisting a peace officer in the performance of his duties; (2) murder by a life term convict; and (3) murder for hire. These proposals were made in 1968 which was a period of increasing public support for the death penalty, terminating a trend of declining public support that had characterized the preceding decade. By leaving the decision as to whether or not to impose the death penalty to the legislature, the professors were, in effect, acquiescing in the virtual certainty that the legislature would include it in any revised penal code. Nor was there any reason to believe that either the public or the legislature would place the limits on the penalty the professors proposed.

In the definition of murder, the professors retained a modified version of the felony-murder rule. The felony-murder rule is a strict liability rule which holds that an offender is guilty of first degree murder when he kills during certain enumerated felonies, even if he did not have the *mens rea* (or moral blameworthiness) for first degree murder. What separates a first degree murder from other killings is the mental element or *mens rea.* The felony-murder rule, however, does away with the *mens rea* requirement for the killings if it was committed during the course of a dangerous enumerated felony. This rule eases the burden of proof for the prosecution in first degree murder cases with the result that an offender can lose his life for an accidental or negligent killing which, in the non-felony-murder situation, would amount only to manslaughter or second degree murder. The professors were well aware of this problem and how it contradicted their moral aversion to strict penal liability. "The felony-murder doctrine," the professors wrote, "is impossible to defend on principle when applied to homicides committed accidentally or negligently."

The professors chose not to follow their principles in this matter, however, and compromised. They proposed a half-way measure, based on the MPC formulation, which would place on the defendant the burden of proof that he was not so reckless as to manifest an extreme indifference to human life which the rule presumed because the killing took place in the context of an enumerated felony. The professors posed the issue in these terms:

> Suppose that *A* shot and killed a store owner during a robbery. *B,* charged as an accomplice, might testify that it was understood between him and *A* that the gun would not be loaded. *B,* if believed, could be said to have raised a reasonable doubt as to the act and rebutted the presumption.

However, the compromise in reality would not significantly change the impact of the felony-murder rule. First, the rule has obvious racial implications since the crime statistics indicate that the most common felony-murder involves a young black offender and a white victim. In most cases the testimony of the offender would not be believed and he would face the death sentence for a possible negligent or accidental killing. In ordinary circumstances this would not be a first degree murder but it is made into one by the strict liability felony-murder rule. The professors, of course, were passionately against strict liability when a businessman might spend a short period in jail but could compromise on the issue when [predominantly] lower class black offenders were involved, who could lose their lives if the legislature did not choose to limit the application of the death penalty. The whole thrust of the penal law has been to place the most stringent limitations on the state when it seeks to take a life except in the case of the felony-murder rule. Second, placing the burden of proof on the defendant, as the professors proposed, in such a life or death situation probably is unconstitutional since it denies the accused due process of law. Professor Herbert Packer was initially an enthusiastic supporter of the formulation of the MPC on felony-murder, calling it "an ingenious solution to the problem." Later, however, after his experience with the [attempted California Penal Code Revision] he changed

his position. Professor Packer died in 1972, and in his last published article he argued that the "doctrine is odious because it can make homicides that are accidental into murder." In addition, he felt that the MPC compromise conceded too much to the prosecutorial lobby.

7. As the previous excerpt notes, the Model Penal Code also abolished the rule as a fixed rule of law, but retained it as a kind of presumption. See §210.2, Chapter 6. What sense, other than political sense, does this solution make?

8. Judicial efforts to limit the scope of the felony-murder rule seen in *Burroughs,* supra page 323, also apply to first degree felony-murder. One court, the Supreme Court of Michigan, has abolished the felony-murder rule outright. See People v. Aaron, 299 N.W.2d 304 (Mich. 1980).

Some courts have elected to narrow the rule's reach through creative reading of felony-murder statutes or by other means, while others have applied the rule rigorously. The following cases map some of the twists and turns of the felony-murder rule that this dissonance has created.

PEOPLE v. GLADMAN

Court of Appeals of New York
41 N.Y.2d 124, 359 N.E.2d 420 (1976)

JASEN, Judge.

On this appeal, defendant argues that his shooting of a police officer did not occur, as a matter of law, in immediate flight from a robbery and that, therefore, his conviction for felony-murder should be set aside. We hold that, under the circumstances presented, the issue of whether the homicide was committed in immediate flight from the robbery was properly presented to the jury as a question of fact. The order of the Appellate Division, therefore, should be affirmed.

At trial, the People submitted overwhelming evidence, largely the confession of the defendant and the testimony of several eyewitnesses, that on the night of December 29, 1971, the defendant shot and killed Nassau County Police Officer Richard Rose in a bowling alley parking lot. The events of that evening can be briefly recited. At approximately 8:00 P.M., defendant obtained a ride to the County Line Shopping Center in Amityville, New York. Ten minutes later, he entered a delicatessen, produced a gun, and demanded money from the clerk. The clerk turned over about $145 in cash and checks. After the robbery, Gladman left the shopping center and walked through the surrounding neighborhood, eventually arriving at the County Line Bowling Alley. In the meantime, the robbery had been reported to the Nassau County Police Department and an alert was transmitted over the police radio. Two officers arrived at the delicatessen at 8:16 P.M., just minutes after the defendant had left. A description of the robber was obtained and broadcast over the police radio. Normal police procedure required that unassigned patrol cars proceed to the vicinity of the crime area and any nearby major intersections in an effort to seal off potential avenues of escape. As Gladman walked onto the parking lot of the bowling alley, he saw a police car turn and enter the lot. He hid under a parked car. Patrolman Rose, the lone officer in the car, emerged from his vehicle and walked over to defendant's hiding place. The defendant got up from underneath the car with his gun concealed between his legs. The officer ordered the defendant to put his weapon on the car hood; instead, the defendant turned and fired. Patrolman Rose, mortally wounded, struggled to his police car and attempted to use the radio to summon the assistance of brother officers. He collapsed on the seat. The defendant commandeered the automobile of a bowling alley patron and made good his escape. An off-duty New York City police officer used Rose's radio to broadcast a signal for help. The report of the shooting went over the police radio at 8:24 P.M. Eyewitnesses fixed the time of the altercation at approximately 8:25 P.M. The bowling alley was located less than one-half mile from the robbed delicatessen.

Defendant was subsequently captured, identified by eyewitnesses, . . . indicted [and convicted]. . . .

. . . The principal issue on this appeal is whether the jury was properly permitted to conclude that the shooting of Officer Rose occurred in the immediate flight from the delicatessen robbery.

A felony murder is committed when a person, acting alone or in concert with others, commits or attempts to commit one of nine predicate felonies, of which robbery is one, and "in the course of and in furtherance of such crime or of immediate flight therefrom, he, or another participant, if there be any, causes the death of a person other than one of the participants." (Penal Law, Sec. 125.25, subd. 3.) By operation of law, the intent necessary to sustain a murder conviction is inferred from the intent to commit a specific, serious, felonious act, even though the defendant, in truth, may not have intended to kill. Here, the jury, by its verdict, found that the defendant did not possess a murderous intent. The question is whether the jury could properly find that the killing of Officer Rose was in the immediate area from the robbery, thus triggering the application of the felony murder doctrine. To resolve the issue, it is first necessary to refer to the checkered case law in this State, applying the felony murder concepts to cases, such as this one, where the fatal wounds were inflicted in the course of escape.

Under old statutes which did not specifically address the issue[20] it was early held that a killing committed during an escape could, under some cir-

20. The Penal Code defined felony murder as a killing "[w]ithout a design to effect death, by a person engaged in the commission of, or in an attempt to commit a felony, either upon or affecting the person or otherwise." (Penal Code, Sec. 183.) The Penal Law of 1909 carried forward this definition in identical language. (Penal Law [1909], Sec. 1044, subd. 2.)

cumstances, constitute a felony murder. In People v. Giro, 197 N.Y. 152, 90 N.E. 432, burglars aroused a slumbering family, the son struggled with one intruder and when the mother went to the aid of her child, she was shot dead. In affirming subsequent convictions, the court stated that the defendants committed actions in furtherance of their design to rob the house and "escape was as much a part thereof as breaking in with the jimmy or stealing the pocketbook. When they armed themselves to enter upon a felonious undertaking, shooting was the natural and probable result in order to get away if discovered, and if either fired the fatal shot both are responsible." *Giro,* however, was a case where the defendants got away with some loot. A different result was reached in People v. Hüter, 184 N.Y. 237, 77 N.E. 6, where the defendant broke into a bake shop and, when discovered, was in the act of removing egg crates from the store and placing them in his wagon. On discovery, defendant and his companion abandoned the wagon and fled on foot. A watchman summoned a police officer, the officer chased the defendant, and was fatally shot. The court held that a felony murder conviction could not be sustained. The hot pursuit of the watchman and the police officer "did not operate to continue the burglary after the defendant had abandoned the property that he undertook to carry away and had escaped from the premises burglarized. In all of the cases to which our attention has been called, in which persons have been convicted of murder in the first degree by reason of the killing of a person while the accused was engaged in the commission of a burglary, the killing took place upon the premises." Although the defendant had armed himself in preparation of a possible escape, this did not serve to continue an "abandoned" crime. Rather, this was a factor that the jury could consider in finding that the defendant had intended to kill anyone who crossed his criminal path, thereby justifying conviction for an intentional killing. These kinds of analyses soon led to the development of some rather arbitrary rules. If the defendant left the premises without the loot, the criminal action was deemed either terminated or abandoned and a subsequent homicide would not be a felony murder. On the other hand, both presence on the premises and retention of loot were not regarded as conclusive proof of felony continuation, but were merely evidence that the felony was continuing. The term premises was rather strictly confined to "within the four walls of the building" and a killing on an immediately adjoining public street would not be a killing on the "premises."

The later New York cases indicate some dissatisfaction with the strict legal rules that had developed and tended to leave the question of escape killings to the jury as a question of fact, under appropriate instructions. The change was to point out "generally that the killing to be felony murder must occur while the actor or one or more of his confederates is engaged in securing the plunder or in doing something immediately connected with the underlying crime, that escape may, under certain unities of time, manner and place, be a matter so immediately connected with the crime as to be part of its commission but that, where there is no reasonable doubt of a complete intervening desistence from the crime, as by the abandonment of the loot and running away, the subsequent homicide is not murder in the first degree without proof of deliberation and intent. The question of termination of the underlying felony was then left to the jury as a fact question.

The New York approach was more rigid than that developed in other jurisdictions. The majority of the States tended to follow the "res gestae" theory—i.e., whether the killing was committed in, about and as a part of the underlying transaction. California had adopted the res gestae theory, at least insofar as robbery is concerned, holding that a robbery is not complete if the "conspirators have not won their way even momentarily to a place of temporary safety and the possession of the plunder is nothing more than a scrambling possession. In such a case the continuation of the use of arms which was necessary to aid the felon in reducing the property to possession is necessary to protect him in its possession and in making good his escape. . . . The escape of the robbers with the loot, by means of arms, necessarily is as important to the execution of the plan as gaining possession of the property. Without revolvers to terrify, or, if occasion requires, to kill any person who attempts to apprehend them at the time of or immediately upon gaining possession of said property, their plan would be childlike." Subsequent case law indicates that, in California, the robbery is ongoing simply if the culprit had failed to reach a place of temporary safety. The comparative rigidity of the New York approach has been explained as stemming from the fact that, at the time, New York, with a minority of other States, provided that all felonies would support a conviction for felony murder. Of course, felony murder was also a capital offense and the cases attempted to narrow the scope of liability particularly where it was an accomplice that did the actual killing.

The 1967 Penal Law limited the application of the felony murder concept to nine serious and violent predicate felonies. At the same time, it was provided that the doctrine would apply to a killing committed in "immediate flight." This change was intended to do away with many of the old technical distinctions relating to "abandonment" or "completion."

Under the new formulation, the issue of whether the homicide occurred in "immediate flight" from a felony is only rarely to be considered as a question of law for resolution by the court. Only where the record compels the inference that the actor was not in "immediate flight" may a felony murder conviction be set aside on the law. Rather, the question is to be submitted to the jury, under an appropriate charge. The jury should be instructed to give consideration to whether the homicide and the felony occurred at the same location or, if not, to the distance separating the two locations. Weight may also be placed on whether there is an interval of time between the commission of the felony and the commission of the homicide. The jury may properly consider such additional factors as whether the culprits had possession of the fruits of criminal activity, whether the police, watchmen or concerned citizens were in close pursuit, and whether the criminals had reached a place of temporary safety. These factors are not exclusive; others may be appropriate in differing factual settings. If anything, past history demonstrates the fruitlessness of attempting to apply rigid rules to virtually limitless factual variations. No single factor is necessarily controlling; it is the combination of several factors that leads to a justifiable inference.

In this case, the jury could properly find, as a question of fact, that the killing of Officer Rose occurred in immediate flight from the delicatessen robbery. The shooting occurred less than 15 minutes after the robbery and less than a half mile away. The defendant had made off with cash proceeds and was attempting to secure his possession of the loot. The police had reason to believe that the robber was still in the immediate vicinity and had taken steps to seal off avenues of escape. In this regard, the absence of proof as to why Officer Rose turned into the bowling alley parking lot is no deficiency. The standard is not whether the police officer subjectively believed that the defendant was the robber. Indeed, the defendant's own apprehension may be more valuable. The defendant's response to the observation of the police car was to seek an immediate hiding place. This indicates that the defendant perceived that the police were on his trail. The record does not indicate that the officer knew or supposed, that defendant committed a crime; it does indicate that the defendant feared that the officer possessed such knowledge. Additionally, the defendant had not reached any place of temporary safety. In short, there is evidence from which the jury could conclude, as it did, that the defendant was in immediate flight from the robbery and that he shot the officer in order to make good his escape with the loot. The jury was properly charged as to the relevant considerations and we see no basis for disturbing its findings. . . .

The order of the Appellate Division should be affirmed.

BREITEL, C.J., and GABRIELLI, JONES, WACHTLER, FUCHSBERG and COOKE, JJ., concur.

Order affirmed.

Notes and Questions

1. Does the court lay down any standards with which to measure the duration of a felony? If not, why not? Is flexibility in this instance good or bad? Why?

2. If a felon is chased by police officers for two hours after committing a crime, is he still in immediate flight? What if the chase is ten hours? Two days? Does it make sense for purposes of the felony-murder rule to say that the felony has ceased if the pursuers lose the felon's trail, allowing the felon to reach a place of temporary safety, even though they regain the trail quickly? In order to answer this kind of question don't we have to know which answer comports best with the policies underlying the felony-murder rule? What are those policies? Why should a felony ever end—at least before the felons have all been brought to justice?

PEOPLE v. CABALTERO
California Court of Appeal
31 Cal. App. 2d 52, 87 P.2d 364 (1939)

KNIGHT, Justice.

The defendants, C. Cabaltero, Benny Flores, Marcella Avelino, Domingo Velasco, [and] Delmacio Dasalla, . . . were accused jointly by an information containing two counts with having committed first degree robbery and first degree murder, it being alleged in the first count that armed with pistols they robbed one J. Nishida of about $1,300, and in the second count that while perpetrating said robbery they killed and murdered one Pedro Ancheta. . . .

The robbery was committed on a farm near Campbell, in Santa Clara county. It was one of several farms operated in that county by Nishida, a Japanese, upon which he employed many Filipino laborers, among them being Fred and Marcella Avelino. Being so employed, the Avelinos knew that it was Nishida's custom to pay the wages of his men in cash about the noon hours on a certain day of the week, in a building on this particular farm near Campbell; and the Avelinos entered into a conspiracy with Dasalla, Flores, Velasco, Cabaltero and Ancheta (all . . . residents of San Francisco), to rob Nishida at that time and place; and the robbery was carried out as planned. Fred Avelino was not on the premises at the time of the robbery, but all of the others were present and actively participated therein, and all except Marcella Avelino were armed. Cabaltero waited nearby with an automobile to provide means of escape; Marcella Avelino entered the farm building with other Filipino laborers ostensibly to receive his wages, but in fact to start an altercation with Nishida, so that during the confusion the robbery could be perpetrated. Velasco and Ancheta stood guard at the outer door, while Dasalla and Flores entered the building, and with drawn pistols held up Nishida, forcibly taking from him approximately $1,200. After seizing the money Dasalla and Flores started for the outer door, but before reaching it two shots were fired from the outside, and as Dasalla made his exit through the door he shot and fatally wounded Ancheta. As a witness in his own behalf he denied having done so, but Nishida testified positively that he saw him fire the shot, and then saw Dasalla, Flores and Velasco assist Ancheta, who had fallen, to the waiting automobile in which they made their escape. From the scene of the robbery they drove to a ranch just north of Gilroy, where they left the wounded Ancheta. Later that same afternoon Cabaltero and Flores were arrested on the highway some little distance from the ranch, but Dasalla and Velasco succeeded in making their way back to San Francisco. Some time during the night Ancheta was removed to the county hospital, and about two weeks later he died from the effects of the gunshot wounds. Shortly after Ancheta's death Dasalla and Velasco were arrested in San Francisco. Part of the evidence introduced by the prosecution against Velasco consisted of a confession made by him to an officer shortly after his arrest, wherein he related the circumstances attending the shooting of Ancheta. In this regard he stated, so the officer testified, that while the robbery was being perpetrated, an automobile drove up in which were two Filipinos; that Ancheta commanded them to stay in the car, but they jumped out and started to run, whereupon Ancheta fired two shots at them; that immediately following the firing of the shots Dasalla emerged through the door of the building and exclaiming to Ancheta, "Damn you, what did you shoot for," fired a shot at Ancheta; that Ancheta fell wounded, and that they, Velasco, Dasalla and Flores picked him up and assisted him to the waiting automobile in which they fled.

The murder charge was based on section 189 of the Penal Code, and all of the essential elements thereof were pleaded in the charge. Said section declares that "All murder which is . . . committed in the perpetration or attempt to perpetrate arson, rape, robbery, burglary, or mayhem, is murder of the first degree . . ."; and it is well settled that one who kills another under such circumstances is guilty of murder of the first degree by force of the statute, altogether regardless of any question of intent. The killing may be willful, deliberate and premeditated, or it may be absolutely accidental; in either case the slayer is equally guilty since the statute applies to all homicide so committed, not merely to such as might be planned as a part of the execution of the felony intended; and it is proper so to instruct the jury. Furthermore, it is well established that if a homicide is committed by one of several confederates while engaged in perpetrating the crime of robbery in furtherance of a common purpose, the person or persons engaged with him in the perpetration of the robbery but who did not actually do the killing, are as accountable to the law as though their own hands had intentionally fired the fatal shot or given the fatal blow, and such killing is murder of the first degree. The jury has no option but to return a verdict of murder of the first degree whether the killing was intentionally or accidentally done, and it is proper so to instruct the jury.

In the present case the jury was instructed in conformity with the foregoing doctrines, and there is no claim made that any of the instructions given in that behalf incorrectly set forth any of the principles of law upon which those doctrines are founded. But appellants argue that because Ancheta, the person killed, was a party to the conspiracy to rob and was fatally shot while actively participating in the perpetration of the robbery, the killing did not fall within the operation of section 189 of the Penal Code; that the prosecution therefore should have been brought under section 187 of said code, and the question of whether the killing was accidental or intentional submitted to the jury under instructions such as they proposed, but which the court refused to give, to the effect that if the jury found that Ancheta was shot accidentally, all of them should be acquitted, notwithstanding the killing was done by one of them during the perpetration of the robbery which all conspired to commit, and in which all were actually participating at the time of the fatal shooting.

It has long since been declared to be the law of the state, however, that *any killing* by one engaged in the commission of any of the felonies enumerated in said section 189 falls within the scope of that section, and constitutes murder of the first degree. As stated in California jurisprudence "The moment one engages in the commission of one of the specified felonies, the law fastens upon him the intent which makes *any killing* in the perpetration of such offense . . . murder of the first degree." All of the cases, and there are many of them, declare to the same effect; and while none of them involved the killing of one conspirator by another, the unqualified language employed in the decisions therein in dealing with the question of the scope of said section 189, makes it clear that said section was designed to include and that its provisions apply to any killing by one engaged in the commission of any of the specified felonies, irrespective of the status of the person killed and regardless of whether the killing is accidental or intentional. . . .

In support of their position appellants cite People v. Ferlin, 203 Cal. 587, 265 P. 230, but an examination of the factual situation there shows it is entirely different from the one here presented, for the reason that there the coconspirator killed himself while he alone was perpetrating the felony he conspired to commit; whereas, here the coconspirator was killed by one of his confederates while all were perpetrating the crime they conspired to commit. To be more specific, the facts of that case were these: The defendant Ferlin hired a young man named Skala to destroy an insured building by fire, and while starting the fire with gasoline (Ferlin not being present) Skala burned himself so severely he died shortly afterwards from the effects of the burns. Ferlin was charged with and found guilty of arson, murder, and destruction of an insured building. The trial court granted a new trial on the murder conviction, and in sustaining the order on appeal it was held in substance and effect that inasmuch as Skala killed himself Ferlin could not be held criminally responsible for his death. [Not all courts subscribe to this reasoning. Under similar facts Pennsylvania has held the felony-murder rule applicable. Commonwealth v. Bolish 391 Pa. 550, 138 A.2d 447 (1958).] In the present case Ancheta did not kill himself and no one makes any such claim. The shot that killed him was fired, as the evidence shows, by Dasalla, a coconspirator, and the fatal shooting occurred during the perpetration of a robbery. Therefore the case falls clearly within the provisions of said section 189; and under the doctrine of the authorities above cited, not only Dasalla, who did the shooting, but all who participated with him in the perpetration of the robbery were guilty of first degree murder regardless of whether Dasalla fired the shot intentionally or accidentally. . . .

The second major point presented by the appeals is made in behalf of Cabaltero, Flores, Marcella Avelino and Velasco, and is based on that portion of Velasco's confession wherein he is purported to have related the circumstances under which the shooting took place. In this connection it is contended that the statements so made by Velasco show that Dasalla shot Ancheta deliberately and with the intention of killing him or doing him great bodily harm; that consequently Dasalla alone is accountable for the killing; and in furtherance of such theory an instruction was proposed by them which the court refused to give, to the effect that if the jury found that Ancheta was a coconspirator and was shot intentionally by his confederate, each of the coconspirators other than the one who fired the shot should be acquitted, despite the fact that the shooting occurred while all were participating in the robbery. In other words, they seek to invoke the benefit of the doctrine that if one member of a conspiracy departs from the original design as agreed upon by all members, and does an act which was not only not contemplated by those who entered into the common purpose but was not in furtherance thereof, and not the natural and probable consequence of anything connected therewith, the person guilty of such act if it was itself unlawful is alone responsible therefor. People v. Kauffman, 152 Cal. 331, 92 P. 861. Such doctrine is not available, however, to coconspirators in cases such as this, where the killing is done during the perpetration of a robbery in which they were participating. As declared in People v. Boss, "The law is also well settled that where two or more persons enter into a conspiracy to commit a robbery or burglary and one of the conspirators commits a murder in the perpetration of the crime, all of said conspirators are equally guilty with said coconspirator of murder of the first degree, and it is no defense that those who did not actually participate in the killing did not intend that life should be taken in the perpetration of the robbery, or had forbidden their associate to kill, or regretted that it had been done." [210 Cal. 245, 290 P. 883.] . . .

It is ordered that each judgment of conviction and each of the orders appealed from be and the same is hereby affirmed.

We concur: Tyler, P.J.; Conlan, Justice pro tem.

Notes and Questions

1. What would the defendants, other than Dasalla, have been guilty of without the felony-murder rule? What would Dasalla be guilty of? Does the felony-murder rule here accord with our sense of justice? Does it have some utilitarian value?

2. Was the felony-murder rule designed to protect felons?

3. Are you persuaded by the Court's attempt to distinguish *Ferlin*? If the felony-murder rule applies here, why not there?

4. As seen in *Stamp* and *Cabaltero,* questions involving the law of complicity often arise in felony-murder cases.

The law of complicity (or "accomplice liability") is rather complex, and is treated at length in Chapter 10. For present purposes, we can stipulate the following general principles of complicity: If person *A* with appropriate *mens rea* aids or abets person *B* in the commission of a crime, he or she is liable for that crime even though he or she did not perform the acts forbidden by the criminal law. Thus, someone who purposely gives a robber a gun to use in a robbery becomes guilty of robbery. In a sense, the felony-murder rule contains an extension of this complicity liability. It generally provides that if because of complicity in the underlying felony, *A* is liable for that felony and a death results from the act of one of *A*'s fellow felons, then *A* is liable for felony-murder along with that felon—even though *A* neither did the killing nor had any culpable *mens rea* with respect to the death.

A few courts have tried to limit the complicity principle in the felony-murder situation where the accomplice not only did not intend the killing, but also where the principal killer did not act "in furtherance of the common design." Consider the Pennsylvania decision in Commonwealth v. Waters, 491 Pa. 85, 418 A.2d 312 (1980):

> On April 13, 1976, Waters and Paul Allen agreed to commit armed robberies in the central Pennsylvania area. The two had recently returned to their joint home in East Berlin, Pennsylvania, from Las Vegas where they had lost most of their money in an attempt to implement Allen's scheme for winning at dice. Allen already owned a .22 calibre pistol, and the two men purchased a rifle. They practiced firing the weapons that afternoon. After placing the weapons in the Allen car, the two men and their families drove to the home of a friend in Williamsport where the family members were dropped off. During the drive and several stops at homes of acquaintances, both men consumed alcoholic beverages.
>
> Allen and Waters then proceeded to the Williamsport apartment of Diane Buck who was known to Allen. Allen suggested they go in "and maybe get a piece of ass and little bit of money." When Allen was unable to break in the door, Waters opened it with a karate kick. Once inside, the men proceeded to a bedroom where they found Diane Buck and Terry Brennan in bed nude. Allen fired a shot between the couple, took Diane Buck from the bed, and, for the next one and one-half hours, pushed, beat, and shoved her around the apartment while attempting, unsuccessfully, to rape her. During this time, Waters kept guard over Brennan and took his cash and watch. At some point, when Waters left the room to get a cigarette, Allen entered the bedroom and shot Brennan in the neck with the pistol. Later, when all four persons were in the bedroom, Allen forced Diane Buck onto the bed with Brennan, who was injured and bleeding, and ordered her to ask him about his injuries. . . . He then took Buck out of the room and continued his efforts to rape her leaving Waters in the room with Brennan.
>
> Waters whispered to Brennan he would get him help and would try to mislead Allen by saying in a loud voice that he was going to finish Brennan off. He did so and shot his weapon into the air. He exited the room, told Allen he had killed Brennan, and encouraged him to leave. Allen went to check whether Brennan was really dead. By Diane Buck's account, Allen threatened to kill both her and Waters if Brennan was not, in fact, dead. As Allen entered the bedroom, Waters shot him from behind. Allen died instantly.
>
> Waters advised Diane Buck to call an ambulance, but, when she could not compose herself sufficiently to complete the call, Waters himself called the police. He remained at the apartment until the police arrived and, later that night, gave a statement to the police concerning the evening's events. Brennan's money was found in Waters' pocket, and his watch was later found in the holding cell in which Waters was detained that evening.

On April 14, 1976, Waters was charged with the murder of Allen, but this charge was later withdrawn by the district attorney who concluded this killing was justifiable homicide. . . . However, when Brennan died on May 29 from the gunshot wound inflicted by Allen, Waters was rearrested and charged with the murder of Brennan. . . .

In support of his position that a new trial is necessary, Waters complains, inter alia, that the trial court erred in refusing a certain requested instruction to the jury. Specifically, Waters requested the court to charge, during its instructions on the law of felony-murder, that the Commonwealth was required to show "the conduct causing the death was done in furtherance of the design to commit the felony."

The court refused to so charge and indicated it would give appropriate instructions. A careful study of the charge in its entirety discloses the court, in both specific and general terms, told the jury that, before Waters could be found guilty of felony-murder in connection with Brennan's killing, it would have to be convinced beyond a reasonable doubt that an act of Allen caused Brennan's death; that this act of Allen was intentional, knowing, reckless or negligent; and, that Allen's act occurred while Waters was an accomplice in the commission of or attempt to commit robbery, rape, or burglary. Waters' complaint is that the court did not instruct that Allen's act which caused Brennan's death had to have been done in furtherance of the felony.[21] We are constrained to agree that the charge did not cover the point requested; that the requested instruction is a correct statement of the law; and, that the failure to so charge constitutes reversible error.

We have indicated that the new Crimes Code, Pa. C.S.A. §101 et seq., has modified prior law with regard to accomplice liability for a felony-murder little, if at all. Under prior law, the responsibility of persons, other than the slayer, for a homicide committed in the perpetration of a felony required proof of a conspiratorial design by the slayer and the others to commit the underlying felony and of an act by the slayer causing death *which was in furtherance of the felony.*[22]

Conceding the point for charge requested by Waters was not covered in the court's jury instructions, the Commonwealth argues the act of the slayer need not be in furtherance of the felony, but need only have occurred while the slayer and others were engaged in a felony, i.e. need only have occurred during the perpetration or commission of a felony. . . .

In Commonwealth v. Legg, —Pa.—, 417 A.2d 1152 (1980) (J. 167 filed this day), we held that henceforth the intent to commit a felony must be formulated when the act of killing occurs in order to apply the felony-murder rule. . . . The same reasoning which compelled our decision in Commonwealth v. Legg, supra, dictates the conclusion that the common design to commit the underlying

21. In so arguing, Waters claims this would have supported a theory that Allen's act of shooting Brennan was not done in furtherance of the felony or felonies to which he was an accomplice and that, hence, he was not guilty of felony-murder.

22. Were it otherwise, an accomplice to a robbery would be guilty of felony-murder if one of his cofelons during the course of the robbery looked out a window, saw a passerby down the street, and shot and killed him even though the passerby had no connection to the robbery whatsoever. Obviously, even though an accomplice knows or should know those connected to a robbery may be killed during the course of a dangerous felony, see Commonwealth v. Legg, —Pa.—, 417 A.2d 1152 (1980) (J. 167, filed this day), he should not be held accountable for that which he cannot *at least foresee.*

> felony must exist when the act of slaying occurs in order to establish an accomplice's liability for felony-murder. But, as with intent, the existence of a common design when the slaying occurred may be inferred from the circumstances or acts of the slayer and accomplice committed shortly after the slaying, but this is far different from saying the common design to commit the underlying felony may be conceived after the act causing death.[23]
>
> Accordingly, Waters must be granted a new trial.

If the felony-murder rule does not require proof that Waters intended or foresaw that Allen would kill Brennan, does the court's restriction of the felony-murder rule make any sense?

The limiting principle in *Waters* does not reflect the felony-murder law in most states. The line of cases that follows examines the consequences of broad application of the felony-murder rule where someone other than the defendant does the shooting.

PEOPLE v. HICKMAN

Appellate Court of Illinois
12 Ill. App. 3d 412, 297 N.E.2d 582 (1973)

Scott, Justice.

[Defendants Rock and Hickman along with several others were surprised by the police as they emerged from a burglary; they attempted to escape and] ran through the bushes while in the meantime Sergeant Cronk ran to the rear of the warehouse where he noticed two people running in a northwesterly direction. Sergeant Cronk yelled "halt—police" several times but his commands were ignored. He lost sight of the two fleeing individuals but within seconds thereafter saw a man carrying a handgun running towards the bushes at the northwest corner of the parking lot. Sergeant Cronk, believing that this approaching individual was one of the burglars . . . and referring to the handgun, ordered the person to "drop it." When there was no compliance to this warning Sergeant Cronk fired his shotgun at the individual, who was later discovered to be Detective William Loscheider of the Joliet police force. Loscheider was killed by this shot from his fellow officer's gun.

Approximately one-half hour later the defendants Rock and Hickman were arrested as they were walking on a street approximately two and a half blocks from the warehouse. Neither of the defendants had a weapon on his person. . . .

The foregoing constitutes a brief summary of the unusual factual situation which led to this appeal and which presents to us the question as to whether or

23. The Commonwealth argues no evidence existed to support a claim that the act was not in furtherance of the felony, and no charge was therefore necessary. We must disagree. The requirement is a necessary finding to establish Waters' guilt, and the facts could have supported an inference that Allen's act was completely independent of the felony in that it was wholly unconnected to the felony.

not the trial court erred when it entered an order arresting a judgment of guilty of murder against the defendants Rock and Hickman which had been returned against them by the jury.

More narrowly presented we must determine whether the actual shooting which caused the death of an innocent victim must have been performed by the defendants or someone acting in concert with them in order to comply with the requirements of the felony-murder doctrine.

Our criminal code contains statutory provisions relating to the felony-murder doctrine, being Ch. 38, Sec. 9-1 (a)(3), Ill. Rev. Stat., which provides:

> (a) A person who kills an individual without lawful justification commits murder if, in performing the acts which cause the death: . . .
>
> (3) He is attempting or committing a forcible felony other than voluntary manslaughter.

The defendants urge an interpretation of this statute to the effect that the person who kills or performs the acts which cause death must be the same person as the one who is attempting or committing a forcible felony before liability for murder can be imposed.

While the syntax of the words involved in our felony-murder statute could be interpreted on the restrictive and narrow lines urged by the defendants, we do not believe that in statutory construction we are bound to consider only the wording used in the statute. The court in construing a statute may consider the notes and reports of the commission pursuant to which the statutory provision was adopted. Turning our attention to the committee comments in regard to the statute in question we find on page 9 of Smith Hurd Ill. Ann. Stat., Ch. 38, the following comments in regard to the application of Sec. 9-1(a)(3), the felony-murder provision:

> It is immaterial whether the killing in such a case is intentional or accidental, or is committed by a confederate without the connivance of the defendant . . . or even by a third person trying to prevent the commission of the felony.

In support of the committee comment that one can be guilty of murder where the killing resulted from the act of third person trying to prevent the commission of a felony, there is cited the case of People v. Payne, 359 Ill. 246, 194 N.E. 539.

In *Payne* we have a factual situation where armed robbers entered the home of two brothers. One of the brothers discharged a weapon to prevent the robbery as did one of the robbers. The other brother was killed and it could not be determined whether he was killed by his brother or the robber. Our Supreme Court in affirming the defendant's conviction of murder stated:

> Where several persons conspire to do an unlawful act, and another crime is committed in the pursuit of the common object, all are alike guilty of the crime committed, if it is a natural and probable consequence of the execution of the

conspiracy. . . . It reasonably might be anticipated that an attempted robbery would meet with resistance, during which the victim might be shot either by himself or someone else in attempting to prevent the robbery, and those attempting to perpetrate the robbery would be guilty of murder.

There are other cases in Illinois where our reviewing courts have recognized that a defendant may be criminally responsible for the killing of another during the commission of a forcible felony even though no certainty exists that the defendant or his cohorts performed the fatal act. Our Supreme Court in the *Payne* case, however, was confronted with a factual situation quite similar to the one presented to us in the instant case and in *Payne* the court clearly adopted the theory that a defendant and co-conspirators acting in concert with him can be held responsible for a killing of an innocent third party during the commission of a forcible felony even though the killing was not actually done by a person acting in concert with the defendant or his co-conspirators.

We hold it to be of no consequence that in the instant case Detective Loscheider was killed at a time when the defendants were attempting to escape. Our Supreme Court has held that the period of time involved in an escape with immediate pursuit after committing a crime becomes part of the crime itself.

The defendants both in the trial court and in this appeal urge that the applicable law is set forth in the case of People v. Morris, 1 Ill. App. 3d 566, 274 N.E.2d 898. In *Morris* the defendant and two cohorts entered a restaurant armed for the purpose of committing a robbery. A struggle ensued between a patron and one of the cohorts during which gunfire erupted and the cohort was killed. The defendant Morris, one of the would-be robbers, was charged with murder of his co-conspirator under the theory of the felony-murder doctrine and was convicted of the crime of murder by the trial court. The reviewing court reversed the trial court holding that the felony-murder doctrine is not applicable against a surviving felon when a co-felon is justifiably killed during commission of a forcible felony.

We do not believe that the rationale of the *Morris* case is controlling in the instant case since *Morris* presented a factual situation which differed in one very significant detail. In *Morris,* unlike the case before us, the victim was not an innocent third party. In *Morris* the victim was not free from culpability but was in fact an individual who was attempting to commit a felony. We do not hold that the character of the victim is controlling merely because he was a felon, nor do we indulge in the fanciful theory that the victim being a felon assumed the risk and thereby constructively consented to his death, but we do hold that he assisted in setting in motion a chain of events which was the proximate cause of his death and therefore in the criminal law as in the civil law there is no redress for the victim.

Clearly the case of People v. Payne, 359 Ill. 246, 194 N.E. 539, and the case now before us are distinguishable from *Morris* in that unlike *Morris,* innocent parties were killed. We interpret *Payne* as setting forth the rule that he whose act causes in any way, directly, or indirectly, the death of an innocent victim is guilty of murder by virtue of the felony-murder doctrine.

We are aware of the conflicting views from other jurisdictions concerning the application of the felony-murder doctrine in cases such as we are now considering, but we are only concerned with following the law as it has been established in our own state, and therefore hold that *Payne* is controlling in the instant case and that the defendants are guilty of the crime of murder. There should be no doubt about the "justice" of holding a felon guilty of murder who engages in a robbery followed by an attempted escape and thereby inevitably calls into action defensive forces against him, the activity of which results in the death of an innocent human being.

Mr. Justice Cardozo in The Nature of the Judicial Process, pages 66, 67, said and we believe wisely, that "When they (Judges) are called upon to say how far existing rules are to be extended or restricted, they must let the welfare of society fix the path, its direction and its distance. . . . The final cause of law is the welfare of society."

Following the precepts of Justice Cardozo we need not extend the existing rules in order to protect society, but are only required to follow the law as set forth in the case of *Payne.* This we do and accordingly direct that the order of the trial court of Will County arresting the judgment of murder as to the defendants in this case be reversed and that further this case is remanded for sentencing of the defendants for the crime of murder.

Reversed and remanded.

Alloy, P.J., and Dixon, J., concur.

Notes and Questions

1. What would the defendants be guilty of in this case without the felony-murder rule?

2. Does it accord more with your sense of justice to convict Hickman of burglary or of murder?

3. New York has, by statute, attempted to solve the *Hickman* problem. Section 125.25 provides for murder in the second degree (murder in the first degree, punishable with life imprisonment, is reserved for intentional killings of police or correctional officers and killings by long-term prisoners) in the following way:

> A person is guilty of murder in the second degree when: . . .
>
> 3. Acting either alone or with one or more other persons, he commits or attempts to commit robbery, burglary, kidnapping, arson, rape in the first degree, sodomy in the first degree, sexual abuse in the first degree, escape in the first degree, or escape in the second degree, and, in the course of and in furtherance of such crime or of immediate flight therefrom, he, or another participant,

if there be any, causes the death of a person other than one of the participants; except that in any prosecution under this subdivision, in which the defendant was not the only participant in the underlying crime, it is an affirmative defense that the defendant:

(a) Did not commit the homicidal act or in any way solicit, request, command, importune, cause or aid the commission thereof; and

(b) Was not armed with a deadly weapon, or any instrument, article or substance readily capable of causing death or serious physical injury and of a sort not ordinarily carried in public places by law-abiding persons; and

(c) Had no reasonable ground to believe that any other participant was armed with such a weapon, instrument, article or substance; and

(d) Had no reasonable ground to believe that any other participant intended to engage in conduct likely to result in death or serious physical injury.

Murder in the second degree is a class A-I felony. (Punishable by from 15 years to life imprisonment.)

PEOPLE v. WASHINGTON

Supreme Court of California
62 Cal. 2d 777, 44 Cal. Rptr. 442, 402 P.2d 130 (1965)

TRAYNOR, Chief Justice.

Defendant appeals from a judgment of conviction entered upon jury verdicts finding him guilty of first degree robbery and first degree murder and fixing the murder penalty at life imprisonment. (Pen. Code, §§187, 189, 190, 190.1) He was convicted of murder for participating in a robbery in which his accomplice was killed by the victim of the robbery.

Shortly before 10 P.M., October 2, 1962, Johnnie Carpenter prepared to close his gasoline station. He was in his office computing the receipts and disbursements of the day while an attendant in an adjacent storage room deposited money in a vault. Upon hearing someone yell "robbery," Carpenter opened his desk and took out a revolver. A few moments later, James Ball entered the office and pointed a revolver directly at Carpenter, who fired immediately, mortally wounding Ball. Carpenter then hurried to the door and saw an unarmed man he later identified as defendant running from the vault with a moneybag in his right hand. He shouted "Stop." When his warning was not heeded, he fired and hit defendant who fell wounded in front of the station.

The Attorney General, relying on People v. Harrison, 176 Cal. App. 2d 330, 1 Cal. Rptr. 414, contends that defendant was properly convicted of first degree murder. In that case defendants initiated a gun battle with an employee in an attempt to rob a cleaning business. In the cross fire, the employee accidentally killed the owner of the business. The court affirmed the judgment convicting defendants of first degree murder, invoking Commonwealth v. Almeida, 362 Pa. 596, 68 A.2d 595, and People v. Podolski, 332 Mich. 508, 52 N.W.2d 201, which held that robbers who provoked gunfire were guilty of first degree murder even though the lethal bullet was fired by a policeman.

Defendant would distinguish the *Harrison, Almeida,* and *Podolski* cases on the ground that in each instance the person killed was an innocent victim, not one of the felons. He suggests that we limit the rule of the *Harrison* case just as the Supreme Court of Pennsylvania and Michigan have limited the *Almeida* and *Podolski* cases by holding that surviving felons are not guilty of murder when their accomplices are killed by persons resisting the felony. A distinction based on the person killed, however, would make the defendant's criminal liability turn upon the marksmanship of victims and policemen. A rule of law cannot reasonably be based on such a fortuitous circumstance. The basic issue therefore is whether a robber can be convicted of murder for the killing of any person by another who is resisting the robbery.

"Murder is the unlawful killing of a human being, with malice aforethought." (Pen. Code, Sec. 187.) Except when the common-law-felony-murder doctrine is applicable, an essential element of murder is an intent to kill or an intent with conscious disregard for life to commit acts likely to kill. The felony-murder doctrine ascribes malice aforethought to the felon who kills in the perpetration of an inherently dangerous felony. That doctrine is incorporated in section 189 of the Penal Code, which provides in part: "All murder . . . committed in the perpetration or attempt to perpetrate . . . robbery . . . is murder of the first degree." Thus, even though §189 speaks only of degrees of "murder," inadvertent or accidental killings are first degree murders when committed by felons in the perpetration of robbery.

When a killing is not committed by a robber or by his accomplice but by his victim, malice aforethought is not attributable to the robber, for the killing is not committed by him in the perpetration or attempt to perpetrate robbery. It is not enough that the killing was a risk reasonably to be foreseen and that the robbery might therefore be regarded as a proximate cause of the killing. Section 189 requires that the felon or his accomplice commit the killing, for if he does not, the killing is not committed to perpetrate the felony. . . . To include such killings within §189 would expand the meaning of the words "murder . . . which is committed in the perpetration . . . [of] robbery . . ." beyond common understanding.

The purpose of the felony-murder rule is to deter felons from killing negligently or accidentally by holding them strictly responsible for killings they commit. This purpose is not served by punishing them for killings committed by their victims.

It is contended, however, that another purpose of the felony-murder rule is to prevent the commission of robberies. Neither the common-law rationale of the rule nor the Penal Code supports this contention. In every robbery there is a possibility that the victim will resist and kill. The robber has little control over such a killing once the robbery is undertaken as this case demonstrates. To impose an additional penalty for the killing would discriminate between robbers, not on the basis of any difference in their own conduct, but solely on the basis of the response by others that the robber's conduct happened to induce. An additional penalty for a homicide committed by the victim would deter robbery haphazardly at best. To "prevent stealing, [the law] would do better to hang one thief in every thousand by lot." (Holmes, The Common Law, p.58.)

A defendant need not do the killing himself, however, to be guilty of murder. He may be vicariously responsible under the rules defining principals and criminal conspiracies. All persons aiding and abetting the commission of a robbery are guilty of first degree murder when one of them kills while acting in furtherance of the common design. Moreover, when the defendant intends to kill or intentionally commits acts that are likely to kill with a conscious disregard for life, he is guilty of murder even though he uses another person to accomplish his objective.

Defendants who initiate gun battles may also be found guilty of murder if their victims resist and kill. Under such circumstances, "the defendant for a base, anti-social motive and with wanton disregard for human life, does an act that involves a high degree of probability that it will result in death" (People v. Thomas, 41 Cal. 2d 470, 480, 261 P.2d 1, 7 (concurring opinion)) and it is unnecessary to imply malice by invoking the felony-murder doctrine.[24] To invoke the felony-murder doctrine to imply malice in such a case is unnecessary and overlooks the principles of criminal liability that should govern the responsibility of one person for a killing committed by another.

To invoke the felony-murder doctrine when the killing is not committed by the defendant or by his accomplice could lead to absurd results. Thus, two men rob a grocery store and flee in opposite directions. The owner of the store follows one of the robbers and kills him. Neither robber may have fired a shot. Neither robber may have been armed with a deadly weapon. If the felony-murder doctrine applied, however, the surviving robber could be convicted of first degree murder, even though he was captured by a policeman and placed under arrest at the time his accomplice was killed.

The felony-murder rule has been criticized on the grounds that in almost all cases in which it is applied it is unnecessary and that it erodes the relation between criminal liability and moral culpability (See, e.g., Model Penal Code (Tent. Draft No. 9, May 8, 1959) Sec. 201.2, comment 4 at pp.37-39) Although it is the law in this state (Pen. Code, Sec. 189), it should not be extended beyond any rational function that it is designed to serve. Accordingly, for a defendant to be guilty of murder under the felony-murder rule the act of killing must be committed by the defendant or by his accomplice's action in furtherance of their common design. Language in People v. Harri-

24. One scholar has commented that "People v. Harrison, 176 Cal. App. 2d 330, 1 Cal. Rptr. 414 (1959), is probably not, strictly speaking, a felony-murder case at all, but rather a case taking a very relaxed view of the necessary causal connection between the defendant's act and the victim's death, an approach which is possibly quite independent of the felony-murder rule." (Packer, The Case for Revision of the Penal Code, 13 Stan. L. Rev. 252, 259 n.39.)

son, 176 Cal. App. 2d 330, 1 Cal. Rptr. 414, inconsistent with this holding, is disapproved. . . .

The judgment is affirmed as to defendant's conviction of first degree robbery and reversed as to his conviction of first degree murder.

Peters, Tobriner, Peek, and White, JJ., concur.

Burke, Justice (dissenting).

I dissent. The unfortunate effect of the decision of the majority in this case is to advise felons:

> Henceforth in committing certain crimes, including robbery, rape and burglary, you are free to arm yourselves with a gun and brandish it in the faces of your victims without fear of a murder conviction unless you or your accomplice pulls the trigger. If the menacing effect of your gun causes a victim or policeman to fire and kill an innocent person or a cofelon, you are absolved of responsibility for such killing unless you shoot first.

Obviously this advance judicial absolution removes one of the most meaningful deterrents to the commission of armed felonies. . . .

I agree with the majority that one purpose of the felony-murder rule is to deter felons from killing negligently or accidentally. However, another equally cogent purpose is to deter them from undertaking inherently dangerous felonies in which, as the majority state, a "killing was a risk reasonably to be foreseen. . . . In every robbery there is a possibility that the victim will resist and kill." As declared in People v. Chavez (1951) 37 Cal. 2d 656, 669, 234 P.2d 632, "The statute [Pen. Code, §189] was adopted for the protection of the community and its residents, not for the benefit of the lawbreaker." Why a felon who has undertaken an *armed* robbery, which this court now expressly notifies him carries a "risk" and "a possibility that the victim will resist and kill," and which "might therefore be regarded as a proximate cause of the killing" should nevertheless be absolved because, fortuitously, the victim can and does shoot first and the lethal bullet comes from the victim's gun rather than from his own, will be beyond the comprehension of the average law-abiding citizen, to say nothing of that of victims of armed robbery. Nor is such a view compatible with the felony-murder doctrine.

But, say the majority, "The robber has little control over such a killing once the robbery is undertaken," and "To impose an additional penalty for the killing would discriminate between robbers, not on the basis of any difference in their own conduct, but solely on the basis of the response by others that the robber's conduct happened to induce." A robber has *no* control over a bullet sent on its way after he pulls the trigger. Certainly his inability to recall it before it kills does not cloak him with innocence of the homicide. The truth is, of course, that the robber may exercise various "controls over" a possible killing from his victim's bullet "once the robbery is undertaken." The robber can drop his own weapon, he can refrain from using it, he can surrender.

Other conduct can be suggested which would tend to reassure the victim and dissuade him from firing his own gun. Moreover, the response by one victim will lead to capture of the robbers, while that of another victim will permit their escape. Is the captured felon to be excused from responsibility for his crime, in order not to "discriminate between robbers . . . solely on the basis of the response by others that the robber's conduct happened to induce"?

The robber's conduct which forms the basis of his criminal responsibility is the undertaking of the *armed* felony, in which a "killing was a risk reasonably to be foreseen" including the "possibility that the victim will resist and kill." If that risk becomes reality and a killing occurs, the guilt for it is that of the felon. And when done, it is murder in the first degree—calling for death or life imprisonment. And to say that the knowledge that this awesome, sobering, terrifying responsibility of one contemplating the use of a deadly weapon in the perpetration of one of the listed offenses is not the strongest possible deterrent to the commission of such offenses belies what is being demonstrated day after day in the criminal departments of our trial courts.

I would hold, in accord with the rationale of People v. Harrison, supra (1959) 176 Cal. App. 2d 330, 1 Cal. Rptr. 414, that the killing is that of the felon whether or not the lethal bullet comes from his gun or that of his accomplice and whether or not one of them shoots first, and would affirm the judgment of conviction of murder in the instant case.

McComb, J., concurs.

Notes and Questions

1. The majority holds that when a killing is not committed by a robber "malice aforethought is not attributable to the robber, for the killing is not committed by him." It therefore precludes use of the felony-murder rule. On the other hand, the majority states that robbers initiating gun battles may "be guilty of murder if their victims resist and kill," without resort to the felony-murder doctrine. Does the majority "imply malice" only if the robber shoots first, but not if he merely creates the foreseeable risk that "the victim will resist and kill"? If so, is this sound?

2. Do you agree with the dissent that the majority in *Washington* has removed a meaningful deterrent to the commission of armed robberies? Review the homicide to felony relationship statistics given in the notes after *Stamp*. Can it be argued that any shooting or gun battle is initiated by the armed robbers, because of their presence, even if a victim or police officer shoots first?

3. In *Stamp,* the accomplices did not have to directly perform the killing to be guilty of felony murder. Why is Washington any less guilty of felony murder than the defendants in *Stamp*? Is the fact that there was an intervening action (the victim shooting the co-felon) sufficient to distinguish *Stamp*?

4. Does it matter that a co-felon was the victim? Should the court be less concerned with giving prosecutors a tool to convict when the victim is a felon, rather than an innocent person? Under *Washington* what would have been the result if Carpenter had missed Ball and killed a passerby? See the solution reached in the New York statute, supra page 408.

5. Which makes more sense to you, the rule in *Hickman* or that in *Washington?*

6. Under *Hickman,* would the defendants in *Cabaltero* not be guilty because the victim was a felon? Why or why not? Should the focus be placed on the shooter or the "shootee"? On whom does *Hickman* place the focus? On whom does *Washington* place the focus?

7. Does not the result in *Hickman* simply depend on the marksmanship of the policeman? On the policeman's mistake? If a co-felon were killed by a policeman's bullet, under *Washington* and implicit in *Hickman*, the defendants would not be guilty of murder. Why does liability depend on this factor?

8. Pennsylvania developed its felony-murder doctrine in a series of cases similar to those in this chapter. In Commonwealth v. Almeida, 362 Pa. 596, 68 A.2d 595 (1949) a police officer was killed by other officers attempting to apprehend robbers. The court expanded the felony-murder doctrine by espousing a doctrine of proximate cause, attaching liability for any death proximately resulting from commission of the felony. If the risk of death was foreseeable and death occurred, the felon was guilty of felony murder.

In Commonwealth v. Thomas, 382 Pa. 639, 117 A.2d 204 (1955) the defendant was charged with the killing of his accomplice by the victim of their robbery. The court, reasoning from *Almeida,* held the defendant liable. *Thomas* was overruled three years later by Commonwealth v. Redline, 391 Pa. 486, 137 A.2d 472 (1958). In *Redline* the defendant initiated a gun battle and his accomplice was killed by a police bullet. Reversing Redline's felony-murder conviction, the court distinguished *Almeida* by distinguishing "excusable" and "justifiable" homicides. The killing of an innocent person, as in *Almeida,* was merely an excusable killing while the killing of a co-felon was a justifiable one.

The court stated:

> The victim of the homicide was one of the robbers who, while resisting apprehension in his effort to escape was shot and killed by a policeman in the performance of his duty. Thus, the homicide was justifiable and, obviously, could not be availed of, on any rational legal theory, to support a charge of murder. How can anyone, no matter how much of an outlaw he may be, have a criminal charge lodged against him for the consequence of the lawful conduct of another person?

The court then held that, "in order to convict for felony murder, the killing must have been done by the defendant or by an accomplice or confederate or by one acting in furtherance of the felonious undertaking." *Almeida* and its proximate cause approach were explicitly overruled in Commonwealth ex rel. Smith v. Meyers, 438 Pa. 218, 261 A.2d 550 (1970), twelve years after *Redline.* The court in *Meyers,* though, rejected *Redline's* distinction between excusable and justifiable killings. Why do you think that distinction was rejected?

TAYLOR v. SUPERIOR COURT

Supreme Court of California
3 Cal. 3d 578, 91 Cal. Rptr. 275, 477 P.2d 131 (1970)

BURKE, Justice.

At the preliminary hearing, the following facts were adduced regarding the murder count: On the evening of January 12, 1969, two men attempted to rob Jax Liquor Store which was operated by Mrs. Linda Lee West and her husband Jack. Mrs. West testified that James Daniels entered the store first and asked Mr. West, who was behind the counter, for a package of cigarettes. While Mr. West was getting the cigarettes, John Smith entered the store and approached the counter. Mrs. West, who was on a ladder at the time the two men entered the store, then heard her husband say something about money. Turning her attention to the counter, she heard Daniels repeatedly saying, "Put the money in the bag," and observed her husband complying with the order.

While Mr. West was putting the money from the register in the bag, Daniels repeatedly referred to the fact that he and Smith were armed. According to Mrs. West, Daniels "chattered insanely" during this time, telling Mr. West "Put the money in the bag. Put the money in the bag. Put the money in the bag. Don't move or I'll blow your head off. He's got a gun. He's got a gun. Don't move or we'll have an execution right here. Get down on the floor. I said on your stomach, on your stomach." Throughout this period, Smith's gun was pointed at Mr. West. Mrs. West testified that Smith looked "intent" and "apprehensive" as if "waiting for something big to happen." She indicated that Smith's apparent apprehension and nervousness was manifested by the way he was staring at Mr. West.

While Daniels was forcing Mr. West to the floor, Mrs. West drew a pistol from under her clothing and fired at Smith, who was standing closest to her. Smith was struck on the right side of the chest. Mrs. West fired four more shots in rapid succession, and observed "sparks" coming from Smith's gun, which was pointed in her direction. A bullet hole was subsequently discovered in the wall behind the place Mrs. West had been standing, approximately eight or nine feet above the floor. During this period, Mr. West had seized a pistol and fired two shots at Smith. Mrs. West's last shot was fired at Daniels as he was going out the door. He "lurched violently and almost went down, [but] picked himself up and kept going." Smith died as the result of multiple gunshot wounds.

The evidence at the preliminary examination indicated that petitioner was waiting outside the liquor store in a getaway car. He was apprehended later and connected with the crime through bills in his possession and through the automobile which was seen by a witness leaving the scene of the robbery.

The information herein charged petitioner with the crime of murder. " 'Murder is the unlawful killing of a human being, with malice aforethought.' (Pen. Code, §187.) Except when the common-law-felony-murder doctrine is applicable, an essential element of murder is an intent to kill or an intent with conscious disregard for life to commit acts likely to kill." (People v. Washington, 62 Cal. 2d 777, 780, 44 Cal. Rptr. 442, 445, 402 P.2d 130, 133.) Petitioner correctly contends that he cannot be convicted under the felony-murder doctrine, since "When a killing is not committed by a robber or by his accomplice but by his victim, malice aforethought is not attributable to the robber, for the killing is not committed by him in the perpetration or attempt to perpetrate robbery." (People v. Washington, supra.) However, apart from the felony-murder doctrine, petitioner could be found guilty of murder on a theory of vicarious liability.

As stated in People v. Gilbert, 63 Cal. 2d 690, 704-705, 47 Cal. Rptr. 909, 917, 408 P.2d 365, 373, "When the defendant or his accomplice, with a conscious disregard for life, intentionally commits an act that is likely to cause death, and his victim or a police officer kills in reasonable response to such act, the defendant is guilty of murder. In such a case, the killing is attributable, not merely to the commission of a felony, but to the intentional act of the defendant or his accomplice committed with conscious disregard for life. Thus, the victim's self-defensive killing or the police officer's killing in the performance of his duty cannot be considered an independent intervening cause for which the defendant is not liable, for it is a reasonable response to the dilemma thrust upon the victim or the policeman by the intentional act of the defendant or his accomplice."

Therefore, if petitioner were an accomplice to the robbery, he would be vicariously responsible[25] for any killing attributable to the intentional acts of his associates committed with conscious disregard for life, and likely to result in death. We must determine whether the committing magistrate had any rational ground for believing that Smith's death was attributable to intentional acts of Smith and Daniels meeting those criteria.

Petitioner relies upon the following language in *Washington,* wherein defendant's accomplice merely pointed a gun at the robbery victim who, without further provocation, shot and killed him: "In every robbery there is a possibility that the victim will resist and kill. The robber has little control over such a killing once the robbery is undertaken as this case demonstrates. To impose an additional penalty for the killing would discriminate between robbers, *not on*

25. "Under the rules defining principals and criminal conspiracies, the defendant may be guilty of murder for a killing attributable to the act of his accomplice. To be so guilty, however, the accomplice must cause the death of another human being by an act committed in furtherance of the common design." Petitioner does not dispute that the conduct of his confederates set forth above was in furtherance of the robbery.

the basis of any difference in their own conduct, but solely on the basis of the response by others that the robber's conduct happened to induce."

As indicated by the italicized words in the foregoing quotation, the central inquiry in determining criminal liability for a killing committed by a resisting victim or police officer is whether the *conduct* of a defendant or his accomplices was sufficiently provocative of lethal resistance to support a finding of implied malice. If the trier of fact concludes that under the particular circumstances of the instant case Smith's death proximately resulted from acts of petitioner's accomplices done with conscious disregard for human life, the natural consequences of which were dangerous to life, then petitioner may be convicted of first degree murder.

For example, we pointed out in *Washington* that "Defendants who initiate gun battles may also be found guilty of murder if their victims resist and kill. Under such circumstances, 'the defendant for a base, anti-social motive and with wanton disregard for human life, does an act that involves a high degree of probability that it will result in death' [citation], and it is unnecessary to imply malice by invoking the felony-murder doctrine."

Petitioner contends that since neither Daniels nor Smith fired the first shot, they did not "initiate" the gun battle which led to Smith's death. However, depending upon the circumstances, a gun battle can be initiated by acts of provocation falling short of firing the first shot. Thus in, People v. Reed, 270 Cal. App. 2d 37, 75 Cal. Rptr. 430, defendant resisted the officers' commands to "put up your hands," and pointed his gun toward the officers and toward the kidnap-robbery victim. The officers commenced firing, wounding defendant and killing the victim. Although defendant did not fire a single shot, his murder conviction was upheld on the theory that his "aggressive actions" were sufficient evidence of implied malice, and that "under these circumstance it may be said that defendant initiated the gunplay. . . ."

Similarly, in Brooks v. Superior Court, 239 Cal. App. 2d 538, 48 Cal. Rptr. 762, petitioner had directed "opprobrious language" to the arresting officer and had grasped the officer's shotgun. The officer, being startled and thinking that petitioner was trying to disarm him, yanked backwards and fired the gun, mortally wounding a fellow officer. In upholding an indictment for murder, the court concluded that under the circumstances, the petitioner's act of reaching for and grasping the officer's shotgun was "fraught with grave and inherent danger to human life," and therefore sufficient to raise an inference of malice.

In the instant case, the evidence at the preliminary hearing set forth above discloses acts of provocation on the part of Daniels and Smith from which the trier of fact could infer malice, including Daniels' coercive conduct toward Mr. West and his repeated threats of "execution," and Smith's intent and nervous apprehension as he held Mr. West at gunpoint. The foregoing conduct was sufficiently provocative of lethal resistance to lead a man of ordinary caution and prudence to conclude that Daniels and Smith "initiated" the gun battle, or that such conduct was done with conscious disregard for human life and with natural consequences dangerous to life.[26] Accordingly, we conclude that the evidence supported the magistrate's finding that reasonable and probable cause existed to charge petitioner with first degree murder.

WRIGHT, C.J., and MCCOMB and SULLIVAN, JJ., concur.

PETERS, Justice (dissenting).

I dissent.

In holding that petitioner can be convicted of murder of John H. Smith, the majority repudiate this court's holdings in People v. Washington and People v. Gilbert that robbers cannot be convicted of murder for a killing by a victim unless the robbers commit malicious acts, in addition to the acts constituting the underlying felony, which demonstrate culpability beyond that of other robbers. The majority . . . purport to distinguish *Washington* from the instant case, resulting in the absurd distinction that robbers who point guns at their victims without articulating the obvious threat inherent in such action cannot be convicted of murder for a killing committed by the victims, whereas robbers who point guns at their victims and articulate their threat can be convicted of murder in the same situation. To hold, as do the majority, that petitioner can be convicted of murder for acts which constitute a first degree robbery solely because the victims killed one of the robbers is in effect to reinstate the felony-murder rule in cases where the victim resists and kills.

In *Washington,* two robbers held up a service station. The owner, Carpenter, was in the office totaling up the receipts and disbursements while an employee was depositing the money in a vault in an adjoining room. Upon hearing someone yell "robbery," Carpenter opened his desk and took out a revolver. A few moments later one of the robbers, Ball, entered the office and pointed a revolver at Carpenter. Carpenter fired immediately, mortally wounding Ball. Washington, the accomplice, was convicted of the murder of Ball. We reversed the murder conviction. We held that the felony-murder doctrine could not be invoked to convict Washington of murder because the killing was not committed by Washington or his accomplice: "When a killing is not committed by a robber or by his accomplice but by his victim, malice

26. Petitioner contends that we should ignore evidence regarding Smith's conduct, on the theory that Smith could not have been held responsible for his own death. We rejected a similar contention in *Washington,* stating that "A distinction based on the person killed, however, would make the defendant's criminal liability turn upon the marksmanship of victims and policemen. A rule of law cannot reasonably be based on such a fortuitous circumstance. The basic issue therefore is whether a robber can be convicted of murder for the killing of *any* person by another who is resisting the robbery." Therefore, the trier of fact may find that Smith set into motion, through the intentional commission of acts constituting the implied malice and in furtherance of the robbery, a gun battle resulting in his own death. Since petitioner may be held vicariously responsible for *any* killing legally attributable to his accomplices, he may be charged with Smith's death.

. . . People v. Ferlin, 203 Ca. 587, 597, 265 P. 230 [is] not apposite for [it] simply held that an accomplice cannot be charged with murder when his confederate accidentally kills himself while committing a felony. The [court in that case was] not faced with a situation involving the intentional commission of acts provoking lethal resistance by victims or police officers.

aforethought is not attributable to the robber, for the killing is not committed by him in the perpetration or attempt to perpetrate robbery."

We further stated that, apart from the felony-murder rule, a defendant may be guilty of murder on a vicarious liability theory for a killing committed by the victim: "Defendants who initiate gun battles may also be found guilty of murder if their victims resist and kill. Under such circumstances, 'the defendant for a base, antisocial motive and with wanton disregard for human life, does an act that involves a high degree of probability that it will result in death' (People v. Thomas, 41 Cal. 2d 470, 480, 261 P.2d 1, 7 . . . [concurring opinion]), and it is unnecessary to imply malice by invoking the felony-murder doctrine. To invoke the felony-murder doctrine to imply malice in such a case is unnecessary and overlooks the principles of criminal liability that should govern the responsibility of one person for a killing committed by another." . . .

To me, it is too obvious to dispute that inherent in the brandishing of a gun in the robbery is the conditional threat of the robber that he will use the gun if his demands are not complied with. The fact that the robber makes his threat express does not serve to distinguish *Washington.* It is unreasonable to assume that, just because the robber in *Washington* did not articulate his threat, the victim in that case had less reason to fear for his safety or, as the majority assert, less "provocation" for shooting the robber than did the victims in the instant case. It is absurd to suggest that the robber's acts in *Washington* were, as a matter of law, not "sufficiently provocative of lethal resistance to support a finding of implied malice," whereas the robbers' acts in the instant case could be so considered.

In sum, the articulation of threats does not without more show that the robber's acts were done "with wanton disregard for human life," involving "a high degree of probability that it will result in death" from which malice can be implied. (See People v. Washington, supra.) The difference between an implied and an express threat furnishes no significant basis for discrimination between robbers. To permit additional punishment for a homicide committed by the victim on the basis of the articulation of the threats would deter robbery "haphazardly at best." (See People v. Washington, supra.) . . .

I would issue prohibition as to the murder count.

TOBRINER, J., concurs.

MOSK, Justice [dissented].

Notes and Questions

1. Where was Taylor when all this happened? Under *Washington,* it would have seemed that Taylor could not have been convicted of first-degree murder. What tool does the court use to uphold the charge? Does this make

sense? Does holding Taylor accountable for the killing have any deterrent effect on robbery? On the behavior of people like Daniels and Smith?

2. Is a robber who articulates conditional threats really more culpable than one who remains silent while pointing a gun at his victim? If the robber was silent and only pointed the gun and then was shot by the storeowner, would not the court find another way to convict Taylor?

3. The holding in *Taylor,* particularly footnote 26, was subsequently modified by People v. Antick, 15 Cal. 3d 79, 123 Col. Rptr. 475, 539 P.2d 43 (1975). Shortly after a residential burglary, police observed an "automobile in traffic with furniture or a stereo in the back seat and furniture in the trunk" occupied by a driver and a passenger. After losing sight of the car for a short time the officers came upon it parked beside the road. Only the driver, Bose, was in the car. Before being frisked, Bose pulled a gun from his waist and fired at the officer. "The officer returned the fire and Bose started running." The officer's partner fired again, killing Bose. The goods in the car were stolen and the police discovered that the defendant had been the other man in the car and had participated in the robbery. Defendant was charged with murder under both the felony-murder and vicarious liability theories and was convicted. On appeal the court held that the conviction could not stand on either theory. First, the felony-murder theory was inapplicable because of *Washington.* Second, the vicarious liability theory did not apply because

> In order to predicate defendant's guilt upon this theory, it is necessary to prove that Bose committed a murder . . . in other words, that he caused the death of another human being [and] that he acted with malice.
>
> It is well settled that Bose's conduct in initiating a shootout with police officers may establish the requisite malice. As we have noted on a number of occasions, a person who initiates a gun battle in the course of committing a felony intentionally and with a conscious disregard for life commits an act that is likely to cause death. However, Bose's malicious conduct did not result in the unlawful killing of *another* human being, but rather in Bose's own death. The only homicide which occurred was the justifiable killing of Bose by the police officer. Defendant's criminal liability certainly cannot be predicated upon the actions of the officer. As Bose could not be found guilty of murder in connection with his own death, it is impossible to base defendant's liability for this offense upon his vicarious responsibility for the crime of his accomplice.

Is there anything wrong with the court's reasoning? If we have already gone as far as *Taylor,* why not extend its doctrine to its logical conclusion?

If in *Antick* the police officer missed Bose but killed another co-felon or an innocent bystander, the defendant would be guilty of murder under *Taylor.* In this situation, though, is the defendant any more or less culpable than when his co-felon is killed?

4. Note a very strange aspect of *Taylor.* If Taylor evinced an abandoned and malignant heart, why should he be charged with first-degree murder (see

p.418) rather than second-degree murder? The reasoning was spelled out in Pizano v. Superior Court, 21 Cal. 3d. 128, 577 P.2d 659 (1977). In *Pizano,* the defendant, in an attempt to escape from a robbery, used the victim as a shield. A neighbor, unaware of the victim's presence, tried to stop the robbery by shooting at the robber as he left the house. The shot killed the victim. Under California law, using a victim as a shield constitutes a conscious disregard for life which can invoke second-degree (extremely reckless) murder liability. The court used California Penal Code §189, however, to determine the degree of murder, stating, "The killing itself, having been committed by the [neighbor] to thwart the robbery, cannot be said to have been committed in perpetration of it. *But the act which made the killing murder attributable to the robber—[using the victim as a shield]—was committed in the perpetration of the robbery.* Therefore . . . section 189 may properly be invoked to determine that the murder is of the first degree." In other words, §189 permits a second-degree nonfelony murder committed during a felony to be aggravated to first-degree murder. Does this make sense?

Chief Justice Bird in dissent argued:

> Assuming, arguendo, the conceptual possibility of the majority's analysis, their goal can be achieved only by writing into section 189 a third "kind" of first degree murder not provided for by the Legislature, i.e., a murder in which "the act which made the killing a murder attributable to the robber . . . was committed in the perpetration of the robbery." To do so, however, expressly contradicts the Legislature's provision that "all other [non-enumerated] kinds of murder are of the second degree."

5. Recall the "merger" cases at the end of the Chapter 6 treatment of felony murder: State v. Thompson and People v. Miller. The "majority rule" is that an assault will merge with a killing to prevent application of the felony-murder rule.

Assume that an armed robber goes into a store and kills the storeowners while in the process of robbing them. What if, as a defense to a felony-murder charge, defendant argues that armed robbery is just assault with a deadly weapon coupled with larceny, and that any charge of murder for a killing arising out of armed robbery necessarily includes assault with a deadly weapon and cannot support a felony-murder instruction? Is this argument to extend the merger rule sound? The court in People v. Burton, 6 Cal. 3d 375, 491 P.2d 793 (1971) said no.

> In the case of armed robbery, as well as the other felonies enumerated in section 189 of the Penal Code, there is an *independent felonious purpose,* namely in the case of robbery to acquire money or property belonging to another. Once a person has embarked upon a course of conduct for one of the enumerated felonious purpose, he comes directly within a clear legislative warning—if a death results from his commission of that felony it will be first degree murder, regard-

less of the circumstances. This court has reiterated numerous times that "The purpose of the felony-murder rule is to deter felons from killing negligently or accidentally by holding them strictly responsible for killings they commit. . . ."

Defendant in this case by embarking upon the venture of armed robbery brought himself within the class of persons who the Legislature has concluded must avoid causing death or bear the consequences of first degree murder. The trial judge quite correctly instructed on felony murder based on homicides directly resulting from the commission of armed robbery.

Is the court correct?

B. CAPITAL MURDER—THE DEATH PENALTY

As the previous sections have shown, the criminal law draws subtle distinctions among types of homicides in order to determine the appropriate punishment, or range of punishment, for a particular killing. Though the difference in punishment between, say, voluntary manslaughter and second-degree murder might be a decade in the defendant's life, no distinction drawn by the criminal law is so important and stark as the one between life imprisonment and the death penalty. Generally, a defendant is not even eligible for the death penalty unless he or she is convicted of the state's equivalent of first-degree murder. Thus the steps between manslaughter and murder, and between second-degree and first-degree murder, help determine whether the defendant may face the death penalty. But under modern American law, the prosecutor who seeks the execution of a defendant convicted of first-degree murder must seek to prove yet a higher degree of murder in a special proceeding, usually called the "penalty trial." The new and unusual doctrines of criminal law applied in the penalty trial are the focus of this section.

1. A Historical Summary

The law of the death penalty has changed dramatically in American history. Roughly, it has passed through three broad phases. At the time of Independence, most homicide, and certainly any murder, was automatically punishable by death. The automatic death penalty, inherited by the colonies from English law, continued in almost all the states well into the nineteenth century, although the states gradually created a two-degree scheme of murder and restricted the death penalty to first-degree murders. Then from roughly the middle of the nineteenth century to the 1970s, the states used their first-degree murder definitions to decide which defendants were eligible for the death penalty but left the choice between life and death to the unguided discretion of the judge or jury that had decided the guilt issue.

After more than a decade of constitutional wrangling, death penalty law has now settled into a fairly stable third phase. Typically, after a jury finds the defendant guilty of "capital" or first-degree murder, it retests the defendant's liability against a still narrower "super-first-degree" murder law by deciding whether the offender or the offense exhibited certain "aggravating" factors. The judge or jury, in the special penalty trial, then "weighs" those aggravating factors against any mitigating factors about the crime or the criminal and decides whether the defendant shall live or die.

Appreciating these developments in American law requires a somewhat more detailed review of the American law of capital punishment, focusing on the complex and tortuous constitutional treatment of capital punishment, with its attendant philosophical and empirical questions. However, in a course in criminal law, as opposed to one in criminology, philosophy, or constitutional law, these broader questions should serve as background to the more concrete question of how the death penalty law actually operates in the states today. Thus, after a summary of the constitutional developments, we will examine capital punishment law as the last step in the continuum of aggravated homicide law.

2. Capital Punishment and the Constitution

The Fifth Amendment to the Constitution says that no person "shall be deprived of life . . . without due process of law." The language obviously suggests that the authors of the Bill of Rights had no categorical objection to the death penalty. And indeed the law in the colonies and in the states after Independence used the death penalty as the major instrument for punishing murders. Borrowing from the English model, early American law normally made the death penalty automatic for anyone convicted of murder. Thus, the jury that believed the defendant to be guilty of murder had no power to relieve the defendant of the death penalty, except by distorting the truth and acquitting him of the murder charge. As American law developed degree distinctions in murder, the state had to win a conviction on an aggravated murder charge to ensure automatic infliction of the death penalty, but the rule of automatic death sentencing persisted.

The only potential constitutional restraint on the death penalty lay in the Eighth Amendment prohibition of cruel and unusual punishments. But the conventional wisdom, at least the wisdom ultimately adopted by the Supreme Court of the United States, Gregg v. Georgia, 428 U.S. 153, 169-70 (1976), is that the authors of the Eighth Amendment, obviously aware of the prevalence of capital punishment, did not believe that the death penalty per se was unconstitutional. Rather, the "cruel and unusual" punishment clause, drawn from the English Bill of Rights of 1689, was concerned with more particular matters. First, it prohibited any punishments not officially authorized by statute or not lying within the sentencing court's jurisdiction. Second, it proscribed brutal, gratuitously painful methods of torture or execution. Although the authors of the Eighth Amendment may have intended to prohibit a severe punishment such as death for a minor crime, they certainly did not view the death penalty as unconstitutionally excessive or disproportionate for the crime of murder, or indeed for such other crimes as rape and kidnapping, which were also frequently punished by death at that time. See generally Granucci, "Nor Cruel and Unusual Punishments Inflicted": The Original Meaning, 57 Calif. L. Rev. 839 (1969).

For more than a century and a half after Independence, capital punishment proceeded in the United States with virtually no constitutional scrutiny. The state law of capital punishment, however, changed significantly. The state legislatures gradually rejected the automatic death penalty scheme for two related reasons. First, many legislators may have simply felt that not all murderers—even first-degree murderers—were equally culpable or that all deserved death. In short, the law of murder did not sufficiently distinguish killers according to the blameworthiness of their crimes or the moral aspects of their characters. Second, the automatic death penalty law had a paradoxically lenient effect. Jurors who believed a defendant was guilty of capital murder but did not believe he or she deserved to die would simply "nullify" the law of homicide by acquitting the defendant of the murder charge.

Slowly but steadily during the nineteenth century, the states changed their death penalty laws to a system that openly and expressly gave juries the discretion they had previously exercised in a subversive fashion. The model was very simple. The judge first instructed the jury in the law of first-degree murder so the jury could determine whether the defendant was "eligible" for the death penalty. If the jury so found, it was then to decide, as part of the same deliberation, whether the defendant should be executed or, instead, sentenced to life imprisonment. The trial court gave the jury absolutely no legal guidance on how to make the choice. Nor did the jury have the benefit of any special information about the defendant's background, character, or previous criminal record, beyond whatever narrow information the state or defendant had offered on the question of the defendant's guilt on the murder charge. The system had changed from one of no jury discretion to one of total—and totally unguided—jury discretion. This new system constituted the American law of the death penalty until 1972. Though a few states had wholly abolished capital punishment late in the nineteenth century or during the twentieth century, the great majority retained the system of jury-discretionary capital punishment until that year.

By the 1950s, the jury-discretion scheme of capital punishment had come under great political and philosophical scrutiny. Many opponents of the death penalty attacked it in absolute terms, arguing that there was no empirical proof that it was superior to life imprisonment in deterring serious crime, and that a morally mature society should not use death as an instrument for revenge or retribution. But the legal attacks on the death penalty during the 1960s also focused on the way the death penalty operated in practice. Though giving discretion to the jury softened the severity of the old automatic death penalty, it also permitted arbitrary and discriminatory administration, since the statutes gave juries no guidance and provided no legal rules by which an appellate court could review a jury sentence. Throughout this century, the states have executed as many as 200 people a year (peaking in the 1930s). Comparing the crimes and criminal records of those executed and those who received life sentences, one is hard put to find a rational pattern in the results. Unfortunately, the one potential pattern that does emerge is one of stark racial discrimination. The likeliest candidate for death was the black defendant convicted of killing a white person or, even more disproportionately, a black man convicted of raping a white woman.

As pressure to end or restrict the death penalty grew, the Supreme Court finally began addressing the constitutionality of capital punishment. In McGautha v. California, 402 U.S. 183 (1971), the petitioner argued unsuccessfully that the standardless jury discretion schemes of the states violated the due process clause of the Fourteenth Amendment. Somewhat hypertechnically, the Court restricted its decision to the application of the due process clause, avoiding any decision on the application of the Eighth Amendment. But Justice Harlan's opinion for the court contained a prescient warning that whatever the constitutional rubric, any effort to impose legal regulation on the morally complex question of capital punishment would be futile:

> To identify before the fact those characteristics of criminal homicides and their perpetrators which call for the death penalty, and to express these characteristics in language which can be fairly understood and applied by the sentencing authority, appear to be tasks which are beyond present human ability. [Id. at 204.]

Justice Harlan believed the Court should not force the state legislatures to devise guiding rules for the death penalty, because the visceral decision of whether to kill a defendant could not be reduced to legal rules.

Just one year later, a majority of the Court rejected Justice Harlan's warning. In the landmark case of Furman v. Georgia, 408 U.S. 238 (1972), the Court, by a vote of 5 to 4, struck down all the death penalty schemes in the United States as they then operated. Unfortunately, there was not a majority opinion in *Furman.* Indeed, each of the five judges in the majority wrote his own opinion. Thus, at best one can glean from the *Furman* opinions some general themes, rather than a single guiding principle. Two of the Justices, Brennan and Marshall, took the view that the death penalty under all circumstances violated the Eighth Amendment, because it served no legitimate deterrent or retributional purpose, and because it violated the "evolving standards of decency." The swing votes, cast by Justices Douglas, Stewart, and White, were more guarded. The consensus of their views was that the wanton, unpredictable infliction of the death penalty under the unguided discretion schemes, as well as the disproportionate infliction of the death penalty on blacks, violated the Eighth Amendment. The result of *Furman,* then, was that the states could restore the death penalty only if they designed new capital punishment laws that so restricted or guided jury discretion as to remove the arbitrary and discriminatory effects decried by the *Furman* plurality.

Immediately after *Furman,* roughly three-quarters of the states did enact new laws aimed at satisfying the somewhat elusive demands of *Furman.* The new capital punishment statutes took two forms, each designed to solve the problem of unguided jury discretion. A handful of states, in an act of historical irony, returned to the mandatory or automatic death penalty. They created special categories of egregious first-degree murder, such as the premeditated murder of a police officer, or premeditated murder in the course of an enumerated felony, and declared the death penalty automatic for anyone convicted of such a murder. Thus, these states "solved" the problem of unguided or excessive jury discretion by eliminating jury discretion altogether. The other type of statute, adopted by the majority of the reenacting states, can be termed "guided discretion" statutes. Under these statutes, the sentencer, usually the jury (though in a few states a judge), holds a separate sentencing hearing after the defendant is convicted of first-degree or "capital" murder. The sentencer then chooses either the death penalty or life imprisonment (sometimes with the possibility of parole, sometimes not) but is guided in that choice by a process of balancing aggravating and mitigating factors. The sentencer must find the presence of certain aggravating factors and weigh them against any apparent mitigating factors. This model of the guided discretion statute has now become the established norm for the death penalty in America, and we will examine it in some detail below.

In 1976, in Gregg v. Georgia, 428 U.S. 153 (1976), and companion cases from Florida, Texas, North Carolina, and Louisiana, the Supreme Court returned to the death penalty to determine whether the new statutes had resolved the problems identified four years earlier in *Furman.* Once again, the Court produced no majority decision, but the holding of *Gregg* was clear. First, over the dissents of Justice Brennan and Marshall, the Court, in a plurality opinion by Justice Stewart, flatly rejected the argument that the death penalty was in all circumstances unconstitutional under the Eighth Amendment. Summarizing the jurisprudence of the Eighth Amendment, Justice Stewart stated that a punishment was constitutional so long as it comported with "evolving standards of human decency," as reflected in "contemporary public attitudes," and with the Eighth Amendment concept of the "dignity of man." The death penalty met the first test because public attitudes, reflected in such objective evidence as the reenactment of death penalty laws by a majority of state legislatures after *Furman* and numerous jury verdicts of death under these new laws, demonstrated that the death penalty did not violate contemporary standards of decency. And the death penalty did not violate the "dignity of man" because it could serve legitimate deterrent and retributive purposes. The

Court acknowledged that the empirical evidence of the deterrent value of the death penalty was inconclusive at best, but in the absence of a clear answer the Justices gave the benefit of the doubt on this issue of penological policy to the legislatures. Moreover, Justice Stewart said that retribution was a legitimate, time-honored justification for the criminal law, especially since retributive action by the state could channel aggressive energies in society that might otherwise lead to lawless, vengeful action by private citizens. Finally, Justice Stewart concluded that whatever the fairness of inflicting death for less serious crimes, the death penalty was not invariably excessive for the crime of murder.

Having concluded that the death penalty did not necessarily violate the Eighth Amendment, the Court proceeded to examine the new post-*Furman* statutes. In Woodson v. North Carolina, 428 U.S. 280 (1976), and Roberts v. Louisiana, 428 U.S. 325 (1976), the Court struck down the revived automatic death penalty statutes. The plurality in *Woodson* and *Roberts* viewed the automatic-death statutes as misguided efforts to solve the problem of jury discretion. The Justices believed that the Eighth Amendment implied a principle of respect for the individuality of all criminal defendants, and were therefore unwilling to tolerate a death penalty law that forbade individualized distinctions of culpability among murderers guilty of a given category of crime. Moreover, the plurality returned to the classic problem of jury nullification that had helped undermine the old automatic statutes more than a century before. It declared that the inevitable tendency of jurors to render "false acquittals" to spare a guilty but sympathetic defendant from death would lead to further arbitrary or capricious administration of the death penalty.

In its key holding in Gregg v. Georgia, however, the Court upheld the guided discretion statutes as constitutionally satisfactory solutions to the problems of unfettered jury discretion diagnosed in *Furman.* In approving the new Georgia statute, Justice Stewart noted several features which supported its constitutionality, though he avoided saying that any of these particular features was constitutionally required: The statute created a separate sentencing proceeding at which the state and the defendant could offer evidence not presented at the guilt phase; the statute offered the jury express guidance in identifying aggravating circumstances and requiring the jury to find at least one of the aggravating circumstances enumerated in the statute before it voted for death; the jury was instructed to consider any individualized mitigating circumstances that might outweigh the aggravating circumstances; the defendant had a right of automatic appeal to the state supreme court for review of the death sentence; and the state supreme court was required to conduct a "proportionality review" of every sentence, ensuring that the sentence was not arbitrary or prejudicial, or disproportionate in comparison to sentences handed down in similar Georgia cases.[27] In companion cases, the Court upheld the constitutionality of similar statutes in Proffitt v. Florida, 428 U.S. 242 (1976), and Jurek v. Texas, 428 U.S. 262 (1976). Though the Florida and

27. In 1984, the Court held that the proportionality review was not constitutionally mandated, Harris v. Pulley, 104 S. Ct. 871 (1984).

Texas statutes differed from the Georgia law in their schemes for establishment of aggravating and mitigating circumstances, the Court found that they provided similarly adequate safeguards against arbitrary and discriminatory application of capital punishment.

The 1976 cases thus restored the death penalty in America under the model of the guided discretion statutes. (States like North Carolina and Louisiana, whose automatic-death laws were struck down in 1976, quickly enacted new death penalty laws to meet the model approved in *Gregg*). One year after *Gregg*, Gary Gilmore was executed in Utah, becoming the first person to suffer the death penalty in America since the pre-*Furman* litigation had effectively suspended the death penalty in 1967.

The Supreme Court has indicated that the death penalty is unconstitutional for any crime other than murder. See, e.g., Coker v. Georgia, 433 U.S. 584 (1977) where the court held that the death penalty was unconstitutionally excessive for the crime of rape of an adult woman. But over 2000 murderers have entered death row under the new statutes. Protracted federal and state appeals have prevented or delayed the execution of the vast majority of these prisoners, but by 1984, more than 20 people had been executed under the new laws, and the rate of execution has been steadily increasing.

The NAACP Legal Defense and Educational Fund, Inc., compiles nationwide statistics on death row inmates. The following are its figures as of May 1, 1985:

Total Number of Death Row Inmates Known to LDF: 1513*

Race:	
Black	627 (41.44%)
White	773 (51.09%)
Hispanic	87 (5.75%)
Native American	18 (1.19%)
Asian	5 (.33%)
Unknown at this issue	3 (.20%)
Sex:	
Male	1494 (98.74%)
Female	19 (1.26%)

Dispositions Since January 1, 1973

Death sentences vacated because of unconstitutional statutes: 558 (rev. est.)
Convictions reversed or sentences vacated on other grounds: 708 (est.)

*Executions: 42
Suicides: 18
Commutations: 43 (including those by the Governor of Texas resulting from favorable court decisions)
Died of natural causes, or killed while under death sentence: 18

Probably the best and most representative example of a modern death penalty law is the one adopted in the Model Penal Code, which won the express approval of Justice Stewart in *Gregg,* 428 U.S. at 193. It reads:

MODEL PENAL CODE

American Law Institute Model Penal Code and Commentaries (1985)

§210.6

(2) *Determination by Court or by Court and Jury.* [The Court] shall conduct a separate proceeding to determine whether the defendant should be sentenced for a felony of the first degree or sentenced to death. The proceeding shall be conducted before the Court alone if the defendant was convicted by a Court sitting without a jury or upon his plea of guilty or if the prosecuting attorney and the defendant waive a jury with respect to sentence. In other cases it shall be conducted before the Court sitting with the jury which determined the defendant's guilt or, if the Court for good cause shown discharges that jury, with a new jury empanelled for the purpose.

In the proceeding, evidence may be presented as to any matter that the Court deems relevant to sentence, including but not limited to the nature and circumstances of the crime, the defendant's character, background, history, mental and physical condition and any of the aggravating or mitigating circumstances enumerated in Subsections (3) and (4) of this Section. Any such evidence, not legally privileged, which the Court deems to have probative force, may be received, regardless of its admissibility under the exclusionary rules of evidence, provided that the defendant's counsel is accorded a fair opportunity to rebut such evidence. The prosecuting attorney and the defendant or his counsel shall be permitted to present argument for or against sentence of death.

The determination whether sentence of death shall be imposed shall be in the discretion of the Court, except that when the proceeding is conducted before the Court sitting with a jury, the Court shall not impose sentence of death unless it submits to the jury the issue whether the defendant should be sentenced to death or to imprisonment and the jury returns a verdict that the sentence should be death. If the jury is unable to reach a unanimous verdict, the Court shall dismiss the jury and impose sentence for a felony of the first degree.

The Court, in exercising its discretion as to sentence, and the jury, in determining upon its verdict, shall take into account the aggravating and mitigating circumstances enumerated in Subsections (3) and (4) and any other facts that it deems relevant, but it shall not impose or recommend sentence of death unless it finds one of the aggravating circumstances enumerated in Subsection (3) and further finds that there are no mitigating circumstances sufficiently substantial to call for leniency. When the issue is submitted to the jury, the Court shall so instruct and also shall inform the jury of the nature of the sentence of imprisonment that may be imposed, including its implication with respect to possible release upon parole, if the jury verdict is against sentence of death.

ALTERNATIVE FORMULATION OF SUBSECTION (2)

(2) *Determination by Court.* [The Court] shall conduct a separate proceeding to determine whether the defendant should be sentenced for a felony of the first degree or sentenced to death. In the proceeding, the Court, in accordance with Section 7.07, shall consider the report of the pre-sentence investigation and, if a psychiatric examination has been ordered, the report of such examination. In addition, evidence may be presented as to any matter that the Court deems relevant to sentence, including but not limited to the nature and circumstances of the crime, the defendant's character, background, history, mental and physical condition and any of the aggravating or mitigating circumstances enumerated in Subsections (3) and (4) of this Section. Any such evidence, not legally privileged, which the Court deems to have probative force, may be received, regardless of its admissibility under the exclusionary rules of evidence, provided that the defendant's counsel is accorded a fair opportunity to rebut such evidence. The prosecuting attorney and the defendant or his counsel shall be permitted to present argument for or against sentence of death.

The determination whether sentence of death shall be imposed shall be in the discretion of the Court. In exercising such discretion, the Court shall take into account the aggravating and mitigating circumstances enumerated in Subsections (3) and (4) and any other facts that it deems relevant but shall not impose sentence of death unless it finds one of the aggravating circumstances enumerated in Subsection (3) and further finds that there are no mitigating circumstances sufficiently substantial to call for leniency.

(3) *Aggravating Circumstances.*

(a) The murder was committed by a convict under sentence of imprisonment.

(b) The defendant was previously convicted of another murder or of a felony involving the use or threat of violence to the person.

(c) At the time the murder was committed the defendant also committed another murder.

(d) The defendant knowingly created a great risk of death to many persons.

(e) The murder was committed while the defendant was engaged or was an accomplice in the commission of, or an attempt to commit, or flight after committing or attempting to commit, robbery, rape or deviate sexual intercourse by force or threat of force, arson, burglary or kidnapping.

(f) The murder was committed for the purpose of avoiding or preventing a lawful arrest or effecting an escape from lawful custody.
(g) The murder was committed for pecuniary gain.
(h) The murder was especially heinous, atrocious or cruel, manifesting exceptional depravity.

(4) *Mitigating Circumstances.*
(a) The defendant has no significant history of prior criminal activity.
(b) The murder was committed while the defendant was under the influence of extreme mental or emotional disturbance.
(c) The victim was a participant in the defendant's homicidal conduct or consented to the homicidal act.
(d) The murder was committed under circumstances which the defendant believed to provide a moral justification or extenuation for his conduct.
(e) The defendant was an accomplice in a murder committed by another person and his participation in the homicidal act was relatively minor.
(f) The defendant acted under duress or under the domination of another person.
(g) At the time of the murder, the capacity of the defendant to appreciate the criminality [wrongfulness] of his conduct or to conform his conduct to the requirements of law was impaired as a result of mental disease or defect or intoxication.
(h) The youth of the defendant at the time of the crime.

Notes and Questions

1. The Model Penal Code proposes both judge and jury death sentencing as plausible procedures for carrying out the mandate of *Furman.* Most states afford the capital defendant the right to a jury determination of sentence in a separate post-conviction hearing. The jury is usually, though not always, the same one that decided the defendant's guilt. In a handful of states, the death penalty decision is made solely by the trial judge, even after conviction by a jury, though the structure of the hearing is virtually identical to that in the jury-sentencing states. See, e.g., Ariz. Rev. Stat. Ann. §703 (Supp. 1983). In a few states, most notably Florida, the jury holds a separate hearing to make a recommendation of sentence, but the jury decision is only advisory: The trial judge has the power to impose life where the jury has recommend death or to choose death where the jury has recommended life. See, e.g., Fla. Stat. §921.141 (West Supp. 1983). The Supreme Court has held that there is no constitutional flaw in a procedure that restricts or eliminates jury death sentencing. Spaziano v. Florida, 104 S.Ct. 3154 (1984).

2. The new laws vary somewhat in their scheme for identifying the most culpable killers. Most of the "guided discretion" states retained their traditional categories of first-degree murder, most obviously premeditated murder and felony murder, and used the aggravating circumstances in the penalty hearing, in effect, to establish an enhanced category, "aggravated first-degree murder." Other states fine-tuned their first-degree murder statutes by requiring the jury *at the guilt stage* to convict the defendant of a new enhanced category of "capital murder," and then added further aggravating circumstances at the penalty stage. See, e.g., Tex. Code Crim. Proc. Ann. art. 37.071 (Vernon 1981). California has taken an intermediate approach: After the jury in the guilt phase convicts the defendant of first-degree murder, it then must find at least one "special circumstance" representing an aggravating factor. If it does, the trial shifts to the penalty phase, at which the jury considers a new list of aggravating circumstances. Cal. Penal Codes §190.2 (West Supp. 1983). Most states created detailed statutory lists of aggravating or mitigating circumstances like the Model Penal Code, but a few states do not enumerate any specific mitigating circumstances, simply requiring the sentencer to consider any mitigating factors that arise from the evidence. See, e.g., Ga. Code Ann. §27-2503, 27-2534.1.

3. The typical aggravating circumstances reflected in Model Penal Code §210.6 bear an interesting relationship to the traditional homicide categories. We will examine them in some detail in State v. Goodman, below, but a few observations may be helpful now. For example, §210.6(3)(e) seems to duplicate the first-degree felony-murder rule. Subsections (f) and (g) seem to overlap slightly with the concerns of the felony-murder rule, but distinguish murders on the basis of "motive," an issue supposedly irrelevant to the criminal law once the required technical *mens rea* is established. See State v. Goodman, below. Subsection (b) enhances punishment on the basis of the defendant's previous criminal record. Under normal rules of evidence, a defendant's earlier crimes cannot be introduced at a criminal trial to help prove the defendant's predisposition to commit a new offense. McCormick's Handbook of The Law of Evidence (Cleary ed. 1972), §190, at 447. Yet in traditional discretionary sentencing by the judge in noncapital cases, the trial judge always looks at the defendant's criminal record. The states have transposed this element of discretionary noncapital sentencing into the new criminal "trial" of the penalty phase. Subsection (d) of Model Penal Code §210.6(3) is curious; it aggravates a first-degree murder where the defendant, in effect, exhibited an "abandoned and malignant heart" with respect to the possible deaths of other people, even if those others were not killed. The most controversial of these factors, the "heinous, atrocious, or cruel" provision in subsection (h), which we will examine later, seems like a vague exhortation to the sentencer to identify whatever aggravating aspects of the particular crime have evaded the other categories.

Finally, note that it is an aggravating circumstance under subsection (a) if the murderer was already under a sentence of life imprisonment. Does that factor make the murder more culpable? Or is it that a prisoner under a life sentence cannot be deterred from killing by any punishment less than death? The Supreme Court has reserved the question of constitutionality of the automatic death sentence in this circumstance alone. Lockett v. Ohio, 438 U.S. 586, 604 n.11 (1978). See People v. Smith, 63 N.Y.2d 41, 468 N.E.2d 879 (1984) (striking down New York's mandatory death sentence for lifers convicted of capital murder).

4. Some of the enumerated mitigating factors, in Model Penal Code §210.4, such as subsection (a) on the absence of a serious criminal record, are simply the obverse of the aggravating circumstances. Others closely resemble various conventional homicide doctrines that would normally serve as defenses to or reduce the grade of the defendant's liability. Thus, subsection (b) is like the diminished capacity or provocation doctrines in voluntary manslaughter; subsections (d) and (f) resemble the justification or duress defenses we will examine later in Part V; subsection (g) obviously resembles the insanity defense, and subsection (e) seems designed to reflect the criminal law's ambivalence about the felony murder rule. (As we will see below in the case of Enmund v. Florida, the Supreme Court itself was beset by this ambivalence.) We will examine the issue of mitigating circumstances in detail below, but note for now that they generally call for the same sort of evidence that might be offered at the guilt phase to reduce the grade of homicide or to serve as a complete defense. If the evidence, by hypothesis, has proved insufficient to save the defendant from a first-degree murder conviction, does it make sense for it to be reconsidered at sentencing?

North Carolina's post-*Woodson* capital punishment statute closely resembles that of the Model Penal Code (though its aggravating circumstances differ slightly from the Code's), and its state supreme court has been unusually thorough and articulate in reviewing the application of the statute in appeals from death sentences. The following case illustrates the operation of the law.

3. Aggravating Circumstances

STATE v. GOODMAN

Supreme Court of North Carolina
298 N.C. 1, 257 S.E.2d 569 (1979)

Principal evidence against defendant was provided by Annie Lois Goins Shamback (Lois) who testified under a grant of immunity pursuant to G.S. 15A-1052. In return for her "truthful testimony" against Charles D. Goins and defendant, the state agreed to dismiss charges against her relating to the murder, robbery and kidnapping of Lester Collins. (Charles was tried prior to the date of the defendant's trial). Her testimony is summarized in pertinent part as follows:

At the time of defendant's trial (October 1978) she was 23 years of age and had been married approximately 6 months. She had two children that were born prior to her marriage. Charles Goins (Charles) was her brother and Collins was married to her sister. On 2 July 1977 her sister was a patient at Dorothea Dix Hospital.

On 2 July 1977 she and her young son lived with defendant at Lumberton, N.C. She and defendant were not married to each other but had lived together for approximately 18 months prior to said date. Charles had been staying with them for about a week, his home being near Fayetteville.

Late in the afternoon of said date she, defendant and Charles went to Fayetteville in her white 1968 Ford Fairlane. Their destination was Charles' home but they stopped at a bar in East Fayetteville, went in and defendant and Charles "had a few beers." When they returned to the car they discovered that a C.B. and scanner belonging to defendant had been taken from the car while they were in the bar. Defendant had reason to believe that Magaline Tyler's brother was one of the persons who stole the C.B. and scanner and insisted on going to her house which was not far from the bar.

When defendant, Lois and Charles left the bar, defendant was driving. After driving a short distance in the neighborhood, defendant and Charles got out of the car and told Lois to circle the area while they looked for the person or persons who stole the equipment from the car. After circling for some 30 minutes, Lois drove the car to Magaline Tyler's home. Defendant came out of the house and Collins was following him, asking defendant to take him home. At first, defendant refused, but Collins kept on asking and eventually defendant said he would take him home. Collins had been drinking.

Defendant got under the wheel, Collins got in the back seat and Lois and Charles rode on the front seat. Defendant was quite angry about his C.B. and scanner being stolen and was also angry with Lois for circling so long.

Defendant then drove the car down Cedar Creek Road east of Fayetteville to Lois' mother's home which was also Charles' home. When they arrived there, Charles went into the house to get some clothes. Collins remained in the back seat of the car and wanted defendant to carry him back to Fayetteville.

The four of them left the Goins home and were situated in the car in the same positions as when they arrived there. They proceeded to drive down Cedar Creek Road and while riding Charles leaned over and whispered something to defendant. Defendant then turned the automobile down a dirt road, went to the end of it and turned around in the direction of Cedar Creek Road. It was then "way after dark."

Defendant stopped the car on the dirt road and got out. He told Collins to get out. Defendant had a gun and as Collins got out of the car, defendant hit Collins on the side of his head with the gun. Collins told defendant he hadn't done anything, but defendant hit him again with the gun, bringing blood from Collins' face. Charles and Lois remained in the car while defendant and Collins went behind the car.

When the two men reached the rear of the car, Lois saw Collins advancing on defendant and then heard three shots fired. Before the shots were fired, Lois could not see what Collins was doing to defendant, "just his body going toward" defendant.

After the shots were fired, Charles got out of the car and went to the back of it. Lois could hear "moaning" and saw that Collins was on the ground. She got out of the car and saw Charles and defendant standing beside Collins who was on the ground a short distance from the trunk of the car. She could tell that Collins' clothing was wet. Defendant and Charles then took Collins and put him in the trunk of the car. They then discussed what to do with Collins.

Defendant said that he knew a place where they could bury Collins and it would take a long time for the police to find him. Collins was alive at that time. Defendant then told Lois to drive the car because he was cut on his left side.

At defendant's instruction, Lois drove the car to Lumberton to defendant's home. Collins was still in the trunk and was "begging for his life." All of the occupants of the car except Collins got out and went into defendant's home. There was a pool of blood on the driver's side of the car. Lois got a washrag and washed the blood off the car. While she was doing that, defendant was looking for a shovel with which to carry out defendant's and Charles' plan to bury Collins.

When Collins begged defendant to let him out of the trunk, defendant and Charles both told him that he might as well shut up because he was going to die anyway. At defendant's request Lois cleaned up his wound and placed a bandage on it. His shirt had blood on it and he took it off after which Lois washed blood off the back of his pants.

While at defendant's home Charles wiped blood off of a knife that he had. After staying at the home for about thirty minutes, they all left with Lois driving and Collins remaining in the trunk. After Lois drove some distance into Robeson County, defendant decided that he would drive. He stated that he had changed his mind about burying Collins and knew where he wanted to carry him.

With defendant driving they proceeded to the village of Buie in Robeson County. At that point defendant drove on to a service road adjacent to the Seaboard Coastline Railroad and proceeded north. After travelling on that road for a reasonable distance, defendant turned the car around and stopped. Defendant got out and opened the trunk of the car after which Charles and Lois got out. Defendant cursed Collins and told him to get out. Defendant and Charles then took Collins out of the trunk and laid him on some rocks. Defendant had a gun which he then pointed down at Collins' head and fired two shots. Lois had reentered the car at the time the shots were fired but immediately got out and Charles had the gun at that time. Charles also had Collins' billfold.

Defendant and Charles then took Collins by his arms and dragged him onto the railroad track. Defendant stated that a train would come along and "do away with him where the police would have a hard time recognizing who he was."

Thereafter, defendant, Lois and Charles got back into the car with defendant driving. Charles had the gun and said that it was a good shooting little gun. Defendant stated that he shot Collins between his eyes and that Charles shot him in the back of his head. . . .

Defendant's evidence consisted of the testimony of Charles Goins. Charles' testimony is substantially consistent with the version of events testified to by Lois with one major exception. He stated that he was the person who shot and cut Collins; that he did so because Collins mistreated his sister; and that defendant had nothing to do with the murder, "wasn't with" him and Lois when the killing occurred and "hadn't done nothing."

On cross-examination, Charles testified that he had been convicted for breaking and entering, larceny, assault with a deadly weapon, driving under the influence, escaping from prison, driving while license permanently revoked and assault inflicting serious injury. He further testified that "I carry a knife and keep it pretty sharp. If somebody messes with me, I will cut them. It don't take much time for me to cut somebody."

The jury returned a verdict finding defendant guilty of first-degree murder by premeditation and deliberation and by the felony murder rule. They also found him guilty of armed robbery and kidnapping.

The court then recessed the trial until the following Monday when proceedings were resumed before the same jury pursuant to G.S. 15A-2000 et seq. to determine if defendant's sentence on the murder conviction would be death or life imprisonment. The state presented evidence summarized as follows:

Gertrude Tyler testified that she was at the Tyler home on the evening of 2 July 1977; that while there she saw Collins, Charles, Lois and defendant; that Collins had been drinking wine and he asked defendant to "run him home"; that defendant appeared not to hear Collins and later he asked him again; that defendant then told Collins "Yeah, I'll run you home. I'll run you to hell, too while I'm at it"; and that Collins then got into the car with defendant and they rode away. Counsel for defendant stipulated that on 31 January 1967 defendant was convicted in the Superior Court for Robeson County of three counts of armed robbery resulting from a single occurrence on 4 January 1966.

Defendant testified as a witness for himself at the sentencing phase of the trial. His version of the events occurring on 2 July 1977 combines elements of the testimony of Lois and Charles. The gist of defendant's testimony is that he was in the car with them when the shooting and cutting of Collins took place, but that he did not participate in the killing and attempted unsuccessfully to prevent Charles from hurting Collins.

Defendant also introduced into evidence a court docket showing that prior to defendant's trial Charles Goins was allowed to plead guilty, and did plead guilty, to the offense of accessory after the fact of murder "in these cases" and received a prison sentence of six years. . . .

Issues as to punishment were submitted to and answered by the jury as follows:

> 1. Do you find beyond a reasonable doubt the presence of one or more of the following aggravated (sic) circumstances?
>
> a. The defendant had been previously convicted of a felony involving the use or threat of violence to the person, to-wit three counts of the felony of armed robbery in Robeson County Superior Court on January 4, 1966.
>
> Answer: *Yes*
>
> b. The capital felony of murder in the first degree was committed for the purpose of avoiding or preventing a lawful arrest.
>
> Answer: *Yes*
>
> c. The capital felony was committed while the defendant was engaged in the commission of or attempt to commit a robbery, or kidnapping, either or both.
>
> Answer: *Yes*
>
> d. The capital felony was committed to disrupt or hinder the lawful exercise of the enforcement of the criminal law, to-wit: the arrest of the defendant for the offense of robbery or kidnapping, either or both.
>
> Answer: *Yes*
>
> e. The capital felony was especially heinous, atrocious, or cruel.
>
> Answer: *Yes*
>
> 2. Do you find that one or more of the following mitigating circumstances existed at the time the murder was committed?
>
> a. The defendant was an accomplice in or accessory to the capital felony committed by another person and his participation was relatively minor.
>
> Answer: *No*
>
> b. The capacity of the defendant to appreciate the criminality of his conduct or to conform his conduct to the requirements of law was impaired.
>
> Answer: *No*
>
> c. Do you find any other circumstance arising from the evidence which the jury deems to have mitigating value?
>
> Answer: *Yes*

3. Do you find beyond a reasonable doubt that the mitigating circumstances are insufficient to outweigh the aggravating circumstance?

Answer: *Yes*

4. Do you find beyond a reasonable doubt that the aggravating circumstance is sufficiently substantial to call for the imposition of the death penalty?

Answer: *Yes*

The jury recommended that a sentence of death be imposed on the defendant. Pursuant thereto the court imposed the death sentence.

As to the armed robbery and kidnapping charges, the court imposed a life sentence in each case, the sentence in the kidnapping case to begin at expiration of sentence in the armed robbery case. . . .

BRITT, Justice.

Pursuant to G.S. 15A-2000 et seq., this case was tried in two phases: (1) to determine the guilt or innocence of defendant and (2) to determine his sentence for first-degree murder following his conviction of that charge. We will discuss the errors assigned under each phase.

[The Court then upheld the jury's conviction of Goodman of first-degree murder on both premeditation and felony-murder grounds].

PHASE II—SENTENCE DETERMINATION . . .

The general scheme of our death penalty statute enacted by the 1977 General Assembly is: Upon conviction or adjudication of guilt of a defendant of a capital felony, the court conducts a separate sentencing proceeding to determine whether the defendant should be sentenced to death or life imprisonment. G.S. 15A-2000(a)(1). Instructions determined by the trial judge to be warranted by the evidence are given in his charge to the jury prior to its deliberation in determining the sentence. The judge should instruct that the jury must consider any aggravating circumstance or circumstances enumerated in G.S. 15A-2000(e) and (f) which are supported by the evidence, and he should furnish to the jury a written list of issues relating to such aggravating or mitigating circumstance or circumstances. After hearing the evidence, arguments of counsel and instructions of the court, the jury must deliberate and render a sentence recommendation based upon (1) whether any sufficient aggravating circumstance or circumstances as enumerated in the statute exist, (2) whether any sufficient mitigating circumstance or circumstances as enumerated in the statute which outweigh the aggravating circumstance or circumstances found, exist, and (3) based on these considerations, whether the defendant should be sentenced to death or to life imprisonment. G.S. 15A-2000(b).

G.S. 15A-2000(d) provides:

(d) Review of Judgment and Sentence.—

(1) The judgment of conviction and sentence of death shall be subject to automatic review by the Supreme Court of North Carolina pursuant to procedures established by the Rules of Appellate Procedure. In its review, the Supreme Court shall consider the punishment as well as any errors assigned on appeal.

(2) The sentence of death shall be overturned and a sentence of life imprisonment imposed in lieu thereof by the Supreme Court upon a finding that the record does not support the jury's findings of any aggravating circumstance or circumstances upon which the sentencing court based its sentence of death, or upon a finding that the sentence of death was imposed under the influence of passion, prejudice, or any other arbitrary factor, or upon a finding that the sentence of death is excessive or disproportionate to the penalty imposed in similar cases, considering both the crime and the defendant. The Supreme Court may suspend consideration of death penalty cases until such time as the court determines it is prepared to make the comparisons required under the provisions of this section.

(3) If the sentence of death and the judgment of the trial court are reversed on appeal for error in the post-verdict sentencing proceeding, the Supreme Court shall order that a new sentencing hearing be conducted in conformity with the procedures of this Article.

Read together, G.S. 15A-2000(d)(1) and (d)(3) empower this court to review errors assigned in the trial and sentencing phases. When prejudicial error is found the court must order a new sentencing hearing.

In the case at hand, after evidence and arguments were presented at the sentencing phase, the court submitted issues upon the aggravating circumstances enumerated in G.S. 15A-2000(e)(3), (e)(4), (e)(5), (e)(7), and (e)(9). We think the court erred in submitting issues under both subsections (e)(4) and (e)(7) and that because thereof defendant should receive a new sentencing hearing. We will examine the various provisions on which issues of aggravating circumstances were submitted.

1

G.S. 15A–2000(e)(3) states that one of the aggravating factors which may justify the imposition of the death penalty is the fact that the "defendant had been previously convicted of a felony involving the use or threat of violence to the person." This section requires that there be evidence that (1) defendant had been convicted of a felony, that (2) the felony for which he was convicted involved the "use or threat of violence to the person," and that (3) the conduct upon which this conviction was based was conduct which occurred prior to the events out of which the capital felony charge arose. If there is no such evidence, it would be improper for the court to instruct the jury on this subsection. . . .

. . . It is improper to instruct the jury upon the factor enumerated in subsection (e)(3) when there is no evidence which tends to show a felony conviction. Also, the felony for which the defendant has been convicted must be one involving threat or use of violence to the person. It cannot, under this provision, be a crime against property.

Finally, we believe that the "previously convicted" language used by the legislature in subsection (e)(3) refers to "criminal activity conducted prior to the events out of which the charge of murder arose." State v. Stewart, 197 Neb. 497, 250 N.W.2d 849 (1977). To decide otherwise would lead to unnecessary duplication within the statute, for G.S. 15A-2000(e)(5) enumerates those felonies which occur simultaneously with the capital felony which the legislature deems worthy of consideration by the jury. It would be improper, therefore, to instruct the jury that this subsection encompassed conduct which occurred contemporaneously with or after the capital felony with which the defendant is charged.

In the case sub judice defendant stipulated at the sentencing phase that he had been convicted on 31 January 1967 of three counts of armed robbery arising from a single incident which occurred on 4 January 1966. Armed robbery, by definition, involves the use or threat of violence to the person of the victim. Defendant was convicted of this crime, and the conduct upon which his conviction was based did not arise out of the incident upon which the capital felony was charged. The trial court properly refrained from instructing the jury that they might consider under this enumeration the convictions of defendant for armed robbery and kidnapping, which convictions were based upon the same events culminating in the murder of Lester Collins. The evidence in this case was clearly sufficient to justify instruction upon this subsection, and the court properly instructed the jury thereon.

2

G.S. 15A-2000(E)(5) states that the jury may consider as an aggravating circumstance justifying the death penalty the fact that the capital felony "was committed *while* the defendant was engaged . . . in the commission of . . . any robbery . . . [or] kidnapping . . ." (emphasis added) or other enumerated felony. In State v. Cherry, 298 N.C. 86, 257 S.E.2d 551 (1979), we have limited the application of this subsection in felony murder cases. This section needs only brief additional comment, for it is otherwise reasonably free from ambiguity. This subsection differs from (e)(3), which we previously discussed, in that it guides the jury's deliberation upon criminal conduct of the defendant which takes place "while" or during the same transaction as the one in which the capital felony occurs. The previous section, as we have already said, deals with prior conduct. Under the rule set forth in *Cherry,* instruction on this provision is appropriate only when the defendant is convicted for first-degree murder upon the theory of premeditation and deliberation.

In instant case, defendant was found guilty upon the theory of premeditation and deliberation as well as by virtue of the felony murder rule. There was ample evidence that Lester Collins was murdered during the course of a kidnapping and armed robbery, and the court was therefore correct in submitting to the jury the aggravating circumstance defined in subsection (e)(5).

3

G.S. 15A-2000(e)(9) states that the jury may consider as an aggravating circumstance justifying the imposition of the death penalty the fact that the "capital felony was especially heinous, atrocious, or cruel." While we recognize that every murder is, at least arguably, heinous, atrocious, and cruel, we do not believe that this subsection is intended to apply to every homicide. By using the word "especially" the legislature indicated that there must be evidence that the brutality involved in the murder in question must exceed that normally present in any killing before the jury would be instructed upon this subsection.

The Florida provision concerning this aggravating factor is identical to ours. Florida's Supreme Court has said that this provision is directed at "the conscienceless or pitiless crime which is unnecessarily torturous to the victim." State v. Dixon, 283 So. 2d 1 (Fla. 1973) cert. denied, 416 U.S. 943 (1974). Nebraska has also adopted the Florida construction of this subsection. Both Florida and Nebraska have limited the application of this subsection to acts done to the victim during the commission of the capital felony itself. We too believe that this is an appropriate construction of the language of this provision. Under this construction, subsection (e)(9) will not become a "catch all" provision which can always be employed in cases where there is no evidence of other aggravating circumstances.

In the case before us the court instructed as follows in his discussion of G.S. 15A-2000(e)(9):

> You are instructed that the words "especially heinous, atrocious or cruel" means extremely or especially or particularly heinous or atrocious or cruel. You're instructed that "heinous" means extremely wicked or shockingly evil. "Atrocious" means marked by or given to extreme wickedness, brutality or cruelty, marked by extreme violence or savagely fierce. It means outrageously wicked and vile. "Cruel" means designed to inflict a high degree of pain, utterly indifferent to or enjoyment of the suffering of others.

We hold that this instruction is in accord with the construction of this subsection which we have adopted and that its submission to the jury was proper in light of the evidence in this case. The evidence reveals that decedent was shot several times and then cut repeatedly with a knife. Still living, he was placed in the trunk of a car where he remained for several hours. His struggle to escape from the trunk could be heard. Decedent, still in the trunk, was then driven into another county where he was taken from the car. He was placed upon the ground with his head resting upon a rock and then shot twice through the head. This murder is marked by extremely vicious brutality.

4

G.S. 15A-2000(e)(4) states that the jury must consider as an aggravating circumstance justifying the imposition of the death penalty the fact that "[t]he capital felony was committed for the purpose of avoiding or preventing a lawful arrest. . . ." This provision, on its face, is unambiguous, but it must also be construed properly so that instructions on this aggravating circumstance will only be given the jury in appropriate cases. In a broad sense every murder silences the victim, thus having the effect of aiding the criminal in the avoidance or prevention of his arrest. It is not accurate to say, however, that in every case this "purpose" motivates the killing.

This provision in the Florida statute, which is identical to North Carolina's statute in this respect, was examined in Riley v. State, supra, a case in which the defendant in the course of an armed robbery at his place of employment shot a witness to the crime who was not a police officer. The Florida court gave this analysis of the provision:

> Appellant urges us to limit this factor to cases where a police officer or other apprehending official is killed. He suggests that unless we do so, every murder could be characterized as an attempt to eliminate a witness, causing another automatic cumulation of factors. The state argues more narrowly, from the evidence in this case, that the only possible motive for the killing was to eliminate an identification witness.
>
> The record supports the state's view, as the facts admit of only one interpretation. The victim, who well knew and could identify appellant, was immobilized and rendered helpless. He was then executed *after one of the perpetrators expressed a concern for subsequent identification.* Plainly appellant killed to avoid identification and arrest. Appellant concedes this view of the evidence in his brief.
>
> Since the facts show this to be an execution-type killing to avoid lawful arrest, we necessarily reach the broader issue of whether the language of the applicable provision encompasses the murder of a witness to a crime as well as law enforcement personnel. We hold that it does. We caution, however, that the mere fact of a death is not enough to invoke this factor when the victim is not a law enforcement official. Proof of the requisite intent to avoid arrest and detection must be very strong in these cases. Here, of course, it was. 366 So. 2d 19 at 22. (Notes and citations omitted, emphasis added.)

We believe that the construction given this subsection by the Florida court is substantially correct. We add, by way of caution, that even the killing of a police officer or other law enforcement official will not automatically trigger this provision. If, for example, a deranged person began randomly firing a weapon into a crowd of people and fortuitously killed a law officer it would not necessarily be true that this factor was present. Absent the existence of other evidence supporting instruction thereon, it would be improper to instruct the jury that they might find that one of the purposes for which the officer was killed under these circumstances was to avoid or prevent the defendant's arrest. Before the trial court can instruct the jury on this aggravating circumstance there must be evidence from which the jury can infer that at least one of the purposes motivating the killing was defendant's desire to avoid subsequent detection and apprehension for his crime. We repeat that "the mere fact of a death is not enough to invoke this factor." Id.

In this case there was evidence from which the jury could infer that defendant killed Lester Collins to avoid or prevent his arrest. There was testimony that after Collins was shot and cut, but before he was killed, defendant stated he "was afraid if the police found Lester he would tell what had been done to him. . . ." Defendant and Charles Goins then planned to bury Collins. At some later point they decided to shoot him and place him on a railroad track where his body would be mangled by a passing train. On this factual basis the court was correct in instructing the jury upon subsection (e)(4).

5

Finally, we direct our attention to G.S. 15A-2000(e)(7). This subsection provides that the jury may consider as an aggravating circumstance the fact that the "capital felony was committed to disrupt or hinder the lawful exercise of any governmental function or the enforcement of laws." This subsection, like subsection (e)(4), might be broadly construed so that its application would be proper in any homicide found to have been committed against a public official, for the purpose of avoiding or preventing a lawful arrest, or for the purpose of escaping from custody.

We can envision the difficulty this court is going to encounter in construing and applying subsections (e)(4) and (e)(7). We can also envision the difficulty the trial courts are having and will have in deciding which of the subsections would be applicable to the evidence in a particular case. Suffice it to say for the purposes of the case at hand, the trial court erred in submitting issues of aggravating circumstances pursuant to *both* subsections.

In submitting the issue under (e)(4), the court reviewed the evidence tending to show that on the night in question while defendant, Lois, Charles and Collins were on Rural Paved Road 2007 in Cumberland County, that Collins was shot and received some cuts to his body; that defendant and Charles then made statements to the effect that they did not want to be arrested for anything; and that they therefore proposed to take Collins to Robeson County so that he could not tell on them. The court then instructed the jury that if they found those to be the facts beyond a reasonable doubt, and believed that to be an aggravating circumstance, then they should answer the issue "yes."

In submitting the issue under (e)(7), the trial court reviewed substantially the same evidence. The court then instructed the jury that if they found those to be the facts beyond a reasonable doubt and believed that to be an aggravating circumstance, then they should answer the issue "yes."

We think the submission of the two issues on the same evidence was improper. This amounted to an unnecessary duplication of the circumstances enumerated in the statute, resulting in an automatic cumulation of aggravating circumstances against the defendant. We now address the question whether the error was prejudicial.

Due to the brief time the statute in question has been in effect, we have no precedent of this court to guide us in answering the question. However, on the question of admitting incompetent evidence, we have held that the test of harmless error is whether there is a *reasonable possibility* that the evidence complained of might have contributed to the conviction.

We believe a similar test should be applied when one of the aggravating circumstances listed in G.S. 15A-2000(e) is erroneously submitted by the court and answered by the jury against the defendant. It follows that in cases coming before us presenting this question we must answer the question based on the evidence in the particular case.

Of course, we have no way of *knowing* if submission of the erroneous issue in the case at hand tipped the scales in favor of the jury finding that the aggravating circumstances were "sufficiently substantial" to justify imposition of the death penalty. We note that the jury answered the issues submitted on five aggravating circumstances against defendant and only one issue on mitigating circumstances in his favor. Ordinarily, this might cause us to conclude that erroneous submission of one of the issues on aggravating circumstances could not have influenced the jury's ultimate decision that defendant should receive the death penalty.

However, due to the highly questionable quality and credibility of the state's primary evidence, we think there is a reasonable possibility that submission of the erroneous issue may have made the difference in the jury's decision. Obviously, the terrible crimes in question were committed by defendant, Charles Goins or Lois Goins or a combination of two or all of them. Through plea bargaining Lois became the key witness for the state and gave testimony damaging to defendant and favorable to her brother Charles. Her character was impeached and Charles' record was shown to be no better than defendant's. Having already received his six-year sentence for participation in the crimes, Charles testified for defendant and stated that he was the chief culprit. Certainly there was more reason for Charles to kill Collins: there was animosity by the Goins family against Collins because of his alleged mistreatment of his wife who was also Charles' sister.

Considering all of the evidence in the case, and in particular the low quality and credibility of Lois' testimony, we hold that submission of the erroneous issue was prejudicial. Therefore, defendant should have a new trial on the sentencing phase.

Before leaving this assignment of error we think that one additional comment needs to be made. We do not intend to imply that the aggravating circumstances enumerated in G.S. 15A-2000(e) can never overlap or that more than one of them can never arise from a single incident. We realize that in some cases the same evidence will support inferences from which the jury might find that more than one of the enumerated aggravating circumstances is present. This duality will normally occur where the defendant's motive is being examined rather than where the state relies upon a specific factual element of aggravation. In such cases it will be difficult for the trial court to decide which factors should be presented to the jury for their consideration. We believe that error in cases in which a person's life is at stake, if there be any, should be made in the defendant's favor, and that the jury should not be instructed upon one of the statutory circumstances in a doubtful case.

In view of the fact that, for the reason aforestated, there must be a retrial of the sentencing phase of this case, we will comment but briefly on defendant's remaining assignments of error. . . .

By his sixth assignment of error defendant contends that the court erred in two respects in instructing the jury upon intoxication as a mitigating factor. Defendant's first argument is that the court limited a finding of mitigation under G.S. 15A-2000(f)(6) by requiring the jury to find that defendant was drunk before finding this circumstance present. Defendant's second argument hereunder is that the court failed to instruct the jury that any intoxication, however slight, might be considered as a mitigating circumstance under G.S. 15A-2000(f)(9). We shall address these arguments separately.

G.S. 15A-2000(f)(6) provides that the jury may consider as a mitigating factor the fact that the "capacity of the defendant to appreciate the criminality of his conduct or to conform his conduct to the requirements of law was impaired." With reference to this provision the court instructed the jury as follows:

> . . . [Y]ou shall take up 2.b. which reads: "The capacity of the defendant to appreciate the criminality of his conduct or to conform his conduct to the requirements of the law was impaired." I instruct you that the defendant has offered evidence which tends to show that he drank approximately eight or more beers from the time he got home from work on that Saturday, July 2, 1977, until approximately 3 A.M. on the Sunday morning of July 3, when he was out on the road by the railroad tracks in Robeson County. The defendant contends that from his drinking beer, he became drunk or intoxicated and that this condition impaired him from having the mental or physical capacity to appreciate the criminality of his conduct or to conform to the requirements of the law.
>
> The State contends that the defendant knew what he was doing and that his capacity was not impaired.
>
> Generally, voluntary intoxication is not a legal excuse for crime. However,

> if you believe that he had been drinking and was drunk or intoxicated and that this impaired his mental and physical capacity to appreciate the criminality of his conduct, or to conform his conduct to the requirements of the law, then you should answer this question 2.b. "Yes." On the other hand if you do not so find it would be your duty to answer 2.b. "No."

We think the instruction adequately explains subsection (f)(6) in context with the evidence in this case.

Because there are a great many factors which might impair the defendant's capacity to appreciate the criminality of his conduct or to conform it to the requirements of the law, the language of this subsection is necessarily broad. Adequate instruction under this provision must be linked to the impairing factor or factors raised by the evidence. In instant case the only such factor was defendant's consumption of alcohol. We do not think that the legislature intended, under this subsection, that the jury might find intoxication, however slight, to be a mitigating circumstance. If this were true, every murderer, conceivably, would consume strong drink before taking his victim's life. Nor is the degree of intoxication so great that it precludes the defendant from being found guilty of crime. When the defendant contends that his faculties were impaired by intoxication, such intoxication must be to a degree that it affects defendant's ability to understand and control his actions before subsection (f)(6) is applicable. We think the instruction now under consideration makes it clear that this state of intoxication is required.

G.S. 15A-2000(f)(9) provides that the jury may consider as a mitigating factor "[a]ny other circumstance arising from the evidence which the jury deems to have mitigating value." We are mindful that a death penalty statute may not restrict the jury's consideration of *any* factor relevant to the circumstances of the crime or the character of the defendant. Lockett v. Ohio 438 U.S. 586 (1978). Even so, we do not believe the court is required to point to every factor arising from the evidence which might conceivably be considered by the jury under this provision. In the instant case the court instructed as follows:

> Again, regardless of how you shall find as to 2.b., you would go and take up 2.c. which reads: "Do you find any other circumstance arising from the evidence which the jury deems to have mitigating value?" The defendant contends that at least you should find the following circumstances to have mitigating value.
>
> First, he contends that the evidence that Charles Goins received a sentence of six years for the offense of accessory after the fact of murder in the first degree is a mitigating circumstance. On the other hand, the State contends that the evidence shows that Charles Goins pled guilty to the offense of accessory after the fact of murder in the first degree by Buck Junior Goodman, and that this was the offense charged against Charles Goins in the bill of information which was the charging instrument against Charles Goins and upon which he entered his plea of guilty.
>
> Second, the defendant contends that he has a limited education and experience and that he stopped school in the 6th grade without completing the same.

> Third, he contends that he was attempting to protect the girl he loved, to wit: Annie Lois Goins, who was the mother of one of his children; and
>
> Fourth, he contends that any other circumstance which you, the jury, find from the evidence is a mitigating value and circumstance ought to be considered by you.
>
> If you simply believe that there are other mitigating circumstances in this case which have mitigating value, then you would answer 2.c. "yes." On the other hand, if you are not so satisfied, it would be your duty to answer 2.c. "no."

This instruction highlights some elements of the evidence which might not have been clearly brought to the attention of the jury. Although the court did not refer to defendant's intoxication, the instruction in no way prevents the jury from considering that circumstance. For this reason we believe the charge is adequate. The court is not required to sift through the evidence and search out every possible circumstance which the jury might find to have mitigating value.

By his seventh assignment of error defendant contends the trial court erred in failing to instruct the jury that they might recommend a sentence of life imprisonment even though they found the aggravating circumstances outweighed those in mitigation. His argument is that without such instruction the jury will mathematically balance the two types of factors against each other and will impose the death penalty whenever aggravating circumstances outnumber mitigating ones. We do not agree that this is the manner in which a jury will reach its decision on this important question or that the instruction for which defendant contends is required by our statute.

It must be emphasized that the deliberative process of the jury envisioned by G.S. 15A-2000 is not a mere counting process. The jury is charged with the heavy responsibility of subjectively, within the parameters set out by the statute, assessing the appropriateness of imposing the death penalty upon a particular defendant for a particular crime. Nuances of character and circumstance cannot be weighed in a precise mathematical formula.

At the same time, we believe that it would be improper to instruct the jury that they may, as defendant suggests, disregard the procedure outlined by the legislature and impose the sanction of death at their own whim. To do so would be to revert to a system pervaded by arbitrariness and caprice. The exercise of such unbridled discretion by the jury under the court's instruction would be contrary to the rules of *Furman* and the cases which have followed it. For these reasons defendant's seventh assignment of error is overruled. . . .

In connection with one of his assignments of error, defendant criticizes the wording of the third issue, namely: Do you find beyond a reasonable doubt that the mitigating circumstances are insufficient to outweigh the aggravating circumstances? Since a new trial on the sentencing phase is being awarded on other grounds, we do not pass upon the validity of defendant's criticism. Suffice it to say, the able trial judge followed the statute in forming this issue.

Nevertheless, at the retrial, we believe the following wording would be more appropriate: Do you find beyond a reasonable doubt that the aggravating circumstances found by you outweigh the mitigating circumstances found by you?

For the reasons stated, the verdict rendered at the sentencing phase of defendant's trial, and the judgment of death predicated thereon, are vacated, and this cause is remanded to the superior court for a new trial on the sentencing phase.

New trial on sentencing phase. . . .

Notes and Questions

1. *Previous felonies.* Why is it an aggravating circumstance that the defendant previously committed another felony involving violence? Doesn't the presence of this factor suggest that in the penalty phase the defendant is being "tried" not just for her crime, but for the culpability of her entire life and character? Note that when the legislature tries to create a new aggravating factor it produces the same sort of problems of statutory interpretation and doctrinal coherence that we encountered in the traditional homicide grading laws. With respect to the "prior violent felony" circumstance, was the legislature careless in the phrase "a felony involving the use or threat of violence to the person"? What if the previous conviction was for burglary of an empty house? Does burglary generally involve violence or the threat of violence? If so, should it matter that this particular defendant committed a burglary in a careful, nonviolent way? Compare the issue of the "inherently dangerous felony" in the discussion of second-degree felony murder in People v. Burroughs, supra page 323.

What if a defendant robs and kills a person, and then as part of the same criminal transaction robs another person, say, a companion of the murder victim? Under *Goodman,* would the second robbery be an aggravating factor with respect to the murder?

One would think that the state could only introduce previous crimes of which the defendant had been formally convicted. But some states permit evidence showing the defendant committed the previous crime even if he or she was never formally convicted. See, e.g., Ark. Crim. Code §41-1303(3) (1983). The ironic result is that the defendant will contest the evidence, so that the penalty phase of the murder trial includes a mini-criminal trial on the previous felony. See, e.g., People v. Haskett, 30 Cal. 3d 841, 640 P.2d 776 (1982). Or if the defendant cannot wholly disprove the previous crime, he or she will introduce evidence in mitigation of it, thus turning the "sideshow" of litigation of the previous crime into a secondary "penalty trial" that may become the "main event" at the penalty trial. See Elledge v. State, 346 So. 2d 998, 1001 (Fla. 1977).

2. *Felony murder as aggravation.* Assume that the defendant in People v. Stamp, supra page 383, faces a death penalty determination after his conviction of first-degree felony murder. When the penalty trial begins, does he have

any way of disproving the aggravating circumstance that the murder was committed during the commission of robbery? Would it be fair for the state to get a "bonus" out of the proof of the robbery, so that the defendant automatically enters the penalty phase with one strike against him? As the court notes, the court in State v. Cherry answered in the negative. Why then, did Goodman not have a claim under *Cherry*? Is that holding sound?

3. *"Heinous, atrocious, or cruel."* In Godfrey v. Georgia, 446 U.S. 420 (1980), the defendant argued to the Supreme Court that the aggravating circumstance that the killing was "outrageously or wantonly vile, horrible or inhuman in that it involved torture, depravity of mind, or an aggravated battery to the victim" was unconstitutionally vague. The facts were this: After a bitter argument with his wife of 28 years, Godfrey threatened her with a knife, and she moved in with her mother and filed assault charges against him:

> At this juncture, the petitioner got out his shotgun and walked with it down the hill from his home to the trailer where his mother-in-law lived. Peering through a window, he observed his wife, his mother-in-law, and his 11-year-old daughter playing a card game. He pointed the shotgun at his wife through the window and pulled the trigger. The charge from the gun struck his wife in the forehead and killed her instantly. He proceeded into the trailer, striking and injuring his fleeing daughter with the barrel of the gun. He then fired the gun at his mother-in-law, striking her in the head and killing her instantly.
>
> The petitioner then called the local sheriff's office, identified himself, said where he was, explained that he had just killed his wife and mother-in-law, and asked that the sheriff come and pick him up. Upon arriving at the trailer, the law-enforcement officers found the petitioner seated on a chair in open view near the driveway. He told one of the officers that "they're dead, I killed them" and directed the officer to the place where he had put the murder weapon. Later the petitioner told a police officer: "I've done a hideous crime, . . . but I have been thinking about it for eight years . . . I'd do it again."

A plurality of the Court declared that on their face, the words of this provision were too vague to impose on the sentencing jury's discretion sufficient control and guidance to meet the demands of *Furman*. The plurality noted that in three recent cases, the Georgia Supreme Court had attempted to give more specific meaning to the provision by establishing certain criteria for its application:

> The first was that the evidence that the offense was "outrageously or wantonly vile, horrible or inhuman" had to demonstrate "torture, depravity of mind, or an aggravated battery to the victim." The second was that the phrase, "depravity of mind," comprehended only the kind of mental state that led the murderer to torture or to commit an aggravated battery before killing his victim. The third . . . was that the word, "torture," must be construed in pari materia with "aggravated battery" so as to require evidence of serious physical abuse of the victim before death. Indeed, the circumstances proved in a number of the Subsection (b)(7) death-sentence cases affirmed by the Georgia Supreme Court have met all three of these criteria.

The Georgia courts did not, however, so limit Subsection (b)(7) in the present case. No claim was made, and nothing in the record before us suggests, that the petitioner committed an aggravated battery upon his wife or mother-in-law or, in fact, caused either of them to suffer any physical injury preceding their deaths. Moreover, in the trial court, the prosecutor repeatedly told the jury—and the trial judge wrote in his sentencing report that the murders did not involve "torture." Nothing said on appeal by the Georgia Supreme Court indicates that it took a different view of the evidence. The circumstances of this case, therefore, do not satisfy the criteria laid out by the Georgia Supreme Court itself in [the prior] cases. In holding that the evidence supported the jury's Subsection (b)(7) finding, the state Supreme Court simply asserted that the verdict was "factually substantiated."

Thus, the validity of the petitioner's death sentences turns on whether, in light of the facts and circumstances of the murders that Godfrey was convicted of committing, the Georgia Supreme Court can be said to have applied a constitutional construction of the phrase "outrageously or wantonly vile, horrible or inhuman in that [they] involved . . . depravity of mind. . . ." We conclude that the answer must be no. The petitioner's crimes cannot be said to have reflected a consciousness materially more "depraved" than that of any person guilty of murder. His victims were killed instantaneously. They were members of his family who were causing him extreme emotional trauma. Shortly after the killings, he acknowledged his responsibility and the heinous nature of his crimes. These factors certainly did not remove the criminality from the petitioner's acts. But . . . it "is of vital importance to the defendant and to the community that any decision to impose the death sentence be, and appear to be, based on reason rather than caprice or emotion."

That cannot be said here. There is no principled way to distinguish this case, in which the death penalty was imposed, from the many cases in which it was not.

Justice White filed a bitter dissent.

[P]etitioner, in coldblooded executioner's style, murdered his wife and his mother-in-law and, in passing, struck his young daughter on the head with the barrel of his gun. The weapon, a shotgun, is hardly known for the surgical precision with which it perforates its target. The murder scene, in consequence, can only be described in the most unpleasant terms. Petitioner's wife lay prone on the floor. Mrs. Godfrey's head had a hole described as "[a]pproximately the size of a silver dollar" on the side where the shot entered, and much less decipherable and more extensive damage on the side where shot exited. Pellets that had passed through Mrs. Godfrey's head were found embedded in the kitchen cabinet.

It will be remembered that after petitioner inflicted this much damage, he took out time not only to strike his daughter on the head, but also to reload his single-shot shotgun and to enter the house. Only then did he get around to shooting his mother-in-law, Mrs. Wilkerson, whose last several moments as a sentient being must have been as terrifying as the human mind can imagine. The police eventually found her face down on the floor with a substantial portion of her head missing and her brain, no longer cabined by her skull, protruding for some distance onto the floor. Blood not only covered the floor and table, but dripped from the ceiling as well.

Who is to say that the murders of Mrs. Godfrey and Mrs. Wilkerson were not "vile," or "inhuman," or "horrible"? In performing his murderous chore, petitioner employed a weapon known for its disfiguring effects on targets, human or other, and he succeeded in creating a scene so macabre and revolting that, if anything, "vile," "horrible," and "inhuman" are descriptively inadequate.

And who among us can honestly say that Mrs. Wilkerson did not feel "torture" in her last sentient moments? Her daughter, an instant ago a living being sitting across the table from Mrs. Wilkerson, lay prone on the floor, a bloodied and mutilated corpse. The seconds ticked by; enough time for her son-in-law to reload his gun, to enter the home, and to take a gratuitous swipe at his daughter. What terror must have run through her veins as she first witnessed her daughter's hideous demise and then came to terms with the imminence of her own. Was this not torture? And if this was not torture, can it honestly be said that petitioner did not exhibit a "depravity of mind" in carrying out this cruel drama to its mischievous and murderous conclusion? I should have thought, moreover, that the Georgia court could reasonably have deemed the scene awaiting the investigating policemen as involving "an aggravated battery to the victim[s]."

With which opinion do you agree? Does the "heinous, atrocious, and cruel" (HAC) factor properly apply to Goodman?

The state courts have struggled to give some coherent meaning to the "heinous, atrocious, or cruel" aggravating circumstance through case-by-case comparison and distinction of facts. The Florida Supreme Court, for example, has held that the "heinous, atrocious, and cruel" circumstance requires that the "horror of the murder is 'accompanied by such additional acts as to set the crime apart from the norm.' " Cooper v. State, 336 So. 2d 1133, 1141 (Fla. 1976), cert. denied 431 U.S. 925 (1977). It has attempted to carry out this nebulous standard by requiring that the killing be "unnecessarily torturous to the victim." State v. Dixon, 283 So. 2d 1, 9 (Fla. 1973). Compare Welty v. State, 402 So. 2d 1159 (Fla. 1981) (circumstance upheld where defendant robbed victim then struck him several times and set his bed afire) with Kampff v. State, 371 So. 2d 1007 (Fla. 1979) (factor reversed where defendant directed pistol shot straight to the victim's head) and Halliwell v. State, 323 So. 2d 557 (Fla. 1975) (factor reversed where mutilation of victim's body occurred after victim died). The circumstance does not apply simply because the killing was "premeditated, cold, and calculated," Lewis v. State, 398 So. 2d 432, 438 (Fla. 1981), or because the defendant killed the victim in the presence of the victim's family, Riley v. State, 366 So. 2d 19, 21 (Fla. 1978).

Does the HAC circumstance overlap significantly with the premeditation formula for first-degree murder? If so, is it fair to make it an aggravating circumstance? Could you imagine a case of HAC that did not meet the premeditation formula? Would it be sensible for the states to narrow the circumstance to such factors as the physical torture of the victim by force beyond that necessary to kill? Or that the killing was knowingly performed in the presence of another person? Only in the presence of a relative of the victim?

4. *Avoiding arrest.* Why is it an aggravating factor that the defendant committed the murder for the purpose of avoiding or preventing arrest? If the defendant acted with intent or purpose (in the Model Penal Code *mens rea* sense), in killing the victim, how does her *motive*—to prevent or avoid arrest—increase her culpability? Would it mitigate an intentional killing that the defendant acted with the purpose or motive of removing from society a person known to be a criminal but not then in the act of committing a serious crime? The *Goodman* court rejected the argument that the legislature intended the provision to apply solely when the defendant kills a police officer in the line of duty. Are you persuaded the court is right? Couldn't the legislature have expressly made it an aggravating circumstance to knowingly kill a police officer in the line of duty? Is the defendant's argument persuasive that under the court's broad construction, the great majority of intentional killers will fall under this circumstance? Don't most intentional killers assume—and hope—that their victims will not survive to call the police and cause their arrest? Would this circumstance apply in virtually every case of an intentional killing of a robbery or burglary or rape victim?

What about Goodman? Are you persuaded that he killed Collins only to avoid being arrested for the crimes he had already committed? In rebutting the argument that its construction is overly broad, the court says the circumstance would not apply where "a deranged person began randomly firing a weapon into a crowd of people and fortuitously killed a law officer." But would such a person be charged with capital murder?

5. *Hindering governmental function.* Why is it an aggravating factor that the defendant committed the murder "to disrupt or hinder the lawful exercise of any governmental function or the enforcement of the laws"? What type of killing was this meant to identify different from the killings captured by the previous circumstance of avoiding arrest? The court strikes this circumstance in *Goodman* because it seems to duplicate the previous circumstance. But if the court therefore suggests that this circumstance would have applied had the "avoiding arrest" circumstance not been in the statute, is it fairly construing the provision in light of the evidence in this case?

6. *Pecuniary gain.* In numerous cases, the apparently discrete categories created by the statutory aggravating circumstances seem to duplicate each other and apply to the exact same evidentiary facts. Some courts have therefore strained to construe the circumstances narrowly and therefore avoid the overlap. A good example is the very common circumstance that the murder was committed for the purpose of "pecuniary gain." If broadly or literally construed, this circumstance will arise any time a murder occurs in the course of a robbery or larceny-based burglary. Seeking to avoid this overlap, a few courts have construed the circumstance to apply only in cases of murder for hire or murder to obtain insurance proceeds or inheritances of bequests. See, e.g., State v. Simants, 197 Neb. 549, 567, 250 N.W.2d 881, 891 (Neb. 1977). The courts have reasoned that in those cases, as opposed to robberies or bur-

glaries, the defendant is "motivated primarily" by the hope of financial gain. Id. But does that principle adequately distinguish the case of the burglar who kills, breaks into a house, steals valuables, and then intentionally shoots the owner to ensure escape? How do you distinguish "primary" and "secondary" intent in these cases? In State v. Tison, 129 Ariz. 526, 633 P.2d 335, 351 (1981), the Arizona Supreme Court held in a case where the murderer stole his victim's car and other property that the state had proved the circumstance that the defendant "committed the offense as consideration for the receipt or in expectation of the receipt, of anything of pecuniary value." The court rejected the defendant's argument that the provision only applied to "contract killing." The Arizona death penalty statute does not contain a "felony murder" aggravating circumstance. Was the court therefore correct?

If the aggravating circumstances are so susceptible to overlap, have the legislatures succeeded in creating new categories of enhanced murder liability to identify criteria of enhanced culpability? Do the courts' difficulties in applying these criteria support Justice Harlan's warning in McGautha v. California, supra page 425?

7. *Other circumstances.* The Florida statute contains an aggravating circumstance that the murder was committed "in a cold, calculated, and premeditated manner without any pretense of moral or legal justification." Fla. Stat. Ann. §921.141(5)(i) (Supp. 1984). What potential overlaps do you perceive between this and other aggravating circumstances? What about the premeditation category for murder liability? In Herzog v. State, 439 So. 2d 1372 (Fla. 1983), the defendant, a drug dealer, murdered his paramour, who shared with him a sordid drug-filled life. Herzog first beat the victim, then suffocated her with a pillow and strangled her with a telephone cord. He then put her body in a plastic bag, drove it to an isolated place, and burned it with gasoline. The Florida Supreme Court held that the "cold, calculated manner" circumstance did not apply. The trial court had found that "the killing was the consummation of prior threats and arguments based on defendant's belief that the victim had previously taken some of his money or drugs." But the appellate court ruled that though "this finding speaks to the issue of premeditation . . . . it is not sufficient to establish [the 5(i) circumstance]." By what definition of premeditation can a premeditated killing be distinguished from a "cold, calculated" killing? As an example of a killing that did fall within the circumstance, the *Herzog* court noted "those murders which are characterized as executions or contract murders." See also Maxwell v. State, 443 So. 2d 967 (Fla. 1983) (premeditated murder not "cold and calculating" where defendant approached victim on golf course, robbed him at knifepoint, and then shot him with special snub-nosed bullets when he refused to hand over his wife's ring).

8. *Nonstatutory aggravating factors.* Though the guided discretion statutes approved in Gregg v. Georgia expressly define certain aggravating circumstances, prosecutors may be inclined to argue the presence of other aggravating circumstances that have a basis in the evidence, but that fall outside the circumstances expressly enumerated in the statute. May the sentencer rely on

such "nonstatutory" aggravating circumstances in reaching a death verdict? In Zant v. Stephens, 103 S. Ct. 2733 (1983) and Barclay v. Florida, 103 S. Ct. 3418 (1983), the Supreme Court found no constitutional flaw in the Georgia and Florida death penalty schemes that permitted the sentencer to rely on such a nonstatutory aggravating factor, so long as the sentencer found at least one statutory factor. For example, in *Barclay,* the trial judge who ordered the defendant's execution over a jury's recommendation of life found an aggravating circumstance that Barclay had been convicted of breaking and entering with intent to commit grand larceny, even though the only prior crimes that constituted statutory aggravating circumstances in Florida were those involving violence.

If the sentencer can rely on nonstatutory aggravating factors, does the death penalty scheme invite the very unguided, arbitrary, and discriminatory death sentencing that prompted *Furman*?

4. Mitigating Circumstances

Goodman appears to have argued for the presence of four mitigating factors in the hopes that they might outweigh the aggravating factors: that he was mentally impaired by intoxication at the time of the killing; that his accomplice, Charles Goins, received a mere six years prison sentence; that he had a limited education; and that he (somewhat implausibly) was acting out of love for Annie Goins. Once Goodman was found guilty of first-degree murder, why should any of these factors affect his sentence? Did the trial judge in any way prevent the jury from considering these factors? What exactly was the error that Goodman attributed to the trial judge?

The instruction on voluntary intoxication suggests that mild involuntary intoxication is not a legal excuse for crime. Obviously, Goodman's intoxication did not prevent the jury from convicting him of first-degree murder. If so, why does the intoxication question arise again at the penalty phase?

The court seems to go to some lengths to hold that the trial judge's instruction on intoxication as mitigation conformed to the legislature's intent in drafting subsection (f)(6). But what is the point of such statutory construction if under (f)(9) the jury is free to consider any other mitigating evidence?

The nature and role of mitigating circumstances are explored below in the Supreme Court's two major pronouncements on this crucial issue.

LOCKETT v. OHIO

United States Supreme Court
438 U.S. 586 (1978)

[Sandra Lockett was the getaway driver in an armed robbery of a pawnshop. While she sat in the car, one of her accomplices accidentally killed the robbery victim. Lockett apparently did not intend or even foresee that anyone would be killed in the robbery, but Ohio's homicide law nevertheless made her guilty of first-degree murder. At her postconviction sentencing hearing, however, she tried to offer as a mitigating circumstance the fact that she had not herself caused or intended the victim's death. At the time of her trial, the Ohio death penalty statute expressly enumerated three mitigating circumstances: That the victim of the killing had helped cause his own death; that the defendant had acted under duress, coercion, or strong provocation; or that the offense primarily resulted from the defendant's mental impairment. Even though the sentencing judge in Lockett's case heard her evidence about her minor participation in the killing, the judge was not allowed to count that evidence as a mitigating factor because it did not fall within any of the enumerated statutory mitigating categories. Lockett then argued to the Supreme Court that the Ohio scheme violated her rights under the Eighth Amendment. The Court upheld her claim and vacated her death sentence. The gist of Chief Justice Burger's opinion follows.]

We begin by recognizing that the concept of individualized sentencing in criminal cases generally, although not constitutionally required, has long been accepted in this country. See William v. New York 337 U.S., at 247-248; Pennsylvania ex rel. Sullivan v. Ashe, 302 U.S. at 55. Consistent with that concept, sentencing judges traditionally have taken a wide range of factors into account. That States have authority to make aiders and abettors equally responsible, as a matter of law, with principals, or to enact felony-murder statues is beyond constitutional challenge. But the definition of crimes generally has not been thought automatically to dictate what should be the proper penalty. See ibid.; Williams v. New York, supra, at 247-248; Williams v. Oklahoma, 358 U.S., at 585. And where sentencing discretion is granted, it generally has been agreed that the sentencing judge's "possession of the fullest information possible concerning the defendant's life and characteristics" is [h]ighly relevant—*if not essential*—[to the] selection of an appropriate sentence. . . ." Williams v. New York, supra, at 247 (emphasis added).

The opinions of this Court going back many years in dealing with sentencing in capital cases have noted the strength of the basis for individualized sentencing. For example, Mr. Justice Black, writing for the Court in Williams v. New York, supra, at 247-248—a capital case—observed that the

> whole country has traveled far from the period in which the death sentence was an automatic and commonplace result of convictions—even for offenses today deemed trivial.

Ten years later in Williams v. Oklahoma, supra, at 585, another capital case, the Court echoed Mr. Justice Black, stating that

> [i]n discharging his duty of imposing a proper sentence, the sentencing judge is authorized, *if not required,* to consider all the mitigating and aggravating circumstances involved in the crime. (Emphasis added.)

See also Furman v. Georgia, 408 U.S., at 245-246 (Douglas, J., concurring); id., at 297-298 (Brennan, J. concurring); id., at 339 (Marshall, J. concurring); id., at 402-403 (Burger, C.J., dissenting); id., at 413 (Blackmun, J. dissenting); McGautha v. California, 402 U.S. at 197-203. Most would agree that "the 19th century movement away from mandatory death sentences marked an enlightened introduction of flexibility into the sentencing process." Furman v. Georgia, supra, at 402 (Burger, C.J., dissenting).

Although legislatures remain free to decide how much discretion in sentencing should be reposed in the judge or jury in noncapital cases, the plurality opinion in *Woodson* after reviewing the historical repudiation of mandatory sentencing in capital cases, 428 U.S., at 289-298, concluded that

> in capital cases the fundamental respect for humanity underlying the Eighth Amendment . . . requires consideration of the character and record of the individual offender and the circumstances of the particular offense as a constitutionally indispensable part of the process of inflicting the penalty of death. Id., at 304.

That declaration rested "on the predicate that the penalty of death is qualitatively different" from any other sentence. Id., at 305. We are satisfied that this qualitative difference between death and other penalties calls for a greater degree of reliability when the death sentence is imposed. The mandatory death penalty statute in *Woodson* was held invalid because it permitted *no* consideration of "relevant facets of the character and record of the individual offender or the circumstances of the particular offense." Id., at 304. The plurality did not attempt to indicate, however, which facets of an offender or his offense it deemed "relevant" in capital sentencing or what degree of consideration of "relevant facts" it would require.

We are now faced with those questions and we conclude that the Eighth and Fourteenth Amendments require that the sentencer, in all but the rarest kind of capital case, not be precluded from considering, *as a mitigating factor,* any aspect of a defendant's character or record and any of the circumstances of the offense that the defendant proffers as a basis for a sentence less than death.[28] We recognize that, in noncapital cases, the established practice of individualized sentences rests not on constitutional commands, but on public policy enacted into statutes. The considerations that account for the wide acceptance of individualization of sentences in noncapital cases surely cannot be thought less important in capital cases. Given that the imposition of death by public authority is so profoundly different from all other penalties, we cannot avoid the conclusion that an individualized decision is essential in capital cases. The need for treating each defendant in a capital case with that degree of respect due the uniqueness of the individual is far more important than in noncapital cases. A variety of flexible techniques—probation, parole,

28. Nothing in this opinion limits the traditional authority of a court to exclude, as irrelevant, evidence not bearing on the defendant's character, prior record, or the circumstances of his offense.

work furloughs, to name a few—and various postconviction remedies may be available to modify an initial sentence of confinement in noncapital cases. The nonavailability of corrective or modifying mechanisms with respect to an executed capital sentence underscores the need for individualized consideration as a constitutional requirement in imposing the death sentence.

There is no perfect procedure for deciding in which cases governmental authority should be used to impose death. But a statute that prevents the sentencer in all capital cases from giving independent mitigating weight to aspects of the defendant's character and record and to circumstances of the offense proffered in mitigation creates the risk that the death penalty will be imposed in spite of factors which may call for a less severe penalty. When the choice is between life and death, that risk is unacceptable and incompatible with the commands of the Eighth and Fourteenth Amendments.

EDDINGS v. OKLAHOMA

United States Supreme Court
455 U.S. 104 (1982)

Justice Powell delivered the opinion of the Court.

Petitioner Monty Lee Eddings was convicted of first degree murder and sentenced to death. Because this sentence was imposed without "the type of individualized consideration of mitigating factor . . . required by the Eighth and Fourteenth Amendment in capital cases," Lockett v. Ohio, 438 U.S. 586, 606 (1978) (opinion of Burger, C.J.), we reverse.

I

On April 4, 1977, Eddings, a 16-year-old youth, and several younger companions ran away from their Missouri homes. They travelled in a car owned by Eddings' brother, and drove without destination or purpose in a southwesternly direction eventually reaching the Oklahoma turnpike. Eddings had in the car a shotgun and several rifles he had taken from his father. After he momentarily lost control of the car, he was signalled to pull over by Officer Crabtree of the Oklahoma Highway Patrol. Eddings did so, and when the Officer approached the car, Eddings stuck a loaded shotgun out of the window and fired, killing the Officer.

Because Eddings was a juvenile, the State moved to have him certified to stand trial as an adult. Finding that there was prosecutive merit to the complaint and that Eddings was not amenable to rehabilitation within the juvenile system, the trial court granted the motion. The ruling was affirmed on appeal. Eddings was then charged with murder in first degree, and the District Court of Creek County found him guilty upon his plea of nolo contendere.

The Oklahoma death penalty statute provides, in pertinent part:

> Upon conviction . . . of guilt of a defendant of murder in the first degree, the court shall conduct a separate sentencing proceeding to determine whether the defendant should be sentenced to death or life imprisonment. . . . In the sentencing proceeding, evidence may be presented as to *any mitigating circumstances* or as to any of the aggravating circumstances enumerated in this act." Okla. Stat., Tit. 211, §701.10 (emphasis added).

Section 701.12 lists seven separate aggravating circumstances; the statute nowhere defines what is meant by "any mitigating circumstances."

At the sentencing hearing, the State alleged three of the aggravating circumstances enumerated in the statute: that the murder was especially heinous, atrocious, or cruel, that the crime was committed for the purpose of avoiding or preventing a lawful arrest, and that there was a probability that the defendant would commit criminal acts of violence that would constitute a continuing threat to society. Okla. Stat., Tit. 21, §701.12(4), (5), and (7).

In mitigation, Eddings presented substantial evidence at the hearing of his troubled youth. The testimony of his supervising Juvenile Officer indicated that Eddings had been raised without proper guidance. His parents were divorced when he was 5 years old, and until he was 14 Eddings lived with his mother without rules or supervision. There is the suggestion that Eddings' mother was an alcoholic and possibly a prostitute. By the time Eddings was 14 he no longer could be controlled, and his mother sent him to live with his father. But neither could the father control the boy. Attempts to reason and talk gave way to physical punishment. The Juvenile Officer testified that Eddings was frightened and bitter, that his father overreacted and used excessive physical punishment: "Mr. Eddings found the only thing that he thought was effectful with the boy was actual punishment, or physical violence—hitting with a strap or something like this."[29]

Testimony from other witnesses indicated that Eddings was emotionally disturbed in general and at the time of the crime, and that his mental and emotional development were at a level several years below his age. A state psychologist stated that Eddings had a sociopathic or anti-social personality and that approximately 30 percent of youths suffering from such a disorder grew out of it as they aged. A sociologist specializing in juvenile offenders testified that Eddings was treatable. A psychiatrist testified that Eddings could be rehabilitated by intensive therapy over a 15 to 20 year period. He testified further that Eddings "did pull the trigger, he did kill someone, but I don't even think he knew that he was doing it."[30] The psychiatrist suggested that, if treated, Eddings would no longer pose a serious threat to society.

29. There was evidence that immediately after the shooting Eddings said, "I would rather have shot an Officer than go back to where I live."

30. The psychiatrist suggested that, at the time of the murder, Eddings was in his own mind shooting his stepfather—a policeman who had been married to his mother for a brief period when Eddings was seven. The psychiatrist stated "I think that given the circumstances and the facts of his life, and the facts of his arrested development, he acted as a seven year old seeking revenge and rebellion; and the act—he did pull the trigger, he did kill someone, but I don't even think he knew that he was doing it."

At the conclusion of all the evidence, the trial judge weighed the evidence of aggravating and mitigating circumstances. He found that the State had proved each of the three alleged aggravating circumstances beyond a reasonable doubt.[31] Turning to the evidence of mitigating circumstances, the judge found that Eddings' youth was a mitigating factor of great weight: "I have given very serious consideration to the youth of the Defendant when this particular crime was committed. Should I fail to do this, I think I would not be carrying out my duty." But he would not consider in mitigation the circumstances of Eddings' unhappy upbringing and emotional disturbance: ". . . the Court cannot be persuaded entirely by the . . . fact that the youth was sixteen years old when this heinous crime was committed. *Nor can the Court in following the law, in my opinion, consider the fact of this young man's violent background.*" (Emphasis added.) Finding that the only mitigating circumstance was Eddings' youth and finding further that this circumstance could not outweigh the aggravating circumstances present, the judge sentenced Eddings to death.

The Court of Criminal Appeals affirmed the sentence of death. Eddings v. State, 616 P.2d 1159 (Okla. Crim. App. 1980). It found that each of the aggravating circumstances alleged by the State had been present. It recited the mitigating evidence presented by Eddings in some detail, but in the end it agreed with the trial court that only the fact of Eddings' youth was properly considered as a mitigating circumstance:

> [Eddings] also argues his mental state at the time of the murder. He stresses his family history in saying he was suffering from severe psychological and emotional disorders, and that the killing was in actuality an inevitable product of the way he was raised. There is no doubt that the petitioner has a personality disorder. But all the evidence tends to show that he knew the difference between right and wrong at the time he pulled the trigger, and that is the test of criminal responsibility in this State. [citation] For the same reason, the petitioner's family history is useful in explaining why he behaved the way he did, but it does not excuse his behavior. Id., at 1170.

In Lockett v. Ohio, 438 U.S. 586 (1978), Chief Justice Burger, writing for the plurality, stated the rule that we apply today.

> [W]e conclude that the Eighth and Fourteenth Amendments require that the sentencer . . . not be precluded from considering, *as a mitigating factor,* any aspect

31. The trial judge found first that the crime was "heinous, atrocious, and cruel" because "designed to inflict a high degree of pain . . . in utter indifference to the rights of Patrolman Crabtree." Second, the judge found that the crime was "committed for the purpose of avoiding or preventing a lawful arrest or prosecution. The evidence was sufficient to indicate that at the time of the offense Eddings did not wish to be returned to Missouri and that in stopping the car the Officer's intent was to make a lawful arrest. Finally, the trial judge found that Eddings posed a continuing threat of violence to society. There was evidence that at one point on the day of the murder, after Eddings had been taken to the county jail, he told two officers that "if he was loose . . . he would shoot" them all. There was also evidence that at another time, when an Officer refused to turn off the light in Eddings' cell, Eddings became angry and threatened the Officer. "Now I have shot one of you people, and I'll get you too if you don't turn this light out." Based on these two "spontaneous utterances," the trial judge found a strong likelihood that Eddings would again commit a criminal act of violence if released.

of a defendant's character or record and any of the circumstances of the offense that the defendant proffers as a basis for a sentence less than death." Id., at 604 (emphasis in original).

[The Court then summarized *Lockett*.]

We now apply the rule in *Lockett* to the circumstances of this case. The trial judge stated that "in following the law," he could not "consider the fact of this young man's violent background." There is no dispute that by "violent background" the trial judge was referring to the mitigating evidence of Eddings' family history.[32] From this statement it is clear that the trial judge did not evaluate the evidence in mitigation and find it wanting as a matter of fact, rather he found that *as a matter of law* he was unable even to consider the evidence.

The Court of Criminal Appeals took the same approach. It found that the evidence in mitigation was not relevant because it did not tend to provide a legal excuse from criminal responsibility. Thus the court conceded that Eddings had a "personality disorder, but cast this evidence aside on the basis that "he knew the difference between right and wrong . . . and that is the test of criminal responsibility. Eddings v. State, supra, at 1170. Similarly, the evidence of Eddings' family history was "useful in explaining" his behavior, but it did not "excuse" the behavior. From these statements it appears that the Court of Criminal Appeals also considered only that evidence to be mitigating which would tend to support a legal excuse from criminal liability.

We find the limitations placed by these courts upon the mitigating evidence they would consider violated the rule in *Lockett*. Just as the state may not by statute preclude the sentencer from considering any mitigating factor, neither may the sentencer, refuse to consider, *as a matter of law*, any relevant mitigating evidence. In this instance, it was as if the trial judge had instructed a jury to disregard the mitigating evidence Eddings proffered on his behalf. The sentencer, and the Court of Criminal Appeals on review, may determine the weight to be given relevant mitigating evidence. But they may not give it no weight by excluding such evidence from their consideration.[33]

Nor do we doubt that the evidence Eddings offered was relevant mitigating evidence. Eddings was a youth of 16 years at the time of the murder. Evidence of a difficult family history and of emotional disturbance is typically introduced by defendants in mitigation. See McGautha v. California, 402 U.S. 183, 187-188 and 193 (1971). In some cases, such evidence may be given little weight. But when the defendant was 16 years old at the time of the offense

32. Brief for Respondent 55 ("the inference that can be drawn is that the court did not consider petitioner's juvenile record and family life to be a mitigating circumstance"); Tr. of Oral Arg. 36 ("the trial court did not consider the fact of his family background as a mitigating circumstance . . . the violent background, which I assume he meant was . . . [that Eddings] was subject to some slapping around and some beating by his father.") (argument of respondent).

33. We note that the Oklahoma death penalty statute permits the defendant to present evidence "as to any mitigating circumstances." Okla. Stat., Tit. 21, §701.10. *Lockett* requires the sentencer to listen.

there can be no doubt that evidence of a turbulent family history, of beatings by a harsh father, and of severe emotional disturbance is particularly relevant.

The trial judge recognized that youth must be considered a relevant mitigating factor. But youth is more than chronological fact. It is a time and condition of life when a person may be most susceptible to influence and to psychological damage. Our history is replete with laws and judicial recognition that minors, especially in their earlier years, generally are less mature and responsible than adults. Particularly "during the formative years of childhood and adolescence, minors often lack the experience, perspective, and judgment" expected of adults. Bellotti v. Baird, 443 U.S. 622, 635 (1979).

Even the normal 16-year-old customarily lacks the maturity of an adult. In this case, Eddings was not a normal 16-year-old; he had been deprived of the care, concern and paternal attention that children deserve. On the contrary, it is not disputed that he was a juvenile with serious emotional problems, and had been raised in a neglectful, sometimes even violent, family background. In addition, there was testimony that Eddings' mental and emotional development were at a level several years below his chronological age. All of this does not suggest an absence of responsibility for the crime of murder, deliberately committed in this case. Rather, it is to say that just as the chronological age of a minor is itself a relevant mitigating factor of great weight, so must the background and mental and emotional development of a youthful defendant be duly considered in sentencing.

We are not unaware of the extent to which minors engage increasingly in violent crime. Nor do we suggest an absence of legal responsibility where crime is committed by a minor. We are concerned here only with the manner of the imposition of the ultimate penalty: the death sentence imposed for the crime of murder upon an emotionally disturbed youth with a disturbed child's immaturity.

On remand, the state courts must consider all relevant mitigating evidence and weigh it against the evidence of the aggravating circumstances. We do not weigh the evidence for them. Accordingly, the judgment is reversed to the extent that it sustains the imposition of the death penalty, and the case is remanded for further proceedings not inconsistent with this opinion.

Notes and Questions

1. In *Lockett* and *Eddings,* has the Court come full circle from *McGautha?* That is, in requiring highly flexible death sentencing procedures with individualized consideration of the offender and the offense, unrestrained by statutory categories, has the Court in effect restored to the sentencer the unguided, subjective discretion that was held illegitimate in *Furman?* Especially after the Court's holding in *Zant* and *Barclay,* supra, that the sentencer can consider nonstatutory aggravating factors as well?

2. *Eddings* makes clear that the sentencer must be free to consider miti-

gating evidence much broader in scope than the evidence that might be introduced as a legal excuse for or defense to the crime. Thus, Eddings presumably could not have claimed as a defense to the murder charge that he had had a troubled childhood (unless that evidence could support a claim of insanity, which seems implausible here). But by permitting the "troubled childhood" claim at the penalty phase, has the Court opened up the whole vexing range of determinist explanations of criminal behavior, which the criminal law has essentially suppressed at the guilt stage? See the discussion in Chapter 1.

By far the most common mitigating circumstances proffered by capital defendants are that they were abused or neglected as children, or suffer from some mental illness short of legal insanity, or were beclouded by drugs or alcohol when they killed their victims. See Goodpaster, The Trial for Life: Effective Assistance of Counsel in Death Penalty Cases, 58 N.Y.U.L. Rev. 299 (1983).

3. Just what is mitigating evidence? In a footnote in *Lockett,* Chief Justice Burger reassured the states that "[n]othing in this opinion limits the authority of a court to exclude, as irrelevant, evidence not bearing on the defendant's character, prior record, or the circumstances of his offense." 438 U.S. at 604 n.12. But is that any limitation at all? Remember that *Lockett* obviously does not force a sentencer to grant mercy on the basis of any proffered mitigating circumstance; it only requires the sentencer to consider and give independent weight to any mitigating circumstance. But is there any definition of the boundaries of mitigating evidence, or must the sentencer consider, and must the jury get a chance to hear, absolutely any evidence that the defendant thinks might sway the jury to mercy?

Judicial attempts to define "mitigation" have proved vapid or circular. See, e.g., Coker v. Georgia, 433 U.S. 584, 591 (1977) (mitigating circumstances are those "which, in fairness and mercy, may be considered as extenuating or reducing the degree of moral culpability"). As a result, the courts have had to struggle to make case-by-case determinations of when a defendant has a right to consideration by the sentencer of particular mitigating circumstances. Of course, under *Eddings,* the defendant can introduce aspects of his or her life or character that would not be admissible at the guilt phase. But *Lockett* seems to encompass any evidence of redeeming character traits, even if it arises after the murder for which the defendant is being sentenced. Thus, the sentencer must hear that the defendant has shown remorse, State v. Arnett, 125 Ariz. 201, 204, 608 P.2d 778 (1980), or that he has behaved admirably in prison after the murder, State v. Schad, 129 Ariz. 557, 573, 633 P.2d 336 (1981), or that the defendant has been born again and has begun a Christian mission in prison, see Southern Poverty Law Center, Trial of the Penalty Phase 129-131 (1981) (penalty trial in Commonwealth v. Lamb).

Apparently, the state cannot bar mitigating evidence on the ground that it is trivial, see, e.g., State v. Arnett, 125 Ariz. 201, 204, 608 P.2d 778 (1980) (defendant showed restraint in not attacking police when he was arrested), or that it is morally equivocal, compare Washington v. Watkins, 655 F.2d 1346,

1375 (1981) (Mississippi trial court wrongly excluded evidence that defendant had carried on a "steady domestic relationship" with a woman and their child), with id. at 1379 (Coleman, J., dissenting) (same "domestic relationship" was criminal adultery or fornication under state law).

Some courts have gone further and required the admission of evidence that might argue for mercy, yet does not refer to the defendant's character, record, or offense, such as evidence that the defendant has a loving family that will suffer terribly if he dies, Cofield v. State, 247 Ga. 98, 110, 274 S.E.2d 530, 542 (1980), or, as in *Goodman,* that the defendant's equally culpable accomplice pleaded guilty to a lesser charge. The final frontier of *Lockett* concerns evidence that has nothing to do with a particular defendant but might sway the jury to mercy. It is common defense practice to offer testimony from social scientists on the dubious deterrent value of the death penalty, Gall v. Commonwealth, 607 S.W.2d 97, 112 (Ky. 1980), or from journalists on the ghastly agonies a person suffers in the electric chair or the gas chamber, id., or from theologians about the questionable religious basis for retribution, Johnson v. State, 416 So. 2d 383, 392 (Miss. 1982). Though courts often say that the sentencer cannot reexamine general questions of criminal law policy decided by the legislature, trial courts often permit this type of testimony out of fear of violating *Lockett.*

Does admission of such "evidence" comport with the traditional principles of the criminal law?

4. Recall that in *Goodman* the defendant argued that the jury should have been instructed that it could recommend a life sentence even if it found that aggravating circumstances outweighed mitigating circumstances. Goodman claimed that without such an instruction, the death penalty decision turns on a mere mathematical comparison of the number of aggravating and mitigating circumstances. Why did the *Goodman* court reject his claim? Would the requested instruction violate the *Furman* principle? Would it raise any greater *Furman* problem than *Lockett* did? On the other hand, does the court's holding violate *Lockett;* that is, does a requirement that the jury *must* vote for death where aggravation exceeds mitigation violate the *Woodson-Lockett* principle of individualized sentencing?

If a jury does not simply tote up and compare the number of aggravating and mitigating circumstances, exactly what is it supposed to do with them? In a later case, State v. McDougall, the North Carolina Supreme Court set out a formal model instruction for death penalty juries.

> We note that the order and form of the issues in capital trials have varied from case to case. The order and form of the issues to be submitted to the jury should be substantially as follows:
>
> (1) Do you find from the evidence beyond a reasonable doubt the existence of one or more of the following aggravating circumstances?
>
> (2) Do you find from the evidence the existence of one more of the following mitigating circumstances?

(3) Do you find beyond a reasonable doubt that the mitigating circumstance or circumstances you have found is, or are, insufficient to outweigh the aggravating circumstance or circumstances you have found?

(4) Do you find beyond a reasonable doubt that the aggravating circumstance or circumstances found by you is, or are, sufficiently substantial to call for the imposition of the death penalty when considered with the mitigating circumstance or circumstances found by you? . . .

Appropriate instructions on the fourth issue should be given to the jury substantially as follows:

> In deciding this issue, you are not to consider the aggravating circumstances standing alone. You must consider them in connection with any mitigating circumstances found by you. After considering the totality of the aggravating and mitigating circumstances, you must be convinced beyond a reasonable doubt that the imposition of the death penalty is justified and appropriate in this case before you can answer the issue "yes." In so doing, you are not applying a mathematical formula. For example, three circumstances of one kind do not automatically and of necessity outweigh one circumstance of another kind. The number of circumstances found is only one consideration in determining which circumstances outweigh others. The jury may very properly emphasize one circumstance more than another in a particular case. You must consider the relative substantiality and persuasiveness of the existing aggravating and mitigating circumstances in making this determination. You, the jury, must determine how compelling and persuasive the totality of the aggravating circumstances are when compared with the totality of the mitigating circumstances found by you. After so doing, if you are satisfied beyond a reasonable doubt that the aggravating circumstances found by you are sufficiently substantial to call for the death penalty, it would be your duty to answer the issue "yes." If you are not so satisfied or have a reasonable doubt, it would be your duty to answer the issue "no." 301 S.E.2d at 327-328.

Does this instruction provide a psychologically realistic alternative to merely counting up the circumstances? Would it be comprehensible to the average juror? Does it provide an objective intellectual process for comparing aggravating and mitigating circumstances so as to satisfy *Furman?*

5. A Reprise on Felony Murder—Enmund v. Florida

Recall that Sandra Lockett was found guilty of capital murder under Ohio's equivalent of the felony-murder rule, and that the mitigating evidence at issue in *Lockett* concerned her actual minor participation in the killing. Though the *Lockett* case was decided on the basis of broader questions of mitigating evidence, the decision may have reflected some of the Supreme Court's ambivalence about felony murder, at least as a basis for the death penalty. In Enmund v. Florida, 458 U.S. 782 (1982), the Court addressed the issue of felony murder more directly.

Enmund was apparently, like Lockett, the classic felony murder "wheelman." He planned a robbery of a farmhouse but stayed in the car while his accomplices, Jeannette and Sampson Armstrong, entered the farmhouse to rob the victims. The Armstrongs seized the owner of the house, Thomas Kersey, and when Mrs. Kersey shot at Jeannette Armstrong in aid of her husband, Sampson Armstrong shot and killed both of the Kerseys. Enmund apparently had not intended that any violence occur and was in the car the entire time. But Enmund was found guilty of first-degree murder, and after considering various aggravating and mitigating circumstances, the sentencing jury and judge imposed the death penalty.

In his opinion for the Court Justice White held that in the case of a felony-murderer such as Enmund, the death penalty was disproportionate to the defendant's culpability and thus unconstitutional under the Eighth Amendment. The Court reached this decision primarily by surveying the various state laws and the pattern of jury verdicts on this issue; it concluded that legislatures and juries had generally opposed the death penalty in these circumstances, and that therefore capital punishment for a defendant like Enmund did not comport with "evolving standards of decency." But Justice White also addressed the criminal law principles underlying the felony-murder rule:

> As recounted above, the Florida Supreme Court held that the record supported no more than the inference that Enmund was the person in the car by the side of the road at the time of the killings, waiting to help the robbers escape. This was enough under Florida law to make Enmund a constructive aider and abettor and hence a principal in first-degree murder upon whom the death penalty could be imposed. It was thus irrelevant to Enmund's challenge to the death sentence that he did not himself kill and was not present at the killings; also beside the point was whether he intended that the Kerseys be killed or anticipated that lethal force would or might be used if necessary to effectuate the robbery or a safe escape. We have concluded that imposition of the death penalty in these circumstances is inconsistent with the Eighth and Fourteenth Amendments. . . .
>
> Although the judgments of legislatures, juries, and prosecutors weigh heavily in the balance, it is for us ultimately to judge whether the Eighth Amendment permits imposition of the death penalty on one such as Enmund who aids and abets a felony in the course of which a murder is committed by others but who does not himself kill, attempt to kill, or intend that a killing take place or that lethal force will be employed. We have concluded, along with most legislatures and juries, that it does not.
>
> We have no doubt that robbery is a serious crime deserving serious punishment. It is not, however, a crime "so grievous an affront to humanity that the only adequate response may be the penalty of death." Gregg v. Georgia, 428 U.S. at 184 (footnote omitted). "[I]t does not compare with murder, which does involve the unjustified taking of human life. Although it may be accompanied by another crime, [robbery] by definition does not include the death of or even the serious injury to another person. The murderer kills; the [robber], if no more than that, does not. Life is over for the victim of the murderer; for the [robbery] victim, life . . . is not over and normally is not beyond repair." Coker v. Georgia, 433 U.S., at 598 (footnote omitted). As was said of the crime of rape in *Coker,* we

have the abiding conviction that the death penalty, which is "unique in its severity and irrevocability," Gregg v. Georgia, supra, at 187, is an excessive penalty for the robber who, as such, does not take human life.

Here the robbers did commit murder; but they were subjected to the death penalty only because they killed as well as robbed. The question before us is not the disproportionality of death as a penalty for murder, but rather the validity of capital punishment for Enmund's own conduct. The focus must be on *his* culpability, not on that of those who committed the robbery and shot the victims, for we insist on "individualized consideration as a constitutional requirement in imposing the death sentence," Lockett v. Ohio, 438 U.S. 586, 605 (1978) (footnote omitted), which means that we must focus on "relevant facts of the character and record of the individual offender." Woodson v. North Carolina, 428 U.S. 280, 304 (1976). Enmund himself did not kill or attempt to kill; and as construed by the Florida Supreme Court, the record before us does not warrant a finding that Enmund had any intention of participating in or facilitating a murder. Yet under Florida law death was an authorized penalty because Enmund aided and abetted a robbery in the course of which murder was committed. It is fundamental that "causing harm intentionally must be punished more severely than causing the same harm unintentionally." H. Hart, Punishment and Responsibility 162 (1968). Enmund did not kill or intend to kill and thus his culpability is plainly different from that of the robbers who killed; yet the state treated them alike and attributed to Enmund the culpability of those who killed the Kerseys. This was impermissible under the Eighth Amendment.

In Gregg v. Georgia the opinion announcing the judgment observed that "[t]he death penalty is said to serve two principal social purposes: retribution and deterrence of capital crimes by prospective offenders." Unless the death penalty when applied to those in Enmund's position measurably contributes to one or both of these goals, it "is nothing more than the purposeless and needless imposition of pain and suffering," and hence an unconstitutional punishment. Coker v. Georgia, supra, at 592. We are quite unconvinced, however, that the threat that the death penalty will be imposed for murder will measurably deter one who does not kill and has no intention or purpose that life will be taken. Instead, it means likely that "captial punishment can serve as a deterrent only when murder is the result of premeditation and deliberation," Fisher v. United States, 328 U.S. 463, 484 (1946) (Frankfurter, J., dissenting), for if a person does not intend that life be taken or contemplate that lethal force will be employed by others, the possibility that the death penalty will be imposed for vicarious felony murder will not "enter into the cold calculus that precedes the decision to act." Gregg v. Georgia, supra, at 186 (footnote omitted).

It would be very different if the likelihood of a killing in the course of a robbery were so substantial that one should share the blame for the killing if he somehow participated in the felony. But competent observers have concluded that there is no basis in experience for the notion that death so frequently occurs in the course of a felony for which killing is not an essential ingredient that the death penalty should be considered as a justifiable deterrent to the felony itself. Model Penal Code §210.2, Comment, p.38, and n.96. This conclusion was based on three comparisons of robbery statistics, each of which showed that only about one-half of one percent of robberies resulted in homicide. The most recent national crime statistics strongly support this conclusion. In addition to the evidence that killings only rarely occur during robberies is the fact, already noted, that however often death occurs in the course of a felony such as robbery, the death penalty is rarely imposed on one only vicariously guilty of the murder, a fact which further attenuates its possible utility as an effective deterrence.

As for retribution as a justification for executing Enmund, we think this very much depends on the degree of Enmund's culpability—what Enmund's intentions, expectations, and actions were. American criminal law has long considered a defendant's intention—and therefore his moral guilt—to be critical to "the degree of [his] criminal culpability," Mullaney v. Wilbur, 421 U.S. 684, 698 (1975), and the Court has found criminal penalties to be unconstitutionally excessive in the absence of intentional wrongdoing. In Robinson v. California, 370 U.S. 660, 667 (1962), a statute making narcotics addiction a crime, even though such addiction "is apparently an illness which may be contracted innocently or involuntarily," was struck down under the Eighth Amendment. Similarly, in Weems v. United States, the Court invalidated a statute making it a crime for a public official to make a false entry in a public record but not requiring the offender to "injur[e] anyone by his act or inten[d] to injure any one." 217 U.S. at 363. The Court employed a similar approach in Godfrey v. Georgia, 446 U.S. 420, 433 (1980), reversing a death sentence based on the existence of an aggravating circumstance because the defendant's crime did not reflect "a consciousness materially more depraved than that of any person guilty of murder."

For purposes of imposing the death penalty, Enmund's criminal culpability must be limited to his participation in the robbery, and his punishment must be tailored to his personal responsibility and moral guilt. Putting Enmund to death to avenge two killings that he did not commit and had no intention of committing or causing does not measurably contribute to the retributive end of ensuring that the criminal gets his just deserts. This is the judgment of most of the legislatures that have recently addressed the matter, and we have no reason to disagree with that judgment for purposes of construing and applying the Eighth Amendment.

Because the Florida Supreme Court affirmed the death penalty in this case in the absence of proof that Enmund killed or attempted to kill, and regardless of whether Enmund intended or contemplated that life would be taken, we reverse the judgment upholding the death penalty and remand for further proceedings not inconsistent with this opinion.

Notes and Questions

1. Read Justice White's opinion carefully. Under *Enmund,* what is the minimum *mens rea* necessary for imposition if the death penalty of the defendant is not the actual killer? Intent? Recklessness? Some other *mens rea?* Has the Supreme Court fully appreciated the subtleties of *mens rea* doctrine?

2. Does *Enmund* establish any minimum *mens rea* for the death penalty where the defendant is the actual killer, either by its literal holding or by the criminal law principles that underlie its holding? What if an armed robber, not intending to hurt anyone, holds a gun and the gun discharges wholly

accidentally, killing the victim or a co-felon? Indeed, recall the facts of People v. Stamp, supra, page 383. Would *Enmund* bar the death penalty in these cases?

3. Almost immediately after *Enmund* was handed down, the state courts began struggling to apply its holding to the diverse facts of the death penalty cases in their jurisdictions. The sequence of cases in the Illinois courts is perhaps the most revealing.

In People v. Ruiz, 94 Ill. 2d 245 (1982), the defendant and three partners kidnapped three youths from a rival gang, beat them, and drove them in the victim's car to the murder spot. While the defendant remained in the car, his cohorts made the three victims lie face down in the snow, brought them one by one into the car, and stabbed them to death. Ruiz was convicted of first-degree murder and sentenced to death. The court rejected his claim under *Enmund,* saying that the defendant "was present throughout the violent episode, actively participated, except for striking a fatal blow, and his conduct was such as to support an inference that he possessed the intent to take the lives of the victims." Justice Seymour Simon, in dissent, argued that Ruiz, as an accomplice, should have been given a lesser sentence than the principal perpetrators. In the present case, the dissent noted, Ruiz not only did not stab the victims but specifically refused to do so. "He had every right to expect," the dissent said, "as a constitutional matter . . . if not as a matter of prosecutorial choice, jury discretion . . . or statutory interpretation that this refusal would make some difference in the punishment he would receive."

In People v. Davis 95 Ill. 2d 1 (1983), the defendant and his partner entered the invalid victim's home while the victim was inside and, as they exited with several items stolen from the house, the defendant's partner shot the victim. The defendant received the death sentence. The Illinois Supreme Court again held that *Enmund* was inapplicable, even though Davis was not the trigger man. The defendant was present during the course of the burglary; was carrying stolen items out to his car while his partner shot the victim; and "certainly had reason to contemplate that a life would be taken, or that lethal force would be employed," based on his experience during a similar previous heist in which the same partner shot the burglary victim. Justice Goldenhersh, dissenting, argued that the death penalty should have been reduced because there was no evidence that the defendant "was present when the murder was committed or that he contemplated it." Justice Simon also took issue with the majority's opinion that Davis must have "contemplated" that life would be taken in the instant case because during a prior similar heist his partner also shot the burglary victim. This, Simon argued was "too artful" a use of the word "contemplate" in deciding whether *Enmund* protected the defendant and was a departure from the *Enmund* holding that the Eighth Amendment forbids imposition of the death penalty on one

> who aids and abets a felony in the course of which a murder is committed by others but who does not himself kill, attempt to kill, or intend that a killing take place or that lethal force will be employed. . . .

> Neither a burglary nor the act of carrying stolen items out of a house that is being burglarized is in itself a murderous act. Such conduct by itself does not intimate an intent to kill. That a murder occurred while defendant was carrying items out of a house on a previous occasion may be enough to convey notice to defendant engaged in similar conduct in a subsequent burglary. He would then be liable for the tort or wrongful death as well as for the crime of felony murder. But foreseeability is not the same as intent, active contemplation, or actual anticipation. To equate the concepts, as the majority does, is to read into negligent or reckless conduct a volitional element that does not exist. Basing an execution on so expansive a definition of the word "contemplate" not only does violence to the clear holding of *Enmund* that a person convicted of felony murder cannot constitutionally be put to death absent a showing that he intended that life be taken, but ignores the fact that our criminal code specifically distinguishes "intent" . . . from "knowledge" . . . , "negligence" . . . , and other states of mind and requires, in order to impose a death sentence, that a defendant convicted of felony murder intend to kill or at least know that as a consequence of his actions a death is likely to occur. . . . I conclude that it is error for the trial court or this court to treat bare forseeability of both *Enmund* and our capital punishment statute that a defendant actually intend a killing or knowingly acquiesce in one.

Two of the most complicated cases arose out of a single crime spree. Freddie Tiller, Andre Jones, and Jones's girlfriend were walking down a street when they saw Richard Stoltz in the distance loading bricks onto a truck. Tiller announced that he wanted to rob Stoltz and asked Jones for his gun. Jones gave it to him, and Tiller walked up to Stoltz, shot him to death, and robbed him. Tiller then suggested that he and Jones rob a cleaners up the street, and Jones agreed. Once inside, Jones shot to death the proprietor and a mail carrier who walked in while the robbery was in progress. People v. Jones, 94 Ill. 2d 275 (1982); People v. Tiller, 94 Ill. 2d 303 (1982). The Illinois Supreme Court upheld the death sentences imposed in Jones's case for his murder of the proprietor and mail carrier, but vacated the death sentence regarding the murder of Stoltz because there was nothing in the record "that shows that defendant killed, attempted to kill, or intended to kill the victim" as required under *Enmund* in order for the death penalty to be imposed. Tiller, appealing his death sentences imposed for all three killings, argued that the evidence failed to show any plan or intent to kill the proprietor or mail carrier or that he performed the acts which resulted in their deaths. The Illinois Supreme Court agreed, saying that unlike the case in *Ruiz,* the defendant was not shown to have planned or in any manner participated in the killings, and thus under *Enmund* the death sentences for the killings of the proprietor and mail carrier had to be vacated. Justice Thomas Moran, dissenting, argued that the majority was interpreting *Enmund* too broadly and that the facts in the instant case were clearly distinguishable:

> In *Enmund,* the two victims were shot to death by defendant's codefendants during the course of a robbery. The murders occurred only after one of the victims shot and wounded a codefendant. Thus, there is every reason to believe that the murders were an unplanned and spontaneous reaction. Defendant En-

> mund participated in the offense to the extent that he drove the getaway car. He was not present at the scene of the crime. The Florida Supreme Court found no evidence that he planned the robbery.
>
> In the instant case, Elem [Jones's girlfriend] testified that defendant suggested the idea of robbing the proprietor of a cleaning store. Although defendant's testimony differed considerably on this point, the jury was not required to believe him. There was evidence from which the jury could infer that defendant participated in planning the offense. Further, unlike Enmund, he was present, at least part of the time, during the commission of the offense. The evidence indicates that he stole the "mail lady's" jeep and a television set. Clearly, defendant participated in the offense to a greater degree than was the case for Enmund.
>
> More importantly, Elem testified that defendant shot Stoltz just prior to the cleaning-shop robbery. That shooting took place during the course of robbing the victim. Shortly thereafter, defendant and Jones entered the cleaning shop, again with the intent of robbing someone. The majority notes defendant's "apparent knowledge of the fact that Jones might harm [the mail lady]." . . . It is difficult to believe that defendant did not anticipate that life would be taken or lethal force employed. . . . Under these circumstances, *Enmund* should not be read to preclude imposition of the death sentence.

Furthermore, the dissent argued, the application of *Enmund* to the instant case "sets an unfortunate precedent":

> It will be difficult indeed to impose the penalty for any unwitnessed murder in which defendant is not the actual "triggerman." This is so despite the fact that defendant just murdered one victim during the course of a separate robbery, and although he was present during, and actively participated in, the offense in question. The position adopted by the majority benefits those defendants who are careful not to leave any witnesses to the crime.

In Carlos v. Superior Court, 35 Cal. 3d 131, 672 P.2d 862, 197 Cal. Rptr. 79 (1983), the California Supreme Court, deriving guidance from *Enmund,* construed the state's death penalty law to bar capital punishment unless the defendant intended the death of the victim.

IV

THE ATTRIBUTION OF CRIMINALITY

8

CAUSATION

A. "BUT FOR" CAUSATION

REGINA v. MARTIN DYOS

Central Criminal Court (1979)
Crim. L. Rev. 660-662 (1979)

CANTLEY, J.

A Friday night dance at a Community Centre was attended by a group of seven youths. The deceased, RM, was one of these as was also SK who at one stage danced near two girls—"he was cocky and showing off."

The boyfriend, BT, of one of the girls was incensed by this; when the seven left shortly before the end of the dance he encouraged the four friends with him to follow to "give us a hand."

At the exit to the dance hall there was some general abuse and threats directed at SK.

The seven went towards the railway station to find a taxi; the five followed at a distance continuing their abuse and threats. When the seven crossed the road the five followed, and were by now closing up.

One of the five, MD, and possibly others, were seen to pick up stones/bricks and throw them. One stone thrown by MD hit PS, one of the seven, on the back of the head. Momentarily stunned, he turned, took off his jacket, challenged the five, advanced, and hit BT.

This immediately turned into a scuffle or fight involving for certain PS, SK, MB, and RM from the seven and BT, IS, and KW of the five. The fight lasted no more than a minute or so as RM was spotted lying in the road by his twin brother GM, bleeding from severe head injuries,—whereupon the five fled and emergency services was called.

One of RM's injuries, that to his right forehead, was caused by a brick held by MD. What had happened, in MD's own words to the police was this:

> Matey threw a punch at me and I ran away . . . I was hit in back by brick as I was going to jump on wall . . . I picked up a brick and started towards one I thought had chucked brick at me . . . he started to run and I went to throw it but I was running and I hit him before I could let it go. I misjudged the distance.

RM survived nine days before succumbing to his injuries; in the meantime all involved were questioned. No evidence was offered against any of the seven; all of the five were indicted with unlawful assembly to which they pleaded guilty, affray which they all denied, MD alone being charged with murder and grievous bodily harm . . . to RM.

At the post mortem it was found that apart from a very few slight marks on the right hand side of the body, legs, and arms, all the injuries were confined to the head, of which the two principal were the one caused by MD to the right forehead and one behind the right ear for which there was no evidence as to the cause.

As to the cause of death the following is a summary of the pathologist's conclusions:

1. The cause of death was cerebral contusion due to a fractured skull.
2. RM received two or more separate blows. There was no evidence as to whether they were caused by the same or different objects, be it metal, wood, masonry, and/or a shod foot.
3. Both principal wounds were potentially fatal.
4. No distinction was made as to the seriousness of either wound.
5. Either wound would "very probably" cause death.
6. There was no certain way of telling which injury came first.
7. There was a "reasonable and sensible" possibility that the deceased might have recovered from the first injury, whichever that was.

In addition to the medical evidence, there was no evidence as to how the second injury was caused, apart from speculation at the time of RM hitting one of the many passing vehicles or of his being swung around and thrown into the traffic. Likewise apart from traces of blood on at least one of the five's shoes (which probably came from kicking SK in the mouth) there was no evidence of blood being found on any blunt object, shoe, brick or kerb. Nor were there any traces of material such as the brick dust in the wounds.

The only evidence against MD was that he struck the one blow to the right forehead; and there was no evidence of joint enterprise as to either wound.

On the count of murder the trial judge upheld the defence submission at the close of the prosecution that it would be unsafe to leave the count to the jury.

These submissions were as follows:

The Crown had failed to prove that MD was responsible for the cause of death because,

> (a) the pathologist's evidence was that it was a reasonable and sensible possibility that the injury behind the ear caused the death, and . . . there was no evidence that MD was responsible for it,

(b) and conversely there was no evidence that the injury which MD (admitted) having caused, was in fact beyond a reasonable doubt the cause of death. MD could only be guilty if death was a natural and probable consequence of his act.

Even if the forehead injury caused by MD was the first injury there was a reasonable and sensible possibility of recovery.

MD's act cannot be held to be the cause of death if that even would or could have occurred without it.

Before the count of murder could go to the jury the Crown had to exclude the possibility . . . that death was not caused by another injury.

It was conceded by the defence that if as a result of what MD did the Crown could show, e.g. that RM was struck by a passing car, then MD's act would have been a substantial cause of death. There was no evidence of this (and in fact the Crown sought to exclude this possibility).

If the ear injury was caused by a brick and that was the cause of death (and the pathologist said both were reasonable possibilities) there was no evidence that MD (or anyone else) did it.

Therefore, in sum:

(1) There was another injury

(2) that injury may reasonably have been the cause of death

(3) that injury cannot be shewn not to have been the cause of death. . . .

After the judge's ruling MD changed his plea to guilty on Count 1 (affray) and Count 4 (grievous bodily harm). . . .

Notes and Questions

1. Certainly MD's action could have caused the death. Why should it make a difference whether or not it actually did? That issue has nothing to do with the moral guilt of the defendant, does it? The comments to Model Penal Code §2.03 defend the causation requirement as follows:

> How far the penal law ought to attribute importance in the grading of offenses to the actual result of conduct, as opposed to results attempted or threatened, presents a significant and difficult issue. Distinctions of this sort are essential, at least when severe sanctions are involved, for it cannot be expected that jurors will lightly return verdicts leading to severe sentences in the absence of the resentments aroused by the infliction of serious injuries. Whatever abstract logic may suggest, a prudent legislator cannot disregard these facts in the enactment of a penal code.

Is this the best defense of the requirement of causation that one can make?

2. Philosophers have debated for centuries about what we mean by "cause." One way of looking at the matter is to regard the question of whether

one event caused another as involving a "thought experiment." To do this, we attempt to envision the world as it would have been if everything had been the same but the allegedly causal event had not occurred. If, in that hypothetical situation, the alleged result would have occurred anyway, we can say that the first event did not cause the second. On the other hand, if, in our hypothetical world, the second event, which is alleged to be the result, would not have occurred, then we can say that the first event was a cause of the second.

A crucial point here is that under this kind of broad definition of cause, every event has many, many causes—the vast majority of which are uninteresting from our point of view. As a result, it simply is not an argument to say that event *A* did not cause a result because event *B* did. Since an event may have many causes, the specification of one does not in any way eliminate others. In other words, when we say that one thing caused another, we have said something—but for the purposes of affixing legal responsibility, we have not said very much.

Professor Glanville Williams has explained the requirement of but-for causation in the following dialogue from his Textbook of Criminal Law 379-381 (1983):

> *Surely the notion of but-for causation is ridiculously wide, because it takes us back to Adam and Eve. The criminal's mother is a but-for cause of his crimes, and so is his grandmother, and all his ancestors to infinity.*
>
> That is perfectly true, but two factors limit the judicial inquiry. First, one starts with the defendant who is charged; his mother does not come into it, much less Adam and Eve. Secondly, but-for causation is only half the story; the defendant who was the but-for cause of the harm is not responsible unless his conduct was also the *imputable* cause. We still have to deal with imputable causation.
>
> *Is the notion of but-for cause a useful one? Where the cause is a positive act, isn't it too obvious to be worth stating? If* D *shoots* V *and* V *drops down dead, surely you don't have to prove that the bullet entering* V's *heart caused him to die?*
>
> When but-for causation is obvious (as it usually is), it is not discussed. Certainly the answer to your last question is in the negative. But occasionally an issue of this kind may require expert assistance.
>
> *D* may administer poison to *V*, who may die shortly afterwards, yet an autopsy may reveal that *V* died not of the poison but of heart disease. There will then be medical evidence at *D*'s trial to the effect that the poison did not cause the death, meaning that *V* would in any case have died at the time and in the way he did, and that the poison did not play any contributory part. If the jury believe this evidence, or, rather, if they are not sure that it is untrue, they must acquit of murder—though *D* may, of course, be convicted of the attempt.
>
> We may summarise, then, by saying that but-for causation is of legal interest only in the comparatively rare cases where, notwithstanding appearances, it is absent; that when it is alleged to be absent, this raises a question of fact for the jury, who may decide by ordinary experience but may have to be assisted by expert evidence; and that the burden is on the Crown to prove beyond reasonable doubt that the defendant's act (or omission) was a but-for cause.

The last point occasions some difficulty in respect of expert evidence, because an expert may not be willing to commit himself to more than the statement that the result would "probably" not have happened as it did apart from the defendant's act or omission. Notwithstanding that the expert will not commit himself to more, the jury (somewhat strangely) are entitled to draw a sure inference of causation from the evidence. Nevertheless, they should be reminded that they themselves must be sure; and the hesitation or reserve of the expert should surely be a factor leading the appeal court to scrutinise a conviction with care. . . .

What about two but-for causes contributed by different defendants? Doesn't your definition imply the paradox that if two persons independently cause an event, neither causes it?

To provide for this, an exception for cases of multiple causation has to be inserted into the definition. It is possible for two sufficient causes, C1 and C2, to be present together, so that E follows both, when usually it follows only one or the other. Both C1 and C2 are causes, even though in the particular situation one or other (as the case may be) was not necessary to be present. An example is where two fatal wounds are given independently at the same time. . . .

Suppose that D1*'s shot entered the lung and would have caused the victim's death in an hour, but* D2*'s entered the heart and killed him instantaneously?*

Then, of course, only *D2* has killed him. *D1* is guilty of an attempt.

The but-for cause is sometimes referred to as the factual cause, or the *de facto* cause, or the scientific cause. The important thing is to distinguish it from cause in another sense, "imputable" (or "legal" or "effective" or "direct" or "proximate") cause. . . .

3. By far, the most commonly litigated crimes requiring a result are those involving homicide. Professor Williams, supra, p.378, describes the state of English law on this subject:

The common law definition of murder, and similarly that of manslaughter, requires that the defendant should have "killed" his victim. . . .

A "killing" can take place by any means. There need be no direct physical act. If the victim asks his way on a dark night, and the defendant, intending to cause his death, directs him to a path that he knows will bring him to the cliff edge, and the victim suffers a fatal fall, this is clearly murder, though the defendant has done nothing more than utter words. So we may say that "killing" means conduct causing death in any way that the law regards as sufficient.[1]

What of accelerating the victim's death?

This is a "killing" in law. Since we are all fated to die at some time, every instance of killing is an instance of accelerating death; and even if death is hastened by as little as five minutes it is still a criminal homicide. So it is no defence to a person who stabs another to death to show that the victim was already dangerously ill. . . .

1. It can even be unlawful homicide to cause a person to catch a disease of which he dies: Castel v. Bambridge (1730) 2 Strange 854, 93 E.R. 894.

4. Actually, causation is not required for guilt under most criminal statutes, which generally require an act, attendant circumstances, and one or more mental states. As Professor Williams, supra, at 378-379 has pointed out:

> [Homicide cases] are the most important [cases involving causation] in practice, but a causal question is capable of arising in other offences, particularly those against the person or property. For example . . . [one] offence . . . [is] *causing* grievous bodily harm. The wording of sections 20 and 47 is different: the one speaks of *inflicting* grievous bodily harm and the other of *occasioning* actual bodily harm, but these verbs, also, imply a requirement of causation.
>
> Similarly, the offences under the Criminal Damage Act [of] 1971 imply that the act of the defendant has caused the damage.

5. Can an omission be a but-for cause of a result? It was assumed in United States v. Jones and People v. Beardsley in Chapter 2 that it could. In those cases, in what sense did the defendants cause the death of the victims? Under that reasoning, don't we all cause any death that takes place while we are alive? If so, why aren't we liable?

B. "LEGAL" CAUSATION

REGINA v. BENGE

Maidstone Crown Court
4 F. & F. 504 (1865)

The prosecution arose out of a fatal railway accident, which occurred on the South Eastern Railway at a place called Staplehurst, where there was a bridge, about two miles in the direction towards London from a station called Headcorn. The tidal trains of that day would be due at Staplehurst at 3:15 P.M., on Friday, the 9th of June. The prisoner Benge was foreman of a gang of plate-layers, who had been employed to repair the rails within a certain distance, including the portion of the line at Staplehurst, and for that purpose it would be necessary to take up and replace the rails. There were eight or nine men employed under the prisoner to do this work, and the other prisoner, Gallimore, was inspector of the line for the distance of 36 miles, comprising the Staplehurst part of the line. The time at which the work was done at any part of the line was left to the direction of the prisoner Benge, as the foreman of the gang. And he was furnished with a time book, in which the precise time of the arrival of the various trains on each day was marked; for each week in columns headed by the name of the day of the week. This book was clear in its arrangement, and printed in good, large, legible type, so that with the least care in its perusal, no mistake would be possible. The hour of arrival of the tidal train varied of course with the tide, and was different on each day. And on the day in question the prisoner Benge had looked at the column for Saturday—the next day—instead of Friday, the 9th. The time of arrival on the Saturday would be 5:20 P.M.; whereas the time for Friday, the day in question, would be 3:15. Thinking that the time would be 5:20, the prisoner Benge, when the last of the trains before the tidal train had passed, which was at 2:50 P.M., directed his gang to take up the rails at Staplehurst bridge, and they were accordingly taken up. There was, it will be seen, barely half an hour between the time at which the 2:50 train passed, and the time—3:15—at which the tidal train would arrive; and half an hour as it turned out, and as indeed was well known, would be far too short a time to allow of the rails taken up being replaced! If the prisoner had read the time of arrival of the tidal train rightly, he would not have thought of taking up the rails, but he did not expect it until 5:20, which would have allowed nearly three hours, and the job would be completed in about an hour. He had no particular directions from the other prisoner, Gallimore, the inspector of the line; nor any particular instructions from any one. Nor was any notice sent on to the next station, Headcorn, from which the tidal trains would arrive. Neither did it appear that it was usual to send such notice, or to give notice to the driver of the trains which were to pass. It was usual, however, to send on one of the gang as a signal man with a flag in his hand, who was to go on at least 1000 yards in the direction in which the expected train was to come, and when he had got that distance he was to stand and raise a flag when it appeared, which would be seen at a distance of above 500 yards, and thus would give a distance of 1500 yards, or nearly a mile, between the train and the spot at which the rails were up, so as to allow of ample time to stop the train. Books of printed rules were in the hands of the foreman of plate-layers, and among others, of the prisoner; and these rules expressly provided that rails should not be taken up without these precautions. On the occasion in question one of the men of the prisoner's gang, named Wills, was sent forward as signal man, but without (as it appeared) any particular directions from the prisoner Benge, and instead of going 1000 yards he went, as he said, only 540 yards; and there he stood till he saw the advancing train, and moved his flag. He was observed, but not until the train was too near to be stopped. The engine-driver was not paying a very sharp look-out, and though so soon as he saw the signal man he gave the signal to stop, and the steam was shut off, and the brakes put on, it was too late to stop the train, which was going at the rate of 50 miles an hour, and it came on to the bridge, and then running off the line at the spot where the rails were up, it dashed on to the bridge, and the catastrophe ensued in which many lives were lost.

There was evidence that at the distance of 1000 yards, the train could easily have been stopped, at any rate of speed. . . .

Ribton, for the prisoner, submitted that there was no evidence of any criminal act or default on his part which had caused the death. It appeared that the accident could not have happened, notwithstanding the mistake which the prisoner had undoubtedly committed, if other servants of the company had done their duty; if for instance, the flagman had gone far enough with the signal, or if the engine-driver had kept a sufficient look-out, and had seen the signal, as then he must have seen it earlier than he did, and in time enough to stop the train.

Pigott, B., said, that assuming culpable negligence on the part of the prisoner which materially contributed to the accident, it would not be material that others also by their negligence contributed to cause it. Therefore he must leave it to the jury whether there was negligence of the prisoner which had been the substantial cause of the accident. In summing up the case to the jury, he said their verdict must depend on whether the death was mainly caused by the culpable negligence of the prisoner. Was the accident mainly caused by the taking up of the rails at a time when an express train was about to arrive, was that the act of the prisoner, and was it owing to culpable negligence on his part? His counsel had urged that it was not so, because the flagman and engine-driver had been guilty of negligence, which had [also] contributed to cause the catastrophe; but they, in their turn, might make the same excuse, and so, if it was valid, no one could be criminally responsible at all. This would be an absurd and unreasonable conclusion, and showed that the contention of the prisoner's counsel could not be sound. Such was not the right view of the law—that if the negligence of several persons at different times and places contributed to cause an accident, any one of them could set up that his was not the sole cause of it. It was enough against any one of them that his negligence was the substantial cause of it. Now, here the primary cause was certainly the taking up of the rails at a time when the train was about to arrive, and when it would be impossible to replace them in time to avoid the accident. And this the prisoner admitted was owing to his own mistake. Was that mistake culpable negligence, and did it mainly or substantially cause the accident? The book was clearly and plainly printed, and must have been read carelessly to admit of such a mistake. Was it not the duty of the prisoner who knew the fearful consequences of a mistake to take reasonable care to be correct? And had he taken such care? Then as to its being the main cause of the accident, it was true that the company had provided other precautions to avoid any impending catastrophe, and that these were not observed upon this occasion; but was it not owing to the prisoner's culpable negligence that the accident was impending, and if so, did his negligence the less cause it, because if other persons had not been negligent it might possibly have been avoided?

Verdict—Guilty.

Notes and Questions

1. Why should we care whether Benge's causal role in the accident was more important than any other causal factor?

2. Probably the most influential work on legal causation is that of H. L. A. Hart and A. M. Honore, Causation and the Law (1959). At page 341

the authors explain the necessity of restricting but-for causation in the criminal context:

> "To consequences no limit can be set": "Every event which would not have happened is the consequence of that earlier event." These two propositions are not equivalent in meaning and are not equally or in the same way at variance with ordinary thought. They have, however, both been urged sometimes in the same breath by the legal theorist and the philosopher: They are indeed sometimes said by lawyers to be "the philosophical doctrine" of causation. It is perhaps not difficult even for the layman to accept the first proposition as a truth about certain physical events; an explosion may cause a flash of light which will be propagated as far as the outer nebulae; its effects or consequences continue indefinitely. It is, however, a different matter to accept the view that whenever a man is murdered with a gun his death was the consequence of (still less an "effect" of or "caused by") the manufacturer of the bullet. The first tells a perhaps unfamiliar tale about unfamiliar events; the second introduces an unfamiliar, though, of course, a possible way of speaking about familiar events. It is not that this unrestricted use of "consequence" is unintelligible or never found; it is indeed used to refer to bizarre or fortuitous connections or coincidences: but the point is that the various causal notions employed for the purposes of explanation, attribution of responsibility or the assessment of contributions to the course of history carry with them implicit limits which are similar in these different employments.
>
> It is, then, the second proposition, defining consequence in terms of "necessary condition," with which theorists are really concerned. This proposition is the corollary of the view that, if we look into the past of any given event, there is an infinite number of events, each of which is a necessary condition of the given event and so, as much as any other, is its cause. This is the "cone" of causation, so called because, since any event has a number of simultaneous conditions, the series fans out as we go back in time. The justification, indeed only partial, for calling this "the philosophical doctrine" of causation is that it resembles Mill's doctrine that "we have no right to give the name of cause to one of the conditions exclusive of the others of them." It differs from Mill's view in taking the essence of causation to be "necessary condition" and not "the sum total" of the sufficient conditions of an event.
>
> Legal theorists have developed this account of cause and consequence to show what is "factual," "objective," or "scientific" in these notions: this they call "cause in fact" and it is usually stressed as a preliminary to the doctrine that any more restricted application of these terms in the law represents nothing in the facts or in the meaning of causation, but expresses fluctuating legal policy or sentiments of what is just or convenient. Moral philosophers have insisted in somewhat similar terms that the consequences of human action are "infinite": this they have urged as an objection against the utilitarian doctrine that the rightness of a morally right action depends on whether its consequences are better than those of any alternative action in the circumstances. "We should have to trace as far as possible the consequences not only for the persons affected directly but also for those indirectly affected and to these no limit can be set." Hence, so the argument runs, we cannot either inductively establish the utilitar-

ian doctrine that right acts are "optimistic" or use it in particular cases to discover what is right. Yet, however vulnerable at other points utilitarianism may be as an account of moral judgment, this objection seems to rest on a mistake as to the sense of "consequence." The utilitarian assertion that the rightness of an action depends on its consequences is not the same as the assertion that it depends on all those later occurrences which would not have happened had the action not been done, to which indeed "no limit can be set." It is important to see that the issue here is not the linguistic one whether the word "consequence" would be understood if used in this way. The point is that, though we could, we do not think in this way in tracing connections between human actions and events. Instead, whenever we are concerned with such connections, whether for the purpose of explaining a puzzling occurrence, assessing responsibility, or giving an intelligible historical narrative, we employ a set of concepts restricting in various ways what counts as a consequence. These restrictions colour *all* our thinking in causal terms; when we find them in the law we are not finding something invented by or peculiar to the law, though of course it is for the law to say when and how far it will use them and, where they are vague, to supplement them.

No short account can be given of the limits thus placed on "consequences" because these limits vary, intelligibly, with the variety of causal connection asserted. Thus we may be tempted by the generalization that consequences must always be something intended or foreseen or at least foreseeable with ordinary care: but counter-examples spring up from many . . . context[s] where causal statements are made. If smoking is shown to cause lung cancer, this discovery will permit us to describe past as well as future cases of cancer as the effect or consequence of smoking even though no one foresaw or had reasonable grounds to suspect this in the past. What is common and commonly appreciated and hence foreseeable certainly controls the scope of consequences in certain varieties of causal statement but not in all. Again the voluntary intervention of a second person very often constitutes the limit. If a guest sits down with a table laid with knife and fork and plunges the knife into his hostess's breast, her death is not in any context thought of as caused by, or the effect or result of the waiter's action in laying the table; nor would it be linked with this action as its consequence for any of the purposes, explanatory or attributive, for which we employ causal notions. Yet as we have seen there are many other . . . case[s] where a voluntary action or the harm it does are naturally attributed to some prior neglect of precaution as its consequence. Finally, we may think that a simple answer is already supplied by Hume and Mill's doctrine that causal connection rests on general laws asserting regular connection; yet, even in the type of case to which this important doctrine applies, reference to it alone will not solve our problem. For we often trace a causal connection between an antecedent and a consequent which themselves very rarely go together: we do this when the case can be broken down into intermediate stages, which themselves exemplify different generalizations, as when we find that the fall of a tile was the cause of someone's death, rare though this be. Here our problem reappears in the form of the question: When can generalizations be combined in this way?

3. In one English case, Hennigan [1971] 3 All E.R. 133, the court held it was error for a judge to direct a jury that the defendant would not be liable if

he were less than one-fifth to blame. What does it mean to say that someone is one-fifth—or any fraction—to blame?

COMMONWEALTH v. RHOADES

Supreme Judicial Court of Massachusetts
401 N.E.2d 342 (1980)

Abrams, Justice.

The first alarm for the three alarm blaze was sounded at 11:03 p.m. Among the firefighters responding to the second alarm was Captain James Trainor. When Trainor entered the burning building in an attempt to rescue persons thought to be trapped inside, he was outfitted in standard firefighting gear: rubber coat, helmet, boots and a self-contained breathing apparatus. The temperature outside was in the 20's. Attempting to assist those fighting the fire, Trainor encountered intense heat and thick smoke, and experienced difficulty in getting air through his face mask. While on the roof of the building, Trainor collapsed; taken to a hospital in Everett, he was pronounced dead on arrival. The Commonwealth's medical expert concluded that the combination of cold weather, stress, and smoke inhalation precipitated the coronary thrombosis which caused Trainor's death.

The trial judge charged the jury that if Captain Trainor died "as a result" of Rhoades' act, or if Rhoades' act "in any way contributed to hasten, or was part of the proximate cause" of Trainor's death, then Rhoades could be liable for second degree murder.[2] The judge charged that if the jury found beyond a reasonable doubt, that Rhoades' act was a "contributing cause" of Trainor's death, then Rhoades would be criminally liable. The overall effect of this charge was to leave the jury with the impression that if Rhoades' act in setting the fire in any way constituted a link, no matter how remote, in the chain of events leading to Trainor's death, Rhoades should be convicted. We conclude that this formulation exposed Rhoades to potential liability for events not proximately caused by his felonious act in setting the fire.[3] See generally, R. Perkins, Criminal Law, 685-738 (2d ed. 1969)

This misimpression is not corrected by the impact of the instructions evaluated as a whole. Nothing said to the jury by the judge indicated that

2. A reading of the record indicates that at trial it was the defendant's theory that the Commonwealth was required to prove that the fire was the sole or exclusive cause of Captain Trainor's death. The defendant claimed an exception to "the Court's explanation that it's not necessary for the Commonwealth to prove—that it [the fire] was the exclusive and sole reason for death, but was a contributing cause." It would have been incorrect for the judge to have instructed the jury that the fire must be the exclusive and sole reason for death.

3. A finding that Rhoades' conduct was the proximate cause of Trainor's death is an inference that a jury could well have drawn from the evidence in this case. On appeal, Rhoades does not contend otherwise. The Commonwealth's medical expert found that Trainor's efforts in fighting the fire "precipitated" the thrombosis that caused his death. The defendant's expert testified that the stress of fighting the fire "contributed to" Trainor's "final thrombosis." Nevertheless, a defendant is entitled to have the law correctly explained to the jury.

proximate cause in Captain Trainor's death "is a cause, which, in the natural and continuous sequence, produces the death, and without which the death would not have occurred." California Jury Instructions, Criminal §8.55 (4th rev. ed. 1979).[4]

The judge, apparently responding to the defendant's theory that he was criminally responsible only if he were the sole cause, merely attempted to instruct the jury that if Rhoades' conduct contributed to Trainor's death, Rhoades could be convicted. §8.58 (4th rev. ed. 1979). He emphasized that the fire need not be the sole cause, but failed to instruct the jury clearly that the defendant's conduct must be the efficient cause, the cause that necessarily sets in operation the factors which caused the death. The judgment on the indictment charging Rhoades with the death of Captain Trainor is therefore reversed, the verdict set aside, and the case remanded to the Superior Court for further proceedings consistent with this opinion.

So ordered.

Notes and Questions

1. What was wrong with the trial judge's instruction in this case?

2. What if Trainor had suffered from a serious heart condition, and his supervisor had violated department rules by failing to put Trainor on medical leave? What if Trainor had violated department guidelines by unnecessarily entering a smoke-filled room or by wearing the wrong equipment?

3. Obviously something else besides mere but-for cause must be necessary before we can impose criminal liability for a result. What help does the court give here? What help does the Model Penal Code give on the issue?

Model Penal Code

Section 2.03. Causal Relationship Between Conduct and Result; Divergence Between Result Designed or Contemplated and Actual Result or Between Probable and Actual Result.

(1) Conduct is the cause of a result when:

(a) It is an antecedent but for which the result in question would not have occurred; and

(b) the relationship between the conduct and result satisfies any additional causal requirements plainly imposed by law.

(2) When purposely or knowingly causing a particular result is a material element of an offense, the element is not established if the actual result is not within the purpose or the contemplation of the actor unless:

4. On this appeal, the defendant does not contest the premise that a person, found to have set a fire in circumstances constituting arson, may be convicted of murder or manslaughter if a firefighter dies in the performance of his duties. See State v. Glover, 330 Mo. 709, 50 S.W.2d 1049 (1932). Rather he claims that the jury should have been clearly instructed that the arsonist's act must constitute not just a cause, but also the proximate cause of the firefighter's death.

(a) the actual result differs from that designed or contemplated, as the case may be, only in the respect that a different person or different property is injured or affected or that the injury or harm designed or contemplated would have been more serious or more extensive than that caused; or

(b) the actual result involves the same kind of injury or harm as that designed or contemplated and is not too accidental in its occurrence to have a just bearing on the actor's liability or on the gravity of his offense.
[Alternative: and it occurs in a manner which the actor knows or should know is rendered substantially more probable by his conduct.]

(3) When recklessly or negligently causing a particular result is a material element of an offense, the element is not established if the actual result is not within the risk of which the actor is aware, or in the case of negligence, of which he should be aware unless:

(a) the actual result differs from the probable result only in the respect that a different person or different property is injured or affected or that the probable injury or harm would have been more serious or more extensive than that caused; or

(b) the actual result involves the same kind of injury or harm as that designed or contemplated and is not too accidental in its occurrence to have a just bearing on the actor's liability or on the gravity of his offense.
[Alternative: and it occurs in a manner which the actor knows or should know is rendered substantially more probable by his conduct.]

UNITED STATES v. HAMILTON

United States District Court, District of Columbia
182 F. Supp 548 (1960)

HOLTZOFF, District Judge.

The evidence in this case establishes the following salient facts. On the afternoon and evening of December 2, 1959, a number of men had gathered in a poolroom on Georgia Avenue near Lamont Street for the purpose of recreation. The defendant and the deceased were in that group. They played several games of pool. They imbibed intoxicating beverages in the rear of the establishment, and they also carried on desultory conversations. There was an exchange of banter between the deceased and the defendant, which developed into an argument, and finally into an acrimonious quarrel. The subject matter of the argument must have been trivial and inconsequential, because the defendant, although he narrated with a great degree of particularity the events of that evening, does not remember what the discussion was about. Both the deceased and the defendant were asked by the person in charge of the poolroom to leave, because it was undesirable that a fight should develop inside.

Accordingly, both of them went outside and a fight started on Lamont Street. In the course of the fight, the deceased was knocked down by the defendant. While he was lying on the ground, the defendant apparently exploded in a fit of ungovernable rage and jumped on the face of the deceased and kicked him in the head as well.

The deceased was taken to the District of Columbia General Hospital, arriving there at 11:30 P.M. No useful purpose would be served by recounting the gory and harrowing details concerning the nature of the injuries sustained by the deceased to his face and head. Suffice it to say that he apparently was in a semi-comatose condition. He was violent and in shock. Blood was coming from his face.

Promptly upon arrival at the hospital, the deceased came into the competent hands of the Chief Resident of the Neurological Service, who impressed the Court as a completely dedicated and entirely devoted physician. He did everything possible that could be done for his patient. A blood transfusion was given to the deceased, his airways were cleansed, and tubes inserted into his nasal passages and trachea in order to maintain the breathing process. In view of the fact that he was violent, it was necessary to restrain the patient by fastening leather handcuffs on him. The doctor saw the patient several times during the night. In addition, the registered nurse in charge of the ward in which the deceased was placed, saw him at least every half hour or every thirty-five minutes. The deceased was in a room with only one other patient. A licensed practical nurse was constantly in attendance in that room. It is obvious that the patient received incessant and continuous care and treatment at the hands of both the medical and nursing staff of the hospital.

During the night it became desirable to change the bed clothes of the deceased, because they had become bloody. To accomplish this result, it was necessary to remove the restraints from the patient. They were not put back, because by that time, the patient was no longer violent and was resting better than when he arrived. About 6:30 in the morning, the patient had a convulsion, and immediately thereafter, he himself, with his own hands, pulled out the tubes. At 7:30 A.M., the patient died.

The Deputy Coroner, who performed the autopsy and who himself is an experienced physician, found the cause of death to be asphyxiation due to aspiration or inhalation of blood caused by severe injuries to the face, including multiple fractures of the nasal bones. The attending physician testified that the cause of death was asphyxia. In other words, the two physicians agree as to the cause of death. It should be said at this point that the purpose of the tubes was to assist in keeping the airways clear in order that the patient might breathe normally. It is claimed by able counsel for the defendant that the immediate cause of death was the fact that the patient pulled out the tubes, and that, therefore, he brought about his own death. This contention requires a consideration of the applicable principles of law.

It is well established that if a person strikes another and inflicts a blow that may not be mortal in and of itself but thereby starts a chain of causation that leads to death, he is guilty of homicide. This is true even if the deceased contributes to his own death or hastens it by failing to take proper treatment.

The principles of the common law on this subject are summarized in Hale's Pleas of the Crown, Volume 1, p.427, in a passage that has been frequently quoted. He says:

> If a man give another a stroke, which it may be, is not in itself so mortal, but that with good care he might be cured, yet if he die of this wound within a year and a day, it is homicide or murder, as the case is, and so it hath been always ruled.

And, again, Hale says:

> But if a man receives a wound, which is not in itself mortal, but either for want of helpful applications, or neglect thereof, it turns to a gangrene, or a fever, and that gangrene or fever be the immediate cause of his death, yet, this is murder or manslaughter in him that gave the stroke or wound, for that wound, tho it were not the immediate cause of his death, yet, if it were the mediate cause thereof, and the fever or gangrene was the immediate cause of his death, yet the wound was the cause of the gangrene or fever, and so consequently is *causa causati.*

Judicial decisions applying this doctrine are too numerous to require a review. Suffice it to say that these principles have been adopted and applied in the District of Columbia, in Hopkins v. United States, 4 App. D.C. 430, 439. In that case, the defendant had struck the deceased. Several weeks later the deceased died, and the autopsy showed that the death was caused by the blow that had been inflicted by the defendant. It was argued that the defendant was not guilty of homicide, because the deceased had neglected to take medical treatment after he was struck and that his failure to do so either caused or contributed to bringing about his death. This contention was overruled, and it was held that the mere fact that the deceased had neglected to procure proper treatment for the effects of the blow or wound did not relieve the defendant of his responsibility for the homicide.

Hawkins' Pleas of the Crown, Volume 1, Chapter 31, Section 10, summarizes this principle very succinctly. He says:

> But if a person hurt by another, die thereof within a year and a day, it is no excuse for the other that he might have recovered, if he had not neglected to take care of himself.

It is urged by defense counsel, however, that this case should not be governed by the principles just discussed, because, in this instance, the deceased was not guilty merely of neglect, but took affirmative action which contributed to his death, namely, pulling out the tubes. The evidence is far from clear whether the action of the deceased in pulling out the tubes was a reflex action, or whether he was then only semi-conscious, or whether it was a conscious, deliberate act on his part. It is not necessary, however, to resolve this question of fact, because even if the act of the deceased in pulling out the tubes was conscious and deliberate, it would not help the defendant. First, there is not sufficient evidence to justify a finding that if the tubes had remained in the trachea and nasal passages of the deceased, he would have continued to live. Second, and quite irrespective of that consideration, even if it were to be assumed, arguendo, that the deceased might have lived if he had not pulled out the tubes, this circumstance would not have any effect on the liability and responsibility of the defendant for the death of the deceased.

In People v. Lewis, 124 Cal. 551, 559, 57 P. 470, 45 L.R.A. 783, the facts were as follows. The defendant inflicted a gunshot wound on the deceased. This would was mortal. The deceased, however, procured a knife and cut his throat, and thereby brought about his death sooner than would have been the case if it had resulted from the original wound. The defendant was convicted of manslaughter, and the conviction was affirmed by the highest court of California.

An even more extreme case is Stephenson v. State, 205 Ind. 141, 183, 179 N.E. 633, 186 N.E. 293. There the defendant attempted to rape the deceased, and seriously, but not mortally, wounded her. She took poison and died as a result of the poisoning. The defendant was convicted of murder in the second degree, and the Supreme Court of Indiana affirmed the conviction. As against the argument in behalf of the defendant that there was no homicide, since the deceased took her own life by committing suicide, the Court held that the jury was justified in finding that the defendant by his acts or conduct rendered the deceased distracted and mentally irresponsible and that her taking poison was a natural and probable consequence of the unlawful and criminal treatment that the defendant had inflicted on the deceased.

Here the question before the Court is whether the defendant should be deemed guilty of homicide or guilty merely of assault with a dangerous weapon. The Court is of the opinion that the injuries inflicted on the deceased by the defendant were the cause of death in the light of the principles of law heretofore discussed, and that, therefore, the defendant should be adjudged guilty of homicide.

Accordingly, the Court finds the defendant guilty of manslaughter.

Notes and Questions

1. To what extent, in the criminal law, should we "take our victims as we find them?" Is that the issue in the *Hamilton* case?

2. If we believe that Hamilton caused his victim's death, can we at the same time believe that the victim intentionally or voluntarily pulled out his life-saving tubes? Or must we believe that the victim did not exercise any volition?

3. Recall the case of People v. Goodman, supra page 212. Did Goodman cause his victim's death, or did she cause her own death?

The *Hamilton* opinion quotes the common law rule (still the rule in many states) that a defendant may be liable for the death of his victim if the victim dies within a year and a day of the injury. How do you explain this rule? What if Hamilton had caused his victim serious internal damage which left the victim unusually susceptible to infection, and the victim, after a long series of infections, and never having left the hospital, died of pneumonia a year and two days after the injury?

4. Glanville Williams, in his Textbook of Criminal Law (1983) at pp.397-399, discusses these "victim aggravated" cases:

> *What if the victim having received an injury foolishly refuses treatment, so that his condition becomes worse?*
>
> The rule excluding from consideration the contributory negligence of the victim leading to his first injury does not necessarily entail the conclusion that the attacker is liable for an aggravation of the injury brought about by the victim. This is a separate question. As a matter of justice, it might be thought that the attacker ought not generally to be liable for the result of the aggravation; but the cases go the other way.
>
> First, it is clear law that if *D* inflicts a serious injury on *V*, and *V* refuses, however unreasonably, to receive medical treatment and so dies from the injury, *D* is responsible for the death. The latest decision is *Blaue*.[5]
>
> > Blaue stabbed *V*, penetrating her lung. She was taken to hospital, but, being a Jehovah's Witness, refused to have a blood transfusion, and died. The transfusion would probably have saved her. The judge directed the jury that they would get some help from the cases to which counsel had referred in their speeches, and said that they might think they had little option but to reach the conclusion that the stab wound was the operative cause of death—or a substantial cause of death. The jury convicted of manslaughter by reason of diminished responsibility (the diminished responsibility, of course, having nothing to do with the question of causation), and the conviction was affirmed on appeal.
>
> Although the case follows certain ancient authorities, preferring them to opinions expressed in "textbooks intended for students or as studies in jurisprudence," it fails to notice that all the cases dated from a time when medical science was in its infancy, and when operations performed without hygiene carried great danger to life. It was therefore open to the court for the benefit of the defendant to consider the question afresh, and there were several reasons for doing so.
>
> We have seen that it was held in *Roberts* that where the victim sustains injury in an attempt to escape, the test of imputable causation is one of reasonable foresight. This is a useful test, and one might have hoped that it would be generalised, but the court refused to apply it to the case where the victim is seriously injured and declines medical assistance.
>
> It had been held in the law of tort that the test of reasonable foresight applies to facts like those in *Blaue*, but the court was not impressed by the

5. [1975] 1 W.L.R. 1411, 3 All E.R. 446, 61 C.A.R. 171.

argument. It thought that on the undisputed evidence the stab wound inflicted by Blaue caused the death, and that the judge could have told the jury so. Of course it was a cause of the death, but *V*'s refusal of treatment was an additional but-for cause. The court described the defendant's act as "the physical cause of death," and regarded that as conclusive. But in cases of multiple causation it is unconvincing to select one cause as "the" cause.

The best reason for the decision, though not one given in the judgment, is that Blaue would have been guilty of unlawful homicide if the victim had had no chance of obtaining medical assistance, and therefore (it may be said) should be equally guilty if the victim chose not to avail herself of such assistance. Still, there is a difference. The decision means that if the death penalty for murder were restored, the attacker might be hanged purely as a result of the unreasonable decision of the victim not to accept proferred medical help. The criminal law should avoid the appearance of harshness, and to make it more stringent than the civil law in the matter of causation is particularly surprising. Lawton L.J., speaking for the court, explained the difference between the criminal and civil law by saying that "the criminal law is concerned with the maintenance of law and order and the protection of the public generally." This overlooks that Blaue was in any event punishable severely for wounding with intent.[6]

Assuming that *Blaue* settles the law, there is doubtless one limitation upon the rule, namely, that it does not apply where the injury inflicted by the defendant was trifling.

What if the victim is guilty of a positive act of foolishness aggravating his injury?

In general the aggravation will again be placed at the door of the defendant, at any rate if the victim's act was within the range of reasonable foresight.

> In *Wall* (1802)[7] the defendant, a colonial governor, sentenced a soldier to an illegal flogging of 800 lashes, from which flogging he died. There was some evidence that the deceased had drunk spirits after the flogging, which would not have helped him; but he was then, according to the evidence, in a dying state. In directing the jury, Macdonald L.C.B. said: "I apprehend there is no apology for a man if he puts another in so dangerous and so hazardous a situation by his treatment of him, that some degree of unskillfulness and mistaken treatment of himself may possibly accelerate the fatal catastrophe." Governor Wall was convicted of murder and executed. Here, the deceased evidently drank the spirits in order to gain some relief from the suffering caused to him by the flogging (alcohol was regularly used as an anaesthetic before the discovery of more effective drugs). The spirits were the ordinary army ration which was placed by the man's bedside each day;[8] and when he drank the spirits he was probably in no condition to exercise a proper judgment. These considerations make the case a somewhat special one, to be used with caution in stating the law.

6. As always, trial courts may act more leniently than the C.A. lays down. In *Urquart,* Daily Telegraph, January 4, 5, 1979, a Jehovah's Witness injured in a road crash refused a blood transfusion and died; the evidence was that he would almost certainly have lived if he had accepted the transfusion. The jury (agreeing with the writers of students' text-books and works on jurisprudence!) acquitted the driver of causing death by dangerous driving but convicted him of dangerous driving.

7. 28 St. Tr. 51 at 145.

8. Though a surgeon testified that it was against orders to allow spirits into the hospital, and that drinking liquor was dangerous for the deceased in his condition.

In another case, where the victim of an attack rode his horse afterwards, and so perhaps contributed to his own death by preventing healing, the attacker was still held guilty of manslaughter.

These authorities show that where the victim took understandable measures to relieve his suffering, or went on with his ordinary life without fully realising the danger caused by the wound, his conduct does not necessarily sever the causal connection that the law sees between the wound and the death. But the cases do not decide that no supervening act of rashness by the deceased affects the responsibility of the defendant. If the victim's acts were not reasonably foreseeable, and particularly if the wound given were not in itself likely to cause death, and the victim by egregious folly introduced infection into it, a jury might well find, and be in effect required to find, that the defendant's act did not substantially contribute to the death.

A dictum in *Blaue* causes some difficulty. Casting around for reasons for its decision, the Court of Appeal prayed in aid the special sensitivity rule, that "those who use violence on other people must take their victims as they find them." The court said:

> This in our judgment means the whole man, not just the physical man. It does not lie in the mouth of the assailant to say that his victim's religious beliefs which inhibited him from accepting certain kinds of treatment were unreasonable.

Probably the dictum was meant only to explain the actual decision; if applied more widely it would have sweeping results. *D* rapes *V* who commits suicide because she is neurotically inclined, or because she hopes to get *D* into more serious trouble by so doing. Or, *D* assaults *V*, cutting his finger; *V* could take medical advice or apply a proper dressing, but he stupidly binds up the wound with a filthy rag, falls ill, still refuses to accept medical assistance, and dies. Are *V*'s neurosis or vengefulness or stupidity to be reckoned as part of the victim that *D* must "take"? It would be carrying the law of constructive manslaughter very far to regard these as cases of manslaughter.

In one respect the dictum is clearly contrary to authority. *D* assaults *V* in some minor way, which would not be very frightening to a normal person, but *V* inexplicably jumps out of the window (which is far above the ground) and dies. According to *Roberts* and previous cases *D* is not guilty of constructive manslaughter by reason of this unforeseeable reaction of the victim. But the dictum in *Blaue* would make him guilty.

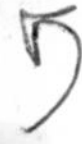

The problem, like others in the theory of causation, would become much easier of solution if constructive manslaughter were abolished, because then it could often be disposed of by saying that the defendant who inflicted only a slight injury was not guilty of gross negligence as to the causing of death.

Similar questions can arise where the death is contributed to by the subsequent acts of third parties. The usual form of the problem relates to negligent (or other improper) medical treatment. . . . When a person has injured another, who dies, the courts are very chary of allowing the assailant to adduce evidence suggesting that the doctors were in some way at fault in their treatment of the victim, in order to escape liability himself for causing the death. The doctors are not on trial, and are not represented; and even if it is alleged that the medical treatment fell short of perfection, whether by act or omission, the court will now generally exclude evidence on the subject, on the ground that it could make no difference to the outcome. However, the court may perhaps be persuaded to admit evidence of gross medical negligence if the injury inflicted by the defendant was demonstrably not serious.

5. Professor Williams's summary of the legal principles which apply where a person injured by the defendant dies after improper treatment by doctors is consistent with the majority approach in American law.

In Baylor v. United States, 407 A.2d 664 (D.C. App. 1979), the defendant struck his wife during an argument, causing a 2-inch laceration in her spleen. She lay in pain while the ambulance was delayed in arriving, and then waited two hours for doctors to diagnose the problem and decide to operate on her spleen. After the operation, she suffered lung problems which led to pneumonia, and she died of cardiac arrest two weeks after her injury. The court of appeals affirmed the husband's conviction of involuntary manslaughter. It held that the hospital's negligence did not negate his liability for homicide, since he could reasonably have foreseen the possibility that the victim would receive negligent treatment.

In *Baylor,* the court noted that the victim had suffered a dangerous wound from which she would have died without treatment. At least one court has held that the defendant might nevertheless be innocent of homicide when the wound inflicted by the defendant would not have caused the victim's death even if left untreated, but the victim received improper or negligent treatment that led to death. Wright v. State, 374 A.2d 824, 829 (Del. Supr. 1977). Does this distinction make sense? Is it more foreseeable that a doctor will be negligent when she treats a dangerous, potentially fatal wound, than when she treats a minor wound? Or is it more foreseeable that any negligent treatment of the dangerous wound will cause the victim's death?

Many courts relieve the defendant of liability where the doctors treating the victim provide "grossly negligent" treatment. The "gross negligence" exception, however, has been applied inconsistently.

In People v. Stewart, 40 N.Y.2d 692, 389 N.Y.S.2d 804, 358 N.E.2d 487 (1976), the defendant stabbed the victim in the stomach. The surgeons succeeded in closing the stomach wound, but while the victim was on the operating table, the surgeons noticed he had an incarcerated hernia, wholly unrelated to the stab wound. While the surgeons treated the stab wound, the anesthesiologist apparently exhibited "gross negligence" in monitoring the victim's intake supply. The victim suffered massive brain and coronary damage and died a month later without ever regaining consciousness. An expert witness testified that it was probably sound medical practice for the surgeons to treat the hernia while they had already opened the victim's abdomen to treat the stab wound, but that the patient would probably have survived the operation to correct the stab wound if the surgeons had left the hernia untreated. On these facts, the court reduced the conviction from manslaughter to assault. The court concluded that the defendant could not be guilty of homicide if the victim's death was "solely attributable to grossly negligent treatment."

Even if the quoted principle is correct, did the court correctly apply the principle to the facts?

In People v. Calvaresi, 546 P.2d 316, 319 (Colo. 1975), a shooting victim died after a doctor confused an exit wound in his shoulder with an entrance wound. The doctor also had made a highly questionable decision to transfer the patient to a new hospital, and the patient had died en route. The court held that the gross negligence of the doctor might negate the defendant's liability, even if the medical mistreatment was not the "sole" cause of the victim's death.

6. Should the defendant be liable for the deaths described in the following news[9] story?

New Hampshire Death Raises Tricky Legal Issues

Sanbornville, N.H.—The scene of the crime—if it's established next month that there was a crime—is now covered with snow. Ruth Moody's trailer is gone, and so is the small wooden shed over which the argument was started. All that's left on the small mobile home lot off Old Stage road is a barren utility pole, a rusty 55-gallon oil drum and a yellow mail box.

But last July 15, a half-dozen people squared off in a confrontation over $75 to $80 of overdue rent money and the possession of the homemade shed. When the dust settled, one man was dead, struck down by a heart attack.

On Jan. 7, three people will go to trial in Carroll County Superior Court on charges of negligent homicide. The state contends they are responsible for the death of Donald Dodier, a 56-year-old one-time auto salesman, contractor and small-time landlord. In a novel application of New Hampshire's negligent homicide law, the prosecution will claim that Perley Ryder, his wife Linda and her brother Daniel Moody knew of Dodier's heart condition and "did negligently provoke an altercation" that lead to Dodier's death.

The case has drawn unusual publicity over the idea that, as one news account put it, someone was "argued to death." One television network has asked to bring TV cameras to the trial, and numerous other news organizations reportedly plan to converge on the small north country town of Ossipee, where the trial will be held.

The case has several unique aspects, according to law professors and prosecutors in other states. Although the legal principle that someone can be held responsible for a freak death during a confrontation is well-established, they said, the notion that words alone can constitute criminal responsibility has not been established.

"The old application of the case is where you aim an unloaded gun at somebody, intending to frighten them, and the person dies of a heart attack," said Alan Dershowitz, a law professor at Harvard University. "You can be held

9. Boston Globe, Dec. 30, 1984 at 41.

guilty. So the principle is not new. But the application of the principle to this kind of case is. . . . It will have interesting implications if there is a conviction."

Dershowitz and others said the crux of the case is likely to hinge on whether there was physical contact during the confrontation, whether the defendants knew Dodier had a heart condition and whether they acted maliciously with that knowledge.

Both the prosecuting and the defense attorneys declined to discuss the facts or strategies behind the case. "You can appreciate that in a small county like ours, any kind of publicity will make if difficult to get an unbiased jury and a fair trial," said Carroll County Atty. William Paine, the prosecutor. Witnesses and the defendants also have been told not to speak with reporters.

Court records, news accounts and interviews with residents who have some knowledge of the case provide some insight into the events of last summer:

In June, Dodier sent an eviction notice to Ruth Moody, who was living in a mobile home on his lot on Old Stage road. She moved the home but left a small storage shed behind.

On July 15, Ruth Moody's son Daniel Moody, her daughter Linda Ryder and her son-in-law Perley Ryder went to get the shed. They found that Dodier had parked a backhoe in a way that prevented the shed's removal. Reportedly, Dodier wanted $75 to $80 in back rent from Mrs. Moody before he would allow the shed to be moved.

Court records indicate witnesses disagree on what transpired next. According to statements made to police by Daniel Moody, 18, Linda Ryder, 31, and Perley Ryder, 27, an unidentified juvenile jumped on the backhoe and started to move it. Dodier came rushing up and took over the driver's seat. (The unidentified juvenile is facing charges in a separate trial.)

Dodier began to move the tractor back, allegedly pinning Linda Ryder between the shed and the machine. Perley Ryder, according to his statements, put his hand on Dodier's shoulder and told him to stop. Dodier and Perley Ryder began talking—or, as the prosecution alleges, arguing. Then, according to Perley Ryder's statement, Dodier abruptly pitched forward onto the ground. Doctors said he had had a fatal heart attack.

At some point during the confrontation, Dodier's wife and daughter arrived. All were described in various degrees of agitation by witnesses.

Interpretation of Facts

The prosecution's success will hinge not only on legal interpretation but on actual events in the case. "The facts of the case are in great dispute," said attorney Harvey Garod, who is representing Moody and the Perleys. In court filings, Garod has made clear he believes Dodier is responsible for his own death and responsible for any disagreement.

Prosecutor Paine contends that Moody and the Perleys are responsible, even if no one touched Dodier. "The law has been developing so that it doesn't take a physical assault [to charge someone with homicide]," Paine said in a telephone interview last week.

Prof. Dershowitz said that if the prosecution can prove physical contact, its case will be far stronger. "Then what is known as the eggshell-skull doctrine might apply," Dershowitz said. "If you assault somebody and he dies because he is weak, you are generally responsible." He cited a case in which a hemophiliac was assaulted, and, although the blow would not have hurt most people, the hemophiliac died. "The man [the defendant] was convicted," Dershowitz said. If physical contact is not proved, Dershowitz said, the constitutional right to free speech should protect the defendants.

Other legal specialists agree that prosecutor Paine's case would be precedent-setting if he wins. "The fact someone tries to pick an argument with you and the fact you lose your cool does not mean he is responsible," said Peter Arenella, a professor of criminal law at Boston University. "That is a very elastic concept of causation."

A Scranton, Pa., prosecutor who recently tried a similar case agreed that the question of physical contact is key. "If you don't have touching, you don't have a strong case," said Ernest Preate Jr., district attorney for Lackawanna County.

Preate said his office was able to convict two men of involuntary manslaughter two years agao after a man they mugged had a heart attack and died. "This was nothing more than a simple assault," said Preate. "The man was grabbed from behind and wrestled to the ground. But the consequence of the robbery was a heart attack, and the two men were ultimately judged guilty of third-degree murder."

At trial the judge directed a verdict of not guilty on the ground that there was no evidence of negligence.

7. What about this one?

Witness's Fatal Heart Attack in Court Is Ruled Homicide

Oklahoma City (AP)—A 67-year-old woman who suffered a fatal heart attack in court as she described how she was robbed at gunpoint has been ruled a homicide victim by Oklahoma's chief medical examiner.

"She was scared to death. I don't mean to be crude, but that's exactly what happened," said Dr. Fred Jordan, who on Wednesday changed the death certificate of Mildred Pruner. "To say that she simply died of a heart attack is not telling the story honestly or accurately." . . .

Pruner, the only witness to the crime, suffered a heart attack May 14 in Oklahoma County district court and died before she could [repeat her identification of] her assailant, despite the prosecutor's attempts to save her with mouth-to-mouth resuscitation.

"She was a 67-year-old lady. She was extremely nervous," Jordan said. "I believe Mrs. Pruner was in court, testifying and frightened, and the stress related to that was what caused her death."

Pruner, who had no history of heart trouble, had been asked by prosecutors to describe her feelings during the robbery when the heart attack occurred.

Her daughter, Glenda Burns, said her mother did not seem upset right after the April 11 robbery, in which $77 was taken. But as the trial date approached, Pruner became shaky.

"She was nervous about going up there to testify," Burns said. "I guess it was just such a strain on her."[10]

10. San Jose Mercury News, May 25, 1984, at 6A.

COMMONWEALTH v. ROOT

Supreme Court of Pennsylvania
403 Pa. 571, 170 A.2d 310 (1961)

Charles Alvin JONES, Chief Justice.

The appellant was found guilty of involuntary manslaughter for the death of his competitor in the course of an automobile race between them on a highway. The trial court overruled the defendant's demurrer to the Commonwealth's evidence and, after verdict, denied his motion in arrest of judgment. On appeal from the judgment of sentence entered on the jury's verdict, the Superior Court affirmed. We granted allocatur because of the important question present as to whether the defendant's unlawful and reckless conduct was a sufficiently direct cause of the death to warrant his being charged with criminal homicide.

The testimony, which is uncontradicted in material part, discloses that, on the night of the fatal accident, the defendant accepted the deceased's challenge to engage in an automobile race; that the racing took place on a rural 3-lane highway; that the night was clear and dry, and traffic light; that the speed limit on the highway was 50 miles per hour; that, immediately prior to the accident, the two automobiles were being operated at varying speeds of from 70 to 90 miles per hour; that the accident occurred in a no-passing zone on the approach to a bridge where the highway narrowed to two directionally-opposite lanes; that, at the time of the accident, the defendant was in the lead and was proceeding in his right hand lane of travel; that the deceased, in an attempt to pass the defendant's automobile, when a truck was closely approaching from the opposite direction, swerved his car to the left, crossed the highway's white dividing line and drove his automobile on the wrong side of the highway head-on into the oncoming truck with resultant fatal effect to himself.

This evidence would of course amply support a conviction of the defendant for speeding, reckless driving and, perhaps, other violations of The Vehicle Code. . . . In any event, unlawful or reckless conduct is only one ingredient of the crime of involuntary manslaughter. Another essential and distinctly separate element of the crime is that the unlawful or reckless conduct charged to the defendant was the *direct* cause of the death in issue. The first ingredient is obviously present in this case but, just as plainly, the second is not.

While precedent is to be found for application of the tort law concept of "proximate cause" in fixing responsibility for criminal homicide, the want of any rational basis for its use in determining criminal liability can no longer be properly disregarded. When proximate cause was first borrowed from the field of tort law and applied to homicide prosecutions in Pennsylvania, the concept connoted a much more direct causal relation in producing the alleged culpable result than it does today. Proximate cause, as an essential element of a tort founded in negligence, has undergone in recent times, and is still undergoing, a marked extension. More specifically, this area of civil law has been progressively liberalized in favor of claims for damages for personal injuries to which careless conduct of others can in some way be associated. To persist in applying the tort liability concept of proximate cause to prosecutions for criminal homicide after the marked expansion of *civil* liability of defendants in tort actions for negligence would be to extend possible *criminal* liability to persons chargeable with unlawful or reckless conduct in circumstances not generally considered to present the likelihood of a resultant death.

The instant case is one of first impression in this State; and our research has not disclosed a single instance where a district attorney has ever before attempted to prosecute for involuntary manslaughter on facts similar to those established by the record now before us. The closest case, factually, would seem to be Commonwealth v. Levin, 1957, 184 Pa. Super. 436, 135 A.2d 764, which affirmed the defendant's conviction of involuntary manslaughter. In the *Levin* case two cars were racing on the streets of Philadelphia at speeds estimated at from 85 to 95 miles per hour. The defendant's car, in the left hand lane, was racing alongside of the car in which the deceased was a passenger when the defendant turned his automobile sharply to the right in front of the other car thereby causing the driver of the latter car to lose control and smash into a tree, the passenger being thrown to the road and killed as a result of the impact. It is readily apparent that the elements of causation in the *Levin* case were fundamentally different from those in the present case. Levin's act of cutting his automobile sharply in front of the car in which the deceased was riding directly forced that car off of the road and into the tree. The defendant's reckless and unlawful maneuver was the direct cause of the crucial fatality. In the instant case, the defendant's conduct was not even remotely comparable. Here, the action of the deceased driver in recklessly and suicidally swerving his car to the left lane of a 2-lane highway into the path of an oncoming truck was not forced upon him by any act of the defendant; it was done by the deceased and by him alone, who thus directly brought about his own demise. The *Levin* case was properly decided but it cannot, by any ratiocination, be utilized to justify a conviction in the present case.

Legal theory which makes guilt or innocence of criminal homicide depend upon such accidental and fortuitous circumstances as are now embraced by modern tort law's encompassing concept of proximate cause is too harsh to be just. A few illustrations should suffice to so demonstrate.

In Mautino v. Piercedale Supply Co. 1940, 338 Pa. 435, 12 A.2d 51,—a civil action for damages—we held that where a man sold a cartridge to a person under 16 years of age in violation of a State statute and the recipient subsequently procured a gun from which he fired the cartridge injuring someone, the injury was proximately caused by the act of the man who sold the cartridge to the underage person. If proximate cause were the test for criminal liability and the injury to the plaintiff in the *Mautino* case had been fatal, the man who sold the bullet to the underage person (even though the boy had the appearance of an adult) would have been guilty of involuntary manslaughter, for his unlawful act would, according to the tort law standard have been the proximate cause of the death.

In Schelin v. Goldberg, 1958, 188 Pa. Super. 341, 146 A.2d 648, it was held that the plaintiff, who was injured in a fight, could recover in tort against the defendants, the owners of a taproom who prior to the fight had unlawfully served the plaintiff drinks while he was in a visibly intoxicated condition, the unlawful action of the defendants being held to be the proximate cause of the plaintiff's injuries. Here, again, if proximate cause were the test for criminal liability and the plaintiff had been fatally injured in the fight, the taproom owners would have been guilty of involuntary manslaughter, for their unlawful act would have been no less the proximate cause of death.

In Marchl v. Dowling & Company, 1945, 157 Pa. Super. 91, 41 A.2d 427, it was held that where a truck driver had double parked his truck and the minor plaintiff was struck by a passing car when she walked around the double parked truck, the truck driver's employer was held liable in tort for the plaintiff's injuries on the ground that the truck driver's act of double parking, which violated both a State statute and a city ordinance, was the proximate cause of the plaintiff's injuries. Here, also, if proximate cause were the test for criminal liability and the plaintiff's injuries had been fatal, the truck driver would have been guilty of involuntary manslaughter since his unlawful act would have been the proximate cause of the death for which his employer was held liable in damages under respondeat superior. To be guilty of involuntary manslaughter for double parking would, of course, be unthinkable, yet if proximate cause were to determine criminal liability, such a result would indeed be a possibility.

Even if the tort liability concept of proximate cause were to be deemed applicable, the defendant's conviction of involuntary manslaughter in the instant case could not be sustained under the evidence. The operative effect of a supervening cause would have to be taken into consideration. . . . But, the trial judge refused the defendant's point for charge to such effect and erroneously instructed the jury that "negligence or want of care on the part of [the deceased] is no defense to the criminal responsibility of the defendant. . . ."

Under the uncontradicted evidence in this case, the conduct of the defendant was not the proximate cause of the decedent's death as a matter of law.

In [Johnson v. Angretti, 361 Pa. 602, 73 A.2d 666 (1950),] while Angretti was driving his truck eastward along a highway, a bus, traveling in the same direction in front of him, stopped to take on a passenger. Angretti swerved his truck to the left into the lane of oncoming traffic in an attempt to pass the bus but collided with a tractor-trailer driven by the plaintiff's decedent, who was killed as a result of the collision. In affirming the entry of judgment n.o.v. in favor of the defendant bus company, we held that any negligence on the part of the bus driver, in suddenly bringing his bus to a halt in order to pick up a passenger, was not a proximate cause of the death of the plaintiff's decedent since the accident "was due entirely to the intervening and superseding negligence of Angretti in allowing his truck to pass over into the pathway of the westbound tractor-trailer. . . ."

In the case now before us, the deceased was aware of the dangerous condition created by the defendant's reckless conduct in driving his automobile at an excessive rate of speed along the highway but, despite such knowledge, he recklessly chose to swerve his car to the left and into the path of an oncoming truck, thereby bringing about the head-on collision which caused his own death.

To summarize, the tort liability concept of proximate cause has no proper place in prosecutions for criminal homicide and more direct causal connection is required for conviction. . . . In the instant case, the defendant's reckless conduct was not a sufficiently direct cause of the competing driver's death to make him criminally liable therefor.

The judgment of sentence is reversed and the defendant's motion in arrest of judgment granted.

BELL, Justice (concurring).

Involuntary manslaughter is an unintentional and nonfelonious killing of another person without malice or passion, which results from conduct by defendant which is so unlawful as to be outrageous, provided such conduct is a direct cause of the killing.

The unlawful racing by this defendant was not only unlawful, it was outrageous, but it was not a direct cause, i.e., one of the direct causes, of the killing.

EAGEN, Justice (dissenting).

The opinion of the learned Chief Justice admits, under the uncontradicted facts, that the defendant, at the time of the fatal accident involved, was engaged in an unlawful and reckless course of conduct. Racing an automobile at 90 miles per hour, trying to prevent another automobile going in the same direction from passing him, in a no-passing zone on a two-lane public highway, is certainly all of that. Admittedly also, there can be more than one direct cause of an unlawful death. To me, this is self-evident. But, says the majority opinion, the defendant's recklessness was not a direct cause of the death. With this, I cannot agree.

If the defendant did not engage in the unlawful race and so operate his automobile in such a reckless manner, this accident would never have occurred. He helped create the dangerous event. He was a vital part of it. The victim's acts were a natural reaction to the stimulus of the situation. The race, the attempt to pass the other car and forge ahead, the reckless speed, all of these factors the defendant himself helped create. He was part and parcel of them. That the victim's response was normal under the circumstances, that his reaction should have been expected and was clearly foreseeable, is to me beyond argument. That the defendant's recklessness was a substantial factor is obvious. All of this, in my opinion, makes his unlawful conduct a direct cause of the resulting collision. . . .

The majority opinion states, "Legal theory which makes guilt or innocence of criminal homicide depend upon such *accidental and fortuitous circumstances* as are now embraced by modern tort law's encompassing concept . . . is too harsh to be just." If the resulting death had been dependent upon "accidental and fortuitous circumstances" or, as the majority also say, "in circumstances not generally considered to present the likelihood of a resultant death," we would agree that the defendant is not criminally responsible. However, acts should be judged by their tendency under the known circumstances, *not* by the actual intent which accompanies their performance. Every day of the year, we read that some teen-agers, or young adults, somewhere in this country, have been killed or have killed others, while racing their automobiles. Hair-raising, death-defying, law-breaking rides, which encompass "racing" are the rule rather than the exception, and endanger not only the participants, but also every motorist and passenger on the road. To call such resulting accidents "accidental and fortuitous," or unlikely to result in death, is to ignore the cold and harsh reality of everyday occurrences. Root's actions were as direct a cause of Hall's death as those in the "shield" cases. Root's shield was his high speed and any approaching traffic in his quest to prevent Hall from passing, which he knew Hall would undertake to do, the first time he thought he had the least opportunity.

Professor Joseph Beale, late renowned member of the Harvard Law School faculty, in an article entitled, The Proximate Consequences of an Act, 33 Harv. L. Rev. 633, 646, said, "Though there is an active force intervening after defendant's act, the result will nevertheless be proximate if the defendant's act actually caused the intervening force. In such a case the defendant's force is really continuing in active operation *by means of the force it stimulated into activity.*" Professor Beale, at 658, sums up the requirements of proximity of result in this manner: "1. The defendant must have acted (or failed to act in violation of a duty). 2. The force thus created must (a) have remained active itself or created another *force* which remained active until it directly caused the result; or (b) have created a new active *risk* of being acted upon by the active force that caused the result." 2 Bishop, New Criminal Law §424 (1913), says: "He whose act causes in any way, directly or indirectly, the death of another, kills him, within the meaning of felonious homicide. It is a rule of both reason and the law that whenever one's will contributes to impel a physical force, whether another's, his own, or a combined force, proceeding from whatever different sources, he is responsible for the result, the same as though his hand, unaided, had produced it." . . . See, Commonwealth v. Hare, 1844, 2 Clark 467. In that case, two separate bands of men were fighting each other with firearms in a public street and, as a result, an innocent citizen was shot and killed. The person firing the fatal shot could not be ascertained. Hare, one of the rioters, was convicted of homicide and the judgment was affirmed. Can anyone question the logic or correctness of this decision? Under the rationale of the majority opinion, what would be the result in the Hare case? Certainly, under its reasoning, if the truck driver met death under the circumstances the case at hand presents, the defendant would not be legally responsible. Again with this conclusion, I cannot agree.

While the victim's foolhardiness in this case contributed to his own death, he was not the only one responsible and it is not he alone with whom we are concerned. It is the people of the Commonwealth who are harmed by the kind of conduct the defendant pursued. Their interests must be kept in mind.

I, therefore, dissent and would accordingly affirm the judgment of conviction.

Notes and Questions

1. The court distinguishes another drag-racing case, *Levin,* where the defendant swerved dangerously in front of his opponent, causing the opponent to smash into a tree. Should there be any difference between the liability attaching to Levin's conduct and Root's? Did not Root act dangerously and recklessly by drag-racing at up to 90 miles an hour? Could he not foresee that his driving—or even that issuing the challenge to race—might cause his opponent's death?

Does the court concede that Root might have foreseen, and hence proximately caused, his opponent's death, and yet demand something more for homicide liability? How would you define the extra element? Does the court's use of the term "direct cause" illuminate the issue? The court says that Root's opponent "directly brought about his own demise," and that his action in swerving into the wrong lane "was not forced upon him by any act of the defendant." Is this reasoning convincing?

The Court summarizes three civil tort cases, *Mautino, Schelin,* and *Marchl,* and says that if Root is guilty of homicide, it would follow that the civil defendants in those cases would themselves be criminally liable. Carefully review the facts of those cases. Is the court correct that the criminal liability of the tort defendants would logically follow from Root's? If so, would punishing them criminally be unjust?

2. In People v. Marshall, 362 Mich. 170, 106 N.W.2d 842 (1961), the defendant loaned his car to a friend he knew was drunk. The friend collided with another car and both drivers were killed. Marshall was at home, asleep, when the accident occurred. The court reversed Marshall's manslaughter conviction, but noted that the result might have been different if Marshall had been sitting in the passenger seat next to his drunken friend. Why?

What if Root's opponent had killed the truck driver with whom he collided, as well as himself? Would that alter the court's view of Root's liability? For a case suggesting just that result, see Jacob v. State, 184 So. 2d 711, 716, 717 (Fla. 1966).

3. The dissent in *Root* vigorously argues for Root's liability. What would

the dissenting judge have said about the homicide liability of friends of the drag-racers who had helped plan the race and had stood by and cheered instead of calling the police or otherwise stopping the dangerous activity. Recall the discussion of omission liability in Chapter 2.

4. Recall the facts of Commonwealth v. Malone, in Chapter 6, where Malone held a gun to the head of Long, and pulled the trigger three times, killing Long the third time. Assume that Malone had merely been playing conventional Russian roulette with Long, with each of the two boys taking turns aiming the revolver at his own head, and that Long had thereby shot himself. Would Malone then be liable for Long's death? Could you distinguish his liability from Root's? For a case upholding a manslaughter conviction on similar facts, see Commonwealth v. Atencio, 345 Mass. 627, 189 N.E.2d 223 (1963).

5. Consider the facts in the *Pinto* case (see page 235) taken from Wheeler, Product Liability, Civil or Criminal—The Pinto Litigation, 17 Forum 250, 250-251 (1981).

> On August 10, 1978, at about six o'clock in the evening, three teenaged girls were driving a 1973 Pinto sedan south on U.S. Highway 33 toward Goshen, Indiana. They stopped for gas at a self-service station, filled up, and drove back onto the highway. The driver, however, had neglected to put the filler cap on tightly. It fell off and rolled across the highway, coming to rest near the curb in the northbound lane.
>
> The girls did a U-turn to retrieve the filler cap, pulled up where it lay, and drew to a stop in the right lane. They could not pull off the road, because it was designed with an eight-inch-high curb running its entire length, only inches from the traffic lane. Neither a shoulder nor periodically spaced turnouts existed to enable a vehicle in trouble to pull off for repairs. The curbed, shoulderless road was so dangerous that Elkhart County's Citizens' Safety Committee had written a letter to the Indiana State Highway Department asking that the road be modified to provide safe stopping spaces for emergencies.
>
> The weather was clear; the road was dry; and visibility was unobstructed for more than a mile in both directions. But, as the girls drew to a stop alongside the filler cap, a Chevrolet van weighing more than 4,000 pounds, modified with a rigid plank in place of the original front bumper, driven by a man carrying open beer bottles, marijuana, and caffeine pills, and travelling at some fifty-five miles per hour, bore down on them. Without touching his brakes, the van driver plowed squarely into the back of the Pinto, knocking it some 170 feet down the road, spinning it around, and causing it to jump the eight-inch curb with its left side wheels.
>
> The Pinto burst into flame. The two passengers died in the car, but the driver was partially ejected. She was rushed to the hospital and died several hours later. Before dying, however, she told two of the hospital employees, an orderly and a nurse, exactly what had happened.
>
> The police inspected the van immediately after the accident. They found the open beer bottles, the marijuana, and what they reported as capsules of speed.

> Based on those facts, one might have expected any of several occurrences. A civil action might have been filed against the Indiana Highway Department and the engineers who designed and approved Highway 33 and who failed to heed the request that it be modified for safety. A civil action might have been filed against the van driver. The van driver might have been criminally prosecuted for reckless homicide, speeding, reckless driving, possession of controlled substances, and driving with open liquor bottles in his possession. Or, because the Pinto driver had neglected to replace the cap and then had stopped her car on a highspeed highway, one might have concluded that, unless comparative negligence applied, no legal action would be brought based on the girls' deaths.
>
> But the prosecutor of Elkhart County, Indiana, chose to seek an indictment against Ford Motor Company for reckless homicide and criminal recklessness, claiming that the cause of the deaths was the design of the Pinto and Ford's failure to "remove [the Pinto] from the highways" before August 10, 1978.

Does this perhaps explain why the jury decided for the Ford Motor Company?

6. The drafters for the California Joint Legislative Committee for Revision of the Penal Code (Tent. Draft No. 2, 1968) suggested one interesting change in the causation rule when they focused on the intervening actions of a person other than the defendant. Note the emphasized clauses below:

> **Section 408. Causation: Responsibility for Causing a Result.**
>
> (1) An element of an offense which requires that the defendant have caused a particular result is established when his conduct is an antecedent but for which the result would not have occurred, and,
>
> (a) if the offense requires that the defendant intentionally or knowingly cause the result, that the actual result, as it occurred,
>
> (i) is within the purpose or contemplation of the defendant, *whether the purpose or contemplation extends to natural events or to the conduct of another. . . .*
>
> (b) if the offense requires that the defendant recklessly or negligently cause the result, that the actual result, as it occurred,
>
> (i) is within the risk of which the defendant was or should have been aware, *whether that risk extends to natural events or to the conduct of another. . . .*

The commentary written by one of the drafters discussed the problem sought to be solved by such a formulation:

> The one substantive departure in my draft appears in subsection (2) dealing with the case in which the offense requires that the actor have recklessly or negligently caused the result. In these cases the test of accountability is whether the result is within the risk of which the actor was or should have been aware. It seemed to me that this was the place to insert a formulation which would deal with the problem which first struck us in discussing [the] complicity material—what I referred to . . . as the complicity-causation overlap. My proposal is that in this category of situations, characterized by the reckless or negligent participation in the causing of a result by another, the actor is liable when the result is

within the risk of which he was or should have been aware "whether that risk extends to the conduct of others or to natural events." . . .

The last mentioned category of situations is a good example of how the Model Penal Code formulation, as modified, would improve the analysis of "causation" questions. The courts in these cases usually overlook the crucial issue of *mens rea* and focus upon the causation issue in factual terms: whether the victim's act was the proximate result of the defendant's conduct, whether it was a dependent or independent intervening cause, etc. . . . Other examples in somewhat different situations in which the superiority of the Model Penal Code formulation, as modified, over present judicial analysis is revealed may be found in other California cases. For present purposes I merely put [forth] two of those cases. . . .

People v. Lewis, 124 Cal. 551, 57 P. 470 (1889). Defendant shot deceased in the abdomen inflicting a mortal wound, a severing of the mesenteric artery, from which he would have died within an hour. Within that time deceased obtained a knife and slit his own throat inflicting a "ghastly" wound from which he must necessarily have died in five minutes. A conviction for manslaughter was affirmed. The court considered the matter first on the assumption, conceded by the attorney general, that the deceased died from the knife wound acting alone. In this event, the court concluded the defendant could be held for the death under a so-called dependent cause theory (not so-called by the court, however): "the defendant would be responsible if it was made to appear and the jury could have found from the evidence, that the knife wound was caused by the wound inflicted by the defendant in the natural course of events. If the relation was causal, and the wounded condition of the deceased was not merely the occasion upon which another cause intervened, not produced by the first wound or related to it in other than a casual way, then defendant is guilty of a homicide. But if the wounded condition only afforded an opportunity for another unconnected person to kill, defendant would not be guilty of a homicide, even though he had inflicted a mortal wound. In such case, I think, it would be true that the defendant was thus prevented from killing."

The court then considered the matter on the assumption that the gunshot wound was contributing to the death at the moment of death, along with the knife wound. On this view, "although other independent causes also contributed, the causal relation between the unlawful acts of the defendant and the death has been made out. . . . Drop by drop the life current went out from both wounds, and at the very instant of death the gunshot wound was contributing to the event. . . . A person dying is still in life, and may be killed, but if he is dying from a wound given by another both may properly be said to have contributed to his death." (124 Cal. 559)

People v. Fowler, 178 Cal. 657, 174 P. 892 (1918). Defendant was convicted of murder by striking the deceased over the head with a blunt instrument. There was evidence that defendant left him for dead in the road and that a car ran over his head inflicting the wound which caused the death. The court concluded that this evidence, even if believed, would not exonerate the defendant, reasoning that if the car was purposely driven over the body the defendant might not have been responsible for the homicide. But since it was not, and was actually "the natural and probable result of the defendant's conduct in leaving [deceased] lying help-

> less and unconscious in a public road, exposed to that danger" the defendant was responsible for the homicide, and his guilt turns on his *mens rea* in striking the blow. (178 Cal. 669).

7. To what extent can it be said that one person causes the act of another human being? If the doctor in charge of a mental institution carelessly leaves the door unlocked when he leaves the padded cell of a homicidal maniac and the maniac escapes and kills someone, should the doctor be criminally liable for having caused the death? Does the fact that the maniac himself would be irresponsible under the insanity defense make it easier to attach liability to the doctor? If so, what about the prison guard who negligently leaves the cell door of a violent (though criminally responsible) murderer open, permitting the criminal to kill his enemy in a nearby cell?

8. Assume that the Model Penal Code standard applied to Henry II of England (which it most certainly did not). Should he be guilty of the reckless or negligent homicide of Thomas à Becket? Angry with the archbishop for having frustrated his plans, Henry II expostulated (apparently with no thought of having the churchman killed), "Will not someone rid me of this meddlesome priest?" Several of his knights, seeking to curry favor with the king and believing that he wished this event to occur, went and murdered Becket in the Canterbury Cathedral.

9. Often questions which appear to involve a quite different issue—the contemporaneity of act and intention—can be better thought of as causation questions. The first sentence of the following excerpt[11] phrases the matter quite abstractly but, seen as a causation question, the issue becomes much simpler:

> Can it be said that if the overt act of the accused which constitutes part of or produces the *actus reus* is not actuated by the relevant *mens rea* the accused must necessarily be acquitted even if there was an earlier *mens rea?* A leading case which prima facie appears to answer this question in the negative is Thabo Meli v. R. decided by the Privy Council in 1954 on appeal from the High Court of Basutoland. The appellants, acting under a preconceived plan first to kill the accused then to fake an "accident," had deliberately given him drink. When he was in a semi-intoxicated state they hit him on the head. The Privy Council assumed for its opinion that the appellants then believed that their victim was dead. They then rolled the body over a low cliff and faked the scene to resemble an accident. The medical evidence showed that the victim's subsequent death was due not to the blow inflicted by the appellants but to exposure.
>
> Lord Reid, who delivered the unreserved advice of a Judicial Committee which also included Lord Goddard, said:[12]
>
> > It is said that two acts were necessary and were separable; first, the attack in the hut; and, secondly, the placing of the body outside afterwards. It is said that, while the first act was accompanied by *mens rea,* it was not the cause of death; but

11. G. Marston, Contemporaneity of Act and Intention in Crime, 86 L.Q.R. 215-219 (1970).
12. [1954] 1 W.L.R. 228, 230, sub nom. Meli v. The Queen; the report at [1954] 1 All E.R. 373, 374 uses the term "one series of acts" instead of "one transaction."

> that the second act, while it was the cause of death, was *not* accompanied by *mens rea;* and on that ground it is said that the accused are not guilty of any crime except perhaps culpable homicide. It appears to their Lordships impossible to divide up what was really one transaction in this way. There is no doubt that the accused set out to do all these acts in order to achieve their plan and as parts of their plan; and it is much too refined a ground of judgment to say that, because they were under a misapprehension at one stage and thought that their guilty purpose had been achieved before in fact it was achieved, therefore they are to escape the penalties of the law.

The case was strongly criticized by Turner who declared:

> This judgment gives no guidance for the decision of any future case in which the basic facts are similar but the interval of time is greater between the end of the conduct inspired by malice aforethought and the beginning of the conduct which led to the death for it leaves the legal argument of the defence unanswered, and does not provide any clear ratio decidendi.[13]

In the English case of R. v. Church[14] the accused claimed that he had struck the deceased during a fight. Believing that she was dead he threw her in a river. The medical evidence showed that although the injuries she had suffered were likely to have caused unconsciousness and eventually death, the deceased was alive when thrown into the water and death was caused by drowning. The jury acquitted the accused of murder but the Court of Criminal Appeal said of the issue:

> [T]he jury should have been told that it was still open to them to convict of murder, notwithstanding that the appellant may have thought his blows and attempt at strangulation had actually produced death when he threw the body into the river, if they regarded the appellant's behaviour from the moment he first struck her to the moment when he threw her into the river as a series of acts designed to cause death or grievous bodily harm. See Meli v. The Queen.

In each of these cases it could have been argued, first, that the earlier act which was actuated by *mens rea* was a *causa sine qua non* of the *actus reus* and, secondly, that the subsequent "guiltless" act of the accused nevertheless did not break the chain of causation. Thus in *Thabo Meli* the blow which rendered the deceased unconscious could be said to have been a causally contributing factor in his death for it made him vulnerable to death by exposure. . . .

If the above cases are regarded as examples of causation instead of coincidence of act and *mens rea* it is submitted that they do not violate the contemporaneity principle. The question is whether or not the chain of causation has been broken. In *Thabo Meli* the answer was no. . . . The danger of the *Thabo Meli* "one transaction" argument is that, by removing the emphasis from the initial act which was actuated by *mens rea* for murder, it may be made easier to convict an accused where the death was really the result of an accident. Thus if an accused attacked his victim with intent to kill but succeeded in inflicting only minor

13. . . . A conclusion contrary to *Thabo Meli* had been reached earlier in the Southern Rhodesian case of R. v. Shorty, 1950 S.R. 280 and the Indian case of R. v. Khandu (1890) I.L.R. 15 Bombay 194. Earlier decisions supporting the result in *Thabo Meli* are the United States' case of Jackson v. Commonwealth, 38 S.W. 422 (1896), and the Indian cases of Re Thavamani, A.I.R. 1943 Madras 571 and Re Kaliappa Goudan, A.I.R. 1933 Madras 798.

14. [1966] 1 Q.B. 59.

> injuries on him, then in his haste to escape from the scene accidentally ran over and killed the victim, he might be found guilty of murder on the basis that the initial attack and the running down were part of one transaction.[15] On the other hand, if the initial attack only is considered, it is probable that the accidental running down would break the chain of causation leading from the initial act. (G. Marston, Contemporaneity of Act and Intention in Crime, 86 L.Q.R. 215-19 (1970).)

Does the metaphor of "chain of causation" really help in these cases?

10. How do we handle the following final examination question based on a hypothetical news story?

Physician to Face Murder Charges

> At his regular weekly news conference, District Attorney Henry S. Ward announced that he was filing homicide charges against Dr. Theodore Blue, a local physician. According to Ward, some ten months ago Blue was visited for a routine examination by a patient, whose name has not been divulged. According to Ward, Blue truthfully informed the patient that she was six weeks pregnant and, a week later, that examination of her intrauterine fluids showed that the child would be born with a rare malady which would prevent it from living for over a month. The patient then returned home and after consultation, asked Blue to perform a therapeutic abortion upon her. Blue consented and scheduled the abortion for one week later.
>
> In his news conference, District Attorney Ward made it clear that under the laws of the State, abortion during the first trimester of pregnancy was not a crime—and indeed is a Constitutionally protected activity. Under State law the child does not come into existence until after the first trimester of pregnancy. Ward, however, said his case is based on the facts that Blue either deliberately or through gross negligence so treated his patient that the abortion was not effective and that by the time the patient realized that she was due to have the child it was too late to terminate the pregnancy, both because of proper medical practice and the laws of the State. The child was born, lived for 26 days and then died of the malady Dr. Blue diagnosed, and it is for causing this death that Blue is being prosecuted.

Is this a causation issue? If not, what is it?

15. R. v. Bernard (1961) 130 Canadian Criminal Cases 165. See also R. v. Ramsay [1967] N.Z.L.R. 1005 where the *Thabo Meli* test was held inapplicable on the wording of the New Zealand Crimes Act.

9

ATTEMPT

A. THE PUNISHMENT FOR ATTEMPT

1. Why Punish Attempt?

MODEL PENAL CODE
American Law Institute, Model Penal Code and Commentaries (1985)

SECTION 5.05. GRADING OF CRIMINAL ATTEMPT. . . .

(1) *Grading.* Except as otherwise provided in this Section, attempt . . . [is a crime] of the same grade and degree as the most serious offense that is attempted. . . . An attempt . . . to commit a [capital crime or a] felony of the first degree is a felony of the second degree.

Consider the Introduction to Article 5 of the Model Penal Code:

> [Attempt is not] the only crime . . . so defined that [its] commission does not rest on proof of the occurrence of the evil that is the object of the law to prevent; many specific, substantive offenses also have a large inchoate aspect. This is true not only with respect to crimes of risk-creation, such as reckless driving, or specific crimes of preparation, like those of possession with unlawful purpose. It is also true, at least in part, of crimes like larceny, forgery, kidnaping and even arson, not to speak of burglary, where a purpose to cause greater harm than that which is implicit in the actor's conduct is an element of the offense. . . .
>
> Since [attempt] always presuppose[s] a purpose to commit another crime, it is doubtful that the threat of punishment for [its] commission can significantly add to the deterrent efficacy of the sanction—which the actor by hypothesis ignores—that is threatened for the crime that is his object. There may be cases where this does occur, as when the actor thinks the chance of apprehension low if he succeeds but high if he should fail in his attempt. . . . These are, however,

special situations. General deterrence is at most a minor function to be served in fashioning provisions of the penal law addressed to . . . inchoate crimes; that burden is discharged upon the whole by the law dealing with the substantive offenses.

Other and major functions of the penal law remain, however, to be served. They may be summarized as follows:

First: When a person is seriously dedicated to commission of a crime, a firm legal basis is needed for the intervention of the agencies of law enforcement to prevent its consummation. In determining that basis, there must be attention to the danger of abuse; equivocal behavior may be misconstrued by an unfriendly eye as preparation to commit a crime. It is no less important, on the other side, that lines should not be drawn so rigidly that the police confront insoluble dilemmas in deciding when to intervene, facing the risk that if they wait the crime may be committed while if they act they may not yet have any valid charge.

Second: Conduct designed to cause or culminate in the commission of a crime obviously yields an indication that the actor is disposed towards such activity, not alone on this occasion but on others. There is a need, therefore, subject again to proper safeguards, for a legal basis upon which the special danger that such individuals present may be assessed and dealt with. They must be made amenable to the corrective process that the law provides.

Third. Finally, and quite apart from these considerations of prevention, when the actor's failure to commit the substantive offense is due to a fortuity, as when the bullet misses in attempted murder . . . his exculpation on that ground would involve inequality of treatment that would shock the common sense of justice. Such a situation is unthinkable in any mature system, designed to serve the proper goals of penal law.

These are the main considerations in the light of which the [provisions on attempt have] been prepared. . . .

The Comments to Section 5.05 explain further:

[Section 5.05 (1)] departs from the law that preceded promulgation of the Model Code by treating attempt . . . on a parity for purposes of sentence and by determining the grade or degree of the inchoate crime by the gravity of the most serious offense that is its object. Only when the object is a capital crime or a felony of the first degree does the Code deviate from this solution, grading the inchoate offense in that case as a felony of the second degree.

The theory of this grading system may be stated simply. To the extent that sentencing depends upon the antisocial disposition of the actor and the demonstrated need for a corrective sanction, there is likely to be little difference in the gravity of the required measures depending on the consummation or the failure of the plan. It is only when and insofar as the severity of sentence is designed for general deterrent purposes that a distinction on this ground is likely to have reasonable force. It is doubtful . . . that the threat of punishment for the inchoate crime can add significantly to the net deterrent efficacy of the sanction threatened for the substantive offense that is the actor's object which he, by hypothesis, ignores. Hence, there is basis for economizing in use of the heaviest and most afflictive sanctions by removing them from the inchoate crimes. The sentencing provisions for second degree felonies, including the provision for extended terms, should certainly suffice to meet whatever danger is presented by the actor.

On the other side of the equation, it is clear that the inchoate crime should not be graded higher than the substantive offense; it is the danger that the actor's conduct may culminate in its commission that justifies creating the inchoate crime.

2. Should the Punishment for Attempts Be Less Than That for the Completed Crime?

BJORN BURKHARDT, IS THERE A RATIONAL JUSTIFICATION FOR PUNISHING AN ACCOMPLISHED CRIME MORE SEVERELY THAN AN ATTEMPTED CRIME?[1]

In 1806 the steward Leopold Wilhelm Leberecht S. was sentenced to death by the law faculty at Halle because he had twice tried to poison his father, his brother, and his uncle. The first attempt failed because the poison, on account of its repulsive smell and its strange appearance, was thrown away without anyone having eaten it. The second attempt also miscarried. Indeed, each victim took a piece of cake that had been sprinkled with poison, but because they immediately experienced a burning pain in their mouth, they spit the cake out without having swallowed it.

The death sentence was annulled by a court of the second instance after obtaining a legal opinion of the law faculty of Frankfurt upon Oder. It was replaced by prison for ten years. The members of the faculty maintained the view that even a very near attempt at committing a murder (even a murder through poisoning, even a patricide), which remains harmless cannot justify the death sentence—neither under statutory law, nor under Roman law, nor under "legal philosophical" viewpoints. This position of the law faculty reasoned as follows:

> a. The evil inflicted by punishment must stand in a strict relationship not only to the intention but also to the harm that the offender has caused by his act. In order to preserve this *idea of proportionality,* one must punish the attempt more leniently than the completed crime. Whoever—with regard to the same fixed criminal intention—wants to punish the attempted murder in the same manner as the completed murder, namely with death, is either compelled to fall into gross abuse—a multiplication—of the death penalty or becomes entangled in contradictions. For, if one only considers viciousness of intention and character, then, for example, one must also punish with the death sentence the person who puts sugar in his father's coffee in the belief that it was arsenic: Hardly a jurist will be found who would plead for the death sentence in this case.

1. For presentation to the German-Anglo-American Workshop on Basic Problems in Criminal Theory, Freiburg, July 19, 1984.

b. The aim of punishment is the prevention of crime. Supposing capital punishment is . . . an emergency measure for the prevention of murders, then it appears to be just and appropriate when comparing the harm that was caused with the evil that must be endured. If, however, it remains a matter of complete indifference, with regard to the prevention of murder, whether harmless and ineffective murder attempts are threatened with the death penalty, then this punishment becomes absolutely *unjust* (principle of the most lenient means). That it remains a matter of complete indifference for the prevention of murder whether murder attempts are punished with death is certainly a consequence of the fact that every premeditating murderer hopes for the success of his act. He does not calculate that perhaps his act could fail and that he would then be more leniently punished. Without the necessity, to decree the death penalty, remains something which is always repugnant to the principles of legal philosophy and natural law.

c. The threat of the death penalty for attempted murder is *unwise.* It prevents under certain circumstances the offender from desisting in his conduct (the incentive to desist): "May it still seldom be the case; a piece of legislation which in itself, and in its arrangement, creates, even for one in a thousand cases, the possibility of an actual murder, remains a piece of legislation that is always incompatible with legal philosophy."

d. The determination of punishment depends above all, on what sort of impression the punishment, on average, makes on people's sentiments. Let us suppose that someone who has indeed intended much detestable harm but has actually not even hurt a hair of his fellow citizen's head is then punished with death. This would rather bring about sympathy in all those with not completely depraved characters and also discontent with the criminal justice system. Such an impression would be completely different from the one which the criminal justice system intends—respect for the moral values of the general public.

Notes and Questions

1. Does this excerpt convince you of the lack of wisdom of punishing an attempt as seriously as we punish the completed crime?

2. Note that, as applied to the death penalty, the above excerpt would be in accord with the Model Penal Code. Are the two approaches the same?

3. Why does the Model Penal Code make one exception to its rule that attempts are punished as severely as completed crimes? Is the exception sensible?

Very few states have adopted the Model Penal Code provision on the punishment of attempts. In most states today the punishment for attempt is lower than that for the completed crime. It may be a fixed fraction of the punishment for the completed crime, or, where state law classifies offenses into grades, the next grade below that of the completed crime.

4. On the other hand, why should we punish attempts at all? Why not apply the rule in most sports, "no harm, no foul"?

B. THE *MENS REA* OF ATTEMPT

PEOPLE v. CASTRO
Supreme Court of Colorado
657 P.2d 932 (1983)

QUINN, Justice.

The defendant was charged in the Pueblo District Court with attempted extreme indifference murder. The charge arose out of the shooting of Alfred Mares on May 31, 1977, in the parking lot of the Heritage House, a bar in Pueblo. During the afternoon of that day Alfred Mares went to the Heritage House Bar for a beer with his uncle, Clovis Velasquez. While inside the bar he spoke to another uncle, John Velasquez, and John's wife. During this conversation a man whom he knew at the time as "Barney," later identified as the defendant, approached him with a young boy at his side and engaged him briefly in conversation. Later an argument developed between the defendant and one Dennis Gonzales over a pool game. The argument became heated and the two men left the bar in an agitated state.

Eventually Mares left the bar and walked to a parking lot where he had previously parked his car. Without warning or apparent reason the defendant, whom Mares had observed just moments before speaking outside the bar with Dennis Gonzales, walked over to his truck and pulled out a shotgun. He aimed the weapon at Mares and started yelling at him. John Velasquez, who had left the bar, stepped between the defendant and Mares and told the defendant to put down the weapon. The defendant lowered the shotgun and walked back towards his truck. Shortly thereafter he fired a shot in the general direction of the bar where several people were still inside. When Mares turned around to see where the shot impacted, the defendant again fired the weapon and shot Mares in the abdomen. Clovis Velasquez wrestled the defendant for the gun but the defendant succeeded in grabbing it away. He reloaded and took aim at Clovis. At this point John Velasquez intervened and told the defendant not to shoot. The defendant's son said "Let's go dad," whereupon the defendant drove away.

Alfred Mares sustained serious injuries to the upper left quadrant of his abdomen, including damage to his kidney, spleen, pancreas, and small intestine. None of the prosecution witnesses was able to offer any reason for the defendant's conduct.

The defendant testified in his own behalf and offered the following version of the shooting. When he left the bar to fight Dennis Gonzales, several other persons followed. Gonzales pulled out a knife and asked the defendant to proceed to an area to the rear of a nearby liquor store. As the defendant moved slowly towards the liquor store, he observed his son being dragged by Alfred Mares and Clovis Velasquez, at which point he ran for his shotgun. After he fired a warning shot in the air, his son was released and ran to the passenger side of his vehicle. Mares, Clovis Velasquez and others approached the vehicle and, according to the defendant, someone jumped him from behind and grabbed him by the throat. In the ensuing struggle the shotgun discharged and struck Mares. . . .

The defendant advances the following argument in support of the proposition that attempted extreme indifference murder is not a cognizable crime under the Colorado Criminal Code: a criminal attempt requires an intent to complete the underlying offense; the element of "intentionally engaging in conduct creating a grave risk of death," as required for the underlying offense of extreme indifference murder, entails an unintentional and inchoate act; therefore, the defendant concludes, an attempt to commit extreme indifference murder requires an intent to commit an unintentional and inchoate act, a logical and legal impossibility. We find this argument to be constructed on a faulty premise, namely, that the crime of extreme indifference murder entails an unintentional and inchoate act.

On May 31, 1977, the date of the offense in question, the crime of criminal attempt was defined as follows:

> A person commits criminal attempt, if, acting with the kind of culpability otherwise required for commission of an offense, he intentionally engages in conduct constituting a substantial step toward the commission of the offense. Section 18-2-101(1), C.R.S. 1973.

A substantial step was defined as any conduct "which is strongly corroborative of the firmness of the actor's intent to complete the commission of the offense." The crime of extreme indifference murder, on May 31, 1977, required the following elements: (1) under circumstances manifesting extreme indifference to the value of human life; (2) "intentionally" engaging in conduct that creates a grave risk of death to another; and (3) thereby causing the death of another. Section 18-3-102(1)(d), C.R.S. 1973. The culpability element of acting "intentionally" was defined to include not only a conscious object to cause a particular result but also, as important here, a conscious object to engage in particular conduct. . . .

Extreme indifference murder is a crime requiring a conscious object to engage in conduct creating a grave risk of death to another. We recognized as much in People ex rel. Russel v. District Court, 185 Colo. 78, 83, 521 P.2d 1254, 1256 (1974), where we stated:

> [T]hough the statute requires that the conduct which creates a grave risk of death be intentional, the use of "intentionally" here does not necessarily mean that the intent be to take the life of a particular person.
>
> Furthermore, our statutes define "intentionally" as "when his conscious object is to cause that result or to engage in that conduct," 1971 Perm. Supp., C.R.S. 1963, 40-1-601(6), which we read to mean that the conduct creating the grave risk of death be consciously done.

In People v. Marcy, 628 P.2d 69 (Colo. 1981), we elaborated further on the culpability requirement of extreme indifference murder, as that crime was originally defined in the Colorado Criminal Code and is applicable here. We pointed out that "[u]nder the initial statutory scheme the *mens rea* for extreme indifference murder—intentionally engaging in conduct which creates a grave risk of death—was not bottomed in the result of the act but in the conduct." Id. at 77. The crime of extreme indifference murder, in other words, while not requiring a conscious object to kill, necessitates a conscious object to engage in conduct that creates a grave risk of death to another. Id. In this sense the culpability element of extreme indifference murder is akin to what traditionally has been known as "general intent."

It is quite obvious that the statutory ingredients of attempted extreme indifference murder do not postulate a logical or legal inconsistency by requiring an intent to engage in an unintentional act. The crime of extreme indifference murder requires an intentional state of mind with respect to proscribed conduct. The actor must be aware of his conduct and have a conscious object to engage in it. This form of consciously directed action is the antithesis of the unintentional conduct which the defendant erroneously ascribes to the crime of extreme indifference murder. Because the underlying offense of extreme indifference murder entails intentional rather than unintentional conduct, the defendant's assertion that the crime of attempted extreme indifference murder requires an intent to commit an unintentional act is without legal foundation.

We also reject the defendant's argument that because the death-causing conduct necessary to the completed offense need only create a grave risk of death (a mere possibility, in the defendant's view, that death will occur), the crime of attempted extreme indifference murder is in effect an attempt to commit an inchoate crime. Extreme indifference murder forbids not what might be characterized as inchoate conduct but, rather, conduct that does in fact result in death. The crime of attempted extreme indifference murder requires quite clearly that the actor's conduct constitute a substantial step towards the completed offense which, by definition, includes the causing of another's death.

Thus, contrary to the defendant's claim, there is neither legal nor logical inconsistency in the statutory proscription of attempted extreme indifference murder. . . .

Notes and Questions

1. Model Penal Code:

Section 5.01. Criminal Attempt.

(1) *Definition of Attempt.* A Person is guilty of an attempt to commit a crime if, acting with the kind of culpability otherwise required for commission of the crime, he:

(a) purposely engages in conduct that would constitute the crime if the attendant circumstances were as he believes them to be; or

(b) when causing a particular result is an element of the crime, does or omits to do anything with the purpose of causing or with the belief that it will cause such result, without further conduct on his part; or

(c) purposely does or omits to do anything that under the circumstances as he believes them to be, is an act or omission constituting a substantial step in a course of conduct planned to culminate in his commission of the crime.

How does the Model Penal Code's "purpose" requirement square with the holding in *Castro*? The common law courts had great difficulty in finding an attempt where the defendant's *mens rea* with respect to the proscribed harm was less than purposeful or knowing. Is this a serious problem? Does the solution depend on the severity of punishment for attempts?

2. Recall the statutory rape cases from Chapter 4. As noted there, a person who purposely has intercourse with a girl under the age of consent may be guilty in some jurisdictions, even if he honestly—or honestly and reasonably—believes she is over the age of consent. What if a man tries to have intercourse with a girl who is in fact 15, but who he honestly (if unreasonably) thinks is 19, but is caught or prevented before he actually has intercourse? Is he guilty of attempted statutory rape, even where, from his point of view, he was "attempting" to have intercourse with a female over the statutory age? See Model Penal Code §5.01. Does it yield a clear result?

Whatever the difficulty of the language of §5.01, the drafters thought the result was clear. According to the Model Penal Code formulation, the purpose requirement does not extend to attendant circumstances. Explaining their choice in the Draft of the Model Penal Code, the drafters wrote:

> This section adopts the view that the actor must have for his purpose to engage in the criminal conduct or accomplish the criminal result which is an element of the substantive crime but that his purpose need not encompass all the surrounding circumstances included in the formal definition of the substantive offense. As to them, it is sufficient that he acts with the culpability that is required for commission of the crime. Suppose, for example, that it is a federal offense to kill or injure an FBI agent and that recklessness or even negligence with respect to the identity of the victim as an agent suffices for commission of the crime. There would be an attempt to kill or injure such an agent under the present formulation if the actor with recklessness or negligence as to the official position of the victim attempts to kill or injure him. Under paragraph (b) the killing or injuring would be the required purpose; the fact that the victim is an agent would be only a circumstance as to which the actor had "the kind of culpability otherwise required for commission of the crime."
>
> It is difficult to say what the result would be in this kind of case under prevailing principles of attempt liability. However, the proposed formulation imposes attempt liability in a group of cases where the normal basis of such liability is present—purposive conduct manifesting dangerousness—and allows the policy of the substantive crime, respecting recklessness or negligence as to surrounding circumstances, to be applied to the attempt to commit that crime.

3. Moreover, the Model Penal Code allows "belief" as well as purpose with respect to the result to be sufficient *mens rea* for attempt. The example given in the Commentary is that if *A* intends to blow up a building, knows people are in the building and believes that they will be killed by the bomb, but does not have a conscious object to kill them; he is still guilty of attempted murder. (Comment to §5.01.) Do you see why a *mens rea* of knowledge cannot be used here?

4. In the following dialogue from his Textbook of Criminal Law 408-409 (2d ed. 1983), Glanville Williams discusses the *mens rea* of attempt:

If a terrorist places a bomb by the front door of a Cabinet Minister, which does damage but fortunately does not kill anybody, could this be an attempt to murder?

If there were evidence that the terrorist hoped to kill, it would be. But if there were no evidence on the intent, and the inference from the evidence could be no more than that the terrorist was completely reckless as to killing, his particular object being to explode a bomb to create a sense of insecurity and to draw attention to his cause, then it would not be an attempt to murder. The terrorist could be dealt with for an offence in relation to explosives, under the Explosives Act of 1983.

Isn't it rather narrow to insist upon intention? Can't one ever attempt recklessly?

Recklessness as to consequence is certainly not enough.

It was held by the Court of Appeal in *Mohan* [[1976] Q.B. 1] that attempt at common law required intention in the true sense, and mere knowledge of the probability or high probability or likelihood of the consequence was not enough. [In Regina v. Mohan, [1975] 2 All E.R. 193, the Court of Appeal quashed a conviction for "attempting by wanton driving to cause grievous bodily harm." Mohan had driven his car at a dangerous speed directly at a policeman who had tried to stop him; the policeman leapt out of the way and was not harmed. The Court held that the attempt conviction could not stand because the jury may have believed that Mohan had merely been reckless with regard to causing the officer harm.] The offence requires "proof of specific intent, a decision to bring about, in so far as it lies within the accused's power, the commission of the offence which it is alleged that the accused attempted to commit." . . . It can be taken for granted that the courts will interpret the Criminal Attempts Act in the same way.

The requirement of intention results in part from the ordinary meaning of the word "attempt." Suppose that *D* is throwing stones in the hope of breaking a window. He knows perfectly well that people are standing near and that he is in danger of hitting one of them instead. He is, therefore, reckless as to hitting a person; but we would not say that he is attempting to hit a person. His object is to break the window. Attempts go with objects, aims and purposes, not with collateral risks. The law of attempt reflects common speech on this matter, or tries to do so. However, there is no reason why "oblique intention" should not be sufficient.[2]

2. See comment in [1975] Crim. L.R. 285-286; Dennis in [1980] Crim. L.R. 763. Contra, Enker in [1977] Am. Bar Foundation Research Jrnl. 864-865. It may be said that oblique intention is included in the formula in *Mohan;* the defendant who foresees a consequence as certainly resulting from his act has taken a "decision" to bring it about (Grubb in [1982] C.L.J. 24).

If you attach importance to the ordinary meaning of "attempt," then surely recklessness as to circumstances (as distinct from consequences) should be enough. If a man tries to have sexual intercourse without knowing or caring whether the woman is consenting, and in fact she does not consent, everyone would say that he has attempted to rape her.

Yes. It was, indeed, held in *Pigg,*[3] just before the Criminal Attempts Act came into force, that the man in such circumstances was guilty of an attempt at common law. In other words, one could attempt at common law if one was reckless as to the circumstances, provided that such recklessness was sufficient for the consummated offence, and that one intended to complete the criminal act (the sexual penetration in rape), and intended any necessary consequence (no consequence is necessary in rape). Whether this is still the position under the Act is not known.

Unfortunately, those responsible for the Criminal Attempts Act failed to incorporate in it the rule of the common law (as it is now settled to have been) or any other rule on this point. . . .

. . . [I]t did not expressly rule out reckless attempts, because it supposed that it had excluded them by the requirement of intention for an attempt. As we have seen, however, there is no certainty that the courts will construe a requirement of intention as meaning that the actor must positively know the circumstances. The same rule will probably be applied to the construction of the Act, and it is in the public interest that it should be. It would mean that the decision in *Pigg* continues to apply under the Act. *Pigg* shows that, in the case of attempt, there is no inconsistency between requiring intention for the crime in general (as *Mohan* did at common law), that is to say intention as to the physical act and its required consequence, if any, and being satisfied with recklessness as to circumstances. If that is so, it must be the same where the requirement of intention is laid down by statute.

Glanville Williams also asks, at 409-410:

Can't one attempt an offence of strict liability?

Yes . . . but the attempt requires intention, even though the offence attempted does not. Whether recklessness as to circumstances is sufficient has just been discussed.

5. Donald Stuart, however, disagrees with Williams and the Model Penal Code, in Mens Rea, Negligence and Attempts, 1968 Crim. L.R. 647, 662:

If a pharmacist is grossly negligent in making up a prescription and the patient dies as a result of taking the dosage on the bottle, the pharmacist is clearly guilty of manslaughter. Surely the policy considerations which dictate such a conviction apply equally if, through chance, the negligent error is discovered before any damage is done. There seems to be every reason for a verdict of attempted manslaughter.

Do you accept Stuart's logic? Would you convict in his hypothetical case?

6. The drafters of the Model Penal Code recognized the gap they had left between a purpose-bound attempt law and the great number of crimes that permit conviction on a lesser *mens rea.* They tried to fill that gap with a reckless endangerment provision, §211.2, which provides:

3. [1982] 1 W.L.R. 762, 2 All E.R. 591, 74 C.A.R. 352.

> A person commits a misdemeanor if he recklessly engages in conduct which places or may place another person in danger of death or serious bodily injury.

The reckless endangerment approach may result in the conviction of some offenders who would have been acquitted of attempted murder. Moreover, because the term "reckless endangerment" is less stigmatic than a term such as "attempted murder," a jury may be more likely to convict when the charge is framed in the less threatening semantic form. But the reckless endangerment approach is not without problems. For example, under the Model Penal Code reckless endangerment is a misdemeanor, while an attempt to commit a first degree felony is a second degree felony. Is this sentencing difference defensible? Moreover, the Model Penal Code has no statute on "*negligent* endangerment." Is there any reason for this omission?

7. Any armed robber creates *some* risk that someone will get shot by someone's gun. Where the robber fires a (nonfatal) shot, should the robber be guility of "attempted felony murder"? For a case holding just that, see Amlotte v. State, 456 So. 2d 448 (Fla. 1984).

8. The elusive concept of "attempted recklessness" has become important in death penalty cases, since many of the new capital punishment statutes make it an aggravating circumstance if the defendant, in addition to killing the victim, also "knowingly created a great risk of death to many persons." See, e.g., Model Penal Code §210(6)(3)(d). Would this circumstance apply whenever the capital defendant commits an armed robbery, since the robber may provoke a gun battle with bystanders or police officers? If not, when would it apply?

The Florida Supreme Court construed this circumstance narrowly in Kampff v. State, 371 So. 2d 1007 (1979). Kampff murdered his former wife; he came to the store where she worked and fired five shots at her, three of which struck her and two of which struck no one. Two other people were in the store at the time and others were nearby. The court held that the finding of an aggravating circumstance was unwarranted, as such a finding requires proof of both a very high possibility of death, *and* a risk to a large number of people.

C. THE *ACTUS REUS* OF ATTEMPT

1. Preparation versus Attempt

PEOPLE v. MURRAY
Supreme Court of California
15 Cal. 160 (1859)

FIELD, C.J., delivered the opinion of the Court—COPE, J., and BALDWIN, J., concurring.

The evidence in this case entirely fails to sustain the charge against the defendant of an attempt to contract an incestuous marriage with his niece. It only discloses declarations of his determination to contract the marriage, his elopement with the niece for that avowed purpose, and his request to one of the witnesses to go for a magistrate to perform the ceremony. It shows very clearly the intention of the defendant, but something more than mere intention is necessary to constitute the offense charged. Between preparation for the attempt and the attempt itself, there is a wide difference. The preparation consists in devising or arranging the means or measures necessary for the commission of the offense; the attempt is the direct movement toward the commission after the preparations are made. To illustrate: a party may purchase and load a gun, with the declared intention to shoot his neighbor; but until some movement is made to use the weapon upon the person of his intended victim, there is only preparation and not an attempt. For the preparation, he may be held to keep the peace; but he is not chargeable with any attempt to kill. So in the present case, the declarations, and elopement, and request for a magistrate, were preparatory to the marriage; but until the officer was engaged, and the parties stood before him, ready to take the vows appropriate to the contract of marriage, it cannot be said, in strictness, that the attempt was made. The attempt contemplated by the statute must be manifested by acts which would end in the consummation of the particular offence, but for the intervention of circumstances independent of the will of the party.

Judgment reversed and cause remanded.

Notes and Questions

1. The court is convinced that the evidence showed "very clearly the intention of the defendant." Moreover, the defendant took steps in the direction of effectuating his intent. Why, then, should he not be punishable by the law? Can he argue that he did not commit an act, when he committed several acts towards the result he intended? Can he argue that he is not blameworthy where his intent was to violate the law? Why, then, should we draw the distinction between preparation and attempt?

2. Although the court was satisfied with the proof of the intent of the defendant in the above case, how do we really know, short of his performing the act, that the defendant *really* intended to commit the crime? Is this the real problem we have in drawing the line between preparation and attempt? Or is the real problem somewhat different?

3. It is black-letter law that the individual who has engaged only in "preparatory activity" is not criminally culpable while the individual who has gone "beyond mere preparation" may be charged with an attempt. Obviously, then, drawing the line between preparation and attempt becomes an important task. As we will explore below, the courts and legislatures have created a great variety of rules for determining when a person has passed from

preparation to attempt: the "last act" test, the "dangerous proximity" test, the "substantial step" test, the "equivocality" test, and others.

How would you evaluate the test proposed by the court in *Murray* in comparison to that of the Model Penal Code test below? How would *Murray* be decided under the Model Penal Code?

4. Model Penal Code:

Section 5.01. Criminal Attempt.

(2) *Conduct That May Be Held Substantial Step Under Subsection (1)(c).* Conduct shall not be held to constitute a substantial step under subsection (1)(c) of this Section unless it is strongly corroborative of the actor's criminal purpose. Without negativing the sufficiency of other conduct, the following, if strongly corroborative of the actor's criminal purpose, shall not be held insufficient as a matter of law:

(a) lying in wait, searching for or following the contemplated victim of the crime;
(b) enticing or seeking to entice the contemplated victim of the crime to go to the place contemplated for its commission;
(c) reconnoitering the place contemplated for the commission of the crime;
(d) unlawful entry of a structure, vehicle or enclosure in which it is contemplated that the crime will be committed;
(e) possession of materials to be employed in the commission of the crime, that are specially designed for such unlawful use or which can serve no lawful purpose of the actor under the circumstances;
(f) possession, collection or fabrication of materials to be employed in the commission of the crime, at or near the place contemplated for its commission, where such possession, collection or fabrication serves no lawful purpose of the actor under the circumstances;
(g) soliciting an innocent agent to engage in conduct constituting an element of the crime.

PEOPLE v. RIZZO

Court of Appeals of New York
246 N.Y. 334, 158 N.E. 888 (1927)

CRANE, J. The police of the city of New York did excellent work in this case by preventing the commission of a serious crime. It is a great satisfaction to realize that we have such wide-awake guardians of our peace. Whether or not the steps which the defendant had taken up to the time of his arrest amounted to the commission of a crime, as defined by our law, is however, another matter. He has been convicted of an attempt to commit the crime of robbery in the first degree, and sentenced to state's prison. There is no doubt that he had the intention to commit robbery, if he got the chance. An examination, however, of the facts is necessary to determine whether his acts were in preparation to commit the crime if the opportunity offered, or constituted a crime in itself, known to our law as an attempt to commit robbery in the first degree. Charles Rizzo, the defendant, appellant, with three others, Anthony J. Dorio, Thomas Milo, and John Thomasello, on January 14th planned to rob one Charles Rao of a pay roll valued at about $1,200 which he was to carry from the bank for the United Lathing Company. These defendants, two of whom had firearms, started out in an automobile, looking for Rao or the man who had the pay roll on that day. Rizzo claimed to be able to identify the man, and was to point him out to the others, who were to do the actual holding up. The four rode about in their car looking for Rao. They went to the bank from which he was supposed to get the money and to various buildings being constructed by the United Lathing Company. At last they came to One Hundred and Eightieth Street and Morris Park Avenue. By this time they were being watched and followed by two police officers. As Rizzo jumped out of the car and ran into the building, all four were arrested. The defendant was taken out from the building in which he was hiding. Neither Rao nor a man named Previti, who was also supposed to carry a pay roll, were at the place at the time of the arrest. The defendants had not found or seen the man they intended to rob. No person with a pay roll was at any of the places where they had stopped, and no one had been pointed out or identified by Rizzo. The four men intended to rob the pay roll man, whoever he was. They were looking for him, but they had not seen or discovered him up to the time they were arrested.

Does this constitute the crime of an attempt to commit robbery in the first degree? The Penal Law, §2, prescribes:

> An act, done with intent to commit a crime, and tending but failing to effect its commission, is "an attempt to commit that crime."

The word "tending" is very indefinite. It is perfectly evident that there will arise differences of opinion as to whether an act in a given case is one tending to commit a crime. "Tending" means to exert activity in a particular direction. Any act in preparation to commit a crime may be said to have a tendency towards its accomplishment. The procuring of the automobile, and searching of the streets looking for the desired victim, were in reality acts tending toward the commission of the proposed crime. The law, however, has recognized that many acts in the way of preparation are too remote to constitute the crime of attempt. The line has been drawn between those acts which are remote and those which are proximate and near to the consummation. The law must be practical, and therefore considers those acts only as tending to the commission of the crime which are so near to its accomplishment that in all reasonable probability the crime itself would have been committed, but for timely interference. The cases which have been before the courts express this idea in different language, but the idea remains the same. The act or acts must come or advance very near to the accomplishment of the intended crime. In People v. Mills, 178 N.Y. 274, 284, 70 N.E. 786, 789 (67 L.R.A. 131), it was said:

> Felonious intent alone in not enough, but there must be an overt act shown in order to establish even an attempt. An overt act is one done to carry out the intention, and it must be such as would naturally effect that result, unless prevented by some extraneous cause.

In Hyde v. U.S., 225 U.S. 347, it was stated that the act amounts to an attempt when it is so near to the result that the danger of success is very great. "There must be dangerous proximity to success." Halsbury in his Laws of England, vol. 9, p.259 says:

> An act in order to be a criminal attempt must be immediately and not remotely connected with and directly tending to the commission of an offense.

Commonwealth v. Peaslee, 177 Mass. 267, 59 N.E. 55, refers to the acts constituting an attempt as coming *very near* to the accomplishment of the crime.

The method of committing or attempting crime varies in each case, so that the difficulty, if any, is not with this rule of law regarding an attempt, which is well understood, but with its application to the facts. As I have said before, minds differ over the requisite proximity and the nearness of the approach.

How shall we apply this rule of immediate nearness to this case? The defendants were looking for the pay roll man to rob him of his money. This is the charge in the indictment. Robbery is defined in section 2120 of the Penal Law as "the unlawful taking of personal property from the person or in the presence of another, against his will, by means of force, or violence, or fear of injury, immediate or future, to his person;" and it is made robbery in the first degree by section 2124 when committed by a person aided by accomplices actually present. To constitute the crime of robbery, the money must have been taken from Rao by means of force or violence, or through fear. The crime of attempt to commit robbery was committed, if these defendants did an act tending to the commission of this robbery. Did the acts above described come dangerously near to the taking of Rao's property? Did the acts come so near to the commission of robbery that there was reasonable likelihood of its accomplishment but for the interference? Rao was not found; the defendants were still looking for him; no attempt to rob him could be made, at least until he came in sight; he was not in the building at One Hundred and Eightieth Street and Morris Park Avenue. There was no man there with the pay roll for the United Lathing Company whom these defendants could rob. Apparently no money had been drawn from the bank for the pay roll by anybody at the time of the arrest. In a word, these defendants had planned to commit a crime, and were looking around the city for an opportunity to commit it, but the opportunity fortunately never came. Men would not be guilty of an attempt at burglary if they had planned to break into a building and were arrested while they were hunting about the streets for the building not knowing where it was. Neither would a man be guilty of an attempt to commit murder if he armed himself and started out to find the person whom he had planned to kill but could not find him. So here these defendants were not guilty of an attempt to commit robbery in the first degree when they had not found or reached the presence of the person they intended to rob.

For these reasons, the judgment of conviction of this defendant appellant must be reversed and a new trial granted.

A very strange situation has arisen in this case. I called attention to the four defendants who were convicted of this crime of an attempt to commit robbery in the first degree. They were all tried together upon the same evidence, and jointly convicted, and all sentenced to state's prison for varying terms. Rizzo was the only one of the four to appeal to the Appellate Division and to this court. His conviction was affirmed by the Appellate Division by a divided court, two of the justices dissenting, and we have now held that he was not guilty of the crime charged. If he were not guilty, neither were the other three defendants. As the others, however, did not appeal, there is no remedy for them through the courts; their judgments stand, and they must serve their sentences. This, of course, is a situation which must in all fairness be met in some way. Two of these men were guilty of the crime of carrying weapons, pistols, contrary to law, for which they could be convicted. Two of them, John Thomasello and Thomas Milo, had also been previously convicted, which may have had something to do with their neglect to appeal. However, the law would fail in its function and its purpose if it permitted these three men whoever or whatever they are to serve a sentence for a crime when the courts subsequently found and declared had not been committed. We therefore suggest to the district attorney of Bronx county that he bring the cases of these three men to the attention of the Governor, to be dealt with as to him seems proper in the light of this opinion.

The judgment of the Appellate Division and that of the county court should be reversed, and a new trial ordered.

Cardozo, C.J., and Pound, Andrews, Lehman, Kellogg, and O'Brien, JJ., concur.

Judgment accordingly.

Notes and Questions

1. If you were the district attorney, would you take any steps toward securing leniency (by pardon, commutation, or otherwise) for Rizzo's co-

defendants? If you were the governor, what would be your position on the issue?

2. What do you think the New York police officers involved in this case had to say about the praise lavished upon them by the court of appeals?

3. If precisely the same situation comes up again, what are the police legally obligated to do?

4. How would *Rizzo* be decided under the Model Penal Code?

5. Examine the following series of events:

a. *A* decides to rob a bank (disclosing this intention in his diary and confiding his plan to two friends).
b. He then contracts to buy a new automobile, the down payment for which is due the next day and for which he presently has no funds.
c. He walks past the bank to get the layout of it and to see when it is open for business.
d. He goes to the five-and-ten-cent store and buys a rubber mask.
e. He goes home and draws a map of the interior of the bank.
f. He takes his old gun (possessed legally) from his attic, cleans it and oils it and loads it for the first time in five years.
g. He then writes a note saying "I have a gun—give me all your money."
h. He leaves his house carrying the gun and note.
i. He steals a car from a parking lot.
j. He parks in front of the bank.
k. He gets out of the car.
l. He enters the bank.
m. He walks up to the teller's cage.
n. He pushes the note across towards the teller.
o. The teller slides the money towards him on the counter.

At what point has *A* become guilty of attempted robbery? Is the question whether *A* really intended to commit the robbery? Whether *A* would have backed out? Whether *A* caused any harm? How does one answer these questions? What question does the Model Penal Code ask? How does the Code answer it? Do you agree with that answer? To appreciate the range of possible answers to this question, consider the next case.

UNITED STATES v. JACKSON

United States Court of Appeals, Second Circuit
560 F.2d 112 (1977)

Frederick van Pelt BRYAN, Senior District Judge.

Robert Jackson, William Scott, and Martin Allen appeal from judgments of conviction entered on November 23, 1976, in the United States District Court for the Eastern District of New York after a trial before Chief Judge Jacob Mishler without a jury.

Count one of the indictment alleged that between June 11 and June 21, 1976, the appellants conspired to commit an armed robbery of the Manufacturer's Hanover Trust branch located at 210 Flushing Avenue, Brooklyn, New York, in violation of 18 U.S.C. §371. Counts two and three each charged appellants with an attempted robbery of the branch on June 14 and on June 21, 1976, respectively. . . .[4]

Appellants' principal contention is that as a matter of law, their conduct never crossed the elusive line which separates "mere preparation" from "attempt." This troublesome question was recently examined by this court in United States v. Stallworth, 543 F.2d 1038 (2d Cir. 1976), which set forth the applicable legal principles. For the reasons which follow, we affirm the convictions.

I

The Government's evidence at trial consisted largely of the testimony of Vanessa Hodges, an unindicted co-conspirator, and of various FBI agents who surveilled the Manufacturers Hanover branch on June 21, 1976. Since the facts are of critical importance in any attempt case, we shall review the Government's proof in considerable detail.

On June 11, 1976, Vanessa Hodges was introduced to appellant Martin Allen by Pia Longhorne. . . .

Hodges wanted to meet someone who would help her carry out a plan to rob the Manufacturer's Hanover branch located at 210 Flushing Avenue in Brooklyn, and she invited Allen to join her. Hodges proposed that the bank be robbed the next Monday, June 14th, at about 7:30 A.M. She hoped that they could enter with the bank manager at that time, grab the weekend deposits, and leave. Allen agreed to rob the bank with Hodges, and told her he had access to a car, two sawed-off shotguns, and a .38 caliber revolver.

The following Monday, June 14th, Allen arrived at Longhorne's house about 7:30 A.M. in a car driven by appellant Robert Jackson. A suitcase in the back seat of the car contained a sawed-off shotgun, shells, materials intended as masks, and handcuffs to bind the bank manager. While Allen picked up Hodges at Longhorne's, Jackson filled the car with gas. The trio then left for the bank.

When they arrived, it was almost 8:00 A.M. It was thus too late to effect the first step of the plan, viz., entering the bank as the manager opened the door. They rode around for a while longer, and then went to a restaurant to get something to eat and discuss their next move. After eating, the trio drove back to the bank. Allen and Hodges left the car and walked over to the bank.

4. Jackson was sentenced to imprisonment for two years on count one, and was given a suspended sentence with concurrent three-year terms of the probation, to commence at the end of the prison sentence, on each of the other counts. Scott was sentenced to imprisonment for five years on count one, and to seven years imprisonment on each of the remaining three counts, all sentences to run concurrently. Allen received a five-year term of imprisonment on count one, and terms of ten years on each of the remaining three counts, all sentences to run concurrently.

They peered in and saw the bulky weekend deposits, but decided it was too risky to rob the bank without an extra man.

Consequently, Jackson, Hodges, and Allen drove to Coney Island in search of another accomplice. In front of a housing project on 33rd Street they found appellant William Scott, who promptly joined the team. Allen added to the arsenal another sawed-off shotgun obtained from one of the buildings in the project, and the group drove back to the bank.

When they arrived again, Allen entered the bank to check the location of any surveillance cameras, while Jackson placed a piece of cardboard with a false license number over the authentic license plate of the car.[5] Allen reported back that a single surveillance camera was over the entrance door. After further discussion, Scott left the car and entered the bank. He came back and informed the group that the tellers were separating the weekend deposits and that a number of patrons were now in the bank. Hodges then suggested that they drop the plans for the robbery that day, and reschedule it for the following Monday, June 21. Accordingly, they left the vicinity of the bank and returned to Coney Island where, before splitting up, they purchased a pair of stockings for Hodges to wear over her head as a disguise and pairs of gloves for Hodges, Scott, and Allen to don before entering the bank.

Hodges was arrested on Friday, June 18, 1976, on an unrelated bank robbery charge, and immediately began cooperating with the Government. After relating the events on June 14, she told FBI agents that a robbery of the Manufacturer's branch at 210 Flushing Avenue was now scheduled for the following Monday, June 21. The three robbers, according to Hodges, would be heavily armed with hand and shoulder weapons and expected to use a brown four-door sedan equipped with a cardboard license plate as the getaway car. She told the agents that Jackson, who would drive the car, was light-skinned with a moustache and a cut on his lip, and she described Allen as short, dark-skinned with facial hair, and Scott as 5′9″, slim build, with an afro hair style and some sort of defect in his right eye.

At the request of the agents, Hodges called Allen on Saturday, June 19, and asked if he were still planning to do the job. He said that he was ready. On Sunday she called him again. This time Allen said that he was not going to rob the bank that Monday because he had learned that Hodges had been arrested and he feared that federal agents might be watching. Hodges nevertheless advised the agents that she thought the robbery might still take place as planned with the three men proceeding without her.

At about 7:00 A.M. on Monday, June 21, 1976, some ten FBI agents took various surveilling positions in the area of the bank. At about 7:39 A.M. the agents observed a brown four-door Lincoln, with a New York license plate on the front and a cardboard facsimile of a license plate on the rear, moving in an

5. Hodges' testimony indicates that, in order to avert suspicion, Jackson would first lift the trunk or hood of the car as though he were working under it before covering or uncovering the genuine license plates.

easterly direction of Flushing Avenue past the bank, which was located on the southeast corner of Flushing and Washington Avenues. The front seat of the Lincoln was occupied by a male driver and a male passenger with muttonchop sideburns. The Lincoln circled the block and came to a stop at a fire hydrant situated at the side of the bank facing Washington Avenue, a short distance south of the corner of Flushing and Washington.

A third male, who appeared to have an eye deformity, got out of the passenger side rear door of the Lincoln, walked to the corner of Flushing and Washington, and stood on the sidewalk in the vicinity of the bank's entrance. He then walked south on Washington Avenue, only to return a short time later with a container of coffee in his hand. He stood again on the corner of Washington and Flushing in front of the bank, drinking the coffee and looking around, before returning to the parked Lincoln.

The Lincoln pulled out, made a left turn onto Flushing, and proceeded in a westerly direction for one block to Waverly Avenue. It stopped, made a U-turn, and parked on the south side of Flushing between Waverly and Washington—a spot on the same side of the street as the bank entrance but separated from it by Washington Avenue. After remaining parked in this position for approximately five minutes, it pulled out and cruised east on Flushing past the bank again. The Lincoln then made a right onto Grand Avenue, the third street east of the bank, and headed south. It stopped halfway down the block, midway between Flushing and Park Avenues, and remained there for several minutes. During this time Jackson was seen working in the front of the car, which had its hood up.

The Lincoln was next sighted several minutes later in the same position it had previously occupied on the south side of Flushing Avenue between Waverly and Washington. The front license plate was now missing. The vehicle remained parked there for close to thirty minutes. Finally, it began moving east on Flushing Avenue once more, in the direction of the bank.

At some point near the bank as they passed down Flushing Avenue, the appellants detected the presence of the surveillance agents. The Lincoln accelerated down Flushing Avenue and turned south on Grand Avenue again. It was overtaken by FBI agents who ordered the appellants out of the car and arrested them. The agents then observed a black and red plaid suitcase in the rear of the car. The zipper of the suitcase was partially open and exposed two loaded sawed-off shotguns,[6] a toy nickelplated revolver, a pair of handcuffs, and masks. A New York license plate was seen lying on the front floor of the car. All of these items were seized.

In his memorandum of decision, Chief Judge Mishler characterized the question of whether the defendants had attempted a bank robbery as charged in counts two and three or were merely engaged in preparations as "a close one." After canvassing the authorities on what this court one month later

6. One of the shotguns proved to be inoperative.

called a "perplexing problem," United States v. Stallworth, supra, at 1039, Chief Judge Mishler applied the following two-tiered inquiry formulated in United States v. Mandujano, 499 F.2d 370, 376 (5th Cir. 1974):

> First, the defendant must have been acting with the kind of culpability otherwise required for the commission of the crime which he is charged with attempting.
>
> Second, the defendant must have engaged in conduct which constitutes a substantial step toward commission of the crime. A substantial step must be conduct strongly corroborative of the firmness of the defendant's criminal intent.

He concluded that on June 14 and again on June 21, the defendants took substantial steps, strongly corroborative of the firmness of their criminal intent, toward commission of the crime of bank robbery and found the defendants guilty on each of the two attempt counts. These appeals followed.

II

"[T]here is no comprehensive statutory definition of attempt in federal law." United States v. Heng Awkak Roman, 356 F. Supp. 434, 437 (S.D.N.Y.). Fed. R. Crim. P. 31(c), however, provides in pertinent part that a defendant may be found guilty of "an attempt to commit either the offense charged or an offense necessarily included therein if the attempt is an offense." 18 U.S.C. §2113(a)[7] specifically makes attempted bank robbery an offense.

Appellant Scott argues that the very wording of 18 U.S.C. §2113(a) precludes a finding that the actions charged in counts two and three reached the level of attempts. Relying on United States v. Baker, 129 F. Supp. 684 (S.D. Cal. 1955), he contends that since the statute only mentions attempted taking and not attempted force, violence, or intimidation, it clearly contemplates that actual use of force, violence, or intimidation must precede an attempted taking in order to make out the offense of attempted bank robbery.

7. The subsection provides:

> Whoever, by force and violence, or by intimidation, takes, or attempts to take, from the person or presence of another any property or money or any other thing of value belonging to, or in the care, custody, control, management, or possession of, any bank, credit union, or any savings and loan association; or
>
> Whoever enters or attempts to enter any bank, credit union, or any savings and loan association, or any building used in whole or in part as a bank, credit union, or as a savings and loan association, with intent to commit in such bank, credit union, or in such savings and loan association, or building, or part thereof, so used, any felony affecting such bank or such savings and loan association and in violation of any statute of the United States or any larceny—
>
> Shall be fined not more than $5,000 or imprisoned not more than twenty years, or both.

The *Stallworth* court faced a similar statutory construction argument which also relied heavily on United States v. Baker, supra. In response to the assertion that the defendants in that case could not be convicted of attempted bank robbery because they neither entered the bank nor brandished weapons, Chief Judge Kaufman stated:

> We reject this wooden logic. Attempt is a subtle concept that requires a rational and logically sound definition, one that enables society to punish malefactors who have unequivocally set out upon a criminal course without requiring law enforcement officers to delay until innocent bystanders are imperiled. (543 F. 2d at 1040)

We conclude that Scott's argument is foreclosed by this *Stallworth* holding, with which we are in entire accord.

Appellants Jackson and Allen, however, seek to distinguish the instant case from *Stallworth.* They claim that while the conduct of the defendants in that case could properly support a finding of attempted bank robbery, this is not true in the case at bar.

In *Stallworth,* the government provided Rodney Campbell, an informant who had participated in numerous bank robberies, with an undercover vehicle outfitted with a tape recorder and monitoring equipment on the understanding that he would aid in apprehending his former accomplices. Campbell rejoined his companions, and he transported the group in his undercover vehicle as they cased several banks in Queens.

On Wednesday, January 21, they began actual preparations for a robbery by stealing ski masks from a department store, surgical gloves from a hospital, and purchasing a hacksaw and roofing nails to "fix" a shotgun. On Thursday, January 22, the gang selected a target bank in Whitestone, had one member enter it and report on its physical layout, and scheduled the robbery for Friday morning.

On Friday morning, January 23, Campbell and company assembled with a revolver, sawed-off shotgun, and other paraphernalia for a hold-up. On their way to the bank in the undercover vehicle they covered their fingers with bandaids, their hands with surgical gloves, and put on the ski masks. Gasoline-soaked newspapers were placed under the seats of the car in preparation for its destruction after the getaway.

The car entered the parking lot of the shopping center in which the bank was located and one Sellers got out. He strolled past the bank several times, peeking in at each opportunity, while the car circled the shopping center. Finally, the vehicle pulled up directly in front of the bank and Sellers, armed with the sawed-off shotgun and positioned at an adjacent liquor store, started to approach the bank. Campbell said "let's go," and the occupants of the car reached for the doors. Immediately, FBI agents and New York City policemen who had staked out the parking lot and were monitoring the gang's conversations moved in and arrested the men.

Chief Judge Kaufman, writing for the court, selected the two-tiered inquiry of United States v. Mandujano,[8] supra, "properly derived from the writings of many distinguished jurists," 543 F.2d at 1040, as stating the proper test for determining whether the foregoing conduct constituted an attempt. He observed that this analysis "conforms closely to the sensible definition of an attempt proffered by the American Law Institute's Model Penal Code." Id.

The draftsmen of the Model Penal Code recognized the difficulty of arriving at a general standard for distinguishing acts of preparation from acts constituting an attempt. They found general agreement that when an actor committed the "last proximate act," i.e., when he had done all that he believed necessary to effect a particular result which is an element of the offense, he committed an attempt. They also concluded, however, that while the last proximate act is *sufficient* to constitute an attempt, it is not *necessary* to such a finding. The problem then was to devise a standard more inclusive than one requiring the last proximate act before attempt liability would attach, but less inclusive than one which would make every act done with the intent to commit a crime criminal. See Model Penal Code §5.01, Comment at 38-39 (Tent. Draft No. 10, 1960).

The draftsmen considered and rejected the following approaches to distinguishing preparation from attempt, later summarized in *Mandujano:*

> (a) The physical proximity doctrine—the overt act required for an attempt must be proximate to the completed crime, or directly tending toward the completion of the crime, or must amount to the commencement of the consummation.
>
> (b) The dangerous proximity doctrine—a test given impetus by Mr. Justice Holmes whereby the greater the gravity and probability of the offense, and the nearer the act to the crime, the stronger is the case for calling the act an attempt.
>
> (c) The indispensable element test—a variation of the proximity tests which emphasizes any indispensable aspect of the criminal endeavor over which the actor has not yet acquired control.
>
> (d) The probable desistance test—the conduct constitutes an attempt if, in the ordinary and natural course of events, without interruption from an outside source, it will result in the crime intended.
>
> (e) The abnormal step approach—an attempt is a step toward crime which goes beyond the point where the normal citizen would think better of his conduct and desist.
>
> (f) The res ipsa loquitur or unequivocality test—an attempt is committed when the actor's conduct manifests an intent to commit a crime.[9]

The formulation upon which the draftsmen ultimately agreed required,

8. The *Mandujano* test was paraphrased as follows:

> Initially, the defendant must have been acting with the kind of culpability otherwise required for the commission of the crime he is charged with attempting. Then, the defendant must have engaged in conduct which constitutes a substantial step toward commission of the crime, conduct strongly corroborative of the firmness of the defendant's criminal intent.

9. 499 F.2d at 373 n.5.

in addition to criminal purpose, that an act be a substantial step in a course of conduct designed to accomplish a criminal result, and that it be strongly corroborative of criminal purpose in order for it to constitute such a substantial step. The following differences between this test and previous approaches to the preparation-attempt problem were noted:

> First, this formulation shifts the emphasis from what remains to be done—the chief concern of the proximity tests—to what the actor *has already done.* The fact that further major steps must be taken before the crime can be completed does not preclude a finding that the steps already undertaken are substantial. It is expected, in the normal case, that this approach will broaden the scope of attempt liability.
>
> Second, although it is intended that the requirement of a substantial step will result in the imposition of attempt liability only in those instances in which some firmness of criminal purpose is shown, no finding is required as to whether the actor would probably have desisted prior to completing the crime. Potentially the probable desistance test could reach very early steps toward the crime—depending upon how one assesses the probabilities of desistance—but since in practice this test follows closely the proximity approaches, rejection of probable desistance will not narrow the scope of attempt liability.
>
> Finally, the requirement of proving a substantial step generally will prove less of a hurdle for the prosecution than the res ipsa loquitur approach, which requires that the actor's conduct must itself manifest the criminal purpose. The difference will be illustrated in connection with the present section's requirement of corroboration. Here it should be noted that, in the present formulation, the two purposes to be served by the res ipsa loquitur test are, to a large extent, treated separately. Firmness of criminal purpose is intended to be shown by requring a substantial step, while problems of proof are dealt with by the requirement of corroboration (although, under the reasoning previously expressed, the latter will also tend to establish firmness of purpose).[10]

The draftsmen concluded that, in addition to assuring firmness of criminal design, the requirement of a substantial step would preclude attempt liability, with its accompanying harsh penalties, for relatively remote preparatory acts. At the same time, however, by not requiring a "last proximate act" or one of its various analogues it would permit the apprehension of dangerous persons at an earlier stage than would the other approaches without immunizing them from attempt liability. Id. at 47-48.

Applying the *Mandujano* test, which in turn was derived in large part from the Model Penal Code's standard, Chief Judge Kaufman concluded that since the *Stallworth* appellants had intended to execute a successful bank robbery and took substantial steps in furtherance of their plan that strongly corroborated their criminal intent, their attempted bank robbery convictions were proper.

In the case at bar, Chief Judge Mishler anticipated the precise analysis which this Court adopted in the strikingly similar *Stallworth* case. He then

10. Model Penal Code §5.01, Comment at 47 (Tent. Draft No. 10, 1960).

found that on June 14 the appellants, already agreed upon a robbery plan, drove to the bank with loaded weapons. In order to carry the heavy weekend deposit sacks, they recruited another person. Cardboard was placed over the license, and the bank was entered and reconnoitered. Only then was the plan dropped for the moment and rescheduled for the following Monday. On that day, June 21, the defendants performed essentially the same acts. Since the cameras had already been located there was no need to enter the bank again, and since the appellants had arrived at the bank earlier, conditions were more favorable to their initial robbery plan than they had been on June 14. He concluded that on both occasions these men were seriously dedicated to the commission of a crime, had passed beyond the stage of preparation, and would have assaulted the bank had they not been dissuaded by certain external factors, viz., the breaking up of the weekend deposits and crowd of patrons in the bank on June 14 and the detection of the FBI surveillance on June 21.

We cannot say that these conclusions which Chief Judge Mishler reached as the trier of fact as to what the evidence before him established were erroneous. As in *Stallworth,* the criminal intent of the appellants was beyond dispute. The question remaining then is the substantiality of the steps taken on the dates in question, and how strongly this corroborates the firmness of their obvious criminal intent. This is a matter of degree. See Model Penal code §5.01, Comments at 47 (Tent. Draft No. 10, 1960).

On two separate occasions, appellants reconnoitered the place contemplated for the commission of the crime and possessed the paraphernalia to be employed in the commission of the crime—loaded sawed-off shotguns, extra shells, a toy revolver, handcuffs, and masks—which was specially designed for such unlawful use and which could serve no lawful purpose under the circumstances. Under the Model Penal Code formulation, approved by the *Stallworth* court, either type of conduct, standing alone, was sufficient as a matter of law to constitute a "substantial step" if it strongly corroborated their criminal purpose. Here both types of conduct coincided on both June 14 and June 21, along with numerous other elements strongly corroborative of the firmness of appellants' criminal intent.[11] The steps taken toward a successful bank rob-

11. After securing the extra man they needed on June 14, the gang returned to the bank with their weapons ready and the car's license plate disguised for the getaway. Hodges' testimony was that they were ready to rob the bank at that time, but eventually postponed the robbery because conditions did not seem favorable. The fact that they then made further preparations by buying the stockings and gloves, an afterthought according to Hodges, does not undercut the firmness of their criminal intent when they were at the bank on June 14. By only postponing execution of the plan, appellants did not renounce their criminal purpose, but reaffirmed it. They reflected further upon the plan and embellished it by acquiring the stockings and gloves.

The actions of the appellants on June 21 might not support a finding, as in *Stallworth,* that "a bank robbery was in progress." 543 F.2d at 1041. Such a finding, however, is not essential to attempt liability, which is designed to "encourag[e] early police intervention where a suspect is clearly bent on the commission of crime." United States v. Stallworth, supra, at 1041. On June 21, the firmness of appellants' criminal intent was again evident. The very fact that they showed up at the bank that day after discovering that the agents had arrested Hodges suggests that they were determined to execute their plan. Moreover, they once again had the necessary weapons, the car prepared for escape, and gave every indication that they were ready to strike.

bery thus were not "insubstantial" as a matter of law, and chief Judge Mishler found them "substantial" as a matter of fact. We are unwilling to substitute our assessment of the evidence for his, and thus affirm the convictions for attempted bank robbery on counts two and three.

Notes and Questions

1. What would you think of a legal system that acquitted the defendants of attempt in the above case?

2. Which of the rules discussed by the Model Penal Code Commentary at page 531 does the *Jackson* court appear to follow?

McQUIRTER v. STATE

Court of Appeals of Alabama
63 So. 2d 388 (1953)

PRICE, Judge.

Appellant, a Negro man, was found guilty of an attempt to commit an assault with intent to rape, under an indictment charging an assault with intent to rape. The jury assessed a fine of $500.

About 8 o'clock on the night of June 29, 1951, Mrs. Ted Allen, a white woman, with her two children and a neighbor's little girl, were drinking Coca-Cola at the "Tiny Diner" in Atmore. When they started in the direction of Mrs. Allen's home she noticed appellant sitting in the cab of a parked truck. As she passed the truck appellant said something unintelligible, opened the truck door and placed his foot on the running board.

Mrs. Allen testified appellant followed her down the street and when she reached Suell Lufkin's house she stopped. As she turned into the Lufkin house appellant was within two or three feet of her. She waited ten minutes for appellant to pass. When she proceeded on her way, appellant came toward her from behind a telephone pole. She told the children to run to Mr. Simmons' house and tell him to come and meet her. When appellant saw Mr. Simmons he turned and went back down the street to the intersection and leaned on a stop sign just across the street from Mrs. Allen's home. Mrs. Allen watched him at the sign from Mr. Simmons' porch for about thirty minutes, after which time he came back down the street and appellant went on home.

Mrs. Allen's testimony was corroborated by that of her young daughter. The daughter testified the appellant was within six feet of her mother as she approached the Lufkin house, and this witness said there was a while when she didn't see appellant at the intersection.

Mr. Lewis Simmons testified when the little girls ran up on his porch and said a Negro was after them, witness walked up the sidewalk to meet Mrs.

Allen and saw appellant. Appellant went on down the street and stopped in front of Mrs. Allen's home and waited there approximately thirty minutes.

Mr. Clarence Bryars, a policeman in Atmore, testified that appellant stated after his arrest that he came to Atmore with the intention of getting him a white woman that night.

Mr. W. E. Strickland, Chief of Police of Atmore, testified that appellant stated in the Atmore jail he didn't know what was the matter with him; that he was drinking a little; that he and his partner had been to Pensacola; that his partner went to the "Front" to see a colored woman; that he didn't have any money and he sat in the truck and made up his mind he was going to get the first woman that came by and that this was the first woman that came by. He said he got out of the truck, came around the gas tank and watched the lady and when she started off he started off behind her; that he was going to carry her in the cotton patch and if she hollered he was going to kill her. He testified appellant made the same statement in the Brewton jail.

Mr. Norvelle Seals, Chief Deputy Sheriff, corroborated Mr. Strickland's testimony as to the statement by appellant at the Brewton jail.

Appellant, as a witness in his own behalf, testified he and Bill Page, another Negro, carried a load of junk-iron from Monroeville to Pensacola; on their way back to Monroeville they stopped in Atmore. They parked the truck near the "Tiny Diner" and rode to the "Front," the colored section, in a cab. Appellant came back to the truck around 8 o'clock and sat in the truck cab for about thirty minutes. He decided to go back to the "Front" to look for Bill Page. As he started up the street he saw prosecutrix and her children. He turned around and waited until he decided they had gone, then he walked up the street toward the "Front." When he reached the intersection at the telegraph pole he decided he didn't want to go to the "Front" and sat around there a few minutes, then went on the "Front" and stayed about 25 or 30 minutes, and came back to the truck.

He denied that he followed Mrs. Allen or made any gesture toward molesting her or the children. He denied making the statements testified to by the officers.

He testified he had never been arrested before and introduced testimony by two residents of Monroeville as to his good reputation for peace and quiet and for truth and veracity.

Appellant insists the trial court erred in refusing the general affirmative charge and in denying the motion for a new trial on the ground the verdict was contrary to the evidence.

"An attempt to commit an assault with intent to rape . . . means an attempt to rape which has not proceeded far enough to amount to an assault." Burton v. State, 8 Ala. App. 295, 62 So. 394, 396.

Under the authorities in this state, to justify a conviction for an attempt to commit an assault with intent to rape the jury must be satisfied beyond a reasonable doubt that defendant intended to have sexual intercourse with prosecutrix against her will, by force or by putting her in fear.

Intent is a question to be determined by the jury from the facts and circumstances adduced on the trial, and if there is evidence from which it may be inferred that at the time of the attempt defendant intended to gratify his lustful desires against the resistance of the female a jury question is presented.

In determining the question of intention the jury may consider social conditions and customs founded upon racial differences, such as that the prosecutrix was a white woman and defendant was a Negro man.

After considering the evidence in this case we are of the opinion it was sufficient to warrant the submission of the question of defendant's guilt to the jury, and was ample to sustain the judgment of conviction.

Defense counsel contends in brief that the testimony of the officers as to defendant's declaration of intent was inadmissible because no attempt or overt act toward carrying that intent into effect had been proven.

Defendant's grounds of objection to this evidence were that it was "irrelevant, incompetent, and immaterial." Proper predicates were laid for the introduction of each of said statements.

Moreover, if any facts are proven from which the jury may reasonably infer that the crime has been committed, proof of the confession is rendered admissible.

We find no reversible error in the record and the judgment of the trial court is affirmed.

Affirmed.

Notes and Questions

1. Is there anything troubling about the *McQuirter* case? Does the punishment imposed by the jury on McQuirter help address the issue? Is the real problem that of race? Is it the reliability of confessions? How would the case be decided under the Model Penal Code? Does this illustrate a defect in the Model Penal Code? Or is the defect somewhere else?

2. Is *McQuirter* an argument for the res ipsa loquitur test? According to the drafters of the Model Penal Code, "[t]he object of this approach is to subject to attempt liability conduct which unequivocally demonstrates that the actor is being guided by a criminal purpose." Comment to §5.01.

One criticism of the test is that instead of eliminating proof problems, the test would compound them, because no act is completely unequivocal. Indeed, there are situations in which an act which seems unequivocal is actually innocent. The Model Penal Code Commentary itself cites the case of Regina v. Chima, 8 Bombay High Ct. R. (Crown Cas.) 164 (1871), in which defendant, an unwed mother, put her baby inside an urn in a way in which it would have suffocated. It was rescued by the police and it turned out that she had only intended to hide it from intruders.

Another example of this type of situation is given by commentator Glanville Williams. He poses the hypothetical that

> a number of haystacks have been set on fire in a particular locality. . . . One night the defendant enters a farmer's field, goes to a haystack, puts a cigarette in his mouth and lights a match. . . . On the one hand, he might have been about to set fire to the stack before lighting the cigarette; on the other hand, he might merely have intended to light the cigarette.[12]

Williams feels that the problem here relates to "proof of *mens rea*" rather than "to the proximity of the *actus reus*." Id. at 382. Is Williams's assessment of the equivocality approach (i.e., that intent can be proved by ways other than unequivocal conduct) convincing? In other words, can you think of examples in which the defendant's actions are equivocal, but because of additional evidence (which would not be heard under a res ipsa/equivocality approach), criminal intent is likely? What of the situation in which the defendant is caught carrying poison? This is an equivocal act—he could be planning to use the poison to kill snails. But assume the defendant confesses that he planned to use the poison to kill *X*. Should this testimony be excluded? Donald Stuart puts it this way:

> If a locksmith is found next to a bank safe with his tools of trade it would be ludicrous to exclude a confession or other evidence that his intent had been to steal.[13]

On the other hand, is the issue whether such a confession should be excluded—or is it whether the confession can make up for defects in the proof of the *actus reus*?

3. McQuirter was convicted of "attempt to commit an assault with intent to rape." Is it fair to say that he was punished for attempting an attempt? If so, is it fair to punish him? Could McQuirter have been prosecuted for attempted rape? What if the Alabama legislature had chosen to punish assault with intent to rape precisely because the uncertainty of the preparation/attempt distinction in traditional law had made it difficult for the state to prove attempted rape? Is it then fair to prosecute McQuirter for attempted assault with intent to rape? The courts have split on this issue, at least in the context of "simple assault," which is essentially an attempt to commit a physical battery on another. Compare Wilson v. State, 53 Ga. 205 (1874) (a metaphysical absurdity to punish attempted assault), with State v. Wilson, 218 Or. 575, 346 P.2d 115 (1959) (upholding conviction of attempted assault with deadly weapon where defendant came to look for his wife at her workplace carrying shotgun and intending to shoot her, but she was saved when her fellow workers hid her).

The problem of "attempted attempt" becomes more complex when we consider other "substantive" crimes which are "preparatory" in the sense that they punish behavior which does not itself cause the ultimate harm the law is

12. Williams, Textbook of Criminal Law 382 (2d ed. 1983).
13. Don Stuart, Canadian Criminal Law 532 (1982).

aimed at preventing. A rough definition of burglary is "entering a dwelling of another at night with intent to commit a felony inside." What if a person is caught just before she enters the victim's dwelling? Should the state punish her for attempted burglary? Numerous cases uphold convictions for this crime. But consider the view in the Comments to the Model Penal Code, §221.1 (1980):

> The initial development of the offense of burglary, as well as much of the later expansion of the offense, probably resulted from an effort to compensate for defects in the traditional law of attempt. The common law of attempt ordinarily did not reach a person who embarked on a course of criminal behavior unless he came very close to his goal. Sometimes it was stated that to be guilty of attempt one had to engage in the final act which would have accomplished his object but for the intervention of circumstances beyond his control. Under that view of the law of attempt, a person apprehended while breaking into a dwelling with intent to commit a felony therein would not have committed an attempt, for he would not have arrived at the scene of his projected theft, rape, or murder. Moreover, even when the actor's conduct reached the stage where an attempt was committed, penalties for attempt were disproportionately low as compared to the penalties for the completed offense.
>
> The development and expansion of the offense of burglary provided a partial solution to these problems. Making entry with criminal intent an independent substantive offense carrying serious sanctions moved back the moment when the law could intervene in a criminal design and authorize penalties more nearly in accord with the seriousness of the actor's conduct.

What if the police are sure that the defendant entered a dwelling with intent to commit a felony therein, but are not sure which felony he intended to commit. What crime should they charge him with?

Do the same issues arise with other crimes that can be viewed as "preparatory" with respect to the ultimate harm feared? If larceny is defined as taking the property of another with the intent permanently to deprive the owner of the property, should the state be able to punish attempted larceny? What of attempted possession of illegal drugs or concealed weapons?

4. The preparation/attempt distinction also affects important issues of constitutional criminal procedure. The police may arrest and fully search a person only if they have "probable cause" to believe that person is committing or has committed a crime. Brinegar v. United States, 338 U.S. 160, 175 (1949). The police may also briefly stop a person and pat him down for weapons on a lesser standard: where they have "reasonable grounds" to believe that the person has committed, is committing, or is about to commit a crime, or that "criminal activity is afoot," Terry v. Ohio, 392 U.S. 1 (1968). Does the combination of these standards for arrest or searches and the modern doctrines of attempt make it too easy for the police to seize people? See R. Misner, The New Attempt Laws: Unsuspected Threat to the Fourth Amendment, 33 Stan. L. Rev. 201 (1981).

2. Abandonment

PEOPLE v. STAPLES

California Court of Appeal
6 Cal. App. 3d 61, 85 Cal. Rptr. 589 (1970)

Reppy, Associate Justice.

Defendant was charged in an information with attempted burglary (Pen. Code, §§664, 459). . . .

In October, 1967, while his wife was away on a trip, defendant, a mathematician, under an assumed name, rented an office on the second floor of a building in Hollywood which was over the mezzanine of a bank. Directly below the mezzanine was the vault of the bank. Defendant was aware of the layout of the building, specifically of the relation of the office he rented to the bank vault. Defendant paid rent for the period from October 23 to November 23. The landlord had 10 days before commencement of the rental period within which to finish some interior repairs and painting. During this pre-rental period defendant brought into the office certain equipment. This included drilling tools, two acetylene gas tanks, a blow torch, a blanket, and a linoleum rug. The landlord observed these items when he came in from time to time to see how the repair work was progressing. Defendant learned from a custodian that no one was in the building on Saturdays. On Saturday, October 14, defendant drilled two groups of holes into the floor of the office above the mezzanine room. He stopped drilling before the holes went through the floor. He came back to the office several times thinking he might slowly drill down, covering the holes with the lineoleum rug. At some point in time he installed a hasp lock on a closet, and planned to, or did, place his tools in it. However, he left the closet keys on the premises. Around the end of November, apparently after November 23, the landlord notified the police and turned the tools and equipment over to them. Defendant did not pay any more rent. It is not clear when he last entered the office, but it could have been after November 23, and even after the landlord had removed the equipment. On February 22, 1968, the police arrested defendant. After receiving advice as to his constitutional rights, defendant voluntarily made an oral statement which he reduced to writing.

Among other things which defendant wrote down were these:

> Saturday, the 14th . . . I drilled some small holes in the floor of the room. Because of tiredness, fear, and the implications of what I was doing, I stopped and went to sleep.
>
> At this point I think my motives began to change. The actutal [sic] commencement of my plan made me begin to realize that even if I were to succeed a fugitive life of living off of stolen money would not give the enjoyment of the life of a mathematician however humble a job I might have.
>
> I still had not given up my plan however. I felt I had made a certain investment of time, money, effort and a certain pschological [sic] commitment to the concept.

> I came back several times thinking I might store the tools in the closet and slowly drill down (covering the hole with a rug of linoleum square). As time went on (after two weeks or so), my wife came back and my life as bank robber seemed more and more absurd.

Our courts have come up with a variety of "tests" which try to distinguish acts of preparation from completed attempts. "The preparation consists in devising or arranging the means or measures necessary for the commission of the offense; the attempt is the direct movement toward the commission after the preparations are made." (People v. Murray, 14 Cal. 159; see also, People v. Franquelin, 109 Cal. App. 2d 777, 784, 241 P.2d 651.) ". . . [T]he act must reach far enough towards the accomplishment of the desired result to amount to the commencement of the consummation." (People v. Miller, supra, 2 Cal. 2d 527, 530, 42 P.2d 308, 309.) ". . . [W]here the intent to commit the substantive offense is . . . clearly established . . . [,] acts done toward the commission of the crime may constitute an attempt, where the same acts would be held insufficient to constitute an attempt if the intent with which they were done is equivocal and not clearly proved." (People v. Berger, 131 Cal. App. 2d 127, 130, 280 P.2d 136, 138.)

None of the above statements of the law applicable to this category of attempts provide a litmus-like test, and perhaps no such test is achievable. Such precision is not required in this case, however. There was definitely substantial evidence entitling the trial judge to find that defendant's acts had gone beyond the preparation stage. Without specifically deciding where defendant's preparations left off and where his activities became a completed criminal attempt, we can say that his "drilling" activity clearly was an unequivocal and direct step toward the completion of the burglary. It was a fragment of the substantive crime contemplated, i.e., the beginning of the "breaking" element. Further, defendant himself characterized his activity as the actual commencement of his plan. The drilling by defendant was obviously one of a series of acts which logic and ordinary experience indicate would result in the proscribed act of burglary.

The instant case provides an out-of-the-ordinary factual situation. . . . Usually the actors in cases falling within [the] category of attempts are intercepted or caught in the act. Here, there was no direct proof of any actual interception. But it was clearly inferable by the trial judge that defendant became aware that the landlord had resumed control over the office and had turned defendant's equipment and tools over to the police. This was the equivalent of interception.

The inference of this nonvoluntary character of defendant's abandonment was a proper one for the trial judge to draw. However, it would seem that the character of the abandonment in situations of this type, whether it be voluntary (prompted by pangs of conscience or a change of heart) or nonvoluntary (established by inference in the instant case), is not controlling. The relevant factor is the determination of whether the acts of the perpetrator have reached such a stage of advancement that they can be classified as an attempt. Once that attempt is found there can be no exculpatory abandonment.

"One of the purposes of the criminal law is to protect society from those who intend to injure it. When it is established that the defendant intended to commit a specific crime and that in carrying out this intention he committed an act that caused harm or sufficient danger of harm, it is immaterial that for some collateral reason he could not complete the intended crime." (People v. Camodeca, 52 Cal. 2d 142, 147, 38 P.2d 903, 906.)

The order is affirmed.

Notes and Questions

1. Did Staples cross the line between preparation and attempt? If he did, why should his subsequent actions negate his criminal liability? If a thief returns the stolen goods undamaged, is he still guilty of larceny? On the other hand, if we are confident that Staples had renounced any intention to burglarize the bank, why would we want to punish him?

2. Unlike the *Staples* court, the Model Penal Code does permit a limited defense of abandonment. Section 5.01(4), dealing with "Renunciation of Criminal Purpose," requires:

> a complete and voluntary renunciation of his criminal purpose. . . . [R]enunciation is not voluntary if it is motivated in whole or in part, by circumstances, not present or apparent at the inception of the actor's course of conduct, which increase the probability of detection or apprehension or which make more difficult the accomplishment of the criminal purpose. Renunciation is not complete if it is motivated by a decision to postpone the criminal conduct until a more advantageous time or to transfer the criminal effort to another but similar objective or victim.

The Model Penal Code Commentary justifies allowing the defense of voluntary abandonment, explaining that the individual who abandons of his or her own volition early on in the course of an attempt lacks dangerousness of character and also that permitting the defense for the individual who abandons later will encourage would-be criminals to desist from their unlawful plans.

Why does the Model Penal Code test depend on the reasons for the person's renunciation? What if Staples had read that the government's arrest and conviction rate for bank crimes had gone up dramatically in recent years, and so he decided not to risk a bank burglary?

3. In practice, the abandonment defense is applied very stringently and there are few reported cases in which the defendant has prevailed on that ground. Of course, some courts dodge the abandonment issue simply by holding that the defendant never crossed the line between preparation and attempt in the first place.

For example, compare the *Staples* case, in which defendant had crossed to the attempt side of the line and was convicted, with Bucklew v. State, 206 So. 2d 200 (Miss. 1968). In *Bucklew* the defendant mayor signed a car repair bill which illegally authorized the city to pay his personal bill. However, he never submitted the bill to a clerk for payment. The court decided he could not be convicted of attempted embezzlement because he abandoned the scheme before taking any overt action and hence had confined himself to preparatory activity.

4. In some instances allowing a defense of voluntary abandonment might lead to disturbing results. In Le Barron v. State, 32 Wis. 2d 294, 145 N.W.2d 79 (1966), the defendant voluntarily abandoned his attempt to rape a woman, after assaulting her, only because he found out she was pregnant. The court rejected the abandonment claim. Would LeBarron have had a defense under the Model Penal Code?

5. Professor Mark Kelman writes:

> [I]t is implausible that a defendant who abandoned his attempted crime because he read a sign, "This Safe Protected by Alarms" could be convicted while one who read a sign, "Safe-crackers will be Apprehended and Prosecuted" would be acquitted. Both are simply being informed of the riskiness of their activity. It is simply unwarranted assertive construction to treat these defendants as renouncing larceny because they renounce this larceny. It is not clear how we would ever know that someone is moving on to a more advantageous time and place for his mischief rather than abandoning a life of crime because he has at last understood the social signals about the costs of crime. It is quite plain we cannot know that, because the social signals concerning the propriety of cost-benefit calculation are ambivalent and uninterpretable. We suppress the recognition of this ambivalence by asserting clear cases of total acceptable renunciation and blocking the knowledge that in a world where selfish calculation is acceptable, all renunciations are in significant senses partial.[14]

Do you agree with Professor Kelman that the voluntary/involuntary distinction rests on faulty premises? If so, can you think of a better way to distinguish between situations in which abandonment should be allowed as a defense and situations in which it should not?

6. One British commentator[15] has pointed out a special problem in the attempt area:

> Whether a defence of abandonment for attempt exists at common law is without direct clear authority in England and the subject of conflicting judicial pronouncements in American jurisdictions. . . . However, certain difficulties peculiar to attempt make the case for introducing a defence of withdrawal in respect of that form of inchoate liability significantly weaker than for conspiracy and in-

14. Kelman, Interpretive Construction in the Substantive Criminal Law, 33 Stan. L. Rev. 591, 649-650 (1981).

15. K. J. M. Smith, Withdrawal from Criminal Liability for Complicity and Inchoate Offences, Anglo-Am. L. Rev. 200, 205 (1983).

citement. Firstly, being the form of inchoate conduct most proximate to the substantive criminal object means the opportunities for repentance induced by the facility of withdrawal are less obvious than with conspiracy or intent. Further, the usually more overt and immediate nature of the act of attempt may cause types of social alarm which cannot be satisfactorily assuaged by withdrawal. However, the most intractable problem is the construction of a principle which convincingly separates cases where withdrawal could acceptably operate from those where it would be commonly thought to be inappropriate. Two classic examples of such situations are where the defendant has fired, with intent to kill, at his victim but misses, and where a woman has unsuccessfully taken a substance to procure an illegal abortion. Should abandonment of the criminal objective at this late stage excuse? Fortuity rather than repentance is responsible in such cases for failure, but is a judgment of this nature capable of being translated into a rule which is likely to be effective in application? Delineation of a point of no return could possibly be approached through a concept of "completed" and "incompleted" attempt, withdrawal being permitted only in the latter situation. An attempt would be "incomplete" when the actor has still to perform a final act, such as pulling the trigger of a gun. But identifying the last or final act is unlikely to prove much more satisfactory than it did when used to determine proximity for the imposition of liability for attempt. In the example of a woman taking a substance with the intent to terminate a pregnancy, should she be debarred from the benefits of the defence if, before waiting for the effects of the abortifacient to show themselves, she takes an antidote? Even if the formula is modified so as not to exclude last acts until failure becomes apparent there remains the problem of identifying the relevant last act. Must it be that of the defendant? If *D* posts a letter containing fraudulent statements with the aim of obtaining money by deception should he be able to withdraw by removing it the following day from the recipient's desk before it is read? Further, supposing in order to kill his wife *D* connects the bathroom towel rail to the main electricity supply. After two days, during which his wife unexpectedly does not touch the rail, *D* experiences remorse and disconnects the rail, reasonably believing that if he had left it a few more days his wife would inevitably have been electrocuted. *D*'s last act was to electrify the towel rail but nothing would happen until the later act of the wife touching the rail occurred, and before this happened *D* withdrew. These hypothetical examples suggest the notion of "complete" attempt could not be relied upon to prevent exculpation from liability in what would probably generally be thought of as unacceptable circumstances. Despite this potential for producing highly anomalous and unsatisfactory results those American jurisdictions which have enacted withdrawal provisions for incitement and conspiracy have also done so in respect of attempt.

3. Solicitation

STATE v. DAVIS

Supreme Court of Missouri, In Banc
6 S.W.2d 609 (1928)

Davis, C. Defendant was convicted on May 29, 1926, after a three days' [sic] trial, of an attempt to commit murder in the first degree. The jury returned a verdict fixing his punishment at imprisonment in the penitentiary for a term of eight years, which the trial court reduced to five years, sentencing him to that term. Defendant duly appealed from the judgment entered accordingly.

On the hearing before us defendant accepted the facts as outlined by the Attorney General in his brief as a true recital of the evidence adduced. The evidence submitted on the part of the state warrants the finding that defendant and Alberdina Lourie resided in Kansas City. They were seemingly infatuated with each other, planning and arranging to have Edmon Lourie, the husband of Alberdina, killed so that they could obtain the insurance on his life, aggregating $60,000, as well as cohabit. Edmon Lourie was absent from home the greater part of the time, returning at intervals of two or three weeks. In furtherance of their plan, defendant, acting for himself and Alberdina, arranged to have one Earl Leverton obtain for them the services of an ex-convict to murder Edmon Lourie for hire. Leverton, instead of procuring the services of an ex-convict for that purpose, disclosed the plot to Joel L. Dill, a member of the Kansas City police force, who agreed to pose as an ex-convict to that end. Several meetings were had between defendant, Leverton, and Dill, defendant stating that he and Alberdina were in love, and desired Edmon Lourie killed. He agreed to pay for the execution of the plot. Defendant outlined his plan, offering Dill the sum of $600, with the further agreement that Alberdina, who was to be with her husband at the time of the contemplated assault, would wear diamonds of the value of $3,000. He further arranged for Alberdina and Dill to see each other that each might recognize the other on sight. Defendant, Dill, and Leverton, during January and the early part of February, 1926, held prearranged conferences on the subject. Prior to February 11, 1926, defendant arranged for Dill to go to Chicago to kill Edmon Lourie there, defendant making and giving Dill a map or drawing showing where Lourie could be found, as well as two photographs of him. The arrangements contemplated that, if Dill was unable to locate Lourie, Alberdina would go to Chicago to aid him. The trip to Chicago was to be made about February 12th.

However, Edmon Lourie telegraphed Alberdina that he would return to Kansas City on February 13, 1926, defendant thereupon notifying Leverton, who in turn communicated the fact to Dill. Defendant paid Dill $600, advising him that Alberdina would persuade Edmon to accompany her to a place of amusement, and that she planned to leave their home at 8 o'clock P.M. on February 13, 1926. It was further planned that Alberdina was to carry the diamonds on her person, and that Dill was to shoot Lourie either as they left their home or as they returned, and that Alberdina was to be mussed up and the diamonds taken from her, so that it might appear the result of a robbery. Alberdina was to appear to faint, giving Dill time to make his escape. However, on the night of February 13, 1926, Dill, accompanied by three other police officers, proceeded about 8 o'clock P.M. to the home of Edmon Lourie as arranged. Edmon and Alberdina Lourie were there found dressed and ready to leave, with the diamonds on her person. As Dill and the officers entered the room, she turned her face to the wall as planned. Two officers took charge of

Edmon and Alberdina; Dill and the other officer going to the home of defendant, where they arrested him. The defendant had previously informed Dill that he would remain at home in order to have an alibi.

Upon his arrest, defendant made and signed a confession in which he stated that he and Alberdina planned to have Edmon Lourie killed. In pursuance of the plan he met Dill, whom he assumed to be an ex-convict and the subject of hire for the purpose intended. The day before the contemplated murder he gave Dill $200 and he gave him $400 the day the murder was to be consummated, together with a picture of Edmon Lourie. It was arranged that Dill was to go to Chicago to kill Lourie. Lourie, however, unexpectedly arranged to go home, notifying Alberdina of his intention by telegram. Thereupon Alberdina informed defendant of the fact, whereupon he notified Dill, resulting that the scene of the contemplated murder was changed to Lourie's home in Kansas City. The arrangements contemplated that Alberdina was to accompany Lourie that night to a picture show, and Dill was to stage a hold-up and kill Lourie. Alberdina agreed to remove the diamond rings from her fingers, giving them to Dill, and he was to retain them as part payment for the murder of Lourie. Lourie masqueraded under different names, among them Lourie, Frank, Payne, and Edmonds, Alberdina telling defendant that she thought he was a master mind among criminals. The confession was made on the night of February 13, 1926. The evidence establishes that all of the acts complained of occurred in Kansas City, Jackson county, Mo., during January and February, 1926.

The evidence on the part of defendant tends to establish that defendant was urged to agree to the arrangement by Dill and Leverton, but that, after paying the money, he abandoned the crime before an overt act was committed. There was also testimony that Alberdina, the coconspirator, abandoned the plot, which abandonment was communicated to Dill and defendant. Defendant was addicted to drink, and had been an inmate of a sanatorium. It was asserted that all these facts were known to Dill and Leverton, who purchased and gave him liquor while persuading him to continue the plot. Such other facts as we find pertinent, if any, will later be noted. . . . The record develops the presence of the inquiry to commit the crime and the failure to consummate its commission. . . . Our sole inquiry then relates to the performance of some act upon the part of defendant toward the commission of the crime.

The physical overt act, which with intent and failure to consummate brings the crime of attempt into existence, is distinguishable from solicitation and preparation. An attempt to commit a crime involves an act on the part of the defendant moving directly toward the commission of the offense. With these concepts in mind we proceed to review the solicitations and preparations by defendant to murder Lourie as constituting an overt act.

In State v. Hayes, 78 Mo. 307, this court, through Philips, C., said:

> It is the recognized law of this country that the solicitation of another to commit a crime is an act toward the commission.

However, the proof in the above case developed, in addition to solicitations, an act on the part of the accused extending beyond solicitation or preparation, that of saturating a portion of the floor with coal oil as well, as the furnishing of plans and an oil can. Conceding that the court reached the proper result in that case, concerning which it is unnecessary to express an opinion, the basic facts there shown extend far beyond the facts here developed. While a few of the courts have treated solicitation to commit a crime as an attempt, the great weight of authority warrants the assertion that mere solicitation, unaccompanied by an act moving directly toward the commission of the intended crime, is not an overt act constituting an element of the crime of attempt. Solicitation of itself is a distinct offense when declared so by law. 16 C.J. 118; 8 R.C.L. 277. Therefore, in conformity with the weight of authority, we hold that merely soliciting one to commit a crime does not constitute an attempt.

The state contends that the arrangement of a plan for the accomplishment of the murder of Lourie and the selecting and hiring of the means or instrumentality by which the murder was to be consummated were demonstrated. We take it that the state means by the foregoing declarations that overt acts were shown. To that we do not agree. The evidence goes no further than developing a verbal arrangement with Dill, the selection of Dill as the one to kill Lourie, the delivery of a certain drawing and two photographs of Lourie to Dill, and the payment of a portion of the agreed consideration. These things were mere acts of preparation, failing to lead directly or proximately to the consummation of the intended crime. In this regard we have found no authority which holds that preparations constitute an overt act. . . .

The plans or arrangements amounted to nothing more than mere preparation. The contract of hiring entered into between defendant and Dill also fails to extend beyond mere preparation. In regard to the hiring, the trial court instructed the jury that the payment of money by defendant to Dill to commit the intended crime did not constitute such an overt act as was tantamount to an attempt. The ruling of the court we think was right, for the payment of money was not an act moving directly toward the consummation of the intended crime. The only case we have found involving the actual payment of money to another as the consideration for the proposed crime is Reg. v. Williams, 1 Car. & K. 589, 1 Den. C.C. 39. In that case the facts showed the actual delivery of money to the agent who straightway went with the poison given him for that purpose to the home of the intended victims. However, on his arrival he disclosed to them the plan to kill, handing over the poison. The fifteen judges who considered the case on appeal held the conviction erroneous.

The employment of Dill as agent to murder Lourie was not tantamount to an attempt. Dill not only had no intention of carrying out the expressed purpose of defendant, but was guilty of no act directly or indirectly moving toward the consummation of the intended crime. He did nothing more than listen to the plans and solicitations of defendant without intending to act upon them. It was not shown that Dill committed an act that could be construed as an attempt. The arrest of Lourie, his wife, and defendant as detailed in the evidence could not be said to have been based upon an act involving the consummation of the crime. . . .

It follows from what we have said that the judgment must be reversed, and the defendant discharged. It is so ordered.

WHITE, J., concurring. . . . In the argument we were directed to the heinous nature of the crime, where one, who is too cowardly to commit the act himself, employs someone else to do it. That is a serious offense, and no doubt many a crime is committed by a hired agent, but the master minds in the criminal world from whom that danger comes never make mistakes such as Davis made. They know their men, and they employ real killers. Davis was not only a coward, but a fool. The entire plan and preparation showed the want of judgment and discretion. He has no criminal record, and he is not a dangerous criminal. If every person who, at some time in his or her life, entertained a criminal impulse, was put in jail, a small minority of us would be at large.

It is said further that the defendant in this case did all he could in furtherance of the plan to have this murder committed. This is incorrect. He failed of many things he might have done—things absolutely necessary for the commission of the crime or its attempt. He might have used the weapon himself. He might have used sense enough to solicit a real criminal to commit the deed. He might have taken precaution to find out who the man was that he employed for the purpose. But blindly he picked . . . the first man who offered his services.

The upshot of the matter is this: The defendant had no intention to kill; that is, to commit the murder himself. Dill had no intention to kill. There can be no crime without a criminal intent, and neither the defendant nor his agent entertained an intent to do the deed. The defendant intended that Dill should do it, but that intent cannot be connected with an act of another which was neither done nor contemplated by the other. The intent to commit the crime must be in the mind of the man who is to commit the crime.

Of course, the defendant was guilty of soliciting another to commit the murder; a serious crime, but he was not charged with that, nor convicted of that offense. We must determine cases upon the law as it is written, and as it has been adjudged for generations.

The judgment is properly reversed.

BLAIR and GANTT, JJ., concur in this opinion.

WALKER, C.J. (dissenting). The charge against the defendant was based upon the following statute, so far as the same is definitory of the offense:

> Every person who shall attempt to commit an offense prohibited by law, and in such attempt shall do any act toward the commission of such offense, but

> shall fail in the perpetration thereof, or shall be prevented or intercepted in executing the same, upon conviction thereof, shall, in cases where no provision is made by law for the punishment of such attempt, be punished as follows: [This is followed by the punishment prescribed]—part of section 3683, R.S. 1919.

Without limitation it may be said that the defendant did everything within the contemplation of malicious human ingenuity to enable the putative murderer to commit the crime, short of actual participation therein. He solicited the detective, Dill, to do the killing. In so doing he was guilty of a constitutive act within the terms of the statute. Thus defined, the act became overt. Despite the contrariety of rulings elsewhere, it is the recognized law in this state that the solicitation of another to commit a felony is an act towards its commission, without any other act being done, to warrant a conviction. The evil intent in the mind of the defendant—the existence of which is shown by all of his acts—imparts to the solicitations their criminality. Incidentally, it may be said in this connection that [a finding] that the party solicited may not have acquiesced or intended to share in the crime will not exonerate the defendant.

I find that our statute was copied from that of New York, where it was held in People v. Bush, 4 Hill, 133, that, where an accused solicited another to commit the crime of arson, and gave him some material for the purpose, this was sufficient to sustain a conviction, although the person solicited did not intend to commit the offense. . . .

The proof of defendant's guilt in the instant case is not limited to solicitations. He and his paramour, the wife of the intended victim, planned and directed with particularity the time, manner, and place of the proposed killing of her husband. A trip to Chicago was even in contemplation to effect that end, when the husband returned home unexpectedly, and the scene of the proposed tragedy was shifted to Kansas City. When it was to occur, the defendant had it understood that he was to remain at his home so as to afford a basis for a plea of alibi. There he waited expectantly for news of the murder. His paramour . . . is not on trial, and the vocabulary of scorn and contempt need not be wasted on her connection with the contemplated murder of her husband.

The chain of proven facts and properly deducible circumstances cannot be otherwise construed than as conclusive of the defendant's guilt. Of what more avail would it have been as proof of his intent or purpose to have shown that he furnished the detective with the weapon he was to use . . . [or] instrumentality he might employ in committing the murder. The limits of human fancy know no horizon; but it is difficult to conceive what more the defendant could have done than he did do towards the attempt to commit the proposed murder without actually participating in its commission.

Ample proof of the presence of those essentials required by our rulings having been adduced to sustain a conviction, the judgment of the trial court should be affirmed.

Notes and Questions

1. Using the doctrines examined above in United States v. Jackson and other cases, would you say that Davis crossed the line from preparation to attempt? What would be the result under the "last act" test? The Model Penal Code test? The "res ipsa loquitur" test?

2. Why should the defendant's guilt depend on (a) the state of mind of Dill, or (b) the acts Dill performed after he left the defendant? Can one argue that Davis poses less of a danger to society because he needed to hire someone else to do the killing, rather than do it himself?

3. Can the decision be defended on the theory that where the legislature has made solicitation a crime, a solicitation must be prosecuted as such even if, under the facts of the case, it also amounts to an attempt? What are the problems with such a rule? What are the problems under the facts of *Davis*?

4. The *Davis* court seems to feel constrained by the fact that Dill was clearly not guilty of any crime. How would you compare the problem of determining attempt liability in *Davis* to that in the following cases?

> a. Stonehouse, a prominent government figure, sought to escape from personal and financial troubles by going to Australia, but only after faking his death so as to enable his wife to receive the proceeds of his life insurance policy. He went to Miami, where he staged his own apparent death by drowning. He was later caught in Australia, just as his wife, who was wholly innocent of his scheme and thought him really dead, was about to file a claim under the policy. Director of Public Prosecutions v. Stonehouse, [1977] 2 All E.R. 909.
>
> b. A storeowner decided to violate a British law setting the maximum legal price for meat. He wrote the excessive price on some price tags and placed the tags in a drawer, assuming that his innocent sales clerk would automatically put the tags on the meat before sale. He was caught before the sales clerk had a chance to do so. Hope v. Brown, [1954] 1 All E.R. 330.

5. To see how the concept of solicitation often does answer questions that raise great difficulties under attempt law, consider the next case.

PEOPLE v. LUBOW

Court of Appeals of New York
29 N.Y.2d 58, 272 N.E.2d 331 (1971)

BERGAN, Judge.

. . . The basic statutory definition of criminal solicitation is that, with intent that another person shall "engage in conduct constituting a crime," the accused "solicits, requests, commands, importunes or otherwise attempts to cause such other person to engage in such conduct." This basic definitory language is continued through three grades of solicitation, the gravity depending on what crime the conduct sought to be induced would effectuate.

If the conduct would be "a crime" it is criminal solicitation in the third degree, a "violation" (§100.00); if the conduct would be "a felony" it is criminal solicitation in the second degree, a class A misdemeanor (§100.05); and if the conduct would be murder or kidnapping in the first degree it is criminal solicitation in the first degree, a class D felony (§100.10).

As it has been noted, nothing need be done under the statute in furtherance of the communication ("solicits, commands, importunes") to constitute the offense. The communication itself, with intent the other person engage in the unlawful conduct, is enough. It needs no corroboration.

And an attempt at communication which fails to reach the other person may also constitute the offense, for the concluding clause "or otherwise attempts to cause such other person to engage in such conduct" would seem literally to embrace as an attempt an undelivered letter or message initiated with the necessary intent.

Appellants have been convicted after a trial by a three-Judge panel in the Criminal Court of the City of New York of violation of section 100.05, which describes solicitation to commit a felony. The information on which the prosecution is based is made by complainant Max Silverman. It describes the charge as criminal solicitation and states that "defendants attempted to cause deponent to commit the crime of grand larceny" in that they "attempted to induce the deponent to obtain precious stones on partial credit with a view towards appropriating the property to their own use and not paying the creditors, said conduct constituting the crime of larceny by false promise."

Although the Penal Law section number is not stated in the information, it was clearly stated in court before the opening of the trial that the charge was a violation of section 100.05 and the facts alleged that the inducement was to commit grand larceny, a felony, which gave adequate notice of the nature of the offense involved.

The evidence showed that complainant Silverman and both defendants were engaged in the jewelry business. It could be found that defendant Lubow owed Silverman $30,000 for diamonds on notes which were unpaid; that Lubow had told Silverman he was associated with a big operator interested in buying diamonds and introduced him to defendant Gissinger.

It could also be found that in October, 1967, Silverman met the two defendants together at their office, demanded his money, and said that because of the amount owed him he was being forced into bankruptcy.

Silverman testified that in response to this Lubow said "Well, let's make it a big one, a big bankruptcy," and Gissinger said this was a good idea. When Silverman asked "how it is done" he testified that Lubow, with Gissinger participating, outlined a method by which diamonds would be purchased partly on credit, sold for less than cost, with the proceeds pyramided to boost Silverman's credit rating until very substantial amounts came in, when there was to be a bankruptcy with Silverman explaining that he had lost the cash gambling in Puerto Rico and Las Vegas. The cash would be divided among the three men. The gambling explanation for the disappearance of cash would be made to seem believable by producing credit cards for Puerto Rico and Las Vegas. Silverman testified that Lubow said "we would eventually wind up with a quarter of a million dollars each" and that Gissinger said "maybe millions."

Silverman reported this proposal to the District Attorney in October, 1967, and the following month a police detective equipped Silverman with a tape recorder concealed on his person which was in operation during conversations with defendants on November 16 and which tends to substantiate the charge. The reel was received in evidence on concession that it was taken from the machine Silverman wore November 16.

A police detective testified as an expert that a "bust out operation" is a "pyramiding of credit by rapid purchasing of merchandise, and the rapid selling of the same merchandise sometimes 10 and 20 per cent the cost of the merchandise itself, and they keep selling and buying until they establish such a credit rating that they are able to purchase a large order at the end of their operation, and at this time they go into bankruptcy or they just leave."

There thus seems sufficient evidence in the record to find that defendants intended Silverman to engage in conduct constituting a felony by defrauding creditors of amounts making out grand larceny and that they importuned Silverman to engage in such conduct. Thus the proof meets the actual terms of the statute.

The statute itself is a valid exercise of legislative power. Commentators closely associated with the drafting of the Model Penal Code of the American Law Institute, from which the New York solicitation statute stems, have observed:

> Purposeful solicitation presents dangers calling for preventive intervention and is sufficiently indicative of a disposition towards criminal activity to call for liability. Moreover, the fortuity that the person solicited does not agree to commit or attempt to commit the incited crime plainly should not relieve the solicitor of liability. . . .

Solicitation to commit a felony was a misdemeanor at common law (People v. Bush, 4 Hill 133, 135; Rex v. Higgins, 2 East 5). Summarizing this historical fact Judge Cardozo observed: "So at common law, incitement to a felony, when it did not reach the stage of an attempt, was itself a separate crime, and like conspiracy, which it resembled, was a misdemeanor, not a felony" (People v. Werblow, 241 N.Y. 55, 66, 148 N.E. 786, 791, citing Higgins and Rex v. Gregory, L.R. 1 C.C.R. 77).

But as People v. Bush demonstrates, the solicitation in early New York cases was treated as closely related to an attempt. There defendant asked another to burn a barn and gave him a match for that purpose. This principle was followed to some extent but there were fundamental difficulties with it under the concept of attempt and it seems not to have been followed.

Although this Penal Law provision is the first statutory enactment regarding criminal solicitation in New York, there have been statutes aimed at criminal solicitation in some other States, notably California.

In commenting on the criminal solicitation enactment of article 100, two lawyers who were active in the work of the State Commission on Revision of the Penal Law and Criminal Code which prepared the present statute observed that article 100 "closes the gap" for those who believe, as apparently the commission and the American Law Institute did, that "solicitation to commit a crime involves sufficient culpability to warrant criminal sanctions."

There are, however, potential difficulties inherent in this penal provision which should be looked at, even though all of them are not decisive in this present case. One, of course, is the absence of any need for corroboration. The tape recording here tends to give some independent support to the testimony of Silverman, but there are types of criminal conduct which might be solicited where there would be a heavy thrust placed on the credibility of a single witness testifying to a conversation. Extraordinary care might be required in deciding when to prosecute; in determining the truth; and in appellate review of the factual decision.

One example would be the suggestion of one person to another that he commit a sexual offense; another is the suggestion that he commit perjury. The Model Penal Code did not require corroboration; but aside from the need for corroboration which is traditional in some sexual offenses, there are dangers in the misinterpretation of innuendos or remarks which could be taken as invitations to commit sexual offenses. These are discussed by Wechsler-Jones-Korn (61 Col. L. Rev., p. 623) with the comment that "it is a risk implicit in the punishment of almost all inchoate crimes."

In two opinions for the California Supreme Court, Justice Traynor has analyzed that State's criminal solicitation statute (Penal Code §653f; Benson v. Superior Ct. of Los Angeles County, 57 Cal. 2d 240, 18 Cal. Rptr. 516, 368 P.2d 116 [1962], and People v. Burt, 45 Cal. 2d 311, 288 P.2d 503 [1955]).

The first case was for solicitation to commit perjury and the second, for solicitation to commit extortion.

The California statute is based on a specific list of serious crimes to which criminal solicitation expressly applies; but as to all of them the statute requires that the offense "must be proved by the testimony of two witnesses, or of one witness and corroborating circumstances."

The basic public justification for legislative enactment is, however, very similar to New York's and was developed in the *Burt* opinion: "Legislative concern with the proscribed soliciting is demonstrated not only by the gravity of the crimes specified but by the fact that the crime, unlike conspiracy, does not require the commission of any overt act. It is complete when the solicitation is made, and it is immaterial that the object of the solicitation is never consummated, or that no steps are taken toward its consummation." The California Legislature was concerned "not only with the prevention of the harm that would result should the inducements prove successful, but with protecting inhabitants of this state from being exposed to inducements to commit or join in the commission of the crimes specified." (45 Cal. 2d 311, supra, p.314, 288 P.2d 503, p.505).

Another potential problem with the statute is that it includes an attempt to commit unlawful solicitation, i.e., solicits . . . "or otherwise attempts to cause" the conduct. This has the same effect as the Model Penal Code, but the language there is different. The Code spells the purpose out more specifically. . . . "It is immaterial . . . that the actor fails to communicate with the person he solicits to commit a crime if his conduct was designed to effect such communication" (Model Penal Code, §5.02, subd. [2], Tent. Draft No. 10, as analyzed by Wechsler-Jones-Korn, op. cit., p. 621). This could be an attempt in the classic sense and might be committed by a telephone message initiated but never delivered. The present Penal Law, stated in different language, has the same effect.

FULD, C.J., and SCILEPPI, BREITEL, JASEN and GIBSON, JJ., concur with BERGAN, J.

BURKE, J., concurs in result only.

Judgment affirmed.

Notes and Questions

1. Model Penal Code:

Section 5.02. Criminal Solicitation.

(1) *Definition of solicitation.* A person is guilty of solicitation to commit a crime if with the purpose of promoting or facilitating its commission he commands, encourages or requests another person to engage in specific conduct that would constitute such crime or an attempt to commit such crime or that would establish his complicity in its commission or attempted commission.

(2) *Uncommunicated solicitation.* It is immaterial under Subsection (1) of this Section that the actor fails to communicate with the person he solicits to commit a crime if his conduct was designed to effect such communication.

(3) *Renunciation of criminal purpose.* It is an affirmative defense that the actor, after soliciting another person to commit a crime, persuaded him not to do so or otherwise prevented the commission of the crime under circumstances manifesting a renunciation of his criminal purpose.

2. For purposes of grading punishment, the Code treats solicitation the same way it treats attempt: Soliciting a crime results in the same penalty as completing that particular crime, except that soliciting a felony of the first degree is punishable as a felony of the second degree. §5.05(1). What if a jurisdiction has a sufficiently flexible attempt law, so that a person can be convicted of both solicitation and attempt for the same behavior? The Code position is that the defendant can be punished for either the solicitation or the attempt, but not both. See §5.05(3).

3. Most state statutes, like the New York statute, are modeled after §5.02 (and quite a few states now have such statutes). But until recently, most states did not have provisions dealing specifically with solicitation (although solicitation *was* a separate offense at common law).

4. By its very nature, the crime of solicitation can raise troublesome political and constitutional issues. What if a person stands on a soapbox in the city park and urges her listeners to take action against the government by refusing to obey unjust laws? When do solicitation laws clash with free speech rights under the First Amendment? See Brandenburg v. Ohio, 395 U.S. 444 (1969) (speech calling for violation of law may be punished only when it is "directed to inciting or producing imminent lawless action and is likely to incite or produce such action").

D. IMPOSSIBILITY

BOOTH v. STATE

Court of Criminal Appeals of Oklahoma
398 P.2d 863 (1964)

Nix, Judge.

John Fletcher Booth, Jr., was charged by information in the District Court of Oklahoma County with the crime of Receiving Stolen Property, and was found guilty of the lesser crime of Attempt to Receive Stolen Property. The jury assessed his penalty at Two Years in the Oklahoma State Penitentiary, and to pay a fine in the amount of $150.00. From said judgment and sentence the defendant appeals.

The record before this Court reveals that this case arose out of a circumstance as testified to by a self-admitted, well-known thief bearing the name of Charley Stanford, whose FBI "rap sheet" covers 8 pages of arrests extending over a period of 15 years. He was obviously braggadocio about his convictions and related from the witness stand that he had been arrested approximately 300 times on everything in the book, short of murder and rape. He admitted serving 4 terms in the penitentiary, and having been committed to a mental institution twice. He testified, in substance, that in the early morning hours he was walking in the parking lot at the YMCA in Oklahoma City and sighted a topcoat in a parked automobile. That he jimmied the window and removed the coat, took it to his home at 308 N.E. 8th Street where he retired until about 7:00, at which time he proceeded down to a pay telephone where he called his attorney (the defendant herein). He testified that he advised him he had the coat he had ordered, and agreed to let him have the coat for $20.00. Arrangements were made for the defendant to meet him at the thief's home at approximately 11:00 A.M., where the transfer was to be made. He returned home, and a friend came by and invited him to go get a drink. He started from his house to his friend's car and was arrested by Lt. Anthony of the Oklahoma City Police Department. He was wearing the stolen coat at the time of his arrest. Lt. Anthony took Stanford to the police station, and asked him where he had gotten the coat and he confessed getting it from the car in the YMCA parking lot.

Lt. Anthony testified, in substance, that he received an anonymous telephone call at approximately 7:00 A.M. on the morning of the day in question, and proceeded to the YMCA and located the owner of the vehicle that had been burglarized. They went then to the vehicle and observed the wing glass had been broken, pried open, and a gray cashmere coat and some shirts were missing. Officer Anthony proceeded to the 300 block on N.E. 8th and saw an ex-convict by the name Charley Stanford leaving his house wearing a gray cashmere coat. Anthony then and there arrested Stanford for Burglary and took him to the police station. He then called Mr. Gothard to the police station, where he identified the coat as his and asked Lt. Anthony for the coat, but was advised that they needed it as evidence. Officer Anthony, Officer Reading and Stanford proceeded to 308 N.E. 8th taking the recovered coat with them. After arriving, they took their position behind a closet door containing "peep-holes" and waited for the arrival of defendant Booth. According to the testimony of Anthony, the following transpired:

A. We then went back to the 300 block on 8th Street and I concealed myself in the closet and Mr. Stanford stayed in the other part of the house which was a combination of or the apartment was a combination of a kitchen with a divan on the west side of the room. He laid the overcoat on the divan. And in the door of this clothes closet there was small pin holes and I left the door ajar slightly. Shortly after eleven o'clock Mr. John Booth came to the front door. . . .

Q. May I ask you and interrupt you at this point. Is that person in the courtroom?

A. Yes sir.

Q. Would you please point him out to the Court and Jury, Officer?

A. That person. (Points to defendant, John Booth)

Q. Go ahead.

A. Booth entered the house, and I heard Charlie say. . . .

By the Court. (Interrupting) Who do you mean by Charlie?

A. Charlie Stanford.

By Mr. Thomas.

Q. Then what?

A. I heard Charlie Stanford say, "John, I got the coat which you wanted. I need the twenty dollars right away." And Mr. Booth said, "this is child support month, Charlie, come to my office later and I will give you a check." There was other conversation. . . .

Q. Officer Anthony, how long was Mr. Booth in the house? With Charlie Stanford?
A. I would judge about ten minutes.
Q. At which time you were in the closet?
A. Yes, sir.
Q. With the door ajar?
A. Yes, sir. But I was looking mostly through the small pin holes.
Q. Were you able to look through the holes?
A. Yes, sir.
Q. Tell us what you observed.
A. They came into this particular room. . . .
Q. Who is "they"?
A. John Booth and Charlie Stanford. They . . . well, Booth picked up the coat in his arms and there was conversation of and he warned him that the thing was "hot."
Q. Who warned who?
A. Charlie Stanford warned John Booth that the thing was "hot."
Q. That the coat was "hot"?
A. Yes, that's the way he termed it.
Q. What did Mr. Booth say?
A. He said, "well, I know how to handle things like this, don't worry about it, Charlie."
Q. Then what happened? . . .
By Mr. Thomas.
Q. You testified that Charlie Stanford told him the coat was "hot."
A. He warned him the coat was hot, it was criminal talk, hot or stolen.
Q. What did Booth say?
A. Booth said, "I know how to handle these things."
Q. "I know how to handle these things"?
A. Yes, and "don't worry about it, Charlie."
Q. Then what happened?
A. At this point they went into a restroom and what went on in there, I didn't hear. Then they came back out, and Booth went to his car and put the coat in the turtle-back of his car and then returned to the house and that is about all that occurred.
Q. Altogether then Mr. Booth was in Charlie Stanford's house about how long?
A. About ten minutes.
Q. Did he leave?
A. Yes, he left.

After taking Stanford to the police station, Anthony obtained a search warrant and then maintained a surveillance of Booth's house until he arrived. He then entered the premises, arrested Booth, and again recovered the coat.

Though defendant Booth was charged with Receiving Stolen Property, at the conclusion of the evidence and after the state and defendant had rested their case, the trial judge gave the following instruction:

> You are instructed that under the law of this case you are at liberty to consider only the included offense of whether the defendant John Fletcher Booth may be guilty of the crime of Attempt to Receive Stolen Property. In this regard you are instructed, an attempt to commit a crime is defined as being the compound of two elements.
>
> (1) The intent to commit a crime.
>
> (2) A direct ineffectual act done towards its commission.
>
> Preparation alone to an attempt to commit a crime is not sufficient.

No doubt this instruction was given based upon the theory that once stolen property has been recovered by the police it loses its character as stolen property. This appears to have been the contention of defense counsel as reflected by the record.

Then the following Motion was made by defense counsel:

> The defendant at this time renews his motion to quash the information for the reason that the evidence introduced in this trial substantially shows that the crime of Receiving Stolen Property could not have been committed under the circumstances of this case, to-wit: The fact that the officers and all of the state's witnesses admitted that the alleged stolen coat had been recovered by the police, that the owner had identified it, that the police checked it and later turned it over to a thief for the purpose of delivery to this defendant.

The trial judge then adjourned court until the following day, stating that there were no guide-lines or guide-posts in this state and that it would take some little time to prepare the instructions. Thus the prepared instruction number two as heretofore recited was given.

In view of said instruction, we are justified in assuming that the trial judge and all parties concerned were in agreement. That under the testimony in the instant case, the coat had lost its character as stolen property when recovered by the police, and the owner apprised of the recovery and identified the coat as the one taken from him.

The general rule evidently adopted by the trial court is stated in 76 C.J.S., Receiving Stolen Goods §5, pg. 7, as follows:

> In order to convict of receiving stolen goods, the goods in question must have retained their stolen character at the time they were received by accused; if they were stolen, they continue to be stolen goods until they are recovered by their owner or some one for him. Hence, where the actual physical possession of stolen goods has been recovered by the owner or his agent and afterwards carried to the receiver either by the original thief or the instrumentality through which the

> thief originally intended to convey it, at the express direction of the owner or his agent, for the purpose of entrapping the receiver, his receiving of the goods is not a receiving of stolen goods.

The law seems to be clear on this point, leaving the only question to be decided as whether or not the defendant could be convicted of an attempt to receive stolen property in such cases. It is the defendant's contention that if he could not be convicted of the substantive charge, because the coat had lost its character as stolen property; neither could he be convicted of an attempt because the coat was not in the category of stolen property at the time he received it.

The briefs filed in the case, and extensive research has revealed that two states have passed squarely on the question—New York and California. It is definitely one of first impression in Oklahoma.

The New York Court, in passing upon the question, laid down the following rule in the case of People v. Jaffe, 185 N.Y. 497, 78 N.E. 169, 6 L.R.A., N.S. 263, on the following facts:

> A clerk stole goods from his employer under an agreement to sell them to accused, but before delivery of the goods the theft was discovered and the goods were recovered. Later the employer redelivered the goods to the clerk to sell to accused, who purchased them for about one-half of their value, believing them to have been stolen.
>
> Held, that the goods had lost their character as stolen goods at the time defendant purchased them, and that his criminal intent was insufficient to sustain a conviction for an attempt to receive stolen property, knowing it to have been stolen.

The Jaffe case, supra, was handed down in 1906, and has prevailed as the law in New York state 58 years without modification.

The State of California has passed upon the question several times and up until 1959, they followed the rule laid down in the Jaffe case, supra.

In 1959, in the case of People v. Comodeca, 52 Cal. 2d 142, 338 P.2d 903, the California Court abandoned the Jaffe rationale that a person accepting goods which he believes to have been stolen, but which was not in fact stolen goods, is not guilty of an attempt to receive stolen goods, and imposed a liability for the attempt, overruling its previous holding to the contrary in the above cited cases. . . .

Though the instant case, insofar as it pertains to the specific crime of attempting to receive stolen property, is one of first impression in Oklahoma, this Court held in Nemecek v. State, 72 Okla. Cr. 195, 114 P.2d 492, 135 A.L.R. 1149, involving attempting to receive money by false pretenses:

> A[n] accused cannot be convicted of an attempt to commit a crime unless he could have been convicted of the crime itself if his attempt had been success-

> ful. Where the act, if accomplished, would not constitute the crime intended, there is no indictable attempt.

In the Nemecek case, supra, the Court quotes with approval In re Schurman, 40 Kan. 533, 20 P. 277; wherein the Kansas Court said:

> With reference to attempt, it has also been said that "if all which the accused person intended would, had it been done, constitute no substantive crime, it cannot be a crime, under the name 'attempt,' to do, with the same purpose, a part of this thing."

. . . The question of "impossibility" was raised for the first time in Regina v. McPherson, Dears. & B. 197, 201 (1857), when Baron Bramwell said:

> The argument that a man putting his hand into an empty pocket might be convicted of an attempt to steal appeared to me at first plausible; but suppose a man, believing a block of wood to be a man who was his deadly enemy, struck it a blow intending to murder, could he be convicted of attempting to murder the man he took it to be?

Subsequently, in Regina v. Collins, 9 Cox C.C. 497, 169 Eng. Rep. 1477 (1864), the Court expressly held that attempted larceny was not made out by proof that the defendant pickpocket actually inserted his hand into the victim's pocket with intent to steal. Chief Justice Cockburn, declaring, at page 499:

> We think that an attempt to commit a felony can only be made out when, if no interruption had taken place, the attempt could have been carried out successfully, and the felony completed of the attempt to commit which the party is charged.

This very broad language, encompassing as it did all forms of "impossibility," was subsequently rejected by the English courts and it was held that the inability of the pickpocket to steal from an empty pocket did not preclude his conviction of an attempted larceny. Regina v. Ring, 17 Cox C.C. 491, 66 L.T. (N.S.) 306 (1892).

In this country it is generally held that a defendant may be charged with an attempt of "physical or factual impossibility," whereas a "legal impossibility" in the completion of the crime precludes prosecution for an attempt.

What is a "legal impossibility" as distinguished from a "physical or factual impossibility" has over a long period of time perplexed our courts and has resulted in many irreconcilable decisions and much philosophical discussion by legal scholars.

The reason for the "impossibility" of completing the substantive crime ordinarily falls into one of two categories: (1) Where the act if completed would not be criminal, a situation which is usually described as a "legal impossibility," and (2) where the basic or substantive crime is impossible of completion, simply because of some physical or factual condition unknown to the defendant, a situation which is usually described as a "factual impossibility."

The authorities in the various states and the text-writers are in general agreement that where there is a "legal impossibility" of completing the substantive crime, the accused cannot be successfully charged with an attempt, whereas in those cases in which the "factual impossibility" situation is involved, the accused may be convicted of an attempt. Detailed discussion of the subject is unnecessary to make it clear that it is frequently most difficult to compartmentalize a particular set of facts as coming within one of the categories rather than the other. Examples of the so-called "legal impossibility" situations are:

(a) A person accepting goods which he believes to have been stolen, but which were not in fact stolen goods, is not guilty of an attempt to receive stolen goods. (People v. Jaffe, 185 N.Y. 497, 78 N.E. 169, 9 L.R.A. N.S. 263).

(b) It is not an attempt to commit subornation of perjury where the false testimony solicited, if given, would have been immaterial to the case at hand and hence not perjurious. (People v. Teal, 196 N.Y. 372, 89 N.E. 1086. 25 L.R.A. N.S. 120).

(c) An accused who offers a bribe to a person believed to be a juror, but who is not a juror, is not guilty of an attempt to bribe a juror. (State v. Taylor, 345 Mo. 325, 133 S.W.2d 336).

(d) An official who contracts a debt which is unauthorized and a nullity, but which he believes to be valid, is not guilty of an attempt to illegally contract a valid debt. (Marley v. State, 58 N.J.L. 207, 33 A. 208).

(e) A hunter who shoots a stuffed deer believing it to be alive is not guilty of an attempt to shoot a deer out of season. (State v. Guffey, 262 S.W.2d 152 (Mo. App.).

Examples of cases in which attempt convictions have been sustained on the theory that all that prevented the consummation of the completed crime was a "factual impossibility" are:

(a) The picking of an empty pocket. (People v. Moran, 123 N.Y. 254, 25 N.E. 412, 10 L.R.A. 109; Commonwealth v. McDonald, 5 Cush. 365 (Mass.); People v. Jones, 46 Mich. 441, 9 N.W. 486).

(b) An attempt to steal from an empty receptacle. (Clark v. State, 86 Tenn. 511, 8 S.W. 145) or an empty house (State v. Utley, 82 N.C. 556).

(c) Where defendant shoots into the intended victim's bed, believing he is there, when in fact he is elsewhere. (State v. Mitchell, 170 Mo. 633, 71 S.W. 175).

(d) Where the defendant erroneously believing that the gun is loaded points it at his wife's head and pulls the trigger. (State v. Damms, 9 Wis. 2d 183, 100 N.W.2d 592, 79 A.L.R.2d 1402).

(e) Where the woman upon whom the abortion operation is performed is not in fact pregnant. (Commonwealth v. Tibbetts, 157 Mass. 519, 32 N.E. 910; People v. Huff, 339 Ill. 328, 171 N.E. 261; and Peckham v. United States, 96 U.S. App. D.C. 312, 266 F.2d 34).

In the case at bar the stolen coat had been recovered by the police for the owner and consequently had, according to the well-established law in this country, lost its character as stolen property. Therefore, a legal impossibility precluded defendant from being prosecuted for the crime of Knowingly Receiving Stolen Property.

It would strain reasoning beyond a logical conclusion to hold contrary to the rule previously stated herein, that,

> If all which the accused person intended would, had it been done, have constituted no substantive crime, it cannot be a crime under the name "attempt" to do, with the same purpose, a part of this thing.

If a series of acts together will not constitute an offense, how can it be said that one of the acts alone will constitute an indictable offense? Bishop Crim. Law §747.

The rule is well stated by the English Court in the case of R. v. Percy, Ltd. 33 Crim. App. R. 102 (1949):

> Steps on the way to the commission of what would be a crime, if the acts were completed, may amount to attempts to commit that crime, to which, unless interrupted, they would have led; but steps on the way to the doing of something, which is thereafter done, and which is no crime, cannot be regarded as attempts to commit a crime.

Sayre, 41 Harvard Law Review 821, 853-854 (1928) states the rationale in this manner:

> It seems clear that cases (where none of the intended consequences is in fact criminal) cannot constitute criminal attempts. If none of the consequences which the defendant sought to achieve constitute a crime, surely his unsuccessful efforts to achieve his object cannot constitute a criminal attempt. The partial fulfillment of an object not criminal cannot itself be criminal. If the whole is not criminal, the part cannot be.

The defendant in the instant case leaves little doubt as to his moral guilt. The evidence, as related by the self-admitted and perpetual law violator indicates defendant fully intended to do the act with which he was charged. However, it is fundamental to our law that a man is not punished merely because he has a criminal mind. It must be shown that he has, with that criminal mind, done an act which is forbidden by the criminal law.

Adhering to this principle, the following example would further illustrate the point.

A fine horse is offered to *A* at a ridiculously low price by *B,* who is a known horse thief. *A,* believing the horse to be stolen, buys the same without inquiry. In fact, the horse had been raised from a colt by *B* and was not stolen. It would be bordering on absurdity to suggest that *A*'s frame of mind, if proven, would support a conviction of an attempt. It would be a "legal impossibility".

Our statute provides that defendant must attempt to *Knowingly* Receive Stolen Property before a conviction will stand. How could one know property to be stolen when it was not? The statute needs to be changed so it would be less favorable to the criminal.

J. C. Smith, a Reader in Law, University of Nottingham, B.A., Cambridge, 1949, LL. B., 1950, M.A., 1954, said in an article (70 Harvard Law Review 422) supporting the *Jaffe* case, supra, and the above reasoning:

> If it appears wrong that the accused should escape unpunished in the particular circumstances, then it may be that there is something wrong with the substantive law and his act ought to be criminal. But the remedy then is to alter the substantive crime. Otherwise "there is no *actus reus* because 'the accident has turned up in his favour' " and the accused ought to be acquitted. When a man has achieved all the consequences which he set out to achieve and those consequences do not, in the existing circumstances, amount to an *actus reus,* it is in accordance both with principle and authority that that man should be held not guilty of any crime.

We earnestly suggest that the Legislature revise the law on Attempts in accordance with The American Law Institute for the adoption of a "Model Penal Code," which Article 5.01 defines "Criminal Attempts" in the following manner.

> (1) *Definition of Attempt.* A person is guilty of an attempt to commit a crime if, acting with the kind of culpability otherwise required for commission of the crime, he:
>
> (a) purposely engages in conduct which would constitute the crime if the attendant circumstances were as he believes them to be; or,
>
> (b) When causing a particular result in an element of the crime, does or omits to do anything with the purpose of causing or with the belief that it will cause such result, without further conduct on his part; or,
>
> (c) purposely does or omits to do anything which, under the circumstances as he believes them to be, is a substantial step in a course of conduct planned to culminate in his commission of the crime.

The Clerk of this Court is requested to send a copy of this decision to the Legislative Council for consideration, as our Court can only adjudicate, it cannot legislate.

In view of our statutory law, and the decisions herein related, it is our duty to Reverse this case, with orders to Dismiss, and it is so ordered. However, there are other avenues open to the County Attorney which should be explored.

JOHNSON, P.J., and BUSSEY, J., concur.

Notes and Questions

1. In *Booth,* did the court appear to be happy with the result it reached? What constrained the court to hold the way it did?

2. Should it make a difference that an attempt to receive stolen property not only did not succeed but, given circumstances unknown to the person receiving the property, could not have succeeded? If one is a true determinist, is there any difference?

3. Carefully review the case summaries cited in the *Booth* opinion to illustrate the purported difference between "legal impossibility" (traditionally a good defense) and "factual impossibility" (traditionally no defense). Can you perceive relevant distinctions between the two groups of cases?

How would you compare the "legal impossibility" and "factual impossibility" cases to that of the classic guilty defendant under conventional attempt law where the "impossibility" issue is never raised—the defendant who shoots his gun at a person intending to kill, but misses because he has pointed the gun in a somewhat wrong direction? How would you distinguish his liability from that of any of the defendants in the "legal impossibility" cases cited by *Booth*?

4. H. L. A. Hart writes in Essays in Jurisprudence and Philosophy (1983): On Attempting the Impossible 388-389:

> When is the law most an ass? Is it an ass when it adopts a narrow conception of a criminal attempt which leads to the acquittal of the pick-pocket in *Collins,* the dishonest clerk in Partington v. Williams, and the would-be handler of stolen goods in Haughton v. Smith? Would it be more of an ass, as Lord Reid thought, if it adopted the wider conception of an attempt embodied in the Intended Steps Model which would lead to a conviction in those cases, but also to the conviction of the would-be murderer who shoots at a corpse believing it to be the living body of his enemy or the would-be thief who takes his own umbrella believing it to be another's?
>
> Two important considerations support the wider conception. The first is that if the punishment of unsuccessful attempts to commit crimes is morally justifiable at all, exactly the same deterrent and retributive justifications are available in the cases of impossibility as in the ordinary cases of attempt. The accused in the impossibility case having done his best to implement his intention to commit a crime is just as much deserving of punishment as the accused in the ordinary case; and the same considerations of general and individual deterrence apply with equal force, whether or not at the relevant time and place the object on which the accused intends to operate exists and has the properties required for the commission of the intended offence.

Secondly, both the narrow conception of an attempt favoured by the House of Lords and the wider conception embodied in the Intended Steps Model have attendant but contrasting disadvantages. If the narrower conception is adopted some "villains" may, as Lord Hailsham said, escape conviction for an attempt; whereas if the wider conception is adopted, this may lead to the conviction of possibly harmless persons like the love-sick girl who tries to kill or disfigure her rival by sticking pins into her wax image. Such persons, entertaining false and possibly superstitious general beliefs about causal laws and physical processes, may often be unlikely to resort to any more dangerous means to accomplish their ends and may be thought harmless. Of these two contrasting disadvantages the second seems to me the less serious and the most amenable to rational legal control. For reasonable provision can be made for such harmless offenders by the exercise of judicial discretion at the sentencing stage, when there will be an opportunity to investigate and assess both the firmness of their intention to harm and the likelihood of their resorting to dangerous means.

By contrast the only consideration that mitigates the disadvantage of the narrower conception is the possibility that the accused in the impossibility cases, who will be acquitted of an attempt, may be convicted of some other offence. But to rely on that is to rely on something entirely haphazard. In many cases there will be no other available charge and even when other charges are available they may be for minor offences not matching the seriousness of the attempts. In any case to rely on the possibility of bringing other charges is to take far too optimistic a view of the resourcefulness of our prosecuting authorities, who in Haughton v. Smith failed to see that the accused who was acquitted could with his accomplices certainly have been convicted of theft and conspiracy to handle stolen goods and possibly of other offences.

Against these two considerations supporting the wider conception, the only support for the narrower conception consists of a highly selective appeal to the alleged intuitions of "common sense" uncorrupted by any consideration of reasonable social aims or penal policy, as if we can just see without thinking that it is "absurd" to convict a would-be thief who takes his own umbrella (however many he has stolen in the past and is likely to steal in the future) and "asinine" to convict the would-be murderer who mistakes a corpse for a living body, however likely he is to get his victim next time. The capricious as well as the unreliable nature of this appeal to "common sense" is made painfully obvious when we are told by judges that the ordinary man's view, that a would-be pickpocket who puts his hand into an empty pocket has attempted to steal, must be rejected because the ordinary man "has not stopped to think." [On Attempting the Impossible at 388-389.]

5. What about the person who attempts to kill using a voodoo doll? Since we regard this attempt as utterly without danger to the purported victim, should we say that the defendant is not guilty? After all, it is in no way dangerous to the purported victim to shoot at a tree trunk which one mistakes for him. Or is the argument that shooting will be dangerous the next time, whereas voodoo will not? On the other hand, how do we know that the attempted voodoo killer will not come around to our way of thinking and look for more efficacious means of accomplishing his or her end?

6. How should we handle the case of the person who attempts to vote, thinking that she is below the appropriate age of 18? In fact, due to a mixup on her birth certificate, she is in fact 19 years old. Is this like the voodoo case? A routine analysis based on factual impossibility grounds would hold her liable because she thought she was committing a crime and, but for the fact that her age was greater than she thought, would have committed it. On the other hand, if the attempt law is based on some degree of social dangerousness—the view that next time the actor will get it right—we know that she will never be below 18 again. Should it make a difference that, based on her actions, we now can conjecture that, should the law raise the voting age to 21, she then would be likely to violate it?

7. The Comments to Model Penal Code Section 5.05 provide:

> 3. *Mitigation.* Any grading system must be based on general evaluations that will not always hold true. Under the Model Code's sentencing system, including its provision for extended terms, there hardly will be need for a corrective mechanism to attain increased severity. A need within this area for a special mitigating mechanism may, however, be perceived. Subsection (2) is designed to meet that problem.
>
> Section 6.12 meets the need for mitigation in general by authorizing the court, when it is of the view that it would be unduly harsh to sentence an offender in accordance with the Code, to enter a judgment of conviction for a lesser degree of felony or for a misdemeanor and to impose sentence accordingly.
>
> The provision has a special relevancy to convictions for inchoate crimes in view of the infinite degrees of danger that attempt, solicitation or conspiracy actually may entail, a variation that the Draft may well increase by its elimination of impossibility as a defense. Section 5.05(2) accordingly directs the court to exercise its power under Section 6.11 if "the particular conduct charged to constitute a criminal attempt, solicitation or conspiracy is so inherently unlikely to result or culminate in the commission of a crime that neither such conduct nor the actor presents a danger warranting the grading of such offense under this Section." If only to dispel such typical objections to broad definitions of inchoate crime as that efforts to kill by incantation are made criminal, the court's power is extended beyond that conferred by Section 6.11; in "extreme cases" it is authorized to "dismiss the prosecution."
>
> It has been argued in objection to this formulation that the court is called upon to make a legislative judgment. We think, with deference, that the judgments demanded by the section are sufficiently subordinate to declared legislative purpose to fall properly within the competence and function of the courts.

8. What about the case where the professor is sitting in the Faculty Club having lunch when it starts raining? He has to go back to class and, rather than getting wet, decides that he will steal from the cloakroom a particularly attractive umbrella. He muses that he has one of the same type at home and that it will keep him very dry and not turn inside-out in the heavy wind. What he does not know is that he left that very umbrella there a week ago when the

rain, which had been falling on his way to have lunch, suddenly stopped. He marches out with the umbrella and, in an excess of guilt, confesses what he regards as his theft to the nearest police officer. Should he be deemed guilty of an attempt? Would he be guilty under the Model Penal Code? Does your answer reveal a defect in the drafting of the Model Penal Code?

9. Professor Glanville Williams in Textbook of Criminal Law 409 (2d ed. 1983) ties the British decision in the Criminal Attempts Act to punish impossible attempts to the view that recklessness as to circumstances is not a sufficient basis for attempt liability:

> The Act for the first time made "impossible attempts" punishable, and the Government thought that it would be going too far to provide for the punishment of attempts that were both impossible and reckless. For example, suppose that a man tries to have sexual intercourse with a woman with her consent. Rape is out of the question on such facts. But suppose that although the woman consents, the man does not know it for sure, and is reckless as to whether she is consenting. If one can commit a reckless impossible attempt, such a man would be guilty of attempted rape!
>
> Because of this type of problem (unlikely as such facts may appear), the Government decided that it had to choose between punishing reckless attempts and impossible attempts, and plumped for the latter.

How does Professor Williams' hypothetical differ from that set out by the court as "bordering on absurdity" on page 562?

PEOPLE v. DLUGASH

Court of Appeals of New York
41 N.Y.2d 725, 363 N.E.2d 1155 (1977)

JASEN, Judge.

The criminal law is of ancient origin, but criminal liability for attempt to commit a crime is comparatively recent. At the root of the concept of attempt liability are the very aims and purposes of penal law. The ultimate issue is whether an individual's intentions and actions, though failing to achieve a manifest and malevolent criminal purpose, constitute a danger to organized society of sufficient magnitude to warrant the imposition of criminal sanctions. Difficulties in theoretical analysis and concomitant debate over very pragmatic questions of blameworthiness appear dramatically in reference to situations where the criminal attempt failed to achieve its purpose solely because the factual or legal context in which the individual acted was not as the actor supposed them to be. Phrased somewhat differently, the concern centers on whether an individual should be liable for an attempt to commit a crime when, unknown to him, it was impossible to successfully complete the crime attempted. For years, serious studies have been made on the subject in an effort to resolve the continuing controversy when, if at all, the impossibility of successfully completing the criminal act should preclude liability for even making the futile attempt. The 1967 revision of the Penal law approached the impossibility defense to the inchoate crime of attempt in a novel fashion. The statute provides that, if a person engages in conduct which would otherwise constitute an attempt to commit a crime, "it is no defense to a prosecution for such attempt that the crime charged to have been attempted was, under the attendant circumstances, factually or legally impossible of commission, if such crime could have been committed had the attendant circumstances been as such person believed them to be." (Penal Law, §110.10.) This appeal presents to us, for the first time, a case involving the application of the modern statute. We hold that, under the proof presented by the People at trial, defendant Melvin Dlugash may be held for attempted murder, though the target of the attempt may have already been slain, by the hand of another, when Dlugash made his felonious attempt.

On December 22, 1973, Michael Geller, 25 years old, was found shot to death in the bedroom of his Brooklyn apartment. The body, which had literally been riddled by bullets, was found lying face up on the floor. An autopsy revealed that the victim had been shot in the face and head no less than seven times. Powder burns on the face indicated that the shots had been fired from within one foot of the victim. Four small caliber bullets were recovered from the victim's skull. The victim had also been critically wounded in the chest. One heavy caliber bullet passed through the left lung, penetrated the heart chamber, pierced the left ventricle of the heart upon entrance and again upon exit, and lodged in the victim's torso. Although a second bullet was damaged beyond identification, the bullet tracks indicated that these wounds were also inflicted by a bullet of heavy caliber. A tenth bullet, of unknown caliber, passed through the thumb of the victim's left hand. The autopsy report listed the cause of death as "[m]ultiple bullet wounds of head and chest with brain injury and massive bilateral hemothorax with penetration of [the] heart." Subsequent ballistics examination established that the four bullets recovered from the victim's head were .25 caliber bullets and that the heart-piercing bullet was of .38 caliber.

Detective Joseph Carrasquillo of the New York City Police Department was assigned to investigate the homicide. On December 27, 1973, five days after the discovery of the body, Detective Carrasquillo and a fellow officer went to the defendant's residence in an effort to locate him. The officers arrived at approximately 6:00 P.M. The defendant answered the door and, when informed that the officers were investigating the death of Michael Geller, a friend of his, defendant invited the officers into the house. Detective Carrasquillo informed defendant that the officers desired any information defendant might have regarding the death of Geller and, since defendant was regarded as a suspect, administered the standard preinterrogation warnings. The defendant told the officers that he and another friend, Joe Bush, had just returned from a four- or five-day trip "upstate someplace" and learned of Geller's death only upon his return. Since Bush was also a suspect in the case and defendant admitted knowing Bush, defendant agreed to accompany the officers to the station house for the purposes of identifying photographs of Bush and of lending assistance to the investigation. Upon arrival at the police station, Detective Carrasquillo and the defendant went directly into an interview room. Carrasquillo advised the defendant that he had witnesses and information to the effect that as late as 7:00 P.M. on the day before the body was found, defendant had been observed carrying a .25 caliber pistol. Once again, Carrasquillo administered the standard preinterrogation statement of rights. The defendant then proceeded to relate his version of the events which culminated in the death of Geller. Defendant stated that, on the night of December 21, 1973, he, Bush and Geller had been out drinking. Bush had been staying at Geller's apartment and, during the course of the evening, Geller several times demanded that Bush pay $100 towards the rent on the apartment. According to defendant, Bush rejected these demands, telling Geller that "you better shut up or you're going to get a bullet." All three returned to Geller's apartment at approximately midnight, took seats in the bedroom, and continued to drink until sometime between 3:00 and 3:30 in the morning. When Geller again pressed his demand for rent money, Bush drew his .38 caliber pistol, aimed it at Geller and fired three times. Geller fell to the floor. After the passage of a few minutes, perhaps two, perhaps as much as five, defendant walked over to the fallen Geller, drew his .25 caliber pistol, and fired approximately five shots in the victim's head and face. Defendant contended that, by the time he fired the shots, "it looked like Mike Geller was already dead." After the shots were fired, defendant and Bush walked to the apartment of a female acquaintance. Bush removed his shirt, wrapped the two guns and a knife in it, and left the apartment, telling Dlugash that he intended to dispose of the weapons. Bush returned 10 or 15 minutes later and stated that he had thrown the weapons down a sewer two or three blocks away.

After Carrasquillo had taken the bulk of the statement, he asked the defendant why he would do such a thing. According to Carrasquillo, the defendant said, "gee, I really don't know." Carrasquillo repeated the question 10 minutes later, but received the same response. After a while, Carrasquillo asked the question for a third time and defendant replied, "well, gee, I guess it must have been because I was afraid of Joe Bush."

At approximately 9:00 P.M., the defendant repeated the substance of his statement to an Assistant District Attorney. Defendant added that at the time he shot at Geller, Geller was not moving and his eyes were closed. While he did not check for a pulse, defendant stated that Geller had not been doing anything to him at the time he shot because "Mike was dead."

Defendant was indicted by the Grand Jury of Kings County on a single count of murder in that, acting in concert with another person actually present, he intentionally caused the death of Michael Geller. At the trial, there were four principal prosecution witnesses: Detective Carrasquillo, the Assistant District Attorney who took the second admission, and two physicians from the office of the New York City Chief Medical Examiner. For proof of defendant's culpability, the prosecution relied upon defendant's own admissions as related by the detective and the prosecutor. From the physicians, the prosecution sought to establish that Geller was still alive at the time defendant shot at him. Both physicians testified that each of the two chest wounds, for which defendant alleged Bush to be responsible, would have caused death without prompt medical attention. Moreover, the victim would have remained alive until such time as his chest cavity became fully filled with blood. Depending on the circumstances, it might take 5 to 10 minutes for the chest cavity to fill. Neither prosecution witness could state, with medical certainty, that the victim was still alive when, perhaps five minutes after the initial chest wounds were inflicted, the defendant fired at the victim's head.

The defense produced but a single witness, the former Chief Medical Examiner of New York City. This expert stated that, in his view, Geller might have died of the chest wounds "very rapidly" since, in addition to the bleeding, a large bullet going through a lung and the heart would have other adverse medical effects. "Those wounds can be almost immediately or rapidly fatal or they may be delayed in there, in the time it would take for death to occur. But I would say that wounds like that which are described here as having gone through the lungs and the heart would be fatal wounds and in most cases they're rapidly fatal."

The jury found the defendant guilty of murder. The defendant then moved to set the verdict aside. He submitted an affidavit in which he contended that he "was absolutely, unequivocally and positively certain that Michael Geller was dead before [he] shot him." This motion was denied.[16]

On appeal, the Appellate Division reversed the judgment of conviction on the law and dismissed the indictment. The court ruled that "the People failed to prove beyond a reasonable doubt that Geller had been alive at the time he was shot by defendant; defendant's conviction of murder thus cannot stand." Further, the court held that the judgment could not be modified to reflect a conviction for attempted murder because "the uncontradicted evidence is that the defendant, at the time that he fired the five shots into the body of the decedent, believed him to be dead, and . . . there is not a scintilla of evidence to contradict his assertion in that regard."

Preliminarily, we state our agreement with the Appellate Division that

16. It should be noted that Joe Bush pleaded guilty to a charge of manslaughter in the first degree. At the time he entered his plea, Bush detailed his version of the homicide. According to Bush, defendant Dlugash was a dealer in narcotic drugs and Dlugash claimed that Geller owed him a large sum of money from drug purchases. Bush was in the kitchen alone when Geller entered and threatened him with a shotgun. Bush pulled out his .38 caliber pistol and fired five times at Geller. Geller slumped to the floor. Dlugash then entered, withdrew his .25 caliber pistol and fired five shots into the deceased's face. Bush, however, never testified at Dlugash's trial.

the evidence did not establish, beyond a reasonable doubt, that Geller was alive at the time defendant fired into his body. To sustain a homicide conviction, it must be established, beyond a reasonable doubt, that the defendant caused the death of another person.

While the defendant admitted firing five shots at the victim approximately two to five minutes after Bush had fired three times, all three medical expert witnesses testified that they could not, with any degree of medical certainty, state whether the victim had been alive at the time the latter shots were fired by the defendant. Thus, the People failed to prove beyond a reasonable doubt that the victim had been alive at the time he was shot by the defendant. Whatever else it may be, it is not murder to shoot a dead body.

The distinction between "factual" and "legal" impossibility is a nice one indeed and the courts tend to place a greater value on legal form than on any substantive danger the defendant's actions pose for society. The approach of the draftsmen of the Model Penal Code was to eliminate the defense of impossibility in virtually all situations. Under the code provision, to constitute an attempt, it is still necessary that the result intended or desired by the actor constitute a crime. However, the code suggested a fundamental change to shift the locus of analysis to the actor's mental frame of reference and away from undue dependence upon external considerations. The basic premise of the code provision is that what was in the actor's own mind should be the standard for determining his dangerousness to society and, hence, his liability for attempted criminal conduct.

In the belief that neither of the two branches of the traditional impossibility arguments detracts from the offender's moral culpability, the Legislature substantially carried the code's treatment of impossibility into the 1967 revision of the Penal Law. Thus, a person is guilty of an attempt when, with intent to commit a crime, he engages in conduct which tends to effect the commission of such crime. (Penal Law, §110.10.) Thus, if defendant believed the victim to be alive at the time of the shooting, it is no defense to the charge of attempted murder that the victim may have been dead.

Turning to the facts of the case before us, we believe that there is sufficient evidence in the record from which the jury could conclude that the defendant believed Geller to be alive at the time defendant fired shots into Geller's head. Defendant admitted firing five shots at a most vital part of the victim's anatomy from virtually point blank range. Although defendant contended that the victim had already been grievously wounded by another, from the defendant's admitted actions, the jury could conclude that the defendant's purpose and intention was to administer the coup de grace.

Defendant argues that the jury was bound to accept, at face value, the indications in his admissions that he believed Geller dead. Certainly, it is true that the defendant was entitled to have the entirety of the admissions, both the inculpatory and the exculpatory portions, placed in evidence before the trier of facts.

However, the jury was not required to automatically credit the exculpatory portions of the admissions. The general rule is, of course, that the credibility of witnesses is a question of fact and the jury may choose to believe some, but not all, of a witness' testimony.

In this case, there is ample other evidence to contradict the defendant's assertion that he believed Geller dead. There were five bullet wounds inflicted with stunning accuracy in a vital part of the victim's anatomy. The medical testimony indicated that Geller may have been alive at the time defendant fired at him. The defendant voluntarily left the jurisdiction immediately after the crime with his coperpetrator. Defendant did not report the crime to the police when left on his own by Bush. Instead, he attempted to conceal his and Bush's involvement with the homicide. In addition, the other portions of defendant's admissions make his contended belief that Geller was dead extremely improbable. Defendant, without a word of instruction from Bush, voluntarily got up from his seat after the passage of just a few minutes and fired five times point blank into the victim's face, snuffing out any remaining chance of life that Geller possessed. Certainly, this alone indicates a callous indifference to the taking of a human life. His admissions are barren of any claim of duress[17] and reflect, instead, an unstinting co-operation in efforts to dispose of vital incriminating evidence. Indeed, defendant maintained a false version of the occurrence until such time as the police informed him that they had evidence that he lately possessed a gun of the same caliber as one of the weapons involved in the shooting. From all of this, the jury was certainly warranted in concluding that the defendant acted in the belief that Geller was yet alive when shot by defendant.

The jury convicted the defendant of murder. Necessarily, they found that defendant intended to kill a live human being. Subsumed within this finding is the conclusion that defendant acted in the belief that Geller was alive. Thus, there is no need for additional fact findings by a jury. Although it was not established beyond a reasonable doubt that Geller was, in fact, alive, such is no defense to attempted murder since a murder would have been committed "had the attendant circumstances been as [defendant] believed them to be." (Penal Law, §110.10.) The jury necessarily found that defendant believed Geller to be alive when defendant shot at him.

The Appellate Division erred in not modifying the judgment to reflect a conviction for the lesser included offense of attempted murder. An attempt to commit a murder is a lesser included offense of murder and the Appellate Division has the authority, where the trial evidence is not legally sufficient to establish the offense of which the defendant was convicted, to modify the judgment to one of conviction for a lesser included offense which is legally

17. Notwithstanding the Appellate Division's implication to the contrary, the record indicates that defendant told the Assistant District Attorney that Bush, after shooting Geller, kept his gun aimed at Geller, and not at Dlugash. As defendant stated, "this was after Joe had his .38 on him, I started shooting on him."

established by the evidence. Thus, the Appellate Division, by dismissing the indictment, failed to take the appropriate corrective action. . . .

Notes and Questions

1. The court takes the view that in convicting the defendant of murder the jury "necessarily . . . found that the defendant intended to kill a live human being." Is that, in fact, true? Examine the New York murder statute on page 293. If it is not true, does this change the result in the case at all? What additional questions of law would we have to answer before we could know?

2. Consider the following "impossible attempt" case. Sally plans to divorce Fred, and then to still claim him as a tax exemption. That would be criminal fraud. She files the divorce papers in February and, thinking the divorce is final in 30 days under state law, files the tax exemption in April (assume you can only claim an exemption for a person who is your spouse at the time you file for the exemption). But Sally has misread the divorce laws, which state that a divorce takes place 120 days after the papers are filed.

Under common law, what kind of "impossibility" is this? Under the revised view of "impossibility" in the Model Penal Code, would Sally be guilty?

In regard to the particular mistake Sally made here, what comparison could you draw to the exculpatory "mistake" cases in Chapter 4 on *mens rea*? What pattern do you see?

3. Now consider another kind of impossible attempt. Ed Emigrant has just moved to Minnesota. He is under the misimpression that the Minnesota Criminal Code contains what he conceives to be a "mopery" law, which, in his view, makes it a misdemeanor to act in a depressed or discouraged fashion on a public highway. Ed wants to engage in an act of civil disobedience in Minnesota, so he purposefully enters a public highway and "mopes."

Is Ed guilty of a crime? What crime? What should his punishment be? This kind of "imaginary crime" is rarely committed—or rather it rarely comes to our attention. Why should the person who commits an imaginary crime be less guilty than the person who "steals" his own umbrella, or someone who "kills" a dead person?

4. As an exercise in the many combinations of the law, the facts, and one's idea of the law and the facts, take the case where Congress has forbidden the delivery of obscene materials to someone under the age of 18. Let us then examine the possible situations with respect to the defendant's knowledge and belief. Assume that in all cases the defendant deliverer knows that the material is obscene.

a) First, with respect to the law, let us assume the deliverer knows that the age specified in the statute is 18. Then the possible combinations of his or her (let us say reasonable) belief in the age of the recipient and the actual age of the recipient can be represented by a box with four cells.

Defendant believes age of recipient is	Age of recipient in fact is: 17	Age of recipient in fact is: 19
17	G.	F.I.
19	N.G.	N.G.

Thus, in the upper lefthand corner where the defendant believes the age of the recipient is 17 and the age of the recipient is in fact 17; the defendant is simply guilty of the offense and the box raises no interesting issue. In the lower lefthand corner, where the defendant thinks the recipient is 19 but he or she in fact is 17, the defendant has made a mistake of fact which prevents him or her from having the *mens rea* required for the crime; hence under our traditional rules the defendant will be not guilty. In the upper righthand corner of the box, where the defendant believes the recipient to be 17 but the recipient is in fact 19, we have our classic factually impossible attempt, and since factual impossibility is generally not regarded as a defense, the defendant would be guilty of attempt. And finally, in the lower righthand corner, the defendant, who thinks that the recipient is 19 years old when the recipient is in fact 19 years old, has not committed any crime and has behaved in a perfectly law-abiding way—thus, the box is not interesting.

b) Now, let us assume that the defendant thinks (wrongly) that the law proscribes delivery of the materials (which he or she knows to be obscene) to anyone over the age of 16. Can you fill in the boxes in such a case?

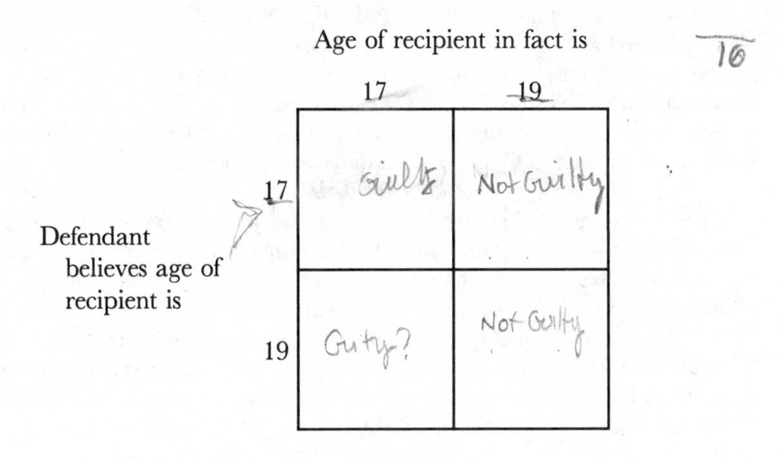

c) Now assume that the defendant believes (again wrongly) that the law makes criminal the delivery of the obscene material to someone under the age of 21.

Defendant believes age of recipient is	Age of recipient in fact is: 17	19
17		
19		

Does the lower lefthand corner of this box reveal an issue that you have not thought of? How should the lower lefthand box be filled in? Do you note anything interesting in comparing the boxes?

How does the following case, Regina v. Taaffe, [1984] 1 A.C. 539, fit into the boxes?

> Before Lord Fraser of Tullybelton, Lord Scarman, Lord Roskill, Lord Bridge of Harwich and Lord Brightman [speeches delivered March 1, 1984].
>
> Where the defendant had mistakenly believed that he was bringing currency into the country and that such importation was prohibited, but had in fact been bringing in cannibis resin the importation of which was prohibited, he was not guilty of an offence under section 170(2) of the Customs and Excise Management Act 1979, of being "knowingly concerned in any fraudulent evasion . . . (b) of any prohibition . . . in force with respect to the goods. . . ."
>
> The House of Lords dismissed an appeal by the Crown from the Court of Appeal (Criminal Division) (Lord Lane, Lord Chief Justice, Mr. Justice McCowan and Mr. Justice Nolan) (The Times, April 16, 1983; [1983] 1 WLR 627) who had allowed an appeal by the defendant, Paul Desmond Patrick Taaffe, from his conviction in the Gravesend Crown Court on November 11, 1982.
>
> On February 12, 1982, the defendant drove a car into the green lane of the Sheerness ferry terminal and said that he had nothing to declare. The car was searched, and in the spare tyre were found five packages containing cannabis resin. The defendant was then searched, and a further three packages were found strapped to his back and under his clothing.
>
> He was cautioned by the customs officer and asked if he knew what the substances in the packages were. He replied: "No, I am waiting to find out, because if it is drugs. . . . " The officer asked him: "What did you think was in the packages?" and he replied: "Money."

On his arraignment at the crown court, he pleaded not guilty. The recorder heard argument on the question whether on agreed facts a defence was afforded.

Those facts were: (a) the defendant had been enlisted by a third party in Holland to import a substance into England in fraudulent evasion of the prohibition on its importation and had so imported it; (b) the substance had in fact been cannabis; (c) the defendant had mistakenly believed it to be currency; (d) currency had not been the subject of any prohibition; (e) the defendant mistakenly believed it was. . . .

The question certified by the Court of Appeal was whether a defendant committed the offence under section 170(2) where he (a) imported prohibited drugs into the United Kingdom, (b) intended to fraudulently evade a prohibition on importation, but (c) mistakenly believed the goods to be money and not drugs and (d) mistakenly believed that money was the subject of a prohibition. . . .

Lord Scarman said that the Lord Chief Justice had construed section 170(2) as creating an offence not of absolute liability but as one of which an essential ingredient was a guilty mind.

To be "knowingly concerned" meant, in his judgment, knowledge not only of the existence of a smuggling operation but also that the substance being smuggled into the country was one the importation of which was prohibited by statute.

The respondent had thought that he was concerned in a smuggling operation but had believed that the substance was currency. The importation of currency was not subject to any prohibition.

The Lord Chief Justice had concluded: "He is to be judged against the fact that he believed them to be. Had this indeed been currency and not cannabis, no offence would have been committed. Does it make any difference that the [respondent] thought wrongly that by clandestinely importing currency he was committing an offence?

The Crown had submitted that it did. The court had rejected the submission: the respondent's mistake of law could not convert the importation of currency into a criminal offence: and that importing currency was what is had to be assumed that the respondent had believed he was doing.

His Lordship found the reasoning of the Lord Chief Justice compelling. He agreed with his construction of section 170(2): and the principle that a man must be judged on the facts as he believed them to be was an accepted principle of the criminal law when the state of a man's mind and his knowledge were ingredients of the offence with which he was charged.

Would it make a difference if smuggling money into England had been a crime?

10

COMPLICITY

A. INTRODUCTION

Traditionally, the common law distinguished among parties to a crime, classifying some as "principals" and others as "accessories." Each of these categories, moreover, was subdivided. A principal in the first degree was the actor or actual perpetrator of the criminal act at the scene of the crime. A principal in the second degree was a person who was "present" at the commission of a felony and provided assistance or encouragement to (aided and abetted) the principal in the first degree in the commission of the felony. A principal in the second degree did not actually commit the felony and his or her "presence" could be constructive instead of actual. Thus, someone who acted as a lookout or kept guard, even at some distance from the scene of the crime, could be convicted as a principal in the second degree.[1]

This concept of presence—actual or constructive—distinguished principals from accessories. An accessory before the fact was someone who commanded, counseled, encouraged, or aided the principal in the first degree in commiting the felony, but who was not actually or constructively present at the scene of the crime. An example would be a person whose only role in the crime was to give the principal a weapon sometime before the crime occurred. By contrast, an accessory after the fact played no role in the preparation or commission of the crime, but rather assisted the felon in eluding capture or destroying evidence. Such assistance had to be an intentional, positive act, rather than a mere failure to notify the authorities.[2]

1. Originally, a principal in the second degree was known as an "accessory at the fact."
2. Accessories after the fact were recognized only in felonies. In treason, all four categories were treated as principals; and in misdemeanors all except the accessory after the fact were treated as principals and the accessory after the fact was not punishable.

These distinctions resulted in the development of a complex system of rules addressing jurisdiction, pleading, trial, and degree of guilt. Most important was the procedural rule that an accessory could not be tried or convicted before the conviction of the principal in the first degree. This rule prevented trial of an accessory if the principal escaped conviction for any reason, including failure to be identified, escape, death, or acquittal.[3] Other rules included a requirement that a party to a crime be tried in the jurisdiction where the aid occurred,[4] and that a person charged as one type of party could not be convicted as another. This last rule was one device used by judges to reduce the number of executions, since, at early common law, all felonies were punishable by death.

Modern statutes have largely eliminated the common law procedural rules and distinctions.[5] Except for the accessory after the fact, all parties to the crime face prosecution for the substantive crime itself, and thus face the same punishment or range of punishments. For example, the federal statute, 18 U.S.C. §22 provides that:

> (a) Whoever commits an offense against the United States or aids, abets, counsels, commands, induces, or procures its commission, is punishable as a principal.
> (b) Whoever willfully causes an act to be done which if directly performed by him or another would be an offense against the United States, is punishable as a principal.

The Model Penal Code (§2.06) has also eliminated the common law distinctions. Accessories after the fact, however, still generally receive lesser punishment than other participants. See, e.g., Va. Code §18.2-19 ("In the case of every felony, every accessory after the fact shall be guilty of a Class 1 misdemeanor. . . .

Generally, accessories can now be convicted regardless of whether the principal is convicted, tried, or even apprehended, although, of course, the state must prove that the acts constituting the crime occurred. The prosecution need not charge a particular type of complicity in order to convict an accomplice, and the jurisdictional complexities have largely vanished.

Nevertheless, as the following materials make clear, we have hardly dispensed with the concept of "aiding and abetting" or "accomplice liability."

The one type of accomplice recognized at common law who obviously

3. At least four states, Maryland, North Carolina, Rhode Island and Tennessee, retain the common law rule where the principal is acquitted of the crime.

4. This rule reduces convictions, since ancient law did not allow the indictment of an accessory if the accessory's actions occurred in one county and the underlying felony took place in another. This limitation was later changed by statute.

5. But see Va. Code §18.2-18, which still retains the terminology of principals and accessories.

played no causal role in the principal's crime was the so-called accessory after the fact, whose offense at common law was often called "misprision of felony."

The origin of the crime is described in Note, 8 U. of Chi. L. Rev. 338 (1940):

> [M]isprision of felony, as defined by Blackstone, is merely one phase of the system of communal responsibility for the apprehension of criminals which received its original impetus from William I, under pressure of the need to protect the invading Normans in hostile country, and which endured up to the Seventeenth Century in England. In order to secure vigilant prosecution of criminal conduct, the vill or hundred in which such conduct occurred was subject to fine, as was the tithing to which the criminal belonged, and every person who knew of the felony and failed to make report thereof was subject to punishment for misprision of felony. Compulsory membership in the tithing group, the obligation to pursue criminals when hue and cry was raised, broad powers of the private arrest, and the periodic visitations of the General Eyre for the purpose of penalizing laxity in regard to crime, are all suggestive of the administrative background against which misprision of felony developed. With the appearance of specialized and paid law enforcement officers, such as constables and justices of the peace in the Seventeenth Century, there was a movement away from strict communal responsibility, and a growing tendency to rely on professional police.

Misprision was essentially defined as the nondisclosure or concealment of a known felony, and did not require any affirmative act by the defendant to aid the principal. Some common law jurisdictions required proof that the person affirmatively concealed the crime. Others made passive concealment a misdemeanor under the misprision statute, but made "active concealers," like true accomplices, guilty of the same crime as the principal.

The United States Code still contains a misprision law, 18 U.S.C. §4:

> Whoever having knowledge of the actual commission of a felony cognizable by a court of the United States, conceals and does not as soon as possible make known the same to some judge or other person in civil or military authority under the United States, shall be fined not more than $500 or imprisoned not more than three years, or both.

Most courts, however, have interpreted the statute to punish only affirmative conduct to conceal the crime or principal from the government. See, e.g., United States v. Davila, 648 F.2d 715 (5th Cir. 1983).

Even in jurisdictions that have eliminated the crime of misprision or accessory after the fact, a person who takes some active steps to prevent the arrest or prosecution of a criminal may face liability under modern statutory charges. See, e.g., Model Penal Code §242.3 (hindering apprehension or prosecution by harboring criminal, providing means of escape, destroying evidence or tampering with witnesses, volunteering false information to the police); §242.4 (aiding consummation of a crime by safeguarding proceeds or converting them into negotiable funds); §242.5 (compounding of a crime by accepting money in exchange for refraining from reporting crime to authorities).

B. THE ACCESSORIAL ACT

PACE v. STATE

Supreme Court of Indiana
248 Ind. 146, 224 N.E.2d 312 (1967)

HUNTER, Judge.

This is an appeal from a jury finding and judgment of conviction of the defendant of the crime of accessory before the fact of robbery by placing in fear.

Viewing the evidence most favorable to the State, the record shows the following: appellant, his wife and two infant children were in a car driving from South Bend to LaPorte. Eugene Rootes was riding with them. The appellant was driving with his wife and one child in the front seat. Rootes and appellant's other child were in the back seat. While in South Bend, appellant after asking his wife for permission stopped to pick up a hitchhiker, Mr. Reppert, who sat next to Rootes in the back seat with one of appellant's infant children. Later Rootes pulled a knife and took Reppert's wallet. After driving further, Reppert got out of the car, Rootes then took his watch. The appellant said nothing during the entire period and they continued driving to LaPorte. This is all of the evidence presented by the record which would have any bearing on the crime charged, i.e., accessory before the fact of robbery by placing in fear.

The main question presented in the facts at bar is what evidence beyond the mere presence of a person at the scene of a crime is sufficient to sustain a conviction as an accessory before the fact? This court has previously stated that negative acquiescence is not enough to constitute a person guilty of aiding and abetting the commission of a crime. Mattingly v. State (1952), 230 Ind. 431, 104 N.E.2d 721. Consequently, this court has always looked for affirmative conduct either in the form of acts or words from which reasonable inferences of a common design or purpose to effect the commission of a crime might be drawn. However, it has been further stated by this court in Mobley v. State (1949), 227 Ind. 335, 344, 85 N.E.2d 489, 492:

> [I]n the absence of anything in his conduct showing a design to encourage, incite, aid, abet or assist in the crime, the trier of the facts may consider failure of such person to oppose the commission of the crime in connection with other circumstances and conclude therefrom that he assented to the commission of the crime, lent his countenance and approval thereto and thereby aided and abetted it.

In the facts at bar we have found no evidence or reasonable inferences therefrom which might demonstrate that the appellant aided and abetted in the alleged crime. While he was driving the car, nothing was said, nor did he act in any manner to indicate his approval or countenance of the robbery. While there is evidence from which a jury might reasonably infer that he knew the crime was being committed, his situation was not one which would demonstrate a duty to oppose it. We do not intend to draw any hard and fast rules in this area of the law. Each case must be reviewed on its own facts; in so doing we hold that the verdict is not sustained by substantial evidence of probative value and is therefore contrary to law.

Judgment reversed.

Notes and Questions

1. The court in *Pace,* citing a generally accepted principle, says that the defendant's "mere presence" was not enough to make him guilty as an aider or abettor of Rootes's crime. Why? What if Pace wanted Rootes to rob Reppert? Once the *mens rea* question is settled, should we care about whether Pace did anything to help Rootes? What if Rootes had only performed the crime because he felt sure that Pace would help him in robbing Reppert if Reppert resisted? Does the treatment of omission liability in Chapter 2 bear on this question? Why does the court say that Pace had no duty to oppose Rootes?

2. If mere presence is not enough, how much affirmative behavior must the state prove? What if, before picking up Reppert, Pace had assured Rootes that he would help Rootes rob Reppert if necessary, but the help proved unnecessary? What if Pace had known Rootes would assault a hitchhiker, but decided to pick up a hitchhiker anyway because he thought hitchhikers deserved what they got?

3. Is it of any relevance that Pace asked his wife for permission to pick up the hitchhiker?

4. Is the following case, Murray v. Commonwealth, 210 Va. 282, 170 S.E.2d 3 (1969), compatible with *Pace*?

> On January 1, 1968 Thomas Grace accosted Adolphus Coltes, knocked him down and stole his wallet. Defendant John Murray, who was with Grace before, during and after that incident, stands convicted of robbing Coltes as a principal in the second degree. The only issue on this appeal is whether the evidence adduced at Murray's trial supports his conviction. . . .
>
> On the morning of January 1, 1968, Murray and Grace were together in the parking lot in the 800 block of West Grace Street in Richmond. They were observed drinking together and attempting to open the doors of vehicles parked in the area.
>
> Shortly before noon, Murray and Grace saw Coltes walking west on Grace Street. When they approached Coltes, Grace tapped him on the shoulder and asked for the loan of a dollar.

A Commonwealth witness, who was standing on a porch across the street, saw Coltes remove his wallet from his pocket. He noticed that Grace was on Coltes's left and Murray on his right—"they were standing real close." A woman who was also standing on the porch said "Watch." Grace then struck Coltes, knocked him down and picked up his wallet. Grace put Coltes's wallet in his pocket, and he and Murray ran away.

The witness who had observed the incident chased Grace and Murray, but he gave up the chase after Grace threw a brickbat at him. Grace and Murray ran into an abandoned building where they were subsequently arrested.

A person cannot be convicted as a principal in the second degree—that is, as an aider or abettor—upon evidence that he was merely present during the commission of a crime and fled from the scene of the crime. Jones v. Commonwealth, 208 Va. 370, 157 S.E.2d 907 (1967). But the trier of fact can consider flight of the accused from the scene of the crime as a circumstance tending to establish his guilt.

A person can be convicted as a principal in the second degree, however, upon evidence that he not only was present, but also committed some overt act—such as inciting, encouraging, advising, or assisting in the commission of the crime—or shared the prime actor's criminal intent.

Murray's counsel contends the evidence showed only that Murray was present when Grace committed the crime and Murray fled from the scene of the crime. The Attorney General contends the evidence supported findings that Murray encouraged and assisted Grace in the criminal act and that he shared Grace's criminal intent. We agree with the Attorney General and affirm the conviction.

The Commonwealth's evidence showed not only circumstances tending to establish Murray's guilt—such as Murray's attempts to open the doors of parked automobiles and his flight with Grace after the robbery. The evidence also showed at least one overt act towards Coltes: Murray's standing "real close" to Coltes immediately before the robbery. From this evidence, the trier of fact could properly infer that Murray, in concert with Grace, intended to intimidate Coltes as a prelude to robbing him.

Jones v. Commonwealth, supra, relied on principally by Murray's counsel, is distinguishable. Jones and another man walked onto a woman's porch, the other man knocked on the door and, when the door was opened, the other man jumped through the door and grabbed the woman. The evidence did not show, directly or by inference, that Jones encouraged or assisted the other man in the criminal act or that Jones knew of the other man's criminal intent.

Affirmed.

Did Murray play any greater role or evince any more overt behavior than Pace did? The court notes testimony that Murray stood "real close" to the victim, Coltes. Would the case have been different if the distance had been ten yards? Wasn't Pace much closer to Reppert?

Murray was observed drinking and trying to pry open car doors along with Grace. What do those acts have to do with the robbery? The court also states that the jury could consider that Murray fled from the scene. Why?

Would you find Pace or Murray guilty of robbery on an individual theory of liability, without any principle of complicity? Do you find that accessorial liability causes us to relax our normal requirements of the *actus reus* specified for the crime?

5. A useful discussion of the concept of "aiding and abetting" appears in the famous case of State v. Tally, 102 Ala. 25, 15 So. 722 (1894) (whose facts and holding we examine later in this chapter):

> It is said . . . that "the words 'aid' and 'abet' are pretty much the synonyms of each other;" and this has doubtless come to be true in the law, though originally a different meaning attached to each. The legal definition of "aid" is not different from its meaning in common parlance. It means "to assist," "to supplement the efforts of another." Rap. & L. Law Dict. p.43. "Abet" is a French word, compounded of the two words "a" and "beter"—"to bait or excite an animal"; and Rapalje and Lawrence thus define it: "To abet is to incite or encourage a person to commit a crime. An abettor is a person who, being present or in the neighborhood, incites another to commit a crime, and thus becomes a principal in the offense." Id. p.4. By the amalgamation of the two words in the meaning—by making synonyms of them—it may be said that to abet has come to mean to aid by presence, actual or constructive, and incitement, and that to aid means not only actual assistance, the supplementing of another's efforts, but also presence for the purposes of such actual assistance as the circumstances may demand or admit of, and the incitement and encouragement which the fact of such presence for such purposes naturally imports and implies. So we have this definition of the two terms by the late Chief Justice Stone:
>
>> The words "aid" and "abet" in legal phrase, are pretty much the synonyms of each other. They comprehend all assistance rendered by acts or words of encouragement or support or presence, actual or constructive, to render assistance should it become necessary. No particular acts are necessary. If encouragement be given to commit the felony, or if, giving due weight to all the testimony, the jury are convinced beyond a reasonable doubt that the defendant was present with a view to render aid should it become necessary, then that ingredient of the offense is made out.
>
> Raiford v. State, 59 Ala. 106. This definition was sufficient for the case then in hand, and it is in the form not infrequently found in the books. But it is incomplete. Mere presence for the purpose of rendering aid obviously is not aid in the substantive sense of assistance by an act supplementary to the act of the principal; nor is it aid in the original sense of abetting, nor abetting in any sense, unless presence with the purpose of giving aid, if necessary, was preconcerted, or in accordance with the general plan conceived by the principal and the person charged as an aider or abettor, or, at the very least, unless the principal knew of the presence, with intent to aid, of such person; for manifestly, in such case, there being no actual, substantive assistance, and no encouragement by words, the only aid possible would be the incitement and encouragement of the fact that another was present for the purpose of assistance, and with the intent to assist if necessary; and, in the nature of things, the fact of presence and purpose to aid could not incite or encourage or embolden the principal unless he knew of the existence of that fact. That kind of aid operates solely upon the mentality of the actual perpetrator. When rendered at all, it is by way of assurance to his mind in

the undertaking he is upon, and it nerves him to the deed, and helps him execute it through a consciousness—a purely mental condition—that another is standing by in a position to help him, if help becomes necessary, who will come to his aid if aid is needed. And how there could be this consciousness without any knowledge of the fact of such other's presence and purpose cannot be conceived. That one may be encouraged or incited to an act by a consideration of which he is wholly oblivious, and which has never addressed itself to his mind, is far beyond the limit of finite comprehension. The definition we have quoted is, as an abstract proposition, clearly at fault. As applied in the concrete to cases of confederacy, as it is, we undertake to say, whenever it is stated in this form, it is free from objection; but in the absence of confederacy, or at least, of knowledge on the part of the actual perpetrator of a crime, one cannot be a principal in the second degree who is present intending to aid, and does not aid by word or deed. The definition must go further. It should appear by it that, to be an aider or abettor when no assistance is given or word uttered, the person so charged must have been present by preconcert, special or general, or at least to the knowledge of the principal, with the intent to aid him. This view is very clearly stated by Mr. Wharton. He says:

> It is not necessary, therefore, to prove that the party actually aided in the commission of the offense. If he watched for his companions in order to prevent surprise, or remained at a convenient distance in order to favor their escape, if necessary or was in such a situation as to be able readily to come to their assistance, the knowledge of which was calculated to give additional confidence to his companions, in contemplation of law he was aiding and abetting. 1 Whart. Cr. Law, §210.

And the same idea is thus expressed by Mr. Stephens in his Summary of Criminal Law:

> The aiding and abetting must involve some participation. Mere presence without participation will not suffice if no act whatever is done in concert, and no confidence intentionally imparted by such presence to the perpetrators. See Connaughty v. State, 1 Wis. 159.

And Mr. Bishop says:

> A principal in the second degree is one who is present lending his countenance and encouragement, or otherwise aiding, while another does the act. Bish. Cr. Law, 648.

And Mr. Wharton further says:

> Something must be shown in the conduct of the bystander which indicates [to the perpetrator, manifestly] a design to encourage, incite, or in some manner afford aid or consent to the particular act, though when the bystander is a friend of the perpetrator, and knows that his presence will be regarded by the perpetrator as an encouragement and protection, presence alone will be regarded as an encouragement. . . . The confederacy must be real. . . . Mere consent to a crime, when no aid is given and no encouragement rendered, does not amount to participation. 1 Whart. Cr. Law §§211a, 211c, 211d.

Thus, in Wicks v. State, 44 Ala. 398, with reference to section 3704 of the Code, it is said: "The testimony must show an actual participation in the commission of the offense, else the party charged cannot be convicted under this statute." And in Cabbell v. State, 46 Ala. 195, a mob had overpowered an officer, and taken his prisoner into a house, where they were assaulting him with intent to murder.

The defendant, coming upon the scene at this juncture, and being informed that the mob was trying to kill the prisoner on account of the offense for which he had been arrested, said: "That is right, kill him. God damn him." The question was whether on this evidence the defendant was an aider and abettor in the assault made by the mob, and upon this the court said:

> It is not pretended that the defendant committed the assault, it was the act of the mob; nor was it seriously contended that he was in fact a member of that unlawful assembly. Consequently, the words uttered by him cannot be held to have encouraged or aided the persons by whom the assault was committed, unless addressed to or at least heard by them or some of them.

Here Cabbell had the guilty intent. He wanted the prisoner killed; and he did an act calculated to contribute to the execution of that intent. He uttered words of encouragement and incitement. But he was adjudged to be not guilty, because what he did, though with criminal intent, and calculated to accomplish or aid in the accomplishment of a criminal result, did not in point of fact contribute to that result. And this proposition is directly supported by Raiford v. State, supra, when the elliptical definition of "aid and abet" is rounded out, as we have shown it must be.

Why do we need the complicity doctrine? How could we decide these cases without it? The following cases explore more deeply the problems of act and causation in accessorial liability and the exceptions that the doctrine of complicity makes to our normal principles of criminal liability.

STATE v. OCHOA

Supreme Court of New Mexico
41 N.M. 589, 72 P.2d 609 (1937)

SADLER, Justice.

The defendants were convicted of murder in the second degree. The victim of the homicide was M. R. Carmichael, sheriff of McKinley county. He was slain while accompanying a prisoner from the office of the local justice of the peace to the county jail.

The homicide occurred about 9:30 o'clock in the forenoon of April 4, 1935. A few days previously one Esiquel Navarro, one Victor Campos, and a Mrs. Lovato had been arrested on warrants charging the unlawful breaking and entering of a certain house. Theretofore the house had been occupied by said Campos who was evicted in forcible entry and detainer proceedings. Following eviction, so the charge ran, the three persons just mentioned forcibly reentered the house and replaced Campos' furniture therein. The preliminary hearing for Navarro, who was confined in jail, was set for 9 A.M., April 4th.

The house in question was located in a section of Gallup known locally as Chiuahuita, largely occupied by former employees of a coal mining company. Considerable excitement had been engendered among them by the eviction proceedings and the approaching trial of Navarro. At a mass meeting held in Spanish-American Hall in Gallup on the afternoon of April 3d, attended by some fifty or sixty people but not shown to have been called especially for the purpose, a committee was appointed to confer with Sheriff Carmichael regarding Navarro. The committee waited upon the sheriff and demanded Navarro's release. This request was denied. Some members of the committee then asked permission to talk with Navarro. This request likewise was denied by the sheriff, who informed the committee Navarro's trial would take place at 9 A.M. the following day and that they then could see him.

The sheriff, accompanied by several deputies, left the jail with the prisoner, Navarro, shortly before 9 o'clock the morning of April 4th and proceeded to the office of Justice of the Peace William H. Bickel on Coal avenue, a distance of one and one-half blocks. Arriving there, they found the justice engaged in the hearing of another matter and were compelled to await the conclusion of that hearing. Soon after they arrived a crowd of approximately 125 people, included in which were many women and children, gathered on the sidewalk and in the street in front of the office of the justice of the peace. The crowd was made up largely of friends of the prisoner, Navarro. The officers, even before leaving the jail with the prisoner, had become apprehensive that an effort might be made to rescue him. So that, when the crowd sought admittance to the justice's chambers which had seating capacity for not more than 25 spectators, none except witnesses were permitted to enter.

The crowd in front grew threatening. They pressed against the plate glass windows to the extent that one of them was cracked; pounded on the windows with their fists; shouted, cursed; and some threatened to kick the door down if they were not admitted. After some delay incident to completion of the other hearing, and upon Navarro's objection that he had no attorney, the hearing of his case was postponed for the purpose of enabling him to secure an attorney to represent him.

Apprehensive of trouble in attempting to make their exit from the office of the justice through the crowd at the front entrance en route back to the jail, the sheriff directed that Navarro should be removed through the rear door. In an endeavor to screen as much as possible this maneuver from the crowd in front, the sheriff directed two of his deputies to stand against the front windows.

As Sheriff Carmichael reached for the prisoner's arm to begin the exit from the building, Navarro communicated with the crowd outside by a motion with his arms suggestive that he was being removed through the rear door. This door opened into a 16-foot paved alley extending from Third street to Second street. Third street intersects Coal avenue, upon which the justice's office is located, only a few doors west of the front entrance to said office. The jail is located on Second street at its intersection with the alley, and it was the plan of the officers to escort the prisoner through the alley to jail, thus avoiding the crowd.

Upon discovering the maneuver of the officers, however, the crowd ran to the corner of Third street and Coal avenue, down Third to the alley, and converged eastwardly upon the rear entrance to the justice's office, forming a semicircle around the entrance. The officers, nevertheless, succeeded in getting their prisoner into the alley, pushing their way through the crowd, and proceeded eastwardly toward the jail with the prisoner. Sheriff Carmichael was on the prisoner's right, holding him by the right arm, and Undersheriff Dee Roberts was on the prisoner's left, holding him by the left arm, walking eastwardly toward the jail. As they proceeded up the alley toward the jail they were surrounded by the crowd, some of whom were ahead of them, some on either side and some to their rear. The officers with the prisoner were followed by Deputies E. L. "Bobcat" Wilson and Hoy Boggess in the order named.

The prisoner was obstinate, holding back and forcing the officers to push or urge him on. An unidentified person in the crowd had been heard to shout: "We want Navarro." When they were about forty feet from the rear exit of the justice's office, Deputy Hoy Boggess observed someone, unknown to him, grab at the prisoner as if to take him from the custody of the officers. Thereupon, he raised his arm and hurled a tear gas bomb to the rear and westwardly into the crowd in the alley. Almost simultaneously with the detonation from explosion of the bomb, a shot was fired somewhat to the rear of the officers accompanying the prisoner. Then a second shot followed the first, apparently fired by Ignacio Velarde, a brother of the defendant Leandro Velarde, from a point at the northeast corner of the Independent Building, some fifteen feet from Sheriff Carmichael. This shot struck the sheriff in the left side of the face and passed out of his body on the right side of his neck. The first shot fired had struck the sheriff in the left side, just under the left arm, passed through his chest and out into his right shoulder. He died instantly, his undersheriff, Dee Roberts, catching hold of his right arm and lowering his body to the pavement. The latter then looking to the west observed two men firing toward him. One was on his left at the corner of the Independent Building, perhaps fifteen feet distant. This proved to be Ignacio Velarde. The other was farther down the alley about twenty feet and to his right. This was Solomon Esquibel. Their fire was returned by Undersheriff Roberts, and both Ignacio Velarde and Solomon Esquibel were killed.

In the meantime the firing had become more general, the total number of shots fired during the affray being twelve to fifteen. When the firing ceased, besides Sheriff Carmichael and the two others named being killed, Deputy Wilson had been seriously wounded by a bullet which entered his body about an inch below the armpit and was later extracted. Two other members of the crowd had received wounds, a woman by a shot through the leg. Both of these wounded, as well as Deputy Wilson, subsequently recovered.

With this general statement of events leading up to the homicide, we shall now particularize in our statement of the facts, detailing the evidence upon which the state relies to show guilty connection of defendants with the resulting homicide. This will require some recapitulation.

About the time it was appreciated by the crowd in front that the prisoner was to be removed through the rear door into the alley, the defendant Leandro Velarde was seen going through the crowd motioning toward the west, the direction to be taken to reach the alley, and he went into the alley practically at the head of the crowd.

The three defendants, Leandro Velarde, Manuel Avitia, and Juan Ochoa, along with certain other defendants acquitted at the trial, were identified as being in the crowd in front of the justice's office and also in the crowd at the rear of the office in the alley after it had hastened there upon discovering that the prisoner, Navarro, was to be removed through the rear door and thence via the alley to the jail. The present defendants, along with Ignacio Velarde and Solomon Esquibel, slain during the affray, were in the forefront of the crowd formed in a semicircle around the rear entrance as the officers prepared to emerge with their prisoner.

Just before they took the prisoner through the rear entrance, former Deputy Fred Montoya, who formed one of the sheriff's party at the justice's office, at the sheriff's request, opened the rear door. He took one step outside. There confronting him among those recognized were Ignacio Velarde, Leandro Velarde, and Solomon Esquibel. Leandro Velarde, clenching his first and raising it in a threatening manner, said to Montoya: "Now you shall see what happens disgraced (one)." Solomon Esquibel, reaching his right hand into a partially open blue jacket worn at the time as if to draw a weapon, said: "You move back, leave them to us alone." Montoya being unarmed immediately moved back inside the office of the justice of the peace.

Contemporaneously with Montoya's return to the inside of the office, Sheriff Carmichael and Undersheriff Dee Roberts emerged therefrom with the prisoner. As they did so and started pushing their way out into the alley, the defendant Juan Ochoa, from a distance of about three feet, struck at Undersheriff Dee Roberts with a claw hammer.

When the officers had advanced a short distance up the alley with their prisoner, the defendant Manuel Avitia drew a pistol from his pocket and rushed from the rear through the crowd toward the officers. After hurling the tear gas bomb, and just before being struck and rendered unconscious, Deputy Boggess observed the defendant Leandro Velarde only a few feet from him on the right; Solomon Esquibel, later slain, not far away; and the defendant Manuel Avitia running toward him (Boggess). When Boggess fell unconscious from a blow on the head delivered by some unidentified person in the crowd, his pistol fell from his belt to the pavement. Two members of the crowd were seen to spring toward same and to be bent over as if to recover it, but, their bodies screening it from view of the witness relating the incident, neither of these persons was seen actually to pick up the pistol.

While Deputy Boggess was down on the paving and after the firing had begun, the defendants Avitia and Ochoa, with two or three other persons, were seen beating and kicking him. When the shooting had ceased Avitia ran west out of the alley with a pistol in his hand.

Juan Ochoa was chairman of the meeting held at Spanish-American Hall the afternoon before the affray at which meeting a committee was named to interview the sheriff regarding Navarro. Leandro Velarde attended the meeting and was named a member of said committee, though it is not established that he actually went with the committee to see the sheriff. Manuel Avitia also was present at the meeting.

On March 29th, preceding the affray, at a gathering at the home of one Mrs. Conception Aurelio about 4 o'clock in the afternoon, Leandro Velarde told the group, there gathered, "to prepare for the following day at 8 o'clock in the morning; that they were to be ready at the house of Victor Campos and to be prepared—to be ready and let the officers take their weapons; that they didn't need anything else but a tooth pick." Also, he said at this time that the first one they wanted to get hold of was Carmichael, "because he had a feeling against Carmichael and Carmichael had a feeling against him." He further said, "that he didn't care to die for the poor; that he had a big body and he was going to stick it out for the poor." The meeting planned evidently had to do with restoring Campos to the house from which he had been evicted. . . .

When Deputy Hoy Boggess regained his feet upon a return of consciousness, he saw Deputy Wilson approaching him in a stooped posture and heard him say: "I'm shot." Finding his own pistol missing, he seized that of Wilson and still in a dazed condition fired twice at two persons he saw fleeing, one of whom he thought was the prisoner Navarro making his escape. He could not say whether either of his shots took effect.

The pistols with which Ignacio Velarde and Solomon Esquibel were seen firing were never located after the affray. The pistol which dropped from Deputy Boggess' belt when he was knocked unconscious was never recovered. Sheriff Carmichael's pistol was removed from its scabbard on his body after his death. It had never been fired. The bullet which had entered the body of Sheriff Carmichael under the left armpit was later extracted from his right shoulder. The bullet which had wounded Deputy Wilson likewise was later extracted. The pistol which Deputy Boggess lost during the affray and which had not been fired by him when lost was a forty-five Smith and Wesson double action. The bullet removed from the body of Sheriff Carmichael and that extracted from Deputy Wilson were both fired from the same pistol and it was of the same make and caliber as that lost by Deputy Boggess, using the same type of ammunition as that then employed in the Boggess gun.

The defendants were proceeded against by information. Ten were thus accused of the murder of Sheriff Carmichael, of whom seven were acquitted by the jury. The three defendants above named having been convicted of second degree murder, they alone prosecute this appeal. The most serious claim of error is directed at the action of the trial court in submitting to the jury the issue of second degree murder. . . . If this claim be good as to all of the defendants it is decisive. Hence, we give it first consideration. The facts as we have recited them are within the verdicts of guilty returned against defendants. Do they support second degree? That is the issue.

Justifying the submission of both first and second degree, the Attorney General in the State's brief says:

> Discarding all of the theories requiring a first degree or nothing verdict, we still have two theories presented by the evidence shown (under) which the jury might find the appellants guilty of second degree murder. First, that one of the appellants actually shot and killed Sheriff Carmichael. Second, that the appellants or

> any of them aided and abetted the person or persons who actually shot and killed Sheriff Carmichael. Under either of the circumstances it was mandatory on the trial judge to submit both first and second degree murder to the jury.

If there be evidence in the record sustaining a conviction of given defendants of second degree on either of the theories thus presented by the State, it will be unnecessary as to such defendants to pass upon sufficiency of the evidence to sustain the other theory. It is the jury's province to say whether the facts sustain either theory. In support of the verdict, we must assume the jury to have adopted a theory sustained by the evidence. In this connection it should be stated that as to the defendant Leandro Velarde there is no effort in the argument before us to connect him with the slaying otherwise than as an aider and abettor. As to the other two defendants, Avitia and Ochoa, it is different. The State urges there is evidence to sustain a finding that either of them actually fired one of the shots entering the body of Sheriff Carmichael, though argued as much more likely under the proof that Ochoa did so, using the gun which fell from the waistband of deputy Boggess when he was assaulted and knocked unconscious. Of course, the theory of aider and abettor also is urged against Avitia and Ochoa. . . .

The return of verdicts of second degree against defendants had the important effect of acquitting them of the charge of first degree upon the theory of a homicide committed in the perpetration of a felony, to wit, the aiding of the prisoner, Navarro, to escape. So, as the matter rests before us, the State must defend the verdict as one finding the defendants guilty of common-law murder, either as principals or as aiders and abettors. This greatly narrows the issue under defendants' contention that second degree was not properly submitted.

We do not understand counsel to contend that the unexplained killing of Sheriff Carmichael with a deadly weapon would not warrant submission of second degree. But, rather, that there is not sufficient evidence to connect them with the slaying, either as the actual slayers or as aiders and abettors. The point now argued is in effect complaint at the trial court's failure to direct a verdict of acquittal as requested.

The distinction between an accessory before the fact and a principal and between principals in the first and second degree, in cases of felony, has been abolished in New Mexico and every person concerned in the commission thereof, whether he directly commits the offense or procures, counsels, aids, or abets in its commission, must be prosecuted, tried, and punished as a principal. The evidence of aiding and abetting may be as broad and varied as are the means of communicating thought from one individual to another; by acts, conduct, words, signs, or by any means sufficient to incite, encourage or instigate commission of the offense or calculated to make known that commission of an offense already undertaken has the aider's support or approval. Mere presence, of course, and even mental approbation, if unaccompanied by outward manifestation or expression of such approval, is insufficient.

Before an accused may become liable as an aider and abettor, he must share the criminal intent of the principal. There must be community of purpose, partnership in the unlawful undertaking.

> To aid and abet another in a crime one must share the intent or purpose of the principal. If two or more acting independently assault another, and one of them inflicts a mortal wound, the other is not guilty as an aider and abettor. An aider and abettor is a partner in the crime, the chief ingredient of which is always intent. There can be no partnership in the act where there is no community of purpose or intent. Landrum v. Commonwealth, 123 Ky. 472, 96 S.W. 587, 588, as quoted in Gill v. Commonwealth, 235 Ky. 351, 31 S.W.2d 608.
>
> To render one an aider or abettor and, as a consequence, guilty in like degree with the principal in the commission of a crime, there should be evidence of his knowledge of the intention or purpose of the principal to commit the assault. In other words, there must have been a "common purpose" by which is meant a like criminal intent in the minds of Mills and the appellant, to render the latter guilty as charged, and hence authorize the giving of the instruction. State v. Porter, 276 Mo. 387, 207 S.W. 774, 776.

With these preliminary observations, we shall proceed to apply them to the facts of the instant case. As to the defendant Leandro Velarde there is no evidence which sufficiently connects him with the unlawful design of the slayer of Sheriff Carmichael. The last time seen prior to the hurling of the tear gas bomb and the firing of the first shot, he was in the crowd a few feet removed from Deputy Boggess. There was nothing about his actions when then seen to excite suspicion. If so, it was not testified to by any witness. . . .

He is not shown to have taken part in the assault on Deputy Boggess, as were Avitia and Ochoa. . . . We do not find in the record evidence supporting the conviction of this defendant as an aider and abettor. Mere suspicion does not furnish the required support.

The defendants Avitia and Ochoa are differently situated. After Deputy Boggess hurled the tear gas bomb, he was knocked down and rendered unconscious for a time. Firing from the party of which they formed a part started almost instantly and continued until a total of as many as 12 or 15 shots had been exchanged between members of the two parties. Even if it be assumed that these two defendants were without previous knowledge of the purpose of the slayer or slayers of deceased to make an attempt on his life, the evidence abundantly supports an inference that with the firing of the first shot they became apprised of that purpose. The intent to kill, or to aid and abet in the commission thereof, may be formed at the scene of the crime, even though the accused may have gone there without such intention. If, with knowledge that one of their party was using or was about to use a deadly weapon, they or either of them rendered aid or assistance to him or them engaged in the deadly assault, they are equally guilty as aiders and abettors. The aider under such circumstances adopts the criminal intent of the principal. Both Avitia and Ochoa are identified in the testimony as being still engaged in an assault upon the fallen Boggess after two bullets had entered the body of the deceased. Boggess was a deputy of the slain sheriff and, of course, would be expected to

come to the aid of his chief in peril. The fact that they were thus engaged in a vicious assault upon him (Boggess), after firing upon the sheriff's party commenced, left it within the jury's province to infer, if it saw fit, not alone that these defendants shared the intent of the slayer, but also that they aided and abetted him in his unlawful undertaking.

Nor would it seem an unwarranted inference, if the jury should elect so to find, that these defendants saw the sheriff's assailant in the act of drawing or aiming his gun and commenced the assault on Deputy Boggess momentarily before or simultaneously with the first outburst of gunfire. Particularly is this true in view of the fact that the assault on Boggess did not cease when it must have become known to the defendants that a member of their party was firing on the sheriff's party. Such an inference, however, is not essential to sustain the verdicts.

The opinion of the Supreme Court of Ohio in Woolweaver v. State, 50 Ohio St. 277, 34 N.E. 352, 353, 40 Am. St. Rep. 667, points out the difficulty frequently presented where a homicide results from a clash between opposing parties and at the moment of the homicide a member of one party is engaged in a struggle with a member of the opposing party other than the deceased. For error in instructing that if what defendant did "tended" to incite the slayer (a substitution by the trial court for the language of the requested instruction that if done "with a view" of inciting him), the Supreme Court awarded a new trial. The opinion makes plain, however, that even though there be opposing parties of several members each, the controlling principles remain the same. The court said:

> In the case under consideration there was evidence tending to show that the plaintiff in error and his two sons composed one party, while the deceased and Mr. Ewing, and probably Mr. Lyons, composed the other party. This difference in the circumstances in no wise affected the principles by which the criminal character of the acts of the parties should be tested . . . upon the springing up of a sudden fight, each should be chargeable only with his own acts, and such acts of the others as he may purposely incite or encourage. The charge, in the form in which it requested, correctly stated this proposition . . . it often becomes a nice and difficult matter to determine the criminal liability of each of a party of friends or kindred for the violent and unlawful acts of his fellows, committed in the course of a conflict, arising upon a sudden quarrel, with one or more antagonists; and in such case, upon the trial of one of them, it is of the first importance that the correct rule of liability should be laid down to the jury, and if the instructions should extend too far as to the liability of the one on trial for the acts of his fellows it would be, necessarily, prejudicial to his rights.

The opinion of the Court of Criminal Appeals of Texas in Bibby v. State (Tex. Cr. App.) 65 S.W. 193, 195, states clearly the rule of responsibility applicable where several members of opposing parties are fighting apart, engaged in separate combats, when one, without previous knowledge by other members of his party of his intention to do so, suddenly begins the use of a deadly weapon on his antagonist. The courts said

> Here the only proof against appellant is that he, with the others, did disturb the meeting, and that he afterwards engaged in the difficulty. There is no proof that he used any weapon, nor is there any proof to show that he knew Wells or Starnes were using their pocketknives. If Wells or Starnes used a knife in the difficulty without the knowledge or consent of appellant, he is not responsible for the homicide. *Or, to put it more strongly, the proof must show beyond a reasonable doubt that he knew Wells was to use the knife beforehand, or that he had knowledge Wells was using the knife at the time he was so using it, and by some act of his aided and abetted him in the use of said knife.* (Emphasis ours.)

The mere statement of the proposition, however, furnishes its own support; for, however free from felonious intent a participant in the combat of opposing parties may have been in the beginning, once it becomes known to him that another member of his party is employing a deadly weapon, he exposes himself to an inference of sharing the latter's intent if, except in necessary defense of his own person, he continues his participation. The question of whether the alleged aider and abettor did share the principal's criminal intent, and whether he knew the latter acted with criminal intent, is one of fact for the jury and may be inferred from circumstances. . . .

Nor is error present in instruction No. 17 given by the court in its relation to the defendant Ochoa. The objection is that it submitted the issue whether Ochoa, himself, killed the deceased. It is claimed Ochoa was prejudiced in submission of this issue in this—that there was no evidence whatever that he did so. Of course, the issue of his aiding and abetting in the killing also was submitted.

We heretofore have pointed out the uncertainty in the evidence as to who fired at least one of the shots contributing to the death of Sheriff Carmichael. It was unnecessary for the State to show who actually fired the fatal shot if the proof was sufficient to warrant the inference as to a given defendant that, if he did not fire it, he aided and abetted him who did.

We are unable to see error as to the defendant Ochoa in submission of the issue whether he actually killed the deceased in view of our conclusion that the evidence supports an inference that he aided and abetted in such killing. Morally, there never has been a distinction in the degree of culpability. The law long since has ceased to recognize any. All are subject to prosecution, trial, and punishment as principals. The aider and abettor may be tried and convicted even though the actual slayer is never apprehended or has been tried and acquitted. Cf. Rule 35-4426. "If *A* be indicted as having given the mortal stroke, and *B* and *C* as present, aiding and assisting, and upon the evidence it appears that *B* gave the stroke and *A* and *C* were only aiding and assisting, the evidence will maintain the indictment, and judgment be given against all the defendants, for it is only a circumstantial variance, as, in law, the mortal blow is the act of all that are present aiding and abetting." 1 Chittys Crim. Law (5th ed.) 259. See, also 1 Wharton's Crim. Law (12th ed.) 345-347, §§259, 260.

The law having so completely abolished the distinction between principals in the first and second degree and the law being that, even though another fired the fatal shot, it is in contemplation of law Ochoa's act if he aided and abetted, we can see no prejudice in the instruction complained of. . . .

It follows from what has been said that the judgment of the district court must stand affirmed as to the defendants Avitia and Ochoa. As to the defendant Velarde, it is reversed, with a direction to the trial court to set aside the judgment of conviction pronounced upon him and to discharge the prisoner.

It is so ordered.

Notes and Questions

1. Did Leandro Velarde, Avitia, or Ochoa cause the death of Carmichael? Must the state prove their causal role beyond a reasonable doubt?

2. Why do you think that the jury found verdicts of second-degree murder? Isn't it likely that they thought that the defendants were guilty of aiding and abetting an attempted escape and that since someone had died as a result, they were technically guilty of first-degree murder—but that considering the equities in the defendants' favor, that verdict was too severe? If so, what should the appellate court do?

3. Why does the court reverse Leandro Velarde's conviction? It states that "there was nothing about his actions when then seen to excite suspicion." Given the nature and purpose of the demonstration near the courthouse, didn't Velarde's presence itself excite suspicion? Would the decision in Murray v. Commonwealth, above, permit Velarde's conviction?

4. How did Avitia and Ochoa aid the sheriff's slayer by their action in attacking the deputy? Would the court have affirmed their convictions if they had attacked the deputy *after* the sheriff had been killed?

5. Must the accomplice communicate to the principal the fact that he is aiding in the crime? The court states: "Before an accused may become liable as an aider and abettor, he must share the criminal intent of the principal. There must be a community of purpose, partnership in the unlawful undertaking." Was it necessary that the actual killer of the sheriff knew Avitia's and Ochoa's intentions? If he didn't, how can the court show a "community of purpose" here?

Conversely, what if Ochoa and Avitia, in attacking the deputy, had no idea that anyone was shooting the sheriff? What if the sheriff's killer knew what Avitia and Ochoa were doing, but Avitia and Ochoa didn't know what the killer was doing?

STATE v. TALLY

Supreme Court of Alabama
102 Ala. 25, 15 So. 722 (1894)

Briefly stated, the information in this case contains two charges against John B. Tally, as judge of the ninth judicial circuit. . . . The second count charges complicity on the part of Tally in the murder of R. C. Ross by the hands of [the] Skeltons. Tally was a brother-in-law of all the Skeltons named. . . . The grievance they had against Ross lay in the fact that the latter had seduced, or been criminally intimate with, a sister of three of them and of Mrs. Tally. . . . Among the facts which the evidence establishes without conflict, direct or inferential, in this case, are the following: About January 6, 1894, Ross left his house in Scottsboro surreptitiously under and because of an apprehension that his life was in imminent peril at the hands of the Skeltons. He remained away from Scottsboro under this apprehension until Tuesday night, January 30th, when he returned on account of the illness of his wife. From that time until Sunday, February 4th, he remained in Scottsboro, secluded in his home. About 6 o'clock on that Sunday morning, just as the train passed Scottsboro going to Stevenson, and beyond there to Chattanooga, Ross left Scottsboro, in a hack, for Stevenson, 18 miles distant, intending to catch a train there on another road, and go on to Chattanooga. With him were his brother-in-law, Bloodwood . . . John Calloway, and the driver, one Hammons. All of the party were armed. Ross had a gun and a pistol, Bloodwood had a gun, and Calloway and Hammons each had a pistol. They arrived in Stevenson about 10:45 that morning, and driving to a point in a public road or street midway between an hotel and the passenger station of the two railroads that connect, or rather unite, there, and 30 or 40 yards from each, all the party alighted from the vehicle, except the driver, and took out their arms and baggage. . . . A person, William Tally, passing at the time from the hotel to the station, walked around the hack, which had stopped immediately in front of him, and met, shook hands, and passed the usual salutations with Ross, who had gotten out on the side next the station. Tally then turned away, and started on towards the station. Just at this juncture a shot was fired at Bloodwood from behind the depot platform. This was followed by another from the same place, and then by other shots from two guns behind the platform, and from a pile of telegraph poles a little way down the road, in the direction from which the hack had come. Some one or more of these succeeding shots took effect in Ross' legs, and he fell. Bloodwood was also wounded, and ran away. The team ran away with Hammons. Calloway does not appear to have been hit, but in some way he fell with and under Ross. They both arose almost immediately. Ross managed to get to the side of a small oil house, a short distance beyond where the hack had stopped, and took a position affording some shelter from persons behind the platform and telegraph poles. While standing there with his gun in his hand, and looking in the direction of the telegraph poles, a man came to the corner of the house behind him, and shot him with a Winchester rifle through the head from back to front. He fell in the throes of death, and died. Then another man came up from behind the platform, and, approaching closely, also shot him through the head with a Winchester rifle. The man who fired the first and two or three other shots from behind the platform was Robert Skelton. The man who fired the other shots from that position was James Skelton. The man who fired from the telegraph poles was Walter Skelton. John Skelton it was who reached the corner of the oil house behind Ross, shot him in the back of the head, and killed him. And it was Robert who came up after he was dead and again shot him in the head. . . . After the killing of Ross, Robert Skelton sent a telegram to the respondent, at Scottsboro, informing him that Ross was dead, and that none of the Skeltons were hurt; and they all surrendered themselves to Huddleston, who was mayor of Stevenson, and were taken back to Scottsboro, and confined in jail. . . .

What connection had the respondent with that murder? Was he, knowing the deadly intent of the Skeltons and their pursuit, bent upon its execution, willfully neglectful of his duty, as a magistrate, in not exercising the power the law had clothed him with to stay their hands? Or did he himself participate in the deed, by commanding, directing, counseling, or encouraging the Skeltons to its execution, or by aiding and abetting them in its commission? The evidence for the prosecution on these issues with be briefly stated: As has been seen, Judge Tally was the brother-in-law of Robert, James, and Walter Skelton, and of Miss Annie Skelton, the wronged girl. It may be supposed, therefore, that he shared with the Skeltons—in some degree, at least—the shame and mortification which had come upon them through Ross, and that the grievance against Ross was common to them all. It was shown that he knew all the facts known to the Skeltons, and came to his knowledge of them soon after they did. They all lived in the same town, with the intimacy usually incident to their relations. James Skelton lived with Judge Tally. On Friday before the Sunday of the homicide, Judge Tally returned to Scottsboro from Ft. Payne, where he had been holding court, by way of Chattanooga, Tenn., and over the Memphis and Charleston Railroad. On the train was Mr. Gregory, a lawyer of Scottsboro, who engaged Judge Tally in conversation. The latter spoke of some interesting murder cases that he had been trying at Ft. Payne; and, in this connection, Gregory remarked to him that he thought they would have one or more killings in Scottsboro in a very short time. "The judge [to quote the witness] asked me why, and I told him that Ross had come back, and that the Skelton boys were on the war path, or some such thing. I don't remember just what it was. The judge said he guessed not; that he supposed Ross would leave, or would not stay there, or something of that kind; and I told him I supposed so. . . ." It was also in evidence that James Skelton left Tally's house that morning before breakfast, went down town, armed and mounted himself, came back to Tally's hitched his horse in front of the house, set his gun against the front gate, went into the dining room to get something to eat before starting, then went out, remounted, and joined Robert and John at the corner. . . . The flight of Ross and the pursuit of the Skeltons at once became generally known in the town of Scottsboro, and was well nigh the sole topic of conversation that Sunday morning. Everybody knew it. Everybody talked about it. Everybody was impressed with the probability of a terrible tragedy to be enacted on the road to Stevenson, or at the latter point. The respondent was soon abroad. He went to the depot, where the telegraph office was. He remained there most of that morning. About nine o'clock that morning Dr. Rorex saw him there, and this, in the language of the witness, passed between them: "I said to Judge Tally that I thought we had better send a hack and a physician to their assistance up the road [referring to the Ross and Skelton parties then on the road to Stevenson]; that these parties might get hurt, and they might need assistance. Judge Tally replied that his folks or friends could take care of themselves. I also said to him that I reckoned we ought to send a telegram to Stevenson and have all of them arrested, to which he made no reply. . . . He said that he was waiting to see if anybody sent a telegram—or words to that effect; waiting and watching, to see if anybody sent a telegram." And he did wait and watch. He was seen there by Judge Bridges just before the passenger train, going west at 10:17, passed. He was seen there after it passed. E. H. Ross, a kinsman of the Ross who had fled, and was being pursued, meeting the telegraph operator, Whitner, at the passenger station, walked with him down to the freight depot, where the telegraph office was. Judge Tally followed them. They went into the telegraph office, and so did he. Ross was sitting at a table, writing a message. It was addressed to R. C. Ross, Stevenson, Ala. Its contents were: "Four men on horseback with guns following. Look out." Ross handed it to the operator to be sent. Tally either saw this message, or in some way accurately divined its contents. He called for paper, and immediately wrote a message himself. Judge Bridges was still in the office. At this juncture, Tally spoke to him, took him into a corner of the room, and, calling him by his given name, said, "What do you reckon that fellow [the operator] would think if I told him I should put him out of that office before he should send that message?" referring to the message quoted above, which E. H. Ross had just given the operator. Judge Bridges replied: "Judge, I wouldn't do that. That might cause you very serious trouble, and, besides that, might cause the young man to lose his position with the company he is working for." Judge Tally then remarked: "I don't want him to send the message he has, and I am going to send this one." He then showed Judge Bridges a message addressed to William Huddleston, containing these words; "Do not let the party warned get away." This message was signed by Tally. The respondent then handed this telegram to the operator, remarking to him, "This message has something to do with that one you just received"; said he wanted it sent, and paid for it. He then started towards the door, but turned to the operator, and said: "Just add to that message, 'say nothing.'" Tally left the office. This message was sent just after that of E. H. Ross to R. C. Ross. The original of it was placed on a file in the office at Scottsboro. . . . These telegrams of Ed Ross and Tally were sent about 10:25 A.M. Tally then, his watch to prevent the sending or delivery of a telegram to R. C. Ross being over, went home. Soon after 11 o'clock, the message before referred to came from Stevenson to Scottsboro, addressed to Judge Tally, and signed by Robert Skelton. It ran: "Ross dead. None of us hurt." This was taken to Judge Tally's house, and there delivered to him. . . .

The second specification charges that the Skeltons "unlawfully, and with malice aforethought, killed Robert C. Ross by shooting him with a gun," and . . . "Tally did aid or abet the said" Skeltons, naming them, "in the commission of the said felony and murder. . . ." These charges of aiding or abetting murder, and of murder direct, which amount to the same thing under our statute (Code, §3704), are, upon considerations to which we have already adverted, to be sustained, if at all, by evidence of the respondent's connection with the homicide after the Skeltons had left Scottsboro in pursuit of Ross, since we do not find any incriminating connection up to that point of time. Being without conviction that Tally knew of the Skelton's intention to take Ross' life until after they had departed on their errand of death, and there being no evidence or pretense that between this time and the homicide any communication passed between them and Tally, we reach and declare the conclusion that the respondent did not command, direct, counsel, instigate, or encourage the Skeltons to take the life of Ross, and that, in whatever and all that was done by them and him, respectively, there was no understanding, preconcert, or conspiracy between them and him.

This narrows the issues to three inquiries—two of fact and one of law: First (a question of fact), did Judge Tally, on Sunday, February 4, 1894, knowing the intention of the Skeltons to take the life of Ross, and after they had gone in pursuit of him, do any act intended to further their design, and aid them in the taking of his life? If he did, then, second (a question of law), is it essential to his guilt that his act should have contributed to the effectuation of their design—to the death of Ross? And, if so, third (another inquiry of fact), did his act contribute to the death of Ross? There can be no reasonable doubt that Judge Tally knew, soon after the Skeltons had departed, that they had gone in pursuit of Ross, and that they intended to take his life. Within a few minutes, he was informed by his wife that Ross had fled, and that the four Skeltons were pursuing him. He had seen three of them mounted and heavily armed. He knew the fourth, even keener on the trail than these, had gone on before. He knew their grievance. The fact that they intended to wreak vengeance, in the way they did, upon overtaking Ross, was known to all men in Scottsboro, as soon as the flight and pursuit became known. It was in the minds and on the tongues of everybody there. Nothing else was thought or talked of. When Dr. Rorex, voicing the universal apprehension, suggested to him that aid be sent up the road to the dead and wounded, Judge Tally, taking in the full force of the implication that there would be a fight to the death, with the Skeltons as assailants, and not dissenting therefrom at all, said with the ken of prophecy, as a reason why he would not be a party to the execution of this humane suggestion, that his folks (the Skeltons) would take care of themselves. How well they took care of themselves—with what exceeding care they conserved their own safety—is shown by the event, and the manner in which it was produced. To the other suggestion of Dr. Rorex—resulting from the universal knowledge that, unless something was done, an awful tragedy would be enacted—that "we telegraph to Stevenson, and have them all arrested," and thus prevent the catastrophe, if perchance Ross should reach that point alive, Judge Tally made no direct response; but in the same connection he said, "I am waiting and watching here to see if anybody sends a telegram." What he meant by this is most clearly demonstrated by his subsequent shadowing and following up Ed Ross, and his conversation with Judge Bridges about putting the operator out of the office before he should send Ed Ross' message of warning to his kinsman, Robert C. Ross. This was the situation: Ross was in what he supposed to be secret flight from the Skeltons. He was unaware that his early departure had been seen by one of them. He did not know they were all in full pursuit to take his life. Under these circumstances, the pursuers had every advantage of the pursued. They could come upon him unawares. Being on horseback, while he was in a vehicle, coming up to him, they could well get beyond and waylay him. This they actually did. Having this tremendous advantage, accentuated by the fact that they were in no danger from Ross even if he saw them, unless he was forced to defend himself—that his effort and intent were to get away, and not to kill—Judge Tally might well feel satisfied with the posture of affairs; he might well feel assured that his folks would take care of themselves, as they did. All he wanted was that this situation, which portended the death of Ross and the safety of his folks, should not be changed. He would not agree that it should be changed so as to save Ross' life, even though at the same time the safety of the Skeltons should be assured, as would have been the result had the authorities at Stevenson been fully advised, at the time Dr. Rorex suggested the sending of a telegram there, to arrest all parties. He was waiting and watching there to see that the situation was not changed by advice to Ross which would or might enable him to escape death at the hands of his folks. He waited long and watched faithfully, and his patience and vigil were rewarded. He saw Ed Ross going towards the telegraph office. He at once concluded Ross was going there to warn his kinsman, and give him a chance for his life. He followed. His purpose was to stop the message; not to let the warning even start on its journey. This he proposed to do by overawing the operator, a mere youth, or by brute force. Judge Bridges dissuaded him from this course, but he adopted another to destroy this one precarious chance of life which was being held out to Robert C. Ross. It would not do, Bridges advised him, to stop the warning by threatening or overpowering him—the operator. The young man was a newcomer, and a stranger there, and a resort to moral suasion with him was therefore unpromising and hazardous. Not so with the operator at the other end of the line. He was Judge Tally's friend of long standing. [Judge Tally] telegraphed his friend (the operator at Stevenson) not to let Ross get away. His language was, as first written, "Do not let party warned get away." This he handed to the operator to be sent to Stevenson, saying, "This message has something to do with the one you have," referring to Ed Ross' message. What then passed through his mind we are left to conjecture; but upon further thought he added to the message these words, "Say nothing." What was the full import of this completed message, looking at its terms and the circumstances under which it was sent? . . . [I]n short, the substance and effect of what Tally said to Huddleston, taking the two dispatches and all the circumstances into the account, was simply this, no more no less: "Ross has fled in the direction of Stevenson. The four Skeltons are following him on horseback, with guns, to take his life. Ross does not know of the pursuit. An effort is being made to get word to Ross through you that he is thus pursued, in order that he may get away from them. If you do not deliver this word to him, he cannot escape them. Do not deliver that message. Say nothing about it, and thereby prevent his getting away from them." A most careful analysis of the voluminous testimony in this case convinces us beyond a reasonable doubt that this was what Tally intended to convey to Huddleston, and that his message means this, and only this, to all reasonable comprehension. . . .

We therefore find and hold that John B. Tally, with full knowledge that the Skeltons were in pursuit of Ross with the intent to take his life, committed acts, namely, kept watch at Scottsboro to prevent warning of danger being sent to Ross; and, with like purpose, sent the message to Huddleston, which were calculated to aid, and were committed by him with the intent to aid, the said Skeltons to take the life of Ross under the circumstances which rendered them guilty of murder.

And we are next to consider and determine the second inquiry above, namely: Whether it is essential to the guilt of Judge Tally, as charged in the second count of the information, that the said acts, thus adapted, intended and committed by him, should, in fact, have aided the said Skeltons to take the life of the said Ross—should have, in fact, contributed to his death at their hands. . . . To be guilty of murder, therefore, not being a common-law principal, and not being an accessory before the fact—to be concerned in the commission of the offense within the meaning of our statute—he must be found to have aided or abetted the Skeltons in the commission of the offense in such sort as to constitute him at common law a principal in the second degree. A principal in this degree is one who is present at the commission of a felony by the hand of the principal in the first degree, and who, being thus present, aids or abets, or aids and abets, the latter therein. The presence which this definition requires need not be actual, physical juxtaposition in respect of the personal perpetrator of the crime. It is enough, so far as presence is concerned, for the principal in the second degree to be in a position to aid the commission of the crime by others. It is enough if he stands guard while the act is being perpetrated by others to prevent interference with them, or to warn them of the approach of danger; and it is immaterial how distant from the scene of the crime his vigil is maintained, provided it gives some promise of protection to those engaged in its active commission. At whatever distance he may be, he is present in legal contemplation if he is at the time performing any act in furtherance of the crime, or is in a position to give information to the principal which would be helpful to the end in view, or to prevent others from doing any act, by way of warning the intended victim or otherwise, which would be but an obstacle in the way of the consummation of the crime, or render its accomplishment more difficult. . . .

We are therefore clear to the conclusion that, before Judge Tally can be found guilty of aiding and abetting the Skeltons to kill Ross, it must appear that his vigil at Scottsboro to prevent Ross from being warned or his danger was by preconcert with them, whereby they would naturally be incited, encouraged, and emboldened—"given confidence"—to the deed, or that he aided them to kill Ross, contributed to Ross' death, in point of physical fact, by means of the telegram he sent to Huddleston. The assistance given, however, need not contribute to the criminal result in the sense that but for it the result would not have ensued. It is quite enough if the aid merely rendered it easier for the principal actor to accomplish the end intended by him and the aider and abettor, though in all human probability the end would have been attained without it. If the aid in homicide can be shown to have put the deceased at a disadvantage, to have deprived him of a single chance of life which but for it he would have had, he who furnishes such aid is guilty, though it cannot be known or shown that the dead man, in the absence thereof, would have availed himself of that chance; as, where one counsels murder, he is guilty as an accessory before the fact, though it appears probable that murder would have been done without his counsel; and as, where one being present by concert to aid if necessary is guilty as a principal in the second degree, though, had he been absent murder would have been committed, so where he who facilitates murder even by so much as destroying a single chance of life the assailed might otherwise have had, he thereby supplements the efforts of the perpetrator, and he is guilty as [a] principal in the second degree at common law, and is [a] principal in the first degree under our statute, notwithstanding it may be found that in all human probability the chance would not have been availed of, and death would have resulted anyway.

We have already said enough to indicate the grounds of the conclusion which we now announce that Tally's standing guard at the telegraph office in Scottsboro to prevent Ross being warned of the pursuit of the Skeltons was not by preconcert with them, and was not known to them. It is even clearer and more certain that they knew neither of the occasion nor the fact of the sending of the message by him to Huddleston; and hence they were not, and could not have been aided in the execution of the purpose to kill by the keeping of this vigil, or by the mere fact of the forwarding of the message to Stevenson, since these facts in and of themselves could not have given them any actual, substantial help, as distinguished from incitement and encouragement, and they could not have aided them by way of incitement and encouragement, because they were ignorant of them; and so we are come to a consideration of the effect, if any, produced upon the situation at Stevenson by the message of Judge Tally to Huddleston, and upon his action in respect of the delivery to Ross of the message of warning sent by Ed Ross. This latter message reached Huddleston for Ross, we suppose, about five minutes—certainly not more than ten minutes—before Ross arrived at Stevenson. Immediately upon the heels of it, substantially at the same time, Tally's message to Huddleston was received by the latter. Ed Ross' message imported extreme urgency in its delivery, and

Tally's to Huddleston, though by no means so intended, emphasized the necessity and importance, from the standpoint of duty, for the earliest possible delivery of Ed Ross' message to Robert C. Ross; and it was the manifest duty of Huddleston to deliver it at the earliest practicable moment of time. Huddleston appears to have appreciated the urgency of the case, and at first to have intended doing his duty. Upon receiving the two messages, he went at once without waiting, to copy them, to the Stevenson Hotel, which is located very near the telegraph office, in quest of Ross, upon the idea that he might have already arrived. We are to presume a purpose to do what duty enjoins until the contrary appears; and we therefore shall assume that Huddleston intended to deliver the message to Ross, or to inform him of its contents, had he been in the hotel. Not finding him there (for he had not yet reached Stevenson), Huddleston returned to the door of the depot, upstairs, in which was the telegraph office. By this time the command which Judge Tally had laid upon him had overmastered his sense of duty, and diverted him from his purpose to deliver Ed Ross' message to Robert. Standing there at the door, he saw a hack approaching from the direction of Scottsboro. He said then that he supposed Ross was in that hack. We do not think it was incumbent upon him, inasmuch as the hack was being driven directly to the depot, to go down the road to meet it, though the situation was then more urgent than was indicated by the telegrams, in that the Skeltons were at that time skulking on the flanks of, and immediately behind, the hack; but there is no evidence that Huddleston knew this. But we do not doubt that it was Huddleston's duty to go out to the road along which the hack was being driven, at a point opposite his own position at the depot, and near to it, and there and then have delivered the message or made known its contents to Ross. The only explanation he offers for not then delivering the message or making known its contents to Ross was not that he could not have done it (that was entirely practicable), but that he had not taken a copy of it—a consideration which did not prevent his going to the hotel for the purpose of delivery before he saw Ross appearing, and which, had his original purpose continued, we cannot believe would have swerved him from his plain duty at this juncture. Presuming that he would have done this, because it was his duty to do it—a duty which he at first appreciated—and finding, as a fact, that he did not do it, the reason for his default is found in the injunction laid upon him by Judge Tally. He did not warn Ross, because he did not want Ross to get away, and this because Judge Tally had asked him not to let Ross get away; so that, as he stood there at the door, he mapped out a course of action. He would not deliver the message immediately, if at all, but he would send off for the town marshal, and in the meantime he would call William Tally from over the way, and confer with him as to what should be done: Ross to be the while wholly unadvised of the contents of the message from his kinsman, and wholly ignorant of the pursuit of the Skeltons. So he sends a man in search of the marshal, whose whereabouts, and, of consequence, the time necessary to find and bring whom to the station, were unknown; beckons to William Tally to come to him; then turns and goes upstairs into the telegraph office. He says he went up there to copy Ross' message for delivery to him. If this be true, this was only another factor, so we have seen, in the delay that Judge Tally's message had determined him upon, for while, at first, he was anxious to deliver the message or its contents uncopied to Ross, when he thought Ross might be at the hotel, and went there to find him for that purpose, when Ross was actually in sight of him, and rapidly approaching him, he deemed it most important to copy the message before advising Ross. It was also into this upstairs office that he invited William Tally, and we cannot escape the conclusion that his purpose in going there before delivering the message was to have a consultation with William Tally as to what should be done before advising Ross, and also to give the marshal time to arrive; so that, should they conclude to adopt that course, they could have Ross arrested; and it cannot, we think, be doubted that he then had no purpose whatever of apprising Ross of the contents of the message, if ever, until he had had this conference with the brother of the man who had asked him not to deliver it at all. That this delay was to conserve such ulterior purpose as might be born of this conference, was wholly unwarranted, and was caused by the telegram of Judge Tally to Huddleston, we believe beyond a reasonable doubt.

It remains to be determined whether the unwarranted delay in the delivery of the message to Ross, or in advising him of its contents, thus caused by Judge Tally, with intent thereby to aid the Skeltons to kill Ross, did in fact, aid them or contribute to the death of Ross, by making it easier than it would otherwise have been for the Skeltons to kill him, by depriving him of some advantage he would have had had he been advised of its contents when his carriage stopped, or immediately upon his alighting from it, or by leaving him without some chance of life which would have been his had Huddleston done his duty. The telegram, we have said, should have been delivered, or its contents made known, to Ross at the time the hack came opposite where Huddleston was, and stopped. Huddleston and William Tally were equidistant from this point when the former called to the latter, at which time also Huddleston had seen the hack approaching this point. Tally, going to Huddleston, reached this middle point between them, unhastened, as Huddleston should have been, by the urgency of the message, just as the carriage got there and stopped. It is therefore clear that had Huddleston, instead of calling Tally and going into the depot, himself gone out to the road along which the carriage was approaching, and which was not more than 100 feet from him, he would have gotten there certainly by the time it stopped, and have acquainted Ross with the contents of the message, with the fact that four men were pursuing him with guns to take his life, before Ross alighted from the hack. Being thus advised, and not knowing of the immediate proximity of the Skeltons, it may be that Ross would have alighted as he did, exposed himself to the Skeltons' fire as he did, and been killed as he was. But, on the other hand, the Skeltons were at that time dismounted, and, two of them at least, a long way from their horses, and none of them were in his front up the road, and he had a chance of escape by continued flight in the vehicle. Again, he might then and there have put himself under the protection of Huddleston, as an officer of the law, and had the bystanders, those in the immediate neighborhood, of whom there were several, summoned to help protect him. This might have saved his life; it was a chance that he had. But, if it be conceded that, as he would not have known of the proximity of the Skeltons from mere knowledge that they were in pursuit, he would have alighted precisely as and when he did; yet when the first shot was fired, Ross would have known that the man who fired it was one of the Skeltons, and that three others of them were present in ambush, armed with guns, to take his life. Knowing this, the hopelessness of standing his ground and attempting to defend himself from his enemies, overpowering in number, and secure in their hiding places, while he stood in the open street, would have been at once manifest to him; and instead of standing there as he did, knowing only as he did that some one man, whom he did not know, had fired a gun, and peering and craning his neck to see whence the shot came, and who fired it, he could, and doubtless would, have sought safety by flight in the opposite direction, in which was the Union Hotel, scarce 100 feet away. And in view of the fact that he was hit only once by the numerous shots that were fired at him while he stood there in the open, and that not in a vital or disabling part, it is very probable that, had he attempted that mode of escape as soon as the first shot was fired, he would have reached the hotel in perfect safety. Certain it is that in making that effort he would have gone away from the lurking places of his enemies, and he would not, as he did in his ignorance of the true situation, have placed himself where John Skelton, at close quarter, could and did shoot him to death from behind his back. But whether he would or would not have reached a place of refuge we need not inquire or find. The knowledge that he would have had if the telegram of Ed Ross had been delivered to him, when it could and should have been delivered, of the pursuit of the Skeltons, together with the knowledge which would have been imparted to him by the report of the first gun in connection with the contents of the message, would instantly have advised him of the extent of his danger—a danger which he could not combat, which was deadly in character, and from which he would naturally have been at once impressed the only hope of escape lay in immediate flight. That was a chance for his life that this knowledge would have given him. That was a chance of which the withholding of this knowledge deprived him. Tally's telegram to Huddleston deprived him of that knowledge. Tally, through Huddleston, deprived him of that chance. Again, after having been shot in the legs, and partially disabled by one of the many shots fired at him by Robert, James, and Walter Skelton as he stood fully exposed to their broadside, he, in his crippled condition, made an effort to find protection behind the oil house, the nearest building to him. Only these three men had fired up to that time. He knew of the presence of these three only. The house sheltered him from two of these men and partially also from the third. He got there, and stood facing the direction these three were; and he called aloud for protection from them, meantime keeping a lookout for them, and intending no doubt to protect himself from them if he could. He knew of the presence of these three only. Nobody had seen John Skelton. He did not know that John Skelton was there. Had he gotten Ed Ross' telegram, this he would have known: that there were four of them; that only three had shot at him; that the other was somewhere hidden in the immediate vicinity. And, while seeking to escape from or guard himself from the other three while he was by the side of the oil house, he would also have sought to guard himself against the fourth. He was off his guard as to this fourth man, John Skelton, because he was ignorant of his presence. This ignorance was directly due to Tally's active interference. Tally's aid to the Skeltons by way of preventing Ross being warned enabled John Skelton to come upon Ross from his rear, and shoot him down. Ross went to his death, guarding himself against the other three, and calling for protection from them, without even knowing that the man who killed him was nearer to him than Scottsboro. Can it be doubted that Ross' utter ignorance of John Skelton's presence with the others at Stevenson made it easier for John Skelton to take his life? Can it be doubted that his ignorance of the presence of all four Skeltons when the first gun was fired by Robert Skelton at Bloodwood, when, had he known it, he could have fled in the appreciable time between the time of the firing of the first and other shots—the next one being fired by the same man—made it easier for them to take his life? Can it be doubted in any case that murder by lying in wait is facilitated by the unconsciousness of the victim? Or in any case that the chances of the intended victim would be improved, and his death rendered more difficult of accomplishment, if the first unfruitful shot apprises him of the number and the identity of his assailants, and the full scope and measure of their motive and purposes? We cannot believe otherwise. It is inconceivable to us after the maturest consideration, reflection, and discussion, but that Ross' predicament was rendered infinitely more desperate, his escape more difficult, and his death of much more easy and certain accomplishment by the withholding from him of the message of Ed Ross. This withholding was the work of Judge Tally. An intent to aid the Skeltons to take the life of Ross actuated him to it. The intent was effectuated. They thereby were enabled to take him unawares, and to send him to his death without, we doubt not, his ever actually knowing who sought his life, or being able to raise a hand in defense, or to take an advised step in retreat. And we are impelled to find that John B. Tally aided and abetted the murder of Robert C. Ross, as alleged in the second specification of the second count of the information, and to adjudge that he is guilty as charged in second count; and judgment deposing him from office will be entered on the records of this court.

Head, J. (dissenting). I am of the opinion the respondent should be acquitted of both charges. I do not believe, beyond a reasonable doubt, that respondent intended, in sending the telegram to Huddleston, to aid or abet in the murder of Ross. I do not believe, beyond a reasonable doubt, that the telegram of warning would have been delivered to Ross by Huddleston before the shooting began if the telegram of the respondent had not been sent.

Notes and Questions

1. What causal role did Tally play in the death of Ross? The court acknowledged that even if Ross had received the warning telegram, he might have been killed. The court speaks of "depriving him of some advantage," but how much deprivation is enough? One chance in a hundred, one in a thousand, or one in a million?

2. How does the court address the problem caused by the fact that the telegraph operator (Huddleston) failed in his legal duty by not delivering the warning telegram? Would it make any difference if Huddleston had known the Skeltons were trying to kill Ross and also wanted Ross dead himself? Can one become an aider and abetter through an omission? Did Huddleston aid and abet the murder? As the court pointed out:

> He did not warn Ross, because he did not want Ross to get away, and this because Judge Tally had asked him not to let Ross get away; so that, as he stood there at the door, he mapped out a course of action. He would not deliver the message immediately, if at all, but he would send off for the town marshal, and in the meantime he would call William Tally from over the way, and confer with him as to what should be done.

What about the guilt of the telegraph operator who sent out Judge Tally's telegram to Huddleston?

3. Consider the following variations on *Tally:*

> a. Tally sends the telegram, but Huddleston ignores it and delivers the warning to Ross. It comes too late, however, and as Ross is fleeing, he is murdered by the Skeltons. Is Tally guilty of attempting to aid a murder, which is identical to attempted murder, or can Tally be convicted of murder regardless of whether his attempts to help had any effect whatsoever? See M.P.C. §2.06(3)(a)(ii):
>
>> A person is an accomplice of another person in the commission of an offense if:
>> (a) with the purpose of promoting or facilitating the commission of the offense, he . . .
>> (ii) aids or agrees or attempts to aid such other person in planning or committing it.
>
> What rationale could justify a conviction for murder, especially since under Part II of the Model Penal Code murder is an exception to the rule that attempt is punished as severely as the completed crime?
>
> b. The same as above, except that Ross escapes. Assuming that the Skeltons could be convicted of attempted murder, could Tally be charged with attempt-

ing to aid an attempted murder? If not, is it because the complicity doctrine is being pushed too far, or because we feel uncomfortable when it is combined with an attempt crime? Is it a stronger case if Huddleston does not deliver the warning but Ross escapes anyway? Why is it stronger when, in both examples, Tally has done all that he can to thwart Ross' escape?

c. The same as in example b above, except that the Skeltons change their minds and make no attempt to kill Ross. Assume that they cannot be convicted of any crime. Examine MCP §5.01(3):

> *Conduct Designed to Aid Another in Commission of a Crime.* A person who engages in conduct designed to aid another to commit a crime which would establish his complicity under Section 2.06 if the crime were committed by such other person, is guilty of an attempt to commit the crime, although the crime is not committed or attempted by such other person.

Does this suggest that Tally could be convicted of attempted murder in both b and c even though in the last example, no substantive crime was committed?

d. Tally changes his mind and sends another telegram, telling Huddleston to ignore his first telegram. This, of course, raises the issue of whether it is possible for an accomplice to recant in such a manner as to negate his criminal liability. In People v. Ortiz, 63 Cal. App. 662, 219 P. 1024 (1923) the defendant was with a group of people drinking at a hotel bar. The victim became angry at one of the group, Doe, and threatened him with a razor. Doe in turn asked the defendant where the gun was. The defendant left and returned immediately with a gun with which he threatened the victim. Doe then took the pistol and shot the victim. The defendant may have tried to prevent Doe from taking the pistol. The court rejected the defendant's proposed instruction that an accessory's responsibility ceases when he abandons the common purpose and withdraws from any further concert. It stated that

> Responsibility of an accessory "does not cease simply because, after starting the ball, he changes his mind, and tries, when too late, to stop it. To emancipate him from the consequences, not only must he have acted in time, and done everything practicable to present the consummation, but the consummation, if it takes place, must be imputable to some independent cause." Wharton's Criminal Law (11th ed.) §267.

The Model Penal Code takes a slightly more generous approach. See MPC §2.06(6)(c)(i) and (ii):

> Unless otherwise provided by the Code or by the law defining the offense, a person is not an accomplice in an offense committed by another person if: . . .
> (c) he terminates his complicity prior to the commission of the offense and
> (i) wholly deprives it of effectiveness in the commission of the offense; or
> (ii) gives timely warning to the law enforcement authorities or otherwise makes proper effort to prevent the commission of the offense.

Does it make sense ever to eliminate an accomplice's liability if the accomplice is unsuccessful in preventing the crime? What if he or she notifies the police in a timely fashion, but they are negligent, or even grossly negligent in preventing the commission of the crime? See also New York Penal Code §40.10(1) and Practice Commentaries:

> In any prosecution for an offense, other than an attempt to commit a crime, in which the defendant's guilt depends upon his criminal liability for the conduct of another person . . . it is an affirmative defense that, under circumstances manifesting a voluntary and complete renunciation of his criminal purpose, the defendant withdrew from participation in such offense prior to the commission thereof and made a substantial effort to prevent the commission thereof.

Consider Hechtman, New York Penal Code §40.10(1), Practice Commentaries:

> The defense of "renunciation," involving the concept of abandonment and related principles, was not dealt with in the former Penal Law, nor did New York case law present any discernible scheme or pattern in this area. This "affirmative defense," which is explained herein largely by means of illustration, applies in the main to anticipatory offenses . . . usually involving two or more participants or culprits, and to multiple offender cases of consummated crime in which the guilt of one or more rest upon principles of accessorial liability. . . .

The operation of §40.10(1) may be illustrated by a case in which *A, B,* and *C,* after carefully planning an armed holdup of a store, finally proceed toward the store to execute the robbery. On the way, *A,* who obtained the guns and otherwise participated in the preparations, decides not to go through with the project, but *B* and *C* continue on and commit the crime.

Upon these facts alone, *A,* having intentionally and materially aided the robbery, is guilty thereof despite his absence at its execution. . . . His liability is not negated by his abandonment or withdrawal "prior to the commission thereof," since he did not make a "substantial effort to prevent" it. While the term "substantial effort" leaves room for construction, it imports considerably more than a mild attempt at verbal dissuasion. It was essential that *A* take earnest and vigorous action, possibly by way of, for example, meaningful warnings to his confederates or notification to the police.

For a judicial interpretation of §40.10, see People v. Nassar, 59 Misc. 2d 1034, 301 N.Y.S.2d 671 (1969).

WILCOX v. JEFFERY

King's Bench Division

[1951] 1 All E.R. 464

Lord GODDARD, C.J. This is a Case stated by the metropolitan magistrate at Bow Street Magistrate's Court before whom the appellant, Herbert William Wilcox, the proprietor of a periodical called "Jazz Illustrated," was charged on an information that "on Dec. 11, 1949, he did unlawfully aid and abet one Coleman Hawkins in contravening art. 1(4) of the Aliens Order, 1920, by failing to comply with a condition to a grant of leave to land, to wit, that the said Coleman Hawkins should take no employment paid or unpaid while in the United Kingdom, contrary to art. 18(2) of the Aliens Order, 1920." Under the Aliens Order, art. 1(1), it is provided that

> . . . an alien coming . . . by sea to a place in the United Kingdom . . . shall not land . . . without the leave of an immigration officer.

It is provided by art 1(4) that:

> An immigration officer, in accordance with general or special directions of the Secretary of State, may, by general order or notice or otherwise, attach such conditions as he may think fit to the grant of leave to land, and the Secretary of State may at any time vary such conditions in such manner as he thinks fit, and the alien shall comply with the conditions so attached or varied.

If the alien fails to comply, he is to be in the same position as if he has landed without permission, i.e., he commits an offence.

The case is concerned with the visit of a celebrated professor of the saxophone, a gentleman by the name of Hawkins who was a citizen of the United States. He came here at the invitation of two gentlemen of the name of Curtis and Hughes, connected with a jazz club which enlivens the neighbourhood of Willesden. They, apparently, had applied for permission for Mr. Hawkins to land and it was refused, but nevertheless, this professor of the saxophone arrived with four French musicians. When they came to the airport, among the people who were there to greet them was the appellant. He had not arranged their visit, but he knew they were coming and he was there to report the arrival of these important musicians for his magazine. So, evidently, he was regarding the visit of Mr. Hawkins as a matter which would be of interest to himself and the magazine which he was editing and selling for profit. Messrs. Curtis and Hughes arranged a concert at the Princes Theatre, London. The appellant attended that concert as a spectator. He paid for his ticket. Mr. Hawkins went on the stage and delighted the audience by playing the saxophone. The appellant did not get up and protest in the name of the musicians of England that Mr. Hawkins ought not be here competing with them and taking the bread out of their mouths or the wind out of their instruments. It is not found that he actually applauded, but he was there having paid to go in, and, no doubt, enjoying the performance, and then, lo and behold, out comes his magazine with a most laudatory description, fully illustrated, of this concert. On those facts the magistrate has found that he aided and abetted.

Reliance is placed by the prosecution on R. v. Coney which dealt with a prize fight. This case relates to a jazz band concert, but the particular nature of the entertainment provided, whether by fighting with bare fists or playing on saxophones, does not seem to me to make any difference to the question which we have to decide. The fact is that a man is charged with aiding and abetting an illegal act, and I can find no authority for saying that it matters what that illegal act is, provided that the aider and abettor knows the facts sufficiently well to know that they would constitute an offence in the principal. In R. v. Coney the prize fight took place in the neighbourhood of Ascot, and four or five men were convicted of aiding and abetting the fight. The conviction was quashed on the ground that the chairman had not given a correct direction to the jury when he told them that, as the prisoners were physically present at the fight, they must be held to have aided and abetted. That direction, the court held, was wrong, it being too wide. The matter was very concisely put by Cave, J., whose judgment was fully concurred in by that great master of the criminal law, Stephen, J. Cave, J., said (8 Q.B.D. 540):

> Where presence may be entirely accidental, it is not even evidence of aiding and abetting. Where presence is prima facie not accidental it is evidence, but no more than evidence, for the jury.

There was not accidental presence in this case. The appellant paid to go to the concert and he went there because he wanted to report it. He must, therefore, be held to have been present, taking part, concurring, or encouraging, whichever word you like to use for expressing this conception. It was an illegal act on the part of Hawkins to play the saxophone or any other instrument at this concert. The appellant clearly knew that it was an unlawful act for him to play. He had gone there to hear him, and his presence and his payment to go there was an encouragement. He went there to make use of the performance, because he went there, as the magistrate finds and was justified in finding, to get "copy" for his newspaper. It might have been entirely different, as I say, if he had gone there and protested, saying: "The musicians' union do [sic] not like you foreigners coming here and playing and you ought to get off the stage." If he had booed, it might have been some evidence that he was not aiding and abetting. If he had gone as a member of a *claque* to try to drown the noise of the saxophone, he might very likely be found not guilty of aiding and abetting. In this case it seems clear that he was there, not only to approve and encourage what was done, but to take advantage of it by getting "copy" for his paper. In those circumstances there was evidence on which the magistrate could find that the appellant aided and abetted, and for these reasons I am of the opinion that the appeal fails.

DEVLIN, J. I agree, and I wish to add only a word on the application of R. v. Coney. Counsel for the appellant sought to distinguish that case on the facts inasmuch as in R. v. Coney the performance, which was a prize fight, was illegal from beginning to end, whereas in the case we are considering the bulk of the concert was quite legal, the only part of the performance which was illegal being that which involved Mr. Hawkins. That, however, is not, in my judgment, a distinction which affects the application to this case of the principle in R. v. Coney. It may well be that if a spectator goes to a concert he may explain his presence during an illegal item by saying that he hardly felt it necessary to get up and go out and then return when the performance resumed its legality, if I may so call it. It is conceivable that in such circumstances (and I should wish to consider it further if it ever arose) the presence of a person during one item might fall within the accidental or casual class which was envisaged by Cave, J. Here there was abundant evidence, apart from the mere fact of the appellant's presence, that he was making use of this item in the performance and that his attendance at that item was, therefore, deliberate. In those circumstances I think the principle in R. v. Coney applies, and that the magistrate was justified in drawing the inference which he did draw.

Appeal dismissed with costs.

Notes and Questions

1. The court emphasizes that Wilcox attended the concert for profit. How is this relevant to the charge that he aided and abetted Hawkins in violating the Aliens Order? The court also states that he paid to see the concert and did nothing to prohibit Hawkins's performance. Does this mean that all spectators who paid and made no attempt to stop the performance are guilty of aiding and abetting? What legal duty did Wilcox have to attempt to prevent Hawkins from playing? Can it seriously be argued that Wilcox's presence caused the performance to occur? What about the other musicians?

2. The statement of facts appended to the court's opinion includes the following:

> The immigration officer gave permission to Hawkins to remain for three days in this country, making it a condition that he should not take any paid or unpaid employment. The appellant was aware that such a condition had been imposed. Later the same day the appellant attended the concert, paying for admission. Hawkins was seated in a box, but after being "spotlighted" he went to the stage and played the saxophone. A description of the performance by Hawkins with several pages of photographs was later published in the appellant's magazine.

Should this make a difference?

3. How should this case have been handled? See pages 564-565.

4. Not all cases where a person clearly aids and abets another's crime will result in criminal liability. In The Queen v. Tyrell, [1893] L.Q.B. 710, the defendant, a minor, was convicted of aiding and abetting her own statutory rape by an adult. The court reversed her conviction, arguing that her conviction contradicted the purpose of the statute, which was to protect young girls:

> I do not see how it would be possible to obtain convictions under the statute if the contention for the Crown were adopted, because nearly every section which deals with offences in respect of women and girls would create an offence in the woman or girl. Such a result cannot have been intended by the legislature. There is no trace in the statute of any intention to treat the woman or girl as criminal.

Although not determinative in itself, *Tyrell* raises the question of accomplice liability in crimes that require two people, but where the legislature appears to have imposed liability on only one of the parties. Assume that the drug laws make selling a drug illegal but not buying it or that the vice laws make selling sex illegal but not buying it. Would the legislature want the courts to make the drug buyer or prostitution customer criminally liable through the complicity doctrine? Why not? The Model Penal Code takes the position in §2.06(6)(b) that

> Unless otherwise provided by the Code or by the law defining the offense, a person is not an accomplice in an offense committed by another person if. . . .
> (b) the offense is so defined that his conduct is inevitably incidental to its commission.

What if the law makes both parties guilty of a "two person" crime? If the buyer and seller are both guilty of crimes, can each be guilty of aiding and abetting the other's crime? Is this a different issue from that in *Tyrell?*

5. Just as one may not be criminally liable even though he or she aids and abets a person who commits a crime, one may be guilty of a crime for aiding and abetting someone who is not guilty of any crime. Although no state has a statute making a successful suicide a crime, most retain criminal liability for aiding and abetting suicide. Three different approaches have developed to deal with aiding and abetting a suicide: the common law position treating such conduct as murder; creating a special form of manslaughter; and by far the most common, creating the substantive crime of aiding and abetting a suicide. For example, the Revised Statutes of Nebraska §28.07 provides:

> (1) A person commits assisting suicide when, with intent to assist another person in committing suicide, he aids and abets him in committing or attempting to commit suicide.
> (2) Assisting suicide is a Class IV felony.

California Penal Code §401 reads:

> Every person who deliberately aids, or advises, or encourages another to commit suicide is guilty of a felony.

Generally, a defendant is not guilty of homicide (murder or manslaughter) when he merely furnishes the means of a suicide, but if he actively participates in causing the death, even at the request of the victim, he is guilty of homicide. What if two people enter into a genuine suicide pact contemplating simultaneous death, but one of the parties survives?

In the case of In re Joseph G., 34 Cal. 3d 429, 194 Cal. Rptr. 193, 667 P.2d 1176 (1983), the defendant, a minor, and a friend, Jeff W., told a group of friends that they intended to kill themselves by driving their car off a nearby cliff:

> The others were skeptical but the minor affirmed their seriousness, stating "You don't believe us that we are going to do it. We are going to do it. You can read it in the paper tomorrow." The minor gave one of the girls his baseball hat, saying firmly that this was the last time he would see her. Jeff repeatedly encouraged the minor by urging, "let's go, let's go" whenever the minor spoke. One

> other youth attempted to get in the car with Jeff and the minor but they refused to allow him to join them "because we don't want to be responsible for you." Jeff and the minor shook hands with their friends and departed. . . .
>
> Two of their fellow students, Keith C. and Craig B., drove up and spoke with Jeff and the minor. The minor said, "Shake my hand and stay cool." Jeff urged, "Let's go," shook their hands and said, "Remember you shook my hand." The minor then drove off in the direction of the cliff with Jeff in the passenger seat; Keith and Craig surreptitiously followed them out of curiosity. The minor and Jeff proceeded up the hill past the cliff, turned around and drove down around the curve and over the steep cliff.
>
> Two other vehicles were parked in the turnout, from which vantage point their occupants watched the minor's car plummeting down the hill at an estimated 50 mph. The car veered off the road without swerving or changing course; the witnesses heard the car accelerate and then drive straight off the cliff. No one saw brake lights flash. The impact of the crash killed Jeff and caused severe injuries to the minor, resulting in the amputation of a foot.

The California Supreme Court held that despite Joseph G.'s active role in the death of Jeff W., he could at most be charged with aiding and abetting a suicide. The court noted the usual rule that a person who "actively participates" in the death of the victim is guilty of murder. But it held that rule inapplicable where the parties make a simultaneous suicide pact, characterizing the "crime" as, in effect, a double attempted suicide.

C. *MENS REA*

WILSON v. PEOPLE
Supreme Court of Colorado
100 Colo. 441, 87 P.2d 5 (1939)

Otto Bock, Justice.

Plaintiff in error was charged and convicted under two counts of having unlawfully and feloniously aided, abetted and assisted one Dwight J. Pierce in the commission of a burglary and larceny. One of his defenses was the absence of felonious intent on his part to commit the crimes in question, because he acted solely as a decoy to detect the commission of the crime and to report it to the proper officers, so that Pierce might be apprehended. Plaintiff in error will hereinafter be referred to as Wilson.

The facts, substantially, are as follows:

On the night of February 19, 1938, Wilson, son of the deputy district attorney of the thirteenth judicial district, and employed by him for several months prior thereto, was in Johnson's Cafe in Sterling, Colorado. Some time after 10 o'clock P.M. Pierce entered. Pierce had been drinking and was looking for a place where he could purchase more liquor. Without previous arrangement, Pierce approached Wilson and prevailed upon him to make an effort to find such a place. The two left the cafe and went to the Commercial Hotel, where Pierce borrowed some money. Wilson left and came back to report to Pierce that no whiskey could be had, but he could get a pint of sloe gin. This was satisfactory to Pierce, and Wilson procured a bottle of the gin which he delivered to Pierce, and both returned to the Johnson Cafe, where they drank some of the liquor. During that time a wrist watch which Wilson had been wearing disappeared while he was in the company of Pierce. When Wilson missed his watch he immediately accused Pierce of taking it. He continued to make the accusation through the evening, and at one time threatened to fight Pierce because of the alleged theft. Pierce denied the theft. The argument about the wrist watch became so noisy that the participants were asked to leave the cafe. They then went to another cafe and Wilson bought Pierce a cup of coffee, and the argument concerning the watch was resumed until Pierce, as he testified, thought they would be thrown out there.

While drinking the liquor at the Johnson Cafe, Pierce first commenced to talk about jobs that he had done and specifically mentioned his burglary of the Wheat Growers Cafe. This talk came up in connection with the disappearance of Wilson's wrist watch. Finally they reached the Commercial Hotel, where Pierce was a janitor, and in the furnace room the conversation about burglaries continued between them. There also was some talk concerning tools, and Pierce procured a piece of paper and wrote down a list of tools that would be needed, not that night, but at some future time, and Wilson said that he could get them for him. The subject of the watch again came up in the furnace room, and Pierce again denied taking it. Wilson suggested that they go to his father's office, to which he had the keys, to start on the jobs, and they there conceived the idea of breaking into Hecker Brothers' Drugstore. Wilson did not first propose the burglarizing, the idea originating with Pierce, and after the latter had told Wilson that he had burglarized the Wheat Growers Cafe several days before. There is some conflict in the evidence as to who first suggested breaking into Hecker Brothers' Drugstore, but they proceeded to the building in which it was located, tried several doors, finally going outside, and effecting an entry through the front transom. After Wilson had boosted Pierce up so that he could break the glass in the transom, and after looking around to see if anyone had heard them, Wilson again lifted Pierce and the latter handed the broken glass to Wilson, who dropped it on the cement. Thereupon Wilson again lifted Pierce up so that he could crawl through the transom. Pierce then proceeded to the cash register. Immediately after Pierce was inside the store Wilson ran to his father's office and telephoned the police to come to Hecker Brothers' Drugstore. He then returned to where the entry had been effected, and a few moments before the police arrived, Pierce handed to Wilson, through the transom, two or three bottles of liquor which he placed on the cement. Pierce noticed after he entered the store that Wilson had disappeared. Immediately after arrival of the police Wilson told them that Pierce was inside, designating him as "that guy from the Commercial Hotel." The police officer asked him how he knew, and he replied, "I boosted him in." Pierce escaped through the back door and Wilson immediately volunteered to track him down, and did so by going to Pierce's room at the Commercial Hotel, where he identified Pierce as the burglar in the presence of the police authorities. Wilson told the police, shortly after the apprehension of Pierce, that his connection with the burglary was for the purpose of getting even with Pierce for taking his watch, and that that was the only way he hoped to recover it. He also stated later that evening that he wanted to apprehend Pierce and turn him over to the authorities—he wanted to catch him in the act.

The record indicates that Wilson was sincere in his belief that Pierce had taken his watch. Moreover, there is evidence in the people's case that tends to support his defense that he acted only as a decoy to apprehend Pierce in the act of committing the crime. Wilson's testimony at the trial substantially supported his defense that he had no criminal intent to feloniously burglarize or steal. . . .

Instruction No. 10, to the giving of which defendant assigns error, reads as follows:

> One may not participate in the commission of a felony and then obtain immunity from punishment on the ground that he was a mere detective or spy. One who attempts to detect the commission of crime in others must himself stop short of lending assistance, or participation in the commission of the crime.

Defendant contends that this instruction is erroneous because it left no question of fact for the determination of the jury on his defense of decoy and detection. Wilson did assist Pierce in entering the drugstore. This he never denied and immediately revealed to the police his part in the transaction when they arrived in response to his call. The instruction inferentially placed guilt upon Wilson, because he did not "stop short of lending assistance," but actually gave assistance. We find the following language in 16 Corpus Juris at page 128, section 115:

> For one to be guilty as principal in the second degree, it is essential that he share in the criminal intent of the principal in the first degree; the same criminal intent must exist in the minds of both.

And on page 129:

> One who participates in a felony as a feigned accomplice, in order to entrap the other, is not criminally liable, and he need not take an officer of the law into his confidence to avoid an imputation of criminal intent.

In this connection we cite also Wharton's Criminal Law (12th ed.) volume 1, section 271, which reads in part as follows: "A detective entering apparently into a criminal conspiracy already formed for the purpose of exploding it is not an accessory before the fact."

It may be that the jury in the instant case placed more stress on the motives that actuated Wilson in his participation in the transaction than they did on the necessity of determining his felonious intent under the circumstances.

Reverting to Instruction No. 10, by judicial fiat this instruction makes any assistance in the perpetration of an offense criminal, whether felonious or not. The determination of whether the assistance by Wilson under the evidence in this case was given with felonious intent was solely the province of the jury, and this instruction erroneously invaded that province. There may be offenses and circumstances when any assistance rendered may make a participant guilty of a criminal offense; but here we are concerned only with the facts, circumstances and defenses in this case. . . . The giving of Instruction No. 10 constituted prejudicial error.

The judgment is reversed and the cause remanded for new trial.

Notes and Questions

1. Assuming that Pierce was guilty of burglary, wasn't Wilson's conduct enough to qualify him as an aider and abettor under the cases we have examined? Can he be acquitted simply because he has a good "motive"? Wasn't his motive to ensure that Pierce committed burglary? Did Wilson have the requisite mental state with regard to the elements of the burglary? For further exploration of the issue as to when a policeman or other citizen can "violate the law" to catch a criminal, see pages 843-856.

How would you define the *mens rea* necessary for complicity?

2. Should we require people like Wilson to stop the "true criminal," the principal, as soon as the principal has crossed the line from preparation to attempt, but before he completes the crime?

Consider the following hypothetical from an examination in criminal law:

> A thug named Andy decided to attack his enemy Victor. On the way to find Victor, Andy stopped at Dan's liquor store. Andy told Dan, who knew Victor, that he was planning to "cut Victor up a little to teach him a lesson," and needed to buy some gin to work up the nerve. He also asked Dan where to find Victor. Dan knew Andy was an undesirable character, but he decided to feign cooperation in order to finally get Andy off the streets. His plan was to set things up so that the police could catch Andy in the act of trying to assault Victor. He sold Andy some gin and directed him to the bar where Victor often hung out. Shortly after Andy left Dan's store, Dan called the police and told them where they could catch Andy in the act of assault. The police arrived just in time to see Andy slash and badly injure Victor.

Is Dan criminally liable? What if Andy, in the course of assaulting Victor, had killed him?

3. Assume the precise facts of *Wilson,* except reverse the roles: Wilson agrees to help Pierce burgle the store, only it is Pierce who assists Wilson in climbing through the window. Would the result be different? Would Wilson

be guilty of burglary? If the court would still hold Wilson not liable, could it hold Pierce liable as an accomplice? How could he be an accomplice to a person who committed no crime? In State v. Hayes, 105 Mo. 76, 16 S.W. 514 (1891), Hill feigned interest in a burglary proposed by Hayes. Hayes assisted Hill in entering a store to steal bacon. After Hill handed Hayes the bacon, he helped the police apprehend Hayes. The court reversed Hayes's conviction, finding no common design to support complicity in burglary, but suggested that Hayes could still be guilty of larceny of the bacon.

4. The jurisdictions vary on the question of whether under complicity doctrine an accomplice may be guilty of a more or less serious crime than the principal (see page 577). But the courts apply a different rule to cases where the criminal uses as an instrument or agent a person who is categorically immune from liability as a principal. Such cases arise where the "principal" (also called the "innocent agent") is a child or a mentally incompetent person, or any person who cannot be convicted under the statute in question. Instead of relying on accessorial liability, the law views the culpable actor as a "perpetrator by means" and treats that person directly as a principal even though he or she may not have actually committed the criminal act.

In State v. Thomas, 619 S.W.2d 513 (Tenn. 1981), "the defendant drew his gun on a married couple and forced the wife to perform 'acts of perversion' upon her husband." The Supreme Court of Tennessee upheld his conviction of criminal sexual conduct commenting on the "perpetration by means" version of complicity:

> The defendant who forces an innocent party to commit armed robbery, burglary, rape, incest, etc., is guilty as the only principal, even though the defendant does not commit the crime with his own hand.
>
> In the situation before us, both husband and wife were victims and both were used as innocent agents of the defendant in the perpetration of the crime. The defendant committed the act of "sexual penetration" by means of these agents and he was properly found guilty.

Why is "perpetration by means" used rather than accessorial liability to convict the defendant? Is it that we do not feel comfortable using accomplice liability when the "principal" is completely innocent? The Model Penal Code also has a specific section to cover these situations. Section 2.06(2)(a) reads:

> A person is legally accountable for the conduct of another person when:
> (a) acting with the kind of culpability that is sufficient for the commission of the offense, he causes an innocent or irresponsible person to engage in such conduct.

Consider the following hypotheticals:

> a. The defendant, a Mansonesque figure, instructs a drug-dependent follower, incapable of forming intent, to shoot the victim for allegedly smashing the defendant's car window. The follower obediently performs her task, with a gun

provided by the defendant. See State v. McCarthy, 179 Conn. 1, 475 A.2d 924 (1979).

b. The defendant packs a bomb in his wife's suitcase in their home and drives her to the airport where she boards an airplane. The bomb is not discovered until she unpacks her suitcase after the airplane has landed. The defendant is charged with willfully causing an explosive device to be placed in an aircraft. The defendant's wife was totally unaware of the bomb's presence. See United States v. Bradley, 540 F. Supp. 690 (D. Md. 1982).

Some cases hold that the fact that the principal's action is constitutionally protected does not prevent the conviction of one who aids and abets him. In Cole v. United States, 329 F.2d 437, 439-440 (9th Cir. 1964), the defendant was under investigation by a grand jury for possible perjury.[6] A former employee of the defendant, Joel Benton, was called to testify. He had previously filed a false affidavit and had come to the defendant for advice about his testimony. Fearing that Benton's testimony might damage him, the defendant suggested that Benton invoke his constitutional privilege against self-incrimination and refuse to answer the grand jury questions. The defendant was subsequently convicted under 18 U.S.C. §1503, which makes it a crime to corruptly influence a witness or obstruct the due administration of justice. In affirming the defendant's conviction, the court of appeals rejected his claim that because a witness has the constitutional right not to testify, one who encourages him to invoke this right cannot be guilty of a crime:

> Many acts which are not in themselves unlawful, and which do not make the actor a criminal, may make another a criminal who sees that the innocent act is accomplished for a corrupt purpose, or by threat of force. . . . It is the witness' privilege which our inspired Constitution protects and which any person in our courts may invoke, whether he be upright citizen or foul criminal; not someone else's privilege to capture by force or threat or bribe; and thus be enabled to prostitute one of the great cornerstones of our freedom under law.
>
> To hold otherwise, would obstruct the due administration of justice, and we refuse to so hold. The sacred right to guard against self-incrimination is not negotiable, any more than is virtue.

Is this a case of aiding and abetting?

PEOPLE v. BEEMAN

Supreme Court of California

35 Cal. 3d 547, 199 Cal. Rptr. 60 (1984)

Reynoso, Justice.

Timothy Mark Beeman appeals from a judgment of conviction of robbery, burglary, false imprisonment, destruction of telephone equipment and assault with intent to commit a felony (Pen. Code, §§211, 459, 236, 591, 221).

6. The perjury was committed when Cole testified at earlier grand jury proceedings concerning the possible deportation of one of Cole's business associates.

Appellant was not present during commission of the offense. His conviction rested on the theory that he aided and abetted his acquaintances James Gray and Michael Burk.

The primary issue before us is whether the standard California Jury Instructions (CALJIC Nos. 3.00 and 3.01) adequately inform the jury of the criminal intent required to convict a defendant as an aider and abettor of the crime.

We hold that instruction No. 3.01 is erroneous. Sound law, embodied in a long line of California decisions, requires proof that an aider and abettor rendered aid with an intent or purpose of either committing, or of encouraging or facilitating commission of, the target offense. . . .

James Gray and Michael Burk drove from Oakland to Redding for the purpose of robbing appellant's sister-in-law, Mrs. Marjorie Beeman, of valuable jewelry, including a 3.5 carat diamond ring. They telephoned the residence to determine that she was home. Soon thereafter Burk knocked at the door of the victim's house, presented himself as a poll taker, and asked to be let in. When Mrs. Beeman asked for identification, he forced her into the hallway and entered. Gray, disguised in a ski mask, followed. The two subdued the victim, placed tape over her mouth and eyes and tied her to a bathroom fixture. Then they ransacked the house, taking numerous pieces of jewelry and a set of silverware. The jewelry included a 3.5 carat, heart-shaped diamond ring and a blue sapphire ring. The total value of these two rings was over $100,000. In the course of the robbery, telephone wires inside the house were cut.

Appellant was arrested six days later in Emeryville. He had in his possession several of the less valuable of the stolen rings. He supplied the police with information that led to the arrests of Burk and Gray. With Gray's cooperation appellant assisted police in recovering most of the stolen property.

Burk, Gray and appellant were jointly charged. After the trial court severed the trials, Burk and Gray pled guilty to robbery. At appellant's trial they testified that he had been extensively involved in planning the crime.

Burk testified that he had known appellant for two and one-half years. He had lived in appellant's apartment several times. Appellant had talked to him about rich relatives in Redding and had described a diamond ring worth $50,000. According to Burk the feasibility of robbing appellant's relatives was first mentioned two and one-half months before the incident occurred. About one week before the robbery, the discussions became more specific. Appellant gave Burk the address and discussed the ruse of posing as a poll taker. It was decided that Gray and Burk would go to Redding because appellant wanted nothing to do with the actual robbery and because he feared being recognized. On the night before the offense appellant drew a floor plan of the victim's house and told Burk where the diamond ring was likely to be found. Appellant agreed to sell the jewelry for 20 percent of the proceeds.

After the robbery was completed, Burk telephoned appellant to report success. Appellant said that he would call the friend who might buy the jewelry. Burk and Gray drove to appellant's house and showed him the "loot." Appellant was angry that the others had taken so much jewelry, and demanded that his cut be increased from 20 percent to one third.

Gray's testimony painted a similar picture. Gray also had known appellant for approximately two years prior to the incident. Gray said Burk had initially approached him about the robbery, supplied the victim's address, and described the diamond ring. Appellant had at some time described the layout of the house to Gray and Burk and had described to them the cars driven by various members of the victim's family. Gray and Burk, but not appellant, had discussed how to divide the proceeds. Both Gray and Burk owed money to appellant. In addition, Burk owed Gray $3,200.

According to Gray appellant had been present at a discussion three days before the robbery when it was mentioned that appellant could not go because his 6 foot 5 inch, 310 pound frame could be too easily recognized. Two days before the offense, however, appellant told Gray that he wanted nothing to do with the robbery of his relatives. On the day preceding the incident appellant and Gray spoke on the telephone. At that time appellant repeated he wanted nothing to do with the robbery, but confirmed that he had told Burk that he would not say anything if the others went ahead.

Gray confirmed that appellant was upset when he saw that his friends had gone through with the robbery and had taken all of the victim's jewelry. He was angered further when he discovered that Burk might easily be recognized because he had not disguised himself. Appellant then asked them to give him all of the stolen goods. Instead Burk and Gray gave appellant only a watch and some rings which they believed he could sell. Gray and Burk then travelled to San Jose where they sold the silverware for $900. Sometime later appellant asked for Gray's cooperation in recovering and returning the property to the victim. On several occasions when Burk called them for more money, appellant stalled and avoided questions about the sale of the jewelry.

Appellant Beeman's testimony contradicted that of Burk and Gray as to nearly every material element of his own involvement. Appellant testified that he did not participate in the robbery or its planning. He confirmed that Burk had lived with him on several occasions, and that he had told Burk about Mrs. Beeman's jewelry, the valuable diamond ring, and the Beeman ranch, in the course of day-to-day conversations. He claimed that he had sketched a floor plan of the house some nine months prior to the robbery, only for the purpose of comparing it with the layout of a house belonging to another brother. He at first denied and then admitted describing the Beeman family cars, but insisted this never occurred in the context of planning a robbery.

Appellant stated that Burk first suggested that robbing Mrs. Beeman would be easy some five months before the incident. At that time, and on the five or six subsequent occasions when Burk raised the subject, appellant told Burk that his friends could do what they wanted but that he wanted no part of such a scheme.

Beeman admitted Burk had told him of the poll-taker ruse within a week before the robbery, and that Burk told him they had bought a cap gun and handcuffs. He further admitted that he had allowed Burk to take some old clothes left at the apartment by a former roomate. At that time Beeman told Burk: "If you're going to do a robbery, you can't look like a bum." Nevertheless, appellant explained that he did not know Burk was then planning to commit this robbery. Further, although he knew there was a possibility Burk and Gray would try to rob Mrs. Beeman, appellant thought it very unlikely they would go through with it. He judged Burk capable of committing the crime but knew he had no car and no money to get to Redding. Appellant did not think Gray would cooperate.

Appellant agreed that he had talked with Gray on the phone two days before the robbery, and said he had then repeated he did not want to be involved. He claimed that Burk called him on the way back from Redding because he feared appellant would report him to the police, but knew appellant would want to protect Gray, who was his closer friend.

Appellant claimed he told the others to come to his house after the robbery and offered to sell the jewelry in order to buy time in which to figure out a way to collect and return the property. He took the most valuable piece to make sure it was not sold. Since Burk had a key to his apartment, appellant gave the diamond ring and a bracelet to a friend, Martinez, for safekeeping.[7] After Burk fled to Los Angeles, appellant showed some of the jewelry to mutual acquaintances in order to lull Burk into believing he was attempting to sell it. During this time Burk called him on the phone several times asking for money and, when appellant told him of plans to return the property, threatened to have him killed.

When confronted with his prior statement to the police that he had given one of the rings to someone in exchange for a $50 loan, appellant admitted making the statement but denied that it was true. He also claimed that his statement on direct examination that "his [Burk's] face was seen. He didn't wear a mask. Didn't do anything he was supposed to do . . ." referred only to the reason Gray had given for wanting to return the victim's property.

Appellant requested that the jury be instructed . . . that aiding and abetting liability requires proof of intent to aid. The request was denied.

After three hours of deliberation, the jury submitted two written questions to the court: "We would like to hear again how one is determined to be an accessory and by what actions can he absolve himself"; and "Does inaction mean the party is guilty?" The jury was reinstructed in accord with the standard instructions, CALJIC Nos. 3.00 and 3.01. The court denied appellant's renewed request that the instructions be modified, explaining that giving another, slightly different instruction at this point would further complicate matters. The jury returned its verdicts of guilty on all counts two hours later.

Penal Code section 31 provides in pertinent part:

7. Martinez corroborated that appellant had given him a diamond ring and other jewelry belonging to appellant's family for this purpose.

> All persons concerned in the commission of a crime, . . . whether they directly commit the act constituting the offense, or aid and abet in its commission, or, not being present, have advised and encouraged its commission, . . . are principals in any crime so committed.

Thus, those persons who at common law would have been termed accessories before the fact and principles in the second degree as well as those who actually perpetrate the offense, are to be prosecuted, tried and punished as principals in California. The term "aider and abettor" is now often used to refer to principals other than the perpetrator, whether or not they are present at the commission of the offense.

CALJIC No. 3.00 defines principals to a crime to include

> Those who, with knowledge of the unlawful purpose of the one who does directly and actively commit or attempt to commit the crime, aid and abet in its commission . . . or . . . who, whether present or not at the commission or attempted commission of the crime, advise and encourage its commission.

CALJIC No. 3.01 defines aiding and abetting as follows:

> A person aids and abets the commission of a crime if, with knowledge of the unlawful purpose of the perpetrator of the crime, he aids, promotes, encourages or instigates by act or advice the commission of such crime.

Prior to 1974 CALJIC No. 3.01 read:

> A person aids and abets the commission of a crime if he knowingly and with criminal intent aids, promotes, encourages or instigates by act or advice, or by act and advice, the commission of such crime.

Appellant asserts that the current instructions, in particular CALJIC No. 3.01, substitute an element of knowledge of the perpetrator's intent for the element of criminal intent of the accomplice, in contravention of common law principles and California case law. He argues that the instruction given permitted the jury to convict him of the same offenses as the perpetrators without finding that he harbored either the same criminal intent as they, or the specific intent to assist them, thus depriving him of his constitutional rights to due process and equal protection of the law. Appellant further urges that the error requires reversal because it removed a material issue from the jury and on this record it is impossible to conclude that the jury necessarily resolved the same factual question that would have been presented by the missing instruction.

The People argue that the standard instruction properly reflects California law, which requires no more than that the aider and abettor have knowledge of the perpetrator's criminal purpose and do a voluntary act which in fact aids the perpetrator. . . . The People further contend that defendants are adequately protected from conviction for acts committed under duress or which inadvertently aid a perpetrator by limitation of the liability of an aider and abettor to those acts knowingly aided and their natural and reasonable consequences [and] because proof of intentional aiding in most cases can be inferred from aid with knowledge of the perpetrator's purpose. Thus, respondent argues, it is doubtful that the requested modification would bring about different results in the vast majority of cases. . . .

There is no question that an aider and abettor must have criminal intent in order to be convicted of a criminal offense. . . . The act of encouraging or counseling itself implies a purpose or goal of furthering the encouraged result. "An aider and abettor's fundamental purpose, motive and intent is to aid and assist the perpetrator in the latter's commission of the crime."

The essential conflict in current appellate opinions is between those cases which state that an aider and abettor must have an intent or purpose to commit or assist in the commission of the criminal offenses, and those finding it sufficient that the aider and abettor engage in the required acts with knowledge of the perpetrator's criminal purpose. . . .

The facts from which a mental state may be inferred must not be confused with the mental state that the prosecution is required to prove. Direct evidence of the mental state of the accused is rarely available except through his or her testimony. The trier of fact is and must be free to disbelieve the testimony and to infer that the truth is otherwise when such inference is supported by circumstantial evidence regarding the actions of the accused. Thus, an act which has the effect of giving aid and encouragement, and which is done with knowledge of the criminal purpose of the person aided, may indicate that the actor intended to assist in fulfillment of the known criminal purpose. However . . . the act may be done with some other purpose which precludes criminal liability.

If the jury were instructed that the law conclusively presumes the intention of the accused solely from his or her voluntary acts, it would "effectively eliminate intent as an ingredient of the offense" and would "conflict with the overriding presumption of innocence with which the law endows the accused and which extends to every element of the crime." (Sandstrom v. Montana (1979) 442 U.S. 510, 522, 99 S. Ct. 2450, 2458, 61 L. Ed. 2d 39, quoting from Morissette v. United States (1952) 342 U.S. 246, 274-275, 72 S. Ct. 240, 255-256, 96 L. Ed. 2d 88; original emphasis omitted.) Where an appellate court employs the same presumption to support the adequacy of a jury instruction, the reviewing court announces its willingness to permit a conviction to stand regardless of whether the trier of fact has found the required criminal intent. Thus at the appellate level, the element of criminal intent is effectively eliminated as an ingredient of the offense. . . .

Thus, we conclude that the weight of authority and sound law require proof that an aider and abettor act with knowledge of the criminal purpose of the perpetrator *and* with an intent or purpose either of committing, or encouraging or facilitating commission of, the offense.

When definition of the offense includes the intent to do some act or achieve some consequence beyond the *actus reus* of the crime . . . the aider and abettor must share the specific intent of the perpetrator. By "share" we mean neither that the aider and abettor must be prepared to commit the offense by his or her own act should the perpetrator fail to do so, nor that the aider and abettor must seek to share the fruits of the crime. Rather, an aider and abettor will "share" the perpetrator's specific intent when he or she knows the full extent of the perpetrator's criminal purpose and gives aid or encouragement with the intent or purpose of facilitating the perpetrator's commission of the crime. The liability of an aider and abettor extends also to the natural and reasonable consequences of the acts he knowingly and intentionally aids and encourages.

CALJIC No. 3.01 inadequately defines aiding and abetting because it fails to insure that an aider and abettor will be found to have the required mental state with regard to his or her own act. While the instruction does include the word "abet," which encompasses the intent required by law, the word is arcane and its full import unlikely to be recognized by modern jurors. Moreover, even if jurors were made aware that "abet" means to encourage or facilitate, and implicitly to harbor an intent to further the crime encouraged, the instruction does not *require* them to find that intent because it defines an aider and abettor as one who "aids, promotes, encourages *or* instigates" (emphasis added). Thus, as one appellate court recently recognized, the instruction would "technically allow a conviction if the defendant knowing of the perpetrator's unlawful purpose, negligently or accidentally aided the commission of the crime. . . ." We suggest that an appropriate instruction should inform the jury that a person aids and abets the commission of a crime when he or she, acting with (1) knowledge of the unlawful purpose of the perpetrator, and (2) the intent or purpose of committing, encouraging, or facilitating the commission of the offense, (3) by act or advice aids, promotes, encourages or instigates, the commission of the crime. . . .

Respondent urges that any instructional error was harmless. . . .

Appellant did not deny that he had given information to Burk and Gray which aided their criminal enterprise, but he claimed his purposes in doing so were innocent.[8] Appellant admitted that he was at some time made aware of his friends' intent to rob Mrs. Beeman, but insisted that he wanted nothing to do with a robbery of his relatives.

He testified that he didn't think Burk would really go through with the robbery or that Gray would help. Two days before the incident, he again told Gray that he didn't want to be involved. Gray's testimony confirmed that appellant had twice said he did not want to be involved. Finally, appellant claimed to have taken possession of the jewelry and feigned attempts to sell it in order to recover the property and return it to the victims. Thus, the essential

8. He testified that he had mentioned the victim's jewels and car only casually and that he had drawn the floor plan only for the purpose of discussing the design of the house.

point of his defense was that although he acted in ways which in fact aided the criminal enterprise, he did not act with the intent of encouraging or facilitating the planning or commission of the offenses.

The jury certainly could have believed Burk and Gray while disbelieving appellant, and thus found that appellant intentionally aided and encouraged his friends in their crimes. However, the fact that the jury interrupted its deliberations to seek further instruction regarding accomplice liability indicates that the jurors did not dismiss appellant's testimony out of hand. Rather, the questions asked indicate the jury's deliberations were focused on the very issue upon which the defense rested and upon which the court's instructions were inadequate: the elements—including the mental element—of aiding and abetting.[9] When it reinstructed the jury according to the standard instructions and again refused the . . . modification requested by appellant, the court repeated its original mistake.

Under these circumstances, where the defense centered on the very element as to which the jury was inadequately instructed and the jurors' communication to the court indicated confusion on the same point, we cannot find the error harmless.

The convictions are reversed.

Notes and Questions

1. If Beeman's testimony were accepted, what would be his *mens rea* for the crimes? If it were knowledge rather than purpose, should that technical distinction make him less culpable than the principals? Recall the discussion of purpose and knowledge in the introduction to *mens rea* in Chapter 4.

2. Do you believe Beeman? How can you judge his credibility?

3. The court rejects criminal liability for "an act which has the effect of giving aid and encouragement, and which is done with the knowledge of the criminal purpose of the person aided." It states that "the act may be done with some other purpose which precludes criminal liability." What could these other purposes have been in Beeman's case?

4. For decades, the American courts and legislatures have debated whether knowledge or "true purpose" should be the required *mens rea* for accomplice liability. Judge Learned Hand authored the definitive opinion adopting the purpose requirement. In United States v. Peoni, 100 F.2d 401, 402 (2d Cir. 1938), the defendant had sold counterfeit money to Regno, who in turn had sold the counterfeit money to Dorsey. Peoni was charged as an accessory to Dorsey's possession of the counterfeit money. Though Peoni had reason to know that Regno would sell the money to a third party, the prosecu-

9. The jury submitted the following questions:
"We would like to hear again how one is determined to be an accessory and by what actions can he absolve himself?" and "Does inaction mean the party is guilty?"

tion could not show that Peoni intended or desired that Regno would sell the counterfeit money again. In reversing the conviction, Judge Hand rejected the government's argument that "the possession of the second buyer was a natural consequence of Peoni's original act, with which he might be charged." Instead, the complicity doctrine required that the defendant "in some sort associate himself with the venture, that he participate in it as something that he wishes to bring about, that he seek by his action to make it succeed. All the words used—even the most colorless 'abet'—carry an implication of purposive attitude towards it."

Even if Judge Hand is right in principle, is it clear that Peoni did not "want" Regno to resell the money? What if Peoni knew Regno always served as middleman in counterfeit transactions?

5. By contrast, in Backun v. United States, 112 F.2d 635, 637 (4th Cir. 1940), Judge Parker stated:

> Guilt as an accessory depends, not on "having a stake" in the outcome of crime . . . but on aiding and assisting the perpetrators; and those who make a profit by furnishing to criminals, whether by sale or otherwise, the means to carry on their nefarious undertakings aid them just as truly as if they were actual partners with them, having a stake in the fruits of their enterprise. To say that the sale of goods is normally a lawful transaction is beside the point. The seller may not ignore the purpose for which the purchase is made if he is advised of that purpose, or wash his hands of the aid that he has given the perpetrator of a felony by the plea that he has merely made a sale of merchandise. One who sells a gun to another knowing that he is buying it to commit a murder, would hardly escape conviction as an accessory to the murder by showing that he received full price for the gun; and no difference in principle can be drawn between such a case and any other case of a seller who knows that the purchaser intends to use the goods which he is purchasing in the commission of a felony. In any such case, not only does the act of the seller assist in the commission of the felony, but his will assents to its commission, since he could refuse to give the assistance by refusing to make the sale.

In *Backun,* the defendant knowingly sold stolen silverware to a third person, Zucker, in New York. Zucker then transported the silverware to North Carolina to sell it. The defendant wanted Zucker to sell the silverware and knew Zucker would go out of state to do so, but the defendant did not specifically desire that Zucker leave the state. Judge Parker upheld his conviction of interstate transportation of stolen merchandise, using the "knowledge" test.

6. The majority of jurisdictions have rejected Parker's analysis in *Backun* and require a showing of purpose. New York, however, has taken a slightly different approach. Although it strictly adheres to the true purpose test for accomplice liability, it has also adopted the lesser included crimes of "criminal facilitation." New York Penal Code §115.05 states:

> A person is guilty of criminal facilitation in the second degree when, believing it is probable that he is rendering aid to a person who intends to commit a class A

> felony, he engages in conduct which provides such person with means or opportunity for the commission thereof and which in fact aids such person to commit such class A felony.

Criminal facilitation in the second degree is a class C felony. Is it now possible in New York to be convicted of aiding and abetting criminal facilitation?

7. The drafters of the Model Penal Code originally suggested that purpose might not be required for accessorial liability. See M.P.C. §2.06(3)(a):

> A person is an accomplice of another person in the commission of an offense if . . . [acting with knowledge that such other person was committing or had the purpose of committing the offense, he knowingly, substantially facilitated its commission; (Alternative: he knowingly provided means or opportunity for the commission of the offense, substantially facilitating its commission;)].

In one of the rare instances where the issue was decided on the floor of the American Law Institute, the drafters determined that purpose be required for complicity liability. Among the arguments put forth in support of the purpose test was the following:

> I line myself up here with Judge Learned Hand of the Second Circuit in believing that liability for misconduct of somebody else should depend upon a sharing of his purpose. I have several reasons for that. In the first place, I want to make it clear that practically we are arguing about very few cases. We are not going to lose a lot of defendants. If you make it clear that the man knows that another man is engaged in crime and provides him substantial help, most juries are going to reach the conclusion that he intended to help him. Therefore, the difference between the two positions is not as wide as you might think. . . ."
>
> I too align myself with Judge Hand's opinion, particularly in the felony cases. We are dealing with crime; and if a person is carrying on, say, a legitimate business and he knows that somebody may be intending to use what he sells for an illicit purpose, I cannot believe that we can make him a party to the crime, unless he shares the purpose and has a stake in the outcome. (American Law Institute Proceedings—Minutes 178, 180 (May 1953) discussion of Model Penal Code §2.04 Tent. Draft No. 1 (1953)).

What is all the fuss about? Did we not already see this sort of problem when we discussed omissions?

8. In United States v. Greer, 467 F.2d 1065, 1069 (7th Cir. 1977), the defendant provided the necessary information for the theft of 40,600 pounds of copper from an interstate freight depot. In addition to being charged with aiding and abetting the actual theft, the defendant was charged with aiding and abetting the interstate transportation of the stolen goods. In reversing his conviction on the transportation charge, the court of appeals stated that:

> [I]n order to prove Greer's complicity with the later stages of the crime—namely the transportation of the goods—the government must show that he intended to

> aid in post-theft plans, or that he knew details of the thieves' travel plans, such as the specific destination of the goods.

Since the government could not show that the defendant knew where the goods were being taken, he did not have the specific intent required for conviction. The court rejected as "far too broad" the government's contention that "an aider and abettor is responsible not only for the immediate acts he facilitates, but for the other likely consequences of his acts." The court, however, did not adopt the true purpose standard:

> We agree, for instance, that a defendant can be held responsible as an aider and abettor of a crime even where there is no direct proof that he intended to aid in the crime, if he is substantially involved in the chain of events leading immediately to it. . . . But where the relationship between the defendant's acts and the ultimate crime for which he is charged is as attenuated as it is in the instant case, we would require some showing of specific intent to aid in, or specific knowledge of, the crime charged.

What does this mean?

9. Although the court rejected the government's theory of liability in *Greer,* accomplice liability has sometimes been expanded to include situations where the so-called accomplice neither intended the crime to occur, nor knew it was going to happen. In People v. Kessler, 57 Ill. 2d 493, 315 N.E.2d 29 (1974), the defendant:

> waited in an automobile outside a tavern while his two unarmed companions entered the building to commit burglary. While inside the tavern, they were surprised by the owner, and one of the burglars shot and wounded him with a gun taken during the burglary. Later while defendant's companions were fleeing on foot, one of them fired a shot at a passing police officer. At that time defendant was sitting in an automobile.

The defendant's conviction for attempted murder was reversed by the appellate court on the grounds that the defendant did not intend the crime to occur. The Supreme Court of Illinois reinstated the conviction, stating that:

> where one aids another in the planning or commission of an offense he is legally accountable for the conduct of the person he aids; and . . . the word "conduct" encompasses any criminal act done in furtherance of the planned and intended act.

Therefore, because the defendant intended to take part in the burglary he is criminally liable for the attempted murder committed by his companions in connection with that crime.

Is this result sound? What is the relationship between this extension of accomplice liability and the felony-murder doctrine? What does the court mean when it refers to "any criminal act done *in furtherance* of the planned and intended act"? When would an additional criminal act *not* be in furtherance of the original crime? Is the accomplice liable for any foreseeable crime? Any *reasonably* foreseeable crime?

10. What *mens rea* must the defendant have with respect to the consequential crime he is charged with aiding and abetting? See M.P.C. §2.06(4). What if the consequential crime is a strict liability offense? Consider the following hypothetical:

> [A] hotel owner rents rooms to individuals he knows are prostitutes, suspecting they have pimps who protect them. One day a "john" fails to pay the prostitute and the pimp kills the john. Wisconsin Law Review 1984: 769 at 795.

Assume that the hotel owner could be found guilty of aiding and abetting prostitution. Under the court's rationale in *Kessler,* could he be convicted of murder? The felony-murder doctrine is, by definition, limited to deaths resulting from certain felonies. Is there any such limitation to the extension of accomplice liability?

11. In many jurisdictions accessories are liable for all subsequent crimes that are reasonably foreseeable as a result of the contemplated crime. Title 17-A §57(3)(A) of the Maine Revised Statutes, for example, specifies that:

> 3. A person is an accomplice of another person in the commission of a crime if:
>
> A. With the intent of promoting or facilitating the commission of the crime, he solicits such other person to commit the crime, or aids or agrees to aid or attempts to aid such other person in planning or committing the crime. A person is an accomplice under this subsection to any crime the commission of which was a reasonably foreseeable consequence of his conduct.

Thus, even in the absence of a felony-murder doctrine, an accomplice could be held liable for a killing committed by the principal during an armed robbery. He would not escape liability even if he did not participate in the actual killing, but waited outside as a lookout.

On the other hand, one court has ruled that "the state cannot hold an accomplice liable for a crime totally unforeseeable." State v. Palermo, 224 Kan. 275, 579 P.2d 718, 720 (1978). In *Palermo,* the defendant sold heroin to a certain Morgan in Missouri. Morgan in turn was persuaded to cross the state border into Kansas, where he sold the heroin to Shrout, a government informant. The state of Kansas prosecuted the defendant for the sale of the drugs to Shrout and claimed jurisdiction on the basis of K.S.A. 21-3104, which states:

> (1) A person is subject to prosecution and punishment under the law of this state if . . .

> (b) Being outside the state, he counsels, aids, [or] abets . . . a crime within this state.

The Kansas Supreme Court held that the trial court had no jurisdiction to try the defendant for the sale of heroin in Kansas. It reasoned that:

> [A] state does not have jurisdiction over an individual for a crime committed within that state when he was located outside the state, did not intend to commit a crime within the state, and could not reasonably foresee that his acts would cause, aid or abet in the commission of a crime within that state. 579 P.2d at 720.

12. Can a person be guilty of complicity where neither he nor the principal acts intentionally or knowingly? In People v. Marshall, 362 Mich. 170, 106 N.W.2d 842 (1961), discussed also at page 501, the defendant voluntarily gave his car keys to a friend whom he knew was drunk. His friend was involved in an accident with another car in which both drivers were killed. At the time of the accident, the defendant was at home, asleep in bed. He was convicted of involuntary manslaughter.[10] The Michigan Supreme Court reversed his manslaughter conviction:

> In the case before us death resulted from the misconduct of driver. The accountability of the owner must rest as a matter of general principle, upon his complicity in such misconduct. In turning his keys over, he was guilty of a specific offense, for which he incurred a specific penalty. Upon these facts he cannot be held a principal with respect to the fatal accident: the killing . . . was not counselled by him, accomplished by another acting jointly with him, nor did it occur in the attempted achievement of some common enterprise.

The court rejected the state's contention that the drunk driving problem was so severe that a new approach was necessary to combat it:

> What the State actually seeks from us in an interpretation that the manslaughter statute imposes an open-end[ed] criminal liability. That is to say, whether the owner may ultimately go to prison for manslaughter or some lesser offense will depend upon whatever unlawful act the driver commits while in the car. Such a theory may be defensible as a matter of civil liability but . . ."[I]t is a basic proposition in a constitutional society that crimes should be defined in advance, and not after action has been taken." We are not unaware of the magnitude of the problem presented, but the new approaches demanded for its solution rest with the legislature, not the courts.

The court also indicated that if the defendant had been sitting next to the drunk driver "an entirely different case would be presented." How would this be different? See State v. Gibbs, 227 N.C. 677, 44 S.E.2d 201, 202 (1947):

10. The defendant was also convicted of violating §625(b) of the Michigan vehicle code which makes it illegal for the owner of an automobile knowingly to permit it to be driven by a legally intoxicated person.

> [W]hen an owner places his motor vehicle in the hands of an intoxicated driver, sits by his side, and permits him without protest, to operate the vehicle on a public highway, while in a state of intoxication, he is as guilty as the man at the wheel.

See also State v. Whitaker, 43 N.C. App. 600, 259 S.E.2d 316, 319 (1979):

> [W]e hold that when a death results from the operation of a motor vehicle by an intoxicated person not the owner of that vehicle, the owner who is present in the vehicle and who with his knowledge and consent permits the intoxicated driver to operate the vehicle, is as guilty as the intoxicated driver.

13. Consider the following ordinance enacted by the city of Trenton, New Jersey:

> It shall be unlawful for any parent to assist, aid, abet, allow, permit, suffer or encourage a minor to commit a violation of the public peace . . . either by overt act, by failure to act or by lack of supervision and control over such minor.

The ordinance further provided that two violations by a minor within a year would lead to the presumption, subject to rebuttal, that the parents allowed the violation to occur. What *mens rea* must the parent have with respect to the minor's conduct? Is mere negligence enough? In Doe v. City of Trenton, 143 N.J. Super. 128, 362 A.2d 1200 (1976) the court invalidated the ordinance on constitutional grounds because of its presumption of parental liability for the second violation.

14. Where the accomplice's *mens rea* differs from that of the principal, the problem of discrepant liability may arise. We have already seen examples (page 613) where the aider and abettor may not be criminally responsible, while the actor is guilty, and cases (page 617) where the actor is not guilty but the aider and abettor is guilty. We now ask whether an accomplice can be convicted of a more serious crime than the principal. In Regina v. Richards, 3 W.L.R. 888 (Ct. of App. 1973), the defendant, Isabelle Richards, persuaded two men to attack her husband. She provided them with the necessary information to effect the assault and signalled from her house at the appropriate time. The defendant explained that she had a bad marriage and was only trying to have her husband hurt so that he would turn to her for affection. She did, however, admit that she told the two men "to beat him up bad enough to put him in a hospital for a month." The two attackers were convicted of the less serious crime of unlawful wounding, a misdemeanor, but the defendant was convicted of unlawful wounding with intent to do grievous bodily harm, a felony. On appeal, the court rejected the prosecution's argument that:

> one can properly look at the *actus reus,* that is the physical blows struck upon Mr. Richards, and separately the intention with which the blows were struck. The defendant . . . is responsible for the blows being struck, the *actus reus,* because they

> were struck at her request by the co-accused. If . . . the specific intention of the defendant was different from the specific intention, if any, proved to be entertained on the part of the co-accused, then it is proper that the defendant should be convicted of the [more serious] offence if that specific intention goes so far as to amount to intent to cause grievous bodily harm, although that intention was never in the minds of the persons who committed the acts at her request.

In reducing the defendant's conviction to one of unlawful wounding, the court reasoned as follows:

> There is proved on the evidence in this case one offence and one offence only, namely the offence of unlawful wounding without the element of specific intent. We do not think it right that one could say that that which was done can be said to be done with the intention of the defendant who was not present at the time and whose intention did not go to the offence which was in fact committed. That is the short point in the case as we see it. If there is only one offence committed, and that is the offence of unlawful wounding, then the person who has requested that offence be committed, cannot be guilty of a graver offence than that in fact which was committed.

Are there any problems with the court's analysis in the *Richards* case? How would it analyze situations where the accomplice exhibited deliberate planning and the principal acted because of provocation? Is this consistent with the case where the principal was immune from prosecution or was an innocent agent of the accomplice? See page 617. In Pendry v. State, 367 A.2d 627 (Del. Supr. 1976) defendant Timothy Pendry shot and killed the victim Clifford Faulkner following an argument between Faulkner, Timothy Pendry, and his codefendant brother Kenneth. The argument concerned the Pendrys' sister, who was being held against her will by the victim. Timothy was convicted of first-degree murder and Kenneth was convicted as his accomplice. On appeal, the Delaware Supreme Court reduced Timothy's conviction to one of manslaughter because he "presented some credible evidence of extreme emotional distress at the time of the shooting." Kenneth, however, did not present such evidence and the court rejected his argument that as an accomplice he could not be convicted of a greater crime than the principal. The court based its decision on Title 11 §272 of the Delaware Code, which reads:

> In any prosecution for an offense in which the criminal liability of the accused is based upon the conduct of another person . . . it is no defense that:
> (1) The other person is not guilty of the offense in question . . . because of other factors precluding the mental state required for the commission of the offense; or
> (2) The other persons . . . has been convicted of a different offense or in a different degree.

15. Now take the case where the accomplice's *mens rea* is more culpable than that of the principal. Let us say that the accomplice, with premeditation, aids and abets a principal who, in the heat of passion, kills in cold blood. Is this an easier question than that raised, and decided, though in opposite ways, by the *Richards* and *Pendry* cases?

Consider the following hypothetical based on Shakespeare's Othello, paying particular attention to Iago's accomplice liability.

> Othello, a mercenary general in the military service of the Venetian Republic, has just married Desdemona, the daughter of a Venetian nobleman. His subordinate, Iago, hates Othello, ostensibly because he has been passed over for promotion in favor of Cassio, actually because he has an abandoned and malignant heart. Iago resolves to bring about Othello's destruction by persuading him that Desdemona is having an affair with Cassio. As Iago knows, Othello is highly susceptible to jealousy. Iago cleverly plays on this jealousy and by a skillful series of innuendoes and deceptions so enrages Othello that he decides to kill Desdemona. Iago does not himself suggest that Othello should kill Desdemona; instead, he occasionally pretends to urge Othello not to do so, but always in terms that he knows will have the opposite effect. Iago is able to make Othello believe anything he wants him to and establishes such an ascendancy over him that on one occasion he causes Othello to collapse in a fit. Iago reinforces his false accusations by "planting" Desdemona's handkerchief, Othello's first present to her, in Cassio's lodgings. He then arranges matters so that Othello sees Cassio with the handkerchief and believes that he now has direct evidence corroborating Iago's accusations. That night Othello smothers Desdemona in her bed.
>
> Assume that after killing Desdemona and then learning that Iago's accusations against her had been false, Othello did not kill himself (as he does in the play).

Of what crime or crimes, on what theory or theories, are Othello and/or Iago liable to be convicted?

The following excerpts from the play are representative of Iago's modus operandi. You may assume that they are in evidence, for whatever relevance they may have on the issues.

> *Oth.* Give me a living reason she's disloyal.
>
> *Iago.* I do not like the office;
> But sith I am enter'd in this cause so far
> (Prick'd to't by foolish honesty and love),
> I will go on. I lay with Cassio lately;
> And, being troubled with a raging tooth,
> I could not sleep.
> There are a kind of men so loose of soul
> that in their sleeps will mutter their affairs.
> One of this kind is Cassio.
> In sleep I heard him say, "Sweet Desdemona,

Let us be wary, let us hide our loves!"
And then, sir, would he gripe and wring my hand,
Cry out "Sweet creature!" and then kiss me hard,
As if he pluck'd up kisses by the roots
That grew upon my lips; then laid his leg
Over my thigh, and sigh'd, and kiss'd; and then
Cried, "Cursèd fate, that gave thee to the Moor!"

Oth. O monstrous! monstrous!

Iago. Nay, this was but his dream.

Oth. But this denoted a foregone conclusion.

Iago. 'Tis but a shrewd doubt, though it be but a dream;
And this may help to thicken other proofs
That do demonstrate thinly.

Oth. I'll tear her to pieces!

Iago. Nay, but be wise. Yet we see nothing done;
She may be honest yet. Tell me but this:
Have you not sometimes seen a handkerchief
Spotted with strawberries in your wife's hand?

Oth. I gave her such a one. 'Twas my first gift.

Iago. I know not that; but such a handkerchief
(I am sure it was your wife's) did I to-day
See Cassio wipe his beard with.

Oth. If't be that,—

Iago. If it be that, or any that was hers,
It speaks against her with the other proofs.

Iago. What
If I had said I had seen him do you wrong?
Or heard him say (as knaves be such abroad,
Who having, by their own importunate suit
Or voluntary dotage of some mistress,
Convinced or supplied them, cannot choose
But they must blab)—

Oth. Hath he said anything?

Iago. He hath, my lord; but be you well assur'd,
No more than he'll unswear.

Oth. What hath he said?

Iago. Faith, that he did—I know not what he did.

Oth. What? what?

Iago. Lie—

Oth. With her?

Iago. With her, on her—what you will.

Oth. Lie with her! Lie on her! We say, lie on her, when they belie her. Lie with her? Zounds, that's fulsome! Handkerchief!—confessions!—Handkerchief! To confess, and be hanged for his labor. First, to be hanged, and then to confess: I tremble at it. Nature would not invest herself in such shadowing passion without some instruction. It is not words that shake me thus. Pish! Noses, ears, and lips. Is't possible?—Confess!—Handkerchief!—O devil!
(*Falls in a trance*)

Iago. Work on,
My medicine, work! Thus credulous fools are caught;
Any many worthy and chaste dames even thus,
All guiltless, meet reproach.

Oth. I would have him nine years a-killing. A fine woman! A fair woman! a sweet woman!

Iago. Nay, you must forget that.

Oth. Ay, let her rot and perish, and be damned to-night, for she shall not live. No, my heart is turned to stone. I strike it, and it hurts my hand. O, the world has not a sweeter creature. She might lie by an emperor's side and command him tasks.

Iago. Nay, that's not your way.

Oth. Hang her! I do but say what she is. So delicate with her needle! An admirable musician! O, she will sing the savageness out of a bear. Of so high and plenteous wit and invention!

Iago. She's the worse for all this.

Oth. O, a thousand, a thousand times. And then, of so gentle a condition!

Iago. Ay, too gentle.

Oth. Nay, that's certain. But yet the pity of it, Iago! O, Iago, the pity of it, Iago!

Iago. If you be so fond over her iniquity, give her patent to offend; for, if it touches not you, it comes near nobody.

Oth. I will chop her into messes. Cuckold me—

Iago. O, tis foul in her.

Oth. With mine officer!

Iago. That's fouler.

Oth. Get me some poison, Iago, this night. I'll not expostulate with her, lest her body and beauty unprovide my mind again. This night, Iago.

Iago. Do it not with poison. Strangle her in her bed, even the bed she hath contaminated.

Oth. Good, good. The justice of it pleases. Very good.

D. LIABILITY WITHIN THE BUSINESS ENTERPRISE

In Chapter 5, on involuntary manslaughter, we examined some of the special problems of applying criminal liability to the business enterprise. In that chapter, though we considered how an enterprise might commit homicide, we postponed the important question of when and how the actions of individual officers, directors, or employees within a business enterprise might make the enterprise itself criminally liable. This section addresses that issue. Although in our legal system the business enterprise—most often the corporation—is theoretically a distinct legal entity, its "behavior" must obviously consist of the behavior of individuals within the enterprise. Thus, the criminal liability of the enterprise is, in effect, a form of accomplice liability—the attribution of the criminal acts of one person to another "person." The relationship of individual to corporate behavior under the criminal law is a complex one that provides an interesting supplement to the larger issue we examine in this chapter, of the relative liability of multiple parties to a crime.

The criminal liability of a corporation for the acts of individuals within it derives in part from the civil law doctrine of respondeat superior, which itself derives from tort law. Before we see how an abstract enterprise such as a corporation can be liable for the acts of an employee or officer, we examine how an individual employer may be criminally liable for the purposeful criminal actions of one of his or her employees.

EX PARTE MARLEY
Supreme Court of California
29 Cal. 2d 525, 175 P.2d 832 (1946)

SCHAUER, Justice.

Petitioner, the proprietor of a meat market, was convicted of a violation of section 12023 of the Business and Professions Code, and sentenced to ninety days in the county jail. The mentioned section provides as follows: "Every

person who by himself or his employee or agent, or as the employee or agent of another, sells any commodity, at, by, or according to gross weight or measure, or at, by, as, of, or according to any weight, measure or count which is greater than the true net weight, . . . is guilty of a misdemeanor." Petitioner seeks release through habeas corpus on the ground that the quoted statute is unconstitutional as it is sought to be applied to the facts here shown. With this position we are compelled to disagree.

The record discloses that on or about March 22, 1945, an employee of the Office of Price Administration, named Mrs. Punteney, accompanied openly by one other woman (named Mrs. Sampson) and surreptitiously by two men (one of them named Delaney), all of the same calling, appeared at the counter of petitioner's meat market in Los Angeles County and requested of petitioner's clerk and employe, one Dennis, that the latter sell her one veal steak and four or five lamb chops. Dennis weighed the selections, told Mrs. Punteney and Mrs. Sampson the respective prices, and wrapped the meat. Mrs. Punteney then showed Dennis her "identification" and summoned Delaney "who was waiting outside the door," and together they checked the weight of the meat, which was found to be less than that which would correspond, according to Office of Price Administration price charts posted in the market, to the prices charged. About two weeks later Delaney signed the complaint upon which petitioner's conviction is based. Dennis was also named as a defendant was convicted, and was penalized by a $100 fine. It is undisputed that petitioner did not participate personally in the transaction here involved, was absent from the premises at the time it occurred, and had at no time instructed Dennis to give short weight.

The general rule of law as repeatedly enunciated and emphasized by the courts of California and of other jurisdictions [is] that a master or principal before he can be held criminally responsible for the act of an employe or agent must be proved to have "Knowingly and intentionally aided, advised, or encouraged the criminal act." Thus, in People v. Green (1913), 22 Cal. App. 45, 50, 133 P. 334, . . . the court declared that

> Before one can be convicted of a crime by reason of the acts of his agent a clear case must be shown. The civil doctrine that a principal is bound by the acts of his agent within the scope of the agent's authority has no application to criminal law. 1 McLain on Criminal Law, §188. While false pretenses may be made to an agent of the person defrauded, yet when made by an agent they must be directly authorized or consented to in order to hold the principal, for authority to do a criminal act, will not be presumed. 1 McLain on Criminal Law, §683 . . .

In limited qualification of the general rule, however, legislative bodies in California as well as in other jurisdictions have adopted various statutes positively forbidding certain acts and imposing criminal liability upon the master if the act is knowingly performed by his servant within the scope of the latter's authority. Such statutes have dealt with the sale of intoxicating liquor; of pure foods and drugs; and with the operating of gaming establishments and of saloons and have been upheld by the courts. . . .

And in the field of weights and measures, the rule is, as stated in 68 Corpus Juris 165-166, sections 24, 25, that where, as here, the statute provides that

> whoever, himself or by a servant or agent, is guilty of giving false or insufficient weight or measure shall be punishable; evidence of giving short weight by defendant's servant in his absence warrants a conviction of defendant. [W]here qualifying words such as knowingly, intentionally, or fraudulently are omitted from provisions creating the offense it is held that guilty knowledge and intent are not elements of the offense. . . . These statutes make the seller the guarantor of the weight and quantity of the commodity sold without regard to his intent or knowledge. . . .

The principle upon which such holdings are based is expressed as follows in State v. Weisberg (1943), supra, at page 95 of 74 Ohio App., at page 872 of 55 N.E.2d:

> There are many acts that are so destructive of the social order, or where the ability of the state to establish the element of criminal intent would be so extremely difficult if not impossible of proof, that in the interest of justice the legislature has provided that the doing of the act constitutes a crime, regardless of knowledge or criminal intent on the part of the defendant.
>
> In these cases it is the duty of the defendant to know what the facts are that are involved or result from his acts or conduct. Statutes punishing the sale of adulterated foods or prohibiting the sale of intoxicating liquor to minors are most frequently found in this class of cases. The use of false weights could well come within this field of the law.

Petitioner complains that he was denied due process and the equal protection of the laws in that he was not permitted to prove that he came within the provisions of subdivisions 4 and 6 of section 26 of the Penal Code. Such provisions are, in material part, as follows:

> All persons are capable of committing crimes except those belonging to the following classes: . . . Four. Persons who committed the act . . . under an ignorance or mistake of fact, which disproves any criminal intent . . . Six. Persons who committed the act . . . through misfortune or by accident, when it appears that there was no evil design, intention, or culpable negligence.

Without any implication as to the legal propriety of his claim, as such, it is to be noted that the petitioner was properly allowed to introduce evidence tending to show that the prohibited act (the short weight element of the sale) was committed by the clerk by accident or mistake of fact, but on this issue the finding was adverse to the two defendants. The facts that petitioner was not present when the short weight sales were made and that he had not instructed the clerk to sell short weight, do not bring petitioner within the code provisions above quoted. He shows no other evidence or offer of evidence to that end. Whether some hypothetical situation (such, for example, as a conspiracy by a clerk with others deliberately to injure an employer) not shown by the record here, might properly be shown and be held to bring an employer within the purview of the code provisions, we do not . . . in the light of the record, have occasion to determine.

Inasmuch as the Legislature of this state has seen fit, in the exercise of its power, to impose upon petitioner criminal liability for the offense which was committed by his employe, we cannot, in the light of the authorities above cited, hold that the statute as written, or as applied here, invades a constitutional right of the petitioner. The seemingly (upon the record before us) disproportionate severity of the penalty assessed by the trial judge against this petitioner, as compared to that meted out against his codefendant, who was the primary actor, does not constitute a legal basis for intervention by habeas corpus. The writ of habeas corpus heretofore issued is discharged and petitioner is remanded to custody.

GIBSON, C.J., and EDMONDS, TRAYNOR, and SPENCE, JJ., concurred.

CARTER, Justice.

I dissent. Broadly speaking this case brings into sharp focus the clash between conflicting social philosophies which are reflected in the interpretation of constitutional and statutory provisions. That is, should the burden be placed upon an innocent and blameless employer, engaged in a business not in itself harmful to the public, of risking conviction of a crime and service of a jail sentence because of the mistake, intentional or not, of his employee? The majority opinion answers this question in the affirmative. With this conclusion I cannot agree. In my opinion there are no considerations of public policy or general welfare which warrant such a departure from the long established rule that criminal intent is a necessary element of a crime. Various situations can be imagined which render intolerable, and shocking to one's sense of justice, the construction placed by the majority opinion on the statute here involved. Similar statutes could be passed relating to the sale of railroad tickets or the cashing of checks which would make criminally liable the officers of a railway or banking corporation for an error made by an employee in overcharging a customer for a ticket or short changing a customer in the cashing of a check. Upon the occurrence of such an event in a remote section of the state where the railroad or bank was operating, the president and other officers of the railroad or bank who might reside in a metropolitan area hundreds of miles from the place where the crime was committed could be arrested and sent to jail for an alleged violation committed by a ticket clerk or bank teller. Likewise a merchant, who had been inducted into military service and who left his business in charge of a manager, could be sent to jail for violation of such a statute committed during his absence in military service when he had no knowledge whatever of what was taking place in his place of business. In such a case there is nothing an employer can do to protect himself, as the act of the employee is one which depends entirely upon use of his own faculties and senses and it is impossible for the employer to determine with any degree of accuracy whether the faculties and senses of the employee are functioning properly and accurately during all his working hours. These considerations, in my opinion, outweigh any benefit or advantage which may be gained to the public by an interpretation of a statute which places upon an innocent and blameless employer criminal responsibility for an act of his employee. . . .

It is clear that [the master or principal is not guilty unless the master or principal assents to, or acquiesces in, the unlawful act of the employee]. The statute condemns unlawful action of a principal by his agent. In other words, the unlawful action of the agent must be authorized specifically not generally under the broad authority to sell his principal's merchandise. It will be remembered that the statute condemns the unlawful act by oneself or by agent. "By oneself" means "alone" "unaided." (Webster's New Int. Dict., p.367.) That expression followed by "or by an agent" must indicate that in the latter case the principal is acting not alone. He has procured and had the aid of his employee. They are acting together—in concert. He is still the one who must commit the unlawful act before he is guilty but he has assistance, that is, he instructs his agents to physically commit the act denounced. . . .

Notes and Questions

1. The court first seems to state that the civil doctrine that a principal is bound by the acts of an agent acting within the scope of the agent's duty does not apply in criminal law. Yet it then proceeds to hold the employer liable on just that theory, relying on the special "regulatory" nature of the crime involved. What if Dennis had offered Mrs. Punteney a bribe if she would ignore his violation of the price regulation? Would Marley be innocent of bribery on the grounds that he lacked any *mens rea* with regard to Dennis's actions, and that vicarious liability does not apply to "true" crimes like bribery? In that case, of course, Marley could argue that Dennis's act fell outside the scope of his duty, since it was no part of his duty to offer bribes. But was it any part of Dennis's duty to violate the price regulation?

2. The court's discussion of "regulatory" crimes recalls, of course, the material on liability without fault in Chapter 3. If Dennis himself had acted inadvertently in overcharging for the meat, Marley might be in the same legal position as were Mr. Dotterweich and Mr. Park in those famous cases on strict liability. But the court in *Marley* notes the jury's determination that Dennis knew he was overcharging, and suggests that Marley therefore does not fall

within the California Code provision protecting from criminal liability "[p]ersons who committed the act . . . through misfortune or by accident, when it appears that there was no evil design, intention, or culpable negligence." But does not holding Marley culpable here constitute a form of strict liability with respect to *him?*

3. Does the application of the tort doctrine of respondeat superior to criminal law overlook important differences between civil and criminal liability? If Dennis had negligently injured a customer, might Marley be liable in tort for Dennis's action on the theory that he provides a better source of compensatory damages for the plaintiff? Is that principle irrelevant to criminal laws such as the one under which Marley was punished?

4. In its imaginative list of the horrible consequences of vicarious criminal liability, the dissent complains that "there is nothing an employer can do to protect himself" in such cases. Is that true?

5. The ambivalence with which the courts have imported vicarious liability into the criminal law finds interesting expression in Commonwealth v. Koczwara, 397 Pa. 575, 155 A.2d 825 (1955). Koczwara, a tavern owner, was sentenced to three months in prison and a $500 fine when one of his bartenders sold liquor to a minor, though Koczwara had not been present at the sale, had known nothing of it, and had never authorized his employees to sell to minors. The Supreme Court of Pennsylvania affirmed his conviction, acknowledging that laws governing the sale of liquor fell within the category of regulatory crimes to which vicarious liability might apply. Nevertheless, the court vacated Koczwara's jail sentence and limited his penalty to the fine:

> As the defendant has pointed out, there is a distinction between the requirement of a *mens rea* and the imposition of vicarious absolute liability for the acts of another. It may be that the courts below, in relying on prior authority, have failed to make such a distinction. In any case, we fully recognize it. Moreover, we find that the intent of the legislature in enacting this Code was not only to eliminate the common law requirement of a *mens rea,* but also to place a very high degree of responsibility upon the holder of a liquor license to make certain that neither he nor anyone in his employ commit any of the prohibited acts upon the licensed premises. Such a burden of care imposed upon the licensee in order to protect the public from the potentially noxious effects of an inherently dangerous business. We, of course, express no opinion as to the *wisdom* of the legislature's imposing vicarious responsibility under certain sections of the Liquor Code. There may or may not be an economic-sociological-justification for such liability on a theory of deterrence. Such determination is for the legislature to make, so long as the constitutional requirements are met.
>
> Can the legislature, consistent with the requirements of the due process, thus establish absolute criminal liability? Were this the defendant's first violation of the Code, and the penalty solely a minor fine of from $100-$300, we would have no hesitation in upholding such a judgment. Defendant, by accepting a liquor license, must bear this financial risk. Because of a prior conviction for violations of the Code, however, the trial judge felt compelled under the mandatory language of the statute, Section 494(a), to impose not only an increased fine of five

hundred dollars, but also a three month sentence of imprisonment. Such sentence of imprisonment in a case where liability is imposed vicariously cannot be sanctioned by this Court consistently with the law of the land clause of Section 9, Article I of the Constitution of the Commonwealth of Pennsylvania., P.S.

The Courts of the Commonwealth have already strained to permit the legislature to carry over the civil doctrine of respondeat superior and to apply it as a means of enforcing the regulatory scheme that covers the liquor trade. We have done so on the theory that the Code established petty misdemeanors involving only light monetary fines. It would be unthinkable to impose vicarious criminal responsibility in cases involving true crimes. Although to hold a principal criminally liable might possibly be an effective means of enforcing law and order, it would do violence to our more sophisticated modern-day concepts of justice. Liability for all true crimes, wherein an offense carries with it a jail sentence, must be based exclusively upon personal causation. It can be readily imagined that even a licensee who is meticulously careful in the choice of his employees cannot supervise every single act of the subordinates. A man's liberty cannot rest on so frail a reed as whether his employee will commit a mistake in judgment.

This Court is ever mindful of its duty to maintain and establish the proper safeguards in a criminal trial. To sanction the imposition of imprisonment here would make a serious change in the substantive criminal law of the Commonwealth, one for which we find no justification. We have found *no* case in any jurisdiction which has permitted a *prison term* for a vicarious offense. The Supreme Court of the United States has had occasion only recently to impose due process limitations upon the actions of a state legislature in making unknowing conduct criminal. Lambert v. People of State of California, 1957, 355 U.S. 225. . . . We would be utterly remiss were we not to so act under these facts.

Does the somewhat guarded criminal law doctrine of respondeat superior that is applied when the employer is a natural person logically extend to the liability of an abstract business entity? Consider the cautious view of the court in Commonwealth v. Beneficial Finance Corp., 360 Mass. 188, 275 N.E.2d 33, 77 (1971):

In fact, Professor Sayre explicitly refrains from dealing with the problem of imposing corporate criminal liability when he states: "The problem of the criminal liability of a corporation for the acts of corporate agents depends upon a consideration of two quite distinct problems, one a problem of agency, and the other a problem of the law of corporations. The first involves the general question of criminal responsibility for the acts of another. Would the principal be criminally liable for the acts of the agent if the principal were a natural person instead of a corporation? The second problem involves the entirely distinct question of when the acts and intent of a natural person, for example of a vice-president or general manager, are to be treated as those of the corporation itself. In [this article], only the first of these two problems is considered." Sayre, Criminal Responsibility for the Acts of Another, 43 Harv. L. Rev. at 689.

. . . [T]he very nature of a corporation as a "person" before the law renders it impossible to equate the imposition of vicarious liability on a human principal

> with the imposition of vicarious liability on a corporate principal. "A corporation can act only through its agents. . . . [C]orporate criminal liability is necessarily vicarious." Note, Criminal Liability of Corporations for Acts of Their Agents, 60 Harv. L. Rev. 283. . . .
>
> . . . Since a corporation is a legal fiction, comprised only of individuals, it has no existence separate and distinct from those whom it has clothed with authority and commissioned to act for it whether such individuals are directors, officers, shareholders or employees. Thus, the issue is not whether vicarious liability should be imposed on a corporation under the "direct participation and assent rule" of the master-servant cases cited above, but rather, whether the acts and intent of natural persons, be they officers, directors or employees can be treated as the acts and intent of the corporation itself.

UNITED STATES v. HILTON HOTELS CORP.

United States Court of Appeals, Ninth Circuit
467 F.2d 100 (1972)

BROWNING, Circuit Judge.

This is an appeal from a conviction under an indictment charging a violation of section 1 of the Sherman Act, 15 U.S.C. §1.

Operators of hotels, restaurants, hotel and restaurant supply companies, and other businesses in Portland, Oregon, organized an association to attract conventions to their city. To finance the association, members were asked to make contributions in predetermined amounts. Companies selling supplies to hotels were asked to contribute an amount equal to one per cent of their sales to hotel members. To aid collections, hotel members, including appellant, agreed to give preferential treatment to suppliers who paid their assessments, and to curtail purchases from those who did not.

I

The jury was instructed that such an agreement by the hotel members, if proven, would be a per se violation of the Sherman Act. Appellant argues that this was error.

We need not explore the outer limits of the doctrine that joint refusals to deal constitute per se violations of the Act, for the conduct involved here was of the kind long held to be forbidden without more. "Throughout the history of the Sherman Act, the courts have had little difficulty in finding unreasonable restraints of trade in agreements among competitors, at any level of distribution, designed to coerce those subject to a boycott to accede to the action or inaction desired by the group or to exclude them from competition." Barber, Refusals to Deal under the Federal Antitrust Laws, 103 U. Pa. L. Rev. 847, 872-873 (1955). . . .

II

Appellant's president testified that it would be contrary to the policy of the corporation for the manager of one of its hotels to condition purchases upon payment of a contribution to a local association by the supplier. The manager of appellant's Portland hotel and his assistant testified that it was the hotel's policy to purchase supplies solely on the basis of price, quality, and service. They also testified that on two occasions they told the hotel's purchasing agent that he was to take no part in the boycott. The purchasing agent confirmed the receipt of these instructions, but admitted that, despite them, he had threatened a supplier with loss of the hotel's business unless the supplier paid the association assessment. He testified that he violated his instructions because of anger and personal pique toward the individual representing the supplier.

Based upon this testimony, appellant requested certain instructions bearing upon the criminal liability of a corporation for the unauthorized acts of its agents. These requests were rejected by the trial court. The court instructed the jury that a corporation is liable for the acts and statements of its agents "within the scope of their employment," defined to mean "in the corporation's behalf in performance of the agent's general line of work," including "not only that which has been authorized by the corporation, but also that which outsiders could reasonably assume the agent would have authority to do." The court added:

> A corporation is responsible for acts and statements of its agents, done or made within the scope of their employment, even though their conduct may be contrary to their actual instructions or contrary to the corporation's stated policies.

Appellant objects only to the court's concluding statement.

Congress may constitutionally impose criminal liability upon a business entity for acts or omissions of its agents within the scope of their employment. Such liability may attach without proof that the conduct was within the agent's actual authority, and even though it may have been contrary to express instructions.

The intention to impose such liability is sometimes express, but it may also be implied. The text of the Sherman Act does not expressly resolve the issue. For the reasons that follow, however, we think the construction of the Act that best achieves its purpose is that a corporation is liable for acts of its agents within the scope of their authority even when done against company orders.

It is obvious from the Sherman Act's language and subject matter that the Act is primarily concerned with the activities of business entities. The statute is directed against "restraint upon commercial competition in the marketing of goods or services." Apex Hosiery Co. v. Leader, 310 U.S. 469, 495

(1940). In 1890, as now, the most significant commercial activity was conducted by corporate enterprises.

Despite the fact that "the doctrine of corporate criminal responsibility for the acts of the officers was not well established in 1890", United States v. Wise, 370 U.S. 405, 408 (1962), the Act expressly applies to corporate entities. 15 U.S.C. §7. The preoccupation of Congress with corporate liability was only emphasized by the adoption in 1914 of section 14 of the Clayton Act to reaffirm and emphasize that such liability was not exclusive, and that corporate agents also were subject to punishment if they authorized, ordered, or participated in the acts constituting the violation. United States v. Wise, supra, 370 U.S. at 411-415.

With such important public interest at stake, it is reasonable to assume that Congress intended to impose liability upon business entities for the acts of those to whom they choose to delegate the conduct of their affairs, thus stimulating a maximum effort by owners and managers to assure adherence by such agents to the requirements of the Act.

Legal commentators have argued forcefully that it is inappropriate and ineffective to impose criminal liability upon a corporation, as distinguished from the human agents who actually perform the unlawful acts, particularly if the acts of the agents are unauthorized. But it is the legislative judgment that controls, and "the great mass of legislation calling for corporate criminal liability suggests a widespread belief on the part of legislators that such liability is necessary to effectuate regulatory policy." ALI Model Penal Code, Comment on §2.07, Tentative Draft No. 4, p.149 (1956). Moreover, the strenuous efforts of corporate defendants to avoid conviction, particularly under the Sherman Act, strongly suggests that Congress is justified in its judgment that exposure of the corporate entity to potential conviction may provide a substantial spur to corporate action to prevent violations by employees.

Because of the nature of Sherman Act offenses and the context in which they normally occur, the factors that militate against allowing a corporation to disown the criminal acts of its agents apply with special force to Sherman Act violations.

Sherman Act violations are commercial offenses. They are usually motivated by a desire to enhance profits.[11] They commonly involve large, complex, and highly decentralized corporate business enterprises, and intricate business processes, practices, and arrangements. More often than not they also involve basic policy decisions, and must be implemented over an extended period of time.

Complex business structures, characterized by decentralization and delegation of authority, commonly adopted by corporations for business purposes,

11. A purpose to benefit the corporation is necessary to bring the agent's acts within the scope of his employment. Standard Oil Co. v. United States, 307 F.2d 120, 128-129 (5th Cir. 1962).

make it difficult to identify the particular corporate agents responsible for Sherman Act violations. At the same time, it is generally true that high management officials for whose conduct the corporate directors and stockholders are the most clearly responsible, are likely to have participated in the policy decisions underlying Sherman Act violations, or at least to have become aware of them.

Violations of the Sherman Act are a likely consequence of the pressure to maximize profits that is commonly imposed by corporate owners upon managing agents and, in turn, upon lesser employees. In the face of that pressure, generalized directions to obey the Sherman Act, with the probable effect of [forgoing] profits, are the least likely to be taken seriously. And if a violation of the Sherman Act occurs, the corporation, and not the individual agents, will have realized the profits from the illegal activity.

In sum, identification of the particular agents responsible for a Sherman Act violation is especially difficult, and their conviction and punishment is peculiarly ineffective as a deterrent. At the same time, conviction and punishment of the business entity itself is likely to be both appropriate and effective.

For these reasons we conclude that as a general rule a corporation is liable under the Sherman Act for the acts of its agents in the scope of their employment, even though contrary to general corporate policy and express instructions to the agent.

Thus the general policy statements of appellant's president were no defense. Nor was it enough that appellant's manager told the purchasing agent that he was not to participate in the boycott. The purchasing agent was authorized to buy all of appellant's supplies. Purchases were made on the basis of specifications, but the purchasing agent exercised complete authority as to source. He was in a unique position to add the corporation's buying power to the force of the boycott. Appellant could not gain exculpation by issuing general instructions without undertaking to enforce those instructions by means commensurate with the obvious risks. . . .

Affirmed.

Notes and Questions

1. Consider the following excerpt from Note, Developments in the Law—Corporate Crime: Regulating Corporate Behavior Through Criminal Sanctions, 92 Harv. L. Rev. 1227, 1247-1251 (1979):

> *1. Respondeat Superior.*—The respondeat superior doctrine of corporate criminal liability, derived from agency principles of tort law, is the common law rule in the federal courts and in most state courts today. The federal criminal code proposed in 1978 also adopts this majority rule. Under the doctrine of respondeat superior, a corporation may be held criminally liable for the acts of any of its agents if an agent (1) commits a crime (2) within the scope of employment (3) with the intent to benefit the corporation.

First, it must be proved than an illegal act was committed by an agent of the corporation, and that the agent acted with the specific intent required by the governing statute. Proving specific intent should be the same for a corporation as for an individual defendant, because under respondeat superior, the intent of the offending agent is imputed directly to the corporation. However, since the corporation is perceived as an aggregation of its agents, it is not necessary to prove that a specific person acted illegally, only that *some* agent of the corporation committed the crime. Thus, proving that a corporate defendant committed the illegal act is in practice substantially easier than an individual prosecution.

Courts have also found the requirement of corporate criminal intent satisfied where no agent's criminal intent has been shown. Corporations have been convicted of crimes requiring knowledge on the basis of the "collective knowledge" of the employees as a group, even though no single employee possessed sufficient information to know that the crime was being committed. For example, in United States v. T.I.M.E.-D.C., Inc., [381 F. Supp. 730 (W.D. Va. 1974)] a trucking company was found guilty of knowingly violating an ICC regulation which forbade truckers from driving when ill. One employee, a dispatcher, knew that the driver in question had telephoned to say he could not work, and then changed his mind after learning of the company's new absentee policy. Corporate officers, the court found, knew that the harsh new policy was likely to encourage truckers to drive despite being ill. Through the collective knowledge of the dispatcher and the officers, the corporation was found to have known that the driver was unfit to drive under the ICC regulation.

In addition, there is some evidence that juries attach less importance to the intent requirement for corporate than for individual defendants. In a number of joint trials where the individual defendants were the only conceivable persons involved in the corporate offense, juries have convicted the corporation while acquitting the individual defendants. Since, under respondeat superior, corporate intent is imputed only from individual intent, it is logically inconsistent under that doctrine to find a corporation guilty when no individual agent is found to have had the requisite intent. Federal courts generally have permitted such inconsistent verdicts to stand, although they have complained at times.

Second, to establish corporate liability under the doctrine of respondeat superior, the prosecution must show that the illegal act was committed within the agent's scope of employment. The traditional agency definition limits scope of employment to conduct that is authorized, explicitly or implicitly, by the principal or that is similar or incidental to authorized conduct. However, courts generally find conduct to fall within the scope of employment even if it was specifically forbidden by a superior and occurred despite good faith efforts on the part of the corporation to prevent the crime. Thus, scope of employment in practice means little more than the act occurred while the offending employee was carrying out a job-related activity. This extension is essential, for if scope of employment were limited to authorized conduct under the doctrine of respondeat superior, a corporation could too easily evade criminal liability. The board of directors, for example, could protect a corporation from liability for the acts of all officers and employees through a simple prohibition of illegal conduct, thus placing such conduct outside the scope of employment.

Third, it must be proved that the agent committed the crime with the intent to benefit the corporation. The corporation may be held criminally liable even if it received no actual benefit from the offense, although the existence or absence of benefit is relevant as evidence of an intent to benefit.

The requirements of scope of employment and intent to benefit the corporation can also be met through ratification. When an employee commits a crime with no intent to benefit the corporation, or while acting outside the scope of his employment, subsequent approval of the act by his supervisor will be sufficient to hold the corporation liable for the employee's criminal act. In a sense, under the doctrine of ratification, a corporation is culpable for approving the criminal act, rather than committing it.

As summarized in this commentary, vicarious liability of a corporation for the acts of its agents is *not* limited to so-called malum prohibitum crimes, while *Marley* and *Koczwara,* above, suggest such a limitation on the vicarious liability of an employer who is a natural person. Is the distinction sound, on the theory that we cannot feel much empathy for a corporation?

2. In United States v. Cincotta, 689 F.2d 238 (1st Cir. 1982), the court examined a key requirement of corporate criminal liability—that the agent of the corporation act to benefit the corporation.

Appellant Mystic Fuel Corporation (Mystic) was engaged in the business of delivering heating oil to oil consumers. It did not own or rent oil storage tanks, but it did own several trucks for transporting oil. It used those trucks to earn money in two different ways: it entered delivery contracts whereby oil suppliers without trucks would pay Mystic a commission to deliver oil to the suppliers' customers; and it entered supply contracts whereby oil consumers would buy oil directly from Mystic, which Mystic would then acquire in its own name from suppliers.

Appellant Cincotta was a major stockholder in Mystic, and its Treasurer. He signed all the company's checks, bids, and contracts. Together with appellant Zero, he made all the major decisions of the company, as well as the rules governing its daily operation.

Appellant Zero was also a major stockholder in Mystic, and its dispatcher. He hired the truck drivers, and issued their daily orders on where to pick up and deliver oil. He also supervised Mystic's billing and accounting.

At trial, the government set forth evidence of a scheme through which Mystic would defraud the United States Department of Defense, inducing it to pay for oil that Mystic would sell in its own name to its own clients. The evidence suggested that during fiscal year 1978 (September 1, 1977, through August 31, 1978) Mystic had a delivery contract giving it a commission for delivering "number four oil" (a moderately heavy oil, generally used to heat small industrial buildings, schools, and medium-sized apartment buildings) from the Union Petroleum Corporation (Union) to Fort Devens in Ayer, Massachusetts. The evidence suggested further that on numerous occasions Mystic picked up a shipment of oil at Union, representing that the oil was for delivery to Fort Devens. Then, Mystic would sell the shipment to its own consumer clients. Finally, it would tell the Fort Devens authorities that it had in fact delivered the shipment to Fort Devens, inducing the Department of Defense to pay Union for the shipment. The net result was that Fort Devens paid for shipments it never received, and Mystic was able to sell oil that it had never paid for.

After a two-week trial, the jury deliberated for ten hours and then found all three defendants guilty of (1) conspiring to defraud the United States in violation of 18 U.S.C. §371, of (2) wilfully causing seven specific false claims to be made against the United States, in violation of 18 U.S.C. §§2, 287, and of (3) knowingly and wilfully making and using seven specific false documents in relation to a matter within the jurisdiction of a United States department, in violation of 18 U.S.C. §§2, 1001.

A corporation may be convicted for the criminal acts of its agents, under a theory of respondeat superior. But criminal liability may be imposed on the corporation only where the agent is acting within the scope of employment. That, in turn, requires that the agent be performing acts of the kind which he is authorized to perform, and those acts must be motivated—at least in part—by an intent to benefit the corporation. United States v. DeMauro, 581 F.2d 50, 54 n.3 (2d Cir. 1978); United States v. Beusch, 596 F.2d 871, 878 & n.7 (9th Cir. 1979). Thus, where intent is an element of a crime (as it is here), a corporation may not be held strictly accountable for acts that could not benefit the stockholders, such as acts of corporate officers that are performed in exchange for bribes paid to the officers personally.

Mystic argues that the trial court erred in denying its motion for acquittal. It contends that the government failed to produce evidence of Cincotta's and/or Zero's intent to benefit the corporation through their scheme to defraud the United States. This argument may be rejected out of hand. The mechanism by which the fraudulent scheme worked required money to pass through Mystic's treasury. When Fort Devens paid Union for the undelivered shipments, the shipments were not resold in Zero's name or Cincotta's name. Rather, they were sold to Mystic's customers in Mystic's name. Mystic—not the individual defendants—was making money by selling oil that it had not paid for.

3. Is it fair to punish Hilton for the criminal acts of its purchasing agent when the corporation established an express policy forbidding such actions? Does the court's rejection of Hilton's defense invoke the concern expressed by the dissent in *Marley*—that vicarious criminal liability for an employer may leave "nothing an employer can do to protect himself"? Or was the court right in suggesting that Hilton could have taken steps to enforce its policy? In any event, is there any legal significance in a corporation's having established a policy against criminal activity by its employees, given the general presumption in our jurisprudence that all citizens know the criminal law?

Assume that the 7-11 Corporation owns 15,000 stores around the country, each operated by a corporation employee (not a franchisee). Assume that the corporation President regularly sends to all store operators vigorous messages reminding the operators that they must comply with all local health and safety codes, adding that the company will fire any operator who is fined or punished for violating a local law. Assume that in addition, the company sends inspectors to visit each store at least four times a year to ensure that the stores are complying with local laws. If one store operator nevertheless violates a local health law just after one of the company inspections, is the corporation criminally liable? What if the store operator bribes a police officer not to ticket customers?

Some recent cases have softened the holding of *Hilton* that a corporation is criminally liable even where its agent violates clear company policy. In United States v. Beusch, 596 F.2d 871 (9th Cir. 1981), Deak & Company, a foreign currency exchange dealer, was convicted of 377 misdemeanor violations when its vice-president, Beusch, failed to make federally required reports of large transactions. The court confirmed that "a corporation *may* be liable for acts of its employees done contrary to express instructions and policies . . . but the existence of such instructions and policies may be considered in determining whether the employee in fact acted to benefit the corporation."

4. The Model Penal Code contains a complex provision establishing when a corporation is criminally liable for the act of a corporate agent.

Section 2.07. Liability of Corporations, Unincorporated Associations and Persons Acting, or Under a Duty to Act, in Their Behalf.

(1) A corporation may be convicted of the commission of an offense if:

(a) the offense is a violation or the offense is defined by a statute other than the Code in which a legislative purpose to impose liability on corporations plainly appears and the conduct is performed by an agent of the corporation acting in behalf of the corporation within the scope of his office or employment, except that if the law defining the offense designates the agents for whose conduct the corporation is accountable or the circumstances under which it is accountable, such provisions shall apply; or

(b) the offense consists of an omission to discharge a specific duty of affirmative performance imposed on corporations by law; or

(c) the commission of the offense was authorized, requested, commanded, performed or recklessly tolerated by the board of directors or by a high managerial agent acting in behalf of the corporation within the scope of his office or employment.

(2) When absolute liability is imposed for the commission of an offense, a legislative purpose to impose liability on a corporation shall be assumed, unless the contrary plainly appears. . . .

(4) As used in this Section:

(a) "corporation" does not include an entity organized as or by a governmental agency for the execution of a governmental program;

(b) "agent" means any director, officer, servant, employee or other person authorized to act in behalf of the corporation or association and, in the case of an unincorporated association, a member of such association;

(c) "high managerial agent" means an officer of a corporation or an unincorporated association, or, in the case of a partnership, a partner, or any other agent of a corporation or association having duties of such responsibility that his conduct may fairly be assumed to represent the policy of the corporation or association.

(5) In any prosecution of a corporation or an unincorporated association for the commission of an offense included within the terms of Subsection (1)(a) or Subsection (3)(a) of this Section, other than an offense for which absolute liability has been imposed, it shall be a defense if the defendant proves by a preponderance of evidence that the high managerial agent having supervisory responsibility over the subject matter of the offense employed due diligence to prevent its commission. This paragraph shall not apply if it is plainly inconsistent with the legislative purpose in defining the particular offense.

The Commentary to §2.07 explains:

The provisions of Subsection (1)(a) identify the offenses for which a corporation may be held criminally liable for the conduct of an agent or employee acting within the scope of his office or employment. This familiar principle of respondeat superior is further qualified by the requirement that the conduct be performed "in behalf of the corporation." The purpose of the latter phrase is to avoid the problem presented in Moore v. Ibresler, Ltd., in which the corporation was held liable for criminal conduct committed by officers within the scope of their duties but for the purpose of concealing a fraud perpetrated by the same officers against the corporation. This limitation appears equitable and is not likely to frustrate the substantial purposes of corporate responsibility.

The provisions of the Model Penal Code dealing with the criminal liability of corporations must be considered both in connection with offenses defined in the Code and offenses defined by other statutes. Subsection (1)(a) deals, in part, with the latter. During the last ninety years a great mass of regulatory legislation imposing criminal liability on corporations for the offenses there defined has been added to the laws of American jurisdictions. Often, perhaps typically, criminal penalties added to such regulatory legislation have been hastily and inadequately considered. In many cases, however, such penal provisions form an integral part of the regulatory policy and are based on considerable pragmatic experience indicating their usefulness. The provisions of Subsection (1)(a) are based on the theory that the criminal code ought not to attempt a pro tanto repeal of such legislation by denying corporate criminal liability under statutes in which it is plainly recognized. The consequences of a general repeal of these provisions could hardly be anticipated and, in an indeterminate number of situations, might produce serious effects on the enforcement of regulatory policy. [T]here are affirmative considerations that tend to justify the recognition of corporate criminal liability for the commission of such regulatory offenses. Moreover, such a case as can be made for its elimination is not strong enough to justify the precipitate step of abolition of a liability that is presently so widespread.

Subsection (1)(a) also recognizes corporate responsibility for the commission of violations, whether defined by the Code or by other statutes. The term "violation," defined in Section 1.04(5) refers generally to those minor offenses that are not classified as crimes and that are punishable only by fine. Subsection (1)(a) is thus a reflection of the judgment that liability for the more serious offenses defined by a criminal code—misdemeanors and felonies—should be ascribed to corporations only after the satisfaction of a more rigorous standard than the one it sets forth. Accordingly, unless the offense is a violation or the offense is defined by a statute other than the criminal code and plainly reflects a legislative purpose to impose liability on corporations, corporate criminal liability will be measured by the standard established in Subsection (1)(c).

. . . Subsection (1)(b) deals with a situation where the criminal law speaks explicitly to corporations, and thus like Subsection (1)(a) leaves the question of more general liability to Subsection (1)(c). The reference to a "specific" duty imposed on corporations by law is designed to make it clear that the provision does not govern in such a case as negligent homicide, where the duty violated is one that the law imposes generally. Rather, the section will apply when there is a failure, for example, to file a report of a kind that the corporation is specifically required to file, or to maintain records that the corporation is required by law to keep. Virtually all revisions with provisions for corporate liability have a similar provision.

. . . Subsection (1)(c) governs the general liability of corporations for crimes defined by the criminal code. In essence, it defines the types of conduct engaged in by corporate officials that will result in charging the offense to the entity.

In approaching the analysis of corporate criminal capacity, it will be observed initially that the imposing of criminal penalties on corporate bodies results in a species of vicarious liability. The direct burden of a corporate fine is visited upon the shareholders of the corporation. In most cases, the shareholders have not participated in the criminal conduct and lack the practical means of supervision of corporate management to prevent misconduct by corporate agents. This is not to say, of course, that all the policy considerations at issue in imposing vicarious responsibility on a human principal are present to the same degree in the corporate cases. Two fundamental distinctions should be noted. First, the fact that the corporation is the party nominally convicted means that the individual shareholders escape the opprobrium and incidental disabilities that normally follow a personal conviction or even indictment. Second, the shareholder's loss is limited to his equity in the corporation. His personal assets are not ordinarily subject to levy and the conviction of the corporation will not result in loss of liberty to the stockholders. Nevertheless, the fact that the direct impact of corporate fines is felt by a group ordinarily innocent of criminal conduct underscores the point that such fines ought not to be authorized except where they clearly may be expected to accomplish desirable social purposes. To the extent that shareholders participate in criminal conduct, or to the extent that there are unlawful transactions involving the shareholders' holdings, they may be reached directly through application of the ordinary principles of criminal liability.

It would seem that the ultimate justification of corporate criminal responsibility must rest in large measure on an evaluation of the deterrent effects of corporate fines on the conduct of corporate agents. Is there a reason for anticipating a substantially higher degree of deterrence from fines levied on corporate bodies than can fairly be anticipated from proceeding directly against the guilty officer or agent or from other feasible sanctions of a noncriminal character?

It may be assumed that ordinarily a corporate agent is not likely to be deterred from criminal conduct by the prospect of corporate liability when, in any event, he faces the prospect of individually suffering serious criminal penalties for his own act. If the agent cannot be prevented from committing an offense by the prospect of personal liability, he ordinarily will not be prevented by the prospect of corporate liability.

Yet the problem cannot be resolved so simply. For there are probably cases in which the economic pressures within the corporate body are sufficiently potent to tempt individuals to hazard personal liability for the sake of company gain, especially where the penalties threatened are moderate and where the offense does not involve behavior condemned as highly immoral by the individual's associates. This tendency may be particularly strong where the individual knows that his guilt may be difficult to prove or where a favorable reaction to his position by a jury may be anticipated even where proof of guilt is strong. A number of appellate opinions reveal situations in which juries have held the corporate defendant criminally liable while acquitting the obviously guilty agents who committed the criminal acts.

This may reflect more than faulty or capricious judgment on the part of the juries. It may represent a recognition that the social consequences of a criminal conviction may fall with a disproportionately heavy impact on the individual defendants where the conduct involved is not of a highly immoral character. It may also reflect a shrewd belief that the violation may have been produced by pressures on the subordinates created by corporate managerial officials even though the latter may not have intended or desired the criminal behavior and even though the pressures can only be sensed rather than demonstrated. Furthermore, the great mass of legislation calling for corporate criminal liability suggests a widespread belief on the part of legislators that such liability is necessary to effectuate regulatory policy. . . .

The case so made out, however, does not demonstrate the wisdom of corporate fines generally. Rather, it tends to suggest that such liability can best be justified in cases in which penalties directed to the individual are moderate and where the criminal conviction is least likely to be interpreted as a form of social moral condemnation. This indicates a general line of distinction between the "malum prohibitum" regulatory offenses, on the one hand, and more serious offenses on the other. The same distinction is suggested in dealing with the problem of jury behavior. The cases cited above involving situations in which individual defendants were acquitted are all cases of economic regulations. It may be doubted that such results would have followed had the offenses involved a more obvious moral element. In any event, it is not clear just what conclusions are to be drawn from the cited cases. In each, the jury had corporate liability available as an alternative to acquittal of all of the defendants. Conceivably, if that alternative had not been available, verdicts against the individuals in some of the cases might have been returned. Thus, it is at least possible that corporate liability encourages erratic jury behavior. It may be true that the complexities of organization characteristic of large corporate enterprise at times present real problems of identifying the guilty individual and establishing his criminal liability. It would be hoped, however, that more could be pointed to in justification of placing the pecuniary burdens of criminal fines on the innocent than the difficulties of proving the guilt of the culpable individual. Where there is concrete evidence that the difficulties are real, however, the effectuation of regulatory policy may be thought to justify the means.

In surveying the case law on the subject of corporate criminal liability one may be struck at how few are the types of common law offenses that have actually resulted in corporate criminal responsibility. They are restricted for the most part to thefts (including frauds) and involuntary manslaughter. Conspiracy might also be included, but generally the cases have involved conspiracies to violate regulatory statutes (such as the antitrust laws), and often these statutes include specific conspiracy provisions made applicable to corporate bodies. No cases have been found in which a corporation was sought to be held criminally liable for such crimes as murder, treason, rape and bigamy. In general, such offenses may be effectively punished and deterred by prosecutions directed against the guilty individuals. One would not anticipate the same reluctance on the part of juries to convict individuals that seems sometimes to be present where the offense is a regulatory crime. Moreover, in may of the situations, such as those involving involuntary manslaughter, there is a strong possibility that the shareholders will be called upon to bear the burden of tort recoveries, a prospect that may also be expected to encourage supervision of subordinate employees by executive personnel.

The burden of this analysis may suggest the conclusion that corporate criminal responsibility should be withheld from serious crimes defined by the criminal code. There are considerations, however, that indicate the prudence of retaining responsibility on a more restricted basis for these crimes. As noted above, the acquisitive offenses, both common law crimes and those defined by special legislation such as the Federal Mail Fraud Act, traditionally have constituted one of the major categories of corporate crime. In a rough way, also, corporate fines in these cases may be employed to deprive a corporation of an unjust enrichment resulting from the commission of offenses by its agents. Moreover, there may be situations in which it is highly desirable to retain a degree of corporate responsibility for the criminal code offenses as when the crime is committed in the state by a foreign corporation but where the guilty individual agent is outside the jurisdiction and hence not amenable to prosecution in the state.

The approach of Subsection (1)(c) is to provide for a more restricted basis of liability for all cases not included within the terms of Subsections (1)(a) and (1)(b). The general respondeat superior approach of Subsection (1)(a) is rejected for these cases, and corporate liability is confined to situations in which the criminal conduct is performed, participated in or recklessly tolerated by the board of directors or by corporate officers or agents sufficiently high in the hierarchy to make it reasonable to assume that their acts are in some substantial sense reflective of the policy of the corporate body. The agents having such power to make the corporation criminally liable are described by the terms of Subsection (1)(c) as the board of directors or any "high managerial agent acting in behalf of the corporation within the scope of his office or employment." The phrase "high managerial agent" is defined in Subsection (4)(c). Given the wide variations in corporate structure, these criteria are necessarily very general. But taken with Subsection (4)(c), they are considerably more precise than those enunciated by many courts as a matter of decisional law. . . .

In practical effect, Subsection (1)(c) would result in corporate liability for the conduct of the corporate president or general manager but not for conduct of a foreman in a large plant or of an insignificant branch manager in the absence of participation at higher levels of corporate authority. The provision thus works a substantial limitation on corporate responsibility in cases in which the deterrent effects of corporate fines are most dubious but preserves it in cases in which the shareholders are most likely to be in a position to bring pressures to bear to prevent corporate crime. . . .

. . . Subsection (2) states a rule of interpretation that has the effect of making corporations liable to prosecution for all offenses that carry absolute liability, unless a contrary legislative intent plainly appears. . . . To impose [criminal] liability on corporations, moreover, results in no greater inequities to the corporation or to the innocent shareholder than to the individual who is held criminally liable despite the absence of the normal requisites of culpability. . . .

. . . Subsection (5) makes an important contribution to the rationalization of corporate criminal responsibility. It is based on the assumption that a primary purpose of the corporate fine is to encourage diligent supervision of corporate personnel by managerial employees in those cases in which the corporation is bound by the conduct of lower echelon employees. Where that diligence can be shown by a preponderance of the evidence, exculpation should follow in all but those cases where such a defense is clearly inconsistent with the legislative purpose manifested in defining the particular offense. If the legislature has imposed strict liability on the corporate agent for the commission of the offense, even where that agent has employed due diligence, there would seem to be no reason to exculpate the corporation on the ground of due diligence on the part of supervisory personnel. Where liability is not strict, however, the defense would seem to comport, as noted, with the objectives of corporate liability.

The same defense, subject to the same limitations, is made available to unincorporated associations. The reasoning in both instances is the same.

5. Model Penal Code §2.07 is a complex and ambivalent compromise. Recall that the cases establishing the vicarious liability of individual employers for the acts of their agents, such as Ex Parte Marley, purport to limit vicarious criminal liability to regulatory or malum prohibitum laws, but that the general development of criminal liability for corporations has not drawn this distinction. The most controversial part of §2.07 is Subsection (1)(c), which greatly limits the liability of the corporation for "true crimes" (or common law offenses or malum in se crimes), by requiring proof that the board of directors or a high managerial agent "authorized, requested, commanded, performed or recklessly tolerated" the offense.

Under §2.07, if in *Hilton Hotels,* the purchasing agent's purposeful antitrust violation were the sort of crime covered by §2.07(1)(c), would the Hilton corporation have been liable? Could the corporation rely on its express policy against illegal "refusals to deal" to invoke the "due diligence" defense of §2.07(5)?

One commentator[12] vigorously applauds the principle of corporate liability for the acts of directors, officers, or high managerial agents on the ground that this principle alone contains a coherent notion of the *mens rea* of an abstract entity:

But section 2.07(1)(c) is entirely right in extending the scope of liability to include the offenses of other high managerial agents. Not the mode of acquisition of a corporate office, but the scope of trust and power is the proper criterion. It

12. Mueller, Mens Rea and the Corporation, 19 U. Pitt. L. Rev. 21, 40-41 (1957).

is entirely proper to argue that all high managerial agents theoretically are equally well known to the shareholders, are part of the corporation's inner circle and are, therefore, equally within the spotlight of scrutiny. We conjecture that if a non-elected high managerial agent shows signs of dereliction, the shareholders will, or ought to, exert pressure in order to cause his removal from a position of command, or at least to restrain him from wrongdoing. Thus, we can call all those officers, whether elected or appointed, who direct, supervise and manage the corporation within its business sphere and policy-wise, the "inner circle." They are the *mens,* the mind or brain, of the corporation. It is this *mens* which is capable of mental self-direction and, because of its human nature, single or composite, there is no reason in the world why this *mens* should not also be capable of harboring a *mens rea.* At least in part, the inner circle may well also be the hands of the man-like phenomenon, the corporation, though more often and more properly the part of the hands is played by the operatives of the corporation.

Thus, it is now this "inner circle" which stands for the corporation for the purpose of the application of the doctrine of criminal liability. The acts of the members of this group, as a matter of policy, convenience and logic, are acts of the corporation which may subject the corporation to criminal liability. The Code is entirely right in recognizing that not only the direct acts of members of this group may create corporate criminal liability, but also acts authorized, requested or commanded by these officers. Likening a corporation to a natural person for the purpose of criminal law administration is not an outgrowth of the "psychological tendency toward personification," as Machen suggested,[13] but is a rational interpretation of the theory of the corporate fiction for purposes of the application of a rational theory of corporate criminal liability on the basis of the guilt—deterrence orientation of the common law of crimes.

On the same principle, Mueller goes on to denounce vicarious corporate liability for the acts of lower-level corporate agents:

As far as discussed in the previous section, the Code is entirely in keeping with orthodox principles of criminal liability. But when the Code goes further, as it does in section 2.07(1)(a), and extends criminal liability of the corporation to independent acts of inferior employees, i.e., not those who are members of the inner circle, it subjects the corporation to liability for acts which "it" (as represented by the inner circle) has not willed, not directed, not authorized. In such a case not only does the corporation lack *mens rea,* it even lacks mental self-direction. Here the hand has moved without order from the brain. To impose liability for such a movement of the corporate hand would be analogous to subjecting an epileptic to criminal liability for the harm done by a motion of his hand, not willed, but solely the reflex of an epileptic fit. Returning to the corporate level, what the Code does in this situation amounts to the imposition of vicarious liability, resting on the assumption of a probability that the crime of the servant could have been prevented by the master through the exercise of due diligence. But this vicarious liability may well lack the *mens rea* of the real defendant, the

13. Machen, Corporate Personality, 24 Harv. L. Rev. 253, 347 (1911).

> corporation, as represented by its inner circle. As long as the probability assumption may be controverted, no injustice can be done, but when the *mens rea* of the inner circle is deemed irrelevant, as it is in many instances under a clause to be discussed below, we wind up with an actual case of absolute liability.

But some courts and commentators have attacked §2.07(1)(c) for taking a wholly unrealistic view of corporate organization. In Commonwealth v. Beneficial Finance Co., 360 Mass. 188, 275 N.E.2d 33 (1971), three loan companies, along with several of their employees, were convicted of bribery and conspiracy to commit bribery, after the employees, hoping to influence officials to set a high maximum interest rate on consumer loans, offered money to state officials. In affirming the convictions of the corporations, the Supreme Judicial Court of Massachusetts refused to adopt the position of the Model Penal Code that the state had to prove that high managerial agents had authorized the bribes.

> Moreover, we do not think that the Model Penal Code standard really purports to deal with the evidentiary problems which are inherent in establishing the quantum of proof necessary to show that the directors or officers of a corporation authorize, ratify, tolerate, or participate in the criminal acts of an agent when such acts are apparently performed on behalf of the corporation. Evidence of such authorization or ratification is too easily susceptible of concealment. As is so trenchantly stated by the judge: "Criminal acts are not usually made the subject of votes of authorization or ratification by corporate Boards of Directors; and the lack of such votes does not prevent the act from being the act of the corporation."
>
> It is obvious that criminal conspiratorial acts are not performed within the glare of publicity, nor would we expect a board of directors to meet officially and record on the corporate records a delegation of authority to initiate, conduct or conclude proceedings for the purpose of bribing a public official. Of necessity, the proof [of] authority to so act must rest on all the circumstances and conduct in a given situation and the reasonable inferences to be drawn therefrom.
>
> Additional factors of importance are the size and complexity of many large modern corporations which necessitate the delegation of more authority to lesser corporate agents and employees. As the judge pointed out: "There are not enough seats on the Board of Directors, nor enough offices in a corporation, to permit the corporation engaged in widespread operations to give such a title or office to every person in whom it places the power, authority, and responsibility for decision and action." This latter consideration lends credence to the view that the title or position of an individual in a corporation should not be conclusively determinative in ascribing criminal responsibility. In a large corporation, with many numerous and distinct departments, a high ranking corporate officer or agent may have no authority or involvement in a particular sphere of corporate activity, whereas a lower ranking corporate executive might have much broader power in dealing with a matter peculiarly within the scope of his authority. Employees who are in the lower echelon of the corporate hierarchy often exercise more responsibility in the *everyday operations* of the corporation than the directors or officers. Assuredly, the title or office that the person holds may be considered,

but it should not be the decisive criterion upon which to predicate corporate responsibility. . . .

To permit corporations to conceal the nefarious acts of their underlings by using the shield of corporate armor to deflect corporate responsibility, and to separate the subordinate from the executive, would be to permit "endocratic" corporations to inflict widespread public harm without hope of redress. It would merely serve to ignore the scramble and realities of the market place.[14] This we decline to do. We believe that stringent standards must be adopted to discourage any attempt by "endocratic" corporations' executives to place the sole responsibility for criminal acts on the shoulders of their subordinates.

We believe that our decision is supported by basic considerations of public policy. The President's Commission on Law Enforcement and Administration of Justice, Task Force Report—Crime and Its Impact—An Assessment (1967) provides a sound rationale for imputing criminal responsibility to the corporation for the acts of lower echelon corporate officials who have the authority to act on behalf of the corporation. The report states at p.104 that "[w]hite collar crime also does serious damage to social and economic institutions. . . . Thus, crimes such as bribery and violation of conflict of interest statutes strike deeply at responsible, impartial government." The report further points out at p.108 that:

> A pervasive problem affecting enforcement is the fact that white collar crime is often business crime and business crime is often corporate crime. Where corporate defendants are involved, the only criminal sanction available is the fine. As noted previously, fines may be inadequate as deterrents for a variety of reasons. There are also serious practical problems in imposing sanctions upon corporate employees. It is very difficult to obtain the conviction of the true policy formulators in large, complex corporations. The top executives do not ordinarily carry out the overt criminal acts—it is the lower or middle management officials who, for example, attend price-fixing meetings.

The President's Commission concluded, at p.108, that:

> where corporate misconduct is involved, the offenders—and particularly the offenders against whom evidence of guilt can be obtained—act as part of a corporate hierarchy and, ordinarily, follow a pattern of corporate behavior. Individual responsibility is therefore reduced—the offenders are often following orders from above, either explicit or implicit. Moreover, the fact that acts are performed to further the interests of the corporation, and not merely the offenders' personal interests, helps to rationalize misconduct. Thus in the *Electrical Equipment* cases, personal explanations for the acts were, for the most part, sought in the structure of corporate pressures. The defendants almost invariably testified that they came new to a job, found price-fixing an established way of life, and simply entered into it as they did into other aspects of their job.

6. The conceptual difficulties of attributing the *mens rea* of an individual agent to an abstract entity have led some commentators to argue that in determining the criminal liability of a corporation, the *mens rea* of individual agents is simply beside the point. Professor Peter French has suggested that in

14. The term "endocratic" was coined by Dean Rostow and means a "large, publicly-held corporation, whose stock is scattered in small fractions among thousands of stockholders." Note, Increasing Community Control Over Corporate Crime—A Problem in the Law of Sanctions, 71 Yale L.J. 280, 281, n.3.

forming policy, corporations manifest a truly "corporate" intent that cannot be reduced to the intent of any of its agents.

> [C]onglomerate collectivities can be justifiably held blameworthy . . . and hence differ significantly from aggregate collectivities. . . . [W]hen we say that a conglomerate collectivity is blameworthy we are saying that other courses of collectivity action were within the province of the collectivity and that had the collectivity acted in those ways the untoward event would not likely have occurred and that no exculpatory excuse is supportable as regards the collectivity. That is not to say that an individual member or even all individual members of the collectivity cannot support excuses. In fact, that is never really at issue.[15]

Professor Brent Fisse has called this concept of conglomerate intent "strategic *mens rea*," and has evaluated it as follows:

> Although strategic *mens rea* is a genuinely corporate concept of mental state, requiring the prosecution to establish a criminal corporate policy at or before the time that the *actus reus* of an offense is committed would make corporate *mens rea* extremely difficult to prove. Corporations almost never endorse criminal behavior by express policy, and boilerplate anticrime policy directives may make it very difficult to establish the existence of implied criminal policies. The difficulty of proving strategic *mens rea,* however, may be significantly reduced if the requisite criminal *mens rea* based on corporate policy need not be shown to have existed at or before the time of the *actus reus* of the offense. If the corporate defendant is given a reasonable opportunity to formulate a legal compliance policy after the *actus reus* of an offense is brought to the attention of the policy-making officials, the corporation's fault can be assessed on the basis of its present reactions rather than its previously designed formal policy directives. . . .
>
> . . . By using only the time prior to and during the commission of the *actus reus* of an offense to measure the blameworthiness of corporate behavior, previous proposals fail to recognize that reactions to socially harmful acts are a common source of public resentment toward corporations. By contrast, the concept of reactive corporate fault directly reflects our attitudes toward corporations which, having engaged in unjustifiably harmful or risky acts, fail to react in a responsible manner.
>
> Consider the well-known Kepone case, United States v. Allied Chemical Corporation, [420 F. Supp. 122 (E.D. Va. 1976)] in which Allied Chemical pled no contest to 940 counts of water pollution resulting from the escape of the pesticide Kepone into the waterways of Virginia. Because Allied was convicted under a statute that imposed strict responsibility, fault was relevant only to gravity of sentence. In the opinion of District Judge Merhige, Allied had been at fault at the time of the *actus reus:* "I disagree with the defendant's position that all of this was so innocently done, or inadvertently done. I think it was done because of what it considered to be business necessities, and money took the forefront." Yet it is not clear that the *corporation* intentionally or recklessly committed illegal acts of pollution. A few middle managers may have possessed *mens rea,* but, as we have seen, managerial *mens rea* alone does not indicate genuinely *corporate* blameworthiness.

15. French, Types of Collective Blame, 56 The Personalist 160, 166 (1975).

Suppose, however, that upon proof of the *actus reus* of the pollution offenses charged, the court had required Allied to prepare a compliance report detailing a program of preventive and restitutionary measures which the company proposed to undertake in response to the violations. Suppose further that the compliance report was unsatisfactory to the court, or bent upon scapegoating rather than reforming. In this situation, public attitudes toward Allied's conduct would focus on its compliance program in response to the prosecution rather than on what it intended at or before the time the *actus reus* was committed. Moreover, if notice were given to the company that its compliance report would be treated as a record of top-level corporate policy, public attitudes would focus on *corporate* intent, rather than on the individual states of mind of one or more middle managers.

If the reactive strategies of corporations represent corporate policy in this way, then unsatisfactory reactive strategies would display strategic *mens rea* and thus, in absence of good excuse, corporate blameworthiness. In other words, if society looks to a corporate defendant to generate a reactive prevention and cure strategy, then an unsatisfactory response would tend to indicate a noncompliant corporate policy and hence arouse attitudes of resentment and blame toward the corporation.

The concept of reactive *mens rea* reflects very sharply the organizational reality of management by exception. An axiom of orthodox management is that routine tasks should be delegated, leaving managers to use their creativity and leadership to the greatest possible corporate advantage. In the normal course of corporate business, top management assumes that compliance with the law is routine. Management typically issues policy directives from time to time, which are implemented by means of standard operating procedures. Only when an "exceptional" event occurs, as when the corporation is alleged to have committed an offense, are questions of compliance referred upwards to managers. For instance, in the Kepone case, there is reason to believe that top managers at Allied Chemical had not even heard of Kepone before the disaster became public news, but, once the problem had surfaced, a program of corrective action was initiated as a matter of high managerial priority.[16]

7. Now consider one final twist on the relationship between individual and corporate culpability. Assume that the corporation is guilty of a crime because of the purposeful criminal acts of one of its agents, acts that are attributed to the corporate entity. What about the high-level officers or directors of the corporation? Are they now *individually* liable? That is, should we now attribute the corporation's liability to them personally, on the ground that they direct the corporation's affairs?

Note that we have already addressed two slightly different versions of this problem. In *Marley* and *Koczwara,* at the beginning of this section, we examined the individual liability of a natural person-employer for the purposeful criminal acts of one of his or her employees. On the other hand, in United States v. Park, in Chapter 3 (on Liability Without Fault), we examined the

16. Fisse, Reconstructing Corporate Criminal Law Deterrence, Retribution, Fault, and Sanctions, 56 S. Cal. L. Rev. 1141, 1191-92, 1197-1200 (1983).

personal liability of the head of a business for the unintentional or nonknowing criminal acts of one of his employees, who was punished under a strict liability statute. Is this situation substantially different? Should we be concerned that a high officer or director of a corporation, who might merit individual vicarious criminal liability for encouraging or tolerating the purposeful criminal acts of his employees, could avoid individual liability by hiding behind the corporate veil, thus letting the corporation "take the rap"?

In Bourgeois v. Commonwealth, 217 Va. 268, 227 S.E.2d 714 (1976), the defendant was president of Revco Tractor-Trailer Training, Inc. Revco contracted with the Department of Vocational Rehabilitation to train disabled students, and the DVR paid Revco for the students' tuition. The Commonwealth discovered that on several occasions, Revco had illegally received duplicate payments, collecting tuition fees from both the students personally and from the DVR. Apparently, someone within the Revco corporation had chosen to defraud the Commonwealth, and the court assumed that the corporation itself could therefore be guilty of grand larceny. It held however, that Bourgeois's role as president of Revco did not make him individually guilty of grand larceny.

> The Assistant Attorney General urged in oral argument that Bourgeois as president of Revco controlled its funds, was responsible for criminal acts perpetrated by the corporation, and cannot now hide behind the corporate shield. However, the general rule is that where the crime charged involves guilty knowledge or criminal intent, it is essential to the criminal liability of an officer of a corporation that he actually and personally did the acts which constitute the offense, or that they were done under his direction or with his permission. An officer cannot avoid criminal responsibility for an illegal act on the ground that it was done in his official capacity or through the instrumentality of the corporation which he controls and dominates and which he has employed for that purpose. And where the business itself involves a violation of the law all who participate in it are liable.
>
> In Revell v. Commonwealth, 215 Va. 708, 213 S.E.2d 756 (1975), an embezzlement case, we considered the status of the accused who, one witness testified, "appeared to be the boss" of the business. In the absence of evidence that his position placed him in control of the other employees or funds of the company which received the benefit of the embezzlement, we reversed the accused's conviction.
>
> In the present case, there is evidence that Bourgeois was president of Revco, but there is no evidence that he controlled its employees or funds, or that he was the alter ego of the corporation. As president he alone signed the Revco check to reimburse DVR for the duplicate payments, but the check contained another signature line for the vice-president, permitting the inference that the vice-president also had authority to sign checks for the corporation. There is no evidence as to the extent of Bourgeois's authority, the number of other officers and employees of Revco and their respective duties, or the business procedures of the corporation, from which knowledge of any wrongdoing by other Revco officers or employees might be imputed to Bourgeois. Therefore, the evidence is insuffi-

cient to hold Bourgeois criminally responsible as a matter of law for the duplicate payments which Revco received for training the 23 DVR clients.

Thus, the courts have walked a fine line in addressing this issue. A corporate agent certainly cannot escape personal criminal liability merely on the ground that all the agent's official actions can be ascribed to a corporate role. On the other hand, at least in the case of "true" or "malum in se" crimes, the courts are loath to impose strict liability on a corporate official for the purposeful criminal acts of corporate agents. The result is that the official may, of course, suffer individual criminal liability where he or she has knowingly commanded, encouraged, or acquiesced in the purposeful criminal acts of an agent working within the official's corporate jurisdiction. This rule roughly correlates with the general principles of accomplice liability we examined in this chapter. But some commentators have suggested that the special social interest in deterring criminal conduct within large corporations and the difficulty of piercing the corporate veil to prove that an official acted purposefully or knowingly, require a compromise standard based on recklessness or even negligence. Thus, a corporate official might face individual criminal liability "whenever [he or she] knew or should have known of a substantial risk that an illegal act was occurring or would occur within [his or her] realm of authority, and failed to take reasonable steps to prevent the offense." Developments—Corporate Crime, [92 Harv. L. Rev. 1270-1271 (1979)].

The Model Penal Code address this issue in §2.07(6):

> (6)(a) A person is legally accountable for any conduct he performs or causes to be performed in the name of the corporation or an unincorporated association or in its behalf to the same extent as if it were performed in his own name or behalf.
>
> (b) Whenever a duty to act is imposed by law upon a corporation or an unincorporated association, any agent of the corporation or association having primary responsibility for the discharge of the duty is legally accountable for a reckless omission to perform the required act to the same extent as if the duty were imposed by law directly upon himself.
>
> (c) When a person is convicted of an offense by reason of his legal accountability for the conduct of a corporation or an unincorporated association, he is subject to the sentence authorized by law when a natural person is convicted of an offense of the grade and the degree involved.

The Code Commentary explains:

> Subsection (6) is designed to overcome certain difficulties in the direct imposition of criminal sanctions on guilty corporate agents. It supplements the provisions of Section 2.06.
>
> Subsection (6)(a) makes certain that the corporate agent will not escape liability because all or part of his conduct is performed through or in the name of the corporation. The difficulties are illustrated by the case of People v. Strong.

[363 Ill. 602, 2 N.E.2d 942 (1936)]. Officers and directors were individually indicted for embezzlement because of the failure of the corporation to turn over to the state certain taxes collected by the company. The state statute provided only imprisonment as a penalty for the embezzlement. The officers, said the Illinois Supreme Court, "were not principals, because they neither received nor possessed the tax money, and they cannot be accessories, because no one can aid or abet a corporation in the commission of a crime of which the corporation is incapable. Without a principal there are no accessories." The provisions of Subsection (6)(a) avoid such substantial failures of justice. Similar provisions are included in the great majority of the revised and proposed codes.

Subsection (6)(b) deals with the case in which the offense consists of an omission by the corporation or association to perform a duty imposed on it by law. Under the antecedent law of accessorial liability, the corporate officer, even though under affirmative obligation to perform the duty on behalf of the corporation, might escape individual liability if his conduct consisted of non-action. The subsection provides for individual liability of the corporate officer having the primary responsibility for performance of the duty on behalf of the corporation. Many revisions include a provision similar to Subsection (6)(b).

Subsection (6)(c) avoids the difficulties suggested by People v. Duncan. In that case, the defendant, a corporate officer, was convicted as an accomplice of the corporation and was fined on certain counts and sentenced to imprisonment on others. The court, in setting aside the defendant's sentence, ruled that since the principal (the corporation) could not be imprisoned, such a penalty could not properly be imposed on the accessory. More than that, even if the individual accessory was fined, the statutory provisions calling for imprisonment to compel payment of the fine would be inapplicable since such sanctions could not be imposed on the corporate principal. This result seems clearly unjustifiable as a matter of policy, and in precluding such a holding the provisions of this subsection are consistent with the objectives of Section 2.06.

After reading these materials do you feel that a criminal conviction has the same meaning for a corporation as for an individual? Given the rules about corporate liability, should the two kinds of liability bear the same stigma? Should the rules be changed so that they do? How?

11

CONSPIRACY

A. THE NATURE OF CONSPIRACY

STATE v. BURLESON

Appellate Court of Illinois
50 Ill. App. 3d 629, 365 N.E.2d 1162 (1977)

REARDON, Justice.

The defendant, Charles Edward Burleson, was charged in a two count information filed December 8, 1975, with conspiracy to commit armed robbery and attempted armed robbery. The two offenses were alleged to have occurred on September 16, 1975. On April 21, 1976, a third count was added to the information charging the defendant with participating in a second conspiracy to commit armed robbery on September 13, 1975. . . .

The facts pertinent to this appeal are reflected in the trial testimony of defendant's alleged co-conspirator, Bruce Brown. Brown testified that he and the defendant agreed to rob the Middletown State Bank. Pursuant to that agreement, the two "cased" the bank on September 11, 1975. They decided to use two cars in the robbery. One would be left on a rural road near Middletown with a change of clothing for each conspirator. From that location, the two would proceed to the bank wearing nylon stockings and stocking caps over their heads. The defendant agreed to secure a shotgun for use in the robbery and Brown agreed to secure the disguises and a container for the money they expected to remove from the bank. They also decided to commit the crime on Saturday, September 13, 1975.

On September 13, 1975, the conspirators initiated their plan, but decided not to rob the bank on that day because they noticed too many people in town and around the bank. Instead, they made a practice run of their approach to and escape from the bank after agreeing that they would try again on Tuesday, September 16, 1975.

On September 16, 1975, the defendant and Brown again parked their cars along a rural road, changed clothing and drove into the town of Middletown in a single car with a white suitcase, shotgun and disguises consisting of the nylon stockings and stocking caps. When they arrived in town, they drove to the Middletown State Bank, exited from the car and approached the bank's front door. Brown carried the suitcase and the defendant carried the shotgun. As the duo neared the front door, however, a man bolted the door from the inside. Thereafter, the defendant and Brown scrambled back into the car and returned to their second car which was still parked along the rural road where they had commenced their escapade. Within minutes, Brown was arrested after being chased by the police. The defendant was arrested a few days later.

On appeal, the defendant raises a single issue for our review: whether his conviction for the September 13, 1975, conspiracy to commit armed robbery should be vacated because the alleged conspiracy arose from the same course of conduct that formed the basis for his attempted armed robbery convictions.

Section 8-2(a) of the Criminal Code of 1961 provides in pertinent part:

> A person commits conspiracy when, with intent that an offense be committed, he *agrees* with another to the commission of that offense. No person may be convicted of conspiracy to commit an offense unless an *act in furtherance* of such agreement is alleged and proved to have been committed by him or by a co-conspirator. (Emphasis added.) (Ill. Rev. Stat. 1973, ch. 38, par. 8-2(a).)

Section 8-4(a) of the Code provides:

> A person commits an attempt when, with intent to commit a specific offense, he does any act which constitutes a substantial step toward the commission of that offense. (Ill. Rev. Stat. 1973, ch. 38, par. 8-4(a).)

Both of the quoted sections are contained in that part of the Code which concerns inchoate or anticipatory offenses. Another of those sections, section 8-5 of the Code, provides that "[n]o person shall be convicted of both the inchoate and the principal offense." Ill. Rev. Stat. 1973, ch. 38, par. 8-5. . . .

In Illinois, in order for a defendant to be convicted for the offense of conspiracy, the State must establish three elements beyond a reasonable doubt: (1) that the defendant intended to commit an offense; (2) that the defendant and another person entered into an agreement to commit the offense; and (3) that one of the co-conspirators committed an act in furtherance of the agreement. In order for a defendant to be convicted for the offense of attempt, the State must only establish two elements beyond a reasonable doubt: (1) that the defendant intended to commit an offense; and (2) that the defendant took a "substantial step" toward committing that offense. (Ill. Rev. Stat. 1973, ch. 38, par. 8-4(a).) In comparing these two sections of our Criminal Code, we note that the attempt provision requires "a substantial step" toward the commission of the offense. In each situation, as in situations involving other inchoate offenses, the law makes possible some preventive action by the police and courts before a defendant has come dangerously close to committing the intended crime. . . .

Here, the defendant and Brown did not enter the bank building on September 16, 1975, although they were in possession of a shotgun, suitcase and disguises which were in place when they approached the bank building. We find these acts sufficient to constitute a "substantial step" toward the commission of an armed robbery in the bank.

As previously noted, section 8-5 of the Code prohibits a defendant's conviction for an inchoate offense and the principal offense. Here, however, the defendant has been convicted for two inchoate offenses and not for a principal offense. Recently, our Supreme Court stated that when more than one offense arises from a single series of closely related acts and when the offenses, by definition, are not lesser included offenses, convictions having concurrent sentences may be entered. Lesser included offenses are defined in section 2-9 of the Code as an offense which:

> (a) Is established by proof of the *same or less than all of the facts* or a less culpable mental state (or both), than that which is required to establish the commission of the offense charged, or (b) Consists of an attempt to commit the offense charged or an offense included therein. (Emphasis added.) Ill. Rev. Stat. 1973, ch. 38, par. 2-9.

Here, as already mentioned, the inchoate offenses of attempt and conspiracy require some act for criminal liability to attach to the actor. For an attempt to be committed, "a substantial step" in furtherance of the criminal objective must occur. For a conspiracy to exist, some act amounting to at least a lesser step is required. In the instant case, however, the State has not relied on the same conduct of the defendant to establish the conspiracy to rob the bank on September 13, 1975, and the attempt to rob which was committed on September 16, 1975. We do not view the conspirators' actions in terms of a single course of conduct. Rather, the conspirators' actions originate in separate agreements or impulses to rob the bank on separate dates. With their attempt to rob the bank on September 13, 1975, the conspirator[s'] first agreement to rob the bank came to an end. The attempt of September 16, 1975, was not the result of the original agreement, but of a fresh agreement which was entered into after the attempt of September 13, 1975. The aforementioned offenses arise from separate courses of conduct, we, accordingly, affirm the defendant's convictions for the conspiracy of September 13, 1975, and for the attempted armed robbery of September 16, 1975. In addition, we reverse defendant's conviction for the conspiracy of September 16, 1975, because it is a lesser included offense of attempt.

Affirmed in part. Reversed in part.

GREEN, P. J., and MILLS, J., concur.

Notes and Questions

1. The court in *Burleson* affirms the defendant's convictions for conspiracy on September 13 and attempt on September 16. Could he also have been convicted for attempt on September 13? Could he have been convicted for conspiracy on September 11, even if he could not have been convicted for attempt on that date?

Conspiracy, as we see, is an inchoate, or preparatory, crime. Though it resembles attempt and solicitation in this respect, conspiracy differs from the other preparatory crimes in important ways. It requires more than attempt, because it requires at least two participants. Yet, it requires less than attempt, because it pushes the line between preparation and criminal liability farther back than attempt law does.

Although conspiracy law aims at conduct further removed from the substantive crime than does attempt, some of the same concerns actuating the dichotomy between preparation and attempt surface again in conspiracy law. Particularly, it is interesting to compare the concept of the "overt act" in conspiracy to the various formulations of the act requirement in attempt law. According to one commentator:[1]

> At common law the crime of conspiracy was indictable upon the formation of the agreement. In enacting conspiracy statutes, several jurisdictions, including the federal government, have required that an overt act in furtherance of the conspiracy be proved. Such a provision has seldom materially increased the difficulty of securing convictions for conspiracy. A noncriminal[2] and relatively minor[3] act is held to satisfy the requirement if it is in furtherance of the conspiracy. An act committed by any one of the conspirators is sufficient both as to all present members of the conspiracy and as to persons subsequently joining the agreement. The act, however, cannot be part of the formation of the agreement, nor can it take place after the termination of the conspiracy. But it may be the step which accomplishes the conspiracy's objective. There need not be an affirmative act, since nonfeasance may in some circumstances satisfy the requirement.
>
> The inclusion of the overt-act requirement in the federal general conspiracy statute was unaccompanied by any indication of the function it was to serve. It may have represented merely a legislative interpretation of what was necessary to prove a conspiracy at common law. The secrecy normally surrounding formu-

1. Developments—Conspiracy, 75 Harvard L. Rev. 945-948 (1959).

2. The contention that the act must be indictable as an attempt has generally been rejected. . . .

3. E.g., Yates v. United States, 354 U.S. 298, 333-334 (1957) (attendance at lawful meeting); Smith v. United States, 92 F.2d 460 (9th Cir. 1937) (telephone call); Kaplan v. United States, 7 F.2d 594 (2d Cir.), cert. denied, 269 U.S. 582 (1925) (interview between two persons); see Pollack, Common Law Conspiracy, 35 Geo. L.J. 328, 338 (1947): "The courts somehow discover an overt act in the slightest action on the part of the conspirators."

lation of criminal plans makes proof of the agreement by direct evidence improbable and usually forces the prosecution to rely upon conduct of the conspirators from which an inference of an agreement can be drawn. Thus, since most conspiracy prosecutions involved proof of an overt act, there emerged a practice of alleging such acts in the indictment. The courts, however, have pragmatically used other rationales of the requirement to justify results which seemed desirable.

In United States v. Donau [25 Fed. Cas. 890 (No. 14983 C.C.S.D.N.Y. 1873)], the defendant sought to quash an indictment on the ground that the overt acts alleged were not reasonably calculated to effect the specific object of the conspiracy. In overruling the motion, the court held that the statutory offense consisted of the agreement alone, the overt act merely affording a *locus poenitentiae* so that before the commission of the act a conspirator might withdraw from the scheme without incurring guilt. The same view was expressed in a widely quoted dictum by the Supreme Court in United States v. Britton [108 U.S. 199, 204 (1883)]. It seems that such a rationale is not very meaningful when the requirement can be satisfied as to all of the conspirators, both present and future, by an overt act on the part of one of them and when even that act may be trivial. . . .

The overt-act requirement may also be interpreted as a legislative determination that a mere agreement does not usually represent a sufficient threat of the specific offense or sufficient evidence of a general danger to warrant criminal prosecution. This rationale seems particularly apparent in the few instances in which legislatures have, for conspiracies to commit certain serious crimes, made specific exceptions to a general rule which requires allegation and proof of an overt act. Should it be thought desirable to limit the liability of conspirators in effect based on mere agreement, the requirement of a more significant act toward the achievement of the ends of the conspiracy would be one means of doing so.

2. Although the court in *Burleson* treats conspiracy as a lesser included offense within attempt, some jurisdictions disagree, primarily because the *Burleson* rule ignores the reasons for treating conspiracy as an aggravating factor (a matter we shall explore later).

One commentator[4] describes the state of the law, as of 1975, on this issue as follows:

> [A] problem emerges when conspirators attempt to commit the crime which is their object, but fail. May they then be convicted of both conspiracy and attempt? Thirteen states and the MPC, answer in the negative. The Hawaii Code Comments offer a concise explanation for this prohibition of multiple inchoate convictions.
>
> > [T]he danger which is represented by inchoate crimes lies in the possibility that the substantive [crime] will be carried to fruition because of [the criminal] disposition of the defendant. Hence any number of stages preparatory to the commission of a

4. Note, Conspiracy: Statutory Reform Since the Model Penal Code, 75 Colum. L. Rev. 1122, 1182-1183.

> given offense, if taken together, still constitute a single danger: that the crime contemplated will be committed. Such a rationale precludes cumulating convictions of attempt . . . and a conspiracy to commit the same offense.
>
> Five additional states occupy the somewhat incongruous position of specifically precluding conviction of both conspiracy and a substantive offense, but remaining silent on multiple inchoate convictions. Almost undoubtedly, convictions of both conspiracy and attempt will not be sanctioned in these jurisdictions either. Where such dual judgments *are* rendered, criminal codes which reject consecutive sentences when several offenses arise out of a single criminal episode, or when one offense is only a conspiracy to commit the other, would require concurrent terms. Many state statutes have not considered the question of multiple inchoate convictions, but the reasoning displayed in the Hawaii Comment above may very well be persuasive, even where conviction of both conspiracy and substantive crime is acceptable.

Can one argue that a conspiracy should not be regarded as a lesser included offense within attempt, on the ground that group pressures among the conspirators increase the likelihood that they will not back down from the ultimate crime. Thus, the presence of more than one actor makes the attempt less likely to be abandoned and the division of labor among the conspirators makes it more likely that the attempt will succeed.

3. In the area of attempt we grappled with the problem of impossibility. As one might expect, we come upon similar problems in the law of conspiracy when the conspirators agree to perform an act that proves impossible. Consider the case of State v. Moretti, 235 A.2d 226 (1967). There, Sylvia Swidler, a special investigator employed in the Essex County Prosecutor's office, arranged, through defendants Schmidt and Moretti, to have an abortion to terminate an unwanted pregnancy. The abortion was to have been performed by defendant Gianettino, an inspector for the New Jersey State Board of Barber Examiners. Gianettino, by appointment, arrived at Mrs. Swidler's home with a bag of instruments to perform the abortion. As soon as Mrs. Swidler paid him $600 in marked money, detectives who were hidden in and about the house arrested him.

The State conceded, and Mrs. Swidler testified, that she was not actually pregnant at the time. The defendants argued that there could not be a criminal conspiracy where attainment of the unlawful object was inherently impossible. Since an essential element of the crime of abortion is the pregnancy of the woman, the defendants argued that it was legally impossible for them to have conspired to commit the act with which they had been charged.

The court stated that the fact that Swidler was not pregnant was not a defense to the conspiracy charge because, "[s]he could have been pregnant, as defendants manifestly thought she was, so that attainment of the unlawful object was not inherently impossible." In other words, factual impossibility does not preclude a conspiracy charge.

The dissent argued that because the defendants could not be convicted of the substantive crime, the case presented an issue of legal, not factual, impossibility.

Should conspiring to commit a crime that proves "impossible," in one of the several senses of that term, be treated differently from an individual "attempt" to do the impossible? Some courts would punish the conspiracy where they would *not* punish the attempt, and some would do the opposite.

4. In addition to the inchoate aspect of conspiracy law, conspiracy seems also to be an aggravating factor in a substantive crime. The criminal law assumes that a group planning to commit a crime poses a special danger to the public welfare. The support and cooperation of co-conspirators supposedly increase the probability of criminal conduct on the part of each participant, increase the social damage the members can do, and make it harder for the police to apprehend them. Consider the next case.

CALLANAN v. UNITED STATES

United States Supreme Court
364 U.S. 587 (1961)

Mr. Justice FRANKFURTER delivered the opinion of the Court.

Petitioner was convicted by a jury in the United States District Court for the Eastern District of Missouri on two counts. Count I charged a conspiracy to obstruct commerce by extorting money, and Count II charged the substantive offense of obstructing commerce by extortion, both crimes made punishable by the Hobbs Anti-Racketeering Act, 18 U.S.C. Sec. 1951.[5] Petitioner was sentenced to consecutive terms of twelve years on each count.

Petitioner thereafter sought a correction of his sentence, invoking Rule 35 of the Federal Rules of Criminal Procedure as well as 28 U.S.C. Sec. 2255. He claimed that the maximum penalty for obstructing interstate commerce under the Act by any means is twenty years and that Congress did not intend to subject individuals to two penalties. The District Court denied relief, holding that the Hobbs Act gave no indication of a departure from the usual rule that a conspiracy and the substantive crime which was its object may be cumulatively punished. The Court of Appeals for the Eighth Circuit affirmed this judgment. Deeming the question raised by petitioner of sufficient importance, we brought the case here.

Under the early common law, a conspiracy—which constituted a misdemeanor—was said to merge with the completed felony which was its object. This rule, however, was based upon significant procedural distinctions be-

5. Section 1951(a) is as follows:

Whoever in any way or degree obstructs, delays, or affects commerce or the movement of any article or commodity in commerce, by robbery or extortion or attempts or conspires so to do, or commits or threatens physical violence to any person or property in furtherance of a plan or purpose to do anything in violation of this section shall be fined not more than $10,000 or imprisoned not more than twenty years, or both.

tween misdemeanors and felonies. The defendant in a misdemeanor trial was entitled to counsel and a copy of the indictment; these advantages were unavailable on trial for a felony. Therefore no conviction was permitted of a constituent misdemeanor upon an indictment for the felony. When the substantive crime was also a misdemeanor, or when the conspiracy was defined by statute as a felony, merger did not obtain. As these common-law procedural niceties disappeared, the merger concept [assumed] less significance, and today it has been abandoned.

Petitioner does not draw on this archaic law of merger. He argues that Congress by combining the conspiracy and the substantive offense in one provision, Sec. 1951, manifested an intent not to punish commission of two offenses cumulatively. Unlike the merger doctrine, petitioner's position does not question that the Government could charge a conspiracy even when the substantive crime that was its object had been completed. His concern is with the punitive consequences of the choice thus open to the Government; it can indict for both or either offense, but, petitioner contends, it can punish only for one.

The distinctiveness between a substantive offense and a conspiracy to commit is a postulate of our law. "It has been long and consistently recognized by the Court that the commission of the substantive offense and a conspiracy to commit it are separate and distinct offenses." Pinkerton v. United States, 328 U.S. 640, 643. Over the years, this distinction has been applied in various situations. For example, in Clune v. United States, 159 U.S. 590, the Court upheld a two-year sentence for conspiracy over the objection that the crime which was the object of the unlawful agreement could only be punished by a $100 fine. The same result was reached when, as in the present case, both offenses were described within the same statute. In Carter v. McClaughry, 183 U.S. 365, cumulative sentences for conspiracy to defraud and fraud were upheld. "Cumulative sentences," the Court pronounced, "are not cumulative punishments, and a single sentence for several offences, in excess of that prescribed for one offence, may be authorized by statute." 183 U.S., at 394.

This settled principle derives from the reason of things in dealing with socially reprehensible conduct: collective criminal agreement—partnership in crime—presents a greater potential threat to the public than individual delicts. Concerted action both increases the likelihood that the criminal object will be successfully attained and decreases the probability that the individuals involved will depart from their path of criminality. Group association for criminal purposes often, if not normally, makes possible the attainment of ends more complex than those which one criminal could accomplish. Nor is the danger of a conspiratorial group limited to the particular end toward which it has embarked. Combination in crime makes more likely the commission of crimes unrelated to the original purpose for which the group was formed. In sum, the danger which a conspiracy generates is not confined to the substantive offense which is the immediate aim of the enterprise.

Affirmed.

Notes and Questions

1. Does the Court in *Callanan* give good reasons for why the conspiracy does not merge into the substantive crime as would attempt? What are the advantages of having conspiracy as a separate crime, even when the substantive offense has been committed?

2. As *Callanan* states, a defendant can suffer consecutive sentences for the substantive crime and the conspiracy. A defendant therefore can receive a sentence in excess of the allowable maximum sentence for the substantive crime. Is this result fair? Does the maximum sentence for the substantive crime provide enough deterrence? Does an extra sentence for conspiracy add more deterrence? If not, can the conspiracy sentence be justified?

3. Punishment schemes in conspiracy statutes vary widely among jurisdictions. Before the influence of the Model Penal Code spread, the variation was even greater. Under some statutes, conspiracy was a misdemeanor. See, e.g., Ark. Stat. Ann. §41-1201 (1947). Others provided a permissible maximum sentence, regardless of the conspiratorial objective. See, e.g., Ariz. Rev. Stat. §13-331 (1956). In still others, the maximum sentence depended on whether the objective of the conspiracy amounted to a misdemeanor or a felony. See, e.g., 18 U.S.C. §371 (1976). (Section 371 is still in effect today). Because these conspiracy statutes usually did not provide for a maximum sentence related to the maximum penalty permitted for the substantive crime objective, it often occurred that the penalty for the conspiracy was greater than the permissible penalty for the crime that was its object. See, e.g., Clune v. United States, 159 U.S. 590 (1895) (conspiracy sentence of two years where maximum penalty for crime which was the object of the conspiracy was $100 fine). This was especially true for less serious crimes.

The Model Penal Code authors criticized these statutes, stating, "there is likely to be little difference in the gravity [of the actors' offense if the plan is consummated or fails]." Section 5.05 of the Code fixes the maximum sentence for the conspiracy equal to the maximum penalty for the criminal objective. The Code influenced a number of states to revise their conspiracy statutes to provide for a maximum sentence that is either equivalent to the maximum sentence for the object of the conspiracy or is a fraction of the maximum sentence. See, e.g., Ariz. Rev. St. Ann. §13-1003 (1978); Mo. Ann. Stat. §564.016 (Vernon 1979). Is this change an improvement?

4. Even if the presence of a conspiracy is an aggravating factor in the commission of a crime, does it follow that the defendant should suffer an additional consecutive sentence, beyond the sentence for the completed crime? It is true that conspiracy aggravates the completed crime, allowing the defendants to enjoy the efficiencies of the division of labor and making it harder for the police to apprehend them. But the legislature usually sets a broad statutory sentencing range, allowing a sentencing judge to account for such aggravating factors as the extreme brutality of the crime or the defendant's lengthy

criminal record. Is there any reason why conspiracy should receive separate treatment as an aggravating factor?

Section 1.07 of the Model Penal Code provides:

> (1) *Prosecution for Multiple Offenses* . . . when the same conduct of a defendant may establish the commission of more than one offense, the defendant may be prosecuted for each offense. He may not, however, be convicted of more than one offense if:
>
> (b) one offense consists only of a conspiracy or other form of preparation to commit the other. . . .

5. According to Burke & Kadish, Conspiracy, 1 Encyclopedia of Crime and Justice 232 (1983):

> Ironically, conspiracy was initially directed neither at preparatory activity nor at group crime in general. Rather, it was a narrowly circumscribed statutory remedy designed to combat abuses against the administration of justice. According to Edward Coke, it consisted of "a consultation and agreement between two or more to appeal or indict an innocent man falsely and maliciously of felony, whom accordingly they cause to be indicted and appealed; and afterward the party is lawfully acquitted." A writ of conspiracy would lie only for this particular offense, and only when the offense (including acquittal of the falsely indicted party) had actually taken place. However, in 1611 the Court of Star Chamber extended the law by upholding a conspiracy conviction even though the falsely accused party was not indicted (Poulterers' Case, 77 Eng. Rep. 813 (K.B. 1611) (Coke)). The court reasoned that the confederating together, and not the false indictment, was the gist of the offense. The ramifications of this decision were twofold. First, if it was not necessary that the intended injury occur, then conspiracy punished the attempted crime. Second, if the agreement and not the false indictment was the target of conspiracy law, then conspiracy was loosed from its mooring: subsequent decisions logically could and in fact did hold that agreement to commit any unlawful act was criminal conspiracy.

6. One of the most remarkable aspects of conspiracy at common law was the rule that the object of the conspiracy need not be a crime itself, or even an unlawful act.

In Commonwealth v. Donoghue, 250 Ky. 343, 63 S.W.2d 3 (1933), the court upheld an indictment charging conspiracy to violate the usury laws, even though Kentucky's usury law was noncriminal and provided as its sole sanction that the lender remit the excessive interest. According to the court,

> The comprehensiveness and indefiniteness of the offense of conspiracy has made an exact definition a very difficult one, as has been often stated. But the broad definition or description everywhere accepted is that conspiracy is a combination between two or more persons to do or accomplish a criminal or unlaw-

ful act, or to do a lawful act by criminal or unlawful means. In the elaborate treatment of the subject in Aetna Insurance Company v. Commonwealth, [106 Ky. 864, 51 S.W.624], the following was taken from the American & English Encyclopedia of Law and approved:

> A criminal conspiracy is (1) a corrupt combination (2) of two or more persons, (3) by concerted action to commit (4) a criminal or unlawful act; (a) or an act not in itself criminal or unlawful, by criminal or unlawful means; (b) or an act which would tend to prejudice the public in general, to subvert justice, disturb the peace, injure public trade, affect public health, or violate public policy; (5) or any act, however innocent, by means neither criminal nor unlawful, where the tendency of the object sought would be to wrongfully coerce or oppress either the public or an individual. . . . It is the corrupt agreeing together of two or more persons to do, by concerted action, something unlawful, either as a means or an end, that constitutes a criminal conspiracy. The unlawful thing must either be such as would be indictable if performed by one alone, or of a nature particularly adapted to injure the public or some individual by reason of the combination. It is not necessary, in order to constitute a conspiracy, that the acts agreed to be done should be acts which, if done, would be criminal. It is enough that they are wrongful; that is, amount to a civil wrong. . . .
>
> Every conspiracy to do an unlawful act, or to do a lawful act for an illegal, fraudulent, malicious, or corrupt purpose, or for a purpose which has a tendency to prejudice the public in general, is an indictable offense, regardless of the means whereby it is to be accomplished. . . .

According to the overwhelming weight of authority the objects of the conspiracy need not be an offense against the criminal law for which an individual could be indicted or convicted, but it is sufficient if the purpose be unlawful. That term "unlawful" in this connection has been expanded beyond its original limits of being only some act punishable as a crime. It is now understood and regarded as a covering act not embraced in the crime of conspiracy as it originally existed. It cannot be said, however—and care must ever be exercised in the application, as all courts recognize—that the term "unlawful" includes every act which violates legal rights of another or such as may create a right of action. The sound attitude to be taken in the premises seems to be as thus well stated in 5 R.C.L. 1069:

> The proper rule undoubtedly is that all such acts as have the necessary tendency to prejudice the public or to injure or oppress individuals by unjustly subjecting them to the power of the conspirators are sufficiently tainted with the quality of the unlawfulness to satisfy the requirements as to conspiracy. It is said that the influence of the act or purpose upon society determines whether a combination to accomplish it is a criminal conspiracy. Purposes or acts which are unlawful, as violative of the rights of individuals, and for which the law will afford a civil remedy to the injured party, and will at the same time by the same process punish the offender for the wrong and outrage done to society by giving exemplary damages beyond the damages actually proved, have in numerous instances been held to be of the quality needed to convert the combination for accomplishing them into a conspiracy.

A more specific distinction is noted by Wharton in . . . his work on Criminal Law. There is a series of acts which have the essence but not the form of crime (e.g., immoral acts, unindictable cheats), which, wanting the necessary objective constituents, escape judicial cognizance as being intrinsically criminal, but which are held to be invested by conspiracy with a garb that exposes them to the penalties of the law. Without the combination of men attempting to accomplish the objects, they had only the essence of crime, but, by means of the conspiracy, an unfair and mischievous advantage of the aggressors is recognized, and the acts are presented in such definiteness that they can be taken hold of and punished. Of this character is a conspiracy to use violence, as a riot, which derives its indictability from the plurality of persons concerned and to conspiracy to injuriously affect the body politic. Another series of acts which become cognizable by reason of the plurality of men or union of forces are those which prejudice the public or the government generally, such as unduly elevating or depressing wages, the price of the necessities of life, or impoverishing a class of individuals. The gist of conspiracies of this class is the unlawfulness of the means used. . . .

It has been said that one of the main objects of the law governing criminal conspiracies is to protect the community at large, and the protection of individuals is subordinate to that end. In section 23 of Brill's Cycl. of Criminal Law, it is written: "It may be laid down as a general rule of the common law that any act or any omission of a legal duty that injures or tended to injure the community at large to such an extent that public policy requires the state to interfere and punish the wrongdoer is a crime and renders the wrongdoer liable to indictment. And this is true although no exact precedent for punishing the particular act in question can be found."

What are the objections to such a rule? One commentator[6] discusses the state of the law on this topic:

A major failing of conventional, i.e., pre-reform, conspiracy statutes involves their vague and overbroad specification of the objectives of a criminal agreement. A typical formulation makes it a crime to agree "to commit any act injurious to the public health, to public morals, or to pervert or obstruct justice, or the due administration of the laws." Though a number of these unsatisfactory[7] statutes remain in force today, the legislative trend is clearly in the direction of major reform suggested by the MPC. Stated simply, the ALI drafters refused to approve the imposition of criminal sanctions on agreements directed toward the

6. Note, Conspiracy: Statutory Reform Since the Model Penal Code, 75 Colum. L. Rev. 1122, 1129-1132.

7. The statutes are unsatisfactory for at least three reasons:

(a) They are too imprecise to fulfill one function which any criminal statute must perform, namely, communication to the citizenry of the bounds of proscribed behavior.

(b) They make criminal a broad range of behavior, not otherwise subject to penal sanctions, for the sole reason that concerted action was involved in such conduct. (This is not to say that the element of combination should never be sufficient to convert behavior, acceptable when undertaken by a single individual, to a criminal offense when performed by a group. The situations where such treatment is proper are limited in number, however, and should be dealt with on an individualized basis. See, e.g., the Sherman Antitrust Act's prohibition of "[e]very contract, combination . . . or conspiracy, in restraint of trade or commerce among the several States. . . ." 15 U.S.C. §1 (1970). Such specialized breeds of illegal conspiracy are outside the scope of this Note.)

(c) By reason of vagueness, they may run afoul of constitutional due process guarantees.

performance of conduct which, if achieved, would not itself constitute a penal violation. With only one exception, each new statute, adopted or proposed, has reflected this conclusion by making criminal only those conspiracies whose objective is the commission of a crime (or, in some states, an offense) as defined elsewhere in the jurisdiction's penal code.

A number of states have gone even further. For an agreement to be criminal in Oregon, either a felony or a class A misdemeanor must be included among its objectives. The laws of New Mexico, Texas, and Virginia do not prohibit conspiracies to commit any sort of misdemeanor; they subject agreements to criminal sanctions only where the goal sought constitutes a felony. Ohio has chosen the most drastic approach of all, making criminal only conspiracies designed to achieve one or more of certain enumerated criminal ends, including murder, kidnapping, compelling or promoting prostitution, arson, robbery, burglary, and felonious use of a vehicle. Such limitation of the range of possible conspiratorial objectives to a set of offenses narrower than the set of all crimes probably reflects a degree of legislative uneasiness with the basic notion of conspiracy as an independent crime. To the extent that certain crimes are rejected as potential bases for making agreements to commit them criminal, a judgment has been made that the societal benefits, measured in terms of prevention of substantive offenses and protection against group criminal endeavor, to be derived from early law enforcement action (and the other procedural advantages offered by conspiracy) are insufficient to counterbalance the likelihood of invasion of individual liberties inherent in a more far-reaching conspiracy statute. Of course, such considerations go to the very heart of the justifications for denominating conspiracy criminal. Widespread acceptance of the recently enacted Ohio statutory pattern would spell the end of conspiracy as a general inchoate crime.

On the other hand, Massachusetts, even in its proposed new provision, clings stubbornly to a definition of conspiracy which includes among the possible objectives of a criminal agreement "conduct . . . which . . . the defendant knows to be substantially and clearly unlawful [but not necessarily criminal], and likely to cause such significant harm to an individual or to the general public as to be seriously contrary to the public interest." The contours of this additional set of conspiratorial goals are derived from the 1966 case of Commonwealth v. Bessette [351 Mass. 148, 217 N.E.2d 893]. That controversy concerned an alleged unauthorized exchange, between private companies, of publicly awarded contracts, in violation of the "Standard Specifications" of the Massachusetts Department of Public Works. Spurning the opportunity to find, as a common law development, that a criminal object is a prerequisite of conspiracy, the Supreme Judicial Court announced two criteria for determining when agreement is criminal, though the acts planned would constitute no offense if performed by a single individual. Assuming a noncriminal objective, said the Court, conspiracy liability may attach only in "a narrow range of situations, (a) where there is a strong probability . . . that the execution of the plan by group actions will cause such significant harm to an individual or to the general public, as to be seriously contrary to the public interest, and (b) where the unlawfulness of objective or contemplated means is substantial and clear." Applying these tests, the Court found no basis for a conspiracy indictment on the facts alleged. The unanimous opinion contained a recommendation for more precise legislative delineation of the possible noncriminal objectives of conspiracy.

B. THE AGREEMENT

GRIFFIN v. STATE
Supreme Court of Arkansas
455 S.W.2d 882 (1970)

FOGLEMAN, Justice.

. . . Evidence upon behalf of the State was as follows:

Appellant's automobile overturned in a ditch. The police were called. Officers Harold Vines and David Ederington arrived at the scene, and saw a crowd of people gathered there. The officers got out of the police car and Vines asked if anyone was hurt. Upon receiving a negative response from an unidentified person, Vines then asked who was driving the vehicle. Appellant, who was standing beside his vehicle, stepped forward, said "I was, I'm not scared, I've been in the war. I wasn't killed over there. I'm not going to be killed here. Take me G. . .d. . .you, if you can," and started toward Vines with his fists. Vines attempted to halt Griffin by use of chemical mace, to no avail. Griffin started hitting the officer, who then attempted to defend himself by striking appellant twice with a "slapper." A group . . . then "swarmed" him. Vines observed that some of the crowd had Ederington down in the street. Griffin was immediately in front of Vines, swinging at and striking him, while the others came up behind the officer and to his side. They knocked Vines down in the ditch, with all of the participants on top of him. Griffin was then on top of Vines, and the others at his side. Griffin was beating the officer with his fists and kicking him and "hollering" all the while. At the same time, the other participants were kicking the policeman about his arms and legs, and striking him about his face, nose, and side. They were also "hollering." Vines, feeling that he and his companion were about to be killed, drew his pistol and fired at appellant, who was still kicking and beating the officer. Griffin was struck about his chest and backed away, as did the others. Vines said, however, that they were all still "hollering" at the police officers, cursing them and saying "that they were going to get us."

As Ederington went to assist Vines, after having heard Griffin's statement to the officer when that officer and Griffin started "scuffling," he was "jumped" by two or three persons from the crowd, and knocked to the street. After he had "scuffed around" with them for three or four seconds he heard the report of a gun and saw everyone start backing away. From his position on the ground, he then saw Vines leaning against a fence over in the ditch with his nose bleeding. Ederington saw Griffin standing about five feet from Vines. He heard Vines "holler" at the people standing around that if they didn't want Griffin shot again they had better come get him. At that time Griffin was still trying to advance toward officer Vines. Appellant's father then came and tried to hold him back. . . .

Appellant seems to take the position that there must be direct evidence of a conspiracy, common design or purpose, and of the intent of the conspirators or joint actors to engage therein. In this he is mistaken. We have long recognized in Arkansas that it is not necessary that an unlawful combination, conspiracy or concert of action to commit an unlawful act be shown by direct evidence, and that it may be proved by circumstances. . . . It may be inferred, even though no actual meeting among the parties is proved, if it be shown that two or more persons pursued by their acts the same unlawful object, each doing a part, so that the acts, though apparently independent, were in fact connected. . . . Where the testimony shows a concert of action, between the persons alleged to have jointly committed a crime, or the person charged and another, it has been held sufficient to establish the necessary common object and intent. . . .

In Dickerson v. State, 105 Ark. 72, 150 S.W. 119, we approved a jury instruction that if the jury found that three persons, charged with an assault, acted with a common and unlawful purpose, and that during the progress of the assault they were all present and participating, and aided and abetted each other, all persons so participating would be guilty of the same offense and each responsible for the other's acts. The basis of objection to the instruction was that there was no evidence of any conspiracy formed between the three. We held that the facts and circumstances connected with the assault and the presence and participation of those charged was sufficient to show an unlawful combination among the parties to make the assault, and the instruction, a correct statement of law.

We find the case of Childs v. State, 98 Ark. 430, 135 S.W. 285, peculiarly applicable here. Dave Childs was convicted of the murder of one Franklin Williams. The crime was committed at a public speaking. There was bad blood between Childs and Williams because Williams's wife, who was Childs's sister, was seeking a divorce and custody of their children, alleging that Williams had cruelly beaten her. There were brief exchanges of words between the two. During the last such exchange Scott Childs, Dave's brother, began cursing Williams, who first threatened trouble, then withdrew, when Dave Childs commenced firing a pistol at Williams, hitting him four times. There was testimony that Scott Childs had a knife in his hands and that a justice of the peace had restrained Williams from advancing on Scott before the attempted withdrawal. It was shown that Scott grabbed the breast yoke of a wagon and struck Williams over the head with it immediately after Dave quit firing. We said the evidence was sufficient to justify the conclusion that Dave and Scott were acting together in making the assault on Williams. . . .

In a murder prosecution, the mere fact that two persons separately approached a third, within a few hours for the purpose of prevailing upon him to kill a fourth person, was held sufficient evidence from which to infer a conspiracy among the three to take the life of the victim. Decker v. State, 185 Ark. 1085, 51 S.W.2d 521. The fact that each of two parties was found to possess portions of stolen goods taken in the same larceny was itself held competent to establish a conspiracy to take the goods and implicate both in the commission of the crime. Wiley v. State, 93 Ark. 586, 124 S.W. 249.

We find that the circumstances shown by the testimony presented by the state were sufficient to pose a jury question as to whether the parties involved in the assault on the officers did so with a common intent and object pursuant to a common plan. It would be extremely difficult, if not impossible, to ever produce direct evidence of a conversation or meeting among the assaulters during the period intervening between the call to the officers and the alleged challenge given them by Griffin, unless one of the participants elected to tell of it. This very problem, arising from the secrecy usually surrounding such understandings, gave rise to the rule, stated by Underhill and often cited by this court, that the existence of the necessary assent of minds may be, and usually must be, inferred from proof of facts and circumstances which, taken together, apparently indicate that they are mere parts of some complete whole. . . .

The judgment is affirmed.

Notes and Questions

1. Recall the facts of *Ochoa* and *Tally* in Chapter 10 on complicity. Did Ochoa, Avitia, or Leandro conspire with the killers of the sheriff? Did Tally conspire with the Skeltons? The issue of just what we mean by an "agreement" has caused considerable confusion. One commentator[8] attempts to explain why:

> The basic principle that a conspiracy is not established without proof of an agreement has been weakened, or at least obscured, by three factors. The first is the courts' unfortunate tendency to overemphasize a rule of evidence at the expense of a rule of law. Conspiracy is by nature a clandestine offense. It is improbable that the parties will enter into their illegal agreement openly; it is not necessary, in fact, that all the parties ever have direct contact with one another, or know one another's identity, or even communicate verbally their intention to agree. It is therefore unlikely that the prosecution will be able to prove the formation of the agreement by direct evidence, and the jury must usually infer its existence from the clear co-operation among the parties. But in their zeal to emphasize that the agreement need not be proved directly, the courts sometimes neglect to say that it need be proved at all. The second factor tending to undermine the strict rule that agreement must be proved is the existence of what are perhaps more liberal requirements in antitrust cases, which, although they may be justified in that area, are ever likely to be extended to the general law of conspiracy.
>
> The third, and perhaps the most important, factor, is another result of the verbal ambiguity which leads courts to deal with the crime of conspiracy as though it were a group rather than an act. If a "conspiracy" consists of the people who are working towards a proscribed object, and if one who aids and abets a substantive offense becomes liable as a principal thereto, then it follows that one who aids and abets these men in the attainment of their object becomes

8. Developments-Conspiracy, 75 Harv. L. Rev. 933-935 (1975).

as liable as a conspirator. It is this reasoning from a faulty premise—a premise difficult to discover since it is assumed rather than articulated—which leads an appellate court to say:

> The [lower] court clearly instructed the jury that, if defendant had knowledge that Jensen and Clark were in a conspiracy . . . and . . . assisted and aided Jensen and Clark by selling and delivering the materials to be used, thus making it possible to carry out the unlawful object of the conspiracy, defendant was a conspirator. This is a correct statement of law. . . . [Pattis v. United States 17 F.2d 562 (9th Cir. 1927).]

But to aid and abet a crime it is necessary not merely to help the criminal, but to help him in the commission of the particular offense. A person does not aid and abet a conspiracy by helping the "conspiracy" to commit a substantive offense, for the crime of conspiracy is separate from the offense which is its object. It is necessary to help the "conspiracy" in the commission of the crime of conspiracy, that is, in the commission of the act of agreement. Only then is it justifiable to dispense with the necessity of proving commission of the act of agreement by the defendant himself. In all other cases, to convict the defendant of conspiracy it is necessary to prove not only knowledge on his part that he was helping in a wrongful enterprise, but also knowledge on another's part that he intended to do so, and at least a tacit agreement to give and accept such help.

2. Just as in the area of attempt, the issue of withdrawal sometimes arises in conspiracy cases. How can one withdraw from a conspiracy? In United States v. Read, 658 F.2d 1225 (7th Cir. 1981) defendants were convicted of conspiracy to commit securities fraud and mail fraud for artificially inflating their company's year-end inventory (to show higher profits) over a five-year period. One of the defendants, Ronald Spiegel, claimed he withdrew from the conspiracy more than five years before the indictment was filed, and hence that the statute of limitations had run.

The trial court in its instruction to the jury gave the following definition of withdrawal:

> A defendant may withdraw by notifying co-conspirators that he will no longer participate in the undertaking. A defendant may also withdraw from a conspiracy by engaging in acts inconsistent with the objects of the conspiracy. These acts or statements need not be known or communicated to all other co-conspirators as long as they are communicated in a manner reasonably calculated to reach some of them. To withdraw from a conspiracy there is no requirement that a conspirator try to convince the other co-conspirators to abandon their undertaking or that he go to public authorities or others to expose the conspiracy or to prevent the carrying out of an act involved in the conspiracy. But a withdrawal defense requires that a defendant completely abandon the conspiracy and that he do so in good faith.

Spiegel claimed that: (1) he instituted a computer program that would improve, not worsen, inventory control; (2) he refused to meet defendant

Read's projections for inflating inventory; and (3) he was terminated because he was "not going to go along with more inflation." Do any of these acts alone constitute withdrawal? What about all the acts together?

The result of a conspirator's withdrawal was explained by the Court of Appeals:

> Withdrawal marks a conspirator's disavowal or abandonment of the conspiratorial agreement. By definition, after a defendant withdraws, he is no longer a member of the conspiracy and the later acts of the conspirators do not bind him. The defendant is still liable, however, for his previous agreement and for the previous acts of his co-conspirators in pursuit of the conspiracy. Withdrawal is not, therefore, a complete defense to the crime of conspiracy. Withdrawal becomes a complete defense only when coupled with the defense of the statute of limitations. A defendant's withdrawal from the conspiracy starts the running of the statute of limitations as to him. If the indictment is filed more than five years after a defendant withdraws, the statute of limitations bars prosecution for his actual participation in the conspiracy. He cannot be held liable for acts or declarations committed in the five years preceding the indictment by other conspirators because his withdrawal ended his membership in the conspiracy. It is thus only the interaction of the two defenses of withdrawal and the statute of limitations which shields the defendant from liability.
>
> Withdrawal, then, directly negates the element of membership in the conspiracy during the period of the statute of limitations. [T]he government should disprove the defense of withdrawal beyond a reasonable doubt.

Some commentators feel that withdrawal should be an affirmative defense to the crime of conspiracy. In fact, the Model Penal Code in Section 5.03(6) states that withdrawal is an affirmative defense, but only when the defendant has "thwarted the success of the conspiracy, under circumstances manifesting a complete and voluntary renunciation of his criminal purpose." Why is this requirement so strict? One reason given is that one conspirator's withdrawal usually will not prevent her co-conspirators from pursuing the objective of the conspiracy.

The withdrawal doctrine played an interesting role in the conspiracy prosecution of Harry Reems, the star of the pornographic movie, Deep Throat. The story of the prosecution is recounted in Alan Dershowitz's The Best Defense 155-174 (1982). When he acted in the film in 1972, Reems allegedly joined a conspiracy to distribute the movie throughout the United States. At that time, the legal definition of obscenity adopted by the Supreme Court gave First Amendment protection to any movie or book that had "redeeming social value." Memoirs v. Massachusetts, 383 U.S. 413 (1966). But in the 1973 decision in Miller v. California, 413 U.S. 15, the Court held that a film could be declared obscene even if it had some "redeeming social value," unless, taken as a whole, it possessed "serious literary, artistic, political, or scientific merit." The withdrawal question became important because Deep Throat was arguably protected under the earlier standard but obscene under the new *Miller* standard. Reems's only role in the conspiracy had been to act in the film in 1972. If he thereafter had withdrawn from the conspiracy, he might have been innocent of any conspiracy charge because the film he had acted in was constitutionally protected before 1973. On the other hand, his co-conspirators, who sustained the conspiracy in an effort to distribute the film, might have been guilty under the *Miller* test after 1973.

C. THE *MENS REA* OF CONSPIRACY

PEOPLE v. LAURIA

California Court of Appeal
251 Cal. App. 2d 471, 59 Cal. Rptr 628 (1967)

FLEMING, J.

In an investigation of call-girl activity the police focused their attention on three prostitutes actively plying their trade on call, each of whom was using Lauria's telephone answering service, presumably for business purposes.

On January 8, 1965, Stella Weeks, a policewoman, signed up for telephone service with Lauria's answering service. Mrs. Weeks, in the course of her conversation with Lauria's office manager, hinted broadly that she was a prostitute concerned with the secrecy of her activities and their concealment from the police. She was assured that the operation of the service was discreet and "about as safe as you can get." It was arranged that Mrs. Weeks need not leave her address with the answering service, but could pick up her calls and pay her bills in person.

On February 11, Mrs. Weeks talked to Lauria on the telephone and told him her business was modelling and she had been referred to the answering service by Terry, one of the three prostitutes under investigation. She complained that because of the operation of the service she had lost two valuable customers, referred to as tricks. Lauria defended his service and said that her friends had probably lied to her about having left calls for her. But he did not respond to Mrs. Weeks' hints that she needed customers in order to make money, other than to invite her to his house for a personal visit in order to get better acquainted. In the course of his talk he said "his business was taking messages."

On February 15, Mrs. Weeks talked on the telephone to Lauria's office manager and again complained of two lost calls, which she described as a $50 and $100 trick. On investigation the office manager could find nothing wrong, but she said she would alert the switchboard operators about slip-ups on calls.

On April 1 Lauria and the three prostitutes were arrested. Lauria complained to the police that this attention was undeserved, stating that Hollywood Call Board had 60 to 70 prostitutes on its board while his own service had only 9 or 10, that he kept separate records for known or suspected prostitutes for the convenience of himself and the police. When asked if his records were available to police who might come to the office to investigate call girls, Lauria replied that they were whenever the police had a specific name. However, his service didn't "arbitrarily tell the police about prostitutes on our board. As long as they pay their bills we tolerate them." In a subsequent voluntary appearance before the Grand Jury Lauria testified he had always cooperated with the police. But he admitted he knew some of his customers were prostitutes, and he knew Terry was a prostitute because he had personally used her services, and he knew she was paying for 500 calls a month.

Lauria and the three prostitutes were indicted for conspiracy to commit prostitution, and nine overt acts were specified. Subsequently the trial court set aside the indictment as having been brought without reasonable or probable cause. The People have appealed, claiming that a sufficient showing of an unlawful agreement to further prostitution was made.

To establish agreement, the People need show no more than a tacit, mutual understanding between coconspirators to accomplish an unlawful act. Here the People attempted to establish a conspiracy by showing that Lauria, well aware that his codefendants were prostitutes who received business calls from customers through his telephone answering service, continued to furnish them with such service. This approach attempts to equate knowledge of another's criminal activity with conspiracy to further such criminal activity, and poses the question of the criminal responsibility of a furnisher of goods or services who knows his product is being used to assist the operation of an illegal business. Under what circumstances does a supplier become a part of a conspiracy to further an illegal enterprise by furnishing goods or services which he knows are to be used by the buyer for criminal purposes?

The two leading cases on this point face in opposite directions. In United States v. Falcone, 311 U.S. 205, the sellers of large quantities of sugar, yeast, and cans were absolved from participation in a moonshining conspiracy among distillers who bought from them, while in Direct Sales Co. v. United States, 319 U.S. 703, a wholesaler of drugs was convicted of conspiracy to violate the federal narcotic laws by selling drugs in quantity to a codefendant physician who was supplying them to addicts. The distinction between these two cases appears primarily based on the proposition that distributors of such dangerous products as drugs are required to exercise greater discrimination in the conduct of their business than are distributors of innocuous substances like sugar and yeast.

In the earlier case, *Falcone,* the sellers' knowledge of the illegal use of the goods was insufficient by itself to make the sellers participants in a conspiracy with the distillers who bought from them. Such knowledge fell short of proof of a conspiracy, and evidence on the volume of sales was too vague to support a jury finding that respondents knew of the conspiracy from the size of the sales alone.

In the later case of *Direct Sales,* the conviction of a drug wholesaler for conspiracy to violate federal narcotic laws was affirmed on a showing that it had actively promoted the sale of morphine sulphate in quantity and had sold codefendant physician, who practiced in a small town in South Carolina, more than 300 times his normal requirements of the drug, even though it had been repeatedly warned of the dangers of unrestricted sales of the drug. The court contrasted the restricted goods involved in *Direct Sales* with the articles of free commerce involved in *Falcone:* "All articles of commerce may be put to illegal ends," said the court. "But all do not have inherently the same susceptibility to harmful and illegal use. . . . This difference is important for two purposes. One is for making certain that the seller knows the buyer's intended illegal use. The other is to show that by the sale he intends to further, promote and cooperate in it. This intent, when given effect by overt act, is the gist of conspiracy. While it is not identical with mere knowledge that another proposes unlawful action, it is not unrelated to such knowledge. . . . The step from knowledge to intent and agreement may be taken. There is more than suspicion, more than knowledge, acquiescence, carelessness, indifference, lack of concern. There is informed and interested cooperation, stimulation, instigation. And there is also a 'stake in the venture' which, even if it may not be essential, is not irrelevant to the question of conspiracy." (319 U.S. at 710-713.)

While *Falcone* and *Direct Sales* may not be entirely consistent with each other in their full implications, they do provide us with a framework for the criminal liability of a supplier of lawful goods or services put to unlawful use. Both the element of *knowledge* of the illegal use of the goods or services and the element of *intent* to further that use must be present in order to make the supplier a participant in a criminal conspiracy.

Proof of *knowledge* is ordinarily a question of fact and requires no extended discussion in the present case. The knowledge of the supplier was sufficiently established when Lauria admitted he knew some of his customers were prostitutes and admitted he knew that Terry, an active subscriber to his service, was a prostitute. In the face of these admissions he could scarcely claim to have relied on the normal assumption an operator of a business or service is entitled to make, that his customers are behaving themselves in the eyes of the law. Because Lauria knew in fact that some of his customers were prostitutes, it is a legitimate inference he knew they were subscribing to his answering service for illegal business purposes and were using his service to make assignations for prostitution. On this record we think the prosecution is entitled to claim positive knowledge by Lauria of the use of his service to facilitate the business of prostitution. . . .

The more perplexing issue in the case is the sufficiency of proof of *intent* to further the criminal enterprise. The element of intent may be proved either by direct evidence, or by evidence of circumstances from which an intent to further a criminal enterprise by supplying lawful goods or services may be inferred. Direct evidence of participation, such as advice from the supplier of legal goods or services to the user of those goods or services on their use for illegal purpose . . . provides the simplest case. When the intent to further and promote the criminal enterprise comes from the lips of the supplier himself, ambiguities of inference from circumstance need not trouble us. But in cases where direct proof of complicity is lacking, intent to further the conspiracy must be derived from the sale itself and its surrounding circumstances in order to establish the supplier's express or tacit agreement to join the conspiracy.

In the case at bench the prosecution argues that since Lauria knew his customers were using his service for illegal purposes but nevertheless continued to furnish it to them, he must have intended to assist them in carrying out their illegal activities. Thus through a union of knowledge and intent he became a participant in a criminal conspiracy. Essentially, the People argue that knowledge alone of the continuing use of his telephone facilities for criminal purposes provided a sufficient basis from which his intent to participate in those criminal activities could be inferred.

In examining precedents in this field we find that sometimes, but not always, the criminal intent of the supplier may be inferred from his knowledge of the unlawful use made of the product he supplies. Some consideration of characteristic patterns may be helpful. . . .

1. Intent may be inferred from knowledge, when the purveyor of legal goods for illegal use has acquired a stake in the venture. (United States v. Falcone, 2 Cir., 109 F.2d 579, 581.) For example, in Regina v. Thomas [1957], 2 All E.R. 181, 342, a prosecution for living off the earnings of prostitution, the evidence showed that the accused, knowing the woman to be a convicted prostitute, agreed to let her have the use of his room between the hours of 9 P.M. and 2 A.M. for a charge of £3 a night. The Court of Criminal Appeal refused an appeal from the conviction, holding that when the accused rented a room at a grossly inflated rent to a prostitute for the purpose of carrying on her trade, a jury could find he was living on the earnings of prostitution.

In the present case, no proof was offered of inflated charges for the telephone answering services furnished the codefendants.

2. Intent may be inferred from knowledge, when no legitimate use for the goods or services exists. The leading California case is People v. McLaughlin, 111 Cal. App. 2d 781, 245 P.2d 1076, in which the court upheld a conviction of the suppliers of horse-racing information by wire for conspiracy to promote bookmaking, when it had been established that wire service information had no other use than to supply information needed by book makers to conduct illegal gambling operations.

In Rex v. DeLaval [1763] 3 Burr. 1434, 97 E.R. 913, the charge was unlawful conspiracy to remove a girl from the control of Bates, a musician to whom she was bound as an apprentice, and place her in the hands of Sir Francis Drake for the purpose of prostitution. Lord Mansfield not only upheld the charges against Bates and Sir Francis, but also against Fraine, the attorney who drew up the indentures of apprenticeship transferring custody of the girl from Bates to Sir Francis. Fraine, said Lord Mansfield, must have known that Sir Francis had no facilities for teaching music to apprentices so that it was impossible for him to have been ignorant of the real intent of the transaction.

In Shaw v. Director of Public Prosecutions, [1962] A.C. 220, the defendant was convicted of conspiracy to corrupt public morals and of living on the earnings of prostitution, when he published a directory consisting almost entirely of advertisements of the names, addresses, and specialized talents of prostitutes. Publication of such a directory, said the court, could have no legitimate use and serve no other purpose than to advertise the professional services of the prostitutes whose advertisements appeared in the directory. The publisher could be deemed a participant in the profits from the business activities of his principal advertisers.

Other services of a comparable nature come to mind: the manufacturer of crooked dice and marked cards who sells his product to gambling casinos; the tipster who furnishes information on the movement of law enforcement officers to known lawbreakers. (Cf. Jackson v. State of Texas, 164 Tex. Cr. R. 276, 298 S.W.2d 837 (1957), where the furnisher of signaling equipment used to warn gamblers of the police was convicted of aiding the equipping of a gambling place.) In such cases the supplier must necessarily have an intent to further the illegal enterprise since there is no known honest use for his goods. . . .

However, there is nothing in the furnishing of telephone answering service which would necessarily imply assistance in the performance of illegal activities. Nor is any inference to be derived from the use of an answering service by women, either in any particular volume of calls, or outside normal working hours. Night-club entertainers, registered nurses, faith healers, public stenographers, photographic models, and free lance substitute employees, provide examples of women in legitimate occupations whose employment might cause them to receive a volume of telephone calls at irregular hours.

3. Intent may be inferred from knowledge, when the volume of business with the buyer is grossly disproportionate to any legitimate demand, or when sales for illegal use amount to a high proportion of the seller's total business. In such cases an intent to participate in the illegal enterprise may be inferred from the quantity of the business done. For example, in *Direct Sales,* supra, the sale of narcotics to a rural physician in quantities 300 times greater than he would have normal use for provided potent evidence of an intent to further the illegal activity. In the same case the court also found significant the fact that the wholesaler had attracted as customers a disproportionately large group of physicians who had been convicted of violating the Harrison Act. In Shaw v. Director of Public Prosecutions, [1962] A.C. 220, almost the entire business of the directory came from prostitutes.

No evidence of any unusual volume of business with prostitutes was presented against Lauria.

Inflated charges, the sale of goods with no legitimate use, sales in inflated amounts, each may provide a fact of sufficient moment from which the intent of the seller to participate in the criminal enterprise may be inferred. In such instances participation by the supplier of legal goods to the illegal enterprise may be inferred because in one way or another the supplier has acquired a special interest in the operation of the illegal enterprise. His intent to participate in the crime of which he has knowledge may be inferred from the existence of his special interest. . . .

Yet there are cases in which it cannot reasonably be said that the supplier has a stake in the venture or has acquired a special interest in the enterprise, but in which he has been held liable as a participant on the basis of knowledge alone. Some suggestion of this appears in *Direct Sales,* supra, where both the knowledge of the illegal use of the drugs and the intent of the supplier to aid that use were inferred. In Regina v. Bainbridge [1959], 3 W.L.R. 656 (CCA 6), a supplier of oxygen-cutting equipment to one known to intend to use it to break into a bank was convicted as an accessory to the crime. . . . It seems apparent from these cases that a supplier who furnishes equipment which he *knows* will be used to commit a serious crime may be deemed from that knowledge alone to have intended to produce the result. Such proof may justify an inference that the furnisher intended to aid the execution of the crime and that he thereby became a participant. For instance, we think the operator of a telephone answering service with positive knowledge that his service was being used to facilitate the extortion of ransom, the distribution of heroin, or the passing of counterfeit money who continued to furnish the service with knowledge of its use, might be chargeable on knowledge alone with participation in a scheme to extort money, to distribute narcotics, or to pass counterfeit money. The same results would follow the seller of gasoline who knew the buyer was using his product to make Molotov cocktails for terroristic use.

Logically, the same reasoning could be extended to crimes of every description. Yet we do not believe an inference of intent drawn from knowledge of criminal use properly applies to the less serious crimes classified as misdemeanors. The duty to take positive action to disassociate oneself from activities helpful to violations of the criminal law is far stronger and more compelling for felonies than it is for misdemeanors or petty offenses. In this respect, as in others, the distinction between felonies and misdemeanors, between more serious and less serious crime, retains continuing vitality. In historically the most serious felony, treason, an individual with knowledge of the treason can be prosecuted for concealing and failing to disclose it. In other felonies, both at common law and under the criminal laws of the United States, an individual knowing of the commission of a felony is criminally liable for concealing it and failing to make it known to proper authority. But this crime, known as misprision of felony, has always been limited to knowledge and concealment of felony and has never extended to misdemeanor. A similar limitation is found in the criminal liability of an accessory, which is restricted to aid in the escape of a principal who has committed or been charged with a *felony.* We believe the distinction between the obligations arising from knowledge of a felony and those arising from knowledge of a misdemeanor continues to reflect basic human feelings about the duties owed by individuals to society. Heinous crime must be stamped out, and its suppression is the responsibility of all. Venial crime and crime not evil in itself present less of a danger to society, and perhaps the benefits of their suppression through the modern equivalent of the posse, the hue and cry, the informant, and the citizen's arrest, are outweighed by the disruption to everyday life brought about by amateur law enforcement and private officiousness in relatively inconsequential delicts which do not threaten our basic security. The subject has been summarized in an English test on the criminal law:

> Failure to reveal a felony to the authorities is now authoritatively determined to be misprision of felony, which is a common-law misdemeanor; misprision of treason is punishable with imprisonment for life. . . . No offence is committed in failing to disclose a misdemeanor. . . .
>
> To require everyone, without distinction as to the nature and degree of the offence, to become an accuser, would be productive of inconvenience in exposing numbers to penal prosecutions, multiplying criminal charges, and engendering private dissension. It may sometimes be more convenient that offences should be passed over, than that all should indiscriminately be made the subject of prosecution; and a law would be considered to be harsh and impolitic, if not unjust, which compelled every party injured by a criminal act, and, still more so, to compel everyone who happened to know that another had been so injured, to make a public disclosure of the circumstances. Here, therefore, there is reason for limiting the law against mere misprisions to the concealment of such crimes as are of an aggravated complexion. . . . (Criminal Law, Glanville Williams (2d ed.) p.423.)

With respect to misdemeanors, we conclude that positive knowledge of the supplier that his products or services are being used for criminal purposes does not, without more, establish an intent of the supplier to participate in the misdemeanors. With respect to felonies, we do not decide the converse, viz., that in all cases of felony, knowledge of criminal use alone may justify an inference of the supplier's intent to participate in the crime. The implications of *Falcone* make the matter uncertain with respect to those felonies which are merely prohibited wrongs. See also Holman v. Johnson, 98 E.R. 1120 (1775) (sale and delivery of tea at Dunkirk known to be destined for smuggling into England not an illegal contract). But decision on this point is not compelled, and we leave the matter open. . . .

From this analysis of precedent we deduce the following rule: the intent of a supplier who knows of the criminal use to which his supplies are put to participate in the criminal activity connected with the use of his supplies may be established by (1) direct evidence, (2) through an inference that he intends to participate based on, (a) his special interest in the activity, or (b) the aggravated nature of the crime itself. . . .

When we review Lauria's activities in the light of this analysis, we find no proof that Lauria took any direct action to further, encourage, or direct the call girl activities of his codefendants and we find an absence of circumstances from which his special interest in their activities could be inferred. Neither excessive charges for standardized services, nor the furnishing of services without a legitimate use, nor an unusual quantity of business with call-girls, are present. The offense which he is charged with furthering is a misdemeanor, a category of crime which has never been made a required subject of positive disclosure to public authority. Under these circumstances, although proof of Lauria's knowledge of the criminal activities of his patrons was sufficient to charge him with that fact, there was insufficient evidence that he intended to further their criminal activities, and hence insufficient proof of his participation in a criminal conspiracy with his codefendants to further prostitution. Since the conspiracy centered around the activities of Lauria's telephone answering service, the charges against his codefendants likewise fail for want of proof.

In absolving Lauria of complicity in a criminal conspiracy we do not wish to imply that the public authorities are without remedies to combat modern manifestations of the world's oldest profession. Licensing of telephone answering services under the police power, together with the revocation of licenses for the toleration of prostitution, is a possible civil remedy. The furnishing of telephone answering service in aid of prostitution could be made a crime. (Cf. Pen. Code §316, which makes it a misdemeanor to let an apartment with knowledge of its use for prostitution.) Other solutions will doubtless occur to vigilant public authorities if the problem of call-girl activity needs further suppression.

The order is affirmed.

Notes and Questions

1. Entirely apart from his *mens rea,* do Lauria's actions satisfy the requirement of an agreement for conspiracy?

2. According to the court, what *mens rea* does one need to become a member of a conspiracy? What does the court mean by intent? Why should we allow the inference of intent when a defendant exhibits knowledge of a serious crime exists but not knowledge of a less serious crime? What does the court mean by a "heinous" crime—any felony? If not, which felonies?

3. The intent required for conspiracy has been the subject of considerable commentary. According to Burke and Kadish, Conspiracy, 1 Encyclopedia of Crime and Justice 235 (1983):

> The two elements of mental state required by conspiracy are the intent to agree and the intent to promote the unlawful objective of the conspiracy. The first of these elements is almost indistinguishable from the act of agreement. Agreement is in any case morally neutral; its moral character depends upon the nature of the objective of agreement. It is the intention to promote a *crime* that lends conspiracy its criminal cast.
>
> Some crimes do not require an intention to cause the prohibited result. Manslaughter, for example, may be committed by a person who kills another by his act of driving carelessly. These crimes may not be the basis of a conspiracy, however, since two people could not be said to agree together to kill another carelessly. The nature of the requirement of agreement, therefore, limits the

objectives of conspiracy to those crimes that are committed by intentional actions.

Problems arise, however, in determining the sense of intention that is required. Does it include acting with knowledge of the probable results of one's action, or is it confined to acting with a purpose to attain such results? The question has most frequently arisen in the case of suppliers who furnish goods to members of a conspiracy with knowledge of their intended illegal use. Examples include the supplying of yeast and sugar to a group known to be using them to engage in illegal production of whiskey (United States v. Falcone, 311 U.S. 205 (1940)) or the furnishing of medical drugs by a manufacturer that knows they will be used for nonmedical and illegal purposes (Direct Sales Co. v. United States, 319 U.S. 703 (1943)).

Some courts have found it enough to convict the supplier for an illegal conspiracy with the user when the supplier knew of the illegal use. The justification for this position is that the supplier has knowingly furthered a crime and has no interest in doing so that is worthy of protection (Model Penal Code, 1960, Commentary on §5.03). However, the majority view is to the contrary; the supplier must be shown to have had a purpose to further the illegal objectives of the user (Model Penal Code, 1962, §5.03 (1)). In the language of Judge Learned Hand, "he must in some sense promote their venture himself, make it his own, have a stake in its outcome" (United States v. Falcone, 109 F.2d 579, 581 (1949)). This might be demonstrated by evidence of the sale of unusually large quantities of goods, particularly where such goods are legally restricted; by evidence of inflated charges or of the sale of goods with no legitimate use; or by evidence that sales to an illegal operation have become a dominant proportion of the seller's business.

The reasons for requiring a stake in the venture are twofold. First, the act of agreement necessarily imports a purpose; indifference to illegal use by another of what one supplies him for otherwise legitimate reasons does not constitute an agreement. Second, making the supplier liable in these situations whenever a jury decides that he knew of the illegal use imposes an undue burden on legitimate business since to avoid liability suppliers would be obliged to police the intended uses of their purchasers. By taking into account the social usefulness of the commercial activity and the magnitude of the seller's contribution to the crime, the majority rule strikes a balance between the needs of business enterprises to operate without oppressive restriction and of society to protect itself against crime.

4. In United States v. Gallishaw, 428 F.2d 760 (2d Cir. 1970), the defendant was convicted of conspiracy to rob a bank for lending the would-be bank robber the machine gun actually used in the robbery. The key testimony was about a conversation between defendant Gallishaw and the bank robber, Thomas.

> Mr. Gallishaw said, "Make sure you bring it back," and Thomas said that he will be sure that he will bring it back and if he didn't pull the bank job, "I will pull something else to give him the money."

During its deliberations the jury asked the judge whether supplying or renting a gun, which is subsequently used in a bank robbery, would be grounds for conviction of a conspiracy if the person who rents the gun does not know how or where it will be used. The judge responded that if the defendant rented the gun and knew that there was a conspiracy to do something wrong, he could be found to have entered the conspiracy.

The court of appeals reversed the defendant's conviction, holding that the defendant would not be guilty of a conspiracy to rob a bank unless he knew a bank was to be robbed and that the judge's answer, therefore, was fatally defective. Note that in *Gallishaw,* the defendant was not charged simply with conspiracy to commit robbery (which would not have been a federal crime) but rather with conspiring to rob a bank.

5. We saw in Chapter 4 on *mens rea* that the legislature can assign requirements of different mental states for different elements of a crime. *Gallishaw* seems to require that the mental state needed for conspiracy not be less than the mental state needed for the substantive crime. This, of course, raises the issues whether conspiracy requires a more culpable mental state than does the substantive crime.

In United States v. Feola, 420 U.S. 671 (1974) the following occurred: Feola and his confederates arranged for a sale of heroin to buyers who turned out to be undercover agents for the Bureau of Narcotics and Dangerous Drugs. The group planned to palm off on the purchasers, for a substantial sum, a form of sugar in place of heroin and, should that ruse fail, simply to surprise their unwitting buyers and relieve them of the cash they had brought along for payment. The plan failed when one agent, his suspicions having been aroused,[9]

> drew his revolver in time to counter an assault upon another agent from the rear. Instead of enjoying the rich benefits of a successful swindle, Feola and his associates found themselves charged, to their undoubted surprise, with conspiring to assault, and with assaulting, federal officers.

The Supreme Court first had to determine the required *mens rea* for the substantive crime of assault on a federal officer. The statute, of course, required purpose with respect to the act element of assault, but the Court held that the attendant circumstance—the identity of the victim as a federal agent—was a strict liability element: If the defendants purposely assaulted the victims, it was no defense under the federal assault statute that they did not know, or did not or even could not reasonably foresee that their victim was a federal officer.

The Court then decided that the identity of the victim remained a strict liability element even on a charge of conspiracy to assault a federal officer.

9. The agent opened a closet door in the Manhattan apartment where the sale was to have taken place and observed a man on the floor, bound and gagged.

The Court found nothing in the principles of conspiracy that warranted changing the *mens rea* requirements established for the substantive offense.

When the defendants are unaware and have no reason to know that their victim is other than a private citizen, can it be said that they conspired to assault a federal officer?

Assume we have a statutory rape law that requires purpose for the act of intercourse, but sets strict liability as the *mens rea* for the circumstance element of the girl's age. Hence, a mistake of fact about age will not exculpate. Two boys agree to go to a 16-year-old's house to persuade her to have intercourse with one or both of them. Both boys mistakenly think the girl is 19. On the statutory rape charge, assume that their mistake will not excuse them. If they are caught before they achieve their goal, can they be convicted of conspiracy? Some courts have held "no," taking the word "conspire" to connote very specific purpose or motive: How can someone "conspire" to have intercourse with a 16-year-old when he thinks she is 19? By now you should be familiar with this problem. The emerging view would be to require no more than that the *mens rea* of the conspirators have symmetry with the substantive crime's *mens rea* requirement. See United States v. Feola, supra.

Consider Model Penal Code §5.03:

> (1) *Definition of Conspiracy.* A person is guilty of conspiracy with another person or persons to commit a crime if with the purpose of promoting or facilitating its commission he:
>
> (a) agrees with such other person or persons that they or one or more of them will engage in conduct which constitutes such crime or an attempt or solicitation to commit such crime.

D. SPECIAL *MENS REA* PROBLEMS

1. Conspiracy and Mistake of Law

Some courts have enunciated what is called the "corrupt motive" doctrine. This means that a mistake of the governing law would exculpate from a charge of conspiracy even where it did not exculpate from the substantive crime itself.

7

In People v. Powell, 63 N.Y. 8 (1875), the defendants were municipal officials charged with conspiring to purchase supplies without advertising for bids. Their defense was that they were unaware of the criminal statute requiring them to solicit bids. The court reversed their convictions, holding that it was "implied in the meaning of the word 'conspiracy' that the agreement must have been entered into with an evil purpose, as distinguished from a purpose to do the act prohibited, in ignorance of the prohibition." Later cases followed the "corrupt motive" doctrine, e.g., Landen v. United States, 299 F. 75 (C.A. 6 1924) (druggists not guilty of conspiracy to violate the prohibition laws where they honestly believed those laws did not apply to their selling methods), some of them applying the doctrine only to charges of conspiracy to violate so-called malum-prohibitum statutes. But the modern trend is to reject the "corrupt motive" doctrine and to equate the *mens rea* requirements for a conspiracy with those for the substantive crime.

The Model Penal Code Commentary to §5.03 (Tent. Draft No. 10, 1960) provides:

> The *Powell* rule, and many of the decisions that rely upon it, may be viewed as a judicial endeavor to import fair *mens rea* requirements into statutes creating regulatory offenses that do not rest upon traditional concepts of personal fault and culpability. We believe, however, that this should be the function of the statutes defining such offenses. Section 2.04(3) specifies the limited situations where ignorance of the criminality of one's conduct is a defense in general. . . . We see no reason why the fortuity of concert should be used as the device for limiting criminality in this area, just as we see no reason for using it as a device for expanding liability through imprecise formulations of objectives that include activity not otherwise criminal.

2. Must There Be Purpose?

Recall our problems with "attempted recklessness" in Chapter 9. Assume two people agree to hold a drag race, knowing it to be dangerous. If a bystander or someone else is killed, one or both the racers may be guilty of involuntary manslaughter, on a recklessness or negligence theory. But what of their conspiracy liability at the point of the original agreement to hold the race? Can we charge them with conspiracy to commit involuntary manslaughter? With respect to the crime's element of requiring *result,* as in homicide, it would seem no conspiracy exists unless the parties have purpose or at least knowledge with respect to result. However, if reckless driving is itself a crime, they are guilty of conspiracy to commit *that* crime.

3. "Malice"

Bill and John are brothers. They both hear that Fred has attacked their sister. In a heat of passion, they agree to kill Fred. Whether or not they succeed, are they guilty of conspiracy to commit murder? If they succeed, the substantive charge might be reduced to voluntary manslaughter because of provocation. Assuming the punishment for conspiracy can be calibrated according to the severity of the object crime, it makes a considerable difference whether they are charged with conspiracy to commit murder or conspiracy to commit voluntary manslaughter. One view is that as long as they have the *mens rea* of purpose for the act of agreement, they should be guilty of conspiracy to murder: provocation diminishes culpability for the killing, but not for the agreement. In People v. Horn, 12 Cal. 3d 290, 524 P.2d 1300 (1974), the California Supreme Court rejected that view and held that the conspiracy charge can be reduced in the same way the substantive crime charge would be.

E. THE INCIDENTS OF CONSPIRACY

STATE v. STEIN

Supreme Court of New Jersey
70 N.J. 369, 360 A.2d 347 (1976)

Conford, P.J.A.D., temporarily assigned.

The evidence adduced on the State's case indicates that defendant, a Trenton lawyer, suggested to a certain underworld figure that the house of one Dr. Gordon in Trenton was a likely target for a successful breaking and entering or burglary, as large amounts of cash were kept there. Defendant expected to share in the gains. As a result, there was an armed robbery at that home about a year later. While attempting to evade the police, who had been alerted to the affair, the perpetrators abducted members of the family and injured two policemen. . . .

As a result of all the foregoing defendant was indicted on counts of (a) conspiracy to steal currency; (b) armed robbery, assaults with an offensive weapon, kidnapping, kidnapping while armed and assaults upon a police officer. . . . Defendant was convicted on all counts and sentenced concurrently to terms of imprisonment aggregating 30 years to 30 years and one day. . . . Subject to amplified comment hereinafter, the factual background of this matter is adequately set out in the Appellate Division opinion as follows:

On March 17, 1972 Testa and Stasio, impersonating police officers, gained entrance to the Trenton home of Dr. Arnold Gordon. The pair produced pistols and demanded money and jewelry. While Testa and Stasio obtained $470 from Gordon and bound him and his wife Edith, a maid telephoned the police. When the police arrived, the robbers took Edith and her 14-year-old daughter Shelly from the house at gunpoint as hostages and attempted an escape at high speed in a getaway car. A chase ensued. Ultimately, the getaway car crashed into a police car barrier, seriously injuring two police officers. . . .

Testa testified before the grand jury as follows: In September 1971 Joe Bradley introduced him to Pontani. Pontani gave Testa particulars about the layout of the Gordon home. Pontani, Testa and Bradley met three times between September and October 18, 1971, the date of Bradley's death. Tassone was present on a few occasions. Testa stated that from the outset it was intended that the crime would be an armed robbery. Although burglary had been initially discussed, it was discarded as an impossibility. After Bradley's death, Pontani spoke to a lawyer who guaranteed the amount of money that would be in the house, the movements of the family and the layout of the telephone system. Pontani had indicated that the lawyer was "Jewish" and a close friend of the Gordons. Testa was present when Pontani telephoned the lawyer. The latter advised Pontani that $200,000 would be found in the house. . . .

The Appellate Division reversed the convictions of the defendant on the substantive charges of assault with an offensive weapon (against Edith and Shelly Gordon), kidnapping, kidnapping while armed and assaults on a police officer. It sustained that of armed robbery. The former were deemed not within the scope of the original conspiracy under the principles stated in State v. Madden, 61 N.J. 377, 294 A.2d 609 (1972). . . .

The question as to the criminal responsibility of a conspirator for the commission by others of substantive offenses having some causal connection with the conspiracy but not in the contemplation of the conspirator has been a matter of considerable debate and controversy. Here there is no question but that Stein did not actually contemplate any criminal consequence of his "tip" to Pontani beyond a burglary and theft of money from the Gordon home. The trial court applied the conventionally stated rule that each conspirator is responsible for "anything done by his confederates which follows incidentally in the execution of the common design as one of its probable and natural consequences, even though it was not intended as part of the original design," citing 15A C.J.S. Conspiracy §74 at 825; and see Pinkerton v. United States, 328 U.S. 640. . . .

The Appellate Division regarded the doctrine as restricted in this State by virtue of State v. Madden. . . . We find ourselves unable to agree with the implication of the Appellate Division, that anything stated in State v. Madden was intended to modify in any substantial sense the rule quoted above as applied by the trial court. *Madden* was not directly concerned with liability of a conspirator for an act consequential to but not specifically the subject of the conspiracy—the problem confronting us here.

In *Madden* there was a prosecution for the murder of a policeman killed in the course of a mob assault upon him consequent upon a racial disturbance. The trial court, in instructing the jury on aiding and abetting, said that if the defendants conspired to do an unlawful act in the course of which there was a killing, they could be held responsible therefor. This court disapproved that instruction, pointing out there was no evidence of an agreement made in advance of the criminal event. If there had been, it would have been "appropriate to tell the jury of the common liability of all with respect to the ensuing substantive offense." Id. The court felt that the defendants were harmed by the possible understanding by the jury, from the charge, that even if the defendants did not participate in inflicting the fatal injuries, there was nevertheless evidence to infer a conspiracy to kill which would then operate to inculpate the defendants with all the acts of the killers. The harm lay in the absence of proof justifying a finding of such a conspiracy by defendants, not in the unacceptability of a rule of law justifying liability for a killing on the part of all who in fact conspired to such a purpose. . . .

The Appellate Division may have been influenced by this court's concern in *Madden* with the possible understanding of the jury from the charge that there would be vicarious liability for murder if the defendants conspired to do any unlawful act, e.g., to pursue the victim, and the killing occurred in the course of that act. But the implication of non-liability for the killing in that context is not at all consistent with the generally held rule, exemplified by the leading *Pinkerton* case cited above, that so long as a conspiracy is still in existence "an overt act of one partner may be the act of all without any new agreement specifically directed to that act," provided the substantive act could "be reasonably foreseen as a necessary or natural consequence of the unlawful agreement." 328 U.S. at 616-647.

We regard the rule as just stated to be sound and viable. We hold it represents the law of this State. . . .

It remains to apply the rule to the instant fact situation. Ordinarily the matter of factual application of the rule would be submitted to the jury under appropriate instructions. Here the matter was for the trial judge in the first instance as factfinder. The Appellate Division found correct the trial ruling that the armed robbery was within the scope of the conspiracy to steal currency from the Gordon home. We are in agreement. The robbery was a "natural or probable" consequence of the conspiracy. But the Appellate Division concluded that the assaults with an offensive weapon on the wife and daughter of Dr. Gordon were "not connected with the robbery as such" but with the preliminary acts of taking the Gordons as hostages and the eventual kidnappings" and therefore "not fairly . . . part of the conspiratorial agreement." The assault convictions were therefore set aside. . . .

We are not in complete agreement with this last determination. The brandishing of handguns by the robbers when they first encountered Dr. and Mrs. Gordon in the house was clearly a foreseeable event in the course of an unlawful invasion of the house for criminal purposes by armed men. That assault on Mrs. Gordon did not merge with the armed robbery, as the Appellate Division suggested might be the case, since the robbery charged was of Dr. Gordon alone, not the members of his family assaulted. Thus the assault conviction as to Mrs. Gordon should not have been set aside as too remote from the conspiracy.

As to the charge of assault with an offensive weapon on Shelly Gordon (daughter of the Gordons), since the evidence indicates that offense occurred only at the time of the attempted escape from the police, its disposition depends on the determination as to the other associated charges, discussed next below. . . .

Liability of the defendant for the kidnapping, kidnapping while armed and assaults on a police officer presents a much closer question. The Appellate Division held that these substantive acts were "offenses committed by the criminals effecting the conspiratorial specific crime after that crime had been committed, as part of a plan to flee when it became evident that they were about to be apprehended" and that defendant could not be charged therefor. On balance, we are satisfied that this is a correct result, particularly in relation to the kidnapping phases of the episode. This holding will also apply to the reversal by the Appellate Division not on the ground that the substantive offenses took place subsequent to the commission of a crime conspired or that the offenses were part of a plan to flee, but rather that it would be unreasonable for a fact-finder to find as a fact beyond a reasonable doubt that they were necessary, natural or probable consequences of the conspiracy, having in mind the unique fact-complex presented. . . .

Notes and Questions

1. There are many incidents or effects of the existence of a conspiracy. The *Stein* case involves one—the rule that all coconspirators are liable for the substantive offenses committed by one of the conspirators if done in furtherance of the conspiracy. This rule is sometimes called the *Pinkerton* rule, after the leading case of Pinkerton v. United States, 328 U.S. 640 (1946). In *Pinkerton,* two brothers were convicted of conspiracy to violate the Internal Revenue Code. Both brothers were also convicted of a number of substantive offenses, namely removing, depositing, and concealing a large quantity of distilled spirits without paying the appropriate tax. At the time some of the substantive offenses were committed, the defendant was in the penitentiary (apparently for violating the liquor laws) and he contended that because of this he could not be implicated in these offenses. The court held, though, that since his brother (a coconspirator) had committed these crimes in furtherance of the conspiracy of which the defendant was a member, the defendant was liable for them, especially since he had made no effort to withdraw from the conspiracy. In *Pinkerton* the brothers lived next to each other, bailed each other out of jail, and helped each other when questioned by the county sheriff. Should the same rule apply in *Stein,* where the existence of a conspiracy was less apparent?

Why does the court in *Stein* reverse the convictions for kidnapping and assault? Is there anything in the *Pinkerton* doctrine to warrant this reversal?

2. Jurisdictions that follow the *Pinkerton* rule have three means of making a person vicariously liable for the act of another. One is the *Pinkerton* rule; another is the rule as to aiding and abetting; and the third is the felony-murder rule. Note that the felony-murder rule is a rule of accessorial liability, in that it could, for example, make a person who is guilty of a robbery also guilty of murder, if an accomplice in the robbery performed an act that resulted in a death.

The *Pinkerton* rule is often phrased in terms of making each conspirator liable for any secondary crimes committed by a coconspirator "in furtherance" of the conspiracy or the primary object crime. Recall the parallel rule for accomplice liability discussed in relation to the *Kessler* case on pp. 628, supra. The rule would make one person liable for secondary crimes committed by an accomplice that, though unintended by the first person, were nevertheless "reasonably foreseeable" results of the common criminal design. The *Pinkerton* rule is usually thought to impose much wider liability. However, given the vagueness of such phrases as "in furtherance" and "reasonably foreseeable," judges and juries may have enough leeway to achieve similar results under the two doctrines. Would the result in *Stein* have been different under the *Kessler* approach?

3. The *Pinkerton* rule has come under considerable attack in recent years. According to one commentator:[10]

> The MPC position . . . is that a conspirator should be measured by the same standard of legal accountability for conduct applicable to any other individual. Therefore, the Code departs from prevailing law in several jurisdictions and establishes no special complicity rules for conspirators. "[L]iability for a substantive crime as an accomplice cannot be predicated on the sole fact of having been a party to a conspiracy; further inquiry must examine a person's real culpability with respect to the substantive offense.[11] This rule stands in stark contrast to current federal practice. Despite the fact that the relevant statute makes no mention of conspiracy as a potential source of complicitous liability, the leading case of Pinkerton v. United States proclaimed, nearly thirty years ago, that a conspirator, by virtue of his participation in a criminal agreement, is responsible for *all* substantive offenses committed by his co-conspirators *in furtherance* of that agreement. Whether reasonable forseeability of such substantive offenses is indispensable to conviction as a principal on the basis of conspiracy alone (i.e., with no showing of actual aiding or abetting) is a subject of some dispute in the federal courts. However, even when this limitation is added to the "in furtherance of the agreement" prerequisite, the embrace of vicarious liability under federal law remains unjustifiably broad. The vast majority of criminal codes

10. Note, Conspiracy: Statutory Reform Since the Model Penal Code, 75 Colum. L. Rev. 1122, 1149-1153.

11. See, e.g., the illuminating comments of the Kentucky Criminal Law Revision Committee:

> The question to be faced by the decision makers in deciding whether to impute liability through a conspiracy is not whether the defendant was a party to the conspiracy; instead, it is whether he aided, counseled, agreed to aid or attempted to aid in the planning or commission of the offense committed. Justification for this approach was put this way in the Model Penal Code: "Conspiracy may prove command, encouragement, assistance or agreement to assist, etc.; it is evidentially important and may be sufficient for that purpose. But whether it suffices ought to be decided by the jury; they should not be told that it establishes complicity as a matter of law." Model Penal Code §2.04(3), Comment (Tent. Draft No. 1 1953).

Ky. Penal Code, Final Draft (1971), Comment to §310, at 29-30.

drafted or adopted since the promulgation of the MPC have, it seems, chosen to make accountability for substantive crimes entirely independent of conspiracy as such. . . .

Crucial in this ointment of legislative enlightenment are the flies of those jurisdictions which have not accepted the MPC wisdom. Especially important is the Senate version of the proposed Federal Criminal Code, which would enact the *Pinkerton* rule, slightly contracted by the overlay of a reasonable foreseeability requirement. The current Wisconsin and Minnesota statutes are of similar design. According to the laws of Kentucky and Ohio, a conspirator is automatically liable as an accomplice, if the criminal agreement's object is achieved by one or more co-conspirators. Probably the most peculiar provision, in form if not in effect, is contained in the Texas complicity section. This statute determines conspirator responsibility for an *object* offense by reference to complicity tests of general applicability (i.e., not dependent on conspiracy membership). Simultaneously, Texas §7.02(b) makes all conspirators vicariously liable for *non-object* offenses which are committed "in furtherance of the unlawful purpose" and which "should have been anticipated as a result" of the agreement's implementation. Thus, where special conspirator accountability for a substantive crime would be most easily defensible, Texas invokes ordinary complicity measures. On the other hand, where questions of intent and causality are most serious, a *Pinkerton*-type rule is imposed.

The conspirator complicity provision of S. 1 has inspired vigorous debate. Professor Louis B. Schwartz, Director of the National Commission on Reform of the Federal Criminal Laws, has been particularly forceful in his opposition. "This formula may implicate a person, on the basis of negligence or stupidity, in very serious offenses which he never contemplated or agreed, expressly or by implication, to have perpetrated." Espousing the Department of Justice view in support of an essentially identical precursor of S. 1's conspirator complicity subsection, Deputy Assistant Attorney General Keeney told a Senate Subcommittee that

> [f]rom the legal standpoint, if we accept the principle that the overt act of one co-conspirator may be used against other members of the conspiracy, then a fortiori there is no reason why the same or other acts in furtherance of the conspiracy should not similarly be attributable to other members for the purpose of rendering them liable for the substantive offenses. Turning to the practical side, the ever increasing sophistication of organized crime presents a compelling reason against abandonment of *Pinkerton.* Complicated and highly refined stock frauds . . . and narcotics conspiracies represent a substantial and ever-increasing threat to society justifying retention of the *Pinkerton* doctrine. Empirical evidence has repeatedly demonstrated that those who form and control illegal enterprises are generally well insulated from prosecutions, with the exception of prosecutions predicated upon the theory of conspiracy. To preclude uniformly their exposure to additional sanctions, regardless of the circumstances, for the very crimes which sustain their illegal ventures, would have the most unfortunate and inequitable consequences.[12]

12. . . . Whatever may be said for his practical argument, Mr. Keeney's legal contention involves an obvious fallacy. The overt act as an element of conspiracy serves a function entirely different from that of imposing liability for substantive offenses. . . . A co-conspirator's overt act may indeed be employed to secure defendant's conviction for a conspiracy in which defendant is shown to have participated. Bannon v. United States, 156 U.S. 464, 468-469 (1895); United

Notwithstanding this testimony, the concerns animating Professor Schwartz and the MPC draftsmen remain convincing.

Recall the discussion of withdrawal from conspiracy, page 681 supra, and apply it to the *Pinkerton* cases. Is there anything the imprisoned *Pinkerton* brother could have done to avoid liability for the substantive crimes committed by his brother? Is there anything Stein could have done to avoid liability for some of the crimes that his co-conspirators committed but that Stein himself had never agreed to?

4. One must first understand the hearsay rule in order to understand another major incident of the existence of a conspiracy. The hearsay rule forbids, subject to various exceptions, the admission of evidence given by a witness on the stand as to what someone said off the stand, when the probative value of that evidence depends on the credibility of the out-of-court declarant (the person who made the statement that the witness is repeating). Thus, a witness's statement on the stand that "my brother-in-law told me he saw the defendant break into the building" would be hearsay. The theory is that the witness's brother-in-law, the person who allegedly observed the defendant, is not in court to be cross-examined. Such cross-examination might reveal defects in his perception (whether his eyesight was good and whether it was light enough when he made his observation); in his memory (even if he had seen correctly, he might not have remembered correctly); in his sincerity (he might have been deliberately lying and spreading untrue stories about the defendant because of a grievance he had against the defendant); and in his ability to relate information (he may have been referring to someone else with the same name as the defendant). The hearsay rule is based on a view that cross-examination is so important that, in general, out-of-court statements should not be admissible.

The law of evidence recognizes many exceptions to the hearsay rule, for the most part premised on a view that certain kinds of hearsay evidence are especially reliable. With respect to conspiracy, one of the most important exceptions to the hearsay rule is that an out-of-court statement made by one co-conspirator in furtherance of the conspiracy may be admissible against another co-conspirator.

The law begins with the view that a person's own statements, made out of court, are admissible against him—as "admissions"—because he has no right to cross-examine himself. From there, the law goes to admit the out-of-court statement of an agent authorized to make such statements. Then, admissions of a member of a partnership are admissible against all partners, on the theory

---

States v. Clay, 495 F.2d 700, 706 (7th Cir.) cert. denied, 419 U.S. 937 (1974). This fact alone, however, hardly justifies the inference that defendant, as conspirator, should be responsible for all substantive offenses committed in furtherance of the criminal agreement, regardless of his culpability with respect to such offenses. Moreover, Mr. Keeney's suggestion that, without the *Pinkerton* doctrine, conspirators would be immune from all accomplice liability is patently absurd. Their behavior would simply be evaluated under general complicity sections, just as the conduct of any suspected criminal would be.

that one partner has the power to bind the other partners by an agreement or act with respect to the business of the partnership. Finally, a conspiracy is viewed, for this purpose, as a partnership in crime. In short, the law has erected the fiction that statements made by a conspirator in the course of or in furtherance of the conspiracy are authorized by all of his or her co-conspirators, and are therefore admissible against them as admissions, so long as the trial judge is satisfied by a preponderance of the evidence that a conspiracy does exist. Thus, if the declarant, a member of a conspiracy, says to you, "Join our burglary ring. We've got Lefty as our safe-cracker," this hearsay statement could be admissible against Lefty if you testified to it. This out-of-court statement, although it is hearsay, is some evidence of Lefty's membership in the conspiracy, and, in conjunction with other evidence, may show his guilt beyond a reasonable doubt.

5. Another incident of conspiracy relates to the likelihood of joint trial. Though the rules of procedure often permit joinder of defendants in situations that do not depend upon the existence of a conspiracy, in practice it is far easier to try defendants together if they are accused of conspiracy. Trying the defendants together gives the prosecutor certain important advantages. If some of the defendants are clearly guilty, the jury may look at the rest and decide that "birds of a feather flock together." Evidence that is admissible against one defendant may be heard by the jury and "informally" considered against another defendant, even though, for one reason or another, the evidence is technically inadmissible against the second defendant. A defendant's privilege against self-incrimination may be impaired if his failure to take the stand is emphasized by the fact that his co-defendants do testify. The prosecutor may even be able to arrange to have each of the defendants accuse the other—while she sits back and argues that they are all correct. Finally, a prosecutor saves resources by having to pick a jury and present witnesses only once in a large trial, rather than often, in many small trials.

The defendant dislikes joint trials for all the reasons that the prosecutor likes them. In addition, defending a case where there are many other defendants requires more resources, because the defendant's attorney in a joint trial will have to sift through far more evidence than concerns her client directly. The very number of defendants may confuse the jury. This is not to say that in all cases joinder favors the prosecution. A defendant who is technically guilty but not very deeply involved in a conspiracy may benefit from comparison with those who are much more deeply involved, and the jury may acquit him either because he looks innocent compared to the others, or because it wishes to maintain an appearance of balance by not convicting everyone.

6. The rules as to venue—where a prosecution may be brought—are another incident of conspiracy. As the Commentary to the Model Penal Code §5.03 points out:

> The Sixth Amendment to the Federal Constitution states that in "all criminal prosecutions, the accused shall enjoy the right to a speedy and public trial,

by an impartial jury of the State and district wherein the crime shall have been committed." The rule is well settled that venue in a conspiracy prosecution may be laid, consistently with these provisions, in any county or district in which the agreement was formed or in which an overt act by any of the conspirators took place. The protection of the constitutional provisions is seriously diluted, however, because of loose present approaches toward unity and scope of a conspiracy. In the words of Justice Jackson, "the leverage of a conspiracy charge lifts this limitation from the prosecution and reduces its protection to a phantom."

In The Best Defense 155-174 (1982), Alan Dershowitz describes how his client Harry Reems, star of the pornographic movie Deep Throat, faced federal conspiracy charges in Memphis, Tennessee, even though Reems had never been in Memphis nor had the movie ever played there. According to Dershowitz, a zealous Assistant United States Attorney charged Reems and others with conspiracy to distribute the film throughout the United States, and persuaded a federal judge that venue could lie in any place where the film *could* have been shown.

7. The overt act in furtherance of a conspiracy is crucial to the running of the statute of limitations. Most jurisdictions provide that the statute of limitations on conspiracy runs not from the time of the agreement, but from the time of the last overt act in furtherance of that agreement.

F. "POLITICAL" CONSPIRACIES

UNITED STATES v. SPOCK

United States Court of Appeals, First Circuit
416 F.2d 165 (1969)

Aldrich, C.J. . . .

As is well known, the war in Vietnam and the draft to support it have engendered considerable animosity and frustration. In August 1967 a number of academic, clerical, and professional persons discussed the need of more vigorous opposition to governmental policies. From their eventually consolidated efforts came a document entitled "A Call to Resist Illegitimate Authority" (hereinafter the Call) and a cover letter requesting signatures and support. The letter was signed by defendant Dr. Benjamin Spock and defendant Rev. William Sloane Coffin, Jr., and two other persons. The Call was originally signed by them, numerous others, and eventually by hundreds. The defendant Mitchell Goodman had been preparing a somewhat similar statement against the war and the draft. In mid-September he learned of the Call, which he also signed. He, Coffin, Spock and others spoke on October 2 at a press conference in New York City to launch the Call. It was there announced by Goodman that further activities were contemplated, including a nationwide collection of draft cards and a ceremonial surrender thereof to the Attorney General. On October 16 a draft card burning and turn-in took place at the Arlington Street Church in Boston, arranged by the defendant Michael Ferber, and participated in by Coffin. Four days afterwards all four defendants attended a demonstration in Washington, in the course of which an unsuccessful attempt was made to present the fruits of that collection and similar gatherings to the Attorney General. . . .

The indictment was framed under section 12 of the Military Selective Service Act of 1967, 50 App. U.S.C. §462(a). It charged that defendants, and others known and unknown, conspired to "counsel, aid and abet diverse Selective Service registrants to . . . neglect, fail, refuse and evade service in the armed forces of the United States and all other duties required of registrants under the Universal Military Training and Service Act . . . and the rules, regulations and directions duly made pursuant to said Act . . . to . . . fail and refuse to have in their personal possession at all times their registration certificates [and] . . . valid notices of classification[13] [and conspired to] . . . unlawfully, willfully and knowingly hinder and interfere, by any means, with the administration of the Universal Military Training and Service Act." . . .

[The court then discussed the evidence of agreement for purposes of conspiracy.]

The government's claim of agreement looks basically to the Call, the cover letter, and the subsequent press conference.[14] Spock participated in drafting the Call, and, as has been stated, he and Coffin were two of the four persons who signed the cover letter. Goodman signed the Call, and was an active participant in the launching press conference which was chaired by Coffin and at which Spock appeared. Ferber did not sign the Call. The Call was addressed "To the young men of America, to the whole of the American people, and to all men of good will everywhere." It observed there was "a growing number of young American men" who, because of their beliefs could not contribute to the war in Vietnam in any way.

After setting forth at some length the signers' belief that the war was unconstitutional and illegal, it stated, "[W]e believe on all these grounds that every free man has a legal right and a moral duty to exert every effort to end this war, to avoid collusion with it, and to encourage others to do the same." There followed a recital of the forms of resistance that young men were exercising, the details of which we will return to, and an assertion of the signers' belief that "each of these forms of resistance . . . is courageous and justified. . . . We will continue to lend our support to those who undertake resistance to this war. We will raise funds to organize draft resistance unions, to supply legal

13. Hereinafter, without distinction, draft cards.

14. Because we are discussing only the evidence of an agreement, the government's vacillation about which part of the evidence it relied on cannot, without some special showing, be taken to have prejudiced the defendants. On the contrary, the government is entitled to rely on whatever agreement is shown by the evidence. Glasser v. United States, 1942, 315 U.S. 60, 80, 625 S. Ct. 457, 86 L. Ed. 680. The defendants do not destroy the government's case by themselves showing a somewhat different but equally illegal agreement.

defense and bail, to support families and otherwise aid resistance to the war in whatever ways may seem appropriate. . . . We call upon all men of good will to join us in this confrontation with immoral authority. . . . Now is the time to resist."

The cover letter, requesting signatures and other response to the Call stated that the signers of the Call "have pledged themselves to extend material and moral support to young men who are directly resisting the war." There followed a "box" containing requests for further signatures of "endorsement," contributions of "$__________ to support the work of RESIST. (Please make checks payable to RESIST.)," and volunteers interested in organizing or joining local groups "to support young men directly resisting the war." A similar "box" appeared in the Call itself, when printed.

At the press conference, in addition to discussing the Call, Goodman advanced his own paper, signed also by Coffin, along strikingly similar lines, entitled "Civil Disobedience Against the War" (hereinafter Civil Disobedience). It announced that the purpose of the signers was to "take away from the government the support and bodies it needs" and contained the following:

> The draft law commands that we shall not aid, abet or counsel men to refuse the draft. But as a group of the clergy has recently said . . . when young men refuse to allow their conscience to be violated by an unjust law and a criminal war, then it is necessary for their elders—their teachers, ministers, friends—to make clear their commitment, in conscience, to *aid, abet and counsel* them against conscription. Most of us have already done this privately. Now publicly we will demonstrate, side by side with these young men, our determination to continue to do so. (emphasis in original)

Goodman described the Call as a first step, and said that further activity was to follow. He announced a demonstration to be held in Washington October 20, as an act of "direct creative resistance," at which time draft cards surrendered at turns-ins that had been planned for October 16 would be delivered to the Attorney General. This announcement, as both conceded, was the result of a prearrangement with Coffin. . . .

Spock argues that there was no "agreement among leaders of an integrated political group. . . . [T]his case presents no more than the publicly expressed coincidence of views on public affairs." No merit, however, lies in the suggestion that there must be a cohesiveness in the group beyond the confines of the agreement itself. See Direct Sales Co. v. United States [319 U.S. 703 (1943)]; cf. United States v. Falcone, 1940, 311 U.S. 205. In the light of all the circumstances the jury was not obliged, in considering the question of agreement, to find a mere coincidence in the appearance of several speakers on the same platform. See Fraina v. United States. . . .

The Call was not what is known in law as an integrated document, limited to the four corners of the instrument. The jury could properly infer that it could not occur in the abstract, with no parents, and no active participants in a joint undertaking. We hold that they could look to Spock as one of the drafters, and to Spock and Coffin as two of the four signers of the solicitation letter, and in the light of the press conference held to publicize the Call in which Goodman took a prominent part, they could find that Goodman included himself as an active member. The evidence disclosed more than parallel conduct, see United States v. Bufalino, 2 Cir., 1960, 285 F.2d 408, 414-415; rather there are several instances of concerted activity from which the jury could infer an agreement.

[The court, to limit the effect of defining agreement so broadly (and to give expression some extra protection), added a requirement that a person must have specific intent to adhere to the illegal acts to be guilty of conspiracy.]

. . . When the alleged agreement is both bifarious and political within the shadow of the First Amendment, we hold that an individual's specific intent to adhere to the illegal portions may be shown in one of three ways: by the individual defendant's prior or subsequent unambiguous statements; by the individual defendant's subsequent commission of the very illegal act contemplated by the agreement; or by the individual defendant's subsequent legal act if that act is "clearly undertaken for the specific purpose of rendering effective the later illegal activity which is advocated." Scales v. United States, 367 U.S. at 234, 81 S. Ct. at 1488.

Application of such a standard should forcefully answer the defendant's protests that conviction of any of them would establish criminal responsibility of all of the many hundreds of persons who signed the Call. Even if the Call included illegal objectives, there is a wide gap between signing a document such as the Call and demonstrating one's personal attachment to illegality. Of greater importance, it responds to the legitimate apprehension of the amicus that the evil must be separable from the good without inhibiting legitimate association in an orderly society. . . .

[The court ultimately ordered an acquittal for Spock and Ferber but not Goodman and Coffin.]

[Circuit Judge Coffin (unrelated to the defendant) dissented:]

I would grant acquittals to all appellants, since, in my view, whatever substantive crimes of aiding, abetting, and counseling, or whatever more specific conspiracies may have been committed, the crime of conspiracy, as charged in the indictment, was not. To apply conspiracy doctrine to these cases is, in my view, not compelled by conspiracy precedents, not consistent with First Amendment principles, not required to deal effectively with the hazard to public security, and not capable of discriminating application as between the culpable and the innocent. . . .

My starting point is the inquiry: how far has the application of conspiracy doctrine reached into the arena of overt associations involving the expression of opinion on public issues? Do reason and authority compel its application to a wholly open, amorphous, and shifting association, having a broad focus of interest in changing public policy, and encompassing a wide spectrum of purposes, legal and illegal? . . .

In the case of public "conspiracies" in the field of opinion, however, the historic rationale for prosecuting the instigators of a group effort loses much of its force. The fact that the group initially places itself at the mercy of the public marketplace of ideas, risking disapproval, recommends that it have the protection of the First Amendment in its effort to gain approval. That a public "agreement" has been arrived at is not so much the genesis of the undertaking or a key to identifying masterminds as it is the manifestation of common concern. There is no possibility of taking society by surprise. There is no difficulty in ascertaining the activists who bear watching. . . .

[W]e face here something quite different from an indictment for an overt promotion of a specific event for an overriding illegal purpose. Here we confront a "conspiracy" where (1) the effort was completely public; (2) the issues were all in the public domain; (3) the group was ill-defined, shifting, with many affiliations; (4) the purposes in the "agreement" are both legal and illegal; and (5) the need for additional evidence to inculcate—notwithstanding the absence of a statutory requirement for an overt act—is recognized.

There is no legal precedent for applying the conspiracy theory to such an effort. This is, to my knowledge, the first attempt to use conspiracy as a prosecutorial device in such circumstances. The attempt to distill the several individual lessons taught by prior cases, mostly old, and combine them in such a case as this is not to apply precedents but to extend them. I would not—for the first time—grant this weapon to the government in this kind of case without the alternative assurance that hazards to individual rights would not be increased or that the interest in the nation's well-being and security cannot be as well served in less repressive ways. So viewing conspiracy law, I ask whether there are hazards to free expression of opinion in extending conspiracy to the cases at bar. The court has attempted to be scrupulously fair and sensitive to the possibility of abuse of the conspiracy weapon. It carefully rejects the use of "the Call" to jeopardize its signers without the proof of specific intent. And equally carefully it delimits the ways in which specific intent can be established: (1) proof of prior or subsequent unambiguous statements; (2) proof of commission of illegal acts; (3) proof of subsequent legal acts clearly undertaken for rendering effective the advocated illegal action.

By so proceeding, the court goes far to depriving the "agreement" of significance. Indeed, it upholds the indictment as to only one of the original four signers of the "Call" and acquits another original signer. But the evil is that such a document is pregnant with any significance at all. . . .

Notes and Questions

1. Would Judge Coffin feel the same way if the "Call" had advocated some form of violence, albeit for political reasons? How can one draw the line on when a charge of conspiracy in the political area is appropriate?

2. One commentator[15] has written:

Much of the difficulty in grappling with the concept of conspiracy to commit a speech crime is a function of the almost total failure of the courts to distinguish between the possible uses of the charge: between conspiracy framed as an inchoate offense before any illegal speech has occurred and its use as a device to prosecute for past illegal utterances. The leading cases involve (or the courts seem to assume they involve) illegal incitement or advocacy which has already occurred, thus suggesting that the conspiracy allegation is relied upon to charge complicity in another completed offense. Nonetheless, the decisions for the most part treat and justify their reliance on conspiracy as if it were being used as an inchoate offense.

So conceived, there is a deep-seated conflict between traditional conspiracy doctrine and the law of free speech. As noted, conspiracy alone requires only agreement, intent, and illegal purpose. When speech is involved, however, the first amendment requires more. There must be a sufficient governmental interest to warrant suppression. Even then, only advocacy of action, actual incitement itself, may be barred. Finally, *some* measure must be taken of the reality of the threat posed by the challenged speech.

When the two doctrines are fused in the context of speech-conspiracy, one would suppose that the constitutional demands would be read to override the more elastic and far-reaching common law concepts—that conspiracy doctrine would be strictly measured against first amendment requirements and the application of traditional conspiracy rules either barred or neatly tailored to preclude intrusion into prohibited areas. This has not been the case. Instead, the courts have created a patchwork. Providing little by way of analysis, they have treated the usual criminal conspiracy rules—developed in other contexts—as largely transferrable to speech cases. With the exception of imprecations about the need to find specific intent, the decisions have done little more than prescribe a meld of basically incompatible legal concepts, leaving both first amendment and conspiracy rules to a dangerous and inarticulate reconciliation in practice.

By definition, proof of criminal conspiracy is complete, and conviction warranted, without any showing of illegal action beyond the agreement itself. Thus, in the case of an alleged conspiracy to incite, for example, there would be no need to show that the defendants delivered themselves of any illegal words; the existence of the combined intent to do so would suffice. Given the fact of agreement, there would be no occasion to await the apprehended danger—prosecution could be initiated before any inflammatory speech were made, before any "illegal" tract or pamphlet were written or published, and before any threatening demonstration were held. Even where the applicable criminal conspiracy statute calls for proof of an overt act, there is no requirement that it be the illegal incitement itself or, indeed, that it be illegal conduct of any kind.

Respect for first amendment standards would seem to require that criminality turn on more than a bare prediction of both the nature and probable consequences of words not yet uttered. Even where speech has crystallized the difficulties of reconciling the first amendment and statutes proscribing advocacy

15. Filvaroff, Conspiracy and the First Amendment, 121 U. Pa. L. Rev. 189, 198-200 (1972).

are inordinate. One would not expect the courts to compound these difficulties and to undertake appraisal of projected or future advocacy. Yet, with but slight variation, the language of speech-conspiracy decisions appears to assume that this may be done.

G. THE PARTIES TO AND OBJECTS OF CONSPIRACY

UNITED STATES v. FOX

United States Court of Appeals, Third Circuit
130 F.2d 56 (1942)

GOODRICH, Circuit Judge.

The appellant, William Fox, was indicted with two other persons, J. Warren Davis and Morgan S. Kaufman, charged with conspiracy to obstruct justice and to defraud the United States. The indictment contained the usual residuary clause charging conspiracy of the named conspirators "with divers other persons whose names are to the Grand Jurors unknown. . . ." The appellant entered a guilty plea and became a witness for the United States at the trial. The first jury, being unable to agree, was discharged without a verdict. Subsequently, a second trial was had which again resulted in a disagreement and this jury was likewise dismissed without a verdict. The appellant was a witness for the government in the second trial also. Sometime thereafter a nolle prosequi was entered upon the application of the government as to the defendants, Davis and Kaufman. The appellant both before and subsequently to the nolle prosequi moved for leave to withdraw his plea of guilty. . . . The District Judge refused both requests and his action is assigned as error upon the appeal.

The case for the appellant in this court . . . concerns the doctrines of the law relating to conspiracy to the facts of his case. . . .

The law of conspiracy has been nearly as proliferative as that of larceny in the development of technical doctrine. The question in this case is limited, however, to the growth of one branch. By definition, conspiracy is a group offense; therefore, two or more people must participate to create the crime. Then it is held that where an indictment for conspiracy names only two, an acquittal or reversal as to one is an acquittal or reversal as to the other. This is no doubt the law announced by the majority of the decisions, including the federal courts, although the New York court says the "contrary view is arguable." This result, however, is not to be expanded into a general "all or none" rule. The conviction of some alleged conspirators does not fall because others named are acquitted, even though the conviction of the others is logically required for the finding of guilty of those held. Nor is the conviction of one alleged conspirator vitiated because of the possible later acquittal of co-defendants not yet tried or even apprehended. Furthermore, one may be convicted and punished for a conspiracy even though his fellow conspirators may be immune from prosecution because of the immunity attaching to representatives of foreign governments, the Fifth Circuit declaring that "The rule that the acquittal of all save one of alleged conspirators results in the acquittal of all applies to acquittals on the merits."

The appellant does not contend that his alleged fellow conspirators were acquitted, but does argue that the nolle prosequi puts an end to charges made by this indictment and so should be treated as having the same effect as an acquittal. This point will be taken up later. Argument for the appellee answers it in part by reference to the charge in the so-called residuary clause alleging a conspiracy with persons unknown. This allegation affords a basis for determining what evidence is admissible and what evidence will support conviction when one of two named defendants is found not guilty. . . . "[A] conspiracy may be established, even though one of the two parties named . . . is not a member, if the evidence shows that there are other persons in existence one or more of whom were parties to such conspiracy." The evidence which was introduced in the two trials referred to is not before this Court. It appears from the affidavits in the record before us that there is, in that evidence, no testimony with regard to a conspiracy participated in by any persons other than the named defendants. The attorney for the appellee, with commendable frankness, stated at the argument that there was no such evidence. We think that this constitutes an abandonment of the residuary clause of the indictment by the government and that the clause is without significance in the case at this stage.

We come then to the actual legal question presented in this appeal. Suppose there is a conviction of one named conspirator and a nolle prosequi as to the other and only two are named? The South Carolina decision in State v. Jackson, 1876, 7 S.C. 283, 24 Am. Rep. 476, squarely holds that a conviction under such circumstances cannot be sustained. This was approved obiter in the Second Circuit and approved, but the question left open, by the Fourth Circuit. In an earlier federal case it was held in the charge of the trial judge that any one of those prosecuted could be found guilty of a conspiracy with another, as to whom a nolle prosequi had been entered, although his co-defendants were acquitted.[16] The result of a conviction of one and a nolle prosequi as to the others of named conspirators is not answered by any authority which we are bound to follow. The South Carolina decision is certainly close to the point. Contra is the Rindskopf case, although the matter appears not to have been given much consideration. The dicta in the other opinions are not, as is obvious from the context, the deliberate thought of the courts upon the point.

We think that to treat a convicted conspirator whose fellow conspirator's

16. United States v. Rindskopf, D.C.W.D. Wis. 1874, 27 Fed. Cas. No. 16, 165.

case has ended by a nolle prosequi like the case where one is convicted and the other is acquitted goes too far. The analogy overlooks the difference between an acquittal and a nolle prosequi. The courts seem to have treated the acquittal in this connection as though the jury had expressly found that the defendant did not participate in the conspiracy charged. Therefore, the defendant who is convicted stands in the situation of having been found to conspire by himself, a manifest impossibility by the definition of conspiracy. One may criticize that rule as being founded upon a false premise, for a not guilty verdict is not necessarily a declaration of innocence by the jury, but simply an indication of lack of proof beyond a reasonable doubt. Be that as it may, the acquittal of the alleged conspirator does free the accused from further prosecution for the offense charged. The nolle prosequi does not. As in the case of disagreement of a jury, "The prisoner has not been convicted or acquitted, and may again be put upon his defense." [United States v. Perez, 9 Wheat. 579 (1824).] It is not a bar to a second indictment covering the same matter, although it does terminate the proceedings in which the nolle prosequi occurs. It is a very considerable step which has to be taken to apply the rule as to acquittal to the termination of proceeding by a nolle prosequi. We are not called upon to take it either by reason or authority. . . .

The judgment of the District Court is affirmed.

Notes and Questions

1. Jim and Mike, agree to commit a crime. Mike is not convicted of conspiracy because: 1) He is an undercover policeman; or 2) he is a private citizen, but never intended that the crime be committed; or 3) he has some special excuse—he is insane, underage, or a foreign ambassador, not subject to the criminal law of the United States. Can Jim be guilty? Can he "agree" by himself? Should it matter why Mike is not guilty?

The common older view of the courts—the "bilateral" view—is as follows:

> Conspiracy is the agreement of two or more to effect an unlawful purpose. Two people cannot agree unless they both intend to carry out the purpose which is stated to be the object of their combination. Therefore there is no agreement, and consequently no conspiracy, where one of the two never intends to carry out the unlawful purpose.[17]

Hence, if there were no one who could be legally responsible for agreeing with Jim, he could not be guilty of conspiracy. More recently, though, a unilateral view of conspiracy has been emerging based on the view that:

> The fact that, unknown to a man who wishes to enter a conspiracy to commit some criminal purpose, the other person has no intention of fulfilling that pur-

17. Friedman, Mens Rea in Conspiracy, 19 Mod. L. Rev. 276 (1956).

pose, ought to be irrelevant as long as the first man does intend to fulfill it if he can because a man who believes he is conspiring to commit a crime and wishes to conspire to commit a crime has a guilty mind and has done all in his power to plot the commission of an unlawful purpose.[18]

The Model Penal Code §5.03(1), adopted the unilateral approach:

> A person is guilty of conspiracy with another person or persons to commit a crime if with the purpose of promoting or facilitating its commission he:
>
> (a) agrees with such other person or persons that they or one or more of them will engage in conduct which constitutes such crime or an attempt or solicitation to commit such crime; or
>
> (b) agrees to aid such other person or persons in the planning or commission of such crime or of an attempt or solicitation to commit such crime.

In Comment 2 to Section 5.03(1), the drafters explained their purpose:

> Attention is directed to each individual's culpability by framing the definition in terms of the conduct which suffices to establish the liability of any given actor, rather than the conduct of a group of which he is charged to be a part—an approach which in this comment we have designated "unilateral."
>
> One consequence of this approach is to make it immaterial to the guilt of a conspirator whose culpability has been established that the person or all of the persons with whom he conspired have not been or cannot be convicted.

Is the unilateral approach consistent with the purposes of conspiracy law? To what extent has Jim's chance of success in carrying out a criminal act been increased by the agreement?

Consider the following facts:

> On March 16, 1974, defendant stated to his cousin, Roger Zobel, that he wanted to kill his mother, Mrs. Marlin Olson, and that he wanted Zobel's help. He would pay him $125,000 over the years, money defendant would get from his father after his mother was dead. Zobel, the key witness against defendant at his trial on the charge of conspiracy, testified that at no time did he ever intend to participate in the murder, but that he discussed the matter with defendant on that and subsequent occasions and acted as if he intended to participate in the plan. On March 18, Zobel contacted the police and told them of defendant's plan and they later told him to continue to cooperate with defendant. The plan, which became definite in some detail as early as March 20, was for Zobel to go to the Olson farmhouse on Saturday, March 23, when defendant's father was at the weekly livestock auction. Since defendant's mother was Zobel's aunt, Zobel could gain entrance readily. The idea was for Zobel to break her neck, hide her body in his automobile trunk, and then attach bricks to it and throw it in a nearby river after dark. Later it developed that defendant's father might not go

18. Id. at 282, 283.

to the sale on Saturday, so a plan was developed whereby defendant would feign car trouble, call his father for help, then signal Zobel when the father was on his way. Police followed defendant on Saturday when he left his apartment and observed him make a number of telephone calls. In one of these he called his father and told him he was having car trouble and asked him to come and help him pay the bill. In a call to Zobel, which was taped, defendant told Zobel that his father was coming and that Zobel should proceed with the plan. Shortly thereafter, police arrested defendant.

The Minnesota Supreme Court adopted the unilateral approach in this case. State v. St. Christopher, 232 N.W.2d 798 (1975).

Instead of the unilateral view, would it be better to say that in cases like *St. Christopher* the defendant is guilty of *attempted* conspiracy?

2. To what extent is the above problem related to that in the *Fox* case? The court there assumed that if Fox's alleged co-conspirators had all been acquitted at his trial, he would have had to be acquitted as well. Does this make sense, even if one does not adopt a unilateral view? Why should the jury not be able to exercise its discretion and give one conspirator a break by acquitting him or her without having to do the same for the other conspirator?

3. In certain cases, one of the persons who agrees to commit a crime is a protected party and not subject to prosecution. For example, in many states, a "bookie," the person who accepts bets, commits a crime but his clients do not; and a man who has intercourse with a woman under the age of consent is guilty of statutory rape but the woman is not.

In Gebardi v. United States, 287 U.S. 112 (1932) the following occurred:

> [A] man and a woman, not then husband and wife, were indicted for conspiring together to transport the woman from one state to another for the purpose of engaging in sexual intercourse with the man. At the trial without a jury there was evidence from which the court could have found that the petitioners had engaged in illicit sexual relations in the course of each of the journeys alleged; that the man purchased the railway tickets for both petitioners for at least one journey, and that in each instance the woman, in advance of the purchase of the tickets, consented to go on the journey and did go on it voluntarily for the specified immoral purpose.

Section 2 of the Mann Act (violation of which was charged as the object of the conspiracy) states:

> Any person who shall knowingly transport or cause to be transported, or aid or assist in obtaining transportation for, or in transporting in interstate or foreign commerce . . . any woman or girl for the purpose of prostitution or debauchery or for any other immoral purpose (commits a punishable act).

The Supreme Court held that the female defendant was not guilty of violating the Mann Act, as she only consented to, but did not "aid or assist" in obtaining her transportation. The Court went on to hold that the female defendant could not be convicted for conspiracy with the man to violate the

Mann Act. The Court reasoned that since Congress did not intend a consenting woman to be punished for violating the Mann Act, she could not be punished by means of a conspiracy charge: "The criminal object [involved] the agreement of the woman to her transportation by the man, which [was] the very conspiracy charged." As a result of the Court's analysis the male defendant was found guilty of violating the Mann Act, but not guilty of conspiracy to violate it.

Could a prostitute be found guilty of conspiring with a client to commit prostitution? If an unmarried person consented to adultery with a married person, where the latter alone is guilty of the substantive offense, can either or both be guilty of conspiracy to commit adultery? What does *Gebardi* say? Does it seem right that a person is not guilty of conspiracy if her co-conspirator is a protected party? Notice that under the unilateral approach, many of these problems disappear.

An important exception to the principle that a conspiracy is a distinct crime from the target substantive offense is the so-called Wharton's Rule. As stated by the scholar after whom it is named:

> [W]hen, to the idea of an offense, plurality of agents is logically necessary, conspiracy, which assumes the voluntary accession of a person to a crime of such a nature that it is aggravated by a plurality of agents, cannot be maintained.[19]

Wharton's Rule

Thus, the two parties to a crime of adultery, incest, bigamy, or duelling cannot be convicted of both the substantive crime and the conspiracy: The definition of the substantive crime assumes that at least two people will agree to commit it, so it would be unfair "double-counting" for the state to charge conspiracy as well.

But what if, for example, the alleged conspiracy consists of more than the number of parties needed to commit the target offense, as where *A*, *B*, *C*, and *D* succeed in arranging a duel between *A* and *B*? Consider the following facts:

> Each of eight petitioners was charged with conspiring to violate and violating a federal gambling statute making it a crime for five or more persons to conduct, finance, manage, supervise, direct, or own a gambling business prohibited by state law. Each petitioner was convicted of both the conspiracy and the substantive offense. On appeal the petitioners argued that the conspiracy should merge into the substantive offense because the substantive offense necessarily requires the participation of a number of petitioners for its commission.

The Supreme Court, in Iannelli v. United States, 420 U.S. 770 (1975), held that Wharton's Rule did not apply to these facts, stating:

> The conduct proscribed by [the federal statute] is significantly different from the offenses to which the Rule traditionally has been applied. Unlike the

19. 2 Wharton, Criminal Law §1604 (12th ed. 1932).

> consequences of the classic Wharton's Rule offenses, the harm attendant upon the commission of the substantive offense is not restricted to the parties to the agreement. Large-scale gambling activities seek to elicit the participation of additional persons—the bettors—who are parties neither to the conspiracy nor to the substantive offense that results from it. Moreover, the parties prosecuted for the conspiracy need not be the same persons who are prosecuted for commission of the substantive offense. An endeavor as complex as a large-scale gambling enterprise might involve persons who have played appreciably different roles, and whose level of culpability varies significantly. It might, therefore, be appropriate to prosecute the owners and organizers of large-scale gambling operations both for the conspiracy and for the substantive offense but to prosecute the lesser participants only for the substantive offense. Nor can it fairly be maintained that agreements to enter into large-scale gambling activities are not likely to generate additional agreements to engage in other criminal endeavors.

Do you agree with the Court's analysis? Would petitioner's argument have been stronger if they had been only five in number?

4. At common law a husband and wife could not be charged as conspirators with each other. The reason was that a husband and wife were seen as one person in law, having one will, while conspiracy required at least two people. In United States v. Dege, 364 U.S. 51 (1960), a husband and wife were indicted for conspiring to bring goods into the United States illicitly. In response to the argument that a husband and wife could not be charged with conspiracy, the Court said:

> For this Court now to act on the medieval view that husband and wife "are esteemed but as one Person in Law, and are presumed to have but one Will" would indeed be "blind imitation of the past." It would require us to disregard the vast changes in the status of woman—the extension of her rights and correlative duties—whereby a wife's legal submission to her husband has been wholly wiped out, not only in the English-speaking world generally but emphatically so in this country. . . . Suffice it to say that we cannot infuse in the conspiracy statute a fictitious attribution to Congress of regard for the medieval notion of woman's submissiveness to the benevolent coercive powers of a husband in order to relieve her of her obligation of obedience to an unqualifiedly expressed Act of Congress by regarding her as a person whose legal personality is merged in that of her husband, making the two one.

Chief Justice Warren, in a dissent joined by Justices Black and Whittaker stated that the husband-wife conspiracy doctrine was well established in the common law and should only have been repudiated by Congress. The dissent went on to state:

> A wife, simply by virtue of the intimate life she shares with her husband, might easily perform acts that would technically be sufficient to involve her in a criminal conspiracy with him, but which might be far removed from the arm's-length agreement typical of that crime. It is not a medieval mental quirk or an attitude

> "unnourished by sense" to believe that husbands and wives should not be subjected to such a risk, or that such a possibility should not be permitted to endanger the confidentiality of the marriage relationship. [T]he concept of the "oneness" of a married couple may reflect an abiding belief that the communion between husband and wife is such that their actions are not always to be regarded by the criminal law as if there were no marriage.

Do you agree with the dissent? Does a conspiracy charge pose a danger to the confidentiality of a marriage relationship? Is the dissent attempting to protect the husband, the wife, or the marriage?

5. Far more litigated than the issue of whether a particular person can be guilty of conspiracy on the basis of her agreement is the problem of determining the extent of the conspiratorial relation—both as to its objectives, where more than one crime is to be committed, and as to its membership, where different people participate in the commissions of different crimes.

One commentator[20] has laid out the problems faced by law enforcement in grappling with the amorphous law in this case:

> Suppose *A* and *B* steal an automobile and sell it to *C,* the owner of a chopshop that fronts as a legitimate automotive repair business. Then a week later, *B* and *D* burglarize a home and sell stolen jewelry to *C.* In addition to the substantive offenses of motor vehicle theft and burglary, does this activity constitute one criminal conspiracy among all three thieves and the fence, or two separate conspiracies, with *A, B,* and *C* participating in a stolen auto conspiracy, and *B, C,* and *D* participating in a burglary conspiracy? From a conspiratorial point of view, does it matter whether the evidence tends to establish one large conspiracy, as opposed to two smaller ones? If it does matter, how does an investigator gather evidence showing one large conspiracy?
>
> The single vs. multiple conspiracy issue raised by these questions is one of the most perplexing problems facing courts in criminal conspiracy cases. The investigation of this crime can be particularly cumbersome when the evidence establishes a large criminal organization with several persons actively participating in a variety of unlawful acts, while others appear only on the periphery of the enterprise. . . .
>
> **Charging a Single Conspiracy**
>
> The evidence may suggest one overall conspiracy, while proof at trial establishes the existence of two or more. It has long been held that in such a case, the variance between the charge and the proof may "affect the substantial rights" of the accused. . . .
>
> [I]n 1946, the Supreme Court identified [a] . . . constitutional guarantee available to attack single conspiracy prosecutions. . . . [T]he leading conspiracy case of Kotteakos v. United States [328 U.S. 750 (1946)], [involved] 32 defendants [who] were charged in a single conspiracy prosecution for defrauding the Federal Government. The defendants used the same loan broker to assist them to

20. Campane, Chains, Wheels, and the Single Conspiracy, FBI Law Enforcement Bulletin, Aug., Sept. 1981, 24-31.

induce various financial institutions and the Federal Housing Administration to grant credit, loans, and advances for housing renovation and modernization. . . . [T]he loan applications contained false and fraudulent information because the proceeds were intended to be used for purposes other than [those] required by the National Housing Act. Seven defendants were eventually found guilty.

The Circuit Court of Appeals believed the trial judge was plainly wrong in supposing that upon the evidence, there could be a single conspiracy, for no connection was shown between any of the defendants other than their mutual use of the same loan broker. The appellate court believed the trial judge should have dismissed the indictment for this material variance between the proof shown and the pleadings, but nevertheless held the error to be nonprejudicial, since guilt was so manifest that it was "proper" to join the conspiracies, and "to reverse the conviction would be a miscarriage of justice." . . .

The Supreme Court disagreed with the lower court and reversed the convictions because due process required the defendant's guilt be proved individually and personally. Although the Court was emphatic in pointing out the necessity of particularized case-by-case analysis on the issue of the materiality of a variance, the opinion showed a shift in emphasis from . . . the criteria of notice of charges and surprise to the equally important factor of transference of prejudicial evidence.

The court recognized that when many conspire, they invite mass trial, but in such cases every effort must be made to individualize and safeguard each defendant in his relation to the mass. The Court pointed out:

> The dangers of transference of guilt from one to another across the line separating conspiracies, subconsciously or otherwise, are so great that no one really can say prejudice to substantial rights has not taken place. . . . That right, in each instance, was the right not to be tried en masse for the conglomeration of distinct and separate offenses committed by others as shown by this record. . . .

In a more recent case, the Second Circuit Court of Appeals in United States v. Bertolotti [529 F.2d 149 (2d Cir. 1975)] reversed the single conspiracy conviction of seven individuals for prejudicial variance when it held that the evidence proved multiple conspiracies. The court cited one item of evidence as a specific example of prejudice suffered by the defendants, as well as an illustration of the inherent dangers of combining unrelated criminal acts under the roof of an alleged single conspiracy. As a part of its investigation, the district attorney's office placed a court-authorized wiretap on the telephone of one suspect. Tapes of 55 intercepted calls were played to the jury and introduced as evidence of narcotics negotiations between two defendants. None of the remaining defendants either participated or was mentioned in any of the 55 taped conversations. As a result, the court stated:

> The prejudicial effect, however, of requiring the jury to spend two entire days listening to obviously shocking and inflammatory discussions about assault, kidnapping, guns and narcotics cannot be underestimated. No defendant ought to have a jury which is considering his guilt or innocence hear evidence of this sort absent proof connecting him with the subject matter discussed.

After a review of the evidence as [a] whole, the court concluded:

> The possibilities of spill-over effect from testimony of these transactions are patent when the number of defendants and the volume of evidence are weighed against the

> ability of the jury to give each defendant the individual consideration our system requires. . . .

Constitutional considerations aside, it tries the patience of a court for a prosecutor to complicate criminal prosecutions of multiple defendants and the inevitable appeals with a joint trial, single conspiracy charge. In United States v. Sperling [566 F.2d 1323 (2d Cir. 1974)], the Federal Government successfully indicted 28 defendants in a single conspiracy prosecution to purchase, process, and resell narcotics from 1971 to 1973. Two defendants were acquitted, two pled guilty, eight were unavailable for trial, three were acquitted by the jury, and two had their cases severed for separate trial.

The convictions of the other eleven defendants were upheld on appeal, but the court warned:

> We take this occasion to caution the government with respect to future prosecutions that it may be unnecessarily exposing itself to reversal by continuing the indictment format reflected in this case. While it is obviously impractical and inefficient for the government to try conspiracy cases one defendant at a time, it has become all too common for the government to bring indictments against a dozen or more defendants and endeavor to force as many of them as possible to trial in the same proceeding on the claim of a single conspiracy when the criminal acts could be more reasonably regarded as two or more conspiracies, perhaps with a link at the top. Little time was saved by the government's having prosecuted the offenses here involved in one, rather than two conspiracy trials. On the contrary, many serious problems were created at the trial level, including the inevitable debate about the single conspiracy charges, which can prove seriously detrimental to the government itself.

Charging Multiple Conspiracies

Adherence to the *Sperling* court's admonition, which suggests prosecution for multiple conspiracies in successive trials or multiple counts in one trial, presents equally hazardous constitutional problems.

The fifth amendment to the Constitution provides, in part, that no person shall be put in jeopardy of life or limb twice for the same offense. This guarantee against double jeopardy protects against a second prosecution for the same offense after acquittal or after conviction, and it protects against multiple punishment for the same offense. The prohibition is not just against being twice punished. It was designed to protect an individual from being subjected to the hazards of trial and possible conviction more than once for an alleged offense.

The same offense requirement becomes particularly significant with conspiracy cases. A prosecutor's attempt to try and convict an individual at successive trials for taking part in two successive conspiracies, when only one overall conspiracy is proved, would result in a conviction for the same offense twice. This prohibited prosecutorial procedure is called fragmentation, and a defendant would be able to bar the second prosecution at the outset by demonstrating that the activities encompassing the allegation were part of one overall conspiracy for which the defendant had already been put in jeopardy in a former prosecution by the same governmental entity.

United States v. Palerma [410 F.2d 468 (7th Cir. 1969)] is a case in point. Joseph Amabile was associated with Melrose Park Plumbing, a subcontractor for the Riley Management Company which built various apartment building complexes in suburban Chicago from 1962 to 1965. He was tried and convicted in Federal court for conspiring to extort $48,500 from the management company by threatening Riley with work stoppages and physical violence, and in doing so, interfering with interstate shipments of construction materials.

In a second prosecution, Amabile was tried and convicted for extorting an additional $64,000 from Riley on a later subcontracted construction project in which Amabile conspired with others, including various public officials in Northlake, Ill. On appeal, Amabile successfully argued his participation in one continuous agreement to extort money from Riley whenever his company was Riley's plumbing subcontractor. The Court held:

> Although the methods of obtaining money from Riley on the various projects may have been different, the overall objective was the same. . . . Even though the incident occurred over a period of years, the overall agreement constituted a continuing conspiracy against Riley. Since Amabile has already been tried and convicted of conspiring to extort money from Riley, Amabile's Fifth Amendment rights were violated by placing him in jeopardy twice for the same criminal act.

Even if the prosecution is able to show multiple conspiracies, a defendant may argue that the prosecutor has overreached and has resorted unfairly to multiple charges and successive trials in order to accomplish indirectly what the double jeopardy clause prohibits. The defendant will attempt to show that the prosecution is trying to wear him out with a succession of trials when the evidence suggests . . . only one prosecution. The question is whether such course has led to fundamental procedural unfairness prohibited by the 5th and 14th amendments, and this is determined by the facts of each case.

The prosecution may be able to avoid double jeopardy and due process claims by establishing evidence of multiple conspiracies, but United States v. Guido [597 F.2d 194 (9th Cir. 1979)] suggests an additional hurdle in the path to successful multiple conspiracy prosecutions. Two defendants pled guilty to Federal drug conspiracy charges in California and were subsequently convicted of similar charges in Arizona. On appeal, the defendants contended that their activities consisted of one conspiracy and the multiple convictions twice put them in jeopardy and deprived them of due process by subjecting them to piecemeal prosecutions. A Federal appellate court agreed that the evidence established only one conspiracy, but a strongly worded opinion devised a differing reasoning:

> Here the defendants were prosecuted twice for the same conspiracy due to the failure of the Arizona prosecutor to evaluate properly the prior California indictment. Guido and Boyle raise double jeopardy and due process claims, but we need not rely upon these constitutional safeguards since, under our supervisory power of the administration of criminal justice, the court has the authority to correct such unfairness.

Another form of fragmentation occurs in conspiracy prosecutions when a defendant is charged at one trial with multiple counts of conspiracy and the proof establishes a lesser number, or only one. The principal vice of this procedure is that it, too, may result in multiple punishment for participation in a single conspiracy. . . .

In Braverman v. United States [317 U.S. 49 (1942)], the defendants were indicted on seven counts, each charging a general conspiracy to violate separate sections of the Internal Revenue Code. The Supreme Court held that the defendants' manufacture and sale of untaxed alcohol was one conspiracy:

> The one agreement cannot be taken to be several agreements and hence several conspiracies because it envisages the violation of several statutes rather than one.

The common remedy for such unconstitutional fragmentation is fortunately less severe than the outright bar to the subsequent prosecution required in multiple trial fragmentation. The court will generally let the trial proceed and ignore the number of charges on which a defendant is subsequently convicted, and impose but a single sentence for the one conspiracy.

Defendants *A, B, C,* and *D,* the burglars, thieves, and fence in our hypothetical case, would thus be able to avail themselves of a variety of legitimate constitutional and equitable claims to defeat an attempt to prosecute them for their participation in either a single conspiracy or two separate conspiracies. A prosecutor may be able to avoid this potential dilemma and proceed with the more frequent and desired conspiracy prosecution if the results of the police officer's investigation are thorough enough to structure the unlawful agreement as either a wheel or a chain conspiracy.

Such structural descriptions are generally well-accepted by the courts, and part two of this article will present an analysis of these configurations and provide the police officer with some examples of the kind of evidence that can join the spokes to the hub of the wheel or weld the links to the chain so that *A, B, C,* and *D* may be jointly tried and successfully prosecuted in a single conspiracy prosecution.

The Party and Object Dimension

One difficulty with analyzing the evidence in conspiracy cases stems from the common law notion that the substance of the offense was the making of an agreement to commit a readily identifiable crime, such as robbery or murder. From this perspective, some courts are inclined to focus on what the individual co-conspirators agreed to. . . . [This is typified] by the case of United States v. Borelli [336 F.2d 376 (2d Cir. 1964)].

In *Borelli,* numerous defendants participated in narcotics transactions extending over a 9-year period, during the course of which some of the principals and sources of supply had changed. Nevertheless, all the defendants were convicted of participating in a single conspiracy. On appeal, a Federal court reversed, holding that the evidence may have suggested multiple conspiracies rather than the single one charged. The defendants were therefore entitled to an instruction requiring the jury to find what the agreements were as to each defendant. The court recognized that it is much more difficult to infer agreement from a series of drug smuggling operations than from the furnishing of guns to a prospective bank robber. This is especially true, the court noted, with numerous drug co-conspirators, where buyers are indifferent to their sources of supply and suppliers are indifferent to the identities of their customers:[21]

21. It may be helpful here to set out at greater length the comments of Judge Henry Friendly in *Borelli.*

> As applied to the long term operation of an illegal business, the common pictorial distinction between "chain" and spoke conspiracies can obscure as much as it clarifies. The

> Although it is usual and often necessary in conspiracy cases for the agreement to be proved by inferences from acts, the gist of the offense remains the agreement, and it is therefore essential to determine what kind of agreement or understanding existed as to each defendant. . . . The view that if the evidence warrants the finding that some defendants were parties to a single agreement to sell contraband for a nine-year period, it necessarily does so as to every defendant who has conspired with them at any time for any purpose, is thus a considerable oversimplification.

Most courts are more sympathetic to the threat posed to society by the kinds of crimes, like narcotics conspiracies, that require complex illegal businesses engaging in prolonged unlawful conduct. This more pragmatic point of view deals with the crime as a group of individuals and thus focuses on their overall operation or objectives rather than the individual acts of agreement. . . .

The U.S. Supreme Court recognized the validity of this perspective many years ago in the leading conspiracy case of Blumenthal v. United States [332

---

chain metaphor is indeed apt in that the links of a narcotics conspiracy are inextricably related to one another, from grower, through exporter and importer, to wholesaler, middleman, and retailer, each depending for his own success on the performance of all the others. But this simple picture tends to obscure that the links at either end are likely to consist of a number of persons who may have no reason to know that others are performing a role similar to theirs—in other words the extreme links of a chain conspiracy may have elements of the spoke conspiracy. Moreover, whatever the value of the chain concept where the problem is to trace a single operation from the start through its various phases to its successful conclusion, it becomes confusing when, over a long period of time, certain links continue to play the same role but with new counterparts, as where importers who regard their partnership as a single continuing one, having successfully distributed one cargo through *X* distributing organization, turn, years later, to moving another cargo obtained from a different source through *Y*. Thus, however reasonable the so-called presumption of continuity may be as to all the participants of a conspiracy which intends a single act, such as the robbing of a bank, or even as to the core of a conspiracy to import and resell narcotics, its force is diminished as to the outer links—buyers indifferent to their sources of supply and turning from one source to another, and suppliers equally indifferent to the identity of their customers.

The basic difficulty arises in applying the seventeenth century notion of conspiracy, where the gravamen of the offense was the making of an *agreement* to commit a readily identifiable crime or a series of crimes, such as murder or robbery, see Developments in the Law—Criminal Conspiracy, 72 Harv. L. Rev. 922, 923 (1959), to what in substance is the conduct of an illegal business over a period of years. There has been a tendency in such cases "to deal with the crime of conspiracy as though it were a group [of men] rather than an act" of agreement. See 72 Harv. L. Rev. at 934. Although it is usual and often necessary in conspiracy cases for the agreement to be proved by inference from acts, the gist of the offense remains the agreement, and it is therefore essential to determine what kind of agreement or understanding existed as to each defendant. It is a great deal harder to tell just *what* agreement can reasonably be inferred from the purchase, even the repeated purchase, of contraband, than from the furnishing of dynamite to prospective bank robbers or the exchange of worthless property for securities to be subsequently distributed. Purchase or sale of contraband may, of course, warrant the inference of an agreement going well beyond the particular transaction. A seller of narcotics in bulk knows that the purchasers will undertake to resell the goods over an uncertain period of time, and the circumstances may also warrant the inference that a supplier or a purchaser indicated a willingness to repeat. But a sale or a purchase scarcely constitutes a sufficient basis for inferring agreement to cooperate with the opposite parties for whatever period they continue to deal in this type of contraband, unless some such understanding is evidenced by other conduct which accompanies or supplements the transaction.

United States v. Borelli, 336 F.2d 376 at 383, 384.

U.S. 539 (1947)]. Five defendants were successfully convicted of participating in a single conspiracy to sell whiskey illegally. In support of the conviction, the Court summarized the bilateral point of view:

> For it is most often true, especially in broad schemes calling for the aid of many persons, that after discovery of enough [evidence] to show clearly the essence of the scheme and the identity of a number participating, the identity and the fact of participation of others remain undiscovered and undiscoverable. Secrecy and concealment are essential features of successful conspiracy. . . . Hence the law rightly gives room for allowing the conviction of those discovered upon showing sufficiently the essential nature of the plan and their connections with it, without requiring evidence of knowledge of all its details or the participation of others. . . .

The Bilateral Perspective

As a result of these divergent views and the possibility of a *Borelli*-like charge to the jury, a successful conspiracy prosecution may depend on the ability of the prosecutor to fashion the proof in such a way as to shift the court['s] and the jury's examination of the evidence away from the agreement of each participant and toward the organization formed to commit the crime. Many courts are willing to accept the bilateral approach and charge the jury to recognize the continuance of a single dominant plan, despite changes in personnel, location, victims, or methods of operation. This shift in focus is often accomplished successfully when the evidence is presented in a form that structures the group's activity as either a chain or wheel conspiracy.

Kotteakos v. United States [supra], decided in 1946, and *Blumenthal*, decided a year later, are the two Supreme Court cases which are generally recognized for their acceptance of such structural metaphors to distinguish the single from the multiple conspiracy.

The Wheel

When a number of persons (the spokes) are engaged in a criminal conspiracy with the same individual or group (the hub), a successful single conspiracy prosecution will depend upon whether the spokes can be drawn together (rim around the wheel) into a single agreement.

The hub generally views his dealings with the spokes as part of a single enterprise, but a spoke may be concerned merely with his own actions, unless it can be shown that the existence and cooperation of other spokes were or should have been known to him. Failing such proof, a court will hold that the other spokes remain individual members of multiple conspiracies. Crimes such as bribery, theft, and fraud particularly lend themselves to a wheel analysis.

In *Kotteakos*, the president of a lumber company, one Brown, having experience in obtaining loans under the National Housing Act (NHA), undertook to act as a broker for others who fraudulently applied to various financial institutions for NHA modernization loans. The undisputed proof showed separate and independent unlawful agreements between eight applicants and Brown. The applicants' only connection with each other was their mutual use of the same broker.

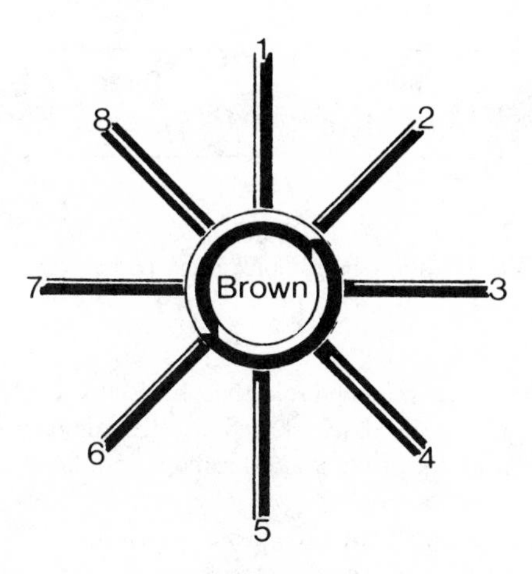

FIGURE 1
The Rimless Wheel
No Single Conspiracy (*Kotteakos*)

The Federal Government claimed the conspiratorial pattern was that of separate spokes meeting at a common center, but the Supreme Court agreed with the Federal appellate court that without the rim of the wheel to enclose the spokes, the proof made out a case of several conspiracies, notwithstanding [the fact that] only one was charged in the indictment. (See fig. 1.)

Kotteakos . . . suggest[s] that the nature of the crime itself generally precludes a wheel analysis. A year later, explaining its conclusion in *Kotteakos,* the Supreme Court pointed out that no two of the fraudulent loan agreements were tied together as stages in the formation of a larger all-inclusive combination, and no spoke gained from the fact that others were involved. Because each loan was an end it itself, the co-conspirators did not know or need to know of each others' existence or involvement:

> The conspiracies therefore were distinct and disconnected, not parts of a larger general scheme. . . . There was no drawing of all together in a single, overall comprehensive plan.

The Chain

Conspiracies suggested by the chain configuration relate to agreements between sellers, middlemen, wholesalers, retailers, and ultimate purchasers. Whether the purpose of the conspiracy is the sale of such commodities as narcotics, counterfeit money, or liquor, the object is to place the goods into the hands of the paying consumer. No one in the chain profits unless each does his part (connects the links) to supply the buyer.

In *Blumenthal,* two whiskey distributors and three of their salesmen were convicted in a single conspiracy prosecution for selling 2,000 cases of whiskey at prices in excess of the ceiling set by the Federal Office of Price Administration. The two distributors operated the Francisco Company as a front for a hidden

FIGURE 2
The Classic Chain Conspiracy (*Blumenthal*)

owner. The three company salesmen sold the whiskey to tavern owners at a price barely above cost, plus a kickback shared by the salesmen, distributors, and hidden owner. The price for product and kickback combined exceeded the mandated ceiling.

Although evidence [at] trial proved an unlawful agreement between the hidden owner and distributors, the three salesmen claimed they did not know of the unknown owner's existence or his part in the plan. The government's case, they argued, proved one conspiracy between the owner and distributors and one between the salesmen and distributors. As such, testimony about the conspiracy between the owner and distributors was inadmissible against them as this was evidence of a conspiracy for which they were not charged.

The Court disagreed, however, and upheld the conviction. It was scarcely conceivable, the Court reasoned, for the salesmen to believe the unknown owner of Francisco Company was giving away his whiskey. It was more appropriate to draw the inference that the salesmen knew an owner, unknown to them, contemplated the entire chain of events:

> All intended to aid the owners, whether Francisco or another, to sell the whiskey unlawfully. . . . All by reason of their knowledge of the plan's general scope, if not its exact limits, sought a common end to aid in disposing of the whiskey. True, each salesman aided in selling only his part. But he knew the lot to be sold was larger and thus that he was aiding in a larger plan.

The Chain-Wheel

Complex conspiratorial plans do not easily lend themselves to chain or wheel structures and are oftentimes a combination of both. For example, in United States v. Perez [489 F.2d 51 (5th Cir. 1973)], a statewide, get-rich-quick scheme involved the staging of fraudulent automobile accidents for the purpose of creating false personal injury claims. Twelve individuals appealed from their convictions in a single mail fraud conspiracy. Each of many phony accidents was organized the same way. "Recruiter" located willing "hitters," who would be liable for a contrived accident with a "target" vehicle. The occupants of the target were "drivers" and "riders" participating in the scheme. The rider would feign injury and be sent to cooperative doctors and lawyers. They, in turn, would contrive to document a bogus medical history in support of a personal injury claim mailed to an insurance company. The rider claimant would then pass the insurance proceeds back through the chain for proportionate disbursement to each cooperating participant. The court held that because each conspirator performed a separate function in a scheme where every participant's cooperation

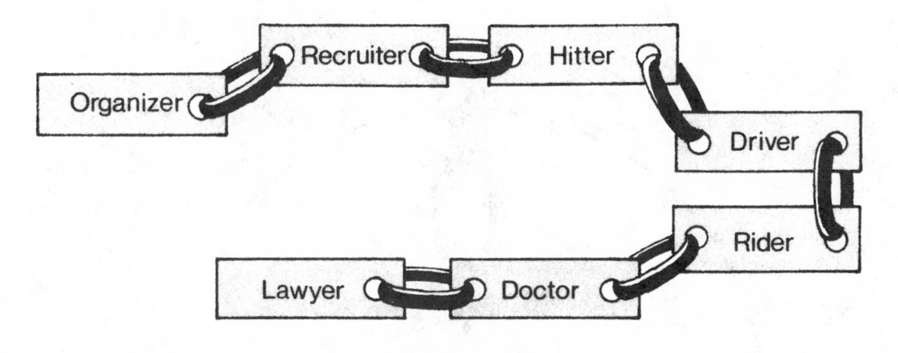

FIGURE 3
A Classic Chain (*Perez*)

was necessary for the plan to succeed, a classic chain had been drawn. (See fig. 3.)

The defendant conceded this much, but argued against the government's attempt to make spokes of a wheel out of numerous chains, and thus bring all the defendants into a single conspiracy prosecution. Absent, they contended, was a common objective or awareness of the other spoke's existence. But the Federal court took a close look at the nature of the enterprise and believed otherwise.

First, unlike the plan in prolonged narcotics conspiracies, the exact chain could not continue in existence for more than one accident for fear that the insurance companies would quickly catch on to the identity of the parties. Second, this conspiracy was fundamentally different from the multiple conspiracies found in *Kotteakos,* where each scheme to obtain a loan was an end in itself from which only separate agreements could be inferred. The nature of the *Perez* agreement contemplated an ongoing scheme that would not persist without the continuing cooperation of numerous conspirators to maintain it. Because various lawyers, doctors, recruiters, and passengers participated in a series of accidents in various combinations, the conspiracy took on the schematic structure of wheel. At the hub were the organizers, whose contacts with cooperating lawyers and doctors were essential ingredients to make the scheme work. The organizers then sent recruiters out to find the other necessary parties. Third, the court believed that each participant, after cooperating in a second phony accident with a similar modus operandi, rimmed the wheel because each knew or should have known that there had to be someone organizing a larger scheme. And fourth, the court appeared impressed with the identity of certain defendants. It believed the participants in each accident must have known that there had to be a series of accidental phony accidents to create rewards high enough to compensate for the risk of loss of professional status for the participating doctors and lawyers.

The court therefore concluded that all the defendants were co-conspirators in a single common scheme to use the mails to defraud the insurance companies. (See fig. 4.) It observed:

> From an operational sense this was not a series of little concoctions to set up a particular collision. . . . It was one big and hopefully profitable enterprise, which

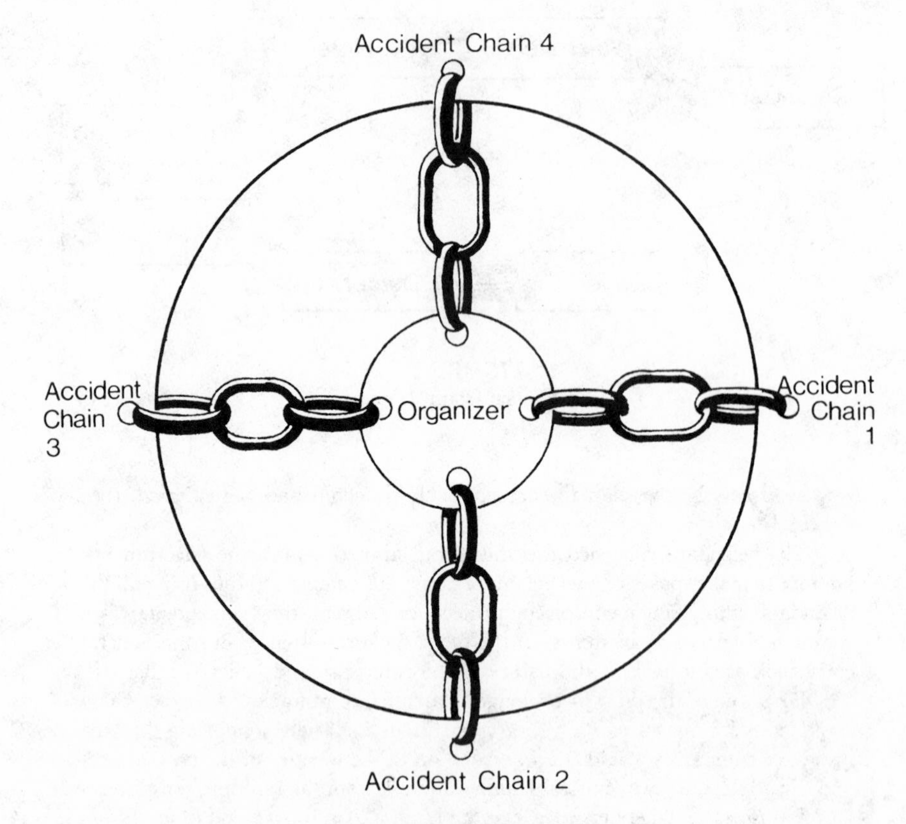

FIGURE 4
The Chain-Wheel (*Perez*)
The Chains Form the Spokes of a Wheel Conspiracy

looked toward successful frequent, but nonetheless discreet, repetitions, and in which each participant was neither innocent nor unrewarded.

The *Kotteakos, Blumenthal,* and *Perez* cases not only illustrate how chain and wheel structures are analyzed but also suggest the kinds of evidence an investigator should be looking for to enable a court to solidify a bilateral view of conspiracy. The nature of the enterprise, its size and volume of business, and the relationship between the participants are all key evidentiary factors in this regard.

Nature of the Enterprise

In United States v. Bruno, [105 F.2d 921 (2d Cir. 1939)], 88 defendants were indicted for a conspiracy to import, sell, and possess narcotics. The smugglers dealt independently with a group of retailers in New York and a group of retailers in Texas and Louisiana. While there was no evidence of cooperation or communication between the diverse groups of retailers, the court held the jury could have found a single, large conspiracy:

> [A]ll the accused were embarked upon a venture in all parts of which each was a participant, and an abettor in the sense that the success of that part with which he was immediately concerned, was dependent upon the success of the whole. . . . [The retailer] knew that he was a necessary link in a scheme of distribution, and the others, whom he knew to be convenient to its execution, were as much parties of a single undertaking or enterprise as two salesmen in the same shop.

The *Bruno* case is recognized for establishing a "stake in the venture" test that has been particularly successful in chain conspiracies where the sale of goods requires the inference that cooperation between producers, distributors, and retailers is necessary for the venture to pay off.

The nature of criminal activity more easily identifiable with the wheel structure can also be used to show mutual dependence among its participants. In the more recent case of United States v. Morado, [454 F.2d 167 (5th Cir. 1972)], eight individuals were convicted in a single conspiracy to violate Texas election laws. The sheriff of Starr County, who was also a physician, directed others to acquire absentee ballots from elderly, illiterate, and infirm voters who were induced to vote a certain way on ballots that were improperly witnessed. A Federal court did not believe that the individual acts of election fraud were separate conspiracies in themselves, but part of a larger plan in which each fraudulent ballot made sense only insofar as it depended upon the others for ultimate success. The court concluded, "Each constituted a mutually beneficial and successive step toward a single common goal—the stealing of an election."

If a legitimate organization is used to cover and coordinate criminal activity, the defendant's association with the organization may be used to draw an inference of a single conspiracy. In United States v. Kenny, [462 F.2d 1205 (3d Cir. 1972)], numerous Jersey City and Hudson County, N.J., politicians were convicted of conspiracy to obstruct justice and affect interstate commerce for accepting kickbacks on city and county construction contracts. All were members of J. V. Kenny's political organization, and all but Kenny held official positions in city or county government. The court believed the evidence reflected a pattern of conduct on the part of an "official family" which repeatedly cooperated closely to achieve the common goal of self-enrichment. The court stated:

> The key to success of all their depravities was their common control over the administration of city and county government under the leadership of J. V. Kenny.

These examples suggest the importance of establishing the nature of the enterprise. An investigator should therefore be prepared to locate witnesses (often immunized co-conspirators) who are willing to testify and are able to explain the complicated or intricate nature of the unlawful activity, and as a consequence, the stake in the venture or mutual dependence each participant has with each other.

Size and Volume of Business

In United States v. Peoni [100 F.2d 401 (2d Cir. 1938)], a Federal court refused to find a single conspiracy based on evidence of the sale of counterfeit money. Defendant Peoni sold the money to one Regno, who in turn sold it to a third party, Dorsey, who passed it on to innocent persons. The court refused to hold Peoni as a co-conspirator with Dorsey, and drew a distinction between knowledge that remote links *must* exist and knowledge that they *may* exist. From

Peoni's point of view, the agreement was to sell to Regno. It was of no moment to him what Regno did with the bills. He could have passed them on to innocent purchasers as easily as passing them on to his accomplice Dorsey.

In a later case [United States v. Agueci, 310 F.2d 817 (2d Cir. 1962)], the same Federal court, citing *Peoni,* noted that had the prosecution been able to establish more than one sale from Peoni to Regno, the inference that Peoni knew that sales beyond his own would be made and that he thus shared a common purpose with Dorsey, Regno's vendee, might well have been strong enough to warrant submission of the single conspiracy issue to the jury.

The case of United States v. LaVechia [513 F.2d 1210 (2d Cir. 1975)] supports the importance of evidence indicating multiple and voluminous sales. A Federal court upheld a single conspiracy among counterfeiters and distributors because it thought the amount of money printed ($450,000) was so large that the success of the conspiracy must have depended on distribution by others. Remote purchasers were also linked to the counterfeiters because the evidence showed: (1) Large ($10,000) purchases suggested a larger operation, (2) The purchasers' negotiations in terms of "points" suggested familiarity with the counterfeit business, and (3) The purchasers' knowledge that additional buys could be made suggested a large-scale operation. In structural form, the counterfeiters should have known they were part of a chain of distribution, and the independent remote purchasers should have suspected that additional chains were working with the same distributors. Evidence regarding the volume of sales, however, was the key to pull the rim around these chains and thus create a wheel conspiracy.

In a similar vein, a Federal court upheld the single conspiracy prosecution of eight defendants involved in a large-scale California drug smuggling operation. The court looked at: (1) The size of the smuggling operation, (2) The quantity and frequency of the retailers' purchases, (3) The efficiency of the distribution system to the retailers, and (4) The efficiency of the retailers in the narcotics sales business. It then concluded that each retailer had reason to know of other retailers' existence even though not aware of each others' identity, numbers, or locations, and that each retailer had reason to believe that his own profits were probably dependent upon the success of the entire venture.

Relationship Between Participants

Specialized functions within group activity can also help establish a single conspiracy. In United States v. Becker [569 F.2d 951 (5th Cir. 1978)], four defendants were convicted of conspiring to defraud investors by misrepresenting that low-grade ore contained enormous quantities of gold and silver capable of low cost extraction. The defendants were divided between two groups, one responsible for handling the scientific aspects and another responsible for marketing the contracts and options. The court held:

> In this case the very structure of the activities supports an inference of an underlying agreement, even if it was unspoken. . . . The division of labor among the various defendants under the supervision of one or two directors supports the existence of a conspiracy.

In United States v. Gleason [616 F.2d 2 (2d Cir. 1979)], three top officials of the Franklin National Bank were convicted of conspiracy to falsify the bank's operating statement in order to cover up a $7 million loss. The scheme relied on the specific and separate expertise of the defendants to evaluate falsely the value of securities and create fictitious foreign exchange transactions. Although there was apparently no direct evidence that each defendant knew the details of what the others were doing, the Federal court believed each defendant should be held to intend the foreseeable consequences of his actions and that it could infer a common objective to falsify the financial statement.

Proof of mere association among the participants may be a helpful indication of a single conspiracy. A single conspiracy conviction to smuggle anti-cancer drugs was upheld where physical surveillance put all the defendants together near the automobile used to smuggle the drugs across the Mexican border. Like conclusions [have been] reached where all the defendants worked in close quarters, or were relatives in a family-run marihuana farm.

6. In Chapter 10 we examined the special problems of determining accomplice liability between an abstract business entity—like a corporation—and its individual agents. By treating the corporation as a separate "person" under the criminal law, we also raise problems under conspiracy law. Can a corporation conspire with its own agents? Can agents within a corporation be guilty of conspiring with each other when they all act for the benefit of the corporation? In United States v. Hartley, 678 F.2d 961 (11th Cir. 1982), Treasure Isle, Inc., a producer of breaded seafood, along with two of its officers, Hartley and Dell, was charged with conspiracy to defraud the government by supplying breaded shrimp that did not meet federal military standards. The court described the complex scheme as follows:

> Apparently the government had begun purchasing shrimp from Treasure Isle in the late 1960's. Pre-1974, military inspectors made individual examinations of each box of raw shrimp as well as every tank of peeled shrimp. If the shrimp satisfied the inspection criteria, an "accept" card was placed on the inspected box or tank. Nonconforming shrimp received a "reject" card.
>
> Testimony revealed that Dell directed Treasure Isle employees to remove "reject" cards from inspected tanks, replace them with "accept" cards from other inspected tanks, and destroy the "reject" cards. In this manner, tanks which had already been "accepted" would be reinspected only to again be approved by the military inspector. Rejected tanks would now bear the "accept" cards and would be placed into the subsequent production process. Treasure Isle's cooler foreman implemented the same plan on the boxes of raw shrimp at the instigation of Dell and Hartley. But, switching cards was just the beginning.
>
> At the direction of Dell and Hartley, a Treasure Isle employee modified a weight used by the inspectors in determining the number of shrimp per pound. The modification was accomplished by cutting two and one-quarter ounces off of a five-pound weight. By doing so, less shrimp were required to balance out the five-pound weight, which now weighed in at four pounds, thirteen and three-quarter ounces.
>
> Treasure Isle employees also falsified production sheets to allow for after-hour processing of shrimp, which would then be packed without having been

inspected. And, employees were directed to inform the inspectors that they miscounted boxes of inspected shrimp permitting additional uninspected boxes to be added during the inspector's absence. . . .

The government changed its inspection system in October, 1974. Rather than inspecting each individual box, the inspectors began a random sampling of the "end product." Under this new system, inspectors selected thirteen boxes of breaded shrimp from each day's production. The boxes were stored overnight in a locked freezer for which only the inspectors supposedly possessed a key. Each box was marked by the inspectors prior to being placed in the locked freezer. The following day, the inspectors would retrieve the samples and conduct an analysis to determine the shrimp's conformance with the requisite specifications. If the sample shrimp conformed, the inspectors approved the entire production lot for that day.

Upon receiving notice that an entire lot had been rejected under the new system, the defendants created a new means by which to accomplish their goal. Not to be outdone by the government's selective sampling, Treasure Isle employees prepared their own sample lot. Each day a "sample run" was made in which the largest shrimp were meticulously processed. Great care was taken to peel and devein the largest shrimp; and extra caution was taken to insure no more than 40 percent of the shrimp's total weight was attributable to breading. The "sample run" was then set aside for special work later that evening. The production then returned to "normal." Smaller shrimp, less careful cleaning and deveining, extra breading, and sloppy freezing became the order of the day.

Reminiscent of Houdini, each night after the inspectors had departed, Treasure Isle employees would sneak into the locked freezer, duplicate the inspector's markings on the "sample run" boxes, and substitute them for the sample lot selected by the inspectors earlier that day. Thus, the next day the inspectors would test only the best of Treasure Isle's production, which unsurprisingly met the military's specifications.

This was not the extent of the defendants' scheme, however. Testimony revealed that chemicals were added to large batches of shrimp which had developed a foul odor to enable the shrimp to be processed and frozen undetected. Rejected shrimp would be secretly added to other production lots. Shrimp received from abroad were also processed in the lots sold to the government. Once again, false counts were given to inspectors to enable Treasure Isle to include uninspected shrimp in government orders. And the company developed signals to alert employees of an inspector's approach.

In upholding the conspiracy convictions, the court reasoned as follows:

The difficulty in accepting the theory of intracorporate conspiracy is conceptual. Under elementary agency principles, a corporation is personified through the acts of its agents. Thus, the acts of its agents become the acts of the corporation as a single entity. The conceptual difficulty is easily overcome, however, by acknowledging the underlying purpose for the creation of this fiction—to expand corporate responsibility.

By personifying a corporation, the entity was forced to answer for its negligent acts and to shoulder financial responsibility for them. See Dussouy v. Gulf Coast Investment Corp., 660 F.2d 594, 608 (5th Cir. 1981). The fiction was never intended to prohibit the imposition of criminal liability by allowing a corporation or its agents to hide behind the identity of the other. We decline to *expand* the fiction only to *limit* corporate responsibility in the context of the criminal conspiracy now before us.

Ours is not the first court to be unpersuaded by the attempted application of this agency principle in the conspiracy context. "In these situations, the action by an incorporated collection of individuals creates the 'group danger' at which conspiracy liability is aimed, and the view of the corporation as a single legal actor becomes a fiction without a purpose." 660 F.2d at 603.

The premier case applying general agency principles to preclude intracorporate conspiracy was Nelson Radio & Supply v. Motorola, 200 F.2d 911 (5th Cir. 1952), cert. denied, 345 U.S. 925, 73 S. Ct. 783, 97 L. Ed. 1356 (1953). In *Nelson Radio* the Fifth Circuit examined an alleged conspiracy among a corporation, its officers and employees in the antitrust context. In its opinion, the Court stated: "A corporation cannot conspire with itself any more than a private individual can, and it is the general rule that the acts of the agent are the acts of the corporation." Id. at 914. . . .

Dissatisfaction with the rule came as early as the *Nelson Radio* opinion itself. In his dissent, Judge Rives referred to an earlier United States Supreme Court decision in which Mr. Justice Burton had acknowledged without concern that the complaint had alleged a conspiracy between a corporation and four of its officials. Judge Rives stated: "My brothers use such strong adjectives as 'unique' and 'absurd' in referring to the contention of a conspiracy to which only the corporation and its own officers and agents are parties. That thought did not occur to Mr. Justice Burton. . . ." 200 F.2d at 918 (Rives, J. dissenting).

Antitrust litigation is a peculiar form of legal action. Indeed, the language of the Sherman Act alone gives pause for consideration of intracorporate conspiracy within its framework. Section one's reference to conspiracies "in restraint of trade" implies a requirement of multiple entities; whereas section two's prohibition of monopolies aims at a single conglomerate. If section one's conspiracy charge was satisfied by a single corporate entity, it would arguably render section two meaningless. But even in the antitrust areas courts have fashioned an exception to the general rule "when the officer has an independent personal stake in achieving the corporation's illegal objective." Greenville Publishing Co., Inc. v. The Daily Reflector, Inc. 496 F.2d 391, 399 (4th Cir. 1974). . . .

Outside the antitrust sphere, the single entity concept has met sterner opposition. The issue has been encountered in §1985 actions concerning conspiracies to discriminate. While the outcomes are far from consistent, it has been held that when more than one act of discrimination is alleged, a cause of action for conspiracy exists between corporate officers.

In United States v. Consolidated Coal Co., 424 F. Supp. 577 (S.D. Ohio 1976), the District Court confronted the single entity fiction in a criminal conspiracy setting. It held "that a corporation *can* be charged with conspiring with its corporate personnel." Id. at 581 (emphasis supplied). The court relied in part on the words of Mr. Justice Harlan in his concurring opinion in United States v. Wise, 370 U.S. 405, 82 S. Ct. 1354, 8 L. Ed. 2d 590 (1962) (Harlan, J. concurring) (see note 12 supra). "[T]he fiction of corporate entity, operative to protect officers from contract liability, had never been applied as a shield against criminal prosecutions. . . ." Id. at 417, 82 S. Ct. at 1362. We find this language most persuasive and in line with the underlying purpose that led to the creation of the fiction of corporate personification. It originated to broaden the scope of corporate responsibility; we will not use it to shield individuals or corporations from criminal liability.

The former Fifth Circuit recognized this exception to the fiction in criminal conspiracy cases in Dussouy v. Gulf Coast Investment Corp., 660 F.2d 594 (5th Cir. 1981) when it stated: "a corporation can be convicted of criminal charges of conspiracy based solely on conspiracy with its own employees." Id. at 603. We now adopt this exception and hold that it is possible for a corporation to conspire with its own officers, agents and employees in violation of 18 U.S.C. §371.

Does the government get a windfall when it can prosecute the corporation for the illegal acts of its individual agents, as well as the individual agents for conspiring with each other and with the corporation? Is there any difference between the law's special concern with crimes by multiple parties and its special concern with the criminal conduct of a complex business entity?

H. THE RICO STATUTE AND THE FRONTIER OF CONSPIRACY

UNITED STATES v. BAGARIC

United States Court of Appeals, Second Circuit
706 F.2d 42 (1983)
cert. denied, 104 S. Ct. 1331 (1983)

KAUFMAN, Circuit Judge.

Milan Bagaric, Mile Markich, Ante Ljubas, Vinko Logarusic, Ranko Primorac, and Drago Sudar appeal from judgments of conviction in the United States District Court for the Southern District of New York, after a trial before Chief Judge Motley and a jury. Appellants urge reversal, relying not only on a series of claimed infirmities of the usual sort, but also upon this court's recent refusal to permit prosecution of a terrorist organization pursuant to the Racketeer Influenced and Corrupt Organizations Act, where the Government failed to allege the group or its activities possessed any financial dimension or purpose. See United States v. Ivic, 700 F.2d 51 (2d Cir. 1983). We are asked to expand that holding to the facts of this case. We decline to do so, since the overwhelming proof at trial showed that the defendants, acting through their criminal enterprise, perpetrated an extensive extortion scheme using the United States and foreign mails. In addition, the defendants directed numerous acts of violence against certain supporters of Yugoslavia. Because we also reject appellants' myriad other contentions, we affirm the convictions.

I

The massive, complex and convoluted record of this thirteen-week trial established that appellants were members of a Croatian terrorist group operating principally in New York, Chicago, and Los Angeles, with participants in Cleveland, San Francisco, Toronto, South America, and Europe. Acting through their criminal enterprise, they perpetrated an international extortion scheme against "moderate Croatians" and persons they believed to be supporters of the government of Yugoslavia, resorting to multiple acts of violence against those not sufficiently sympathetic to their cause. We chronicle the history of their activities in some detail.

Operating from his home base in Chicago, Ante Ljubas began in late 1974 to recruit and hire persons to commit murders and bombings. In each case, the intended victim was to be an individual considered unsympathetic to the cause of Croatian independence from Yugoslavia. In time, Ljubas approached a long-time acquaintance, Frank Korenic, inquiring whether Korenic could obtain explosives, and requesting that Korenic introduce Ljubas to one Joe Neary. Neary, a notorious Chicago gangster, was a frequent customer at a restaurant where Korenic's ex-wife was a waitress, and the two men had known one another since 1973. Korenic took Ljubas to Neary's home, where Ljubas was introduced to Neary and another local gangster, Louis Almeida. Ljubas told these men he "was working with other people," and would be willing to pay well for a series of contract killings. He offered $20,000 for the first murder, and $10,000 for each of approximately ten additional assassinations. Neary and Almeida agreed to perform the killings. Accordingly, Ljubas gave them a photograph and the address of the first intended victim, John Badovinac. At that time, Badovinac was president of the Croatian Fraternal Union in Pittsburgh, Pennsylvania, an organization Ljubas regarded as pro-Yugoslavian.

In February, 1975, Neary and Almeida travelled to Pittsburgh, and went to Badovinac's office. Uncertain whether that was the best locale at which to carry out the murder, they drove to Badovinac's home address and "look[ed] the place over[,] trying to figure out how . . . to assassinate him there." Still undecided, they telephoned Badovinac's office, only to discover, from his secretary, that Badovinac was out of town attending a meeting. Neary and Almeida returned to Chicago to tell Ljubas of their frustration. The three men met at a restaurant near Ljubas's home, where Ljubas expressed his unhappiness that Neary and Almeida had not "[gotten] the job done."

In March, Neary and Almeida set off to Pittsburgh a second time. En route, they were stopped by Ohio police for speeding. A search of their car turned up a .38 Colt firearm with a four-inch barrel, a .380 automatic Barretta, a .380 Walther PPKS with silencer, and a photograph of Badovinac. Shortly after his arrest on firearms charges, Almeida told Illinois state police that Ante Ljubas had approached Neary and Almeida and hired them to murder a man in Pittsburgh.

Undeterred by the intervention of fate which spared Badovinac, Ljubas sought out co-appellant Milan Bagaric, and had Bagaric introduce him to Ante Caran. Bagaric and Ljubas demonstrated to Caran the nature and seriousness of their endeavor. Bagaric showed him explosives the two men were storing in Bagaric's basement, and Ljubas instructed Caran on techniques of bomb construction. Shortly thereafter, apparently convinced of Caran's bona fides, Ljubas asked Caran if he would be willing to recruit two men to bomb the Pittsburgh home of Milan Vranes, an officer of the Croatian Fraternal Union. Ljubas provided Caran with the address of Vrane's home in Pittsburgh and told Caran to pick up the bomb at Bagaric's apartment. Caran acquired the services of two friends, Andrija Skrabo and Vjelko Jaksic. The three men went to Bagaric's home, where they were shown a bomb and timer device built by Bagaric. Skrabo and Jaksic drove to Pittsburgh with the bomb.

In Pittsburgh, the two men had difficulty locating Vranes's home. After consulting a local telephone directory, they drove to an address other than that provided by Ljubas. They set the timer on the bomb and left it in a snowbank near the sidewalk of that house, later learning from a radio broadcast that the bomb had exploded. Soon after, Bagaric informed them they had bombed the wrong house.

This series of misadventures in Pittsburgh seems reminiscent of Inspector Clouseau-style bumbling. Unfortunately, tragedy soon replaced what had appeared to be a comedy of errors. Ljubas and Bagaric, undaunted, continued their private war, taking on new soldiers along the way. Beginning in early 1977, the members of the criminal enterprise began an operation to stockpile dynamite in the United States and to transport it for use in various cities.[22] Ljubas asked Caran to arrange for the use of an automobile "to go to Canada to bring some explosive[s]." Caran secured the assistance of Mico Jaksic, brother of Vjelko. Ljubas, Caran, and Mico Jaksic drove to Canada in Jaksic's car. Their destination was a small rural town, Elliott Lake, Ontario, site of the huge Dennison uranium mines, the ex-employer of appellant Mile Markich.

Upon arrival in Elliott Lake, Ljubas departed alone in the car. He rejoined Caran and Mico Jaksic twenty minutes later, with a bag containing approximately twenty sticks of dynamite which he showed the two men. The dynamite was manufactured by CIL Inc., a Canadian company, bore the coded manufacturing date D7 (signifying April, 1977 manufacture), and had been shipped in April and May of 1977 to Dennison Mines. Ljubas, Caran, and Jaksic then drove to the Toronto area, where they stopped at the home of Milan Rukavina, a Croatian acquaintance of Caran. To ensure they would not be observed, they drove into Rukavina's garage, where Jaksic packed the dynamite into the door panels of the car. Blasting caps, also obtained by

22. Simultaneously, appellants conceived and began the execution of an extortion scheme, alleged to have involved "[i]n excess of fifty individual acts of extortion of victims residing in Manhattan, Westchester, Queens, the vicinity of Chicago, the vicinity of Los Angeles and elsewhere, through letters posted in West Germany, in June, 1978." Indictment SS 81 Cr. 402, ¶5. E., *reprinted in* Joint App. at A-57.

Ljubas, were separated from the dynamite and were stored "underneath the dashboard so they would blend in with the rest of the wires." Ljubas left the two men at this point, after instructing them to transport the contraband across the United States-Canada border and deliver it to Markich in Skokie, Illinois. Several days later, Caran travelled to Skokie, telephoned Markich to receive directions to the latter's home, and brought most of the dynamite and blasting caps to Markich, retaining some for his own use.[23] After Markich hid the explosives, the two men spoke briefly "[a]bout Croatia and [the] Croatian cause." Caran returned to his home in Milwaukee, and later travelled to San Francisco. There, he went to the home of one Mile Boban, and left the explosives he had not given Markich. Bagaric came to San Francisco and wired the explosives into bombs.[24]

Also in mid-1977, appellants formalized and commenced their principal operation, a scheme to extort money from so-called "moderate" Croatians in the United States. Ljubas travelled to West Germany, where he and others committed to the violent overthrow of the Belgrade government determined to adopt a tactic which had previously been employed by Algerian terrorists seeking independence from France. They would send letters to "bad Croatians," demanding they provide financial support for appellants' criminal enterprise and also stating that, if they balked, reprisals would be carried out against them.

Appellant Ranko Primorac headed up the extortion operation in the Los Angeles area, where a number of successful Croatians resided. Primorac compiled a list of potential wealthy victims, and threatened "to squeeze that [sic] people financially, and if they refuse, to be punished [sic] for example for rest of Croatians." Among other possible targets, Primorac named Steven Bubalo, Krizan Brkic, Marko Zubcic, Frank Striskovitch, and Walter Rasic, all of whom later received extortion letters. The letters demanded that a specified sum of money, generally between $5,000 and $20,000, be mailed to a post office box in Asuncion, Paraguay, or "you will . . . compel us to set a horrible example by making you the first object of the disciplinary rules." Miro Baresic, an unindicted co-racketeer, who participated in the enterprise's affairs during 1977 and 1978, *see infra,* maintained a box in the same postal office.

Having established, and set in motion, the extortion scheme, appellants proceeded on two fronts. First, they continued their bombing activities, as well as trafficking in firearms, committing arsons, and attempting additional murders independent of the extortions. At the same time, they began to carry out reprisals against a number of persons who had failed to heed the warnings in the extortion letters.

In April, 1978, Caran received a telephone call from Los Angeles. The

23. Prior to leaving Canada, Caran had sought and received permission from Ljubas to retain several sticks of the dynamite for use against the Yugoslavian Consulate in San Francisco.

24. Due to an apparent malfunctioning of the device, Caran's attempt to bomb the Yugoslavian Consulate in February, 1978 failed. Caran retrieved the dynamite and kept it in his home, having separated the dynamite from the blasting caps.

caller instructed Caran to retrieve the explosives he had first stored at Boban's home, and later used in the unsuccessful attempt on the Yugoslavian Consulate, and to deliver them to Primorac and two other men, Miro Biosic and Baresic, in Los Angeles. Skrabo and a man named Ante Sisko delivered the bomb materials on Caran's behalf. After making the delivery, Skrabo joined Baresic, Primorac and several others, and together these men set fire to the Yugoslavian American Club in San Pedro, California.

Several months later, some of the Canadian dynamite turned up on the East Coast. On August 14, 1978, members of the New York City Bomb Squad disarmed and dismantled two bombs which had been placed in a library at the United Nations and in a locker at Grand Central Station. In a communique left with both bombs, a Croatian terrorist group claimed credit for the attempted bombings, and indicated they were intended to protest West Germany's decision to extradite to Yugoslavia one Stipe Bilandzic, a Croatian nationalist and close associate of Ljubas, Markich, and Primorac. The nine sticks of dynamite used in the two New York bombs were Cilgel D7 dynamite, a rare brand, yet precisely the one obtained by Ljubas during the Elliott Lake trip, and bearing the same date code. The electrical tape on the United Nations bomb was discovered to exhibit an "end match" with tape utilized in a bombing of the factory of one of the extortion victims, see infra, that is, both bombs were made with contiguous pieces cut from a single roll of black electrical tape.

In mid-1978, Vjelko Jaksic, then residing in Milwaukee, planned a summer vacation in the San Francisco area. Caran asked him to pick up "something," which turned out to be a handgun equipped with silencer which Ljubas had offered to provide Caran. Ljubas had arranged for Bagaric to turn over the gun in Chicago. Vjelko and Mico Jaksic left Milwaukee for Chicago. Upon arrival, they spoke with Ljubas and Bagaric, and were informed that the weapon had been hidden in Markich's apartment. The Jaksics picked up the gun silencer from Markich. In June, 1978, Vjelko Jaksic went to San Francisco for his holiday, stopping long enough to meet with Caran to deliver the gun and silencer. Caran later tried to use the gun, unsuccessfully, in an attempt to kill the Yugoslavian consul.

Nor did Vjelko Jaksic return to the midwest empty handed. In late May or early June, Primorac had met with Caran in California, and asked Caran to transport weapons to New York. Primorac provided a Westchester telephone number, which Caran was to call upon arrival in the metropolitan area, to be informed of the exact destination for the assorted rifles, machineguns, and ammunition he would be carrying. If Caran were unable to travel to the East Coast, he was to deliver the arsenal to the home of Ivan Misetic in Chicago. As it turned out, Vjelko Jaksic was the courier, rather than Caran. He brought the weapons to Chicago, en route to his home in Milwaukee. Eventually, the cache made its way to Irvington, a town in Westchester, and to Bridgeport, Connecticut. After Primorac had attempted to use one of the guns to murder a New York critic of the extortion scheme, Joseph Badurina, agents of the

Joint Terrorism Task Force seized the weapons from Caran's home in Bridgeport, and from the Irvington home of Ivan Cale and Stipe Ivkosic, associates and fellow terrorists involved in the principal New York based faction of appellants' enterprise.[25]

The violence threatened in the extortion letters began in the fall of 1978, several months after their mailing. On September 28, Westchester businessman Anthony Cikoja, who had received a letter but refused to pay, was shot and killed on his front lawn. Six weeks after Cikoja's murder, Chicago factory owner Danilo Nikolic, who had also received an extortion demand, narrowly missed becoming the second victim when a bomb exploded near the section of his plant where flammable liquids were stored. The bomb used in this attempt was prepared in the identical fashion, using the same roll of electrical tape, as the bombs made of Canadian Cilgel dynamite discovered at the United Nations and Grand Central Station.

In Los Angeles, attacks were carried out on several targets of the extortion scheme. Just after Labor Day, 1978, Primorac had asked Caran to leave his work in Sacramento for one week, to kill one Mario Forgiarini, a wealthy recipient of an extortion letter. Three weeks later, Primorac's roommate, Miro Biosic, met Caran at the Los Angeles airport, and after informing Caran that Primorac had decided to remain out of town because "he don't [sic] want to be around if anything is happening," handed Caran a gun and silencer and drove him to Forgiarini's house. Forgiarini never appeared. Despite Caran's failure to carry out the attempt on the life of Forgiarini, Primorac paid him the $700 week's wages Caran lost.

In November, 1978, Caran moved to Los Angelos. There, he was introduced by Primorac to another Croatian named Marijan Rudela. Acting on Primorac's instructions, Rudela asked Caran to assist him in murdering Forgiarini. This time, Caran declined, apparently having decided the proper approach was to "kill some Yugoslavs, some enemy of our people, not the Croatians." Caran did not balk several days later, however, when Rudela suggested an alternative target, Marko Zubcic, another successful businessman who had been the recipient of an extortion letter. Caran and Rudela waited near Zubcic's place of business, intending to ambush him, but Zubcic never emerged.

The next morning, Rudela suggested yet another victim, Krizan Brkic. Rudela drove to Brkic's residence and handed Caran the same gun and silencer that had previously been provided Caran by Primorac's roommate, Biosic, for the unsuccessful attempt on Forgiarini. Caran hid in bushes outside Brkic's home, and when Brkic appeared in the yard, Caran shot and killed him.

Over the next several months, a new form of violence was employed

25. Cale and Ivkosic were convicted, along with Caran and several others, in the earlier trial before Judge Pollack. The RICO convictions of Cale, Ivkosic, Franjo Ivic, and Nedjelko Sovulj have since been reversed. See Part II infra.

against the Los Angeles victims. On April 6, 1979, identical pipe bombs, constructed to explode upon impact and scatter metal shrapnel, caused property damage to the homes of Forgiarini and Frank Striskovitch, both of whom, along with Brkic and Zubcic, had been threatened by Primorac. On May 23, 1979, Rudela and another Croatian were killed in the process of arming yet another pipe bomb which detonated prematurely. At the time, Rudela was sitting in an automobile parked seventy feet from the home of extortion victim Martin Balov. According to Bagaric, "We had made a mistake."

In 1979, appellants conceived of still an additional reprisal tactic, the mailing of "book bombs," that is, hardcover books hollowed out, filled with a stick of dynamite and a blasting cap, and wired in such a fashion that the two naked wire ends would join as the book was opened, setting off a powerful explosion designed, in the words of Richard M. Rogers, a special agent examiner in the FBI Explosives Unit, simply "to kill a human being."

On February 19, 1979, two of these book bombs were mailed, from Akron, Ohio, to Joseph Badurina, a Queens, New York journalist, and Father Timothy Majic, a Catholic priest in Milwaukee. Both men were Croatian nationalists, of significant influence in their home communities, who had taken explicit and adamant editorial positions against the use of violence. Remarkably, Father Majic was being interviewed by an FBI agent on the morning of February 26, when his mail arrived. The agent, seeing the priest about to open the cover of a black book and observing what appeared to be wires inside, seized the book instantly and threw it into a snowbank in the church courtyard. A police officer from the Milwaukee bomb squad separated the blasting cap from the dynamite, losing part of his hand in the process.

One week later, Badurina received a similar package. Aware of the unsuccessful attempt to kill Majic, Badurina alerted the FBI. The New York City bomb squad removed the package and disarmed the book.

On April 4, detectives of the Cleveland Police Department obtained a warrant and searched the residence of appellant Vinko Logarusic. The search turned up a metal toolbox containing more than eight hundred rounds of ammunition and batteries, as well as a hollowed out book containing wires, a battery and a light bulb. This book, described by an FBI expert as the "prototype, or perhaps test book, which was manufactured prior to the other two book bombs," was the same size as the ones mailed to Badurina and Father Majic, with a depth of exactly one and one-half inches, permitting a stick of dynamite to be placed flat inside. The glue in all three books was of the same chemical composition, the wire was the same gauge, the wires in all three were twisted into loops and L-shaped hooks, and, finally, all three books employed solder, rather than standard battery connectors, to hook the wire to the power source. Laboratory tests showed the same pair of pliers had been used to cut a wire in the bomb sent to Badurina and the one found in Logarusic's home.

In August, 1979, Caran moved his family to Bridgeport, Connecticut. That autumn, he was approached by Ljubas in the Croatian Center in Manhattan. Ljubas asked whether Caran would be interested in learning to make bombs and teaching others, apparently primarily for use in Europe but in this country as well. Caran assented. Several months later, Caran was telephoned at work by appellant Drago Sudar, who informed Caran he had been sent by Ljubas. After Caran picked up Sudar at the Croatian Center, the two men drove to Fairfield, Connecticut to purchase wires, a clock, a soldering iron, and gloves. From there they went to the apartment of a friend of Caran's in Bridgeport, where Sudar taught Caran how to put together a time bomb.

Caran's lesson could not be completed, however, because the two men had been unable to purchase blasting caps in Fairfield. Several weeks later, Ljubas, who had come to the East Coast, offered to have blasting caps delivered to Caran (as well as arranging for Caran to be paid $2,000 to travel to Europe to pass on the skills he had acquired from Sudar). On July 5, 1980, Bagaric's wife delivered to Caran, at the latter's Bridgeport home, two blasting caps.

In September, 1980, Sudar returned to Bridgeport to resume the bomb construction lessons. After detailing his recent trip to California to teach bombmaking to other Croatians (including the brother of Marijan Rudela), Sudar described to Caran "how to make bombs in the drawer, in the door, in the car, and in the book. In the book . . . is most dangerous, you got to be very, very careful to make a bomb." Sudar demonstrated to Caran the preparation of time bombs.

On June 25, 1981, Sudar was arrested at his home in Toronto, Canada, on an extradition warrant. Detectives of the Peel Regional Police Department searched his home, discovering and seizing a watch, batteries, light bulbs for automobile directional signals, tape, and coiled and color coded wires. One of the nine-volt batteries seized had its terminals filled with solder, in a manner similar to that used in the book bombs from the United Nations, Grand Central Terminal, and Logarusic's home.

By indictment S 81 Cr. 402, superseding and consolidating two earlier instruments and filed on June 30, 1981, Bagaric, Markich, Ljubas, Logarusic, Primorac, and Sudar were charged with violations of the Racketeer Influenced and Corrupt Organizations Act ("RICO"). Count One charged conspiracy to violate the racketeering statute, 18 U.S.C. §§1961, 1962(d), and Count Two alleged a substantive violation, id. §§1961, 1962(c).[26] . . .

26. The relevant portions of RICO provide as follows:

§1961. Definitions

As used in this chapter—

(1) "Racketeering activity" means (A) any act or threat involving murder, kidnaping, gambling, arson, robbery, bribery, extortion, or dealing in narcotic or other dangerous drugs, which is chargeable under State law and punishable by imprisonment for more than one year; (B) any act which is indictable under . . . the following provision[] of title 18, United States Code: . . . section 1952 (relating to racketeering) . . .;

(2) "State" means any State of the United States, the District of Columbia, the Commonwealth of Puerto Rico, any territory or possession of the United States, any political subdivision, or any department, agency, or instrumentality thereof;

(3) "person" includes any individual or entity capable of holding a legal or beneficial interest in property;

Trial commenced on February 16, 1982, and continued for thirteen weeks. On May 15, after approximately six days of deliberations, the jury returned guilty verdicts on both counts against Ljubas, Markich, Primorac, and Bagaric. Sudar was convicted of the single conspiracy count on which he was tried. Logarusic was convicted of conspiracy and acquitted on the substantive offense. The district court sentenced Ljubas and Primorac to terms of imprisonment of twenty years on each count, to run consecutively. Markich and Bagaric received prison terms of twenty years under Count One and ten years under Count Two, such terms also to be served consecutively. Logarusic and Sudar were both sentenced to terms of imprisonment of twenty years on the conspiracy count. All convicted defendants have appealed, raising a multitude of contentions.

II

The difficult threshold question posed for consideration is whether, in light of our recent decision in United States v. Ivic, supra, the conduct charged in the indictment and proved at trial constituted an offense under RICO. In *Ivic,* a panel of this court concluded that a prosecution may not properly be brought pursuant to §1962(c) when the Government does not charge that either the enterprise, 18 U.S.C. §1961(4), or the predicate acts which make up the alleged pattern of rackettering activity, id. §1961(1), (5), possess some financial purpose. United States v. Ivic, supra, at 64. In this case the charges and proof all relate to a terrorist organization, "motivated"[27] by political as

(4) "enterprise" includes any individual, partnership, corporation, association, or other legal entity, or any union or group of individuals associated in fact although not a legal entity;

(5) "pattern of racketeering activity" requires at least two acts of racketeering activity, one of which occurred after the effective date of this chapter and the last of which occurred within ten years (excluding any period of imprisonment) after the commission of a prior act of racketeering activity: . . .

§1962. Prohibited activities . . .

(c) It shall be unlawful for any person employed by or associated with any enterprise engaged in, or the activities of which affect, interstate or foreign commerce, to conduct or participate, directly or indirectly, in the conduct of such enterprise's affairs through a pattern of racketeering activity or collection of unlawful debt.

(d) It shall be unlawful for any person to conspire to violate any of the provisions of subsection[] . . . (c) of this section.

27. We purposely highlight our use of the word "motivated." As the text makes clear, we are troubled by the notion, advanced by appellants, that the Government will be required to prove the animating or long-run objective of a RICO enterprise was economic, apparently to the exclusion of other, collateral "motives."

It is clear that §1962 does not, by its terms, require proof of ultimate improper economic motive, as does, for example, 18 U.S.C. §1503 ("corrupt" motive to obstruct investigation). We think it simplifies matters to state at the outset our belief that the term "motive" has been used imprecisely throughout these proceedings, as it suggests an inquiry into mens rea. See text infra. The issue is whether an objective assessment of the crimes charged and proved in this case demonstrates an economic dimension sufficient to bring them within the language and intention of §1962.

well as economic goals, and claimed to have engaged in economic crimes "to obtain money to further [its] activities," id. at 61 n.6 (reserving issue of applicability of RICO to such cases). We are called upon to decide whether this case, falling somewhere between the complete absence of financial purpose or activity, on the one hand, and an enterprise engaged solely in siphoning monies from, and infiltrating, legitimate businesses, e.g., United States v. Scotto, 641 F.2d 47 (2d Cir. 1980), cert. denied, 452 U.S. 961, 101 S. Ct. 3109, 69 L. Ed. 2d 971 (1981), on the other, is within the purview of RICO. For several reasons, we conclude it is.

A

Relying on isolated language in *Ivic,* appellants argue the Government is required to prove an ultimate and overriding financial motive to secure a RICO conviction. The *Ivic* court nowhere stated, however, that economic gain must be the sole motive of every RICO enterprise. Such a rule, we believe, would run counter to fundamental principles of criminal law and risk the politicization of criminal trials. We reject appellants' contention.

Although evidence of motives or purposes underlying criminal behavior is normally admissible, provided certain criteria of reliability are met, motive itself is not generally an element of a particular offense. And, when Congress has required proof of motive, it has generally done so for behavior not deemed blameworthy absent the immoral motive, and not otherwise punishable. So, for example, it may be permissible under various circumstances to communicate with a judge to offer mitigating information relevant to sentence, but "an endeavor to exploit" a friendship with the judge may be found to be a "corrupt" motive. (18 U.S.C. §1503).

RICO demands no such inquiry. The offenses it proscribes are, in the main, activities punishable irrespective of motives for performance, and accordingly they are provable by showing mens rea in the typical fashion. Hence, no additional scienter requirement is imposed by the statute. . . .

. . . To carry out a deeper inquiry into long-term or ultimate motive would be to require adjudication of a factor traditionally deemed not exculpatory. E.g., United States v. Starks, 515 F.2d 112, 124 (3d Cir. 1975) (Hobbs Act applies to extortions committed for religious "purposes"), aff'd sub nom. Abney v. United States, 431 U.S. 651, 97 S. Ct. 2034, 52 L. Ed. 2d 651 (1977); United States v. Cullen, 454 F.2d 386, 392 (7th Cir. 1971) (Stevens, J.) ("Appellant's professed unselfish motivation, rather than a justification, actually identifies a form of arrogance which organized society cannot tolerate."). Moreover, such an exercise would embroil courts and jurors in a controversy essentially irrelevant to the purpose of the statute under consideration. Whether appellants extorted money for the long-term political purpose of effecting the separation of Croatia from Yugoslavia, whether this formed part, but not all, of their "motivation," or whether the freedom of their former province is an issue they care about not at all, the effect of their activities on the national economy is identical. The *Ivic* court described RICO as a device to prevent (and reverse) "the drain[ing of] billions of dollars from America's economy by unlawful conduct," United States v. Ivic, supra, at 62. This effect is accomplished whatever considerations compel the creation and execution of an extortion scheme.

RICO's liberal construction provision, Pub. L. No. 91-452, §904(a), 84 Stat. 922, 947, was deemed irrelevant in *Ivic,* "since . . . construing RICO to cover terrorist activities . . . would in no way 'effectuate its remedial purposes,' " id. at 65 n.8, where there is no allegation or proof the enterprise's "activities generate monies which can serve as a 'springboard into the sphere of legitimate [business],' " id. at 63. In the case before us today, it is clear that, irrespective of the motive which appellants would have us believe spurred them to action, the remedial purposes of RICO are directly implicated. Pursuant to the direction of section 904(a), we decline to add an element of proof which would hamper the effective implementation of the statute.

Further, investigation into motive would serve only to politicize, and otherwise inflame, RICO prosecutions. As discussed in greater detail infra, defense counsel sought to inject peripheral political and religious considerations into the trial of this case, implying that appellants' anti-Communism or Catholicism, or their persecution by American and Yugoslavian officials acting in concert, justifiably drove them to commit the acts of extortion and violence charged in the indictment. These suggestions—which ultimately formed no part of the defense case of appellants who testified or presented witnesses—were, viewed charitably, misguided. They can only have served to patronize the jury and to add a distracting element of emotionalism to the proceedings. An interpretation of RICO requiring proof of long-term pecuniary objectives which in some sense can be said to supersede accompanying political or religious ones would invite a repetition of this conduct. It would authorize the admission of evidence of political beliefs, racial animosities, and family and blood feuds as justifications for criminal acts. Because we believe Congress, and the traditions of our criminal law, contemplate trials free of consideration of such issues, we reject appellants' argument that economic motive must surmount all others.

B

Appellants appear to argue also that the enterprise itself, rather than the predicate acts of racketeering, must be shown to yield financial gain. This contention is supported neither by a careful reading of the *Ivic* opinion nor by reference to the underlying purposes of RICO.

The literal terms of the narrow *Ivic* holding require no more than an objective appraisal that some economic purpose was to be accomplished by the crime charged: "We hold that when an indictment does not charge that an enterprise *or* the predicate acts have *any* financial purpose, it does not state a crime under [RICO]." Id. at 65 (emphasis supplied). Additionally, this court has recognized that the nature of the misconduct often provides the best clue toward defining the enterprise. We have upheld application of RICO to situations where the enterprise was, in effect, no more than the sum of the predicate racketeering acts. . . . These decisions reflect the common sense recognition that a group of individuals may join together, and therefore be "associated in fact," §1961(4), although not a legally cognizable entity in one of the traditional forms, id., solely for the purpose of conducting their activities. That is, it is logical to characterize any associative group in terms of what it *does*, rather than by abstract analysis of its structure. See also United States v. Chovanec, 467 F. Supp. 41, 44-45 (S.D.N.Y. 1979) (enterprise need not be a group having characteristics of "organized crime," since Congress enumerated acts "with no restrictions limiting [RICO] to persons with particular affiliations"); cf. United States v. Roselli, 432 F.2d 879, 885-886 (9th Cir. 1970) (rejecting contention that "business enterprise," 18 U.S.C. §1952, reaches only "business[es] . . . associated with or controlled by a clandestine criminal organization").

Moreover, even where the enterprise is one of the legal entities listed in §1961(4), and proof of that element diverges from the proof of a pattern of racketeering, we think the requisite economic dimension may be demonstrated through the latter. Section 1961(4) appears to contemplate application of RICO to enterprises which, for example, are not themselves profit-making, or reinvest all their funds. Cf. United States v. Turkette, 452 U.S. 576, 580-581, 101 S. Ct. 2524, 2527, 69 L. Ed. 2d 246 (1981) (in §1961(4), use of word "any" in clause dealing with unions and individuals associated in fact signals congressional intent to impose no restriction upon associations embraced by definition; illegitimate associations therefore included); United States v. Angelilli, 660 F.2d 23, 30-31 (2d Cir. 1981) (New York City Civil Court held a RICO "enterprise"; use of word "any" indicates intent to make list all-inclusive, and "any being whose existence is recognized by law is within the term 'enterprise' "), cert. denied, 455 U.S. 945, 102 S. Ct. 1442, 71 L. Ed. 2d 657 (1982). The situation reached by §1962 may thus not always be one in which the enterprise "makes money" for its members. Yet, even absent a requirement that the enterprise be a profit-making one, the section implements the principal congressional purpose, "the elimination of the infiltration of organized crime and racketeering into legitimate organizations operating in interstate commerce," S. Rep. No. 617, 91st Cong., 1st Sess. 76 (1969), in two significant ways. First, by "striking at the source of the problem," United States v. Turkette, supra, 452 U.S. at 593, 101 S. Ct. at 2533, that is, proscribing the racketeering activities demonstrably capable of providing "a springboard into the sphere of legitimate enterprise[s]," id. at 591, 101 S. Ct. at 2533, whether "profit-making" or otherwise, Congress sought to make RICO preventive as well as remedial. Second, since non-profit corporations (as well as entirely illegitimate associations of individuals, see id. at 588-593, 101 S. Ct. at 2531-2533; United States v. Mazzei, supra, at 88-90) compete within the economy for funds and services, it would have been counter-productive to exempt from the statute those invested in, acquired, or maintained through a pattern of racketeering activity.

Accordingly, the Government may meet its obligation to show "financial purpose" through either the enterprise or the predicate acts of racketeering.

We recognize that, read in isolation, language in *Ivic* can be taken to support a requirement that, quite apart from the nature of the predicate acts, the enterprise itself must be "the sort of entity one joins to make money." United States v. Ivic, supra, at 60. The court noted the usage of "enterprise" in other parts of §1962, concluded it referred to "the sort of entity in which funds can be invested and a property interest of some sort acquired," id., and applied the same definition to subsection (c). Initially, we note this language is dictum, and differs from the holding of the case, which stated only that because *neither* the acts charged *nor* the purpose of the enterprise was economic, the indictment was outside the scope of §1962(c). More significantly, the context in which it was employed persuades us the panel had no intention of insisting the necessary showing of economic purpose be confined to the enterprise.

Ivic involved a group of individuals associated in fact. That phrase is defined in the portion of §1961(4) designed to bring within §1962 the commission of criminal acts related, in any one of several ways, 18 U.S.C. §1962(a), (b), (c), to enterprises with ascertainable associative structures but not one of those enumerated in the other part of §1961(4). See, e.g., United States v. Huber, 603 F.2d 387, 394 (2d Cir. 1979) (group of corporations not legally related may be "group of individuals associated in fact;" otherwise "[o]ne could simply transfer assets from the corporation whose affairs had been conducted through a pattern of racketeering activity to another corporation whose affairs had up to that point not been so conducted"), cert. denied, 445 U.S. 927, 100 S. Ct. 1312, 63 L. Ed. 2d 758 (1980). If the statute did not include this definition of enterprise, there might occur "the anomolous [sic] result that a large scale underworld operation which engaged solely in trafficking of heroin would not be subject to RICO's enhanced sanctions, whereas small-time criminals jointly engaged in infrequent sales of contraband drugs and illegal handguns arguably could be prosecuted under RICO." United States v. Mazzei, supra, at 89. And, as noted, we have sanctioned RICO prosecutions where the enterprise and the predicate acts of racketeering, although of course separate and necessary elements of §1962(c), need not be proved by distinct and independent proof. The *Ivic* panel's consideration of the meaning of "enterprise" in subsections (a) and (b) therefore amounted to no more than support for its ultimate conclusion that economic purpose must be shown in *either* the proof of enterprise *or* the proof of predicate acts. In *Ivic,* the two were functionally equivalent, and "the proof used to establish [them] . . . coalesce[d]," United States v. Turkette, supra, 452 U.S. at 583, 101 S. Ct. at 2528. The problem for the Government was that no proof established (nor did the indictment allege) that the group's "activities [were] designed to obtain,

[or] in fact yield[ed], any money whatsoever." United States v. Ivic, supra, at 63.[28]

C

This case fits well within the principles we have enunciated. The core of the enterprise was the commission of more than fifty acts of the classic economic crime of extortion, and many of the violent crimes perpetrated were in aid of the extortion scheme. They were carried out either to compel payment or in retaliation for refusal to meet appellants' extortionate demands. Indeed, the Assistant United States Attorney said in his opening statement to the jury that appellants sought to extort money from "moderate Croatians [to] help finance [their] criminal enterprise," and emphasized that "this extortion scheme . . . is one of the centerpieces of this criminal case." The first ten Government witnesses were extortion victims or widows of murdered extortion victims and proof of economic crimes continued throughout the lengthy trial.

The indictment and proof in this prosecution were consistent with the language and purposes of RICO. We decline to impose upon the Government an obligation to show pure or ultimate economic motive in any of the various formulations urged by appellants. Although we have previously noted, United States v. Huber, supra, 603 F.2d at 395-396, and we repeat the admonition here, "that the potentially broad reach of RICO poses a danger of abuse [when the statute is] appl[ied] . . . to situations for which it was not primarily

28. Other factors, relied upon in *Ivic,* comport with this reading. The title of the statute, "Racketeer Influenced and Corrupt Organizations," see United States v. Ivic, supra, at 61, insofar as it "may furnish some aid in showing what was the mind of the legislature." United States v. Palmer, 16 U.S. (3 Wheat.) 610, 631, 4 L. Ed. 471 (1818), supports inclusion of terrorist groups which finance their violent activities through extortionate means. "Corrupt" is defined in Webster's New Collegiate Dictionary (5th ed. 1977) as "characterized by bribery, the selling of political favors, or other improper conduct." Even more directly on point, a "racketeer" is "one who extorts money or advantages by *threats of violence,* by blackmail, or *by unlawful interference with business or employment"* (emphasis supplied). Precisely these tactics were employed by appellants.

Similarly, the statement of findings which prefaces RICO evinces an intent to put a halt to the "widespread" illicit operation of groups, made more powerful by the sophistication and diversification which accompany organization. Their activities were said to "drain[] billions of dollars from America's economy by unlawful conduct and the illegal use of force, fraud, and corruption." Apart from the reference to "organized crime," an amorphous concept popularly associated with groups different from the one in the instant case, but not meant to limit applicability of the statute to persons within its ranks, see, e.g., United States v. Vignola, supra, and other cases cited, this description of congressional concern clearly covers the conduct of appellants in this case.

Finally, the contention advanced at oral argument by Ljubas's counsel, that because Congress was primarily concerned with the "infiltration" of legitimate businesses, the Government must prove more than either the potential for such penetration or the diversion of monies from the legitimate sphere, has been rejected by this court, United States v. Barton, 647 F.2d 224, 227 (2d Cir.) (struggle between rival illegal underworld factions to gain control of unlawful enterprises), cert. denied, 454 U.S. 857, 102 S. Ct. 307, 70 L. Ed. 2d 152 (1981), and, in a slightly different context, by the Supreme Court, United States v. Turkette, supra, 452 U.S. at 593, 101 S. Ct. at 2533 (wholly illegitimate criminal organizations whose "activities . . . give rise to . . . concerns about infiltration" within RICO).

intended," our obligation is "to rule on actual, as opposed to hypothetical, applications of the statute," United States v. Weisman, 624 F.2d 1118, 1123 (2d Cir.), cert. denied, 449 U.S. 871, 101 S. Ct. 209, 66 L. Ed. 2d 91 (1980), and it is clear to us that the present one was appropriate. . . .

III . . .

The Jury Charge

Several elements of the jury charge are said to have been in error. First, appellants contend the jury was led to believe that conspiracy to commit the predicate acts constituted conspiracy to violate §1962(c). We think Chief Judge Motley's instruction on conspiracy to violate RICO, which appears in large part to have followed the Supreme Court's recent elucidation of the statutory elements, see generally United States v. Turkette, supra, 452 U.S. at 578-583, 101 S. Ct. at 2526-2528, was correct.

The court first charged that "a criminal enterprise as defined in the statute [must have] existed," and that "the defendant you have under consideration [must have been] associated with that enterprise." "Enterprise" was defined in detail. The jury was informed that the enterprise need not have a name, or be a commonly recognized legal entity, but could be a "group of individuals who are associated in fact although not a legal entity. Thus, any group of persons who associate together in order to achieve common illegal purposes can constitute a criminal enterprise under the statute." Compare id. at 583, 101 S. Ct. at 2528 ("The enterprise is an entity, for present purposes a group of persons associated together for a common purpose of engaging in a course of conduct.") And, the court stated that the jury "must find that a group of individuals in fact associated together for the purposes charged in the indictment—that is, to carry out a pattern of murders, arsons, extortions, and racketeering travel—and that the defendant you have under consideration was one such individual who associated himself with that criminal enterprise."

Turning to the conspiracy element here under attack, the judge stated that this necessitated the defendant "unlawfully, knowingly and willfully conspired with others to conduct the enterprise's affairs through a pattern of racketeering activity," language derived directly from 18 U.S.C. §1962(d), and further distinguished from conspiracy merely to commit predicate acts of racketeering by the language which immediately followed: "that is, that the defendant conspired to commit at least two acts or threats . . . in aid of racketeering in the course of the activities of the enterprise." This instruction was well within the meaning of our cases. See United States v. Scotto, supra, 641 F.2d at 54 (one conducts activities of enterprise through pattern of racketeering when predicate offenses are simply related to activities of enterprise);

United States v. Weisman, supra, 624 F.2d at 1122 (pattern of racketeering activity must be done "in the conduct of the affairs of an 'enterprise' ").[29]

Appellants also argue the court was obliged to charge the elements of the penal codes of the various states where acts of racketeering occurred, and was not permitted to rely upon generic definitions of murder, arson, and extortion. We disagree. Under RICO, as under the Travel Act, 18 U.S.C. §1952; see United States v. Nardello, 393 U.S. 286, 289-295, 89 S. Ct. 534, 536-539, 21 L. Ed. 2d 487 (1969), "[s]tate offenses are included by generic designation." H.R. Rep. No. 1549, 91st Cong., 2d Sess. (1970), reprinted in 1970 U.S. Code Cong. & Ad. News 4007, 4032. "Courts construing the racketeering statutes have found that the references to state law serve a definitional purpose, to identify generally the kind of activity made illegal by the federal statute." United States v. Salinas, 564 F.2d 688, 690 (5th Cir. 1977), cert. denied, 435 U.S. 951, 98 S. Ct. 1577, 55 L. Ed. 2d 800 (1978); see United States v. Frumento, 563 F.2d 1083, 1087 n.8A (3d Cir. 1977) ("Section 1961 requires, in our view, only that the *conduct* on which the federal charge is based be typical of the serious crime dealt with by the state statute, not that the particular defendant be 'chargeable under State law,' at the time of the federal indictment.") (emphasis in original), cert. denied, 434 U.S. 1072, 98 S. Ct. 1256, 55 L. Ed. 2d 775 (1978). Absent an allegation that the racketeering act is not prohibited *at all* under state law, cf. United States v. Nardello, supra, 393 U.S. at 295, 89 S. Ct. at 539, a claim obviously not available to appellants here, accurate generic definitions of the crimes charged were sufficient.

Finally, the court's charges on "pattern of racketeering activity" and the "knowledge" element of conspiracy were detailed and correct. The language for the former came from the statute, and was similar to instructions we have upheld. E.g., United States v. Scotto, supra, 641 F.2d at 53-54. As to "knowledge," the charge provided precisely the protection appellants now claim was lacking, since the district court first defined the objective of the "overall" conspiracy, United States v. Tramunti, 513 F.2d 1087, 1111-1112 (2d Cir.), cert. denied, 423 U.S. 832, 96 S. Ct. 54, 46 L. Ed. 2d 50 (1975), and then required the Government to demonstrate "an agreement as to the objective of the conspiracy. This does not mean that the conspirators must be shown to have agreed on the details of their criminal enterprise, but it does mean that the essential nature of the plan must be shown to have been agreed upon." And, "mere knowledge by a defendant of the conspiracy or any illegal act on

29. Similarly without merit is appellants' related argument. They note the Government charged, as part of the alleged conspiracy, but not in the substantive RICO allegations, acts agreed to in the course of the enterprise's activities but never completed. Based upon this difference, they claim the Government's theory under §1962(d) was a conspiracy merely to perform the individual acts. But, in charging only completed racketeering acts in the substantive RICO count, the Government was simply following the dictum in United States v. Weisman, supra, 624 F.2d at 1123-1124, that a §1962(c) conviction must include proof of consummated acts of racketeering and not conspiracies or attempts, unless conspiracies or attempts to commit the substantive crimes included within §1961(1)(D).

the part of an alleged co-conspirator is not sufficient to establish his relationship in the conspiracy. You must find . . . actual knowing participation of [the] defendant [under consideration] in the agreement . . . ." See United States v. Gleason, 616 F.2d 2, 16-17 (2d Cir. 1979), cert. denied, 444 U.S. 1082, 100 S. Ct. 1037, 62 L. Ed. 2d 767 (1980).[30]

Notes and Questions

1. The Statement of Findings and Purpose attached to the RICO statute reads as follows:

> The Congress finds that (1) organized crime in the United States is a highly sophisticated, diversified, and widespread activity that annually drains billions of dollars from America's economy by unlawful conduct and the illegal use of force, fraud, and corruption; (2) organized crime derives a major portion of its power through money obtained from such illegal endeavors as syndicated gambling, loan sharking, the theft and fencing of property, the importation and distribution of narcotics and other dangerous drugs, and other forms of social exploitation; (3) this money and power are increasingly used to infiltrate and corrupt legitimate business and labor unions and to subvert and corrupt our democratic processes; (4) organized crime activities in the United States weaken the stability of the Nation's economic system, harm innocent investors and competing organizations, interfere with free competition, seriously burden interstate and foreign commerce, threaten the domestic security, and undermine the general welfare of the Nation and its citizens; and (5) organized crime continues to grow because of defects in the evidence-gathering process of the law inhibiting the development of the legally admissible evidence necessary to bring criminal and other sanctions or remedies to bear on the unlawful activities of those engaged in organized crime and because the sanctions and remedies available to the Government are unnecessarily limited in scope and impact.

30. . . Concerning the claim that the proof at trial demonstrated multiple conspiracies, we have long held that the issue is a "question of fact for a properly instructed jury." United States v. Alessi, 638 F.2d 466, 472 (2d Cir. 1980) (collecting cases). Long duration, change in membership, or "a shifting emphasis in its locale of operation," United States v. Vila, 599 F.2d 21, 24 (2d Cir.), cert. denied, 444 U.S. 837, 100 S. Ct. 73, 62 L. Ed. 2d 48 (1979), do not transform a single conspiracy into several. Here, the jury was correctly instructed, and the evidence amply supported its conclusion that the mailing of a series of identical extortion letters—followed by reprisals engineered by various of the appellants; the common exchange of weaponry and explosives; the scientific evidence demonstrating most bombs were constructed in the same fashion; the numerous meetings and phone conversations among appellants, and their employment of various other persons to transport weapons and messages from one appellant to another, all taken together, established a common criminal enterprise in which each played a role.

Finally . . . the plain language and different elements of §1962(c) and §1962(d), see Blockburger v. United States, 284 U.S. 299, 304, 52 S. Ct. 180, 182, 76 L. Ed. 306 (1932), combined with the absence of evidence of a contrary legislative intention, support the imposition of consecutive sentences for violation of both subsections. See Albernaz v. United States, 450 U.S. 333, 336-342, 101 S. Ct. 1137, 1140-43, 67 L. Ed. 2d 275 (1981); United States v. Barton, supra, 647 F.2d at 234-238 (cumulative sentences proper for RICO conspiracy and general conspiracy, 18 U.S.C. §371).

> It is the purpose of this Act to seek the eradication of organized crime in the United States by strengthening the legal tools in the evidence-gathering process, by establishing new penal prohibitions, and by providing enhanced sanctions and new remedies to deal with the unlawful activities of those engaged in organized crime. [Public Law 91-452; 84 Stat. 922.]

Did Congress pass a statute adapted to its ends?

2. Why shouldn't Bagaric be prosecuted as a conspiracy case? What difference does RICO make?

V

JUSTIFICATION AND EXCUSE

The defenses of justification and excuse cut across the entire criminal law. In both cases, the actor concedes that she has caused the harm the law sought to prevent, and done so with the *mens rea* established in the definition of the elements of the crime. Nevertheless, the actor offers a plausible argument why she should not suffer punishment. In theory, the difference between justification and excuse is simple. An actor can claim justification when, in causing the harm, she has nevertheless advanced some social interest, so that we do not want the criminal law to discourage her action. An actor claims excuse, but not justification, when, in causing the proscribed harm, she has not advanced any important social interest, but when she nevertheless merits exculpation because special circumstances surrounding her action demonstrate that she is not morally blameworthy.

In this part, we will begin, in Chapter 12, with a justification claim, "choice of evils"—and continue in Chapter 13 with an excuse, duress. Then, in Chapter 14, we consider a group of defenses that somewhat blur the line between justification and excuse: the use of force in self-defense, defense of another, defense of property, and law enforcement. We normally regard an objectively valid claim of such defenses as a justification. Yet many of the cases involve defendants who claim that they acted on the mistaken but honest or reasonable belief that they were justified, and who therefore are essentially pleading a form of excuse. Finally, we consider a pure excuse defense—insanity—whose voluminous materials require a separate treatment in Chapter 15, the end of this part.

The distinction between justification and excuse, though perhaps important in theory, is often difficult to apply in practice. The introduction to Article 3 of the Model Penal Code, in fact, defends the drafters' decision not to draw a bright line between the two:

> The plan of the Code makes a rough analytical distinction between excuse and justification as defenses to a criminal prosecution, even when their proce-

dural significance is the same. Thus, such matters as compulsion, duress, consent and entrapment are not dealt with in this article. They are treated in Article 2, which concerns general principles of liability.

The Model Code does not, however, attempt to draw a fine line between all those situations in which a defense might more precisely be labelled a justification and all those situations in which a defense might more precisely be labelled an excuse. Thus, it treats in justification sections those cases in which an actor mistakenly perceives the circumstances or the necessity for force; in some of the cases, at least, it might be said that the actor is really offering an excuse for his conduct rather than a full-fledged justification. The Code's approach is based on a skepticism that any fine line between excuse and justification can sensibly be drawn, and on the belief that any possible value of attempting such a line would be outweighed by the cost of complicating the content of relevant provisions.

To say that someone's conduct is "justified" ordinarily connotes that the conduct is thought to be right, or at least not undesirable; to say that someone's conduct is "excused" ordinarily connotes that the conduct is thought to be undesirable but that for some reason the actor is not to be blamed for it. Usually one can say whether a defense that is offered is justificatory or excusatory, but there are some troublesome borderline cases. Suppose an actor makes a mistake of fact that is not only reasonable but also consistent with the highest standards of perception and apprehension. For example, relying on the consistently prevailing wind, a person sets a fire that will destroy private property but will also stop the advance of a large forest fire that looks as if it will destroy much more property. A sudden unexpected shift in the wind renders the forest fire harmless, while the set fire does the expected amount of property damage. In retrospect it is regrettable that the second fire was set, and one might consider a defense of setting it an "excuse" for an unfortunate occurrence. But based on all available information, the act of setting the fire was appropriate, and society would hope that similar fires would be set by persons with similar available information; thus the conduct of setting the fire was justified. Whether in this circumstance, one speaks of "justification" or "excuse" is a question of vague linguistic boundary lines rather than of substantive judgment.

In other circumstances there may be genuine doubt as to how behavior should be judged. Self-defense serves as an acceptable reason for the use of deadly force both because it is often desirable that people defend their lives and because it is thought that people will "naturally" defend themselves if they believe their lives are in danger. For many cases of self-defense it would probably be generally agreed that the use of deadly force was actually desirable, but for others, e.g., resistance by one family member to attack by another, there would be disagreement whether the use of deadly force was actually desirable or should merely be accepted as a natural response to a grave threat.

There is little point in trying to "purify" justification provisions of all situations in which it might be said that the defense offered is really an excuse. The main aim of a criminal code is to differentiate conduct that warrants criminal sanctions from conduct that does not. If it is clear that conduct will not be subject to criminal sanctions, the effort to establish precisely in each case whether that conduct is actually justified or only excused does not seem worthwhile, especially since, in regard to the difficult cases, members of society may disagree over the appropriate characterization. Moreover, insofar as determinations of justification and excuse are made by juries and both sorts of defenses are offered in difficult cases, a general verdict of acquittal would conceal the precise defense accepted even if the criminal code drew a fine line between justification and excuse.

12

CHOICE OF EVILS—NECESSITY

THE QUEEN v. DUDLEY AND STEPHENS

Queen's Bench Division
14 Q.B.D. 273 (1884)

INDICTMENT for the murder of Richard Parker on the high seas within the jurisdiction of the Admiralty.

At the trial before Huddleston, B., at the Devon and Cornwall Winter Assizes, November 7, 1884, the jury, at the suggestion of the learned judge, found the facts of the case in a special verdict which stated "that on July 5, 1884, the prisoners, Thomas Dudley and Edward Stephens, with one Brooks, all able-bodied English seamen, and the deceased also an English boy, between seventeen and eighteen years of age, the crew of an English yacht, a registered English vessel, were cast away in a storm on the high seas 1600 miles from the Cape of Good Hope, and were compelled to put into an open boat belonging to the said yacht. That in this boat they had no supply of water and no supply of food, except two 1 lb. tins of turnips, and for three days they had nothing else to subsist upon. That on the fourth day they caught a small turtle, upon which they subsisted for a few days, and this was the only food they had up to the twentieth day when the act now in question was committed. That on the twelfth day the remains of the turtle were entirely consumed, and for the next eight days they had nothing to eat. That they had no fresh water, except such rain as they from time to time caught in their oilskin capes. That the boat was drifting on the ocean, and was probably more than 1000 miles away from land. That on the eighteenth day, when they had been seven days without food and five without water, the prisoners spoke to Brooks as to what should be done if no succour came, and suggested that some one should be sacrificed to save the rest, but Brooks dissented, and the boy, to whom they were understood to refer, was not consulted. That on the 24th of July, the day before the act now in question, the prisoner Dudley proposed to Stephens and Brooks that lots should be cast who should be put to death to save the rest, but Brooks refused to consent, and it was not put to the boy, and in point of fact there was no drawing of lots. That on that day the prisoners spoke of their having families, and suggested it would be better to kill the boy that their lives should be saved, and Dudley proposed that if there was no vessel in sight by the morrow morning the boy should be killed. The next day, the 25th of July, no vessel appearing, Dudley told Brooks that he had better go and have a sleep, and made signs to Stephens and Brooks that the boy had better be killed. The prisoner Stephens agreed to the act, but Brooks dissented from it. That the boy was then lying at the bottom of the boat quite helpless, and extremely weakened by famine and by drinking sea water, and unable to make any resistance, nor did he ever assent to his being killed. The prisoner Dudley offered a prayer asking forgiveness for them all if either of them should be tempted to commit a rash act, and that their souls might be saved. That Dudley, with the assent of Stephens, went to the boy, and telling him that his time was come, put a knife into his throat and killed him then and there; that the three men fed upon the body and blood of the boy for four days; that on the fourth day after the act had been committed the boat was picked up by a passing vessel, and the prisoners were rescued, still alive, but in the lowest state of prostration. That they were carried to the port of Falmouth, and committed for trial at Exeter. That if the men had not fed upon the body of the boy they would probably not have survived to be so picked up and rescued, but would within the four days have died of famine. That the boy, being in a much weaker condition, was likely to have died before them. That at the time of the act in question there was no sail in sight, nor any reasonable prospect of relief. That under these circumstances there appeared to the prisoners every probability that unless they then fed or very soon fed upon the boy or one of themselves they would die of starvation. That there was no appreciable chance of saving life except by killing some one for the others to eat. That assuming any necessity to kill anybody, there was no greater necessity for killing the boy than any of the other three men." But whether upon the whole matter by the jurors found the killing of Richard Parker by Dudley and Stephens be felony and murder the jurors are ignorant, and pray the advice of the Court thereupon, and if upon the whole matter the Court shall be of opinion that the killing of Richard Parker be felony and murder, then the jurors say that Dudley and Stephens were each guilty of felony and murder as alleged in the indictment."

The learned judge then adjourned the assizes until the 25th of November at the Royal Courts of Justice. On the application of the Crown they were again adjourned to the 4th of December, and the case ordered to be argued before a Court consisting of five judges.

[The court first discussed certain procedural issues.]

There remains to be considered the real question in the case—whether killing under the circumstances set forth in the verdict be or be not murder. The contention that it could be anything else was, to the minds of us all, both new and strange, and we stopped the Attorney General in his negative argument in order that we might hear what could be said in support of a proposition which appeared to us to be at once dangerous, immoral, and opposed to all legal principle and analogy. All, no doubt, that can be said has been urged before us, and we are now to consider and determine what it amounts to. . . . Though law and morality are not the same, and many things may be immoral which are not necessarily illegal, yet the absolute divorce of law from morality would be of fatal consequence; and such divorce would follow if the temptation to murder in this case were to be held by law an absolute defence of it. It is not so. To preserve one's life is generally speaking a duty, but it may be the plainest and the highest duty to sacrifice it. War is full of duty, in instances in which it is a man's duty not to live, but to die. The duty, in case of shipwreck, of a captain to his crew, of the crew to the passengers, of soldiers to women and children, as in the noble case of the *Birkenhead*; these duties impose on men the moral necessity, not of the preservation, but of the sacrifice of their lives for others, from which in no country, least of all, it is to be hoped, in England, will men ever shrink, as indeed, they have not shrunk. It is not correct, therefore, to say that there is any absolute or unqualified necessity to preserve one's life. . . . It would be a very easy and cheap display of commonplace learning to quote from Greek and Latin authors, from Horace, from Juvenal, from Cicero, from Euripides, passage after passage, in which the duty of dying for others has been laid down in glowing and emphatic language as resulting from the principles of heathen ethics; it is enough in a Christian country to remind ourselves of the Great Example whom we profess to follow. It is not needful to point out the awful danger of admitting the principle which has been contended for. Who is to be the judge of this sort of necessity? By what measure is the comparative value of lives to be measured? Is it to be strength, or intellect, or what? It is plain what the principle leaves to him who is to profit by it to determine the necessity which will justify him in deliberately taking another's life to save his own. In this case the weakest, the youngest, the most unresisting, was chosen. Was it more necessary to kill him than one of the grown men? The answer must be "No"—

> So spake the Fiend, and with necessity,
> The tryant's plea, excused his devilish deeds.

It is not suggested that in this particular case the deeds were "devilish," but it is quite plain that such a principle once admitted might be made the legal cloak for unbridled passion and atrocious crime. There is no safe path for judges to tread but to ascertain the law to the best of their ability and to declare it according to their judgment; and if in any case the law appears to be too severe on individuals, to leave it to the Sovereign to exercise that prerogative of mercy, which the Constitution has intrusted to hands fittest to dispense it.

It must not be supposed that in refusing to admit temptation to be an excuse for crime it is forgotten how terrible the temptation was; how awful the suffering; how hard in such trials to keep the judgment straight and the conduct pure. We are often compelled to set up standards we cannot reach ourselves, and to lay down rules which we could not ourselves satisfy. But a man has no right to declare temptation to be an excuse, though he might himself have yielded to it, nor allow compassion for the criminal to change or weaken in any manner the legal definition of the crime. It is therefore our duty to declare that the prisoner's act in this case was wilful murder, that the facts as stated in the verdict are no legal justification of the homicide; and to say that in our unanimous opinion the prisoners are upon this special verdict guilty of murder.[1]

The Court then proceeded to pass sentence of death upon the prisoners.[2]

Solicitors for the Crown: The Solicitors for the Treasury.

Solicitors for the prisoners: Irvine & Hodges.

Notes and Questions

1. Assuming that the three seamen and the cabin boy all would have died if the seamen had not killed and eaten the cabin boy, what reason is there to prefer four deaths to one? The problem is more general than the extreme case of *Dudley and Stephens* might suggest:

> Unlike failure of proof and offense modification defenses, justification defenses do not define the harm sought to be prevented or punished by an offense. The harm caused by the justified behavior remains a legally recognized harm that is to be avoided whenever possible. Under the special justifying circumstances, however, that harm is outweighed by the need to avoid an even greater harm or to further a greater societal interest.
>
> A forest fire rages toward a town of 10,000 unsuspecting inhabitants. The actor burns a field of corn located between the fire and the town; the burned field then serves as a firebreak, saving 10,000 lives. By setting fire to the field with the purpose of destroying it, the actor satisfies all elements of the offense of arson. The immediate harm he has caused—the destruction of the field—is precisely the harm that the statute serves to prevent and punish. Yet the actor is likely to have a complete defense, because his conduct and its harmful consequences are justified. The conduct in this instance is tolerated, even encouraged, by society.
>
> The forest fire case provides an example of the "lesser evils" or "choice of evils" justification (also called "necessity" when the threat of greater harm stems from natural forces). This type of justification defense, not always recognized in American criminal codes, most clearly reflects the general principle of all justification defenses. [1 P. Robinson, Criminal Law Defenses 83 (1984).]

1. My brother Grove has furnished me with the following suggestion, too late to be embodied in the judgment but well worth preserving: "If the two accused men were justified in killing Parker, then if not rescued in time, two of the three survivors would be justified in killing the third, and of the two who remained the stronger would be justified in killing the weaker, so that three men might be justifiably killed to give the fourth a chance of surviving."

2. This sentence was afterwards commuted by the Crown to six months' imprisonment.

2. Is the problem in *Dudley and Stephens* that the seamen did not use a "fair" method to choose the one to die? Would the result have been different if the seamen had drawn straws or cut cards, rather than simply killed the weakest and youngest?

Would the seamen have been justified in basing their choice on principles of social utility? Was it fair to kill the boy on the ground that, because of his weakened condition, he had the shortest life expectancy anyway? If they had all been in the same physical condition, would it have been fair to kill the oldest? Was it relevant that the cabin boy was the only person on board who did not have a family dependent on him? If three cancer researchers were adrift on a lifeboat with a skid-row drunk, would the researchers be justified in killing the drunk to advance social utility?

The notion of letting the strongest decide who shall live raises many problems. Consider the treatment of the problem offered by Don Marquis in Archy and Mehitabel 40-42 (1973):

a spider and a fly

i heard a spider
and a fly arguing
wait said the fly
do not eat me
i serve a great purpose
in the world

you will have to
show me said the spider

i scurry around
gutters and sewers
and garbage cans
said the fly and gather
up the germs of
typhoid influenza
and pneumonia on my feet
and wings
then i carry these germs
into the household of men
and give them diseases
all the people who
have lived the right
sort of life recover
from the diseases

and the old soaks who
have weakened their systems
with liquor and iniquity
succumb it is my mission
to help rid the world
of these wicked persons
i am a vessel of righteousness
scattering seeds of justice
and serving the noblest uses

it is true said the spider
that you are more
useful in a plodding
material sort of way
than i am but i do not
serve the ultilitarian deities
i serve the gods of beauty
look at the gossamer webs
i weave they float in the sun
like filaments of song
if you get what i mean
i do not work at anything
i play all the time
i am busy with the stuff
of enchantment and the materials
of fairyland my works
transcend utility
i am the artist
a creator and a demi god
it is ridiculous to suppose
that i should be denied
the food i need in order
to continue to create
beauty i tell you
plainly mister fly it is all
damned nonsense for that food
to rear up on its hind legs
and say it should not be eaten

you have convinced me
said the fly say no more
and shutting all his eyes
he prepared himself for dinner
and yet he said i could

have made out a case
for myself too if i had
had a better line of talk

of course you could said the spider
clutching a sirloin from him
but the end would have been
just the same if neither of
us had spoken at all

boss i am afraid that what
the spider said is true
and it gives me to think
furiously upon the futility
of literature

archy

3. By the way, why didn't the court hold that Dudley and Stephens were justified? If they were not justified, why wasn't Brooks convicted as well?

4. The Model Penal Code contains a general "choice of evils" justification defense:

Section 3.02. Justification Generally: Choice of Evils.

(1) Conduct that the actor believes to be necessary to avoid a harm or evil to himself or to another is justifiable, provided that:

(a) the harm or evil sought to be avoided by such conduct is greater than that sought to be prevented by the law defining the offense charged; and

(b) neither the Code nor other law defining the offense provides exceptions or defenses dealing with the specific situation involved; and

(c) a legislative purpose to exclude the justification claimed does not otherwise plainly appear.

(2) When the actor was reckless or negligent in bringing about the situation requiring a choice of harms or evils or in appraising the necessity for his conduct, the justification afforded by this Section is unavailable in a prosecution for any offense for which recklessness or negligence, as the case may be, suffices to establish culpability.

Comment

1. *Codification of a Principle of Necessity.* This section accepts the view that a principle of necessity, properly conceived, affords a general justification for con-

duct that would otherwise constitute an offense. It reflects the judgment that such a qualification on criminal liability, like the general requirements of culpability, is essential to the rationality and justice of the criminal law, and is appropriately addressed in a penal code. Under this section, property may be destroyed to prevent the spread of a fire. A speed limit may be violated in pursuing a suspected criminal. An ambulance may pass a traffic light. Mountain climbers lost in a storm may take refuge in a house or may appropriate provisions. Cargo may be jettisoned or an embargo violated to preserve the vessel. An alien may violate a curfew in order to reach an air raid shelter. A druggist may dispense a drug without the requisite prescription to alleviate grave distress in an emergency. A developed legal system must have better ways of dealing with such problems than to refer only to the letter of particular prohibitions, framed without reference to cases of this kind.

2. *Limitations on Scope of Defense* . . . the necessity must arise from an attempt by the actor to avoid an evil or harm that is greater than the evil or harm sought to be avoided by the law defining the offense charged. An equal or a lesser harm will not suffice. Thus, a ship's captain may enter a forbidden port if medical treatment on shore is necessary to save a crewman's life. On the other hand, one who takes a life in order to avoid financial ruin does not act from a justifying necessity.

[T]he balancing of evils is not committed to the private judgment of the actor; it is an issue for determination at the trial. Thus, even if the defendant genuinely believes that the life of another is less valuable than his own financial security, his conduct would not be justified under Subsection (1)(a); for it requires that the harm or evil sought to be avoided be greater than that which would be caused by the commission of the offense, not that the defendant believe it to be so. What is involved may be described as an interpretation of the law of the offense, in light of the submission that the special situation calls for an exception to the criminal prohibition that the legislature could not reasonably have intended to exclude, given the competing values to be weighed. The Code does not resolve the question of how far the balancing of values should be determined by the court as a matter of law or submitted to the jury. There was disagreement in the Council of the Institute over the proper distribution of responsibility and it was decided that this question was best remitted to the law that generally governs the respective functions of the court and jury.

[U]nder Subsections (1)(b) and (1)(c), the general choice of evils defense cannot succeed if the issue of competing values has been previously foreclosed by a deliberate legislative choice, as when some provision of the law deals explicitly with the specific situation that presents the choice of evils or a legislative purpose to exclude the claimed justification otherwise appears. It was one thing, for example, for a court to face the question of justification for therapeutic abortion under a statute of the earlier British type, which merely condemned the "unlawful" termination of a pregnancy, without attention to exceptions. It was quite another to face the question under a statute that purported to delineate the therapeutic abortions excluded from the ambit of the prohibition. In the former case, the problem of the choice of value was remitted to the governance of the general law, including the principle of necessity. In the latter case, the legislature had itself canvassed the issue and determined what the choice should be. The legislature, so long as it acts within constitutional limits,[3] is always free to make such a choice and have its choice prevail. Subsections (1)(b) and (1)(c) accordingly so provide.

The [next] limitation is dealt with in Subsection (2). As noted above, the question of whether a proper choice of values has been made by the defendant is determined by a judge or jury rather than left to the judgment of the defendant. But even if the actor has made a proper choice of values, the necessity for his conduct in order to serve the higher goal may not be clear. If an actor rushes through a red light to get a passenger more quickly to a hospital, it may be questioned, for example, whether getting to the hospital faster did help or was likely to help save the passenger's life.

When the actor has made a proper choice of values, his belief in the necessity of his conduct to serve the higher value will exculpate—unless the crime involved can be committed recklessly or negligently. When the latter is the case, recklessness or negligence in bringing about the situation requiring the choice of evils or in appraising the necessity for his conduct may be the basis for conviction. This treatment of the matter thus precludes conviction of a purposeful offense when the actor's culpability inheres in recklessness or negligence, while sanctioning conviction for a crime for which that level of culpability is otherwise sufficient to convict.

How would the Model Penal Code resolve *Dudley and Stephens?* Does it address the question of how to choose the person to die?

5. How would the Model Penal code handle this case from the San Jose Mercury, May 31, 1984, at 10A:

Judge Upholds Woman's Right to Nurse Her Baby

Presque Isle, Maine (UPI)—A woman's right to breast-feed her baby in a moving automobile supersedes a state law requiring children be buckled into special car safety-seats, a Maine judge has ruled.

"The need to feed the child comes first," District Court Judge Julian W. Turner said Tuesday in suspending a $25 dollar fine against Dale Nickerson, 27, of Presque Isle.

Nickerson was pulled over by a state police officer for violating the state's mandatory child safety-seat law when his wife was breast-feeding their infant in a moving car. The year-old law requires children under the age of 4 to be restrained in special seats.

6. The alleged health benefits of marijuana have given rise to a number of justification defenses. In State v. Diana, 24 Wash. App. 908, 604 P.2d 1312 (1979) the court held it to be a defense to a charge of marijuana possession that the defendant believed that marijuana was a sedative for frustration resulting from multiple sclerosis (from which he suffered). The court held:

3. Of course, since Roe v. Wade. 410 U.S. 113 (1973), the range of legislative choice in dealing with abortion is greatly limited in the United States on constitutional grounds.

Although the defense of necessity has been variously applied, only one trial court decision had been called to our attention where the defense was recognized to a charge of possession of marijuana. That case is United States v. Randall, 104 Daily Wash. L. Rptr. 2249 (D.C. Super. Ct. Nov. 24, 1976). There, a defendant grew marijuana plants and used them to treat his own glaucoma. Expert testimony revealed that conventional glaucoma medications were ineffective and that defendant's experimental use of marijuana normalized inner-ocular pressure and lessened visual distortions caused by the disease. In determining whether the evil to be avoided by the defendant's act was greater than that inherent in the possession and personal use of marijuana, the court balanced the defendant's interest in preserving his sight against the government's interest in controlling the drug. The court concluded that Mr. Randall's right to preserve his sight outweighed the government's interest in outlawing the drug. Special emphasis was placed upon the importance of an individual's right to preserve and protect his own health and body. Roe v. Wade, 410 U.S. 113, 93 S. Ct. 705, 727, 35 L. Ed. 2d 147 (1973); Doe v. Bolton, 410 U.S. 179, 93 S. Ct. 739, 35 L. Ed. 2d 201 (1973) (abortion cases). . . .

We believe that the defendant here should be given the opportunity to demonstrate the alleged beneficial effect, if any, of marijuana on the symptoms of multiple sclerosis. Accordingly, we remand his case to the trial court, here the trier of fact, for determination of whether medical necessity exists.

In making that determination, the court should refer to the authorities cited in this opinion. To summarize, medical necessity exists in this case if the court finds that (1) the defendant reasonably believed his use of marijuana was necessary to minimize the effects of multiple sclerosis; (2) the benefits derived from its use are greater than the harm sought to be prevented by the controlled substances law; and (3) no drug is as effective in minimizing the effects of the disease. To support the defendant's assertions that he reasonably believed his actions were necessary to protect his health, corroborating medical testimony is required. In reaching its decision, the court must balance the defendant's interest in preserving his health against the State's interest in regulating the drug involved.[4]

In State v. Tate, 477 A.2d 462, 194, N.J. Super. 622 (1984) the defendant was a quadriplegic charged with unlawful possession of marijuana. The court, citing *Diana,* held:

[The defendant must] be able to demonstrate, by competent evidence, (1) his condition: (2) that it is "sense-threatening"—in his case, that the involuntary spastic episodes are real and painful; (3) that physiological relief (that is, by way of muscle relaxation, "pain-blocking" of the nervous system or the like) does occur and (4) that there is no other licit substance which can be prescribed affording the same benefits but without other deleterious side effects.

The allocation of the burden of proof concerning the defense of justification by reason of necessity is made by the Criminal Code. It is an "affirmative defense" which requires that the defendant first produce evidence supporting it.

4. On retrial, Diana's medical necessity defense was accepted, and he was found not guilty.—Eds.

Once he has done that the ultimate burden falls upon the State to disprove its existence. N.J.S.A. 2C:1-13(b)(1)—and it must disprove it beyond a reasonable doubt—N.J.S.A. 2C:1-13(a) and N.J.S.A. 2C:1-14(b), (c). The finder of fact will be required to determine whether the elements set forth have been disproved. If tried to a jury, the judge, before submitted the case to the jury, will have to determine whether sufficient evidence has been produced on the required elements to raise a factual issue. The underlying value judgment (assuming the required elements do have factual underpinning) as to whether the individual's need outweighs society's interest in enforcing the criminal law must be made by the judge after hearing the proofs.

7. The Model Penal Code §3.02 gives several hypotheticals to illustrate the position taken in its justification defense:

Suppose, for example, that the actor makes a breach in a dike, knowing that this will inundate a farm, but taking the only course available to save a whole town. If he is charged with homicide of the inhabitants of the farm house, he can rightly point out that the object of the law of homicide is to save life, and that by his conduct he has effected a net saving of innocent lives. The life of every individual must be taken in such a case to be of equal value and the numerical preponderance in the lives saved compared to those sacrificed surely should establish legal justification for the act. So too, a mountaineer, roped to a companion who has fallen over a precipice, who holds on as long as possible but eventually cuts the rope, must certainly be granted the defense that he accelerated one death slightly but avoided the only alternative, the certain death of both. Although the view is not universally held that it is ethically preferable to take one innocent life than to have many lives lost,[5] most persons probably think a net saving of lives is ethically warranted if the choice among lives to be saved is not unfair. Certainly the law should permit such a choice.

8. So far, all of our hypotheticals have involved weighing human lives against one another, weighing one property value against another, or weighing some value against a technical breach of the law that does no one any

5. Roman Catholic moralists have generally taken the position that one should not cause effects that are directly evil even if they are thought to be a necessary means to a greater good. See Ford, The Morality of Obliteration Bombing, in War and Morality 15, 26-28 (R. Wasserstrom ed. 1970); D. Callahan, Abortion: Law, Choice and Morality 422-24 (1970). Thus, it is considered wrong to terminate the life of a fetus even if that is the only way the mother can be saved and even if the fetus will die in any event. On the other hand, an ordinary operation designed directly to protect the mother's health is permissible, even if an inevitable effect is the death of the fetus, under the so-called principle of "double effect" that death is only permitted, not intended and is not itself a means to saving the mother's life.

Many acts justifiable under this section would also be justifiable under the principle of "double effect." Diverting a flood to destroy a farmhouse instead of a town would be acceptable since the destruction of the farmhouse is not intended and is not a means of saving the town. Suppose, however, the citizens of a town receive a credible threat, say from a foreign invader, that everyone in the town will be killed unless the townspeople themselves kill their mayor, who is hiding. If the townspeople accede, they would have a substantial argument against criminal liability under this section but their act would be immoral under the double effect analysis, since they have intended to kill the mayor and it is his death that is the means to their safety.

obvious harm. Should we conclude that human life is always more valuable than property? Can you conceive of any property that you could honestly say was more valuable than a human life?

It is generally understood in the heavy construction industry that for every $85 million of heavy construction, one worker will be killed accidentally. Insurance premiums, for instance, are set on such a basis. Why then is not the owner of a construction firm which undertakes the building of a dam or aqueduct, with full knowledge that fatalities will result, guilty of homicide?

What if an excessive build-up of water threatened the destruction of a dam, but did not imminently endanger lives? Would the operator of the dam be justified in opening the flood gates to save the dam, knowing that this action would kill one person caught under the dam? What if rebuilding the dam entailed the predictable loss of several lives?

What about taking a human life to save a priceless work of art? A member of a nonhuman species threatened with extinction? What if the entire species is threatened, as where a pilot, before bailing out, must choose between aiming her plane at a hermit's shack (which she knows is occupied) or at the breeding ground of the world's entire population of whooping cranes? Giant pandas?

STATE v. WARSHOW

Supreme Court of Vermont
410 A.2d 1000 (1980)

BARNEY, Chief Justice.

The defendants were part of a group of demonstrators that travelled to Vernon, Vermont, to protest at the main gate of a nuclear power plant known as Vermont Yankee. The plant had been shut down for repairs and refueling, and these protestors had joined a rally designed to prevent workers from gaining access to the plant and placing it on-line.

They were requested to leave the private premises of the power plant by representatives of Vermont Yankee and officers of the law. The defendants were among those who refused, and they were arrested and charged with unlawful trespass.

The issue with which this appeal of their convictions is concerned relates to a doctrine referred to as the defense of necessity. At trial the defendants sought to present evidence relating to the hazards of nuclear power plant operation which, they argued, would establish that defense. After hearing the defendants' offer of proof the trial court excluded the proffered evidence and refused to grant compulsory process for the witnesses required to present the defense. The jury instruction requested on the issue of necessity was also refused, and properly preserved for appellate review.

In ruling below, the trial court determined that the defense was not available. It is on this basis that we must test the issue.

The defense of necessity is one that partakes of the classic defense of "confession and avoidance." It admits the criminal act, but claims justification. It has a counterpart in civil litigation, recognized in Vermont in the case of Ploof v. Putnam, 81 Vt. 471, 71 A. 188 (1908).

The doctrine is one of specific application insofar as it is a defense to criminal behavior. This is clear because if the qualifications for the defense of necessity are not closely delineated, the definition of criminal activity becomes uncertain and even whimsical. The difficulty arises when words of general and broad qualification are used to describe the special scope of this defense.

In the various definitions and examples recited as incorporating the concept of necessity, certain fundamental requirements stand out:

> (1) there must be a situation of emergency arising without fault on the part of the actor concerned;
>
> (2) this emergency must be so imminent and compelling as to raise a reasonable expectation of harm, either directly to the actor or upon those he was protecting;
>
> (3) this emergency must present no reasonable opportunity to avoid the injury without doing the criminal act; and
>
> (4) the injury impending from the emergency must be of sufficient seriousness to outmeasure the criminal wrong. . . .

There is no doubt that the defendants wished to call attention to the dangers of low-level radiation, nuclear waste, and nuclear accident. But low-level radiation and nuclear waste are not the types of imminent danger classified as an emergency sufficient to justify criminal activity. To be imminent, a danger must be, or must reasonably appear to be, threatening to occur immediately, near at hand, and impending. . . . We do not understand the defendants to have taken the position in their offer of proof that the hazards of low-level radiation and nuclear waste buildup are immediate in nature. On the contrary, they cite long-range risks and dangers that do not presently threaten health and safety. Where the hazards are long term, the danger is not imminent, because the defendants have time to exercise options other than breaking the law. . . .

Nor does the specter of nuclear accident as presented by these defendants fulfill the imminent and compelling harm element of the defense. The offer does not take the position that they acted to prevent an impending accident. Rather, they claimed that they acted to foreclose the "chance" or "possibility" of accident. This defense cannot lightly be allowed to justify acts taken to foreclose speculative and uncertain dangers. Its application must be limited to acts directed to the prevention of harm that is reasonably certain to occur. . . .

These acts may be a method of making public statements about nuclear power and its dangers, but they are not a legal basis for invoking the defense of necessity. Nor can the defendants' sincerity of purpose excuse the criminal nature of their acts.

Judgment affirmed.

HILL, Justice, concurring.

While I agree with the result reached by the majority, I am unable to agree with their reasoning. As I see it, the sole issue raised by this appeal is whether the trial court erred in not allowing the defendants to present the defense of necessity. . . . Based upon their belief that nuclear power presented real and substantial dangers, defendants blocked the entrance to the power station to prevent its further operation.

At trial defendants sought to raise the affirmative defense of necessity. arguing that they were faced with a choice of evils—either violate the literal terms of the law or comply with the law and allow the commission of a more egregious wrong, i.e., the proliferation of nuclear power—and that they chose the course which would result in the least harm to the public, even though it meant violating the criminal law. The trial court refused to allow the defendants to present the defense, stating that it was not available "in Vermont at this time." . . .

The defense of necessity proceeds from the appreciation that, as a matter of public policy, there are circumstances where the value protected by the law is eclipsed by a superseding value, and that it would be inappropriate and unjust to apply the usual criminal rule. . . .

The balancing of competing values cannot, of course, be committed to the private judgment of the actor, but must, in most cases, be determined at trial with due regard being given for the crime charged and the higher value sought to be achieved.

Determination of the issue of competing values and, therefore, the availability of the defense of necessity is precluded, however, when there has been a deliberate legislative choice as to the values at issue. The common law defense of necessity deals with imminent dangers from obvious and generally recognized harms. It does not deal with non-imminent or debatable harms, nor does it deal with activities that the legislative branch has expressly sanctioned and found not to be harms.

Both the state of Vermont and the federal government have given their imprimatur to the development and normal operation of nuclear energy and have established mechanisms for the regulation of nuclear power. Implicit within these statutory enactments is the policy choice that the benefits of nuclear energy outweigh its dangers.

If we were to allow defendants to present the necessity defense in this case we would, in effect, be allowing a jury to redetermine questions of policy already decided by the legislative branches of the federal and state governments. This is not how our system of government was meant to operate. . . .

In my opinion the majority puts the cart before the horse. It measures the offer made against the requisite elements of the defense of necessity and concludes that the defendants failed to show a likelihood of imminent danger; yet it reserves judgment on the legislative policy exception to the defense. It is illogical to consider whether the necessary elements of a defense have been shown before determining whether the defense is even available in the particular situation.

The dissent, on the other hand. assumes that defendants' offer was sufficient to show not only imminent danger but also a failure of the regulatory scheme. I cannot agree with this assumption because the offer failed to show a danger not contemplated by the legislative scheme. The legislative framework was set up to deal with the very situation defendants offered to prove "might" happen. But because neither the state legislature nor Congress acted to shut down the power plant based on speculative possibilities does not, in my opinion, give rise to the questionable inference that there was an emergency which the regulatory scheme failed to avert. . . .

Since defendants' defense of necessity was foreclosed by a deliberate legislative policy choice, there was no error on the trial court's part in not allowing the defense to be presented.

BILLINGS, Justice, dissenting. . . .

The majority states that the danger of low-level radiation and nuclear waste, which the defendants offered to prove, are "not the types of imminent danger classified as an emergency sufficient to justify criminal activity." Furthermore, the majority dismisses those portions of the proof dealing with the threat of a nuclear accident by characterizing them as mere "speculative and uncertain dangers." In doing so the majority has decided to so read the evidence as to give credibility only to that evidence offered on the effects of low-level radiation. . . . The defendants also stated that "there was reasonable belief that it would have been an emergency had they started that reactor up. . . . there was a very good chance of an accident there for which there is no insurance coverage or very little." Specifically, the defendants offered to show by expert testimony that there were defects in the cooling system and other aspects of the power plant which they believed could and would result in a meltdown within seven seconds of failure on the start up of the plant. In addition, the defendants went to great lengths to base their defense on the imminent danger that would result from the hazardous radiation emitted from the plant and its wastes when the plant resumed operations.

While the offer made by the defendants was laced with statements about the dangers they saw in nuclear power generally, it is clear that they offered to show that the Vermont Yankee facility at which they were arrested was an imminent danger to the community on the day of the arrests; that, if it commenced operation, there was a danger of meltdown and severe radiation damage to persons and property. . . .

Furthermore, the defendants offered to show that, in light of the imminent danger of an accident, they had exhausted all alternative means of preventing the start up of the plant and the immediate catastrophe it would bring. Under the circumstances of imminent danger arising from the start up of the plant, coupled with the resistance of Vermont Yankee and government officials, which the defendants offered to prove, nothing short of preventing the workers access to start up the plant would have averted the accident that the defendants expected. . . .

I would also dissent from the concurring opinion in so far as it attempts to hide behind inferences that the legislature precluded the courts from hearing the defense of necessity in the instant case. . . . Even assuming that such inferences can be drawn from the regulatory schemes cited, they have no bearing on this case. We were asked to infer under the facts, which the defendants offered to prove (that they were acting to avert an imminent nuclear disaster), that the legislative branch of government would not permit the courts of this state to entertain the defense of necessity because it had legislatively determined nuclear power to be safe. Were the defense raised without any offer to show an imminent danger of serious accident, it might fail both because defendants did not offer evidence on imminent danger and on the basis of legislative preclusion. But, where, as here, the defendants offer to prove an emergency which the regulatory scheme failed to avert, the inference of preclusion is unwarranted. The defendants are entitled to show that although there is a comprehensive regulatory scheme, it had failed to such an extent as to raise for them the choice between criminal trespass and the nuclear disaster which the regulatory scheme was created to prevent. . . .

I am of the opinion that the defendants are entitled to present evidence on the defense of necessity as it exists at common law. To deny them this opportunity is to deny them a fair trial merely because they express unpopular political views. . . .

Notes and Questions

1. Does this kind of "political" justification defense raise different issues from those in the cases discussed previously? Do you think that the protesters should have had a justification defense? Should the issue have been submitted to the jury for their decision?

2. How would you analyze the following case from the Boston Globe, Nov. 17, 1984, at 21?

Jury Acquits Vt. Protesters of Trespass

Burlington, Vt.—A jury agreed last night with 26 protesters who had argued that their occupation of the Vermont office of US Sen. Robert Stafford (R-Vt.) was an essential part of their campaign against US policies in Central America.

The jury found the protesters innocent of criminal trespass, accepting the so-called necessity defense used by the protesters, which said the trespassing was necessary to prevent the greater evil of US involvement in Central America.

"This is a call to the American people to deliver a very strong message to their elected representatives that the US government is paying for a war in Central America that we do not want," said Celia Oyler of South Burlington, one of those arrested last March, after the verdict.

The group had called in a number of national authorities on Central America, including two ex-CIA agents, as defense lawyers sought to prove to the jury of Vermonters that the policies of President Ronald Reagan were wrong.

Judge Frank Mahady had allowed the protesters to use the necessity defense, which is rarely invoked, permitted or used successfully.

The prosecutors had dismissed the notion of the necessity defense, charging that the demonstrators broke the law by refusing to leave when asked.

"What one feels about Central America is really not at issue in this case," said Kevin Bradley; state's attorney for Chittenden County. "Senator Stafford had a right to run that office. The question is, was that right violated?"

The trial began Monday and ran until late yesterday as defense lawyers tried to establish US war crimes in Central America as part of their case that the crime of trespassing was necessary to prevent the greater evil of US involvement.

The protesters made it clear from the start that they wanted the trial to be a forum on Central America.

"We fully intend to use our trial to put the Reagan Administration's Central American war policy on trial." protester Jeanne Keller said when the trial started. "We will show that a state of emergency exists, that our democracy is in jeopardy due to the misinformation campaign out of the White House, that the lives of our brothers and sisters in Central America are in danger and that our alleged criminal act was necessary to bring to light the illegal wars being waged in El Salvador and Nicaragua."

The controversy began in late March when the demonstrators showed up at Stafford's office and staged a peaceful protest against the senator's support of administration policy in Central America.

The group felt it could pressure Stafford into changing his position for an upcoming vote in the Senate on emergency military aid to El Salvador. The protesters arrived on a Friday and were allowed to remain inside the senator's office complex over the weekend while Stafford's aides went home. On March 26, Stafford's top Vermont aide, Rey Post, asked the group to leave. They refused.

The protesters were arrested and processed at a nearby State Police barracks. Forty-four were arrested, but only 31 faced charges because the rest gave false names.

Charges against 26 of them were consolidated into one case which was before the jury. Five of the demonstrators went to trial earlier and were found guilty.

What should happen to the five protesters who happened to have been tried first and convicted?

As a juror, would your attitude toward the defense depend upon your view in the debate over Central American policy? If so, should policy on this issue be decided by the national government or by local juries? Or is the point that this is one way of getting the issue decided by the national government?

Would you feel different if the case involved a protest against a Senator who opposed our Central American policies? Would it be different if the issue were funding for abortions?

Are you influenced by the fact that the defendants caused no physical harm at the sit-in in Senator Stafford's office? Would your answer then be different if one of those sitting in, without the knowledge or authorization of the others, had used the confusion to destroy valuable property? What if the stress of the event had caused the Senator's elderly secretary to suffer a heart attack?

Would there be a difference in the way you would analyze these questions in the United States today and in Germany in 1938?

3. How do you distinguish the case below from that of the protesters in the Senator's office?

Man Accused of Arson Says Fires Helped Tregor Bill Pass

A member of a Boston arson ring that allegedly set 219 building fires claimed on the witness stand yesterday the fires were responsible for passage of legislation which forced the rehiring of laidoff firefighters and police officers in the city.

The witness, Gregg M. Bemis, spent his fourth day testifing at the US District Court trial of a codefendant, Donald Stackpole, 28, of Scituate. Stackpole is charged with arson, conspiracy, manufacturing incendiary devices, perjury and obstruction of justice.

Bemis said the ring was composed of "sparkles"—fire enthusiasts—who wanted to become Boston firefighters but saw their hopes dashed by the passage of Proposition 2½, the state's taxcutting measure, which led to municipalities laying off public employees.

Under cross-examination by defense lawyer John F. Herlihy, Bemis said the group set the fires in hopes of creating a public outcry to repeal Proposition 2½.

Q. So when you got started back in February 1982, you . . . had some idea that you might . . . have some conceivable impact on the law of the land, but after a while it became clear that you were not having any?

A. No . . . We were, I believe, the sole responsibility the Tregor bill did pass in Boston.

[The so-called Tregor bill provided the city with new revenues and required reinstatement of all police officers and firefighters laid off following implementation of Proposition 2½.]

Q. You think you did a good public service. You're proud of yourself?

A. No, I'm not proud of myself.

Q. But you think . . . you are the sole reason, one of the major reasons for the Tregor Bill passing?

A. Yes.

[Boston Globe, Nov. 15, 1984 at 49.]

Does your view as to the merits of the case depend upon how good and important you think the Tregor bill was?

What happens if rather than pressing for legislative action that she knows would be held unconstitutional, a person takes more direct action? Should a sit-in at an abortion clinic be more or less subject to a justification defense than a sit-in in a senator's office? What about the following story from the Boston Globe, Dec. 28, 1984, at 5?

Woman Says She Bombed Abortion Clinics Out of Guilt

Pensacola, Fla.—A newspaper got an anonymous letter yesterday from a woman claiming she participated in the bombings of three abortion clinics because "even deadly force is justifiable in saving innocent lives."

The locally postmarked letter received by the Pensacola News-Journal was given to the US Bureau of Alcohol, Tobacco and Firearms, which is investigating the blasts that destroyed one clinic and heavily damaged two others on Christmas.

The writer said she got pregnant, was unmarried, and had an abortion in Pensacola. Later, she realized she had made a mistake and wrote she did not want "what happened to me to happen to anyone else."

The typewritten letter also hinted if the clinics are reopened, more trouble may occur.

"I did not act alone," the writer said, "And if these clinics are opened again, we will see that they are closed again."

Bureau agent Dan Conroy said "appropriate" laboratory tests will be made on the letter, which the bureau is taking seriously.

"It is a well-established principle of justice that force, even deadly force, is justified in order to save innocent lives if necessary. So, I do not feel that I have done anything wrong," said the writer, who signed the letter "A Woman Who Knew What She Was Doing."

4. In Stahl v. State, 665 P.2d 839 (Okla. Ct. Crim. App. 1983), the defendants were newspaper reporters who trespassed on the site of a prospective nuclear power plant to cover a demonstration there. They argued that their entry was justified by the first amendment, regardless of whether the protestors also had a first amendment right to be there. The court, however, did not even discuss the criminal law doctrine of justification. Rather, it focused entirely on whether the first amendment protected the reporters' right to gather the news in this case, and affirmed the convictions after concluding that the first amendment gave the reporters no protection here.

If we treat the *Stahl* opinion solely as an interpretation of the first amendment, did the defendants still have a good justification claim under state criminal law? What if the state argued that it had to bar all outsiders from the site to protect them from injury and to protect the site from vandalism?

13

DURESS

DIRECTOR OF PUBLIC PROSECUTIONS FOR NORTHERN IRELAND v. LYNCH

House of Lords, N.I.
1 All E.R. 913 (1975)

Appeal from the Court of Criminal Appeal in Northern Ireland. . . .

On June 20, 1972, after a trial which began on June 12, 1972, before Gibson J. and a jury of the Belfast City Commission, Joseph Lynch was convicted by a unanimous verdict "for that he, the said Joseph Lynch, with others on January 28, 1972, in the county and city of Belfast murdered Raymond Norman Carroll." The deceased was a police constable. Lynch, who was convicted as an aider and abettor, was sentenced to life imprisonment. His appeal to the Court of Criminal Appeal in Northern Ireland having been dismissed, he appealed to the House of Lords.

Two other men, William Bates and William Whelan, were tried with the appellant. Bates was unanimously convicted and sentenced to life imprisonment. Whelan, who was said by the prosecution to have been an accessory before the fact, was acquitted at the close of the case for the Crown.

Gibson J. ruled that the defence of duress was not available to the appellant. The Court of Criminal Appeal dismissed his appeal. He appealed to the House of Lords by leave of the court, which certified that two points of law of general public importance were involved in its decision:

> (1) On a charge of murder is the defence of duress open to a person who is accused as a principal in the second degree (aider and abettor)?
>
> (2) Where a person charged with murder as an aider and abettor is shown to have intentionally done an act which assists in the commission of the murder with knowledge that the probable result of his act, combined with the acts of those whom his act is assisting, will be the death or serious bodily injury of another, is his guilt thereby established without the necessity of proving his willingness to participate in the crime?

The facts described or asserted by the appellant, many of them set out in a signed statement which he made to the police, were summarised by Lord Morris of Borth-y-Gest as follows: He said that while at his house he had received a message that one Sean Meehan required his presence. It was in the forefront of his case that Sean Meehan was and was known to be both a member of the I.R.A. and a ruthless gunman. The appellant had not previously know Meehan personally but had known of him. He said that what Meehan asked to be done had to be done. "You have no other option. I firmly believe that I would have been shot for defying him." So he went with the messenger to an address in Belfast and there saw Meehan and two other men. Meehan, he said, had a rifle in his hand. After it was learned that the appellant could drive a car he was told to go with another man named Mailey (who had a small automatic gun) and seize a car. They went away. Mailey held up a car and ordered its driver to get out. The appellant was told to drive the car to the address where Meehan had remained. The appellant did so. He parked the car and was told that he would not be doing any more driving. So he returned to his own house. Some half-hour later the messenger returned and told the appellant that Meehan wanted him. He went to the same house as before. Meehan, Bates, Mailey and another man were there. Meehan, who had a rifle, told the appellant that he was to drive the car which he then did after Mailey (who had a gun in his pocket) had got in beside him and after Bates and Meehan had got into the back. Meehan, Bates and Mailey had combat jackets and balaclava helmets. The appellant was told to go to a particular road. He asked Meehan what he was going to do and was told: "Bates knows a policeman." Following directions given to him he drove past a garage (at which point Bates said: "That's him") and then stopped near to the garage. Meehan told him to stay there. The other three pulled up their woollen helmets and left the car and ran across the road. Then there were a number of shots fired in quick succession. The three men came running back to the car and got into it. The appellant was told to drive on—which he did. They returned to their starting point.

Witnesses gave evidence that the three men who got out of the car driven by the appellant moved swiftly towards the service bay of the garage where Constable Carroll was doing work on his own car: that shots were fired: that the constable was fatally wounded: that the three men made off towards the waiting car which was then driven away. . . .

Lord Morris of Borthy-y-Gest. . . . [T]he question presents itself whether the issue of duress should have been left to the jury. If on the facts the conclusion could be that the appellant only participated to the extent that he did because he was forced to participate should he be held guilty? There are two aspects of the question, viz., (a) whether there was evidence upon which it would be open to a jury to say that there was duress and (b) if there was, and if a jury considered that there had been duress, whether duress can avail as a defence to a charge which is presented as a charge of murder.

It is important to remember that in this case we are concerned with an alleged principal in the second degree, and that the particular points of law which are raised are framed in reference to an aider and abettor. We are concerned with duress in the form of threats (either expressly made or by conduct indicated) to kill the person threatened or to cause serious personal physical injury to him. I limit my decision to the facts of the present case. The view of the learned judge at the trial was that duress is not available as a defence to a charge of murder: he considered that he was precluded by the weight of authority from holding that it could be and, furthermore, he concluded that the defence was no more available in the case of a principal in the second degree than in the case of a principal in the first degree.

Counsel for the Crown indicated that they would have been prepared to embark before us upon an examination of the evidence with a view to making a submission that the evidence did not have the weight which would warrant a finding that there was duress: they would then have submitted that in any event there could be an application of the proviso. The Court of Appeal have, however, held, as expressly stated in their judgment, that there was on the facts a clear issue as to duress. In view of this it would in my view have been quite inappropriate for us to go beyond the issues of law which are raised. At the same time it is to be remembered, as I have indicated, that the facts as to duress have not been considered by the jury and that because the learned judge withdrew the issue he naturally found it unnecessary to deal with various questions which would have been or might have been most pertinent had the matter been left for the consideration of the jury.

In a series of decisions and over a period of time courts have recognised that there can be circumstances in which duress is a defence. In examining them and more particularly in approaching the issue raised in this appeal the question naturally presents itself—why and on what basis can duress be raised? If someone acts under duress—does he intend what he does? Does he lack what in our criminal law is called *mens rea?* If what he does amounts to a criminal offence ought he to be convicted but be allowed in mercy and in mitigation to be absolved or relieved from some or all of the possible consequences?

The answer that I would give to these questions is that it is proper that any rational system of law should take fully into account the standards of honest and reasonable men. By those standards it is fair that actions and reactions may be tested. If then someone is really threatened with death or serious injury unless he does what he is told to do is the law to pay no heed to the miserable, agonising plight of such a person? For the law to understand not only how the timid but also the stalwart may in a moment of crisis behave is not to make the law weak but to make it just. In the calm of the court-room measures of fortitude or of heroic behaviour are surely not to be demanded when they could not in moments for decision reasonably have been expected even of the resolute and the well disposed.

In posing the case where someone is "really" threatened I use the word "really" in order to emphasise that duress must never be allowed to be the easy answer of those who can devise no other explanation of their conduct nor of those who readily could have avoided the dominance of threats nor of those who allow themselves to be at the disposal and under the sway of some gangster-tyrant. Where duress becomes an issue courts and juries will surely consider the facts with care and discernment.

In my view the law has recognised that there can be situations in which duress can be put forward as a defence. Someone who acts under duress may have a moment of time, even one of the utmost brevity, within which he decides whether he will or will not submit to a threat. There may consciously or subconsciously be a hurried process of balancing the consequences of disobedience against the gravity of the wickedness of the action that is required. The result will be that what is done will be done most unwilling but yet intentionally. Terminology may not, however, much matter. The authorities show that in some circumstances duress may excuse and may therefore be set up as a special defence.

A tenable view might be that duress should never be regarded as furnishing an excuse from guilt but only where established as providing reasons why after conviction a court could mitigate its consequences or absolve from punishment. Some writers including Stephen (see History of the Criminal Law in England (1883), vol. 2, pp.107-108) have so thought. It is, however, much too late in the day, having regard to the lines of authority, to adopt any such view. But apart from this—would such an approach be just? I think not. It is said that if duress could not be set up as a defence there would be difficulties in the way of bringing evidence of the relevant facts and circumstances before the court. I am not greatly impressed by this. A judge could ensure that after a conviction full opportunity would be given to adduce all material evidence. If, however, what a person has done was only done because he acted under the compulsion of a threat of death or of serious bodily injury it would not in my view be just that the stigma of a conviction should be cast on him. As Blackstone put it (Commentaries on the Laws of England (1862), vol. 4, p.23):

> . . . it is highly just and equitable that a man should be excused for those acts which are done through unavoidable force and compulsion.

The law must, I think, take a common sense view. If someone is forced at gun-point either to be inactive or to do something positive—must the law not remember that the instinct and perhaps the duty of self-preservation is powerful and natural? I think it must. A man who is attacked is allowed within reason to take necessary steps to defend himself. The law would be censorious and inhumane which did not recognise the appalling plight of a person who perhaps suddenly finds his life in jeopardy unless he submits and obeys.

The issue in the present case is therefore whether there is any reason why the defence of duress, which in respect of a variety of offences has been recognised as a possible defence, may not also be a possible defence on a charge of being a principal in the second degree to murder. I would confine my decision to that issue. It may be that the law must deny such a defence to an actual killer, and that the law will not be irrational if it does so.

Though it is not possible for the law always to be worked out on coldly logical lines there may be manifest factual differences and contrasts between the situation of an aider and abettor to a killing and that of the actual killer. Let two situations be supposed. In each let it be supposed that there is a real and effective threat of death. In one a person is required under such duress to drive a car to a place or to carry a gun to a place with knowledge that at such place it is planned that *X* is to be killed by those who are imposing their will. In the other situation let it be supposed that a person under such duress is told that he himself must there and then kill *X*. In either situation there is a terrible agonising choice of evils. In the former to save his life the person drives the car or carries the gun. He may cling to the hope that perhaps *X* will not be found at the place or that there will be a change of intention before the purpose is carried out or that in some unforeseen way the dire event of a killing will be averted. The final and fatal moment of decision has not arrived. He saves his own life at a time when the loss of another life is not a certainty. In the second (if indeed it is a situation likely to arise) the person is told that to save his life he himself must personally there and then take an innocent life. It is for him to pull the trigger or otherwise personally to do the act of killing. There, I think, before allowing duress as a defence it may be that the law will have to call a halt. May there still be force in what long ago was said by Hale?

> Again, if a man be desperately assaulted, and in peril of death, and cannot otherwise escape, unless to satisfy his assailant's fury he will kill an innocent person then present, the fear and actual force will not acquit him of the crime and punishment of murder, if he commit the fact; for he ought rather to die himself, than kill an innocent

(see Hale's Pleas of the Crown, vol. 1, p.51). Those words have over long periods of time influenced both thought and writing but I think that their application may have been unduly extended when it is assumed that they were intended to cover all cases of accessories and aiders and abettors.

Writers on criminal law have generally recorded that whatever may be the extent to which the law has recognised duress as a defence it has not been recognised as a defence to a charge of murder (see Russell on Crime, 12th ed. (1964), p.90; Kenny's Outlines of Criminal Law, 19th ed. (1966), p.70; Glanville Williams, Criminal Law, 2nd ed. (1961), p.759, and Smith and Hogan, Criminal Law, 3rd ed. (1973), pp.164-168).

It may be a matter for consideration whether the offences of being accessory before the fact to murder and of aiding and abetting murder might not be constituted as separate offences involving a liability to the imposition of life imprisonment but not as a mandatory sentence.

I fully appreciate that, particularly at the present time, situations may arise where the facts will be much less direct and straightforward than those which, as examples, I have described. I see no advantage in giving illustrations of them. They will be situations presenting greater difficulties of fact than those presented in the present case. But where there have been threats of the nature that really have compelled a person to act in a particular way and he has only acted because of them I think that the approach of the law should be to recognise that the person may be excused in the cases that I have supposed.

It is most undesirable that, in the administration of our criminal law, cases should arise in which, if there is a prosecution leading to a conviction, a just conclusion will only be attained by an exercise thereafter of the prerogative of granting a pardon. I would regret it, therefore, if upon an application of legal principles such cases could arise. Such principles and such approach as will prevent them from arising would seem to me to be more soundly based. . . .

We are only concerned in this case to say whether duress could be a possible defence open to Lynch who was charged with being an aider and abettor. Relying on the help given in the authorities we must decide this as a matter of principle. I consider that duress in such a case can be open as a possible defence. Both general reasoning and the requirements of justice lead me to this conclusion.

The second certified point of law would seem on a first study of it to raise questions closely allied to those raised under the first: that would appear to be so when the question of the necessity to prove "willingness" to participate is raised. In regard to the matters discussed in the judgments on this second point I am content to say that I am in general agreement with the conclusion reached by the majority as expressed in the judgment of the Lord Chief Justice. The words "aid" and "abet" are, I think, synonymous. If in the present case the jury were satisfied that the car was driven towards the garage in pursuance of a murderous plan and that the appellant knew that that was the plan and intentionally drove the car in execution of that plan, he could be held to have aided and abetted even though he regretted the plan or indeed was horrified by it. However great his reluctance, he would have intended to aid and abet. But if that intention and all that he did only came about because of the compulsion of duress of the nature that I have described he would, in my view, have a defence.

The question arises as to what is the proper course to follow. The appellant did not have the opportunity of having his defense of duress considered. I think that he should have it. His conviction should be quashed but having regard to all the circumstances. I consider that the interests of justice require that there should be a re-trial. I would remit the case to the Court of Criminal Appeal to make the appropriate order.

I would allow the appeal accordingly.

Lord Wilberforce. . . . The principle upon which dureess is admitted as a defence is not easy to state. Professor Glanville Williams indeed doubts whether duress fits in to any accepted theory: it may, in his view, stand by itself altogether outside the definition of will and act. The reason for this is historical. Duress emerged very early in our law as a fact of which account has to be taken, particularly in times of civil strife where charges of treason were the normal consequence of defeat, long before the criminal law had worked out a consistent or any theory of "mens rea" or intention. At the present time, whatever the ultimate analysis in jurisprudence may be, the best opinion, as reflected in decisions of judges and in writers, seems to be that duress per minas is something which is superimposed upon the other ingredients which by themselves would make up an offence, i.e., upon act and intention. . . . Heinousness is a word of degree, and that there are lesser degrees of heinousness, even of involvement in homicide, seems beyond doubt. An accessory before the fact, or an aider or abettor, may (not necessarily must) bear a less degree of guilt than the actual killer: and even if the rule of exclusion is absolute, or nearly so in relation to the latter, it need not be so in lesser cases. Nobody would dispute that the greater the degree of heinousness of the crime, the greater and less resistible must be the degree of pressure, if pressure is to excuse. Questions of this kind where it is necessary to weigh the pressures acting upon a man against the gravity of the act he commits are common enough in the criminal law, for example with regard to provocation and self-defence: their difficulty is not a reason for a total rejection of the defence. To say that the defence may be admitted in relation to some degrees of murder, but that its admission in cases of direct killing by a first degree principal is likely to be attended by such great difficulty as almost to justify a ruling that the defence is not available, is not illogical. It simply involves the recognition that by sufficiently adding to the degrees, one may approach an absolute position.

So I find no convincing reason, on principle, why, if a defence of duress in the criminal law exists at all, it should be absolutely excluded in murder charges whatever the nature of the charge; hard to establish, yes, in case of direct killing so hard that perhaps it will never be proved: but in other cases to be judged, strictly indeed, on the totality of facts. . . .

The conclusion which I deduce is that although, in a case of actual killing by a first degree principal the balance of judicial authority at the present time is against the admission of the defence of duress, in the case of lesser degrees of participation, the balance is, if anything, the other way. At the very least, to admit the defence in such cases involves no departure from established decisions. . . .

. . . The authority quoted as regards murder is, as usual that of Hale: ". . . he ought rather to die himself, than kill an innocent." (Hale's Pleas of the Crown, vol. 1, p.51.)

In the same category, perhaps, is a provision (also found in English law) in the law of Northern Ireland, the Criminal Justice Act (Northern Ireland) 1945, section 37 (cf. the Criminal Justice Act 1925, section 47). This provides:

> Any presumption of law that an offence committed by a wife in the presence of her husband is committed under the coercion of the husband is hereby abolished,

> but on a charge against a wife for any offence other than treason or murder it shall be a good defence to prove that the offence was committed in the presence of, and under the coercion of, the husband.

This section has given me some difficulty for it seems to reflect a parliamentary opinion that murder and treason are exceptions to the defence of coercion: and if so it may seem difficult to differentiate the case of duress.

But there is considerable obscurity as to the meaning of this provision. A leading writer says of it that it raises an almost insoluble problem of interpretation and states that it may be regarded as an incomplete statement of the common law which still exists to supplement its deficiency (Glanville Williams, Criminal Law, section 249). As a guide to the principle on which duress should be admitted as a defence to a charge of the various degrees of murder, such light as it shed is too dim to read by. I conclude that these statutory provisions leave the common law of this country untouched. . . .

It is said that such persons as the appellant can always be safeguarded by action of the executive which can order an imprisoned person to be released. I firmly reject any such argument. A law, which requires innocent victims of terrorist threats to be tried for murder and convicted as murderers, is an unjust law even if the executive, resisting political pressures, may decide, after it all, and within the permissible limits of the prerogative to release them. Moreover, if the defence is excluded in law, much of the evidence which would prove the duress would be inadmissible at the trial, not brought out in court, and not tested by cross-examination. The validity of the defence is far better judged by a jury, after proper direction and a fair trial, than by executive officials; and if it is said that to allow the defence will be to encourage fictitious claims of pressure I have enough confidence in our legal system to believe that the process of law is a better safeguard against this than inquiry by a government department.

I would allow the appeal and answer the first certified question in the affirmative. This involves no more than saying that a defence of duress was admissible in law. Since, as I have explained, that defence has yet to be made good in fact, and since a number of elements have to be proved to a jury's satisfaction, I would. . . . order a new trial and remit the case. . . .

Lord Simon of Glaisdale. . . .

My Lords, the first question that arises is whether duress is a defence to a charge of murder as a principal in the second degree. The law has never recognised such a defence; and there is considerable authority that duress, and closely cognate juridical concepts (such as "necessity" and "coercion"), do not extend to being defences to a charge of murder as a principal—if, indeed, to murder in any degree of participation. But it is argued on behalf of the appellant, first, that the law has already recognised duress as a defence to some crimes, and that there is no logical reason for its limitation; and, secondly, that a criminal law which exacts sanctions against persons who are terrorised into performing prohibited acts is making excessive demands on human nature and imposing penalties in circumstances where they are unjustified as retribution and irrelevant as deterrent.

Before turning to examine these considerations, it is convenient to have a working definition of duress—even though it is actually an extremely vague and elusive juristic concept. I take it for present purposes to denote such [well-grounded] fear, produced by threats, of death or grievous bodily harm [or unjustified imprisonment] if a certain act is not done, as overbears the actor's wish not to perform the act, and is effective, at the time of the act, in constraining him to perform it. I am quite uncertain whether the words which I have put in square brackets should be included in any such definition. It is arguable that the test should be purely subjective, and that it is contrary to principle to require the fear to be a reasonable one. . . . Then the law leaves it also quite uncertain whether the fear induced by threats must be of death or grievous bodily harm, or whether threatened loss of liberty suffices: cases of duress in the law of contract suggest that duress may extend to fear of unjustified imprisonment; but the criminal law returns no clear answer. It also leaves entirely unanswered whether, to constitute such a general criminal defence, the threat must be of harm to the person required to perform the act, or extends to the immediate family of the actor (and how immediate?), or to any person. Such questions are not academic, in these days when hostages are so frequently seized. Is it worse to have a pistol thrust into your back and a grenade into your hand, or to have your child (or a neighbour's child) seized by terrorists and held at peril until you have placed in a public building a parcel which you believe to contain a bomb?

I shall have to consider such situations in another connection in a moment. As of now I refer to them to demonstrate the uncertainty of the proffered rule of law in critical and far from fanciful situations. Surely, certainty in the law is hardly less important in the rules which exonerate from criminal responsibility than in those which impose it. Candid recognition, at the outset, of the vague and amorphous nature of the proffered rule should have at least three consequences: first, to cast doubt on whether there is, or should be, any general defence of duress; secondly, to encourage exploration whether the law has not other means of mitigating its rigours towards those who commit prohibited acts under threats which call for far more than ordinary courage to resist; and, thirdly, to cause hesitation before, in deference to logic, extending the defence beyond where it has been heretofore recognised.

And not only do your Lordships meet with uncertainty at the very outset of your inquiry, you also meet with anomaly. Where so little is clear, this at least seems to be established: that the type of threat which affords a defence must be one of human physical harm (including, possibly, imprisonment), so that threat of injury to property is not enough. The criminal law . . . is here at one with the law of contract. But a threat to property may, in certain circumstances, be as potent in overbearing the actor's wish not to perform the prohibited act as a threat of physical harm. For example, the threat may be to burn down his house unless the householder merely keeps watch against interruption while a crime is committed. Or a fugitive from justice may say, "I have it in my power to make your son bankrupt. You can avoid that merely by driving me to the airport." Would not many ordinary people yield to such threats, and act contrary to their wish not to perform an action prohibited by law? Faced with such anomaly, is not the only answer, "Well, the law must draw a line somewhere; and, as a result of experience and human valuation, the law draws it between threats to property and threats to the person"? But if an arbitrary line is thus drawn, is not one between murder and traditionally lesser crimes equally justifiable? How can an arbitrary line drawn between murder as a principal in the first degree and murder as a principal in the second degree be justified either morally or juridically? Faced with anomaly and uncertainty, may it not be that a narrow, arbitrary and anomalous general defence of duress, negativing the crime, is far less acceptable in practice and far less justifiable in juristic theory than a broadly based plea which mitigates the penalty?

Any sane and humane system of criminal justice must be able to allow for all such situations as the following, and not merely for some of them. A person, honestly and reasonably believing that a loaded pistol is at his back which will in all probability be used if he disobeys, is ordered to do an act prima facie criminal. Similarly, a person whose child has been kidnapped, and whom as a consequence of threats he honestly and reasonably believes to be in danger of death or mutilation if he does not perform an act prima facie criminal. Or his neighbour's child in such a situation. Or any child. Or any human being. Or his home, a national heritage, threatened to be blown up. Or a stolen masterpiece of art destroyed. Or his son financially ruined. Or his savings for the old age of himself and his wife put in peril. In other words, a sane and humane system of criminal justice needs some general flexibility, and not merely some quirks of deference to certain odd and arbitrarily defined human weaknesses. In fact our own system of criminal justice has such flexibility, provided that it is realised that it does not consist only in the positive prohibitions and injunctions of the criminal law, but extends also to its penal sanctions. May it not be that the infinite variety of circumstances in which the lawful wish of the actor is overborne could be accommodated with far greater flexibility, with much less anomaly, and with avoidance of the social evils which would attend acceptance of the appellant's argument (that duress is a general criminal defence), by taking those circumstances into account in the sentence of the court? Is not the whole rationale of duress as a criminal defence that it recognises that an act prohibited by the criminal law may be morally innocent? Is not an absolute discharge just such an acknowledgment of moral innocence? . . .

I spoke of the social evils which might be attendant on the recognition of a general defence of duress. Would it not enable a gang leader of notorious violence to confer on his organisation by terrorism immunity from the criminal law? Every member of his gang might well be able to say with truth, "It was as much as my life was worth to disobey." Was this not in essence the plea of the appellant? We do not, in general, allow a superior officer to confer such immunity on his subordinates by any defence of obedience to orders: why should we allow it to terrorists? Nor would it seem to be sufficient to stipulate that no one can plead duress as a defence who had put himself into a position in which duress could be exercised on himself. Might not his very initial involvement with, and his adherence to, the gang be due to terrorism? Would it be fair to exclude a defence of duress on the ground that its subject should have sought police protection, were the police unable to guarantee immunity, or were co-operation with the police reasonably believed itself to be a warrant for physical retribution? . . . In my respectful submission your Lordships should hesitate long lest you may be inscribing a charter for terrorists, gang-leaders and kidnappers.

As Stephen pointed out, coercion lies at the very basis of the criminal law itself. The criminal law is itself a system of threats of pains and penalties if its commands are disregarded. Is it to abdicate because some subject institutes a countervailing system of threats? The answer might well be a reluctant Yes, if the only alternative were to require something more than ordinary human nature can reasonably be expected to bear. But is that the only alternative? Are prosecutors bound to indict? Have English courts no power and duty to reflect moral guilt in the sentence? (I shall deal later with murder, where the penalty is a fixed one.) . . .

My Lords, I have ventured so far to deal with the policy of any sane and humane system of criminal justice as regards the problem which faces your Lordships, and with its juristic implications. But, of course, no discussion can have any claim to adequacy which does not extend to the authorities. Fortunately, I am absolved from reviewing them in detail, since that has been done by my noble and learned friends. My only misgiving is that such an impressive muster should be sent packing so ignominiously. Poor Hale, poor Blackstone; wretched Russel and Kenny; poor, poor Lord Denman. But at least they are in good company. There are all those famous jurists, headed by Stephen, who drew up the draft code of 1879 under the fond belief that they were codifying the common law. And all those framers of the Commonwealth codes, and the commentators on them, under the same illusion. And Americans too. They are like the denizens of the first circle of Hell, who, for all their wisdom and virtue, lived in such benighted times as to have forfeited salvation. So, too, these great lawyers are too eminent to go altogether unacknowledged: they are recognised with a courtly bow, but their words are lost in the gale of juristic change. For, in truth their voices were unanimous that duress is no defence to murder. . . .

A sane system of criminal justice does not permit a subject to set up a countervailing system of sanctions or by terrorism to confer criminal immunity on his gang. A humane system of criminal justice does not exact retribution from those who infringe the substantive provisions of its code under stresses greater than ordinary human nature can bear, nor attempt, by making an example of them, to deter those who in the nature of things are beyond deterrent. A sane and humane system of criminal justice is sufficiently flexible to reconcile such considerations, and to allow for all their infinite degrees of interaction. I have ventured to suggest that our own system of criminal justice is capable of such sanity and humanity—provided always that it is recognised to extend beyond the mere injunctions and prohibitions and immunities of the substantive criminal code.

There is, however, an apparent exception to such flexibility. This is constituted where a crime has a fixed penalty—specifically, murder with its fixed penalty of life imprisonment. It is true that prosecutors have a discretion whether to indict; but such discretion is hardly real in the circumstances which fall for your Lordships' instant consideration. It is true that the Home Secretary can advise exercise of the royal prerogative of mercy, and that the Parole Board can mitigate the rigour of the penal code: but these are executive not forensic processes, and can only operate after the awful verdict with its dire sentence has been pronounced. Is a sane and humane law incapable of encompassing this situation? I do not believe so.

An infraction of the criminal code under duress does not involve that the conduct is either involuntary or unintentional. The actor is therefore responsible for his act. But his responsibility is diminished by the duress. Provocation operates similarly to diminish the responsibility, transmuting the great crime of murder to the lesser crime of manslaughter with no fixed penalty.

The English common law evolved the concept of provocation. Since the Homicide Act 1957 the provocation may originate in a third pary, making the doctrine even closer to that of duress. The Scottish common law evolved another concept of diminished responsibility for homicide (H.M. Advocate v. Dingwall (1867) 5 Irv. 466). In my judgment the English common law is well capable of accommodating duress under the concept of diminished responsibility reducing murder to manslaughter. . . .

Your Lordships have therefore, as it seems to me, three courses open: (1) to approve of the various cases where duress has been allowed to be a defence negativing the crime, and then extend the doctrine to the crime of murder as a principal; (2) to overrule the cases where duress has been allowed to be a defence negativing the crime, leaving duress as a matter of mitigation of sentence in crimes other than homicide, and in homicide as a defence reducing murder to manslaughter; (3) to affirm the cases where duress has been allowed to be a defence negativing the crime, but to refuse to extend it to murder as a principal.

I have, I hope, sufficiently indicated the juridical, practical and constitutional considerations which have caused me decisively to reject the first course.

Were it not for two considerations I would strongly urge your Lordships to adopt the second course. The first such consideration is that the Great Britain Parliament in 1925 and the Northern Irish Parliament as recently as 1945 affirmed the existence of the strictly cognate concept of "coercion" as a general defence available to married women who commit what would otherwise be criminal offences (except murder or treason) in the presence of their husbands. These seem to me to have been policy decisions by Parliament with implications as to both the existence and limitations of the defence of duress:

they should be respected by the courts, which should leave it to Parliament to alter, develop or confirm the existing law as so advised. That is strongly reinforced by the second consideration. This branch of the law is closely bound up with matters of policy relating to public safety. Such matters are far more fitly weighed in Parliament on the advice of the Executive than developed in courts of law. In fact, the law of duress is currently subject to the examination of the Law Commission (see Working Paper No. 55), which will shortly be reporting to Parliament.

In these circumstances, I have no doubt that the proper course for your Lordships is merely to accept the law as it has heretofore developed, and to declare that the defence of duress is not available to a person accused of murder as a principal. I would therefore answer the first certified question, No. . . .

. . . I would dismiss the appeal.

Lord KILBRANDON. My Lords, the learned trial judge directed the jury to the effect that the defence of duress is not available as exculpation in a charge of murder, whether the accused has been charged as a principal in the first or in the second degree. In my opinion, that direction correctly stated the law as it then stood and now stands. . . . It will not do to claim that judges have the duty—call it the privilege—of seeing to it that the common law expands and contracts to meet what the judges conceive to be the requirements of modern society. Modern society rightly prefers to exercise that function for itself, and this it conveniently does through those who represent it in Parliament. And its representatives nowadays demand, or should demand, that they be briefed by all those who can qualify an interest to advise them. The fascinating discussions of policy which adorn the speeches of your Lordships—and to which I intend to make a short and undistinguished addition—are themselves highly illustrative of what I mean. They may perhaps be taken as the ultimate in the distillation of legal policy-opinion. But that is not enough. I will not take time to enumerate the various other disciplines and interests whose views are of equal value in deciding what policy should inform the legislation, necessary if reform of the law is really called for, giving effect to the defence of duress per minas in all crimes including murder. In the absence of such consultations I do not think it would be right to decide an appeal in such a way as to set aside the common understanding of the law.

I will say a word as to the law as presently understood, because thorough examinations of the history and progression of the doctrine have already been made. The content of duress I will look at briefly later on, in so far as that is necessary. Duress is recognised as a defence to crime. It has never been laid down judicially as a matter of decision that murder is an exception to that rule, though many judges have expressed the opinion that it is. The whole weight of opinion in common law jurisdiction has always been to that effect. For sheer economy of citation I will select two examples only, one academic, the other judicial. Professor Kenny in his Outlines of Criminal Law, at p.74—

I quote from the 12th edition (1926) since it was prepared by him—says, "It (sc. duress per minas) certainly will not excuse murder." This is what the master must have taught Cambridge law students over many years. I will select as my second authority that of Bray C.J. in Reg. v. Brown and Morley [1968] S.A.S.R. 467, since in his dissenting opinion he allows, as I myself would not, duress as a defence to a charge of murder as a principal in the second degree. He says at p.499: "as at present advised I do not think duress could constitute a defence to one who actually kills or attempts to kill the victim."

I do not think the fact that duress may excuse treason is relevant—see M'Growther's Case, 18 St. Tr. 391—on the argument that treason is an even graver crime than murder. I do not agree with that. The crime of treason always seems grave to an injured or threatened executive. But no one could classify George Washington or Flora Macdonald—undoubted traitors—as heinous criminals. . . .

The next aspect of the matter leads me to the little I have to say on policy. The difference between the defence of duress, which comes from coercion by the act of man, and that of necessity, which comes from coercion by the forces of nature, is narrow and unreal. Counsel for the appellant was, in my opinion, right to concede that if his argument succeeded, the case of Reg. v. Dudley and Stephens, 14 Q.B.D. 273 must be held to have been wrongly decided. It seems clear that, if the argument for the appellant is sound, the judge in that case ought to have directed the jury that in law the defence of necessity was available, and to have taken a plain verdict of "guilty" or "not guilty." If that be so it will then become essential, at some time or other, to decide how far the doctrine of necessity is to extend. Unless, for example, want is to be allowed to excuse theft, a strange situation would arise. Suppose that in the instant case the accused had acted under the threat of violence to his family. Then, although if he had taken a loaf from a supermarket to feed his starving children he would have been a thief, he is guiltless if, for his own family's safety, he kills the father of Constable Carroll's children. Again, it is impossible not to be deeply impressed by the circumstances, dramatically figured by your Lordships, which are especially liable to occur at this moment in Northern Ireland; the coercion of otherwise law-abiding citizens could, under present law, turn them into unwilling murderers. On the other hand, if the present law be altered, coercion will be a good defence to one who, at the behest of a mafia or I.R.A. boss, places a bomb in an aircraft and 250 people are killed. It is more likely, too, that the accused will have assisted by preparing and delivering the bomb knowing its intended use; in that case the question would be, is coercion a good defence to murder as a principal in the second degree or as accessory? This situation was long ago foreseen. The closing passage of the judgment in Reg. v. Dudley and Stephens points out that, if the defence were a good one, the strongest man on board the boat might have eaten his way through all the crew, killing them one by one, and after his rescue have been held guiltless. How many may a man kill in order to save his own life? I pose such a question for the purpose of suggesting that it cannot be answered in this place. It raises issues, some legal, others social, even more ethical, upon which the public will clamour to be heard. It would probably be necessary, too, to lay down that coercion would not avail one who, e.g., took orders from the head of the gang of which he was a voluntary member. Such a provision figures in the codes; I do not see how it could become part of English law save by legislation. In short, the policy questions are so deeply embedded in the legal doctrines we are being asked to review that we may be in danger of reforming the law upon an inadequate appreciation of public needs and public opinion. What would purport to be a judgment declaratory of the common law would in reality be a declaration of public policy.

On the question whether it is possible, in this context, to distinguish between the defences open to a principal in the first degree and those open to a principal in the second degree I have had the advantage of seeing the speech of my noble and learned friend Lord Simon of Glaisdale. I agree with him that no distinction can be made. . . .

On the view which I have taken, it is not truly necessary to go into the meaning of the word duress, that is, the sense in which it may exhibit an admissible defence to crime. Our learned forebears who used the word knew what they meant by it, and they were capable of expressing themselves as clearly as we can do. But I must confess to great difficulty in seeing how, in a reformed situation (by which I mean a situation in which all crimes are treated as regards duress in the same way), duress should exculpate rather than mitigate. The effect of a threat upon its recipient may be said to be to reduce his constancy, so that he is forced to do what he knows to be wrong and would not have done unless he had been threatened. He is not like the infant or the insane, who are disqualified or disabled from forming a criminal intention. He has decided to do a wrong thing, having balanced in his mind, perhaps unconsciously, the consequences to himself of refusal against the consequences to another of acquiescence. But the agonising nature of the decision he has to make may render it impossible for a civilised system of criminal law to hold him fully responsible for what followed from that decision. Much of our difficulty in assessing his responsibility at law stems from the "black-or-white" nature of that unfortunate expression *mens rea,* which is none the better for concealing itself "in the decent obscurity of a learned language." Our minds, whatever we are doing, are neither wholly wicked nor wholly virtuous. To elaborate upon that proposition would be to encourage the wrong kind of debate. The practical importance, for present purposes, is that the decision of the threatened man whose constancy is overborne so that he yields to the threat, is a calculated decision to do what he knows to be wrong, and is therefore that of a man with, perhaps to some exceptionally limited extent, a "guilty mind." But he is at the same time a man whose mind is less guilty than is his who acts as *he* does but under no such constraint. The law must give effect to that distinction.

This would be easy except in a charge of murder, whether against a principal in the first or the second degree, or against an accessory before the fact, upon all of whom the court was always, on conviction, obliged to impose the extreme penalty of the law. It seems to me probable, therefore, that if the solution ultimately found is the allowing of duress, or necessity, as defence to all crimes, in the sense only of mitigating penalty, and if murder is to continue as a crime visited upon conviction with a mandatory sentence, it would be perfectly reasonable, for the reasons I have indicated, to make duress or necessity ground for declaring diminished responsibility, so that in cases of murder where the defence was established a verdict of manslaughter would be returned and the penalty left at large. . . .

Lord Edmund-Davies. . . .

The facts of the case have alread been related in the speeches of my noble and learned friends. I restrict myself to quoting a passage from the judgment of the Lord Chief Justice:

> It was . . . proved that, before the date of the shooting, six policemen had already been murdered in the Ardoyne area, which was a stronghold of the Provisional I.R.A., and where the appellant lived, and that Sean Meehan was a well-known and ruthless gunman, and the appellant and Bates gave evidence that Meehan was the kind of person whom it would be perilous to defy or disobey and who, on the occasion in question, gave his instructions in a manner which indicated to them that he would tolerate no disobedience. There was no evidence of a direct threat by Meehan or any other person against the life or personal safety of the appellant or any member of his family, but both the appellant and Bates testified to their fear of Meehan and their clear view that their disobedience of his instructions would cause them to be shot.

The Lord Chief Justice proceeded to consider the various submissions of the prosecution that the available evidence did not constitute a triable issue fit to go to the jury on the plea of duress. The court accepted that "mere apprehension" of death or serious bodily injury is not enough, and that "the duress must be constraint exercised by one person on another." But they added that,

> The constraint . . . can be implied, as well as express, and, once there is evidence that A has somehow caused B to fear for himself or his family, it is a question of fact whether the reasonable possibility of this having occurred has been disproved by the Crown. We consider that the evidence in this case raised a question for the jury whether Meehan impliedly threatened the appellant with death or serious personal injury.

The court next considered the submission of the Crown that,

> . . . the defence of duress is not available to an accused who voluntarily joins in a criminal enterprise and its afterwards subjected to threats of violence in order to ensure that he does not withdraw, even if the enterprise becomes more gravely criminal than the accused foresaw.

This may well have been an echo of Stephen's History of the Criminal Law of England, vol. 2, p.108, that:

> If a man chooses to expose and still more if he chooses to submit himself to illegal compulsion, it may not operate even in mitigation of punishment. It would surely be monstrous to mitigate the punishment of a murderer on the ground that he was a member of a secret society by which he would have been assassinated if he had not committed murder.

But, in the light of Lynch's police statement and his evidence that at no time was he a member of the I.R.A. or any other organisation, and in the absence of any prosecution evidence to the contrary, the appellate court not surprisingly held that the point did not arise for consideration and expressly reserved it for determination if on any future occasion it became relevant.

As to the imminence of the threat of death or serious bodily injury, and the Crown's submission that the plea of duress is never available if the accused has not taken advantage of an opportunity to escape from its influence, the Lord Chief Justice said:

> We consider it to be a question of fact (assuming duress to be a proper issue for the jury) whether the Crown could successfully invoke this principle, bearing in mind that if the effect of the threat is felt at the material time, this is enough to keep duress in issue: Reg. v. Hudson [1971] 2 Q.B. 202, Subramaniam v. Public Prosecutor [1956] 1 W.L.R. 965. The same authorities are relevant to the immediacy of the threat, because the question is not when the threats are made, but whether they overbore the will of the accused at a material time.

Having thus considered the main elements of duress, and having apparently adopted the subjective test of the effect on the mind of this appellant of the alleged implied threat, the Lord Chief Justice concluded:

> There was, in our opinion, on the facts a clear issue of duress in this case, and therefore the question in this appeal as to whether duress may afford a defence to a person accused of murder as a principal in the second degree is material.

It is manifestly impossible to arrive at an acceptable answer to that question without first examining the raison d'être and limits of the plea of duress. . . .

Of the two theories regarding the nature of the plea of duress canvassed below and before this House, I prefer the view of Professor Glanville Williams (Criminal Law, p.751 para. 242) that:

> True duress is not inconsistent with act and will as a matter of legal definition, the maxim being coactus volui. Fear of violence does not differ in kind from fear of economic ills, fear of displeasing others, or any other determinant of choice, it would be inconvenient to regard a particular type of motive as negativing will.

The alternative theory advanced ("Theory 2") is that, as a result of his will being overborne by threats of grave violence, the transgressor never forms the criminal intent necessary to constitute the offence with which he is charged, whatever be its nature, which would thus exculpate an actual killer who would otherwise be a principal in the first degree to murder. In my judgment, this will not do. Duress is properly to be regarded as a plea in confession and avoidance, and I respectfully adopt the view of the Lord Chief Justice that:

> Apart altogether from philosophical argument, it seems clear that the defendants Whelan, Gill, Subramaniam, and Hudson intentionally received stolen goods, stole, took possession of ammunition and committed perjury, even though the reason that they did so was that their respective wills were overborne by threats. Their prima facie criminal acts were the result of a conscious choice, although the choice was made unwillingly and because of the threats to which they were subjected.

At the end of the day, the defence of duress is probably best evaluated without reference to its supposed relation to either *actus reus* or *mens rea,* for, in the words of Professor Turpin [1972] C.L.J. 205, "not every morally exculpatory circumstance has a necessary bearing on these legal ingredients of crime. . . .

If the circumstances are such that "the ordinary power of human resistance" is overborne, why should they not render excusable even the unlawful killing of an innocent person? Several reasons have been advanced for asserting that no duress, however terrible, can save such a participator in unlawful killing as the appellant from being convicted of murder. One of these has already been referred to and is epitomised by the observation of Lord Coleridge C.J., in Reg. v. Dudley and Stephens, 14 Q.B.D. 273, 287 that: "To preserve one's life is generally speaking a duty, but it may be the plainest and the highest duty to sacrifice it." Such an approach was elaborately dealt with in S. v: Goliath, 1972 (3) S.A. 1; S.A.L.R. (1972) (3) 465 where the Appellate Division held that on a charge of murder compulsion can be a complete defence. In giving the majority judgment, Rumpff J. developed the submission of defence counsel, at p.6 that, "the criminal law, should not be applied as if it were a blueprint for saintliness but rather in a manner in which it can be obeyed by the reasonable man," by saying:

> It is generally accepted . . . that for the ordinary person in general his life is more valuable than that of another. Only those who possess the quality of heroism will intentionally offer their lives for another. Should the criminal law then state that compulsion could never be a defence to a charge of murder, it would demand that a person who killed another under duress, whatever the circumstances, would have to comply with a higher standard than that demanded of the average person. I do not think that such an exception to the general rule which applies in criminal law is justified. (S.A.L.R. (1973) (3) 465, 480.)

It has also to be remembered that lack of "heroism" may not necessarily be selfishly self-directed, for the duress exerted may well extend to and threaten the lives and safety of others, and, as has been said, ". . . when a third person's life is also at stake even the path of heroism is obscure" (Wechsler and Michael, A Rationale of the Law of Homicide (1937) 37 Col. L.R. 738). That these are not idle considerations is demonstrated by Reg. v. Hurley and Murray [1967] V.R. 526, where the wife of one of two accused (charged with having been accessories after the fact to the felony of escape) was already a hostage of the oppressors. In such circumstances, what, it may be asked, is the nature of the "heroism" which the law may properly demand?

A second ground advanced in support of the proposition that duress affords no defence in murder is said to have public policy as its basis. Murder, it is rightly said, is a crime so grave that no facilities should be afforded to the murderer to escape conviction and punishment. It is then added that duress is a plea easy to raise and that (the onus to destroy it being upon the prosecution) it may prove impossible to rebut it, however dark the suspicion that it is not well-founded, and that in this way the murderer may well escape retribution. But this is true of many other pleas which extenuate or even extinguish criminal culpability—drunkenness, for example, as destroying criminal intent, or an alibi which may serve to eliminate criminal involvement of any kind—and no course is open other than to repose confidence in the tribunal of fact to discharge its duty of scrutinising with care the evidence adduced. In this respect, the risk of a miscarriage of justice by a guilty man being acquitted is no greater in murder trials than in those cases in which the plea of duress is, on the authorities, clearly available, despite their gravity—for example, even in attempted murder, where an intent actually to kill is an essential ingredient. Nor should the present grave state of affairs prevailing in Northern Ireland, to which prosecuting counsel very understandably referred, lead this House to arrive at a conclusion different from that which would be proper were Ireland trouble-free. . . .

Prosecuting counsel urged upon this House that, even were we to regard it as possibly appropriate to allow duress as a defence to murder, we should leave the matter to be dealt with by Parliament, and in this context invoked certain observations of the Lord Chancellor in Reg. v. Hyam [1975] A.C. 55, 69. But my noble and learned friend Lord Hailsham of St. Marylebone was there dealing with a topic (the criminal intent necessary to constitute murder) upon which authoritative pronouncements have several times been made by this House, whereas the questions certified in the present appeal have never hitherto been considered here and, as far as I am aware, have never even been the subject of obiter dicta. We are therefore called upon for the first time to make an unfettered decision on a point of pure common law in accordance with basic common law principles. In these circumstances, with respect, I find it quite unacceptable to hold that, were this House otherwise inclined to adopt a view favourable to the appellant, it should dismiss his appeal and, presumably, any other appeals of a like kind until the legislature dealt with the matter.

I therefore turn at long last to consider whether, as the learned trial judge thought, "The whole weight of judicial writing is against the availability of duress as a defence on a charge of murder," and whether, if so, that should lead this House to the same conclusion. The speeches of my noble and learned friends amply illustrate the frequency with which judges in this country have observed that duress does not extend as a defence to murder, but, with but one solitary exception, these observations were all obiter dicta, being made in cases where murder was not charged. The one exception cited to this House is Reg. v. Tyler, 8 C. & P. 616, where two men accused of murder sought to excuse their participation in the act of killing performed by one Thom on the ground of duress. I quoted at an earlier stage the widely expressed observations of Lord Denman C.J. in charging the jury, and they amount to a direction that duress was no defence. But, as Professor Glanville Williams has pointed out (Criminal Law, pp.759-760, para. 247).

> . . . the same result could have been reached in *Tyler* even if murder is not excepted from the defence of duress. There appears to have been no evidence that Tyler went in fear of death (which would be the minimum necessary to justify murder); nor was any attempt made to show that Tyler could not escape from the gang. Also, the evidence seemed to show that Tyler had voluntarily joined a criminal organisation knowing of its purpose; and one who does this has no cause for complaint if he is debarred from the defence of duress in respect of threats afterwards made to him. . . .

Having considered the available material to the best of my ability, I find myself unable to accept that any ground in law, logic, morals or public policy has been established to justify withholding the plea of duress in the present case. To say, as Murnaghan J. did in Attorney-General v. Whelan [1934] I.R. 518, 526, that " . . . murder is a crime so heinous that . . . in such a case the strongest duress would not be any justification" is, with respect, to beg the whole question. That murder has a unique gravity most would regard as not open to doubt, but the degree of legal criminality or blameworthiness involved in participation therein depends upon all the circumstances of the particular case, just as it does whenever the *actus reus* and the *mens rea* necessary to constitute any other offence are established. In homicide, the law already recognises degrees of criminality, notwithstanding that unlawful killing with malice aforethought has unqestionably taken place. In non-homicidal cases, the degree of criminality or blameworthiness can and should be reflected in the punishment meted out, a course which the mandatory life sentence for murder prohibits. . . . Professor J. C. Smith has rightly observed ([1974] Crim. L. R. 352) that: "To allow a defence to crime is not to express approval of the action of the accused person but only to declare that it does not merit condemnation and punishment." For the reasons I have sought to advance, I can find no valid ground for preventing the appellant Lynch from presenting the plea of duress, and I would therefore be for allowing his appeal. By doing so, I consider that this House would be paying due regard to those "contemporary views of what is just, what is moral, what is humane" which my noble and learned friend, Lord Diplock, described in Reg. v. Hyam [1975] A.C. 55, 89 as constituting "the underlying principle which is the justification for retaining the common law as a living source of rules binding upon all members of contemporary society in England." . . .

Appeal allowed.

Notes and Questions

1. Is Lynch arguing that he should be excused in this case because he did the right thing? Or is his argument based on an entirely different theory? Section 2.09 of the Model Penal Code provides a duress defense as follows:

Section 2.09. Duress.

(1) It is an affirmative defense that the actor engaged in the conduct charged to constitute an offense because he was coerced to do so by the use of, or a threat to use, unlawful force against his person or the person of another, that a person of reasonable firmness in his situation would have been unable to resist.

(2) The defense provided by this Section is unavailable if the actor recklessly placed himself in a situation in which it was probable that he would be subjected to duress. The defense is also unavailable if he was negligent in placing himself in such a situation, whenever negligence suffices to establish culpability for the offense charged.

(3) It is not a defense that a woman acted on the command of her husband, unless she acted under such coercion as would establish a defense under this Section. [The presumption that a woman acting in the presence of her husband is coerced is abolished.]

(4) When the conduct of the actor would otherwise be justifiable under Section 3.02, this Section does not preclude such defense.

Explanatory Note

Subsection (1) establishes the affirmative defense of duress, which is applicable if the actor engaged in criminal conduct because he was coerced to do so by the use or threat of unlawful force against himself or another, that a person of reasonable firmness in his situation would have been unable to resist. The standard is thus partially objective; the defense is not established simply by the fact that the defendant was coerced; he must have been coerced in circumstances under which a person of reasonable firmness in his situation would likewise have been unable to resist.

Subsection (2) deprives the actor of his defense if he recklessly placed himself in a situation in which it was probable that he would be subjected to duress. Thus, an actor reckless in this respect can be liable for offenses that carry a higher culpability standard than recklessness. In the case of negligent exposure to the possibility of duress, however, Subsection (2) only permits an offense to be charged for which negligence is sufficient to establish culpability.

Subsection (3) abolishes special rules that still obtained in some jurisdictions concerning the effect of marriage as an automatic basis for claims of coercion. The bracketed sentence is included for those jurisdictions where silence on the point might be construed as continuing present law.

Subsection (4) assures that this section will not be construed to narrow the effect of the choice of evils defense afforded by Section 3.02. This intention is that the defenses of duress and choice of evils will be independently considered, and that the fact that a defense is unavailable under one section will not be relevant to its availability under the other. . . .

Comment . . .

2. *Proper Scope of Defense*. . . . The case of concern here is that in which the actor makes a choice, but claims in his defense that he was so intimidated that he was unable to choose otherwise. Should such psychological incapacity be given the same exculpative force as the physical incapacity that may afford a defense under Section 2.01? Given the other provisions of the Model Code, this is the concrete issue to be faced in judging whether and how far duress ought to be recognized as a distinct defense.

In favor of allowing the defense, it may be argued that the legal sanction cannot be effective in the case supposed and that the actor may not properly be blamed for doing what he had to choose to do. It seems clear, however, that the argument in its full force must be rejected. The crucial reason is the same as that which elsewhere leads to an unwillingness to vary legal norms with the individual's capacity to meet the standards they prescribe, absent a disability that is both gross and verifiable, such as the mental disease or defect that may establish irresponsibility. The most that it is feasible to do with lesser disabilities is to accord them proper weight in sentencing. To make liability depend upon the fortitude of any given actor would be no less impractical or otherwise impolitic than to permit it to depend upon such other variables as intelligence or clarity of judgment, suggestibility or moral insight.

Moreover, the legal standard may gain in its effectiveness by being unconditional in this respect. It cannot be known what choices might be different if the actor thought he had a chance of exculpation on the ground of his peculiar disabilities instead of knowing that he does not. No less important, legal norms and sanctions operate not only at the moment of climactic choice, but also in the fashioning of values and of character.

Though, for the foregoing reasons, the submission that the actor lacked the fortitude to make the moral choice should not be entertained as a defense, a different situation is presented if the claimed excuse is based upon the incapacity of men in general to resist the coercive pressures to which the individual succumbed. Here the essential principle is that which Henry Hart has put as follows: "Obligations of conduct fixed by a fair appraisal of the minimum requirements for the maintenance and fostering of community life will, by hypothesis, be obligations which normal members of the community will be *able* to comply with, given the necessary awareness of the circumstances of fact calling for compliance." This is to say that law is ineffective in the deepest sense, indeed that it is hypocritical, if it imposes on the actor who has the misfortune to confront a dilemmatic choice, a standard that his judges are not prepared to affirm that they should and could comply with if their turn to face the problem should arise. Condemnation in such a case is bound to be an ineffective threat; what is, however, more significant is that it is divorced from any moral base and is unjust. Where it would be both "personally and socially debilitating" to accept the actor's cowardice as a defense, it would be equally debilitating to demand that heroism be the standard of legality. The proper treatment of the hero is not merely to withhold a social censure; it is to give him praise and just reward.

3. *Approach of Model Penal Code.* The Model Code accordingly provides for the defense in cases where the actor was coerced by force or threats of force "that a person of reasonable firmness in his situation would have been unable to resist." The standard is not, however, wholly external in its reference; account is taken of the actor's "situation," a term that should here be given the same scope it is accorded in appraising recklessness and negligence. Stark, tangible factors that differentiate the actor from another, like his size, strength, age, or health, would be considered in making the exculpatory judgment. Matters of temperament would not.

Given the nature of the problem and the criteria proposed for its solution, it is reasonable to confine the exculpation to the case where force against the person of the actor or another, or the threat thereof, is the instrument of coercion. Perils to property alone may sometimes justify upon a proper choice of evils and they are not excluded by the terms of Section 3.02. But when the claimed excuse is that duress was irresistible, threats to property or even reputation cannot exercise sufficient power over persons of "reasonable firmness" to warrant consideration in these terms.

Beyond this limitation to coercive force or threats against the person, no valid reason was perceived for demanding that the threat be one of death or even of great bodily harm, that the imperiled victim be the actor rather than another,[1] or that the injury portended be immediate in point of time. It is sufficient that factors such as these be given evidential weight, along with other circumstances in the application of the statutory standard that a person of "reasonable firmness" would have succumbed to the pressure. They must be weighed, of course, together with other factors, since persons of reasonable firmness surely break at different points depending on the stakes that are involved. It is obvious that even homicide may sometimes be the product of coercion that is truly irresistible, that danger to a loved one may have greater impact on a person of reasonable firmness than a danger to himself, and, finally, that long and wasting pressure may break down resistance more effectively than a threat of immediate destruction. This section is framed on these assumptions.

The typical situation in which the section will be invoked is one in which the actor is told that unless he performs a particular criminal act a threatened

1. *Compare* Judge Magruder's comment in R.I. Recreation Center v. Aetna Cas. & Sur. Co., 177 F.2d 603, 606-607 (1st Cir. 1949): "As to fear for the bodily safety of a third person, even a close relative, there is a surprising dearth of authority; but if the question were ever presented under sufficiently strong, dramatic and convincing circumstances, I am fairly sure the courts would sanction the defense of coercion."

> harm will occur and he yields to the pressure of the threat, performing the forbidden act. The applicability of the language to [another kind] of [situation] merits brief review. First, suppose that by the continued use of unlawful force, persons effectively break down the personality of the actor, rendering him submissive to whatever suggestions they make. They then, using neither force nor threat of force on that occasion, suggest that he perform a criminal act; and the actor does what they suggest. The "brainwashed" actor would not be barred from claiming the defense of duress, since he may assert that he was "coerced" to perform the act by the use of unlawful force on his person.[2] He might also argue that he is responding to earlier threats to use unlawful force that have rendered him submissive to those who made the threats because he still subconsciously fears they will be carried out. Of course, it may be very difficult to persuade a jury that an act willingly performed at the time was truly the product of unlawful force and would have been performed by a person of reasonable firmness subjected to similar conditions, but as framed, the section is broad enough to permit such an argument.[3]

2. Would the Model Penal Code duress defense exculpate Lynch—or, more precisely, would the Code require that the issue be submitted to the jury? On retrial, Lynch was again convicted of murder and thereafter made his imprisonment a cause celebre by deliberately starving himself to death in a British prison. It now seems undisputed that he was an active member of the IRA. Is this a reason to reject the concept of a duress defense? Is it a reason to be cautious in adopting such a defense?

3. Is the point of the duress defense, and indeed of all excuses to criminal culpability, that in these cases the law cannot deter, since those with excuses cannot be "threatened" into obeying the law? Thus, the argument goes, we cannot deter those under duress because the threat of punishment later cannot outweigh the immediate threat that has produced the duress. Note Professor H. L. A. Hart's answer to this argument:

2. The psychological phenomenon referred to commonly as "brainwashing" is a process by which an individual's capacity to act of his own volition is impaired. Such a mind-control scheme might, for example, consist of physical and emotional assaults upon the individual, occasional rewards for responding to directions, a demand for renunciation of past values, and reeducation (indoctrination) to the new ideas of the brainwasher. The effects of such brainwashing efforts upon a defendant might be severe enough to give rise to other defenses to a charge of crime, such as insanity, involuntary action (to the extent the person brainwashed was hypnotized), intoxication (if drugs were used in the brainwashing process) or mistake of fact (if the actor was convinced of the reality of something illusory). The duress defense may be appropriate in certain circumstances where a defendant was "so far in thrall to some power" that the choices he made were not really his. Although there have been declarations that the defense of duress is inapplicable to purely internal psychic incapacity, the wording of Subsection (1) leaves open its possible use in some such cases.

3. If it were asserted that the actor had been permanently "programmed" to commit crimes, it would, of course, not be tolerable simply to excuse the actor on the basis of duress without counteractive treatment. In that event, he would merely repeat the crimes, again invoking the defense. It might be appropriate that such thorough "brainwashing," if it is possible, be treated as the cause of a particular kind of mental disease or defect, giving the state power to commit and treat the actor on grounds of his dangerousness to others.

It is questionable, however, whether such a thorough "brainwashing" is possible. . . .

Bentham's argument was a reply to Blackstone who, in expounding the main excusing conditions recognized in the criminal law of his day, claimed that "all the several pleas and excuses which protect the committer of a forbidden act from punishment which is otherwise annexed thereto may be reduced to this single consideration: "the want or defect of Will" [and to the principle] "that to constitute a crime . . . there must be first, a vicious will." In his Introduction to the Principles of Morals and Legislation, under the heading, "main excusing conditions" [Bentham] then undertakes to show that the infliction of punishment on those who have done, while in any of these conditions, what the law forbids "must be inefficacious: it cannot act so as to prevent the mischief." All the common talk about want or defect of will or lack of a "vicious" will is, he says, "nothing to the purpose," except so far as it implies the reason (inefficacy of punishment) which he himself gives for recognizing these excuses.

Bentham's argument is in fact a spectacular non sequitur. He sets out to prove that to punish the mad, the infant child or those who break the law unintentionally or under duress or even under "necessity" must be inefficacious; but all that he proves (at the time) is the quite different proposition that the *threat* of punishment will be ineffective so far as the class of persons who suffer from these conditions is concerned. Plainly it is possible that though (as Bentham says) the *threat* of punishment could not have operated on them, the actual *infliction* of punishment on those persons, may secure a higher measure of conformity to law on the part of normal persons than is secured by the admission of excusing conditions. If this is so and if Utilitarian principles only were at stake, we should, without any sense that we were sacrificing any principle of value or were choosing the lesser of two evils, drop from the law the restriction on punishment entailed by the admission of excuses: unless, of course, we believed that the terror or insecurity or misery produced by the operation of law so Draconic was worse than the lower measure of obedience to law secured by the law which admits excuses.

This objection to Bentham's rationale of excuses is not merely a fanciful one. Any increase in the number of conditions required to establish criminal liability increases the opportunity for deceiving courts or juries by the pretence that some condition is not satisfied. When the condition is a pyschological factor the chances of such pretence succeeding are considerable. Quite apart from the provision made for mental disease, the cases where an accused person pleads that he killed in his sleep or accidentally or in some temporary abnormal state of unconsciousness show that deception is certainly feasible. From the Utilitarian point of view this may lead to two sorts of "losses." The belief that such deception is feasible may embolden persons who would not otherwise risk punishment to take their chance of deceiving a jury in this way. Secondly, a criminal who actually succeeds in this deception will be left at large, though belonging to the class which the law is concerned to incapacitate. [Punishment and Responsibility 18-20 (1968)].

According to most modern scholars, the defense of duress is based on the view that, even though the harm evisaged by the law has taken place, the actor was not morally blameworthy in doing what he did, and hence should not be criminally punished. If duress is an excuse, why should not absence of the appropriate *mens rea* equally be an excuse? Is there any particular reason why we define a *mens rea* as necessary to guilt and duress as an excuse? Note that a mistake of the governing law, in those cases where it does exculpate (see page 172), is regarded as an excuse.

4. Could not *Dudley and Stephens* have put forth a defense of duress in addition to one of justification? If not, does that show an error in the drafting of the duress provision? Why must duress be conceived of as applicable only when one is threätened with deliberate force by another? Why should a duress defense be unavailable where a life-threatening natural force would "coerce . . . a person of reasonable firmness" into committing a crime? The commentary to Section 2.09 of the Model Penal Code attempts to answer this objection to the duress defense its drafters have formulated:

> The section, though plainly more liberal toward the victims of coercion than traditional law, does not reach one other situation that is arguably similar in principle to those it does reach. That is the case in which the danger to oneself or another arises from the effect of natural causes and an otherwise criminal act is performed to meet the danger. Professors Kadish and Paulsen illustrate the point in the following way:
>
> > (a) *X* is unwillingly driving a car along a narrow and precipitous mountain road, falling off sharply on both sides, under the command of *Y*, an armed escaping felon. The headlights pick out two persons, apparently and actually drunk, lying across the road in such a position as to make passage impossible without running them over. *X* is prevented from stopping by the threat of *Y* to shoot him dead if he declines to drive straight on. If *X* does go on and kills the drunks in order to save himself he will be excused under §2.09 if the jury should find that "a person of reasonable firmness in his situation would have been unable to resist," although he would not be justified under the lesser evil principle of §3.02.
> >
> > (b) The same situation as above except that *X* is prevented from stopping by suddenly inoperative brakes. His alternatives are either to run down the drunks or to run off the road and down the mountainside. If *X* chooses the first alternative to save his own life and kills the drunks he will not be excused under §2.09 even if a jury should find that a person of reasonable fortitude would have been unable to do otherwise.
>
> Whether or not *X* would actually have a duty to leave the road in example (b),[4] it is clear that other hypotheticals may be constructed in which actors perform criminal acts in response to the "coercive" effect of natural forces.
>
> At the time the Model Code was drafted, the Wisconsin Code contained a defense of necessity that, in effect, established a defense of duress from natural causes.[5] The judgment of the Institute, however, was that such a defense should not be included. The general justification defense of Section 3.02 does apply to choices of evils required by natural causes. It will be an extraordinarily rare case

4. Remaining on the road might be viewed as an omission to act and it might be doubted that the driver had any civil duty to leave the road in these circumstances. See Section 2.01(3). However, it would seem more accurate to describe driving down the road as an act insofar as one needs to steer to stay on the road.

5. Wis. §939.47, entitled "Necessity," reads:

> Pressure of natural physical forces which causes the actor reasonably to believe that his act is the only means of preventing imminent public disaster, or imminent death or

in which a person will not be able to claim successfully that a response to natural causes was a choice of a lesser evil but could successfully claim that the choice was one a person of reasonable firmness would make. And there is a significant difference between the situations in which an actor makes the choice of an equal or greater evil under the threat of unlawful human force and when he does so because of a natural event. In the former situation, the basic interests of the law may be satisfied by prosecution of the agent of unlawful force; in the latter circumstance, if the actor is excused, no one is subject to the law's application.

Does this explanation satisfy you?

PEOPLE v. UNGER

Supreme Court of Illinois
362 N.E.2d 319 (1977)

RYAN, Justice.

Defendant, Francis Unger, was charged with the crime of escape (Ill. Rev. Stat. 1971, ch. 108, par. 121), and was convicted following a jury trial before the circuit court of Will County. Defendant was sentenced to a term of three to nine years to be served consecutively to the remainder of the sentence for which he was imprisoned at the time of the escape. The conviction was reversed upon appeal and the cause was remanded for a new trial over the dissent of one justice. . . .

We granted leave to appeal and now affirm the judgment of the appellate court.

At the time of the present offense, the defendant was confined at the Illinois State Penitentiary in Joliet, Illinois. Defendant was serving a one- to three-year term as a consequence of a conviction for auto theft in Ogle County. Defendant began serving this sentence in December of 1971. On February 23, 1972, the defendant was transferred to the prison's minimum security, honor farm. It is undisputed that on March 7, 1972, the defendant walked off the honor farm. Defendant was apprehended two days later in a motel room in St. Charles, Illinois.

At trial, defendant testified that prior to his transfer to the honor farm he had been threatened by a fellow inmate. This inmate allegedly brandished a

---

great bodily harm to himself or another and which causes him so to act, is a defense to a prosecution for any crime based on that act except that if the prosecution is for murder the degree of the crime is reduced to manslaughter.

This provision is distinguishable from the ordinary necessity provision in that the actor may be excused thereunder even though he does not choose the lesser of evils. For example, if an actor diverted water coming through a dike in order to save himself, thereby risking the lives of many other people, but actually caused only property damage and physical injury short of death, this provision would give him a complete defense to any prosecution for his actions. Compare MPC Section 3.02. It will also be noted that the Wisconsin provision, unlike Section 2.09, does not require that a person of reasonable firmness in the actor's situation would have been unable to resist.

six-inch knife in an attempt to force defendant to engage in homosexual activities. Defendant was 22 years old and weighed approximately 155 pounds. He testified that he did not report the incident to the proper authorities due to fear of retaliation. Defendant also testified that he is not a particularly good fighter.

Defendant stated that after his transfer to the honor farm he was assaulted and sexually molested by three inmates, and he named the assailants at trial. The attack allegedly occurred on March 2, 1972, and from that date until his escape defendant received additional threats from inmates he did not know. On March 7, 1972, the date of the escape, defendant testified that he received a call on an institution telephone. Defendant testified that the caller, whose voice he did not recognize, threatened him with death because the caller had heard that defendant had reported the assault to prison authorities. Defendant said that he left the honor farm to save his life and that he planned to return once he found someone who could help him. None of these incidents were reported to the prison officials. As mentioned, defendant was apprehended two days later still dressed in his prison clothes.

The State introduced prior statements made by the defendant which cast some doubt on his true reasons for leaving the prison farm. In these statements, defendant indicated that he was motivated by a desire for publicity concerning the sentence on his original conviction, which he deemed to be unfair, as well as fear of physical abuse and death.

Defendant's first trial for escape resulted in a hung jury. The jury in the second trial returned its verdict after a five-hour deliberation. The following instruction (People's Instruction No. 9) was given by the trial court over defendant's objection.

> The reasons, if any, given for the alleged escape are immaterial and not to be considered by you as in any way justifying or excusing, if there were in fact such reasons.

The appellate court majority found that the giving of People's Instruction No. 9 was reversible error. Two instructions which were tendered by defendant but refused by the trial court are also germane to this appeal. Defendant's instructions Nos. 1 and 3 were predicated upon the affirmative defenses of compulsion and necessity. (Ill. Rev. Stat. 1971, ch. 38, pars. 7-11 (compulsion), 7-13 (necessity).) Defendant's instructions Nos. 1 and 3 read as follows:

> It is a defense to the charge made against the Defendant that he left the Honor Farm of the Illinois State Penitentiary by reason of necessity if the accused was without blame in occasioning or developing the situation and reasonably believed such conduct was necessary to avoid a public or private injury greater than the injury which might reasonably result from his own conduct.
>
> It is a defense to the charge made against the Defendant that he acted under the compulsion of threat or menace of the imminent infliction of death or great bodily harm, if he reasonably believed death or great bodily harm would

> be inflicted upon him if he did not perform the conduct with which he is charged. . . .

The State contends that, under the facts and circumstances of this case, the defenses of compulsion and necessity are, as a matter of law, unavailable to defendant. . . . Traditionally, the courts have been reluctant to permit the defenses of compulsion and necessity to be relied upon by escapees. This reluctance appears to have been primarily grounded upon considerations of public policy. Several recent decisions, however, have recognized the applicability of the compulsion and necessity defenses to prison escapes. In People v. Harmon (1974), 53 Mich. App. 482, 220 N.W.2d 212, the defense of duress was held to apply in a case where the defendant alleged that he escaped in order to avoid repeated homosexual attacks from fellow inmates. In People v. Lovercamp (1974), 43 Cal. App. 3d 823, 118 Cal. Rptr. 110, a limited defense of necessity was held to be available to two defendants whose escapes were allegedly motivated by fear of homosexual attacks. . . .

As illustrated by *Harmon* and *Lovercamp*, different courts have reached similar results in escape cases involving sexual abuse, though the question was analyzed under different defense theories. A certain degree of confusion has resulted from the recurring practice on the part of the courts to use the terms "compulsion" (duress) and "necessity" interchangeably, though the defenses are theoretically distinct. It has been suggested that the major distinction between the two defenses is that the source of the coercive power in cases of compulsion is from human beings, whereas in situations of necessity the pressure on the defendant arises from the forces of nature. (LaFave and Scott, Handbook on Criminal Law 381 (1972).) Also, as noted in the dissenting opinion in the appellate court, the defense of compulsion generally requires an impending, imminent threat of great bodily harm together with a demand that the person perform the specific criminal act for which he is eventually charged. Additionally, where the defense of compulsion is successfully asserted the coercing party is guilty of the crime. LaFave and Scott, Handbook on Criminal Law 380 (1972).

It is readily discernible that prison escapes induced by fear of homosexual assaults and accompanying physical reprisals do not conveniently fit within the traditional ambits of either the compulsion or the necessity defense. However, it has been suggested that such cases could best be analyzed in terms of necessity. (LaFave and Scott, Handbook on Criminal Law 381-82 n. 2 (1972).) One commentator has stated that the relevant consideration should be whether the defendant chose the lesser of two evils, in which case the defense of necessity would apply, or whether he was unable to exercise a free choice at all, in which event compulsion would be the appropriate defense. . . .

In our view, the defense of necessity, as defined by our statute (Ill. Rev. Stat. 1971, ch. 38, par. 7-13), is the appropriate defense in the present case. In a very real sense, the defendant here was not deprived of his free will by the threat of imminent physical harm which, according to the Committee Comments, appears to be the intended interpretation of the defense of compulsion as set out in section 7-11 of the Criminal Code. (Ill. Ann. Stat., ch. 38, par. 7-11, Committee Comments, at 423-433 (Smith-Hurd 1972).) Rather, if defendant's testimony is believed, he was forced to choose between two admitted evils by the situation which arose from actual and threatened homosexual assaults and fears of reprisal. Though the defense of compulsion would be applicable in the unlikely event that a prisoner was coerced by the threat of imminent physical harm to perform the specific act of escape, no such situation is involved in the present appeal. We, therefore, turn to a consideration of whether the evidence presented by the defendant justified the giving of an instruction on the defense of necessity.

The defendant's testimony was clearly sufficient to raise the affirmative defense of necessity. That defense is defined by statute (Ill. Rev. Stat. 1971, ch. 38, par. 7-13):

> Conduct which would otherwise be an offense is justifiable by reason of necessity if the accused was without blame in occasioning or developing the situation and reasonably believed such conduct was necessary to avoid a public or private injury geater than the injury which might reasonably result from his own conduct.

Defendant testified that he was subjected to threats of forced homosexual activity and that, on one occasion, the threatened abuse was carried out. He also testified that he was physically incapable of defending himself and that he feared greater harm would result from a report to the authorities. Defendant further testified that just prior to his escape he was told that he was going to be killed, and that he therefore fled the honor farm in order to save his life. Through the State's evidence cast a doubt upon the defendant's motives for escape and upon the reasonableness of defendant's assertion that such conduct was necessary, the defendant was entitled to have the jury consider the defense on the basis of his testimony. It is clear that defendant introduced some evidence to support the defense of necessity. As previously mentioned, that is sufficient to justify the giving of an appropriate instruction.

The State, however, would have us apply a more stringent test to prison escape situations. The State refers to the *Lovercamp* decision, where only a limited necessity defense was recognized. In *Lovercamp,* it was held that the defense of necessity need be submitted to the jury only where five conditions had been met. (43 Cal. App. 3d 823, 831, 118 Cal. Rptr. 110, 115.) Those conditions are:

> (1) The prisoner is faced with a specific threat of death, forcible sexual attack or substantial bodily injury in the immediate future;
> (2) There is no time for a complaint to the authorities or there exists a history of futile complaints which make any result from such complaints illusory;
> (3) There is no time or opportunity to resort to the courts;

> (4) There is no evidence of force or violence used towards prison personnel or other "innocent" persons in the escape; and
>
> (5) The prisoner immediately reports to the proper authorities when he has attained a position of safety from the immediate threat.

The State correctly points out that the defendant never informed the authorities of his situation and failed to report immediately after securing a position of safety. Therefore, it is contended that, under the authority of *Lovercamp,* defendant is not entitled to a necessity instruction. We agree with the State and with the court in *Lovercamp* that the above conditions are relevant factors to be used in assessing claims of necessity. We cannot say, however, that the existence of each condition is, as a matter of law, necessary to establish a meritorious necessity defense.

The preconditions set forth in *Lovercamp* are, in our view, matters which go to the weight and credibility of the defendant's testimony. The rule is well settled that a court will not weigh the evidence where the question is whether an instruction is justified. The absence of one or more of the elements listed in *Lovercamp* would not necessarily mandate a finding that the defendant could not assert the defense of necessity.

By way of example, in the present case defendant did not report to the authorities immediately after securing his safety. In fact, defendant never voluntarily turned himself in to the proper officials. However, defendant testified that he intended to return to the prison upon obtaining legal advice from an attorney and claimed that he was attempting to get money from friends to pay for such counsel. Regardless of our opinion as to the believability of defendant's tale, this testimony, if accepted by the jury, would have negated any negative inference which would arise from defendant's failure to report to proper authorities after the escape. The absence of one of the *Lovercamp* preconditions does not alone disprove the claim of necessity and should not, therefore, automatically preclude an instruction on the defense. We therefore reject the contention that the availability of the necessity defense be expressly conditioned upon the elements set forth in *Lovercamp.*

In conclusion, we hold that under the facts and circumstances of the present case the defendant was entitled to submit his defense of necessity to the jury. It was, therefore, reversible error to give People's Instruction No. 9 to the jury and to refuse to give an appropriate instruction defining the defense of necessity, such as the instruction tendered by the defendant. In light of our disposition of this appeal, we need not consider contentions raised by defendant as to the propriety of his sentence. . . .

Affirmed and remanded.

UNDERWOOD, Justice, dissenting.

My disagreement with my colleagues stems from an uneasy feeling that their unconditional recognition of necessity as a defense to the charge of escape carries with it the seeds of future troubles. Unless narrowly circumscribed, the availability of that defense could encourage potential escapees, disrupt prison discipline, and could even result in injury to prison guards, police or private citizens. For these reasons courts have been quite reluctant to honor the defenses of duress, necessity or compulsion in prison escapes, and, until recent years, they were uniformly held insufficient to justify escapes. . . .

I am not totally insensitive to the sometimes brutal and unwholesome problems faced by prison inmates, and the frequency of sexually motivated assaults. Prisoner complaints to unconcerned or understaffed prison administrations may produce little real help to a prisoner or may actually increase the hazard from fellow inmates of whose conduct complaint has been made. Consequently, and until adequate prison personnel and facilities are realities, I agree that a necessity defense should be recognized. The interests of society are better served, however, if the use of that defense in prison-escape cases is confined within well-defined boundaries such as those in *Lovercamp*. In that form it will be available, but with limitations precluding its wholesale use.

It is undisputed that defendant here did not meet those conditions. He did not complain to the authorities on this occasion even though, following an earlier threat and demand by a fellow inmate that defendant submit to homosexual activity, defendant had requested and been granted a transfer to the minimum security honor farm. Nor did he immediately report to the authorities when he had reached a place of safety. Rather, he stole a truck some nine hours after his escape, drove to Chicago, and later drove to St. Charles, using the telephone to call friends in Canada. . . .

Since defendant's conduct does not comply with conditions such as those in *Lovercamp* which, in my judgment, should be required before a necessity defense may be considered by a jury, I believe the trial court did not err in its instructions.

I would accordingly reverse the appellate court and affirm the judgment of the trial court.

Notes and Questions

1. Should cases like *Unger* be handled as raising issues of duress or of justification? Does it matter? What would the liability be of someone who aided and abetted Unger if Unger's conduct were justified? What if it were only excused? What would be the liability of a guard who prevented Unger's escape? Assuming the guard knew all the facts, would it matter whether Unger were justified, or merely excused?

2. In United States v. Contento-Pachon 723 F.2d 691 (9th Cir. 1984), the defendant claimed a duress defense. According to the defendant:

> [He] is a native of Bogota, Colombia and was employed there as a taxicab driver. He asserts that one of his passengers, Jorge, offered him a job as the driver of a privately-owned car. Contento-Pachon expressed an interest in the job and agreed to meet Jorge and the owner of the car the next day.

> Instead of a driving job, Jorge proposed that Contento-Pachon swallow cocaine-filled balloons and transport them to the United States. Contento-Pachon agreed to consider the proposition. He was told not to mention the proposition to anyone, otherwise he would "get into serious trouble." Contento-Pachon testifed that he did not contact the police because he believes that the Bogota police are corrupt and that they are paid off by drug traffickers.
>
> Approximately one week later, Contento-Pachon told Jorge that he would not carry the cocaine. In response, Jorge mentioned facts about Contento-Pachon's personal life, including private details which Contento-Pachon had never mentioned to Jorge. Jorge told Contento-Pachon that his failure to cooperate would result in the death of his wife and three-year-old child.
>
> The following day the pair met again. Contento-Pachon's life and the lives of his family were again threatened. At this point, Contento-Pachon agreed to take the cocaine into the United States.
>
> The pair met two more times. At the last meeting, Contento-Pachon swallowed 129 balloons of cocaine. He was informed that he would be watched at all times during the trip, and that if he failed to follow Jorge's instruction he and his family would be killed.
>
> After leaving Bogota, Contento-Pachon's plane landed in Panama. Contento-Pachon asserts that he did not notify the authorities there because he felt that the Panamanian police were as corrupt as those in Bogota. Also, he felt that any such action on his part would place his family in jeopardy.
>
> When he arrived at the customs inspection point in Los Angeles, Contento-Pachon consented to have his stomach x-rayed. The x-rays revealed a foreign substance which was later determined to be cocaine.

The trial judge refused to submit the issue of duress to the jury on the ground that the defendant had shown neither the immediacy of the threat nor its inescapability. The court of appeals held that, under the facts, the defendant had presented a jury question as to whether he had been under duress:

> Contento-Pachon presented credible evidence that he acted under an immediate and well-grounded threat of serious bodily injury, with no opportunity to escape. Because the trier of fact should have been allowed to consider the credibility of the proffered evidence,[6] we reverse.

Judge Coyle dissented from this view, arguing that:

> Moreover, the trial court found that the defendant and his family enjoyed an adequate and reasonable opportunity to avoid or escape the threats of the drug dealers in the weeks before his flight. Until he went to the house where he

6. The dissent takes the position that the trial court made findings adverse to the duress defense which were supported by the record. That would be an appropriate test if the case had been tried by the judge without a jury. We acknowledge that the record in this case will support a finding of guilty. The problem is that there has been evidence tendered which, if found credible by the jury, would justify a determination that Contento-Pachon acted under duress. A defendant has the right to have a jury resolve the disputed factual issues. See Sandstrom v. Montana, 442 U.S. 510, 523, 99 S. Ct. 2450, 2459, 61 L. Ed. 2d 39 (1974).

ingested the balloons containing cocaine, defendant and his family were not physically restrained or prevented from seeking help. The record supports the trial court's findings that the defendant and his family could have sought assistance from the authorities or have fled. Cases considering the defense of duress have established that where there was a reasonable legal alternative to violating the law, a chance to refuse to do the criminal act and also to avoid the threatened danger, the defense will fail. Duress is permitted as a defense only when a criminal act was committed because there was no other opportunity to avoid the threatened danger.

Should the issue of duress have been submitted to the jury?

14

DEFENSIVE FORCE

STATE v. LEIDHOLM
Supreme Court of North Dakota
334 N.W.2d 811 (1983)

VANDE WALLE, Justice.

Janice Leidholm was charged with murder for the stabbing death of her husband, Chester Leidholm, in the early morning hours of August 7, 1981, at their farm home near Washburn. She was found guilty by a McLean County jury of manslaughter and was sentenced to five years' imprisonment in the State Penitentiary with three years of the sentence suspended. Leidholm appealed from the judgment of conviction. We reverse and remand the case for a new trial.

I

According to the testimony, the Leidholm marriage relationship in the end was an unhappy one, filled with a mixture of alcohol abuse, moments of kindness toward one another, and moments of violence. The alcohol abuse and violence was exhibited by both parties on the night of Chester's death.

Early in the evening of August 6, 1981, Chester and Janice attended a gun club party in the city of Washburn where they both consumed a large amount of alcohol.[1] On the return trip to the farm, an argument developed between Janice and Chester which continued after their arrival home just after midnight. Once inside the home, the arguing did not stop; Chester was shouting, and Janice was crying.

At one point in the fighting, Janice tried to telephone Dave Vollan, a

1. A Breathalyzer test administered to Janice shortly after the stabbing, at approximately 3:30 A.M., showed her blood-alcohol content was .17 of 1 percent. The analysis of a blood sample from Chester showed his blood-alcohol content was .23 of 1 percent.

deputy sheriff of McLean County, but Chester prevented her from using the phone by shoving her away and pushing her down. At another point, the argument moved outside the house, and Chester once again was pushing Janice to the ground. Each time Janice attempted to get up, Chester would push her back again.

A short time later, Janice and Chester re-entered their home and went to bed. When Chester fell asleep, Janice got out of bed, went to the kitchen, and got a butcher knife. She then went back into the bedroom and stabbed Chester. In a matter of minutes Chester died from shock and loss of blood.

II

. . . The first, and controlling, issue we consider is whether or not the trial court correctly instructed the jury on self-defense. Our resolution of the issue must of necessity begin with an explanation of the basic operation of the law of self-defense as set forth in Chapter 12.1-05 of the North Dakota Century Code.

Our criminal code is the product of a massive revision which began in 1971 and culminated in 1973 with the legislative enactment of Senate Bill No. 2045. Although remnants of the "old code" survived revision and remain in the present code, most of its provisions are in substantial part modeled after the Proposed New Federal Criminal Code[2] which in turn relies heavily on the American Law Institute Model Penal Code. Both the Proposed Code and the Model Penal Code are highly integrated codifications of the substantive criminal law which exhibit close interrelationships between their respective parts.

This integration is especially apparent in Chapter 12.1-05 of the North Dakota Century Code, which is an almost complete adoption of Chapter 6 of the Proposed Code dealing with defenses involving justification and excuse. It is to Chapter 12.1-05, N.D.C.C., that we now turn.

Conduct which constitutes self-defense may be either justified [Section 12.1-05-03, N.D.C.C.] or excused [Section 12.1-05-08, N.D.C.C.]. Although the distinction between justification and excuse may appear to be theoretical and without significant practical consequence, because the distinction has been made in our criminal statutes we believe a general explanation of the difference between the two concepts—even though it requires us to venture briefly into the pathway of academicism—is warranted.

A defense of justification is the product of society's determination that the *actual existence* of certain circumstances will operate to make proper and legal what otherwise would be criminal conduct. A defense of excuse, contrarily, does not make legal and proper conduct which ordinarily would result in criminal liability; instead, it openly recognizes the criminality of the conduct but excuses it because the actor believed that circumstances actually existed

2. The Proposed New Federal Criminal Code ("Proposed Code") with annotations comprises the Final Report of the National Commission on Reform of Federal Criminal Laws (1971) ("Final Report") and is supplemented by three volumes of the Working Papers of the National Commission on the Reform of Federal Criminal Laws (1970-1971) ("Working Papers") which contain materials used by the Commission in drafting the Proposed Code.

which would justify his conduct when in fact they did not. In short, had the facts been as he supposed them to be, the actor's conduct would have been justified rather than excused. . . .

In the context of self-defense, this means that a person who believes that the force he uses is necessary to prevent imminent unlawful harm is *justified* in using such force if his belief is a *correct* belief; that is to say, if his belief corresponds with what actually is the case. If, on the other hand, a person *reasonably* but incorrectly believes that the force he uses is necessary to protect himself against imminent harm, his use of force is *excused.*

The distinction is arguably superfluous because whether a person's belief is correct and his conduct justified, or whether it is merely reasonable and his conduct excused, the end result is the same, namely, the person avoids punishment for his conduct. Furthermore, because a correct belief corresponds with an actual state of affairs, it will always be a reasonable belief; but a reasonable belief will not always be a correct belief, viz., a person may reasonably believe what is not actually the case.[3] Therefore, the decisive issue under our law of self-defense is not whether a person's beliefs are correct, but rather whether they are reasonable and thereby excused or justified. . . .

Section 12.1-05-08, N.D.C.C., which sets forth the general conditions that excuse a person's conduct, states:

> A person's conduct is excused if he believes that the facts are such that his conduct is necessary and appropriate for any of the purposes which would establish a justification or excuse under this chapter, even though his belief is mistaken. However, if his belief is negligently or recklessly held [i.e., unreasonably], it is not an excuse in a prosecution for an offense for which negligence or recklessness, as the case may be, suffices to establish culpability. Excuse under this section is a defense or affirmative defense according to which type of defense would be established had the facts been as the person believed them to be.

The first sentence of Section 12.1-05-08, N.D.C.C., in combination with Section 12.1-05-03, N.D.C.C., which contains the kernel statement of self-defense, yields the following expanded proposition: A person's conduct is excused if he *believes* that the use of force upon another person is necessary and appropriate to defend himself against danger of imminent unlawful harm, even though his belief is mistaken.[4] Thus we have a statement of the first element of self-defense, i.e., a person must actually and sincerely believe that the conditions exist which give rise to a claim of self-defense. . . .

From the next sentence of Section 12.1-05-08 we may infer that, besides being actual and sincere, a person's belief that the use of force is necessary to

3. For example, a person may reasonably, but mistakenly, believe that a gun held by an assailant is loaded.

4. If the danger against which a person uses force to defend himself is "death, serious bodily injury, or the commission of a felony involving violence," the person may use deadly force [Section 12.1-05-07, N.D.C.C.], which is defined as that force "which a person uses with the intent of causing, or which he knows creates a substantial risk of causing, death or serious bodily injury." Sec. 12.1-05-12(2), N.D.C.C.

protect himself against imminent unlawful harm must be reasonable. Here, we have the second element of self-defense, namely, a person must reasonably believe that circumstances exist which permit him to use defensive force. . . .

If, therefore, a person has an actual and reasonable belief that force is necessary to protect himself against danger of imminent unlawful harm, his conduct is justified or excused. If, on the other hand, a person's actual belief in the necessity of using force to prevent imminent unlawful harm is unreasonable, his conduct will not be justified or excused. Instead, he will be guilty of an offense for which negligence or recklessness suffices to establish culpability. For example, if a person recklessly believes that the use of force upon another person is necessary to protect himself against unlawful imminent serious bodily injury *and* the force he uses causes the death of the other person, he is guilty of manslaughter. And if a person's belief is negligent in the same regard, he is guilty of negligent homicide.

We are not the only State to make distinctions like this in the law of self-defense. Other States distinguish between reasonable and unreasonable beliefs when attaching liability for acts assertedly committed in self-defense. However, they do not further subdivide the class of unreasonably held beliefs, as our Legislature has done, into the subclass of recklessly held beliefs and the subclass of negligently held beliefs. Still, such interpretations do not significantly differ from our own.

Under both approaches, if a person reasonably believes self-defense is necessary, his conduct is excused or justified. And even though under our view an unreasonable belief may result in a conviction for either manslaughter or negligent homicide, and under theirs an unreasonable belief may result only in a conviction for manslaughter, they are the same to the extent that an honest but unreasonable belief will never result in a conviction for murder.

It must remain clear that once the factfinder determines under a claim of self-defense that the actor honestly and sincerely held the belief that the use of defensive force was required to protect himself against imminent unlawful injury, the actor may not be convicted of more than a crime of recklessness or negligence; but, if the factfinder determines, to the contrary, that the actor did not honestly and sincerely hold the requisite belief under a claim of self-defense, the actor may not appeal to the doctrine of self-defense to avoid punishment, but will be subject to conviction for the commission of an intentional and knowing crime.

As stated earlier, the critical issue which a jury must decide in a case involving a claim of self-defense is whether or not the accused's belief that force is necessary to protect himself against imminent unlawful harm was reasonable. However, before the jury can make this determination, it must have a standard of reasonableness against which it can measure the accused's belief.

Courts have traditionally distinguished between standards of reasonableness by characterizing them as either "objective" or "subjective." An objective standard of reasonableness requires the factfinder to view the circumstances surrounding the accused at the time he used force from the standpoint of a hypothetical reasonable and prudent person. Ordinarily, under such a view, the unique physical and psychological characteristics of the accused are not taken into consideration in judging the reasonableness of the accused's belief.

This is not the case, however, where a subjective standard of reasonableness is employed. See State v. Wanrow, 88 Wash. 2d 221, 559 P.2d 548 (1977). Under the subjective standard the issue is not whether the circumstances attending the accused's use of force would be sufficient to create in the mind of a reasonable and prudent person the belief that the use of force is necessary to protect himself against immediate unlawful harm, but rather whether the circumstances are sufficient to induce in *the accused* an honest and reasonable belief that he must use force to defend himself against imminent harm.

Neither Section 12.1-05-03, N.D.C.C., nor Section 12.1-05-08, N.D.C.C., explicitly states the viewpoint which the factfinder should assume in assessing the reasonableness of an accused's belief. Moreover, this court has not yet decided the issue of whether Sections 12.1-05-03 and 12.1-05-08 should be construed as requiring an objective or subjective standard to measure the reasonableness of an accused's belief under a claim of self-defense. Finally, the legislative history of our self-defense statutes, as well as the commentaries to the codified criminal statutes which form the basis of the North Dakota Criminal Code, give no indication of a preference for an objective standard of reasonableness over a subjective standard, or vice versa.[5]

We do, however, find guidance for our decision on this issue from past decisions of this court which developed the law of self-defense prior to the adoption in 1975 of Chapter 12.1-05, N.D.C.C. In 1907, the members of this court, confronted with the same issue whether to adopt an objective or subjective standard of reasonableness, unanimously decided to accept the latter standard for judging the reasonableness of an accused's belief because they believed it to be more just than an objective standard. *Hazlett,* 113 N.W.2d at 380-381. As late as 1974, this court has confirmed that early decision. *Jacobs,* 222 N.W.2d at 588-589.

Because (1) the law of self-defense as developed in past decisions of this court has been interpreted to require the use of a subjective standard of reasonableness, and (2) we agree with the court in *Hazlett* that a subjective standard is the more just, and (3) our current law of self-defense as codified in Sections 12.1-05-03, 12.1-05-07, and 12.1-05-08 does not require a contrary conclusion, that is to say, our current law of self-defense is consistent with either a subjective or objective standard, we now decide that the finder of fact must view the circumstances attending an accused's use of force from the standpoint of the accused to determine if they are sufficient to create in the accused's mind an honest and reasonable belief that the use of force is necessary to protect himself from imminent harm. . . .

5. One defense in Chapter 12.1-05, N.D.C.C., which involves an objective standard is entrapment. In Section 12.1-05-11(2), N.D.C.C., the Legislature, by the specific words "likely to cause *normally law-abiding persons* to commit the offense," eliminated the subjective test for that defense. . . .

The practical and logical consequence of this interpretation is that an accused's actions are to be viewed from the standpoint of a person whose mental and physical characteristics are like the accused's and who sees what the accused sees and knows what the accused knows. For example, if the accused is a timid, diminutive male, the factfinder must consider these characteristics in assessing the reasonableness of his belief. If, on the other hand, the accused is a strong, courageous, and capable female, the factfinder must consider these characteristics in judging the reasonableness of her belief.

In its statement of the law of self-defense, the trial court instructed the jury:

> The circumstances under which she acted must have been such as to produce in the mind of reasonably prudent persons, regardless of their sex, similarly situated, the reasonable belief that the other person was then about to kill her or do serious bodily harm to her.

In view of our decision today, the court's instruction was a misstatement of the law of self-defense. A correct statement of the law to be applied in a case of self-defense is:

> [A] defendant's conduct is not to be judged by what a reasonably cautious person might or might not do or consider necessary to do under the like circumstances, but what he himself in good faith honestly believed and had reasonable ground to believe was necessary for him to do to protect himself from apprehended death or great bodily injury.

The significance of the difference in viewing circumstances from the standpoint of the "defendant alone" rather than from the standpoint of a "reasonably cautious person" is that the jury's consideration of the unique physical and psychological characteristics of an accused allows the jury to judge the reasonableness of the accused's actions against the accused's subjective impressions of the need to use force rather than against those impressions which a jury determines that a hypothetical reasonably cautious person would have under similar circumstances. . . .

Hence, a correct statement of the law of self-defense is one in which the court directs the jury to assume the physical and psychological properties peculiar to the accused, viz., to place itself as best it can in the shoes of the accused, and then decide whether or not the particular circumstances surrounding the accused at the time he used force were sufficient to create in his mind a sincere and reasonable belief that the use of force was necessary to protect himself from imminent and unlawful harm. . . .

Leidholm argued strongly at trial that her stabbing of Chester was done in self-defense and in reaction to the severe mistreatment she received from him over the years. Because the court's instruction in question is an improper statement of the law concerning a vital issue in Leidholm's defense, we conclude it amounts to reversible error requiring a new trial.

III

Although we decide that this case must be sent back to the district court for a new trial, there still remain several other issues raised by Leidholm on appeal which must be addressed to ensure a proper disposition of the case on remand.

Expert testimony was presented at trial on what has come to be commonly referred to as the "battered woman syndrome." Such testimony generally explains the "phenomenon" as one in which a regular pattern of spouse abuse[6] creates in the battered spouse low self-esteem and a "learned helplessness," i.e., a sense that she cannot escape from the abusive relationship she has become a part of. See Comment, The Admissibility of Expert Testimony on the Battered Woman Syndrome in Support of a Claim of Self-Defense, 15 Conn. L. Rev. 121 (1982).

The expert witness in this case testified that Janice Leidholm was the victim in a battering relationship which caused her to suffer battered woman syndrome manifested by (1) a psychological condition of low self-esteem and (2) a psychological state of "learned helplessness." On the basis of the expert testimony, Leidholm offered the following proposed instruction on battered woman syndrome:

> A condition known or described by certain witnesses as the "battered wife syndrome" if shown by the evidence to have existed in the accused at the time she allegedly committed the crime charged, is not of itself a defense. However, as a general rule, whether an accused was assaulted by the victim of the homicide prior to the commission of a fatal act by the accused may have relevance in determining the issue of self-defense.
>
> Whenever the actual existence of any particular purpose, motive or intent is a necessary element to the commission of any particular species or degree of crime, you may take into consideration evidence that the accused was or had been assaulted by the victim in determining the purpose, motive or intent with which the act was committed.
>
> Thus, in the crime of murder of which the accused is charged in this case, specific intent is a necessary element of the crime. So, evidence the accused acted or failed to act while suffering the condition known as the "battered wife syndrome" may be considered by the jury in determining whether or not the accused acted in self-defense. The weight to be given the evidence on that question, and the significance to attach to it in relation to all the other evidence in the case, are for you the jury to determine.[7]

6. Typically, the pattern begins with a tension-building phase, followed by an intermediate phase where one spouse physically, with undoubted psychological effects, abuses the other, and a final phase where the battering spouse feels remorse for his actions and then attempts to "make up" with the battered spouse.

7. Leidholm's counsel in his brief indicates that an instruction almost identical with this one was given in United States v. Mary Ann Ironshield, No. C1-81-40 (D.N.D. 1982), and United States v. Vicki Starr, No. C1-79-33 (D.N.D. 1980).

The court's refusal to include the proposed instruction in its charge to the jury, Leidholm contends, was error.

The instruction on battered woman syndrome was designed to support Leidholm's claim of self-defense by focusing the jury's attention on the psychological characteristics common to women who are victims in abusive relationships, and by directing the jury that it may consider evidence that the accused suffered from battered woman syndrome in determining whether or not she acted in self-defense. The instruction correctly points out that battered woman syndrome is *not of itself* a defense. In other words, "The existence of the syndrome in a marriage does not of itself establish the legal right of the wife to kill the husband, the evidence must still be considered in the context of self-defense."[8]. . .

There is nothing in the proposed instruction at issue which would add to or significantly alter a correct instruction on the law of self-defense. The jury's use of a subjective standard of reasonableness in applying the principles of self-defense to the facts of a particular case requires it to consider expert testimony, once received in evidence, describing battered woman syndrome and the psychological effects it produces in the battered spouse when deciding the issue of the *existence* and *reasonableness* of the accused's belief that force was necessary to protect herself from imminent harm. If an instruction given is modeled after the law of self-defense which we adopt today, the court need not include a specific instruction on battered woman syndrome in its charge to the jury.

IV

An inseparable and essential part of our law of self-defense limits the use of deadly force to situations in which its use is necessary to protect the actor against death or serious bodily injury. However, the use of deadly force by an actor in self-defense is not justified if a retreat from the assailant can be accomplished with safety to the actor and others. Thus, before, it can be said that the use of deadly force is "necessary" to protect the actor against death or serious injury, it must first be the case that the actor cannot retreat from the assailant with safety to himself and others. In short, the use of deadly force is not

8. And, if the particular facts of a defendant's case do not fit well with a claim of self-defense, the defendant perhaps should consider abandoning any such claim because the law of self-defense will not be judicially orchestrated to accommodate a theory that the existence of battered woman syndrome in an abusive relationship operates in and of itself to justify or excuse a homicide. When a battered spouse argues that a killing was committed in self-defense, the issue raised is not whether the battered spouse believes that homicide or suicide are the only available solutions to the problems she faces in her relationship with the abusive spouse, nor is it whether the cumulative effect of a series of beatings caused the battered spouse to react violently "under the influence of extreme emotional disturbance" by killing the batterer; under a claim of self-defense the only issue is whether the circumstances surrounding the killing were sufficient to create in the accused's mind *an honest and sincere belief that the use of deadly force is necessary to defend herself against imminent unlawful harm.* See *Kelly,* supra, 655 P.2d at 1203.

necessary (and therefore not justified) within the meaning of our law of self-defense unless the actor has no safe avenue of retreat.[9]

The practical effect of this statement is that the jury must first satisfy itself that an actor could not safely retreat before it can find that the actor's use of deadly force was necessary to protect himself against death or serious injury. And the way in which the jury determines whether or not the actor could not retreat safely is by considering whether or not the actor honestly and reasonably believed that he could not retreat from his attacker with safety. . . .

The duty to retreat, however, is not a rule without exceptions. Section 12.1-05-07(2)(b), N.D.C.C., provides, in part:

> (2) *no person is required to retreat from his dwelling,* or place of work, *unless he* was the original aggressor or *is assailed by a person who he knows also dwells* or works *there.* (Emphasis added.)

Included within the trial court's instruction to the jury on the law of self-defense was a statement roughly equivalent to the underscored language above. Leidholm maintains that the principle stated by this language violates the Equal Protection Clause, the Due Process Clause, and the Privileges and Immunities Clause of Article 14, Section 1, of the Amendments to the United States Constitution. Her argument seems to be that making an individual's duty to retreat from his dwelling dependent upon the status of the assailant unduly discriminates against the accused if the attacker is a cohabitant. We find no merit in this argument.

If the facts and circumstances attending a person's use of deadly force against an assailant who is a cohabitant are sufficient to create in his own mind an honest and reasonable belief that he cannot retreat from the assailant with safety to himself and others, his use of deadly force is justified or excused, and his failure to retreat is of no consequence.

This is a certain corollary to the guiding principle in our law of self-defense that the reasonableness of an accused's belief is to be measured against the accused's subjective impressions and not against the impressions which a jury might determine to be objectively reasonable.

Leidholm also argues it was error for the trial court to instruct the jury that manslaughter is a lesser included offense of murder.

Whether or not a lesser included offense instruction on manslaughter is appropriate in a murder trial depends upon the particular facts and circumstances of the case. We have no question that the court's instruction on manslaughter was warranted in this case.

9. This principle follows strictly from the language of Section 12.1-05-07(2)(b). It states that the use of deadly force is *justified* if such force is *necessary* to protect the actor against death or serious injury. It also states that the use of deadly force is *not justified* if the actor *can retreat* with safety to himself and others. Therefore, if the actor *can retreat* (and the use of deadly force is not justified), the use of deadly force cannot be necessary (i.e., justified); otherwise, the use of such force would be at the same time both "not justified" and "justified."

Moreover, any time the court instructs a jury on self-defense, it must of necessity include a special instruction on manslaughter as well as an instruction on negligent homicide. The difference between self-defense and manslaughter is the reasonableness of the accused's belief that the use of force is necessary to prevent imminent unlawful harm. If the accused's belief is reasonable, he will be found to have acted in self-defense. If unreasonable, he is guilty of either manslaughter or negligent homicide, depending upon whether his belief was held recklessly or negligently, respectively. . . .

The judgment of conviction is reversed and the case is remanded to the district court of McLean County for a new trial.

Notes and Questions

1. According to the court, when is a killing in "self-defense" justified and when is it merely excused? Does the distinction make any difference in this context?

After the case was reversed, Mrs. Leidholm worked out a plea agreement under which she would plead guilty to manslaughter but could not be sentenced to more than one year imprisonment with three months suspended. She would also get credit for the time she had already spent in jail, some 76 days. A sentencing hearing was then held at which she presented evidence to the judge that her sentence should be less than specified in the agreement. The judge agreed and gave her a suspended sentence.

2. Self-defense is only one of a number of related "defensive force justifications." According to one commentator:[10]

> Defensive force justifications differ from general justifications in that they always concern threats of harm from a human aggressor to the particular interest that is the subject of the defense—to the actor himself in self-defense, to other persons in the defense of others, and to property in the defense of property. Defensive force justifications rely on the same balancing of evils that is the basis of the lesser evils defense. Where a gang of thugs, rather than a natural forest fire, threatens the lives of the inhabitants of a town, the defense of others will permit defensive force against the attackers, just as the lesser evils justification permits the setting of a fire to create a firebreak. In the former case, however, an innocent person, such as the owner of the firebreak field, need not bear the harm of the justified conduct; rather, it is born by the culpable attackers. Consequently, there is not as strong a need for the strict balancing of *physical* harms commonly done in lesser evils; that is, the actor may be permitted to kill three attacking thugs in order to save three innocent townspeople even though the physical harm caused (three lives) is not less than the physical harm threatened (three lives). One may even permit the killing of three attacking thugs to save

10. 2 P. Robinson, Criminal Law Defenses 69-73 (1984).

one innocent person, though the harm caused is clearly greater, because society highly values the protection of innocents and deplores unjustified aggression.

Permitting the actor to cause greater physical harm than he avoids does not mean that the balancing of harms of the general justification defense has been rejected. The aggressors' culpability may be seen as discounting the value of their lives in the balance. Or, what is perhaps a better characterization of the process, one may properly add to the evil of physical harm to an innocent, a variety of intangible evils that arise from such aggression, evils that may well be more significant to society than the physical harm threatened. In the case of the thugs, for example, the lives of the three thugs are balanced against the lives of the three townspeople *plus* the compelling societal interest in preserving the right of bodily autonomy and condemning unjustified aggression.

The same process occurs in the protection of property. The harm of physical injury to a thief is balanced against the owner's interest in retaining the threatened property *plus* the societal interest in preserving a right to property ownership and condemning unjustified aggression. Again, the more intangible societal interests may be more significant than the particular owner's interest in retaining the particular item threatened. But even the weight of these societal interests has a limit—the limit is generally surpassed when human life is taken in defense of property. A human life, even a culpable aggressor's, is still likely to be assigned a more significant value than property.[11]

The same balancing principles apply when the actor kills another to save his own life. But self-defense is unique among defensive force justifications, and is sometimes theoretically troublesome. First, by definition only one human life can be at stake on the side of the actor; if there are more, a defense of others is available. This forces difficult choices because the frequent situation of one life for one life demands complete reliance on intangible societal interests to break the deadlock. There is no reason, however, that the analysis should vary. The community is generally willing to give sufficient weight to the intangible interests to permit the killing of the aggressor.

Self-defense is also unique among defensive force situations because the actor makes the justification decision at a moment when he is in a difficult position. Taking this into account, it seems appropriate that many jurisdictions provide liberal excuse provisions for an actor who makes a mistake as to a self-defense justification, as well as liberal rules governing the admission of evidence relevant to those mistakes, such as evidence concerning the battered-wife syndrome. Some jurisdictions have gone further to say that an attack on a person

11. Evidence of a concern for the value of human life, even an aggressor's life is found in the retreat rule. . . . and in the specific limitations on deadly force. . . . There are other examples. Despite a property owner's interest in enjoyment of his property, he may not exclude a trespasser if it will expose the trespasser to substantial danger of bodily harm. See Model Penal Code §3.06(3)(b). This view is not universal, however. It has been argued, for example, that when the choice is between the poacher and the game "the least worthy of God's creatures must fall—the rustic without a soul,—not the Christian partridge—not the immortal pheasant—not the rational woodcock, or the accountable hare." The Selected Writings of Sidney Smith 230-231 (Auden ed. 1956). To reach a similar conclusion, some would argue that a threatened actor's right to autonomy is absolute. No balancing is needed under this view, and the victim may use whatever force is necessary. See G. Fletcher, Rethinking Criminal Law 871-872 (1978) (describing the German and Soviet "hostility" toward a proportionality requirement, even where the interest in autonomy is merely the interest in undisturbed possession of property).

may produce a state of coercion in him that should be recognized as duress. If the actor is in fact justified, however, there is no need for such excuses. Just because the self-defense situation may give rise to an excuse does not, as some commentators suggest, change the fact that it may also provide a justification.[12] If *A* is permitted to intervene to save the life of *another* by killing an unjustified attacker, one can hardly deny *A* a justification when *A* is the intended victim, simply because *A* would *also* be excused for having acted in a state of confusion or coercion.

If *A* is mistaken in his self-defense and is not in fact justified, recognition of a coercion-like excuse, in addition to mistake, might be useful. But to avoid the confusion of justification and excuse, it seems advisable to use a name different than self-defense when providing such an excuse. Because such a condition is in many ways similar to duress or provocation/extreme emotional disturbance, it might be included under either of those defenses. In fact, a duress defense, properly drafted, should exculpate such an actor without any modification of its provisions.

Defensive force justifications are generally formulated as separate justifications, each protecting different interests—the actor, another person, or property. There is some precedent, however, for a single general defensive force justification.[13] Such a general provision could have the advantage of providing broader coverage, to include all defensive action in protection of any legitimate legal interest, not just the interests of security from physical harm to persons and property. Such a general provision might take the following form, which is also the archetype for the more common specialized formulations of defensive force justifications:

12. See, e.g., State v. Boyce, 284 Minn. 242, 170 N.W.2d 104 (1969) (finding of an intentional killing under heat of passion does not preclude a finding that the killing was in self-defense: the two defenses raise distinct issues).

Fletcher provides an elaborate discussion of competing "models" of self-defense (and indeed seems to include all defensive force defenses). They are, essentially, self-defense as an excuse, as a justification with normal balancing of interests, and as a justification where the right to personal autonomy of the defender is absolute thus eliminating the proportionality requirement of the justification. G. Fletcher, Rethinking, supra note [11], at §§10.51 to 10.5.3. His conclusion, after reviewing instances where these different "models" create different results (id. at §10.5.4), is apparently that we must simply tolerate continuing instability and unending debate about the nature of self-defense. Id. at 874. But this conclusion follows only if we insist that there be only one defense of self-defense, which is either an excuse or a justification or a hybrid. The obvious solution is to create two defenses, as was done with necessity (see id. at §10.4.1), in other words, to provide a self-defense justification *and* a self-defense excuse, each of which would operate like other defenses of that group. Thus, if an actor's force in self-defense is necessary and proportional, the actor is justified and no one may resist or intervene and all may assist. If the force used is more than is justified, but the circumstances and their effect on the defendant suggest that an excuse is appropriate (in the form of mistake as to a justification), then no one may assist and all may intervene. . . .

13. Fletcher notes that the German and Soviet systems recognize a general defensive force privilege. G. Fletcher, Rethinking, supra note [11], at 855-856. The German and Soviet systems extend the defensive force privilege to the defense of "virtually all the rights and interests recognized by the law." G. Fletcher, Rethinking, supra note [11], at 863-864. Iowa, although codifying separate provisions for defense of persons and property, comes close to providing a general defensive force statute. Iowa Code Ann. §704.1 (West Cum. Supp. 1983-84) provides that reasonable force may be used to prevent injury or loss, and this section apparently applies regardless of whether one of the specific justifications applies.

Defensive Force Justification. Conduct constituting an offense is justified if:

(1) an aggressor unjustifiably threatens harm to any legally-protected interest; and

(2) the actor engages in conduct harmful to the aggressor,

(a) when and to the extent necessary to protect that interest,

(b) that is reasonable in relation to the harm or evil threatened.

3. The Model Penal Code contains an elaborate formula for determining when the use of force in self-defense is noncriminal. Note that the MPC rules seem to parallel those used by the court in the *Leidholm* case. Note too, how the right to use deadly force is subject to more stringent rules than is the right to use force in general. To what extent is the explanatory note that follows the MPC section helpful in understanding the provision?

Section 3.04. Use of Force in Self-Protection.

(1) Use of Force Justifiable for Protection of the Person. Subject to the provisions of this Section . . . the use of force upon or toward another person is justifiable when the actor believes that such force is immediately necessary for the purpose . . . of protecting himself against the use of unlawful force by such other person on the present occasion.

(2) Limitations on Justifying Necessity for Use of Force.

(a) The use of force is not justifiable under this Section:

(i) to resist an arrest that the actor knows is being made by a peace officer, although the arrest is unlawful; or

(ii) to resist force used by the occupier or possessor of property or by another person on his behalf, where the actor knows that the person using the force is doing so under a claim of right to protect the property, except that this limitation shall not apply if:

(A) the actor is a public officer acting in the performance of his duties or a person lawfully assisting him therein or a person making or assisting in a lawful arrest; or

(B) the actor has been unlawfully dispossessed of the property and is making a re-entry or recaption justified by Section 3.06; or

(C) the actor believes that such force is necessary to protect himself against death or serious bodily injury.

(b) The use of deadly force is not justifiable under this Section unless the actor believes that such force is necessary to protect himself against death, serious bodily injury, kidnapping or sexual intercourse compelled by force or threat; nor is it justifiable if:

(i) the actor, with the purpose of causing death or serious bodily injury, provoked the use of force against himself in the same encounter; or

(ii) the actor knows that he can avoid the necessity of using such force with complete safety by retreating or by surrendering possession of a thing to a person asserting a claim of right thereto or by complying with a demand that he abstain from any action that he has no duty to take, except that:

(A) the actor is not obliged to retreat from his dwelling or place of work, unless he was the initial aggressor or is assailed in his place of work by another person whose place of work the actor knows it to be; and

(B) a public officer justified in using force in the performance of his duties or a person justified in using force in his assistance or a person justified in using force in making an arrest or preventing an escape is not obliged to desist from efforts to perform such duty, effect such arrest or prevent such escape because of resistance or threatened resistance by or on behalf of the person against whom such action is directed.

(c) Except as required by paragraphs (a) and (b) of this Subsection, a person employing protective force may estimate the necessity thereof under the circumstances as he believes them to be when the force is used, without retreating, surrendering possession, doing any other act that he has no legal duty to do or abstaining from any lawful action.

(3) Use of Confinement as Protective Force. The justification afforded by this Section extends to the use of confinement as protective force only if the actor takes all reasonable measures to terminate the confinement as soon as he knows that he safely can, unless the person confined has been arrested on a charge of crime.

Explanatory Note

Subsection (1) states the basic principle that is to govern the use of force in self-protection. The actor is justified in using force toward another person when he believes that such force is immediately necessary for the purpose of protecting himself against the use of unlawful force by the other person on the present occasion. Under this subsection, the actor's actual belief is sufficient to support the defense; if his belief is mistaken and is recklessly or negligently formed, he may then be prosecuted for an offense of recklessness or negligence under Section 3.09. In other words, if an actor makes a negligent mistake in assessing the need for self-defensive action, he cannot be prosecuted for an offense that requires purpose to establish culpability.

Subsection (2) provides a series of additional limitations on the use of self-defensive force. Three situations are dealt with.

First, the actor is not privileged to use force for the purpose of resisting an arrest that he knows is being made by a peace officer, irrespective of the legality of the arrest.

Second, the actor is not privileged to use force for the purpose of resisting force used by one who is the occupant or possessor of property, where the actor knows that the person using the force is doing so under a claim of right to protect the property. This limitation, however, is not applicable in any of three situations: when the actor is a public officer acting in the performance of his duties, or a person lawfully assisting him; when the actor has been unlawfully dispossessed of the property and is making a reentry or recaption that is itself justified by Section 3.06; or when the actor believes that his use of force is necessary to protect himself against death or serious bodily injury.

The third limitation on the use of self-defensive force relates to the occasions when deadly force may be used. Deadly force is not justified unless the actor believes that such force is necessary to protect himself against death, serious bodily injury, kidnapping or sexual intercourse compelled by force or threat. Deadly force is also not justified if the actor provoked the use of force in the same encounter, with the purpose of causing death or serious bodily injury. Finally, deadly force is not justified if the actor can avoid the necessity of using such force with complete safety by taking certain alternative steps: by retreating, by surrendering possession of a thing to a person asserting a claim of right thereto, or by complying with a demand that he abstain from action that he has no duty to take. The requirement that one of these alternatives be pursued does not apply, however, in two very narrow circumstances: an actor is not obliged to retreat from his dwelling or place of work, unless he was the initial aggressor or the attack is at the actor's place of work and is by another person whose place of work the actor knows it to be; and public officers seeking to effect an arrest or prevent an escape are not obliged to desist from such efforts because of resistance by the person against whom such action is directed. Finally, Subsection (2)(c) clarifies the point that retreat, the surrender of possession, etc., are not required except when specifically contemplated by Paragraphs (ii)(A) and (ii)(B) of Subsection (2)(b). Where there is no such requirement, the actor may estimate the necessity of his self-defensive force under the circumstances as he believes them to be when the force is used. Mistakes, as noted, are governed by Section 3.09.

Subsection (3) speaks to the use of confinement as self-defensive force. Confinement may be used only if the actor takes all reasonable measures to terminate the confinement as soon as he knows that he may safely do so, unless the confinement is in the form of an arrest. In the latter case, the processes of the law will determine the point at which release should occur.

4. What does the court in *Leidholm* think is the difference between the subjective and the objective standards of reasonableness? What does it mean to say, as does the court, that the issue is not whether a reasonable person would have believed something, but rather whether the defendant *reasonably* believed it? What does it mean to say someone reasonably believed something? Is the court simply saying that the reasonableness of a person's belief must be determined from the viewpoint of that person? Would that be anything startling? Or is the court, rather, saying that the reasonableness of a decision must be determined with respect to the standard we can reasonably expect of a person with the personal qualities of the defendant? What if one of the personal qualities of the defendant is that he or she is unreasonably timid or fearful? What if the defendant is just plain unreasonable?

5. Of course, the fact that the defendant was a woman is relevant to the right to use self-defense. In the leading case on this issue, State v. Wanrow, 88 Wash. 2d 221, 559 P.2d 548 (1977), cited by the court in *Leidholm*, the court held:

The second paragraph of instruction No. 10 contains an . . . erroneous and prejudicial statement of the law. That portion of the instruction reads:

> However, when there is no reasonable ground for the person attacked to believe that *his* person is in imminent danger of death or great bodily harm, and it appears to *him* that only an ordinary battery is all that is intended, and all that *he* has reasonable grounds to fear from *his* assailant, *he* has a right to stand *his* ground and repel such threatened assault, yet *he* has no right to repel a threatened assault with naked hands, by the use of a deadly weapon in a deadly manner, unless *he* believes, *and has reasonable grounds* to believe that *he* is in imminent danger of death or great bodily harm.

(Italics ours.) In our society women suffer from a conspicuous lack of access to training in and the means of developing those skills necessary to effectively repel a male assailant without resorting to the use of deadly weapons. Instruction No. 12 does indicate that the "relative size and strength of the persons involved" may be considered; however, it does not make clear that the defendant's actions are to be judged against her own subjective impressions and not those which a detached jury might determine to be objectively reasonable. State v. Miller [141 Wash. 104, 250 p.645 (1926)]. The applicable rule of law is clearly stated in *Miller:*

> If the appellants, at the time of the alleged assault upon them, as reasonably and ordinarily cautious and prudent men, honestly believed that they were in danger of great bodily harm, they would have the right to resort to self-defense, and their conduct is to be judged by the condition appearing to them at the time, not by the condition as it might appear to the jury in the light of testimony before it.

The second paragraph of instruction No. 10 not only establishes an objective standard, but through the persistent use of the masculine gender leaves the jury with the impression the objective standard to be applied is that applicable to an altercation between two men. The impression created—that a 5′4″ woman with a cast on her leg and using a crutch must, under the law, somehow repel an assault by a 6′2″ intoxicated man without employing weapons in her defense, unless the jury finds her determination of the degree of danger to be objectively reasonable—constitutes a separate and distinct misstatement of the law and, in the context of this case, violates the respondent's right to equal protection of the law. The respondent was entitled to have the jury consider her actions in the light of her own perceptions of the situation, including those perceptions which were the product of our nation's "long and unfortunate history of sex discrimination." Frontiero v. Richardson, 411 U.S. 677, 684, 93 S. Ct. 1764, 1769, 36 L. Ed. 2d 583 (1973). Until such time as the effects of that history are eradicated, care must be taken to assure that our self-defense instructions afford women the right to have their conduct judged in light of the individual physical handicaps which are the product of sex discrimination. To fail to do so is to deny the right of the individual woman involved to trial by the same rules which are applicable to male defendants. . . . The portion of the instruction above quoted misstates our law in creating an objective standard of "reasonableness." It then compounds that error by utilizing language suggesting that the respondent's conduct must be measured against that of a reasonable male individual finding himself in the same circumstances.

We conclude that the instruction here in question contains an improper statement of the law on a vital issue in the case, is inconsistent, misleading and

> prejudicial when read in conjunction with other instructions pertaining to the same issue, and therefore is a proper basis for a finding of reversible error.

In determining whether the jury would be moved by the sexism the court found in instruction number 10, would it make a difference what portion of the jury consisted of women?

6. Cases involving defensive force by battered women do not only deal with problems of jury instructions. In Ibn-Tamas v. United States, 407 A.2d 626 (D.C. Ct. App. 1979) the defendant had shot her husband to death. Although her plea was self-defense, the prosecutor argued that she had "simply decided that she had endured enough of her husband's abuse; lured him back into the house with a telephone call; ambushed him on the stairs; and followed him downstairs shooting him in the forehead at point blank range." The prosecutor also suggested that she stood to gain financially from her husband's death and was "jealous of the other women he had told her he had dated during the last few weeks before the shooting." The defendant attempted to introduce expert testimony that Dr. Walker, her expert witness,

> had studied 110 women who had been beaten by their husbands. Her studies revealed three consecutive phases in the relationships: "tension building," when there are small incidents of battering; "acute battering incident," when beatings are severe; and "loving-contrite," when the husband becomes very sorry and caring. Dr. Walker then testified that women in this situation typically are low in self-esteem, feel powerless, and have few close friends, since their husbands commonly "accuse[] them of all kinds of things with friends, and they are embarrassed. They don't want to cause their friends problems, too." Because there are periods of harmony, battered women tend to believe their husbands are basically loving, caring men; the women assume that they, themselves, are somehow responsible for their husbands' violent behavior. They also believe, however, that their husbands are capable of killing them, and they feel there is no escape. Unless a shelter is available, these women stay with their husbands, not only because they typically lack a means of self-support but also because they fear that if they leave they will be found and hurt even more. Dr. Walker stressed that wife batterers come from all racial, social and economic groups (including professionals), and that batterers commonly "escalate their abusiveness" when their wives are pregnant. She added that battered women are very reluctant to tell anyone that their husbands beat them. Of those studied, 60 percent had never done so before (Dr. Walker typically found them in hospitals), 40 percent had told a friend, and only 10 percent had called the police.
>
> When asked about appellant, whom she had interviewed, Dr. Walker replied that Mrs. Ibn-Tamas was a "classic case" of the battered wife. Dr. Walker added her belief that on the day of the killing, when Dr. Ibn-Tamas had been beating his wife despite protests that she was pregnant, Mrs. Ibn-Tamas' pregnancy had had a "major impact on the situation. . . . [T]hat is a particularly crucial time."
>
> Dr. Walker's testimony, therefore, arguably would have served at least two basic functions: (1) it would have enhanced Mrs. Ibn-Tamas' general credibility

> in responding to cross-examination designed to show that her testimony about the relationship with her husband was implausible; and (2) it would have supported her testimony that on the day of the shooting her husband's actions had provoked a state of fear which led her to believe she was in imminent danger ("I just knew he was going to kill me"), and thus responded in self-defense. Dr. Walker's contribution, accordingly, would have been akin to the psychiatric testimony admitted in the case of Patricia Hearst "to explain the effects kidnapping, prolonged incarceration, and psychological and physical abuse may have had on the defendant's mental state at the time of the robbery, insofar as such mental state is relevant to the asserted defense of coercion or duress." Dr. Walker's testimony would have supplied an interpretation of the facts which differed from the ordinary lay perception ("she could have gotten out, you know") advocated by the government.

The court reversed the trial judge's exclusion of Dr. Walker's testimony as a matter of law, and sent the matter back for further hearings on the admissibility of her study.

The problem of the battered wife does not, in any event, fit neatly into our rules of self-defense. According to Professor George E. Dix, writing in the Encyclopedia of Crime and Justice 948, 948-950 (1983):

> Special problems are presented when one spouse, usually the wife, assaults and perhaps kills the other as the culmination of a situation involving abuse by the ultimate victim. It has been urged (Schneider, Jordan, and Arguedas) that self-defense doctrine provides a reasonable vehicle for determining whether such women should be criminally liable for their conduct, but only if adequate effect is given to women's perceptions and the manner in which past experience causes them to respond to threatening situations. Two major problems are presented.
>
> If the defendant used deadly force, there is often doubt as to whether the victim's conduct threatened sufficiently serious harm to justify response with deadly force, especially where the victim showed no inclination to use a weapon. Schneider, Jordan, and Arguedas, however, urge that the reasonableness of a woman's perception that her spouse posed a threat of serious injury must be considered in the light of a number of factors. These include women's smaller size, their lack of training and experience in hand-to-hand fighting, and the traditional social pressure on women to respond with apprehension and fear to threatening situations. Further, consideration must be given to the victim's history of assaultiveness and to the frequent ineffectiveness of efforts by women to seek assistance from law enforcement and the courts in dealing with assaultive husbands.
>
> Whether or not deadly force was used, doubt may frequently exist as to whether the woman could reasonably perceive the threat posed by the husband as imminent enough to meet self-defense requirements. From some perspectives, these situations would appear to have offered no barrier to the woman's avoiding the need to use force by terminating her relationship with the husband. Again, however, Schneider, Jordan, and Arguedas stress the need to consider the woman's perception concerning alternatives. Assistance from police or courts may be

unavailable. Cultural pressures may preclude a woman from forfeiting the financial and social security provided by even a battering husband. Sex discrimination in employment may make abandonment of the situation impractical. Threatened harm can usefully be regarded as nonimminent if the period before the harm will occur permits utilization of alternatives to self-defense. Battered women may assault and even kill their husbands at a time when anticipated injuries may be hours or even days in the future. Further, use of force in some of these situations, objectively considered, appears to be quite inappropriate; a dead husband (especially if he was uninsured) provides no financial and social security. But the cultural and social influences to which some women have been subjected may cause them reasonably to perceive no actual and practical alternative to a violent attack upon the husband. Perhaps, in such situations, the threatened harm can be regarded as sufficiently imminent to support self-defense.

7. What should the defendant in *Leidholm* be guilty of if on retrial the jury determines that she honestly believed her life was in imminent danger but was unreasonable in so believing? Doesn't the Model Penal Code flatly provide in the first few lines of Section 3.04(1) and again in the first few lines of Section 3.04(2)(b) that the defense is proper when the "actor believes" the force is necessary? Comments to the Model Penal Code §3.04 explain this apparent error:

> The basic formulation of Subsection (1) requires that the actor believe that the circumstances create the necessity for using some protective force and that the force that he employs does not exceed what he believes to be essential to relieve his peril. Prevailing rules respecting self-defense, both common law and statutory, similarly demanded belief in the necessity of the defensive action. They usually added, however, a requirement of a reasonable ground for the belief, the precise statement of which varied somewhat with the jurisdiction. Two consequences followed from this requirement: (1) a mistaken belief in the necessity of force or the degree of force employed might suffice to exculpate; but (2) the actor's negligence in making the mistake might strip him of any defensive claim, thus permitting his conviction of a purposeful offense, even of murder.
>
> The Model Code sections are grounded on the belief that the second consequence is wrong. Compare, for example, the actor who purposely kills in order to reap financial reward and the actor who purposely kills while believing in the existence of circumstances that would, if they actually existed, exonerate on self-defense grounds. If the second actor was mistaken—if the circumstances were not in fact as he believed them to be—it is unjust to view him as having the same level of culpability as the first actor. It is unjust to put him at that level even if he was negligent or reckless in forming his belief, though to be sure in that case it would be appropriate to view him as culpable. This lesser degree of culpability should not be left merely to influence prosecutorial decisions to seek lesser charges or judicial decisions to mitigate sentences, but should be reflected in the criminal code. If the actor was reckless or negligent as to the existence of circumstances that would justify his conduct, he should then be subject to conviction of

a crime for which recklessness or negligence, as the case may be, is otherwise sufficient to establish culpability. Negligence in this context would permit a conviction of negligent homicide rather than purposeful murder, while recklessness would permit a conviction of manslaughter. The defendant should thus be classified according to the culpability he actually manifested toward the material elements[14] of his offense. This solution is worked out for Article 3 by Sections 3.09(2) and 3.02(2), and is also embodied as a general principle of liability in Section 2.02(10).

Recent legislative revisions have maintained the requirement that the actor believe that the force he uses is necessary to protect himself. Some jurisdictions have followed the Model Code and permitted negligent or reckless mistaken beliefs to serve as a defense to offenses requiring purpose or knowledge, but others have adhered to the old rule that an unreasonable mistake about the necessity for self-defense does not exculpate at all. It is often unclear whether this resolution is the consequence of a disagreement with the Institute's view of the culpability of the negligently mistaken actor, a belief that in real cases it will be too difficult to ascertain whether the actor actually entertained an unreasonable belief, a generalized disposition not to expand defenses, or a failure to understand the issue.[15] Since determining an actor's belief about self-defense is not peculiarly more difficult than determining his belief about other facts, there does not appear to be any good reason for a jurisdiction that makes liability turn largely on the actor's actual perceptions to refuse to do so in respect to the use of force in self-defense.

. . . The Model Code takes a consistent approach to different justifications for the use of force, requiring actual belief in its necessity and treating unreasonably mistaken belief uniformly. The statutory and common law that preceded the Code often contained anomalies lacking rational support.

While the rules dealing explicitly with self-defense required a belief in the necessity of the defensive action and made allowance for mistake, the overlapping rules establishing justification for the use of force in crime prevention sometimes differed on both points. There are decisions in which this privilege was extended, even to the use of deadly force, whenever the victim was engaged in the commission of a felony or of specified felonies, without regard to the necessity of the force used or even to the actor's view of the necessity.[16] There were also jurisdictions where, under this privilege, the actor's belief in the necessity sufficed

14. The term "material element," as established by Section 1.13(9) and (10), includes such conduct, circumstances or results as negative an excuse or justification.

15. For discussion of provisions retaining the requirement that the actor's belief be reasonable, see commentary accompanying Ill. ch. 38, §7-1; La. §14:19; Minn. §609.06; Mont. §94-3-102; N.Y. §35.15; Tex §9.31; Alas. (p) §11.21.130(a) (T.D., pt. 2); Md. (p) §35.15(1); S.C. (p) §12.1.

16. See, e.g., State v. Bonofiglio, 67 N.J.L. 239, 52 A. 712 (1902), overruled, State v. Fair, 45 N.J. 77, 211 A.2d 359 (1965); People v. Ligouri, 284 N.Y. 309, 31 N.E.2d 37 (1940) (based on a statutory formulation that has since been repealed), discussed in Note, 41 Colum. L. Rev. 733 (1941); cf. Commonwealth v. Foster, 364 Pa. 288, 72 A.2d 279 (1950).

It should be added, however, that some of the prevention of crime statutes, though silent in respect to the initial question of the necessity for using force, provided that the amount of force employed must not exceed that which is sufficient to prevent the commission of the crime. For recent revisions to similar effect, see, e.g., S.D. §22-18-4; Wash. §9A.16.020(3).

for the defense and, per contra, where the actor's belief, however reasonably grounded, did not exculpate unless a felony was actually threatened or committed.[17]

8. The defendant in *Leidholm* argued that the trial judge's instruction on retreat was defective. What did retreat have to do with that case, when the defendant stabbed her husband to death while he was asleep? Is it a retreat case? Under what theory? Aren't the real issues the "imminence" and gravity of the harm? Can't one argue that the entire rule on retreat is unnecessary, since if one can retreat safely, the harm the defendant fears cannot be imminent? Did the drafters of the Model Penal Code agree with this view? Why have a retreat rule anyway? Again according to Professor Dix:

> Perhaps the most hotly disputed issue in self-defense law can be put in deceptively simple terms: Should one faced with attack have a duty, subject to certain exceptions, to exercise any such opportunity as exists to retreat in safety before using deadly force?
>
> The rationale for the retreat rule is not difficult to ascertain, at least in part. It rests upon the view that human life, even the life of an aggressor, is sufficiently important that it should be preserved when to do so requires only the sacrifice of the much less important interest in standing one's ground (Model Penal Code, 1958, §3.04).
>
> Opponents of a retreat requirement urge that, at least on some occasions, compelling a threatened person to retreat or punishing such a person for not retreating involves an exceptionally grievous insult to the person's dignity that should be avoided. Further, while human life is unquestionably of major value, one who assaults another under circumstances justifying deadly force in response can reasonably be regarded as having forfeited as least some of the respect to which most persons and their lives are entitled.
>
> *When retreat is required.* The traditional retreat rule contains a clear exception for attack in one's own residential premises—one's "castle." A person assaulted in his dwelling need not retreat before using deadly force, even if a safe opportunity exists. Modern developments have raised significant question as to the meaning of this exception and its scope. Perhaps the most frequent question is whether one is required to retreat when assaulted in one's business premises. A majority of courts have expanded the "castle" exception to cover business premises, apparently on the assumption that the indignity of being compelled to flee one's place of business is little different from being forced to flee from one's home. When one is attacked on the porch of one's home, must one, under the rule, retreat at least into the structure? In State v. Bonano, 59 N.J. 515, 284 A.2d 345 (1971) the court held no retreat was required, reasoning that a porch or similar appurtenance is within the concept of one's dwelling house. Modern apartment

17. The most common type of provision relating to the prevention of felony was in two subdivisions. The first subdivision, which may be called the self-defense provision, justified homicide when: "in the lawful defense of such person [and certain enumerated others] . . . when there is reasonable ground to apprehend a design on the part of the person slain to commit a felony . . . and there is imminent danger of such design being accomplished."

living presents further difficulties. For example, must one who is accosted in an apartment-house hallway at least retreat into his or her own apartment? In Commonwealth v. Daniels, 451 Pa. 163, 301 A.2d 841 (1973), the court, over vigorous dissent, held that retreat is not required in such circumstances.

Requirement of safe retreat. Those jurisdictions requiring retreat apply the requirement only when the defendant has an opportunity to retreat in safety. The case of Commonwealth v. Eberle, 474 Pa. 548, 379 A.2d 90 (1977) illustrates the tendency to hold the prosecution to a substantial showing of a safe opportunity. Eberle's assailant, while intoxicated, lunged at her, and she stabbed him with the knife she had in her hand. Evidence introduced at trial showed that to reach the door of the apartment in which the assault occurred, she would have had to go around a corner. The apartment was cluttered, and diagrams introduced into evidence showed that there were some objects between the defendant and the doorway. There was no indication that the door was unlocked and could be easily opened in a hurry, and no evidence demonstrated that once Eberle got into the hallway outside the apartment she would be in a place of safety. In light of these considerations, and assuming a duty to retreat existed, the court concluded that the prosecution had failed to show that an opportunity to retreat in safety had been presented.

The Model Penal Code and the retreat rule. Although the retreat rule remains a minority one among American jurisdictions, it received significant impetus when it was incorporated into the Model Penal Code (1962) as Section 3.04(2)(b)(ii). Modern American statutory formulations of self-defense vary. A number embody the retreat requirement; others do not. The English courts have held that a failure to retreat before using any force, whether deadly force or not, is to be considered along with all other factors in determining whether the use of force was reasonable under the circumstances (*Regina v. McInnes,* [1971] 1 W.L.R. 1600 (C.A.)). The matter is thus posed to the jury in assault prosecutions as well as homicide cases (*Regina v. Julien,* [1969] 1 W.L.R. 839 (C.A.)).

Despite the Model Penal Code's effort to breathe new vigor into the traditionally minority position, the retreat rule seems likely to wither. While society is undoubtedly developing greater sensitivity for human life and less sympathy for extrajudicial battles to resolve disputes, there is also an increasing willingness to trust juries and to avoid complex and arguably inflexible rules designed to reduce jury discretion. It is likely that the position of the English courts will attract increased favor. No absolute duty to retreat will be formally imposed. Juries, however, will be told to consider any failure to make use of retreat opportunities in evaluating the reasonableness of responding to attacks with deadly force. [3 Encyclopedia of Crime and Justice, at 948-949 (1983).]

9. What about the person who brings about the necessity of using force in self-defense by his own unreasonable behavior? In one case, United States v. Peterson, 483 F.2d 1222 (D.C. Cir. 1973) the court held that this issue was raised by the following facts:

The events immediately preceding the homicide are not seriously in dispute. The version presented by the Government's evidence follows. Charles Keitt, the deceased, and two friends drove in Keitt's car to the alley in the rear of Peterson's house to remove the windshield wipers from the latter's wrecked car.[18] While Keitt was doing so, Peterson came out of the house[19] into the back yard to protest. After a verbal exchange,[20] Peterson went back into the house, obtained a pistol, and returned to the yard.[21] In the meantime, Keitt had reseated himself in his car, and he and his companions were about to leave.

Upon his reappearance in the yard, Peterson paused briefly to load the pistol.[22]

"If you move," he shouted to Keitt, "I will shoot." He walked to a point in the yard slightly inside a gate in the rear fence and, pistol in hand, said, "If you come in here I will kill you." Keitt alighted from his car, took a few steps toward Peterson and exclaimed, "What the hell do you think you are going to do with that?"[23] Keitt then made an about-face, walked back to his car and got a lug wrench. With the wrench in a raised position, Keitt advanced toward Peterson, who stood with the pistol pointed toward him. Peterson warned Keitt not to "take another step" and, when Keitt continued onward shot him in the face from a distance of about ten feet.[24] Death was apparently instantaneous. Shortly thereafter, Peterson left home and was apprehended 20-odd blocks away.

This description of the fatal episode was furnished at Peterson's trial by four witnesses for the Government.[25] Peterson did not testify or offer any evidence, but the Government introduced a statement which he had given the police after his arrest, in which he related a somewhat different version. Keitt had removed objects from his car before, and on the day of the shooting he had told Keitt not to do so. After the initial verbal altercation, Keitt went to his car for the lug wrench, so he, Peterson, went into his house for his pistol. When Keitt was about ten feet away, he pointed the pistol "away of his right shoulder"; adding that Keitt was running toward him, Peterson said he "got scared and fired the gun.

18. The car was characterized by some witnesses as "wrecked" and by others as "abandoned." The testimony left it clear that its condition was such that it could not be operated. It was parked on one side of the alley about fifteen feet from a gate in the rear fence which opened into Peterson's back yard. Keitt's car was stopped in the alleyway about four feet behind it.

19. Peterson, inside the house, had been told that Keitt was removing something from his car.

20. There were testimonial differences as to the content and intensity of the exchange. Ricky Gray, Peterson's brother, who had followed him into the yard, stated that Peterson "told Charley he oughtn't to take something off his car. . . ." Donald Dyson, one of Keitt's companions in the car, said "[t]hey were just arguing," Peterson complaining that Keitt "had been taking stuff off his car and hadn't been paying . . . for anything. . . ." Richard Hilliard, Keitt's other companion, characterized the argument as much more vigorous and profane.

21. Although the time lapse between Peterson's reentrance into the house and his subsequent reappearance in the yard is not precisely fixed, the testimony indicates that it was very short.

22. Richard Hilliard testified that Peterson inserted three bullets. Ricky Gray said there was only one. That there was some loading is uncontradicted.

23. There was abundant evidence that Keitt was intoxicated or nearly so. His companions readily admitted to a considerable amount of drinking earlier that day, and an autopsy disclosed that he had a .29 percent blood-alcohol content.

24. Keitt fell in the alley about seven feet from the gate. No powder burns were discernible.

25. Dyson and Hilliard who were seated in Keitt's car; Gray, who was in Peterson's back yard; and Murray Simon, a neighbor.

He ran right into the bullet." "I did not mean to shoot him," Peterson insisted, "I just wanted to scare him."

At trial, Peterson moved for a judgment of acquittal on the ground that as a matter of law the evidence was insufficient to support a conviction. The trial judge denied the motion. After receiving instructions which in two respects are challenged here, the jury returned a verdict finding Peterson guilty of manslaughter. Judgment was entered conformably with the verdict, and this appeal followed.

The court affirmed the conviction, holding:

It has long been accepted that one cannot support a claim of self-defense by a self-generated necessity to kill. The right of homicidal self-defense is granted only to those free from fault in the difficulty; it is denied to slayers who incite the fatal attack, encourage the fatal quarrel or otherwise promote the necessitous occasion for taking life. The fact that the deceased struck the first blow, fired the first shot or made the first menacing gesture does not legalize the self-defense claim if in fact the claimant was the actual provoker. In sum, one who is the aggressor in a conflict culminating in death cannot invoke the necessities of self-preservation. Only in the event that he communicates to his adversary his intent to withdraw and in good faith attempts to do so is he restored to his right of self-defense.

This body of doctrine traces its origin to the fundamental principle that a killing in self-defense is excusable only as a matter of genuine necessity. Quite obviously, a defensive killing is unnecessary if the occasion for it could have been averted, and the roots of that consideration run deep with us. A half-century ago, in Laney v. United States [54 App. D.C. 56, 294 F. 412 (1923)], this court declared

> that, before a person can avail himself of the plea of self-defense against the charge of homicide, he must do everything in his power, consistent with his safety, to avoid the danger and avoid the necessity of taking life. If one has reason to believe that he will be attacked, in a manner which threatens him with bodily injury, he must avoid the attack if it is possible to do so, and the right of self-defense does not arise until he has done everything in his power to prevent its necessity.

And over the many years since *Laney,* the court has kept faith with its precept.

In the case at bar, the trial judge's charge fully comported with these governing principles. The remaining question, then, is whether there was evidence to make them applicable to the case. A recapitulation of the proofs shows beyond peradventure that there was.

It was not until Peterson fetched his pistol and returned to his back yard that his confrontation with Keitt took on a deadly cast. Prior to his trip into the house for the gun, there was, by the Government's evidence, no threat, no display of weapons, no combat. There was an exchange of verbal aspersions[26] and a misdemeanor[27] against Peterson's property[28] was in progress but, at this junc-

26. See note [25] supra, and accompanying text.

27. It is well settled that deadly force cannot be employed to arrest or prevent the escape of a misdemeanant. . . .

28. The law never tolerates the use of deadly force in the protection of one's property. . . .

ture, nothing more. Even if Peterson's post-arrest version of the initial encounter were accepted—his claim that Keitt went for the lug wrench before he armed himself—the events which followed bore heavily on the question as to who the real aggressor was.[29]

The evidence is uncontradicted that when Peterson reappeared in the yard with his pistol,[30] Keitt was about to depart the scene. Richard Hilliard testified that after the first argument, Keitt reentered his car and said "Let's go." This statement was verified by Ricky Gray, who testified that Keitt "got in the car and . . . they were getting ready to go"; he, too, heard Keitt give the direction to start the car. The uncontroverted fact that Keitt was leaving shows plainly that so far as he was concerned the confrontation was ended. It demonstrates just as plainly that even if he had previously been the aggressor, he no longer was.

Not so with Peterson, however, as the undisputed evidence made clear. Emerging from the house with the pistol, he paused in the yard to load it,[31] and to command Keitt not to move. He then walked through the yard to the rear gate and, displaying his pistol, dared Keitt to come in, and threatened to kill him if he did. While there appears to be no fixed rule on the subject, the cases hold, and we agree, that an affirmative unlawful act reasonably calculated to produce an affray foreboding injurious or fatal consequences is an aggression which, unless renounced, nullifies the right of homicidal self-defense. We cannot escape the abiding conviction that the jury could readily find Peterson's challenge to be a transgression of that character.

The situation at bar is not unlike that presented in *Laney*. There the accused, chased along the street by a mob threatening his life, managed to escape through an areaway between two houses. In the back yard of one of the houses, he checked a gun he was carrying and then returned to the areaway. The mob beset him again, and during an exchange of shots one of its members was killed by a bullet from the accused's gun. In affirming a conviction of manslaughter, the court reasoned:

> It is clearly apparent . . . that, when defendant escaped from the mob into the back yard . . . he was in a place of comparative safety, from which, if he desired to go home, he could have gone by the back way, as he subsequently did. The mob had turned its attention to a house on the opposite side of the street. According to Laney's testimony, there was shooting going on in the street. His appearance on the street at that juncture could mean nothing but trouble for him. Hence, when he adjusted his gun and stepped out into the areaway, he had every reason to believe that his presence there would provoke trouble. We think his conduct in adjusting his revolver and going into the areaway was such as to deprive him of any right to invoke the plea of self-defense.

Similarly, in Rowe v. United States [125 U.S. App. D.C. 218, 370 F.2d 240 (1966)], the accused was in the home of friends when an argument, to which the

29. Notwithstanding that the deceased provoked the original quarrel, the accused cannot, after that quarrel has ended or the deceased has withdrawn, invoke the right of self-defense in a subsequent difficulty which he himself causes or brings on. . . .

30. One may deliberately arm himself for purposes of self-defense against a pernicious assault which he has good reason to expect. On the other hand, the true significance of the fact of arming can be determined only in the context of the surrounding circumstances.

31. One of Keitt's companions and Ricky Gray testified that Peterson "broke open" the pistol and inserted one or more bullets immediately upon his exit from the house.

friends became participants, developed in the street in front. He left, went to his nearby apartment for a loaded pistol and returned. There was testimony that he then made an insulting comment, drew the pistol and fired a shot into the ground. In any event, when a group of five men began to move toward him, he began to shoot at them, killing two, and wounding a third. We observed that the accused "left an apparently safe haven to arm himself and return to the scene," and that "he inflamed the situation with his words to the men gathered there, even though he could have returned silently to the safety of the [friends'] porch." We held that

> [t]hese facts could have led the jury to conclude that [the accused] returned to the scene to stir up further trouble, if not actually to kill anyone, and that his actions instigated the men into rushing him. Self-defense may not be claimed by one who deliberately places himself in a position where he has reason to believe "his presence . . . would provoke trouble."

We noted the argument "that a defendant may claim self-defense if he arms himself in order to proceed upon his normal activities, even if he realizes that danger may await him"; we responded by pointing out "that the jury could have found that the course of action defendant here followed was for an unlawful purpose." We accordingly affirmed his conviction of manslaughter over his objection that an acquittal should have been directed.

We are brought much the readier to the same conclusion here. We think the evidence plainly presented an issue of fact as to whether Peterson's conduct was an invitation to and provocation of the encounter which ended in the fatal shot. We sustain the trial judge's action in remitting that issue for the jury's determination.

Do you agree that Peterson should forfeit what would otherwise have been his right to self-defense? Did he do anything illegal? Did he do anything wrong? What about *Laney,* cited by the court; what did Laney do that was wrong?

According to one commentator,[32] this issue is but one facet of a much broader problem:

> [T]he current treatment of an actor who is culpable in causing the conditions of his defense is inadequate in many troubling respects. Moreover, current law imposes liability on the actor through the theoretically unsound method of denying him a defense. This Part suggests an analysis that would continue to allow the actor a defense for the immediate conduct constituting the offense, but would separately impose liability on the basis of the actor's earlier conduct in culpably causing the conditions of his defense.
>
> This alternative, "conduct-in-causing" analysis avoids the problems arising from current law treatment and has several advantages. It avoids the anomaly of denying a justification or excuse to an actor who satisfies the conditions of those defenses. It avoids the improper assumption that an actor who intends to cause (or risks causing) the conditions under which an offense is committed necessarily

32. Robinson, Causing the Condition of One's Own Defense: A Study in the Limits of Theory in Criminal Law Doctrine, 71 Va. L. Rev. 1, 27-43 (1985).

intends to commit (or risks committing) the offense. It also properly distinguishes among levels of culpability at the time of causing one's defense in determining the level of liability to be imposed. . . .

Where conduct is justified because it avoids a net harm for society, it provides little basis on which to fasten blame and it is against society's interest to deter it. Where a forest fire has been set, for whatever reason, society wants any and all persons to set a firebreak and save a threatened town. To withdraw a defense for such conduct is to punish and to discourage it.

Assume that an actor sets a fire that threatens a nearby town to create the conditions that will justify his using his enemy's farm as a firebreak. Denying a justification defense might dissuade him from undertaking such a scheme, but if it fails to dissuade him, the unavailability of the defense may reduce his incentive to set the firebreak and save the town. Once the justifying conditions exist, regardless of the cause, society benefits if the actor undertakes the justified conduct. Moreover, if the defense is denied, the owner of the field, who values his crop more than he does the lives of the townspeople, may lawfully interfere with the actor's attempt to set fire to the field.

Denying the defense to the actor who has created the justifying circumstances also creates an anomalous situation in which the actor and another person may work side-by-side engaging in the same conduct—here, setting fire to the same field—yet one will be justified and the other will not. It is the nature of justified conduct that it either is or is not justified—depending on whether it causes a net societal benefit—regardless of the particular state of mind, past or present, of the actor.

These problems may be avoided, however, and such a grand schemer may be properly punished, if his liability is based on his initial conduct in causing the justifying circumstances and on his culpable state of mind, at that time, as to causing the justified harm. In the culpably-caused-need-for-a-firebreak case, the actor might be liable for setting the forest fire in the first place and for the damage it caused. His subsequent conduct in saving the town by setting the firebreak would remain justified, and thus would be encouraged and protected.[33] Indeed, the actor retains a special incentive to set the firebreak, for if the town burns down and kills or injures someone, he may be liable for this additional harm.

As with justifications, there is a fundamental flaw in an approach that denies an excuse because the actor culpably causes the conditions of his excuse. Just as causing one's defense does not alter the justified nature of otherwise justified conduct, it does not erase the excusing conditions that exculpates the actor for the offense conduct. If an actor is not responsible when a recognized disability causes an excusing condition for his actions, it follows that he is equally not responsible at the moment of the same offense conduct under similar conditions, even though he has contributed to their creation. To punish an actor for

33. Similarly, where a speeder must choose between hitting two pedestrians or damaging a grocery store, he may be justified in veering off toward the store. He should not escape liability entirely, however, because his speeding is properly viewed as an intentional creation of a risk of injury to persons or property. He may properly be held liable for reckless destruction of property. The destruction itself is justified; it is his earlier creation of the risk on which liability may be imposed.

conduct performed when he is not responsible is to punish him for conduct that society has determined to be beyond his control and thus blameless. . . .

Where an actor brings about the conditions of his defense but at the time has no culpability, not even negligence, as to causing or risking the commission of the subsequent offense, it is appropriate to limit his liability to that imposed by existing statutes. If his conduct constitutes negligent property destruction or being drunk in public, then such offenses are properly the extent of his liability. If his conduct does not constitute an offense, he faces no liability.

Where the actor is not only culpable as to causing the defense conditions, but also has a culpable state of mind *as to causing himself to engage in the conduct constituting the offense,* the state should punish him for causing the ultimate justified or excused conduct.[34] His punishment, however, is properly based on his initial conduct of causing the defense conditions with his accompanying scheming intention, not on the justified or excused conduct that he subsequently performs.

Under this analysis, one need simply consider whether, at the time that the actor engages in his initial conduct in causing the defense conditions (for example, starting the forest fire), he has a culpable state of mind as to causing the conduct constituting the offense (i.e., burning the firebreak). For example, if when the defendant sets the forest fire, his ultimate objective is to create the conditions that will permit him (or anyone else) to burn the firebreak, he is properly held liable for intentionally causing the burning of the firebreak. His liability is based on his conduct of setting the forest fire with his accompanying intention to cause the burning of the firebreak, not on his justified burning of the firebreak. He is then liable for the result that he has intentionally caused, yet all persons are still justified in burning the firebreak.[35]

34. This occurs in a "grand schemer" case, for example, where the actor intends to create the defense conditions to then commit the defense. It is no doubt the concern for the "grand schemer" that creates a hesitation to provide an excuse when an actor has culpably caused the disability and excusing conditions. As one court complained: "All that the crafty criminal would require for a well-planned murder . . . would be a revolver in one hand to commit the deed, and a quart of intoxicating liquor in the other with which to build his excusable defense." State v. Arsenault, 152 Me. 121, 130-131, 124 A.2d 741, 746 (1956). Perhaps the "grand schemer" best known in the popular culture is the vigilante character of the 1974 movie "Death Wish," who deliberately takes late-night walks and subway rides to place himself in threatening situations where he could kill the muggers who tried to attack him.

35. There is some legislation designed to punish the grand schemer in the manner suggested here. At least one jurisdiction punishes as a murderer one who perjures himself with intent to bring about circumstances justifying the execution of an innocent person. Colo. Rev. Stat. §18-3-102(1)(c) (1978). . . .

One might argue that the conduct of a grand schemer in causing the justified burning of the field should give rise to liability for only *attempted* property destruction. Like the unknowingly justified actor, this actor intended to cause a legally-recognized net harm and acted upon that intention, but caused only a justified harm. . . .

There are valid objections, however, to imposing only attempt liability on one who culpably creates justifying circumstances. First, it would give to an actor bent on crime a device to limit his liability to *an attempt* to commit the offense, simply by creating circumstances that would justify his conduct constituting the offense. (He would also be liable for any offense committed while creating the justifying circumstances, for example, setting a forest fire, but as noted in the text of this subsection, the conduct in causing is not always an offense.)

Second, the situation is not really analogous to that of the unknowingly justified actor. There, no net harm has been caused, except for the harm or evil of the bad intention that the unknowingly justified actor acted upon. Here, however, in considering whether there is a *net* harm, one must look at the time *before* the actor engaged in the conduct creating the justifying circumstances.

This approach has the additional advantage of holding an actor liable for burning the firebreak when his grand scheme causes *others* to burn the firebreak, rather than limiting such liability, as current law tends to do, to the situation where he personally burns it.[36] In addition, under this analysis the actor and all others are encouraged to perform the justified conduct.[37] Finally, this analysis accounts for different degrees of culpability as to the ultimate offense. If at the time of starting the forest fire the actor is only aware of a risk that his conduct will cause him (or others) to burn the firebreak, he is properly held liable only for recklessly causing the destruction of the firebreak.

The same analysis is appropriate when an actor causes the conditions of an excuse. He may properly be held liable for the ultimate offense on the basis of his causing the excused conduct and his accompanying culpable state of mind with respect to his commission of the ultimate offense. . . .

[The] focus on the actor's earlier conduct and his accompanying culpability as to the ultimate offense, rather than on the conduct and culpability most immediately associated with the offense, is analogous to liability for causing a crime by an innocent. The analysis simply generalizes the latter principle and treats the justified, excused, or unaware actor as the "innocent actor" who was caused to engage in the criminal conduct by the actor's prior, culpable actions. Thus, the statutes and cases imposing liability for such causing-crime-by-an-innocent provide a certain measure of support for the principle proposed here of liability for causing the conditions of one's defense.

The present analysis is also entirely consistent with the normal operation of criminal liability rules of causation. Assume that the actor's car accelerator has recently been sticking momentarily. Being a seasoned auto mechanic, she realizes that the accelerator could become stuck in the full-throttle position. In such an emergency, she would need at least thirty seconds to slow her car and would

---

From this perspective, the actor's conduct in creating the justifying circumstances *did create a net harm*—he engaged in conduct that ultimately caused the burning of the firebreak at a time when there was no justification for such conduct. He has thus caused two harms: (1) the immediate harm—the forest fire, and (2) the harm of the justified conduct necessary to combat the forest fire—the firebreak. The burning of the firebreak is justified because under the circumstances as they *then* exist, the harm of the firebreak avoids a greater harm. The firebreak, however, is a harm necessitated by the actor's initial conduct. Nor would attempt liability be sufficient where the actor culpably causes an excusing condition; excused conduct does cause a harm or evil. . . .

36. For example, the Model Penal Code provides a justification defense to one who believes the person whom he assists is entitled to protect himself. Model Penal Code §3.05(1)(b) (Proposed Official Draft 1962). There is no readily apparent means of holding a provoker liable for the conduct of one who comes to the provoker's assistance when the person provoked attacks the provoker. One might, however, argue that id. §2.06(2)(a) ("Liability for Conduct of Another; Complicity") imposes liability on the theory that the provoker caused an innocent person to engage in the conduct and is therefore accountable for the conduct.

37. The actor generally has an incentive to engage in the justified conduct himself and assure that the greater harm is avoided. If he fails to do so, he will increase his own liability. Where the firebreak is not burned, for example, he may be held liable for the death and destruction of the entire town. Liability will be based either on his initial conduct in setting the forest fire and creating a risk of such death and destruction or, under an omission theory, on his failure to act to avoid the harm when he could have done so at little risk to himself and where he had a duty to do so because he created the danger. The Model Penal Code contains a provision to cover this situation. Id. §220.1(3)(b) (actor who starts a fire commits a misdemeanor if he knows that the fire is endangering life or substantial amounts of property and fails to take reasonable steps to put it out).

therefore be unable to respond if another car or a pedestrian suddenly crossed her path. She reasons that because she will be driving on a straight and open highway she is unlikely to face any emergency that will require her to react quickly. In the middle of her excursion, the accelerator becomes stuck, and while she is trying to release it, she sees a line of school children crossing the highway during a nature outing. Because of her rapidly increasing speed, she cannot avoid the children and kills four of them. Assume that at the time of the killing she is truly helpless to avoid the children. Although she is not affirmatively "taking a risk" at the time of the offense (in the sense that she is consciously choosing to drive that fast—she has no choice at that point), we can nevertheless hold her liable for reckless, or at least negligent, homicide. This liability would be based on her earlier conduct of setting in motion the chain of events—culpably causing the conditions—that led to the four deaths.

From a narrow time perspective the driver is blameless for the deaths, because the car was out of her control at the time of the offense. Her preceding act of driving with the defective accelerator was reckless, however, as to causing the deaths of pedestrians. By broadening the time perspective to include the earlier conduct and its accompanying culpability as to the ultimate harm, one may then properly impose liability for the deaths despite the driver's inability to avoid the harm at the time it actually occurred. This use of traditional causation rules is analogous to the proposed causing-the-conditions analysis.

There is case law precedent for the causing-one's-defense analysis proposed here.[38] . . .

[One] case where the court relied on the defendant's culpability in causing the conditions of his excuse is State v. Gooze [14 N.J. Super. 277, 81 A.2d 811 (App. Div. 1951)]. Gooze had a history of blackouts from Ménière's Syndrome. While he was driving, he suffered a blackout and ran over a pedestrian. He was convicted of "caus[ing] the death of another by driving [a] vehicle carelessly and heedlessly in willful or wanton disregard of the rights or safety of others." The court noted that "[i]t was reasonably foreseeable that if he 'blacked out' or became dizzy without warning, its probable consequence might well be injury or

38. See, e.g., State v. Butner, 66 Nev. 127, 135, 206 P.2d 253, 257 (1949) (person who drinks to nerve himself before committing a crime cannot maintain that he was too drunk at the time of the offense to entertain the requisite intent), cert. denied, 338 U.S. 950 (1950); see generally R. Perkins and R. Boyce, Criminal Law 1008-09 (3d ed. 1982) (where premeditation and deliberation occur before the defendant causes his excusing intoxication, the defendant is properly held liable for the offense perpetrated); Model Penal Code §2.08 comment 3, at 7 (Tent. Draft No. 9, 1959) (noting that those who objected to the Model Penal Code formulation of the intoxication negating an element defense . . . argued that the voluntarily intoxicated actor's liability could be based on the actor's awareness of the harm risked at the time he became intoxicated).

In Taylor v. Superior Court, 3 Cal. 3d 578, 477 P.2d 131, 91 Cal. Rptr. 275 (1970), the court would not hold the defendant directly liable under the felony-murder rule for the justifiable killing of one of his co-felons by the owner of a store that the defendant and his co-felons were robbing. The court *was* willing, however, to permit an imputation of liability under a theory of vicarious liability. It focused on the co-felon's earlier conduct of initiating the gun battle that caused the justifying circumstances. Under the analysis proposed in the text, however, where the actor intentionally causes the justifying circumstances but is only reckless as to whether a justified killing will result, as the *Taylor* court conceded to be the case there, id. at 582-83, 477 P.2d at 133, 91 Cal. Rptr. at 277, the defendant may properly be held liable only for reckless homicide. The contrary result in *Taylor* may be due to the special aggravation of culpability aspect inherent in the felony-murder rule. . . .

death to others." The court then reasoned, "while one cannot be liable for what he does during the unconsciousness of sleep, he is responsible for allowing himself to go to sleep" while driving. . . .

Where an actor's conduct that causes the conditions of his defense is an offense—for example, negligent burning or public drunkenness—there is little difficulty in imposing additional liability, as proposed in this Part, if the actor causes those conditions with some culpability toward causing himself thus to engage in further proscribed conduct, albeit justified or excused. Where the conduct causing the conditions of a defense is otherwise lawful, however, there may be some question as to whether the actor's lawful conduct may be used as the basis for criminal liability; after all, his conduct does not appear to satisfy the conduct requirements of any specified offense. In the hardest case, his conduct may be of a nature that is constitutionally protected.

Assume that a known member of the Palestine Liberation Organization enters a meeting of the Jewish Defense League being held in a public place. Assume further that his purpose in doing so is to induce, by his mere presence, the attendees to assault him, thereby creating the circumstances that will justify his use of force against them in self-defense. One might be inclined not to punish his conduct in causing the circumstances justifying his use of force because that conduct—entering the public meeting—is otherwise lawful. Courts have said, for example, in speaking of *fault* in causing the conditions of justifications, that "[f]ault implies misconduct," such as being where one has no legal right to be.[39]

This attitude, however, betrays a conception of criminal law according to which conduct is per se either legal or illegal, and fails to accept the relevance of context in assessing an act's criminality. Almost any act, even a homicidal one, may be legal in certain situations; an execution is an obvious example, as is self-defense. Similarly, an act that is usually legal may be criminal in certain situations; for example, driving along a highway may be illegal if it causes the death of a pedestrian standing in the middle of the road.

Even when similar acts are performed in similar situations, the actor's state of mind as to the consequences can be determinative of criminality. An actor who comes into control of property that he knows was lost by another but who fails to report his finding is not guilty of theft unless he intended to deprive the owner of the property. A person who "antiques" his dining room furniture is not guilty of a crime unless he intends to defraud someone into buying it at an inflated price. A more important example of where otherwise legal acts can be the basis for criminal liability if performed with a particular state of mind is criminal attempt. An actor who has tools in his possession can be convicted of attempt if he intends to use them to commit a burglary. By analogy, therefore, an actor may be criminally liable for entering a room of hostile people and eventually causing a justified killing if he did so with the appropriate state of mind as to causing that consequence.

To take a less dramatic example than the P.L.O./J.D.L. case, consider the actor, *D*, who sends *T* a false letter claiming that he, *D*, is in possession of a watch that *T* treasures. *D* knows that the watch was recently stolen and that *T*, a person of violent temper, will on receipt of the letter unjustifiably attack him in an attempt to recover the watch. *D* knows nothing of the whereabouts of the

39. State v. Jackson, 94 Ariz. 117, 122, 382 P.2d 229, 232 (1963).

watch, but has devised this grand scheme to permit him to kill *T* in self-defense. *D*'s conduct in sending the letter is not itself unlawful. Because he did it with the intent to kill *T*,[40] however, one may be inclined to hold him liable for murder, or at least attempted murder.[41] His liability would be based on his conduct in causing the attack, not on his justified defensive force.

One might have the same view toward the P.L.O. member who enters the J.D.L. meeting with a grand scheme of injuring the attendees in self-defense. The letter-sending case may seem a stronger one for criminal liability because the P.L.O. member is exercising an affirmative right of all citizens to go where they choose in public places, whereas the letter-sender has no affirmative right to mail false letters. It seems questionable, however, to distinguish noncriminal acts according to how offensive or desirable they may be.[42] The better conclusion may be that although one may generally sympathize with the P.L.O. member's exercise of his rights to move freely in a public place, he has, by his intention to kill, acted just as improperly as the sender of the false letter. It may be more difficult to prove a grand scheme intention by the P.L.O. member than by the letter-sender, whose actions may speak for themselves, but where such an intent is proven, it is an adequate basis for liability, even though the underlying conduct is otherwise lawful. . . .

Defenses to Liability for Causing One's Own Defense

Like conduct constituting an offense, an actor's conduct in causing the conditions of his defense may be blameless under a variety of defenses. If his conduct is entirely accidental—as when an actor provokes an attack when he takes property that he mistakenly but reasonably believes to be his own—his accidental conduct will not satisfy the culpability requirements of the liability principle proposed here. This outcome is analogous to the typical failure of proof "defense" where an actor's lack of culpability negates a culpable state of mind required by an offense definition. Here, the liability principle requires a culpable state of mind as to causing the resulting offense.[43]

Even if the actor does satisfy the culpability requirements for causing-one's-defense liability, he should nonetheless be entitled to any appropriate general defense to such liability. For example, an actor may have set a forest fire as a justification for later burning a firebreak, but may have done so only because he was coerced, thereby meriting a duress excuse for his causing the justificatory circumstances. A C.I.A. agent may provoke an attack to conceal, under the guise

40. Note that if the letter-sender or the P.L.O. member intends only to create the opportunity for a justified *assault* in self-defense, but ends up killing in self-defense, he may be held liable for the degree of homicide consistent with his culpable state of mind with regard to causing the death. For example, by intending an assault, he may be aware of a risk of causing death, and thus be liable for reckless homicide.

41. Although one might argue that his conduct is only of the *attempt* variety because he has not at the time of the offense caused a net harm that the law punishes as a substantive offense, this argument is easily countered by considering the course of conduct.

42. Travel in interstate or foreign commerce is generally lawful, and interstate travel is often considered a constitutional right, but such travel becaomes a federal crime when done with the intent to avoid prosecution for a state felony. 18 U.S.C. §1073 (1982).

43. No culpability is required for the underlying offense, however, where it is a strict liability crime.

of self-defense, a homicide justified by a spy's imminent attempt to leave the country with information that will lead to nuclear war. The agent would be entitled to a justification defense for creating the circumstances justifying the homicide.

Do you agree with Professor Robinson's handling of the problem? Particularly, if the PLO member does not wish to be assaulted at the JDL meeting but reasonably should know that he will be, should he then be guilty of negligent homicide if he kills in self defense? What would happen if, to the PLO members' great surprise, no one from the JDL assaulted him? Would he nonetheless be guilty of attempted murder?

10. Why should we be entitled to kill in self-defense anyway? A prominent moral philosopher, Judith Thomson, grapples with this issue in the context of several interesting hypotheticals:[44]

1. Suppose Aggressor has got hold of a tank. He had told Victim that if he gets a tank, he's going to get in it and run Victim down. Victim sees Aggressor get in his tank and start towards Victim. It is open country, and Victim can see that there is no place to hide, and nothing he can put between himself and Aggressor which Aggressor cannot circle round. Fortunately, Victim happens to have an anti-tank gun with him, and it is in good working order, so he can use it to blow up the tank, thereby saving his life, but of course thereby also killing Aggressor. I think that most people would say that it is morally permissible for Victim to use that anti-tank gun: surely it is permissible to kill a man if that is the only way in which you can prevent him from killing you!

On the other hand, one of the things we are firmly wedded to is the belief that human beings have a right to life, and this presumably includes the right to not be killed. Aggressor is a human being; so he, like the rest of us, has a right to life, and presumably, therefore, the right to not be killed. So how *can* Victim kill him? Precisely *why* is it permissible for Victim to use that anti-tank gun on Aggressor? I propose we look at three replies which I think come fairly readily to mind.

2. The first reply I am going to call "forfeit," and it goes like this. "We good folk all do have a right to life, and that does include the right to not be killed. But there is such a thing as forfeiting a right. We say such things as that the right to life, liberty, and the pursuit of happiness are 'natural rights,' and therefore unconditionally possessed by all people; but that is just so much high-minded rhetoric. What has happened in the case described is that Aggressor, by virtue of his attack on Victim, has forfeited his right to not be killed, and therefore his right to life. And *that* is why Victim may use his anti-tank gun on Aggressor, thereby killing him: he violates no right of Aggressor's in doing so."

But the fact is that this very natural first reply is not at all satisfactory. Suppose that as Victim raises his anti-tank gun to fire it, Aggressor's tank stalls. Aggressor gets out to examine the engine, but falls and breaks both ankles in the process. Victim (let us suppose) now has time to get away from Aggressor, and is

44. Thomson, Self-Defense and Rights, The Lindley Lecture, University of Kansas, April 5, 1976.

in no danger. I take it you will not think that Victim may all the same go ahead and kill Aggressor. But why not?—if Aggressor really has forfeited his right to not be killed by virtue of his attack on Victim.[45]

It could, of course, be said that at this point utilitarian considerations come into play. I.e., it could be said that yes, Aggressor has forfeited his right to life, but no, Victim cannot now kill him, and that this latter is true because Victim now has no need to kill Aggressor—indeed, because killing Aggressor would mean the loss of a life, whereas not killing Aggressor would mean no loss at all.

But I think this cannot be right. Suppose Victim is a great transplant surgeon. There is Aggressor, lying helpless next to his tank, with two broken ankles—but the rest of him physically fine and healthy. Can Victim now cart Aggressor off to surgery, cut him up, and give his one heart, two kidneys, and two lungs to five who need the parts? If Aggressor now has no right to not be killed (having forfeited it by his attack on Victim), so that utilitarian considerations are all we have to weigh here, it is hard to see why not. After all, five lives would be saved at a cost of only one. Yet surely Victim cannot do this.

I am inclined to think that it would no more be permissible for Victim to cut Aggressor up and parcel out his parts to save five than it would be for Victim to cut *you* up and parcel out *your* parts to save five. He cannot do this to you; and it is often said that the reason why he cannot (despite the fact that utilities might be maximized by doing so) is the fact that you have a right to life, and thus, presumably, the right to not be killed.[46] I should imagine that the very same thing makes it impermissible for Victim to do this to Aggressor, viz., the fact that Aggressor, now helpless and no danger to anyone, has a right to life, and thus, presumably, the right to not be killed. . . .

There are two moves open to a friend of "forfeit." He can say (1) that the fact that the tank stalled and Aggressor broke both ankles shows that it never was necessary for Victim to kill Aggressor, so that Aggressor never did forfeit his right to not be killed. Or he can say (2) that Aggressor did forfeit his right to not be killed when he launched his attack on Victim, but that he regained this right at the moment at which he ceased to pose a threat to Victim's life.

(1) would be an unfortunate choice for the purpose of "forfeit." For surely Victim could, permissibly, have killed Aggressor at any time between the launching of Aggressor's attack and the stall of the tank. (Who in such circumstances could be expected to know that the tank would stall? Who in such circumstances could be expected to wait in hopes of so freakish an accident?) That indeed was where we began: i.e., with the fact that it was then permissible for Victim to shoot. "Forfeit" proposed to explain this fact by saying that Aggressor forfeited a right; yet (1) denies that he did.

(2) seems preferable for the purposes of this reply. If Aggressor did forfeit his right to not be killed when he launched the attack, that would explain why, between the launching of it and the stall of the tank, Victim could shoot; and if Aggressor re-acquired that right when he ceased to pose a threat to Victim, that would explain why, after the stall of the tank, Victim could no longer shoot.

45. This question is asked by Sanford H. Kadish, in "Respect for Life and Regard for Rights in the Criminal Law," forthcoming. (In fact, this paper was caused by that one.)

46. But it is not at all obvious that this is what explains the fact that Victim cannot cut you up and parcel out your parts to save five. . . .

But it is a far from happy choice. If it were by virtue just of the launching of that attack that Aggressor forfeited his right, then it would seem possible to say that when the attack ceases, Aggressor re-acquires his right—the right being, as it were, in abeyance throughout the time of the attack. But it surely cannot be said to have been by virtue *just* of the launching of that attack that Aggressor forfeited his right. Compare a second aggressor and a second victim. Suppose that Second Aggressor launches a similar attack on Second Victim, but that Second Aggressor (by contrast with Aggressor) is innocent: Second Aggressor, let us suppose, is a schizophrenic, and he is under a hallucination that Second Victim is in a tank of his own, driving towards Second Aggressor's home and family, so that, as Second Aggressor sees it, he is merely trying to ward off an attack. Morality may not protect us from getting run down by lunatics in tanks, but it does permit our protecting ourselves from such a fate; and it seems plain that poor Second Victim, who is himself innocent, may permissibly us his anti-tank gun on Second Aggressor. Why is this permissible? It is an excellent question. But presumably "forfeit" would be a most implausible reply in this case.[47] Perhaps Aggressor, being a villain, can be thought to have forfeited a right; Second Aggressor, however, being himself innocent, cannot. But then it is not by virtue *just* of launching an attack on Victim that Aggressor forfeits his right; Aggressor's bad intention figures too. Yet Aggressor's bad intention may be supposed to remain, even after he becomes helpless—we may imagine him continuing to plot as he is carried off to jail—and if that remains, how can he be thought to have re-acquired the right he forfeited at least in part because of that bad intention?

There is room for maneuver here. It could be said that the point is this: both Aggressor and Second Aggressor simply cease to have a right to not be killed when they launch their attacks on their victims, and both of them re-acquire that right when their tanks stall. (On this view, while Aggressor is guilty and Second Aggressor is not, this does not matter: launching an attack by itself—whether guilty or not—is what makes one lose the right to not be killed.) I shall come back to this idea later. For the moment, it should be noted that saying that Aggressor simply ceased to have the right is not the same as saying that Aggressor has forfeited the right. . . .

Again, consider a case . . . of an "innocent shield of a threat." Third Aggressor is driving his tank at you. But he has taken care to arrange that a baby is strapped to the front of the tank, so that if you use your anti-tank gun, you will not only kill Third Aggressor, you will kill the baby. Now Third Aggressor, admittedly, is in process of trying to kill you; but that baby isn't. Yet you can presumably go ahead and use the gun, even though this involves killing the baby as well as Third Aggressor.

If Professor Thomson can convince us that self-defense is not a justification under a choice-of-evils standard, would this prevent us from regarding it as an excuse under a "reasonable firmness" standard, such as the one we rely on in duress cases?

11. Aside from self-defense, the most litigated questions involving the use

47. Cf. again Kadish, [n.45 supra].

of force in defense arise in the area of law enforcement and the prevention of crime. According to Professor Ronald Boyce, writing in the Encyclopedia of Crime and Justice, 953, 953-957 (1983):

> In certain defined circumstances, persons are privileged to employ force against others in order to enforce the law. This justification is in addition to other justifications that may exist for the use of force against the person or property of another and is an independent basis upon which to assess the legality of the use of force.
>
> **Common Law**
>
> At common law a peace officer or a private citizen could employ force to prevent the commission of, or to apprehend for, a felony or breach of the peace. Force could not be used to prevent the commission of a misdemeanor that did not constitute a breach of the peace. Force that was short of deadly force could be used to prevent felonies or misdemeanors involving a breach of the peace; deadly force was reserved for use in cases involving felonies and a few special misdemeanors. The common-law standard on the use of deadly force in felony cases was said to encompass "any felony" . . . However, this is probably an overstatement of the common-law position, since most felonies at common law were dangerous or forcible felonies. It is more probable that the rule was actually limited to felonies for which the death penalty could be imposed, which included most common-law felonies, or to felonies which were themselves perceived as dangerous (Storey v. State, 71 Ala. 329, 339 (1883)). William Blackstone observed that "such homicide as is committed for the prevention of any forcible and atrocious crime is justifiable by the law of nature and also by the law of England." It may be concluded that the common law did not sanction the use of deadly force to prevent any crime that was classified as a felony, but it was not clear when deadly force could and could not be used in felony cases.
>
> The common-law standard on the use of force for law enforcement purposes was carried over in court decisions and statutory codifications of the law in the United States. Several states adopted rules or statutes that stated the standard on use of force for law enforcement purposes as the judges and lawyers of the particular jurisdiction read the English law, or as it was believed the standard ought to be.
>
> The common law authorized private persons as well as law officers to use force for law enforcement purposes. Police departments as they are known today did not exist in early England or during the early period of the United States, and private persons played an important and sometimes primary role in enforcing the law and ensuring that law violators were apprehended and punished. The private citizen was obligated to respond to a "hue and cry" raised by a crime victim or others and to aid in apprehending a burglar, robber, murderer, or other offender. The citizen-enforcer was sanctioned by law in all American jurisdictions and was popularly supported in legislation authorizing the assembly of a posse by peace officers to aid in the apprehension of criminals or enforcement of the law. Since police departments and large public enforcement agencies are of modern origin, it is not surprising that citizens in the United States were accorded common-law or similar authority to use force to arrest or to prevent

crime. The importance of the citizen law enforcement authority has been reduced because of the expansion of public enforcement agencies, but most jurisdictions still recognize some citizen enforcement power. In numerous jurisdictions legislation has refined the common-law standards, and more precise criteria have been formulated as guides to the use of force. However, in several jurisdictions in the United States, the common-law standard is still applicable.

Classifications of Force

Two classifications of force, deadly and nondeadly, are recognized by the courts as available for law enforcement purposes.

Nondeadly force. Nondeadly force is force against a person short of that likely to result in death or serious bodily harm. Generally, nondeadly force must be reasonable and necessary under the circumstances in which it is employed. In most jurisdictions, nondeadly force may be used to prevent the commission, or to arrest the perpetrator, of a felony or a misdemeanor constituting a breach of the peace (LaFave and Scott, p.402). Where reasonably necessary, it may be used to enforce the legal process in the case of other misdemeanors.

Deadly force. Deadly force is force that is likely to cause death or serious bodily harm. The right to use deadly force for law enforcement purposes is limited in all jurisdictions, and the applicable standard varies from state to state. In several jurisdictions, the use of deadly force for such purposes has been narrowed over that sanctioned at common law. Some jurisdictions limit the right to use deadly force to law officers or law enforcement personnel. Others allow the use of deadly force by any person when necessary for prevention of, or apprehension for, certain serious or violent crimes (La. Rev. Stat. §14:20 (1974 and 1982 Supp.)). Several jurisdictions have codified the common-law standard (as seen, for example, in Cal. Penal Code §196 (1970)). A number of states have taken a more restrictive position, limiting the use of deadly force to enumerated, dangerous, or forcible felonies. Illinois, for example, limits deadly force to the crimes of "treason, murder, voluntary manslaughter, rape, robbery, burglary, arson, kidnapping, aggravated battery" and to other felonies involving "use or threat of physical force or violence against any individual" (Ill. Ann. Stat. 38, §§2-8, 7-1, 7-5 (1972)). Arizona limits deadly force in preventing crime to arson, burglary, kidnapping, murder, manslaughter, robbery, aggravated assault, sexual assault, and child molestation (Ariz. Rev. Stat. §13-410 (1978)).

The American Law Institute's Model Penal Code states a restrictive view of the circumstances justifying the use of deadly force for law enforcement purposes. The use of deadly force to make an arrest or to prevent the commission of a crime is limited to situations in which such force was thought necessary to avoid a substantial risk of death or serious injury to innocent persons. The Code's approach has influenced a number of jurisdictions.

In addition to statutory restraints on the use of deadly force, many law enforcement agencies impose administrative limitations and guidelines on the use of deadly force by their personnel. . . . Illustrative of the approach taken by some law enforcement agencies in restricting the use of deadly force is that of the Federal Bureau of Investigation, which prohibits shooting except where necessary in self-defense or defense of another. . . . The administrative trend of most police departments is toward substantially restricting the use of deadly force.

Situations in Which Force May Be Used

In addition to the division of use of force into deadly and nondeadly categories, various situational classifications determine when, and to what degree, force may be used for law enforcement purposes. These may be generally stated as (1) force to stop and arrest, (2) force to prevent escape from custody, (3) force to prevent the commission of a crime, and (4) force to suppress riots and disorders.

Stop and arrest. At common law, private persons as well as peace officers were privileged to make arrests. An arrest by a private person was proper for a felony actually committed when the arresting person had probable cause to believe a particular person had committed the offense, or for a misdemeanor constituting a breach of the peace when it was committed in the presence of the arresting person. A peace officer could arrest pursuant to a warrant or where the officer had probable cause to believe a felony had been committed and the arrested person had committed it. If the person arrested had, in fact, not committed the offense, the arrest by an officer, if based on probable cause, was still lawful (Hill v. California, 401 U.S. 797 (1971)). A peace officer could arrest for any offense with a warrant but could arrest without a warrant only for a misdemeanor when the offense was committed in his presence. A private person or peace officer was privileged to use reasonable force to effect an arrest. Deadly force could be used where necessary to arrest for a felony—at least for a violent felony, as indicated above—or to apprehend a fleeing felon under the same standard.

In most jurisdictions today, the power to arrest, and the persons and force authorized to arrest, are governed by statute. A peace officer usually has the authority to arrest for a felony if he has probable cause. Several jurisdictions, as that of New York, have given the officer the same power to arrest for a misdemeanor (N.Y. Crim. Proc. Law (McKinney) §140. 10 (1971)). Private persons are still accorded the authority to arrest in most jurisdictions, although the trend has been to limit their power to employ deadly force in making an arrest (Model Penal Code §3.07). The justification of the use of force to overcome resistance to arrest has been asserted to be that of self-defense. It has been held in jurisdictions applying the retreat rule, that an officer need not retreat before using deadly force in self-defense or to overcome resistance. However, the justification for the use of force to arrest, overcome resistance, capture a fleeing felon, or otherwise enforce the law stands on a policy of not only protecting the arresting person but of ensuring proper enforcement of the law and protecting the societal interests in a well-regulated community. In support of this conclusion, the Supreme Court has held that peace officers have the authority to use force to stop a person on the basis of reasonable suspicion, short of probable cause, and to conduct a protective frisk of the person where there is reasonable belief that the person is armed (Terry v. Ohio, 392 U.S. 1 (1968)). Although this power involves some self-defense considerations, it is actually a more expansive authority to protect society from potential lawbreakers.

Escape from custody. An officer having custody of a person is empowered to exercise force to prevent the person's escape. Generally, a person may not use greater force to prevent an individual from escaping than would be allowed in the original arrest. However, in several jurisdictions, where a person is escaping from a jail or a penal facility, the use of deadly force is authorized. Some jurisdictions also limit the use of such force to peace officers. Section 3.07(3) of the Model Penal Code grants limited authority for use of deadly force by a peace officer to prevent an escape from certain institutions. An officer "is justified in using any force, including deadly force, which he believes to be immediately necessary to prevent the escape of a person from a jail, prison, or other institution for the detention of persons charged with or convicted of a crime." In this instance, society's interest in confining law violators prevails over the competing concern for human life. Deadly force necessary to prevent escape is proper even though the escaping person may not in the first instance have committed a forcible or dangerous felony.

Crime prevention. The law allows a person to use force, and at times deadly force, to prevent the commission of an offense. The authority to use force to prevent offenses has been codified in several jurisdictions (Ariz. Rev. Stat. §§13-409, -410 (1978); Idaho Code §19-201 (1979)). Section 3.07(5)(a) of the Model Penal Code provides that the use of force is justifiable "when the actor believes that such force is immediately necessary to prevent [another] . . . from committing or consummating the commission of a crime involving or threatening bodily harm, damage to or loss of property or a breach of the peace." The use of deadly force for crime prevention has been changed in some jurisdictions from the common-law standard of "any felony" to felonies involving death or serious bodily harm to another. Other state statutes appear to adhere to the common-law rule. The critical element in justifying the application of force to prevent crime is the reasonable belief, by the user of force, in the necessity of its use (State v. Terrell, 55 Utah 314, 186 P. 108 (1919)). Therefore, killing because a person was committing a petty theft or minor battery would not be justified. The force must at the time be directed to crime prevention and not for revenge, or asserted after the fact as a possible defense or justification.

Suppression of riots and disorders. The common law authorized any person to use force to suppress riots or civil disorders. This authority was supplemented by English statutes. The most prominent and influential statute was the Riot Act of 1714, which allowed authorities, after commanding dispersal of an unlawful assemblage, to use force, including deadly force, against those resisting public order. An English authority observed that "the intentional infliction of death or bodily harm is not a crime when it is done either by justices of the peace, peace officers, or private persons, whether such persons are, and whether they act as, soldiers under military discipline or not for the purpose of suppressing a general and dangerous riot which cannot otherwise be suppressed." This form of force is not necessarily limited to effecting an arrest, and may be used for the purposes of protecting property interests as well as persons and for suppressing general disorders. Further, because in some instances deadly force is authorized in the suppression of a riot, a situation could occur in which deadly force would be authorized when it would not be allowed if the law violator were not involved in a riot.

Statutes patterned on the English concept of allowing force to suppress a riot have been adopted in the United States, and the authority to use force by a private person or the police under such circumstances is accepted law. The California Penal Code provides that a homicide is justifiable when it is committed "in lawfully suppressing any riot, or in lawfully keeping and preserving the peace" (Cal. Penal Code §197 (1970)). One Florida statute authorizes the suppression of affrays and riots (Fla. Stat. Ann. §870.04 (1976 and 1981 Supp.)), and another provides that "if, by reason of the efforts made by any of said officers or by their direction to disperse such assembly, or to seize and secure the persons composing the same, who have refused to disperse, any such person or other person present is killed or wounded, the said officers and all persons acting by their order or under their direction, shall be held guiltless and fully justified in law" (Fla. Stat. Ann. §870.05 (1976 and 1981 Supp.)). The Model Penal Code provisions that have been adopted in some states provide that deadly force may be justifiable if "the actor believes that the use of such force is necessary to suppress a riot or mutiny after the rioters or mutineers have been ordered to disperse and warned, in any particular manner that the law may require, that such force will be used if they do not obey" (§3.07(5)).

Additionally, military force is frequently authorized to suppress civil disorders and insurrections (U.S. Const. art. I, §8, cl. 15). In emergencies of an extremely serious nature, the right to employ special enforcement techniques, including use of military force, has been recognized (Moyer v. Peabody, 212 U.S. 78, 85 (1909)). Special statutory authority to suppress civil disorders exists in several states and on the federal level (10 U.S.C. §§331-333 (1976): Tenn. Code Ann. §38-901 (1975)). The authority is not without limitation, and when it is abused, a public official may be held accountable (Scheuer v. Rhodes, 416 U.S. 232 (1974)).

The danger of authorizing special power to deal with civil disorders is that it may be abused by excessive and indiscriminate exercise. The law on this subject has not crystallized as precisely as one would like, but it can be stated that where there is no necessity for the exercise of special arrest powers or force authority, the right to use such measures ceases.

Constitutional Limitations

The Constitution has been held to impose restraints on the use of force for law enforcement purposes. The use of excessive force against a person may, for example, amount to a violation of his right to protection against deprivation of life or liberty without due process of law. This may be so even if a statute or the common law authorizes the use of such force. . . .

TENNESSEE v. GARNER

United States Supreme Court
105 S. Ct. 1694

Justice White delivered the opinion of the Court.

This case requires us to determine the constitutionality of the use of deadly force to prevent the escape of an apparently unarmed suspected felon. We conclude that such force may not be used unless it is necessary to prevent the escape and the officer has probable cause to believe that the suspect poses a significant threat of death or serious physical injury to the officer or others. . . .

At about 10:45 P.M. on October 3, 1974, Memphis Police Officers Elton Hymon and Leslie Wright were dispatched to answer a "prowler inside call." Upon arriving at the scene they saw a woman standing on her porch and gesturing toward the adjacent house.[48] She told them she had heard glass breaking and that "they" or "someone" was breaking in next door. While Wright radioed the dispatcher to say that they were on the scene, Hymon went behind the house. He heard a door slam and saw someone run across the back yard. The fleeing suspect, who was appellee-respondent's decedent, Edward Garner, stopped at a 6-feet-high chain link fence at the edge of the yard. With the aid of a flashlight, Hymon was able to see Garner's face and hands. He saw no sign of a weapon, and, though not certain, was "reasonably sure" and "figured" that Garner was unarmed. He thought Garner was 17 or 18 years old and about 5′ 5″ or 5′ 7″ tall.[49] While Garner was crouched at the base of the fence, Hymon called out "police, halt" and took a few steps toward him. Garner then began to climb over the fence. Convinced that if Garner made it over the fence he would elude capture,[50] Hymon shot him. The bullet hit Garner in the back of the head. Garner was taken by ambulance to a hospital, where he died on the operating table. Ten dollars and a purse taken from then house were found on his body.[51]

In using deadly force to prevent the escape, Hymon was acting under the authority of a Tennessee statute and pursuant to Police Department policy. The statute provides that "[i]f, after notice of the intention to arrest the defendant, he either flee or forcibly resist, the officer may use all the necessary means to effect the arrest."[52]

Garner's father . . . brought this action in the Federal District Court for the Western District of Tennessee, seeking damages under 42 U. S. C. §1983

48. The owner of the house testified that no lights were on in the house, but that a back door light was on. Officer Hymon, though uncertain, stated in his deposition that there were lights on in the house. Record 209.

49. In fact, Garner, an eighth-grader, was 15. He was 5′ 4″ tall and weighed somewhere around 100 or 110 pounds.

50. When asked at trial why he fired, Hymon stated:

> Well, first of all it was apparent to me from the little bit that I knew about the area at the time that he was going to get away because, number 1, I couldn't get to him. My partner then couldn't find where he was because, you know, he was late coming around. He didn't know where I was talking about. I couldn't get to him because of the fence here, I couldn't have jumped this fence and come up, consequently jumped this fence and caught him before he got away because he was already up on the fence, just one leap and he was already over the fence, and so there is no way that I could have caught him.

He also stated that the area beyond the fence was dark, that he could not have gotten over the fence easily because he was carrying a lot of equipment and wearing heavy boots, and that Garner, being younger and more energetic, could have outrun him.

51. Garner had rummaged through one room in the house, in which, in the words of the owner, "[a]ll the stuff was out on the floors, all the drawers was pulled out, and stuff was scattered all over." The owner testified that his valuables were untouched but that, in addition to the purse and the 10 dollars, one of his wife's rings was missing. The ring was not recovered.

52. Although the statute does not say so explicitly, Tennessee law forbids the use of deadly force in the arrest of a misdemeanant. See Johnson v. State, 173 Tenn. 134, 114 S.W.2d 819 (1938).

for asserted violations of Garner's constitutional rights. The complaint alleged that the shooting violated the Fourth, Fifth, Sixth, Eighth, and Fourteenth Amendments of the United States Constitution. . . . After a 3-day bench trial, the District Court entered judgment for all defendants.

The District Court found that the statute, and Hymon's actions, were constitutional.

The Court of Appeals reversed and remanded. It reasoned that the killing of a fleeing suspect is a "seizure" under the Fourth Amendment,[53] and is therefore constitutional only if "reasonable." The Tennessee statute failed as applied to this case because it did not adequately limit the use of deadly force by distinguishing between felonies of different magnitudes—"the facts, as found, did not justify the use of deadly force under the Fourth Amendment." Officers cannot resort to deadly force unless they "have probable cause . . . to believe that the suspect [has committed a felony and] poses a threat to the safety of the officers or a danger to the community if left at large."[54]

The State of Tennessee appealed to this Court. . . .

. . . [T]here can be no question that apprehension by the use of deadly force is a seizure subject to the reasonableness requirement of the Fourth Amendment. . . .

. . . To determine the constitutionality of a seizure "[w]e must balance the nature and quality of the intrusion on the individual's Fourth Amendment interests against the importance of the governmental interests alleged to justify the intrusion."

. . . [T]he question [is] whether the totality of the circumstances justifie[s] a particular sort of search or seizure.

. . . The intrusiveness of a seizure by means of deadly force is unmatched. The suspect's fundamental interest in his own life need not be elaborated upon. The use of deadly force also frustrates the interest of the individual, and of society, in judicial determination of guilt and punishment. Against these

53. "The right of the people to be secure in their persons . . . against unreasonable searches and seizures, shall not be violated. . . ." U.S. Const., Amdt. 4.

54. The Court of Appeals concluded that the rule set out in the Model Penal Code "accurately states Fourth Amendment limitations on the use of deadly force against fleeing felons." The relevant portion of the Model Penal Code provides:

> The use of deadly force is not justifiable . . . unless (i) the arrest is for a felony; and (ii) the person effecting the arrest is authorized to act as a peace officer or is assisting a person whom he believes to be authorized to act as a peace officer, and (iii) the actor believes that the force employed creates no substantial risk of injury to innocent persons; and (iv) the actor believes that (1) the crime for which the arrest is made involved conduct including the use or threatened use of deadly force; or (2) there is a substantial risk that the person to be arrested will cause death or serious bodily harm if his apprehension is delayed. American Law Institute, Model Penal Code §3.07(2)(b) (Proposed Official Draft 1962).

The court also found that "[a]n analysis of the facts of this case under the Due Process Clause" required the same result, because the statute was not narrowly drawn to further a compelling state interest. The court considered the generalized interest in effective law enforcement sufficiently compelling only when the suspect is dangerous. . . .

interests are ranged governmental interests in effective law enforcement.[55] . . . The use of deadly force is a self-defeating way of apprehending a suspect and so setting the criminal justice mechanism in motion. . . . And while the meaningful threat of deadly force might be thought to lead to the arrest of more live suspects by discouraging escape attempts,[56] the presently available evidence does not support this thesis. The fact is that a majority of police departments in this country have forbidden the use of deadly force against nonviolent suspects. . . . Petitioners and appellant have not persuaded us that shooting nondangerous fleeing suspects is so vital as to outweigh the suspect's interest in his own life.

The use of deadly force to prevent the escape of all felony suspects, whatever the circumstances, is constitutionally unreasonable. It is not better that all felony suspects die than that they escape. Where the suspect poses no immediate threat to the officer and no threat to others, the harm resulting from failing to apprehend him does not justify the use of deadly force to do so. It is no doubt unfortunate when a suspect who is in sight escapes, but the fact that the police arrive a little late or are a little slower afoot does not always justify killing the suspect. A police officer may not seize an unarmed, nondangerous suspect by shooting him dead. The Tennessee statute is unconstitutional insofar as it authorizes the use of deadly force against such fleeing suspects.

55. The dissent emphasizes that subsequent investigation cannot replace immediate apprehension. We recognize that this is so, indeed, that is the reason why there is any dispute. If subsequent arrest were assured, no one would argue that use of deadly force was justified. Thus, we proceed on the assumption that subsequent arrest is not likely. Nonetheless, it should be remembered that failure to apprehend at the scene does not necessarily mean that the suspect will never be caught.

In lamenting the inadequacy of later investigation, the dissent relies on the report of the President's Commission on Law Enforcement and Administration of Justice. It is worth noting that, notwithstanding its awareness of this problem, the Commission itself proposed a policy for use of deadly force arguably even more stringent than the formulation we adopt today. See President's Commission on Law Enforcement and Administration of Justice, Task Force Report: The Police 189 (1967). The Commission proposed that deadly force be used only to apprehend "perpetrators who, in the course of their crime threatened the use of deadly force, or if the officer believes there is a substantial risk that the person whose arrest is sought will cause death or serious bodily harm if his apprehension is delayed." In addition, the officer would have "to know, as a virtual certainty, that the suspect committed an offense for which the use of deadly force is permissible." Ibid.

56. We note that the usual manner of deterring illegal conduct—through punishment—has been largely ignored in connection with flight from arrest. Arkansas, for example, specifically excepts flight from arrest from the offense of "obstruction of governmental operations." The commentary notes that this "reflects the basic policy judgment that, absent the use of force or violence, a mere attempt to avoid apprehension by a law enforcement officer does not give rise to an independent offense." Ark. Stat. Ann. §41-2802(3)(a) (1977) and commentary. . . .

This lenient approach does avoid the anomaly of automatically transforming every fleeing misdemeanant into a fleeing felon—subject, under the common-law rule, to apprehension by deadly force—solely by virtue of his flight. However, it is in real tension with the harsh consequences of flight in cases where deadly force is employed. For example, Tennessee does not outlaw fleeing from arrest. The Memphis City Code does, §30-15, subjecting the offender to a maximum fine of $50, §1-8. Thus, Garner's attempted escape subjected him to (a) a $50 fine, and (b) being shot.

It is not, however, unconstitutional on its face. Where the officer has probable cause to believe that the suspect poses a threat of serious physical harm, either to the officer or to others, it is not constitutionally unreasonable to prevent escape by using deadly force. Thus, if the suspect threatens the officer with a weapon or there is probable cause to believe that he has committed a crime involving the infliction or threatened infliction of serious physical harm, deadly force may be used if necessary to prevent escape, and if, where feasible, some warning has been given. As applied in such circumstances, the Tennessee statute would pass constitutional muster. . . .

It is insisted that the Fourth Amendment must be construed in light of the common-law rule, which allowed the use of whatever force was necessary to effect the arrest of a fleeing felon, though not a misdemeanant. . . .

It has been pointed out many times that the common-law rule is best understood in light of the fact that it arose at a time when virtually all felonies were punishable by death.[57] . . . Courts have also justified the common-law rule by emphasizing the relative dangerousness of felons.

Neither of these justifications makes sense today. Almost all crimes formerly punishable by death no longer are or can be. And while in earlier times "the gulf between the felonies and the minor offences was broad and deep," today the distinction is minor and often arbitrary. . . . Indeed, numerous misdemeanors involve conduct more dangerous than many felonies.[58]

There is an additional reason why the common-law rule cannot be directly translated to the present day. The common-law rule developed at a time when weapons were rudimentary. Deadly force could be inflicted almost solely in a hand-to-hand struggle during which, necessarily, the safety of the arresting officer was at risk. Handguns were not carried by police officers until the latter half of the last century. As a practical matter, the use of deadly force under the standard articulation of the common-law rule has an altogether different meaning—and harsher consequences—now than in past centuries. . . .

In evaluating the reasonableness of police procedures under the Fourth Amendment, we have also looked to prevailing rules in individual jurisdictions. . . . Nonetheless, the long-term movement has been away from the rule that deadly force may be used against any fleeing felon, and that remains the rule in less than half the States. . . .

57. The roots of the concept of a "felony" lie not in capital punishment but in forfeiture. 2 F. Pollock & F. Maitland, The History of English Law 465 (2d ed. 1909) (hereinafter Pollock & Maitland). Not all felonies were always punishable by death. See id., at 466-467, n. 3. Nonetheless, the link was profound. Blackstone was able to write that "[t]he idea of felony is indeed so generally connected with that of capital punishment, that we find it hard to separate them; and to this usage the interpretations of the law do now conform. And therefore if a statute makes any new offence felony, the law implies that is shall be punished with death, viz. by hanging, as well as with forfeiture. . . ." 4 W. Blackstone *98. See also R. Perkins & R. Boyce, Criminal Law 14-15 (3d ed. 1982); 2 Pollock & Maitland 511.

58. White collar crime, for example, poses a less significant physical threat than, say, drunken driving.

Actual departmental policies are important. . . . We would hesitate to declare a police practice of long standing "unreasonable" if doing so would severely hamper effective law enforcement. But the indications are to the contrary. There has been no suggestion that crime has worsened in any way in jurisdictions that have adopted, by legislation or departmental policy, rules similar to that announced today. *Amici* note that "[a]fter extensive research and consideration, [they] have concluded that laws permitting police officers to use deadly force to apprehend unarmed, non-violent fleeing felony suspects actually do not protect citizens or law enforcement officers, do not deter crime or alleviate problems caused by crime, and do not improve the crime-fighting ability of law enforcement agencies." . . .

Nor do we agree with petitioners and appellant that the rule we have adopted requires the police to make impossible, split-second evaluations of unknowable facts. . . . The highly technical felony/misdemeanor distinction is equally, if not more, difficult to apply in the field. An officer is in no position to know, for example, the precise value of property stolen, or whether the crime was a first or second offense. Finally, as noted above, this claim must be viewed with suspicion in light of the similar self-imposed limitations of so many police departments. . . .

The District Court concluded that Hymon was justified in shooting Garner because state law allows, and the Federal Constitution does not forbid, the use of deadly force to prevent the escape of a fleeing felony suspect if no alternative means of apprehension is available. . . .

In reversing, the Court of Appeals accepted the District Court's factual conclusions and held that "the facts, as found, did not justify the use of deadly force." . . . We agree. . . . Hymon did not have probable cause to believe that Garner, whom he correctly believed to be unarmed, posed any physical danger to himself or others.

The judgment of the Court of Appeals is affirmed, and the case is remanded for further procedings consistent with this opinion.

Justice O'CONNOR, with whom THE CHIEF JUSTICE and Justice REHNQUIST join, dissenting. . . .

The public interest involved in the use of deadly force as a last resort to apprehend a fleeing burglary suspect relates primarily to the serious nature of the crime. Household burglaries represent not only the illegal entry into a person's home, but also "pos[e] real risk of serious harm to others." Solem v. Helm, 463 U. S. 277, 315-316 (1983) (Burger, C. J., dissenting). According to recent Department of Justice statistics, "[t]hree-fifths of all rapes in the home, three-fifths of all home robberies, and about a third of home aggravated and simple assaults are committed by burglars." Bureau of Justice Statistics Bulletin, Household Burglary 1 (January 1985). During the period 1973-1982, 2.8 million such violent crimes were committed in the course of burglaries. Ibid. Victims of a forcible intrusion into their home by a nighttime prowler will find little consolation in the majority's confident assertion that "burglaries only rarely involve physical violence." Moreover, even if a particular burglary, when viewed in retrospect, does not involve physical harm to others, the "harsh potentialities for violence" inherent in the forced entry into a home preclude characterization of the crime as "innocuous, inconsequential, minor, or 'nonviolent.' " Solem v. Helm, supra, at 316 (Burger, C. J., dissenting). See also Restatement of Torts §131, Comment *g* (1934) (burglary is among felonies that normally cause or threaten death or serious bodily harm); R. Perkins and R. Boyce, Criminal Law 1110 (3d ed. 1982) (burglary is dangerous felony that creates unreasonable risk of great personal harm).

Because burglary is a serious and dangerous felony, the public interest in the prevention and detection of the crime is of compelling importance. Where a police officer has probable cause to arrest a suspected burglar, the use of deadly force as a last resort might well be the only means of apprehending the suspect. With respect to a particular burglary, subsequent investigation simply cannot represent a substitute for immediate apprehension of the criminal suspect at the scene. See Report of President's Commission on Law Enforcement and Administration of Justice, The Challenge of Crime in a Free Society 97 (1967). Indeed, the Captain of the Memphis Police Department testified that in his city, if apprehension is not immediate, it is likely that the suspect will not be caught. App. in No. 81-5605 (CA6), at 334. Although some law enforcement agencies may choose to assume the risk that a criminal will remain at large, the Tennessee statute reflects a legislative determination that the use of deadly force in prescribed circumstances will serve generally to protect the public. Such statutes assist the police in apprehending suspected perpetrators of serious crimes and provide notice that a lawful police order to stop and submit to arrest may not be ignored with impunity.

The Court unconvincingly dismisses the general deterrence effects by stating that "the presently available evidence does not support [the] thesis" that the threat of force discourages escape and that "there is a substantial basis for doubting that the use of such force is an essential attribute to the arrest power in all felony cases." There is no question that the effectiveness of police use of deadly force is arguable and that many States or individual police departments have decided not to authorize it in circumstances similar to those presented here. But it should go without saying that the effectiveness or popularity of a particular police practice does not determine its constitutionality. Cf. Spaziano v. Florida, 468 U. S. —, — (1984) ("The Eighth Amendment is not violated every time a State reaches a conclusion different from a majority of its sisters over how best to administer its criminal laws") (slip op. 16). Moreover, the fact that police conduct pursuant to a state statute is challenged on constitutional grounds does not impose a burden on the State to produce social science statistics or to dispel any possible doubts about the necessity of the conduct. This observation, I believe, has particular force where the challenged practice both predates enactment of the Bill of Rights and continues to be accepted by a substantial number of the States.

Against the strong public interests justifying the conduct at issue here must be weighed the individual interests implicated in the use of deadly force by police officers. The majority declares that "[t]he suspect's fundamental interest in his own life need not be elaborated upon." This blithe assertion hardly provides an adequate substitute for the majority's failure to acknowledge the distinctive manner in which the suspect's interest in his life is even exposed to risk. For purposes of this case, we must recall that the police officer, in the course of investigating a nighttime burglary, had reasonable cause to arrest the suspect and ordered him to halt. The officer's use of force resulted because the suspected burglar refused to heed this command and the officer reasonably believed that there was no means short of firing his weapon to apprehend the suspect. Without questioning the importance of a person's interest in his life, I do not think this interest encompasses a right to flee unimpeded from the scene of a burglary. Cf. Payton v. New York, 445 U. S. 573, 617, n.14 (1980) (White, J., dissenting) ("[T]he policeman's hands should not be tied merely because of the possibility that the suspect will fail to cooperate with legitimate actions by law enforcement personnel"). The legitimate interests of the suspect in these circumstances are adequately accommodated by the Tennessee statute: to avoid the use of deadly force and the consequent risk to his life, the suspect need merely obey the valid order to halt.

A proper balancing of the interests involved suggests that use of deadly force as a last resort to apprehend a criminal suspect fleeing from the scene of a nighttime burglary is not unreasonable within the meaning of the Fourth Amendment. Admittedly, the events giving rise to this case are in retrospect deeply regrettable. No one can view the death of an unarmed and apparently nonviolent 15-year old without sorrow, much less disapproval. Nonetheless, the reasonableness of Officer Hymon's conduct for purposes of the Fourth Amendment cannot be evaluated by what later appears to have been a preferable course of police action. The officer pursued a suspect in the darkened backyard of a house that from all indication had just been burglarized. The police officer was not certain whether the suspect was alone or unarmed; nor did he know what had transpired inside the house. He ordered the suspect to halt, and when the suspect refused to obey and attempted to flee into the night, the officer fired his weapon to prevent escape. The reasonableness of this action for purposes of the Fourth Amendment is not determined by the unfortunate nature of this particular case; instead, the question is whether it is constitutionally impermissible for police officers, as a last resort, to shoot a burglary suspect fleeing the scene of the crime.

[Moreover, the] Court's silence on critical factors in the decision to use deadly force simply invites second-guessing of difficult police decisions that must be made quickly in the most trying of circumstances. Cf. Payton v. New York, supra, at 619 (White, J., dissenting). Police are given no guidance for determining which objects, among an array of potentially lethal weapons ranging from guns to knives to baseball bats to rope, will justify the use of deadly force. The Court also declines to outline the additional factors necessary to provide "probable cause" for believing that a suspect "poses a significant threat of death or serious physical injury," when the officer has probable cause to arrest and the suspect refuses to obey an order to halt. But even if it were appropriate in this case to limit the use of deadly force to that ambiguous class of suspects, I believe the class should include nighttime residential burglars who resist arrest by attempting to flee the scene of the crime. We can expect an escalating volume of litigation as the lower courts struggle to determine if a police officer's split-second decision to shoot was justified by the danger posed by a particular object and other facts related to the crime. . . .

. . . Whatever the constitutional limits on police use of deadly force in order to apprehend a fleeing felon, I do not believe they are exceeded in a case in which a police officer has probable cause to arrest a suspect at the scene of a residential burglary, orders the suspect to halt, and then fires his weapon as a last resort to prevent the suspect's escape into the night. I respectfully dissent.

PEOPLE v. CEBALLOS

Supreme Court of California

12 Cal. 3d 470, 116 Cal. Rptr. 233, 526 P.2d 241 (1974)

BURKE, Justice.

Don Ceballos was found guilty by a jury of assault with a deadly weapon. Imposition of sentence was suspended and he was placed on probation. He appeals from the judgment, contending primarily that his conduct was not unlawful because the alleged victim was attempting to commit burglary when hit by a trap gun mounted in the garage of defendant's dwelling and that the court erred in instructing the jury. We have concluded that the former argument lacks merit, that the court did not commit prejudicial error in instructing the jury, and that the judgment should be affirmed.

Defendant lived alone in a home in San Anselmo. The regular living quarters were above the garage, but defendant sometimes slept in the garage and had about $2,000 worth of property there.

In March 1970 some tools were stolen from defendant's home. On May 12, 1970, he noticed the lock on his garage doors was bent and pry marks were on one of the doors. The next day he mounted a loaded .22 caliber pistol in the garage. The pistol was aimed at the center of the garage doors and was connected by a wire to one of the doors so that the pistol would discharge if the door was opened several inches.

The damage to defendant's lock had been done by a 16-year-old boy named Stephen and a 15-year-old boy named Robert. On the afternoon of May 15, 1970, the boys returned to defendant's house while he was away. Neither boy was armed with a gun or knife. After looking in the windows and seeing no one, Stephen succeeded in removing the lock on the garage doors with a crowbar, and, as he pulled the door outward, he was hit in the face with a bullet from the pistol.

Stephen testified: He intended to go into the garage "[f]or musical equipment" because he had a debt to pay to a friend. His "way of paying that debt would be to take [defendant's] property and sell it" and use the proceeds to pay the debt. He "wasn't going to do it [i. e., steal] for sure, necessarily." He was there "to look around," and "getting in, I don't know if I would have actually stolen."

Defendant, testifying in his own behalf, admitted having set up the trap gun. He stated that after noticing the pry marks on his garage door on May 12, he felt he should "set up some kind of a trap, something to keep the burglar out of my home." When asked why he was trying to keep the burglar out, he replied, ". . . Because somebody was trying to steal my property . . . and I don't want to come home some night and have the thief in there . . . usually a thief is pretty desperate . . . and . . . they just pick up a weapon . . . if they don't have one . . . and do the best they can."

When asked by the police shortly after the shooting why he assembled the trap gun, defendant stated that "he didn't have much and he wanted to protect what he did have."

As heretofore appears, the jury found defendant guilty of assault with a deadly weapon. An assault is "an unlawful attempt, coupled with a present ability, to commit a violent injury on the person of another."

Defendant contends that had he been present he would have been justified in shooting Stephen since Stephen was attempting to commit burglary [and] defendant had a right to do indirectly what he could have done directly, and that therefore any attempt by him to commit a violent injury upon Stephen was not "unlawful" and hence not an assault. The People argue . . . that as a matter of law a trap gun constitutes excessive force, and that in any event the circumstances were not in fact such as to warrant the use of deadly force.

The issue of criminal liability . . . where the instrument employed is a trap gun or other deadly mechanical device appears to be one of first impression in this state,[59] but in other jurisdictions courts have considered the question of criminal and civil liability for death or injuries inflicted by such a device.

At common law in England it was held that a trespasser, having knowledge that there are spring guns in a wood, cannot maintain an action for an injury received in consequence of his accidentally stepping on the wire of such

59. The parties have cited no California statute specifically dealing with trap guns, except Fish and Game Code section 2007, which provides: "It is unlawful to set, cause to be set, or placed any trap gun. [¶] A 'trap gun' is a firearm loaded with other than blank cartridges and connected with a string or other contrivance contact with which will cause the firearm to be discharged." Even if the Legislature in enacting this section intended merely to regulate the taking of wild life, defendant's attempt to commit a violent injury upon Stephen, as we shall see, was unlawful.

gun. That case aroused such a protest in England that it was abrogated seven years later by a statute, which made it a misdemeanor to set spring guns with intent to inflict grievous bodily injury but excluded from its operation a spring gun set between sunset and sunrise in a dwelling house for the protection thereof.

In the United States, courts have concluded that a person may be held criminally liable under statutes proscribing homicides and shooting with intent to injure, or civilly liable, if he sets upon his premises a deadly mechanical device and that device kills or injures another. . . . However, an exception to the rule that there may be criminal and civil liability for death or injuries caused by such a device has been recognized where the intrusion is, in fact, such that the person, were he present, would be justified in taking the life or inflicting the bodily harm with his own hands. The phrase "were he present" does not hypothesize the actual presence of the person but is used in setting forth in an indirect manner the principle that a person may do indirectly that which he is privileged to do directly.

Allowing persons, at their own risk, to employ deadly mechanical devices imperils the lives of children, firemen and policemen acting within the scope of their employment, and others. Where the actor is present, there is always the possibility he will realize that deadly force is not necessary, but deadly mechanical devices are without mercy or discretion. Such devices "are silent instrumentalities of death. They deal death and destruction to the innocent as well as the criminal intruder without the slightest warning. The taking of human life [or infliction of great bodily injury] by such means is brutally savage and inhuman."

It seems clear that the use of such devices should not be encouraged. Moreover, whatever may be thought in torts, the foregoing rule setting forth an exception to liability for death or injuries inflicted by such devices "is inappropriate in penal law for it is obvious that it does not prescribe a workable standard of conduct; liability depends upon fortuitous results." (See Model Penal Code (Tent. Draft No. 8), §3.06, com. 15.) We therefore decline to adopt that rule in criminal cases.

Furthermore, even if that rule were applied here, as we shall see, defendant was not justified in shooting Stephen. Penal Code section 197 provides: "Homicide is . . . justifiable . . . 1. When resisting any attempt to murder any person, or to commit a felony, or to do some great bodily injury upon any person; or, 2. When committed in defense of habitation, property, or person, against one who manifestly intends or endeavors, by violence or surprise, to commit a felony. . . ." (See also Pen. Code, §198.) Since a homicide is justifiable under the circumstances specified in section 197, a fortiori an attempt to commit a violent injury upon another under those circumstances is justifiable.

By its terms subdivision 1 of Penal Code section 197 appears to permit killing to prevent any "felony," but in view of the large number of felonies today and the inclusion of many that do not involve a danger of serious bodily harm, a literal reading of the section is undesirable. [In] People v. Jones, 191 Cal. App. 2d 478, 481, 12 Cal. Rptr. 777, [the court,] rejecting the defendant's theory that her husband was about to commit the felony of beating her (Pen. Code, §273d) and that therefore her killing him to prevent him from doing so was justifiable, stated that Penal Code section 197 "does no more than codify the common law and should be read in light of it." *Jones* read into section 197, subdivision 1, the limitation that the felony be "some atrocious crime attempted to be committed by force." [*Jones*] further stated, "the punishment provided by a statute is not necessarily an adequate test as to whether life may be taken for in some situations it is too artificial and unrealistic. We must look further into the character of the crime, and the manner of its perpetration. *When these do not reasonably create a fear of great bodily harm,* as they could not if defendant apprehended only a misdemeanor assault, *there is no cause for the exaction of a human life.*" . . .

Jones involved subdivision 1 of Penal Code section 197, but subdivision 2 of that section is likewise so limited. The term "violence or surprise" in subdivision 2 is found in common law authorities and, whatever may have been the very early common law the rule developed at common law that killing or use of deadly force to prevent a felony was justified only if the offense was a forcible and atrocious crime. "Surprise" means an unexpected attack—which includes force and violence . . . and the word thus appears redundant.

Examples of forcible and atrocious crimes are murder, mayhem, rape and robbery. In such crimes "from their atrocity and violence human life [or personal safety from great harm] either is, or is presumed to be, in peril." . . .

Burglary has been included in the list of such crimes. However, in view of the wide scope of burglary under Penal Code section 459, as compared with the common law definition of that offense, in our opinion it cannot be said that under all circumstances burglary under section 459 constitutes a forcible and atrocious crime.[60]

Where the character and manner of the burglary do not reasonably create a fear of great bodily harm, there is no cause for exaction of human life or for the use of deadly force (see generally 13 Stan. L. Rev. 566, 577). The character and manner of the burglary could not reasonably create such a fear unless the burglary threatened, or was reasonably believed to threaten, death or serious bodily harm.

In the instant case the asserted burglary did not threaten death or serious bodily harm, since no one but Stephen and Robert was then on the premises. A defendant is not protected from liability merely by the fact that the intrud-

60. At common law burglary was the breaking and entering of a mansion house in the night with the intent to commit a felony. Burglary under Penal Code section 459 differs from common law burglary in that the entry may be in the daytime and of numerous places other than a mansion house . . . and breaking is not required. For example, under section 459 a person who enters a store with the intent of committing theft is guilty of burglary. It would seem absurd to hold that a store detective could kill that person if necessary to prevent him from committing that offense.

er's conduct is such as would justify the defendant, were he present, in believing that the intrusion threatened death or serious bodily injury.[61] There is ordinarily the possibility that the defendant, were he present, would realize the true state of affairs and recognize the intruder as one whom he would not be justified in killing or wounding.

We thus conclude that defendant was not justified under Penal Code section 197, subdivisions 1 or 2, in shooting Stephen to prevent him from committing burglary. Our conclusion is in accord with dictum indicating that there may be no privilege to use a deadly mechanical device to prevent a burglary of a dwelling house in which no one is present. . . .

In support of his position that had he been present he would have been justified in shooting Stephen, defendant cites Nakashima v. Takase, 8 Cal. App. 2d 35, 46 P.2d 1020, a case in which the decedent's mother was seeking damages. The defendant, a cafe proprietor, suspected a burglary might be committed, returned to the cafe after dark, and hid inside. The decedent and a companion broke into the cafe intending to commit larceny, and after they entered, the defendant, who was secreted in a position where he could not be seen or heard, shot the decedent without warning. *Nakashima,* in reversing the judgment in the plaintiff's favor, concluded that the defendant's act was a justifiable homicide under Penal Code section 197, subdivision 2. That case manifestly differs on its facts from the present one in that, among other things, here no one except the asserted would-be burglar and his companion was on the premises when the gun was fired. . . .[62]

Several cases contain broad language relating to justification for killing where a person acts in defense of his habitation or property to prevent "a felony" but in those cases also it does not appear that any issue was raised or decided as to the nature of the felony coming within that doctrine.

We recognize that our position regarding justification for killing under Penal Code section 197, subdivisions 1 and 2, differs from the position of

61. Restatement Second of Torts, section 85, comment d, states, "The user of a device likely to cause death or serious bodily harm is not protested from liability merely by the fact that the intruder's conduct is such as would justify the actor, were he present, in believing that his intrusion is so dangerous or criminal as to confer upon the actor the privilege of killing or maiming him to prevent it. The actor is relieved from liability only if the intruder is, in fact, one whose intrusion involves danger of life and limb of the occupants of the dwelling place or is for the purpose of committing certain serious crimes, as to which see §§142(2) and 143(2). . . ." Section 142, subdivision (2) concerns a riot "which threatens death or serious bodily harm." As hereinafter appears, section 143, subdivision (2), contains a broader rule with respect to the type crime for the prevention of which deadly force is privileged than the rule followed herein.

62. *Nakashima* cited Brooks v. Sessagesimo, 139 Cal. App. 679, 34 P.2d 766, another tort action case. In *Brooks* the defendant, without warning, shot and killed a man who was attempting to burglarize the defendant's chickencoop at night. *Brooks,* in affirming the judgment in the defendant's favor, concluded that the homicide was justifiable. (Pen. Code, §§197 and 198.) *Brooks* stated, inter alia, that there was evidence that the defendant was in fear of his life, that under the circumstances it could not be said that the fear was unreasonable, and that, although no gun was found on the decedent an open pocket knife was in his pocket and a burglar is apt to be armed with a gun. That case also manifestly differs from the present one in that here no one but the asserted would-be burglar and his companion was on the premises when the gun was fired.

section 143, subdivision (2), of the Restatement Second of Torts, regarding the use of deadly force to prevent a "felony . . . of a type . . . involving the breaking and entry of a dwelling place."[63] (see also Perkins on Criminal Law, p.1030, which is in accord with the foregoing section of the Rest. 2d Torts) but in view of the supreme value of human life we do not believe deadly force can be justified to prevent all felonies of the foregoing type, including ones in which no person is, or is reasonably believed to be, on the premises except the would-be burglar.

Defendant also argues that had he been present he would have been justified in shooting Stephen under subdivision 4 of Penal Code section 197, which provides, "Homicide is . . . justifiable . . . 4. When necessarily committed in *attempting,* by lawful ways and means, *to apprehend* any person for any felony committed. . . ." (Italics added.) The argument cannot be upheld. The words "attempting . . . to apprehend" contain the idea of acting for the purpose of apprehending. An attempt to commit a crime includes, inter alia, the specific intent to commit a particular crime and "In statutes and in cases other than criminal prosecutions an 'attempt' ordinarily means an intent combined with an act falling short of the thing intended." (Black's Law Dictionary (4th ed.) p.162.) Here no showing was made that defendant's intent in shooting was to apprehend a felon. Rather it appears from his testimony and extrajudicial statement heretofore recited that his intent was to prevent a burglary, to protect his property, and to avoid the possibility that a thief might get into defendant's house and injure him upon his return. . . .

Defendant also does not, and could not properly, contend that the intrusion was in fact such that, were he present, he would be justified under Civil Code section 50 in using deadly force. That section provides, "Any necessary force may be used to protect from wrongful injury the person or property of oneself. . . ." This section also should be read in the light of the common law, and at common law in general deadly force could not be used solely for the protection of property. (See Model Penal Code, supra, §3.06, com. 8; Perkins on Criminal Law, p. 1026, fn. 6; 13 Stan. L. Rev. 566, 575-576.) " 'The preservation of human life and limb from grievous harm is of more importance to society than the protection of property.' " (Commonwealth v. Emmons, 157 Pa. Super. 195, 43 A. 2d 568, 569. . . .) Thus defendant was not warranted under Civil Code section 50 in using deadly force to protect his personal property. . . .

We conclude that as a matter of law the exception to the rule of liability

63. Section 143, subdivision (2), of Restatement Second of Torts, reads, "The use of force . . . intended or likely to cause death or serious bodily harm is privileged if the actor reasonably believes that the commission or consummation of the felony cannot otherwise be prevented and the felony for the prevention of which the actor is intervening is of a type threatening death or serious bodily harm or *involving the breaking and entry of a dwelling place.*" (Italics added.)

The comment to that subsection states: "The Statement in this Subsection permits the use of means intended or likely to cause death or serious bodily harm for the purpose of preventing such crimes as murder, voluntary manslaughter, mayhem, robbery, common law rape, kidnapping, and *burglary.*" (Italics added.)

for injuries inflicted by a deadly mechanical device does not apply under the circumstances here appearing. . . .

The judgment is affirmed.

Notes and Questions

1. How does *Ceballos* differ from the occasions where one is entitled to use deadly force? What if I am a very heavy sleeper and fear that my enemy may come through my window to kill me? Would I be entitled to put up a spring gun at the foot of my bed? If it did kill my enemy as he approached me, hatchet in hand, of what crime, if any, would I be guilty? If it instead killed a burglar merely looking for my wallet, would the answer be different? If nobody was hurt, would I be guilty of attempt?

2. Cases such as *Ceballos* are relatively rare. Cases like the following one described in the San Jose Mercury News, May 3, 1984 at 2G are more common.

> San Diego (AP)—A young policeman accused of being "trigger-happy" in the shotgun death of a bank robber's hostage went on trial Wednesday on a charge of involuntary manslaughter.
>
> Escondido police officer David DeLange, 24, does not dispute that it was a blast from his shotgun that killed Leslie Landersman, 22, a newlywed and former hometown beauty queen.
>
> "I'm going to relate to you a tragic tale," deputy district attorney Richard Neely told jurors as he described 20 minutes of confusion and shooting in the streets of Escondido the day of the robbery. He said he would show that DeLange should have heard police radio reports that Landersman was a hostage before he saw her bolt from her commandeered truck and run from her abuctor.
>
> "She was home free. She had made it, and officer DeLange fired his shotgun at her and hit her with the full force," Neely said. "Nine pellets hit her in the right side. She started slowing down, and she finally . . . slumped to the ground."
>
> Landersman died soon afterward at Palomar Hospital.
>
> DeLange's attorney, Richard Mills, told Superior Court Judge James Malkus he will reserve his opening argument until later in the case.
>
> Earlier in the day, Neely had told jurors, "There's no evil motive or purpose in this case. It's negligence, criminal negligence."
>
> Timothy Robert Harding, 34, of Daytona Beach, Fla., was identified by police as the man who masterminded the robbery last Aug. 26 of the Escondido branch of Crocker National Bank. After the robbery, he abandoned his cohorts, kidnapped Landersman, and commandeered her pickup truck. He and the hostage were killed on a dead-end street by police fire 15 minutes after the bank was robbed.
>
> Landersman's hostage status had been broadcast over a police radio during the chase and shootout. But Lt. Chuck Askegreen, a 17-year department veteran who was demoted for his own actions in the shooting, said on Aug. 27, "There was a shift change. There were officers going on duty at 4 P.M. who may not have been on the radio when this thing was first going down."
>
> John Morlan, 20, of San Diego, and Bernadette Borgas-Garcia, 26, driver of the getaway van, were convicted of bank robbery and sentenced last month in

> federal court to 16 years and six years, respectively. Garcia's 2-year-old son was in the van with her during the bank robbery, which netted $9,000.
>
> Five of the 20 Escondido police officers who participated in the chase and shootout last August, including Askegreen, have been disciplined.

Under what conditions should the police officer be guilty? Of what?

3. Finally, how would you assess the conduct of Bernhard Hugo Goetz, the notorious subway vigilante? From the New York Times, Jan. 6, 1985, at E-1:

> Bernhard Hugo Goetz worked out of his apartment on West 14th Street in Manhattan calibrating electrical equipment, leading the kind of quiet life that would make him an unlikely candidate for notoriety. That was before the 37-year-old engineer walked into police headquarters in Concord, N.H., one afternoon last week and said that he was the gunman who had shot four teenagers in a New York subway car nine days before.
>
> The case had already aroused extraordinary public passions. The shootings occurred on a train near Chambers Street, in lower Manhattan, about 1:30 P.M. on the Saturday before Christmas. The four teen-agers—two of whom are still hospitalized, one paralyzed from the waist down—told the police they had approached a slim blond man wearing wire-rimmed glasses and asked him for the time, then a match and, finally, for $5. "Yes," they said he had responded. "I have $5 for each of you." The man fired four times with a .38-caliber handgun, wounding each of the youths. Then he jumped from the halted train and vanished into the subway tunnel.
>
> After the police set up a special telephone line for tips in the case, they received hundreds of calls from people praising the vigilante and offering to pay his legal fees. Governor Cuomo and Mayor Koch denounced the gunman's actions, but the incident seemed to have tapped deep emotions in a population that feels vulnerable to criminals and insufficiently protected by the criminal justice system. A tip on the phone line had led the police to consider Mr. Goetz a suspect, but he apparently turned himself in before New York detectives could locate him.
>
> On Wednesday, Mr. Goetz agreed to waive extradition and to return to New York City. A New Hampshire attorney who advised him said that Mr. Goetz "feels justified in what happened and believes the justice system will take care of it." The next day in New York, Mr. Goetz was arraigned on four counts of attempted murder and one count of illegal weapon possession. He was held on $50,000 cash bail, and offers poured in from people willing to pay his bail or help underwrite his legal defense.
>
> Mr. Goetz, who had worked with a group seeking to rid his neighborhood of drug dealers and had organized petition drives for increased police protection, was attacked in a subway station four years ago. After the incident, he applied for a gun permit, but was denied. The son of the manager of Mr. Goetz's apartment building described him as a "very quiet and a very smart guy." "He's not the violent type," the man said, "but he's also not the type to let people abuse him."

Should there be a "battered citizen" self-defense doctrine?

15

MENTAL ILLNESS AS AN EXCUSE

The existence of a mental disease or defect can be relevant to the decision of many kinds of cases. In the noncriminal context, for instance, the fact that a testator was mentally ill at the time he or she made a will may cause the will to be ineffective if the mental disease prevented the testator from "recognizing the natural objects of his bounty." A mental disease that does not have this effect does not, in general, destroy testamentary capacity. Similarly, a parent may lose custody of a child if the parent's mental disease prevents him or her from fulfilling the physical or emotional needs of the child or otherwise being a "fit" parent. A mental disease that does not have this effect will not cause a parent to lose custody of his or her child. So too, where the state tries to subject a patient to involuntary civil commitment because of a mental disease, that disease must either make the patient dangerous to him or herself or others, or cause the patient to be gravely disabled. Any mental disease that does not cause these effects will not prove an appropriate ground for civil commitment.

In the criminal area mental disease may be relevant at various points. An accused who has a mental disease may be found not competent to stand trial, if the mental disease is so severe that it "prevents the accused from cooperating with his attorney in his defense." A mental disease that does not have this effect will not prevent an accused from being put on trial. An accused who becomes insane while in prison may be transfered to a mental institution if because of the mental disease the person can be "more appropriately treated" in the confines of such an institution or if because of the mental disease the accused cannot be controlled by the processes of the correctional institution. In many jurisdictions an accused who is mentally ill cannot be executed even though properly convicted of a capital offense, if mental illness prevents the accused from appreciating the connection between the punishment and the crime he or she has committed. Mental illness that does not have this effect is ineffective for postponing an execution.

The major question we shall grapple with in this chapter is when someone with a mental disease should be held not morally responsible for a crime. We have already seen one case in which a mental disease would prevent an accused from being responsible for his or her crime—where the mental disease prevented the accused from having the *mens rea* required by the criminal statute (see p.159). In one sense, however, this inquiry involves a play on words because if one does not have the *mens rea* for the commission of a crime, one has not committed a crime to begin with. The issue of criminal responsibility of the mentally ill cuts across the entire criminal law and typically applies even when the accused did have the *mens rea* for a crime.

UNITED STATES v. BRAWNER

United States Court of Appeals, District of Columbia Circuit
471 F.2d 969 (1972)

LEVENTHAL, Circuit Judge.

The principal issues raised on this appeal from a conviction for second degree murder and carrying a dangerous weapon relate to appellant's defense of insanity. After the case was argued to a division of the court, the court *sua sponte* ordered rehearing en banc. We identified our intention to reconsider the appropriate standard for the insanity defense, authorized counsel to file supplemental briefs. . . . We advised a number of organizations of our action, and invited briefs amicus curiae. Subsequently we directed the Clerk to notify all concerned of questions the court requested be discussed (Appendix A).

In the course of our reconsideration of the rule governing the insanity defense, we have studied the opinions of other courts, particularly but not exclusively the opinions of the other Federal circuits, and the views of the many scholars who have thoughtfully pondered the underlying issues. Our file includes presentations of counsel, both Government lawyers and counsel appointed to represent defendant, and submissions of those who have responded to the invitation to comment as amicus curiae on a considerable number of inter-related matters.

We have stretched our canvas wide; and the focal point of the landscape before us is the formulation of the American Law Institute. The ALI's primary provision is stated thus in its Model Penal Code, see §4.01(1).

Section 4.01 Mental Disease or Defect Excluding Responsibility

(1) A person is not responsible for criminal conduct if at the time of such conduct as a result of mental disease or defect he lacks substantial capacity either to appreciate the criminality [wrongfulness] of his conduct or to conform his conduct to the requirements of the law.

We have decided to adopt the ALI rule as the doctrine excluding responsibility for mental disease or defect, for application prospectively to trials begun after this date.

The interest of justice that has called us to this labor bids us set forth comments in which we review the matters we concluded were of primary consequence—though we cannot practicably retraverse all the ground covered in our reflection. These comments also contain features of the rule in which we, like other courts, have recorded our adjustments of the rule and understandings concerning its application that are stated as part of the adoption of the rule, to improve its capacity to further its underlying objectives. We highlight, as most notable of these, our decision to retain the definition of "mental illness or defect" that we evolved in our 1962 *McDonald*[1] opinion en banc. Others are prompted by the submissions which raised, as points of objection to the ALI rule, matters that we think can be fairly taken into account by clarifying comments. . . .

A. The Trial Record

Passing by various minor disagreements among the witnesses, the record permits us to reconstruct the events of September 8, 1967, as follows: After a morning and afternoon of wine-drinking, appellant Archie W. Brawner, Jr. and his uncle Aaron Ross, went to a party at the home of three acquaintances. During the evening, several fights broke out. In one of them, Brawner's jaw was injured when he was struck or pushed to the ground. The time of the fight was approximately 10:30 P.M. After the fight, Brawner left the party. He told Mr. Ross that some boys had jumped him. Mr. Ross testified that Brawner "looked like he was out of his mind." Other witnesses who saw him after the fight testified that Brawner's mouth was bleeding and that his speech was unclear (but the same witness added, "I heard every word he said"); that he was staggering and angry; and that he pounded on a mailbox with his fist. One witness testified that Brawner said, "[I'm] going to get my boys" and come back, and that "someone is going to die tonight."

Half an hour later, at about eleven P.M., Brawner was on his way back to the party with a gun. One witness testified that Brawner said he was going up there to kill his attackers or be killed.

Upon his arrival at the address, Brawner fired a shot into the ground and entered the building. He proceeded to the apartment where the party was in progress and fired five shots through the closed metal hallway door. Two of the shots struck Billy Ford, killing him. Brawner was arrested a few minutes later, several blocks away. The arresting officer testified that Brawner appeared normal, and did not appear to be drunk, that he spoke clearly, and had no odor of alcohol about him.

After the Government had presented the evidence of its non-expert witnesses, the trial judge ruled that there was insufficient evidence on "deliberation" to go to the jury: accordingly, a verdict of acquittal was directed on first degree murder.

1. McDonald v. United States, 114 U.S. App. D.C. 120, 312 F.2d 847 (en banc 1962).

The expert witnesses, called by both defense and prosecution, all agreed that Brawner was suffering from an abnormality of a psychiatric or neurological nature. The medical labels were variously given as "epileptic personality disorder," "psychologic brain syndrome associated with a convulsive disorder," "personality disorder associated with epilepsy," or, more simply, "an explosive personality." There was no disagreement that the epileptic condition would be exacerbated by alcohol, leading to more frequent episodes and episodes of greater intensity, and would also be exacerbated by a physical blow to the head. The experts agreed that epilepsy per se is not a mental disease or defect, but a neurological disease which is often associated with a mental disease or defect. They further agreed that Brawner had a mental, as well as a neurological, disease.

Where the experts disagreed was on the part which that mental disease or defect played in the murder of Billy Ford. The position of the witnesses called by the Government is that Brawner's behavior on the night of September 8 was not consistent with an epileptic seizure, and was not suggestive of an explosive reaction in the context of a psychiatric disorder. In the words of Dr. Platkin of St. Elizabeths Hospital, "He was just mad."

The experts called by the defense maintained the contrary conclusion. Thus, Dr. Eugene Stanmeyer, a psychologist at St. Elizabeths, was asked on direct by counsel for defense, whether, assuming accused did commit the act which occurred, there was a causal relationship between the assumed act and his mental abnormality. Dr. Stanmeyer replied in the affirmative, that there was a cause and effect relationship.

Later, the prosecutor asked the Government's first expert witness Dr. Weickhardt: "Did you . . . come to any opinion concerning whether or not the crimes in this case were causally related to the mental illness which you diagnosed?" An objection to the form of the question was overruled. The witness then set forth that in his opinion there was no causal relationship between the mental disorder and the alleged offenses. Brawner claims that the trial court erred when it permitted a prosecution expert to testify in this manner. He relies on our opinion in Washington v. United States, 129 U.S. App. D.C. 29, 390 F.2d 444 (1967).

B. Prior Developments of the Insanity Defense in this Jurisdiction

History looms large in obtaining a sound perspective for a subject like this one. But the cases are numerous. And since our current mission is to illuminate the present, rather than to linger over the past, it suffices for our purposes to review a handful of our opinions on the insanity defense.

1. The landmark opinion was written by Judge Bazelon in Durham v. United States, 94 U.S. App. D.C. 228, 214 F.2d 862 (1954). Prior to *Durham* the law of the District of Columbia was established by United States v. Lee, 15

D.C. (4 Mackey) 489, 496 (1886) and Smith v. United States, 59 App. D.C. 144, 36 F.2d 548 (1929), which, taken together, stated a traditional test of insanity, in terms of right and wrong[2] and irresistible impulse.[3] *Durham* adopted the "product rule," pioneered in State v. Pike, 49 N.H. 399, 402 (1869-1870), and exculpated from criminal responsibility those whose forbidden acts were the product of a mental disease or defect.

Few cases have evoked as much comment as *Durham.* It has sparked widespread interest in the legal-judicial community and focused attention on the profound problems involved in defining legal responsibility in case of mental illness. It has been hailed as a guide to the difficult and problem-laden intersection of law and psychiatry, ethics and science. It has been scored as an unwarranted loophole through which the cunning criminal might escape from the penalty of the law. We view it more modestly, as the court's effort, designed in the immemorial manner of the case method that has built the common law, to alleviate two serious problems with the previous rule.

The first of these was a problem of language which raised an important symbolic issue in the law. We felt that the language of the old right-wrong/irresistible impulse rule for insanity was antiquated, no longer reflecting the community's judgment as to who ought to be held criminally liable for socially destructive acts. We considered the rule as restated to have more fruitful, accurate and considered reflection of the sensibilities of the community as revised and expanded in the light of continued study of abnormal human behavior.

The second vexing problem that *Durham* was designed to reach related to the concern of the psychiatrists called as expert witnesses for their special knowledge of the problem of insanity, who often and typically felt that they were obliged to reach outside of their professional expertise when they were asked, under the traditional insanity rule established in 1843 by *M'Naghten's* Case,[4] whether the defendant knew right from wrong. They further felt that the narrowness of the traditional test, which framed the issue of responsibility solely in terms of cognitive impairment, made it impossible to convey to the judge and jury the full range of information material to an assessment of defendant's responsibility.

2. Discerning scholarship now available asserts that the experts' fears and concerns reflected a misapprehension as to the impact of the traditional standard in terms of excluding relevant evidence.

2. United States v. Lee, 15 D.C. 489, 496 (1886):

> The rule of law is very plain that in order that the plea of insanity shall prevail, there must have been that mental condition of the party which disabled him from distinguishing between right and wrong in respect of the act committed.

3. Smith v. United States, 59 App. D.C. 144, 145, 36 F.2d 548, 549 (1929):

> [it must be found that defendant's] reasoning powers were so far dethroned by his diseased mental condition as to deprive him of the will power to resist the insane impulse to perpetrate the deed, though knowing it to be wrong.

4. 10 Clark & F. 200, 2 Eng. Rep. 718 (H.L. 1843).

> Wigmore states the rule to be that when insanity is in issue, "any and all conduct of the person is admissible in evidence." And the cases support Wigmore's view. The almost unvarying policy of the courts has been to admit *any* evidence of abberational behavior so long as it is probative of the defendant's mental condition, without regard to the supposed restrictions of the test used to define insanity for the jury.[5]

Moreover if the term "know" in the traditional test of "know right from wrong" is taken as denoting affective knowledge, rather than merely cognitive knowledge, it yields a rule of greater flexibility than was widely supposed to exist. Livermore and Meehl, The Virtues of M'Naghten, 51 Minn. L. Rev. 789, 800-808 (1967).

We need not occupy ourselves here and now with the question whether, and to what extent, the *M'Naghten* rule, ameliorated by the irresistible impulse doctrine, is susceptible of application to include medical insights and information as justice requires. In any event, the experts felt hemmed in by the traditional test; they felt that they could not give the jury and judge the necessary information in response to the questions which the traditional test posed, see 37 F.R.D. 365, 387 (1964).

The rule as reformulated in *Durham* permitted medical experts to testify on medical matters properly put before the jury for its consideration, and to do so without the confusion that many, perhaps most, experts experienced from testimony structured under the *M'Naghten* rule. That was a positive contribution to jurisprudence—and one that was retained when the American Law Institute undertook to analyze the problem and proposed a different formulation.

3. A difficulty arose under the *Durham* rule in application. The rule was devised to facilitate the giving of testimony by medical experts in the context of a legal rule, with the jury called upon to reach a composite conclusion that had medical, legal and moral components.[6] However the pristine statement of

5. A. Goldstein. The Insanity Defense 54 (1967), citing 1 Wigmore Evidence §228 (1940) and numerous cases.

6. *Durham* contemplated from the start that the jury would have the guidance of "wider horizons of knowledge" from the medical experts than was available under the prior rule, but that in the last analysis the ultimate question is left to the jury "to perform its traditional function . . . to apply 'our inherited ideas of moral responsibility to individuals prosecuted for crime.' [Juries will] continue to make moral judgments. . . ." 94 U.S. App. D.C. at 242, 214 F.2d at 876. See also, King v. United States, 125 U.S. App. D.C. 318 at 323-324, 372 F.2d 383 at 388-389.

> The question for the jury requires the application to medical knowledge, and the lay evidence as well, of the understanding and judgment of the community as reflected in the jury. . . . [In] view of the complicated nature of the decision to be made—intertwining moral, legal, and medical judgments—it will require an unusually strong showing to induce us to reverse a conviction because the judge left the critical issue of responsibility with the jury.

Holloway v. United States, 80 U.S. App. D.C. 3, 4, 148 F.2d 665, 666 (1945):

> Legal tests of criminal insanity are not and cannot be the result of scientific analysis or objective judgment. . . . They must be based on the instinctive sense of justice of ordinary men. This sense of justice assumes that there is a faculty called reason which is separate

the *Durham* rule opened the door to "trial by label." *Durham* did distinguish between "disease," as used "in the sense of a condition which is considered capable of either improving or deteriorating," and "defect," as referring to a condition not capable of such change "and which may be either congenital or the result of injury, or the residual effect of a physical or mental disease." 94 U.S. App. D.C. at 241, 214 F.2d at 875. But the court failed to explicate what abnormality of mind was an essential ingredient of these concepts. In the absence of a definition of "mental disease or defect," medical experts attached to them the meanings which would naturally occur to them—medical meanings—and gave testimony accordingly. The problem was dramatically highlighted by the weekend flip flop case. In re Rosenfield, 157 F. Supp. 18 (D.D.C. 1957). The petitioner was described as a sociopath. A St. Elizabeths psychiatrist testified that a person with a sociopathic personality was not suffering from a mental disease. That was Friday afternoon. On Monday morning, through a policy change at St. Elizabeths Hospital, it was determined as an administrative matter that the state of a psychopathic or sociopathic personality did constitute a mental disease.[7]

The concern that medical terminology not control legal outcomes culmintated in McDonald v. United States, 114 U.S. App. D.C. 120, 312 F.2d 847, 851 (en banc, 1962), where this court recognized that the term, mental disease or defect, has various meanings, depending upon how and why it is used, and by whom. Mental disease means one thing to a physician bent on treatment, but something different, if somewhat overlapping, to a court of law. We provided a legal definition of mental disease or defect, and held that it included "any abnormal condition of the mind which substantially affects mental or emotional processes and substantially impairs behavior controls." (312 F.2d at 851). "Thus the jury would consider testimony concerning the development, adaptation and functioning of these processes and controls." Id.

While the *McDonald* standard of mental disease was not without an attribute of circularity, it was useful in the administration of justice because it made plain that clinical and legal definitions of mental disease were distinct, and it helped the jury to sort out its complex task and to focus on the matters given it to decide.

4. The *Durham* rule also required explication along other lines, notably

---

> and apart from instinct, emotion, and impulse, that enables an individual to distinguish between right and wrong and endows him with moral responsibility for his acts. . . . Our collective conscience does not allow punishment where it cannot impose blame.

Sauer v. United States, 241 F.2d 640, 649 (9th Cir. 1957), quoting *Holloway*, refers to the court's "awareness that the jury will eventually exercise a moral judgment as to the sanity of the accused."

United States v. Wilson, 399 F.2d 459, 463 (4th Cir. 1968): "There is enough doubt about a sociopath such as [defendant] to call for an exercise of the jury's moral judgment. . . ."

7. Compare Campbell v. United States, 113 U.S. App. D.C. 260, 261, 307 F.2d 597, 598 (1962):

> As an administrative matter, "emotionally unstable personality" has been regarded by the staff at St. Elizabeths as a mental disease only since November 1957.

the resolution of the ambiguity inherent in the formulation concerning actions that were the "product" of mental illness. It was supplemented in Carter v. United States, 102 U.S. App. D.C. 227 at 234, 235, 252 F.2d 608 at 615-616 (1957):

> The simple fact that a person has a mental disease or defect is not enough to relieve him of responsibility for a crime. There must be a relationship between the disease and the criminal act; and the relationship must be such as to justify a reasonable inference that the act would not have been committed if the person had not been suffering from the disease.

Thus *Carter* clarified that the mental illness must not merely have entered into the production of the act, but must have played a necessary role. *Carter* identified the "product" element of the rule with the "but for" variety of causation.

The pivotal "product" term continued to present problems, principally that it put expert testimony on a faulty footing. Assuming that a mental disease, in the legal sense, had been established, the fate of the defendant came to be determined by what came to be referred to by the legal jargon of "productivity." On the other hand, it was obviously sensible if not imperative that the experts having pertinent knowledge should speak to the crucial question whether the mental abnormality involved is one associated with aberrant behavior. But since "productivity" was so decisive a factor in the decisional equation, a ruling permitting experts to testify expressly in language of "product" raised in a different context the concern lest the ultimate issue be in fact turned over to the experts rather than retained for the jurors representing the community.

The problem was identified by then Circuit Judge Burger in his concurring opinion in *Blocker:*[8]

> The hazards in allowing experts to testify in precisely or even substantially the terms of the ultimate issue are apparent. This is a course which, once allowed, risks the danger that lay jurors, baffled by the intricacies of expert discourse and unintelligible technical jargon may be tempted to abdicate independent analysis of the facts on which the opinion rests. . . .

As early as *Carter,* we had warned that the function of an expert was to explain the origin, development and manifestations of mental disorders, in terms that would be coherent and meaningful to the jury. "Unexplained medical labels . . . are not enough." (102 U.S. App. D.C. at 236, 252 F.2d at 617). Even after *McDonald,* however, we continued to see cases where the testimony of the experts was limited to the use of conclusory labels, without the explication of the underlying analysis. We do not say this was deliberated by the experts. It seems in large measure to have reflected tactical decisions of counsel, and perhaps problems of communications between the disciplines.

8. Blocker v. United States, 110 U.S. App. D.C. 41, 51, 288 F.2d 853, 863 (en banc 1961).

It was in this context that the court came to the decision in Washington v. United States, 129 U.S. App. D.C. 29, 390 F.2d 444 (1967), which forbade experts from testifying as to productivity altogether. Chief Judge Bazelon's opinion illuminates the basis of the ruling, as one intended "to help the psychiatrists understand their role in court, and thus eliminate a fundamental cause of unsatisfactory expert testimony," namely, the tendency of the expert to use "concepts [which] can become slogans, hiding facts and representing nothing more than the witness's own conclusion about the defendant's criminal responsibility." (at 41, 390 F.2d at 456).

[The court then discussed the standards for an insanity defense in other circuits.]

D. Comments Concerning Reason for Adoption of ALI Rule and Scope of Rule as Adopted by This Court

In the foreglimpse stating that we had determined to adopt the ALI rule we undertook to set forth comments stating our reasons, and also the adjustments and understandings defining the ALI rule as adopted by this Court. Having paused to study the rulings in the other circuits, we turn to our comments, and to our reflections following the extensive, and intensive, exposure of this court to insanity defense issues.[9]

1. NEED TO DEPART FROM "PRODUCT" FORMULATION AND UNDUE DOMINANCE BY EXPERTS

A principal reason for our decision to depart from the *Durham* rule is the undesirable characteristic, surviving even the *McDonald* modification, of undue dominance by the experts giving testimony. The underlying problem was identified, with stress on different facets, in the *Carter, Blocker* (concurring), and *Washington* opinions. The difficulty is rooted in the circumstance that there is no generally accepted understanding, either in the jury or the community it represents, of the concept requiring that the crime be the "product" of the mental disease.

When the court used the term "product" in *Durham* it likely assumed that this was a serviceable, and indeed a natural, term for a rule defining criminal responsibility—a legal reciprocal, as it were, for the familiar term "proximate cause," used to define civil responsibility. But if concepts like "product" are, upon refinement, reasonably understood, or at least appreciated, by judges and lawyers, and perhaps philosophers, difficulties developed when it emerged that the "product" concept did not signify a reasonably identifiable common

9. Ten years ago Judge Burger said: "While the time span since 1954 is brief, our total study and collective case consideration of the problem is equal perhaps to as much as a half century of case review of this problem in most jurisdictions." Blocker v. United States, 110 U.S. App. D.C. at 52, 288 F.2d at 864 (en banc, 1961) (concurring opinion).

ground that was also shared by the nonlegal experts,[10] and the laymen serving on the jury as the representatives of the community.

The doctrine of criminal responsibility is such that there can be no doubt "of the complicated nature of the decision to be made—intertwining moral, legal, and medical judgments," see King v. United States, 125 U.S. App. D.C. 318, 324, 372 F.2d 383, 389 (1967) and *Durham* and other cases cited supra, note 6. Hence, as *King* and other opinions have noted, jury decisions have been accorded unusual deference even when they have found responsibility in the face of a powerful record, with medical evidence uncontradicted, pointing toward exculpation.[11] The "moral" elements of the decision are not defined exclusively by religious considerations but by the totality of underlying conceptions of ethics and justice shared by the community, as expressed by its jury surrogate. The essential feature of a jury "lies in the interposition between the accused and his accuser of the commonsense judgment of a group of laymen, and in the community participation and shared responsibility that results from that group's determination of guilt or innocence." Williams v. Florida, 399 U.S. 78, 100, 90 S. Ct. 1893, 1906, 26 L. Ed. 2d 446 (1970).

The expert witnesses—psychiatrists and psychologists—are called to adduce relevant information concerning what may for convenience be referred to as the "medical" component of the responsibility issue. But the difficulty—as emphasized in *Washington*—is that the medical expert comes, by testimony given in terms of a non-medical construct ("product"), to express conclusions that in essence embody ethical and legal conclusions. There is, indeed, irony in a situation under which the *Durham* rule, which was adopted in large part to permit experts to testify in their own terms concerning matters within their domain which the jury should known, resulted in testimony by the experts in terms not their own to reflect unexpressed judgments in a domain that is properly not theirs but the jury's. The irony is heightened when the jurymen, instructed under the esoteric "product" standard, are influenced significantly

10. A difference in language perception probably contributed to the development that psychiatric testimony concerning "product" causal relationship did not develop along the lines presaged by legal students of the problem. Early critiques in journals asserted that a but-for test of "product" would rarely, if ever, permit a psychiatrist to testify as to the existence of mental illness coexisting with a lack of "product" causal relationship to the crime. See, e.g., Wechsler, The Criteria of Criminal Responsibility, 22 U. Chi. L. Rev. 367, 371 (1955); De Grazia, The Distinction of Being Mad, 22 U. Chi. L. Rev. 339, 343 (1955). Presumably, the force of this analysis was strengthened when "mental disease or defect" was defined and tightened in *McDonald.* As events have developed, however, it has become almost commonplace that psychiatrists testifying as to the presence of mental disease have nevertheless found an absence of "product" causal relation with the crime, or at least expressed substantial doubt as to such relationship. Perhaps more to the point, it has become commonplace for psychiatrists called by Government and defense to be in agreement on the mental disease aspects of their testimony and to differ on the issue of "product" relationship. This is not intended, in any way, as a criticism of any particular testimony. There is often a genuine and difficult question as to the relationship between a particular mental disease and particular offense. What is our concern, however, is that the inherent difficulty of this core problem has been intensified, and the sources of confusion compounded, by a kind of mystique that came to surround the "product" test, and testimony cast in that language.

11. E.g., Hawkins v. United States, 114 U.S. App. D.C. 44, 310 F.2d 849 (1962); Isaac v. United States, 109 U.S. App. D.C. 34, 284 F.2d 168 (1960).

by "product" testimony of expert witnesses really reflecting ethical and legal judgments rather than a conclusion within the witnesses' particular expertise.

It is easier to identify and spotlight the irony than to eradicate the mischief. The objective of *Durham* is still sound—to put before the jury the information that is within the expert's domain, to aid the jury in making a broad and comprehensive judgment. But when the instructions and appellate decisions define the "product" inquiry as the ultimate issue, it is like stopping the tides to try to halt the emergence of this term in the language of those with a central role in the trial—the lawyers who naturally seek to present testimony that will influence the jury who will be charged under the ultimate "product" standard, and the expert witnesses who have an awareness, gained from forensic psychiatry and related disciplines, of the ultimate "product" standard that dominates the proceeding.

The experts have meaningful information to impart, not only on the existence of mental illness or not, but also on its relationship to the incident charged as an offense. In the interest of justice this valued information should be available, and should not be lost or blocked by requirements that unnaturally restrict communication between the experts and the jury. The more we have pondered the problem the more convinced we have become that the sound solution lies not in further shaping of the *Durham* "product" approach in more refined molds, but in adopting the ALI's formulation as the linchpin of our jurisprudence.

The ALI's formulation retains the core requirement of a meaningful relationship between the mental illness and the incident charged. The language in the ALI rule is sufficiently in the common ken that its use in the courtroom, or in preparation for trial, permits a reasonable three-way communication—between (a) the law-trained, judges and lawyers; (b) the experts and (c) the jurymen—without insisting on a vocabulary that is either stilted or stultified, or conducive to a testimonial mystique permitting expert dominance and encroachment on the jury's function. There is no indication in the available literature that any such untoward development has attended the reasonably widespread adoption of the ALI rule in the Federal courts and a substantial number of state courts.

2. RETENTION OF MCDONALD DEFINITION OF "MENTAL DISEASE OR DEFECT"

Our ruling today includes our decision that in the ALI rule as adopted by this court the term "mental disease or defect" includes the definition of that term provided in our 1962 en banc *McDonald* opinion, as follows:

> [A] mental disease or defect includes any abnormal condition of the mind which substantially affects mental or emotional processes and substantially impairs behavior controls.

McDonald v. United States, 114 U.S. App. D.C. at 124, 312 F.2d at 851.

We take this action in response to the problem, identified by amicus comments of Mr. Dempsey and the D.C. Bar Association, that the ALI's rule, lacking definition of "mental disease or defect," contains an inherent ambiguity. These comments consider this a reason for avoiding the ALI rule. We find more merit in the suggestion of Mr. Flynn, counsel appointed to represent appellant, that the *McDonald* definition be engrafted on to the ALI rule.[12]

In our further discussion of ALI and *McDonald,* we shall sometimes refer to "mental disease" as the core concept, without specifically referring to the possibility of exculpation by reason of a non-altering "mental defect."

The *McDonald* rule has helped accomplish the objective of securing expert testimony needed on the subject of mental illness, while guarding against the undue dominance of expert testimony or specialized labels. It has thus permitted the kind of communication without encroachment, as between experts and juries, that has prompted us to adopt the ALI rule, and hence will help us realize our objective. This advantage overrides the surface disadvantage of any clumsiness in the blending of the *McDonald* component, defining mental disease, with the rest of the ALI rule, a matter we discuss further below.

3. INTEREST OF UNIFORMITY OF JUDICIAL APPROACH AND VOCABULARY, WITH ROOM FOR VARIATIONS AND ADJUSTMENTS

Adoption of the ALI rule furthers uniformity of judicial approach—a feature eminently desirable, not as a mere glow of "togetherness," but as an appreciation of the need and value of judicial communication. In all likelihood, this court's approach under *Durham,* at least since *McDonald,* has differed from that of other courts in vocabulary more than substance. Uniformity of vocabulary has an important value, however, as is evidenced from the familiar experience of meanings that "get lost in translation." No one court can amass all the experience pertinent to the judicial administration of the insanity defense. It is helpful for courts to be able to learn from each other without any blockage due to jargon. It is an impressive virtue of the common law, that its distinctive reliance on judicial decisions to establish the corpus of the law furthers a multiparty conversation between men who have studied a problem in various places at various times.

The value of uniformity of central approach is not shattered by the circumstance that in various particulars the different circuits have inserted variations in the ALI rule. Homogeneity does not mean rigidity, and room for local variation is likely a strength, providing a basis for comparison,[13] not a weakness. Nor is the strength of essential uniformity undercut by the caution of our appointed amicus that the formulation of the ALI rule provides extremely

12. This was also the suggestion of the National District Attorneys Association, subject to caveats, as the test recommended if the court did not accept its submission that the insanity defense should be abolished entirely.

13. Compare New State Ice Co. v. Liebmann, 285 U.S. 262, 280, 52 S. Ct. 371, 76 L. Ed. 747 (1932) (dissenting opinion of Brandeis, J.).

broad flexibility.[14] Flexibility and ductility are inherent in the insanity defense, as in any judicial rule with an extensive range—say, negligence, or proximate cause—and the ALI rule permits appropriate guidance of juries.

In prescribing a departure from *Durham* we are not unmindful of the concern that a change may generate uncertainties as to corollaries of the change.[15] While the courts adopting the ALI rule have stated variations, as we have noted, these were all, broadly, in furtherance of one or more of the interrelated goals of the insanity defense:

(a) a broad input of pertinent facts and opinions
(b) enhancing the information and judgment
(c) of a jury necessarily given latitude in light of its functioning as the representative of the entire community.

We are likewise and for the same objectives defining the ALI rule as adopted by the court, with its contours and corollaries given express statement at the outset so as to minimize uncertainty. We postpone this statement to a subsequent phase of the opinion in order that we may first consider other alternatives, for in some measure our adaptation may obviate or at least blunt objections voiced to the ALI rule.

4. CONSIDERATION AND REJECTION OF OTHER SUGGESTIONS

a. Proposal to Abolish Insanity Defense

A number of proposals in the journals recommend that the insanity defense be abolished altogether.[16] This is advocated in the amicus brief of the National District Attorneys Association as both desirable and lawful.[17] The amicus brief of American Psychiatric Association concludes it would be desirable, with appropriate safeguards, but would require a constitutional amendment. That a constitutional amendment would be required is also the conclusion of others, generally in opposition to the proposal.[18]

14. Amicus points out that in *Freeman* the Second Circuit referred to the fact that the Third and Tenth Circuits "have employed their own language approaching the objectives of the Model Penal Code formulation," and then offered a discussion of guiding policy considerations, including Senator Dodd's espousal of an approach sending "marginal" cases to a hospital rather than prison, that, as amicus puts it, "strikes quite a different tone than, say, the analogous discussion of the Tenth Circuit in Wion."

15. See, e.g., Report of President's D.C. Crime Commission at pp.550 ff. A majority of the members of the Commission preferred the ALI rule, but were concerned lest departure from *Durham-McDonald* spawn confusion.

16. "[I]t may be that psychiatry and the other social and behavioral sciences cannot provide sufficient data relevant to a determination of criminal responsibility no matter what our rules of evidence are. If so, we may be forced to eliminate the insanity defense altogether, or refashion it in a way which is not tied so tightly to the medical model." Washington v. United States, 129 U.S. App. D.C. at 42, n.33, 390 F.2d at 457 (1967).

17. It suggests that a mental condition be exculpatory solely as it negatives *mens rea.*

18. E.g., Mr. Dempsey. To the same general effect is the position in the research memorandum from the University of Virginia Law School Research Group to Mr. Flynn, appellant's appointed counsel attached to his brief.

This proposal has been put forward by responsible judges for consideration, with the objective of reserving psychiatric overview for the phase of the criminal process concerned with disposition of the person determined to have been the actor.[19] However, we are convinced that the proposal cannot properly be imposed by judicial fiat.

The courts have emphasized over the centuries that "free will" is the postulate of responsibility under our jurisprudence. 4 Blackstone's Commentaries 27. The concept of "belief in freedom of the human will and a consequent ability and duty of the normal individual to choose between good and evil" is a core concept that is "universal and persistent in mature systems of law." Morissette v. United States, 342 U.S. 246, 250, 72 S. Ct. 240, 243, 96 L. Ed. 288 (1952). Criminal responsibility is assessed when through "free will" a man elects to do evil. And while, as noted in *Morissette,* the legislature has dispensed with mental element in some statutory offenses, in furtherance of a paramount need of the community, these instances mark the exception and not the rule, and only in the most limited instances has the mental element been omitted by the legislature as a requisite for an offense that was a crime at common law.

The concept of lack of "free will" is both the root of origin of the insanity defense and the line of its growth.[20] This cherished principle is not undercut by difficulties, or differences of view, as to how best to express the free will concept in the light of the expansion of medical knowledge. We do not concur in the view of the National District Attorneys Association that the insanity defense should be abandoned judicially, either because it is at too great a variance with popular conceptions of guilt[21] or fails "to show proper respect for the personality of the criminal [who] is liable to resent pathology more than punishment."[22]

These concepts may be measured along with other ingredients in a legislative re-examination of settled doctrine of criminal responsibility, root, stock and branch. Such a reassessment, one that seeks to probe and appraise the society's processes and values, is for the legislative branch, assuming no constitutional bar. The judicial role is limited, in Justice Holmes's figure, to action that is molecular, with the restraint inherent in taking relatively small steps,

19. See, e.g., Burger, then Circuit Judge, Proceedings of the Sixth Annual Meeting of the National Conference of State Trial Judges, Chicago, Illinois, Aug. 9-11, 1963, quoted in Wion v. United States, 325 F.2d at 428, n.10; Bazelon, Chief Judge, in Washington v. United States, 129 U.S. App. D.C. at 42, n.33, 390 F.2d at 457 (1967); Haynesworth, Chief Judge, in en banc opinion in United States v. Chandler, 393 F.2d at 928 (1968); see also remarks of Chief Justice Weintraub (of New Jersey) in Insanity as a Defense—Panel Discussion, Annual Judicial Conference, Second Circuit, 37 F.R.D. 365, 369 (1964).

20. Davis v. United States, 160 U.S. 469, 484-485, 16 S. Ct. 353, 40 L. Ed. 499 (1895); Durham v. United States, supra, 94 U.S. App. D.C. at 242, 214 F.2d at 876.

21. Amicus argues that penal systems can only survive so long as they "accord substantially with the popular estimate of the enormity of guilt," citing 1 W. Lecky, History of the Rise and Influence of the Spirit of Rationalism in Europe 336-337 (1891).

22. Citing Harris, Respect for Persons in Ethics and Society 129-130 (R. De George ed. 1966).

leaving to the other branches of government whatever progress must be made with seven-league leaps. Such judicial restraint is particularly necessary when a proposal requires, as a mandatory ingredient, the kind of devotion of resources, personnel and techniques that can be accomplished only through whole-hearted legislative commitment.

To obviate any misunderstanding from our rejection of the recommendation of those proposing judicial abolition of the insanity defense, we expressly commend their emphasis on the need for improvement of dispositional resources and programs. The defense focuses on the kind of impairment that warrants exculpation, and necessarily assigns to the prison walls many men who have serious mental impairments and difficulties. The needs of society—rooted not only in humanity but in practical need for attempting to break the recidivist cycles, and halt the spread of deviant behavior—call for the provision of psychiatrists, psychologists and counselors to help men with these mental afflictions and difficulties, as part of a total effort toward a readjustment that will permit re-integration in society.

b. Proposal for Defense If Mental Disease Impairs Capacity to Such an Extent That the Defendant Cannot "Justly Be Held Responsible"

We have also pondered the suggestion that the jury be instructed that the defendant lacks criminal responsibility if the jury finds that the defendant's mental disease impairs his capacity or controls to such an extent that he cannot "justly be held responsible."

This was the view of a British commission,[23] adapted and proposed in 1955 by Professor Wechsler, the distinguished Reporter for the ALI's Model Penal Code, and sustained by some, albeit a minority, of the members of the ALI's Council.[24] In the ALI, the contrary view prevailed because of a concern over presenting to the jury questions put primarily in the form of "justice."

The proposal is not to be condemned out of hand as a suggestion that the jury be informed of an absolute prerogative that it can only exercise by flatly disregarding the applicable rule of law. It is rather a suggestion that the jury

23. In 1953 the British Royal Commission on Capital Punishment proposed:

> [A person is not responsible for his unlawful act if] at the time of the act the accused was suffering from disease of the mind (or mental deficiency) *to such a degree that he ought not to be held responsible.*

24. The minority, together with the Reporter for the Model Penal Code (Professor Herbert Wechsler), proposed the following test of insanity:

> A person is not responsible for criminal conduct if at the time of such conduct as a result of mental disease or defect his capacity either to appreciate the criminality of his conduct or to conform his conduct to the requirements of law is *so substantially impaired that he cannot justly be held responsible.*

This proposal appears as alternative (a) to paragraph (1) of Model Penal Code §4.01 (Tent. Draft No. 4, 1955) (emphasis added).

be informed of the matters the law contemplates it will take into account in arriving at the community judgment concerning a composite of factors.[25]

However, there is a substantial concern that an instruction overtly cast in terms of "justice" cannot feasibly be restricted to the ambit of what may properly be taken into account but will splash with unconfinable and malign consequences. The Government cautions that "explicit appeals to "justice" will result in litigation of extraneous issues and will encourage improper arguments to the jury phrased solely in terms of 'sympathy' and 'prejudice.' "

Nor is this solely a prosecutor's concern.

Mr. Flynn, counsel appointed to represent defendant, puts it that even though the jury is applying community concepts of blameworthiness "the jury should not be left at large, or asked to find out for itself what those concepts are."

The amicus submission of the Public Defender Service argues that it would be beneficial to focus the jury's attention on the moral and legal questions intertwined in the insanity defense. It expresses concern, however, over a blameworthiness instruction without more, saying (Br. 19) "it may well be that the 'average' American condemns the mentally ill."[26] It would apparently accept an approach not unlike that proposed by the ALI Reporter, under which the justice standard is coupled with a direction to consider the individual's capacity to control his behavior. Mr. Dempsey's recommendation is of like import, with some simplification.[27] But the problem remains, whether, assuming justice calls for the exculpation and treatment of the mentally ill, that is more likely to be gained from a jury, with "average" notions of mental illness, which is explicitly set at large to convict or acquit persons with impaired mental capacity according to its concept of justice.

The brief of the D.C. Bar Association as amicus submits that with a "justly responsible" formulation the test of insanity "would be largely swallowed up by this consideration." And it observes that the function of giving to the jury the law to be applied to the facts is not only the duty of the court, see Sparf v. United States, 156 U.S. 51, 102, 15 S. Ct. 273, 39 L. Ed. 343 (1895), but is also "a bedrock right of every citizen"—and, possibly, his "only protection," citing Justice Story in United States v. Battiste, 2 Sumn. 240, 244, Fed. Cas. No. 14,545 (C.C.D. Mass. 1835).

We are impressed by the observation of Professor Abraham S. Goldstein, one of the most careful students of the problem:

25. See authorities cited supra, note 6.

26. See, e.g., Szasz, Psychiatry, Ethics and the Criminal Law, 58 Colum. L. Rev. 183, 195 (1958) "[To] have a 'psychopathic' personality is only a more elegant way of expressing moral condemnation." See also, Star, The Public's Ideas About Mental Illness (National Opinion Research Center, 1955); H. Kalven and H. Zeisel, The American Jury 405 (1966).

27. He proposes (Br. 78) an instruction with this crucial sentence: "It is up to you to decide whether defendant had such an abnormal mental condition, and if he did whether the impairment was substantial enough, and was so related to the commission of the crime, *that he ought not be held responsible.*" (Emphasis added.)

> [The] overly general standard may place too great a burden upon the jury. If the law provides no standard, members of the jury are placed in the difficult position of having to find a man responsible for no other reason than their personal feeling about him. Whether the psyches of individual jurors are strong enough to make that decision, or whether the "law" should put that obligation on them, is open to serious question. It is far easier for them to perform the role assigned to them by legislature and courts if they know—or are able to rationalize—that their verdicts are "required" by law.[28]

Professor Goldstein was referring to the broad "justice" standard recommended by the Royal Commission. But the problems remain acute even with the modifications in the proposal of the ALI Reporter, for that still leads to "justly responsible" as the ultimate and critical term.

There may be a tug of appeal in the suggestion that law is a means to justice and the jury is an appropriate tribunal to ascertain justice. This is a simplistic syllogism that harbors the logical fallacy of equivocation, and fails to take account of the different facets and dimensions of the concept of justice. We must not be beguiled by a play on words. The thrust of a rule that in essence invites the jury to ponder the evidence on impairment of defendant's capacity and appreciation, and then do what to them seems just, is to focus on what seems "just" as to the particular individual. Under the centuries-long pull of the Judeo-Christian ethic, this is likely to suggest a call for understanding and forgiveness of those who have committed crimes against society, but plead the influence of passionate and perhaps justified grievances against that society, perhaps grievances not wholly lacking in merit. In the domain of morality and religion, the gears may be governed by the particular instance of the individual seeking salvation. The judgment of a court of law must further justice to the community, and safeguard it against undercutting and evasion from overconcern for the individual. What this reflects is not the rigidity of retributive justice—an eye for an eye—but awareness how justice in the broad may be undermined by an excess of compassion as well as passion. Justice to the community includes penalties needed to cope with disobedience by those capable of control, undergirding a social environment that broadly inhibits behavior destructive of the common good. An open society requires mutual respect and regard, and mutually reinforcing relationships among its citizens, and its ideals of justice must safeguard the vast majority who responsibly shoulder the burdens implicit in its ordered liberty. Still another aspect of justice is the requirement for rules of conduct that establish reasonable generality, neutrality and constancy. Cf. L. Fuller, The Morality of Laws 33-94 (1964). This concept is neither static nor absolute, but it would be sapped by a rule that invites an ad hoc redefinition of the "just" with each new case.

It is the sense of justice propounded by those charged with making and declaring the law—legislatures and courts—that lays down the rule that persons without substantial capacity to know or control the act shall be excused.

28. A. Goldstein, The Insanity Defense 81-82 (1967).

The jury is concerned with applying the community understanding of this broad rule to particular lay and medical facts. Where the matter is unclear it naturally will call on its own sense of justice to help it determine the matter. There is wisdom in the view that a jury generally understands well enough that an instruction composed in flexible terms gives it sufficient latitude so that, without disregarding the instruction, it can provide that application of the instruction which harmonizes with its sense of justice.[29] The ALI rule generally communicates that meaning. Wade v. United States, supra, 426 F.2d at 70-71. This is recognized even by those who might prefer a more explicit statement of the matter.[30] It is one thing, however, to tolerate and even welcome the jury's sense of equity as a force that affects its application of instructions which state the legal rules that crystallize the requirements of justice as determined by the lawmakers of the community. It is quite another to set the jury at large, without such crystallization, to evolve its own legal rules and standards of justice. It would likely be counter-productive and contrary to the larger interest of justice to become so explicit—in an effort to hammer the point home to the very occasional jury that would otherwise be too rigid—that one puts serious strains on the normal operation of the system of criminal justice.

Taking all these considerations into account we conclude that the ALI rule as announced is not productive of injustice, and we decline to proclaim the broad "justly responsible" standard.

5. ALI RULE IS CONTEMPLATED AS IMPROVING THE PROCESS OF ADJUDICATION, NOT AS AFFECTING NUMBER OF INSANITY ACQUITTALS

Amicus Dempsey is concerned that a change by this court from *Durham-McDonald* to ALI will be taken as an indication that this court intends that the number and percentage of insantity acquittals be modified. That is not the intendment of the rule adopted today, nor do we have any basis for forecasting that effect.

a. Statistical data concerning the use of insanity in criminal trials in this jurisdiction were presented in the December 15, 1966, Report of the President's Commission on Crime in the District of Columbia.[31] These data have been up-dated in Mr. Dempsey's brief, with the aid of data helpfully supplied by the United States Attorney's office. At least since *Durham* was modified by *McDonald,* insanity acquittals have run at about 2 percent of all cases terminated. In the seven years subsequent to *McDonald* jury verdicts of not guilty by

29. See H. Kalven and H. Zeisel, The American Jury (1966), passim, and particularly Chapters 5, 8, 12, 15 et seq. See also, Rifkind, Follow-up: The Jury, The Center Magazine 59, 64 (July, 1970).

30. See, e.g., the response of the Attorney General in Ramer v. United States, 390 F.2d 564, 575, n.10 (9th Cir. en banc, 1968).

31. See ch. 7, section III: The Mentally Ill Offender, subsection "Experience Under the Durham Rule," at p.534 ff. of the Report, including Tables 1-10.

reason of insanity averaged only 3 per annum.[32] In trials by the court, there has been an annual average of about 38 verdicts of not guilty by reason of insanity; these typically are cases where the Government psychiatrists agreed that the crime was the product of mental illness.[33] We perceive no basis in these data for any conclusion that the number of percentage of insanity acquittals has been either excessive or inadequate.

We have no way of forecasting what will be the effect on verdicts, of juries or judges, from the reduction in influence of expert testimony on "productivity" that reflects judgments outside the domain of expertise.[34] Whatever its effect, we are confident that the rule adopted today provides a sounder relationship in terms of the giving, comprehension and application of expert testimony. Our objective is not to steer the jury's verdict but to enhance its deliberation.[35]

b. Some judges have viewed the ALI test as going beyond *Durham* in enlarging the category of persons who may win acquittals.[36] The 1966 report of the President's Crime Commission (supra note 15) apparently concludes that the debate over *Durham* was stilled by *McDonald,* and that *Durham-McDonald* is not significantly different in content from the ALI test. In contrast, Mr. Dempsey is concerned that a person's ability to control his behavior could be "substantially impaired" by mental condition, thus qualifying the defense under *McDonald,* while still leaving him with "substantial capacity," rendering the defense unavailable under the ALI rule. We have no way of knowing whether psychiatrists giving testimony would draw such a distinction, and

32. *McDonald* was decided in 1962. For fiscal years ending June 30, 1964-1970, there were 21 verdicts of not guilty by reason of insanity in trials by jury, 265 such verdicts in trials by court. These data appear in Appendix C of Mr. Dempsey's brief, as revised by submission of Sept. 21, 1971.

Mr. Dempsey provides data on all terminations for fiscal 1964-1968. The data for these five years show 7,537 terminations, and 194 verdicts of not guilty by reason of insanity. The other terminations are: 3,500 verdicts of guilty on plea, 1,567 verdicts of guilty after trial, and 629 verdicts of not guilty.

33. These trials are discussed in the amicus submission of David Chambers, consultant, who prepared a report on the John Howard Pavilion at St. Elizabeths Hospital, submitted to the Hospital and the National Institutes of Mental Health.

Professor Chambers characterizes most insanity trials to the courts as more nearly comparable to the taking of guilty pleas—consisting of a stipulated statement of facts; a conclusory Hospital report that the crime was the product of mental illness; and brief supporting testimony from a single John Howard psychiatrist—all in a context of a "tacit or explicit understanding" that the defendant will not contest his indefinite commitment to the Hospital.

34. Any such analysis of the productivity testimony and verdicts not only would require prodigious time and effort, but might well be inconclusive in view of the way experts testifying on the "product" issues come to diametric differences in the same trial.

35. We do not share the cynical view that treats the instruction as devoid of consequence. In a study of the reactions of more than a thousand jurors to two experimental trials involving a defense of insanity, it was found that juries deliberated significantly longer when instructed under *Durham* than under *M'Naghten.* Yet this did not undercut consensus; there was no significant difference in the percentages of hung juries. R. Simon, The Jury and the Defense of Insanity 213 ff. (1967).

36. See the opinion of Trask, J., for six of the 13 judges on the Ninth Circuit, in Wade v. United States, 426 F.2d 64, 75, 79.

moreover there would be no difference in result unless one also indulges the assumption, which is dubious, that the jury would reason that the crime may have been the "product" of the mental condition of a man even though he retained substantial capacity.

In the last analysis, however, if there is a case where there would be a difference in result—and it would seem rare—we think the underlying freedom of will conception renders it just to assign responsibility to a person, even though his controls have been impaired, if his residual controls give him "substantial capacity" both to appreciate the wrongfulness of his conduct and to conform it to the requirement of law. Whether the ALI standard is to be given a narrow or broad conception rests not on abstract analysis[37] but on the application reflecting the underlying sense of responsibility of the jury, as the community's surrogate.[38]

6. ELEMENTS OF THE ALI RULE ADOPTED BY THIS COURT

Though it provides a general uniformity, the ALI rule leaves room for variations. Thus, we have added an adjustment in the *McDonald* definition of mental disease, which we think fully compatible with both the spirit and text of the ALI rule. In the interest of good administration, we now undertake to set forth, with such precision as the subject will permit, other elements of the ALI rule as adopted by this court.

The two main components of the rule define (1) mental disease, (2) the consequences thereof that exculpate from responsibility.

a. *Intermesh of Components*

The first component of our rule, derived from *McDonald,* defines mental disease or defect as an abnormal condition of the mind, and a condition which substantially (a) affects mental or emotional processes and (b) impairs behavioral controls. The second component, derived from the Model Penal Code, tells which defendant with a mental disease lacks criminal responsibility for particular conduct: it is the defendant who, as a result of this mental condition, at the time of such conduct, either (i) lacks substantial capacity to appreciate that his conduct is wrongful, or (ii) lacks substantial capacity to conform his conduct to the law.

The first component establishes eligibility for an instruction concerning

37. Mr. Dempsey is concerned lest the ALI test assigns responsibility unless capacity has been reduced "to the vagrant and trivial dimensions characteristic of the most severe afflictions of the mind," see Wechsler, Codification of Criminal Law in the United States: The Model Penal Code, 68 Colum. L. Rev. 1425, 1443 (1968). But the application in fact will depend in the last analysis on the jury's application of community standards to the evidence adduced.

38. Even under *McDonald* the jury has frequently brought in a verdict of guilty, when the exculpatory rules would plainly permit, or even contemplate, a verdict of not guilty by reason of insanity. King v. United States, supra.

the defense for a defendant who presents evidence that his abnormal condition of the mind has substantially impaired behavioral controls. The second component completes the instruction and defines the ultimate issue, of exculpation, in terms of whether his behavioral controls were not only substantially impaired but impaired to such an extent that he lacked substantial capacity to conform his conduct to the law.[39]

b. The "Result" of the Mental Disease

The rule contains a requirement of causality, as is clear from the term "result." Exculpation is established not by mental disease alone but only if "as a result" defendant lacks the substantial capacity required for responsibility. Presumably the mental disease of a kleptomaniac does not entail as a "result" a lack of capacity to conform to the law prohibiting rape.

c. At the Time of the Conduct

Under the ALI rule the issue is not whether defendant is so disoriented or void of controls that he is never able to conform to external demands, but whether he had that capacity at the time of the conduct. The question is not properly put in terms of whether he would have capacity to conform in some untypical restraining situation—as with an attendant or policeman at his elbow. The issue is whether he was able to conform in the unstructured condition of life in an open society, and whether the result of his abnormal mental condition was a lack of substantial internal controls. These matters are brought out in the ALI's comments to §4.01 of the Model Penal Code Tentative Draft No. 4, p.158:

> The schizophrenic . . . is disoriented from reality; the disorientation is extreme; but it is rarely total. Most psychotics will respond to a command of someone in authority within the mental hospital; they thus have some capacity to conform to a norm. But this is very different from the question whether they have the capacity to conform to requirements that are not thus immediately symbolized by an attendant or policeman at the elbow. Nothing makes the inquiry into responsibility more unreal for the psychiatrist than limitation of the issue to some ultimate extreme of total incapacity, when clinical experience reveals only a graded scale with marks along the way.

d. Capacity to Appreciate Wrongfulness of His Conduct

As to the option of terminology noted in the ALI code, we adopt the formulation that exculpates a defendant whose mental condition is such that he lacks substantial capacity to appreciate the wrongfulness of his conduct. We prefer this on pragmatic grounds to "appreciate the criminality of his con-

39. Defendant is also exculpated if he lacks substantial capacity to appreciate the conduct is wrongful.

duct" since the resulting jury instruction is more like that conventionally given to and applied by the jury. While such an instruction is of course subject to the objection that it lacks complete precision, it serves the objective of calling on the jury to provide a community judgment on a combination of factors. And since the possibility of analytical differences between the two formulations is insubstantial in fact in view of the control capacity test, we are usefully guided by the pragmatic considerations pertinent to jury instructions.[40]

In adopting the ALI formulation, this court does not follow the *Currens* opinion of the Third Circuit, which puts it that the sole issue in every case is defendant's capacity to control his behavior, and that as a matter of analysis a person who lacks substantial capacity to appreciate the wrongfulness [criminality] of his conduct necessarily lacks substantial capacity to control his behavior. Like the other circuits, we resist the *Currens* lure of logic in order to make certain that the jury will give heed to the substantiality of a defense of lack of substantial capacity to appreciate wrongfulness, a point that may elude a jury instructed solely in terms of control capacity. In a particular case, however, defendant may have reason to request omission of the phrase pertaining to lack of capacity to appreciate wrongfulness, if that particular matter is not involved on the facts, and defendant fears that a jury that does not attend rigorously to the details of the instruction may erroneously suppose that the defense is lost if defendant appreciates wrongfulness. Here again, it is not enough to rely solely on logic, when a simple change will aid jury understanding. In such a case, if defendant requests, the judge should limit the instruction to the issue involved in that case, and charge that the jury shall bring in a verdict of not guilty if as a result of mental illness defendant lacked substantial capacity to conform his conduct to the requirements of the law.

40. In *M'Naghten's* case, 10 Cl. & F. 200, 211, 8 Eng. Rep. 718, 722 (H.L. 1843), the majority opinion of Lord Chief Justice Tindal ruled that the jury should be instructed in terms of the ability of the accused "to know that he was doing an act that was wrong," adding: "If the question were to be put as to the knowledge of the accused solely and exclusively with reference to the law of the land, it might tend to confound the jury, by inducing them to be believe that an actual knowledge of the law of the land was essential in order to lead to a conviction."

When the question arose as to whether "wrong" means moral or legal wrong, the American courts split. One group, following *M'Naghten,* held the offender sane if he knew the act was prohibited by law. A second group, following the lead of Judge Cardozo in People v. Schmidt, 216 N.Y. 324, 110 N.E. 945, 948-950 (1915) ruled that, e.g., the defense was available to a defendant who knew the killing was legally wrong but thought it morally right because he was so ordered by God. The issue is discussed and authorities collected in A. Goldstein, The Insanity Defense, and notes thereto. In Sauer v. United States, 241 F.2d 640, 649 (9th Cir. 1957), Judge Barnes summed up the practicalities: "[The] practice has been to state merely the word 'wrong' and leave the decision for the jury. While not entirely condonable, such practice is explained in large measure by an awareness that the jury will eventually exercise a moral judgment as to the sanity of the accused."

This issue rarely arose under *M'Naghten,* and its substantiality was reduced if not removed by the control capacity test, since anyone under a delusion as to God's mandate would presumably lack substantial capacity to conform his conduct to the requirements of the law.

We are not informed of any case where a mental illness left a person with capacity to appreciate wrongfulness but not a capacity to appreciate criminality. If such a case ever arises, supported by credible evidence, the court can then consider its correct disposition more meaningfully, in the light of a concrete record.

e. Caveat Paragraph

Section 4.01 of the Model Penal Code as promulgated by ALI contains in subsection (2) what has come to be known as the "caveat paragraph":

> (2) The terms "mental disease or defect" do not include an abnormality manifested only by repeated criminal or otherwise anti-social conduct.

The purpose of this provision was to exclude a defense for the so-called "psychopathic personality."[41]

There has been a split in the Federal circuits concerning this provision. Some of the courts adopting the ALI rule refer to both subsections but without separate discussion of the caveat paragraph—as in the *Chandler* and *Blake* opinion. As to the decisions considering the point, those of the Second and Third Circuits conclude the paragraph should be retained (in *Freeman* and *Currens*), while the *Smith* and *Wade* decisions, of the Sixth and Ninth Circuits, conclude it should be omitted. The Sixth Circuit's position is (404 F.2d at 727, fn. 8) that there is "great dispute over the psychiatric soundness" of the caveat paragraph. The *Wade* opinion considers the matter at great length and puts forward three grounds for rejecting the caveat paragraph: (1) As a practical matter, it would be ineffectual in keeping sociopaths out of the definition of insanity; it is always possible to introduce some evidence, other than past criminal behavior, to support a plea of insanity. (2) The criminal sanction ought not be sought for criminal psychopaths—constant recidivists—because such people should be taken off the streets indefinitely, and not merely for a set term of years. (3) Its third ground is stated thus (426 F.2d at 73):

> It is unclear whether [the caveat paragraph] would require that a defendant be considered legally sane if, although the only overt acts manifesting his disease or defect were "criminal or otherwise anti-social," there arises from his acts a reasonable inference of mental derangement either because of the nature of the acts or because of credible medical or other evidence.

Our own approach is influenced by the fact that our rule already includes a definition of mental disease (from *McDonald*). Under that definition, as we

41. See Comments to Fourth Draft, p.160:

> 6. Paragraph (2) of section 4.01 is designed to exclude from the concept of "mental disease or defect" the case of so-called "psychopathic personality." The reason for the exclusion is that, as the Royal Commission put it, psychopathy "is a statistical abnormality; that is to say, the psychopath differs from a normal person only quantitatively or in degree, not qualitatively; and the diagnosis of psychopathic personality does not carry with it any explanation of the causes of the abnormality." While it may not be feasible to formulate a definition of "disease," there is much to be said for excluding a condition that is manifested only by the behavior phenomena that must, by hypothesis, be the result of disease for irresponsibility to be established. Although British psychiatrists had agreed, on the whole, that psychopathy should not be called "disease," there is considerable difference of opinion on the point in the United States. Yet it does not seem useful to contemplate the litigation of what is essentially a matter of terminology; nor is it right to have the legal result rest upon the resolution of a dispute of this kind.

have pointed out, the mere existence of "a long criminal record does not excuse crime." Williams v. United States, 114 U.S. App. D.C. 135, 137, 312 F.2d 862, 864 (1962). We do not require the caveat paragraph as an insurance against exculpation of the deliberate and persistent offender.[42] Our *McDonald* rule guards against the danger of misunderstanding and injustice that might arise, say, from an expert's classification that reflects only a conception[43] defining all criminality as reflective of mental illness. There must be testimony to show both that the defendant was suffering from an abnormal condition of the mind and that it substantially affected mental or emotional processes and substantially impaired behavioral controls.

In this context, our pragmatic approach is to adopt the caveat paragraph as a rule for application by the judge, to avoid miscarriage of justice, but not for inclusion in instructions to the jury.

The judge will be aware that the criminal and antisocial conduct of a person—on the street, in the home, in the ward—is necessarily material information for assessment by the psychiatrist. On the other hand, rarely if ever would a psychiatrist base a conclusion of mental disease solely on criminal and anti-social acts. Our pragmatic solution provides for reshaping the rule, for application by the court, as follows: The introduction or proffer of past criminal and anti-social actions is not admissible as evidence of mental disease unless accompanied by expert testimony, supported by a showing of the concordance of a responsible segment of professional opinion, that the particular characteristics of these actions constitute convincing evidence of an underlying mental disease that substantially impairs behavioral controls.

This formulation retains the paragraph as a "caveat" rather than an inexorable rule of law. It should serve to obviate distortions of the present state of knowledge that would constitute miscarriages of justice. Yet it leaves the door open—on shouldering the "convincing evidence" burden—to accommodate our general rule to developments that may lie ahead. It is the kind of imperfect, but not unfeasible, accommodation of the abstract and pragmatic that is often found to serve the administration of justice.

We do not think it desirable to use the caveat paragraph as a basis for instructions to the jury. It would be difficult for a juryman—or anyone else—to reconcile the caveat paragraph and the basic (*McDonald*) definition of mental disease if a psychiatrist testified that he discerned from particular past criminal behavior a pattern that established defendant as suffering from an abnormal condition of the mind that substantially impaired behavioral controls. If there is no such testimony, then there would be no evidence that mere misconduct betokens mental illness, it would be impermissible for defense

42. We note that the Second Circuit adopted the caveat paragraph on the ground that a contrary holding would reduce to absurdity a test designed to encourage full analysis of all psychiatric data and would exculpate those who knowingly and deliberately seek a life of crime. (*Freeman,* 357 F.2d at 625).

43. See, e.g., D. Abrahamsen, Who Are the Guilty? 125 (1952).

counsel to present such a hypothesis to the jury, and there would be very little likelihood that a jury would arrive at such a proposition on its own. On the other hand, an instruction along the lines of the caveat paragraph runs the risk of appearing to call for the rejection of testimony that is based materially, but only partially, on the history of criminal conduct.

f. Broad Presentation to the Jury

Our adoption of the ALI rule does not depart from the doctrines this court has built up over the past twenty years to assure a broad presentation to the jury concerning the condition of defendant's mind and its consequences. Thus we adhere to our rulings admitting expert testimony of psychologists,[44] as well as psychiatrists, and to our many decisions contemplating that expert testimony on this subject will be accompanied by presentation of the facts and premises underlying the opinions and conclusions of the experts,[45] and that the Government and defense may present, in Judge Blackmun's words, "all possibly relevant evidence" bearing on cognition, volition and capacity.[46] We agree with the amicus submission of the National District Attorneys Association that the law cannot "distinguish between physiological, emotional, social and cultural sources of the impairment"—assuming, of course, requisite testimony establishing exculpation under the pertinent standard—and all such causes may be both referred to by the expert and considered by the trier of fact.[47]

Breadth of input under the insanity defense is not to be confused with breadth of the doctrines establishing the defense. As the National District Attorneys Association brief points out, the latitude for salient evidence of, e.g., social and cultural factors pertinent to an abnormal condition of the mind significantly affecting capacity and controls, does not mean that such factors may be taken as establishing a separate defense for persons whose mental condition is such that blame can be imposed. We have rejected a broad "injustice" approach that would have opened the door to expositions of, e.g., cultural deprivation, unrelated to any abnormal condition of the mind.

We have recognized that "Many criminologists point out that even normal human behavior is influenced by such factors as training, environment, poverty and the like, which may limit the understanding and options of the individual." King v. United States, supra, 125 U.S. App. D.C. at 323, 372 F.2d at 388. Determinists may contend that every man's fate is ultimately sealed by his genes and environment, over which he has no control. Our jurisprudence, however, while not oblivious to deterministic components, ultimately rests on a premise of freedom of will. This is not to be viewed as an

44. Jenkins v. United States, 113 U.S. App. D.C. 300, 307 F.2d 637 (en banc, 1962) (assuming substantial experience in the diagnosis of disease in association with psychiatrists or neurologists).

45. E.g., the opinions in *Durham, Carter, McDonald* and *Washington,* and Judge Burger's concurring opinion in *Blocker.*

46. Pope v. United States, 372 F.2d 710, 736 (8th Cir. 1967).

47. The Association points out that "the effects of poverty, historical factors and prejudice may well have an adverse effect upon an individual's mental condition."

exercise in philosophic discourse, but as a governmental fusion of ethics and necessity, which takes into account that a system of rewards and punishments is itself part of the environment that influences and shapes human conduct. Our recognition of an insanity defense for those who lack the essential, threshold free will possessed by those in the normal range is not to be twisted, directly or indirectly, into a device for exculpation of those without an abnormal condition of the mind.

Finally, we have not accepted suggestions to adopt a rule that disentangles the insanity defense from a medical model, and announces a standard exculpating anyone whose capacity for control is insubstantial, for whatever cause or reason. There may be logic in these submissions, but we are not sufficiently certain of the nature, range and implications of the conduct involved to attempt an all-embracing unified field theory. The applicable rule can be discerned as the cases arise in regard to other conditions—somnambulism or other automatisms; blackouts due, e.g., to overdose of insulin; drug addiction. Whether these somatic conditions should be governed by a rule comparable to that herein set forth for mental disease would require, at a minimum, a judicial determination, which takes medical opinion into account, finding convincing evidence of an ascertainable condition characterized by "a broad consensus that free will does not exist." Salzman v. United States, 131 U.S. App. D.C. 393, 400, 405 F.2d 358, 365 (1968) (concurring opinion of Judge Wright).

E. Inter-related Doctrines and Implementing Instructions

For sake of clarity, and to obviate misunderstanding and unnecessary litigation, we undertake by today's ruling to accompany our definition of the underlying doctrine on insanity as a defense negativing criminal responsibility, with comments on implementing instructions and certain inter-related doctrines as they will stand hereafter.

1. Suggested Instruction

Appendix B contains a suggested instruction in the thought that the trial judges may consider it useful for their consideration and guidance in the task of making the adjustments in practices and routines required by our ruling.

Burden of Proof

Appendix B contains alternate wordings on burden of proof. One wording conforms to the doctrine of Davis v. United States, 160 U.S. 469, 16 S. Ct. 353, 40 L. Ed. 499 (1895), that the Government has the burden of proving beyond a reasonable doubt that the defendant was not entitled to exculpation as a result of his mental disease or defect. The other version is cast in the wording of the last sentence of 24 D.C. Code §301(j), as added to the law in 1970:[48] "No person accused of an offense shall be acquitted on the ground that he was insane at the time of its commission unless his insanity, regardless of who raises the issue, is affirmatively established by a preponderance of the evidence."

Questions have been raised as to the constitutionality of this 1970 provision,[49] its applicability to offenses committed prior to the 1970 enactment, and its applicability to offenses committed in the District of Columbia which are not violations of the D.C.Code but are violations of the United States Code.[50] We do not think it appropriate to decide such questions at this time, and accordingly have provided alternate versions in the instruction suggested in Appendix B.

2. THE "LYLES" INSTRUCTION—AS TO EFFECT OF VERDICT OF NOT GUILTY BY REASON OF INSANITY

By a statute of August 9, 1955, passed in the wake of *Durham,* Congress added to 24 D.C.Code §301, provisions on mandatory commitment of persons acquitted by reason of insanity, set forth in subsection (d), and provisions governing the release of persons so committed, set forth in subsection (e).

In Lyles v. United States, 103 U.S. App. D.C. 22, 254 F.2d 725 (en banc, 1957), the majority of the court concurred in Part I of the opinion filed by Judges Prettyman and Burger that the jury, which knows the meaning of a verdict of guilty and not guilty, "has a right to know the meaning of [the insanity] verdict as accurately as it knows by common knowledge the meaning of the other two possible verdicts." The court said, 103 U.S. App. D.C. at 25, 254 F.2d at 728:

> We think that when the instruction is given the jury should simply be informed that a verdict of not guilty by reason of insanity means that the accused will be confined in a hospital for the mentally ill until the superintendent has certified, and the court is satisfied, that such person has recovered his sanity and will not in the reasonable future be dangerous to himself or others, in which event and at which time the court shall order his release either unconditionally or under such conditions as the court may see fit.

48. By §207(6) of the D.C. Court Reform and Criminal Procedure Act of 1970, P.L. 91-358.

49. E.g., Bazelon, C. J., concurring in United States v. Eichberg, 142 U.S. App. D.C. 110, 114, 439 F.2d 620, 624 (1971), where the vitality of Leland v. Oregon, 343 U.S. 790, 72 S. Ct. 1002, 96 L. Ed. 1302 (1952) is questioned in view of In re Winship, 397 U.S. 358, 90 S. Ct. 1068, 25 L. Ed. 2d 368 (1970).

See also Report of the President's D.C. Crime Commission (1966) 553: "The majority of the Commission also believes that the views of the dissenting justices in Leland v. Oregon are grounds for caution. . . . We believe that there is at least a substantial question whether requiring the defendant to prove insanity in a Federal court would be upheld by the Supreme Court."

50. United States v. Thompson, 147 U.S. App. D.C. 1, 452 F.2d 1333 (1971).

The court provided for omission of such an instruction on the affirmative request of a defendant.

Bolton v. Harris, 130 U.S. App. D.C. 1, 395 F.2d 642 (1968) read §301(d) as permitting mandatory commitment for the purpose of a mental examination, but as containing a requirement of a judicial hearing, on the question of whether the defendant involved ought to be retained in custody on the basis of his current mental condition, with procedures substantially similar to those in proceedings, under 21 D.C.Code §545(b), for civil commitment of the dangerous mentally ill. The court also construed §301(e) to entitle the patient to periodic examinations by the hospital staff, to an examination by an outside psychiatrist, and to a court hearing if any one of the examining physicians believes he should no longer be hospitalized.

Finally, the court construed §301(g), reserving the right of a confined person to establish eligibility for release under this section by habeas corpus, to require the person confined to prove by a preponderance of the evidence that his detention is illegal. "Thus, the court must find, by the preponderance of the evidence, that the patient's commitment is no longer valid—i.e., that he is no longer 'likely to injure himself or other persons' due to 'mental illness.' " (130 U.S. App. D.C. at 12, 395 F.2d at 653.) The Court referred to its ruling as similar to that in the concurring opinion of Judge Fahy in Ragsdale v. Overholser, 108 U.S. App. D.C. 308, 315, 281 F.2d 943, 950 (1960).

As to the *Lyles* instruction, the *Bolton* opinion (at note 50) held that it should be changed to comport with the procedures then construed to be required under the law. The D.C. Court Reform and Criminal Procedure Act of 1970, P.L. 91-358, retained what was formerly §301(d) as §301(d)(1) of 24 D.C. Code, and retained a §301(e) unchanged. Accordingly, the 1970 law retains the Bolton v. Harris construction of what is now §301(d)(1), as providing mandatory commitment for the purpose of examination, and its construction of §301(e), as to provisions for release. However, the 1970 law adds a new provision, see 24 D.C. Code §301(d)(2):

> (2) A person confined pursuant to paragraph (1) shall have a hearing, unless waived, within 50 days of his confinement to determine whether he is entitled to release from custody. At the conclusion of the criminal action referred to in paragraph (1) of this subsection, the court shall provide such person with representation by counsel—
>
> (A) in the case of a person who is eligible to have counsel appointed by the court, by continuing any appointment of counsel made to represent such person in the prior criminal action or by appointing new counsel; or
>
> (B) in the case of a person who is not eligible to have counsel appointed by the court, by assuring representation by retained counsel. If the hearing is not waived, the court shall cause notice of the hearing to be served upon the person, his counsel, and the prosecuting attorney and hold the hearing. Within ten days from

> the date the hearing was begun, the court shall determine the issues and make findings of fact and conclusions of law with respect thereto. The person confined shall have the burden of proof. If the court finds by a preponderance of the evidence that the person confined is entitled to his release from custody, either conditional or unconditional, the court shall enter such order as may appear appropriate.

Section 301(d)(2), as added in 1970, gives specific implementation to the construction of Bolton v. Harris, which requires a judicial hearing, following the initial examination, prior to an order of mandatory commitment under 301(d). It differs to the extent that Bolton v. Harris contemplated a burden of proof on the Government in 301(d) commitment proceedings, like that in civil commitment proceedings. Section 301(d)(2) now provides that the person confined "shall have the burden of proof"—to establish eligiblity for release under the standards of §301(e). Accordingly the *Lyles* instruction must be recast as to persons governed by the 1970 law. This is a suggested form:

> If the defendant is found not guilty by reason of insanity, it becomes the duty of the court to commit him to St. Elizabeths Hospital. There will be a hearing within 50 days to determine whether defendant is entitled to release. In that hearing the defendant has the burden of proof. The defendant will remain in custody, and will be entitled to release from custody only if the court finds by preponderance of the evidence that he is not likely to injure himself or other persons due to mental illness.

As to the possibility of an attack on the constitutionality of §301(d)(2), that question has not been briefed or argued, and it is not now being decided.[51]

3. MENTAL CONDITION, THOUGH INSUFFICIENT TO EXONERATE, MAY BE RELEVANT TO SPECIFIC MENTAL ELEMENT OF CERTAIN CRIMES OR DEGREES OF CRIME.

Our decision accompanies the redefinition of when a mental condition exonerates a defendant from criminal responsibility with the doctrine that expert testimony as to a defendant's abnormal mental condition may be received and considered, as tending to show, in a responsible way, that defendant did not have the specific mental state required for a particular crime or degree of crime—even though he was aware that his act was wrongful and was able to control it, and hence was not entitled to complete exoneration.

51. In *Bolton* the court relied in part on the circumstances that an acquittal by reason of insanity might reflect only a doubt as to sanity. This may be affected by the 1970 provision putting the trial burden on defendant to establish his insanity.

We are not addressing ourselves to the procedure that would result if a court concludes that §301(d)(2) is unconstitutional.

Some of the cases following this doctrine use the term "diminished responsibility," but we prefer the example of the cases that avoid this term, for its convenience is outweighed by its confusion: Our doctrine has nothing to do with "diminishing" responsibility of a defendant because of his impaired mental condition,[52] but rather with determining whether the defendant had the mental state that must be proved as to all defendants. . . .

F. Disposition of the Case

1. ISSUE OF CAUSALITY TESTIMONY

We are urged to reverse appellant's conviction on the ground that the trial court erred in allowing Government experts to testify in terms of "causality."

The rule of Washington v. United States, 129 U.S. App. D.C. 29, 390 F.2d 444 (1967) that experts must not frame their testimony in terms of "product," was aimed at relieving a stubborn and recurring problem—that of experts using their facility with the esoteric and imprecise language of mental disease to exert an undue dominion over the jury's deliberations. The *Washington* opinion did not refer to the prior opinion in Harried v. United States, 128 U.S. App. D.C. 330, 389 F.2d 281 (1967), wherein the court stated that narrowly drawn, concrete questions addressed to the experts on the causal connection between the forbidden act and alleged mental disease were permissible.

Since both *Washington* and *Harried* are superseded—on this point—by our change today of the ultimate rule, it would be bootless to consider to what extent *Washington* superseded *Harried.* It suffices for disposition of this case to say only: (1) Under the rule of *Harried* the questioning of Government experts on the question of the causal connection between appellant's crime and his mental disease or defect was proper. (2) Assuming, arguendo, that these questions were not consonant with *Washington* we are unable, on this record, to discern prejudice. We think the expert testimony in this case adequately and lucidly ventilated the issues, there was no use of the term "product," and we see no sign of overreaching.[53]

52. Our doctrine is different from the doctrine of "partial responsibility" that permits a jury to find that a defendant's mental condition was such that he is only "partly responsible," and therefore entitled to a verdict reducing the degree of the offense. See Model Penal Code, Comments to Art. 201. app. B at 111 (Tentative Draft No. 9, 1959), quoting the English Homicide Act of 1957, 5 & 6 Eliz. 2, c. 11.

53. Compare Washington v. United States, 129 U.S. App. D.C. 29, 35, 390 F.2d 444, 450 (1967):

> [T]he persistent use of conclusory labels may have hindered the jury in getting to the underlying facts. But we think the jury obtained enough concrete information to preclude us from disturbing the verdict. The defense psychiatrists and, on cross-examination, the Government psychiatrists gave some meaningful descriptions of defendant's mental and emotional processes. . . . [T]aken as a whole, the testimony in this case was, if anything, a little better than in most insanity cases. Under these circumstances, reversal seems inappropriate.

Our conclusion is also impelled by the fact that it was defendant himself who first sought expert testimony on the question of causal connection. The doctrine of curative admissibility rests upon "the necessity of removing prejudice in the interest of fairness," United States v. Winston, 145 U.S. App. D.C. 67, 447 F.2d 1236, 1240 (1971), quoting Crawford v. United States, 91 U.S. App. D.C. 234, 237, 198 F.2d 976, 979 (1952). In this case, the interests of fairness were served by permitting additional inquiry on the subject of the relationship between the murder and the appellant's mental status. Defense questioning established that, in the opinion of defense experts, there was a causal connection between the act and the defendant's mental disorder. It would be unfair, and against the interest of justice, for us to hold that the jury had to retire to consider the case believing that this question was beyond medical dispute.

2. PROSECUTOR'S CONDUCT

It is also urged upon us that reversal of appellant's conviction is required because the prosecutor went beyond the limits of the permissible in his summation, by attempting to discredit the projective tests the St. Elizabeths psychologist had given to the defendant. Excerpts from this summation are set out in a footnote.[54]

It is unfortunate that the prosecutor's summation incorporated, as an approach to the projective tests: "After all, they are just blots of ink." The prosecutor, who speaks in court in behalf of the public interest, has a respon-

54. "Now, another one, you remember on the same test, that drawing test, the doctor said he had ten of those little things and they had squiggles and lines and angles, and he was asked to draw those, ten of them separately. And the doctor said he rotated, he rotated one. And I said, well, what was the significance of that. Well, the significance is that shows that there is organic brain damage. That is a very hard indicator of organic brain damage. Why organic brain damage. He said he meant structural damage, something physically wrong with the brain, a part missing, a dead cell, something like that, a lesion in the brain.

"And I asked the doctor how many of them did he rotate, how many of them did he turn the picture a little bit. I asked him how many did he rotate 90 degrees, and I think he said it was, how many out of those ten—one. That is a hard indicator, that is a hard indicator of organic brain damage.

"Ladies and gentlemen, then we came to that ink blot, and the doctor said, well, the usual thing about that was those anatomical things, and how many of them were there. Well, let's see, and he counts, and there are four. How many responses. Fourteen of them. Fourteen responses and four of them turn out to be anatomical things—hearts or whatever it happened to be.

"Is there something unusual about that? Is a man crazy when he sees a heart or something else four times, four different anatomical things or maybe the same things in those little drawings, these little ink blots. And [after] all, they are just blots of ink. Is a man crazy when he sees them? And how about that last one, that rocket one. He says he sees a rocket going off.

"I asked him doctor, was there any rocket fired during that period of time that might stick in a man's brain and might suggest it to him. The doctor doesn't know. But there is something explosive about a personality if he sees a rocket on a little ink blot.

"Well, ladies and gentlemen, there is not much I can say about that; I am not an expert. You heard the expert on the stand and he testified about that.

"But I can say one thing: that it is a jury decision. It is your province. It is your function to take that evidence and weigh that evidence and decide whether what that doctor said as far as you are concerned made any sense at all."

sibility to refrain from know-nothing appeals to ignorance. The prosecutor is not free to offer his own opinions and attitudes on matters of expert knowledge, even in camouflaged form. The prosecutor was free to adduce appropriate expert testimony, on direct or cross-examination, to attack the validity of such tests, or perhaps to adduce limitations on their value and significance. However, in this trial the prosecutor's cross-examination was not oriented in that manner, but sought rather to probe the basis for the expert's conclusion, and his use of the tests. That was an entirely permissible course, particularly since the witness agreed that interpretation of the tests involves a subjective evaluation, over and above the underlying training and expertise of the expert. But there was neither testimony adduced on cross-examination, nor testimony of a prosecutor's witness, to support a disparagement of the very concept of projective tests, as based on mere ink blots.

While the prosecutor's summation contains an approach we do not expect to recur, it was neither as aggravated nor as prolonged as that in *King.*[55] And the record context includes clarifying questions by the trial judge that brought out for the jury both the long and widespread use of projective tests, and their use as a basis for this expert's conclusions. We do not find reversible error.

3. REMAND

Our action today in stating a new rule for insanity, and for receipt and consideration of expert testimony on abnormal mental condition that does not establish an insanity defense but is material to a substantive element of the offense, is effective prospectively for all trials beginning after this date. However, under established doctrines of the judicial function we conclude that the benefit of the rule cannot wholly be withheld from the defendant in whose case it was established. We do not, however, think it appropriate for us to determine at this juncture whether a jury which convicted under our old insanity standard might have acquitted under the new standard. While we hesitate to burden the trial judge further, we are remanding to the trial judge to determine whether a new trial is appropriate in the interest of justice, rather than considering that question at the appellate level in the first instance, because the trial judge has a superior vantage point for assessing whether there is a substantial possibility that the jury, if instructed under our new rule, would have found that appellant should be acquitted by reason of insanity. If a new trial is denied, the trial judge will re-enter a judgment on the verdict of guilty. . . .

55. In King v. United States, we pointed out (at 125 U.S. App. D.C. 325, 372 F.2d 390):

[T]he prosecutor persistently drummed into the jury—without evidentiary basis, and contrary to the uncontradicted testimony of the Government psychiatrists called by the defense—the assertion that organic [brain] damage was negatived by the failure to detect it by physical tests, and that psychological tests could not establish organic brain damage. . . .

The case is remanded for further consideration by the District Court in accordance with this opinion.

So ordered.

Appendix A

Letter of February 5, 1971, from the Clerk to organizations invited to make a submission amicus curiae.

The Court has directed me to request you to discuss in your briefs the following question:

1. In this case all four expert witnesses testified on the issue of "productivity." Assuming arguendo that this testimony violated the rule of Washington v. United States, 129 U.S. App. D.C. 29, 390 F.2d 444 (1967), is the *Washington* rule a viable device for limiting the role of the expert and preserving the ultimate question of criminal responsibility for the jury? Would it be more effective simply to eliminate the separate inquiry into productivity from our test of responsibility? See United States v. Eichberg, 142 U.S. App. D.C. 110 at 117, 118, 439 F.2d 620 at 627, 628 (Decided Jan. 21, 1971) concurring opinion).
2. What are the theoretical and practical differences between the *Durham-McDonald* test of criminal responsibility, the ALI test, and the various other tests that have been proposed in recent years by courts and commentators?
3. Should the *Durham-McDonald* formulation be retained as it is?
4. Should the ALI formulation be adopted?
5. If so, should the *McDonald* definition of "mental disease or defect" be applied to the ALI formulation?
6. If a defendant's behavior controls are impaired, should a test of criminal responsibility distinguish between physiological, emotional, social, and cultural sources of the impairment? Is it appropriate to tie a test of criminal responsibility to the medical model of mental illness? See United States v. Eichberg, supra, 142 U.S. App. D.C. at 116, 117, 439 F.2d at 626, 627.
7. Should the results of psychological tests such as the Rorschach test be admissible in evidence? If so, what kind of testimony is necessary or appropriate in order to put the test results in proper perspective?
8. Have we departed in practice, if not in theory, from the rule that the government has the burden of proving criminal responsibility beyond a reasonable doubt? See United States v. Eichberg, supra, 142 U.S. App. D.C. at 113-116, 439 F.2d at 623-626.
9. Would it be sound as a matter of policy to abolish the insanity defense? Possible as a matter of law? If so, what are the possible alternatives? Should the issues presently treated under that heading be subsumed under the inquiry

into *mens rea*? Should we reconsider the possibility of "diminished" or "partial" responsibility?

Should you wish a copy of the transcript, I should be pleased to furnish it to you if you intend to submit and file a brief.

Sincerely yours,
Nathan J. Paulson
Clerk

APPENDIX B

SUGGESTION FOR INSTRUCTION ON INSANITY*

The defendant in this case asserts the defense of insanity.

You are not to consider this defense unless you have first found that the Government has proved beyond a reasonable doubt each essential element of the offense. One of these elements is the requirement [of premeditation and deliberation for first degree murder] [or of specific intent for ___________], on which you have already been instructed. In determining whether that requirement has been proved beyond a reasonable doubt you may consider the testimony as to the defendant's abnormal mental condition.

If you find that the Government has failed to prove beyond a reasonable doubt any one or more of the essential elements of the offense, you must find the defendant not guilty, and you should not consider any possible verdict relating to insanity.

If you find that the Government has proved each essential element of the offense beyond a reasonable doubt, then you must consider whether to bring in a verdict of not guilty by reason of insanity.

The law provides that a jury shall bring in a verdict of not guilty by reason of insanity if, at the time of the criminal conduct, the defendant, as a result of mental disease or defect, either lacked substantial capacity to conform his conduct to the requirements of the law, or lacked substantial capacity to appreciate the wrongfulness of his conduct.

Every man is presumed to be sane, that is, to be without mental disease or defect, and to be responsible for his acts. But that presumption no longer controls when evidence is introduced that he may have a mental disease or defect.

The term insanity does not require a showing that the defendant was disoriented as to time or place.

* Note: In addition to this instruction, for submission of the insanity issue to the jury, the judge will have given the jury the guidance provided by reading in its presence the instruction to the expert witness required by Washington v. United States, 129 U.S. App. D.C. 29, 42, 390 F.2d 444, 457 (1967), revised in accordance with note 82 of the opinion in United States v. Brawner, 153 U.S. App. D.C. at —, 471 F.2d at 1006.

Mental disease [or defect] includes any abnormal condition of the mind, regardless of its medical label, which substantially affects mental or emotional processes and substantially impairs behavior controls. The term "behavior controls" refers to the processes and capacity of a person to regulate and control his conduct and his actions.

In considering whether the defendant had a mental disease [or defect] at the time of the unlawful act with which he is charged, you may consider testimony in this case concerning the development, adaptation and functioning of these mental and emotional processes and behavior controls.

[The term "mental disease" differs from "mental defect" in that the former is a condition which is either capable of improving or deteriorating and the latter is a condition not capable of improving or deteriorating.]

[Burden of proof—alternate versions:

(a) The burden of proof is on the defendant to establish by a preponderance of the evidence that, as a result of mental disease or defect, he either lacked substantial capacity to conform his conduct to the requirements of the law or lacked substantial capacity to appreciate the wrongfulness of his conduct. If defendant has met that burden you shall bring in a verdict of not guility by reason of insanity. If he has not met that burden you shall bring in a verdict of guilty of the offenses you found proved beyond a reasonable doubt.

(b) The burden is on the Government to prove beyond a reasonable doubt either that the defendant was not suffering from a mental disease or defect, or else that he nevertheless had substantial capacity both to conform his conduct to the requirements of the law and to appreciate the wrongfulness of his conduct. If the Government has not established this beyond a reasonable doubt, you shall bring in a verdict of not guilty by reason of insanity.]

Evaluation of Testimony

In considering the issue of insanity, you may consider the evidence that has been admitted as to the defendant's mental condition before and after the offense charged, as well as the evidence as to defendant's mental condition on that date. The evidence as to the defendant's mental condition before and after that date was admitted solely for the purpose of assisting you to determine the defendant's condition on the date of the alleged offense.

You have heard the evidence of psychiatrists [and psychologists] who testified as expert witnesses. An expert in a particular field is permitted to give his opinion in evidence. In this connection, you are instructed that you are not bound by medical labels, definitions, or conclusions as to what is or is not a mental disease [or defect]. What psychiatrists [and psychologists] may or may not consider a mental disease [or defect] for clinical purposes, where their concern is treatment, may or may not be the same as mental disease [or defect] for the purpose of determining criminal responsibility. Whether the defendant had a mental disease [or defect] must be determined by you under the explanation of those terms as it has been given to you by the Court.

There was also testimony of lay witnesses, with respect to their observations of defendant's appearance, behavior, speech, and actions. Such persons are permitted to testify as to their own observations and other facts known to them and may express an opinion based upon those observations and facts known to them. In weighing the testimony of such lay witnesses, you may consider the circumstances of each witness, his opportunity to observe the defendant and to know the facts to which he had testified, his willingness and capacity to expound freely as to his observations and knowledge, the basis for his opinion and conclusions, and the nearness or remoteness of his observations of the defendant in point of time to the commission of the offense charged.

You may also consider whether the witness observed extraordinary or bizarre acts performed by the defendant, or whether the witness observed the defendant's conduct to be free of such extraordinary or bizarre acts. In evaluating such testimony, you should take into account the extent of the witness's observation of the defendant and the nature and length of time of the witness's contact with the defendant. You should bear in mind that an untrained person may not be readily able to detect mental disease [or defect] and that the failure of a lay witness to observe abnormal acts by the defendant may be significant only if the witness had prolonged and intimate contact with the defendant.

You are not bound by the opinions of either expert or lay witnesses. You should not arbitrarily or capriciously reject the testimony of any witness, but you should consider the testimony of each witness in connection with the other evidence in the case and give it such weight as you believe it is fairly entitled to receive.

You may also consider that every man is presumed to be sane, that is, to be without mental disease [or defect], and to be responsible for his acts. You should consider this principle in the light of all the evidence in the case and give it such weight as you believe it is fairly entitled to receive.

Effect of Verdict of Not Guilty by Reason of Insanity

If the defendant is found not guilty by reason of insanity, it becomes the duty of the court to commit him to St. Elizabeths Hospital. There will be a hearing within 50 days to determine whether defendant is entitled to release. In that hearing the defendant has the burden of proof. The defendant will remain in custody, and will be entitled to release from custody only if the court finds by preponderance of the evidence that he is not likely to injure himself or other persons due to mental illness.

Note: If the defendant so requests, this instruction need not be given. . . .

Notes and Questions

1. The court in *Brawner* begins its historical treatment of the insanity defense rather late, with the *M'Naghten,* or "right-wrong," test. In fact, the insanity defense goes back much further than this.

The requirement of moral culpability for criminal condemnation reaches back to the origins of Western ethical and legal thought. Commentary on the Jewish scriptures and Hebrew law distinguished between the harmful act that was traceable to fault and that which occurred without fault. Aside from one who harms by pure accident, the immature child, incapable of weighing the moral implications of his behavior even when willful, was the paradigm of the actor whose harmful act was without fault. Likened to the child was the retarded (idiot) and the insane. (See: Platt and Diamond, The Origins and Development of the "Wild Beast" Concept of Mental Illness and its Relation to Theories of Criminal Responsibility, 1 Journal of History of the Behavioral Sciences 355, 366 (1965)). The Greek moral philosophers, at least as far back as the fifth century B.C., considered the distinction between a culpable and non-culpable act to be among the "unwritten laws of nature supported by the universal moral sense of mankind." . . . The same view pervaded Roman law and appears in the moral teaching of the early Christian Church Fathers. It emerges in Anglo-Saxon law no later than the twelfth century, the result of the "mutual influences and interaction of Christian theology and Anglo-Saxon law". . . . With the Norman invasion had come continental legal thought, strongly influenced by Christian ethics and Canon law which had already in turn absorbed Jewish ethical thought, classical philosophy, and Roman law. The first comprehensive legal treatise on law in England was that of Bracton, De Legibus et Consuetudinibus Angliae, completed in 1256. Bracton was an ecclesiastic as well as a jurist. [American Bar Association, First Tentative Draft, Criminal Justice Mental Health Standards, 271 (1983).]

An early surviving reference to an insanity defense under English law involves Hugh de Misyn, in 1278.

Calendar of Close Rolls, Edward I
7 Edw. I 518 (1278)

To the sheriff of Nottingham. Order to deliver Hugh de Misyn of Leyton [sic], imprisoned at Noting[ham] for the death of Cicely, his daughter, in bail to twelve men of that county who shall mainpern to have him before the King to stand to right if any one wish to speak against him, and who shall maintain that he shall not hereafter injure anyone, as the King learns by inquisition taken by the justices to deliver Noting[ham] gaol that Hugh hanged his daughter whilst suffering from madness, and not by felony or of malice aforethought.

One of the earliest tests by which English law determined when someone who was mentally ill should be regarded as criminally irresponsible appears in a charge to the jury dating from 1724. For obvious reasons, it is called "Wild Beast" test.

Trial of Edward Arnold
Kingston Assizes, 1724. 16 How. St. Tr. 695, 764

Justice TRACY, charging the jury: . . . If a man be deprived of his reason, and consequently of his intention, he cannot be guilty; . . . punishment is intended for example, and to deter other persons from wicked designs; but the

> punishment of a madman, a person that hath no design, can have no example. This is on one side. On the other side, we must be very cautious; it is not every frantic and idle humour of a man, that will exempt him from justice, and the punishment of the law. When a man is guilty of a great offence, it must be very plain and clear, before a man is allowed such an exemption; therefore it is not every kind of frantic humour or something unaccountable in a man's actions, that points him out to be such a madman as is to be exempted from punishment: it must be a man that is totally deprived of his understanding and memory, and doth not know what he is doing, no more than an infant, than a brute, or a wild beast, such a one is never the object of punishment. . . .

Apparently, though the picture of a wild beast calls to mind defects in both cognition, in the sense that an animal does not understand the existence of any moral laws, and volition, in that the image suggests frenzied loss of control, the judges gradually came to charge exclusively in terms of whether the accused knew the difference between right and wrong. The *M'Naghten* test, it is sometimes said, made an advance over this kind of standard, since the court there focused on the particular criminal act of which the defendant was accused and held that insanity would exculpate if the accused did not know that his or her act was wrong.

One commentator[56] attempts to place this movement in a broader perspective:

> The general drift of history runs from thinking of insanity as a general condition to thinking of insanity as an excuse for a particular act. It is fairly clear that prior to the nineteenth century, lunatics—like witches—were thought to be a special class of people. They were thought possessed, compared to brutes and "wild beasts" and treated as generally incapable of evil.[57] The image of the insane began to change in the nineteenth century and by the time of M'Naghten's Case in 1843,[58] the conception of insanity as a particularized excuse had taken hold. In his speech to the House of Lords after the acquittal of Daniel M'Naghten, Lord Chief Justice Tindal commented on the general practice at the time of instructing the jury to find whether "at the time of doing the act the accused knew the difference between right and wrong."[59] This generalized inquiry continued to treat insanity as an undifferentiated moral incapacity. A weak-minded person might grasp that some things are wrong, but not others. Therefore, as Tindal, L.C.J., reasoned, the apt question for the criminal law is not whether the actor knows the difference between right and wrong in general,

56. George Fletcher, Rethinking Criminal Law 837-843 (1978).

57. See Platt and Diamond, The Origins and Development of the "Wild Beast" Concept of Mental Illness and Its Relation to Theories of Criminal Responsibility, 1 J. of Hist. of Behavioral Sciences 355 (1965) (noting that the "wild beast test" was not formulated in those precise terms until the eighteenth century).

58. 8 Eng. Rep. 718 (1843).

59. Id. at 722-723. But note that Tindal, L.C.J., himself had instructed the jury in M'Naghten's trial to find "whether at the time [of] the act . . . the prisoner had or had not the use of his understanding, so as to know that he was doing a wrong or wicked act." Id. at 719.

but whether he knows that a particular act is wrong.[60] Thus this speech to the Lords (whence we derive the famous *M'Naghten* test) confirmed the ascendant practice of treating insanity as an excuse bearing on the actor's accountability at a particular moment for a particular act.[61]

M'Naghten also marked the culmination of another trend in understanding insanity, a trend related to, but logically independent of the transition from insanity as a condition to insanity as an excuse. For centuries lunacy was treated as a condition discernible to the untutored eye. If a person's behavior was bizarre, if it was like that of a person possessed, then he or she was insane. There was little that experts could say about the subject. But the conception of insanity began to change when, for example, "insane delusions" began to constitute a form of legal insanity.[62] Delusions come and go; and their onset may not be visible to the untrained observer. At some point in the nineteenth century, insanity ceased to be a matter of common discernment and became an issue on which counsel from medical experts was indispensable. How this transition occurred is not clear, but we do know that by the time of *M'Naghten* the medical conception of insanity was ready for absorption into the law. Amending the instructions he gave in M'Naghten's trial, Tindal, L.C.J., concluded that insanity must be based on a "disease of the mind." In a revealing admission, the Lord Chief Justice said that when the facts are well established, "the question becomes substantially one of science only."

The two themes that intersected in *M'Naghten* are of continuing concern. We have yet to abandon the notion that insanity is a condition rather than an excuse, and the question of the extent to which the issue is "scientific" is even more perplexing. Though we have moved in the direction of treating insanity as an excuse for wrongdoing, we remain ambivalent about the issue. This is evident in the practice of automatic commitment after jury determination of insanity (or even a reasonable doubt as to insanity). It is only in recent years that we have begun to question the practice of automatic commitment. The current mood is insistent on a supplementary hearing to determine whether the acquitted defendant is sufficiently dangerous to himself or others to be justifiably committed. It remains to be seen, however, whether these hearings will become an arena of dispute or a ritual preceding routine orders of commitment.

60. Though Tindal, L.C.J., explicitly disavowed the generalized inquiry whether accused knew the difference between right and wrong, the *M'Naghten* test is still called "the right-wrong test" and criticized as though the test inquires simply whether the accused knew the difference between right and wrong. See Durham v. United States, 214 F.2d 862, 870, 869-872 (D.C. Cir. 1954). For example, the passage from I. Ray, Medical Jurisprudence of Insanity 32 (1838), quoted 214 F.2d at 870 n.22, supports rather than detracts from the *M'Naghten* test.

61. The full test is stated 8 Eng. Rep. at 722: "it must be clearly proved that, at the time of the committing of the act, the party accused was labouring under such a defect of reason, from disease of the mind, as not to know the nature and quality of the act he was doing; or, if he did know it, that he did [not] know he was doing what was wrong."

Compare the version of the test currently employed in California, CALJIC §4.00: "Legal insanity . . . means a diseased or deranged condition of the mind which makes a person incapable of knowing or understanding the nature and quality of the act, or makes a person incapable of knowing or understanding that his act was wrong."

62. In the Trial of James Hadfield for attempting to assassinate the King, 27 How. State Trials 1281 (1800), Thomas Erskine argued effectively that insanity did not require a "total deprivation of reason" but that intermittent delusions should suffice. Id. at 1311-1314. The Court directed an acquittal for Hadfield on the condition that he be committed. Id. at 1354-1355.

If people once knew a lunatic when they saw one, that sense of confidence in indentifying the criminally insane has long since disappeared. There may be nothing in the accused's behavior that reveals his incapacity. Thus the investigation of insanity has come to presuppose expert diagnosis. With the application of expertise to the issue of guilt or innocence, the nagging question has become whether the ultimate issue of criminal responsibility can be reduced to a scientific inquiry.

There are three distinct senses in which insanity might be thought to be a medical or scientific issue. First, the notion of "insanity" might be thought to be a diagnostic category like "psychosis" or "paranoia." Today, however, it is readily conceded that insanity is a legal and not medical category. Secondly, the information necessary to analyze insanity—namely, whether the accused suffers from a "defect of reason" or a "disease of the mind" might be thought to be medical data accessible to scientific investigation. The appropriate analogy would be to establishing blood alcohol content in assessing whether the accused was subject to the influence of alcohol at the time of a deed. The data are scientific, but the inference from the data is a matter of judgment and interpretation. The analogy is not entirely apt. For there is considerable disagreement about whether particular diagnostic categories—such as the "sociopathic personality"—constitute a "mental disease or defect." Thus even the basic categories of the insanity test are affected by legal dispute and potential tension between judges and the experts.

Thirdly, insanity might be reduced to a scientific question if it is officially defined so as to minimize the relevance of moral judgment. This was implicitly the ambition of the *Durham* test, adopted in 1954 by the Court of Appeals in the District of Columbia. The test reduced the question of insanity and non-responsibility to a determination whether the act was "the product of a mental disease or defect."

Durham identified the moral issue of accountability with the seemingly scientific issues of diagnosis and causation. As with other arguments reducing value to fact, the affirmation of the fact carries more power than it should. The judges administering *Durham* soon discovered that psychiatric affirmation of the facts of disease and of causation "unduly" influenced the jury on the suppressed issue of value—namely, whether the accused was fairly to blame for a criminal act. The response was to convert the supposedly neutral issues of fact into legal issues beyond the competence of psychiatric expertise. This occurred first with the concept of "mental disease"[63] and finally with the concept of "causation." Whatever the initial reductionistic ambition, the courts eventually returned to the issues of value implicit in judgments of insanity. By 1972 the disaffection from the pseudo-science of *Durham* was complete, and the Circuit Court of Appeals was prepared to formulate a new set of instructions on insanity that would be patently more judgmental.

The problem in 1972 was whether the judges would swing to the opposite extreme and adopt a test that required jurors to assess whether the accused was

63. McDonald v. United States, 312 F.2d 847, 850-851 (D.C. Cir. 1962) ("mental disease or defect" as "any abnormal condition of the mind which substantially affects mental or emotional processes and substantially impairs behavior controls").

suffering from a mental disease to the extent that he could not "justly be held responsible" or that "he ought not to be held responsible." Eschewing this extreme, which arguably burdened the jury with an unstructured moral inquiry, the Court adopted the highly conventional test proposed by the Model Penal Code.[64] This latter test, which is fast becoming the dominant rule in the United States, conforms to the definition of insanity used in Germany since 1871[65] and which is codified as well in the Soviet Union.[66] All of these tests consist of the following elements:

1) a recitation of relevant categories of "mental illness,"[67]
2) a statement linking the "mental illness" to a particular deficiency in the execution of the criminal act,
3) a definition of two types of deficiency in executing the criminal act:
   a) a cognitive deficiency: e.g., not "appreciat[ing] the wrongfulness of the act;"[68]
   b) a volitional deficiency: e.g., not being "able to conform [one's] conduct to the requirements of the law."[69]

It is curious that after the tortuous history of the insanity defense in the United States, the courts and legislatures should gravitate toward a mode of inquiry that has long prevailed on the Continent.[70] This is particularly odd in view of important procedural differences in the adjudication of insanity in the United States and, say, in Germany. Though a more detailed comparative procedural analysis is required, I will mention two differences that might lead one to expect a different test of insanity in commonlaw courts. First, German law, as well as other Continental systems, recognizes the prosecutor's right to appeal a finding of insanity at trial. Not only is the state entitled to a trial de novo at the first level of appeal,[71] but even after the trial de novo, the state can appeal errors of law (including mistaken analysis in the trial court's opinion) to the Supreme Court. One might expect the absence of this prerogative in the common law to lead to a narrow, safer definition of insanity.

64. MPC §4.01.

65. StGB 1871, §51; StGB §20.

66. Ugol. kod. (RSFSR) §11.

67. *Brawner* requires a "mental disease or defect"; StGB §20 lists the following specific conditions: "a diseased mental disturbance, a deep disturbance to consciousness (*Bewusstseinseinstörung*), weak-mindedness or a serious mental defect"; the Soviet test requires "a chronic mental illness, a temporary disturbance of mental activity, weak-mindedness, or any other diseased condition."

68. *Brawner* requires a finding that the accused "lacked substantial capacity to appreciate the wrongfulness of his conduct"; StGB §20 requires that the actor be "incapable of seeing the wrong he has done"; the Soviet provision requires that the actor "not be able to account to himself for his actions."

69. *Brawner* requires the actor "lacked substantial capacity to conform his conduct to the requirements of law"; StGB §20 requires that the actor be "incapable of acting according to his perception" that the conduct is wrong; the Soviet provision requires that the actor "not be able to control his actions."

70. Note that the French Code lacks a definition of insanity; Code Pénal §64 requires simply that the actor be in a "state of insanity at the time of the act." The literature suggests that insanity (*démence*) consists primarily of diseases bearing on the capacity of self-control. Merle and Vitu 619-620.

71. StPO §§312-327 (*Berufungsinstanz*).

The second procedural difference should have the opposite effect. The insanity defense arises in a common-law trial only if the accused is sufficiently sane to stand trial. German law employs a system of compulsory legal representation, one implication of which is that the insanity of the accused is not a reason for suspending the trial. It follows that common-law courts hear the insanity defense only in a subset of cases, while German courts hear the claim in all cases. It should follow (but does not), that American courts would fashion a standard of insanity oriented to forms of psychological aberration less serious than those that disable the defendant from standing trial.

In light of these differences, how do we explain the tendency of American thinking about insanity to dovetail with established Continental formulae? Perhaps the procedural differences simply offset each other. But another explanation might be that the resolution of concrete cases is less important than the ideological importance of the insanity test in conveying our conception of personal responsibility. The negative implication of the insanity test is that "all others are sane and responsible." The message that the law conveys on that issue is critical. Thus if the common test of insanity in Germany, the Soviet Union and the United States conveys a shared Western conception of personal responsibility, the procedural differences among the systems pale in significance.

2. The Model Penal Code rule for the insanity defense has been widely adopted by the states, with little or no change, and has become the dominant test for legal insanity in America. Nevertheless, the Comprehensive Crime Control Act of 1984, signed by President Reagan on October 12, 1984, significantly curtails the insanity defense in all prosecutions under federal criminal statutes. The 1984 statute was a partial victory for opponents of the insanity defense, who found political support in the public reaction to the acquittal of John Hinckley, who shot President Reagan and several other people in 1981, but who won an insanity verdict.

Thus, ironically, the *Brawner* holding no longer applies when federal courts conduct federal criminal prosecutions. Nevertheless, the Model Penal Code test remains the dominant standard in state criminal prosecutions. Since defendants most commonly raise the insanity defense in prosecutions for the common crimes against persons and property that are largely the subject of state criminal law, the *Brawner* opinion remains an accurate statement of the nature and rationale of the insanity defense in this country.

The changes the new federal statute makes in the Model Penal Code test are described in United States v. Kowal, 596 F. Supp. 375 (D. Conn. 1984):

> The government has moved that the court require that defendant's duly-noticed insanity defense comport with the requirements of the Insanity Defense Reform Act of 1984 (Act) signed into law by the President on October 12, 1984. While the Act is in effect, its revised and curtailed grounds of insanity and reallocation of the burden of proof to the defendant may not be applied to defendant's trial. As the offenses charged were allegedly committed by defendant before the effective date of the legislation, application of the Act in these respects is prohibited by the ex post facto clause of the Constitution. . . .

Defendant is charged with two counts of traveling in interstate commerce with intent to further an unlawful activity, in violation of 18 U.S.C. §1952. The indictment, returned on January 12, 1984, charges that on or about December 6, 1982, and again on or about June 16, 1983, with intent to further an attempted extortion and an extortion of money from his former employer and principal, in violation of the law of the State of New York, the defendant traveled in interstate commerce and thereafter performed and attempted to perform the unlawful activity of extortion.

Originally scheduled to commence on May 22, 1984, trial was aborted by reason of defendant's then incompetence, since alleviated, and then continued for psychiatric testing and evaluation. On July 31, 1984, defendant filed notice of his reliance on the defense of insanity. Fed. R. Crim. P. 12.2(a). Trial is presently scheduled for October 29, 1984.

On October 12, 1984, the President signed the Comprehensive Crime Control Act of 1984, of which Sections 401 through 406 constitute a sweeping overhaul of the nature and presentation of the insanity defense in the federal courts.

Aimed at redressing "a glaring deficiency in our—federal criminal justice system—the abuse of the insanity defense," 130 Cong. Rec. 13, H 381 (daily ed. 2/8/83) (Statement of Rep. Gekas), the Act is a multi-pronged attack on "a long-developing problem that we have permitted to confuse and misguide that [sic] fact finding process of criminal trials." Id. The Act substantially changes: the definition of insanity, the allocation of the burden of proof; the limits of expert testimony; the forms of verdict; and procedures for disposition of the mentally ill offender. The present motion provides a sufficiently clear record to consider the applicability of two principal provisions of the Act, the revised definition of insanity and the allocation of the burden of proving insanity.

Section 402 of the Act provides as follows:

> (a) Affirmative Defense.—It is an affirmative defense to a prosecution under any Federal statute that, at the time of the commission of the acts constituting the offense, the defendant, as a result of severe mental disease or defect, was unable to appreciate the nature and quality or the wrongfulness of his acts. Mental disease or defect does not otherwise constitute a defense.
>
> (b) Burden of Proof.—The defendant has the burden of proving the defense of insanity by clear and convincing evidence. . . .

The standard for criminal responsibility first promulgated by the American Law Institute (ALI) and incorporated into the Model Penal Code has, during the last two decades, come to supplant the once dominant common law *McNaughten* test.

The ALI standard, approved for use in nearly all federal courts, was adopted in this circuit as follows: "A person is not responsible for criminal conduct if at the time of such conduct as a result of mental disease or defect he lacks substantial capacity *either* to appreciate the wrongfulness of his conduct *or* to conform his conduct to the requirements of the law." United States v. Freeman, 357 F.2d 606, 622 (2d Cir. 1966) (emphasis added). The ALI standard thus has a cognitive and a volitional prong.

The Act narrows the definition of insanity and includes only the inability to appreciate the nature and quality or the wrongfulness of his acts. The inability, as a result of a mental disease or defect, to conform one's conduct to the requirements of the law has thus been eliminated.

Under the ALI standard, a finding that defendant met either the cognitive or volitional test would result in an acquittal. The Act, premised on the view "that it is impossible with any degree of fairness or accuracy to determine whether a defendant acted because he chose to or because he was driven by uncontrollable psychological forces," and that maintenance of the volitional prong of the test "merely perpetuates an inviting arbitrary loophole for those with the resources to avail themselves of it," (130 Cong. Rec. 13) sanctions only a unitary, cognitive standard.

The adoption, in Freeman, of the ALI standard (and its retroactive effect to cases pending on appeal) changed the legal definition of insanity in a manner noted to be substantive in nature. United States v. Tarrago, 398 F.2d 621, 623 (2d Cir. 1968). The change effectuated by the Act is likewise substantive. Retrospective application of the Act's standard to this defendant would deprive him of one prong of the ALI insanity defense to wit, that at the time of his conduct, as a result of mental disease or defect, he lacked substantial capacity to conform his conduct to the requirements of the law. As the Act, if applied, would deprive one charged with crime of a defense available at the time when the act was committed, it cannot be so applied in the face of the ex post facto clause. *Beazell,* 269 U.S. at 169-170, 46 S. Ct. at 68-69. . . .

The Act's changes with respect to the burden of proof of the insanity defense if imposed on defendant would also violate the ex post facto clause. Under prior federal law, the government has borne the ultimate burden of persuasion on the issue of insanity. Once a federal defendant notified the government of his intention to rely upon the insanity defense, Fed. R. Crim. P. 12.2(a), and introduced some evidence of insanity, it was incumbent on the government to prove defendant's sanity beyond a reasonable doubt. That burden has been criticized as "entirely inappropriate since it is the defendant who possesses the secrets of his own mind and it is he who claims that these mysterious impulses were responsible for his conduct. It is not excessive to place the burden on the defendant to show that which he best knows." 130 Cong. Rec. 13.

Prior to the Act, evidence short of proof of sanity beyond a reasonable doubt would entitle defendant to an acquittal. The Act, by allocating the burden of proof to defendant, results in an acquittal by reason of insanity only if insanity is proven clearly and convincingly.

There is a substantial middle ground or "grey area" between government proof of sanity (beyond a reasonable doubt) and clear and convincing proof of insanity. Prior to the Act, if the evidence raised a reasonable doubt as to defendant's sanity or showed him to be possibly insane, he should be acquitted. Under the Act, the same state of the evidence, where his sanity is in doubt or he is possibly but not clearly and convincingly insane, i.e. in the same middle ground, he would not be entitled to an acquittal. The Act thus denies a defendant acquittal if he falls in the middle ground or grey area whereas the pre-Act law would require acquittal in such circumstances. . . .

The legal definition of insanity and the burden of proving insanity established and assigned by the Insanity Defense Reform Act of 1984 may not, constitutionally, be applied to this defendant by reason of the ex post facto prohibition. Defendant's trial shall proceed in accordance with the legal definition and burden of proof with respect to insanity in effect at the time of the conduct alleged in the indictment.

So ordered.

3. The *M'Naghten* test spoke in terms of whether the accused had "knowledge" of right and wrong, while the Model Penal Code provision adopted by the court in *Brawner* refers to whether the accused can "appreciate" the wrongfulness of his or her act. However, in most jurisdictions the treatment of the *M'Naghten* rule has brought the two concepts into agreement. Thus in State v. Cameron, 100 Wash. 2d 520, 674 P.2d 650 (1983), the court was confronted by the following situation:

Petitioner, Gary Cameron, was charged with the premeditated first degree murder of his stepmother, Marie Cameron. His principal defense was that he was insane at the time he committed the offense. The Court of Appeals affirmed a guilty verdict and this court granted Cameron's petition for review. We reverse the trial court and the Court of Appeals. In doing so, we shall discuss only those issues on which reversal is granted.

At the outset it should be noted that petitioner does not challenge the charge that he stabbed Marie Cameron numerous times or that she died as a result of those wounds. Further, there does not seem to be any serious question that, except for the defense of insanity, the stabbing was done with an intent to kill. Rather, the challenge focuses on three errors alleged to have denied him a fair trial: (1) the definition of insanity in such a way as to prevent the jury's consideration of his insanity defense; (2) the admission of foreign pubic hairs found on the victim's body; and (3) the admission of hearsay evidence of an alleged statement made by the victim 2 months prior to her murder. . . .

Turning first to the insanity defense, it is clear there is evidence running counter to petitioner's contention. This, however, does not detract from petitioner's challenge to the trial court's insanity instruction. The question is whether there is evidence of insanity which the jury could have considered but for the court's instruction. We hold there is.

The basic facts reveal that on the morning of June 9, 1980, petitioner stabbed Marie Cameron in excess of 70 times, leaving the knife sticking in her heart. The body was left in the bathtub with no apparent attempt to conceal it. Later that day a police officer saw petitioner in downtown Shelton wearing only a pair of women's stretch pants, a woman's housecoat, a shirt and no shoes. He was stopped and questioned. After first giving a false name, he corrected it and explained he was dressed that way because "I just grabbed what I could . . . My mother-in-law turned vicious." He also stated he was headed for California. Having no known reason to detain petitioner, the officer released him to continue hitchhiking.

The next day petitioner was detained by the Oregon State Police as he wandered along the shoulder of Interstate 5 near Salem. Since he was wearing only the stretch pants and one shoe he was thought to be an escapee from a nearby mental hospital. A check revealed petitioner was wanted in Shelton for the death of Marie Cameron.

Petitioner was arrested and informed of his constitutional rights. He then gave two confessions, the first being a tape-recorded oral confession and the second a signed written confession. Neither is challenged by petitioner.

In the oral confession petitioner stated generally that he was living in or about the home of his father and stepmother. He left home dressed as he was because his stepmother had become violent. "[S]he's into different types of sorcery. She's just strictly a very evil person . . . and she became very violent with me, with a knife in her hand, and so, uh, I don't deny that I'm the one that did what went on out there." He indicated that when he walked into the bathroom he had not expected her. When he saw her, she had the knife which he was able to take from her easily by bending her wrist back. Then, as he stated: "I took the knife and really stabbed her."

In describing the stabbing, petitioner related: "I just kept stabbing her and stabbing her, because she wasn't feeling . . . it was as if she was laughing . . . as if she was up to something that morning, and I don't know . . . she plays around with witchcraft and that stuff . . ." The last place he saw her was in the bathtub about which he said "she kept moving and moving and moving, and kind of grabbed me like this, but laughing, as if she was enjoying . . . and it was kind of sickening, but it was really maddening to me, because of her offense towards me, it was like . . . you know, it was almost like she was mechanical . . . I mean, the thing was set up that, that's what she wanted to happen. . . . I feel that deep inside she was asking somebody to put her out of her misery . . . she was very symbolic with the 'Scarlet Whore Beast' she was very much into sorcery very, uh, anti-God, not really anti-God but takes the God's truth and twists it into sorcery."

Concerning his feelings about the incident petitioner said: "I felt confused . . . I felt no different from the beginning than the end there was no difference . . . legally I know, that it is against the law, but as far as right and wrong in the eye of God, I would say I felt no particular wrong."

When asked further about the incident petitioner responded: "I washed the blood off me, and I changed clothes, and then I looked back at her and she was, uh, she was still moving around, after being stabbed, what I thought was in the heart, and the throat . . . about seven or eight times, and she just . . . she kept moving. It was like, . . . there was a smile on her face, she kept lunging for me, while she was dead . . . I wasn't trying to be vicious . . . it would look that way, but that wasn't the intent, but she kept lunging at me, over and over again, and the nature of her attack, I was, ah, mad enough I wanted to kill her, I felt that I was justified in self defense at that point . . ." The last petitioner saw of the knife "I tried to stick it in her heart . . . she's some kind of an animal."

Petitioner explained further "she's into a very strong sorcery trip, and that's why so many stab wounds . . . I'm not a goring [sic] person . . . I've never been violent in my life, but for some reason . . . there was some evil spirit behind her that was . . . it was like, it was like there was something within her that, that wasn't really part of her body . . . she was smiling . . . she was almost like enjoying playing and it was disgusting."

When petitioner subsequently gave the written confession he added: "My attack wasn't a vicious attack the first time. I was trying to stop the spirit that was moving in her. She kept saying, 'Gary, Gary, Gary,' as if she was enjoying it." When she stopped moving he washed himself, changed his clothes and then "My stepmother started moving again as if a spirit was in her. I took the knife and started stabbing her again. When I realized there was something in her that wouldn't stop moving, I started stabbing her in the head and heart. I wanted to kill the spirit that seemed to be attacking my spirit." Once again he changed his clothes but again found her moving and again stabbed her numerous times until all movement stopped. He then changed clothes once more and left.

As with the petitioner's testimony we note the testimony of the psychiatrists and psychologists is not without some disparity. Nevertheless, there is ample evidence which, under a proper insanity instruction, could have been considered by the jury as a matter of defense.

Prior to trial, petitioner made a motion to acquit on the ground of insanity pursuant to RCW 10.77.080. Three psychiatrists, Doctors Jarvis, Allison and Bremner and a psychologist, Dr. Trowbridge, were called to testify. They agreed petitioner suffered from paranoid schizophrenia both at the time of the killing and at the time of trial. Although stating it differently, all four appeared to agree that petitioner believed he was an agent of God, required to carry out God's directions. They also agreed that petitioner believed God commanded him to kill his stepmother and that he was therefore obligated to kill the "evil spirit." Consequently, all doctors concurred he was legally insane at the time of the murder.

The trial court denied the motion for acquittal and submitted the issue of insanity to the jury. At trial, the four doctors repeated their earlier testimony. All agreed that at the time of the killing, and at the time of trial, petitioner suffered from the mental disease of paranoid schizophrenia. While expressing their views in slightly different ways, they agreed petitioner understood that, as a mechanical thing, he was killing his stepmother and knew it was against the laws of man. They stressed, however, that at the time, he was preoccupied with the delusional belief that his stepmother was an agent of satan who was persecuting him, as were others like Yasser Arafat and the Ayatollah Khomeini. He believed he was being directed by God to kill satan's angel and that by so doing, he was obeying God's higher directive or law. At this time he believed himself to be a messiah and in fact compared himself with Jesus Christ.

The doctors pointed out, in different ways, that because of his delusional beliefs, petitioner felt God had directed him to send her from this life to another. He had no remorse over the killing. He felt it was justified by God and that he was merely doing a service. "He felt he would generally be protected from any difficulties . . . because 'God would not allow it to happen.' "

Concerning the legal tests for insanity the mental health experts opined that while he understood it was against the law to kill, he believed he was responding to God's directive and thus had an obligation to rid the world of this "demon," "sorceress" or "evil spirit." Thus, while technically he understood the mechanical nature of the act, he did not have the capacity to discern between right and wrong with reference to the act. Some of the doctors expressed the clear view that at the time of the killing, he was unable to appreciate the nature and quality of his acts. No doctor contended otherwise.

Concerning petitioner's insanity defense the trial court gave standard WPIC pattern jury instruction 20.01, but, over petitioner's exception, added a last paragraph which defines "right and wrong."

> In addition to the plea of not guilty, the defendant has entered a plea of insanity existing at the time of the act charged.

> Insanity existing at the time of the commission of the act charged is a defense.
>
> For a defendant to be found not guilty by reason of insanity you must find that, as a result of mental disease or defect, the defendant's mind was affected to such an extent that the defendant was unable to perceive the nature and quality of the acts with which the defendant is charged or was unable to tell right from wrong with reference to the particular acts with which defendant is charged.
>
> *What is meant by the terms "right and wrong" refers to knowledge of a person at the time of committing an act that he was acting contrary to the law.*

(Italics ours.) Petitioner, on the other hand, proposed the use of WPIC pattern jury instruction 20.01 which does not contain the last paragraph.

Petitioner argues that the trial court should have left the term "right and wrong" undefined as provided by the Legislature in RCW 9A.12.010. At the very least, it is urged, "right and wrong" should not have been defined in such a way as to exclude from the jury's deliberation the consideration of "right and wrong" in terms of one's ability to understand the moral qualities of the act.

[The court held that the instruction was wrong:]

At the time this case was tried, the Court of Appeals had just issued State v. Crenshaw, 27 Wn. App. 326, 617 P.2d 1041 (1980) which approved the instruction challenged herein. Subsequent thereto this court affirmed the Court of Appeals opinion in State v. Crenshaw, 98 Wn. 2d 789, 659 P.2d 488 (1983). . . .

Insofar as the instant case is concerned, however, our discussion of *Crenshaw* also recognized an exception to the alternative grounds set forth therein. That exception is controlling here:

> A narrow exception to the societal standard of moral wrong has been drawn for instances wherein a party performs a criminal act, knowing it is morally and legally wrong, but believing, because of a mental defect, that the act is ordained by God: such would be the situation with a mother who kills her infant child to whom she is devotedly attached, believing that God has spoken to her and decreed the act. Although the woman knows that the law and society condemn the act, it would be unrealistic to hold her responsible for the crime, since her free will has been subsumed by her belief in the deific decree.

(Citations omitted.) *Crenshaw,* at 798. Consequently, as we held in *Crenshaw,* one who believes that he is acting under the direct command of God is no less insane because he nevertheless knows murder is prohibited by the laws of man. Indeed, it may actually emphasize his insanity. People v. Schmidt, 216 N.Y. 324, 110 N.E. 945 (1915).

In the instant case there is considerable evidence (although not unanimous) from which the jury could have concluded that petitioner suffered from a mental disease; that he believed his stepmother was satan's angel or a sorceress; that he believed God directed him to kill his stepmother; that because of the mental disease it was impossible for him to understand that what he was doing was wrong; and, as stated in *Crenshaw* at page 798, that his free will had "been subsumed by [his] belief in the deific decree." The last paragraph of the trial court's challenged instruction precluded the jury's consideration of these factors and thus runs afoul of the *Crenshaw* exception. In short, the instruction prevented the jury from considering those essential relevant facts that formed petitioner's theory of the case. To this extent the trial court erred by adding the definitional paragraph to the instruction.

4. Note that the Model Penal Code standard adopted by the court in *Brawner* involves a volitional as well as a cognitive element. The comments to Section 4.01 of the Model Penal Code explain this:

> The part of the Model Code test relating to volition is cast in terms of capacity to conform one's conduct to the requirements of the law.[72] Application of the principle calls for a distinction, inevitable for a standard addressed to impairment of volition, between incapacity and mere indisposition.[73] In drawing this distinction, the Model Code formulation effects a substantial improvement over pre-existing standards.
>
> In contrast to the M'Naghten and "irresistible impulse" criteria, the Model Code formulation reflects the judgment that no test is workable that calls for complete impairment of ability to know or to control. The extremity of these conceptions had posed the largest difficulty for the administration of the old standards. Disorientation, psychiatrists indicated, might be extreme and still might not be total; what clinical experience revealed was closer to a graded scale with marks along the way. Hence, an examiner confronting a person who had performed a seemingly purposive act might helpfully address himself to the extent of awareness, understanding and control. If, on the other hand, he had to speak to utter incapacity vel non under the M'Naghten test, his relevant testimony would be narrowly limited to the question of whether the defendant suffered from delusional psychosis, where the act would not be criminal if the facts were as the defendant deludedly supposed them to be. A test requiring an utter incapacity for self-control imposes a comparably unrealistic restriction on the

72. Compare the test for proceedings in courts martial at the time the Model Code was proposed: whether the accused was "at the time [of the alleged offense], so far free from mental defect, disease, or derangement as to be able concerning the particular act charged both to distinguish right from wrong and to adhere to the right." Manual for Courts-Martial, United States, 1951, ¶120b, at 200. See also United States v. Smith, 5 C.M.A. 314, 320, 17 C.M.R. 314, 320 (1954).

73. The Institute considered but did not approve an alternative formulation supported by a minority of its Council. See ALI Proceedings 206-221 (1955). Under that formulation:

> A person is not responsible for criminal conduct if at the time of such conduct as a result of mental disease or defect he lacks substantial capacity to appreciate the criminality of his conduct or is in such state that the prospect of conviction and punishment cannot constitute a significant restraining influence upon him.

MPC T.D. 4, at 27 (alternative (b)).

Instead of asking whether the defendant had capacity to conform his conduct to the requirements of law, this alternative formulation asks whether, in consequence of mental disease or defect, the threat of punishment could not exercise a significant restraining influence upon him. To some extent, of course, these are the same inquiries. To the extent that they diverge, the latter asks a narrower and harder question, involving the assessment of capacity to respond to a single influence, the threat of punishment. Both Dr. Guttmacher and Dr. Overholser considered the assessment of responsiveness to this one influence too difficult for psychiatric judgment. See ALI Proceedings 209 (1955). Hence, though the issue framed by the alternative may well be thought to state the question that is most precisely relevant for legal purposes, the inquiry was deemed impolitic on this ground. Insofar as nondeterrability is the determination that is sought, it must be reached by probing general capacity to conform to the requirements of law.

The alternative formulation has not been adopted in any jurisdiction.

scope of the relevant inquiry.[74] To meet these difficulties, it was thought that the criterion should ask if the defendant, as a result of mental disease or defect, was deprived of "substantial capacity" to appreciate the criminality (or wrongfulness) of his conduct or to conform his conduct to the requirements of law, meaning by "substantial" a capacity of some appreciable magnitude when measured by the standard of humanity in general, as opposed to the reduction of capacity to the vagrant and trivial dimensions characteristic of the most severe afflictions of the mind.

The adoption of the standard of substantial capacity may well be the Code's most significant alteration of the prevailing tests. It was recognized, of course, that "substantial" is an open-ended concept, but its quantitative connotation was believed to be sufficiently precise for purposes of practical administration.[75]

74. Such a strict standard was explicitly proposed by Stephen, who suggested a test of "whether the impulse to commit a crime was so violent that the offender would not be prevented from doing the act by knowing that the greatest punishment permitted by law for the offence would be instantly inflicted." However, whether the defendant could have controlled himself in an imaginary situation of automatic and instantaneous punishment is a very different question from whether he could have refrained from criminal conduct in the situation in which he actually found himself. For defendants who are in fact incapable of conforming their conduct to the law's requirements, the normal deterrent function of criminal punishment is inoperative, and posing the test of responsibility, in terms of hypothetical conduct under other circumstances requires speculation that may be of limited relevance to the real issue.

At the time of the drafting of Section 4.01, military law used a comparably strict standard of volitional incapacity, which was elaborated as the inquiry whether the presence of a policeman at the defendant's elbow would have caused him to refrain from committing the offense. See United States v. Kunak, 5 C.M.A. 346, 357-358, 17 C.M.R. 346, 357-358 (1954). This test has the same deficiency as Stephen's standard—the answer under the test has limited bearing on the defendant's capacity to conform to norms not immediately represented by an authority figure possessing the power of enforcement. In criticizing the "policeman" test, Dr. Guttmacher observed: "Even the very severe impulse neurotic and obsessive-compulsive neurotic can momentarily postpone acting out until the certainty of immediate capture is gone." . . .

75. In connection with the work of the New York State Governor's Committee on the Insanity Defense, Herbert Wechsler drafted a model jury charge, reproduced infra in Appendix C to this Comment, illustrating how a standard like that of the Model Code should be employed. The Institute considered but did not approve an alternative formulation supported by the Reporter and a minority of the Council. See ALI Proceedings 206-221 (1955). Under that formulation:

> A person is not responsible for criminal conduct if at the time of such conduct as a result of mental disease or defect his capacity either to appreciate the criminality of his conduct or to conform his conduct to the requirements of law is so substantially impaired that he cannot justly be held responsible.

MPC T.D. 4, at 27 (alternative (a)).

This alternative formulation would submit the issue squarely to the jury's sense of justice, asking expressly whether the capacity of the defendant was "so substantially impaired that he cannot justly be held responsible." Some members of the Council deemed it unwise to present questions of justice to the jury, preferring a submission that in form, at least, confined the inquiry to the fact. The proponents of this alternative contended that since the jury normally will feel that it is just to exculpate only if the disorder is extreme, and that otherwise conviction is demanded, it is safer to invoke the jury's sense of justice than to rest entirely on the single word "substantial," imputing no specific measure of degree. Judge Bazelon wrote approvingly of this formulation in his dissent in United States v. Brawner, 471 F.2d 969, 1033-1034 (D.C. Cir. 1972), the case in which the Court of Appeals for the District of Columbia abandoned the Durham rule and accepted the Model Penal Code formulation. This alternative formulation has recently been adopted by judicial decision in Rhode Island, with the substitution of the word "wrongfulness" for "criminality." See State v. Johnson, 399 A.2d 469 (1979).

The law is full of instances in which courts and juries are explicitly authorized to confront an issue of degree. Such an approach was deemed to be no less essential and appropriate in dealing with this issue than in dealing with the questions of recklessness and negligence.

5. Note that the court in *Brawner* considers whether it should simply abolish the insanity defense. Why does it not do so? One of the most interesting arguments in favor of abolition is that of Professors Norval Morris and Gordon Hawkins:[76]

> Historically the defense of insanity made good sense. The executioner infused it with meaning. And in a larger sense, all criminal sanctions did so too, since they made no pretense of being rehabilitative. In the present context of the expressed purposes and developing realities of both the criminal justice system and the mental health system this defense is an anachronism. In the future, this defense would be not only anachronistic, it would be manifestly inefficient as well.
>
> Let us offer a small statistical point before turning to the moral issue. In this country the defense of insanity is pleaded in about 2 percent of the criminal cases which come to jury trial. Overwhelmingly, of course, criminal matters are disposed of by pleas of guilty and trials by a judge sitting without a jury. Only the exceptional case goes to trial by jury. And of these exceptional cases, in only two of every hundred is this defense raised. In the United Kingdom, for the period on which the Royal Commission on Capital Punishment reported, the situation was very similar. The verdict of "guilty but insane" was returned, over a five-year period, in 19.8 percent of murder trials, whereas over the same period it was returned in only 0.1 percent of trials for other offenses. Does anyone believe that this measures the significance of gross psychopathology to crime? Let him visit the nearest criminal court or penitentiary if he does. Is not this defense clearly a sop to our conscience, a comfort for our failure to address the difficult arena of psychopathology and crime?
>
> The practical difference between traditional tests of insanity and modern revisions was recently empirically tested. Various juries were given instructions based on the M'Naughten rules, the Durham test, and the following simple and uncluttered formula: "If you believe the defendant was insane at the time he committed the act of which he is accused, then you must find the defendant not guilty by reason of insanity." The juries failed to see any operative differences in the three instructions. Do we need to labor another century and a half to produce a mouse of such inconsequence?
>
> Yet the moral issue remains central. Should we exculpate from criminal responsibility, or from "accountability" to use the preferable European concept, those whose freedom to choose between criminal and lawful behavior has been curtailed by mental illness? It is too often overlooked that the exculpation of one group of "criminal actors" confirms the inculpation of others. Why not a defense of "dwelling in a Negro ghetto"? This defense would not be morally indefensible.

76. N. Morris and G. Hawkins, The Honest Politician's Guide to Crime Control 178-185 (1970).

Such an adverse social and subcultural background is statistically *more* criminogenic than is psychosis, and it also severely circumscribes the freedom of choice which a nondeterministic criminal law (and that describes all present criminal law systems) attributes to accused persons.

True, a defense of social adversity would be politically intolerable; but that does not vitiate the analogy for our purposes. Insanity, it is said, destroys, undermines, or diminishes man's capacity to reject the wrong and adhere to the right. So does the ghetto—more so. But surely, you might ask, you would not have us punish the sick? Indeed we would, if you insist on punishing the grossly deprived. To the extent that criminal sanctions serve punitive purposes we fail to see the difference between these two defenses; to the extent that they serve rehabilitative, treatment, and curative purposes, we fail to see the need for the difference. Some reply: it is not a question of freedom or morality, it is a question of stigmatization, and to this we shall return; but let us not brush aside the moral issue so lightly.

In Shavian terms: Vengeance is mine, saith the Lord—which means that it is not the Lord Chief Justice's! It seems to us clear that there *are* different degrees of moral turpitude in criminal conduct and that the mental health or illness of an actor is relevant to an assessment of that degree—as are many other factors in the social setting and historical antecedents of a crime. This does not mean, however, that society is obliged to measure any or all of these pressures for purposes of a moral assessment which will lead to conclusions concerning criminal responsibility.

In a few cases the question of moral irresponsibility is so clear that there is no purpose in invoking the criminal process. The example of accident, in its purest and least subconscious accident-prone form, is a situation where there is little utility in invoking the criminal process. The same is true of a person who did not know what he was doing at the time of the alleged crime. But to exculpate him there is no need for the M'Naughten or Durham rules for he falls clearly within general criminal law exculpatory rules. He simply lacks the *mens rea* of the crime. Thus, it seems to us that all we need to achieve within the area of criminal responsibility and psychological disturbance is already achieved by existing and long-established rules of mental intent and crime, and we would allow a sane or insane *mens rea* to suffice for guilt.

Perhaps an example of this principle may help. The *Hadfield* case will serve our purpose admirably. Hadfield had been severely wounded in the head in the Napoleonic wars and subsequently decided that it was necessary for the salvation of the world that he kill George III. He equipped himself with a blunderbuss and secreted himself in the Drury Lane Theatre in a position from which he hoped to shoot George III as he waddled into the royal box. Hadfield saw the flabby creature in the royal box and discharged his blunderbuss in the direction of the king, unfortunately missing him.

There was no doubt of Hadfield's brain damage or of his psychosis, his gross psychological disturbance. He did, however, clearly intend to kill the king. He had the insane *mens rea* of murder, and indeed of treason. We do not regard the phrase "insane *mens rea*" as a contradiction in terms. Had his psychological disturbance led him to think that he was discharging the blunderbuss to start the performance on the stage, or to burst a balloon, he would have lacked the *mens rea* of murder and of treason. But he saw himself as sacrificing himself for the good of the world—and he may not have been far wrong. We do not deplore the fact that Hadfield was held to be not guilty on the grounds of insanity. We do, however, maintain that there would be no greater injustice involved in convicting in such a case and applying the psychological diagnosis to the decision how to treat the offender than in convicting in any of the other thousands of cases that daily flow through our criminal courts.

Clearly the crucial question in this context is: what are the consequences of the defense of insanity? Is there an operative difference between peno-correctional and psychiatric-custodial processes which renders benefit to the accused who is found not guilty on the grounds of insanity? To this important inquiry we offer two replies. First, the differences if they exist are marginal; and second, the defense of insanity is an extraordinarily inefficient mechanism of deciding on the allocation of psychiatric treatment resources. . . .

A more sophisticated critic might suggest that we are missing the point. . . . Criminal processes are, he might say, public morality plays. They have deterrent purposes, perhaps, but they certainly aim dramatically to affirm the minimum standards of conduct society will tolerate. By public ceremonial and defined liturgy, criminal trials stigmatize those who fail to conform to society's standards. In short, the criminal justice system is a name-calling, stigmatizing, community superego reinforcing system. And, it could be urged, we should not stigmatize the mentally ill. They are mad not bad, sick not wicked; it is important that we not misclassify them. Is there a rebuttal to this defense of the defense of insanity? . . .

For our part, we look toward a future in which moral outrage and name-calling will not so significantly influence our reaction to the behavior of others. This is a generation that despoils our natural resources and prepares to terminate human life on this planet; but if the ruination of our environment and the eliminating of our species are avoided, if aggressions are controlled in favor of decency and creativity, we do not believe that systems of justice in which name-calling and vengeance figure so prominently can long survive. If this be so, then the issue becomes one of how we can, as rapidly as the traffic will allow, destigmatize our criminal law processes.

There is a choice. We could follow the pattern of a gradual extension of the exculpatory and allegedly destigmatizing processes of the defense of insanity, opening it more and more widely to cover larger and larger slices of criminal conduct until most criminal behavior is encompassed. Many of those working in this field, men whom we respect, favor that engulfing process. We do not oppose their purpose; but we think their political judgment wrong. It seems to us that we should not make an artificial and morally unjustifiable exception to a false general rule and allow the exception to swallow the rule. It seems to us better to support the advance that is now taking place, certainly in theory and rhetoric, in the treatment of all criminal conduct, and to a degree in correctional practice. In other words, to put it aggressively, we think society will move faster toward a rational system of criminal justice through honesty than by self-deception; and we think it dishonest to create an artificial, morally unjustifiable, practically ineffective exception to the general rules of criminal responsibility. We think the English judges went wrong in the nineteenth century and that it is time we got back to earlier and truer principles.

We find it impossible morally to distinguish the insane from others who may be convicted though suffering deficiencies of intelligence, adversities of social circumstances, indeed all the ills to which the flesh and life of man is prey. It seems to us that our approach better accords with the total role of the criminal law in society than does a system which makes a special exculpatory case out of one rare and unusual criminogenic process, while it determinedly denies exculpatory effects to other, more potent processes. In the long run we will better handle these problems, as well as the whole and more complex problem of criminality in the community, if we will recognize that within crime itself there lies the greatest disparity of human wickedness and the greatest range of human capacities for self-control.

Our perennial perseverations about the defense of insanity impede recognition of this diversity, since they push us to a false dichotomy between the responsible and the irresponsible. They should be abandoned. One occupation for the energies thus released might be suggested, a task in which the psychiatrist has an important role to play: the defining of those categories of psychologically disturbed criminals who are serious threats to the community and to whom special treatment measures should therefore be applied.

Professor Alan Stone, M.D.,[77] has answered these objections in a qualified defense of the insanity defense:

So, finally, why not abolish the insanity defense? Who is standing in the way? My answer is the law itself. By the law, I mean those people—lawyers, judges, legislatures, and citizens—who have a profound concern for the morality of the law itself and who believe that the law should reflect our most basic human intuitions of morality. I maintain that every moral philosopher in every culture has realized that morality requires that man has free will. Our legal system and the law are inspired by that moral intuition. At the same time, I maintain that every moral philosopher who has thought about human nature has also concluded that at *some* time in a man's life, he feels he has no choice; he acts without choice. The contradiction between this experience of being without choice and the moral intuition of free will is one of the inescapable contradictions of human existence. That contradiction is expressed and denied by the insanity defense. The insanity defense is the exception that "proves" the rule of law. I bowdlerize the maxim because today the insanity defense does more than test the law, it *demonstrates* that all other criminals had free will—the ability to choose between good and evil—but that they chose evil and therefore deserve to be punished.

It is not psychiatrists, it is not criminals, it is not the insane who need the insanity defense. The insanity defense is the exception that "proves" the rule of free will. It is required by the law itself, and it is this vision of law which has throughout history required resistance to abolition of the insanity defense. It is not for psychiatrists to choose between this vision of law and the new loss of protection to society. Members of Congress, outraged by the Hinckley decision, have discovered that the insanity defense has been the creation of judges overly influenced by academics. After two hundred years, they have decided it is time for the elected members of the legislature to shape the insanity defense. Although a few states will abolish the insanity defense, the most likely result is that Con-

77. 33 Harv. L. Sch. Bull. 21 (Fall 1982).

gress and the majority of state legislatures will enact a variety of legal reforms to narrow the standard on the theory that some form of insanity defense is probably constitutionally required.

But if there is to be even a narrow insanity defense, there must be psychiatric testimony or some equivalent. Someone will be asked to help the court do the impossible, to distinguish the few who do not have free will from the multitude who do. So, in the end, I suggest that it is the law that cannot do without psychiatry. The marriage between law and psychiatry is therefore just like many other marriages in which one hears it said at time of crisis, "I don't know what to do. I can't live with her, and I can't live without her."

6. Professor David Wexler[78] has suggested an intriguing form of partial abolition of the insanity defense. He notes that when people call for abolition of the defense, they have in mind a particular frightening image of the "insane" criminal—the criminal who commits a violent crime at random, directed at a total stranger.

We should, therefore, be able rather easily to dissipate public fear over and objection to the insanity defense if, through legislation, we render the defense *unassertable in the prosecution of specified crimes* (e.g., homicide, attempted homicide, and perhaps aggravated assault) *unless the victim of the offense is somehow "related to" the defendant.*

Conventional wisdom holds that the insanity defense is successfully asserted only in homicide cases. In fact, however, the relevant research indicates that jurisdictions vary widely regarding the seriousness of the criminal acts committed by insanity acquittees. In some jurisdictions, it is clear that insanity acquittals occur overwhelmingly in prosecutions for non-homicidal offenses. In any event, an appreciable percentage of homicides involve victims who are related to the offender, and this intrafamilial pattern holds true even when we limit our attention to killers who are mentally ill. Accordingly, an "offense-victim" limitation on the assertability of the insanity defense will disallow the defense in instances (e.g., homicides against non-family members) that may well exceed bounds of public tolerance, but will nonetheless allow the defense to be asserted for most offenses and even for a large segment of homicide cases.

Apart from its pragmatics, the offense-victim limitation may be acceptable because the familial/non-familial distinction seems, in many ways, to be a meaningful one. In terms of the public protection interest, the distinction is particularly potent. Surely, the public at large will be less fearful of one who has killed a family member than of one who has killed a stranger. Moreover, although this is an area that can profit from empirical research, a person who has killed a non-relative seems in actuality to be more likely to pose a threat—particularly to the general public—than does a person who has killed a family member. Research by Paul Meehl, for example, "failed to reveal one single instance of a psychotically depressed patient who, after an altruistic homicide of a family member

78. Wexler, An Offensive-Victim Approach to Insanity Defense Reform, 26 Ariz. L. Rev. 18, 21-23 (1984).

(unlike paranoid schizophrenics, depressed patients don't kill strangers or neighbors) was a repeater.[79] Even more to the point, Monahan, in his monograph regarding the clinical prediction of violent behavior, notes that violence is an interactional concept and that murderers may range from "indiscriminate" to very "specific" in their choice of victims. Spouse murderers, he notes, "have a very low recidivism rate. . . ." After all, they have "removed their source of irritation."[80]

For many people, the real issue is not who should have an insanity defense but rather what should be done with those whose defense "succeeds." The crucial question then becomes that asked by Professor Alan Stone, M.D.:[81]

From Fiction to Reality

"Are there some people, even a few, who, for example, kill and then invoke the plea of insanity and thereby avoid or spend less time confined?" We deal now with a very narrow question, and for the first time, we hit on a charge against the insanity defense that is, in my opinion, quite justified.

However, until 30 years ago, the answer to even this narrow charge would have been not true. Persons found not guilty by reason of insanity were usually confined for the rest of their lives in institutions for the criminally insane. Such institutions were even more awful than prisons. Unfortunately, the public was not aware of this reality. They believed that a successful plea of insanity meant that the defendant had escaped punishment. The fantasy of comfortable hospitals and the fiction of temporary insanity gave a completely incorrect impression.

Norval Morris, former dean of the University of Chicago Law School and a distinguished professor of criminal law who did know the realities, wrote an article in 1968 calling for the abolition of the insanity defense. Along with other arguments for abolition, he suggested that the only humane value the insanity defense had served through history was to avoid capital punishment. Since, at the time he wrote, capital punishment had been virtually abolished de facto if not de jure, it seemed to him that defendants found guilty of a capital offense would get a better deal in prison than if found not guilty by reason of insanity and condemned to live out their lives in these horrible institutions. But Professor Morris did not fully anticipate subsequent developments either in law or in psychiatry.

First, consider the law. In a series of decisions mainly predicated on constitutional grounds, the law has made it more difficult to confine and keep confined persons found not guilty by reason of insanity. These legal developments, which again are not well understood by the public, are part of the great recent legal reforms of mental health law. Essentially, what these particular legal reforms did was to reject the traditional practice of automatic indefinite confinement of persons found not guilty by reason of insanity. Such persons, it was decided, have rights; after trial, they must be given a new hearing, and it must be determined

79. Meehl, The Insanity Defense, Minn. Psychologist 11 (Summer 1983).
80. J. Monahan, The Clinical Prediction of Violent Behavior 96, 113-114 (1981).
81. 33 Harv. L. Sch. Bull., supra, at 15-21.

that they are civilly commitable, that is, they are still mentally ill and dangerous. If they are then committed, they are entitled to periodic review of their status so that they will not be needlessly confined. For example, in People vs. McQuillan, the Supreme Court of Michigan found that the state's automatic commitment of insanity acquittals was a violation of due process and equal protection. Such people could be held for only 60 days. After that time, they had exactly the same procedural rights as any civilly committed patient. It was this decision which led the Michigan legislature to pass the first guilty but mentally ill legislation.

These developments took place at the same time that civil libertarians were making it much more difficult to civilly commit or to retain in confinement any mentally ill person whether a crime had been committed or not. Although temporary insanity as a defense had been mainly a fiction, these legal developments began to make it a reality. This was the work not of psychiatrists but of civil libertarians. They and federal judges agreed that psychiatrists had too much influence over the law in determining who should be confined in mental hospitals. The law decided psychiatry was too subjective, and that it needed an objective standard. The objective standard announced by the courts and relevant to these cases was imminent, likely or probable danger to others.

Ironically, this objective standard is totally without empirical foundation. No one—not psychiatrists, not psychologists, not sociologists, not computers—can provide valid evidence about who does or does not meet this objective standard. Both the American Psychiatric Association and the American Psychological Association have concluded that no scientific or clinical basis exists for making long-term predictions of violence. This problem is particularly acute when a decision has to be made whether a person who was once dangerous is still dangerous. This is exactly the question that arises after a person like Hinckley is found not guilty by reason of insanity. No one can answer yes or no to this objective standard, which most courts insist must be proven beyond a reasonable doubt. In its quest for objectivity the law has lost touch with reality.

These legal developments take on even greater import when we examine what happened in psychiatry during these same three decades. Until the second half of this century, long-term custodial confinement was an accepted practice of institutional psychiatry. Whether patients were dangerous or not, whether they came from the criminal courts or by ordinary civil commitment, the length of hospital stay could often be measured in years rather than in days. In 1958, the average length of hospitalization in the United States for schizophrenia was 13.1 years. As long as psychiatry endorsed or accepted the practice of long-term custodial confinement, mental institutions provided an extra measure of protection for the criminal justice system. Psychiatry, by calling this custodial confinement "treatment," gave legitimacy to the notion that the insanity defense was humane.

Later, when the community mental health approach began to dominate the therapeutic imagination, when effective drug treatments became available, and when psychiatrists finally opened their eyes to the evils of long-term institutionalization, a process began that, even without legal reform, might well have ended many of the abuses the civil libertarians decried. But these changes also radically altered the mental health system's ability to protect society. Institutions with revolving doors offer little security to the public. When therapeutic considerations alone determine the length of hospital stay, patients who formerly would have been hospitalized for years are now released after only a few days.

These psychiatric developments eventually reached even into the institutions for the criminally insane. Before a seriously mentally ill offender can be tried and plead insanity, he must first, as a requirement of law, be restored to competency. Thus, if someone kills, who is actually psychotic, he is confined, treated, restored to competency, and then goes to trial. From the psychiatrist's current perspective, almost everyone who has had sufficient treatment to be restored to competency has had as much in-hospital treatment as is necessary for therapeutic reasons. Therefore, if his insanity plea is successful, there will be no compelling therapeutic justification for his continued confinement. Indeed, the more we improve conditions in institutions for the criminally insane, the more competent psychiatrists we hire, the greater pressure there will be from the psychiatrists not to keep these patients confined. What this two-sided development means is that the law created by the civil libertarians and the methods of treatment developed by psychiatrist now both push in the same direction, and the traditional way of dealing with persons found not guilty by reason of insanity has been drastically transformed.

Confronting the Hypocrisy

For the last two hundred years, the insanity defense was a profound hypocrisy. The courts found defendants not guilty by reason of insanity and then relied on psychiatry to confine them for the rest of their lives. Thus, there was no loss of protection to society. But beginning 30 years ago with the developments I have described, this hypocrisy was confronted. Perhaps for the first time in history, a successful plea of insanity has real bite. That is why the public should be concerned about the insanity defense and the Hinckley verdict. At his initial hearing Hinckley in effect "confessed" that he was dangerous, but he is now entitled to a new hearing every six months as long as he is confined. At one of those future hearings, a judge may have to decide without a recent confession whether Hinckley will be dangerous in the "reasonable future." We all know that Hinckley has been dangerous, but no one can really predict whether he will be dangerous as the years go by. The psychiatrists and the judge have been given an impossible responsibility to fulfill. Those who are now reassuring the public that Hinckley will be confined for the rest of his life can only be assuming that the judge will ignore the impossible requirements of the statute and instead look to public opinion for guidance. But in less notorious cases, judges are releasing people whose history of violence is much worse than Hinckley's.

Because the consequences of a successful plea of insanity have changed, it is now becoming increasingly attractive to criminal defendants, even defendants who have committed lesser crimes. For example, an average of eight insanity acquittals a year occurred in New York between 1965 and 1971. Then in 1972, there were 25 cases; in 1973, 37 cases; in 1974, 55 cases; in 1975, 61 cases. Furthermore, 31 persons charged with murder and given insanity acquittals had been discharged within a year. In addition, many insanity acquittals were given to defendants charged with less serious offenses, where there was no possibility of capital punishment or a lengthy sentence. However, practice in different states varies enormously. Some states still have few insanity defenses. Some states have made increasing use of not guilty by reason of insanity for less serious offenses in uncontested cases. But in every state, as a result of the legal reforms of civil commitment, the public has no guarantee that persons who have done violence to others and been found not guilty by reason of insanity will be confined for a substantial period of time.

Compared with the debacle of the entire criminal justice system and the threat posed to the public by its failures, the insanity defense is trivial, notwithstanding these recent developments. If, on the other hand, we compare the consequences of the insanity defense 30 years ago and the consequences today, a watershed change has taken place. The insanity defense, once a legal hypocrisy, has become a legal reality. It is this new legal reality that understandably has led to legislation that seeks to change the consequences of the insanity defense so as to restore the old hypocrisy.

What shall we do then—invent some new hypocrisy such as guilty but insane, or shall we once and for all abolish the insanity defense? In order to consider the question, one final, critical issue must be faced. Psychiatrists treat mental illness, often with great benefit to very sick patients, but that is not the same as curing them. Psychiatry certainly has not found a permanent cure for violence. We can treat people and return them to the community. They will function better, but we cannot guarantee that they are cured, and we certainly can make no promises that they will not be violent in the future.

The best evidence currently available is that of those defendants found not guilty by reason of insanity and, subsequently, released, 20 to 30 percent will be rearrested for some type of crime. As the law now stands, then, there can be no guarantee that these potential recidivists will be identified and confined. Even under the Michigan statute providing the verdict, guilty but mentally ill, half of such defendants are treated by the correctional system on an out-patient parole basis.

For those who still support the insanity defense in 1982, it is not enough to say that it is morally wrong to punish an insane person. They must also be willing to submit to further risks at the hands of the insane rather than punish them or deprive them of due process and equal protection. Jesus Christ asked us to turn the other cheek. The American Civil Liberties Union proclaims that due process and equal protection are supreme legal values. But whether the American public will endorse either of these positions is another matter. The Michigan experience with guilty but mentally ill, demonstrates again that it is the disposition after the verdict, rather than the verdict itself, which is critical. This underlines the hypocrisy of changing the insanity verdict because of its supposed symbolic significance for the public. If only the label changes and not the underlying reality, the public is being misled.[82]

82. From my perspective the best resolution of these problems is that introduced by the state of Oregon. There the "symbolic" verdict is not responsible by reason of mental disease or defect. Such defendants are under the jurisdiction of a special board for a time equal to the length of confinement if convicted. The board can confine using criteria different from those for civil commitment.

8. One commentator, the head of a Mental Health Clinic attached to the criminal courts in a California county gives us a view of how the insanity defense works (or should work) in practice.[83]

> It is usually a mistake for forensic mental health experts to poach on the preserve of judge or jury. Many an expert in the early stages of his forensic career has been admonished by an exasperated judge not to overreach, to *Please,* Doctor, confine yourself to the matter of your expertise: present the natural history of the defendant's pathological mental condition and draw a line connecting that history to the point in time that is the focus of the proceeding; do not pre-try the case according to the lights of your own moral sensibility, and do not argue, or even consider, the relative advantages of different sentences and dispositions. *Having done what is his to do, the expert should retire gracefully to let the judge and jury do what is theirs.*
>
> That, at least, is the theory, and in a jury trial, theory and practice come closest to being one. But despite memorable exceptions, psychiatric defenses are rarely raised in front of a jury. They are infrequently raised at all, but when the occasions arise the odds are better than 10 to 1 that the principals will opt for a bench trial, a trial before a judge without a jury.
>
> The significance of this proportion for a mental health professional appointed to do a forensic evaluation is this: when the expert comes to write his report, the vast majority of the time his audience will be the judge and the two opposing attorneys rather than a jury. Submitting his opinions and conclusions to professional officers of the court, the expert will be free to ignore evidentiary conventions he would be forced to respect were he testifying before the twelve amateur fact-finders of the jury.
>
> Judges, considering themselves relatively immune to the corrupting influence of irrelevant, unsubstantiated or prejudicial evidence, will generally admit for their own scrutiny testimony which they would hold inadmissible in a jury trial. They will take the evidence "for what it's worth," assigning it as much or as little weight as they think it deserves. As for the attorneys, they are supposed to be biased to begin with because of their role as advocates. In that sense, they are beyond corrupting by expert testimony (although not beyond persuading, as I will argue later).
>
> In a bench trial, therefore, the forensic mental health expert can approach his job in the role of an advisor presenting an unbowdlerized overview to a broadly empowered professional administrator rather than in the role of a technical assistant presenting carefully edited material to a fact-finding committee of amateurs—amateurs, moreover, much of whose naïveté it is legally necessary to maintain intact.
>
> The forensic mental health report that follows, addressing a judge in a bench trial, takes this broad advisory approach. It combines elements of clinical report, legal brief, and a type of dispositional analysis and recommendation one might expect to find in the post-conviction reports written by probation officers to aid judges at sentencing time. The report is full of material that would have

83. C. J. Meyers, An Alternative Approach to Writing Forensic Mental Health Reports, 13 J. Psychiatry and L.—(1985).

been inadmissible in a jury trial, but which the judge, free to take or leave alone, accepted into evidence.

Background. This case was referred to me by the father of a chronically mentally ill young man who had been arrested and charged with over 50 counts of molesting children. If the young man was convicted, which seemed likely considering the overwhelming evidence against him, he faced many years in prison, an experience the father felt sure his son would be unable to survive.

The defendant had already been examined by a veteran forensic examiner retained by the son's defense attorney, but the expert's report had been discouraging: he wrote that the young man fit California's Mentally Disordered Sex Offender category perfectly, but regretted that the legislature had recently seen fit to make that category an historical curiosity and to phase out the treatment program that had accompanied it. Since the defendant apparently knew he was molesting children ("knew the nature and quality of his act") and from his attempts to avoid detection presumably knew that what he was doing was wrong, he did not seem to fit California's recently adopted modified M'Naghten standard. Hence he could not avoid prison and get admitted to a security hospital via the still existing route of a successful insanity defense.

(In many jurisdictions, hospitals for mentally ill criminals are uglier institutions than prisons, but in California mentally ill criminals who are diverted from the prison system to the mental hospital system are not just dumped in a big hole with a high fence and a euphemistic name. The treatment available to them in the hospital systems meets a higher standard than that available within the prison system, and the mentally ill offenders committed there are better protected from themselves and from other inmates than they would be in prison. This safety advantage is particularly significant for child molesters who in prison are often the focus of more conventional inmates' vindictive ire. The father's concern about the life-expectancy of his son was realistic.)

After examining the young man in jail, I became convinced a) that he was severely mentally impaired, b) that his mental impairment contributed to his criminality by clouding his moral understanding and c) that it would be advantageous both to the defendant and to the public if he were committed to the mental hospital system rather than to the prison system. Since it was a bench trial that was impending rather than a jury trial, I wrote the following report, divided into three sections:

The first section is the most conventional: it documents the impairment, listing the symptoms and explaining the diagnoses. I am unaware of any statements in the first section of the report that would be considered legally objectionable or excludable under current California law.

The second section blends a legal analysis of California's current insanity test with an application of the test to the defendant's offences. My testimony to the ultimate conclusion—my statement that I think the defendant should be found Not Guilty By Reason of Insanity—is currently admissible in California jury trials, although if reformers have their way, the law may soon be changed to restrict expert testimony to clinical presentation alone. It is unlikely, however, that my legal analysis would be admissible in a jury trial, although the defense attorney could request something on this order be made part of the judge's instructions to the jury before the jury retired to consider their verdict. Since this was a bench trial, I felt free to expand the range of my forensic presentation. The judge, in turn, was free to take it or leave it.

The third and final section "testifies to the disposition." If "testifying to the conclusion" is controversial, "testifying to the disposition" is universally abjured. Testifying to the disposition is using the tail to wag the dog: it is telling the trier of fact what will happen to the defendant if the facts are found one way or the other, and urging the trier to make a finding that yields the most pragmatically satisfying outcome. The general rule is that juries are not to consider disposition. *Theirs is to decide what happened, not to ask what will happen once they decide.* A consideration of the future is deemed an impediment to the determination of the past. The rule is taken seriously and strictly enforced. A defense attorney who turns a jury's attention to the disposition that attends its verdict risks rebuke. A prosecutor who does the same thing flirts with mistrial.

But again, this is a bench trial. There is no jury on the case whose purity of function must be preserved. Because of my experience working with mentally ill offenders in a public forensic mental health clinic, I am in a position to know about the dispositions contingent on a finding of Not Guilty By Reason of Insanity. I have no desire to keep this information to myself. The judge, sharing the normal human concern about the practical effects of his decisions, probably will be willing to listen to what I have to say.

The dispositional section of the report had a function other than getting the judge to think about the long-term practical consequences of his finding. It was also written with an eye to persuading the prosecutor to think about those consequences and to try to persuade him that it would be in the interest of justice to stipulate to a finding of Not Guilty By Reason of Insanity—*to dispense with a trial altogether.* It seems to be a well-kept secret of the criminal justice system that 9 out of 10 findings of insanity are made with the blessing of the prosecution and are in fact a type of plea-bargain rather than the outcome of a trial. I was trying to persuade the prosecutor to join the 9 out of 10, but in this I was unsuccessful. The prosecutor is said to have stated that he considered the arguments in the report carefully, but, given the notoriety of the case, he thought it would look unseemly if he just "rolled over."

Nevertheless, the report may have had some of the intended effect. The prosecutor contested the insanity plea, but his cross-examination was the most cordial and respectful I have yet experienced on the witness stand. I think that he may have been persuaded that the State had nothing to lose from a verdict of Not Guilty By Reason of Insanity, but that for political reasons he was obliged to put up a fight. The case, therefore, came to trial. The report, which formed the basis of my subsequent testimony, was admitted into evidence without objection.

Forensic Mental Health Report: The Case of Harold Prince

I. Evaluation of the Defendant's Mental Capacities: The Defendant Is Severely Impaired by a Combination of Organic Brain Damage and Schizophrenia

Harold Prince is a 34-year-old chronic mental patient, stabilized on antipsychotic medications. For the past ten years he has carried a diagnosis of schizophrenia, been supported by social security disability payments, and resided at the same board and care home in Capital City. For the past five years he has supplemented his disability payments with earnings from his job as janitor at the local day care program. Until recently, he appeared to be a model community mental health patient: although carrying one of the most severe psychiatric diagnoses, paranoid schizophrenia, it seemed that he was being treated successfully and economically as an outpatient in the community instead of as an inpatient on the ward of a State mental hospital.

It then became apparent that Mr. Prince had been molesting children at the day care program. From statements in the police reports, it appears that he would follow some of the children into the lavatory, then entice and/or coerce them into allowing him to wipe, rub and poke their anuses with his gloved or newspaper-wrapped hand.

On June 8, 1984, Mr. Prince entered a dual plea in Superior Court: (1) Guilty of molesting two of the children; and (2) Not guilty by reason of insanity. The next day, I spent four hours interviewing and testing Mr. Prince at the county jail. Prior to the examination, I familiarized myself with police reports of interviews with witnesses, with suspected victims and with the defendant (including his partial confession). I also read some miscellaneous material provided by Mr. Prince's father, including a psychiatric evaluation, performed last December by Dr. Nancy Lisbon, giving evidence to the Department of Social Services about the defendant's continuing mental disability. Subsequent to interviewing Mr. Prince, I was made privy to the record of his two hospitalizations at Napa State Hospital.

Briefly, Prince's history as derived from official records, family and the defendant himself is as follows: He is the second son in a family that includes five children. His father is a minister who was hoping that this son would become a physician. Young Prince, however, abandoned his premedical studies in the late 1960's and dropped out of college to experiment with drugs in the subculture of the Haight-Ashbury. Prince admits that he tried various hallucinogens, including LSD and psilocybin, plus "uppers, downers, glue, chloroform—anything I could get my hands on," although he carefully points out that he never sampled heroin or cocaine. Massive drug abuse was followed by the destabilization of his mind and a career as a chronic mental patient. It is unclear at this remove in time to what extent the drug abuse was cause, effect or coincidental concomitant of his "nervous breakdown."

Prince was admitted to Napa State Hospital in 1975 and in 1976. Two years earlier he was admitted to a mental hospital in Fresno. The Fresno records are unavailable to me, but the Napa records, which chronicle a flare-up of his illness and are the aftermath of a near fatal intentional overdose of highly toxic anti-depressant medication, indicate that the schizophrenia diagnosis has been Prince's burden for at least a decade. Currently, per the December 1983 evaluation of Dr. Lisbon, Prince is diagnosed as suffering from schizophrenia, paranoid type, and he is being treated accordingly with anti-psychotic medication.

That Prince is mentally impaired is obvious to an examiner, professional or layman. He forgets questions and loses the threads of his own thoughts so that his statements, unless his interrogator keeps bringing him back to point, tend to wander on tangents. His speech resembles that of a punch-drunk boxer: it is hesitant and laborious, seeming to be produced one word at a time. His difficulty in thinking, child-like manner and nervous hunger for approval from his audience remind one of the way Lon Chaney, Jr., played Lenny, the gigantic simpleton in Steinbeck's "Of Mice and Men." Prince is small and frail, however, giving an impression of both physical and mental weakness. His wrists are as thin as a girl's, his movements are poorly coordinated and when he walks, especially on the day I interviewed him, when his natural jerkiness was emphasized by the limp of an injured foot, he calls to mind a bird with a broken wing.

The clinical impression that Prince suffers from brain damage is sustained by his performance on psychological tests. On the revised Wechsler Adult Intelligence Scale, Prince did best on those sub-sections which test abilities resistant to the effects of brain damage, and he did relatively poorly on those sub-sections which test abilities susceptible to those effects. For instance, on the Information and Vocabulary subtests, measures of funds of knowledge acquired before he began abusing drugs, Prince scored in the 37th and 25th percentile respectively, lowish scores within the normal range. On the Block Design and Digit Span subtests, measures of current spatial relations skills and short term memory, Prince scored in 9th and 5th percentile respectively, scores within the borderline retarded range.

The MMPI profile, derived from a long questionnaire designed to test personality characteristics rather than neurological deficits, is nevertheless consistent with a diagnosis of brain damage. It is the profile of a mental cripple, reflecting a sense of weakness, helplessness, and self-contempt along with an intense suspiciousness towards a world he finds incomprehensible and overwhelming.

The brain damage appears to be diffuse, rather than localized, moderate rather than extreme, chronic and stable rather than acute and deteriorating. A diagnosis of brain damage is consistent with the defendant's years of chemical self-assault, but brain damage alone does not account for the degree of the defendant's disability, nor even for the major part of his impairment.

According to the records, Prince suffers from schizophrenia, a severe mental disease characterized by gross disturbances of thinking, perceiving, feeling and action. Schizophrenia is like a bad drug trip that starts spontaneously, lasts weeks or months instead of hours, then abates as mysteriously as it began, leaving part of the patient's mind burned away. Attacks are usually recurrent, and the patient is left with less and less, until he bottoms out on a low plateau.

Typically, after an onset in late adolescence or early adulthood, the disease goes through three phases:

(1) *Prodromal Phase.* There is a marked, though often insidiously gradual, deterioration of functioning. Increasing social isolation, strange behavior, bizarre imaginings, poor grooming and hygiene, roller-coaster emotional instability in some cases, in other cases, an apparent inability to respond with normal emotional intensity or warmth to any stimulus—all these morbid signs herald the patient's withdrawal into a private reality. Prince may have gone through such a phase in 1968, but the symptoms would have been masked by the overlapping effects of his hallucinogenic drug use.

(2) *Active Phase.* The patient goes mad: he becomes classically crazy. Judgment is nil, ideas are absurd, hallucinatory voices intrude, and communication verges on the incoherent. The patient is psychotic, and if the prodromal phase is recognized retrospectively as having gone on for six months or more, the diagnosis will be schizophrenia. Schizophrenics generally perceive their condition as being imposed upon them from outside themselves. If they develop lunatic theories about the source of their tribulation and either plan or try to fight back, their

schizophrenia will be classified as "paranoid type." If the patient passively acquiesces in his affliction, he is more likely to be classified as "undifferentiated type." Prince, at different times in his career as a mental patient, has been classified as a chronic undifferentiated schizophrenic (Napa State Hospital, 1975) and as a paranoid schizophrenic (Dr. N. Lisbon, 1983).

(3) *Residual Phase.* The patient returns to his prodromal state, except that he is more likely to be emotionally flat and apathetic rather than erratically intense. Delusional theories and even hallucinations may persist, unfueled by the emotional energy of the active phase. Currently, with the help of anti-psychotic medications, Mr. Prince's schizophrenia is stabilized in the residual phase.

Schizophrenic psychosis is generally distinguishable from a psychosis generated by an extended drug intoxication, but there are exceptions to this rule. A long run of amphetamine abuse, for instance, can precipitate a paranoid psychosis with symptoms indistinguishable on psychiatric interview from the symptoms of paranoid schizophrenia. Bad PCP and LSD trips can also mimic a schizophrenic psychosis. Without knowledge of the patient's recent past, the clinician will have to wait to see how the psychosis resolves itself before he can feel confident of the label he appends to it.

Hallucinogen- or amphetamine-induced psychoses last a matter of hours, days or, sometimes, weeks, but schizophrenia, unless treated by an as yet undiscovered cure, is a lifetime affliction. If the onset of a schizophrenic psychosis and a drug-induced psychosis coincide, as they sometimes do in our polydrug-ridden society, teasing out which psychotic symptom is attributable to which drug and which is attributable to the concurrent schizophrenic process is a task beyond the capacity of current diagnostic technology. Mr. Prince in 1984 shows signs of two sorts of organic impairment, schizophrenic and drug-induced. He is a "burned out case," and it is impossible to say which cause is responsible for which part of the ruin, or even to document physiologically what parts of his brain have been damaged. It is possible, however, to describe his current behavior and to point to its shortfall from normality.

Aside from the mental stumblings that, regardless of their content, constitute the *form* of his thinking, Prince's two most striking pathological characteristics are his sexual immaturity and his ignorance of what real people do and expect others to do in the real world. I assume that Prince has regressed from a pre-morbid level of functioning and that his regression is attributable to the massive chemical assaults on his brain cells and to his schizophrenia, but however he got where he is, he now responds to life like a precociously sexual but otherwise socially backward pre-teen, rather than like a man with the biologic age of 34.

He lusts after women, finds them unattainable and makes do with Playboy centerfolds and masturbation. To his muddled way of thinking, the child molestation seems to have been a thing apart from his habitual auto-erotic sex leading to orgasm. He seems to be unaware that what he was doing with the children was a sexual act. He wanted to scratch them where he thought they itched, where in the past he had scratched himself and found relief and pleasure. He knew what he was doing was not allowed, but he knew it the way a child knows he should not explore the private parts of his classmates but then naughtily colludes with them anyway, expecting a frown, a harsh word and, perhaps, a spanking if he gets caught. He had no sense of the magnitude of the emotions he might be arousing in the children or in the adults who cared for them. He still lacks that sense, although he realizes that the penalties the world attaches to what he still perceives as playful and affectionate naughtiness are terrifyingly severe.

Unfortunately, for his victims and for Prince, he genuinely likes children. They are the only people he can come close to understanding. Such true guilt as he feels comes from his acknowledgment that he liked some children more than others and was not evenhanded in bestowing what he considered his favors. He feels he deprived some of the children because, while liking them, he selfishly spent time with those he liked more. In his own mind, Prince was following some sort of primitive golden rule, doing unto others what he would have them do unto him.

We can take some solace from the fact that, unlike those cases where a child-molester robs his victims of their childhood by imposing adult forms of sexuality on the children before their time, in this case a childlike adult engaged in childlike "potty games," with real children rather than in the frighteningly intense or anatomically traumatic acts of adult sexuality. For all their aesthetic and moral repugnance, there is a good chance that his acts did not leave the children who engaged in them seriously scarred.

Prince's lack of ability to appreciate what people expect of one another in the real world is exemplified by his answers on the "Comprehension" subtest of the Wechsler Adult Intelligence Scale, a section of the exam that measures a kind of common sense. On this subtest Prince scores lower than 99 percent of the general population. Although he is not mentally retarded, he does no better here than those who used to be labeled "congenital morons" before the most recent wave of official euphemism relabelled them "developmentally disabled."

"What is the thing to do if you find an envelope in the street that is sealed, and addressed, and has a new stamp?" asks the test.

"I might pick it up and look at the letter," answers Prince, "or I might just leave it there."

"Why are child labor laws needed?" asks the test.

"Pregnant women can't do as much work," Prince says, picking up on the word "labor." He then veers off on another tack: "It would be good if children *could* work. They learn real fast and could do a lot."

Question: "Why do some people prefer to borrow money from a bank rather than from a friend?"

Answer: "You know you can get money from the bank right away. I don't like to borrow. I forget to pay back."

Question: "Why does the state require people to get a license before they get married?"

Answer: "I don't know. (Smiles.) I trip back to Roman days. And then God comes into the picture. I'm not too sure."

Question: "What should you do if while in the movies you are the first person to see smoke and fire?"

Answer: "I'd get help. You know, (cups hands to make megaphone) say, *'Help!'* Or I'd try to put it out."

Prince grabs on to the wrong end of every stick, then pokes himself in the eye with it. His unerring sense of the inappropriate carries over to his jail experiences. If some psychologist ever devises a "Competency to Survive in Jail Test," Prince will fail it. If presented with the question, "What is the thing to do if you are arrested and charged with multiple counts of child molesting?" a good answer is not, "Tell all the guys in the holding cell what I'm in for." Prince was not asked such a question, but when presented with the situation in his life, he acted true to form: he told all the guys in the holding cell what he was in for. "They said they would kill me, but then they didn't." A cellmate had second thoughts, wrapped a sock around Prince's neck and twisted until "everything started to get dark." Then the cellmate thought yet again, and let the defendant recover. "He said I wasn't worth it." (Smiles). Perhaps God does indeed look out for children and idiots, both of whom are related in spirit to the defendant.

II. The Relationship of the Defendant's Mental Incapacities to the Validity of His Not Guilty by Reason of Insanity Plea: Prince Was Impaired Enough at the Time of His Offenses to Meet California's Modified M'Naghten Standard

Mr. Prince has pled not guilty by reason of insanity. In the California state courts, an accused entering a plea of Not Guilty by Reason of Insanity must prove that he was incapable of knowing or understanding the nature and quality of his act and of distinguishing right from wrong at the time of the offense. Prince can meet the conditions of this stringent test.

It is my opinion that at the time of the acts, Mr. Prince was suffering from a diseased and permanently drug-scarred mind to such a degree that he should not be held criminally responsible for his actions. He was unable to appreciate the criminality of his acts, and he is still unable. He had a sense that what he did was wrong, but the sense of wrongness was akin to that of a child who knows that potty games are wrong but who tries to play with his peers in bathroom or bushes anyway. In sexual matters, as in most matters, (recall the answers from the IQ test) much of what Mr. Prince thinks right, is wrong. Mr. Prince's moral and intellectual capacities are so impaired that he cannot attain the level of understanding necessary to assert that he "understood the nature and quality of his act." He does not appear to have been aware that he was wiping and rubbing the children for sexual gratification. Sexual gratification was something he did in the privacy of his room.

Historically, we are informed, the California trial courts have placed "a commendably broad interpretation upon the M'Naghten knowledge test." People v. Wolf, 394 P.2d 959, 961-962 (Calif. 1964). Prince did not appear to have the "capacity to appreciate the character and to comprehend the probable or possible consequences of his act[s] [at the time he committed them.]" A. Goldstein, The Insanity Defense (1967).

A broad construction of "know" carries with it a broad reading of "nature and quality." "To know the quality of an act, with all its social and emotional implications, requires more than an abstract, purely intellectual knowledge. Likewise, to talk of appreciating the full significance of an act means that 'nature and quality' must be understood as including more than the physical nature of the act." Id. at 51. Prince knew that he was not squeezing or rubbing a lemon when he squeezed or rubbed his child victims, but his social and emotional appreciations of the implications of his acts were so deficient that he was unaware that he was molesting them. "In those situations where the accused does not know the nature and quality of his act, in the broad sense, he will not know that it was wrong, no matter what construction 'wrong' is given." Id. at 51.

In light of the foregoing analysis, I believe that Prince lacked the necessary capacity to understand what he was doing and that he did not "know" or "distinguish" the rightness or wrongness of his acts. If called upon, I will so testify.

III. Dispositional Comments: Both the Public and the Defendant Will Benefit If the Defendant Is Detained Indefinitely in a Maximum Security State Hospital Rather Than Sentenced Determinately to State Prison

A jury's only concern is determination of fact. A prosecutor has a broader mission. To a jury, it is supposed to be irrelevant whether the defendant acquitted by reason of insanity spends more or less time in custody than the defendant convicted of crime; or whether the quality of care that the defendant receives while he is in custody can have an effect on the likelihood that he will reoffend once he is released; or whether the quality of the parole program available to a state prison parolee is better or worse than the quality of the parole program available to a state hospital parolee. All these considerations are relevant to an officer of the court pledged to protect the public, however, and it is to these matters that I will now address myself.

If Prince is convicted of the charges against him and is *not* found Not Guilty by Reason of Insanity (NGI), he faces a sentence of 8 years. With credit for time served and with time off for good behavior he should be out in closer to 3½. If Prince is found NGI, his "sentence" will be indeterminate and theoretically extendable indefinitely if it can be proved that he remains dangerous. Studies of averages indicate that it is likely that he will spend approximately the same amount of time in the mental institution as he would spend in prison. There is therefore not much to gain in the way of time by sending Prince to prison, and there may even be something to lose. If Prince continues to be a threat, as one presumes him to be now, the public will not be safe from him for long if he merely goes to prison.

Prince would be treated differently in prison, however, than he would be treated if he were sent to a hospital for the criminally insane, like Atascadero. The Department of Corrections would probably domicile him at Vacaville where the treatment he would receive would be inferior to the treatment he would receive in the hospital, and the security would be no better. Vacaville could treat his schizophrenia adequately—the medication is available everywhere—but Atascadero is the only institution that has elaborate and intensive programs designed to treat pedophiles. Currently, Prince is even unaware that he has a problem in this area. By putting him in a group with other more mentally stable pedophiles, it can be hammered home to him that he shares his inclinations with others, that the inclination is sexual in nature and, when expressed toward children, it is shameful. He can then try to learn how to restrain himself.

At Atascadero, he may prove suitable for admission to their unique aversive conditioning program, and if so he would be subject to tests of his sexual arousal to potentially exciting pictures and tapes of children before a decision was made whether or not to recommend his release. Atascadero also has an experimental program using *depo provera,* a female hormone that inhibits male sexuality and which has sometimes been called "chemical castration." If Prince remains persistently arousable by children, he may wish to volunteer for the experimental program, if it could give him a chance to be paroled.

It should also be mentioned that Prince has a better chance of surviving unmolested and unassaulted himself at Atascadero than he does in prison, regardless of the treatment he receives. The Department of Mental Hygiene has a better record of protecting its pedophiles from the rough injustice of avenging fellow inmates than does the Department of Corrections. And Prince, with his combination of tactlessness and helplessness, needs more protection than most.

If Prince eventually would be paroled from Atascadero, he would be paroled to a program that provides much closer supervision and control than he would get from a conventional prison parole program. Mental health parole programs for penal code commitments (sometimes called "AB1229 programs," after the assembly bill of 1975 that mandated their existence) use psychiatric social workers and psychologists to monitor and coordinate treatment and living arrangements when the patients leave the hospital. Any backsliding does not have to await a *Morrissey* hearing before the patient can be returned to the hospital for further treatment, but usually depends on the recommendation of the supervisor/coordinator or his designee.

Conclusion

Clinically, Prince is brain-damaged and schizophrenic and has carried these diagnoses for a decade. I believe he is so impaired by his condition that he could be considered Not Guilty by Reason of Insanity, if the California test is construed broadly. Such a construction would be kinder to Prince, since his crime and his simpleton's impulsiveness make him vulnerable in a prison. It would also be considerate of the public, since Prince would be likely to spend as much time in hospital as in prison, and he might spend much more. The superior treatment available to Prince in the mental hospital would decrease his chances of reoffending, and, were he paroled from the mental hospital, he would be under closer surveillance than he would be were he paroled from prison. Considerations of substantial justice, of public safety, and of best available treatment for the defendant, therefore, all coincide in a finding of Not Guilty by Reason of Insanity.

Postscript. This case eventually came to a satisfying conclusion, at least from my perspective: in a contested bench trial, where two psychologists and a psychiatrist testified that they considered the defendant sane—sane because he was afraid to admit what he did and hence demonstrated that he knew what he did was wrong, and sane because he was intact enough to realize that he was touching his victims bottoms and not their tops (and hence knew "the nature and quality of his act")—the judge, nevertheless, found persuasive my testimony to the contrary.

To give credit where it is due, the Not Guilty by Reason of Insanity verdict would never have been possible without a relatively fair-minded and non-vindictive prosecutor, conscientious investigation and honest testimony by the police, and, above all, a judge who had the courage, in this time of mounting hysteria about child abuse and of post-*Hinckley* hostility toward the insanity defense, to make the right rather than the politically popular decision.

9. *"Guilty But Mentally Ill."* Several states have given juries the choice between the traditional verdict of "not guilty by reason of insanity" (NGI) and a special new verdict of "guilty but mentally ill" (GBMI). This new verdict differs from the conventional insanity verdict in one crucial way: the defendant is legally convicted of and sentenced for a crime. After the trial court sentences the defendant to a prison term authorized by the regular criminal statute, state authorities then examine the defendant and may choose to confine him in a mental hospital for all or part of his prison term. Typically, the jury is instructed to hand down the GBMI verdict rather than the NGI verdict when it finds the defendant mentally ill, but not so mentally ill as to win full exculpation from criminal responsibility. Thus, the GBMI test in most states defines mental illness more broadly than does the regular insanity defense test. For example, in some states that use the Model Penal Code insanity test, the jury may hand down a GMBI verdict if it finds the defendant was "unable to appreciate the nature and quality of his act."

Does the GBMI verdict serve any useful purpose, when all jurisdictions already provide mental health treatment to prisoners within the regular prison system? Does it represent a rational compromise between total criminal responsibility and no criminal responsibility at all? If juries are offered the GBMI alternative, how often do you think they will hand down an NGI verdict?

10. In Jones v. United States, 103 S. Ct. 3043 (1983), the Supreme Court upheld a District of Columbia law under which a person acquitted by reason of insanity is automatically committed for 50 days and then may gain release only if he proves by a preponderance of the evidence that he is no longer mentally ill or dangerous. The court found no constitutional problem in the lack of correlation between the acquittee's civil commitment and the hypothetical maximum sentence he could have received if convicted. Justice Powell noted that some acquittees might suffer civil commitment for a shorter time than the hypothetical sentence and others might suffer a longer confinement than the hypothetical sentence. However, he found justification for the law in the different purposes underlying civil commitment and criminal imprisonment, the former being concerned with present and future dangerousness, the latter with punishment for a completed act.

11. Mental impairment other than a mental disease has led to an interesting line of cases. Note how a relatively newly recognized clinical phenomenon interacts with a relatively new legal treatment of the problem of criminal responsibility.

Premenstrual Syndrome: A Disease of the Mind?[84]

R. v. Craddock

A woman of 30 was convicted of a first offence in 1970. Her subsequent uncontrolled behaviour resulted in some 30 convictions. Psychiatric reports concluded that she had an unstable personality disorder and that she was troublesome and attention-seeking. In May, 1979, when she was working at a pub, a fight broke out and a barmaid was stabbed to death. She was charged with murder and taken into custody.

It was noticed that her uncontrollable disruptive behaviour followed a definite pattern each month, which was not curbed or corrected by spells in prison or psychiatric wards. Dr. Katherina Dalton visited her in prison during her trial and diagnosed PMS [premenstrual syndrome] which could be treated by daily injections of progesterone. When she was convicted of manslaughter due to diminished responsibility brought about by PMS, her case was set back to allow a period of treatment so that an appropriate sentencing order could be made. On May 1, 1980, Dr. Dalton reported that she could be completely stabilised on progesterone. Her condition improved on 50 mg/day, but stabilised fully only on 100 mg/day. [The judge] made a probation order of three years (the maximum possible), with a condition that she should receive such treatment as Dr. Dalton prescribed. She was to be given progesterone injections by the district nursing service. In October, 1980, because of a failure of communication, she did not receive progesterone for four days. On the fourth day she did not eat; she took a train to Southend, and threw a brick through a window and then reported herself to the police. She was arrested and taken into custody. Her condition was explained and progesterone given, and she became calm once again. She was released by the magistrates.

Efforts were made to reduce the daily dose, since 100 mg injections were painful and there was of risk of abscess. By April, 1981, she was on four 100 mg injections weekly, supplemented by suppositories. After 3½ weeks of this lower dosage, she erupted without warning. She tried to slash her wrists; and she wrote to a police sergeant whom she claimed had insulted her in 1978, threatening to kill him. Four days later she went to a police station carrying a knife, to wait for him to come on duty, and was arrested. While in prison she was given 100 mg of progesterone daily and stabilised. After being charged with three offences relating to having intent to kill and carrying an offensive weapon, she was tried at the Old Bailey and convicted. Another probation order of three years was imposed, subject to treatment.

R. v. English

On November 10, 1981, a woman of 37 was convicted of the manslaughter of her lover . . . because of diminished responsibility owing to PMS. She had no previous convictions and no history of uncontrolled violence. . . . She had married in 1963, and had two sons. . . . The marriage was not happy and in 1972 she was divorced. In 1976, she met a married man six years younger than herself. He was an alcoholic who subsequently lost both his driving license and his job. Her

84. D. Brahams, 11 *The Lancet* No. 8257 pp.1238-1240 (November 28, 1981).

relationship with him was stormy and fraught with jealousy on both sides. On December 16, 1980, there was a bitter row about his intention to meet another woman and he attacked her physically and left the house. She was worried about him and telephoned him during the late afternoon, and asked him not to meet the other woman and not to go out drinking but to contact Alcoholics Anonymous as he had done in the past. He refused. He went drinking and during the evening Mrs. English found him in a pub. He was aggressive and quarrelsome. He bought a quarter bottle of whiskey and went to wait at the bus stop. She collected him in her car. He said he wanted to meet the other woman: she drove him round Colchester, but they did not find her. He became angry and violent and they had a further bitter row. He drank some of the whiskey and left the car when they reached another pub. She waited in the car park. He emerged very drunk and got back in the car asking her to take him home with her. She refused. There was another violent row and he got out of her car saying "I hate you and I never want to see you again." She drove away, but then was unhappy about parting on such bad terms and turned back to look for him. It was about 9:40 P.M. when she saw him. He made a V sign as she approached slowly in the car. She then drove her car at him, pinning him between the bonnet and a lamp post. He suffered severe leg, foot, and pelvic injuries, and died in the hospital on December 31. She was charged forthwith with causing grievous bodily harm (and later with murder), was able to recount clearly what had happened, and began menstruating on leaving the police station.

At her trial she pleaded guilty to manslaughter on the grounds of diminished responsibility caused by PMS. The plea was accepted by the prosecution subject to the judge's acceptance of it. Mr. Justice Purchas accepted that plea after consulting reports from Dr. Dalton and Dr. John Hamilton, a consultant psychiatrist at Broadmoor, for the defence, and from Dr. Paul D'Orban, a consultant psychiatrist from Holloway Prison, for the prosecution. Dr. Dalton said . . . as early as 1966, symptoms of PMS, though not necessarily labelled and recognized as such, had been recorded. In 1971 [English] had been sterilised. Sterilisation increased the severity of PMS. By the evening of December 16 she had not eaten for 9 hours owing to emotional stress; she was expecting her period (which started at 5 A.M. the next morning) and knew that alcohol was bad for her, so she had drunk only orange juice. It was Dr. Dalton's opinion that sufferers from PMS have raised glucose tolerance so that they are not able to tolerate long food gaps. When their blood sugar drops, there is an automatic surge of adrenaline to raise the blood sugar level so that hypoglycaemia does not occur. It was this accumulation of adrenaline after a long food gap which was responsible for the violence, irritability, and impulsive behaviour.

Dealing with the psychological implications of diminished responsibility, Dr. Hamilton gave evidence that at the crucial moment when she snapped, she was suffering from PMS. She was in a state of anxiety, and, to a degree, provoked by the deceased; she had not eaten for 9 hours, and was probably hypoglycaemic. The converging circumstances, and the fact that she found herself in possession of an offensive weapon, her car, caused her to do what she did. PMS was a factor to be taken into account.

Dr. Dalton gave evidence that PMS is a disease of the body and therefore a disease of the mind in that the bodily metabolism is upset and that upsets the mental processes. Dr. Hamilton agreed.

How Far Has the Door Been Opened?

[I]n 1957 the Homicide Act, s.2, introduced a new defence to murder, known as "diminished responsibility. . . ."

S.2 provides:

> (1) Where a person kills or is a party to the killing of another, he shall not be convicted of murder if he was suffering from such abnormality of mind (whether arising from a condition of arrested or retarded development of mind or any inherent causes or induced by disease or injury) as substantially impaired his mental responsibility for his acts and omissions in doing or being a party to the killing. . . .
> (3) A person who but for this section would be liable . . . to be convicted of murder shall be liable instead to be convicted of manslaughter.

Looking at the cases of English and Craddock from the point of view of a lawyer . . . it seems to me that the cases are very far apart. In Craddock there is a history of criminal disruptive behaviour, and regular treatment with progesterone apparently controls these outbursts. Whereas English, who snapped under stress, was able to recount fully and comprehensively what happened before and after the killing, Craddock had no clear recollection at all of her behaviour, and is, it appears, unable to appreciate her own deterioration into a state of uncontrolled behaviour, much less curb it by will. Her crimes were random violent acts often so extraordinary as to appear to the lay outsider, motiveless . . . or plain mad.

Critics of the inclusion of PMS should bear in mind that diminished responsibility has been pleaded with success in cases where one would have thought there was no chance of a defence of insanity succeeding—mercy killers, deserted spouses, or disappointed lovers who killed while in a state of depression, persons with chronic anxiety states. It is surprising that there has been no spectacular increase in the number of persons escaping conviction for murder on the ground of their mental abnormality. Has the door been pushed open too far now, however? Should a person with severe and chronic migraine be included as suffering from abnormality of the mind? Or toothache? Or back trouble? . . .

12. In United States v. Gould, 741 F.2d 45 (4th Cir. 1984), the defendant, charged with attempted bank robbery and larceny, pleaded insanity on the ground that he suffered from a "pathological gambling disorder." Addressing the general problem of "new" insanity defenses, the court said that it would only recognize a specific disorder as a defense where there is "substantial acceptance in the relevant [scientific] discipline" that the disorder causes specific forms of antisocial conduct. The court found no such consensus among psychiatrists on the "gambling" disorder and did not even reach the question whether the defendant met the then prevailing Model Penal Code test of insanity.

VI

FURTHER REQUISITES OF JUST PUNISHMENT

16

LEGALITY

COMMONWEALTH v. KELLER

Pennsylvania Court of Common Pleas
35 D. & C. 2d 615 (1964)

Gates, P.J. Violet Miller Keller married Elton Ray Keller on June 29, 1957, and she was not divorced from him until the first week of December, 1963. From 1961 until the time of the trial, Elton Ray Keller was in the military service, and the parties were living separate and apart from each other. From August of 1961, defendant had illicit and regular sexual relations with one Roy Schaeffer. In April of 1962, defendant secretly gave birth to a female child which, defendant said, was born dead. She wrapped the dead body in a towel and wrapped a plastic sheet around the towel and put the body in this manner into a paper carton and put the carton on a shelf in the basement of the premises wherein she had her apartment, where the body remained until discovered in August of 1963. When found, the body was badly decomposed, and only small pieces of skin and bones remained. Inside the box was evidence of the presence of maggots. A forensic pathologist examined the remains, but, due to the extensive decomposition of the body, he was unable to determine the cause of death or whether the child was born dead or alive. Defendant never told anyone of her pregnancy or of the birth of this child, neither did she tell anyone what she had done with the child before she was arrested.

In March of 1963, she again gave birth to a child secretly in the bathroom of her apartment, after leaving her bed, which she was then sharing with Roy Schaeffer. She signed a confession, wherein she stated that the child was born alive, and that she put the child's head into the commode, intending to drown it. Using bathroom towels, she cleaned the blood from the floor and put the towels and the body of the dead baby in a sanitary napkin box and stuffed other towels in the box and put the box in the bathroom closet. This was in the early morning hours of March 15, 1963. She did not tell Roy Schaeffer or anyone else what had happened or what she had done with the child's body. Later in the day, she was taken to the hospital, and, at first, denied having recently given birth to a child and did not admit it until the child's body was discovered as a result of a police search of her apartment on March 23, 1963.[1]

Following the discovery of the bodies of these dead children, defendant was indicted for adultery and two counts of a common law misdemeanor, characterized as the "indecent disposition of a dead body." Following a three day trial, defendant was convicted on all three charges. In due course, defendant properly filed a motion in arrest of judgment and a motion for a new trial. . . .

From the present posture of the record, and from defendant's brief, the following issues are raised: . . .

4. Did the court err in refusing defendant's motion to quash the indictment, because it did not charge defendant with a crime cognizable under the laws of the Commonwealth of Pennsylvania?. . .

Common Law Crimes in Pennsylvania

Defendant does not contend, nor does she argue, that the evidence is insufficient to convict her of adultery. She does, however, argue, at least in support of her demurrer to the indictment and motion to quash the indictment, that the indictment does not charge defendant with a crime under the laws of this Commonwealth. However, at oral argument and in the brief submitted to us by defendant, there is a tacit admission that it would be a crime at common law to indecently dispose of a dead body.

We consider the matter of common law crimes both gravely and carefully. We have considered authorities on the subject, both under the laws of the Commonwealth of Pennsylvania and in other common law jurisdictions. We conclude that this bill of indictment does properly charge the defendant in two separate and distinct counts with committing an offense cognizable under the common law.

There is no statute in this Commonwealth which would make the acts chargeable to the defendant a misdemeanor. However, the Criminal Code of June 24, 1939, P. L. 872, sec. 1101, 18 PS §5101, provides as follows:

> Every offense now punishable either by the statute or common law of this Commonwealth and not specifically provided for by this act, shall continue to be an offense punishable as heretofore.

This statute was merely a reenactment of prior statutes which have pre-

1. Defendant was prosecuted for murder as a result of this confession. However, the Commonwealth was unable to establish the corpus delicti, because the pathologist testified that his autopsy produced no evidence that the child was born alive. He did testify that the child did not die from drowning. The confession, therefore, was rendered inadmissible, and the Commonwealth thereby unable to make out a case of infanticide.

served common law crimes and made them part of our jurisprudence. We are a community, indeed a nation, with but one exception,[2] that has embraced the concepts and principles of the common law. The essential characteristic of the common law, which distinguishes it as a system of law from the civil law, is its flexibility. Under the common law, we are not powerless to cope with novel situations not comprehended or contemplated by the legislators. In his work on the common law, Justice Holmes noted that, "The first requirement of a sound body of law is that it should correspond with the actual feelings and demands of the community, whether right or wrong." The landmark case in this Commonwealth which enounces the principle of preserving common law offenses is Commonwealth v. McHale, 97 Pa. 397. After analyzing and determining that common law crimes are preserved, Mr. Justice Paxton, at page 408, asks the question, "What is a common-law offense?"

> The highest authority upon this point is Blackstone. In chap. 13, of vol. 4, of Sharswood's edition, it is thus defined: "The last species of offenses which especially affect the Commonwealth are those against the public police or economy. By the public police and economy I mean the due regulation and domestic order of the kingdom, whereby the individuals of the state, like members of a well-governed family, are bound to conform their general behavior to the rules of propriety, good neighborhood and good manners, and to be decent, industrious and inoffensive in their respective stations. This head of offenses must therefore be very miscellaneous, as it comprises all such crimes as especially affect public society, and are not comprehended under any of the four preceding series. These amount some of them to felony, and other to misdemeanors only."

Thus, from the McHale case in 1881 down to the present time, our courts have consistently recognized common law offenses under the doctrine set forth in the McHale case. This is so even in the absence of specific common law precedent or statutory declaration. The McHale doctrine has been held to be applicable to any conduct which is inherently offensive to the public peace, decency, morals, and economy. It is true that there is no precedent in this Commonwealth that is on all fours with the facts in this case. Indeed, there is no case at all dealing with the indecent or immoral disposition of a dead body. This does not surprise us. Perhaps for the same reason that the legislators have not passed a criminal statute proscribing such conduct, we have been able to find few factual authorities. It is undeniably the sentiment of people throughout the world that it would be unthinkable to ill treat a dead body. However, our research into the matter has disclosed two factually similar cases, one occurring in the State of Maine and another in the State of Arkansas.

The Maine case is reported in State v. Bradbury, 136 Me. 347, 9 A.2d 657 (1939). Frank E. Bradbury lived with his unmarried sister Harriet. They were old people. Harriet was in bad health and suffered injuries in a fall on

2. Louisiana, with its historic ties to France has adopted the civil law or code system, patterned in part after the Napoleonic Code. Its rigidity has been frequently criticized by legal writers.

June 9th, resulting in her death at 4 A.M. on June 10th at her home. Shortly thereafter, Frank went into the cellar and built a hot fire in the cellar furnace. He tied a rope around his sister's dead body and dragged it down the cellar steps and shoved it into the furnace and burned it. Being impossible to get it all in at one time, he waited for the head and shoulders to be first consumed and then he forced the remaining body further and further into the furnace until he at last got the door shut. Neighbors complained of disagreeable odors emanating from the Bradbury home, and an investigation resulted in the discovery of this grisly deed. Defendant was indicted and convicted of the common law offense of indecently disposing of a dead body. The Maine court in appellate review carefully considered the proposition: Wharton on Criminal Law, Vol. 2, §1704, wherein it is said, "Indecency in treatment of a dead human body is an offense at common law, as an insult to public decency. Hence, it is indictable to expose such a body without proper burial; to wantonly or illegally disturb it . . ." In examining section 1704, Wharton also continues as follows, "A person, also, is indictable who buries or otherwise disposes of any dead body on which an inquest ought to be taken, without giving notice to a coroner, or, who, being under a legal duty to do so, fails to give notice to the coroner that a body on which an inquest ought to be held is lying unburied, before such body has putrefied." Footnote 20 of section 1704 contains a number of English and American cases holding it to be an offense at common law even to bury a body in such a way as to obstruct the coroner in his duties. Thus, it is an offense at common law to obstruct or pervert public justice.

The other case examined by us was Baker v. State, 223 S.W.2d 809 (Ark.) (1949). Ed White was an aged and old man drawing old age assistance from the State of Arkansas. His check for $30 came on the first day of the month. Defendant Mrs. Baker provided Ed with room, board, and personal attention, and, in turn, Ed would endorse the check to her by making a mark, he being illiterate. Ed lived in a cabin on defendant's premises and a short distance from her home. Ed's December 1st check was received and cashed by defendant on December 2nd, bearing Ed's purported mark. At 9 P.M., on December 2nd, defendant reported Ed's death to a funeral home. Experts who later examined Ed's body testified that he was dead at least five days. Decomposition and other ghastly conditions of the body had occurred. Defendant and her witnesses had testified that they saw Ed alive as late as 3 in the afternoon of December 2nd. Mrs. Baker was indicted and convicted of the common law offense characterized as "treating a dead body indecently." The court in its consideration of the case not only determined that defendant violated a duty to promptly report Ed's death but also considered the indecent aspects of so using his dead body to get a $30 public assistance check.

Ever since the existence of man has been evidenced there is also evidence that there existed a standard of decency and respect for the dead and their resting places. The Holy Scripture discloses that it was a disgrace not to bury the dead: Jeremiah 16:4. See also Genesis 50:1-7. Archaeologists have unearthed graves of prehistoric men indicating that they had a religious, or at least respectful, concern for dead bodies and the way and manner in which they were treated and buried. The renowned pyramids of Egypt are but resting places for the dead and memorials to them. Resort to American Indian lore will reveal a whole body of custom dealing with the Indian's attitude and concept of decency with respect to dead bodies and places of burial. Much of the Indian's day's activities were performed with a view to earning a sacred and hallowed resting place upon their death. The Code of Justinian provided that, ". . . Directly the body or bones of a dead person, whether slave or free, were buried, the grounds in which they were buried became religious. . . ." Carved on the tomb of William Shakespeare is a reflection upon early English people's attitude toward the sanctity of the grave. It says, "Curst be he that moves my bones." In the English case of Regina v. Stewart, 12 A. & E. 773, p.778, it is declared, "We have no doubt, therefore, that the common law casts on someone the duty of carrying to the grave, decently covered, the dead body of any person dying in such a state of indigence as to leave no funds for that purpose. The feelings and interests of the living require this and create the duty." So universal is the right of sepulture that the common law, as it seems, casts the duty of providing it, and of carrying to the grave the dead body, decently covered, upon the person under whose roof the death takes place; for such person cannot keep the body unburied nor do anything which prevents Christian burial; he cannot, therefore, cast it out so as to expose the body to violation, or to offend the feeling or injure the health of the living, and for the same reason, he cannot carry the dead body uncovered to the grave.

It would seem unnecessary for a further extension of this opinion to rationalize the existence in this community of a well-established and known standard of decency and morality with respect to the disposition and treatment of dead bodies. Yet, the importance of this matter commands one further observation. From our childhood, we have all been accustomed to pay a reverential respect to the sepulchres of our fathers and to attach a character of sacredness to the grounds dedicated and enclosed as the cemeteries of the dead. This standard of decency has been recognized by our legislators through the years, and they have made statutory provisions governing cemeteries, cemetery companies, reinterment and abandonment, crypts, burial permits, cremation, mutilation of graves and tombstones, mausoleums and vaults. At both common law and under the statutory law of this Commonwealth, it is an offense to dig up or disturb or desecrate bodies which have been buried. It is an outrage upon the public feelings and torturing to the afflicted relations of the deceased. If it be a crime thus to disturb the ashes of the dead, it must also be a crime to deprive them of a decent burial, by disgracefully exposing or disposing of the body, contrary to usages so long sanctioned by people and which are so grateful to the wounded hearts of friends and mourners, and this is so, irrespective of their religious aspects of burial and life hereafter, be it Christian, Jew, or Agnostic. We thus consider the common law as being sufficiently broad to punish as a misdemeanor, although there may be no exact precedent, any act which directly injures or tends to injure the public to such an extent as to require the state to interfere and punish the wrongdoer, as in the case of acts which injuriously affect public morality or obstruct or pervert public justice, or the administration of government. It is the common law of this Commonwealth that whatever openly outrages decency and is injurious to public morals is a misdemeanor and punishable at law.

We have little difficulty therefore in concluding that this bill of indictment does properly charge the defendant with a crime cognizable under the laws of the Commonwealth, and the court did not err in refusing the defendant's motion to quash the indictment assigning therefor this reason. . . .

[Conviction affirmed.]

Notes and Questions

1. Did the court infer that "indecent disposition of a dead body" is a crime in Pennsylvania, or did it make a normative decision that this conduct should be a crime? If this conduct was "inherently offensive to the public peace, decency, morals, and economy," why didn't the state legislature forbid it?

2. Did Keller have fair notice that her conduct was criminal? If a state statute had expressly forbidden this conduct, the law certainly would have presumed that Keller knew what the statute said. Is it any less fair—or realistic—to presume that she knew her conduct was forbidden by the common law, as reflected in the case law of Maine and Arkansas?

3. The court cites various religious and cultural authorities for its holding. By what means did they become part of the law of Pennsylvania?

4. In Commonwealth v. Mochan, 177 Pa. Super. 454, 110 A.2d 788 (1955), the defendant was charged with making obscene phone calls. No statute forbade such conduct expressly, but the indictment charged him with "devising, contriving and intending the morals and manners of the good citizens of this Commonwealth then and there being, to debauch and corrupt and further devising and intending to harass, embarrass and vilify divers citizens of this Commonwealth. . . ." The court affirmed the conviction, finding the conduct was forbidden by the common law because "its nature scandalously affects the morals or health of the community." The dissent said:

> Not unmindful of the reprehensible conduct of the appellant, I nevertheless cannot agree with the majority that what he did was a crime punishable under the laws of this Commonwealth.
>
> The majority is declaring something to be a crime which was never before known to be a crime in this Commonwealth. They have done this by the application of such general principles as "it is a crime to do anything which injures or tends to injure the public to such an extent as to require the state to interfere and punish the wrongdoer"; and "whatever openly outrages decency and is injurious to public morals is a misdemeanor."

Not only have they declared it to be a crime to do an act "injuriously affecting public morality," but they have declared it to be a crime to do any act which has a "potentially" injurious effect on public morality.

Under the division of powers in our constitution it is for the legislature to determine what "injures or tends to injure the public."

One of the most important functions of a legislature is to determine what acts "require the state to interfere and punish the wrongdoer." There is no reason for the legislature to enact any criminal laws if the courts delegate to themselves the power to apply such general principles as are here applied to whatever conduct may seem to the courts to be injurious to the public.

There is no doubt that the common law is a part of the law of this Commonwealth, and we punish many acts under the common law. But after nearly two hundred years of constitutional government in which the legislature and not the courts have been charged by the people with the responsibility of deciding which acts do and which do not injure the public to the extent which requires punishment, it seems to me we are making an unwarranted invasion of the legislative field when we arrogate that responsibility to ourselves by declaring now, for the first time, that certain acts are a crime.

When the legislature invades either the judicial or the executive fields, or the executive invades either the judicial or legislative fields, the courts stand ready to stop them. But in matters of this type there is nothing to prevent our invasion of the legislative field except our own self restraint. There are many examples of how carefully the courts, with admirable self restraint, have fenced themselves in so they would not romp through the fields of the other branches of government. This case is not such an example.

Until the legislature says that what the defendant did is a crime, I think the courts should not declare it to be such.

5. Pennsylvania is one of the few jurisdictions that retains common law crimes. The vast majority of the states, as well as the federal system, have followed the evolution of the criminal law from common law to statutory law, and from piecemeal statutory law to comprehensive codification and reform. Nonetheless, this is not the only way one could look at the matter. One commentator points out:

The Confucian element of Chinese legal thought . . . attacks what Westerners consider the rule of law as subversive of good government. Under the Confucian view the ruler should rule primarily by example and not rely upon threat of enforcement to compel obedience to particular standards of behavior.

In perhaps an extreme example of this position, scholars denounced one early king because he had "caused the laws to be written down." Instead of leading by his example of virtue, he had caused his subjects simply to look at the law to see how much they could get away with. . . .

The ancient Chinese way of looking at things remains a strain in modern Chinese thought. It helps explain both what one scholar has called "the low regard the Chinese traditionally held for law and legal procedure" and the importance of accommodation and proper behavior, as opposed to the exercise of individual rights. [Kaplan, The Court-Martial of the Kaohsiung Defendants 71 (1981).]

What are the problems inherent in such a view of the law?

The next case sets out the dominant contemporary American view of the principle of legality. Does it carry the principle too far?

KEELER v. SUPERIOR COURT

Supreme Court of California

2 Cal. 3d 619, 87 Cal. Rptr. 481, 470 P.2d 617 (1970)

Mosk, J. In this proceeding for writ of prohibition we are called upon to decide whether an unborn but viable fetus is a "human being" within the meaning of the California statute defining murder (Pen. Code, §187). We conclude that the Legislature did not intend such a meaning, and that for us to construe the statute to the contrary and apply it to this petitioner would exceed our judicial power and deny petitioner due process of law.

The evidence received at the preliminary examination may be summarized as follows: Petitioner and Teresa Keeler obtained in interlocutory decree of divorce on September 27, 1968. They had been married for 16 years. Unknown to petitioner, Mrs. Keeler was then pregnant by one Ernest Vogt, whom she had met earlier that summer. She subsequently began living with Vogt in Stockton, but concealed the fact from petitioner. Petitioner was given custody of their two daughters, aged 12 and 13 years, and under the decree Mrs. Keeler had the right to take the girls on alternate weekends.

On February 23, 1969, Mrs. Keeler was driving on a narrow mountain road in Amador County after delivering the girls to their home. She met petitioner driving in the opposite direction; he blocked the road with his car, and she pulled over to the side. He walked to her vehicle and began speaking to her. He seemed calm, and she rolled down her window to hear him. He said, "I hear you're pregnant. If you are you had better stay away from the girls and from here." She did not reply, and he opened the car door; as she later testified, "He assisted me out of the car. . . . '[I]t wasn't roughly at this time." Petitioner then looked at her abdomen and became "extremely upset." He said, "You sure are. I'm going to stomp it out of you." He pushed her against the car, shoved his knee into her abdomen, and struck her in the face with several blows. She fainted, and when she regained consciousness petitioner had departed.

Mrs. Keeler drove back to Stockton, and the police and medical assistance were summoned. She had suffered substantial facial injuries, as well as extensive bruising of the abdominal wall. A Caesarian section was performed and the fetus was examined in utero. Its head was found to be severely fractured, and it was delivered stillborn. The pathologist gave as his opinion that the cause of death was skull fracture with consequent cerebral hemorrhaging, that death would have been immediate, and that the injury could have been the result of force applied to the mother's abdomen. There was no air in the fetus' lungs, and the umbilical cord was intact.

Upon delivery the fetus weighed five pounds and was 18 inches in length. Both Mrs. Keeler and her obstetrician testified that fetal movements had been observed prior to February 23, 1969. The evidence was in conflict as to the estimated age of the fetus; the expert testimony on the point, however, concluded "with reasonable medical certainty" that the fetus had developed to the stage of viability, i.e., that in the event of premature birth on the date in question it would have had a 75 percent to 96 percent chance of survival.

An information was filed charging petitioner, in count I, with committing the crime of murder (Pen. Code, §187) in that he did "unlawfully kill a human being, to wit Baby Girl Vogt, with malice aforethought.". . . His motion to set aside the information for lack of probable cause (Pen. Code, §995) was denied, and he now seeks a writ of prohibition; as will appear, only the murder count is actually in issue. Pending our disposition of the matter, petitioner is free on bail. . . .

Penal Code section 187 provides: "Murder is the unlawful killing of a human being, with malice aforethought." The dispositive question is whether the fetus which petitioner is accused of killing was, on February 23, 1969, a "human being" within the meaning of the statute. If it was not, petitioner cannot be charged with its "murder" and prohibition will lie.

Section 187 was enacted as part of the Penal Code of 1872. Inasmuch as the provision has not been amended since that date, we must determine the intent of the Legislature at the time of its enactment. But section 187 was, in turn, taken verbatim from the first California statute defining murder, part of the Crimes and Punishments Act of 1850. (Stats. 1850, ch. 99, §19, p.231).[3] Penal Code section 5 (also enacted in 1872) declares: "The provisions of this code, so far as they are substantially the same as existing statutes, must be construed as continuations thereof, and not as new enactments." We begin, accordingly, by inquiring into the intent of the Legislature in 1850 when it first defined murder as the unlawful and malicious killing of a "human being."

It will be presumed, of course, that in enacting a statute the Legislature was familiar with the relevant rules of the common law, and, when it couches its enactment in common law language, that its intent was to continue those rules in statutory form. This is particularly appropriate in considering the work of the first session of our Legislature: its precedents were necessarily drawn from the common law, as modified in certain respects by the Constitution and by legislation of our sister states.

We therefore undertake a brief review of the origins and development of the common law of abortional homicide [Discussion omitted.]

We conclude that in declaring murder to be the unlawful and malicious

3. Murder is the unlawful killing of a human being, with malice aforethought, either express or implied. The unlawful killing may be effected by any of the various means by which death may be occasioned." . . .

killing of a "human being" the Legislature of 1850 intended that term to have the settled common law meaning of a person who had been born alive, and did not intend the act of feticide—as distinguished from abortion—to be an offense under the laws of California.

Nothing occurred between the years 1850 and 1872 to suggest that in adopting the new Penal Code on the latter date the Legislature entertained any different intent. The case law of our sister states, for example, remained consonant with the common law. . . .

It is the policy of this state to construe a penal statute as favorably to the defendant as its language and the circumstances of its application may reasonably permit; just as in the case of a question of fact, the defendant is entitled to the benefit of every reasonable doubt as to the true interpretation of words or the construction of language used in a statute. We hold that in adopting the definition of murder in Penal Code section 187 the Legislature intended to exclude from its reach the act of killing an unborn fetus. . . .

The People urge, however, that the sciences of obstetrics and pediatrics have greatly progressed since 1872, to the point where with proper medical care a normally developed fetus prematurely born at 28 weeks or more has an excellent chance of survival, i.e., is "viable"; that the common law requirement of live birth to prove the fetus had become a "human being" who may be the victim of murder is no longer in accord with scientific fact, since an unborn but viable fetus is now fully capable of independent life; and that one who unlawfully and maliciously terminates such a life should therefore be liable to prosecution for murder under section 187. We may grant the premises of this argument; indeed, we neither deny nor denigrate the vast progress of medicine in the century since the enactment of the Penal Code. But we cannot join in the conclusion sought to be deduced: we cannot hold this petitioner to answer for murder by reason of his alleged act of killing an unborn—even though viable—fetus. To such a charge there are two insuperable obstacles, one "jurisdictional" and the other constitutional.

Penal Code section 6 declares in relevant part that "No act or omission" accomplished after the code has taken effect "is criminal or punishable, except as prescribed or authorized by this code, or by some of the statutes which it specifies as continuing in force and as not affected by its provisions, or by some ordinance, municipal, county, or township regulation. . . ." This section embodies a fundamental principle of our tripartite form of government, i.e., that subject to the constitutional prohibition against cruel and unusual punishment, the power to define crimes and fix penalties is vested exclusively in the legislative branch. Stated differently, there are no common law crimes in California. . . . In order that a public offense be committed, some statute, ordinance or regulation prior in time to the commission of the act, must denounce it; likewise with excuses or justifications—if no statutory excuse or justification apply as to the commission of the particular offense, neither the common law nor the so-called 'unwritten law' may legally supply it." (People v. Whipple (1929) 100 Cal. App. 261, 262 [279 P. 1008].)

Settled rules of construction implement this principle. Although the Penal Code commands us to construe its provisions "according to the fair import of their terms, with a view to effect its objects and to promote justice" (Pen. Code, §4), it is clear the courts cannot go so far as to create an offense by enlarging a statute, by inserting or deleting words, or by giving the terms used false or unusual meanings. Penal statutes will not be made to reach beyond their plain intent; they include only those offenses coming clearly within the import of their language. Indeed, "Constructive crimes—crimes built up by courts with the aid of inference, implication, and strained interpretation—are repugnant to the spirit and letter of English and American criminal law." (Ex parte McNulty (1888) 77 Cal. 164, 168 [19 P. 237].)

Applying these rules to the case at bar, we would undoubtedly act in excess of the judicial power if we were to adopt the People's proposed construction of section 187. As we have shown, the Legislature has defined the crime of murder in California to apply only to the unlawful and malicious killing of one who has been born alive. We recognize that the killing of an unborn but viable fetus may be deemed by some to be an offense of similar nature and gravity; but as Chief Justice Marshall warned long ago, "It would be dangerous, indeed, to carry the principle, that a case which is within the reason or mischief of a statute, is within its provisions, so far as to punish a crime not enumerated in the statute, because it is of equal atrocity, or of kindred character, with those which are enumerated." (United States v. Wiltberger (1820) 18 U.S. (5 Wheat.) 76, 96.) Whether to thus extend liability for murder in California is a determination solely within the province of the Legislature. For a court to simply declare, by judicial fiat, that the time has now come to prosecute under section 187 one who kills an unborn but viable fetus would indeed be to rewrite the statute under the guise of construing it. Nor does a need to fill an asserted "gap" in the law between abortion and homicide—as will appear, no such gap in fact exists—justify judicial legislation of this nature: to make it "a judicial function 'to explore such new fields of crime as they may appear from time to time' is wholly foreign to the American concept of criminal justice" and "raises very serious questions concerning the principle of separation of powers." (In re Davis (1966) 242 Cal. App. 2d 645, 655-656 and fn.12.)

The second obstacle to the proposed judicial enlargement of section 187 is the guarantee of due process of law. Assuming arguendo that we have the power to adopt the new construction of this statute as the law of California, such a ruling, by constitutional command, could operate only prospectively, and thus could not in any event reach the conduct of petitioner on February 23, 1969.

The first essential of due process is fair warning of the act which is made punishable as a crime. "That the terms of a penal statute creating a new offense must be sufficiently explicit to inform those who are subject to it what conduct on their part will render them liable to its penalties, is a well-recognized requirement, consonant alike with ordinary notions of fair play and the settled rules of law." (Connally v. General Construction Co. (1926) 269 U.S.

385, 391.) "No one may be required at peril of life, liberty or property to speculate as to the meaning of penal statutes. All are entitled to be informed as to what the State commands or forbids." (Lanzetta v. New Jersey (1939) 306 U.S. 451, 453.)

This requirement of fair warning is reflected in the constitutional prohibition against the enactment of ex post facto laws (U.S. Const., art. I, §§9, 10; Cal. Const., art I. §16). When a new penal statute is applied retrospectively to make punishable an act which was not criminal at the time it was performed, the defendant has been given no advance notice consistent with due process. And precisely the same effect occurs when such an act is made punishable under a preexisting statute but by means of an unforeseeable *judicial* enlargement thereof. (Bouie v. City of Columbia (1964) 378 U.S. 347.)

In *Bouie* two Negroes took seats in the restaurant section of a South Carolina drugstore; no notices were posted restricting the area to whites only. When the defendants refused to leave upon demand, they were arrested and convicted of violating a criminal trespass statute which prohibited entry on the property of another "after notice" forbidding such conduct. Prior South Carolina decisions had emphasized the necessity of proving such notice to support a conviction under the statute. The South Carolina Supreme Court nevertheless affirmed the convictions, construing the statute to prohibit not only the act of entering after notice not to do so but also the wholly different act of remaining on the property after receiving notice to leave.

The United States Supreme Court reversed the convictions, holding that the South Carolina court's ruling was "unforeseeable" and when an "unforeseeable state-court construction of a criminal statute is applied retroactively to subject a person to criminal liability for past conduct, the effect is to deprive him of due process of law in the sense of fair warning that his contemplated conduct constitutes a crime." (378 U.S. at pp.354-355.) Analogizing to the prohibition against retrospective penal legislation, the high court reasoned

> Indeed, an unforeseeable judicial enlargement of a criminal statute, applied retroactively, operates precisely like an ex post facto law, such as Art. I, §10, of the Constitution forbids. An ex post facto law has been defined by this Court as one 'that makes an action done before the passing of the law, and which was *innocent* when done, criminal; and punishes such action,' or 'that *aggravates* a *crime,* or makes it *greater* than it was, when committed.' Calder v. Bull, 3 Dall. 386, 390, 1 L. Ed. 648, 650. If a state legislature is barred by the Ex Post Facto Clause from passing such a law, it must follow that a State Supreme Court is barred by the Due Process Clause from achieving precisely the same result by judicial construction. The fundamental principle that 'the required criminal law must have existed when the conduct in issue occurred,' Hall, General Principles of Criminal Law (2d ed. 1960), at 58-59, must apply to bar retroactive criminal prohibitions emanating from courts as well as from legislatures. . . .

The court remarked in conclusion that "Application of this rule is particularly compelling where, as here, the petitioners' conduct cannot be deemed improper or immoral." (Id. at p.362.) In the case at bar the conduct with which petitioner is charged is certainly "improper" and "immoral," and it is not contended he was exercising a constitutionally favored right. But the matter is simply one of degree, and it cannot be denied that the guarantee of due process extends to violent as well as peaceful men. The issue remains, would the judicial enlargement of section 187 now proposed have been foreseeable to this petitioner?. . .

We conclude that the judicial enlargement of section 187 now urged upon us by the People would not have been foreseeable to this petitioner, and hence that its adoption at this time would deny him due process of law. . . .

Notes and Questions

1. Consider this excerpt from Giovanetti, The Principle of Analogy in Sino-Soviet Criminal Laws, 8 Dal. L.J. 321, 381-382, 399-400 (1984).

> "Analogy" is a principle of substantive criminal law which permits the conviction of an accused despite the absence of any defined criminal behavior. If the actions of the accused are perceived to be inimical to the socio-political order then he may be found guilty of a defined crime which prohibits analogous behavior. Analogy may also be employed in a more restrained fashion as a principle of sentencing law. If the accused has committed a defined crime which is now perceived to be more deleterious his punishment may exceed the maximum legislatively mandated sentence. Analogy is, therefore, one method of defining and punishing acts which are perceived to be iniquitous. In this application, analogy is qualitatively distinguished from liberal statutory interpretation, and it frequently includes or accompanies the retroactive application of law.
>
> The principle of analogy is neither the product of twentieth century jurisprudence, nor is its application confined to regimes which Westerners characterize as totalitarian. However, it was employed until 1958 in the Soviet Union and it is still in use in the People's Republic of China. Our focus will be primarily on these modern applications.
>
> The use of analogy is anathema to the Western tradition. The contrasting philosophy in Europe is expressed in the maxim *Nulla crimen sine lege, Nulla poena sine lege,* the essence of which is that no person may be punished except under the authority of a statute which defines the act as criminal and prescribes the permissible punishment. This maxim is usually found to exist concomitantly with the requirement that penal statutes must be strictly construed and not applied retroactively. A similar tradition exists in Anglo-American law, where the principle *nulla poena sine lege* is included within the group of principles known as the rule of law. The dichotomy between analogy and *nulla poena sine lege* is our second and subsidiary enquiry.
>
> The doctrinal justifications and actual applications of analogy have been

protean. Analogy permits and encourages flexibility. It imbues the administration of criminal law with a chameleon character. Westerners view this chameleon character as corrosive to our concept of justice. The study of analogy may therefore provide one method of contrasting fundamental beliefs. . . .

The principle *nulla poena sine lege* has been dominant in Western Europe at least since the French Declaration of the Rights of Man in 1789. Article 8 provides: "The law may establish only such punishments as are strictly necessary. No one may be punished except according to a law enacted and promulgated before the commission of the offence and lawfully applied". In England, the rule of law has been established since the time of the promulgation of the Charter of Henry the First, and Canada has, of course, received this tradition. And in the United States the "void-for-vagueness" doctrine and the constitutional prohibition against ex post facto laws have established a rule of law.

This is not to assert that the history of the principle of rule of law demonstrates an unbroken or pure application of its central concept, viz., the concept that behaviour should not be considered criminal unless precisely defined as criminal in a penal law of prospective effect only. This is certainly not the case. But the dominant Western theme has been the rule of law, the central achievement of which is the establishment of "a definite limitation on the power of the State."

There is, however, one challenge to the purity of the rule of law in the Anglo-American tradition which could be made and which is of particular interest in a comparative study of analogy. This is the creation of crime at common law, a matter of contemporary interest because it still may occur in the State law of the United States. This does not raise an issue of pragmatic importance. In England, Professor Glanville Williams wrote in 1961 that "the creative powers of the judges in the realm of criminal law have almost withered away" and common law crimes have been abolished in Canada. In the United States "the trend in the twentieth century . . . is to enact comprehensive new criminal codes, abolishing common law crimes in the process." However, from the doctrinal point of view, is the creation of crime at common law distinct from analogy?

The answer to the question posed lies in the meaning of the term analogy. It is clear that in the socialist applications we have examined, analogy is an instrument of flexibility, a means of enforcing whatever ideology is currently valued. In the application it has received, socialist analogy has denied any role of certainty and predictability in law. In this sense it is definitely qualitatively distinguished from the process of creating crimes at common law. That process has been described by Professor Hall, thus:

> The necessary use of analogy, especially by Anglo-American judges, is a process that is so minute in the changes effected as to be hardly perceptible. Excepting occasional leaps that undoubtedly occur, it reflects the day-by-day growth of criminal law which, for the most part keeps pace with change in the language institution itself. It has thus amounted largely to an all-but-unnoticed bringing up-to-date of old terms so that, filled with new content, they referred more adequately to the changed conditions. When American judges speak of expanding criminal law by "analogy," they certainly do not mean the so-called "legal analogy," the deliberate lawmaking, avowed and apparent to all, which was required in the Russian and German innovations . . . , they are speaking of necessary analogy, limited by the

> traditional judicial function to apply, not to make, law and restricted by the canon of strict construction illustrated in a vast number of decided cases.[4]

2. Could the court have found support for Keeler's conviction within the confines of California's statutory murder law? If section 187 forbids the killing of a human being, could one simply interpret the statutory term "human being" broadly in terms of modern medical developments, as well as contemporary scientific and philosophical views of when life begins? Perhaps the common law refused to treat the killing of a quickened fetus as a homicide because it presumed that the fetus would be born dead. Could the court have found that twentieth-century science has rendered that presumption false?

Is it possible, however, that the court, which had previously agreed with the Supreme Court's abortion decision, did not want to appear inconsistent by calling the killing of a fetus in this context homicide? The California legislature filled the gap that the court had found by adding "or a fetus" after "human being" in section 189 (see p.290).

3. Would Keeler have had any reasonable claim that he had been denied fair warning that his act was illegal? If the court had affirmed his conviction, could he have argued that its decision was unforeseeable when he set out on his course of conduct?

4. In Leffel v. Municipal Court, 54 Cal. App. 3d 569, 126 Cal. Rptr. 773 (1976), the defendant was charged with bidding for the services of a prostitute. The statutory prohibition referred to anyone who "solicits or engages in any act of prostitution," but Leffel argued that judicial and prosecutorial decisions had limited the prohibition to the acts of the prostitute herself, and not her customer. The court discussed the *Keeler* principle and rejected its application to Leffel's conduct:

> In People v. Sobiek (1973), 30 Cal. App. 3d 458; 473-474, 106 Cal. Rptr. 519, the question was whether the judicial interpretation of Penal Code section 487 to make a partner guilty of grand theft when he steals from the partnership resulted in an ex post facto application to the defendant by making criminal an act innocent when done. (30 Cal. App. 3d at p. 472, 106 Cal. Rptr. 519.) In holding that the defendant had fair notice under the statute and that the judicial interpretation holding a partner guilty of grand theft when he steals from the partnership was not unforeseeable, the court quoted from United States ex rel. Almeida v. Rundle (E.D. Pa. 1966), 255 F. Supp. 936, as follows:
>
> > This is not a case where an act clearly not criminal at the time of its occurrence, is so declared to be at some subsequent time. Nor is it a case where criminal responsibility should not attach because the actor could not reasonably understand that his contemplated conduct was proscribed. . . . It is not always true that where the definition of a crime is extended by judicial construction, a conviction which results therefrom is a denial of due process . . . the law is full of instances where a man's fate depends on his estimating rightly, that is, as the jury subsequently estimates it, some

4. J. Hall, General Principles of Criminal Law 48-49 (1960).

> matter of degree. If his judgment is wrong, not only may he incur a fine or a short imprisonment, as here; he may incur the penalty of death. . . . *The criterion in such cases is to examine whether common social duty would, under the circumstances, have suggested a more circumspect conduct.* (30 Cal. App. 3d at pp.474-475, 106 Cal. Rptr. at p.530.) (Emphasis added.)
>
> *Sobiek* distinguished Keeler v. Superior Court, 2 Cal. 3d 619, 87 Cal. Rptr. 481, 470 P.2d 617. *Keeler* had held that the killing of a viable fetus did not violate section 187 of the Penal Code which defines murder as "the unlawful killing of a human being" because the Legislature clearly intended by section 187 to restrict the crime of murder to the killing of one who had been born alive. (2 Cal. 3d at pp. 628-629, 87 Cal. Rptr. 481, 470 P.2d 617.) *Sobiek* noted that under the facts of *Keeler,* prior to the killing, the defendant had no notice from any source that destroying a viable fetus might be murder, whereas, under the Grand Theft Statute, section 487, "there is no indication that the Legislature did not intend to include in 'property of another' the property of partners other than the one stealing such property, or of the partnership itself." (30 Cal. App. 3d at p.475, 106 Cal. Rptr. at p.531.)
>
> In the present case, appellant must have realized that his conduct was not entirely innocent. He presumably was aware that prostitution was illegal and that his actions with the prostitute could result in her prosecution. Any past reluctance on the part of public authorities to arrest and prosecute the customer cannot rescue appellant from his presumed knowledge that what he was doing was wrong; hence, our interpretation that customers are within the ambit of section 647, subdivision (b), was foreseeable.

5. In People v. Van Alstyne, 46 Cal. App. 3d 900, 121 Cal. Rptr. 363 (1975), the defendant was convicted of selling marijuana. He claimed that the Cal. Health and Safety Code §11018 prohibited the sale of only "Cannabis sativa L." rather than such other forms as "Cannabis indica," "Cannabis ruderalis," and "Cannabis gigantea," and that there was no evidence that he had sold "Cannabis sativa L." in particular. The court rejected the defendant's claim. It noted that all forms of cannabis contain the "hallucinogenic" tetrahydrocannabinol (THC), and, after examining the legislative history of the statute, it concluded:

> We are satisfied on the basis of this survey that from 1929 to the present day the Legislature has always meant to outlaw all plants popularly known as marijuana. . . .
>
> Accordingly, we hold that the term "Cannabis sativa L." in section 11018 must be construed as a general term which includes all plants popularly known as marijuana that contain the toxic agent THC. . . . While the Legislature with the wisdom of hindsight could have been clearer in its definition of marijuana, we do not doubt that the Legislature intended to proscribe possession of and dealings in all species of marijuana and that section 11018 must be read to effectuate this underlying legislative purpose.

The court also rejected the defendant's claim that the statute's definition of marijuana failed to give him fair notice that his conduct was criminal.

Right or wrong, the monotypic classification of marijuana has had considerable currency, until very recently at least, and the term "Cannabis sativa L." in section 11018 was, we think, sufficient . . . to put a seller of marijuana on notice that he acted at his peril. The proscription of marijuana, after all, is directed to the public at large and not to botanists alone. Appellant has made no attempt to demonstrate that members of the general public "of common intelligence" would have had to guess as to the meaning of our marijuana statute in early 1973 and would have differed as to its application.

Had the question before us arisen in connection with a drug less widely publicized than marijuana, the definition set forth in section 11018 might well have created a substantial due process problem. Here, though, we think it too obvious for further discussion that appellant, as a man presumed to be of common intelligence, understood in advance that his clandestine sale of marijuana, whatever the species, constituted a crime.

Nevertheless, we take this occasion to state that in future cases we undoubtedly will have to consider whether the term "Cannabis sativa L." has so changed in general usage and understanding since the time of the 1972 enactment of section 11018 that the section no longer provides fair notice to potential violators of the nature of the acts prohibited thereunder and thereby denies to them constitutional due process of law. In other words, while the legislative intent behind section 11018 is, to our mind, perfectly clear, and was expressed in words entirely adequate to convey that intent, scientific advances have since rendered these words obsolete for that purpose. In our opinion, section 11018 as now worded constitutes a potential trap for the unwary and the Legislature would be well advised to rewrite the section so that it plainly says what it means. Otherwise enforcement of the policy of the section will be imperiled.

Do you find this reasoning persuasive? What does the court mean when it speaks of "notice that he acted at his peril"? His peril of what? Peril that what he sold might be Cannabis sativa L. or that it might not matter whether it was Cannabis sativa L.?

17

SPECIFICITY

RICKS v. DISTRICT OF COLUMBIA

United States Court of Appeals, District of Columbia Circuit
414 F.2d 1097 (1967)

Spottswood W. ROBINSON, III, Circuit Judge.

Nearly every state in the Union has ventured to regulate in a criminal context an assortment of conduct characteristically grouped under the denomination "vagrancy." Congress, in like vein, has enacted the two statutes currently in operation in the District of Columbia commonly referred to as the "general vagrancy" and "narcotic vagrancy" laws. On this appeal we came face-to-face with claims of unconstitutionality directed toward the former.

The legislation now before us categorizes eight "classes of persons" who "shall be deemed vagrants in the District of Columbia," and specifies fine and imprisonment as the punishment for vagrancy. The District's police department has administratively implemented these provisions with procedures, called "vagrancy observations," which are utilized prior to vagrancy arrests. An observation, as the word connotes, consists in police surveillance of an individual, followed by questioning and the assembly of information on a vagrancy observation form. The form is turned in at a precinct station and circulated to other precincts with substantial vice problems. At least three observations within a 45-day period are customarily made before the person observed is arrested for vagrancy.

On January 22, 1966, at 3:08 A.M., two police officers, patrolling a section of the inner city described as a "den of vice," saw appellant standing in the doorway of a "known house of ill fame." The officers recognized appellant as a "known and convicted felon, thief, prostitute, vagrant, and narcotics user." She was "observed" approaching a male pedestrian and walking with him toward a neighboring "house of ill fame." The officers intercepted the pair and asked appellant a battery of questions concerning her reasons for being on the streets at that hour, to which appellant responded that she was on her way to "Slim's room" to get clothes which she left there. Inquiry was also made as to her employment status, the last time she had "turned a trick," and her use of "junk." Appellant said that she was not employed, was no longer using "junk," and had not "turned tricks" since the previous month. Compliably with the officers' request, she rolled up her sleeves, thereby revealing two needle marks on her left arm.

Four days later, an around-the-clock police vigil again focused on appellant. At 1:04 A.M. she was spotted "flagging several automobiles" carrying male occupants, and was overheard using the jargon of professional prostitutes soliciting customers. She asked one male driver if he was "sporting" and invited him to accompany her to a house because she "didn't turn any tricks in any car." She was again questioned by the police and, for the second time, her answers intimated nothing. Marks were perceived on appellant's left arm when, in response to an officer's request, she exposed it.

On January 29, 1966, seven days after the first observation, appellant was seen at 4:10 in the morning walking back and forth from a street corner. Her meandering apparently aroused the interest of a police officer who kept her in view for approximately ten minutes. Then followed another round of interrogation, and appellant was informed of the vagrancy law and told to go home.

The final observation of appellant was made by the officer who had conducted the first. On February 11, 1966, between 1:30 and 3:00 A.M., he detected appellant standing on a street corner and stopping male pedestrians as they passed. This time the officer placed appellant under arrest.

The information upon which appellant was prosecuted charged that appellant was a vagrant within three of the statute's definitions of the term:

> The following classes of persons shall be deemed vagrants in the District of Columbia:
>
> (1) Any person known to be a pickpocket, thief, burglar, confidence operator, or felon, either by his own confession or by his having been convicted in the District of Columbia or elsewhere of any one of such offenses or of any felony, and having no lawful employment and having no lawful means of support realized from a lawful occupation or source, and not giving a good account of himself when found loitering around in any park, highway, public building, or other public place, store, shop, or reservation, or at any public gathering or assembly. . . .
>
> (3) Any person leading an immoral or profligate life who has no lawful employment and who has no lawful means of support realized from a lawful occupation or source. . . .
>
> (8) Any person who wanders about the streets at late or unusual hours of the night without any visible or lawful business and not giving a good account of himself. . . .

Appellant advances skillfully a number of bases upon which it is urged that the vagrancy law is unconstitutional, but we find it necessary to consider but one. The pervading difficulty, as we see it, is the legislative omission to provide a reasonable degree of guidance to citizens, the police and the courts as to just what constitutes the offenses with which appellant was charged. We reverse, holding that each of the statutory provisions upon which appellant's conviction rests is so vague as to infringe rights secured by the Fifth Amendment.

I

Reasonable precision in the definition of crime has been regarded as a desideratum by free people since the early days of the common law. That precept, virtually from the birth of the Nation, has occupied a position of honor in the scheme of constitutional values, and for justifications of the highest order. Fluid language which sweeps citizens under the penumbra of penal legislation without warning is abhorrent. The imposition of criminal liability for behavior which a person could not reasonably understand to be prohibited offends the most rudimentary considerations of fairness. "No one may be required at peril of life, liberty or property to speculate as to the meaning of penal statutes. All are entitled to be informed as to what the State commands or forbids." Thus "a statute which either forbids or requires the doing of an act in terms so vague that men of common intelligence must necessarily guess at its meaning and differ as to its application violates the first essential of due process of law."

Statutory vagueness has a distinctive impact, too, on human activity not essentially wicked and on the processes by which its criminality is to be appraised. "Liberty under law extends to the full range of conduct which the individual is free to pursue."[1] Since most people shy away from legal violations, personal liberty is unconstitutionally dampened when one can but doubt whether he is actually free to pursue particular conduct. Moreover, definitional uncertainty is an open invitation, if indeed not inevitably an antecedent, to virtually unrestrained administration. "[A] law fails to meet the requirements of the Due Process Clause" not only "if it is so vague and standardless that it leaves the public uncertain as to the conduct it prohibits," but also if it "leaves judges and jurors free to decide, without any legally fixed standards, what is prohibited and what is not in each particular case."[2] And legislation of that character "does not provide for government by clearly defined laws, but rather for government by the moment-to-moment opinions of a policeman on his beat."[3]

So it is that a criminal statute perishes on constitutional grounds when it leaves speculative the tests for ascertaining the line separating guilty from innocent acts. A reasonable degree of certainty is prerequisite. Fair notice to

1. Bolling v. Sharpe, 347 U.S. 497, 499 (1954).
2. Giaccio v. Pennsylvania, 382 U.S. 399, 402-403 (1966).
3. Shuttlesworth v. City of Birmingham, 382 U.S. 87, 90 (1965), quoting Cox v. Louisiana, 379 U.S. 536, 579 (1965) (separate opinion of Mr. Justice Black).

those of ordinary intelligence is necessary. It is essential that the statutory language "conveys sufficiently definite warnings as to the proscribed conduct when measured by common understanding and practices."[4]

These are the critical elements of the void-for-vagueness doctrine; these are the criteria by which we must measure the statute at bar. "Vague laws in any area suffer a constitutional infirmity,"[5] and what the Constitution demands of other laws it exacts imperatively of those which undertake to punish vagrancy.[6]

II

Appellant was prosecuted and convicted under three of the statutory subsections—(1), (3) and (8) of Section 22-3302—defining independent concepts of vagrancy. Perusal of these subsections discloses that each incorporates language precipitating problems in terms of the void-for-vagueness doctrine. These provisions we must now individually scrutinize, in the light of pertinent constitutional principles, to ascertain whether they can pass muster.

D.C. Code §22-3302(1)

The first type of vagrancy with which appellant was charged has four elements. "Any person [1] known to be a . . . thief, . . . by his having been convicted in the District of Columbia . . . of . . . such [offense] . . . and [2] having no lawful employment and having no lawful means of support realized from a lawful occupation or source, and [3] not giving a good account of himself [4] when found loitering around in any . . . public place" is a vagrant. Appellant's prior conviction of petit larceny supplies the first element, and there was evidence on which the trial judge could find the second. But this subsection requires additionally that the accused be found loitering, and that he fail to give a good account of himself. We are unable to perceive in these two elements the degree of specificity which due process enjoins upon legislative enactments that specify criminal offenses.

"LOITERING"

"Loitering" has not been defined legislatively. The District of Columbia Court of Appeals, . . . has construed "loitering" in the vagrancy statute as meaning "to be slow in moving, to delay, to linger, to be dilatory, to spend time idly, to saunter, to lag behind."[7] In contrast to such seemingly innocuous conduct, however, the court has also read subsection (1) to mean that "when

4. United States v. Petrillo, [332 U.S. 1, 8 (1947)].

5. Ashton v. Kentucky, 384 U.S. 195, 200 (1966).

6. Vagrancy often includes within its sweep conduct which is otherwise innocuous and which involves no knowing violation of the law. . . .

7. Williams v. District of Columbia, 65 A.2d 924, 926 (D.C. Mun. App. 1949).

one's wandering and conduct on the streets at late or unusual hours is such as to give reasonable grounds for a belief that his purpose for being on the street is not a legitimate one, we think that the law may validly require that he be called upon to account for his actions."[8] Further evidencing the susceptibility of the statutory language to divergent understandings, witnesses at appellant's trial likewise voiced widely differing interpretations of "loitering," ranging from the ostensibly innocent to the potentially criminal.[9] In the complete absence of statutory criteria by which the one can be objectively distinguished from the other, we find a fatal constitutional flaw. . . .

We encounter difficulty not only with "loitering" but equally with the mandate of subsection (1) that the person loitering explain his activity in a manner that amounts to "giving a good account of himself." The statute furnishes no standard by which it can be ascertained whether an explanation for particular conduct is "good," and decisions addressing "good account" provisions are but little more definitive. A refusal to account . . . is a failure to give a good account, and what the statute demands is not "a *mere account*" but "one which is reasonably credible." . . .

The record discloses disparate opinions on "good account" entertained by those to whom enforcement of the statute is entrusted. Two police officers testified that a declination to answer questions is a failure to give a good account, but another officer said that this was a matter which the judge would have to decide. An officer avowed that "[g]ood account means that you are not out there for an illegal purpose," but another declared that the accounting is not good if the answers to an officer's questions do not satisfy the officer. To the Corporation Counsel's chief prosecutor whether a good account is given is a matter determinable only on the facts of the particular case.

We deem the "good account" provision much too loose to satisfy constitutional requirements. It takes but little reflection to bring to mind almost immediately the magnitude of the guesswork its application commonly entails. As one court recently put it:

> [T]he term "good account" . . . leaves too much discretion in the hands of the police and the courts. It does not involve a certain standard, for what may be a good account to one person may very easily not be one to another. The word "good" is especially subjective in nature and is used in our parlance in many different ways and contexts. Does it mean "morally good" or does it mean "lawful" in the sense that if one does not admit to a crime he has given a good account of himself? On the other hand, "good account" may mean an account

8. Harris v. District of Columbia [132 A.2d 152, 154 (D.C. Mun. App. 1957)].

9. One police officer considered loitering to consist in "walking back and forth from the corner and standing idle in a doorway." Another felt that it was "standing around in one spot, not going anywhere. Just standing there flagging automobiles." Still another said it was "[s]tanding idle in a doorway." The Chief of the Law Enforcement Division of the Corporation Counsel's office defined loitering as "a man hanging around a street corner he has been hanging around for an hour, we will say, there is no apparent purpose or motive for his being there. But, now, loitering in and of itself doesn't make me a vagrant. . . . You have got to have some acts on his part to indicate that he has an ulterior motive."

> which puts the accused above suspicion or it may mean that his statement must give the officer sufficient credible information so as to negate probable cause.
>
> In addition, the statute imposes no time limit on "good account." Does it require a person to give a "good account" of himself as of the moment the officer stops him or must he be prepared to explain and defend his conduct and whereabouts since he entered the state? One cannot tell how far back in time he may have to justify himself or his activities in order to avoid the criminal penalties of the statute.[10]

However viewed, subsection (1) is an investiture of enormous discretion in those who must administer it. Interdicted persons may tarry in public places only if willing to answer questions by police officers as to why they are there, and then only at the risk that their explanations might not appeal to their inquisitors. In Shuttlesworth v. City of Birmingham, [supra] the Supreme Court held invalid an ordinance making it "unlawful for any person . . . to so stand, loiter, or walk upon any street or sidewalk . . . after having been requested by any police officer to move on," saying:

> Literally read, therefore, the second part of this ordinance says that a person may stand on a public sidewalk in Birmingham only at the whim of any police officer of that city. The constitutional vice of so broad a provision needs no demonstration. It "does not provide for government by clearly defined laws, but rather for government by the moment-to-moment opinions of a policeman on his beat."[11]

We discern no significant difference from a constitutional standpoint between a law licensing one's presence on a public street upon a police officer's favorable judgment and one conditioning it upon the officer's satisfaction with the explanation as to why the person is there.

"LEADING AN IMMORAL OR PROFLIGATE LIFE"

The second statutory provision appellant allegedly violated denominates a vagrant "[a]ny person [1] leading an immoral or profligate life [2] who has no lawful employment and who has no lawful means of support realized from a lawful occupation or source." Our concern here is with the first specification. Immorality and profligateness are not terms of art, at least in common understanding, and the definitional problems they pose are quite readily apparent.

The record in this case contains an instance in point. A police officer testified that he made approximately 470 arrests for vagrancy in 1965, yet he was uncertain as to the reach of the statutory words. He was sure that "leading an immoral and profligate life means being a known prostitute." When ques-

10. United States v. Margeson, 259 F. Supp. 256, 268-269 (E.D. Pa. 1966). . . .
11. 382 U.S. at 90.

tioned, however, as to whether the statutory language is limited to prostitution, this veteran responded "No, I imagine it means other things," but commendably admitted that "I don't know what they might mean."

Turning to prior judicial construction, we discover that the dilemma is not lessened but magnified. The District of Columbia Court of Appeals considers the provision under examination to be so elastic as to prohibit any conduct that is not "decent, upright, good, [or] right."[12] Elaborating, it says:

> Webster's Dictionary defines "profligate" as "completely given up to dissipation and licentiousness; broken down in morals and decency." It has been said that "Immorality" is not necessarily confined to matters sexual in their nature; it may be that which is contra bonos mores; or not moral, inconsistent with rectitude, purity, or good morals; contrary to conscience or moral law; wicked; vicious; licentious, as, an immoral man or deed. Its synonyms are: Corrupt, indecent, depraved, dissolute; and its antonyms are: Decent, upright, good, right.[13]

We are in no position to debate this interpretation, for the statutory language leaves an open field for speculation. And given this meaning, subsection (3) affords an almost boundless area for individual assessment of the morality of another's behavior.

. . . Opposing segments of the general public may agree as to the immorality or profligateness of many activities.[14] But, more importantly, it is expectable, if indeed not inevitable, that they will disagree on many others without approaching absurdity. Not only does the phrase under scrutiny fail to chart for the individual citizen the course that is proscribed, but it also fails to mark out reasonably distinct boundaries for the judges, juries and police officers who are required to administer the law. We hold that the first element of subsection (3)—"leading an immoral and profligate life"—necessitates so much guesswork as to its coverage as to incur the condemnation of the Fifth Amendment.

D.C. Code §22-3302(8)

Subsection (8), the final provision invoked against appellant, extends the vagrancy definition to "[a]ny person [1] who wanders about the streets at late or unusual hours of the night [2] without any visible or lawful business and [3] not giving a good account of himself." The last component—failure to render "a good account"—alone suffices to invalidate this subsection on vagueness grounds. Upon analysis, we find that the first two elements of subsection (8) afflict it with the same malady.

12. Davenport v. District of Columbia, 61 A.2d 486, 488 (D.C. Mun. App. 1948).
13. Id. at 488.
14. We do not, of course, imply that prostitution is a subject on which opinion is apt to be divided, but this is beside the point. Constitutional specificity must be found in the statute defining the offense, and the particular conduct involved, though constitutionally punishable, does not save the statute.

"WANDERS . . . WITHOUT ANY VISIBLE OR LAWFUL BUSINESS"

The proscription against wandering has no built-in criterion whatever for ascertainment of the kind or degree of movement prohibited. Nor does the statute attempt to give content to the expression "without any visible or lawful business." As construed by the District of Columbia Court of Appeals, this phrase "does not refer to the ordinary vocation of the person but has reference to the purpose of being on the street, and business is not limited to the pursuit of monetary gain. One may have lawful business on the street even though he is there merely for exercise or recreation or any other proper purpose."[15]

This appears to be a logical reading of the statutory language, but what it means is that law enforcement officers may arrest a person who "wanders" on the streets late at night without "any proper purpose."[16] A police officer must first make an unguided determination as to whether in one's activity on the streets he "wanders." Coupled with the requirement that the wanderer give "a good account" of himself, it is evident that the officer must then make an equally unassisted judgment as to whether the purpose is "proper." Subsection (8) is thus a grant of an unfettered discretion—to administrative and judicial authorities alike—to regulate movement on the public streets. This is plainly much more than the Constitution tolerates.

III

The role of statutory vagueness in the aberrations of vagrancy administration appears vividly from the testimony regarding appellant's arrest and the enforcement policies generally in vogue in the District. One of the officers who arrested appellant testified that it "appeared" to him that she had been soliciting prostitution, but that for lack of evidence he "could not make a proper arrest or a proper prosecution on grounds of prostitution." "Instead," he arrested her for vagrancy, in accordance with what seems to be common practice. The other officer participating in the arrest opined that appellant is leading an immoral and profligate life because "I believe she is currently soliciting prostitution," but, since "all the elements of soliciting prostitution were not there," admitted that he "could not prove it." This officer, too, in taking appellant into custody, was simply following his usual procedure in such situations.

Definitions of crime traditionally combine a wrongful intent with a guilty act in a causal relationship to a consummated social harm. None of these characteristics is to be found in vagrancy prosecutions, which present instead "the astounding spectacle" of "criminality with no misbehavior at all."[17] Into

15. Beail v. District of Columbia [82 A.2d 765 (D.C. Mun. App. 1951)].

16. "I have known judges and lawyers who, afflicted with insomnia, have wandered the streets at night." Douglas, Vagrancy and Arrest On Suspicion, 70 Yale L.J. 1, 4 (1960).

17. President's Commission on Law Enforcement and Administration of Justice, Task Force Report: The Courts 102.

the making of "vagrancy" go such formless ingredients as "loitering," "wandering," "leading an immoral and profligate life," and "good account," concepts featuring a suspicion that a crime is being or might be committed.[18] Essentially all that has to be proved beyond a reasonable doubt in a vagrancy prosecution is that the accused was observed under circumstances deemed questionable. Charges of vagrancy thus make possible criminal convictions based on conjecture rather than on evidence of criminality, contrary to the most fundamental principles of our criminal jurisprudence.

The record exposes vagrancy enforcement as a device utilized not only to inflict punishment for suspected but unprovable violations in progress but also, through preventive conviction and incarceration, to suppress crime in the future. By this theory of vagrancy administration, a police officer testified, "undesirables" are swept from the streets into prison because "if they are not out there, the crime can't be committed." "[I]n practical effect," the witness acknowledged, "vagrancy is used as a charge or ground for arrest in cases where you feel there is prostitution or sodomy going on but you cannot make a case. . . . It is used to get the undesirables off the street." "[T]he good effect of this statute," the witness continued, "is that it puts people in jail who might be about to commit a crime or who might commit a crime in the near future," and "helps to lower the crime rate of the precinct."

According to another officer, a vagrancy arrest may be preferred to an arrest for another crime, though known to be in commission, because the arrested "person might be a real smooth operator and I might not be able to catch them doing these other things." The Corporation Counsel's chief prosecutor testified that "you certainly don't have to wait until a person goes in and engages in the act of prostitution before you can see fit to arrest that person for being a vagrant."

We agree with Judge Greene that the "basic design [of the vagrancy law] is one of preventive conviction imposed upon those who because of their background and behavior are more likely than the general public to commit crimes, and that the statute contemplates such convictions even though no overt criminal act has been committed or can be proved." . . .

We do not gainsay the importance of crime prevention or the need for effective measures to combat transgression of the criminal law. But as desirable as these goals are they cannot be achieved through techniques that trample on constitutional rights. Many years ago this court held that a citizen cannot be punished merely for being "a suspicious person." Statistical likelihood that a particular societal segment will engage in criminality is not permissible as an all-out substitute for proof of individual guilt. And not even past violation of the criminal law authorizes one's subjection to innately vague statutory specifications of crime.

18. Thus, in the case at bar, "leading an immoral and profligate life," an element of the vagrancy charged, was proved by the opinions of witnesses that appellant was soliciting prostitution, a matter which itself could not be proved. . . .

We conclude, then, that subsections (1), (3) and (8) of the general vagrancy statute must fall for unconstitutional vagueness. . . .

Reversed.

Notes and Questions

1. In a famous opinion in Papachristou v. Jacksonville, 405 U.S. 110, 162-172 (1972), striking down a similar vagrancy law, Justice Douglas offered an essay on vagrancy and the void-for-vagueness principle:

> Living under a rule of law entails various suppositions, one of which is that "[all persons] are entitled to be informed as to what the State commands or forbids." Lanzetta v. New Jersey, 306 U.S. 451, 453, 59 S. Ct. 618, 619, 83 L. Ed. 888.
>
> *Lanzetta* is one of a well-recognized group of cases insisting that the law give fair notice of the offending conduct. In the field of regulatory statutes governing business activities, where the acts limited are in a narrow category, greater leeway is allowed.
>
> The poor among us, the minorities, the average householder are not in business and not alerted to the regulatory schemes of vagrancy laws; and we assume they would have no understanding of their meaning and impact if they read them. Nor are they protected from being caught in the vagrancy net by the necessity of having a specific intent to commit an unlawful act.
>
> The Jacksonville ordinance makes criminal activities which by modern standards are normally innocent. "Nightwalking" is one. Florida construes the ordinance not to make criminal one night's wandering, Johnson v. State, 202 So. 2d, at 855, only the "habitual" wanderer or, as the ordinance describes it, "common night walkers." We know, however, from experience that sleepless people often walk at night, perhaps hopeful that sleep-inducing relaxation will result.
>
> Luis Munoz-Marin, former Governor of Puerto Rico, commented once that "loafing" was a national virtue in his Commonwealth and that it should be encouraged. It is, however, a crime in Jacksonville.
>
> "[P]ersons able to work but habitually living upon the earnings of their wives or minor children"—like habitually living "without visible means of support"—might implicate unemployed pillars of the community who have married rich wives.
>
> "[P]ersons able to work but habitually living upon the earnings of their wives or minor children" may also embrace unemployed people out of the labor market, by reason of a recession or disemployed by reason of technological or so-called structural displacements.
>
> Persons "wandering or strolling" from place to place have been extolled by Walt Whitman and Vachel Lindsay.[19] The qualification "without any lawful

19. And see Reich, Police Questioning of Law Abiding Citizens, 75 Yale L.J. 1161, 1172 (1966): "If I choose to take an evening walk to see if Andromeda has come up on schedule, I think I am entitled to look for the distant light of Almach and Mirach without finding myself staring into the blinding beam of a police flashlight."

purpose or object" may be a trap for innocent acts. Persons "neglecting all lawful business and habitually spending their time by frequenting . . . places where alcoholic beverages are sold or served" would literally embrace many members of golf clubs and city clubs.

Walkers and strollers and wanderers may be going to or coming from a burglary. Loafers or loiterers may be "casing" a place for a holdup. Letting one's wife support him is an intra-family matter, and normally of no concern to the police. Yet it may, of course, be the setting for numerous crimes.

The difficulty is that these activities are historically part of the amenities of life as we have known them. They are not mentioned in the Constitution or in the Bill of Rights. These unwritten amenities have been in part responsible for giving our people the feeling of independence and self-confidence, the feeling of creativity. These amenities have dignified the right of dissent and have honored the right to be nonconformists and the right to defy submissiveness. They have encouraged lives of high spirits rather than hushed, suffocating silence.

They are embedded in Walt Whitman's writings, especially in his "Song of the Open Road." They are reflected too, in the spirit of Vachel Lindsay's "I Want to Go Wandering," and by Henry D. Thoreau.[20]

This aspect of the vagrancy ordinance before us is suggested by what this Court said in 1876 about a broad criminal statute enacted by Congress: "It would certainly be dangerous if the legislature could set a net large enough to catch all possible offenders, and leave it to the courts to step inside and say who could be rightfully detained, and who should be set at large." United States v. Reese, 92 U.S. 214, 221, 23 L. Ed. 563.

While that was a federal case, the due process implications are equally applicable to the States and to this vagrancy ordinance. Here the net cast is large, not to give the courts the power to pick and choose but to increase the arsenal of the police. In Winters v. New York, 333 U.S. 507, 68 S. Ct. 665, 92 L. Ed. 840, the Court struck down a New York statute that made criminal the distribution of a magazine made up principally of items of criminal deeds of bloodshed or lust so massed as to become vehicles for inciting violent and depraved crimes against the person. The infirmity the Court found was vagueness—the absence of "ascertainable standards of guilt" (id., at 515, 68 S. Ct., at 670) in the sensitive First Amendment area.[21] Mr. Justice Frankfurter dissented.

20. "I have met with but one or two persons in the course of my life who understood the art of Walking, that is, of taking walks,—who had a genius, so to speak, for *sauntering:* which word is beautifully derived 'from idle people who roved about the country, in the Middle Ages, and asked charity, under pretence of going *à la Sainte Terre,'* to the Holy Land, till the children exclaimed, 'There goes a *Sainte Terrer,'* a Saunterer, a Holy-Lander. They who never go to the Holy Land in their walks, as they pretend, are indeed mere idlers and vagabonds; but they who do go there are saunterers in the good sense, such as I mean. Some, however, would derive the word from *sans terre,* without land or a home, which, therefore, in the good sense, will mean, having no particular home, but equally at home everywhere. For this is the secret of successful sauntering. He who sits still in a house all the time may be the greatest vagrant of all; but the saunterer, in the good sense, is no more vagrant than the meandering river, which is all the while sedulously seeking the shortest course to the sea. But I prefer the first, which, indeed, is the most probable derivation. For every walk is a sort of crusade, preached by some Peter the Hermit in us, to go forth and reconquer this Holy Land from the hands of the Infidels." Excursions 251-252 (1893).

21. For a discussion of the void-for-vagueness doctrine in the area of fundamental rights see Note, The Void-For-Vagueness Doctrine in the Supreme Court, 109 U. Pa. L. Rev. 67, 104 et seq.; Amsterdam, Federal Constitutional Restrictions on the Punishment of Crimes of Status,

But concerned as he, and many others, had been over the vagrancy laws, he added:

> Only a word needs to be said regarding Lanzetta v. New Jersey, 306 U.S. 451, 59 S. Ct. 618, 83 L. Ed. 888. The case involved a New Jersey statute of the type that seek to control "vagrancy." These statutes are in a class by themselves, in view of the familiar abuses to which they are put. . . . Definiteness is designedly avoided so as to allow the net to be cast at large, to enable men to be caught who are vaguely undesirable in the eyes of police and prosecution, although not chargeable with any particular offense. In short, these "vagrancy statutes" and laws against "gangs" are not fenced in by the text of the statute or by the subject matter so as to give notice of conduct to be avoided." Id., at 540, 68 S. Ct., at 682.

Where the list of crimes is so all-inclusive and generalized as the one in this ordinance, those convicted may be punished for no more than vindicating affronts to police authority:

> The common ground which brings such a motley assortment of human troubles before the magistrates in vagrancy-type proceedings is the procedural laxity which permits "conviction" for almost any kind of conduct and the existence of the House of Correction as an easy and convenient dumping-ground for problems that appear to have no other immediate solution. Foote, Vagrancy-Type Law and Its Administration, 104 U. Pa. L. Rev. 603, 631.[22]

Another aspect of the ordinance's vagueness appears when we focus, not on the lack of notice given a potential offender, but on the effect of the unfettered discretion it places in the hands of the Jacksonville police. Caleb Foote, an early student of this subject, has called the vagrancy-type law as offering "punishment by analogy." Id., at 609. Such crimes, though long common in Russia,[23] are not compatible with our constitutional system. We allow our police to make arrests only on "probable cause," a Fourth and Fourteenth Amendment standard appli-

---

Crimes of General Obnoxiousness, Crimes of Displeasing Police Officers, and the Like, 3 Crim. L. Bull. 205, 224 et seq. (1967).

22. Thus, "prowling by auto," which formed the basis for the vagrancy arrests and convictions of four of the petitioners herein, is not even listed in the ordinance as a crime. But see Hanks v. State, 195 So. 2d 49, 51, in which the Florida District Court of Appeal construed "wandering or strolling from place to place" as including travel by automobile.

23. J. Hazard, The Soviet Legal System 133 (1962):

> The 1922 code was a step in the direction of precision in definition of crime, but it was not a complete departure from the concept of punishment in accordance with the dictates of the social consciousness of the judge. Laying hold of an old tsarist code provision that had been in effect from 1864 to 1903 known by the term "analogy," the Soviet draftsmen inserted an article permitting a judge to consider the social danger of an individual even when he had committed no act defined as a crime in the specialized part of the code. He was to be guided by analogizing the dangerous act to some act defined as crime, but at the outset the analogies were not always apparent, as when a husband was executed for the sadistic murder of a wife, followed by dissection of her torso and shipment in a trunk to a remote railway station, the court arguing that the crime was analogous to banditry. At the time of this decision the code permitted the death penalty for banditry but not for murder without political motives or very serious social consequences.
>
> On the traditionally important subject of criminal law. Algeria is rejecting the flexibility introduced in the Soviet criminal code by the "analogy" principle, as have the East-Central European and black African states. Hazard, The Residue of Marxist Influence in Algeria, 9 Colum. J. of Transnatl. L. 194, 224 (1970).

cable to the States, as well as to the Federal Government. Arresting a person on suspicion, like arresting a person for investigation, is foreign to our system, even when the arrest is for past criminality. Future criminality, however, is the common justification for the presence of vagrancy statutes. See Foote, supra, at 625. Florida has, indeed, construed her vagrancy statute "as necessary regulations," inter alia, "to deter vagabondage and prevent crimes." Johnson v. State, Fla., 202 So. 2d 852; Smith v. State, Fla., 239 So. 2d 250, 251.

A direction by a legislature to the police to arrest all "suspicious" persons would not pass constitutional muster. A vagrancy prosecution may be merely the cloak for a conviction which could not be obtained on the real but undisclosed grounds for the arrest. People v. Moss, 309 N.Y. 429, 131 N.E.2d 717. But as Chief Justice Hewart said in Frederick Dean, 18 Crim. App. 133, 134 (1924):

> It would be in the highest degree unfortunate if in any part of the country those who are responsible for setting in motion the criminal law should entertain, connive at or coquette with the idea that in a case where there is not enough evidence to charge the prisoner with an attempt to commit a crime, the prosecution may, nevertheless, on such insufficient evidence, succeed in obtaining and upholding a conviction under the Vagrancy Act, 1824.

Those generally implicated by the imprecise terms of the ordinance—poor people, nonconformists, dissenters, idlers—may be required to comport themselves according to the life style deemed appropriate by the Jacksonville police and the courts. Where, as here, there are no standards governing the exercise of the discretion granted by the ordinance, the scheme permits and encourages an arbitrary and discriminatory enforcement of the law. It furnishes a convenient tool for "harsh and discriminatory enforcement by local prosecuting officials, against particular groups deemed to merit their displeasure." Thornhill v. Alabama, 310 U.S. 88, 97-98, 60 S. Ct. 736, 742, 84 L. Ed. 1093. . . .

A presumption that people who might walk or loaf or loiter or stroll or frequent houses where liquor is sold, or who are supported by their wives or who look suspicious to the police are to become future criminals is too precarious for a rule of law. The implicit presumption in these generalized vagrancy standards—that crime is being nipped in the bud—is too extravagant to deserve extended treatment. Of course, vagrancy statutes are useful to the police. Of course, they are nets making easy the roundup of so-called undesirables. But the rule of law implies equality and justice in its application. Vagrancy laws of the Jacksonville type teach that the scales of justice are so tipped that even-handed administration of the law is not possible. The rule of law, evenly applied to minorities as well as majorities, to the poor as well as the rich, is the great mucilage that holds society together.

The Jacksonville ordinance cannot be squared with our constitutional standards and is plainly unconstitutional.

2. Could any of the defendants in *Ricks* or *Papachristou* be prosecuted on another theory—that they attempted more specific crimes such as theft, drug-dealing, or prostitution? Recall that contemporary attempt laws, like the Model Penal Code's "substantial step" formulation in §5.01, reject the rigid "last act" requirement of the common law and permit the police to intervene fairly early in a criminal transaction without fear of losing a prosecution.

Would this modern kind of attempt law serve as a proxy for a vagrancy law?

3. Is it still possible to draft a constitutionally valid vagrancy law? Consider the following effort by the drafters of the Model Penal Code:

Section 250.6. Loitering or Prowling.

> A person commits a violation if he loiters or prowls in a place, at a time, or in a manner not usual for lawabiding individuals under circumstances that warrant alarm for the safety of persons or property in the vicinity. Among the circumstances which may be considered in determining whether such alarm is warranted is the fact that the actor takes flight upon appearance of a peace officer, refuses to identify himself, or manifestly endeavors to conceal himself or any object. Unless flight by the actor or other circumstance makes it impracticable, a peace officer shall prior to any arrest for an offense under this section afford the actor an opportunity to dispel any alarm which would otherwise be warranted, by requesting him to identify himself and explain his presence and conduct. No person shall be convicted of an offense under this Section if the peace officer did not comply with the preceding sentence, or if it appears at trial that the explanation given by the actor was true and, if believed by the peace officer at the time, would have dispelled the alarm.

Does the Code's emphasis on "alarming" loitering solve the void-for-vagueness problem? The comments to §250.6 (Commentaries, Pt. II (1980)), suggest that the following conduct would be covered by the provision:

> [A] known professional pickpocket is seen loitering in a crowded railroad station; a person not recognized as a local resident is seen lurking in a doorway and furtively looking up and down the street to see if he is being watched; an unknown man is seen standing for some time in a dark alley where he has no apparent business.

Is it clear that the statute covers these cases? If it does cover them, is it constitutional? Compare City of Portland v. White, 9 Crt. App. Ore. 239, 495 P.2d 778 (1972) (holding a similar law void for vagueness), with City of Seattle v. Drew, 70 Wash. 2d 405, 423 P.2d 522 (1967) (upholding similar law).

4. In Paris Adult Theatre I v. Slaton, 413 U.S. 49, 84-89, Justice Brennan, in dissent, discussed the peculiar susceptibility of obscenity laws to void-for-vagueness problems:

> But after 16 years of experimentation and debate I am reluctantly forced to the conclusion that none of the available formulas, including the one announced today, can reduce the vagueness to a tolerable level while at the same time striking an acceptable balance between the protections of the First and Fourteenth Amendments, on the one hand, and on the other the asserted state interest in regulating the dissemination of certain sexually oriented materials. Any effort to draw a constitutionally acceptable boundary on state power must resort to

such indefinite concepts as "prurient interest," "patent offensiveness," "serious literary value," and the like. The meaning of these concepts necessarily varies with the experience, outlook, and even idiosyncrasies of the person defining them. Although we have assumed that obscenity does exist and that we "know it when [we] see it," Jacobellis v. Ohio, 378 U.S., at 197, 84 S. Ct., at 1683 (Stewart, J., concurring), we are manifestly unable to describe it in advance except by reference to concepts so elusive that they fail to distinguish clearly between protected and unprotected speech.

We have more than once previously acknowledged that "constitutionally protected expression . . . is often separated from obscenity only by a dim and uncertain line." Bantam Books, Inc. v. Sullivan, 372 U.S., at 66, 83 S. Ct., at 637. Added to the "perhaps inherent residual vagueness" of each of the current multitude of standards, Ginzburg v. United States, supra, 383 U.S., at 475 n.19, 86 S. Ct., at 950, is the future complication that the obscenity of any particular item may depend upon nuances of presentation and the context of its dissemination. . . . As Mr. Chief Justice Warren stated in a related vein, obscenity is a function of the circumstances of its dissemination:

> It is not the book that is on trial; it is a person. The conduct of the defendant is the central issue, not the obscenity of a book or picture. The nature of the materials is, of course, relevant as an attribute of the defendant's conduct, but the materials are thus placed in context from which they draw color and character. *Roth,* 354 U.S., at 495, 77 S. Ct., at 1314 (concurring opinion).

I need hardly point out that the factors which must be taken into account are judgmental and can only be applied on "a case-by-case, sight-by-sight" basis. Mishkin v. New York, 383 U.S., at 516, 86 S. Ct., at 968 (Black, J., dissenting). These considerations suggest that no one definition, no matter how precisely or narrowly drawn, can possibly suffice for all situations, or carve out fully suppressible expression from all media without also creating a substantial risk of encroachment upon the guarantees of the Due Process Clause and the First Amendment.[24]

24. Although I did not join the opinion of the Court in Stanley v. Georgia, 394 U.S. 557, 89 S. Ct. 1243, 22 L. Ed. 2d 542 (1969), I am now inclined to agree that "the Constitution protects the right to receive information and ideas," and that "this right to receive information and ideas, regardless of their social worth . . . is fundamental to our free society." Id., at 564, 89 S. Ct., at 1247. See Martin v. City of Struthers, 319 U.S. 141, 143, 63 S. Ct. 862, 863, 87 L. Ed. 1313 (1943); Winters v. New York, 333 U.S. 507, 510, 68 S. Ct. 665, 667, 92 L. Ed. 840 (1948); Lamont v. Postmaster General, 381 U.S. 301, 307-308, 85 S. Ct. 1493, 1496-1497, 14 L. Ed. 2d 398 (1965) (concurring opinion). This right is closely tied, as *Stanley* recognized, to "the right to be free, except in very limited circumstances, from unwarranted governmental intrusions into one's privacy." 394 U.S. at 564, 80 S. Ct. at 1247. See Griswold v. Connecticut, 381 U.S. 479, 85 S. Ct. 1678, 14 L. Ed. 2d 510 (1965); Olmstead v. United States 277 U.S. 438, 478, 48 S. Ct. 564, 572, 72 L. Ed. 944 (1928) (Brandeis, J., dissenting). It is similarly related to "the right of the individual, married or single, to be free from unwarranted governmental intrusion into matters so fundamentally affecting a person as the decision whether to bear or beget a child" (italics omitted), Eisenstadt v. Baird, 405 U.S. 438, 453, 92 S. Ct. 1029, 1038, 31 L. Ed. 2d 349 (1972), and the right to exercise "autonomous control over the development and expression of one's intellect, interests, tastes, and personality." (Italics omitted.) Doe v. Bolton, 410 U.S. 179, 211, 93 S. Ct. 739, 757, 35 L. Ed. 2d 201 (1973) (Douglas, J., concurring). It seems to me that the recognition of the validity of the two-level approach is recognized in *Roth.* After all, if a person has the right to receive information without regard to its social worth—that is, without regard to its obscenity—

The vagueness of the standards in the obscenity area produces a number of separate problems, and any improvement must rest on an understanding that the problems are to some extent distinct. First, a vague statute fails to provide adequate notice to persons who are engaged in the type of conduct that the statute could be thought to proscribe. The Due Process Clause of the Fourteenth Amendment requires that all criminal laws provide fair notice of "what the State commands or forbids." Lanzetta v. New Jersey, 306 U.S. 451, 453 (1939). In the service of this general principle we have repeatedly held that the definition of obscenity must provide adequate notice of exactly what is prohibited from dissemination. While various tests have been upheld under the Due Process Clause, I have grave doubts that any of those tests could be sustained today. For I know of no satisfactory answer to the assertion by Mr. Justice Black, "after the fourteen separate opinions handed down" in the trilogy of cases decided in 1966, that "no person, not even the most learned judge much less a layman, is capable of knowing in advance of an ultimate decision in his particular case by this Court whether certain material comes within the area of 'obscenity'. . . ." Ginzburg v. United States, 383 U.S., at 480-481, 86 S. Ct., at 952-953 (dissenting opinion). In this context, even the most painstaking efforts to determine in advance whether certain sexually oriented expression is obscene must inevitably prove unavailing. For the insufficiency of the notice compels persons to guess not only whether their conduct is covered by a criminal statute, but also whether their conduct falls within the constitutionally permissible reach of the statute. The resulting level of uncertainty is utterly intolerable, not alone because it makes "[b]ookselling . . . a hazardous profession," Ginsberg v. New York, 390 U.S., at 674, 88 S. Ct., at 1298 (Fortas, J., dissenting), but as well because it invites arbitrary and erratic enforcement of the law.

In addition to problems that arise when any criminal statute fails to afford fair notice of what it forbids, a vague statute in the areas of speech and press creates a second level of difficulty. We have indicated that "stricter standards of permissible statutory vagueness may be applied to a statute having a potentially inhibiting effect on speech; a man may the less be required to act at his peril here, because the free dissemination of ideas may be the loser." That proposition draws its strength from our recognition that

> [t]he fundamental freedoms of speech and press have contributed greatly to the development and well-being of our free society and are indispensable to its continued growth. Ceaseless vigilance is the watchword to prevent their erosion by Congress or by the States. The door barring federal and state intrusion into this area cannot be left ajar. . . . *Roth,* 354 U.S., at 488, 77 S. Ct., at 1311. . . .[25]

---

then it would seem to follow that a State could not constitutionally punish one who undertakes to provide this information to a willing, adult recipient. See Eisenstadt v. Baird, supra, 405 U.S. at 443-446, 92 S. Ct., at 1033-1035. . . . Whether or not a class of "obscene" and thus entirely unprotected speech does exist, I am forced to conclude that the class is incapable of definition with sufficient clarity to withstand attack on vagueness grounds. Accordingly, it is on principles of the void-for-vagueness doctrine that this opinion exclusively relies.

25. . . . Barenblatt v. United States, 360 U.S. 109, 137-138:

> This Court . . . has emphasized that the "vice of vagueness" is especially pernicious where legislative power over an area involving speech, press, petition and assembly is involved. . . . For a statute broad enough to support infringement of speech, writings, thoughts and public assemblies, against the unequivocal command of the First Amend-

5. Even relatively uncontroversial criminal laws, such as the homicide laws, give juries broad moral and political discretion to define criminal conduct under vague categories such as "reasonableness." If the involuntary manslaughter law requires the jury to determine whether the victim's death was "reasonably foreseeable," or if the voluntary manslaughter law requires it to find that a "reasonable" person in the defendant's position would have been provoked into the heat of passion, are these laws void for vagueness? In a famous antitrust opinion in Nash v. United States, 229 U.S. 373, 376-378, Justice Holmes said:

> And thereupon it is said that the crime thus defined by the statute contains in its definition an element of degree as to which estimates may differ, with the result that a man might find himself in prison because his honest judgment did not anticipate that of a jury of less competent men. . . .
>
> But apart from the common law as to restraint of trade thus taken up by the statute the law is full of instances where a man's fate depends on his estimating rightly, that is, as the jury subsequently estimates it, some matter of degree. If his judgment is wrong, not only may he incur a fine or a short imprisonment, as here; he may incur the penalty of death. "An act causing death may be murder, manslaughter, or misadventure according to the degree of danger attending it" by common experience in the circumstances known to the actor. "The very meaning of the fiction of implied malice in such cases at common law was, that a man might have to answer with his life for consequences which he neither intended nor foresaw." Commonwealth v. Pierce, 138 Mass. 165, 178. Commonwealth v. Chance, 174 Mass. 245, 252. "The criterion in such cases is to examine whether common social duty would, under the circumstances, have suggested a more circumspect conduct." 1 East P.C. 262. If a man should kill another by driving an automobile furiously into a crowd he might be convicted of murder however little he expected the result. If he did no more than drive negligently through a street he might get off with manslaughter or less. And in the last case he might be held although he himself thought that he was acting as a prudent man should. . . . We are of opinion that there is no constitutional difficulty in the way of enforcing the criminal part of the act.

In State v. Musser, 118 Utah 537, 223 P.2d 193 (1950), the defendants, charged with counseling and practicing polygamy, were convicted under a statute making it a crime "to commit any act injurious . . . to public morals. . . ." In striking the act as void for vagueness, the concurring judge explained the ruling as follows:

---

ment necessarily leaves all persons to guess just what the law really means to cover, and fear of a wrong guess inevitably leads people to forego the very rights the Constitution sought to protect above all others. Vagueness becomes even more intolerable in this area if one accepts, as the Court today does, a balancing test to decide if First Amendment rights shall be protected. It is difficult at best to make a man guess—at the penalty of imprisonment—whether a court will consider the State's need for certain information superior to society's interest in unfettered freedom. It is unconscionable to make him choose between the right to keep silent and the need to speak when the statute supposedly establishing the "state's interest" is too vague to give him guidance.

I might pose the question: How all-inclusive is the phrase "contrary to public morals"? It must be conceded it has wide coverage unless limited by other judicial or legislative pronouncements. It has been suggested that the phrase can be interpreted so as to indicate a legislative intent to limit its effect to those acts which are specified by the legislature in other sections of the statutes as being injurious to public morals. . . .

In interpreting a statute, the legislature will be presumed to have inserted every part for a purpose and to have intended that every part be given effect. Significance and meaning should, if possible, be accorded every phrase, and a construction is favored which will render every word operative rather than one which makes some phrases or subsections nugatory. If we adopt the foregoing rule of construction we must hold that subsection (5) is a catch-all provision without guides, standards or limits.

There are situations when conspiracies to teach certain dogmas, tenets, or beliefs might be deemed inimical to public morals by some jurists and by some jurors, and yet not be defined by the legislature as crimes. The teaching of card-playing might be considered by some as being in that category, although the legislature may not have made such teaching a crime. It is in this aspect that subsection (5) becomes vagrant and wandering and has no limits. Courts and juries might determine that certain teachings offend against public morals and yet the parties doing the teaching might not be advised by statute or otherwise that they were committing a crime. The standards for an offense would thus be fixed by those who heard the evidence and not by the legislature, whose duty it is to define the crime with some degree of particularity.

In the final analysis, each individual has his own moral codes, private and public, and what acts might be considered as injurious to public morals are as numerous as the opinions of man. The law requires that crimes be defined with more certainty than that.

18

PROPORTIONALITY

In Hart v. Coiner, 483 F.2d 136 (4th Cir. 1973), the defendant was sentenced to life imprisonment under West Virginia's recidivist statute. Hart was convicted of writing a check on insufficient funds for $50 in 1949, transporting forged checks worth $140 across state lines in 1955, and perjury in 1968. The recidivist statute required the trial court to impose a life sentence on anyone convicted three separate times of crimes punishable by imprisonment in a penitentiary. Although the court of appeals acknowledged the facial validity of the recidivist statute, it nevertheless felt obliged to examine "whether the recidivist mandatory life sentence *in this case* is so excessive as to constitute cruel and unusual punishment" under the Eighth Amendment.

In trying to reach a coherent standard by which to decide such cases, the court stated:

> [T]here are several objective factors which are useful in determining whether the sentence in this case is constitutionally disproportionate. The last to be used is a cumulative one focusing on an analysis of the combined factors. . . .
>
> The initial element to be analyzed . . . is the nature of the offense itself. . . . In assessing the nature and gravity of an offense, courts have repeatedly emphasized the element of violence and danger to the person. . . .
>
> Another factor to be examined is the legislative purpose behind the punishment. . . .
>
> A third objective factor is comparison of [the defendant's] punishment with how he would have been punished in other jurisdictions. . . .
>
> A comparison of punishment available in the same jurisdiction for other offenses is likewise a factor.

Applying these factors to Hart's conviction, the Court noted that none of his crimes were offenses against the person. Indeed the bad check conviction "was very nearly trivial"—one penny less and it would have been a petty misdemeanor. The court also criticized the state's deterrence rationale, calling it impractical to attempt to jail all Hart-like criminals for life and suggesting that such a punishment should be reserved for violent criminals who pose a danger to others. In examining comparative provisions in other states, the court found West Virginia's scheme "among the top four in the nation" (in terms of severity) and said that "[c]onsideration of the penalties provided for grave crimes of violence in West Virginia reveals the irrationally disparate treatment visited upon Hart." It then reversed Hart's sentence and remanded for resentencing solely on the basis of the perjury conviction.

Notes and Questions

1. What does the court mean when it refers to "objective factors"? Was its decision, in fact, based on any form of objectivity? How manageable is the four-part test devised by the court? Is it even possible to devise an objective test?

2. How would you decide whether a sentence was unconstitutionally disproportionate?

3. At what point do you think that the difference of the sentencing policy of a given state from that of most other states should become a constitutional factor? The court noted that West Virginia's statute was among the top four in severity. What if it had only been number ten, fifteen, or twenty?

4. The analysis in *Hart* is very similar to that undertaken a year earlier by the California Supreme Court in In re Lynch, 8 Cal. 3d 410, 105 Cal. Rptr. 217, 503 P.2d 921 (1972). The defendant was convicted of a second offense of indecent exposure in 1967; the first occurred in 1958 and was punished by two years on probation. The California Penal Code provided that for a second conviction, the offender is subject to an indeterminate sentence of one year to life, with the precise length of sentence to be determined by the Adult Authority, an administrative agency within the Department of Corrections. Since the prisoner had no legally enforceable claim to early release, the court treated the sentence as one of life imprisonment. It then concluded that a prison sentence could violate the California constitutional guarantee against cruel or unusual punishment if "it is so disproportionate to the crime for which it is inflicted that it shocks the conscience and offends fundamental notions of human dignity." To administer this somewhat nebulous standard, the court pointed to several factors: "the nature of the offense and/or offender, with particular regard to the degree of danger both present to society"; "the nonviolent nature of the offense"; a comparison between the challenged penalty and punishments in the same jurisdiction for more serious offenses; and a comparison with punishments for the same offense in other jurisdictions with a similar constitutional provision. In finding that the recidivist portion of the indecent exposure statute was unconstitutionally disproportionate, the court was particularly affected by the circumstances of Lynch's second conviction:

> This is not a case, for example, in which an exhibitionist forced himself on large numbers of the public by cavorting naked on a busy street at high noon. Instead, a very different picture emerges. The prosecuting witness was a "carhop" or waitress on the night shift at a drive-in restaurant. She testified that between midnight and 1 A.M. petitioner drove into the restaurant area, alone in his car. He first parked in the rear lot, where no car service was provided. Subsequently he moved his vehicle closer and asked the waitress for a cup of coffee. When she returned with a second cup he inquired what time the restaurant would close, and she told him 2:45 A.M. He instructed her to bring him a fresh cup of coffee whenever she thought the previous cup might be cold, explaining that he didn't want to "bother" her. Accordingly, about half an hour later and without being called, the waitress approached petitioner's car with another cup of coffee. A siren happened to be sounding in the street at that moment, and petitioner was looking in its direction, away from the waitress. As she stood by his window she saw the fly of his pants open, his hand on his erect penis, and a "pin-up" magazine open on the front seat next to him. When petitioner heard her put the coffee down on his tray he turned, saw her, and said "Oops." The waitress left immediately. Some 15 minutes later, however, she assertedly observed him from a distance through a rearview mirror on his car and saw he was still exposed. The incident was then reported to the police, and petitioner was placed under arrest. . . .
>
> For this single act petitioner has now spent more than five years in state prison—three and a half of those years in the maximum security confines of Folsom. The Adult Authority has four times denied him release on parole, and has never fixed his sentence at any term less than the life maximum.

Lynch was extended in In re Wells, 46 Cal. App. 3d 542, 121 Cal. Rptr. 23 (1975) to invalidate a similar recidivist provision in the child molestation statute. See also People v. Keogh, 46 Cal. App. 3d 919, 120 Cal. Rptr. 817 (1975) (four consecutive 1 to 14 year sentences for four counts of forgery involving checks with a total value of less than $500 "is so severely disproportionate as to violate the California Constitution." 46 Cal. App. 3d at 932); In re Grant, 18 Cal. 3d 1, 132 Cal. Rptr. 430, 553 P.2d 590 (1976) ("[T]hose provisions of the Health and Safety Code which preclude parole consideration for a minimum of five years or more for recidivist narcotics offenders constitute both cruel and unusual punishment in violation of [the California Constitution]").

RUMMEL v. ESTELLE

United States Supreme Court
445 U.S. 263 (1980)

Mr. Justice REHNQUIST delivered the opinion of the Court.

Petitioner William James Rummel is presently serving a life sentence imposed by the State of Texas in 1973 under its "recidivist statute," . . . which provided that "[w]hoever shall have been three times convicted of a felony less than capital shall on such third conviction be imprisoned for life in the penitentiary." On January 19, 1976, Rummel sought a writ of habeas corpus in the United States District Court for the Western District of Texas, arguing that life imprisonment was "grossly disproportionate" to the three felonies that formed the predicate for his sentence and that therefore the sentence violated the ban on cruel and unusual punishments of the Eighth and Fourteenth Amendments. The District Court and the United States Court of Appeals for the Fifth Circuit rejected Rummel's claim, finding no unconstitutional disproportionality. We granted certiorari, 441 U.S. 960, and now affirm.

I

In 1964 the State of Texas charged Rummel with fraudulent use of a credit card to obtain $80 worth of goods or services. Because the amount in question was greater than $50, the charged offense was a felony punishable by a minimum of 2 years and a maximum of 10 years in the Texas Department of Corrections. Rummel eventually pleaded guilty to the charge and was sentenced to three years' confinement in a state penitentiary.

In 1969 the State of Texas charged Rummel with passing a forged check in the amount of $28.36, a crime punishable by imprisonment in a penitentiary for not less than two nor more than five years. Rummel pleaded guilty to this offense and was sentenced to four years' imprisonment.

In 1973 Rummel was charged with obtaining $120.75 by false pretenses. Because the amount obtained was greater than $50, the charged offense was designated "felony theft," which, by itself, was punishable by confinement in a penitentiary for not less than 2 nor more than 10 years. The prosecution chose, however, to proceed against Rummel under Texas' recidivist statute, and cited in the indictment his 1964 and 1969 convictions as requiring imposition of a life sentence if Rummel were convicted of the charged offense. A jury convicted Rummel of felony theft and also found as true the allegation that he had been convicted of two prior felonies. As a result, on April 26, 1973, the trial court imposed upon Rummel the life sentence mandated by Art. 63 [of the Texas Penal Code].

II

Initially, we believe it important to set forth two propositions that Rummel does not contest. First, Rummel does not challenge the constitutionality of Texas' recidivist statute as a general proposition. . . . Here, Rummel attacks only the result of applying this concededly valid statute to the facts of his case.

Second, Rummel does not challenge Texas' authority to punish each of his offenses as felonies, that is, by imprisoning him in a state penitentiary. . . . Under Texas law Rummel concededly could have received sentences totaling

25 years in prison for what he refers to as his "petty property offenses." Indeed, when Rummel obtained $120.75 by false pretenses he committed a crime punishable as a felony in at least 35 States and the District of Columbia. Similarly, a large number of States authorized significant terms of imprisonment for each of Rummel's other offenses at the times he committed them. Rummel's challenge thus focuses only on the State's authority to impose a sentence of life imprisonment, as opposed to a substantial term of years, for his third felony.

This Court has on occasion stated that the Eighth Amendment prohibits imposition of a sentence that is grossly disproportionate to the severity of the crime. In recent years this proposition has appeared most frequently in opinions dealing with the death penalty. Rummel cites these latter opinions dealing with capital punishment as compelling the conclusion that his sentence is disproportionate to his offenses. But as Mr. Justice Stewart noted in [Furman v. Georgia, 408 U.S. 238 (1972)]:

> The penalty of death differs from all other forms of criminal punishment, not in degree but in kind. It is unique in its total irrevocability. It is unique in its rejection of rehabilitation of the convict as a basic purpose of criminal justice. And it is unique, finally, in its absolute renunciation of all that is embodied in our concept of humanity. . . .

Because a sentence of death differs in kind from any sentence of imprisonment, no matter how long, our decisions applying the prohibition of cruel and unusual punishments to capital cases are of limited assistance in deciding the constitutionality of the punishment meted out to Rummel.

Outside the context of capital punishment, successful challenges to the proportionality of particular sentences have been exceedingly rare. In Weems v. United States [217 U.S. 349 (1910)], a case coming to this Court from the Supreme Court of the Philippine Islands, petitioner successfully attacked the imposition of a punishment known as "cadena temporal" for the crime of falsifying a public record. . . . The mandatory "remedy" for this offense was *cadena temporal,* a punishment described graphically by the Court:

> Its minimum degree is confinement in a penal institution for twelve years and one day, a chain at the ankle and wrist of the offender, hard and painful labor, no assistance from friend or relative, no marital authority or parental rights or rights of property, no participation even in the family council. These parts of his penalty endure for the term of imprisonment. From other parts there is no intermission. His prison bars and chains are removed, it is true, after twelve years, but he goes from them to a perpetual limitation of his liberty. He is forever kept under the shadow of his crime, forever kept within voice and view of the criminal magistrate, not being able to change his domicil without giving notice to the "authority immediately in charge of his surveillance," and without permission in writing. Id., at 366.

Although Rummel argues that the length of Weems' imprisonment was, by itself, a basis for the Court's decision, the Court's opinion does not support such a simple conclusion. The opinion consistently referred jointly to the length of imprisonment and its "accessories" or "accompaniments." . . .

Thus, we do not believe that *Weems* can be applied without regard to its peculiar facts: the triviality of the charged offense, the impressive length of the minimum term of imprisonment, and the extraordinary nature of the "accessories" included within the punishment of *cadena temporal.*

Given the unique nature of the punishments considered in *Weems* and in the death penalty cases, one could argue without fear of contradiction by any decision of this Court that for crimes concededly classified and classifiable as felonies, that is, as punishable by significant terms of imprisonment in a state penitentiary, the length of the sentence actually imposed is purely a matter of legislative prerogative.[1] . . .

As was noted by Mr. Justice White, writing for the plurality in Coker v. Georgia, [433 U.S. 584, 592 (1977)], our Court's "Eighth Amendment judgments should not be, or appear to be, merely the subjective views of individual Justices; judgment should be informed by objective factors to the maximum possible extent." . . .

In an attempt to provide us with objective criteria against which we might measure the proportionality of his life sentence, Rummel points to certain characteristics of his offenses that allegedly render them "petty." He cites, for example, the absence of violence in his crimes. But the presence or absence of violence does not always affect the strength of society's interest in deterring a particular crime or in punishing a particular criminal. A high official in a large corporation can commit undeniably serious crimes in the area of antitrust, bribery, or clean air or water standards without coming close to engaging in any "violent" or short-term "life-threatening" behavior. Additionally, Rummel cites the "small" amount of money taken in each of his crimes. But to recognize that the State of Texas could have imprisoned Rummel for life if he had stolen $5,000, $50,000, or $500,000, rather than the $120.75 that a jury convicted him of stealing, is virtually to concede that the lines to be drawn are indeed "subjective," and therefore properly within the province of legislatures, not courts. Moreover, if Rummel had attempted to defraud his victim of $50,000, but had failed, no money whatsoever would have changed hands; yet Rummel would be no less blameworthy, only less skillful, than if he had succeeded.

In this case, however, we need not decide whether Texas could impose a life sentence upon Rummel merely for obtaining $120.75 by false pretenses. Had Rummel only committed that crime, under the law enacted by the Texas Legislature he could have been imprisoned for no more than 10 years. In fact, at the time that he obtained the $120.75 by false pretenses, he already had

1. This is not to say that a proportionality principle would not come into play in the extreme example mentioned by the dissent if a legislature made overtime parking a felony punishable by life imprisonment.

committed and had been imprisoned for two other felonies, crimes that Texas and other States felt were serious enough to warrant significant terms of imprisonment even in the absence of prior offenses. Thus the interest of the State of Texas here is not simply that of making criminal the unlawful acquisition of another person's property; it is in addition the interest, expressed in all recidivist statutes, in dealing in a harsher manner with those who by repeated criminal acts have shown that they are simply incapable of conforming to the norms of society as established by its criminal law. By conceding the validity of recidivist statutes generally, Rummel himself concedes that the State of Texas, or any other State, has a valid interest in so dealing with that class of persons.

Nearly 70 years ago, and only 2 years after *Weems,* this Court rejected an Eighth Amendment claim that seems factually indistinguishable from that advanced by Rummel in the present case. In Graham v. West Virginia, 224 U.S. 616 (1912), this Court considered the case of an apparently incorrigible horsethief who was sentenced to life imprisonment under West Virginia's recidivist statute. In 1898 Graham had been convicted of stealing "one bay mare" valued at $50; in 1901 he had been convicted of "feloniously and burglariously" entering a stable in order to steal "one brown horse, named Harry, of the value of $100"; finally, in 1907 he was convicted of stealing "one red roan horse" valued at $75 and various tack and accessories valued at $85. Upon conviction of this last crime, Graham received the life sentence mandated by West Virginia's recidivist statute. This Court did not tarry long on Graham's Eighth Amendment claim, noting only that it would not be maintained "that cruel and unusual punishment [had] been inflicted." Id., at 631.

. . . Rummel attempts to ground his proportionality attack on an alleged "nationwide" trend away from mandatory life sentences and toward "lighter, discretionary sentences." According to Rummel, "[n]o jurisdiction in the United States or the Free World punishes habitual offenders as harshly as Texas." In support of this proposition, Rummel offers detailed charts and tables documenting the history of recidivist statutes in the United States since 1776.

Before evaluating this evidence, we believe it important to examine the exact operation of Art. 63 as interpreted by the Texas courts. In order to qualify for a mandatory life sentence under that statute, Rummel had to satisfy a number of requirements. First, he had to be convicted of a felony and actually sentenced to prison.[2] Second, at some time subsequent to his first conviction, Rummel had to be convicted of another felony and again sentenced to imprisonment.[3] Finally, after having been sent to prison a second time, Rummel had to be convicted of a third felony. Thus, under Art. 63, a three-time felon receives a mandatory life sentence, with possibility of parole,

2. Texas courts have interpreted the recidivist statute as requiring not merely that the defendant be convicted of two prior felonies, but also that he actually serve time in prison for each of those offenses.

3. As the statute has been interpreted, the State must prove that each succeeding conviction was subsequent to both the commission of and the conviction for the prior offense.

only if commission and conviction of each succeeding felony followed conviction for the preceding one, and only if each prior conviction was followed by actual imprisonment. Given this necessary sequence, a recidivist must twice demonstrate that conviction and actual imprisonment do not deter him from returning to crime once he is released. One in Rummel's position has been both graphically informed of the consequences of lawlessness and given an opportunity to reform, all to no avail. Article 63 thus is nothing more than a societal decision that when such a person commits yet another felony, he should be subjected to the admittedly serious penalty of incarceration for life, subject only to the State's judgment as to whether to grant him parole.[4]

In comparing this recidivist program with those presently employed in other States, Rummel creates a complex hierarchy of statutes and places Texas' recidivist scheme alone on the top rung. This isolation is not entirely convincing. Both West Virginia and Washington, for example, impose mandatory life sentences upon the commission of a third felony. Rummel would distinguish those States from Texas because the Supreme Court of Washington and the United States Court of Appeals for the Fourth Circuit, which includes West Virginia, have indicated a willingness to review the proportionality of such sentences under the Eighth Amendment. See State v. Lee, 87 Wash. 2d 932, 937, n.4, 558 P.2d 236, 240, n.4 (1976) (dictum); Hart v. Coiner, 483 F.2d 136 (CA4 1973). But this Court must ultimately decide the meaning of the Eighth Amendment. If we disagree with the decisions of the Supreme Court of Washington and the Court of Appeals for the Fourth Circuit on this point, Washington and West Virginia are for practical puposes indistinguishable from Texas. If we agree with those courts, then of course sentences imposed in Texas, as well as in Washington and West Virginia, are subject to a review for proportionality under the Eighth Amendment. But in either case, the legislative judgment as to punishment in Washington and West Virginia has been the same as that in Texas.

Rummel's charts and tables do appear to indicate that he might have received more lenient treatment in almost any State other than Texas, West Virginia, or Washington. The distinctions, however, are subtle rather than gross. A number of States impose a mandatory life sentence upon conviction of four felonies rather than three. Other States require one or more of the felonies to be "violent" to support a life sentence. Still other States leave the imposition of a life sentence after three felonies within the discretion of a judge or jury. It is one thing for a court to compare those States that impose capital punishment for a specific offense with those States that do not. It is quite another thing for a court to attempt to evaluate the position of any particular recidivist scheme within Rummel's complex matrix.

[The Court then discussed Texas's relatively liberal policy of granting good time credits to reduce sentences and noted that Rummel could become eligible for parole after 12 years.]

4. Thus, it is not true that, as the dissent claims, the Texas scheme subjects a person to life imprisonment "merely because he is a three-time felon." On the contrary, Art. 63 mandates such a sentence only after shorter terms of actual imprisonment have proved ineffective.

. . . If nothing else, the possibility of parole, however slim, serves to distinguish Rummel from a person sentenced under a recidivist statute like Mississippi's, which provides for a sentence of life without parole upon conviction of three felonies including at least one violent felony.

Another variable complicating the calculus is the role of prosecutorial discretion in any recidivist scheme. It is a matter of common knowledge that prosecutors often exercise their discretion in invoking recidivist statutes or in plea bargaining so as to screen out truly "petty" offenders who fall within the literal terms of such statutes. . . .

We offer these additional considerations not as inherent flaws in Rummel's suggested interjurisdictional analysis but as illustrations of the complexities confronting any court that would attempt such a comparison. Even were we to assume that the statute employed against Rummel was the most stringent found in the 50 States, that severity hardly would render Rummel's punishment "grossly disproportionate" to his offenses or to the punishment he would have received in the other States. As Mr. Justice Holmes noted in his dissenting opinion in Lochner v. New York, 198 U.S. 45, 76 (1905), our Constitution "is made for people of fundamentally differing views. . . ." Until quite recently, Arizona punished as a felony the theft of any "neat or horned animal," regardless of its value; California considers the theft of "avocados, olives, citrus or deciduous fruits, nuts and artichokes" particularly reprehensible. In one State theft of $100 will earn the offender a fine or a short term in jail; in another State it could earn him a sentence of 10 years' imprisonment. Absent a constitutionally imposed uniformity inimical to traditional notions of federalism, some State will always bear the distinction of treating particular offenders more severely than any other State.[5]

5. The dissent draws some support for its belief that Rummel's sentence is unconstitutional by comparing it with punishment imposed by Texas for crimes other than those committed by Rummel. Other crimes, of course, implicate other societal interests, making any such comparison inherently speculative. Embezzlement, dealing in "hard" drugs, and forgery, to name only three offenses, could be denominated "property related" offenses, and yet each can be viewed as an assault on a unique set of societal values as defined by the political process. The notions embodied in the dissent that if the crime involved "violence" a more severe penalty is warranted under objective standards simply will not wash, whether it be taken as a matter of morals, history, or law. Caesar's death at the hands of Brutus and his fellow conspirators was undoubtedly violent; the death of Hamlet's father at the hands of his brother, Claudius, by poison, was not. Yet there are few, if any, States which do not punish just as severely murder by poison (or attempted murder by poison) as they do murder or attempted murder by stabbing. The highly placed executive who embezzles huge sums from a state savings and loan association, causing many shareholders of limited means to lose substantial parts of their savings, has committed a crime very different from a man who takes a smaller amount of money from the same savings and loan at the point of a gun. Yet rational people could disagree as to which criminal merits harsher punishment. By the same token, a State cannot be required to treat persons who have committed three "minor" offenses less severely than persons who have committed one or two "more serious" offenses. If nothing else, the three-time offender's conduct supports inferences about his ability to conform with social norms that are quite different from possible inferences about first- or second-time offenders.

In short, the "seriousness" of an offense or a pattern of offenses in modern society is not a line, but a plane. Once the death penalty and other punishments different in kind from fine or imprisonment have been put to one side, there remains little in the way of objective standards for judging whether or not a life sentence imposed under a recidivist statute for several separate felony convictions not involving "violence" violates the cruel-and-unusual-punishment prohibition of the

Perhaps, as asserted in *Weems,* "time works changes" upon the Eighth Amendment, bringing into existence "new conditions and purposes." We all, of course, would like to think that we are "moving down the road toward human decency." Within the confines of this judicial proceeding, however, we have no way of knowing in which direction that road lies. Penologists themselves have been unable to agree whether sentences should be light or heavy, discretionary or determinate. This uncertainty reinforces our conviction that any "nationwide trend" toward lighter, discretionary sentences must find its source and its sustaining force in the legislatures, not in the federal courts.

III

The most casual review of the various criminal justice systems now in force in the 50 States of the Union shows that the line dividing felony theft from petty larceny, a line usually based on the value of the property taken, varies markedly from one State to another. We believe that Texas is entitled to make its own judgment as to where such lines lie, subject only to those strictures of the Eighth Amendment that can be informed by objective factors. Moreover, given Rummel's record, Texas was not required to treat him in the same manner as it might treat him were this his first "petty property offense." Having twice imprisoned him for felonies, Texas was entitled to place upon Rummel the onus of one who is simply unable to bring his conduct within the social norms prescribed by the criminal law of the State.

The purpose of a recidivist statute such as that involved here is not to simplify the task of prosecutors, judges, or juries. Its primary goals are to deter repeat offenders and, at some point in the life of one who repeatedly commits criminal offenses serious enough to be punished as felonies, to segregate that person from the rest of society for an extended period of time. This segregation and its duration are based not merely on that person's most recent offense but also on the propensities he has demonstrated over a period of time during which he has been convicted of and sentenced for other crimes. Like the line dividing felony theft from petty larceny, the point at which a recidivist will be deemed to have demonstrated the necessary propensities and the amount of time that the recidivist will be isolated from society are matters largely within the discretion of the punishing jurisdiction.

We therefore hold that the mandatory life sentence imposed upon this petitioner does not constitute cruel and unusual punishment under the Eighth and Fourteenth Amendments. The judgment of the Court of Appeals is affirmed.

Eighth Amendment. As Mr. Justice Frankfurter noted for the Court in Gore v. United States, 357 U.S. 386, 393 (1958), "[w]hatever views may be entertained regarding severity of punishment, whether one believes in its efficacy or its futility, . . . these are peculiarly questions of legislative policy."

Mr. Justice STEWART, concurring.

I am moved to repeat the substance of what I had to say on another occasion about the recidivist legislation of Texas:

> If the Constitution gave me a roving commission to impose upon the criminal courts of Texas my own notions of enlightened policy, I would not join the Court's opinion. For it is clear to me that the recidivist procedures adopted in recent years by many other States . . . are far superior to those utilized [here]. But the question for decision is not whether we applaud or even whether we personally approve the procedures followed in [this case]. The question is whether those procedures fall below the minimum level the [Constitution] will tolerate. Upon that question I am constrained to join the opinion and judgment of the Court. Spencer v. Texas, 385 U.S. 554, 569 (concurring opinion).

Mr. Justice POWELL, with whom Mr. Justice BRENNAN, Mr. Justice MARSHALL, and Mr. Justice STEVENS join, dissenting.

The question in this case is whether petitioner was subjected to cruel and unusual punishment in contravention of the Eighth Amendment, made applicable to the States by the Fourteenth Amendment, when he received a mandatory life sentence upon his conviction for a third property-related felony. Today, the Court holds that petitioner has not been punished unconstitutionally. I dissent.

. . . I dissent because I believe that (i) the penalty for a noncapital offense may be unconstitutionally disproportionate, (ii) the possibility of parole should not be considered in assessing the nature of the punishment, (iii) a mandatory life sentence is grossly disproportionate as applied to petitioner, and (iv) the conclusion that this petitioner has suffered a violation of his Eighth Amendment rights is compatible with principles of judicial restraint and federalism. . . .

II

A

The Eighth Amendment prohibits "cruel and unusual punishments." . . .

B

The scope of the Cruel and Unusual Punishments Clause extends not only to barbarous methods of punishment, but also to punishments that are grossly disproportionate. Disproportionality analysis measures the relationship between the nature and number of offenses committed and the severity of the punishment inflicted upon the offender. The inquiry focuses on whether a person deserves such punishment, not simply on whether punishment would serve a utilitarian goal. A statute that levied a mandatory life sentence for overtime parking might well deter vehicular lawlessness, but it would offend our felt sense of justice. The Court concedes today that the principle of disproportionality plays a role in the review of sentences imposing the death penalty, but suggests that the principle may be less applicable when a noncapital sentence is challenged. Such a limitation finds no support in the history of Eighth Amendment jurisprudence.

The principle of disproportionality is rooted deeply in English constitutional law. The Magna Carta of 1215 insured that "[a] free man shall not be [fined] for a trivial offence, except in accordance with the degree of the offence; and for a serious offence he shall be [fined] according to its gravity." By 1400, the English common law had embraced the principle, not always followed in practice, that punishment should not be excessive either in severity or length. . . .

In Weems v. United States, 217 U.S. 349 (1910), a public official convicted for falsifying a public record claimed that he suffered cruel and unusual punishment when he was sentenced to serve 15 years' imprisonment in hard labor with chains. The sentence also subjected Weems to loss of civil rights and perpetual surveillance after his release. This Court agreed that the punishment was cruel and unusual. The Court was attentive to the methods of the punishment, but its conclusion did not rest solely upon the nature of punishment. The Court relied explicitly upon the relationship between the crime committed and the punishment imposed:

> Such penalties for such offenses amaze those who have formed their conception of the relation of a state to even its offending citizens from the practice of the American commonwealths, and believe that it is a precept of justice that punishment for crime should be graduated and proportioned to offense. Id., at 366-367.

In both capital and noncapital cases this Court has recognized that the decision in Weems v. United States "proscribes punishment grossly disproportionate to the severity of the crime."

In order to resolve the constitutional issue, the *Weems* Court measured the relationship between the punishment and the offense. The Court noted that Weems had been punished more severely than persons in the same jurisdiction who committed more serious crimes, or persons who committed a similar crime in other American jurisdictions. . . .

In Furman v. Georgia, the Court held that the death penalty may constitute cruel and unusual punishment in some circumstances. The special relevance of *Furman* to this case lies in the general acceptance by Members of the Court of two basic principles. First, the Eighth Amendment prohibits grossly excessive punishment. Second, the scope of the Eighth Amendment is to be measured by "evolving standards of decency." . . .

In Coker v. Georgia, this Court held that rape of an adult woman may not be punished by the death penalty. The plurality opinion of Mr. Justice White stated that a punishment is unconstitutionally excessive "if it (1) makes no measurable contribution to acceptable goals of punishment and hence is nothing more than the purposeless and needless imposition of pain and suffering; or (2) is grossly out of proportion to the severity of the crime." The plurality concluded that the death penalty was a grossly disproportionate punishment for the crime of rape. The plurality recognized that "Eighth Amendment judgments should not be, or appear to be, merely the subjective views of individual Justices; judgment should be informed by objective factors to the maximum possible extent." To this end, the plurality examined the nature of the crime and attitudes of state legislatures and sentencing juries toward use of the death penalty in rape cases. In a separate opinion, I concurred in the plurality's reasoning that death ordinarily is disproportionate punishment for the crime of raping an adult woman. Nothing in the *Coker* analysis suggests that principles of disproportionality are applicable only to capital cases. Indeed, the questions posed in *Coker* and this case are the same: whether a punishment that can be imposed for one offense is grossly disproportionate when imposed for another.

In sum, a few basic principles emerge from the history of the Eighth Amendment. Both barbarous forms of punishment and grossly excessive punishments are cruel and unusual. A sentence may be excessive if it serves no acceptable social purpose, or is grossly disproportionate to the seriousness of the crime. The principle of disproportionality has been acknowledged to apply to both capital and noncapital sentences.

III

Under Texas law, petitioner has been sentenced to a mandatory life sentence. . . .

It is true that imposition in Texas of a mandatory life sentence does not necessarily mean that petitioner will spend the rest of his life behind prison walls. If petitioner attains sufficient good-time credits, he may be eligible for parole within 10 or 12 years after he begins serving his life sentence. But petitioner will have no right to early release; he will merely be eligible for parole. And parole is simply an act of executive grace.

Last Term in Greenholtz v. Nebraska Penal Inmates, 442 U.S. 1 (1979), we held that a criminal conviction extinguishes whatever liberty interest a prisoner has in securing freedom before the end of his lawful sentence. The Court stated unequivocally that a convicted person has "no constitutional or inherent right . . . to be conditionally released before the expiration of a valid sentence." Of course, a State may create legitimate expectations that are entitled to procedural protection under the Due Process Clause of the Fourteenth Amendment, but Texas has not chosen to create a cognizable interest in parole. The Court of Appeals for the Fifth Circuit has held that a Texas prisoner has no constitutionally enforceable interest in being freed before the expiration of his sentence.

A holding that the possibility of parole discounts a prisoner's sentence for the purposes of the Eighth Amendment would be cruelly ironic. The combined effect of our holdings under the Due Process Clause of the Fourteenth Amendment and the Eighth Amendment would allow a State to defend an Eighth Amendment claim by contending that parole is probable even though the prisoner cannot enforce that expectation. Such an approach is inconsistent with the Eighth Amendment. The Court has never before failed to examine a prisoner's Eighth Amendment claim because of the speculation that he might be pardoned before the sentence was carried out.

Recent events in Texas demonstrate that parole remains a matter of executive grace. In June 1979, the Governor of Texas refused to grant parole to 79 percent of the state prisoners whom the parole board recommended for release. . . . As this case comes to us, petitioner has been deprived by operation of state law of his right to freedom from imprisonment for the rest of his life. We should judge the case accordingly.

IV

The Eighth Amendment commands this Court to enforce the constitutional limitation of the Cruel and Unusual Punishments Clause. In discharging this responsibility, we should minimize the risk of constitutionalizing the personal predilictions of federal judges by relying upon certain objective factors. Among these are (i) the nature of the offense, (ii) the sentence imposed for commission of the same crime in other jurisdictions, and (iii) the sentence imposed upon other criminals in the same jurisdiction.

A

Each of the crimes that underlies the petitioner's conviction as a habitual offender involves the use of fraud to obtain small sums of money ranging from $28.36 to $120.75. In total, the three crimes involved slightly less than $230. None of the crimes involved injury to one's person, threat of injury to one's person, violence, the threat of violence, or the use of a weapon. Nor does the commission of any such crimes ordinarily involve a threat of violent action against another person or his property. It is difficult to imagine felonies that pose less danger to the peace and good order of a civilized society than the three crimes committed by the petitioner. Indeed, the state legislature's recodification of its criminal law supports this conclusion. Since the petitioner was convicted as a habitual offender, the State has reclassified his third offense, theft by false pretext, as a misdemeanor.[6]

6. The Court suggests that an inquiry into the nature of the offense at issue in this case inevitably involves identifying subjective distinctions beyond the province of the judiciary. Yet the distinction between forging a check for $28 and committing a violent crime or one that threatens violence is surely no more difficult for the judiciary to perceive than the distinction between the gravity of murder and rape. I do not suggest that all criminal acts may be separated into precisely identifiable compartments. A professional seller of addictive drugs may inflict greater bodily harm upon members of society than the person who commits a single assault. But the difficulties of line-drawing that might be presented in other cases need not obscure our vision here.

B

Apparently, only 12 States have ever enacted habitual offender statutes imposing a mandatory life sentence for the commission of two or three nonviolent felonies and only 3, Texas, Washington, and West Virginia, have retained such a statute. Thus, three-fourths of the States that experimented with the Texas scheme appear to have decided that the imposition of a mandatory life sentence upon some persons who have committed three felonies represents excess punishment. Kentucky, for example, replaced the mandatory life sentence with a more flexible scheme "because of a judgment that under some circumstances life imprisonment for an habitual criminal is not justified. An example would be an offender who has committed three Class D felonies, none involving injury to person." The State of Kansas abolished its statute mandating a life sentence for the commission of three felonies after a state legislative commission concluded that "[t]he legislative policy as expressed in the habitual criminal law bears no particular resemblance to the enforcement policy of prosecutors and judges."

. . . In Washington, which retains the Texas rule, the State Supreme Court has suggested that application of its statute to persons like the petitioner might constitute cruel and unusual punishment. See State v. Lee, 87 Wash. 2d 932, 937, n.4, 558 P.2d 236, 240, n.4 (1976).

More than three-quarters of American jurisdictions have never adopted a habitual offender statute that would commit the petitioner to mandatory life imprisonment. The jurisdictions that currently employ habitual offender statutes either (i) require the commission of more than three offenses,[7] (ii) require the commission of at least one violent crime, (iii) limit a mandatory penalty to less than life, or (iv) grant discretion to the sentencing authority.[8] In none of the jurisdictions could the petitioner have received a mandatory life sentence merely upon the showing that he committed three nonviolent property-related offenses.[9]

The federal habitual offender statute also differs materially from the Texas statute. Title 18 U.S.C. §3575 provides increased sentences for "dangerous special offenders" who have been convicted of a felony. A defendant is a "dangerous special offender" if he has committed two or more previous felo-

7. Four States impose a mandatory life sentence upon the commission of a fourth felony. Thus, even if the line between these States and Texas, West Virginia, and Washington, is "subtle rather than gross," ante, at 279, the most that one can say is that 7 of the 50 States punish the commission of four or fewer felonies with a mandatory life sentence.

8. See, e.g., D.C. Code §22-104a (1973) (Persons who commit three felonies may be sentenced to life); Idaho Code §19-2514 (1979). . . .

9. A State's choice of a sentence will, of course, never be unconstitutional simply because the penalty is harsher than the sentence imposed by other States for the same crime. Such a rule would be inconsistent with principles of federalism. The Eighth Amendment prohibits grossly disproportionate punishment, but it does not require local sentencing decisions to be controlled by majority vote of the States. Nevertheless, a comparison of the Texas standard with the sentencing statutes of other States is one method of "assess[ing] contemporary values concerning the infliction of a challenged sanction." The relevant objective factors should be considered together and, although the weight assigned to each may vary, no single factor will ever be controlling.

nies, one of them within the last five years, if the current felony arose from a pattern of conduct "which constituted a substantial source of his income, and in which he manifested special skill or expertise," or if the felony involved a criminal conspiracy in which the defendant played a supervisory role. Federal courts may sentence such persons "to imprisonment for an appropriate term not to exceed twenty-five years and not disproportionate in severity to the maximum term otherwise authorized by law for such felony." Thus, Congress and an overwhelming number of state legislatures have not adopted the Texas scheme. These legislative decisions lend credence to the view that a mandatory life sentence for the commission of three nonviolent felonies is unconstitutionally disproportionate.

C

Finally, it is necessary to examine the punishment that Texas provides for other criminals. First and second offenders who commit more serious crimes than the petitioner may receive markedly less severe sentences. The only first-time offender subject to a mandatory life sentence is a person convicted of capital murder. A person who commits a first-degree felony, including murder, aggravated kidnaping, or aggravated rape, may be imprisoned from 5 to 99 years. Persons who commit a second-degree felony, including voluntary manslaughter, rape, or robbery, may be punished with a sentence of between 2 and 20 years. A person who commits a second felony is punished as if he had committed a felony of the next higher degree. Thus, a person who rapes twice may receive a 5-year sentence. He also may, but need not, receive a sentence functionally equivalent to life imprisonment.

The State argues that these comparisons are not illuminating because a three-time recidivist may be sentenced more harshly than a first-time offender. Of course, the State may mandate extra punishment for a recidivist. In Texas a person convicted twice of the unauthorized use of a vehicle receives a greater sentence than a person once convicted for that crime, but he does not receive a sentence as great as a person who rapes twice. Such a statutory scheme demonstrates that the state legislature has attempted to choose a punishment in proportion to the nature and number of offenses committed.

Texas recognizes when it sentences two-time offenders that the amount of punishment should vary with the severity of the offenses committed. But all three-time felons receive the same sentence. In my view, imposition of the same punishment upon persons who have committed completely different types of crimes raises serious doubts about the proportionality of the sentence applied to the least harmful offender. Of course, the Constitution does not bar mandatory sentences. I merely note that the operation of the Texas habitual offender system raises a further question about the extent to which a mandatory life sentence, no doubt a suitable sentence for a person who has committed three violent crimes, also is a proportionate punishment for a person who has committed the three crimes involved in this case.

D

Examination of the objective factors traditionally employed by the Court to assess the proportionality of a sentence demonstrates that petitioner suffers a cruel and unusual punishment. Petitioner has been sentenced to the penultimate criminal penalty because he committed three offenses defrauding others of about $230. The nature of the crimes does not suggest that petitioner ever engaged in conduct that threatened another's person, involved a trespass, or endangered in any way the peace of society. A comparison of the sentence petitioner received with the sentences provided by habitual offender statutes of other American jurisdictions demonstrates that only two other States authorize the same punishment. A comparison of petitioner to other criminals sentenced in Texas shows that he has been punished for three property-related offenses with a harsher sentence than that given first-time offenders or two-time offenders convicted of far more serious offenses. The Texas system assumes that all three-time offenders deserve the same punishment whether they commit three murders or cash three fraudulent checks.

The petitioner has committed criminal acts for which he may be punished. He has been given a sentence that is not inherently barbarous. But the relationship between the criminal acts and the sentence is grossly disproportionate. For having defrauded others of about $230, the State of Texas has deprived petitioner of his freedom for the rest of his life. The State has not attempted to justify the sentence as necessary either to deter other persons or to isolate a potentially violent individual. Nor has petitioner's status as a habitual offender been shown to justify a mandatory life sentence. My view, informed by examination of the "objective indicia that reflect the public attitude toward a given sanction," is that this punishment violates the principle of proportionality contained within the Cruel and Unusual Punishments Clause.

V

The Court today agrees with the State's arguments that a decision in petitioner's favor would violate principles of federalism and, because of difficulty in formulating standards to guide the decision of the federal courts, would lead to excessive interference with state sentencing decisions. Neither contention is convincing.

Each State has sovereign responsibilities to promulgate and enforce its criminal law. In our federal system we should never forget that the Constitution "recognizes and preserves the autonomy and independence of the States—independence in their legislative and independence in their judicial departments." But even as the Constitution recognizes a sphere of state activity free from federal interference, it explicitly compels the States to follow certain constitutional commands. When we apply the Cruel and Unusual Punishments Clause against the States, we merely enforce an obligation that the Constitution has created. As Mr. Justice Rehnquist has stated, "[c]ourts are exercising no more than the judicial function conferred upon them by Art. III of the Constitution when they assess, in a case before them, whether or not a particular legislative enactment is within the authority granted by the Constitution to the enacting body, and whether it runs afoul of some limitation placed by the Constitution on the authority of that body."

Because the State believes that the federal courts can formulate no practicable standard to identify grossly disproportionate sentences, it fears that the courts would intervene into state criminal justice systems at will. Such a "floodgates" argument can be easy to make and difficult to rebut. But in this case we can identify and apply objective criteria that reflect constitutional standards of punishment and minimize the risk of judicial subjectivity.

I do not suggest that each of the decisions in which the Court of Appeals for the Fourth Circuit applied Hart v. Coiner is necessarily correct. But I do believe that the body of Eighth Amendment law that has developed in that Circuit constitutes impressive empirical evidence that the federal courts are capable of applying the Eighth Amendment to disproportionate noncapital sentences with a high degree of sensitivity to principles of federalism and state autonomy.

VI

I recognize that the difference between the petitioner's grossly disproportionate sentence and other prisoners' constitutionally valid sentences is not separated by the clear distinction that separates capital from noncapital punishment. "But the fact that a line has to be drawn somewhere does not justify its being drawn anywhere." The Court has, in my view, chosen the easiest line rather than the best.[10]

It is also true that this Court has not heretofore invalidated a mandatory life sentence under the Eighth Amendment. Yet our precedents establish that the duty to review the disproportionality of sentences extends to noncapital cases. The reach of the Eighth Amendment cannot be restricted only to those claims previously adjudicated under the Cruel and Unusual Punishments Clause. "Time works changes, brings into existence new conditions and purposes. Therefore a principle to be vital must be capable of wider application than the mischief which gave it birth. This is particularly true of constitutions. They are not ephemeral enactments, designed to meet passing occasions. They are, to use the words of Chief Justice Marshall, 'designed to approach immortality as nearly as human institutions can approach it.' " Weems v. United States, 217 U.S., at 373.

10. The Court concedes, as it must, that a mandatory life sentence may be constitutionally disproportionate to the severity of an offense. Yet its opinion suggests no basis in principle for distinguishing between permissible and grossly disproportionate life imprisonment.

We are construing a living Constitution. The sentence imposed upon the petitioner would be viewed as grossly unjust by virtually every layman and lawyer. In my view, objective criteria clearly establish that a mandatory life sentence for defrauding persons of about $230 crosses any rationally drawn line separating punishment that lawfully may be imposed from that which is proscribed by the Eighth Amendment. I would reverse the decision of the Court of Appeals.

Notes and Questions

1. Although Rummel lost his appeal to the Supreme Court, he was in fact released within eight months of the Court's decision. Rummel then pled guilty to theft by false pretenses and was sentenced to time served under the terms of a plea bargaining agreement. Two-Bit Lifer Finally Freed—After Pleading Guilty, Chicago Tribune, Nov. 15, 1980, at 2, col. 3.

2. In footnote 1, the Court acknowledges that in extreme examples, such as life imprisonment for overtime parking, the proportionality principle would "come into play." How would the Court define such extreme examples? Given its implicit rejection of the *Hart* factors, what standards would it apply?

3. Justice Rehnquist emphasizes the distinction between the death penalty and imprisonment, while minimizing the differences based on sentence length. Is this realistic? Is it possible to draw a meaningful distinction between life imprisonment without the possibility of parole and a life sentence with a parole possibility? What about between imprisonment and probation? With the exception of the extreme example of overtime parking, would Rehnquist ever declare a sentence unconstitutional based on its length?

4. *Rummel* was applied in Hutto v. Davis, 454 U.S. 370 (1982). In 1973 the defendant was convicted of possession of nine ounces of marihuana with intent to distribute and distribution of marijuana. At the time of his conviction, Virginia law authorized fines up to $25,000 and prison terms from 5 to 40 years for each offense. The jury imposed a fine of $10,000 and a 20-year prison term on each count, with the sentences to run consecutively. Following its decision in *Rummel,* the Supreme Court vacated the Fourth Circuit's decision declaring the punishment unconstitutional and remanded. Once again the court of appeals affirmed the district court's original find of unconstitutionality, and Virginia appealed. In a per curiam decision the Supreme Court reversed, chastising the court of appeals for "sanction[ing] an intrusion into the basic line drawing process that is 'properly within the legislatures, not courts.' " In reluctantly concurring, Justice Powell pointed out two important features that could serve to distinguish Davis's situation from *Rummel.* First, the commonwealth attorney who prosecuted Davis wrote a letter in 1976 urging that Davis's sentence be changed to a suspended one: "[T]he sentences now being imposed throughout the majority of the Commonwealth and the nation

for *comparable* acts of drug distribution are extremely light and in most cases insignificant. In view of such, I think a *gross injustice* would be done should I not recommend his immediate release with the remainder of his term suspended." Id. at 378, n.7. Furthermore, in 1979, the Virginia State Legislature reduced the maximum penalty for those offenses to 10 years on each count.

5. At least two states have rejected the *Rummel* approach in interpreting state constitutional provisions barring cruel and unusual punishment. In Wanstreet v. Bordenkircher, 276 S.E.2d 205 (W. Va. 1981) the West Virginia Supreme Court of Appeals considered the same recidivist statute examined in *Hart.* Here, the defendant's convictions consisted of forging a check for $18.62 in 1951, burning a hay barn worth $490 in 1955, violating parole by driving without a license in 1963, and forging a check for $43.00 in 1967. West Virginia's constitution contains an explicit provision guaranteeing that "Penalties shall be proportional to the character and degree of the offence." In reversing Wanstreet's life sentence the court ignored *Rummel* and essentially relied on the "objective standards" enunciated in Hart v. Coiner:

> In determining whether a given sentence violates the proportionality principle, consideration is given to the nature of the offense, the legislative purpose behind the punishment, a comparison of the punishment with what would be inflicted in other jurisdictions, and a comparison with other offenses within the same jurisdiction. We give initial emphasis to the nature of the final offense which triggers the recidivist life sentence, although consideration is also given to the other underlying convictions. The primary analysis of these offenses is to determine if they involve actual or threatened violence to the person since crimes of this nature have traditionally carried the more serious penalties and therefore justify application of the recidivist statute. A further analysis is then made of our recidivist statute in relation to other states' recidivist statutes to determine their treatment of similar offense.

Similarly in State v. Fain, 94 Wash. 2d 387, 617 P.2d 720 (1980) the Supreme Court of Washington reversed the defendant's life sentence based on the Washington recidivist statute. Fain's violations included a 1960 grand larceny conviction stemming from a $30 check written on insufficient funds, a 1965 California forgery conviction based on another $30 check and a 1977 second-degree theft conviction resulting from a series of 24 bad checks worth a total value of $408. Although the court agreed that *Rummel* barred a federal constitutional claim based on the Eighth Amendment, it felt free to "interpret the Washington Constitution as more protective than its federal counterpart." Relying considerably on Hart v. Coiner, the court examined three of its suggested four factors: the nature of the offense; punishment in other jurisdictions for the same offense; and punishment in Washington for other offenses. It concluded that Fain's life sentence was "entirely disproportionate to the seriousness of his crimes" and violated the Washington State Constitution.

SOLEM v. HELM
United States Supreme Court
463 U.S. 277 (1983)

Justice POWELL delivered the opinion of the Court.

The issue presented is whether the Eighth Amendment proscribes a life sentence without possibility of parole for a seventh nonviolent felony.

I

By 1975 the State of South Dakota had convicted respondent Jerry Helm of six nonviolent felonies. In 1964, 1966, and 1969 Helm was convicted of third-degree burglary. In 1972 he was convicted of obtaining money under false pretenses. In 1973 he was convicted of grand larceny. And in 1975 he was convicted of third-offense driving while intoxicated. The record contains no details about the circumstances of any of these offenses, except that they were all nonviolent, none was a crime against a person, and alcohol was a contributing factor in each case.

In 1979 Helm was charged with uttering a "no account" check for $100. The only details we have of the crime are those given by Helm to the state trial court:

> "I was working in Sioux Falls, and got my check that day, was drinking and I ended up here in Rapid City with more money than I had when I started. I knew I'd done something I didn't know exactly what. If I would have known this, I would have picked the check up. I was drinking and didn't remember, stopped several places." State v. Helm, 287 N.W.2d 497, 501 (S.D. 1980) (Henderson, J., dissenting) (quoting Helm). After offering this explanation, Helm pleaded guilty.

Ordinarily the maximum punishment for uttering a "no account" check would have been five years imprisonment in the state penitentiary and a $5,000 fine. As a result of his criminal record, however, Helm was subject to South Dakota's recidivist statute:

> When a defendant has been convicted of at least three prior convictions [sic] in addition to the principal felony, the sentence for the principal felony shall be enhanced to the sentence for a Class 1 felony. S.D. Codified Laws §22-7-8 (1979) (amended 1981).

The maximum penalty for a "Class 1 felony" was life imprisonment in the state penitentiary and a $25,000 fine. Moreover, South Dakota law explicitly provides that parole is unavailable: "A person sentenced to life imprisonment is not eligible for parole by the board of pardons and paroles." S.D. Codified

Laws §24-15-4 (1979). The Governor is authorized to pardon prisoners, or to commute their sentences, but no other relief from sentence is available even to a rehabilitated prisoner.

Immediately after accepting Helm's guilty plea, the South Dakota Circuit Court sentenced Helm to life imprisonment under §22-7-8. The court explained:

> I think you certainly earned this sentence and certainly proven that you're an habitual criminal and the record would indicate that you're beyond rehabilitation and that the only prudent thing to do is to lock you up for the rest of your natural life, so you won't have further victims of your crimes, just be coming back before Courts. You'll have plenty of time to think this one over. State v. Helm, 287 N.W.2d, at 500 (Henderson, J., dissenting) (quoting S.D. Circuit Court, Seventh Judicial Circuit, Pennington County (Parker, J.)).

[The South Dakota Supreme Court rejected Helm's Eighth Amendment argument. He sought habeas relief in the district court, but his writ was denied by the district judge relying on Rummel v. Estelle. The Court of Appeals for the Eighth Circuit reversed distinguishing *Rummel* on the grounds that it involved the possibility of parole while Helm's sentence did not.]

. . . We now affirm.

II

The Eighth Amendment declares: "Excessive bail shall not be required, nor excessive fines imposed, nor cruel and unusual punishments inflicted." The final clause prohibits not only barbaric punishments, but also sentences that are disproportionate to the crime committed.

[Justice Powell then detailed the history of the principle of proportionality from the Magna Carta in 1215 to the present day.]

When the Framers of the Eighth Amendment adopted the language of the English Bill of Rights, they also adopted the English principle of proportionality. . . .

[W]e hold as a matter of principle that a criminal sentence must be proportionate to the crime for which the defendant has been convicted. Reviewing courts, of course, should grant substantial deference to the broad authority that legislatures necessarily possess in determining the types and limits of punishments for crimes, as well as to the discretion that trial courts possess in sentencing convicted criminals.[11] But no penalty is per se constitutional. As

11. Contrary to the dissent's suggestions, we do not adopt or imply approval of a general rule of appellate review of sentences. Absent specific authority, it is not the role of an appellate court to substitute its judgment for that of the sentencing court as to the appropriateness of a particular sentence; rather, in applying the Eighth Amendment the appellate court decides only whether the sentence under review is within constitutional limits. In view of the substantial deference that must be accorded legislatures and sentencing courts, a reviewing court rarely will be required to engage in extended analysis to determine that a sentence is not constitutionally disproportionate.

the Court noted in Robinson v. California, 370 U.S. at 667, a single day in prison may be unconstitutional in some circumstances.

III

A

When sentences are reviewed under the Eighth Amendment, courts should be guided by objective factors that our cases have recognized.[12]

[A] court's proportionality analysis under the Eighth Amendment should be guided by objective criteria, including (i) the gravity of the offense and the harshness of the penalty; (ii) the sentences imposed on other criminals in the same jurisdiction; and (iii) the sentences imposed for commission of the same crime in other jurisdictions.

B

Application of these factors assumes that courts are competent to judge the gravity of an offense, at least on a relative scale. In a broad sense this assumption is justified, and courts traditionally have made these judgments—just as legislatures must make them in the first instance. Comparisons can be made in light of the harm caused or threatened to the victim or society, and the culpability of the offender. . . .

There are other accepted principles that courts may apply in measuring the harm caused or threatened to the victim or society. The absolute magnitude of the crime may be relevant. Stealing a million dollars is viewed as more serious than stealing a hundred dollars—a point recognized in statutes distinguishing petty theft from grand theft. Few would dispute that a lesser included offense should not be punished more severely than the greater offense. Thus a court is justified in viewing assault with intent to murder as more serious than simple assault. . . .

Turning to the culpability of the offender, there are again clear distinctions that courts may recognize and apply. . . . Most would agree that negligent conduct is less serious than intentional conduct. South Dakota, for example, ranks criminal acts in ascending order of seriousness as follows: negligent acts, reckless acts, knowing acts, intentional acts, and malicious acts. A court, of course, is entitled to look at a defendant's motive in committing a

12. The dissent concedes—as it must—that some sentences of imprisonment are so disproportionate that they are unconstitutional under the Cruel and Unusual Punishments Clause. It offers no guidance, however, as to how courts are to judge these admittedly rare cases. We reiterate the objective factors that our cases have recognized. As the Court has indicated, no one factor will be dispositive in a given case. The inherent nature of our federal system and the need for individualized sentencing decisions result in a wide range of constitutional sentences. Thus no single criterion can identify when a sentence is so grossly disproportionate that it violates the Eighth Amendment. But a combination of objective factors can make such analysis possible.

crime. Thus a murder may be viewed as more serious when committed pursuant to a contract.

This list is by no means exhaustive. It simply illustrates that there are generally accepted criteria for comparing the severity of different crimes on a broad scale, despite the difficulties courts face in attempting to draw distinctions between similar crimes.

C

Application of the factors that we identify also assumes that courts are able to compare different sentences. This assumption, too, is justified. The easiest comparison, of course, is between capital punishment and noncapital punishments, for the death penalty is different from other punishments in kind rather than degree.[13] For sentences of imprisonment, the problem is not so much one of ordering, but one of line-drawing. It is clear that a 25-year sentence generally is more severe than a 15-year sentence,[14] but in most cases it would be difficult to decide that the former violates the Eighth Amendment while the latter does not. Decisions of this kind, although troubling, are not unique to this area. The courts are constantly called upon to draw similar lines in a variety of contexts.

IV

It remains to apply the analytical framework established by our prior decisions to the case before us. We first consider the relevant criteria, viewing Helm's sentence as life imprisonment without possibility of parole. We then consider the State's argument that the possibility of commutation is sufficient to save an otherwise unconstitutional sentence.

A

Helm's crime was "one of the most passive felonies a person could commit." State v. Helm, 287 N.W.2d, at 501 (Henderson, J., dissenting). It involved neither violence nor threat of violence to any person. The $100 face value of Helm's "no account" check was not trivial, but neither was it a large amount. One hundred dollars was less than half the amount South Dakota required for a felonious theft. It is easy to see why such a crime is viewed by society as among the less serious offenses.

Helm, of course, was not charged simply with uttering a "no account"

13. There is also a clear line between sentences of imprisonment and sentences involving no deprivation of liberty.

14. The possibility of parole may complicate the comparison, depending upon the time and conditions of its availability.

check, but also with being an habitual offender.[15] And a State is justified in punishing a recidivist more severely than it punishes a first offender. Helm's status, however, cannot be considered in the abstract. His prior offenses, although classified as felonies, were all relatively minor.[16] All were nonviolent and none was a crime against a person. Indeed, there was no minimum amount in either the burglary or the false pretenses statutes, and the minimum amount covered by the grand larceny statute was fairly small.

Helm's present sentence is life imprisonment without possibility of parole. Barring executive clemency, Helm will spend the rest of his life in the state penitentiary. This sentence is far more severe than the life sentence we considered in Rummel v. Estelle. Rummel was likely to have been eligible for parole within 12 years of his initial confinement, a fact on which the Court relied heavily. See 445 U.S., at 280-281, 100 S. Ct., at 1142-1143. Helm's sentence is the most severe punishment that the State could have imposed on any criminal for any crime. Only capital punishment, a penalty not authorized in South Dakota when Helm was sentenced, exceeds it.

We next consider the sentences that could be imposed on other criminals in the same jurisdiction. When Helm was sentenced, a South Dakota court was required to impose a life sentence for murder, and was authorized to impose a life sentence for treason, first degree manslaughter, first degree arson, and kidnapping. No other crime was punishable so severely on the first offense.

Helm's habitual offender status complicates our analysis, but relevant comparisons are still possible. . . .

In sum, there were a handful of crimes that were necessarily punished by life imprisonment: murder, and, on a second or third offense, treason, first degree manslaughter, first degree arson, and kidnapping. There was a larger group for which life imprisonment was authorized in the discretion of the sentencing judge, including: treason, first degree manslaughter, first degree arson, and kidnapping; attempted murder, placing an explosive device on an aircraft, and first degree rape on a second or third offense; and any felony after three prior offenses. Finally, there was a large group of very serious offenses for which life imprisonment was not authorized, including a third offense of heroin dealing or aggravated assault.

Criminals committing any of these offenses ordinarily would be thought more deserving of punishment than one uttering a "no account" check—even when the bad-check writer had already committed six minor felonies. Moreover, there is no indication in the record that any habitual offender other than

15. We must focus on the principal felony—the felony that triggers the life sentence—since Helm already has paid the penalty for each of his prior offenses. But we recognize, of course, that Helm's prior convictions are relevant to the sentencing decision.

16. Helm, who was 36 years old when he was sentenced, is not a professional criminal. The record indicates an addiction to alcohol, and a consequent difficulty in holding a job. His record involves no instance of violence of any kind. Incarcerating him for life without possibility of parole is unlikely to advance the goals of our criminal justice system in any substantial way. Neither Helm nor the State will have an incentive to pursue clearly needed treatment for his alcohol problem, or any other program of rehabilitation.

Helm has ever been given the maximum sentence on the basis of comparable crimes. It is more likely that the possibility of life imprisonment under §22-7-8 generally is reserved for criminals such as fourth-time heroin dealers, while habitual bad-check writers receive more lenient treatment. In any event, Helm has been treated in the same manner as, or more severely than, criminals who have committed far more serious crimes.

Finally, we compare the sentences imposed for commission of the same crime in other jurisdictions. The Court of Appeals found that "Helm could have received a life sentence without parole for his offense in only one other state, Nevada," and we have no reason to doubt this finding. At the very least, therefore, it is clear that Helm could not have received such a severe sentence in 48 of the 50 States. But even under Nevada law, a life sentence without possibility of parole is merely authorized in these circumstances. We are not advised that any defendant such as Helm, whose prior offenses were so minor, actually has received the maximum penalty in Nevada. It appears that Helm was treated more severely than he would have been in any other State. . . .

[The Court also rejected the state's claim that the possibility of executive clemency is sufficient to sustain an otherwise unconstitutional punishment.]

V

The Constitution requires us to examine Helm's sentence to determine if it is proportionate to his crime. Applying objective criteria, we find that Helm has received the penultimate sentence for relatively minor criminal conduct. He has been treated more harshly than other criminals in the State who have committed more serious crimes. He has been treated more harshly than he would have been in any other jurisdiction, with the possible exception of a single State. We conclude that his sentence is significantly disproportionate to his crime, and is therefore prohibited by the Eighth Amendment.[17] The judgment of the Court of Appeals is accordingly

Affirmed.

Notes and Questions

1. Is Solem v. Helm closer to Hart v. Coiner or Rummel v. Estelle in its approach?

17. Contrary to the suggestion in the dissent, our conclusion today is not inconsistent with Rummel v. Estelle. The *Rummel* Court recognized—as does the dissent—that some sentences of imprisonment are so disproportionate that they violate the Eighth Amendment. . . . But since the *Rummel* Court—like the dissent today—offered no standards for determining when an Eighth Amendment violation has occurred, it is controlling only in a similar factual situation. Here the facts are clearly distinguishable. Whereas Rummel was eligible for a reasonably early parole, Helm, at age 36, was sentenced to life with no possibility of parole.

2. What do you make of Justice Powell's statement that although sentences must be proportionate to the crime, reviewing courts should grant "substantial deference" to legislative authority? How does this formula compare with Justice Rehnquist's in *Rummel*?

3. Is it possible to reconcile the refusal to overrule *Rummel*, which itself disapproved Hart v. Coiner, and the adoption of objective criteria almost identical to those used in Hart? Has *Solem* clarified the proportionality issue? Is it applicable generally, or does *Rummel* still apply to those cases that do not involve a life sentence without the possibility of parole?

4. In Seritt v. Alabama, 731 F.2d 728 (11th Cir. 1984), the defendant was sentenced to life without parole under the Alabama Habitual Offender Statute. His earlier convictions involved four separate violations of the Alabama Uniform Controlled Substance Act in 1975 and drug selling in 1973. His latest offense was first-degree armed robbery in 1980, in which he threatened to shoot the victim and placed a knife against the victim's side in the course of stealing $200. The court of appeals distinguished *Solem* on its facts, paying particular attention to the crime of violence committed by Seritt. In applying the "objective criteria" set forth in *Solem*, the Court pointed out that under the Alabama statute "no criminal will receive the sentence of life imprisonment without parole, as a habitual offender, unless he has been convicted of three prior felonies and then commits a life-endangering offense." In making comparisons to other criminals in the same jurisdiction and the same crime in other jurisdictions, the court concluded that the defendant was treated in the same way as defendants who committed equally dangerous felonies, whereas nonviolent offenders were treated more leniently. Further, his punishment was no more severe than it would have been in other southern states. Consequently, the court affirmed his sentence of life without parole.

5. In Moreno v. Estelle, 717 F.2d (5th Cir. 1983), the defendant was sentenced to life imprisonment with the possibility of parole after 20 years. His three felonies were unlawful possession of narcotics paraphernalia, theft of personal property, and aggravated assault. The court emphasized that *Solem* did not purport to overrule *Rummel* in factually similar situations, and found that the facts in Moreno's case were not distinguishable:

> Therefore, because we do not find Moreno's case to be "clearly distinguishable" from the facts of *Rummel*, we deny the petitioner's request for a remand to the district court for a *Solem* analysis. Thus, bound by *Rummel*, we reject the petitioner's Eighth Amendment claim.

6. State constitutional provisions barring cruel and unusual punishments have also been applied in contexts other than recidivist statutes. Consider the majority opinion in People v. Dillon, 194 Cal. Rptr. 390, 668 P.2d 697 (1983).

> Defendant appeals from a judgment convicting him of first degree felony murder and attempted robbery. . . .

We . . . hold . . . that the penalty for first degree felony murder, like all statutory penalties, is subject to the constitutional prohibition against cruel or unusual punishments (Cal. Const. art. I, §17), and in particular to the rule that a punishment is impermissible if it is grossly disproportionate to the offense as defined or as committed, and/or to the individual culpability of the offender. . . .

At the time of these events defendant was a 17-year-old high school student living in the Santa Cruz Mountains not far from a small, secluded farm on which Dennis Johnson and his brother illegally grew marijuana. Told by a friend about the farm, defendant set out with two schoolmates to investigate it and to take some of the marijuana if possible. . . . In an effort to avoid being seen by Johnson, who was guarding the property, the boys tried several different approaches, then hid in a hollow tree stump. Johnson appeared with a shotgun, cocked the weapon, and ordered them out. . . . He warned them that his brother would have shot them if he had met them, adding that the next time the youths came on his property he might shoot them himself. . . .

After the school term began, defendant and a friend discussed the matter further and decided to attempt a "rip-off" of the marijuana with the aid of reinforcements. Various plans were considered for dealing with Johnson; defendant assertedly suggested that they "just hold him up. Hit him over the head or something. Tie him to a tree." They recruited six other classmates, and on the morning of October 17, 1978, the boys all gathered for the venture. Defendant had prepared a rough map of the farm and the surrounding area. Several of the boys brought shotguns, and defendant carried a .22 caliber semi-automatic rifle. They also equipped themselves with a baseball bat, sticks, a knife, wirecutters, tools for harvesting the marijuana, paper bags to be used as masks or for carrying plants, and rope for bundling plants or for restraining the guards if necessary. . . .

The boys climbed a hill towards the farm. There they saw one of the Johnson brothers tending the plants; discretion became much the better part of valor, and they made little or no progress for almost two hours. Although the testimony of the various participants was not wholly consistent, if appears that two of the boys abandoned the effort altogether, two others were chased away by dogs but began climbing the hill by another route, and defendant and his companion, with the remaining pair, watched cautiously just outside the field of marijuana.

One of the boys returning to the farm then accidentally discharged his shotgun, and the two ran back down the hill. While the boys near the field reconnoitered and discussed their next move, their hapless friend once more fired his weapon by mistake. In the meantime Dennis Johnson had circled behind defendant and the others, and was approaching up the trail. They first heard him coming through the bushes, then saw that he was carrying a shotgun. When Johnson drew near, defendant began rapidly firing his rifle at him. After Johnson fell, defendant fled with his companions without taking any marijuana. Johnson suffered nine bullet wounds and died a few days later.

[The Court held that Section 189 of the California Penal Code enacts the first degree felony-murder rule.]

. . . [F]irst degree felony murder encompasses a far wider range of individual culpability than deliberate and premeditated murder. It includes not only the latter, but also a variety of unintended homicides resulting from reckless behavior, or ordinary negligence, or pure accident; it embraces both calculated conduct and acts committed in panic or rage, or under the dominion of mental illness, drugs, or alcohol; and it condemns alike consequences that are highly probable, conceivably possible, or wholly unforeseeable.

Despite this broad factual spectrum, the Legislature has provided only one punishment scheme for all homicides occurring during the commission of or attempt to commit an offense listed in section 189: regardless of the defendant's individual culpability with respect to that homicide, he must be adjudged a first degree murderer and sentenced to death or life imprisonment with or without possibility of parole—the identical punishment inflicted for deliberate and premeditated murder with malice aforethought. . . .

. . . We adopted in *Lynch* [People v. Lynch, 8 Cal. 3d 410, 105 Cal. Rptr. 217, 503 P.2d 921 (1972)] the rule that a statutory punishment may violate the [State] constitutional prohibition [against cruel or unusual punishment] not only if it is inflicted by a cruel or unusual method, but also if it is grossly disproportionate to the offense for which it is imposed.[18]. . .

Undertaking to define that limit for future cases, we explained that the state must exercise its power to prescribe penalties within the limits of civilized standards and must treat its members with respect for their intrinsic worth as human beings. . . .

Under this standard we held in *Lynch* that an indeterminate life-maximum sentence for second-offense indecent exposure was unconstitutionally excessive. In succeeding years we have invoked the proportionality rule to strike down legislation barring recidivist narcotic offenders from being considered for parole for 10 years (In re Foss (1974) [112 Cal. Rptr. 649, 519 P.2d 1073]; In re Grant (1976) [132 Cal. Rptr. 430, 553 P.2d 590]), to order the release of a defendant who served 22 years for a nonviolent act of child molestation, and to invalidate the statutory requirement that persons convicted of misdemeanor public lewdness must register with the police as sex offenders. . . .

In each such decision the court used certain "techniques" identified in *Lynch* to aid in determining proportionality. Especially relevant here is the first of these techniques, i.e., an examination of "the nature of the offense and/or the offender, with particular regard to the degree of danger both present to society."

With respect to "the nature of the offense," . . . the courts are to consider not only the offense in the abstract—i.e., as defined by the Legislature—but also "the facts of the crime in question." . . .

Secondly, it is obvious that the courts must also view "the nature of the offender." . . . This branch of the inquiry therefore focuses on the particular person before the court, and asks whether the punishment is grossly disproportionate to the defendant's individual culpability as shown by such factors as his age, prior criminality, personal characteristics, and state of mind. . . .

18. The United States Supreme Court has recently reaffirmed a similar rule applicable to the corresponding provision of the federal Constitution: "The Cruel and Unusual Punishment Clause of the Eighth Amendment is directed, in part, 'against all punishments which by their excessive length or severity are greatly disproportioned to the offenses charged.' [Citations.]" (Enmund v. Florida (1982) 458 U.S. 782, 788 [73 L. Ed. 2d 1140, 1146, 102 S. Ct. 3368, 3372]; accord, Solem v. Helm (1983) U.S.—, —[77 L. Ed. 2d 637, 645-647, 103 S. Ct. 3001].)

We proceed [using this] analysis. . . . As noted at the outset, when he committed the offenses herein defendant was a 17-year-old high school student.[19] At trial he took the stand in his own behalf and told the jury his side of the story. From that testimony a plausible picture emerged of the evolution of defendant's state of mind during these events—from youthful bravado, to uneasiness, to fear for his life, to panic. Although such an explanation is often discounted as self-serving, in this case the record repeatedly demonstrates that the judge and jury in fact gave defendant's testimony large credence and substantial weight.

Called as an expert witness, a clinical psychologist testified that [in his opinion] when confronted by the figure of Dennis Johnson armed with a shotgun in the circumstances of this case, defendant probably "blocked out" the reality of the situation and reacted reflexively, without thinking at all. There was no expert testimony to the contrary.

In his final remarks before discharging the jurors . . . the judge . . . told the jurors that defendant could either be sent to state prison to serve a life sentence or be committed to the Youth Authority, and the prosecutor advised them that any observations they may have about the disposition of the case would be welcomed.

In response to that invitation, the foreman of the jury wrote to the judge two days later, . . . "The felony-murder law is *extremely* harsh but with the evidence and keeping 'the law, the law,' we the jury had little choice but to bring in a verdict of guilty of 1st degree murder. . . ."[20]

[The foreman implored] the judge to give defendant "his best opportunity in life" by committing him to the Youth Authority rather than sentencing him to state prison. . . .

. . . After the trial court committed defendant to the Youth Authority and he took this appeal, the People collaterally attacked the commitment order on the ground of excess of jurisdiction. The Court of Appeal held that at the time of the offense herein a minor convicted of first degree murder was ineligible as a matter of law for commitment to the Youth Authority. It therefore issued a writ of mandate directing the trial court to vacate the order of commitment,[21] and that court was left with no alternative but to sentence defendant to life imprisonment in state prison.

Because of his minority no greater punishment could have been inflicted on defendant if he had committed the most aggravated form of homicide known to our law—a carefully planned murder executed in cold blood after a calm and mature deliberation.[22] Yet despite the prosecutor's earnest endeavor throughout

19. In the rural setting in which he lived, it was apparently common for youths of his age to have .22 caliber rifles. Defendant also held a hunting license.

20. This letter was lodged with the superior court, and a copy thereof was appended as an exhibit to defendant's opening brief on appeal. Defendant requests that the record on appeal be augmented to include the letter, and the Attorney General has not opposed the request. Pursuant to California Rules of Court, rule 12(a), we order the record to be so augmented.

21. A trial court has jurisdiction to set aside a void order even while an appeal in the case is pending.

22. This contrast implicates the second technique noted in *Lynch* for determining proportionality, i.e., a comparison of the challenged penalty with those prescribed in the same jurisdiction for more serious crimes. (8 Cal. 3d at pp.426-427.) While such a comparison is particularly striking when a more serious crime is punished *less* severely than the offense in question, it remains instructive when the latter is punished *as* severely as a more serious crime. (See, e.g., In re Foss (1974) supra, 10 Cal. 3d 910, 925-926.) That is the case here.

the trial to prove a case of premeditated first degree murder, the triers of fact squarely rejected that view of the evidence.

The record fully supports the triers' conclusion. . . .

Finally, the excessiveness of defendant's punishment is underscored by the petty chastisements handed out to the six other youths who participated with him in the same offenses.[23] It is true that it was only defendant who actually pulled the trigger of his gun; but several of his companions armed themselves with shotguns, and the remainder carried such weapons as a knife and a baseball bat. Because their raid on the marijuana plantation was an elaborately prepared and concerted attempt evidenced by numerous overt acts, it appears they were all coconspirators in the venture. At the very least they were aiders and abettors and hence principals in the commission of both the attempted robbery and the killing of Johnson. (Pen. Code, §31.) Yet none was convicted of any degree of homicide whatever, and none was sentenced to state prison for any crime. . . . In short, defendant received the heaviest penalty provided by law while those jointly responsible with him received the lightest—the proverbial slap on the wrist.

For the reasons stated we hold that in the circumstances of this case the punishment of this defendant by a sentence of life imprisonment as a first degree murder violates article I, section 17, of the Constitution. Nevertheless, because he intentionally killed the victim without legally adequate provocation, defendant may and ought to be punished as a second degree murderer.

. . . The cause is remanded to the trial court with directions to arraign and pronounce judgment on defendant accordingly.

We need not invoke the third *Lynch* technique—a comparison of the challenged penalty with those prescribed for the same offense in other jurisdictions—in order to complete our analysis. We discussed these techniques in *Lynch* only as examples of the ways in which courts approach the proportionality problem; we neither held nor implied that a punishment cannot be ruled constitutionally excessive unless it is disproportionate in all three respects. (See. e.g., In re Rodriguez (1975) supra, 14 Cal. 3d 639, 656 ["Petitioner has already served a term which by *any* of the *Lynch* criteria is disproportionate to his offense" (italics added)]. The sole test remains, as quoted above, whether the punishment "shocks the conscience and offends fundamental notions of human dignity." (*Lynch,* 8 Cal. 3d at p.424.)

23. The remaining member of the group was granted immunity for giving evidence against all the others.

VII

ADDITIONAL CRIMES

19

THEFT AND EXTORTION

A. THEFT

COMMONWEALTH v. MITCHNECK

Superior Court of Pennsylvania
130 Pa. Super. 433, 198 A. 463 (1938)

KELLER, P.J.

The appellant was convicted of the offense of fraudulently converting the money of another person to his own use. . . .

The evidence produced on the part of the commonwealth would have warranted the jury in finding that the defendant, Mitchneck, operated a coal mine in Beaver township, Columbia county; that he employed certain persons, Hunsinger, Derr, Steeley, and others, as workers in and about his mine; that these employees dealt at the store of A. Vagnoni and signed orders directing their employer to deduct from their wages the amounts of their respective store bills and pay the same to Vagnoni; that the defendant agreed to do so, and pursuant to said agreement deducted from the wages due the eleven workmen, named in the indictment, an aggregate of $259.26, which he agreed to pay Vagnoni, but had failed and neglected to do so.

We are of the opinion that the evidence was insufficient to support a conviction under the Fraudulent Conversion Act of 1917, and that the court erred in refusing the defendant's point for a directed verdict of acquittal.

The gist of the offense of fraudulent conversion is that the defendant has received into his possession the money or property of another person, firm, or corporation, and fraudulently withholds, converts, or applies the same to or for his own use and benefit, or to the use and benefit of any person other than the one to whom the money or property belonged. If the property so withheld or applied to the defendant's use and benefit, etc., did not belong to some other person, etc., but was the defendant's own money or property, even though obtained by borrowing the money, or by a purchase on credit of the property, the offense has not been committed. "Whatever may have been the intention of the legislature in the enactment of the statute under which the indictment in this case was drawn, it was clearly not intended to make criminal the act of one who sells his own property, and it is not to be so applied as to make it an effective substitute for an action at law in the collection of a debt." Com. v. Hilpot, [84 Pa. Super. 424, 458]. . . .

The defendant in the present case had not received, nor did he have in his possession, any money *belonging* to his employees. True he owed them money, but that did not transfer to them the title to and ownership of the money. His deduction from their wages of the amounts of the store bills which they had assigned to Vagnoni did not change the title and ownership of the money thus withheld, nor did his agreement to pay to Vagnoni the amounts thus deducted constitute the latter the owner of the money. It effected only a change of creditors. The money, if Mitchneck actually had it, of which there was no proof, was still his own, but, after he accepted the assignments, he owed the amount due his employees to Vagnoni instead of to them. A novation had been effected. The defendant had been discharged of his liability to his employees by contracting a new obligation in favor of Vagnoni. But failure to pay the amount due the new creditor was not fraudulent conversion within the Act of 1917. Otherwise, it would be a very dangerous thing to agree to a novation. Defendant's liability for the unpaid wages due his employees was, and remained, civil, not criminal. His liability for the amount due Vagnoni after his agreement to accept or honor the assignments of his employees' wages was likewise civil and not criminal. . . .

The judgment is reversed, and the appellant is discharged.

Notes and Questions

1. See MPC §223 in Appendix C. Of what form of theft did the lower court convict Mitchneck? What provisions of the Model Penal Code would it have invoked? Section 223.2? Section 223.3? Section 223.8? Would Mitchneck have been found guilty under Model Penal Code §223.8? Would he be more clearly guilty if the word "retains" were added after the word "obtains"?

2. Would the result in the case have been the same if Mitchneck's employees had drawn their pay and immediately handed the money back to Mitchneck to pay their store bills to Vagnoni? *Should* the case turn on the fact that the employees did *not* do so? Is that too subtle or formal a distinction? Didn't Mitchneck in any event unlawfully deprive the employees of their property?

3. Should creditors be given the power of the State, including the power to imprison, in enforcing contract obligations? If Mitchneck were criminally liable, would criminal liability also extend to the installment buyer who fails to

make her payments? Would it make a difference that Mitchneck agreed to make payments on behalf of others, to whom he owed money?

4. Why does the Code need any theft provision other than §223.2?

The *Mitchneck* case nicely illuminates some of the central problems that have influenced the complex development of theft law in British and American history. For a rich and concise summary of that development, consider this excerpt by Professor Louis B. Schwartz, Theft, Encyclopedia of Crime and Justice 1537-1551 (1983).

> *Theft* is a general term embracing a wide variety of misconduct by which a person is improperly deprived of his property. The purpose of theft law is to promote security of property by threatening aggressors with punishment. Property security is valued as part of the individual's enjoyment of his belongings and because the community wishes to encourage saving and economic planning, which would be jeopardized if accumulated property could be plundered with impunity. Another function of the law of theft is to divert the powerful acquisitive instinct from nonproductive preying on others to productive activity.
>
> One problem that dogs the law of theft, as will be seen below, is that in a commercial society no clear line can be drawn between greedy antisocial acquisitive behavior on the one hand and, on the other hand, aggressive selling, advertising, and other entrepreneurial activity that is highly regarded or at least commonly tolerated. Here two important principles of constitutional and criminal law come into play to restrict the scope of the law of theft. A criminal law must not be so comprehensive as to jeopardize the ordinary behavior of decent citizens. Nor may a criminal law be so vague that it fails to warn the citizen what is forbidden and leaves to the discretion of enforcement officers or judges whether certain behavior should be punishable. The tension between these principles, and the impulse to penalize all egregious greed, account for the fact that theft law inevitably falls short of penalizing all rascality. At the same time—such are the refractory problems of legislative drafting—it is impossible, even with the most painstaking draftsmanship, to avoid overpenalizing in some cases. For example, obviously trivial peculations such as using an employer's stationery for writing personal notes quite clearly fall within theft law; yet it has proved impossible to articulate exceptions that will exclude this and a myriad of other trivial violations. Such things remain, therefore, within the province of prosecutorial and judicial discretion.
>
> Within the broad category of theft, the law has long made important distinctions according to the particular means employed to appropriate the property, the nature and value of the property, the "criminal intent" or its absence, and other circumstances. These variables are reflected in the number of distinct criminal offenses that the law developed to deal with theft—for example, larceny, embezzlement, false pretense, fraudulent conversion, cheating, robbery, extortion, shoplifting, and receiving stolen goods. . . .
>
> **Larceny**
>
> Larceny, not an original common-law felony, must have emerged as the royal courts extended their jurisdiction beyond robbery to reflect increasing cen-

tral concern for property security generally and to control the imposition of capital punishment, a sanction often employed in the illusory hope of repressing theft. As might be expected, the initial excursion of the royal courts into the law of theft was sharply limited. Larceny was defined as taking and carrying away tangible personal property of another by trespass and without his consent with the purpose of stealing or permanently depriving the owner of possession. Consideration of the technical limits that the courts derived from, or built into, this seemingly simple definition will throw light on the way law evolves and on the process that ultimately made it necessary for Parliament and other legislatures to take up the task of extending the law of theft.

A property offense. Larceny deals with tangible property. There are many ways of inflicting pecuniary injury on another apart from taking his tangible property. For example, one can cheat another out of services due him, as where a municipal or corporate officer causes underlings to labor for the officer's private benefit on time paid for by the municipality or corporation. One can cause an actor, physician, architect, or other professional to provide valuable service by false promises or representations. One can bypass the electric meter to obtain power service without paying for it. One can plagiarize another's book or music, or "steal" technical information that has been entrusted in confidence. Only much later and by explicit legislation did such frauds become punishable, usually as offenses distinct from larceny. . . .

Tangible property. The requirement that the personal property be "tangible" served to exclude many forms of interpersonal economic claims from the larceny offense, including debts, contract rights, promissory notes, trade secrets, and patents. Controversies over such commercial interests, like controversies over land, were generally between identifiable rivals, not with sneak thieves, the prime target of larceny law, and these controversies could ordinarily be resolved by civil law suits. Perhaps one can see here also the beginnings of that special tolerance for what was later to be identified as white-collar crime, that is, middle-class nonviolent peculation, often by persons of the same social class as the legislators, judges, and prosecutors.

Take and carry away; attempted larceny. . . .

What . . . is the quantum of actual misbehavior that will suffice for a larceny conviction? The answer was found in the definition of larceny insofar as it requires proof that the actor did "take and carry away," that is, exercise physical dominion over the property, thus interfering with the possession of the true owner. Such interference constitutes the "trespass" discussed below; but more is required. The actor must move the property, however slightly; that is, begin to remove it or carry it away. A culprit, observing a packing case on the loading platform of a warehouse, might go so far as to tip the case up on one corner without actually committing larceny; only if there was additional movement resulting in the displacement of "every atom" of the object would the offense be complete.

On the other hand, the significance of these intriguing technicalities is diminished by the fact that the suspect may be convicted of *attempted* larceny if he has not gone far enough to "complete" the crime. The law of attempt has its own requirements with regard to how far criminal action must proceed in order to cross the line between "mere preparation," which is not criminal, and criminal attempt. One may therefore be guilty of attempted larceny although the larceny requirement of carrying away is not satisfied. Grave consequences turn on whether there has been a completed larceny or only an attempt. In the eighteenth century, when some larcenies were capital offenses, life or death might depend on whether the suspect had merely tipped the case on end or had moved it entirely. In modern law, criminal codes frequently set lower sentence maxima for attempts than for completed offenses.

Making important differences in potential sentence turn on nice distinctions between attempted larceny and completed larceny is additionally curious when one perceives that many "completed" larcenies prove, on analysis, to be frustrated, rather than successful, efforts to steal—in other words, attempts. Our culprit of the warehouse loading platform, having indeed moved the case a few inches, may desist from his nefarious purpose upon observing the arrival of a policeman. A pickpocket, having the victim's wallet already in his grasp and having partly removed it from the pocket, may find that the alert victim has grasped him firmly by the wrist. Abandoning the tempting wallet, the pickpocket seeks only to escape. The law would hold this to be larceny rather than attempt.

Confusion is further confounded when it is observed that the "aggravated larcenies," robbery and burglary, are analytically attempts, although centuries of treatment as distinct substantive offenses obscure this analytic truth. Assaults *for the purpose* of larceny are robbery. The slightest intrusion into a building *for the purpose* of larceny is burglary, although the burglar has succeeded only in inserting his screwdriver or crowbar under the window. Activity that has not accomplished its purpose falls logically into the category of attempt. There may be good reason to treat these particular inchoate larcenies more severely than the ordinary "completed" larceny, since the culprit manifests special dangerousness by embarking on larceny in specially frightening circumstances. Moreover, since the preliminary steps taken for the purpose of larceny, that is, assault and trespass, are themselves criminal offenses, it is possible to regard the purpose to steal as merely an aggravating circumstance attending the commission of those "completed" offenses. But these explanations leave undisturbed the perception that the mere distinction between attempt and completed larceny hardly suffices to justify special leniency toward culprits who do not fully accomplish their larcenous purposes.

By trespass and without consent. Extraordinary extensions of larceny law were accomplished by daring judicial pronouncements in the eighteenth century with regard to the central concept of larceny—that an owner's possession must be shown to have been disturbed without his consent, a disturbance known in law as "trespass" (Rex v. Pear, 168 Eng. Rep. 208 (Crown Cases 1780)). The one thing the old English judges did not want to be involved in as administrators of the criminal law was quarrels between an owner and one to whom the owner had entrusted his property for such purposes as to sell, store, transport, repair, process, or invest. These relationships, known in law as bailments, were perceived as quintessentially civil matters of contract. A merchant must take his chances and could minimize his risks by care in selecting those to whom he entrusted goods. Moreover, if criminality were to depend on the bailee's having done something not authorized by the contract of bailment, there was the difficulty of proving exactly how far that authority went. This would depend on customs of the trade and, frequently, on verbal understandings of ambiguous import. The circumstances, in short, were altogether different from the typical larceny involving a thief without a shadow of claim of right. . . .

"Custody" versus "possession." Consider, then, what is to be done with the butler who, while polishing his master's silver, is overcome by the temptation of illicit gain and absconds with the family plate. Is this to be regarded as "bailment"? Has milord, who may reside in distant London, voluntarily transferred "possession" to the trusted butler, so that the butler's misappropriating what is rightfully in his own possession cannot amount to a "trespass" against his master's possession? As early as the sixteenth century, the lordly gentlemen of the bench sought to find their way past such obstacles so as to convict the butler of larceny. They did so by perceiving or inventing a distinction between "possession" and mere "custody." A servant had mere custody; he held the master's belongings only as a proxy for the master. Thus the master retained "possession," and the servant committed trespass against the master's possession when he carried off the plate. A similar extension was easily made in favor of merchants, whose clerks and apprentices in stores, banks, and factories were treated as holding mere custody of goods that remained in possession of the employers.

Trespass by bailee in possession. Economic and social pressures mounted in favor of applying theft sanctions to bailees. With increasing specialization of labor and increasing nationalization of the market, more and more goods were unavoidably entrusted to other participants in the process of production, transportation, and marketing—participants who most certainly were not servants but "independent contractors," that is, bailees. Theft law began to respond as early as the fifteenth century, but fitfully. A hauler entrusted with a case of goods was convicted of larceny when he broke the case open and helped himself to the contents (The Carrier's Case, Y. B. Pasch. 13 Edw. IV, f. 9, pl. 5 (Star Chamber 1473)). The judges could bring themselves to say that the case, but not the contents, had been delivered into the possession of the hauler by consent of the owner. The contents thus remained in the possession of the owner, against which possession the hauler had committed trespass.

Larceny by trick. A famous prosecution in the eighteenth century involved an accused who hired a coach and horses for a specified trip and duration, although his real purpose was to make off with the coach and dispose of it. There could be no question that the transaction began as a bailment. But the court was willing to say that "possession" reverted to the lessor upon breach of the bailment contract, so that the lessee trespassed on the lessor's possession. Moreover, in the court's view, the voluntary aspect of the initial delivery of the car to the bailee was vitiated by the bailee's fraudulent misrepresentation of his intentions. Fraud in inducing a transfer of possession vitiated the apparent "consent" of the bailor to the change of possession. This was the famous "larceny by trick," a far cry from the archetypal covert snatch, and ancestor of the legislation to come that would penalize obtaining property by false pretenses even when the transaction induced was a transfer of money or other property, a change of ownership rather than merely possession as in larceny—in short, a sale.

Lost or abandoned property. If an owner abandons or loses, that is, loses possession of, his property, another's taking of it is not a trespass against the owner's possession; hence no larceny. However, the interests of property losers eventually received some criminal law protection. It had long been recognized that an owner possessed goods, in the sense that he asserted continued dominion over them even if he were far from them and thus in no position to exert immediate physical control. Ingenious judges availed themselves of this idea by drawing a distinction between lost and "mislaid" property. Thus, a cab driver who appropriates a wallet that a passenger has inadvertently left on the seat or dropped to the floor takes "mislaid" rather than "lost" property, trespassing against the owner's continued "possession." Nevertheless, there was reluctance to extend the harsh penalties of larceny to finders, who do not aggressively act against the property security of others. Their misbehavior, if it be such, consists of a failure to take steps to restore property to its true owners. Anglo-American law has traditionally been averse to penalizing inaction, and in the lost-property situation, to make a thief out of a finder runs counter to the folk wisdom of "finders, keepers." Special legislation has been passed to define the affirmative action required and to penalize only egregious departures from ordinary standards of behavior, as where the property has substantial value, the identity of the owner is manifest, and the property can be restored to the owner without disproportionate effort and expense. Violation of such a duty of affirmative action would not ordinarily be characterized as theft, and the maximum authorized sentence would be much lower. . . .

The larcenous intent. Generally speaking, serious crimes such as larceny cannot be committed unknowingly or innocently. There is a requirement of *mens rea* (wickedness or evil intent). Three aspects of this psychological component of larceny are worth discussing here: (1) purpose to appropriate; (2) claim of right; and (3) permanence of intended deprivation.

Purpose to appropriate. Purpose to appropriate serves to differentiate acquisitive misbehavior from destructive behavior—that is, larceny from malicious mischief. The classic Latin formulation was *lucri causa* ("for the sake of gain"). Vandalism of property has always been regarded as a less serious offense, although that is by no means a self-evident proposition, considering that stolen goods remain part of the social stock, since they are merely redistributed, whereas destroyed things are irretrievably lost. On the other hand, the temptation to acquire illicitly seems to be much more pervasive. Yielding to it leads readily to the adoption of thievery as a way of life. A clever thief can become a professional criminal and make a living without the labor endured by his honest and indignant fellow citizens. Accordingly, if I take my neighbor's vase meaning to make it my own or to sell it, I am guilty of the felony of larceny (or one of the modern composite theft offenses of which larceny becomes a component); but if I merely toss it to the floor, shattering it, that amounts only to the misdemeanor of property destruction or malicious mischief. Interesting variants can occur, as where the culprit first "appropriates"—that is, takes and carries away—and thereafter destroys. He is guilty of both offenses even if the original taking was with purpose to destroy.

Purpose to appropriate means that one cannot be guilty of larceny by taking what he believes, however unreasonably, to be his own, for one does not intend to "appropriate" what is already his own, or to deprive another. There is lacking the thievish state of mind that would identify the taker as a threat to the property of others. In some connections, such as homicide, the law recognizes "recklessness" as a sufficient mens rea; but in the case of larceny even the most careless mistake as to ownership will absolve the accused. In the jargon of the law, larceny is a crime requiring "specific intent," that is, the conscious purpose to trespass against another's right of possession.

Yet there is a class of situations involving "claim of right" where the accused's subjective good faith will not save him from conviction for larceny. If a man appropriates property that he knows to belong to another, he commits larceny even if he takes the property to satisfy a real or supposed obligation that is due from the owner. Thus an employee who believes that the employer has illegally withheld wages may not with impunity help himself to a corresponding amount of the employer's cash or goods. A farmer who thinks or, for that matter, knows that his neighbor has stolen one of his calves violates the larceny law if he helps himself to an equivalent calf belonging to the neighbor. In sum, the defense of claim of right requires a showing of belief that the actor owned (or otherwise had the right to possession of) the specific article, not merely that he was entitled to some form of compensation. It seems doubtful whether creditors' self-help is sufficiently analogous to the basic misbehavior condemned by the law of theft, or sufficiently identifies the actor as an egregious threat to the property interests of others, to warrant social castigation as a thief. Yet in the absence of alternative categories of minor crime into which creditor self-help might be fitted, society has chosen to leave to prosecutorial discretion whether such over-zealous creditors should be prosecuted as thieves.

Intent to deprive permanently. This aspect of the definition of larceny serves to exclude unauthorized borrowing from larceny. In general, temporary takings ought to be excluded from larceny, although it is worth noting by way of anticipation that when the issue is embezzlement rather than larceny, even temporary misappropriation by a trustee, agent, or other fiduciary leads to conviction. The courts have shown no disposition to hear a lawyer or stockbroker say, "I took my clients' securities or cash only briefly to meet an urgent need of my own and with full intent to return the property." Larceny borrowings, however, would ordinarily not involve large sums of liquid assets that can readily disappear, nor is there involved the aggravating circumstance that the culprit breached a strong duty of fidelity he owed to the owner who had entrusted property to him. The harm done when an ordinary tool, article of clothing, or bicycle is borrowed without permission is minimal if the object is returned promptly in good condition. The possibility of professional thievery based on illicit borrowing is remote.

Criminal borrowing. However, there are many situations in which borrowing without the owner's consent presents a serious enough risk of substantial loss as to warrant excluding a defense that the taking was without intent to deprive permanently. The courts readily convicted of larceny where the taker had only a conditional intent to restore the property, that is, if the owner would pay a reward. So also where the taker, although abjuring any purpose to appropriate permanently and, indeed, professing hope that the property will be regained by the owner, deals with the property in a way that reveals his essential indifference to returning the property. Having "borrowed" a shotgun from his neighbor's barn to go hunting, he abandons it in the woods. Such recklessness regarding restoration of the property was held sufficient *mens rea* for larceny.

A second category identified by modern reformers as appropriate for larceny conviction despite the alleged intention of the taker to restore the property is where the property is withheld "under such circumstances that a major portion of its economic value or its use and benefit has in fact been appropriated." This formulation was adopted in the Model Penal Code of the American Law Institute (§223.0) and in the Proposed New Federal Criminal Code of the United States National Commission on Reform of Federal Criminal Laws (§1741(b)). Thus, the draftsmen sought to extend larceny to cases such as the prolonged "borrowing" of an art treasure or the surreptitious "borrowing" of a mowing machine precisely for the season in which the owner would need it.

"Joyride" statutes. A third category of criminal borrowing, of great practical importance, is dealt with by the so-called joyride statutes. These laws penalize unauthorized borrowing of automobiles or other vehicles. One of the commonest offenses committed by youths in an automobile civilization is to take an available car for a fast (and risky) drive, without any intention of keeping the vehicle. When abandoned, it will soon be restored to the owner by the police. The great risk presented by this activity—not only to valuable property but also to the lives of those encountered on the highway—led to penal legislation against it, sometimes by way of expanding larceny, and sometimes under a nonthievery designation. How far should the principle be extended? To boats, motorcycles, and airplanes, clearly. But should it also be extended to other motor-propelled vehicles, including snowmobiles, motor scooters, parachutes, and hang gliders? Should special laws be enacted to penalize unauthorized borrowing of dangerous machines, nuclear materials, or guns? Does the number of exceptions from the principle of penalizing only permanent deprivations multiply so uncontrollably that the principle itself should be abandoned except for the most trivial borrowing of personal belongings, thus leaving it to the discretion of prosecutors and judges which illegal borrowings should be prosecuted and punished? . . .

Embezzlement

In the eighteenth and nineteenth centuries the pressures to extend theft law beyond the "trespass" limits of common larceny became irresistible. An offense had to be created to penalize the defalcations of bailees, trustees, and the like who clearly did *not* wrongfully infringe on the possession of others, since they had themselves been put in possession either by the owners or by authority of law, as where an executor, administrator, or trustee took property under a will subject to a fiduciary obligation to administer for the benefit of heirs. Embezzlement is, then, misappropriation of the property of another when that property is already in the possession of the embezzler. The law expanded cautiously, as might be expected, since the objections to an expansive theft law, which had been felt in connection with larceny, did not evaporate. Initially only a few of the numerous classes of potential embezzlers, such as fiduciaries and haulers, were named in the statutes. Eventually the coverage of the embezzlement statutes was enlarged to cover anyone who had property of another in his own possession.

One of the objections to expanding theft law—the harshness of larceny penalties—was met by providing milder although still heavy sanctions for embezzlement, thus introducing the somewhat surprising phenomenon that different forms of theft would be treated with varying degrees of severity depending on the historic moment when a particular expansion of theft law was effectuated. A major peculation by a trustee or bank official might carry a lesser penalty than a minor trespassory larceny, although many would consider that the former was the more heinous and harmful behavior. Over a period of time the severity of larceny penalties gradually moderated; and ultimately, when various forms of theft were consolidated into a single offense, the same statutory maximum would become applicable to both larceny and embezzlement.

Misappropriation. "Misappropriation" is the criminal act that characterizes embezzlement, just as "taking" characterizes larceny. It is generally more difficult to decide whether misappropriation occurred than to decide whether property was unlawfully taken. A real estate broker or a lawyer, for example, may receive the proceeds of a sale of property or money recovered in a lawsuit. It is easy to say that such monies are misappropriated if the broker or lawyer pockets the whole fund and spends it for his personal needs. But what if the broker deposits the buyer's check in the broker's personal bank account, meaning to write a check later payable to the client for the amount of the proceeds less commission? That way of handling the transaction may violate standards of professional behavior which explicitly require clients' funds to be deposited and held in separate accounts; but it would be a harsh rule that transformed every violation of prophylactic professional regulations into a severely punishable theft. Ethical codes of the professions generally provide lesser sanctions, such as reprimand or suspension from practice, and no ethics committee of a professional association should have the power to redefine crime by changing its rules of ethics. On the other hand, the mere fact that an act violates professional standards should not immunize professional misbehavior from criminal sanctions that apply to identical conduct engaged in by nonprofessionals.

Perhaps the resolution of this dilemma lies in the proposition that identical acts have different significance in different circumstances. If I give my friend $1,000 with which to pay my bills while I am on a long journey, and he deposits the money in his own account to avoid the inconvenience of opening a separate account, it would be unreasonable to conclude that he is misappropriating my property. However, if I give money to my lawyer to pay a judgment against me and the lawyer deposits it in his own account, quite different implications may arise. For the lawyer, having a separate account for clients' funds is no temporary or occasional need but part of the normal way of doing business, explicitly mandated by codes of professional ethics. Accordingly, the commingling of client funds with personal funds ordinarily represents not merely a lazy avoidance of minor inconvenience, but rather a significant and, for the professional, unusual choice among available accounts. In short, the lawyer appears to have taken the first step toward applying the client's money to his own private use. One could call that preparation or attempt to misappropriate the money, the offense becoming complete later when the lawyer draws checks on the account to pay his personal bills. However, the law chooses to treat the initial deposit in the lawyer's account as already an exercise of hostile dominion over the entrusted fund. Just as has been seen above in the case of larceny, the logical distinction between attempted and completed theft is not always maintained.

The ambiguity of "misappropriation" is further illustrated by cases where an agent has been convicted of misappropriating a check made out to his principal *even though he deposits that check in his principal's account.* This result has been reached in situations where the agent, owing the principal money on account of earlier transactions, covers up the shortage by depositing current checks with vouchers falsely attributing them to the earlier transactions. Because of the false accounting, the agent is seen as having applied the current checks *to his own purposes,* squaring himself with the company, and thus misappropriating.

An extreme and dubious extension of the concept of misappropriation is expressed in some statutes that make any shortage in the accounts of a public official a basis for convicting him of embezzlement. The reasoning goes as follows. There is proof that the official received X amount, as tax collector. He has on hand only X minus Y. Thus he must have misappropriated Y, or at least failed to exercise proper care in collecting, conserving, or disbursing tax monies. Such reasoning and legislation confounds theft with negligence, or, even more at variance with Anglo-American traditions, seeks to facilitate convicting an official of a *presumed* embezzlement by eliminating the necessity of proving misappropriation.

Property of another. The embezzlement statutes transcended the difficulties experienced in larceny law over the kinds of property covered. One can embezzle real as well as personal property, negotiable instruments and securities as well as tangible physical goods. But limiting embezzlement to "property" plays an important role in one class of situations, namely, where it may be necessary to decide whether a defendant exerted control over property belonging to another or whether instead he merely failed to pay a contracted debt owed to the other. The distinction is of constitutional importance where imprisonment for debt is constitutionally forbidden. It is, in any event, important from a policy viewpoint because putting the force of the criminal law behind fulfillment of contracts would have immense social and economic implications. Department stores, banks, credit card agencies, and other creditors would then be able to call upon prosecuting attorneys to aid in collections, the threat of jail for defaulting debtors would be legitimated, and creditors, especially of the poor, would be partially relieved of the necessity of carefully screening their extensions of credit.

Distinguishing property from contract obligations is not always easy. One tends to think of "having" money in a bank, whereas the true relationship is that depositing money "in" one's bank account, unlike stashing it in a safe-deposit box, is in effect a transfer of ownership to the bank. Thereafter the bank merely owes money to the depositor. That means that the banker may, the moment he has the depositor's cash in hand, use that cash as he will. He does not misappropriate it even though he proceeds forthwith to the racetrack, where he loses it all at the betting windows. That may violate certain banking laws; it is not theft.

The niceties to which the distinction between property and contract can give rise are illustrated by Commonwealth v. Mitchneck, 130 Pa. Super. 433, 198 A. 463 (1938). . . .

Intention and motives. The statutory definitions of embezzlement include no express requirement that the culprit means to deprive the owner permanently. Accordingly, unauthorized "borrowing" of trust funds by a trustee or of a customer's securities by his broker is embezzlement. It will be observed, however, that these examples involve valuable liquid assets that are jeopardized by deviation from propriety in handling them. The cases thus resemble larceny cases where, despite a professed intention to deprive the owner only temporarily, the borrower disposes of the property in a way that creates a high risk that it will not be restored. Moreover, cash or fungible securities "temporarily" borrowed are unlikely to be literally returned; the borrower intends to return *equivalent* money or securities, which is to say that the intent is to pay at some time in the future for what is presently taken. The kind of trivial borrowing that escapes punishment as larceny might also be excluded from embezzlement by finding that no "appropriation" had occurred. The executor of an estate who lets his daughter take a ride on a bicycle that is part of the estate is not only unlikely to be indicted, as a matter of the prosecutor's discretion, but also is probably immune under the law of embezzlement. . . .

We have come a long way from the core concept of thievery to a kind of penal sanction against violation of codes of good behavior for fiduciaries. Perhaps a completely rational—that is, ahistorical—theft law would be cut back to the old common-law notion of *lucri causa.* That is, theft would be limited to acquisitive behavior for the sake of gain. But doing this would entail creating additional penal offenses, outside of or auxiliary to the theft legislation, to deal with specific property offenses not for the purpose of gain: compare the traditional "malicious mischief" law.

False Pretenses and Fraud

Larceny and embezzlement deal with takings and appropriations without the consent of the true owner. It is necessary now to confront the question of how far the penal law should go where the owner is not merely deprived of possession or enjoyment of his property, but voluntarily transfers his title to the property, as where he is induced to sell the property or to part with money as a result of trickery or misrepresentation by the other party to the transaction. The expansion of common-law larceny to include "larceny by trick" in cases where the thief obtained possession by deception has already been noted. But this covered a small fraction of the domain of fraud because it was limited to transfers of *possession.* If the swindler induced the owner to part with title, that is, to sell or otherwise transfer ownership, the transaction was seen as falling within the realm of contract or commerce.

A number of reasons conjoined to delay the advance of penal regulation in this area. With regard to controversies between merchants, there was a long history of special tribunals and guild regulation that must have seemed to them preferable to the heavy-handed intrusion of national law and officials. With regard to protection of the ordinary citizen and consumer, the ancient common-law misdemeanor of "cheating" might have been cited as filling most of the need. That reached the use of false weights and measures or other devices by which *the public generally* was mulcted. It did not, in principle, inquire into single transactions, where bargainers were supposed to protect themselves ("Let the buyer beware!"). To a cautious eighteenth-century legislator or judge, it would have seemed dangerous, paternalist, and a nuisance to involve the high courts in such trivial, nonviolent controversies. Dangerous, because conviction would so often depend on appraisal of the complaining victim's credibility and that of the defendant, who in the early days at least could not testify in his own defense and enjoyed limited or no assistance of counsel. Moreover, it would have been evident to opponents of penalizing "private" fraud that there would be serious difficulties in distinguishing substantial deception from sellers' exaggeration of value and other conventional puffing of wares (Rex v. Wheatley, 96 Eng. Rep. 151 (K.B. 1761)). Such concerns would manifest themselves during the eighteenth and nineteenth centuries in the first penal laws against private fraud by the very narrow limits placed on the kind of misrepresentation that would be criminal. To this day, under the Penal Code of France mere lying by one party to bargaining is not criminal. To prove criminal fraud the prosecution must also show a "mise-en-scène," that is, a stage setting for the lie such as would inveigle even skeptics.

False representation. The first false-pretense statutes were couched in terms of obtaining money or other property by means of a knowingly false and fraudulent misrepresentation of fact. We may pass without further comment the conventional restriction of this new theft law to theft of "property," and defer for a moment discussion of "knowingly false and fraudulent." What would constitute a sufficient "misrepresentation of fact"? That question may best be answered by specifying what was *not* included.

Misleading omissions. The false-pretense laws did not create an affirmative obligation to tell the other party to a bargain everything that he might like to know. Silence is not misrepresentation, even when it is obvious that the other party labors under a misunderstanding. The antique dealer may acquire grandma's rocking chair for one-tenth of its market value, she being manifestly ignorant of the fact that it is a rare piece of seventeenth-century Americana. The oil company may send its disguised agent to buy Farmer Brown's land cheap without telling him that oil has been discovered on adjoining land. Not until the enactment of the twentieth-century "blue sky laws" and the federal Securities Act of 1933 did affirmative disclosure become an obligation enforced by penal law, and then the obligation was particularized by specific questions that the promoter was obliged to answer in the registration forms drafted by the enforcement agency. The principle has been extended to other kinds of promotions, such as land sales and franchising.

Opinions and promises. Opinions, including most certainly the seller's expressed opinion of the value of his goods, were not treated as punishable misrepresentations of fact under the typical false-pretense statute, however clear the proof might be that the seller did not hold that opinion. Promises, predictions, and statements of intention were not covered, however clear the proof that the promisor did not intend to perform or did not believe his prediction. Although modern courts are willing to regard such deception as factual misrepresentation of the state of mind of the swindler, the earlier attitude was that the true state of mind of the accused with respect to promises and intentions incident to a bargain seemed too chancy an issue for a criminal trial. Moreover, penalizing false promises would be seen as dangerously close to using criminal law to enforce debts and other contracts. True, such a law would reach only promisors who did not *at the time of promising* mean to abide by the promise, so that honest promisors would, theoretically, not be imperiled. But again, who could judge reliably the subjective good faith of a promisor? Every user of a credit card, every borrower from a small-loan company, every purchaser on deferred payment, would be in jeopardy if at the time of the transaction his financial condition and prospects were so unfavorable as to give rise to an inference that he knew he would be unable to pay the obligation when it came due. . . .

Materiality of misrepresentation. Since the false-pretense statute speaks in terms of obtaining property "by means of" misrepresentation, a causal relation between the swindler's deception and the victim's loss must be shown. For example, if the victim knew the true facts, it could not be said that he parted with his money as a result of the misrepresentation, although the swindler might in such situations be guilty of attempt to obtain by false pretense. It was not necessary that the false pretense be the sole cause of the harm to the victim: deception by others, false rumor, or the victim's greed or self-deception might be contributory causes without immunizing the swindler's fraud.

The idea that the misrepresentation must be material is linked to the causation element of the offense. A salesman may feign a joviality or enthusiasm he does not feel. He may assume a name other than his own, pretend to be rich or pious, or falsely claim membership in a lodge or a veterans' association. Except where such identifications are relevant to an extension of credit to him, they would be held immaterial to the transaction, that is, presumptively not causative. This would be the case even if it could be proved conclusively that the victim would not have entered into the transaction but for a deception of this sort, as where the victim was intensely prejudiced against the race or religion of the salesman, who consequently misrepresented himself in that respect while avoiding all deception as to the mercantile aspects of the deal.

It is thus apparent that the requirement of materiality goes beyond the question of actual causation, and enables the courts to disregard some effective deception for reasons of policy. In effect, it is held that some methods of advertising and "hard sell," although possibly reprehensible, are so pervasive and so uncertainly separable from laudable business activity as to call for repression by less drastic methods than the penal law, for example, by affirmative administrative regulation of competitive practices.

Transcending the limitations of the early false-pretense statutes. Beginning in the nineteenth century, mounting social pressures to penalize all sorts of swindling led to judicial evasion of the limits fixed by the false-pretense statutes and to supplementary legislation, culminating in the federal Mail Fraud Act, which reaches every trick, artifice, or scheme to defraud (18 U.S.C. §§1341-1342 (1976)). Judicial expansion of the concept of criminal false pretense often rested on the incontrovertible proposition that misrepresentation need not be express but can be implied. Thus, granting that omission is not to be penalized, the stock salesman who garnishes his expressed rosy view of the company's profitability (mere "opinion" and "puffery") with the reassuring statistic that the stock has earned an *average* profit of 20 percent for the last ten years might nevertheless be convicted on a showing that he omitted to state that all the earnings had been in the first year, with steady losses thereafter. Notwithstanding the literal truth of the "average" figure, there would be a finding of an "implicit" misrepresentation that 20 percent was typical of recent earnings. . . .

Mail fraud. The Mail Fraud Act incorporates the broadest definition of criminal fraud. Any "trick, scheme or device" suffices for conviction, and false promises are explicitly included. Opinion, value, or law may be the subject of material deception. Materiality does not totally disappear as a criterion, but a misrepresentation that, standing alone, would have been held immaterial under a false-pretense statute may figure as one element of a "scheme to defraud." The Mail Fraud Act is not confined to obtaining property; a "scheme to defraud" obviously may be directed at defrauding others of valuable services. Indeed, it has been held that the government is defrauded where its normal administrative processes are vitiated through the exercise of improper influences upon officials.

Even the criminal-intent requirement has been somewhat diluted so as to come very close to penalizing reckless as well as knowingly false representations. This result was reached by holding that a promisor's state of mind is a fact which may be misrepresented. Thus, a promoter who makes confident predictions of profit in order to sell securities may be convicted of mail fraud if he is far less confident than he represents himself to be and omits to disclose circumstances which impugn that confidence. Being sanguine himself, he actually believes what he asserts, so that he acts in good faith and without intent to deceive. The prediction is honest but reckless. Or, stated more cautiously, the promoter, aware of his own secret doubts, knowingly misrepresents the extent of his confidence. (Knickerbocker Merchandising Co. v. United States, 13 F.2d 544 (2d Cir. 1926)).

Mail fraud is a peculiarly American phenomenon that deserves a word of explanation. In principle, under American federalism ordinary crime is the concern of the states rather than of the federal government. The federal government would naturally promulgate penal law relating to treason against the United States, to enforcement of federal tax and customs laws, and to perjury committed before the federal courts and agencies. Theft law, under this concept, would fall within the domain of the states, as do murder, rape, arson, burglary, and assault. But the line begins to blur. Theft of *federal* property seems to demand uniform national law and enforcement, and appropriate legislation is enacted. As the interstate rail and highway system developed, protection of this national network similarly evoked federal penal legislation against train robbery, stealing of goods moving in interstate commerce, transportation of stolen goods across state lines, and even transportation of women "for immoral purposes." Thus arose a dual jurisdiction whereby a great many local crimes could be prosecuted either by the state or by the national government if some federal "peg" could be proved.

In the case of mail fraud, the federal peg was use of the mails to carry out the scheme to defraud. This was more than a technicality. The mails were extensively employed to conduct fraudulent public promotions extending far beyond the bounds of the state or foreign country where the enterprise was operated. The federal government, by making the subsidized facilities of the postal service available to swindlers, would be perceived as aiding in the exploitation of the victims. State officials where the victims resided would be hampered in investigating operations thousands of miles away, and there would be overlapping and wasteful enforcement effort when numerous state investigations were initiated. Within the postal service, enforcement officers called postal inspectors were employed to determine when the mails were being used for noxious purposes (including not only fraud but extortion, dissemination of pornography, and the like) and to assemble evidence for prosecuting those who thus exploited the federal facilities. Unfortunately, once this enforcement apparatus was created, it followed the tradition of bureaucratic expansionism and involved itself in a great deal of petty local misconduct where, for example, the culprit used the mail, however peripherally, in writing to the victim in the same city or state. . . .

Receiving Stolen Goods

The law generally penalizes an accessory to a crime only if he conspired or aided in its commission or if, after the commission, he harbors or conceals the offender, that is, obstructs law enforcement. The objective encouragement that a "fence," or professional receiver, gives to theft does not amount to conspiring or aiding in the theft, although a receiver can easily cross the line and become a conspirator, for example, by entering into a continuing relationship with the thief, promising to buy regularly, or suggesting what had best be stolen and where. Merely buying the loot does not amount to harboring the thief. These limits of accessorial liability gave rise to special legislation penalizing those who buy stolen goods or otherwise aid the thief in disposing of them.

In principle, the receiving, like other theft offenses, should be confined to situations where the offender knows he is dealing with property that does not belong to the person bringing it to him. The difficulty of proving such knowledge led to broadening the statutes to cover recklessness or negligence with respect to the true ownership. Sometimes the statutes created a presumption of knowledge where the receiver bought at far less than the market value of the goods, although such a presumption appears to contradict the constitutional requirement that conviction of infamous crime be based on proof beyond a reasonable doubt. An alternative approach to the problem of the professional receiver is to license and regulate pawnshops, junk dealers, and secondhand stores. The regulations may require the dealer to keep record of the identity of sellers, to report certain purchases to the police, to submit to police inspections, and the like. Violations lead to suspension or revocation of license and of the right to do business, or to misdemeanor penalties for breach of regulations.

Grading of Theft Offenses

. . . One might initially expect that if "theft" is a rational category of behavior, the legislature would content itself with providing a maximum sentence, say, ten years' imprisonment, for theft of the greatest scale under the most aggravating circumstances. Within the ten-year legislative maximum, the sentencing judge would have discretion to impose individual sentences that reflect the infinite variety of circumstances and offenders. Actual duration of imprisonment under an indeterminate sentence imposed by the judge would be determined at the discretion of a parole board, which may judge that the prisoner has been sufficiently reoriented by his prison experience to be safely returned to the community.

Sentence limits expressed in categories as gross as larceny or theft are unacceptable. Already in the eighteenth century, the extreme penalty authorized for larceny led to statutes barring capital punishment where only petty values were involved. By the twentieth century, the grading of theft offenses by value had become more complex. There would be not only "grand" and "petty" larceny, but ladders of value with three or more rungs, for example, at $100, $500, $5,000, and $100,000. Petty-value grading might be denied in the case of particular classes of property, the misappropriation of which was especially to be discouraged. Examples are guns, drugs, public records, vehicles, mail, and keys. Similarly, legislative downgrading based on low value might be denied because of aggravating circumstances, such as theft of public property by a civil servant, theft by means of certain threats, or theft of property by one to whom it was entrusted in a fiduciary capacity. Of special interest is the development of statutes dealing uniquely with shoplifting, or stealing merchandise from stores, carrying very low maximum sentences. It seems strange that merchants would seek legislation reducing the penalties for stealing their goods. They recognized, however, that lower penalties, which can be imposed in less formal proceedings before magistrates, would be a more effective deterrent than cumbersome prosecution for conventional larceny.

Apart from different maxima corresponding to amounts stolen, there were differences depending on the manner in which the theft was effectuated. The historic evolution of theft legislation had the consequence that every time a legislature added a new category of theft, such as embezzlement or false pretense, it made a contemporary judgment of the appropriate maximum for that "new" offense without aligning that maximum with older, more rigorous sanctions applicable to larceny. After the consolidation of theft offenses, discussed below, these differences tended to disappear, leaving only traces in the value-grading where certain betrayals of trust, such as embezzlement, may carry higher legislative maxima than a corresponding larceny.

Modern criminal law reform projects lay the basis for some retreat from the effort to grade theft and other offenses too complexly. The sentencing schemes of such reforms include provision for "sentencing commissions" to formulate "guidelines" for judicial sentences. Guideline sentences would be based on a scoring system in which many separate features of the offense and the offender would be rated. Such a system would facilitate a rational integration of such diverse factors as value of the property, nature of the property, breach of fiduciary relationship, use of force or threat, youth of the offender, mental condition of the offender, prior record, and the offender's way of life insofar as it is crime-dependent. These reforms seem to hold promise of greater consistency of sentence and more flexible adaptation to changing community attitudes and needs.

The Commentary to the Model Penal Code §223.1 (Official Draft and Revised Comments 1980), explains the purpose behind the latest stage in the development of theft law: the consolidation of theft offenses:

. . . If history were the whole explanation of the existence of distinctive theft crimes, there would be little reason to preserve differentiations whose subtleties have occasioned serious procedural difficulties. The problem is not so simple. History has its own logic. The criminal law reached larceny first and embezzlement later because of real distinctions between theft by a stranger and the peculations of a trusted agent. If the move to punish embezzlement was a natural one, it was nevertheless a momentous step when the exceptional liability of servants for stealing from their masters was generalized into fraudulent conversion by anyone who had goods of another in his possession. The ordinary trespass-theft was committed by a stranger, an intruder with no semblance of right even to touch the object taken. The offender was easily recognized by the very taking, surreptitious or forceful, and so set apart from the law-abiding community. No bond of association in joint endeavor linked criminal and victim. In contrast, the embezzler stands always in a lawful as well as in an unlawful relation to the victim and the property. He is respectable; indeed, some tend to identify with him rather than with the bank or insurance company from which he embezzles. The line between lawful and unlawful activity is for the embezzler a question of the scope of his authority, which may be ill-defined. Not every deviation from the authority conferred will be civilly actionable, much less a basis for criminal liability. Sometimes the scope of the authority may be so broad, e.g., as in the case of a revocable inter-vivos trust where the grantor is trustee, as to be hardly distinguishable from ownership. The agent or bailee may actually be part of a co-proprietorship, being entitled to a commission or satisfaction of a lien out of funds in his hands. A man who is psychologically the absolute "owner" may be in the legal position of a bailee with extremely circumscribed freedom to deal with the property, as a result of modern methods of selling consumer goods on credit arrangements involving retention of title by the seller.

The embezzlement problem is complicated further by the necessity of distinguishing between defalcation by one who has "property of another" and failure of a debtor to pay his debts. Modern society is opposed to imprisonment for debt, however committed it may be to punishment for betrayal of trust. Yet when property is entrusted to a dealer for sale, with the expectation that he will receive the proceeds, deduct his commission, and remit the balance, the dealer's criminal liability if he fails to remit may turn on refinements of the civil law of contracts, agency, sales, or trusts. Such refinements, designed to allocate financial risks or to determine priorities among creditors of an insolvent, are hardly a relevant index to the harm done the owner or to the character of the defaulting dealer and thus may be entirely inappropriate as a measure of criminal liability.

It may nevertheless be true that theft by a stranger and a suitably delimited offense of theft by a fiduciary represent similar dangers requiring approximately the same treatment and characterization. Similarly, while there are significant differences between a larcenous taking and a cheat or swindle, it also may be that for the purposes of a legislative classification of offenses these alternative techniques for pursuit of unlawful gain may be advantageously fitted into a single category. Prevailing moral standards do not differentiate sharply between the swindler and other "thieves." To that extent, at least, consolidation conforms to the common understanding of what is substantially the same kind of undesirable conduct. Consolidation also has advantages in the administration of the criminal law if it eliminates procedural problems arising from nice distinctions between closely related types of misbehavior. Differences in the treatment of thieves can be determined on an individual basis by taking into account many factors which are at least as significant as whether fraud or stealth was the means employed to deprive another of his property.

Nevertheless, consolidation cannot eliminate the necessity for careful drafting, nor can it avoid the necessity for a properly specific delineation of the various types of property deprivations that should be punished by the criminal law. In relation to taking by stealth, there are difficulties in identifying the degree of control which the thief must achieve, and care must be taken to exclude from liability a mere unconsented occupation of another's property or an infringement of his patent. With respect to fraud or extortion, the criminal law still must define carefully what constitutes the "deception" or "coercion" that may safely be penalized. Moreover, consolidation cannot be regarded, as has sometimes been supposed, as a solution for shortcomings in the definition of any branch of theft. For example, a rule that a false promise is not a criminal false pretense will not be changed merely by consolidating false pretenses with larceny. The common law developed elaborate distinctions with respect to the role that a false promise could play in the law of theft. In cases where the actor secured temporary possession of a chattel by a false promise, it was said to be larceny by trick if he subsequently converted the property to his own permanent use. By fiction, the law was prepared in this case to regard the offense as one that was committed against the possession of the owner, as was required for larceny. In cases where the actor secured full ownership rather than temporary custody, however, the offense-category was shifted from larceny to false pretenses, and it was established that a false promise would not suffice for liability. Experience in New York establishes the point that mere consolidation of larceny, embezzlement, and false pretenses into a single crime called larceny did not result in the elimination of this anomalous distinction from the law.

The purpose of consolidation, therefore, is not to avoid the need to confront substantive difficulties in the definition of theft offenses. The appropriate objective is to avoid procedural problems. Even a consolidated offense, as reflected in Sections 223.2 to 223.8, will retain distinctions among methods of acquisition and appropriation. The real problem arises from a defendant's claim that he did not misappropriate the property by the means alleged but in fact misappropriated the property by some other means and from the combination of such a claim with the procedural rule that a defendant who is charged with one offense cannot be convicted by proving another.

Examples come readily to mind where an unwary prosecutor might stumble in distinguishing larceny, false pretenses, extortion, and embezzlement. An offender who is prosecuted for fraud might escape by proving that the victim did not believe the representations made to him but was merely frightened by them.[1] Similarly, one who gives a bad check as a down payment on an automobile which is thereupon delivered to him on conditional sale may defeat criminal prosecution for obtaining by false pretenses by arguing that the vendor reserved title and that the vendee could therefore only be guilty of larceny, the offense against possession. The intricacies of distinguishing between stealing and receiving stolen goods and of the proper procedure for presenting these alternative views of the defendant's involvement may also lead to needless reversals of convictions.

These problems can be partially solved by more modern definitions of the offenses involved, though it will still be necessary to draw what will often be subtle distinctions. There remains a necessity for some device to prevent a charge based on one method of wrongfully obtaining property from being defeated by the defense that the property was acquired by a different wrongful method. While consolidation is not the only way to accomplish this objective, it does seem

1. In Norton v. United States, 92 F.2d 753 (9th Cir. 1937), the defendant was convicted under the mail-fraud statute of scheming to defraud Clark Gable by representing in letters to him that as a result of illicit relations with him she had given birth to a child for whom she sought support. The indictment charged that the representations were false in that no such relations had ever occurred and that Gable had not even been in England during the year in which they were alleged to have occurred. Conviction was reversed on the ground that although the scheme employed a false pretense, and although no threat to make the charge public was involved, the method employed was a resort to coercion or fear rather than trickery or deception. Cf. Fasulo v. United States, 272 U.S. 620 (1926) (coercion is not a scheme to defraud within the federal mail-fraud statute); Huff v. United States, 301 F.2d 760 (5th Cir.), cert. denied, 371 U.S. 922 (1962) (scheme involving trickery is within wire-fraud statute although coercion is employed to secure the property).

the most effective way. This judgment is confirmed by the extent to which consolidation has been accepted in recent legislation dealing with theft.

During the period when the Model Code was being drafted, there were a few states that had adopted consolidations embracing larceny, embezzlement, and false pretenses but not extortion. There are at least 30 states, however, that have adopted comprehensive consolidation provisions since the publication in 1962 of the Proposed Official Draft of the Model Code. In addition, proposed legislation embracing the more complete consolidation has been drafted in at least eight states and at the federal level. . . .

Implementing Consolidation. Article 223 recognizes the substantive problems inherent in the different forms of theft by dealing in Sections 223.2 through 223.8 with different methods of acquisitive behavior. Section 223.1(1), however, creates the single offense of "theft" which is committed by violation of any one of the succeeding sections. It was specifically stated in the text of Subsection (1) as published in the Proposed Official Draft of the Model Code, that the consolidated offense was designed to embrace the offenses that were "heretofore known as larceny, embezzlement, false pretense, extortion, blackmail, fraudulent conversion, receiving stolen property, and the like." This language has been omitted so as not to suggest that the common-law content of these offenses is meant to be carried forward. The omission is not intended to change the basic objective of the consolidation—namely, to subsume various forms of acquisitive behavior into a single theft offense and to redefine the scope of conduct that was formerly treated in the separate categories mentioned above.

The second sentence of Subsection (1) provides that an accusation of theft may be supported by evidence that it was committed in any manner that would be theft under Article 223, even though a different manner was specified in the indictment or information. The defendant is thus foreclosed from defending on the basis that his conduct was not larceny as charged but extortion. These offenses are abolished as separate categories of crime and are to be charged as the single theft offense created by this article.

There is, however, the problem of fair notice to the defendant. In general, the Model Code does not deal with the degree of specificity that an indictment or information must contain but reflects the view that the matter is one of procedure beyond the scope of the penal code itself. On the other hand, account must be taken of the possibility that too great a variance between charge and proof may render an indictment or information insufficient to apprise the defendant of the case he must meet. Accordingly, the last clause of Subsection (1) refers to the inherent power of the court to ensure a fair trial by granting a continuance or other appropriate relief where the conduct of the defense would be prejudiced by lack of fair notice or by surprise.

The problem of lack of fair notice in an indictment or information is not, of course, unique to charges of theft. If overly specific charging is required, technical defenses based on inevitable minor variances can be made to a charge of any type of offense. It should be noted here, however, that the success of the effort to consolidate the various forms of theft into a single offense is limited by the extent to which highly detailed charging is perceived to be mandated by constitutional limitations or the fair notice requirement. It is the premise of Subsection (1) that postcharge relief should in most cases suffice to fill in the details of an accusation of theft that the defendant must know in order to meet the case against him.

Such relief can come in the form of a bill of particulars or other specification of information following the formal charge or in the form of a continuance of the trial to allow additional time for preparation. If recharging is consistently required, the advantages of consolidation will be significantly impaired.

B. EXTORTION

PEOPLE v. DIOGUARDI

Court of Appeals of New York
8 N.Y.2d 260, 203 N.Y.S.2d 870 (1960)

FROESSEL, Judge.

The Appellate Division has reversed defendants' convictions for extortion and conspiracy to commit extortion, dismissed the indictment and discharged them from custody. In addition to the conspiracy count, the indictment charged defendants with extorting $4,700 from the officers of two corporations. Said corporations were nonunion, conducted a wholesale stationery and office supply business in Manhattan, did an annual business of several million dollars, and their stock was wholly owned by a family named Kerin. Anthony Kerin, Sr., president and "boss" of the Kerin companies, made all the important corporate policy decisions. The other two corporate officers were his son Kerin, Jr., and one Jack Shumann.

Defendant McNamara, the alleged "front man" in the extorsive scheme, was an official of Teamster Local 295 and 808, as well as a member of the Teamsters Joint Council. Defendant Dioguardi, the immediate beneficiary of the payments and the alleged power behind the scene, was sole officer of Equitable Research Associates, Inc.—a *publishing house,* according to its certificate of incorporation, a *public relations concern,* according to its bank account and the Yellow Pages of the telephone directory, a *labor statistics concern,* according to its office secretary and sole employee, and a *firm of labor consultants,* according to its business card and alternate listing in the aforesaid directory. . . .

Between November, 1955 and mid-January, 1956, the Kerin companies were confronted with organizational activities on the part of four unions. A CIO local first contacted management by letter. Two visiting representatives from Teamster Local 210 then threatened to organize the companies by "putting pickets out" and "stopping shipments" if management did not agree to organize the employees on behalf of their local. Some six weeks later a picket appeared at the delivery and shipping entrance in the rear of the Kerin premises, carrying a placard reciting that one of the Kerin companies was unfair to members of Teamster Local 138. No representative from that local ever contacted management, and all its officials testified that they had not authorized a picket line at the premises.

Finally, during the week in which the picket was parading at the rear, two organizers from Local 1601 of the Retail Clerks International Association appeared in the front lobby distributing literature to the companies' employees. . . .

The appearance of the picket line—which truck drivers from two companies refused to cross—thoroughly alarmed the Kerin officers, since they were in an "extremely competitive business," and a cessation of incoming or outgoing truck deliveries for as short a period as two weeks would effectively force them out of business. Their attorney, William Coogan, advised them that filing a petition with the National Labor Relations Board (NLRB) for an election among the competing unions would not constitute a solution, since such proceeding might take anywhere from two weeks to three months, and peaceful picketing could not be enjoined before, during, or even after the election. He felt that a *consent* election was the best way to settle the matter, and informed them that he might be able to meet with a prominent teamster official on a higher level, who would call a halt to the "ridiculous" situation of two teamster locals competing with each other.

Coogan had previously been in touch with his brother-in-law, William White, a labor law professor who had met McNamara socially and, after the Kerin management agreed, White contacted McNamara and arranged a meeting with him and Coogan. At the meeting, McNamara was generally discouraging as to the feasibility of a consent election. However, after joining Coogan in a men's room, McNamara suggested privately "that something might be done, but that it would be expensive . . . it could run five to ten thousand dollars." After Coogan vetoed that possibility, and McNamara made several phone calls, the three adjourned to a Chinese restaurant recommended by McNamara for dinner, during the course of which one Milton Holt approached the table and was introduced by McNamara as an attorney, although, in fact, he was an officer of Teamster Local 805 and not a member of the Bar. After Holt was apprised of the labor difficulties confronting the Kerin companies, McNamara stated: "This looks to me to be the kind of a situation which Equitable can help out," to which Holt nodded an affirmative. Neither White nor Coogan had ever heard of Equitable before that day, and they neither sought nor received enlightenment.

The following morning Coogan reported to the Kerin officers that he had had "a very rough evening" with McNamara—whom he described as a "tough-talking man" who "was obviously a high official in the labor movement," "had a grasp of the whole situation," and "knew what was going on"—and that "the gist of the conversation was that . . . for a payment of ten thousand, the whole matter could be settled, and settled almost immediately." . . .

On Friday afternoon, January 20, 1956, McNamara, accompanied by Holt—whom he again introduced as his attorney—met with the three Kerin officers in a private diningroom at the Manhattan Club. Holt soon suggested that Kerin, Sr., and McNamara "step outside and have a chat" and, after adjourning to another room, McNamara assured Kerin, Sr., that his troubles could be ended, and *would be,* if he did three things: (1) "joined up" with McNamara's local 295, (2) paid $3,500 to Equitable to defray the "out-of-pocket" expenses incurred by the various unions that had sought to organize the companies, and (3) retained Equitable as labor consultant at $100 per month for each company for the period of the collective bargaining contract to be signed with Local 295, for which the companies "would get counsel and advice . . . in any matter that was pertinent or related to labor or labor relationships." McNamara repeatedly assured Kerin, Sr., that the picketing would stop immediately and the companies would be guaranteed labor peace if his program were accepted.

Kerin, Sr., stated that he was not adverse to having his employees organized by Local 295, if it was a good honest union, and that he could "accept the idea of a hundred dollars a month as a retainer fee for labor counsel and advice." He protested against the proposed payment of $3,500, however, as an "extraordinary charge" that sounded "like a hold-up," to which McNamara replied: " 'It may seem that way to you, Mr. Kerin, but that is the amount of money that these unions that have sought to organize you . . . have expended, and *if we are going to avoid further trouble and further difficulties, it is my suggestion that you pay that to the Equitable Associates. If you don't pay it, we can't go through with the program.'* That was either said or implied, . . . I better withdraw that. *That was the point.*" (Emphasis supplied.) Kerin, Sr., finally agreed, after insisting upon a written contract with Equitable and payment by check. Upon returning to the rest of the group, he advised his son and Shumann of the terms of McNamara's program. He emphasized that the payments to Equitable were necessary "in order to get rid of [the] picket," who "was going to be removed immediately," and that McNamara has assured him "that our troubles and difficulties would be at an end" and that "we would be guaranteed labor peace for the term of the contract." Kerin, Jr., and Shumann assented to the program. . . .

. . . The Kerin companies continued to pay Equitable $200 a month until July, 1956, when they were instructed by the District Attorney's office to discontinue the payments. A total of $4,700 had been paid to Equitable, which was the amount defendants were charged in the indictment with extorting. In August, 1957, pursuant to a petition filed by a Kerin employee and following an election conducted by the NLRB, Local 295 was "deauthorized" as bargaining agent for the Kerin employees.

Upon the proof in this record, a jury could properly conclude that defendants were guilty of extortion—cleverly conceived and subtly executed, but extortion nonetheless. The essence of the crime is obtaining property by a wrongful use of fear, induced by a threat to do an unlawful injury (Penal Law, Consol. Laws, c.40, §§850, 851). It is well-settled law in this State that fear of *economic loss or harm* satisfies the ingredient of fear necessary to the crime.

Moreover, it is not essential that a defendant *create* the fear existing in the mind of his prospective victim so long as he succeeds in persuading him that he possesses the power to remove or continue its cause, and instills a new fear by threatening to misuse that power as a device to exact tribute. Our statute, as well as the Hobbs or Federal Anti-Racketeering Act (U.S. Code, tit. 18, §1951, subd. [b], par. [2]) which was patterned after it, talks in terms of a wrongful *use of* fear, and the ultimate issue " 'is not much the cause of the victim's fear, as it is whether or not defendants played upon that fear, in other words, made use of that fear to extort money or property' " (Callanan v. United States, 8 Cir., 223 F.2d 171, 174, supra).

The Kerin management unmistakably feared that the continued existence of the picket line and the perpetuation of the ostensible organizational struggle between competing locals would put their companies out of business. The failure to establish that this fear was *initially* induced by or attributable to either defendant, or someone acting in concert with them, is not determinative, so long as there was proof that defendants "seized upon the opportunity presented by" that fear "to line their own pockets by implanting in the minds of the company officials the idea that unless and until the tribute demanded was paid the defendants," the picketing and labor war would continue. . . .

As to the element of a *threat,* the crux of defendant's position is that McNamara was under no duty to intervene to alter the existing situation, and a threat to do nothing to aid the Kerin management if they did not assent to the terms of his proposal is not tantamount to a threat to do an unlawful injury within the contemplation of the statute. However, section 858 of the Penal Law expressly makes it "immaterial" to the crime of extortion "whether a threat . . . is of things to be done *or omitted* by the offendor, or by any other person" (emphasis supplied), and we long ago held: "No precise words are needed to convey a threat. *It may be done by innuendo or suggestion.* To ascertain whether a letter [or oral proposal] conveys a threat, all its language, together with the circumstances under which it was written [or spoken], and the relations between the parties may be considered, and if it can be found that *the purport and natural effect* of the letter [or oral proposal] is to convey a threat, then the mere form of words is unimportant." People v. Thompson, 97 N.Y. 313, 318. (Emphasis supplied). If McNamara, acting for himself and Dioguardi's alter ego, Equitable, professed to have control over the labor problems besetting the Kerin companies, i.e., if he instilled the belief in the minds of the Kerin officers that the continuance or discontinuance of the picket line and the labor war rested with him and Equitable, and he demanded tribute for the exercise of that control, then he effectively conveyed a threat to do an unlawful injury, and he and those acting in concert with him could properly be convicted of extortion.

Local 210, which threatened to organize the Kerin companies by picket lines if necessary, and Local 138, which ostensibly commenced the potentially ruinous picket line, were both teamster unions and from the beginning McNamara was pictured to Coogan, and, in turn, to the Kerin management, as a powerful and high-ranking figure in the teamster organization. McNamara effectively heightened this image by displaying to Coogan a familiarity with the labor difficulties faced by his client, and by suggesting that the matter could be "settled almost immediately" by the payment of as much as $10,000. He discouraged resort to a consent election, since Locals 210 and 138 were "old-line unions" who would press their organizational efforts to the utmost, and not willingly forgo their investment in organizational expenses. He further darkened the picture by informing Coogan that it was "entirely probable" that other unions would respect the organizational picket line, and there was no "real hope" that even partial deliveries would continue. There is also evidence that McNamara left Coogan with the impression—thereafter conveyed to the Kerin officers—that he had the power to intensify the picket line by having the Joint Council issue orders to all teamster locals to make the picket line 100 percent effective, with the necessary result of putting the Kerin companies out of business.

It seems clear, at all events, that the "furious" Kerin, Sr., as well as the other officers, agreed to meet with McNamara because they believed he possessed the power to cure the labor situation which threatened their business with potential ruin. During the private chat suggested by the bogus attorney Holt, McNamara confidently assured Kerin, Sr., that his troubles not merely "could be ended" but "would be ended" if his (McNamara's) package deal were accepted. McNamara flatly stated that the picket "would be out of there by Monday morning" and, if any other union attempted to organize, "all we had to do was tell them that we were members of his local, and that that should be enough for them, and advise the Equitable Research Associates of our problem." All the Kerin officers testified, in substance, that McNamara induced them to believe that they would be guaranteed labor peace if they made the suggested payments. . . .

. . . The picketing here . . . may have been perfectly lawful in its inception (assuming it was part of a bona fide organizational effort) and may have remained so—despite its potentially ruinous effect on the employer's business—so long as it was employed to accomplish the legitimate labor objective of organization. Its entire character changed from legality to criminality, however, when it was used as a pressure device to exact the payment of money as a condition of its cessation (see People v. Hughes, 137 N.Y. 29, 39, 32 N.E. 1105, 1107). The fact that McNamara, unlike Weinseimer [see below], was not an official of the particular local engaging in the injurious activity is immaterial, so long as he and Equitable professed to have power to eliminate or continue it, and used that purported power as a lever to exact tribute. Although McNamara "did not *expressly* represent that he controlled" the picket and Kerin, Sr., "did not *expressly* testify that he believed that the defendant would keep the [picket line going] unless his demands were acceded to," the evidence "fairly warranted the jury in finding those facts" (People v. Weinseimer, 117 App. Div. 603, 614, 102 N.Y.S. 579, 587, supra). While he "did not expressly threaten [management] that he would do anything himself," McNamara "asserted himself to be in such a relation to the [picket] . . . as to control [its] movements" (People v. Barondess, 61 Hun 571, 579, 584, 16

N.Y.S. 436, 443, supra), and instilled the belief that the picketing would continue unless his monetary demands were met. The power to remove a picket clearly implies the power to maintain it. The jury could properly infer that the substance of McNamara's proposal was: "You have got to pay Equitable $3,500 down and $200 a month to have the picket removed and labor peace guaranteed." . . .

Moreover, in the present case, we have not only "the pretense of control," but clear evidence of *actual* control. On the business day next following the Manhattan Club meeting, *before any money was paid* and before any written contract with Equitable had been signed by management, no picket or organizer appeared at the Kerin premises. McNamara promptly reminded management to notice "you have no more picket," and, so long as the monthly payments to Equitable continued, labor peace ensued. Any doubt concerning the "control" flavor of the entire transaction seems dissipated by the necessity of $200 monthly payments to the labor consultant who never advised and was never consulted. As the People contend, the jury could reasonably infer that the Kerin companies continued to make these payments "because of a plain implication that [Equitable's] demonstrated influence and control could and doubtless would be exerted to restore and even intensify the labor predicament just as readily as it could be and was employed to terminate it." . . .

The orders appealed from should be reversed, the indictments reinstated, and a new trial ordered.

Notes and Questions

1. The court makes much of the fact that the defendants claimed to be able to remove the picket line and were able to do so. Why is this relevant? The court also implies that there was no proof that the picket line was initiated by the defendants or by a confederate of theirs. If so, what distinguishes the defendants' conduct from normal fee-for-service negotiations? Is the conduct in this case different from that of a doctor who threatens to let a patient die unless the patient pays the doctor a fee? Isn't there a difference between a threat to commit an injurious act and a threat not to come to another's aid?

2. Should it matter that the complainants approached the defendants first and requested their aid in ending the picket line?

3. *Common law and statutory extortion.* At common law, extortion was the corrupt collection of an unlawful payment by an official under color of office. Neither threat nor coercion was an element of the offense. United States v. Williams, 621 F.2d 123, 124 (5th Cir. 1980). Statutory extortion, also sometimes referred to as blackmail, is a broader offense. A person is guilty of statutory extortion if she obtains, or attempts to obtain, the property of another by means of a threat.

4. *Nature of the threat.* The act threatened by the extortionist need not itself be illegal. Indeed, the actor may be privileged or even required to perform the

threatened act. For example, a police officer is guilty of extortion if he threatens to arrest a person whom he has caught committing a crime unless that person pays $100 to the officer. Nor need the threat involve a commission by the actor; as *Dioguardi* demonstrates, omissions and refusals to act are also included.

The wide scope of actionable threats under the extortion statutes creates a number of potential problems in distinguishing extortion from tolerable, or even desirable, behavior. A merchant who is unable to collect a debt owed by a customer should, for example, be allowed to threaten suit if payment is not made, even though the suit would tend to impair the credit of the customer. Extortion statutes like the one in the Model Penal Code eliminate many of these difficulties by creating an affirmative defense where the defendant "honestly" claims the property sought as restitution for harm done "in the circumstances to which such accusation, exposure, lawsuit or other official action relates." Thus, an employer who discovers that one of his employees has been stealing from him is not guilty of extortion for threatening to bring theft charges unless the employee pays restitution. State v. Burns, 161 Wash. 362, 297 P. 212 (1931). However, if the employer demands an amount greater than that stolen by the employee, he may be guilty of extortion. People v. Fichtner, 281 App. Div. 159, 118 N.Y.S.2d 392 (1952). Nonetheless, distinguishing extortion from lawful, consensual exchanges can sometimes be difficult, particularly when the threatened act is not in itself unlawful.

5. *Threats to reveal secrets.* The defendant in State v. Harrington, 128 Vt. 242, 260 A.2d 692 (1969), was convicted for extortion because he had threatened to use incriminating photos in a divorce action. Harrington had obtained the photos on behalf of his client, Mrs. Morin, who wished to divorce her husband. Harrington hired a woman, Mrs. Mazza, who was instructed to make herself " 'receptive and available' but not aggressive" to the advances of Mr. Morin. Harrington and his associates were subsequently able to take several photographs of Mr. Morin and Mrs. Mazza undressed and in bed. Harrington then contacted Mr. Morin and informed him that Mrs. Morin desired a divorce and $175,000 in alimony. In return, she would relinquish all her other marital rights. Mr. Morin was told that if he did not consent to these terms, Mrs. Morin would sue him for divorce on grounds of adultery, and introduce the photos as evidence. In upholding Harrington's conviction, the court emphasized that the incriminating evidence was "wilfully contrived and procured." Should this be relevant? What purpose is served by punishing as extortion threats to reveal essentially accurate information of wrongdoing? For an argument that such threats constitute a desirable sanction against misconduct, see Stigler, An Introduction to Privacy in Economics and Politics, 9 J. Legal Studies 623, 643-644 (1980).

20

RAPE AND KIDNAPPING

A. RAPE

MODEL PENAL CODE

American Law Institute, Model Penal Code and Commentaries (1985)

§213.1 . . . Rape. . . .

Force and resistance. The central element in the definition of rape is the absence of the female's consent. Current statutes invariably make force or the threat of force an element of the crime. To prove that force was used and that she did not consent, the alleged victim, or "prosecutrix," traditionally had to show that she resisted her attacker. For centuries, courts required that "the female must resist to the utmost of her ability, and such resistance must continue till the offense is complete" Reidhead v. State, 31 Ariz. 70, 72, 250 P. 366, 367 (1926). More recently, many courts have begun to recognize that such resistance can be futile as well as dangerous for the female, and in any event may have little to do with proving that she did not consent to intercourse. Determining how much resistance the woman must offer presents both substantive and evidentiary questions.

STATE v. RUSK

Court of Appeals of Maryland
289 Md. 230, 424 A.2d 720 (1981)

Murphy, Chief Judge.

Edward Rusk was found guilty by a jury in the Criminal Court of Baltimore (Karwacki, J. presiding) of second degree rape in violation of Maryland Code (1957, 1976 Repl. Vol., 1980 Cum. Supp.), Art. 27, §463(a)(1), which provides in pertinent part:

> A person is guilty of rape in the second degree if the person engages in vaginal intercourse with another person:
>
> (1) By force or threat of force against the will and without the consent of the other person; . . .

On appeal, the Court of Special Appeals, sitting en banc, reversed the conviction; it concluded by an 8-5 majority that in view of the prevailing law as set forth in Hazel v. State, 221 Md. 464, 157 A.2d 922 (1960), insufficient evidence of Rusk's guilt had been adduced at the trial to permit the case to go to the jury. Rusk v. State, 43 Md. App. 476, 406 A.2d 624 (1979). We granted certiorari to consider whether the Court of Special Appeals properly applied the principles of *Hazel* in determining that insufficient evidence had been produced to support Rusk's conviction.

At the trial, the 21-year-old prosecuting witness, Pat, testified that on the evening of September 21, 1977, she attended a high school alumnae meeting where she met a girl friend, Terry. After the meeting, Terry and Pat agreed to drive in their respective cars to Fells Point to have a few drinks. On the way, Pat stopped to telephone her mother, who was baby sitting for Pat's two-year-old son; she told her mother that she was going with Terry to Fells Point and would not be late in arriving home.

The women arrived in Fells Point about 9:45 P.M. They went to a bar where each had one drink. After staying approximately one hour, Pat and Terry walked several blocks to a second bar, where each of them had another drink. After about thirty minutes, they walked two blocks to a third bar known as E. J. Buggs. The bar was crowded and a band was playing in the back. Pat ordered another drink and as she and Terry were leaning against the wall, Rusk approached and said "hello" to Terry. Terry, who was then conversing with another individual, momentarily interrupted her conversation and said "Hi, Eddie." Rusk then began talking with Pat and during their conversation both of them acknowledged being separated from their respective spouses and having a child. Pat told Rusk that she had to go home because it was a week-night and she had to wake up with her baby early in the morning.

Rusk asked Pat the direction in which she was driving and after she responded, Rusk requested a ride to his apartment. Although Pat did not know Rusk, she thought that Terry knew him. She thereafter agreed to give him a ride. Pat cautioned Rusk on the way to the car that "I'm just giving a ride home, you know, as a friend, not anything to be, you know, thought of other than a ride"; and he said, "Oh, okay." They left the bar between 12:00 and 12:20 A.M.

Pat testified that on the way to Rusk's apartment, they continued the general conversation that they had started in the bar. After a twenty-minute drive, they arrived at Rusk's apartment in the 3100 block of Guilford Avenue. Pat testified that she was totally unfamiliar with the neighborhood. She parked the car at the curb on the opposite side of the street from Rusk's apartment but left the engine running. Rusk asked Pat to come in, but she refused. He invited her again, and she again declined. She told Rusk that she could not go into his apartment even if she wanted to because she was separated from her husband and a detective could be observing her movements. Pat said that Rusk was fully aware that she did not want to accompany him to his room. Notwithstanding her repeated refusals, Pat testified that Rusk reached over and turned off the ignition to her car and took her car keys. He got out of the car, walked over to her side, opened the door and said, "Now, will you come up?" Pat explained her subsequent actions:

> At that point, because I was scared, because he had my car keys. I didn't know what to do. I was someplace I didn't even know where I was. It was in the city. I didn't know whether to run. I really didn't think at that point, what to do.
>
> Now, I know that I should have blown the horn. I should have run. There were a million things I could have done. I was scared, at that point, and I didn't do any of them.

Pat testified that at this moment she feared that Rusk would rape her. She said: "[I]t was the way he looked at me, and said 'Come on up, come on up'; and when he took the keys, I knew that was wrong."

It was then about 1 A.M. Pat accompanied Rusk across the street into a totally dark house. She followed him up two flights of stairs. She neither saw nor heard anyone in the building. Once they ascended the stairs, Rusk unlocked the door to his one-room apartment, and turned on the light. According to Pat, he told her to sit down. She sat in a chair beside the bed. Rusk sat on the bed. After Rusk talked for a few minutes, he left the room for about one to five minutes. Pat remained seated in the chair. She made no noise and did not attempt to leave. She said that she did not notice a telephone in the room. When Rusk returned, he turned off the light and sat down on the bed. Pat asked if she could leave; she told him that she wanted to go home and "didn't want to come up." She said, "Now, [that] I came up, can I go?" Rusk, who was still in possession of her car keys, said he wanted her to stay.

Rusk then asked Pat to get on the bed with him. He pulled her by the arms to the bed and began to undress her, removing her blouse and bra. He unzipped her slacks and she took them off after he told her to do so. Pat removed the rest of her clothing, and then removed Rusk's pants because "he asked me to do it." After they were both undressed Rusk started kissing Pat as she was lying on her back. Pat explained what happened next:

> I was still begging him to please let, you know, let me leave. I said, "you can get a lot of other girls down there, for what you want," and he just kept saying, "no"; and then I was really scared, because I can't describe, you know, what was said. It was more the look in his eyes; and I said, at that point—I didn't know what to say; and I said, "If I do what you want, will you let me go without killing me?" Because I didn't know, at that point, what he was going to do; and I started to cry; and when I did, he put his hands on my throat, and

> started lightly to choke me; and I said, "If I do what you want, will you let me go?" And he said, yes, and at that time, I proceeded to do what he wanted me to.

Pat testified that Rusk made her perform oral sex and then vaginal intercourse.

Immediately after the intercourse, Pat asked if she could leave. She testified that Rusk said, "Yes," after which she got up and got dressed and Rusk returned her car keys. She said that Rusk then "walked me to my car, and asked if he could see me again; and I said, 'Yes;' and he asked me for my telephone number; and I said, 'No, I'll see you down Fells Point sometime,' just so I could leave." Pat testified that she "had no intention of meeting him again." She asked him for directions out of the neighborhood and left.

On her way home, Pat stopped at a gas station, went to the ladies room, and then drove "pretty much straight home and pulled up and parked the car." At first she was not going to say anything about the incident. She explained her initial reaction not to report the incident: "I didn't want to go through what I'm going through now [at the trial]." As she sat in her car reflecting on the incident, Pat said she began to "wonder what would happen if I hadn't of done what he wanted me to do. So I thought the right thing to do was to go report it, and I went from there to Hillendale to find a police car." She reported the incident to the police at about 3:15 A.M. Subsequently, Pat took the police to Rusk's apartment, which she located without any great difficulty.

Pat's girlfriend Terry corroborated her testimony concerning the events which occurred up to the time that Pat left the bar with Rusk. Questioned about Pat's alcohol consumption, Terry said she was drinking screwdrivers that night but normally did not finish a drink. Terry testified about her acquaintanceship with Rusk: "I knew his face, and his first name, but I honestly couldn't tell you—apparently I ran into him sometime before. I couldn't tell you how I know him. I don't know him very well at all."

Officer Hammett of the Baltimore City Police Department acknowledged receiving Pat's rape complaint at 3:15 A.M. on September 22, 1977. He accompanied her to the 3100 block of Guilford Avenue where it took Pat several minutes to locate Rusk's apartment. Officer Hammett entered Rusk's multi-dwelling apartment house, which contained at least six apartments, and arrested Rusk in a room on the second floor. . . .

At the close of the State's case-in-chief, Rusk moved for a judgment of acquittal. In denying the motion, the trial court said:

> There is evidence that there is a taking of automobile keys forcibly, a request that the prosecuting witness accompany the Defendant to the upstairs apartment. She described a look in his eye which put her in fear.
>
> Now, you are absolutely correct that there was no weapon, no physical threatening testified to. However, while she was seated on a chair next to the bed, the Defendant excused himself, and came back in five minutes; and then she testifies, he pulled her on to the bed by reaching over and grabbing her wrists, and/or had her or requested, that she disrobe, and assist him in disrobing.

> Again, she said she was scared, and then she testified to something to the effect that she said to him, she was begging him to let her leave. She was scared. She started to cry. He started to strangle her softly she said. She asked the Defendant, that if she'd submit, would he not kill her, at which point he indicated that he would not; and she performed oral sex on him, and then had intercourse." . . .

Rusk, the 31-year-old defendant, testified that he was in the Buggs Tavern for about thirty minutes when he noticed Pat standing at the bar. Rusk said: "She looked at me, and she smiled. I walked over and said, hi, and started talking to her." He did not remember either knowing or speaking to Terry. When Pat mentioned that she was about to leave, Rusk asked her if she wanted to go home with him. In response, Pat said that she would like to, but could not because she had her car. Rusk then suggested that they take her car. Pat agreed and they left the bar arm-in-arm.

Rusk testified that during the drive to her apartment, he discussed with Pat their similar marital situations and talked about their children. He said that Pat asked him if he was going to rape her. When he inquired why she was asking, Pat said that she had been raped once before. Rusk expressed his sympathy for her. Pat then asked him if he planned to beat her. He inquired why she was asking and Pat explained that her husband used to beat her. Rusk again expressed his sympathy. He testified that at no time did Pat express a fear that she was being followed by her separated husband.

According to Rusk, when they arrived in front of his apartment Pat parked the car and turned the engine off. They sat for several minutes "petting each other." Rusk denied switching off the ignition and removing the keys. He said that they walked to the apartment house and proceeded up the stairs to his room. Rusk testified that Pat came willingly to his room and that at no time did he make threatening facial expressions. Once inside his room, Rusk left Pat alone for several minutes while he used the bathroom down the hall. Upon his return, he switched the light on but immediately turned it off because Pat, who was seated in the dark in a chair next to the bed, complained it was too bright. Rusk said that he sat on the bed across from Pat and reached out

> and started to put my arms around her, and started kissing her; and we fell back into the bed, and she—we were petting, kissing, and she stuck her hand down in my pants and started playing with me; and I undid her blouse, and took off her bra; and then I sat up and I said "Let's take our clothes off"; and she said, "Okay"; and I took my clothes off, and she took her clothes off; and then we proceeded to have intercourse.

Rusk explained that after the intercourse, Pat "got uptight."

> Well, she started to cry. She said that—she said, "You guys are all alike," she says, "just out for," you know, "one thing."

> She started talking about—I don't know, she was crying and all. I tried to calm her down and all; and I said, "What's the matter?" And she said, that she just wanted to leave; and I said, "Well, okay"; and she walked out to the car. I walked out to the car. She got in the car and left.

Rusk denied placing his hands on Pat's throat or attempting to strangle her. He also denied using force or threats of force to get Pat to have intercourse with him.

In reversing Rusk's second degree rape conviction, the Court of Special Appeals, quoting from *Hazel,* 221 Md. at 469, 157 A.2d 922, noted that:

> Force is an essential element of the crime [of rape] and to justify a conviction, the evidence must warrant a conclusion either that the victim resisted and her resistance was overcome by force or that she was prevented from resisting by threats to her safety.

Writing for the majority, Judge Thompson said:

> In all of the victim's testimony we have been unable to see any resistance on her part to the sex acts and certainly can we see no fear as would overcome her attempt to resist or escape as required by *Hazel.* Possession of the keys by the accused may have deterred her vehicular escape but hardly a departure seeking help in the rooming house or in the street. We must say that "the way he looked" fails utterly to support the fear required by *Hazel.* 43 Md. App. at 480, 406 A.2d 624.

The Court of Special Appeals interpreted *Hazel* as requiring a showing of a reasonable apprehension of fear in instances where the prosecutrix did not resist. It concluded:

> [W]e find the evidence legally insufficient to warrant a conclusion that appellant's words or actions created in the mind of the victim a reasonable fear that if she resisted, he would have harmed her, or that faced with such resistance, he would have used force to overcome it. The prosecutrix stated that she was afraid, and submitted because of "the look in his eyes." After both were undressed and in the bed, and she pleaded to him that she wanted to leave, he started to lightly choke her. At oral argument it was brought out that the "lightly choking" could have been a heavy caress. We do not believe that "lightly choking" along with all the facts and circumstances in the case, were sufficient to cause a reasonable fear which overcame her ability to resist. In the absence of any other evidence showing force used by appellant, we find that the evidence was insufficient to convict appellant of rape." Id. at 484, 406 A.2d 624.

In argument before us on the merits of the case, the parties agreed that the issue was whether, in light of the principles of *Hazel,* there was evidence before the jury legally sufficient to prove beyond a reasonable doubt that the intercourse was "[b]y force or threat of force against the will and without the consent" of the victim in violation of Art. 27, §463(a)(1). . . .

The vaginal intercourse once being established, the remaining elements of rape in the second degree under §463(a)(1) are, as in a prosecution for common law rape (1) force—actual or constructive, and (2) lack of consent. The terms in §463(a)(1)—"force," "threat of force," "against the will" and "without the consent"—are not defined in the statute, but are to be afforded their "judicially determined meaning" as applied in cases involving common law rape. In this regard, it is well settled that the terms "against the will" and "without the consent" are synonymous in the law of rape.

Hazel, which was decided in 1960, long before the enactment of §463(a)(1), involved a prosecution for common law rape, there defined as "the act of a man having unlawful carnal knowledge of a female over the age of ten years by force without the consent and against the will of the victim." 221 Md. at 468-469, 157 A.2d 922. . . . It recognized that force and lack of consent are distinct elements of the crime of rape. It said:

> Force is an essential element of the crime and to justify a conviction, the evidence must warrant a conclusion either that the victim resisted and her resistance was overcome by force or that she was prevented from resisting by threats to her safety. But no particular amount of force, either actual or constructive, is required to constitute rape. Necessarily, that fact must depend upon the prevailing circumstances. As in this case force may exist without violence. If the acts and threats of the defendant were reasonably calculated to create in the mind of the victim—having regard to the circumstances in which she was placed—a real apprehension, due to fear, of imminent bodily harm, serious enough to impair or overcome her will to resist, then such acts and threats are the equivalent of force. Id. at 469, 157 A.2d 922.

As to the element of lack of consent, the Court said in *Hazel*:

> [I]t is true, of course, that however reluctantly given, consent to the act at any time prior to penetration deprives the subsequent intercourse of its criminal character. There is, however, a wide difference between consent and a submission to the act. Consent may involve submission, but submission does not necessarily imply consent. Furthermore, submission to a compelling force, or as a result of being put in fear, is not consent. Id.

The Court noted that lack of consent is generally established through proof of resistance or by proof that the victim failed to resist because of fear. The degree of fear necessary to obviate the need to prove resistance, and thereby establish lack of consent, was defined in the following manner:

> The kind of fear which would render resistance by a woman unnecessary to support a conviction of rape includes, but is not necessarily limited to, a fear of death or serious bodily harm, or a fear so extreme as to preclude resistance, or a fear which would well nigh render her mind incapable of continuing to resist, or

a fear that so overpowers her that she does not dare resist. Id. at 470, 157 A.2d 922.

Hazel thus made it clear that lack of consent could be established through proof that the victim submitted as a result of fear of imminent death or serious bodily harm. In addition, if the actions and conduct of the defendant were reasonably calculated to induce this fear in the victim's mind, then the element of force is present. *Hazel* recognized, therefore, that the same kind of evidence may be used in establishing both force and non-consent, particularly when a threat rather than actual force is involved.

The Court noted in *Hazel* that the judges who heard the evidence, and who sat as the trier of fact in Hazel's non-jury case, had concluded that, in light of the defendant's acts of violence and threats of serious harm, there existed a genuine and continuing fear of such harm on the victim's part, so that the ensuing act of sexual intercourse under this fear "amounted to a felonious and forcible act of the defendant against the will and consent of the prosecuting witness." In finding the evidence sufficient to sustain the conviction, the Court observed that "[t]he issue of whether the intercourse was accomplished by force and against the will and consent of the victim was one of credibility, properly to be resolved by the trial court." 221 Md. at 470, 157 A.2d 922.

Hazel did not expressly determine whether the victim's fear must be "reasonable." Its only reference to reasonableness related to whether "the acts and threats of the defendant were reasonably calculated to create in the mind of the victim . . . a real apprehension, due to fear, of imminent bodily harm. . . ." 221 Md. at 469, 157 A.2d 922. Manifestly, the Court was there referring to the calculations of the accused, not to the fear of the victim. While *Hazel* made it clear that the victim's fear had to be genuine, it did not pass upon whether a real but unreasonable fear of imminent death or serious bodily harm would suffice. The vast majority of jurisdictions have required that the victim's fear be reasonably grounded in order to obviate the need for either proof of actual

force on the part of the assailant or physical resistance on the part of the victim. We think that, generally, this is the correct standard.

As earlier indicated, the Court of Special Appeals held that a showing of a reasonable apprehension of fear was essential under *Hazel* to establish the elements of the offense where the victim did not resist. The Court did not believe, however, that the evidence was legally sufficient to demonstrate the existence of "a reasonable fear" which overcame Pat's ability to resist. In support of the Court's conclusion, Rusk maintains that the evidence showed that Pat voluntarily entered his apartment without being subjected to a "single threat nor a scintilla of force"; that she made no effort to run away nor did she scream for help; that she never exhibited a will to resist; and that her subjective reaction of fear to the situation in which she had voluntarily placed herself was unreasonable and exaggerated. Rusk claims that his acts were not reasonably calculated to overcome a will to resist; that Pat's verbal resistance was not resistance within the contemplation of *Hazel;* that his alleged menacing look did not constitute a threat of force; and that even had he pulled Pat to the bed, and lightly choked her, as she claimed, these actions, viewed in the context of the entire incident—no prior threats having been made—would be insufficient to constitute force or a threat of force or render the intercourse non-consensual.

We think the reversal of Rusk's conviction by the Court of Special Appeals was in error for the fundamental reason so well expressed in the dissenting opinion by Judge Wilner when he observed that the majority had "trampled upon the first principle of appellate restraint . . . [because it had] substituted [its] own view of the evidence (and the inferences that may fairly be drawn from it) for that of the judge and jury . . . [and had thereby] improperly invaded the province allotted to those tribunals." 43 Md. App. at 484-485, 406 A.2d 624. In view of the evidence adduced at the trial, the reasonableness of Pat's apprehension of fear was plainly a question of fact for the jury to determine. . . .

. . . Applying the constitutional standard of review . . . [i.e.]—whether after considering the evidence in the light most favorable to the prosecution, any rational trier of fact could have found the essential elements of the crime beyond a reasonable doubt—it is readily apparent to us that the trier of fact could rationally find that the elements of force and non-consent had been established and that Rusk was guilty of the offense beyond a reasonable doubt. Of course, it was for the jury to observe the witnesses and their demeanor, and to judge their credibility and weigh their testimony. Quite obviously, the jury disbelieved Rusk and believed Pat's testimony. From her testimony, the jury could have reasonably concluded that the taking of her car keys was intended by Rusk to immobilize her alone, late at night, in a neighborhood with which she was not familiar; that after Pat had repeatedly refused to enter his apartment, Rusk commanded in firm tones that she do so; that Pat was badly frightened and feared that Rusk intended to rape her; that unable to think clearly and believing that she had no other choice in the circumstances, Pat entered Rusk's apartment; that once inside Pat asked permission to leave but Rusk told her to stay; that he then pulled Pat by the arms to the bed and undressed her; that Pat was afraid that Rusk would kill her unless she submitted; that she began to cry and Rusk then put his hands on her throat and began " 'lightly to choke' " her; that Pat asked him if he would let her go without killing her if she complied with his demands; that Rusk gave an affirmative response, after which she finally submitted.

Just where persuasion ends and force begins in cases like the present is essentially a factual issue, to be resolved in light of the controlling legal precepts. That threats of force need not be made in any particular manner in order to put a person in fear of bodily harm is well established. Indeed, conduct, rather than words, may convey the threat. That a victim did not scream out for help or attempt to escape, while bearing on the question of consent, is unnecessary where she is restrained by fear of violence.

Considering all of the evidence in the case, with particular focus upon the actual force applied by Rusk to Pat's neck, we conclude that the jury could rationally find that the essential elements of second degree rape had been established and that Rusk was guilty of that offense beyond a reasonable doubt.

Cole, Judge, dissenting. . . .

The majority . . . concludes that "[i]n view of the evidence adduced at the trial, the reasonableness of Pat's apprehension of fear was plainly a question of fact for the jury to determine." In so concluding, the majority has skipped over the crucial issue. It seems to me that whether the prosecutrix's fear is reasonable becomes a question only after the court determines that the defendant's conduct under the circumstances was reasonably calculated to give rise to a fear on her part to the extent that she was unable to resist. In other words, the fear must stem from his articulable conduct, and equally, if not more importantly, cannot be inconsistent with her own contemporaneous reaction to that conduct. The conduct of the defendant, in and of itself, must clearly indicate force or the threat of force such as to overpower the prosecutrix's ability to resist or will to resist. In my view, there is no evidence to support the majority's conclusion that the prosecutrix was forced to submit to sexual intercourse, certainly not fellatio. . . .

While courts no longer require a female to resist to the utmost or to resist where resistance would be foolhardy, they do require her acquiescence in the act of intercourse to stem from fear generated by something of substance. She may not simply say, "I was really scared," and thereby transform consent or mere unwillingness into submission by force. These words do not transform a seducer into a rapist. She must follow the natural instinct of every proud female to resist, by more than mere words, the violation of her person by a stranger or an unwelcomed friend. She must make it plain that she regards such sexual acts as abhorrent and repugnant to her natural sense of pride. She must resist unless the defendant has objectively manifested his intent to use physical force to accomplish his purpose. The law regards rape as a crime of violence. The majority today attenuates this proposition. It declares the innocence of an at best distraught young woman. It does not demonstrate the defendant's guilt of the crime of rape.

My examination of the evidence in a light most favorable to the State reveals no conduct by the defendant reasonably calculated to cause the prosecutrix to be so fearful that she should fail to resist and thus, the element of force is lacking in the State's proof.

Here we have a full grown married woman who meets the defendant in a bar under friendly circumstances. They drink and talk together. She agrees to give him a ride home in her car. When they arrive at his house, located in an area with which she was unfamiliar but which was certainly not isolated, he invites her to come up to his apartment and she refuses. According to her testimony he takes her keys, walks around to her side of the car, and says

"Now will you come up?" She answers, "yes." The majority suggests that "from her testimony the jury could have reasonably concluded that the taking of her keys was intended by Rusk to immobilize her alone, late at night, in a neighborhood with which she was unfamiliar. . . ." But on what facts does the majority so conclude? There is no evidence descriptive of the tone of his voice; her testimony indicates only the bare statement quoted above. How can the majority extract from this conduct a threat reasonably calculated to create a fear of imminent bodily harm? There was no weapon, no threat to inflict physical injury.

She also testified that she was afraid of "the way he looked," and afraid of his statement, "come on up, come on up." But what can the majority conclude from this statement coupled with a "look" that remained undescribed? There is no evidence whatsoever to suggest that this was anything other than a pattern of conduct consistent with the ordinary seduction of a female acquaintance who at first suggests her disinclination.

After reaching the room she described what occurred as follows:

> I was still begging him to please let, you know, let me leave. I said, "you can get a lot of other girls down there, for what you want," and he just kept saying, "no," and then I was really scared, because I can't describe, you know, what was said. It was more the look in his eyes; and I said, at that point—I didn't know what to say; and I said, "If I do what you want, will you let me go without killing me?" Because I didn't know, at that point, what he was going to do; and I started to cry; and when I did, he put his hands on my throat and started lightly to choke me; and I said "If I do what you want, will you let me go?" And he said, yes, and at that time, I proceeded to do what he wanted me to.

The majority relies on the trial court's statement that the defendant responded affirmatively to her question "If I do what you want, will you let me go without killing me?" The majority further suggests that the jury could infer the defendant's affirmative response. The facts belie such inference since by the prosecutrix's own testimony the defendant made *no* response. *He said nothing*!

She then testified that she started to cry and he "started lightly to choke" her, whatever that means. Obviously, the choking was not of any persuasive significance. During this "choking" she was able to talk. She said "If I do what you want will you let me go?" It was at this point that the defendant said yes.

I find it incredible for the majority to conclude that on these facts, without more, a woman was *forced* to commit oral sex upon the defendant and then to engage in vaginal intercourse. In the absence of any verbal threat to do her grievous bodily harm or the display of any weapon and threat to use it, I find it difficult to understand how a victim could participate in these sexual activities and not be willing.

What was the nature and extent of her fear anyhow? She herself testified she was "fearful that maybe I had someone following me." She was afraid because she didn't know him and she was afraid he was going to "rape" her.

But there are no acts or conduct on the part of the defendant to suggest that these fears were created by the defendant or that he made any objective, identifiable threats to her which would give rise to this woman's failure to flee, summon help, scream, or make physical resistance. . . .

The record does not disclose the basis for this young woman's misgivings about her experience with the defendant. The only substantive fear she had was that she would be late arriving home. The objective facts make it inherently improbable that the defendant's conduct generated any fear for her physical well-being.

In my judgment the State failed to prove the essential element of force beyond a reasonable doubt and, therefore, the judgment of conviction should be reversed. . . .

Notes and Questions

1. The opinion of the dissenting judge in the lower court case that was reversed in *Rusk,* 43 Md. App. 476, 406 A.2d 624 (1979), offers an interesting perspective on the issues of force and consent:

> Unfortunately, courts . . . often tend to confuse . . . two elements—force and lack of consent—and to think of them as one. They are not. They mean, and require, different things. What seems to cause the confusion—what, indeed, has become a common denominator of both elements—is the notion that the victim must actively resist the attack upon her. If she fails to offer sufficient resistance (sufficient to the satisfaction of the judge), a court is entitled, or at least presumes the entitlement, to find that there was no force or threat of force, or that the act was not against her will, or that she actually consented to it, or some unarticulated combination or synthesis of these elements that leads to the ultimate conclusion that the victim was not raped. Thus it is that the focus is almost entirely on the extent of resistance—*the victim's acts, rather than those of her assailant.* Attention is directed not to the wrongful stimulus, but to the victim's reactions to it. Right or wrong, that seems to be the current state of the Maryland law; and, notwithstanding its uniqueness in the criminal law, and its illogic, until changed by statute or the Court of Appeals, I accept it as binding.
>
> But what is required of a woman being attacked or in danger of attack? How much resistance must she offer? Where is that line to be drawn between requiring that she either risk serious physical harm, perhaps death, on the one hand, or be termed a willing partner on the other?
>
> [The dissent then reviewed the facts of the case.]
>
> At this point, appellant returned her car keys and escorted her to her car. She then drove off:
>
>> I stopped at a gas station, that I believe was Amoco or Exon (sic), and went to the ladies' room. From there I drove home. I don't know—I don't know if I rode around for a while or not; but I know I went home, pretty much straight home and pulled up and parked the car.
>>
>> I was just going to go home, and not say anything.

Q. Why?
A. *Because I didn't want to go through what I'm going through now.*
Q. What, in fact did you do then?
A. I sat in the car, thinking about it a while, and I thought I wondered what would happen if I hadn't of done what he wanted me to do. So I thought the right thing to do was to go report it, and I went from there to Hillendale to find a police car. (Emphasis supplied.)

How does the majority Opinion [in the lower court] view these events? It starts by noting that Pat was a 21-year-old mother who was separated from her husband but not yet divorced, as though that had some significance. To me, it has none, except perhaps (when coupled with the further characterization that Pat and Terry had gone "bar hopping") to indicate an underlying suspicion, for which there is absolutely no support in the record, that Pat was somehow "on the make." Even more alarming, and unwarranted, however, is the majority's analysis of Pat's initial reflections on whether to report what had happened. Ignoring completely her statement that she "didn't want to go through what I'm going through now," the majority, in footnote 1, cavalierly and without any foundation whatever, says:

> If, in quiet contemplation after the act, she had to wonder what would have happened, her submission on the side of prudence seems hardly justified. Indeed, if *she* had to wonder afterward, how can a fact finder reasonably conclude that she was justifiably in fear sufficient to overcome her will to resist, at the time." (Emphasis in the original.)

It is this type of reasoning—if indeed "reasoning" is the right word for it—that is particularly distressing. The concern expressed by Pat . . . is one that is common among rape victims, and largely accounts for the fact that most incidents of forcible rape go unreported by the victim. See F.B.I. Uniform Crime Reports (1978), p.14; Report of Task Force on Rape Control, Baltimore County (1975); The Treatment of Rape Victims In The Metropolitan Washington Area, Metropolitan Washington Council of Governments (1976), p.4. See also Rape and Its Victims: A Report for Citizens, Health Facilities, and Criminal Justice Agencies, LEAA (1975). If appellant had desired, and Pat had given, her wallet instead of her body, there would be no question about appellant's guilt of robbery. Taking the car keys under those circumstances would certainly have supplied the requisite threat of force or violence and negated the element of consent. No one would seriously contend that because she failed to raise a hue and cry she had consented to the theft of her money. Why then is such life-threatening action necessary when it is her personal dignity that is being stolen?

Rape has always been considered a most serious crime, one that traditionally carried the heaviest penalty. But until recently, it remained shrouded in the taboos and myths of a Victorian age, and little real attention was given to how rapes occur, how they may be prevented, and how a victim can best protect herself from injury when an attack appears inevitable. The courts are as responsible for this ignorance and the misunderstandings emanating from it as any other institution in society, and it is high time that they recognize reality.

Rape is on the increase in the United States. The Uniform Crime Reports compiled by the FBI show more than a doubling in both the absolute number of forcible rapes and in the rate per 100,000 population between 1965 and 1974.

Between 1973 and 1977, forcible rape has increased 19 percent.[1] As the result of the Battelle Study,[2] we now know some things about this crime that we could only guess at before. Nearly half of the rapes occur when this one did, between 8:00 P.M. and 2:00 A.M., and, as in this case, approximately one-third of rape victims had come into contact with their assailants voluntarily, under circumstances other than hitchhiking.[3] *Physical force is absent in over half of reported cases and, in a third of the cases, no weapon is involved.* In rapes occurring in large cities (over 500,000 population), the statistics showed:[4]

Use of physical force	47.4%
Use of weapon:	
none	34.6%
firearms	21.1%
sharp instrument	24.7%
blunt instrument	7.3%
other	11.6%

Of particular significance is what was learned about *resistance.* The most common type of resistance offered by victims is *verbal.* Note: verbal resistance *is* resistance! In cases arising in the large cities, only 12.7 percent of the victims attempted flight, and only 12 percent offered physical resistance.[5] The reason for this is apparent from the next thing learned: that *"[r]ape victims who resisted were more likely to be injured than ones who did not."*[6] (Emphasis supplied.) The statistics showed, for rapes in large cities, that, where physical resistance was offered, over 71 percent of the victims were physically injured in some way, 40 percent requiring medical treatment or hospitalization.[7]

Said the Report: *"These results indicate one possible danger of the popular notion (and some statutory requirements) that a victim of an attack should resist to her utmost."* (Emphasis supplied.)

In a second volume of the Report, intended for prosecutors, some of the social attitudes about rape were discussed. With respect to resistance, it was noted (p.4):

> Perhaps because most women's experience and expertise with violence tends to be minimal, they are unlikely to engage in physical combat or succeed when they do. Many women employ what is referred to as "passive resistance." This can include crying, being slow to respond, feigning an inability to understand instructions or telling the rapist they are pregnant, diseased or injured. *While these techniques may not always be successful, their use does suggest that the victim is surely not a willing partner.* (Emphasis supplied.)

1. See FBI Uniform Crime Reports (1978), p.14. See also Battelle Study, infra, note [2], Prosecutors' Volume 1 (1977), p.7.

2. This was a study conducted by the Battelle Memorial Institute Law and Justice Study Center under grant from the LEAA (National Institute of Law Enforcement and Criminal Justice). The Report of the study was published during 1977 and 1978. I shall refer to it hereafter as "Battelle Study."

3. Battelle Study, Police Volume 1, p.20.

4. Id., p.21. These figures, of course, are not cumulative. Weapons may accompany physical force, or there may be an absence of both.

5. Id., p.21.

6. Id., p.22.

7. Id., p.22.

. . . [T]he Report further points out (Prosecutor's Volume I, p.5):

> Rather than expressing their emotions, some victims respond to a rape with a calm, composed demeanor or "controlled reaction." [Footnote omitted.] These victims do not wish to exhibit emotions, especially in front of a stranger or authority figure like the prosecutor. Psychologically it is important for these victims to demonstrate that they can handle stress in a mature and adult manner. *The appearance of casualness hides and may avoid true and often intense emotions.* This "control" may result in victim responses which are considered inappropriate such as giggling, smiling or even laughing. *Unfortunately this type of response can cause others to doubt the victims account of the rape.* (Emphasis supplied.)

Finally, perhaps in response to the oft-quoted comment of Matthew Hale that still pervades societal thinking about rape ("[Rape] is an accusation easily to be made and hard to be proved, and harder to be defended by the party accused, tho never so innocent"),[8] the Report observes (Vol. II, p.4):

> *On a national average, 15 percent of all forcible rapes reported to the police were "determined by investigation" to be unfounded. Given the inherent skepticism of many criminal justice personnel to rape victims and the harassment and invasion of privacy that a reporting victim is likely to confront, it is doubtful that many false accusations proceed past the initial report.* Curtis (1974) asserts that "contrary to widespread opinion, there is in fact little hard empirical evidence that victims in rape lie more than, say victims in robbery." Undoubtedly, there are false reports. However, the danger posed by the myth that women "cry rape" is that police officers and prosecutors will believe it and then place the burden on the victims to prove the contrary. (Emphasis supplied.)

Law enforcement agencies throughout the country warn women not to resist an attack haphazardly, not to antagonize a potential attacker, but to protect themselves from more serious injury. The United States Department of Justice, for example, has published a pamphlet warning, among other things:[9]

> If you are confronted by a rapist, stay calm and maximize your chances for escape. *Think* through what you will do. You should not *immediately* try to fight back. Chances are, your attacker has the advantage. Try to stay calm and take stock of the situation." . . .

I close with this comment taken from 13 Western Australian Law Rev. at 75 (1977), written half a world away, but precisely for this case:

> Courts have sought to enunciate legal standards for consent with respect to allegations of rape, rather than leaving the issue as a question of fact for the jury.

8. 1 Hale, *The History of the Pleas of the Crown* 635 (1847).

9. Be on the Safe Side, LEAA, U.S. Department of Justice. The pamphlet also advises: "Be selective about new acquaintances; don't *invite* a forcible sexual encounter." See also Let Prevention Be Your Guide, a pamphlet published by the (Baltimore City) Mayor's Coordinating Council on Criminal Justice; Rape Prevention, a pamphlet distributed by the Prince George's County Police Department. That pamphlet specifically warns:

> Extensive research into thousands of rape cases indicates that attempts at self defense, such as screaming, kicking, scratching and use of tear gas devices and other weapons, usually have provoked the rapist into inflicting severe bodily harm on the victim. Since it is unlikely you will be able to overcome the rapist by force, you must think about what he will do after you try and fail. Before you do anything, remember . . . IF WHATEVER YOU DO DOES NOT HELP YOU, MAKE SURE THAT IT WILL NOT HARM YOU.

Thus, judges have intruded into an area which in terms of the common law definition of rape should be dealt with by the jury. This appears to suggest that juries are incompetent to do their job, that is, to review the facts as impartially as possible, and to make findings beyond a reasonable doubt without being led astray by prejudices or irrelevancies. The jury is indispensible to the common law justice system. If rape is defined as "carnal knowledge of a woman without her consent," then it makes nonsense of the proposition that the jury is the trier of fact if the judge takes it upon himself to tell the jury what is or is not consent.

If the purpose of the law is to protect women from acts of sexual intercourse to which they have not in fact consented, whether by reason of force actually applied, physical or other threat, or fear induced by accused or by others, then the relevant question would appear to be: Did this particular woman, in these particular circumstances, submit to this particular man; or did she in fact freely consent to have intercourse with him? If, on the contrary, the law requires a woman to react in a particular way, that is, by fighting back against her attacker and sustaining a certain degree of damage inflicted by the accused in order to signify the lack of consent, and if the law deems the woman to have consented to the act despite ample evidence of threats which rendered her submissive but nonconsenting, then the law cannot be said to be serving its true function of protecting individuals from the imposition of nonconsensual sexual intercourse.

Whether the relevant threats do or do not measure up to standards which appear to be set in current rape cases—that the threat be immediate, physical, violent, interpreted on a reasonable-man standard—the accused is amply protected. He cannot be convicted unless the prosecution has proved beyond a reasonable doubt the requisite state of mind: that he intended to have intercourse with the woman without her consent, and did so; or that he was reckless thereto. By imposing an artificial standard of consent, by requiring the woman concerned to resist or at least not simply to suffer the imposition of the act as a lesser evil, the criminal law would seem to require a measure of "self-help" which it does not require in any other area of criminal law—and indeed which is usually frowned upon by the law.

2. *Mens rea.* What if Rusk conceded, in retrospect, that Pat had not consented to have intercourse, but he nevertheless argued that at the time of the alleged rape he honestly, and perhaps reasonably, had believed that she was consenting? Does a claim of mistake of fact seem plausible in a case like this? If the use of force (or the absence of consent) is an element of the crime of rape, isn't the defendant entitled to argue that he lacked the requisite *mens rea* for that element?

In People v. Mayberry, 15 Cal. 3d 143, 542 P.2d 1337, 125 Cal. Rptr. 745 (1975), the defendant was convicted of forcing a woman to come with him to his apartment and raping her there. On appeal to the California Supreme Court, Mayberry argued that the woman had consented to intercourse. Mayberry relied on his trial testimony that the woman had not immediately reported the alleged rape to the police, that she had not physically resisted him after their initial encounter, that she had failed to take advantage of several opportunities to flee, that she had, with apparent casualness, lighted a cigarette just before she left his apartment. The Court rejected this argument and sustained the jury's finding that the woman had not consented, holding that the jury could reasonably have found the woman's contrary testimony more credible. But in the court's view, the defendant's *mens rea* argument was another matter altogether:

> The [trial] court refused to give requested instructions that directed the jury to acquit Franklin of the rape and kidnaping if the jury had a reasonable doubt as to whether Franklin reasonably and genuinely believed that Miss B. freely consented to her movement from the grocery store to his apartment and to sexual intercourse with him. Franklin contends that the court thereby erred. The Attorney General argues that the court properly refused to give the instructions because "mistake of fact instruction[s] as to consent should be rejected as against the law and public policy." . . .
>
> Penal Code section 26 recites, generally, that one is incapable of committing a crime who commits an act under a mistake of fact disproving any criminal intent. Penal Code section 20 provides, "In every crime . . . there must exist a union, or joint operation of act and intent, or criminal negligence." The word "intent" in section 20 means "wrongful intent." (See People v. Vogel, 46 Cal. 2d 798, 801, fn. 2, 299 P.2d 850.) "So basic is this requirement [of a union of act and wrongful intent] that it is an invariable element of every crime unless excluded expressly or by necessary implication." (Id., at p.801, 299 P.2d at p.853.)
>
> In People v. Hernandez, 61 Cal. 2d 529, 39 Cal. Rptr. 361, 393 P.2d 673 we considered the matter of intent within a context similar to that presented in the instant case. The defendant in *Hernandez* was convicted of statutory rape under former subdivision 1 of Penal Code section 261, which provided "Rape is an act of sexual intercourse, accomplished with a female not the wife of the perpetrator . . . 1. Where the female is under the age of eighteen years." On appeal the defendant contended that the court erred in excluding evidence that he had in good faith a reasonable belief that the prosecutrix was 18 years or more in age, and in *Hernandez* we upheld the contention.
>
> *Hernandez* emphasized that we gave recognition to the legislative declarations in Penal Code sections 20 and 26 when we held in People v. Vogel, supra, 46 Cal. 2d 798, 299 P.2d 850, that "a [reasonable and] good faith belief that a former wife had obtained a divorce was a valid defense to a charge of bigamy arising out of a second marriage when the first marriage had not in fact been terminated." *Hernandez* quoted from *Vogel,* " 'Nor would it be reasonable to hold that a person is guilty of bigamy who remarries in good faith in reliance on a judgment of divorce . . . that is subsequently found not to be the "judgment of a competent Court." . . . Since it is often difficult for laymen to know when a judgment is not that of a competent court, we cannot reasonably expect them always to have such knowledge and make them criminals if their bona fide belief proves to be erroneous.' " *Hernandez* then declared, "Certainly it cannot be a greater wrong to entertain a bona fide but erroneous belief that a valid consent to an act of sexual intercourse has been obtained." *Hernandez* had theretofore noted that, although in one sense the lack of the female's consent is not an element of statutory rape, in a broader sense the lack of consent is deemed to remain an element but the law creates a conclusive presumption of the lack thereof. (61 Cal. 2d at p.535, 39 Cal. Rptr. 361, 393 P.2d 673.)
>
> *Hernandez* further stated, "Equally applicable to the instant case are the following remarks [in *Vogel*]: 'The severe penalty imposed for bigamy, the serious loss of reputation conviction entails, . . . and the fact that it has been re-

garded for centuries as a crime involving moral turpitude, make it extremely unlikely that the Legislature meant to include the morally innocent to make sure the guilty did not escape.' [¶] We are persuaded that the reluctance to accord to a charge of statutory rape the defense of a lack of criminal intent has no greater justification than in the case of other statutory crimes, where the Legislature has made identical provision with respect to intent. . . ." *Hernandez* also indicated that the defendant's belief must be, inter alia, reasonable in order to negate criminal intent. (61 Cal. 2d at pp.534-536, 39 Cal. Rptr. 361, 365, 393 P.2d 673, 677).

Although *Hernandez* dealt solely with statutory rape, its rationale applies equally to rape by means of force or threat (Pen. Code, §261, subds. 2 & 3) and kidnaping (Pen. Code, §207). Those statutory provisions, like that involved in *Hernandez,* neither expressly nor by necessary implication negate the continuing requirement that there be a union of act and wrongful intent. The severe penalties imposed for those offenses (Pen. Code, §207 [1 to 25 years in prison (see Pen. Code, §208)]; Pen. Code. §261, subds. 2 & 3 [3 years to life (Pen. Code, §§264, 671)]) and the serious loss of reputation following conviction make it extremely unlikely that the Legislature intended to exclude as to those offenses the element of wrongful intent. If a defendant entertains a reasonable and bona fide belief that a prosecutrix voluntarily consented to accompany him and to engage in sexual intercourse, it is apparent he does not possess the wrongful intent that is a prerequisite under Penal Code section 20 to a conviction of either kidnaping (§207) or rape by means of force or threat (§261, subds. 2 & 3). . . .

The Attorney General further argues that a defense based on mistake of fact as to the prosecutrix' consent in prosecutions for kidnaping or rape should not be permitted because it will promote greater resistance by the victim to assure there is no misunderstanding as to consent and that such resistance could result in harm to the victim. The Attorney General notes that utmost resistance by the female to establish lack of consent to intercourse is not required. Such an argument, in our view, invokes a policy consideration for the Legislature—adoption of the argument would result in effective nullification of Penal Code sections 20 and 26 when applied to cases of kidnaping (Pen. Code, §207) and rape (Pen. Code, §261, subds. 2 & 3).

The Attorney General next argues that, even if instructions regarding mistake of fact as to consent are appropriate in some cases of kidnaping (Pen. Code, §207) and rape (Pen. Code, §261, subds. 2 & 3), here the court properly determined that the evidence did not warrant such instructions. However, Franklin's testimony . . . could be viewed as indicating that he reasonably and in good faith believed that Miss B. consented to accompany him to the apartment and to the subsequent sexual intercourse. In addition, part of Miss B's testimony furnishes support for the requested instructions. It appears from her testimony that her behavior was equivocal. Although she did not want Franklin to think she was consenting, her "act" and admitted failure physically to resist him after the initial encounter or to attempt to escape or obtain help might have misled him as to whether she was consenting. We by no means intimate that such is the *only* reasonable interpretation of her conduct, but we do conclude that there was some evidence "deserving of . . . consideration" which supported his contention that he acted under a mistake of fact as to her consent both to the movement and to intercourse. It follows, accordingly, that the requested instructions, if correctly worded, should have been given.

On retrial, what evidence could Mayberry offer to persuade the jury that he honestly and reasonably believed the woman was consenting, if the jury must treat as an established fact that the woman did not in fact consent? Could he argue that he was drunk? That he was socially or sexually inexperienced, or not very psychologically insightful?

In *Mayberry,* the prosecution argued that the mistake of fact instruction requested by the defendant "should be rejected as against . . . public policy." What "public policy" supports making the absence of consent a strict liability element?

Return to the Model Penal Code rape provision, §213.1. Using the general *mens rea* structure of §2.02, what is the required *mens rea* for the element "compels her to submit by force"?

3. The focus of the rape laws on the behavior of the victim is unique. This feature of rape law is obviously tied to the central role played by the issue of consent. But theoretically, consent could play an equally central role in such crimes as robbery and kidnapping. The special treatment given to the behavior and character of the victim may derive more specifically from a fear that the prosecutrix may have consented to intercourse and brought the charge of rape because of guilt, fantasy, or a desire for revenge. These concerns have been vigorously challenged by Martha A. Field, Rape: Legal Aspects, Encyclopedia of Crime and Justice 1361-1362 (1983).

> [The assumption that the prosecutrix is lying] is buttressed by nothing more substantial than a view that women are foolish creatures who do not have a good grasp of reality. " 'Fantasies of being raped are exceedingly common in women, indeed one may almost say that they are universal' " (Wigmore, p.744, quoting Karl Menninger). Alternatively, women are depicted as bitter, vengeful creatures who use sex to manipulate or punish men. As late as 1970 a respected law review, without any empirical support, declared: "Women often falsely accuse men of sexual assault to extort money, to force marriage, to satisfy a childish desire for notoriety, or to attain personal revenge. Their motives include hatred, a sense of shame after consenting to illicit intercourse, especially when pregnancy results, and delusion. In cases of delusion, the woman may describe the attack in remarkable detail, for she herself believes her story but fails to appreciate the significance and consequences of the accusation" [Comment. The Corroboration Rule and Crimes Accompanying Rape, 118 U. Pa. L. Rev. 458-472]. No one has shown that the system's presupposition of falsity with regard to rape charges has any foundation in reality. Nor is it more suitable for rape than for other crimes. The theft victim often has a more obvious motive to falsify charges than does the rape victim.

4. The concerns described above help explain some unusual evidentiary issues in the traditional rape laws.

Evidence of the victim's prior sexual history. Rape has been almost unique among crimes in that, at least until the 1970s, the accuser was treated as an immoral person and her morality was litigated for all to see. The total exposure of the private lives of rape victims has led to the remark that they are raped twice, once by the perpetrator and again in the courtroom. Traditionally, a woman's entire prior sexual history was admissible in evidence, either to prove that the victim had consented to sexual activity in the past and therefore was likely to have consented in this instance, or to challenge the woman's credibility as a witness. This general rule of admissibility arose, first, from men's fear of false charges by vindictive women. Second, it is often said that females fantasize being raped. (That belief itself is a male fantasy.) Third, lack of chastity was considered a character trait supporting an inference that the unchaste woman had consented to intercourse with the defendant. Fourth, there existed the widespread view that premarital sex was immoral and, as such, reflected upon one's credibility as a witness.

Evidence of prior sexual relations between victim and defendant has always been admitted because "it simply ignores reality to suggest that past practice with the accused is not relevant to the issue of consent on a given occasion, though it is equally a distortion to regard proof of such experience as dispositive" (Model Penal Code, commentary on §213.1). More troublesome were the cases where "propensity to consent" was shown by evidence of the woman's sexual activity with persons other than the accused or by the victim's general reputation for chastity and sexual virtue. Many jurisdictions also allowed evidence of the victim's specific and reputed sexual activity to be introduced to challenge her credibility. Thus, the victim was treated as if she were the one on trial and, unless a virgin, she was presumed a liar. Perhaps this reflects an attitude that rape is most heinous when those defiled are the most pure; a woman who has engaged consensually in sexual intercourse outside of marriage cannot successfully prosecute a rape case.

During the 1970s the unfairness to women inherent in the prevailing rules came to be recognized. A new federal rule of evidence (Fed. R. Evid. 412(b)(2)(B)) and "rape shield" statutes in forty-six states were enacted to prohibit or limit the use of evidence concerning the rape victim's sexual history. In addition to substantive rules concerning admissibility, many of the statutes provide procedural protections, such as in camera (confidential) review, for determining what evidence is admissible.

These statutes represent better treatment of rape victims by the judicial system and reflect some recognition of the problem of victimization of women. It is questionable, however, how much change has occurred in practice. Almost every rape-shield statute allows substantial exceptions to the presumptive rule against admissibility. Even the most exclusionary statutes admit evidence of prior sexual conduct with the defendant (La. Rev. Stat. Ann. §15:498 (1981)). Other statutes allow the defendant to make admissible some instances of prior sexual behavior by asserting that someone else was the source of semen or of other physical evidence of the rape (Mich. Stat. Ann. §28.788(10) (1982-1983 Supp.); Fed. R. Evid. 412(b)(2)(A); Minn. Stat. Ann. §609.347(3)(b) (1982 Supp.)). Some go further, giving the trial judge discretion to admit any relevant evidence (N.Y. Crim. Proc. Law (McKinney) §60.42(5) (1972-1981 Supp.)), or any evidence that is not more prejudicial to the victim than it is probative of an issue for the defendant (Tex. Penal Code Ann. tit. 5, §21.13(a) (1982 Supp.)).

The exclusionary effect of the rape-shield laws can also be circumvented through exceptions included in many of the statutes for attacking the credibility of the complaining witness. Some jurisdictions allow past sexual conduct to be admitted as evidence for the purpose of impeaching a witness, even though the evidence cannot be introduced for proof of consent (Cal. Evid. Code §1103(b)(3) (1982 Supp.)). Some allow evidence of prior sexual conduct if it is relevant, material, and not outweighed by its prejudicial nature, and if the evidence supports a claim that the victim has an ulterior motive in accusing the defendant of the crime (Md. Code Ann. art. 27, §461A(a)(3) (1982)).

In sum, the rape-shield statutes represent an improvement; but given the exceptions, there remains room for concern that the system deals unjustly with rape victims.

Is this an area where justice for victims can be reconciled with the criminal defendant's due process rights to a fair trial and to confrontation of witnesses? In particular cases, the interests are reconcilable. Thus, the Michigan Court of Appeals repudiated a challenge to the constitutionality of the Michigan rape-shield statute, saying that the statute serves a legitimate state interest in encouraging the rape victim to come forward and prosecute the crime. Moreover, the court reasoned, it does not impinge upon a defendant's right of confrontation when it deprives him of the opportunity to question the rape victim concerning her general sexual behavior, because this behavior simply is not relevant; it is not probative of her general credibility, nor is it more than minimally relevant to the question of whether she consented to intercourse with the defendant (People v. Thompson, 76 Mich. App. 705, 711-713, 257 N.W.2d 268, 272 (1977)). The court might have added that even if the evidence is of some relevance, its potential prejudicial effect may outweigh its probative value. In other contexts, evidence is regularly excluded for such reasons—hearsay evidence, privileged information, and opinion evidence, to name but a few examples.

In particular cases, therefore, the conflicting interests can be reconciled. There will be instances, however, where the evidence is sufficiently relevant that fairness to the defendant compels invasion of the victim's privacy. In other cases when the right of confrontation has come into conflict with important private and public interests in nondisclosure, such as the interest in preserving the anonymity of government informants, the United States Supreme Court has held that the right to confrontation prevails (Roviaro v. United States, 353 U.S. 53 (1957); Davis v. Alaska, 415 U.S. 308 (1974)). In the American system, the fear that takes precedence is that an innocent defendant will be unable to demonstrate his innocence (Chambers v. Mississippi, 410 U.S. 284 (1973)). In those instances where evidence embarrassing to the victim must be considered, use of in camera procedures can help minimize evidence that must be heard in open court and can help prevent illegitimate forms of cross-examination that are designed to badger and embarrass the witness.

Special requirements of corroboration. Just as the focus on victim consent and her prior sexual history reflects the system's distrust of women, so do some of the evidentiary rules peculiar to rape. Although it was much more common before the 1970s, some of the states and the Model Penal Code, for example, retain special requirements of corroboration for rape offenses. Basically, they state that the rape victim's testimony must be corroborated to sustain a charge. The earlier New York law was the most extreme, demanding corroboration for each material element of the offense—force, penetration, and identity of the accused (N.Y. Penal Law (McKinney) §130.15 (repealed)). Such corroboration can be impossible to produce. Faced with a weapon-wielding assailant, many women decide not to resist physically and thereby avoid the bruises and torn clothing that would corroborate the use of force. Women frequently do not submit to medical examination immediately upon completion of the rape since obtaining corroboration of penetration may not be foremost in their minds. It is rare to have eyewitnesses to corroborate identification of the accused.

During the 1970s such rules became a focus of feminist criticism. New York eliminated its corroboration requirement for forcible rape, sodomy, and sexual abuse, keeping the requirement only for consensual sodomy and for those situations where the alleged victim is deemed by law to be incapable of consenting to the act. Some jurisdictions require corroboration only for statutory rape, or only where complaint to the authorities was belated. Others have repealed their statutory corroboration requirements.

For the most part, both courts and state legislatures have come to recognize that a special corroboration rule for rape cases is unjustified. Rape defendants, like other criminal defendants, are fully protected by the general principle that guilt must be proved beyond a reasonable doubt. [Field, supra, at 1359-1360]

5. *Purpose of the laws against rape.* The major function of the laws against rape would seem to be to protect women against unwanted and coerced intimacy. As such, rape laws reflect the social value favoring an individual's right to control her own mind and body. Yet a number of commentators have argued that the traditional rape laws may have a more cynical goal: to protect the virtue of chastity, which may be a male creation and a male concern. Hence, rape laws may have emerged to enforce male rights to control sexual access to females. This historical theory may explain why rape laws rarely prohibit homosexual rape, at least at the same level of punishment. See Field, supra note 3, at 1362. It may also explain one traditional limitation in rape laws, which was addressed, and overturned, in the following case.

PEOPLE v. LIBERTA

New York Court of Appeals

64 N.Y. 2d 152, 485 N.Y. S.2d 207 (1984)

WACHTLER, J.

The defendant, while living apart from his wife pursuant to a Family Court order, forcibly raped . . . her in the presence of their 2½ years old son. Under the New York Penal Law a married man ordinarily cannot be prosecuted for raping . . . his wife. The defendant, however, though married at the time of the incident, is treated as an unmarried man under the Penal Law because of the Family Court order. On this appeal, he contends that because of the exemption for married men, the statutes for rape in the first degree (Penal Law §130.35) . . . violate the equal protection clause of the federal constitution (U.S. Const., Amend. 14). The defendant also contends that the rape statute violates equal protection because only men, and not women, can be prosecuted under it.

I

Defendant Mario Liberta and Denise Liberta were married in 1978. Shortly after the birth of their son, in October of that year, Mario began to beat Denise. In early 1980 Denise brought a proceeding in the Family Court in Erie County seeking protection from the defendant. On April 30, 1980 a temporary order of protection was issued to her by the Family Court. Under this order, the defendant was to move out and remain away from the family home, and stay away from Denise. The order provided that the defendant could visit with his son once each weekend.

On the weekend of March 21st, 1981, Mario, who was then living in a motel, did not visit his son. On Tuesday, March 24, 1981 he called Denise to ask if he could visit his son on that day. Denise would not allow the defendant to come to her house, but she did agree to allow him to pick up their son and her and take them both back to his motel after being assured that a friend of his would be with them at all times. The defendant and his friend picked up Denise and their son and the four of them drove to defendant's motel.

When they arrived at the motel the friend left. As soon as only Mario, Denise, and their son, were alone in the motel room, Mario attacked Denise, threatened to kill her, and forced her . . . to engage in sexual intercourse with him. The son was in the room during the entire episode, and the defendant forced Denise to tell their son to watch what the defendant was doing to her.

The defendant allowed Denise and their son to leave shortly after the incident. Denise, after going to her parents' home, went to a hospital to be treated for scratches on her neck and bruises on her head and back, all inflicted by her husband. She also went to the police station, and on the next day she swore out a felony complaint against the defendant. On July 15, 1981 the defendant was indicted for rape in the first degree and sodomy in the first degree.

II

Section 130.35 of the Penal Law provides in relevant part that "A male is guilty of rape in the first degree when he engages in sexual intercourse with a female . . . by forcible compulsion." "Female," for purposes of the rape statute, is defined as "any female person not married to the actor" (Penal Law §130.00, subd. 4). . . . Thus, due to the "not married" language in the definitions of "female" . . . there is a "marital exemption" for . . . forcible rape. . . . The marital exemption itself, however, has certain exceptions. For purposes of the rape . . . [statute], a husband and wife are considered to be "not married" if at the time of the sexual assault they "are living apart . . . pursuant to a valid and effective (i) order issued by a court of competent jurisdiction which by its terms or in its effect requires such living apart, or (ii) decree or judgment of separation, or (iii) written agreement of separation . . ." (Penal Law §130.00, subd. 4).

Defendant moved to dismiss the indictment, asserting that because he and Denise were still married at the time of the incident[10] he came within the "marital exemption." . . . The People opposed the motion, contending that the temporary order of protection required Mario and Denise to live apart, and they in fact were living apart, and thus were "not married" for purposes of the statutes. The trial court granted the defendant's motion and dismissed the indictment, concluding that the temporary order of protection did not require Mario and Denise to live apart from each other, but instead required only that he remain away from her, and that therefore the "marital exemption" applied.

On appeal by the People, the Appellate Division reversed the trial court, reinstated the indictment, and remanded the case for trial. The Appellate Division held that a Family Court Order of Protection is within the scope of "[an] order . . . which by its terms or in its effect requires such living apart" even though it is directed only at a husband, and thus found that Mario and Denise were "not married" for purposes of the statute at the time of the incident.

The defendant was then convicted of rape in the first degree . . . and the conviction was affirmed by the Appellate Division. Defendant asserts on this appeal that the temporary order of protection is not the type of order which enables a court to treat him and Denise as "not married" and that thus he is within the marital exemption. Defendant next asserts, assuming that because of the Family Court Order he is treated just as any unmarried male would be, that he cannot be convicted of . . . rape in the first degree . . . because [the statute is] unconstitutional. Specifically, he contends that [the statute] violate[s] equal protection because [it] burden[s] some, but not all males (all but those within the "marital exemption"), and that the rape statute also violates equal protection for burdening only men, and not women. The lower courts rejected the defendant's constitutional arguments, finding that [the] statute [did not] violate the equal protection clause in the Fourteenth Amendment. Although we affirm the conviction of the defendant, we do not agree with the constitutional analysis of the lower courts and instead conclude that the marital and gender exemptions must be read out of the statutes prohibiting forcible rape. . . .

10. The defendant and Denise were divorced several months after the assault in the motel room.

III

We first address the defendant's argument that, despite the Order of Protection, he was within the "marital exemption" to rape . . . and thus could not be prosecuted for either crime. [The court then held that defendant was not within the marital exception.]

IV

The defendant's constitutional challenges to the rape . . . statute are premised on his being considered "not married" to Denise and are the same challenges as could be made by any unmarried male convicted under [this statute]. The defendant's claim is that [the statute] violate[s] equal protection because [it is an] underinclusive classification which burden[s] him, but not others similarly situated. A litigant has standing to raise this claim even though he does not contend that under no circumstances could the burden of the statute be imposed upon him. This rule of standing applies as well to a defendant in a criminal prosecution who, while conceding that it is within the power of a state to make criminal the behavior covered by a statute, asserts that the statute he is prosecuted under violates equal protection because it burdens him but not others. Thus, defendant's constitutional claims are properly before this court.

A. THE MARITAL EXEMPTION

As noted above, under the Penal Law a married man ordinarily cannot be convicted of forcibly raping . . . his wife. This is the so-called marital exemption for rape (see, 1881 Penal Code, Title X, Ch II, §278). Although a marital exemption was not explicit in earlier rape statutes, an 1852 treatise stated that a man could not be guilty of raping his wife (O. L. Barbour, Treatise on the Criminal Law of the State of New York, 69). The assumption, even before the marital exemption was codified, that a man could not be guilty of raping his wife, is traceable to a statement made by the seventeenth century English jurist Lord Hale, who wrote: "[T]he husband cannot be guilty of a rape committed by himself upon his lawful wife, for by their mutual matrimonial consent and contract the wife hath given up herself in this kind unto her husband, which she cannot retract" (1 M. Hale, The History of the Pleas of the Crown, 629). Although Hale cited no authority for his statement it was relied on by state legislatures which enacted rape statutes with a marital exemption and by courts which established a common law exemption for husbands.

The first American case to recognize the marital exemption was decided in 1857 by the Supreme Judicial Court of Massachusetts, which stated in dictum that it would always be a defense to rape to show marriage to the victim (Commonwealth v. Fogerty, 74 Mass. 489). Decisions to the same effect by other courts followed, usually with no rationale or authority cited other than Hale's implied consent view. In New York, a 1922 decision noted the marital exemption in the Penal Law and stated that it existed "on account of the matrimonial consent which (the wife) has given, and which she cannot retract" (People v. Meli, 193 N.Y.S. 365, 366 [Sup. Ct.]).

Presently, over forty states still retain some form of marital exemption for rape.[11] While the marital exemption is subject to an equal protection challenge, because it classifies unmarried men differently than married men, the equal protection clause does not prohibit a state from making classifications, provided the statute does not arbitrarily burden a particular group of individuals. Where a statute draws a distinction based upon marital status, the classification must be reasonable and must be based upon "some ground of difference that rationally explains the different treatment . . . (Eisenstadt v. Baird, 405 U.S. 437, 447.)

We find that there is no rational basis for distinguishing between marital rape and non-marital rape. The various rationales which have been asserted in defense of the exemption are either based upon archaic notions about the consent and property rights incident to marriage or are simply unable to withstand even the slightest scrutiny. We therefore declare the marital exemption for rape in the New York statute to be unconstitutional.

Lord Hale's notion of an irrevocable implied consent by a married woman to sexual intercourse has been cited most frequently in support of the marital exemption. Any argument based on a supposed consent, however, is untenable. Rape is not simply a sexual act to which one party does not consent. Rather, it is a degrading, violent act which violates the bodily integrity of the victim and frequently causes severe, long-lasting physical and psychic harm. To ever imply consent to such an act is irrational and absurd. Other than in the context of rape statutes, marriage has never been viewed as giving a husband the right to coerced intercourse on demand. Certainly, then, a marriage license should not be viewed as a license for a husband to forcibly

11. Statutes in nine states provide a complete exemption to rape as long as there is a valid marriage (Alabama, Arkansas, Kansas, Montana, South Dakota, Texas, Vermont, Washington, West Virginia). In twenty-six other states, statutes provide for a marital exemption but with certain exceptions, most typically where the spouses are living apart pursuant to either a court order or a separation agreement (Alaska, Arizona, Colorado, Idaho, Indiana, Kentucky, Louisiana, Maine, Maryland, Michigan, Minnesota, Missouri, Nevada, New Mexico, New York, North Carolina, North Dakota, Ohio, Oklahoma, Pennsylvania, Rhode Island, South Carolina, Tennessee, Utah, Wyoming, Wisconsin). In three other states (Georgia, Mississippi, Nebraska) and the District of Columbia the exemption appears to still exist as a common law doctrine, and it may still have a limited application in Virginia (see Weishaupt v. Commonwealth, 315 S.E.2d 847). Finally, in Connecticut, Delaware, Hawaii, and Iowa, there is a marital exemption for some, but not all degrees of forcible rape (see generally, for statutory references, Schwartz, The Spousal Exemption for Rape Prosecutions, 7 Vt. L. Rev. 33, 38-41, [hereafter cited as Rape Prosecution]; Note, Equal Protection Considerations of the Spousal Sexual Assault Exclusion, 16 N. Eng. L. Rev. 1, 2-3 n.4 [hereafter cited as Equal Protection Considerations]. . . .

rape his wife with impunity. A married woman has the same right to control her own body as does an unmarried woman. If a husband feels "aggrieved" by his wife's refusal to engage in sexual intercourse, he should seek relief in the courts governing domestic relations, not in "violent or forceful self-help."

The other traditional justifications for the marital exemption were the common law doctrines that a woman was the property of her husband and that the legal existence of the woman was "incorporated and consolidated into that of the husband" (1 Blackstone, Commentaries on the Laws of England, 430 [1966 ed.]. Both these doctrines, of course, have long been rejected in this state. Indeed, "[n]owhere in the common-law world—[or] in any modern society—is a woman regarded as chattel or demeaned by denial of a separate legal identity and the dignity associated with recognition as a whole human being" (Trammel v. United States, 445 U.S. 40, 52).

Because the traditional justifications for the marital exemption no longer have any validity, other arguments have been advanced in its defense. The first of these recent rationales, which is stressed by the People in this case, is that the marital exemption protects against governmental intrusion into marital privacy and promotes reconciliation of the spouses, and thus that elimination of the exemption would be disruptive to marriages. While protecting marital privacy and encouraging reconciliation are legitimate state interests, there is no rational relation between allowing a husband to forcibly rape his wife and these interests. The marital exemption simply does not further marital privacy because this right of privacy protects consensual acts, not violent sexual assaults. Just as a husband cannot invoke a right of marital privacy to escape liability for beating his wife,[12] he cannot justifiably rape his wife under the guise of a right to privacy.

Similarly, it is not tenable to argue that elimination of the marital exemption would disrupt marriages because it would discourage reconciliation. Clearly, it is the violent act of rape and not the subsequent attempt of the wife to seek protection through the criminal justice system which "disrupts" a marriage. Moreover, if the marriage has already reached the point where intercourse is accomplished by violent assault it is doubtful that there is anything left to reconcile. This, of course, is particularly true if the wife is willing to bring criminal charges against her husband which could result in a lengthy jail sentence.

Another rationale sometimes advanced in support of the marital exemption is that marital rape would be a difficult crime to prove. A related argument is that allowing such prosecutions could lead to fabricated complaints by "vindictive" wives. The difficulty of proof argument is based on the problem of showing lack of consent. Proving lack of consent, however, is often the most difficult part of any rape prosecution, particularly where the rapist and the victim had a prior relationship. Similarly, the possibility that married women

12. A wife may sue her husband for torts he commits against her, including assault and battery (General Obligations Law 3-313).

will fabricate complaints would seem to be no greater than the possibility of unmarried women doing so.[13] The criminal justice system, with all of its built-in safeguards, is presumed to be capable of handling any false complaints. Indeed, if the possibility of fabricated complaints were a basis for not criminalizing behavior which would otherwise be sanctioned, virtually all crimes other than homicides would go unpunished.

The final argument in defense of the marital exemption is that marital rape is not as serious as offense as other rape and is thus adequately dealt with by the possibility of prosecution under criminal statutes, such as assault statutes, which provide for less severe punishment. The fact that rape statutes exist, however, is a recognition that the harm caused by a forcible rape is different, and more severe, than the harm caused by an ordinary assault. "[S]hort of homicide, [rape] is the ultimate violation of self" (Coker v. Georgia, 433 U.S. 584, 597 [citation omitted]). Under the Penal Law, assault is generally a misdemeanor unless either the victim suffers "serious physical injury" or a deadly weapon or dangerous instrument is used (Penal Law §§120.05, 120.06, 120.10). Thus, if the defendant had been living with Denise at the time he forcibly raped . . . her he probably could not have been charged with a felony, let alone a felony with punishment equal to that for rape in the first degree.[14]

Moreover, there is no evidence to support the argument that marital rape has less severe consequences than other rape. On the contrary, numerous studies have shown that marital rape is frequently quite violent and generally has *more* severe, traumatic effects on the victim than other rape.

Among the recent decisions in this country addressing the marital exemption, only one court has concluded that there is a rational basis for it (see People v. Brown, 632 P.2d 1025 [Colo.]).[15] We agree with the other courts which have analyzed the exemption, which have been unable to find any present justification for it. Justice Holmes wrote: "It is revolting to have no better reason for a rule of law than that so it was laid down in the time of Henry IV. It is still more revolting if the grounds upon which it was laid down have vanished long since, and the rule simply persists from blind imitation of the past" (Holmes, The Path of the Law, 10 Harv. L. Rev. 457, 469). This

13. The stigma and other difficulties associated with a woman reporting a rape and pressing charges probably deter most attempts to fabricate an incident; rape remains a grossly underreported crime.

14. Rape in the first degree [is a] "Class B violent felony offense," the minimum sentence for which is a jail term of 2-6 years, and the maximum sentence for which is a jail term of 8⅓-25 years (Penal Law §70.02). The defendant possibly could have been charged with coercion in the first degree, a class D felony (Penal Law 135.65), but not all forcible rapes meet all the elements of the coercion statute, (see People v. Greer, 42 N.Y.2d 170, 174-175), and thus if a husband cannot be prosecuted under the rape statute when he forcibly rapes his wife he may be able to escape prosecution for any felony.

15. The Colorado Supreme Court, relying on a 1954 Law Review comment, stated that the marital exemption "may remove a substantial obstacle to the resumption of normal marital relations" and "averts difficult emotional issues and problems of proof inherent in this sensitive area" (632 P.2d at 1027). We have considered, and rejected, both of these arguments.

statement is an apt characterization of the marital exemption; it lacks a rational basis, and therefore violates the equal protection clauses of both the federal and state constitutions (U.S. Const., 14th Amend., §1; N.Y. Const., Art I, §11).

B. THE EXEMPTION FOR FEMALES

Under the Penal Law only males can be convicted of rape in the first degree. Insofar as the rape statute applies to acts of "sexual intercourse," which, as defined in the Penal Law (see Penal Law §130.00) can only occur between a male and a female, it is true that a female cannot physically rape a female and that therefore there is no denial of equal protection when punishing only males for forcibly engaging in sexual intercourse with females.[16] The equal protection issue, however, stems from the fact that the statute applies to males who forcibly rape females but does not apply to females who forcibly rape males.

Rape statutes historically applied only to conduct by males against females, largely because the purpose behind the proscriptions was to protect the chastity of women and thus their property value to their fathers or husbands. New York's rape statute has always protected only females, and has thus applied only to males (see Penal Law §130.35; 1909 Penal Law §2010; 1881 Penal Code, Title X, Ch II §278). Presently New York is one of only ten jurisdictions that does not have a gender-neutral statute for forcible rape.[17]

A statute which treats males and females differently violates equal protection unless the classification is substantially related to the achievement of an important governmental objective. This test applies whether the statute discriminates against males or against females. The People bear the burden of showing both the existence of an important objective and the substantial relationship between the discrimination in the statute and that objective. This burden is not met in the present case, and therefore the gender exemption also renders the statute unconstitutional.

The first argument advanced by the People in support of the exemption for females is that because only females can become pregnant the state may constitutionally differentiate between forcible rapes of females and forcible rapes of males. This court and the United States Supreme Court have upheld statutes which subject males to criminal liability for engaging in sexual intercourse with underage females without the converse being true (People v.

16. A female can, however, be convicted under the present statute as an accomplice to forcible rape of a female (Penal Law §§20.00, 20.05[3]; People v. Evans, 58 A.D.2d 919).

17. The other nine jurisdictions are Alabama, Delaware, District of Columbia, Georgia, Idaho, Kansas, Mississippi, Oregon, and Virginia. Some of these other states, like New York (see Penal Law §130.65), have other statutes which proscribe conduct including the forcible rape of a male by a female and which have less severe punishments than for forcible rape of a female by a male.

Whidden, supra; Michael M. v. Superior Court of Sonoma County, 450 U.S. 464). The rationale behind these decisions was that the primary purpose of such "statutory rape" laws is to protect against the harm caused by teenage pregnancies, there being no need to provide the same protection to young males.

There is no evidence, however, that preventing pregnancies is a primary purpose of the statute prohibiting forcible rape, nor does such a purpose seem likely. Rather, the very fact that the statute proscribes "forcible compulsion" shows that its overriding purpose is to protect a woman from an unwanted, forcible, and often violent sexual intrusion into her body. Thus, due to the different purposes behind forcible rape laws and "statutory" (consensual) rape laws, the cases upholding the gender discrimination in the latter are not decisive with respect to the former, and the People cannot meet their burden here by simply stating that only females can become pregnant.

The People also claim that the discrimination is justified because a female rape victim "faces the probability of medical, sociological, and psychological problems unique to her gender." This same argument, when advanced in support of the discrimination in the statutory rape laws, was rejected by this court in People v. Whidden, supra (51 N.Y.2d at 461), and it is no more convincing in the present case. "An 'archaic and overbroad generalization,' which is evidently grounded in long-standing stereotypical notions of the differences between the sexes, simply cannot serve as a legitimate rationale for a penal provision that is addressed only to adult males."

Finally, the People suggest that a gender-neutral law for forcible rape is unnecessary, and that therefore the present law is constitutional, because a woman either cannot actually rape a man or such attacks, if possible, are extremely rare. Although the "physiologically impossible" argument has been accepted by several courts (see, People v. Reilly, 85 Misc. 2d 702, 706-707; Brooks v. State, 24 Md. App. 334; Finley v. State, 527 S.W.2d 553 [Tex. Crim. App.]), it is simply wrong. The argument is premised on the notion that a man cannot engage in sexual intercourse unless he is sexually aroused, and if he is aroused then he is consenting to intercourse. "Sexual intercourse" however, "occurs upon any penetration, however slight" (Penal Law §130.00); this degree of contact can be achieved without a male being aroused and thus without his consent.

As to the "infrequency" argument, while forcible sexual assaults by females upon males are undoubtedly less common than those by males upon females this numerical disparity cannot by itself make the gender discrimination constitutional. Women may well be responsible for a far lower number of all serious crimes than are men, but such a disparity would not make it permissible for the state to punish only men who commit, for example, robbery.

To meet their burden of showing that a gender-based law is substantially related to an important governmental objective the People must set forth an "exceedingly persuasive justification" for the classification, which requires, among other things, a showing that the gender-based law serves the governmental objective better than would a gender-neutral law. The fact that the act of a female forcibly raping a male may be a difficult or rare occurrence does not mean that the gender exemption satisfies the constitutional test. A gender-neutral law would indisputably better serve, even if only marginally, the objective of deterring and punishing forcible sexual assaults. The only persons "benefitted" by the gender-exemption are females who forcibly rape males. As the Supreme Court has stated, "[a] gender-based classification which, as compared to a gender-neutral one, generates additional benefits only for those it has no reason to prefer cannot survive equal protection scrutiny" (Orr v. Orr, supra, 440 U.S. at 283).

Accordingly, we find that section 130.35 of the Penal Law violates equal protection because it exempts females from criminal liability for forcible rape.

V

Having found that the [statute] for rape in the first degree [is] unconstitutionally underinclusive, the remaining issue is the appropriate remedy for [the] equal protection [violation]. When a statute is constitutionally defective because of underinclusion, a court may either strike the statute, and thus make it applicable to nobody, or extend the coverage of the statute to those formerly excluded. Accordingly, the unconstitutionality of one part of a criminal statute does not necessarily render the entire statute void.

This court's task is to discern what course the Legislature would have chosen to follow if it had foreseen our conclusions as to underinclusiveness. As Judge Cardozo wrote over 50 years ago, "The question is in every case whether the Legislature, if partial invalidity had been foreseen, would have wished the statute to be enforced with the invalid part exscinded, or rejected altogether." . . . These principles of severance apply as well where elimination of an invalid exemption will impose burdens on those not formerly burdened by the statute, and where the exemption is part of a criminal statute.

The question then is whether the Legislature would prefer to have statutes which cover forcible rape . . . with no exemption for married men who rape . . . their wives and no exception made for females who rape males, or instead to have no statutes proscribing forcible rape. . . . In any case where a court must decide whether to sever an exemption or instead declare an entire statute a nullity it must look at the importance of the statute, the significance of the exemption within the overall statutory scheme, and the effects of striking down the statute. Forcible sexual assaults have historically been treated as serious crimes and certainly remain so today. Statutes prohibiting such behavior are of the utmost importance, and to declare such statutes a nullity would have a disastrous effect on the public interest and safety. The inevitable conclusion is that the Legislature would prefer to eliminate the exemptions and thereby preserve the [statute]. Accordingly we choose the remedy of striking the marital exemption . . . and the gender exemption from Penal Law 130.35, so that it is now the law of this state that any person who engages in sexual intercourse . . . with any other person by forcible compulsion is guilty of . . . rape in the first degree. . . . Because the [statute] under which the defendant was convicted [is] not being struck down, his conviction is affirmed.

Though our decision does not "create a crime," it does, of course, enlarge the scope of two criminal statutes. We recognize that a court should be reluctant to expand criminal statutes, due to the danger of usurping the role of the Legislature, but in this case overriding policy concerns dictate our following such a course in light of the catastrophic effect that striking down the [statute] and thus creating a hiatus would have. Courts in other states have in numerous cases applied these same principles in eliminating an unconstitutional exception from a criminal statute and thereby enlarging the scope of the statute. The decision most similar factually to the present one comes from the Alaska Supreme Court in Plas v. United States, (598 P.2d 966). That court addressed an equal protection challenge by a female prostitute to a statute which criminalized prostitution, and defined it as a female offering her body for sexual intercourse for hire. The court agreed with the defendant that the statute violated equal protection because it covered only females, but chose to remedy this underinclusion by striking the definition, thereby expanding the statute to cover any person who engaged in prostitution, and affirmed her conviction.

The defendant cannot claim that our decision to retain the rape [statute], and thereby affirm his conviction, denies him due process of the law. The due process clause of the Fourteenth Amendment requires that an accused have had fair warning at the time of his conduct that such conduct was made criminal by the state. Defendant did not come within any of the exemptions which we have stricken, and thus his conduct was covered by the [statute as it] existed at the time of his attack on Denise.

Neither can it be said that by the affirmance of his conviction the defendant is deprived of a constitutionally protected right to equal protection. The remedy chosen by our opinion is to extend the coverage of the provisions for forcible rape . . . to all those to whom these provisions can constitutionally be applied. While this remedy does treat the defendant differently than, for example, a married man who, while living with his wife, raped her prior to this decision, the distinction is rational inasmuch as it is justified by the limitations imposed on our remedy by the notice requirements of the due process clause (U.S. Const. Amend. 14), and the prohibition against ex post facto laws (U.S. Const., Art I, §10). Thus, for purposes of choosing the proper remedy, the defendant is simply not similarly situated to those persons who were not within the scope of the statutes as they existed prior to our decision.

To reverse the defendant's conviction would mean that all those persons now awaiting trial for forcible rape . . . would be entitled to dismissal of the indictment. Indeed if we were to reverse no person arrested for forcible rape . . . prior to the date of this decision could be prosecuted for that offense, and every person already convicted of forcible rape . . . who raised the equal protection challenge would be entitled to have the conviction vacated. As the equal protection clause does not require us to reach such a result, we decline to do so.

Accordingly, the order of the Appellate Division should be affirmed.

B. KIDNAPPING

Consider the following from the commentary to Model Penal Code §212.1 (1980):

> The central problem in the law of kidnapping is to restrict the drastic sanctions authorized for this offense to instances of misbehavior warranting such punishment. The challenge, in other words, is to define the crime in terms that identify a distinct kind of wrongful act. This goal requires avoidance of two related dangers.
>
> First, the entire range of misconduct based on unlawful confinement of another must not be lumped together in one undifferentiated offense for purposes of grading. The person who physically restrains another on a public street in order to drive a point home is guilty of wrongful interference with the other's personal liberty, but a rational penal code must distinguish such conduct from prolonged confinement and isolation from the protection of the law. Even instances of more serious misbehavior, such as locking another in a closet for several hours, should be treated differently from abduction for ransom. Finally, the extreme gravity of sanctions authorized under existing law is related to the prospect that the victim will not emerge alive. This danger is precluded if the kidnapper voluntarily releases his captive alive, and the law should take some account of such action. . . .
>
> The other potential danger which a rational penal code must avoid is that the definition of kidnapping will sweep within its scope conduct that is decidedly wrongful but that should be punished as some other crime. Thus, for example, the robber who forces his victim to move from one room to another in order to find a cashbox or open a safe technically may commit kidnapping as well as robbery. This reasoning raises the possibility of cumulative penalties or of higher sanctions for kidnapping, even though the "removal" of the victim to another place was part and parcel of the robbery and not an independent wrong. Similarly, many instances of forcible rape involve some coerced movement of the victim or unlawful restraint for enough time to complete the sex act. Again, the actor may be liable for both kidnapping and rape, even though such asportation or detention of the victim is a criminologically insignificant circumstance in a course of conduct constituting rape. Definition of kidnapping to exclude such cases is a task of special subtlety for, unless some particular care is taken, trivial aspects of robbery, rape, or some other crime will end up classified as the most serious version of kidnapping.
>
> The concerns expressed here are not merely hypothetical. Experience reveals numerous instances of abusive prosecution under expansive kidnapping

> statutes for conduct that a rational and mature penal law would have treated as another crime. Furthermore, the harms occasioned thereby are more important than mere aesthetic distaste for conceptual confusion. The availability of kidnapping as an alternative to robbery or rape may mean imposition of higher penalties on grounds that must be termed haphazard. Where the underlying crime is not completed, prosecution for kidnapping instead of attempt may amount to an end run around the special doctrinal protections designed for uncompleted crimes. Improper use of kidnapping statutes may also involve de facto negation of legislative decisions in other contexts. For example, some states bar conviction for rape on the uncorroborated testimony of the complaining witness. That requirement is a controversial issue that should be debated and resolved on its own merits. If the legislative judgment favors retention of such a requirement, that choice should not be nullified by prosecutorial discretion to deal with the same course of conduct as kidnapping, which has no parallel evidentiary rule.

Committing certain offenses, such as robbery or rape, often entails forcibly moving the victim. The law may therefore find it difficult at times to determine whether the robber or rapist has also kidnapped the victim. The courts have sustained convictions for kidnapping where the forced movement of the victim appears to be incidental to the commission of another offense. See, e.g., State v. Ayers, 198 Kan. 723, 426 P.2d 21 (1967) (convictions for kidnapping and rape were sustained where defendant moved victim about 11 feet). As noted in the Commentary to the Model Penal Code, the severe penalties for kidnapping may be excessive where the movement of the victim seems clearly incidental to the commission of another crime. Many states (as well as the MPC) attempt to avoid this problem by allowing conviction for kidnapping only if the movement, or asportation, of the victim was "substantial." Consider how the following case addresses this central issue.

COMMONWEALTH v. HUGHES

Superior Court of Pennsylvania
399 A.2d 694 (1979)

CERCONE, Judge:

Appellant was convicted following a jury trial of rape, kidnapping, unlawful restraint, terroristic threats and possession of instruments of a crime. On appeal, appellant claims that the evidence was insufficient to support the definition of the statutory crime of kidnapping and that the trial court abused its discretion in refusing the appellant's request at trial for a continuance. We disagree and affirm the conviction.

The facts . . . are essentially as follows. On August 11, 1976, Cynthia Lee Helfrich drove Howard Harrison to Media, Pennsylvania for an appointment with his attorney. Arriving early before the law offices opened, the two waited outside on a public bench. While they were waiting, appellant approached them and attempted to engage them in conversation. When appellant's conversation was not encouraged, he left. Mr. Harrison then went to his attorney's office to keep the scheduled appointment. Ms. Helfrich did not accompany Mr. Harrison into the office building because she was casually dressed and without shoes. Once Ms. Helfrich was alone, appellant returned, sat beside her and resumed his one-sided conversation. Appellant asked Ms. Helfrich if she wanted to go for a ride or smoke marijuana with him. When Ms. Helfrich refused, appellant left. Minutes later, the appellant returned, placed a sharp kitchen knife to her throat and stated, "I think you are going for a ride." Appellant forced Ms. Helfrich to walk to his car one and one-half blocks away and threatened to kill her if she resisted. Once in the car, he drove around the Media area in a reckless manner for approximately two miles and stopped his car in an abandoned lot surrounded by trees. He then forced Ms. Helfrich into the wooded area where he raped her. He then returned her to a place near the attorney's office and fled. The abduction occupied somewhat less than thirty minutes.

The statutory crime of kidnapping is defined in 18 Pa. C.S.A. §2901 in pertinent part as follows: "A person is guilty of kidnapping if he unlawfully removes another a substantial distance under the circumstances from the place where he is found or if he unlawfully confines another for a substantial period in a place of isolation, with any of the following intentions: . . . (2) to facilitate commission of any felony or flight thereafter." Appellant contends that the jury was unable to conclude as a matter of law that the victim was removed a "substantial distance under the circumstances" or "confine[d] . . . for a substantial period." Appellant focuses in on the word "substantial" and asserts that two miles and thirty minutes is not "substantial" within the statutory framework.

In attempting to ascertain the legislative meaning of the word "substantial," we find that legal authority is sparse. Two cases and no legislative history in this jurisdiction offer little guidance. In Commonwealth v. Ruehling, 232 Pa. Super. 378, 334 A.2d 702 (1975), this court held that thirty miles was a "substantial distance." In Commonwealth v. Larry, 467 Pa. 501, 359 A.2d 388 (1976), the defendant forcefully abducted the victim from her home one night after stabbing her three times. The defendant delivered the victim to the hospital the following morning when [sic] she was pronounced dead. At trial in Commonwealth v. Larry supra, a medical examiner testified that the victim suffered numerous blows with a blunt instrument in addition to the three knife wounds. The Supreme Court held that the evidence was sufficient to sustain a conviction of criminal homicide which occurred during the perpetration of a kidnapping. Implicit in its holding was the fact that the elements of the statutory definition of kidnapping had been met although there was no discussion of the length of time involved nor the distance which the defendant had transported the victim.

In these cases, the courts have not attempted to establish a definition of the concepts of "substantial distance" nor "unlawfully confine[d] . . . for a substantial period." These definitions cannot be confined to a given linear distance nor a certain time period. This is clear from a consideration of the most obvious evil at which the statute is aimed—the abduction of a victim to hold for ransom. Certainly the guilt of an abductor cannot depend upon the fortuity of the distance he has transported his victim nor the length of time elapsed before the ransom is paid. "Substantial" is a limitation within the statutory framework of kidnapping, and in ascertaining the proper construction of that limitation it is useful to consider the experience of other jurisdictions and §212.1 of the Model Penal Code which is essentially similar to the Pennsylvania kidnapping statute.

In most states, as in Pennsylvania, kidnapping is one of the most serious crimes carrying with it extremely severe criminal sanctions. It developed that in other jurisdictions which had a broader definition of kidnapping than Pennsylvania, the prosecutors would charge a defendant with kidnapping in order to obtain a higher permissible sentence whenever there was any forcible movement of the victim. Convictions were upheld even when the movement was incidental to the commission of a separate crime. . . . This position was taken to extremes in People v. Wein, 50 Cal. 2d 383, 326 P.2d 457 (1958). In that case, the defendant was convicted of kidnapping when he forced his victim to go from room to room within her house until she found her wallet, he then robbed and raped her. A later case citing *Wein* held that "*any* carrying away is sufficient." State v. Ingland, 278 N.C. 42, 51, 178 S.E.2d 577, 583 (1971) [emphasis in original]. This equivocal situation was clarified in a California case when the Supreme Court of that state reversed its line of cases which held that any movement constituted kidnapping. In reversing a conviction for kidnapping, the Supreme Court instructed that "movements of the victim [which] are merely incidental . . . [to] the robbery and do not substantially increase the risk of harm over and above that necessarily present in the crime of robbery itself" are outside the scope of the kidnapping statute. People v. Daniels, 71 Cal. 2d 1119, 80 Cal. Rptr. 897, 459 P.2d 225, 238 (1969). . . .

The framers of the Model Penal Code were aware of the experience of other jurisdictions when they drafted the model kidnapping statute. They recognized that "[w]hen an especially outrageous crime is committed there will be a public clamor for the extreme penalty and it is asking too much of public officials and juries to resist such pressures." Model Penal Code §212.1, Comment (Tent. Draft No. 11, p.14, 1960). To combat the undesirable situation of charging kidnapping to obtain a higher permissible sentence, the framers of the Model Penal Code drafted the kidnapping statute restrictively. The statute reads in part as follows: "A person is guilty of kidnapping if he unlawfully removes another from his place of residence or business, or a substantial distance from the vicinity where he is found, or if he unlawfully confines another for a substantial period in a place of isolation . . . (b) to facilitate commission of any felony. . . ." Model Penal Code §212.1. The drafters made explicit their "purpose to preclude kidnapping convictions based on trivial changes of location having no bearing on the evil at hand." Model Penal Code §212.1, Comment (Tent. Draft No. 11, p.16, 1960).

Drawing from the experience of other jurisdictions, the comments to the Model Code, and the fact that the Pennsylvania statute is similar to the Model Penal Code Statute of kidnapping, it is clear to us that the legislature intended to exclude from kidnapping the incidental movement of a victim during the commission of a crime which does not substantially increase the risk of harm to the victim.

Turning to the case at hand, we find that the movement of the victim was not a trivial incident to the other crime charged. Although the victim was removed only a distance of two miles, the wooded area to which she was brought was in an isolated area, seemingly beyond the aid of her friends and police. Under the circumstances, two miles is a substantial enough distance to place the victim in a completely different environmental setting removed from the security of familiar surroundings. (In addition, the movement itself seriously endangered the victim as she was subject to a knife poised at her throat and to the reckless driving of appellant. At one point, appellant drove onto a one-way street in the wrong direction.) Furthermore, once isolated, the appellant was free to deal with his victim at will. The fact that appellant returned his victim after raping her says nothing of the terrifying and desperate reaction that such a removal might have upon a victim. In such a case, the singular fact of removal compounded the risk of harm to the victim which was distinct from the risk inherent in the crimes which the movement accompanied. Under these circumstances, it is evidently clear that the jury had adequate grounds for finding that the victim was removed a "substantial distance." We need not decide whether the 30 minutes involved constitutes a "substantial period" under the Model Penal Code. We will state, however, that what is a "substantial period" in time can depend on the mental state of the victim. The fright that can be engendered in 30 minutes can have the same debilitating effect on one person as 30 hours may have on another. Accordingly, the conviction is sustained.

Notes and Questions

1. *Asportation.* Note that the court focused on the fact that Hughes took his victim to a "completely different environmental setting" where she was isolated from the aid of friends and police. What relevance does this fact have to the question of whether Hughes should be punished for one crime or two? Would it have made any difference if Ms. Helfrich had been familiar with the area to which she was taken? If she had been taken to her own home? If she had been moved only 2 blocks, or held only 10 minutes? Is the court defining "substantial distance," or is it interpreting the subjective experience of the victim?

2. *Secrecy.* Some states have rejected the asportation requirement. In these states, the court may sustain a kidnapping conviction even though the defendant did not move the victim at all. Instead, kidnapping is defined as the

unlawful seizure of another with the intent to detain him secretly against his will.

> [P]rolonged restraint without asportation may be as penologically significant as asportation and, under certain circumstances, will support a conviction for kidnapping as a separate act or animus from that of rape. Secret confinement, such as in an abandoned building or nontrafficked area, without the showing of any substantial asportation, may, in a given instance, also signify a separate animus and support a conviction for kidnapping apart from the commission of an underlying offense.

State v. Logan, 60 Ohio St. 2d 126, 397 N.E.2d 1345, 1351 (1979).

In the case of many offenses against the person, the defendant necessarily restrains the victim, often with a measure of secrecy in mind. See, e.g., Cowan v. State, 208 Tenn. 52, 347 S.W.2d 37 (1961) (conviction for kidnapping of a defendant who had held two teenage couples in their car for seven hours, in an unsuccessful attempt to rape two of the victims). What distinguishes a crime of this sort from kidnapping, in a state that has eliminated the asportation requirement?

3. *Consent.* Note that the Model Penal Code provision for kidnapping is defined in terms of *unlawful* removal, rather than forcible removal. The defendant cannot be guilty of kidnapping if the alleged victim consented to his or her movement. But the defendant may be convicted of kidnapping where he gains the victim's consent unlawfully, or where the victim is unable to give informed consent. In State v. Ware, 63 Ohio St. 2d 84, 406 N.E.2d 1112 (1980), the defendant offered to permit the victim the use of his telephone in his residence. When the two arrived at the defendant's home, the defendant stated that he had no telephone. He thereupon carried the victim to his bedroom, where he raped her. The court stated that the defendant's act of carrying the victim to his bedroom was an insufficient asportation to sustain a kidnapping conviction. However, the court held that the victim's travel to the defendant's home constituted kidnapping because her consent was obtained by deceit for the purpose of commiting a felony. Does a conviction for kidnapping seem appropriate under these circumstances?

4. *Related offenses.*

Model Penal Code §212.2. Felonious Restraint.

A person commits a felony of the third degree if he knowingly:

(a) restrains another unlawfully in circumstances exposing him to risk of serious bodily injury; or

(b) holds another in a condition of involuntary servitude.

Model Penal Code §212.3. False Imprisonment.

A person commits a misdemeanor if he knowingly restrains another so as to interfere substantially with his liberty.

The Code treats felonious restraint as an intermediate offense between kidnapping and false imprisonment. Unlike kidnapping, it does not require that the victim be restrained for a specified purpose, or for a substantial period of time. False imprisonment is "a residual misdemeanor for instances of illegal restraint that do not merit felony sanctions." MPC commentary to §212.3 (1980).

Appendix A

A NOTE ON THE CRIMINAL JUSTICE SYSTEM

G. HAZARD, CRIMINAL JUSTICE SYSTEM; OVERVIEW

2 Encyclopedia of Crime and Justice 450-469 (1983)

INTRODUCTION

The criminal justice system may be considered from at least three perspectives. First, it can be considered a normative system, that is, a body of legal rules expressing social values through prohibitions backed by penal sanctions against conduct viewed as seriously wrong or harmful. Second, the criminal justice system can be regarded as an administrative system. This view comprehends the official apparatus for enforcing the criminal law, including the police and other frontline enforcement agencies, prosecutorial authorities, the judiciary, and penal and correctional facilities and services. A third view of criminal justice is that of a social system. In this perspective, defining and responding to criminal conduct involves all elements of society. This definition of criminal conduct includes not only the penal law enacted by the legislature but also the way in which these provisions are interpreted by the citizenry at all levels. For example, if particular communities do not regard simple assaults taking place within the family as fully criminal, those communities are unlikely to summon the police when one family member beats up another. So also, prosecutors generally do not pursue white-collar crime with the same intensity as they pursue violent crime, even if the actual harms are comparable, because the constituencies to which prosecutors generally respond are more concerned with violent crime. By taking into account such societal views of criminal behavior, it is possible to explain many apparent anomalies in the administration of criminal justice, for example, why many criminal provisions are in some degree "dead letters." Another example is the phenomenon of "acquittal of the guilty," that is, the fact that juries and judges often return findings of not guilty of accused persons with respect to whom the proof of technical guilt is clear and uncontroverted.

These three aspects of the criminal justice system may be integrated in examining particular phases of criminal justice and in interpreting the system as a whole. Hence, the arrest and prosecution of an offender for theft can be considered simultaneously as a manifestation of a legislative prohibition against knowingly taking another's property, as a response by the police, prosecutor, judiciary, and penal-correctional system to conduct that appears to be criminal, and as a community interpretation of the behavior in question. Criminal justice as a whole results from the interaction between legal rules, administrative practice, and societal attitudes and behavior.

Some caution is required in using the term *system* to refer to the myriad complexities contained in this framework. The term may imply a series of transactions that are arranged in a rational and efficient way to produce specified results within more or less consciously perceived constraints. The criminal justice system does indeed have a substantial degree of coherence in this sense. Thus, in the law of crimes itself the penalties for deliberate homicide are much more severe than the penalties for assault. This differential is rationally coherent if one assumes that the underlying value is protection of human life and that an attack resulting in death is a more serious impairment of that value than an attack which leaves the victim alive. Similarly, it is rational that adjudication of guilt by the court system should follow *after* investigation of an offense by the police, if the underlying value is that guilt should be determined on the basis of a disinterested weighing of evidence and not upon predisposition.

Nevertheless, it must be recognized that the criminal justice system is pervaded by anomalies and discontinuities. For example, although law and public opinion attach high value to human life, as expressed in the penalties for willful homicide, measures to control the distribution of weapons, particularly handguns, are modest to the point of being virtually nominal. So also, great efforts are made to control industrial pollutants at the same time that subsidies are provided for the production of tobacco, even though cigarette smoke probably has worse immediate effects on health than any other pollutant. Still another example of discontinuity is the phenomenon of street drunks being arrested, jailed overnight, and then released in a never-ending cycle, rather than being handled in some nonpenal way. When full account is taken of such anomalies, the criminal justice process is a "system" in only a limited sense. Although a comprehensive view of criminal justice can be projected only in terms of some conceptual system, it is important to remember that concepts are merely constructs for interpreting profoundly ambiguous and endlessly complex social events.

In the following analysis, attention will focus on the penal law as a normative system and on the police, the prosecutor, the judiciary, and the penal agencies as constituting an administrative system. The system of criminal procedural law and the larger social system that envelops the whole are considered only incidentally.

The Penal Law

Common law. Taken together, the legislative provisions defining crimes and prescribing punishments are usually referred to as the penal law, although they are also called the criminal law. The penal law in virtually all states in the United States is legislative in origin. That is, conduct is not criminally punishable unless it has been proscribed by statute.

The situation was not always thus. In the original common law, which began its development with the Norman domination of England after 1066, crimes and civil wrongs were not clearly distinguished. Moreover, there was no systematic body of criminal prohibitions. Rather, the original common-law offenses consisted of the use of force by the offender in violation of the King's peace and could result in both punitive and compensatory sanctions. It was the use of violence as such, rather than the particular consequences of a violent act, that constituted the wrong. From this foundation, the common law of crimes evolved over the course of centuries. Development took place through judicial decisions interpreting and elaborating the concept of violence into such specific categories as homicide, robbery, arson, and assault. In the later years of the common law's development, particularly from the sixteenth century onward, enactments of Parliament added specific crimes to the array of common-law offenses.

There was, however, no penal code or official systemization of the law of crimes. Commentaries by jurists, such as Matthew Hale's History of the Pleas of the Crown and the fourth volume of William Blackstone's Commentaries on the Laws of England, undertook to group the array of offenses, common-law and statutory, into coherent order according to the nature of the harm inflicted and the intensity and severity of the violation. The law of crimes thus unofficially systematized was nevertheless essentially common law, that is, the pronouncements of courts defining conduct that constituted a crime. In the colonization of British North America, the common law of crimes was received and applied. With the rupture of sovereignty in the colonies at the time of the American Revolution, however, a strong movement arose to establish all law, including the criminal law, on the foundation of legislative enactment. Initially, this took the form of legislative enactments that simply declared the common law, including the common law of crimes, to be in effect except as displaced by particular statutory provisions. However, the principle was established in many states that the definition of crimes was the province of the legislature and not of the courts.

Legislation. The period of social and political upheaval after the American and French revolutions engendered, among many other legal changes, a strong movement toward legislative codification of law, particularly the criminal law. Reform efforts aimed both to order and clarify the law and to ameliorate its severity, for in English law by 1800 more than one hundred different kinds of offenses were punishable by death. A leading reformer was Jeremy Bentham, whose utilitarianism afforded a coherent basis for ordering the law of crimes according to the principle of degrees of social harm. Many reform efforts were launched in the United States, paralleling and to some extent inspired by those of Bentham, as a result of which the law of crimes in many states was recast into more or less coherent penal codes. At least since the late nineteenth century, the criminal law has been expressed in a penal code in all but a few American jurisdictions.

Today the paradigm of penal legislation, both in substance and format, is the Model Penal Code, promulgated by the American Law Institute in 1962. The Code is a comprehensive reformulation of the principles of criminal liability that is drawn from previous codes, decisional law, and scholarly commentary. It has been substantially adopted in many states and is the preeminent source of guidance in revision and reform of substantive criminal law in the United States.

The Model Penal Code establishes a hierarchy of substantive criminal proscriptions and a corresponding hierarchy of social values. It can be considered as having two dimensions. The first consists of the principles of criminal liability; the second, of the definition of various specific crimes.

Principles of liability. The principles of liability express the fundamental notion that an individual is responsible for conforming his behavior to the standards prescribed in the criminal law. Quite different fundamental conceptions of criminal responsibility might be imagined. An individual could be considered responsible under the criminal law, and hence subject to condemnation and punishment, for causing any kind of substantial injury to another person, even for an accidental act on his own part. Some offenses actually are defined in this way, so that a violator is subject to criminal penalties even though he did not intend the result or indeed made an effort to avoid it. A familiar example is that of parking violations, which are penalized without regard to the actor's intention and for the purpose of allocating the use of street parking. However, in American law, as in Western cultures generally, such strict liability under criminal law usually is limited to monetary penalties in various regulatory schemes governing business and financial transactions. Aside from these "regulatory" offenses—which in modern society are widespread—Anglo-American criminal law generally reflects the principle that criminal liability should depend on an intention to commit wrong, or at least an awareness that serious wrong will result from a course of action.

Closely related to the principle of intentionality is that of justification or excuse. The essential notion is that a serious harm to another is not criminally punishable if it resulted from conduct that was necessary to preserve some other equal or superior interest. The most obvious examples is self-defense as a basis for avoiding liability for homicide or assault on another. Other defenses include protection of third persons, protection of property, and necessity in the carrying out of official responsibilities, for example, where a policeman uses physical force to subdue a person resisting arrest. The criminal law thus holds the individual responsible for the consequences of his intended acts, but it authorizes him in a limited way to exercise judgment to vindicate fundamental interests of social safety and order. However, popular sentiment—that is, the principles of criminal responsibility embedded in popular culture—is often more lenient. As a result, there is tension between the norms of responsibility expressed in the penal law and those shared by the ordinary citizenry. Where there is a serious discrepancy between the legal concept of responsibility and the common notions of responsibility, the result is often erratic enforcement. This tendency, in turn, compromises to some extent the legitimacy of the criminal law and therefore the legitimacy of the administration of criminal justice.

The principle of responsibility has a corollary concerning the effect of mental incapacity or immaturity on the individual's accountability. This aspect of the problem includes the endlessly debatable question of the "insanity defense." Fundamentally, the question is whether an individual under given circumstances "could but did not" control his behavior or "could not" control it. In extreme cases, everyone would recognize that a given individual is "really crazy"—that is, obviously demented. On the other hand, to excuse one who acted on the basis of impulse or passion would be to say that crimes consist only of wrongs that were definitely premeditated and committed without emotion. A society could function with a criminal law of this limited scope, relying on communal control, persuasion, and inhibition to protect its members. But our society is inhospitable to communal control, for individual autonomy holds a high place in our values. Our system therefore relies on a combination of self-control and criminal penalties for breach of self-control. The conflicting tendencies of this policy are perhaps most fully revealed in the dilemma as to how intense and how pervasive must a mental or emotional disorder be before it excuses an actor from criminal responsibility for inflicting serious harm on another.

For similar reasons, intense conflict attends the question of immaturity as a basis for limiting or precluding criminal responsibility. The notion that a youth is not fully responsible for his acts is the basis of the law governing juvenile offenders. The law provides that juveniles below a very young age are not criminally responsible at all, for example, a five-year-old who kills a playmate. Above that age but below the level of adulthood, a youthful offender is treated as responsible but with less severity than an adult under the same circumstances. The central issues are the definition of immaturity, particularly the age below which prosecution as an adult is not permitted, and the degree to which sanction against a youthful offender should emphasize rehabilitation rather than punishment. In popular terminology, this conflict presents itself as the question of whether a youthful offender is "a kid" or "a young thug." Such conflicting epithets reveal both the importance of the concept of responsibility in the criminal law and the difficulties of giving specific legal definition to the concept. A legally specified age of responsibility is, at the margin, necessarily arbitrary, and it also necessarily contradicts some segments of popular opinion.

Specific offenses. On the foundation of these basic concepts of criminal liability, the penal law defines specific offenses. The crimes established in the law are enormous in number and variety. There is a classical distinction between fundamentally or intrinsically criminal types of misbehavior, and misbehavior that is only formally criminal. This distinction is expressed in the terms malum in se and malum prohibitum: wrongs in themselves, and wrongs that are such only because they have been so declared. In this classification, homicide, assault, and theft are mala in se—acts that would be regarded as serious wrongs in any legal system in any culture. In contrast, the crime of driving on the wrong side of the street can be regarded as malum prohibitum; with much less confidence the same can be said of the crimes of failing to conform to pollution control requirements and violating building and zoning codes. However, it is evident that many offenses in the latter category are designed to induce patterns of behavior that will in turn minimize risks of serious social harms. Traffic regulations are intended, among other things, to prevent death and injury from highway accidents, and pollution controls are intended to prevent the accretion of toxic substances to lethal or injurious levels. Although it is therefore possible loosely to classify criminal offenses as mala in se and mala prohibita, it is impossible to use such a distinction for refined classification.

Among serious crimes there is an ordering that reflects fundamental social values. At one time in Western cultures, treason headed the list of crimes. It may be inferred that this positioning expressed a strong sense of insecurity about the stability of government. In modern society the state is relatively stable except under extraordinary circumstances of turmoil or revolution, and the penal law of the modern state characteristically places homicide at the head of the list of crimes. Such is the arrangement of the Model Penal Code, which begins with homicide and then proceeds to other offenses against the person: assault, including threat of assault; kidnapping; and sexual offenses, including rape, sexual molestation of minors, and related offenses. The next general category encompasses offenses against property, including arson, burglary, robbery, various forms of theft, and forgery and other frauds committed by manipulation of documents. A third general category is that of offenses against public administration, including bribery and corruption, perjury, obstruction of justice, and abuse of office. There is also a category of offenses against the family, including incest and abortion. These offenses perhaps could better have been classified as offenses against the person, but they can be viewed as addressed to the protection of the family as a social institution. Finally comes the category of offenses against public order, such as riot, disorderly conduct, and violation of privacy. Within each category there are comparable gradations. Thus, the provisions dealing with homicide begin with willful murder and end with negligent homicide, and the offenses against property begin with arson, burglary, and robbery, all of which involve an element of threat to human safety, and proceed to simple theft of various forms, where that element is absent.

This classification expresses a system of values in which individual human life stands highest and public decorum stands relatively low. A rather different hierarchy of values can be conceived. Preservation of decorum, for example, could be given far greater relative weight. Some differences in value are conspicuous. American penal law places high value on human life as compared with protection from fraud; accordingly, the fact that an attacker has previously been defrauded by the person assaulted is not a justification for an assault. However, a penal code would be intelligible which provided that assault is excusable in these circumstances, since it would thus express a high societal value on integrity in exchange transactions as compared with the value of immunity from physical violence. In any event, the relative weight attached to these specific values as expressed in the penal code is not the relative value in which they are held by some members of society. Specifically, it seems probable that the poor more than the rich regard fraud as comparable in wrongfulness to assault, and perhaps even more wrongful.

The relative order of social values in the criminal law manifests itself in still another way. In some societies, and certainly in contemporary America, the resources available to enforce the criminal law fall considerably short of those required to suppress crime completely. The administration of criminal justice therefore entails allocating resources in such a way that suppression of some crimes is pursued intensely whereas other crimes are more or less ignored. Allocation of resources may take place at the micro level, as when a policeman on patrol decides, in response to an unfolding situation, whether to chase a purse-snatcher or to respond to a burglary alert. The process also occurs at the macro level, in the way in which police, prosecution, and other agencies are organized and deployed. Thus, all police departments apparently devote a great deal of effort to following up homicides—effort that is probably disproportionate to the actual effect on the incidence of homicide. Meanwhile, they give only sporadic attention to those norms whose systematic enforcing might substantially affect behavior, for example, the incidence of muggings. The deployment of criminal justice resources is a complex mixture of efficiency and symbolism. But both calculation of efficiency and projection of symbols are intelligible only by reference to the system of values that society seeks to realize.

The Administrative System in General

Subsystems. The system of criminal justice can be considered as an administrative bureaucracy consisting of four principal subsystems: police, prosecution, judiciary, and corrections. Broadly speaking, the police are responsible for prevention of crime through patrol, and for detection of crime after it has taken place. The prosecution is responsible for assembling evidence gathered by the police, determining whether prosecution is warranted, and, where it is, presenting the evidence and the law to establish the accused person's guilt. The judiciary is responsible for deciding the questions of law and fact relevant to determination of guilt and imposition of sentence; and the correctional system provides imprisonment and monitoring of offenders who are released on probation or parole.

The functional divisions between these subsystems are not tidy. The police not only investigate crimes but may exercise considerable influence in the determination of which crimes are prosecuted. Prosecutorial policies influence police practices regarding patrol and detection. Judge-made law pervasively influences the whole criminal process and apparatus, and the judicial attitude toward sentencing affects dispositions at every point in the system. The capacity and competence of the correctional system to provide either incarceration or rehabilitation constrain the effectiveness of the criminal law as an instrument of deterrence and rehabilitation. As in all complex administrative systems, there is continuous intercommunication and influence among the components of the system and the people within them.

Influential constituencies. There are other groups, not officially part of the administrative system, who strongly interact with it. Among these is the legal profession, particularly the lawyers who regularly represent criminal defendants. They continually monitor and check the enforcement apparatus, influence the development of the law in the courts and legislatures, and mediate impressions of the system to various sectors of the general population. Another highly influential group is the news media. It is an ancient maxim that justice must not only be done, but must be seen to be done. The modern public sees the criminal justice system chiefly as the media present it, in what is published, ignored, or withheld. Another important influence in many communities, a semiofficial constituency, are the labor organizations of which police and corrections officers are members.

Also influencing the system are the accused persons themselves. Most criminal suspects are young, male, and relatively poor. They are disproportionately members of ethnic minorities. In some sense they are official participants in the criminal justice process, for their status as such is legally recognized and defined. They are permitted by law to express their attitudes and inclinations in certain key decisions by the system. Furthermore, although the resources of the prosecution are formidable when compared with those of an individual defendant, the criminal defendant group as a whole has resources that the administrative system cannot ignore. It is well recognized that the inmate population of a penal institution strongly influences the operation of the institution; similar influence operates, although in a less obvious manner, in the functions of the police, prosecution, and judiciary.

Other agencies. The exposition here focuses primarily on the ordinary criminal justice system as it exists at the state and local level. In addition to that system, there is a federal law enforcement apparatus, which includes such police agencies as the Federal Bureau of Investigation and the Customs Bureau; the prosecutorial authority of the attorney general of the United States and the local United States district attorneys; the United States courts, particularly the district courts that have trial jurisdiction and are located throughout the country; and the Federal Probation Service and the Federal Bureau of Prisons, constituting the federal correctional system.

In addition, at both the federal and state levels there are many specialized law enforcement agencies having important criminal responsibilities. These include the state police and motor-vehicle bureaus, revenue enforcement agencies such as the Internal Revenue Service at the federal level and tax commission agencies at the state and local level, and a myriad of specialized regulatory agencies having authority to investigate and prosecute violations of penal prohibitions governing health, safety, environment, and the like. The functions of these specialized agencies are not considered here. It may be noted, however, that the offenses with which these agencies deal generally are classified as white-collar offenses, for which the typically employed sanction is a monetary penalty rather than either imprisonment or probation.

System characteristics. *Mass production and discretion.* Several general observations should be made about the administrative system. First, it is required to deal with a large and never-ending flow of cases. Even though the system attempts to individualize its response to each offender, and in theory is supposed to treat each case as though it stood alone under the law, the process is in fact one of mass production. This is not to say that the system was planned as a mass-production system. Quite the contrary, many difficulties with it arise from the discrepancy between the fact of mass production and the ideal that each case be considered on its own merit.

A second general observation is that the system is pervaded by exercise of loosely controlled discretion, which is both systemic and particular. Systemically, discretion is exercised to mediate between the high incidence of crime and the modest resources available to respond to it. Decisions must be made as to the allocation of the system's resources. These decisions are made officially and to some degree publicly, but often they are not based upon open deliberation. Thus, for example, no legislative act or mayoral directive says that the police shall devote intensive effort to investigating crimes against police officers, or that they shall deal with rape only where the victim is willing to carry the prosecution all the way through, but such policies in fact exist in most communities. They are necessary simply so that the system may deal with the overload of demand that would exist if it attempted to enforce the criminal law across the board.

Exercise of discretion is particular in that subsystems and individual officials within the system have a high degree of autonomy in performing their functions. A policeman is assigned a beat, but the patrol of the beat is usually under minimal supervision from superior police officers; the patrolman's allocation of time and effort is not subject to anything like the direction given an ordinary office or production-line worker, for example. In prosecutor's offices, individual deputy prosecutors generally have considerable discretion in deciding on the types and quality of cases that should be fully prosecuted. This discretion results partly from loose administration and partly from the fact that the prosecuting staff consists of lawyers who regard themselves as having the right and duty to exercise professional judgment in the performance of their functions. At the judicial stage, judges are the principal officials and have broad professional discretion in the exercise of their functions, particularly in sentencing. Moreover, the courts are very loosely administered in most localities, so that individual judges have administrative autonomy to an important degree. So also in the correctional system, discretion is both formal and de facto. Broad official discretion is exercised with regard to whether imprisonment will be terminated and parole granted, whether "good time" allowance (resulting in the shortening of imprisonment) will be denied for violation of prison regulations, and so on. Lower-level, informal discretion is exercised by prison guards in responding to prisoner behavior of all kinds.

Taken as a whole, the system is subject to pervasive formal legal controls, but it is also characterized by the pervasive exercise of unsupervised discretion. There are dynamic relationships between these two phenomena; because legal rules so thoroughly govern official action, it is assumed that the official actions are under control and that higher administrative controls are unnecessary; and the rigidity of legal controls creates incentives to seek waivers, a fact that in turn entails exercise of discretion.

Balkanization. The administrative structure of the criminal justice system is extremely decentralized. There are about forty thousand different public police forces in the United States, one for almost every city and for many villages, and usually a separate one in every county. In some large cities there are several different police agencies, such as transit police or housing police, in addition to the municipal police as such. In virtually all states, the prosecutorial function is centered at the county level in the office of the district attorney. Many large cities have a further division of prosecutorial authority in that municipal legal departments prosecute misdemeanors. The judiciary is usually organized along county lines, although in rural areas in most states the counties are grouped into judicial districts. In a few states the judiciary is organized on a statewide basis, but even there the daily operations of calendars and judicial assignments usually is handled separately in each courthouse. In any case, the work load of judges and supporting court staff is unbalanced and poorly managed in many jurisdictions.

The correctional system is sharply divided in almost all states between local authorities and state authorities. At the local level, except in very thinly populated rural areas, virtually all counties maintain a jail. All cities of substantial size have their own jails. Jails are used for temporary incarceration of persons awaiting prosecution and for punishment of offenders sentenced to short jail sentences. Also at the local level, but usually attached to the court system rather than the jail system, is the probation service, which performs essentially two functions. The first is investigating an offender's background immediately after conviction and before sentence for the purpose of providing information on which to base the sentence. The second is supervising offenders who are given a sentence of probation. The correctional system at the state level consists of the prison system, including institutions for the incarceration of juveniles, and the parole service. The parole service is usually attached to the state prison administration and provides supervision of offenders who have served a prison term and are released on parole.

The administrative autonomy of these various administrative organizations has two dimensions. First, each of the components—police, prosecution, judiciary, and corrections—generally is administratively autonomous from the others. (In a few states the courts and the prosecutor's office are under one administrative authority.) Second, the various local subdivisions of each of these functions are administratively separated from one another. Thus, police units of different cities, even those in a single metropolitan area, are subject to no common administrative control, although they often have various formal and informal working arrangements. The same is true of prosecutor's offices from one county to the other and, to a lesser extent, of courts and probation services.

The foregoing description if anything understates the lack of administrative coordination in criminal justice. A complete account would require describing the separation between various federal criminal justice agencies and their state counterparts, and between state-level criminal justice agencies, such as the state police and the state attorney general's office, and their local counterparts. It would also describe how these separations impede vital routines, such as controlling the flow of cases from one subsystem to another, coordinating allocation of resources, and using common terminology and comparable statistics. On the other hand, the fact that these organizations are not well orchestrated has certain important benefits. Most obvious is the maintenance of the independence of the judiciary, with the resulting governance of the functions of police, prosecution, and corrections by independent judicial review. This legal control of the criminal justice system is unparalleled anywhere else in the world. Moreover, the tensions arising between autonomous agencies result in public visibility of fundamental issues in criminal justice that otherwise would be submerged within a bureaucracy. For example, the fundamental issue of allocating police and prosecutorial resources is manifested in conflicts between police and prosecutorial agencies over priorities regarding specific crimes. Making the issues visible subjects them in some degree to resolution in accordance with public opinion, rather than simply with the preference of the agencies involved.

Another generalization is that the degree of professionalism and competence in the broadest sense varies considerably throughout the country. The variance is probably much less than it was around 1960, and certainly less than it was in 1930. The day of the bumpkin sheriff or of the judge who is law unto himself has virtually passed. Modern communication and interaction disseminate techniques and standards of performance despite administrative boundaries. Nevertheless, variance remains and has important consequences. "Professionalism" implies certain values, particularly impersonality, neutrality, and formal rationality in goals and techniques. The fact that professionalism is unevenly distributed among various elements in the system indicates, among other things, that there are corresponding differences of public opinion on the underlying issues of value. It seems fair to say, for example, that some communities prefer an "old boy" police force.

POLICE

Organization. Of the two basic police functions, prevention and detection, prevention—patrolling streets and other places where crime may happen—is the most visible.

Prevention and detection. Patrolling is a "proactive" technique, that is, it consists of planned anticipatory maneuvers which frustrate potential criminal activity. Detection consists of investigating crimes that already have taken place, and may be described as a reactive technique, in that it is mobilized after, and in response to, criminal activity initiated by an offender. In strategic terms, prevention and detection obviously reinforce each other. Effective prevention makes unnecessary the laborious process of identifying and prosecuting criminal offenders, whereas effective detection provides a deterrent to crime that would take place beyond the scrutiny of a preventive patrol.

From an organizational and tactical point of view, however, prevention and detection are generally fairly distinct. Characteristically, preventive police patrol is carried out by more or less widely dispersed police officers, operating individually or in pairs and patrolling on foot or in patrol cars. The number and distribution of patrols is worked out, mainly on the basis of continuously trial and error, with the aim of reducing crime in public spaces (such as street assaults), and in places accessible from public spaces (such as burglaries in residential districts). Police departments rarely patrol purely private locations, such as apartment houses or office buildings, partly because of legal limitations on such patrols and partly because responsibility for such locations is deemed a matter of private concern. Hence, there has been an enormous expansion of private policing of private locations through all kinds of guards and "security officers" in stores, office buildings, shopping areas, apartment houses, and residential areas, where private police forces are employed to supplement public patrol. The number of private police engaged in various forms of patrol is now substantially larger than the number of public police engaged in that function. Whether patrol is performed by public or private police, however, it is characteristically performed by low-ranking officers assigned to cruise a particular territory and to keep an eye out for criminal eventuality. In most urban localities it is very dangerous work.

Specialized squads. The detective function is usually performed by specialized squads. Many police departments have several detective squads dealing specifically with such crimes as homicide, burglary, rape, and narcotic trafficking. The detective function is so organized because detection essentially involves compiling and sifting through background information. For certain types of crime, particularly homicide, the useful information relates chiefly to the facts of the immediate crime and the identity of persons having a motive, since that crime typically involves people who have had a relationship with each other. With respect to other crimes, particularly burglary and robbery, the investigative task consists of comparing prior police records with what is known about the immediate offense to derive a suspect or set of suspects upon whom more intensive investigation may then focus. The key to any suspect is a pattern of repeated offenses, that is, his modus operandi (M/O). In either case, the detection focus is largely a historical investigation, dealing with records, photographs, fingerprints, and the like, whereas patrol is a face-to-face "action" interchange.

In general, detection is performed by police who are older, higher in rank, longer in service, and more knowledgeable about patterns of crime and the criminal process than are patrol officers. However, virtually all detectives are former patrolmen, a consequence of the fact that virtually all police forces hire at the patrolman rank and promote from within. The detection function is thus carried out by officers who have first established their ability to perform the more rough-and-ready functions of patrol. Few police departments directly recruit and train experts in detection, although in urban centers there are specialists in such fields as ballistics and fingerprint analysis. Few police departments have officers trained in detection of white-collar crime, a circumstance that contributes to relegating responsibility for controlling such crime to specialized administrative agencies.

Most urban police departments have specialized units that deal with victimless crimes, including narcotic violations, gambling, and prostitution. Characteristically, these offenses involve consensual participants, and hence no unwilling victims. For this reason, these offenses cannot be suppressed by either patrol or the usual detective function, since these methods presuppose either that the offense is directly observable by the police or that persons injured by the offense will cooperate in supplying information about the offender. In dealing with victimless crimes the police therefore must be both aggressive and surreptitious, using such methods as hidden surveillance and informers. Because concealment and deception necessarily must be used, this kind of police work is morally ambiguous and often crosses the border of legal restrictions on police search, interrogation, and entrapment. In addition, victimless crimes constitute a commerce often involving large sums of money, a circumstance which makes police operations directed against such crimes very vulnerable to corruption.

Police operations addressing crime, whether through patrol or detection, in fact occupy only a fraction of the effort and attention of police departments. Most police departments spend the bulk of their time in various helping services to the public, such as traffic control, crowd control, emergency ambulance and other health and safety care, physical rescue, and emergency taxi service. In addition, all police departments devote a substantial amount of effort to traffic offenses and to the routine arrest and temporary jailing of drunks, both motorists and pedestrians.

Arrest. The term *arrest* is ambiguous. Legally, an arrest includes a temporary involuntary interception of a person's otherwise intended movement, for example, stopping a pedestrian or motorist to ask a question. Arrest also means the more formal and complete act of taking a suspect into custody for purposes of detention and possible prosecution. Many of the legal rules defining police authority to make an arrest apply to both forms of arrest, although it is recognized that the threshold of suspicion sufficient for stopping and questioning is much lower than the threshold for taking a person into custody. Nevertheless, the basic law of arrest is founded on the premise that the involuntary suspension of a person's movements usually requires the same justification as a full-blown arrest and detention.

Probable cause. Authority to arrest depends upon the existence of "probable cause"—the existence of a substantial factual basis for supposing that an offense was committed and that the arrested person committed it. If such facts are evident to the police officer, an arrest may be made without a warrant. If the crime involved is a felony, the police officer need not have directly witnessed the required facts. The same rule generally applies to misdemeanors, but in some states a misdemeanor arrest is authorized only if the offense took place in the officer's presence. Alternatively, if the police have evidence constituting probable cause, they can seek a judicial warrant for arrest. If the court determines that probable cause exists, it issues the warrant, and the police arrest on the basis of the warrant. The judicial determination that probable cause exists constitutes a prior adjudication that there is sufficient evidentiary basis for arrest.

Most arrests made on police patrol are made without warrants, for the obvious reason that an encounter with crime on a patrol requires immediate response. Warrants for arrest therefore are more often used where the suspect is identified through detection, when emergency conditions have subsided. Arrest warrants are awkward to use with regard to victimless crime because successful prosecution usually requires that the offense actually has been committed, as distinct from being in preparation. Apart from the problem of maintaining secrecy, it is generally difficult to show that such a crime will probably be committed.

Search warrant. An arrest warrant must be distinguished from a search warrant. A warrant for arrest authorizes taking the person in question into custody. A search warrant authorizes the police to enter premises and to search for specified evidence of criminality such as weapons, stolen goods, or narcotics, and it requires a showing of reasonable cause to believe that the evidence will be found at the specified premises. Without a search warrant, the police may search a person, a vehicle, or premises only under very limited circumstances. Arrest without a warrant and search without a warrant are governed by rules developed by the United States Supreme Court under the Bill of Rights and the Fourteenth Amendment. The rules involve many fine distinctions and render the process of arrest and search a highly technical exercise except where an offense is committed in the presence of a policeman. This fact is a powerful inducement for police to assert that an offense was committed before their very eyes when this is not true—that is, to lie. The legal controls on arrest and search serve to protect individual rights, but they also carry the risk of morally corrupting the police.

An arrest in the course of patrol is usually made on the basis of the individual officer's judgment, but sometimes upon radio consultation with a supervisory officer. An arrest by detectives or upon warrant by definition is usually based on a decision by a higher authority. In either case, the arrested person is taken to a police facility, either a central jail or a precinct station. For some types of less serious offenses, a policeman who observes the offense is permitted, rather than making an arrest, to issue a citation requiring the offender to appear in court at a specified time. The procedure is adapted from, and is essentially similar to, the issuing of a "ticket" for a motor-vehicle violation.

Police follow-up. *Scope and criteria.* Where an arrest has been made by a patrol officer, the question arises whether prosecution should be followed through. A chief issue is whether the evidence is sufficient to carry the case through to the prosecutor's office. From their continuous dealings with the prosecutor, the police know the standards of proof that the prosecutor will require to commence judicial proceedings, and if they believe that the standard of proof has been met, they forward the case to the prosecutor. After having made an arrest the police rarely presume to decide not to prosecute a case; discretion at this stage is reserved to the prosecutor and the judiciary. On the other hand, if the evidence does not meet the standard required by the prosecutor, the police have to decide whether further investigatory effort is justified. That decision will be based on the seriousness of the crime, whether a victim is willing to pursue the case, whether there appear to be sources of additional evidence, whether the offender has a prior record, and other circumstances. The additional investigation may be relatively intensive or virtually perfunctory. For example, the killing of a police officer will be pursued relentlessly even in the face of few promising leads. On the other hand, muggings not involving serious injury generally are given sufficient attention to placate the victim, thereby pacifying public opinion about the police, but are given no more attention unless the crime fits a pattern pointing to a specific suspect. The police have a realistic sense of the futility of trying to identify a snatch thief from the portfolio of hundreds of plausible suspects whose photographs are on file from previous arrests.

An essentially similar calculation is made in the detective units responsible for investigating crimes reported to the police. Serious offenses against the person receive relatively intensive pursuit, particularly if the victim actively participates and if serious injury was involved. On the other hand, routine cases of breaking and entering dwellings are pursued by reviewing files on past offenses for clues to a pattern associated with a particular offender.

Booking. A person who is taken into custody to be charged is "booked" by the police. In the era before tight legal restrictions were imposed on arrest, patrol officers confronted with doubtful cases could take a suspect into custody and leave it to the station officer to decide whether the accused should be booked or simply released. Now that a patrol arrest can have serious legal consequences, including possible civil litigation against the arresting officer, the police resolve doubtful cases on patrol in favor of releasing the suspect, subject to the possibility of follow-up investigation. Indeed, the patrol officer may simply let the suspect go or ignore the situation. These frontline decisions, made rapidly and according to the officer's personal judgment, often determine whether a suspect will be virtually untouched or will be caught up in the prosecutorial apparatus coming into play after an arrest.

Release pending prosecution. *Bail.* An arrested suspect is generally entitled to release after booking. Where the charge is a misdemeanor, the suspect ordinarily becomes automatically eligible for release upon his promise to appear in court to answer the charge against him; sometimes he must also post bail. When the charge is a felony, the accused generally may obtain release from custody only by posting bail. Bail is a deposit of cash or a cash-equivalent asset, or the posting of bond. A bond is a written promise to pay the bail sum and is posted in lieu of bail by a person whose financial credit is recognized by the court, such as a professional bondsman. Until after 1960, bail typically was high, so that indigent suspects simply stayed in jail until their cases came before the court. A bail reform movement led to a radical reduction of bail, and by the early 1980s bail had been dramatically reduced except in serious offenses where there was a demonstrated risk that the offender would fail to appear for trial.

Preventive detention. The desuetude of bail has led to a search for alternatives. The underlying concern is not that the suspect will flee but that he will commit more offenses pending prosecution and conviction. To deal with this problem, the procedure of "preventive detention" has been widely proposed and in some places adopted. In preventive detention a judicial hearing is held to determine whether the suspect is likely to commit more offenses if released. Preventive detention procedure juxtaposes two fundamental but contradictory ideas. On the one hand, many suspects arrested in the modern criminal justice system have had repeated encounters with the police. They are almost certainly guilty of something and are quite possibly guilty of the offense for which they have been arrested; they may well commit other offenses if they are let go. At the same time, it is a principle of law that no person should be held in jail unless he has been convicted according to law. Preventive detention authorizes the court to estimate whether an arrested but legally innocent person is likely to commit another offense, and on the basis of such an estimate to order his detention. As a technique of public protection, preventive detention serves much the same function as high bail and has the additional merit of focusing on the question of the accused's present dangerousness. Nevertheless, it has proved impossible to make very accurate estimates of dangerousness, and there is an inevitable tendency in actual administration to err on the side of caution. As a practical matter, suspects with a prior record are likely to be held if they are charged with a serious offense. In any event, the decision whether to insist on bail or preventive detention rests with the court rather than the police.

Aiding prosecution. After the police develop a case sufficiently for formal prosecution, they relinquish control of the matter to the prosecution and the courts. However, the police participate in the prosecution. Police officers are often important witnesses, particularly in cases encountered on patrol, and they usually have responsibility for conserving evidence and conducting such supplemental investigation as the prosecutor determines to be necessary. This division of authority between police and prosecution is not necessary in the nature of things. In other countries the police have substantial responsibility for prosecution: in some, the prosecuting attorney is essentially a legal representative of the police, and in others, the police are subject to administrative supervision by the prosecutor. The division of function between police and prosecution in the American criminal justice system means that there can be continuing unresolved conflict over enforcement policy and practice. Furthermore, there is often conflict between the police and the courts, the police perceiving that their cases disappear into the prosecutor's office and become ensnarled in judicial technicalities.

Prosecution and Defense

Adversary system. A criminal proceeding moves along through the mechanism of the adversary system. In the adversary system the accused is presumed innocent until proved guilty, and under modern American criminal procedure he has a right to assistance to counsel from the point where he is arrested. The procedure for determining guilt is that of competitive presentations by the prosecuting attorney as legal representative of the state, countered by the defense counsel as representative of the defendant. Although only a small fraction of all charges originating from the police actually go to trial, the adversary process dominates criminal prosecutions from the point of arrest and even before that point. A criminal charge can become a conviction only through an adversary trial or by guilty plea on the part of the defendant. Although it may be said that the police function is administratively self-contained and operates by a system of quasi-military command, the prosecutorial function proceeds by a dialectic between the prosecuting attorney and the defense counsel. Hence, the most fundamental practical problem confronting a prosecution is whether the proceedings leading to trial, and trial itself, can be successfully sustained in face of challenge and resistance by the defendant through his legal counsel.

The adversary system may be contrasted with the inquisitorial, or investigatory, system of prosecution that prevails in most of Europe and in such countries as Japan, whose legal system is patterned on that of Western Europe. In the investigatory system, the prosecutor has more authority, but also more responsibility, for determining the charge and the evidence that will be presented to the court. In some versions of the European system the prosecutor is regarded as a member of the court. By contrast, in the adversary system, prosecutor and defense counsel stand as equals. However, even in the Anglo-American system the prosecutor is required to be not only advocate for the state but a guardian against unfair or unwarranted prosecution. This dual responsibility obliges a prosecutor continually to balance between overcoming the defendant's resistance to conviction, and terminating the prosecution if he himself is not satisfied that the defendant is legally guilty.

Prosecutor. *Office of the prosecutor.* The prosecuting attorney is a full-time public official, except in very sparsely populated rural counties. In most jurisdictions he is chosen by election in the county in which he serves; in a few jurisdictions the prosecutor is appointed by a state-level authority. In urban areas the prosecutor has a supporting staff, which in large cities may run to hundreds of lawyers, along with paralegals, investigators, and clerical staff. The legal and paralegal staff is largely professionalized, in contrast to the patronage system once prevalent. In some states, members of the legal staff hold merit-rated positions, and a substantial percentage of the incumbents serve as such during their entire professional career. On the other hand, top-level deputies are often discretionary appointments and are often selected on political or patronage grounds. There is also a relatively high turnover at junior-level staff positions, with lawyers entering to gain rapid, intensive trial experience and then moving on to private practice. This pattern results in many cases being handled by deputy prosecutors who are young in years and limited in experience.

The prosecutor's office is responsible for a case from the point where it is received from the police through its termination by trial, guilty plea, or dismissal. The prosecutor is responsible for determining whether a formal charge should be lodged, and, if so, what specific crime should be charged; for conducting settlement negotiations where a plea of guilty may be in prospect; for deciding to abandon prosecutions that cannot be proved or settled; and for trying cases that go to trial. Particularly in the charging and negotiating processes, the prosecutor has [a] very broad range of discretion.

Decision to charge. A complex set of factors is involved in the decision to charge. The single most important factor is the seriousness of the crime, if it is serious, only a dearth of evidence or extraordinary circumstances would warrant a prosecutor's refusing to proceed. The decision to charge is strongly influenced by the strength of the evidence available to the prosecutor. Where the offense is heinous but the evidence is weak, the prosecutor may be obliged to charge a lesser offense that can be proved. Another relevant factor is the defendant's criminal record. If he has a prior record, the prosecutor will be much more inclined to charge—and to charge the maximum offense that the evidence will permit—than if the accused has no prior record. The theory is simply that the accused with a criminal record deserves further punishment and is also more dangerous to the community.

Still another factor is the attitude of the victim. Victim attitude influences the availability of evidence, obviously so where a conviction can be obtained only if the victim will testify. But beyond this, the fact that the victim wants prosecution is morally and politically influential, for the prosecutor's office must sustain public confidence that it is seriously interested in vindicating the criminal law. On the other hand, if the accused has no criminal record and is a provably good citizen, if the crime was in some sense a response to provocation, or if the victim is a provably evil person, the prosecutor normally will be inclined to a lesser charge or, in some circumstances, will simply let the matter go without prosecution.

Alternatives to prosecution. Also relevant in formulating the charge is the possibility of redress outside the criminal justice system. For example, if an offense appears to have been the product of violent emotion, and if the accused has agreed to submit to psychological therapy or supervision, the prosecutor may suspend prosecution or moderate the charge. Prosecutions for possession or use of narcotics are often terminated in a disposition that involves voluntarily submitting to rehabilitative therapy. Where the offense involves actual harm to the victim, the fact that the defendant can make restitution is a relevant circumstance, particularly if restitution is made voluntarily. Basically, the charging decision consists of selecting the appropriate criminal component of a suitable overall resolution of the transaction. This reflects the fact that the conduct in question results from a complex transaction in which the involvement of a crime is only a part of the picture, although of course often the most important part.

This perspective reveals the practical importance of whether the accused has economic and social resources to commit in closing the transaction. Noncriminal redress is, up to a point, a substitute for criminal redress. In an extreme case, a wealthy offender may be able to buy off a victim. Less dramatically, the community, speaking through the prosecutor, may be propitiated by gestures of contrition and acts of redress outside criminal prosecution. These gestures and acts generally are more feasible for the relatively affluent and literate than for the poor and inarticulate. Hence, there is an inherently unequal capacity among the affluent and the poor to participate in the "closing" of a transaction involving a crime. The resulting tendency is that the poor submit to heavier criminal sanctions, or have their offenses treated on a lower moral plane, than do the affluent.

Constituencies. Serving to moderate and channel the prosecutor's discretion are influences from various constituencies to which the prosecutor must be responsive. These include (1) the courts, whose past decisions have to be taken into account and whose future decisions have to be anticipated; (2) the police, who in some sense are the prosecutor's clients and who certainly can influence the esteem in which the prosecutor's office is held by the general public; (3) the press; (4) victims, bystanders, neighbors, and other more or less proximately involved elements of the public; (5) other agencies of government, particularly mayors and city councilmen; and (6) the legal profession, of which the lawyers in the prosecutor's office are members. These cumulative surveillances place the charging decision in something of a goldfish bowl, so that its exercise is only in a formal sense ungoverned by outside controls. The prosecutor's decisions also are influenced by the limited resources available to deal with the steady flow of incoming cases.

Only a fraction of the cases booked by the police are charged at about the same offense level by the prosecutor. Many potential prosecutions are abandoned, and most others go forward on a reduced charge, which may be reduced still further through settlement or at trial.

Negotiation of pleas. A substantial majority of all prosecutions filed by the prosecutor's office are resolved by a negotiated plea of guilty. The prosecution agrees that the original charge will be reduced to a somewhat lesser offense, thus reducing the range of penalties that the judge may impose. In addition, or alternatively, the prosecutor may agree to make a specific recommendation to the court regarding the sentence. The defendant agrees in return to abandon resistance to the accusation and to plead guilty. Generally, and appropriately, this process is called plea bargaining.

Resource constraints. Plea bargaining is a practical necessity in the criminal justice system. The prosecution does not have the resources to develop evidence and conduct trials to convert every accusation into a conviction through a trial. Similar considerations constrain the defense. Where a defendant has retained his own counsel, the cost of conducting a defense is a relevant factor in all but those crimes for which the penalty is so severe that monetary considerations become irrelevant. The cost factor is particularly relevant if the state's evidence is strong, for then the probability of success in defense is correspondingly small. It would make little sense for a defendant to spend five or ten thousand dollars pursuing a one-in-fifty chance of acquittal when conviction means a probable prison sentence and a negotiated plea of guilty will result in probation. Where the defendant is represented by publicly employed counsel, for example, a public defender, these economic constraints still exist but fall directly on the lawyer rather than on the client. That is, a public defender's legal staff cannot afford to spend five or ten thousand dollars' worth of its resources on behalf of a defendant who is simply being stubborn, where the consequence is to reduce the assistance that could be provided to other defendants whose cases are more meritorious.

The guilty plea purports to be a voluntary concession of guilt by the defendant. Expressions of contrition are relevant in a moral calculation of the wrongfulness of an offender's conduct. This moral factor is a part of plea bargaining, for the prosecutor, the court, and public opinion are constrained to leniency toward a defendant who has, at least ostensibly, acknowledged his responsibility for wrong. This explains and justifies the fact, often officially denied, that courts on the average are less severe with defendants who plead guilty than with those who defend their innocence to the end. However, this tendency also vitiates to some degree the presumption of innocence, for it results in the imposition of heavier sentences on offenders who have insisted on their right to trial than on offenders who acquiesce in the accusation against them. Furthermore, the possibility of a plea bargain is an incentive for a person who sincerely believes himself innocent to acquiesce in a negotiated plea of guilty in order to eliminate the risk of a severe sentence that may result from conviction following a trial. The incentive is particularly strong where the flood of cases is so great that the system makes many mistakes. A system of plea bargaining therefore inevitably creates inducements for innocent persons to plead guilty. Furthermore, the exaction of disingenuous guilty pleas undermines the morality of contrition.

Guilty pleas and innocence. Plea bargaining also results in anomalous guilty pleas. For example, a case involving homicide may yield a negotiated plea to the offense of manslaughter when the facts of the killing show that it was almost certainly murder. Such a plea is perfectly intelligible where the evidence for the prosecution is sufficient to go to trial, but insufficient, in the prosecutor's estimation, to be clearly convincing to a jury. In such a situation, and especially if the defendant's prior record and personal situation warrant only a modest sentence, both parties have strong incentives to reach the plea bargain. The prosecution faces a serious risk of failure to obtain any conviction at all; the defense faces the risk that a trial will result in conviction of the much more serious crime of murder. Both parties agree to conviction of a lesser crime, even though that crime certainly did not occur. Negotiated pleas in such situations, and endless varieties of a less dramatic type, are a part of the routine of criminal justice administration. They violate the premises both of the substantive penal law, which attempts to apportion blame according to the nature of the offense, and of the rules of criminal procedure and evidence, which seek to ensure that criminal punishment will be imposed only on those who are proved guilty beyond a reasonable doubt.

Plea bargaining is perhaps the most controversial and disparaged aspect of modern criminal justice administration. Yet some process is necessary by which to discount a criminal charge to reflect the value of the evidence that supports it, for not all charges stand on the same quality of proof. The variability of proof in turn reflects several more fundamental propositions about criminal law: it can never be certain that an accused is guilty or innocent; the criminal law cannot be fully enforced because the state has limited resources to enforce it: defendants cannot insist on ultimate efforts to determine whether they are really innocent, again because of resource constraints; an accused person who acknowledges guilt is morally more worthy than one who attempts to escape responsibility before the law and should be treated with corresponding leniency; and it is morally outrageous that a person who is actually innocent should have to plead guilty in order to avoid the greater injustice of being wrongly convicted of a serious crime. All these propositions are both true and intractable.

It seems evident that charge discounting in some form has existed for as long as there has been a system of criminal justice, that is, a system where guilt is determined only in accordance with law and a standard of objective proof.

The biblical story of King Solomon's threat to cut the baby in half can be interpreted as the use of a coercive method to obtain a guilty plea from the false mother, thus obviating a dismissal for lack of sufficient evidence. The fundamental question, then, is where and by whom the business of charge discounting is to be done. In many criminal justice systems, it is done at the police interrogation stage, with charges formulated after it is established how the defendant will respond to a particular accusation. In the present American system, it is conducted at the prosecution stage by lawyers on behalf of the state and the defense. Charge discounting goes on, overtly or tacitly, from the point the case arrives in the prosecutor's hands until trial, indeed until the matter is submitted for decision by the judge or jury.

Procedure. *Post-arrest stage.* The prosecution stage begins at the transition between arrest and formal accusation. There are two basic pathways, depending on whether the defendant has been arrested upon a warrant or without a warrant. An arrest upon a warrant presupposes a hearing before a magistrate, who is a judge or a parajudicial officer, in order to obtain the warrant. Obtaining a warrant for arrest requires a charge and a showing of probable cause that a crime was committed and that the defendant committed it. A prosecutor ordinarily will not have sought an arrest warrant unless the evidence is also sufficient to carry through the prosecution, that is, unless the evidence easily meets the standard of probable cause. However, notwithstanding the fact that an arrest warrant was obtained, it may be open to the defendant to object that probable cause has not been established.

In most criminal cases the accused is arrested without a warrant. After an arrest, if the prosecutor is satisfied that the evidence is sufficient, a charge is filed against the offender. The technical purpose of the charge is to justify holding the accused in custody (subject to the right to bail) pending further proceedings. Custody is justified if there is probable cause to believe that a crime was committed and that the defendant commited it. Whether probable cause exists is determined by a judicial officer at a preliminary hearing. The preliminary hearing thus is functionally similar to a hearing on an application for an arrest warrant, but it takes place after the arrest rather than before.

The procedure in prosecutions beyond this point depends on whether the accusation is a felony or a misdemeanor, and whether a grand jury is involved. Where the crime charged is a misdemeanor, the charging document is denominated a complaint. If the defendant has been arrested, probable cause must be established at a preliminary hearing; if the defendant was not arrested, he will have been, or will be, summoned to answer. In either case, the defendant responds through a plea of guilty or not guilty. This simple form of procedure is used for lesser crimes and for petty offenses.

Preliminary hearing. In some jurisdictions, the preliminary hearing is a relatively superficial review of the evidence. In other jurisdictions, it is a "mini-trial" where the prosecution's evidence is fully developed and the defendant's counsel may challenge the evidence through cross-examination. In either event, but particularly where the preliminary hearing is relatively extensive, prosecution and defense are able to assess their cases with greater realism, having seen how the evidence will come across in open court. The more realistic assessments may change the parties' positions, resulting in either a reduction or dismissal of the charge or an acceleration of a guilty plea.

Assuming that the prosecution sustains its burden of showing probable cause, the defendant is "bound over" on the charge. This means that he remains obligated to appear to respond to the charge and may be required to post bail.

Felony and misdemeanor. The procedure from this point forward depends on whether the charge is a felony or a lesser offense. Where the charge is a misdemeanor or petty offense, the defendant responds through a plea of guilty or not guilty, and the issue thus joined goes on the trial calendar. The procedure for charging a felony is more complicated. Under common-law procedure, a felony could be charged only by an indictment of a grand jury. The grand jury is a criminal investigation body composed of laymen selected under the auspices of the court in much the same way that an ordinary (petit) jury is assembled. In the earlier common law, before professional police had been established, community knowledge of a crime was transformed by the grand jury into accusations that were then tried before judges riding on circuit. A vestige of this original function remains in the many states in which a felony accusation still requires a grand jury indictment. In these jurisdictions, after the police have investigated a crime and the prosecutor has been satisfied that sufficient evidence exists to justify prosecution, a presentation is made to the grand jury to obtain an indictment. The process usually is wholly routine, for in appearance, and to a considerable extent in fact, the grand jury is simply a rubber stamp for the prosecution. However, the grand jury serves as something of a check on the prosecutor's freedom to go forward with prosecution.

Grand jury. Grand juries nevertheless can exercise a very important investigative function. A grand jury has authority to subpoena witnesses and documents, a power that the prosecutor ordinarily does not have. Hence, where crime is involved that requires extensive investigation, particularly crimes involving conspiracy or the conduct of illegal businesses, the grand jury is a powerful investigative mechanism and its function as such is anything but routine.

Because the procedure for grand jury indictment is redundant in routine cases, many states provide an alternative method of accusation, known as the information. An information is an accusation made on the authority of the prosecutor; instead of a grand jury affirming its belief that the accused is guilty, the prosecutor himself does so. Abuse of the power to proceed by information is constrained by the right to a preliminary hearing and by the fact that in most jurisdictions the defendant can demand that there be a grand jury indictment instead.

After an indictment or information is filed, the defendant makes a further appearance, which is called the arraignment. The arraignment is simply a summoning of the defendant to respond formally to the charge. The defendant pleads guilty or not guilty. If he pleads guilty, the matter proceeds to the sentencing stage. If the defendant pleads not guilty, it proceeds to trial.

Trial. *Prosecution's case.* A trial begins with the selection of the jury, unless a jury trial is waived. The charge is formally read by the judge, and a record is made of the fact that the defendant has pleaded not guilty. Thereupon the prosecution begins its presentation. The presentation commences with an opening statement, which is a narrative of the nature of the offense, the identity of the victim and the defendant, the facts and circumstances of the crime, and the evidence that will be offered. The defendant at this point is permitted, but not required, to make an opening statement corresponding in subject matter to that of the prosecution. However, the defendant may reserve making an opening statement until the conclusion of the prosecution's case.

The prosecution then presents the evidence constituting its "case in chief," that is, all of its case except what may later be added as a rebuttal of the defendant's evidence. This consists of testimonial evidence and may include real evidence such as a weapon, documents, and expert testimony. Upon completing its evidence, the prosecution rests.

Defense. When the prosecution has rested, the defendant may move for dismissal of the charge on the ground that the evidence does not establish proof of the crime beyond a reasonable doubt. The court may dismiss all or some of the charges, depending on its assessment of the evidence. If the matter is tried before a jury, the court's function is to determine whether the jury properly could find guilt beyond a reasonable doubt with respect to the various offenses charged. Charges not established by this quantum of evidence are dismissed by the court. The charges for which the required evidentiary standard has been met are open for consideration by the jury, subject to the right of the defendant to present his own contradicting evidence. In a case tried by the judge without a jury, the motion to dismiss may be treated as a request to find the defendant not guilty.

The defendant has the privilege of introducing contradictory evidence, but he may simply rest on the prosecution's evidence. Under the Fifth Amendment privilege against self-incrimination, the defendant is not required to testify but has a right to do so. He also has the right to offer evidence other than his own testimony. For example, in the case in wich ballistics is the central issue, the defendant may have his own ballistics expert. After the defendant has presented his evidence, he rests. The prosecution then may introduce rebuttal evidence, limited to proof contradicting new matter offered by the defendant; the prosecution is not allowed simply to offer evidence additional to that initially presented.

After all the evidence has been received, counsel for each side may address the jury or, in a nonjury case, the judge. This address is called the final argument, or summation, and is an opportunity for the prosecution and defense in turn to review the evidence and argue it cogency and weight. At the conclusion of the summations, the judge instructs the jury as to the governing legal principles and may review and comment upon the evidence. A standard instruction in a jury case is that questions of fact, including questions of credibility and of the weight of the evidence, are for the jury to decide. The jury then retires for deliberation and a verdict. If the case is tried without a jury, the court simply takes the matter under deliberation.

Verdict and judgment. The verdict may be one of acquittal or conviction, or the jury may become deadlocked and reach no verdict. If the verdict is an acquittal, that is the end of the matter, for the state has no right of appeal from an acquittal. If a jury returns a verdict of guilty, the defendant may request a new trial on the ground either of procedural error during the trial or of the evidence being insufficient to sustain the conviction. If the jury is deadlocked, a mistrial is declared and a new trial may be held.

When the defendant has been found guilty, a judgment of conviction is entered. The defendant is thereupon sentenced. After sentence, the defendant may simply accept the disposition and proceed to serve whatever penalty is imposed, but he has the right of appeal. In modern procedure, where a defendant is provided with the assistance of publicly compensated counsel, appeals are routine where a prison sentence is imposed. Not infrequently, a court imposes a sentence of "time served" where the offense is not heinous and where the defendant has been compelled to stay in jail for want of bail during prosecution.

Courts

Court systems. *Federal and state systems.* The American judiciary includes a system of federal courts and a separate system of courts in each state. The federal courts are organized on a nationwide basis. In each state there is a federal trial court, the United States District Court. Above the district courts in the federal hierarchy are the twelve United States courts of appeals, organized by geographical regions called circuits. At the apex of the federal court system is the United States Supreme Court, which has appellate jurisdiction over the lower federal courts and also authority to review issues of federal law that arise in state courts.

State courts. Each state has its own court system. The structure in most states is essentially similar to the federal court system—a trial court level, an intermediate appellate court, and a state supreme court. The trial courts in most states are organized along county lines, with a separate trial court in each county, although in some rural areas several counties are grouped together to form a trial court district. In most states the trial courts are in two divisions, an upper one of general jurisdiction and a lower one of limited authority. The trial court of general jurisdiction is variously called the district court, circuit court, or superior court; the court of limited jurisdiction had its origin in the justice-of-the-peace courts and municipal courts of an earlier era and is now called by various names. Generally speaking, felony prosecutions are conducted in the trial court of general jurisdiction, whereas the courts of limited jurisdiction conduct preliminary hearings in felony cases, and trials in cases involving misdemeanors and minor offenses.

Procedural standards. *Federal due process.* All offenses against federal law are prosecuted in federal courts. All prosecutions for offenses against state law are prosecuted in state courts, with exceptions concerning offenses that involve federal activity. However, the federal courts have important supervisory authority with regard to the administration of criminal justice in the state courts. Since about 1930, the Supreme Court has been interpreting the due process clause of the Fourteenth Amendment to imply procedural requirements that state courts must observe in criminal prosecutions. These federally imposed procedural requirements now include (1) the right to jury trial in all serious offenses; (2) the right to assistance of counsel in any case in which a jail sentence may be imposed; (3) the privilege against self-incrimination, including the right not to testify against oneself and a prohibition against comment by the prosecution on the defendant's failure to testify; (4) a requirement that proof of guilt be established beyond a reasonable doubt; (5) the right to refuse to respond to police interrogation and the right to demand the presence of a lawyer during such interrogation; and (6) freedom from racial and sex discriminatory provisions in substantive and procedural criminal law.

These federally created procedural rights must be observed by the state courts. An accused who contends that [these rights have] been denied or improperly interpreted has a right to appeal through the state court system to the Supreme Court. Although this right of appeal to the Supreme Court is important in principle, its practical effect is limited because the Court is able to consider only a small fraction of state court cases involving federal questions. However, the Court has also developed doctrines protecting these federal rights through habeas corpus proceedings in the United States district courts. After a state court conviction has become final, the state prisoner petitions the federal court to determine whether the state court observed his federal procedural rights.

Although basic criminal procedure in state courts is prescribed by state law, procedural protections established by federal law amount to a supplemental code of criminal procedure. Enforcing these protections results in federal trial court review of the procedural regularity of criminal prosecutions that have already been reviewed by state appellate courts. The total effect of federal procedural protections has been virtually revolutionary. As late as 1950, state criminal process, except in unusually serious or complex cases, consisted of relatively free police investigation, charging based on the prosecutor's estimate of the sufficiency of the evidence, defense without the assistance of counsel in the case of indigents, and convictions that were rarely appealed. By the 1980s, police investigatory methods were stringently regulated, particularly concerning interrogation and search of premises; prosecution was restricted by the requirement that evidence be legally obtained and by the stricter enforcement of standards of proof; defense counsel was provided to the indigent; and conviction was almost routinely followed by appeal if a substantial sentence had been imposed. The proceedings as a whole became subject to the possibility of still additional review through federal habeas corpus proceedings.

Technical complexity. Criminal procedure has probably become more complicated and technical than any other body of procedural law. Additional complexity results from the fact that much of this law has evolved through case law decisions over time, rather than through comprehensive legislative enactment. As a result, at any given time it is often difficult to say what the law is, particularly since the Supreme Court has shifted its approach from time to time and because lower courts have inevitably overinterpreted or underinterpreted Supreme Courts trends. In addition, a number of state supreme courts have themselves been very active in elaborating procedural rights for defendants. In some states, the procedural protections established by state courts are considerably more exacting than those established by the Supreme Court in interpretation of the federal Constitution. These developments have changed the whole tenor of criminal proceedings and have reduced the risk of unjust conviction, particularly the disproportionateness of the risks to which minorities are subject.

In modern criminal procedure the trial court judiciary is responsible for applying a highly complex body of procedural law to a very high volume of cases. Giving full-scale treatment to all cases is simply impossible. In heinous offenses, particularly ones that have attracted public attention, the full panoply of procedures unfolds, so that it can cost literally hundreds of thousands of dollars to try a major felony where the evidence is in serious dispute and the defendant is determined to seek acquittal. The criminal justice system adapts with shortcuts in routine cases, including waiver of various formalities, dispositions by stipulation, and postponement. These cases constitute virtually a system of consensual justice, in which prosecution goes forward on the basis of the defendants' acquiescence. The low-visibility cases that flow endlessly through the criminal justice system are resolved by "slow plea" and "delayed dismissal." The slow plea is a guilty plea to a relatively minor offense, elicited from the defendant through the persuasion of his own counsel in response to alternating threats and cajolery from the prosecution. A delayed dismissal is a dismissal obtained from the prosecutor by defense threats and cajolery but withheld for a time—perhaps three to six months—as a stern warning to the defendant and to allow the victim to be placated or at least reconciled to the fact that a severe sanction will not be forthcoming. Prosecutor and defense counsel work out the slow pleas and delayed dismissals while the lower courts record and monitor.

Juvenile courts. Brief mention should be made of the juvenile court system. In all states, offenders under a specified age, typically sixteen or eighteen, are proceeded against in juvenile courts, except in the most heinous offenses such as murder. The proceedings nominally are civil rather than criminal, the theory being that the respondent is to be rehabilitated rather than punished. However, the basis of the proceedings is an act which if committed by an adult would be a criminal offense. In some states, the juvenile court is a separate trial court; in others, it is a specialized branch of the regular trial court. In any event, juvenile court procedure roughly corresponds to criminal procedure; however, it is less formal and less technical and, in almost all jurisdictions, trials are held with a judge alone rather than with a jury. Until about 1960, juvenile court procedure was quite informal, intended to be mediatory and protective rather than accusatory and concerned with the question of guilt. Procedural changes, many of them required by Supreme Court interpretations of the due process requirement, have subsequently made juvenile court procedure quite formal. It is now required that there be a written accusation, proof beyond a reasonable doubt, and the assistance of counsel. The aim and character of juvenile courts nevertheless remain more amelioratory than is so in the criminal courts. However, as serious offenses have come to be committed by younger and younger persons, the case pattern in juvenile courts has come increasingly to resemble that of criminal courts. The cases include a high proportion of assaults and thefts by young males who are predominantly from poor families and ethnic minorities.

Sentencing and Corrections

An offender who has been convicted, whether by trial or by plea of guilty, is subject to sentencing. Imposing sentence is the responsibility of the judge, except in a few jurisdictions where the jury is authorized to impose the penalty for felonies. Sentence may consist of confinement in jail or prison, release under supervision, a fine, or a combination of these sanctions. Every state has a cluster of penal facilities for the incarceration of offenders, and a cluster of agencies responsible for the supervision of convicted offenders.

Jails and prisons. The most familiar penal institution is the local jail. Jails are maintained in all urban communities, operated by cities or counties or both. A jail provides temporary custody for arrested persons pending prosecution, and a place of punishment for persons sentenced to short periods of confinement. In most urban communities the jail is part of a facility that also serves as police headquarters or subheadquarters. A jail is thus a police administration center, an intake facility, a holding place, and a facility for local punishment. Its inmate population at any given time commingles the legally innocent, the legally guilty, and people whose legal and life situation is in disarray. It is a population that is above all transient. Jails in large urban centers generally have a mildly chaotic atmosphere, stabilized by the facts that all inmates have an interest in getting out and that most have excellent prospects of doing so soon if they do not seriously misbehave. In general, urban jails are chronically overcrowded and have few services beyond preserving order and providing food, a bunk, and a common room with a television set. In all but very rural communities, separate facilities are provided for women and for juveniles. Generally, the level of services in juvenile detention centers is somewhat higher, but those facilities have the same characteristic atmosphere of transience and boredom.

All states operate penal institutions at the state level. These institutions include a state prison and a state juvenile training facility. Separate wings or facilities are provided for female adult prisoners and for female juveniles. For adult males, and sometimes for other categories of offenders, facilities are graduated according to tightness of security and rigor of regimen, ranging from maximum security to fairly liberal conditions. Most states, including all those with large populations, have a number of separate facilities graduated in this way. The total number of prison facilities in the country, excluding the federal system, exceeds five hundred. The total prison and jail population in 1981 was estimated at more than five hundred thousand.

Sentencing purposes. *Multiple purposes.* Sentence to imprisonment is designed to fulfill a mixed set of objectives. The most immediate and popular purpose is punishment. Since about 1800, prisons have been a substitute in this respect for capital punishment, corporal punishment such as whipping or disfigurement, and enslavement or banishment, which were the forms of punishment used in earlier times. The will to punish is a strong one, animated by the outrage and desire for revenge that are aroused by the offenses for which offenders are typically given prison sentence[s]—murder, rape, assault, and robbery. A second and rather different theory of imprisonment is that isolation in confinement provides occasion for an offender to reconsider his life and mend his ways. This theory is the origin of the term *penitentiary,* that is, a place in which to be penitent. It may be doubted whether there was ever much realistic possibility that convicts would undergo transformation through penitence, but there is little doubt that the prison experience brings home the lesson that committing crime can interfere with one's life. A third objective, also associated with prisons reforms of the nineteenth century, is that a prison should be a place of rehabilitation, where the prisoner undergoes a change in outlook and acquires the capacity to live a law-abiding life through education and training provided in the institution. A fourth theory is that incarceration simply keeps the offender out of circulation, so that as long as he remains in prison he cannot do further injury to society. Finally, it is said that the foregoing consequences of imprisonment serve as examples to others and thus deter them from committing crime.

Conflict among purposes. It seems obvious, although it is not always recognized, that this set of purposes is internally inconsistent in several important ways. The purpose of punishment and deterrence is served by making prison as brutal and bleak an experience as possible; however, making prisons brutal and bleak has the effect of making them poor places in which to conduct moral education and technical training for the purposes of rehabilitation. The theory of penitence holds that an offender through his own will can come to understand and control himself; however, placing him involuntarily in custody presumes his inability to govern himself. Furthermore, if the prisoner really is meditating, it is inconsistent to punish him for doing so. The rehabilitation of offenders would require that they be taught job skills through which they can earn a satisfactory living; however, given the typically low level of achievement and educability of most prison populations, attaining such an objective would entail creating an educational program far more extensive than is afforded to persons of similar background who are not in prison, resulting in an anomalous distribution of social benefits. At the same time, truly effective rehabilitation and training would require long periods of incarceration, although those who perform well in rehabilitation programs deserve to be released early. Finally, if the aim of prison is to keep the offender out of circulation, it is not clear why investment should be made in rehabilitation until shortly before he is ready for release.

These inconsistencies reflect a deeper contradiction in the attitude toward crime that seems always to have prevailed. This is the dilemma of whether to condemn an offender as an outlaw and treat him as absolutely or provisionally subhuman, or instead to regard him as an autonomous being who can be brought around to behave himself. This fundamental ambivalence seems unavoidable. If it is, inconsistency in the administration of penal policy is also unavoidable. At any rate, the contemporary prison system in the United States reflects these contradictions.

Prisons. *Conditions.* Prisons are elaborate and expensive, but the number of places in prison is low compared to the demand. Hence at least since the 1960s prisons have been chronically overcrowded. For most prisoners in the United States, the prison term is nominally long but actually short through allowance for "good time" and parole. As a result, productive training programs are extremely difficult to manage. Physical brutality is prohibited but, particularly in the case of violence by inmates against other inmates, is inadequately controlled and sometimes unofficially condoned. Psychological brutality is pervasive. Rehabilitation programs are elaborate in ambition and are the subject of continuously reborn experimental and demonstration programs, but they are generally underfunded and often technically obsolete and pedagogically dispirited. The moral ambivalence and technical mediocrity that characterize modern American prisons help explain the state of demoralization and danger generally prevailing within them. The environment is literally vicious, involving pervasive use of drugs, physical exploitation between prisoners including rampant homosexuality, and a culture dominated by prisoners with long criminal records and serving long sentences. The overwhelming majority of prisoners in most American prisons are black or Hispanic, whereas the guards are white lower-level civil servants. The growing legal protection of prisoner rights has considerably restricted the extent to which prison authorities can use arbitrary administrative methods to control inmates. The improved legal status of prisoners has reduced the degree of official lawlessness in handling prisoners, but it may also have contributed to increased lawlessness among prisoners. As a result, life in modern prisons is subject to less discrimination and arbitrary official action, but it also seethes with repressed unrest that periodically bursts out in riots and rampage.

The condition of prisons is largely the result of a desire by governmental authorities, particularly at the state level, to have a criminal justice system that provides rigorous sanctions at low operating cost. The combination of growing rates of crime and growing incidence of prison sentences increases demand for prison places. Relentless inflation, higher building costs, and rising staff compensation rates increase the cost of each place. The transformation of the prison population from predominantly white to predominately black reduces the empathy of the general population with the prison population. As a result, almost all prisons are overcrowded and understaffed but are subject to unremitting pressures to accept more inmates.

Federal legal intervention. Partly in response to this deterioration, the courts, and particularly the federal courts, have become actively involved in scrutinizing the administration of prisons. Expansion of prisoners' legal rights, a major legal development since the late 1960s, has taken place along two related lines. The first is procedural—the decision procedures used by prison authorities in such matters as imposing prison punishments or withholding good time, granting or refusing parole, and dealing with disputes between prisoners and prison personnel. In general, there has been expansion of rights to a hearing or at least to statements of the reason for official action. The other line of development has concerned prison programs and facilities. Under the rubric in the Bill of Rights forbidding "cruel and unusual punishments," the courts have prohibited the use of brutal corporal punishment, the unregulated use of solitary confinement, and the arbitrary restriction of outside communication. Affirmatively, the courts have regulated the availability and quality of medical care and access to legal services and law books. Taken as a whole, these legal standards, enforceable by proceedings in federal court, have considerably raised the legally required level of administration in prisons.

This improvement, welcome insofar as it has been given actual effect, results in two additional discrepancies in contemporary prison policy. The first is between the level of legally prescribed conditions in penal institutions, and the level of conditions that actually exist. In general, prisons are probably not much worse than they were in 1960, and many of them are considerably better. In the meantime, however, the legally prescribed standards have risen still farther, so that the gap between aspiration and fulfillment may have widened. This generates a legitimate sense of injustice among prisoners that is not conducive to their acceptance of their sentences. The second discrepancy concerns the theory of prison management. Both the old-style lockup prison and the reformed rehabilitative penal institution were administered on principles of hierarchical authority, in which prisoners were told what to do. This concept of management remains, but is now intersected by what amounts to management with the participation of prisoners, who use legal proceedings as leverage.

Probation and parole. *Probation policy.* The alternative to jail or prison is release under supervision. Most persons convicted of crimes are sentenced neither to jail nor to prison but are released back into the community under obligation to report periodically to a probation officer charged with supervising their behavior. Probation is the most frequent disposition of a first offender convicted of anything but murder or murderous assault. The period of probation usually is proportional to the length of the prison sentence that would have been imposed for the crime in question. Since penalties of imprisonment average perhaps a nominal five years, and involve an actual term of something less than two years, probation usually is imposed for a period of one to three years. While on probation, the convicted person is required to stay out of trouble, to avoid association with previous companions in crime, to attempt to find a job, to avoid use of alcohol or narcotics, and to report periodically to the probation officer. Theoretically, the probation service provides psychological, social, and employment counseling. In idealized form the relationship between probation officer and offender is avuncular.

Probation practice. However, probation resources in manpower and auxiliary services generally are insufficient to live up to the stated aims. As a result, probation in fact generally consists merely of nominal supervision in which the probation officer keeps in occasional touch with the convicted person and becomes actively involved only when a new offense has been committed, which happens in a substantial fraction of cases. At that point, the offender's performance while on probation, so far as it can be established from information available to the probation service, will become a highly relevant factor in determining whether probation will be revoked and whether the offender will be prosecuted for his subsequent offense. Often a subsequent offense will result in a proceeding before the court at which revocation is threatened but where probation is actually continued. The records of many offenders, particularly those who avoid really heinous offenses, consist of a series of convictions, probation, brief revocations, and reprobation. All these determinations are made on the basis of proof falling considerably short of the standard required for conviction, but they result in treating the offender as a repeater. At some point along the line, if the pattern of behavior continues, prison will result. The hope, however, is that prison can be avoided, to spare the offender a harsh disposition and the system additional expense.

Some form of probation must always have existed in the criminal justice system. That is, offenders, particularly those who admitted their guilt, were simply let go on a promise to behave themselves. In the modern system, the probation decision is made by the judge on the basis of a presentence investigation conducted by the probation service. Theoretically, this investigation includes a full account of the circumstances surrounding the offense (including details not admissible in a trial), a biography of the offender, and a scientific psychological appraisal of his predisposition to further criminal behavior. In fact, the information provided the court generally falls short of this ideal, partly because diagnostic technique is very imperfect and partly because resources generally do not exist to permit a full professional workup of each case. Nevertheless, an attempt is made to provide the court with information so that it can formulate a sentence with regard not only to the offense but also to the offender.

An offender who has served a jail sentence is usually simply discharged at the conclusion of the specified period; one sentenced to prison is subject to a more complicated set of adjustments in his sentence. While in prison he is entitled to reduction of the nominal sentence on the basis of good time: for every interval in prison in which he avoids breaking rules, the offender receives a proportionate reduction in his sentence. An offender who maintains steady good time can shorten his sentence by about two-thirds. On top of this, the rules fixing eligibility for parole generally permit a person to be considered for parole at regular intervals after the commencement of his sentence. If the prisoner is regarded as a safe bet for parole, he may be paroled ahead of the normal time, and this is frequently done in the case of persons without prior records.

Parole. Supervision on parole is essentially similar to probation supervision, except that the parole service is an agency of the state correctional system, whereas probation services are connected administratively to the court system. If a parolee violates parole, the consequences are the same as for violation of probation. Parole may be revoked, with the parolee returned to prison, or it may simply be continued with a warning. In general, violation of parole is more likely to lead to reimprisonment than is violation of probation, because the population that has found its way into parole by way of imprisonment is made up of persons with more serious criminal records.

Although the criminal justice system seeks at all points to consider each offender as an individual, it functions on the supposition that the best indicator of an offender's future behavior is his pattern of behavior in the past. This is no doubt a realistic supposition, although in practice if not in theory it contradicts the legal presumption of innocence.

Appendix B

A NOTE ON THE MODEL PENAL CODE

C. McCLAIN, CRIMINAL LAW REFORM: HISTORICAL DEVELOPMENT IN THE UNITED STATES

2 Encyclopedia of Crime and Justice 510-512 (1983)

The Model Penal Code. The American Law Institute, an organization of lawyers, judges, and legal scholars, was founded in 1923 for the purpose of clarifying and improving the law. One of the major causes that had led to its establishment was dissatisfaction with the state of the criminal law, and thus it is no surprise that criminal law reform occupied a high place on its agenda from the outset. However, it proved difficult to translate this concern into action. The institute was quick to decide that the method of restatement which seemed the appropriate way to proceed in other fields of law was inappropriate for the law of crime. As Herbert Wechsler, a leading theorist of penal jurisprudence, later explained, "The need . . . was less for a description and reaffirmation of existing law than for a guide to long delayed reform." . . . A proposal for a model penal code was advanced in 1931, but the project was large in scope, and the funding to carry it out was not forthcoming during the Depression years.

In 1950 the infusion of a large grant from the Rockefeller Foundation stirred the model penal code project to life again. An advisory committee, made up of distinguished scholars in the field of criminal law, was assembled by the American Law Institute. Wechsler was appointed chief reporter of the enterprise, and Louis Schwartz, another eminent authority in the field, was named co-reporter.

Early in the project's life, Wechsler made it clear that he and his colleagues were confronting a task of immense magnitude. In Wechsler's view, American society had entered the twentieth century without having ever rationally articulated "the law on which men placed their ultimate reliance for protection against all the deepest injuries that human conduct can inflict on individuals and institutions." . . . Instead, the penal law of the various states was a hopelessly disorganized and internally inconsistent mass of common and statute law—with the statutes often more important in their gloss than in their text—less the product of informed, deliberate choice than of accident, chance, and unreflecting imitation. As Wechsler put it, American penal law was "a combination of the old and the new that only history explains." . . .

From beginning to end, Wechsler was the code project's guiding spirit, and he deserves most of the credit for leading the enterprise to successful completion. But the drafting of the Model Penal Code was no solo performance by Wechsler. It was very much a collaborative effort, drawing on the talent of virtually the whole of the academic criminal law establishment, of a goodly number of judges, and of a handful of practitioners. It was also an effort that proceeded carefully and deliberately. The writing of the Code took ten years, from 1952 to 1962, during which time thirteen tentative drafts were circulated for general discussion and comment after debate in the project's advisory committee and on the floor of the American Law Institute.

In 1962 the institute's Proposed Official Draft of the Model Penal Code was promulgated, the greatest attempt since Livingston's time to put the house of penal jurisprudence into some kind of rational order. In truth, the Proposed Official Draft was in many respects a very Livingstonian document. This was seen particularly in its commitment to the principle that the sole purpose of the criminal law was the control of harmful conduct, and in its adherence to the notion that clarity of concept and expression were essential to that purpose's fulfillment. The draft was wholly lacking, however, in that ideological smugness and imperiousness which at times had tarnished the work of Livingston and of his mentor, Bentham. As befitted a product of the mid-twentieth-century American mind, the draft was suffused with a spirit of pragmatism, albeit a pragmatism tempered by principle.

The Code was divided into four parts: general provisions, definitions of specific crimes, treatment and correction, and organization of correction. Each contained significant innovations with respect to existing law. In keeping with the principle that the criminal law's only purpose was to deter blameworthy, harmful conduct, and the converse principle that faultless conduct should be shielded from punishment, new standards of criminal liability were established in the Code's general provisions. In the area of inchoate crimes, for example, the law of attempt was rewritten to sweep away all questions as to factual impossibility and to focus attention on the actor's perception of the circumstances surrounding the commission of his act (§5.01). In conspiracy, on the other hand, the traditional common-law rule that made every member of the conspiracy liable for any reasonably foreseeable crime committed by any other member of the conspiracy was rejected. Instead, an accomplice's liability was limited to those crimes of the principal that the accomplice intended to assist or encourage (§5.03). Thus too, in the interest of protecting faultless conduct, the use of defensive force was declared justifiable in cases of apparent, as opposed to actual, necessity (§3.04). Reasonable mistake of fact was affirmed as a defense in crimes such as bigamy (§230.1). In addition, a limited defense of *ignorantia legis* was made available to defendants who harbored good faith beliefs regarding the innocence of their conduct as a result of reliance on official opinion or as a result of the unavailability to them of the enactment they were accused of violating (§§2.02, 2.04).

The most striking provisions in the Code's general part were those that sought to articulate a new definition of the mental element in crime. The common law used a bewildering variety of terms to designate the mental blameworthiness (mens rea) that had to be present if a person were to be convicted of a criminal offense. For this profusion of terms the Code drafters substituted four modes of acting with respect to the material elements of offenses—purposely, knowingly, recklessly, and negligently—one of which would have to be present for criminal liability to attach (§2.02). The Code achieved a creative compromise in the area of strict liability, allowing for the possibility of such offenses by classifying them as violations punishable only by fines.

In addition to attempting to order and rationalize the general, underlying principles of criminal liability, the Model Penal Code wrought numerous innovations in the definitions of specific offenses. Perhaps the most signal achievement in this regard was its substitution of a unified law of theft for the potpourri of common-law offenses that went under the names of larceny, larceny by trick, false pretenses, and embezzlement. It sought, too, to bring greater rationality and fairness to the sentencing of those convicted of crimes. It proposed a scheme of determinate sentencing, under which felonies were classified into three punishment categories and all misdemeanors into two. Upper and lower limits of sentences were set out for each category, with the determination of the exact length left to the discretion of the judge (§§6.06, 6.08). Extended terms were authorized for persistent offenders and professional criminals (§§7.03, 7.04).

The American Law Institute neither expected nor intended that its Model Penal Code would be adopted in toto anywhere, or that it would lead to the establishment of a uniform national penal law. Diversity of political history and of population makeup in the various states made that kind of expectation quite unrealistic. Rather, the institute hoped that the Code would spark a fresh and systematic reevaluation of the penal law in many jurisdictions and that its provisions would be liberally drawn on. The institute was not to be disappointed in this hope. By 1980, in large part owing to the Model Penal Code's example, some thirty states had adopted revised criminal codes, and another nine had code revisions either under way or completed and awaiting enactment. It is no exaggeration to say, as did Sanford Kadish, that within three decades of the time when Code drafts began to be circulated, the Model Penal Code had "permeated and transformed" American substantive law.

A final salutary impact of the Model Penal Code must be mentioned, namely, the impetus that it gave to the effort to codify—for the first time in the true sense of the word—the federal penal law. In 1962, when the Code's Proposed Official Draft was promulgated, the federal criminal law was in a sorrier condition than that of most of the states. It had grown up in an unsystematic, piecemeal fashion since the beginnings of the republic, and the several efforts that had been previously undertaken to place it on a more rational basis had not come to very much. In 1866 Congress, alarmed at the uncontrolled manner in which the corpus of federal criminal law seemed to have been growing since 1800, had impaneled a commission to introduce some order into the confusion. The work of this commission led to the passage of a body of revised statutes, which at least had the virtue of arranging federal penal provisions into some sort of coherent order (U.S. Congress). In 1897 and later in 1909, revisions and rearrangements of federal penal statutes were again undertaken (Appropriations Act of June 4, 1897, ch. 2, 30 Stat. 11; Act of March 4, 1909, ch. 321, 35 Stat. 1088 (codified in scattered sections of 18 U.S.C.)). Finally, in 1948, after eight years of work by another commission, Congress enacted Title 18 of the United States Code, which purported to be the first codification of the federal criminal law. If it was a codification, it was one in the Fieldian rather than the Benthamite-Livingstonian sense—and even that may be a charitable overstatement.

In 1966 Congress established the National Commission on Reform of Federal Criminal Laws to examine the state of the federal penal law and to propose a reformulation. The action was in part taken to appease an anxious public which was insisting that Congress do something about dramatically escalating crime rates, but it was motivated as well by an authentic desire to reform and improve the law. Congress left no doubt that it wished to see a thorough rethinking of the federal law of crimes, and its mandate was heeded. In due course the commission produced a thorough revision of the federal substantive law of crimes, and several bills were promptly introduced for the enactment of some version of it into law.

Appendix C

THE MODEL PENAL CODE

PART I. GENERAL PROVISIONS

Article 1. Preliminary

Section 1.01. Title and Effective Date. [Omitted.]

Section 1.02. Purposes; Principles of Construction.

(1) The general purposes of the provisions governing the definition of offenses are:

- (a) to forbid and prevent conduct that unjustifiably and inexcusably inflicts or threatens substantial harm to individual or public interests;
- (b) to subject to public control persons whose conduct indicates that they are disposed to commit crimes;
- (c) to safeguard conduct that is without fault from condemnation as criminal;
- (d) to give fair warning of the nature of the conduct declared to constitute an offense;
- (e) to differentiate on reasonable grounds between serious and minor offenses.

(2) The general purposes of the provisions governing the sentencing and treatment of offenders are:

- (a) to prevent the commission of offenses;
- (b) to promote the correction and rehabilitation of offenders;
- (c) to safeguard offenders against excessive, disproportionate or arbitrary punishment;
- (d) to give fair warning of the nature of the sentences that may be imposed on conviction of an offense;
- (e) to differentiate among offenders with a view to a just individualization in their treatment;
- (f) to define, coordinate and harmonize the powers, duties and functions of the courts and of administrative officers and agencies responsible for dealing with offenders;

(g) to advance the use of generally accepted scientific methods and knowledge in the sentencing and treatment of offenders;
(h) to integrate responsibility for the administration of the correctional system in a State Department of Correction [or other single department or agency].

(3) The provisions of the Code shall be construed according to the fair import of their terms but when the language is susceptible of differing constructions it shall be interpreted to further the general purposes stated in this Section and the special purposes of the particular provision involved. The discretionary powers conferred by the Code shall be exercised in accordance with the criteria stated in the Code and, insofar as such criteria are not decisive, to further the general purposes stated in this Section.

Section 1.03. Territorial Applicability. [Omitted.]

Section 1.04. Classes of Crimes; Violations.

(1) An offense defined by this Code or by any other statute of this State, for which a sentence of [death or of] imprisonment is authorized, constitutes a crime. Crimes are classified as felonies, misdemeanors or petty misdemeanors.

(2) A crime is a felony if it is so designated in this Code or if persons convicted thereof may be sentenced [to death or] to imprisonment for a term which, apart from an extended term, is in excess of one year.

(3) A crime is a misdemeanor if it is so designated in this Code or in a statute other than this Code enacted subsequent thereto.

(4) A crime is a petty misdemeanor if it so designated in this Code or in a statute other than this Code enacted subsequent thereto or if it is defined by a statute other than this Code which now provides that persons convicted thereof may be sentenced to imprisonment for a term of which the maximum is less than one year.

(5) An offense defined by this Code or by any other statute of this State constitutes a violation if it is so designated in this Code or in the law defining the offense or if no other sentence than a fine, or fine and forfeiture or other civil penalty is authorized upon conviction or if it is defined by a statute other than this Code which now provides that the offense shall not constitute a crime. A violation does not constitute a crime and conviction of a violation shall not give rise to any disability or legal disadvantage based on conviction of a criminal offense.

(6) Any offense declared by law to constitute a crime, without specification of the grade thereof or of the sentence authorized upon conviction, is a misdemeanor.

(7) An offense defined by any statute of this State other than this Code shall be classified as provided in this Section and the sentence that may be imposed upon conviction thereof shall hereafter be governed by this Code.

Section 1.05. All Offenses Defined by Statute; Application of General Provisions of the Code.

(1) No conduct constitutes an offense unless it is a crime or violation under this Code or another statute of this State.

(2) The provisions of Part I of the Code are applicable to offenses defined by other statutes, unless the Code otherwise provides.

(3) This Section does not affect the power of a court to punish for contempt or to employ any sanction authorized by law for the enforcement of an order or a civil judgment or decree.

Section 1.06. Time Limitations. [Omitted.]

Section 1.07. Method of Prosecution When Conduct Constitutes More Than One Offense.

(1) *Prosecution for Multiple Offenses; Limitation on Convictions.* When the same conduct of a defendant may establish the commission of more than one offense, the defendant may be prosecuted for each such offense. He may not, however, be convicted of more than one offense if:

(a) one offense is included in the other, as defined in Subsection (4) of this Section; or

(b) one offense consists only of a conspiracy or other form of preparation to commit the other; or

(c) inconsistent findings of fact are required to establish the commission of the offenses; or

(d) the offenses differ only in that one is defined to prohibit a designated kind of conduct generally and the other to prohibit a specific instance of such conduct; or

(e) the offense is defined as a continuing course of conduct and the defendant's course of conduct was uninterrupted, unless the law provides that specific periods of such conduct constitute separate offenses.

(2) *Limitation on Separate Trials for Multiple Offenses.* Except as provided in Subsection (3) of this Section, a defendant shall not be subject to separate trials for multiple offenses based on the same conduct or arising from the same criminal episode, if such offenses are known to the appropriate prosecuting officer at the time of the commencement of the first trial and are within the jurisdiction of a single court.

(3) *Authority of Court to Order Separate Trials.* When a defendant is charged with two or more offenses based on the same conduct or arising from the same criminal episode, the Court, on application of the prosecuting attorney or of the defendant, may order any such charge to be tried separately, if it is satisfied that justice so requires.

(4) *Conviction of Included Offense Permitted.* A defendant may be convicted of an offense included in an offense charged in the indictment [or the information]. An offense is so included when:

(a) it is established by proof of the same or less than all the facts required to establish the commission of the offense charged; or

(b) it consists of an attempt or solicitation to commit the offense charged or to commit an offense otherwise included therein; or

(c) it differs from the offense charged only in the respect that a less serious injury or risk of injury to the same person, property or public interest or a lesser kind of culpability suffices to establish its commission.

(5) *Submission of Included Offense to Jury.* The Court shall not be obligated to charge the jury with respect to an included offense unless there is a rational basis for a verdict acquitting the defendant of the offense charged and convicting him of the included offense.

Section 1.08. When Prosecution Barred by Former Prosecution for the Same Offense. [Omitted.]

Section 1.09. When Prosecution Barred by Former Prosecution for Different Offense. [Omitted.]

Section 1.10. Former Prosecution in Another Jurisdiction: When a Bar. [Omitted.]

Section 1.11. Former Prosecution Before Court Lacking Jurisdiction or When Fraudulently Procured by the Defendant. [Omitted.]

Section 1.12. Proof Beyond a Reasonable Doubt; Affirmative Defenses; Burden of Proving Fact When Not an Element of an Offense; Presumptions.

(1) No person may be convicted of an offense unless each element of such offense is proved beyond a reasonable doubt. In the absence of such proof, the innocence of the defendant is assumed.

(2) Subsection (1) of this Section does not:

(a) require the disproof of an affirmative defense unless and until there is evidence supporting such defense; or

(b) apply to any defense which the Code or another statute plainly requires the defendant to prove by a preponderance of evidence.

(3) A ground of defense is affirmative, within the meaning of Subsection (2)(a) of this Section, when:

(a) it arises under a section of the Code which so provides; or

(b) it relates to an offense defined by a statute other than the Code and such statute so provides; or

(c) it involves a matter of excuse or justification peculiarly within the knowledge of the defendant on which he can fairly be required to adduce supporting evidence.

(4) When the application of the Code depends upon the finding of a fact which is not an element of an offense, unless the Code otherwise provides:

(a) the burden of proving the fact is on the prosecution or defendant, depending on whose interest or contention will be furthered if the finding should be made; and

(b) the fact must be proved to the satisfaction of the Court or jury, as the case may be.

(5) When the Code establishes a presumption with respect to any fact which is an element of an offense, it has the following consequences:

(a) when there is evidence of the facts which give rise to the presumption, the issue of the existence of the presumed fact must be submitted to the jury, unless the Court is satisfied that the evidence as a whole clearly negatives the presumed fact; and

(b) when the issue of the existence of the presumed fact is submitted to the jury, the Court shall charge that while the presumed fact must, on all the evidence, be proved beyond a reasonable doubt, the law declares that the jury may regard the facts giving rise to the presumption as sufficient evidence of the presumed fact.

(6) A presumption not established by the Code or inconsistent with it has the consequences otherwise accorded it by law.

Section 1.13. General Definitions.

In this Code, unless a different meaning plainly is required:

(1) "statute" includes the Constitution and a local law or ordinance of a political subdivision of the State;

(2) "act" or "action" means a bodily movement whether voluntary or involuntary;

(3) "voluntary" has the meaning specified in Section 2.01;

(4) "omission" means a failure to act;

(5) "conduct" means an action or omission and its accompanying state of mind, or, where relevant, a series of acts and omissions;

(6) "actor" includes, where relevant, a person guilty of an omission;

(7) "acted" includes, where relevant, "omitted to act";

(8) "person," "he" and "actor" include any natural person and, where relevant, a corporation or an unincorporated association;

(9) "element of an offense" means (i) such conduct or (ii) such attendant circumstances or (iii) such a result of conduct as

(a) is included in the description of the forbidden conduct in the definition of the offense; or

(b) establishes the required kind of culpability; or

(c) negatives an excuse or justification for such conduct; or

(d) negatives a defense under the statute of limitations; or

(e) establishes jurisdiction or venue;

(10) "material element of an offense" means an element that does not relate exclusively to the statute of limitations, jurisdiction, venue or to any other matter similarly unconnected with (i) the harm or evil, incident to conduct, sought to be prevented by the law defining the offense, or (ii) the existence of a justification or excuse for such conduct;

(11) "purposely" has the meaning specified in Section 2.02 and equivalent terms such as "with purpose," "designed" or "with design" have the same meaning;

(12) "intentionally" or "with intent" means purposely;

(13) "knowingly" has the meaning specified in Section 2.02 and equivalent terms such as "knowing" or "with knowledge" have the same meaning;

(14) "recklessly" has the meaning specified in Section 2.02 and equivalent terms such as "recklessness" or "with recklessness" have the same meaning;

(15) "negligently" has the meaning specified in Section 2.02 and equivalent terms such as "negligence" or "with negligence" have the same meaning;

(16) "reasonably believes" or "reasonable belief" designates a belief which the actor is not reckless or negligent in holding.

Article 2. General Principles of Liability

Section 2.01. Requirement of Voluntary Act; Omission as Basis of Liability; Possession as an Act.

(1) A person is not guilty of an offense unless his liability is based on conduct which includes a voluntary act or the omission to perform an act of which he is physically capable.

(2) The following are not voluntary acts within the meaning of this Section:

(a) a reflex or convulsion;

(b) a bodily movement during unconsciousness or sleep;

(c) conduct during hypnosis or resulting from hypnotic suggestion;

(d) a bodily movement that otherwise is not a product of the effort or determination of the actor, either conscious or habitual.

(3) Liability for the commission of an offense may not be based on an omission unaccompanied by action unless:

(a) the omission is expressly made sufficient by the law defining the offense; or

(b) a duty to perform the omitted act is otherwise imposed by law.

(4) Possession is an act, within the meaning of this Section, if the possessor knowingly procured or received the thing possessed or was aware of his control thereof for a sufficient period to have been able to terminate his possession.

Section 2.02. General Requirements of Culpability.

(1) *Minimum Requirements of Culpability.* Except as provided in Section 2.05, a person is not guilty of an offense unless he acted purposely, knowingly, recklessly or negligently, as the law may require, with respect to each material element of the offense.

(2) *Kinds of Culpability Defined.*

(a) *Purposely.*

A person acts purposely with respect to a material element of an offense when:

(i) if the element involves the nature of his conduct or a result thereof, it is his conscious object to engage in conduct of that nature or to cause such a result; and

(ii) if the element involves the attendant circumstances, he is aware of the existence of such circumstances or he believes or hopes that they exist.

(b) *Knowingly.*

A person acts knowingly with respect to a material element of an offense when:

(i) if the element involves the nature of his conduct or the attendant circumstances, he is aware that his conduct is of that nature or that such circumstances exist; and

(ii) if the element involves a result of his conduct, he is aware that it is practically certain that his conduct will cause such a result.

(c) *Recklessly.*

A person acts recklessly with respect to a material element of an offense when he consciously disregards a substantial and unjustifiable risk that the material element exists or will result from his conduct. The risk must be of such a nature and degree that, considering the nature and purpose of the actor's conduct and the circumstances known to him, its disregard involves a gross deviation from the standard of conduct that a law-abiding person would observe in the actor's situation.

(d) *Negligently.*

A person acts negligently with respect to a material element of an offense when he should be aware of a substantial and unjustifiable risk that the material element exists or will result from his conduct. The risk must be of such a nature and degree that the actor's failure to perceive it, considering the nature and purpose of his conduct and the circumstances known to him, involves a gross deviation from the standard of care that a reasonable person would observe in the actor's situation.

(3) *Culpability Required Unless Otherwise Provided.* When the culpability sufficient to

establish a material element of an offense is not prescribed by law, such element is established if a person acts purposely, knowingly or recklessly with respect thereto.

(4) *Prescribed Culpability Requirement Applies to All Material Elements.* When the law defining an offense prescribes the kind of culpability that is sufficient for the commission of an offense, without distinguishing among the material elements thereof, such provision shall apply to all the material elements of the offense, unless a contrary purpose plainly appears.

(5) *Substitutes for Negligence, Recklessness and Knowledge.* When the law provides that negligence suffices to establish an element of an offense, such element also is established if a person acts purposely, knowingly or recklessly. When recklessness suffices to establish an element, such element also is established if a person acts purposely or knowingly. When acting knowingly suffices to establish an element, such element also is established if a person acts purposely.

(6) *Requirement of Purpose Satisfied if Purpose Is Conditional.* When a particular purpose is an element of an offense, the element is established although such purpose is conditional, unless the condition negatives the harm or evil sought to be prevented by the law defining the offense.

(7) *Requirement of Knowledge Satisfied by Knowledge of High Probability.* When knowledge of the existence of a particular fact is an element of an offense, such knowledge is established if a person is aware of a high probability of its existence, unless he actually believes that it does not exist.

(8) *Requirement of Wilfulness Satisfied by Acting Knowingly.* A requirement that an offense be committed wilfully is satisfied if a person acts knowingly with respect to the material elements of the offense, unless a purpose to impose further requirements appears.

(9) *Culpability as to Illegality of Conduct.* Neither knowledge nor recklessness or negligence as to whether conduct constitutes an offense or as to the existence, meaning or application of the law determining the elements of an offense is an element of such offense, unless the definition of the offense or the Code so provides.

(10) *Culpability as Determinant of Grade of Offense.* When the grade or degree of an offense depends on whether the offense is committed purposely, knowingly, recklessly or negligently, its grade or degree shall be the lowest for which the determinative kind of culpability is established with respect to any material element of the offense.

Section 2.03. Causal Relationship Between Conduct and Result; Divergence Between Result Designed or Contemplated and Actual Result or Between Probable and Actual Result.

(1) Conduct is the cause of a result when:

(a) it is an antecedent but for which the result in question would not have occurred; and

(b) the relationship between the conduct and result satisfies any additional causal requirements imposed by the Code or by the law defining the offense.

(2) When purposely or knowingly causing a particular result is an element of an offense, the element is not established if the actual result is not within the purpose or the contemplation of the actor unless:

(a) the actual result differs from that designed or contemplated, as the case may be, only in the respect that a different person or different property is injured or affected or that the injury or harm designed or contemplated would have been more serious or more extensive than that caused; or

(b) the actual result involves the same kind of injury or harm as that designed or contemplated and is not too remote or accidental in its occurrence to have a [just] bearing on the actor's liability or on the gravity of his offense.

(3) When recklessly or negligently causing a particular result is an element of an offense, the element is not established if the actual result is not within the risk of which the actor is aware or, in the case of negligence, of which he should be aware unless:

(a) the actual result differs from the probable result only in the respect that a different person or different property is injured or affected or that the probable injury or harm would have been more serious or more extensive that that caused; or

(b) the actual result involves the same kind of injury or harm as the probable result and is not too remote or accidental in its occurence to have a [just] bearing on the actor's liability or on the gravity of his offense.

(4) When causing a particular result is a material element of an offense for which absolute liability is imposed by law, the element is not established unless the actual result is a probable consequence of the actor's conduct.

Section 2.04. Ignorance or Mistake.

(1) Ignorance or mistake as to a matter of fact or law is a defense if:

(a) the ignorance or mistake negatives the purpose, knowledge, belief, recklessness or negligence required to establish a material element of the offense; or

(b) the law provides that the state of mind established by such ignorance or mistake constitutes a defense.

(2) Although ignorance or mistake would otherwise afford a defense to the offense charged, the defense is not available if the defendant would be guilty of another offense had the situation been as he supposed. In such case, however, the ignorance or mistake of the defendant shall reduce the grade and degree of the offense of which he may be convicted to those of the offense of which he would be guilty had the situation been as he supposed.

(3) A belief that conduct does not legally constitute an offense is a defense to a prosecution for that offense based upon such conduct when:

(a) the statute or other enactment defining the offense is not known to the actor and has not been published or otherwise reasonably made available prior to the conduct alleged; or

(b) he acts in reasonable reliance upon an official statement of the law, afterward determined to be invalid or erroneous, contained in (i) a statute or other enactment; (ii) a judicial decision, opinion or judgment; (iii) an administrative order or grant of permission; or (iv) an official interpretation of the public officer or body charged by law with responsibility for the interpretation, administration or enforcement of the law defining the offense.

(4) The defendant must prove a defense arising under Subsection (3) of this Section by a preponderance of evidence.

Section 2.05. When Culpability Requirements Are Inapplicable to Violations and to Offenses Defined by Other Statutes; Effect of Absolute Liability in Reducing Grade of Offense to Violation.

(1) The requirements of culpability prescribed by Sections 2.01 and 2.02 do not apply to:

(a) offenses which constitute violations, unless the requirement involved is included in the definition of the offense or the Court determines that its application is consistent with effective enforcement of the law defining the offense; or

(b) offenses defined by statutes other than the Code, insofar as a legislative purpose to impose absolute liability for such offenses or with respect to any material element thereof plainly appears.

(2) Notwithstanding any other provision of existing law and unless a subsequent statute otherwise provides:

(a) when absolute liability is imposed with respect to any material element of an offense defined by a statute other than the Code and a conviction is based upon such liability, the offense constitutes a violation; and

(b) although absolute liability is imposed by law with respect to one or more of the material elements of an offense defined by a statute other than the Code, the culpable commission of the offense may be charged and proved, in which event negligence with respect to such elements constitutes sufficient culpability and the classification of the offense and the sentence that may be imposed therefor upon conviction are determined by Section 1.04 and Article 6 of the Code.

Section 2.06. Liability for Conduct of Another; Complicity.

(1) A person is guilty of an offense if it is committed by his own conduct or by the conduct of another person for which he is legally accountable, or both.

(2) A person is legally accountable for the conduct of another person when:

(a) acting with the kind of culpability that is sufficient for the commission of the offense, he causes an innocent or irresponsible person to engage in such conduct; or

(b) he is made accountable for the conduct of such other person by the Code or by the law defining the offense; or

(c) he is an accomplice of such other person in the commission of the offense.

(3) A person is an accomplice of another person in the commission of an offense if:

(a) with the purpose of promoting or facilitating the commission of the offense, he

(i) solicits such other person to commit it; or

(ii) aids or agrees or attempts to aid such other person in planning or committing it; or

(iii) having a legal duty to prevent the commission of the offense, fails to make proper effect so to do; or

(b) his conduct is expressly declared by law to establish his complicity.

(4) When causing a particular result is an element of an offense, an accomplice

in the conduct causing such result is an accomplice in the commission of that offense, if he acts with the kind of culpability, if any, with respect to that result that is sufficient for the commission of the offense.

(5) A person who is legally incapable of committing a particular offense himself may be guilty thereof, if it is committed by the conduct of another person for which he is legally accountable, unless such liability is inconsistent with the purpose of the provision establishing his incapacity.

(6) Unless otherwise provided by the Code or by the law defining the offense, a person is not an accomplice in an offense committed by another person if:

(a) he is a victim of that offense; or

(b) the offense is so defined that his conduct is inevitably incident to its commission; or

(c) he terminates his complicity prior to the commission of the offense and

(i) wholly deprives it of effectiveness in the commission of the offense; or

(ii) gives timely warning to the law enforcement authorities or otherwise makes proper effort to prevent the commission of the offense.

(7) An accomplice may be convicted on proof of the commission of the offense and of his complicity therein, though the person claimed to have committed the offense has not been prosecuted or convicted or has been convicted of a different offense or degree of offense or has an immunity to prosecution or conviction or has been acquitted.

Section 2.07. Liability of Corporations, Unincorporated Associations and Persons Acting, or Under a Duty to Act, in Their Behalf.

(1) A corporation may be convicted of the commission of an offense if:

(a) the offense is a violation or the offense is defined by a statute other than the Code in which a legislative purpose to impose liability on corporations plainly appears and the conduct is performed by an agent of the corporation acting in behalf of the corporation within the scope of his office or employment, except that if the law defining the offense designates the agents for whose conduct the corporation is accountable or the circumstances under which it is accountable, such provisions shall apply; or

(b) the offense consists of an omission to discharge a specific duty of affirmative performance imposed on corporations by law; or

(c) the commission of the offense was authorized, requested, commanded, performed or recklessly tolerated by the board of directors or by a high managerial agent acting in behalf of the corporation within the scope of his office or employment.

(2) When absolute liability is imposed for the commission of an offense, a legislative purpose to impose liability on a corporation shall be assumed, unless the contrary plainly appears.

(3) An unincorporated association may be convicted of the commission of an offense if:

(a) the offense is defined by a statute other than the Code which expressly provides for the liability of such an association and the conduct is performed by an agent of the association acting in behalf of the association within the scope of his office or employment, except that if the law defining the offense designates the agents for whose conduct the association is accountable or the circumstances under which it is accountable, such provisions shall apply; or

(b) the offense consists of an omission to discharge a specific duty of affirmative performance imposed on associations by law.

(4) As used in this Section:

(a) "corporation" does not include an entity organized as or by a governmental agency for the execution of a governmental program;

(b) "agent" means any director, officer, servant, employee or other person authorized to act in behalf of the corporation or association and, in the case of an unincorporated association, a member of such association;

(c) "high managerial agent" means an officer of a corporation or an unincorporated association, or, in the case of a partnership, a partner, or any other agent of a corporation or association having duties of such responsibilities that his conduct may fairly be assumed to represent the policy of the corporation or association.

(5) In any prosecution of a corporation or an unincorporated association for the commission of an offense included within the terms of Subsection (1)(a) or Subsection (3)(a) of this Section, other than an offense for which absolute liability has been imposed, it shall be a defense if the defendant proves by a preponderance of evidence that the high managerial agent having supervisory responsibility over the subject matter of the offense employed due diligence to prevent its commission. This paragraph shall not apply if it is plainly inconsistent with the legislative purpose in defining the particular offense.

(6) (a) A person is legally accountable for any conduct he performs or causes to be performed in the name of the corporation or an unincorporated association or in its behalf to the same extent as if it were performed in his own name or behalf.

(b) Whenever a duty to act is imposed by law upon a corporation or an unincorporated association, any agent of the corporation or association having primary responsibility for the discharge of the duty is legally accountable for a reckless omission to perform the required act to the same extent as if the duty were imposed by law directly upon himself.

(c) When a person is convicted of an offense by reason of his legal accountability for the conduct of a corporation or an unincorporated association, he is subject to the sentence authorized by law when a natural person is convicted of an offense of the grade and the degree involved.

Section 2.08. Intoxication.

(1) Except as provided in Subsection (4) of this Section, intoxication of the actor is not a defense unless it negatives an element of the offense.

(2) When recklessness establishes an element of the offense, if the actor, due to self-induced intoxication, is unaware of a risk of which he would have been aware had he been sober, such unawareness is immaterial.

(3) Intoxication does not, in itself, constitute mental disease within the meaning of Section 4.01.

(4) Intoxication which (a) is not self-induced or (b) is pathological is an affirmative defense if by reason of such intoxication the actor at the time of his conduct lacks

substantial capacity either to appreciate its criminality [wrongfulness] or to conform his conduct to the requirements of law.

(5) *Definitions.* In this Section unless a different meaning plainly is required:

(a) "intoxication" means a disturbance of mental or physical capacities resulting from the introduction of substances into the body;

(b) "self-induced intoxication" means intoxication caused by substances which the actor knowingly introduces into his body, the tendency of which to cause intoxication he knows or ought to know, unless he introduces them pursuant to medical advice or under such circumstances as would afford a defense to a charge of crime;

(c) "pathological intoxication" means intoxication grossly excessive in degree, given the amount of the intoxicant, to which the actor does not know he is susceptible.

Section 2.09. Duress.

(1) It is an affirmative defense that the actor engaged in the conduct charged to constitute an offense because he was coerced to do so by the use of, or a threat to use, unlawful force against his person or the person of another, which a person of reasonable firmness in his situation would have been unable to resist.

(2) The defense provided by this Section is unavailable if the actor recklessly placed himself in a situation in which it was probable that he would be subjected to duress. The defense is also unavailable if he was negligent in placing himself in such a situation, whenever negligence suffices to establish culpability for the offense charged.

(3) It is not a defense that a woman acted on the command of her husband, unless she acted under such coercion as would establish a defense under this Section. [The presumption that a woman, acting in the presence of her husband, is coerced is abolished.]

(4) When the conduct of the actor would otherwise be justifiable under Section 3.02, this Section does not preclude such defense.

Section 2.10. Military Orders.

It is an affirmative defense that the actor, in engaging in the conduct charged to constitute an offense, does no more than execute an order of his superior in the armed services which he does not know to be unlawful.

Section 2.11. Consent.

(1) *In General.* The consent of the victim to conduct charged to constitute an offense or to the result thereof is a defense if such consent negatives an element of the offense or precludes the infliction of the harm or evil sought to be prevented by the law defining the offense.

(2) *Consent to Bodily Harm.* When conduct is charged to constitute an offense because it causes or threatens bodily harm, consent to such conduct or to the infliction of such harm is a defense if:

(a) the bodily harm consented to or threatened by the conduct consented to is not serious; or

(b) the conduct and the harm are reasonably foreseeable hazards of joint participation in a lawful athletic contest or competitive sport; or

(c) the consent establishes a justification for the conduct under Article 3 of the Code.

(3) *Ineffective Consent.* Unless otherwise provided by the Code or by the law defining the offense, assent does not constitute consent if:

(a) it is given by a person who is legally incompetent to authorize the conduct charged to constitute the offense; or

(b) it is given by a person who by reason of youth, mental disease or defect or intoxication is manifestly unable or known by the actor to be unable to make a reasonable judgment as to the nature or harmfulness of the conduct charged to constitute the offense; or

(c) it is given by a person whose improvident consent is sought to be prevented by the law defining the offense; or

(d) it is induced by force, duress or deception of a kind sought to be prevented by the law defining the offense.

Section 2.12. De Minimis Infractions.

The Court shall dismiss a prosecution if, having regard to the nature of the conduct charged to constitute an offense and the nature of the attendant circumstances, it finds that the defendant's conduct:

(1) was within a customary license of tolerance, neither expressly negatived by the person whose interest was infringed nor inconsistent with the purpose of the law defining the offense; or

(2) did not actually cause or threaten the harm or evil sought to be prevented by the law defining the offense or did so only to an extent too trivial to warrant the condemnation of conviction; or

(3) presents such other extenuations that it cannot reasonably be regarded as envisaged by the legislature in forbidding the offense.

The Court shall not dismiss a prosecution under Subsection (3) of this Section without filing a written statement of its reasons.

Section 2.13. Entrapment.

(1) A public law enforcement official or a person acting in cooperation with such an official perpetrates an entrapment if for the purpose of obtaining evidence of the commission of an offense, he induces or encourages another person to engage in conduct constituting such offense by either:

(a) making knowingly false representations designed to induce the belief that such conduct is not prohibited; or

(b) employing methods of persuasion or inducement which create a substantial risk that such an offense will be committed by persons other than those who are ready to commit it.

(2) Except as provided in Subsection (3) of this Section, a person prosecuted for an offense shall be acquitted if he proves by a preponderance of evidence that his conduct occurred in response to an entrapment. The issue of entrapment shall be tried by the Court in the absence of the jury.

(3) The defense afforded by this Section is unavailable when causing or threatening bodily injury is an element of the offense charged and the prosecution is based on conduct causing or threatening such injury to a person other than the person perpetrating the entrapment.

Article 3. General Principles of Justification

Section 3.01. Justification an Affirmative Defense; Civil Remedies Unaffected.

(1) In any prosecution based on conduct which is justifiable under this Article, justification is an affirmative defense.

(2) The fact that conduct is justifiable under this Article does not abolish or impair any remedy for such conduct which is available in any civil action.

Section 3.02. Justification Generally: Choice of Evils.

(1) Conduct which the actor believes to be necessary to avoid a harm or evil to himself or to another is justifiable, provided that:

(a) the harm or evil sought to be avoided by such conduct is greater than that sought to be prevented by the law defining the offense charged; and

(b) neither the Code nor other law defining the offense provides exceptions or defenses dealing with the specific situation involved; and

(c) a legislative purpose to exclude the justification claimed does not otherwise plainly appear.

(2) When the actor was reckless or negligent in bringing about the situation requiring a choice of harms or evils or in appraising the necessity for his conduct, the justification afforded by this Section is unavailable in a prosecution for any offense for which recklessness or negligence, as the case may be, suffices to establish culpability.

Section 3.03. Execution of Public Duty.

(1) Except as provided in Subsection (2) of this Section, conduct is justifiable when it is required or authorized by:

(a) the law defining the duties or functions of a public officer or the assistance to be rendered to such officer in the performance of his duties; or

(b) the law governing the execution of legal process; or

(c) the judgment or order of a competent court or tribunal; or

(d) the law governing the armed services or the lawful conduct of war; or

(e) any other provision of law imposing a public duty.

(2) The other sections of this Article apply to:

(a) the use of force upon or toward the person of another for any of the purposes dealt with in such sections; and

(b) the use of deadly force for any purpose, unless the use of such force is otherwise expressly authorized by law or occurs in the lawful conduct of war.

(3) The justification afforded by Subsection (1) of this Section applies:

(a) when the actor believes his conduct to be required or authorized by the judgment or direction of a competent court or tribunal or in the lawful execution of legal process, notwithstanding lack of jurisdiction of the court or defect in the legal process; and

(b) when the actor believes his conduct to be required or authorized to assist a public officer in the performance of his duties, notwithstanding that the officer exceeded his legal authority.

Section 3.04. Use of Force in Self-Protection.

(1) *Use of Force Justifiable for Protection of the Person.* Subject to the provisions of this Section and of Section 3.09, the use of force upon or toward another person is justifiable when the actor believes that such force is immediately necessary for the purpose of protecting himself against the use of unlawful force by such other person on the present occasion.

(2) *Limitations on Justifying Necessity for Use of Force.*

(a) The use of force is not justifiable under this Section:

(i) to resist arrest which the actor knows is being made by a peace officer, although the arrest is unlawful; or

(ii) to resist force used by the occupier or possessor of property or by another person on his behalf, where the actor knows that the person using the force is doing so under a claim of right to protect the property, except that this limitation shall not apply if:

(1) the actor is a public officer acting in the performance of his duties or a person lawfully assisting him therein or a person making or assisting in a lawful arrest; or

(2) the actor has been unlawfully dispossessed of the property and is making a re-entry or recaption justified by Section 3.06; or

(3) the actor believes that such force is necessary to protect himself against death or serious bodily harm.

(b) The use of deadly force is not justifiable under this Section unless the actor believes that such force is necessary to protect himself against death, serious bodily harm, kidnapping or sexual intercourse compelled by force or threat; nor is it justifiable if:

(i) the actor, with the purpose of causing death or serious bodily harm, provoked the use of force against himself in the same encounter; or

(ii) the actor knows that he can avoid the necessity of using such force with complete safety by retreating or by surrendering possession of a thing to a person asserting a claim of right thereto or by complying with a demand that he abstain from any action which he has no duty to take, except that:

(1) the actor is not obliged to retreat from his dwelling of place or work, unless he was the initial aggressor or is assailed in his place of work by another person whose place of work the actor knows it to be; and

(2) a public officer justified in using force in the performance of his duties or a person justified in using force in his assistance or a person justified in using force in making an arrest or preventing an escape is not obliged to desist from efforts to perform such duty, effect such arrest or prevent such escape because of resistance or threatened resistance by or on behalf of the person against whom such action is directed.

(c) Except as required by paragraphs (a) and (b) of this Subsection, a person employing protective force may estimate the necessity thereof under the circumstances as he believes them to be when the force is used, without retreating, surrendering possession, doing any other act which he has no legal duty to do or abstaining from any lawful action.

(3) *Use of Confinement as Protective Force.* The justification afforded by this Section extends to the use of confinement as protective force only if the actor takes all reasonable measures to terminate the confinement as soon as he knows that he safely can, unless the person confined has been arrested on a charge of crime.

Section 3.05. Use of Force for the Protection of Other Persons.

(1) Subject to the provisions of this Section and of Section 3.09, the use of force upon or toward the person of another is justifiable to protect a third person when:

(a) the actor would be justified under Section 3.04 in using such force to protect himself against the injury he believes to be threatened to the person whom he seeks to protect; and

(b) under the circumstances as the actor believes them to be, the person whom he seeks to protect would be justified in using such protective force; and

(c) the actor believes that his intervention is necessary for the protection of such other person.

(2) Notwithstanding Subsection (1) of this Section:

(a) when the actor would be obliged under Section 3.04 to retreat, to surrender the possession of a thing or to comply with a demand before using force in self-protection, he is not obliged to do so before using force for the protection of another person, unless he knows that he can thereby secure the complete safety of such other person; and

(b) when the person whom the actor seeks to protect would be obliged under Section 3.04 to retreat, to surrender the possession of a thing or to comply with a demand if he knew that he could obtain complete safety by so doing, the actor is obliged to try to cause him to do so before using force in his protection if the actor knows that he can obtain complete safety in that way; and

(c) neither the actor nor the person whom he seeks to protect is obliged to retreat when in the other's dwelling or place of work to any greater extent than in his own.

Section 3.06. Use of Force for the Protection of Property.

(1) *Use of Force Justifiable for Protection of Property.* Subject to the provisions of this Section and of Section 3.09, the use of force upon or toward the person of another is justifiable when the actor believes that such force is immediately necessary:

(a) to prevent or terminate an unlawful entry or other trespass upon land or a trespass against or the unlawful carrying away of tangible, movable property, provided that such land or movable property is, or is believed by the actor to be, in his possession or in the possession of another person for whose protection he acts; or

(b) to effect an entry or re-entry upon land or to retake tangible movable property, provided that the actor believes that he or the person by whose authority he acts or a person from whom he or such other person derives title was unlawfully dispossessed of such land or movable property and is entitled to possession, and provided, further, that:

(i) the force is used immediately or on fresh pursuit after such dispossession; or

(ii) the actor believes that the person against whom he uses force has no claim of right to the possession of the property and, in the case of land, the circumstances, as the actor believes them to be, are of such urgency that it would be an exceptional hardship to postpone the entry or re-entry until a court order is obtained.

(2) *Meaning of Possession.* For the purposes of Subsection (1) of this Section:

(a) a person who has parted with the custody of property to another who refuses to restore it to him is no longer in possession, unless the property is movable and was and still is located on land in his possession;

(b) a person who has been dispossessed of land does not regain possession thereof merely by setting foot thereon;

(c) a person who has a license to use or occupy real property is deemed to be in possession thereof except against the licensor acting under claim of right.

(3) *Limitations on Justifiable Use of Force.*

(a) *Request to Desist.* The use of force is justifiable under this Section only if the actor first requests the person against whom such force is used to desist from his interference with the property, unless the actor believes that:

(i) such request would be useless; or

(ii) it would be dangerous to himself or another person to make the request; or

(iii) substantial harm will be done to the physical condition of the property which is sought to be protected before the request can effectively be made.

(b) *Exclusion of Trespasser.* The use of force to prevent or terminate a trespass is not justifiable under this Section if the actor knows that the exclusion of the trespasser will expose him to substantial danger of serious bodily harm.

(c) *Resistance of Lawful Re-entry or Recaption.* The use of force to prevent an entry or re-entry upon land or the recaption of movable property is not justifiable under this Section, although the actor believes that such re-entry or recaption is unlawful, if:

(i) the re-entry or recaption is made by or on behalf of a person who was actually dispossessed of the property; and

(ii) it is otherwise justifiable under paragraph (1)(b) of this Section.

(d) *Use of Deadly Force.* The use of deadly force is not justifiable under this Section unless the actor believes that:

(i) the person against whom the force is used is attempting to dispossess him of his dwelling otherwise than under a claim of right to its possession; or

(ii) the person against whom the force is used is attempting to commit or consummate arson, burglary, robbery or other felonious theft or property destruction and either:

(1) has employed or threatened deadly force against or in the presence of the actor; or

(2) the use of force other than deadly force to prevent the com-

mission or the consummation of the crime would expose the actor or another in his presence to substantial danger of serious bodily harm.

(4) *Use of Confinement as Protective Force.* The justification afforded by this Section extends to the use of confinement as protective force only if the actor takes all reasonable measures to terminate the confinement as soon as he knows that he can do so with safety to the property, unless the person confined has been arrested on a charge of crime.

(5) *Use of Device to Protect Property.* The justification afforded by this Section extends to the use of a device for the purpose of protecting property only if:

(a) the device is not designed to cause or known to create a substantial risk of causing death or serious bodily harm; and

(b) the use of the particular device to protect the property from entry or trespass is reasonable under the circumstances, as the actor believes them to be; and

(c) the device is one customarily used for such a purpose or reasonable care is taken to make known to probable intruders the fact that it is used.

(6) *Use of Force to Pass Wrongful Obstructor.* The use of force to pass a person whom the actor believes to be purposely or knowingly and unjustifiably obstructing the actor from going to a place to which he may lawfully go is justifiable, provided that:

(a) the actor believes that the person against whom he uses force has no claim of right to obstruct the actor; and

(b) the actor is not being obstructed from entry or movement on land which he knows to be in the possession or custody of the person obstructing him, or in the possession or custody of another person by whose authority the obstructor acts, unless the circumstances, as the actor believes them to be, are of such urgency that it would not be reasonable to postpone the entry or movement on such land until a court order is obtained; and

(c) the force used is not greater than would be justifiable if the person obstructing the actor were using force against him to prevent his passage.

Section 3.07. Use of Force in Law Enforcement.

(1) *Use of Force Justifiable to Effect an Arrest.* Subject to the provisions of this Section and of Section 3.09, the use of force upon or toward the person of another is justifiable when the actor is making or assisting in making an arrest and the actor believes that such force is immediately necessary to effect a lawful arrest.

(2) *Limitations on the Use of Force.*

(a) The use of force is not justifiable under this Section unless:

(i) the actor makes known the purpose of the arrest or believes that it is otherwise known by or cannot reasonably be made known to the person to be arrested; and

(ii) when the arrest is made under a warrant, the warrant is valid or believed by the actor to be valid.

(b) The use of deadly force is not justifiable under this Section unless:

(i) the arrest is for a felony; and

(ii) the person effecting the arrest is authorized to act as a peace officer or is assisting a person whom he believes to be authorized to act as a peace officer; and

(iii) the actor believes that the force employed creates no substantial risk of injury to innocent persons; and

(iv) the actor believes that:

(1) the crime for which the arrest is made involved conduct including the use or threatened use of deadly force; or

(2) there is a substantial risk that the person to be arrested will cause death or serious bodily harm if his apprehension is delayed.

(3) *Use of Force to Prevent Escape from Custody.* The use of force to prevent the escape of an arrested person from custody is justifiable when the force could justifiably have been employed to effect the arrest under which the person is in custody, except that a guard or other person authorized to act as a peace officer is justified in using any force, including deadly force, which he believes to be immediately necessary to prevent the escape of a person from a jail, prison, or other institution for the detention of persons charged with or convicted of a crime.

(4) *Use of Force by Private Person Assisting an Unlawful Arrest.*

(a) A private person who is summoned by a peace officer to assist in effecting an unlawful arrest, is justified in using any force which he would be justified in using if the arrest were lawful, provided that he does not believe the arrest is unlawful.

(b) A private person who assists another private person in effecting an unlawful arrest, or who, not being summoned, assists a peace officer in effecting an unlawful arrest, is justified in using any force which he would be justified in using if the arrest were lawful, provided that (i) he believes the arrest is lawful, and (ii) the arrest would be lawful if the facts were as he believes them to be.

(5) *Use of Force to Prevent Suicide or the Commission of a Crime.*

(a) The use of force upon or toward the person of another is justifiable when the actor believes that such force is immediately necessary to prevent such other person from committing suicide, inflicting serious bodily harm upon himself, committing or consummating the commission of a crime involving or threatening bodily harm, damage to or loss of property or a breach of the peace, except that:

(i) any limitations imposed by the other provisions of this Article on the justifiable use of force in self-protection, for the protection of others, the protection of property, the effectuation of an arrest or the prevention of an escape from custody shall apply notwithstanding the criminality of the conduct against which such force is used; and

(ii) the use of deadly force is not in any event justifiable under this Subsection unless:

(1) the actor believes that there is a substantial risk that the person whom he seeks to prevent from committing a crime will cause death or serious bodily harm to another unless the commission or the consummation of the crime is prevented and that the use of such force presents no substantial risk of injury to innocent persons; or

(2) the actor believes that the use of such force is necessary to suppress a riot or mutiny after the rioters or mutineers have been ordered to disperse and warned, in any particular manner that the law may require, that such force will be used if they do not obey.

(b) The justification afforded by this Subsection extends to the use of confinement as preventive force only if the actor takes all reasonable measures to terminate the confinement as soon as he knows that he safely can, unless the person confined has been arrested on a charge of crime.

Section 3.08. Use of Force by Persons with Special Responsibility for Care, Discipline or Safety of Others.

The use of force upon or toward the person of another is justifiable if:

(1) The actor is the parent or guardian or other person similarly responsible for the general care and supervision of a minor or a person acting at the request of such parent, guardian or other responsible person and:

(a) the force is used for the purpose of safeguarding or promoting the welfare of the minor, including the prevention or punishment of his misconduct; and

(b) the force used is not designed to cause or known to create a substantial risk of causing death, serious bodily harm, disfigurement, extreme pain or mental distress or gross degradation; or

(2) the actor is a teacher or a person otherwise entrusted with the care or supervision for a special purpose of a minor and:

(a) the actor believes that the force used is necessary to further such special purpose, including the maintenance of reasonable discipline in a school, class or other group, and that the use of such force is consistent with the welfare of the minor; and

(b) the degree of force, if it had been used by the parent or guardian of the minor, would not be unjustifiable under Subsection (1)(b) of this Section; or

(3) the actor is the guardian or other person similarly responsible for the general care and supervision of an incompetent person; and:

(a) the force is used for the purpose of safeguarding or promoting the welfare of the incompetent person, including the prevention of his misconduct, or, when such incompetent person is in a hospital or other institution for his care and custody, for the maintenance of reasonable discipline in such institution; and

(b) the force used is not designed to cause or known to create a substantial risk of causing death, serious bodily harm, disfigurement, extreme or unnecessary pain, mental distress, or humiliation; or

(4) the actor is a doctor or other therapist or a person assisting him at his direction, and:

(a) the force is used for the purpose of administering a recognized form of treatment which the actor believes to be adapted to promoting the physical or mental health of the patient; and

(b) the treatment is administered with the consent of the patient or, if the patient is a minor or an incompetent person, with the consent of his parent or guardian or other person legally competent to consent in his behalf, or the treatment is administered in an emergency when the actor believes that no one competent to consent can be consulted and that a reasonable person, wishing to safeguard the welfare of the patient, would consent; or

(5) the actor is a warden or other authorized official of a correctional institution, and:

(a) he believes that the force used is necessary for the purpose of enforcing the lawful rules or procedures of the institution, unless his belief in the lawfulness of the rule or procedure sought to be enforced is erroneous and his error is due to ignorance or mistake as to the provisions of the Code, any other provision of the criminal law or the law governing the administration of the institution; and

(b) the nature or degree of force used is not forbidden by Article 303 or 304 of the Code; and

(c) if deadly force is used, its use is otherwise justifiable under this Article; or

(6) the actor is a person responsible for the safety of a vessel or an aircraft or a person acting at his direction, and

(a) he believes that the force used is necessary to prevent interference with the operation of the vessel or aircraft or obstruction of the execution of a lawful order, unless his belief in the lawfulness of the order is erroneous and his error is due to ignorance or mistake as to the law defining his authority; and

(b) if deadly force is used, its use is otherwise justifiable under this Article; or

(7) the actor is a person who is authorized or required by law to maintain order or decorum in a vehicle, train or other carrier or in a place where others are assembled, and:

(a) he believes that the force used is necessary for such purpose; and

(b) the force used is not designed to cause or known to create a substantial risk of causing death, bodily harm, or extreme mental distress.

Section 3.09. Mistake of Law as to Unlawfulness of Force or Legality of Arrest; Reckless or Negligent Use of Otherwise Justifiable Force; Reckless or Negligent Injury or Risk of Injury to Innocent Persons.

(1) The justification afforded by Sections 3.04 to 3.07, inclusive, is unavailable when:

(a) the actor's belief in the unlawfulness of the force or conduct against which he employs protective force or his belief in the lawfulness of an arrest which he endeavors to effect by force is erroneous; and

(b) his error is due to ignorance or mistake as to the provisions of the Code, any other provision of the criminal law or the law governing the legality of an arrest or search.

(2) When the actor believes that the use of force upon or toward the person of another is necessary for any of the purposes for which such belief would establish a

justification under Sections 3.03 to 3.08 but the actor is reckless or negligent in having such belief or in acquiring or failing to acquire any knowledge or belief which is material to the justifiability of his use of force, the justification afforded by those Sections is unavailable in a prosecution for an offense for which recklessness or negligence, as the case may be, suffices to establish culpability.

(3) When the actor is justified under Sections 3.03 to 3.08 in using force upon or toward the person of another but he recklessly or negligently injures or creates a risk of injury to innocent persons, the justification afforded by those Sections is unavailable in a prosectution for such recklessness or negligence towards innocent persons.

Section 3.10. Justification in Property Crimes.

Conduct involving the appropriation, seizure or destruction of, damage to, intrusion on or interference with property is justifiable under circumstances which would establish a defense of privilege in a civil action based thereon unless:

(1) the Code or the law defining the offense deals with the specific situation involved; or

(2) a legislative purpose to exclude the justification claimed otherwise plainly appears.

Section 3.11. Definitions.

In this Article, unless a different meaning plainly is required:

(1) "unlawful force" means force, including confinement, which is employed without the consent of the person against whom it is directed and the employment of which constitutes an offense or actionable tort or would constitute such offense or tort except for a defense (such as the absence of intent, negligence, or mental capacity; duress; youth; or diplomatic status) not amounting to a privilege to use the force. Assent constitutes consent, within the meaning of this Section, whether or not it otherwise is legally effective, except assent to the infliction of death or serious bodily harm.

(2) "deadly force" means force which the actor uses with the purpose of causing or which he knows to create a substantial risk of causing death or serious bodily harm. Purposely firing a firearm in the direction of another person or at a vehicle in which another person is believed to be constitutes deadly force. A threat to cause death or serious bodily harm, by the production of a weapon or otherwise, so long as the actor's purpose is limited to creating an apprehension that he will use deadly force if necessary, does not constitute deadly force;

(3) "dwelling" means any building or structure, though movable or temporary, or a portion thereof, which is for the time being the actor's home or place of lodging.

Article 4. Responsibility

Section 4.01. Mental Disease or Defect Excluding Responsibility.

(1) A person is not responsible for criminal conduct if at the time of such conduct as a result of mental disease or defect he lacks substantial capacity either to appreciate the criminality [wrongfulness] of his conduct or to conform his conduct to the requirements of law.

(2) As used in this Article, the terms "mental disease or defect" do not include an abnormality manifested only by repeated criminal or otherwise anti-social conduct.

Section 4.02. Evidence of Mental Disease or Defect Admissible When Relevant to Element of the Offense; [Mental Disease or Defect Impairing Capacity as Ground for Mitigation of Punishment in Capital Cases].

(1) Evidence that the defendant suffered from a mental disease or defect is admissible whenever it is relevant to prove that the defendant did or did not have a state of mind which is an element of the offense.

[(2) Whenever the jury or the Court is authorized to determine or to recommend whether or not the defendant shall be sentenced to death or imprisonment upon conviction, evidence that the capacity of the defendant to appreciate the criminality [wrongfulness] of his conduct or to conform his conduct to the requirements of law was impaired as a result of mental disease or defect is admissible in favor of sentence of imprisonment.]

Section 4.03. Mental Disease or Defect Excluding Responsibility Is Affirmative Defense; Requirement of Notice; Form of Verdict and Judgment When Finding of Irresponsibility Is Made.

(1) Mental disease or defect excluding responsibility is an affirmative defense.

(2) Evidence of mental disease or defect excluding responsibility is not admissible unless the defendant, at the time of entering his plea of not guilty or within ten days thereafter or at such later time as the Court may for good cause permit, files a written notice of his purpose to rely on such defense.

(3) When the defendant is acquitted on the ground of mental disease or defect excluding responsibility, the verdict and the judgment shall so state.

Section 4.04. Mental Disease or Defect Excluding Fitness to Proceed.

No person who as a result of mental disease or defect lacks capacity to understand the proceedings against him or to assist in his own defense shall be tried, convicted or sentenced for the commission of an offense so long as such incapacity endures.

Section 4.05. Psychiatric Examination of Defendant with Respect to Mental Disease or Defect.

(1) Whenever the defendant has filed a notice of intention to rely on the defense of mental disease or defect excluding responsibility, or there is reason to doubt his fitness to proceed, or reason to believe that mental disease or defect of the defendant will otherwise become an issue in the cause, the Court shall appoint at least one qualified psychiatrist or shall request the Superintendent of the ________ Hospital to designate at least one qualified psychiatrist, which designation may be or include himself, to examine and report upon the mental condition of the defendant. The Court may order the defendant to be committed to a hospital or other suitable facility for the purpose of the examination for a period of not exceeding sixty days or such longer period as the Court determines to be necessary for the purpose and may direct that a qualified psychiatrist retained by the defendant be permitted to witness and participate in the examination.

(2) In such examination any method may be employed which is accepted by the medical profession for the examination of those alleged to be suffering from mental disease or defect.

(3) The report of the examination shall include the following: (a) a description of the nature of the examination; (b) a diagnosis of the mental condition of the defendant; (c) if the defendant suffers from a mental disease or defect, an opinion as to his capacity to understand the proceedings against him and to assist in his own defense; (d) when a notice of intention to rely on the defense of irresponsibility has been filed, an opinion as to the extent, if any, to which the capacity of the defendant to appreciate the criminality [wrongfulness] of his conduct or to conform his conduct to the requirements of law was impaired at the time of the criminal conduct charged; and (e) when directed by the Court, an opinion as to the capacity of the defendant to have a particular state of mind which is an element of the offense charged.

If the examination can not be conducted by reason of the unwillingness of the defendant to participate therein, the report shall so state and shall include, if possible, an opinion as to whether such unwillingness of the defendant was the result of mental disease or defect.

The report of the examination shall be filed [in triplicate] with the clerk of the Court, who shall cause copies to be delivered to the district attorney and to counsel for the defendant.

Section 4.06. Determination of Fitness to Proceed; Effect of Finding of Unfitness; Proceedings if Fitness is Regained [; Post-Commitment Hearing].

(1) When the defendant's fitness to proceed is drawn in question, the issue shall be determined by the Court. If neither the prosecuting attorney nor counsel for the defendant contests the finding of the report filed pursuant to Section 4.05, the Court may make the determination on the basis of such report. If the finding is contested, the Court shall hold a hearing on the issue. If the report is received in evidence upon such hearing, the party who contests the finding thereof shall have the right to summon and to cross-examine the psychiatrists who joined in the report and to offer evidence upon the issue.

(2) If the Court determines that the defendant lacks fitness to proceed, the proceeding against him shall be suspended, except as provided in Subsection (3) [Subsections (3) and (4)] of this Section, and the Court shall commit him to the custody of the Commissioner of Mental Hygiene [Public Health or Correction] to be placed in an appropriate institution of the Department of Mental Hygiene [Public Health or Correction] for so long as such unfitness shall endure. When the Court, on its own motion or upon the application of the Commissioner of Mental Hygiene [Public Health or Correction] or the prosecuting attorney, determines, after a hearing if a hearing is requested, that the defendant has regained fitness to proceed, the proceeding shall be resumed. If, however, the Court is of the view that so much time has elapsed since the commitment of the defendant that it would be unjust to resume the criminal proceeding, the Court may dismiss the charge and may order the defendant to be discharged or, subject to the law governing the civil commitment of persons suffering from mental disease or defect, order the defendant to be committed to an appropriate institution of the Department of Mental Hygiene [Public Health].

(3) The fact that the defendant is unfit to proceed does not preclude any legal objection to the prosecution which is susceptible of fair determination prior to trial and without the personal participation of the defendant.

[Alternative: (3) At any time within ninety days after commitment as provided in Subsection (2) of this Section, or at any later time with permission of the Court granted for good cause, the defendant or his counsel or the Commissioner of Mental Hygiene [Public Health or Correction] may apply for a special post-commitment hearing. If the application is made by or on behalf of a defendant not represented by counsel, he shall be afforded a reasonable opportunity to obtain counsel, and if he lacks funds to do so, counsel shall be assigned by the Court. The application shall be granted only if the counsel for the defendant satisfies the Court by affidavit or otherwise that as an attorney he has reasonable grounds for a good faith belief that his client has, on the facts and the law, a defense to the charge other than mental disease or defect excluding responsibility.

[(4) If the motion for a special post-commitment hearing is granted, the hearing shall be by the Court without a jury. No evidence shall be offered at the hearing by either party on the issue of mental disease or defect as a defense to, or in mitigation of, the crime charged. After hearing, the Court may in an appropriate case quash the indictment or other charge, or find it to be defective or insufficient, or determine that it is not proved beyond a reasonable doubt by the evidence, or otherwise terminate the proceedings on the evidence or the law. In any such case, unless all defects in the proceedings are promptly cured, the Court shall terminate the commitment ordered under Subsection (2) of this Section and order the defendant to be discharged or, subject to the law governing the civil commitment of persons suffering from mental disease or defect, order the defendant to be committed to an appropriate institution of the Department of Mental Hygiene [Public Health].]

Section 4.07. Determination of Irresponsibility on Basis of Report; Access to Defendant by Psychiatrist of His Own Choice; Form of Expert Testimony When Issue of Responsibility Is Tried.

(1) If the report filed pursuant to Section 4.05 finds that the defendant at the time of the criminal conduct charged suffered from a mental disease or defect which substantially impaired his capacity to appreciate the criminality [wrongfulness] of his conduct or to conform his conduct to the requirements of law, and the court, after a hearing if a hearing is requested by the prosecuting attorney or the defendant, is satisfied that such impairment was sufficient to exclude responsibility, the Court on motion of the defendant shall enter judgment of acquittal on the ground of mental disease or defect excluding responsibility.

(2) When, notwithstanding the report filed pursuant to Section 4.05, the defendant wishes to be examined by a qualified psychiatrist or other expert of his own choice, such examiner shall be permitted to have reasonable access to the defendant for the purposes of such examination.

(3) Upon the trial, the psychiatrists who reported pursuant to Section 4.05 may be called as witnesses by the prosecution, the defendant or the Court. If the issue is being tried before a jury, the jury may be informed that the psychiatrists were designated by the Court or by the Superintendent of the ______________________ Hospital at the request of the Court, as the case may be. If called by the Court, the witness shall be subject to cross-examination by the prosecution and by the defendant. Both the prosecution and the defendant may summon any other qualified psychiatrist or other expert to testify, but no one who has not examined the defendant shall be competent to testify to an expert opinion with respect to the mental condition or responsibility of the defendant, as distinguished from the validity of the procedure followed by, or the general scientific propositions stated by, another witness.

(4) When a psychiatrist or other expert who has examined the defendant testifies concerning his mental condition, he shall be permitted to make a statement as to the nature of his examination, his diagnosis of the mental condition of the defendant at the time of the commission of the offense charged and his opinion as to the extent, if any, to which the capacity of the defendant to appreciate the criminality [wrongfulness] of his conduct or to conform his conduct to the requirements of law or to have a particular state of mind which is an element of the offense charged was impaired as a result of mental disease or defect at that time. He shall be permitted to make any explanation reasonably serving to clarify his diagnosis and opinion and may be cross-examined as to any matter bearing on his competency or credibility or the validity of his diagnosis or opinion.

Section 4.08. Legal Effect of Acquittal on the Ground of Mental Disease or Defect Excluding Responsibility; Commitment; Release or Discharge.

(1) When a defendant is acquitted on the ground of mental disease or defect excluding responsibility, the Court shall order him to be committed to the custody of the Commissioner of Mental Hygiene [Public Health] to be placed in an appropriate institution for custody, care and treatment.

(2) If the Commissioner of Mental Hygiene [Public Health] is of the view that a person committed to his custody, pursuant to paragraph (1) of this Section, may be discharged or released on condition without danger to himself or to others, he shall make application for the discharge or release of such person in a report to the Court by which such person was committed and shall transmit a copy of such application and report to the prosecuting attorney of the county [parish] from which the defendant was committed. The Court shall thereupon appoint at least two qualified psychiatrists to examine such person and to report within sixty days, or such longer period as the Court determines to be necessary for the purpose, their opinion as to his mental condition. To facilitate such examination and the proceedings thereon, the Court may cause such person to be confined in any institution located near the place where the Court sits, which may hereafter be designated by the Commissioner of Mental Hygiene [Public Health] as suitable for the temporary detention of irresponsible persons.

(3) If the Court is satisfied by the report filed pursuant to paragraph (2) of this Section and such testimony of the reporting psychiatrists as the Court deems necessary that the committed person may be discharged or released on condition without danger to himself or others, the Court shall order his discharge or his release on such conditions as the Court determines to be necessary. If the Court is not so satisfied, it shall promptly order a hearing to determine whether such person may safely be discharged or released. Any such hearing shall be deemed a civil proceeding and the burden shall be upon the committed person to prove that he may safely be discharged or released. According to the determination of the Court upon the hearing, the committed person shall thereupon be discharged or released on such conditions as the Court determines to be necessary, or shall be recommitted to the custody of the Commissioner of Mental Hygiene [Public Health], subject to discharge or release only in accordance with the procedure prescribed above for a first hearing.

(4) If, within [five] years after the conditional release of a committed person, the Court shall determine, after hearing evidence, that the conditions of release have not been fulfilled and that for the safety of such person or for the safety of others his conditional release should be revoked, the Court shall forthwith order him to be recom-

mitted to the Commissioner of Mental Hygiene [Public Health], subject to discharge or release only in accordance with the procedure prescribed above for a first hearing.

(5) A committed person may make application for his discharge or release to the Court by which he was committed, and the procedure to be followed upon such application shall be the same as that prescribed above in the case of an application by the Commissioner of Mental Hygiene [Public Health]. However, no such application by a committed person need be considered until he has been confined for a period of not less than [six months] from the date of the order of commitment, and if the determination of the Court be adverse to the application, such person shall not be permitted to file a further application until [one year] has elapsed from the date of any preceding hearing on an application for his release or discharge.

Section 4.09. Statements for Purposes of Examination or Treatment Inadmissible Except on Issue of Mental Condition.

A statement made by a person subjected to psychiatric examination or treatment pursuant to Sections 4.05, 4.06 or 4.08 for the purposes of such examination or treatment shall not be admissible in evidence against him in any criminal proceeding on any issue other than that of his mental condition but it shall be admissible upon that issue, whether or not it would otherwise be deemed a privileged communication [, unless such statement constitutes an admission of guilt of the crime charged].

Section 4.10. Immaturity Excluding Criminal Conviction; Transfer of Proceedings to Juvenile Court.

(1) A person shall not be tried for or convicted of an offense if:

- (a) at the time of the conduct charged to constitute the offense he was less than sixteen years of age [, in which case the Juvenile Court shall have exclusive jurisdiction]; or
- (b) at the time of the conduct charged to constitute the offense he was sixteen or seventeen years of age, unless:
  - (i) the Juvenile Court has no jurisdiction over him, or,
  - (ii) the Juvenile Court has entered an order waiving jurisdiction and consenting to the institution of criminal proceedings against him.

(2) No court shall have jurisdiction to try or convict a person of an offense if criminal proceedings against him are barred by Subsection (1) of this Section. When it appears that a person charged with the commission of an offense may be of such an age that criminal proceedings may be barred under Subsection (1) of this Section, the Court shall hold a hearing thereon, and the burden shall be on the prosecution to establish to the satisfaction of the Court that the criminal proceeding is not barred upon such grounds. If the Court determines that the proceeding is barred, custody of the person charged shall be surrendered to the Juvenile Court, and the case, including all papers and processes relating thereto, shall be transferred.

Article 5. Inchoate Crimes

Section 5.01. Criminal Attempt.

(1) *Definition of Attempt.* A person is guilty of an attempt to commit a crime if, acting with the kind of culpability otherwise required for commission of the crime, he:

- (a) purposely engages in conduct which would constitute the crime if the attendant circumstances were as he believes them to be; or

(b) when causing a particular result is an element of the crime, does or omits to do anything with the purpose of causing or with the belief that it will cause such result without further conduct on his part; or

(c) purposely does or omits to do anything which, under the circumstances as he believes them to be, is an act or omission constituting a substantial step in a course of conduct planned to culminate in his commission of the crime.

(2) *Conduct Which May Be Held Substantial Step Under Subsection (1)(c).* Conduct shall not be held to constitute a substantial step under Subsection (1)(c) of this Section unless it is strongly corroborative of the actor's criminal purpose. Without negativing the sufficiency of other conduct, the following, if strongly corroborative of the actor's criminal purpose, shall not be held insufficient as a matter of law:

(a) lying in wait, searching for or following the contemplated victim of the crime;

(b) enticing or seeking to entice the contemplated victim of the crime to go to the place contemplated for its commission;

(c) reconnoitering the place contemplated for the commission of the crime;

(d) unlawful entry of a structure, vehicle or enclosure in which it is contemplated that the crime will be committed;

(e) possession of materials to be employed in the commission of the crime, which are specially designed for such unlawful use or which can serve no lawful purpose of the actor under the circumstances;

(f) possession, collection or fabrication of materials to be employed in the commission of the crime, at or near the place contemplated for its commission, where such possession, collection or fabrication serves no lawful purpose of the actor under the circumstances;

(g) soliciting an innocent agent to engage in conduct constituting an element of the crime.

(3) *Conduct Designed to Aid Another in Commission of a Crime.* A person who engages in conduct designed to aid another to commit a crime which would establish his complicity under Section 2.06 if the crime were committed by such other person, is guilty of an attempt to commit the crime, although the crime is not committed or attempted by such other person.

(4) *Renunciation of Criminal Purpose.* When the actor's conduct would otherwise constitute an attempt under Subsection (1)(b) or (1)(c) of this Section, it is an affirmative defense that he abandoned his effort to commit the crime or otherwise prevented its commission, under circumstances manifesting a complete and voluntary renunciation of his criminal purpose. The establishment of such defense does not, however, affect the liability of an accomplice who did not join in such abandonment or prevention.

Within the meaning of this Article, renunciation of criminal purpose is not voluntary if it is motivated, in whole or in part, by circumstances, not present or apparent at the inception of the actor's course of conduct, which increase the probability of detection or apprehension or which make more difficult the accomplishment of the criminal purpose. Renunciation is not complete if it is motivated by a decision to postpone the criminal conduct until a more advantageous time or to transfer the criminal effort to another but similar objective or victim.

Section 5.02. Criminal Solicitation.

(1) *Definition of Solicitation.* A person is guilty of solicitation to commit a crime if with the purpose of promoting or facilitating its commission he commands, encourages

or requests another person to engage in specific conduct which would constitute such crime or an attempt to commit such crime or which would establish his complicity in its commission or attempted commission.

(2) *Uncommunicated Solicitation.* It is immaterial under Subsection (1) of this Section that the actor fails to communicate with the person he solicits to commit a crime if his conduct was designed to effect such communication.

(3) *Renunciation of Criminal Purpose.* It is an affirmative defense that the actor, after soliciting another person to commit a crime, persuaded him not to do so or otherwise prevented the commission of the crime, under circumstances manifesting a complete and voluntary renunciation of his criminal purpose.

Section 5.03. Criminal Conspiracy.

(1) *Definition of Conspiracy.* A person is guilty of conspiracy with another person or persons to commit a crime if with the purpose of promoting or facilitating its commission he:

(a) agrees with such other person or persons that they or one or more of them will engage in conduct which constitutes such crime or an attempt or solicitation to commit such crime; or

(b) agrees to aid such other person or persons in the planning or commission of such crime or of an attempt or solicitation to commit such crime.

(2) *Scope of Conspiratorial Relationship.* If a person guilty of conspiracy, as defined by Subsection (1) of this Section, knows that a person with whom he conspires to commit a crime has conspired with another person or persons to commit the same crime, he is guilty of conspiring with such other person or persons, whether or not he knows their identity, to commit such crime.

(3) *Conspiracy With Multiple Criminal Objectives.* If a person conspires to commit a number of crimes, he is guilty of only one conspiracy so long as such multiple crimes are the object of the same agreement or continuous conspiratorial relationship.

(4) *Joinder and Venue in Conspiracy Prosecutions.*

(a) Subject to the provisions of paragraph (b) of this Subsection, two or more persons charged with criminal conspiracy may be prosecuted jointly if:

(i) they are charged with conspiring with one another; or

(ii) the conspiracies alleged, whether they have the same or different parties, are so related that they constitute different aspects of a scheme of organized criminal conduct.

(b) In any joint prosecution under paragraph (a) of this Subsection:

(i) no defendant shall be charged with a conspiracy in any county [parish or district] other than one in which he entered into such conspiracy or in which an overt act pursuant to such conspiracy was done by him or by a person with whom he conspired; and

(ii) neither the liability of any defendant nor the admissibility against him of evidence of acts or declarations of another shall be enlarged by such joinder; and

(iii) the Court shall order a severance or take a special verdict as to any defendant who so requests, if it deems it necessary or appropriate to promote the fair determination of his guilt or innocence, and shall take any other proper measures to protect the fairness of the trial.

(5) *Overt Act.* No person may be convicted of conspiracy to commit a crime, other

than a felony of the first or second degree, unless an overt act in pursuance of such conspiracy is alleged and proved to have been done by him or by a person with whom he conspired.

(6) *Renunciation of Criminal Purpose.* It is an affirmative defense that the actor, after conspiring to commit a crime, thwarted the success of the conspiracy, under circumstances manifesting a complete and voluntary renunciation of his criminal purpose.

(7) *Duration of Conspiracy.* For purposes of Section 1.06(4):

(a) conspiracy is a continuing course of conduct which terminates when the crime or crimes which are its object are committed or the agreement that they be committed is abandoned by the defendant and by those with whom he conspired; and

(b) such abandonment is presumed if neither the defendant nor anyone with whom he conspired does any overt act in pursuance of the conspiracy during the applicable period of limitation; and

(c) if an individual abandons the agreement, the conspiracy is terminated as to him only if and when he advises those with whom he conspired of his abandonment or he informs the law enforcement authorities of the existence of the conspiracy and of his participation therein.

Section 5.04. Incapacity, Irresponsibility or Immunity of Party to Solicitation or Conspiracy.

(1) Except as provided in Subsection (2) of this Section, it is immaterial to the liability of a person who solicits or conspires with another to commit a crime that:

(a) he or the person whom he solicits or with whom he conspires does not occupy a particular position or have a particular characteristic which is an element of such crime, if he believes that one of them does; or

(b) the person whom he solicits or with whom he conspires is irresponsible or has an immunity to prosecution or conviction for the commission of the crime.

(2) It is a defense to a charge of solicitation or conspiracy to commit a crime that if the criminal object were achieved, the actor would not be guilty of a crime under the law defining the offense or as an accomplice under Section 2.06(5) or 2.06(6)(a) or (b).

Section 5.05. Grading of Criminal Attempt, Solicitation and Conspiracy; Mitigation in Cases of Lesser Danger; Multiple Convictions Barred.

(1) *Grading.* Except as otherwise provided in this Section, attempt, solicitation and conspiracy are crimes of the same grade and degree as the most serious offense which is attempted or solicited or is an object of the conspiracy. An attempt, solicitation or conspiracy to commit a [capital crime or a] felony of the first degree is a felony of the second degree.

(2) *Mitigation.* If the particular conduct charged to constitute a criminal attempt, solicitation or conspiracy is so inherently unlikely to result or culminate in the commission of a crime that neither such conduct nor the actor presents a public danger warranting the grading of such offense under this Section, the Court shall exercise its power under Section 6.12 to enter judgment and impose sentence for a crime of lower grade or degree or, in extreme cases, may dismiss the prosecution.

(3) *Multiple Convictions.* A person may not be convicted of more than one offense

defined by this Article for conduct designed to commit or to culminate in the commission of the same crime.

Section 5.06. Possessing Instruments of Crime; Weapons.

(1) *Criminal Instruments Generally.* A person commits a misdemeanor if he possesses any instrument of crime with purpose to employ it criminally. "Instrument of crime" means:

(a) anything specially made or specially adaptated [sic] for criminal use; or

(b) anything commonly used for criminal purposes and possessed by the actor under circumstances which do not negative unlawful purpose.

(2) *Presumption of Criminal Purpose from Possession of Weapon.* If a person possesses a firearm or other weapon on or about his person, in a vehicle occupied by him, or otherwise readily available for use, it shall be presumed that he had the purpose to employ it criminally, unless:

(a) the weapon is possessed in the actor's home or place of business;

(b) the actor is licensed or otherwise authorized by law to possess such weapon; or

(c) the weapon is of a type commonly used in lawful sport.

"Weapon" means anything readily capable of lethal use and possessed under circumstances not manifestly appropriate for lawful uses which it may have; the term includes a firearm which is not loaded or lacks a clip or other component to render it immediately operable, and components which can readily be assembled into a weapon.

(3) *Presumptions as to Possession of Criminal Instruments in Automobiles.* Where a weapon or other instrument of crime is found in an automobile, it is presumed to be in the possession of the occupant if there is but one. If there is more than one occupant, it shall be presumed to be in the possession of all, except under the following circumstances:

(a) where it is found upon the person of one of the occupants;

(b) where the automobile is not a stolen one and the weapon or instrument is found out of view in a glove compartment, car trunk, or other enclosed customary depository, in which case it shall be presumed to be in the possession of the occupant or occupants who own or have authority to operate the automobile;

(c) in the case of a taxicab, a weapon or instrument found in the passenger's portion of the vehicle shall be presumed to be in the possession of all the passengers, if there are any, and, if not, in the possession of the driver.

Section 5.07. Prohibited Offensive Weapons.

A person commits a misdemeanor if, except as authorized by law, he makes, repairs, sells, or otherwise deals in, uses or possesses any offensive weapon. "Offensive weapon" means any bomb, machine gun, sawed-off shotgun, firearm specially made or specially adapted for concealment or silent discharge, any blackjack, sandbag, metal knuckles, dagger, or other implement for the infliction of serious bodily injury which serves no common lawful purpose. It is a defense under this Section for the defendant to prove by a preponderance of evidence that he possessed or dealt with the weapon solely as a curio or in a dramatic performance, or that he possessed it briefly in consequence of having found it or taken it from an aggressor, or under circumstances similarly negativing any purpose or likelihood that the weapon would be used unlawfully. The presumptions provided in Section 5.06(3) are applicable to prosecutions under this Section.

Article 6. Authorized Disposition of Offenders

Section 6.01. Degrees of Felonies.

(1) Felonies defined by this Code are classified, for the purpose of sentence, into three degrees, as follows:

(a) felonies of the first degree;
(b) felonies of the second degree;
(c) felonies of the third degree.

A felony is of the first or second degree when it is so designated by the Code. A crime declared to be a felony, without specification of degree, is of the third degree.

(2) Notwithstanding any other provision of law, a felony defined by any statute of this State other than this Code shall constitute for the purpose of sentence a felony of the third degree.

Section 6.02. Sentence in Accordance with Code; Authorized Dispositions. [Omitted.]

Section 6.03. Fines.

A person who has been convicted of an offense may be sentenced to pay a fine not exceeding:

(1) $10,000, when the conviction is of a felony of the first or second degree;
(2) $5,000, when the conviction is of a felony of the third degree;
(3) $1,000, when the conviction is of a misdemeanor;
(4) $500, when the conviction is of a petty misdemeanor or a violation;
(5) any higher amount equal to double the pecuniary gain derived from the offense by the offender;
(6) any higher amount specifically authorized by statute.

Section 6.04. Penalties Against Corporations and Unincorporated Associations; Forfeiture of Corporate Charter or Revocation of Certificate Authorizing Foreign Corporation to Do Business in the State.

(1) The Court may suspend the sentence of a corporation or an unincorporated association which has been convicted of an offense or may sentence it to pay a fine authorized by Section 6.03.

(2) (a) The [prosecuting attorney] is authorized to institute civil proceedings in the appropriate court of general jurisdiction to forfeit the charter of a corporation organized under the laws of this State or to revoke the certificate authorizing a foreign corporation to conduct business in this State. The Court may order the charter forfeited or the certificate revoked upon finding (i) that the board of directors or a high managerial agent acting in behalf of the corporation has, in conducting the corporation's affairs, purposely engaged in a persistent course of criminal conduct and (ii) that for the prevention of future criminal conduct of the same character, the public interest requires the charter of the corporation to be forfeited and the corporation to be dissolved or the certificate to be revoked.

(b) When a corporation is convicted of a crime or a high managerial agent of a corporation, as defined in Section 2.07, is convicted of a crime committed in the conduct of the affairs of the corporation, the Court, in sentencing the corporation or the agent, may direct the [prosecuting attorney] to institute proceedings authorized by paragraph (a) of this Subsection.

(c) The proceedings authorized by paragraph (a) of this Subsection shall be conducted in accordance with the procedures authorized by law for the involuntary dissolution of a corporation or the revocation of the certificate authorizing a foreign corporation to conduct business in this State. Such proceedings shall be deemed additional to any other proceedings authorized by law for the purpose of forfeiting the charter of a corporation or revoking the certificate of a foreign corporation.

Section 6.05. Young Adult Offenders.

(1) *Specialized Correctional Treatment.* A young adult offender is a person convicted of a crime who, at the time of sentencing, is sixteen but less than twenty-two years of age. A young adult offender who is sentenced to a term of imprisonment which may exceed thirty days [alternatives: (1) ninety days; (2) one year] shall be committed to the custody of the Division of Young Adult Correction of the Department of Correction, and shall receive, as far as practicable, such special and individualized correctional and rehabilitative treatment as may be appropriate to his needs.

(2) *Special Term.* A young adult offender convicted of a felony may, in lieu of any other sentence of imprisonment authorized by this Article, be sentenced to a special term of imprisonment without a minimum and with a maximum of four years, regardless of the degree of the felony involved, if the Court is of the opinion that such special term is adequate for his correction and rehabilitation and will not jeopardize the protection of the public.

[(3) *Removal of Disabilities; Vacation of Conviction.*

(a) In sentencing a young adult offender to the special term provided by this Section or to any sentence other than one of imprisonment, the Court may order that so long as he is not convicted of another felony, the judgment shall not constitute a conviction for the purposes of any disqualification or disability imposed by law upon conviction of a crime.

(b) When any young adult offender is unconditionally discharged from probation or parole before the expiration of the maximum term thereof, the Court may enter an order vacating the judgment of conviction.]

[(4) *Commitment for Observation.* If, after pre-sentence investigation, the Court desires additional information concerning a young adult offender before imposing sentence, it may order that he be committed, for a period not exceeding ninety days, to the custody of the Division of Young Adult Correction of the Department of Correction for observation and study at an appropriate reception or classification center. Such Division of the Department of Correction and the [Young Adult Division of the] Board of Parole shall advise the Court of their findings and recommendations on or before the expiration of such ninety-day period.]

Section 6.06. Sentence of Imprisonment for Felony; Ordinary Terms.

A person who has been convicted of a felony may be sentenced to imprisonment, as follows:

(1) in the case of a felony of the first degree, for a term the minimum of which shall be fixed by the Court at not less than one year nor more than ten years, and the maximum of which shall be life imprisonment;

(2) in the case of a felony of the second degree, for a term the minimum of which shall be fixed by the Court at not less than one year nor more than three years, and the maximum of which shall be ten years;

(3) in the case of a felony of the third degree, for a term the minimum of which shall be fixed by the Court at not less than one year nor more than two years, and the maximum of which shall be five years.

Alternate Section 6.06. Sentence of Imprisonment for Felony; Ordinary Terms.

A person who has been convicted of a felony may be sentenced to imprisonment, as follows:

(1) in the case of a felony of the first degree, for a term the minimum of which shall be fixed by the Court at not less than one year nor more than ten years, and the maximum at not more than twenty years or at life imprisonment;

(2) in the case of a felony of the second degree, for a term the minimum of which shall be fixed by the Court at not less than one year nor more than three years, and the maximum at not more than ten years;

(3) in the case of a felony of the third degree, for a term the minimum of which shall be fixed by the Court at not less than one year nor more than two years, and the maximum at not more than five years.

No sentence shall be imposed under this Section of which the minimum is longer than one-half the maximum, or, when the maximum is life imprisonment, longer than ten years.

Section 6.07. Sentence of Imprisonment for Felony; Extended Terms.

In the cases designated in Section 7.03, a person who has been convicted of a felony may be sentenced to an extended term of imprisonment, as follows:

(1) in the case of a felony of the first degree, for a term the minimum of which shall be fixed by the Court at not less than five years nor more than ten years, and the maximum of which shall be life imprisonment;

(2) in the case of a felony of the second degree, for a term the minimum of which shall be fixed by the Court at not less than one year nor more than five years, and the maximum of which shall be fixed by the Court at not less than ten nor more than twenty years;

(3) in the case of a felony of the third degree, for a term the minimum of which shall be fixed by the Court at not less than one year nor more than three years, and the maximum of which shall be fixed by the Court at not less than five nor more than ten years.

Section 6.08. Sentence of Imprisonment for Misdemeanors and Petty Misdemeanors; Ordinary Terms.

A person who has been convicted of a misdemeanor or a petty misdemeanor may be sentenced to imprisonment for a definite term which shall be fixed by the Court and shall not exceed one year in the case of a misdemeanor or thirty days in the case of a petty misdemeanor.

Section 6.09. Sentence of Imprisonment for Misdemeanors and Petty Misdemeanors; Extended Terms.

(1) In the cases designated in Section 7.04, a person who has been convicted of a misdemeanor or a petty misdemeanor may be sentenced to an extended term of imprisonment, as follows:

(a) in the case of a misdemeanor, for a term the minimum of which shall be fixed by the Court at not more than one year and the maximum of which shall be three years;

(b) in the case of a petty misdemeanor, for a term the minimum of which shall be fixed by the Court at not more than six months and the maximum of which shall be two years.

(2) No such sentence for an extended term shall be imposed unless:

(a) the Director of Correction has certified that there is an institution in the Department of Correction, or in a county, city [or other appropriate political subdivision of the State] which is appropriate for the detention and correctional treatment of such misdemeanants or petty misdemeanants, and that such institution is available to receive such commitments; and

(b) the [Board of Parole] [Parole Administrator] has certified that the Board of Parole is able to visit such institution and to assume responsibility for the release of such prisoners on parole and for their parole supervision. . . .

PART II. DEFINITION OF SPECIFIC CRIMES

Offenses Involving Danger to the Person

Article 210. Criminal Homicide

Section 210.0. Definitions.

In Articles 210-213, unless a different meaning plainly is required:

(1) "human being" means a person who has been born and is alive;

(2) "bodily injury" means physical pain, illness or any impairment of physical condition;

(3) "serious bodily injury" means bodily injury which creates a substantial risk of death or which causes serious, permanent disfigurement, or protracted loss or impairment of the function of any bodily member or organ;

(4) "deadly weapon" means any firearm, or other weapon, device, instrument, material or substance, whether animate or inanimate, which in the manner it is used or is intended to be used is known to be capable of producing death or serious bodily injury.

Section 210.1. Criminal Homicide.

(1) A person is guilty of criminal homicide if he purposely, knowingly, recklessly or negligently causes the death of another human being.

(2) Criminal homicide is murder, manslaughter or negligent homicide.

Section 210.2. Murder.

(1) Except as provided in Section 210.3(1)(b), criminal homicide constitutes murder when:

(a) it is committed purposely or knowingly; or

(b) it is committed recklessly under circumstances manifesting extreme indifference to the value of human life. Such recklessness and indifference are presumed if the actor is engaged or is an accomplice in the commission of, or an attempt to commit, or flight after committing or attempting to commit robbery, rape or deviate sexual intercourse by force or threat of force, arson, burglary, kidnapping or felonious escape.

(2) Murder is a felony of the first degree [but a person convicted of murder may be sentenced to death, as provided in Section 210.6].

Section 210.3. Manslaughter.

(1) Criminal homicide constitutes manslaughter when:

(a) it is committed recklessly; or

(b) a homicide which would otherwise be murder is committed under the influence of extreme mental or emotional disturbance for which there is reasonable explanation or excuse. The reasonableness of such explanation or excuse shall be determined from the viewpoint of a person in the actor's situation under the circumstances as he believes them to be.

(2) Manslaughter is a felony of the second degree.

Section 210.4. Negligent Homicide.

(1) Criminal homicide constitutes negligent homicide when it is committed negligently.

(2) Negligent homicide is a felony of the third degree.

Section 210.5. Causing or Aiding Suicide.

(1) *Causing Suicide as Criminal Homicide.* A person may be convicted of criminal homicide for causing another to commit suicide only if he purposely causes such suicide by force, duress or deception.

(2) *Aiding or Soliciting Suicide as an Independent Offense.* A person who purposely aids or solicits another to commit suicide is guilty of a felony of the second degree if his conduct causes such suicide or an attempted suicide, and otherwise of a misdemeanor.

Section 210.6. Sentence of Death for Murder; Further Proceedings to Determine Sentence.[1]

(1) *Death Sentence Excluded.* When a defendant is found guilty of murder, the Court shall impose sentence for a felony of the first degree if it is satisfied that:

(a) none of the aggravating circumstances enumerated in Subsection (3) of this Section was established by the evidence at the trial or will be established if further proceedings are initiated under Subsection (2) of this Section; or

(b) substantial mitigating circumstances, established by the evidence at the trial, call for leniency; or

1. . . . The brackets are meant to reflect the fact that the Institute took no position on the desirability of the death penalty. . . .

(c) the defendant, with the consent of the prosecuting attorney and the approval of the Court, pleaded guilty to murder as a felony of the first degree; or
(d) the defendant was under 18 years of age at the time of the commission of the crime; or
(e) the defendant's physical or mental condition calls for leniency; or
(f) although the evidence suffices to sustain the verdict, it does not foreclose all doubt respecting the defendant's guilt.

(2) *Determination by Court or by Court and Jury.* Unless the Court imposes sentence under Subsection (1) of this Section, it shall conduct a separate proceeding to determine whether the defendant should be sentenced for a felony of the first degree or sentenced to death. The proceeding shall be conducted before the Court alone if the defendant was convicted by a Court sitting without a jury or upon his plea of guilty or if the prosecuting attorney and the defendant waive a jury with respect to sentence. In other cases it shall be conducted before the Court sitting with the jury which determined the defendant's guilt or, if the Court for good cause shown discharges that jury, with a new jury empanelled for the purpose.

In the proceeding, evidence may be presented as to any matter that the Court deems relevant to sentence, including but not limited to the nature and circumstances of the crime, the defendant's character, background, history, mental and physical condition and any of the aggravating or mitigating circumstances enumerated in Subsections (3) and (4) of this Section. Any such evidence not legally privileged, which the Court deems to have probative force, may be received, regardless of its admissibility under the exclusionary rules of evidence, provided that the defendant's counsel is accorded a fair opportunity to rebut any hearsay statements. The prosecuting attorney and the defendant or his counsel shall be permitted to present argument for or against sentence of death.

The determination whether sentence of death shall be imposed shall be in the discretion of the Court, except that when the proceeding is conducted before the Court sitting with a jury, the Court shall not impose sentence of death unless it submits to the jury the issue whether the defendant should be sentenced to death or to imprisonment and the jury returns a verdict that the sentence should be death. If the jury is unable to reach a unanimous verdict, the Court shall dismiss the jury and impose sentence for a felony of the first degree.

The Court, in exercising its discretion as to sentence, and the jury, in determining upon its verdict, shall take into account the aggravating and mitigating circumstances enumerated in Subsections (3) and (4) and any other facts that it deems relevant, but it shall not impose or recommend sentence of death unless it finds one of the aggravating circumstances enumerated in Subsection (3) and further finds that there are no mitigating circumstances sufficiently substantial to call for leniency. When the issue is submitted to the jury, the Court shall so instruct and also shall inform the jury of the nature of the sentence of imprisonment that may be imposed, including its implication with respect to possible release upon parole, if the jury verdict is against sentence of death.

Alternative formulation of Subsection (2):

(2) *Determination by Court.* Unless the Court imposes sentence under Subsection (1) of this Section, it shall conduct a separate proceeding to determine whether the defendant should be sentenced for a felony of the first degree or sentenced to death. In the proceeding, the Court, in accordance with Section 7.07, shall consider the report of the

presentence investigation and, if a psychiatric examination has been ordered, the report of such examination. In addition, evidence may be presented as to any matter that the Court deems relevant to sentence, including but not limited to the nature and circumstances of the crime, the defendant's character, background, history, mental and physical condition and any of the aggravating or mitigating circumstances enumerated in Subsections (3) and (4) of this Section. Any such evidence not legally privileged, which the Court deems to have probative force, may be received, regardless of its admissibility under the exclusionary rules of evidence, provided that the defendant's counsel is accorded a fair opportunity to rebut any hearsay statements. The prosecuting attorney and the defendant or his counsel shall be permitted to present argument for or against sentence of death.

The determination whether sentence of death shall be imposed shall be in the discretion of the Court. In exercising such discretion, the Court shall take into account the aggravating and mitigating circumstances enumerated in Subsections (3) and (4) and any other facts that it deems relevant but shall not impose sentence of death unless it finds one of the aggravating circumstances enumerated in Subsection (3) and further finds that there are no mitigating circumstances sufficiently substantial to call for leniency.

(3) *Aggravating Circumstances.*

(a) The murder was committed by a convict under sentence of imprisonment.

(b) The defendant was previously convicted of another murder or of a felony involving the use or threat of violence to the person.

(c) At the time the murder was committed the defendant also committed another murder.

(d) The defendant knowingly created a great risk of death to many persons.

(e) The murder was committed while the defendant was engaged or was an accomplice in the commission of, or an attempt to commit, or flight after committing or attempting to commit robbery, rape or deviate sexual intercourse by force or threat of force, arson, burglary or kidnapping.

(f) The murder was committed for the purpose of avoiding or preventing a lawful arrest or effecting an escape from lawful custody.

(g) The murder was committed for pecuniary gain.

(h) The murder was especially heinous, atrocious or cruel, manifesting exceptional depravity.

(4) *Mitigating Circumstances.*

(a) The defendant has no significant history of prior criminal activity.

(b) The murder was committed while the defendant was under the influence of extreme mental or emotional disturbance.

(c) The victim was a participant in the defendant's homicidal conduct or consented to the homicidal act.

(d) The murder was committed under circumstances which the defendant believed to provide a moral justification or extenuation for his conduct.

(e) The defendant was an accomplice in a murder committed by another person and his participation in the homicidal act was relatively minor.

(f) The defendant acted under duress or under the domination of another person.

(g) At the time of the murder, the capacity of the defendant to appreciate the criminality [wrongfulness] of his conduct or to conform his conduct to the requirements of law was impaired as a result of mental disease or defect or intoxication.
(h) The youth of the defendant at the time of the crime.]

Article 211. Assault; Reckless Endangering; Threats

Section 211.0. Definitions.

In this Article, the definitions given in Section 210.0 apply unless a different meaning plainly is required.

Section 211.1. Assault.

(1) *Simple Assault.* A person is guilty of assault if he:
(a) attempts to cause or purposely, knowingly or recklessly causes bodily injury to another; or
(b) negligently causes bodily injury to another with a deadly weapon; or
(c) attempts by physical menace to put another in fear of imminent serious bodily injury.

Simple assault is a misdemeanor unless committed in a fight or scuffle entered into by mutual consent, in which case it is a petty misdemeanor.

(2) *Aggravated Assault.* A person is guilty of aggravated assault if he:
(a) attempts to cause serious bodily injury to another, or causes such injury purposely, knowingly or recklessly under circumstances manifesting extreme indifference to the value of human life; or
(b) attempts to cause or purposely or knowingly causes bodily injury to another with a deadly weapon.

Aggravated assault under paragraph (a) is a felony of the second degree; aggravated assault under paragraph (b) is a felony of the third degree.

Section 211.2. Recklessly Endangering Another Person.

A person commits a misdemeanor if he recklessly engages in conduct which places or may place another person in danger of death or serious bodily injury. Recklessness and danger shall be presumed where a person knowingly points a firearm at or in the direction of another, whether or not the actor believed the firearm to be loaded.

Section 211.3. Terroristic Threats.

A person is guilty of a felony of the third degree if he threatens to commit any crime of violence with purpose to terrorize another or to cause evacuation of a building, place of assembly, or facility of public transportation, or otherwise to cause serious public inconvenience, or in reckless disregard of the risk of causing such terror or inconvenience.

Article 212. Kidnapping and Related Offenses; Coercion

Section 212.0. Definitions.

In this Article, the definitions given in section 210.0 apply unless a different meaning plainly is required.

Section 212.1. Kidnapping.

A person is guilty of kidnapping if he unlawfully removes another from his place of residence or business, or a substantial distance from the vicinity where he is found, or if he unlawfully confines another for a substantial period in a place of isolation, with any of the following purposes:

(a) to hold for ransom or reward, or as a shield or hostage; or
(b) to facilitate commission of any felony or flight thereafter; or
(c) to inflict bodily injury on or to terrorize the victim or another; or
(d) to interfere with the performance of any governmental or political function.

Kidnapping is a felony of the first degree unless the actor voluntarily releases the victim alive and in a safe place prior to trial, in which case it is a felony of the second degree. A removal or confinement is unlawful within the meaning of this Section if it is accomplished by force, threat or deception, or, in the case of a person who is under the age of 14 or incompetent, if it is accomplished without the consent of a parent, guardian or other person responsible for general supervision of his welfare.

Section 212.2. Felonious Restraint.

A person commits a felony of the third degree if he knowingly:

(a) restrains another unlawfully in circumstances exposing him to risk of serious bodily injury; or
(b) hold another in a condition of involuntary servitude.

Section 212.3. False Imprisonment.

A person commits a misdemeanor if he knowingly restrains another unlawfully so as to interfere substantially with his liberty.

Section 212.4. Interference with Custody.

(1) *Custody of Children.* A person commits an offense if he knowingly or recklessly takes or entices any child under the age of 18 from the custody of its parent, guardian or other lawful custodian, when he has no privilege to do so. It is an affirmative defense that:

(a) the actor believed that his action was necessary to preserve the child from danger to its welfare; or
(b) the child, being at the time not less than 14 years old, was taken away at its own instigation without enticement and without purpose to commit a criminal offense with or against the child.

Proof that the child was below the critical age gives rise to a presumption that the actor knew the child's age or acted in reckless disregard thereof. The offense is a misdemeanor unless the actor, not being a parent or person in equivalent relation to the child, acted with knowledge that his conduct would cause serious alarm for the child's safety, or in reckless disregard of a likelihood of causing such alarm, in which case the offense is a felony of the third degree.

(2) *Custody of Committed Persons.* A person is guilty of a misdemeanor if he knowingly or recklessly takes or entices any committed person away from lawful custody when he is not privileged to do so. "Committed person" means, in addition to anyone committed under judicial warrant, any orphan, neglected or delinquent child, mentally defective or insane person, or other dependent or incompetent person entrusted to

another's custody by or through a recognized social agency or otherwise by authority of law.

Section 212.5. Criminal Coercion.

(1) *Offense Defined.* A person is guilty of criminal coercion if, with purpose unlawfully to restrict another's freedom of action to his detriment, he threatens to:

(a) commit any criminal offense; or

(b) accuse anyone of a criminal offense; or

(c) expose any secret tending to subject any person to hatred, contempt or ridicule, or to impair his credit or business repute; or

(d) take or withhold action as an official, or cause an official to take or withheld action.

It is an affirmative defense to prosecution based on paragraphs (b), (c) or (d) that the actor believed the accusation or secret to be true or the proposed official action justified and that his purpose was limited to compelling the other to behave in a way reasonably related to the circumstances which were the subject of the accusation, exposure or proposed official action, as by desisting from further misbehavior, making good a wrong done, refraining from taking any action or responsibility for which the actor believes the other disqualified.

(2) *Grading.* Criminal coercion is a misdemeanor unless the threat is to commit a felony or the actor's purpose is felonious, in which cases the offense is a felony of the third degree.

Article 213. Sexual Offenses

Section 213.0. Definitions.

In this Article, unless a different meaning plainly is required.

(1) the definitions given in Section 210.0 apply;

(2) "Sexual intercourse" includes intercourse per os or per anum, with some penetration however slight; emission is not required;

(3) "Deviate sexual intercourse" means sexual intercourse per os or per anum between human beings who are not husband and wife, and any form of sexual intercourse with an animal.

Section 213.1. Rape and Related Offenses.

(1) *Rape.* A male who has sexual intercourse with a female not his wife is guilty of rape if:

(a) he compels her to submit by force or by threat of imminent death, serious bodily injury, extreme pain or kidnapping, to be inflicted on anyone; or

(b) he has substantially impaired her power to appraise or control her conduct by administering or employing without her knowledge drugs, intoxicants or other means for the purpose of preventing resistance; or

(c) the female is unconscious; or

(d) the female is less than 10 years old.

Rape is a felony of the second degree unless (i) in the course thereof the actor inflicts serious bodily injury upon anyone, or (ii) the victim was not a voluntary social companion of the actor upon the occasion of the crime and had not previously permitted him sexual liberties, in which cases the offense is a felony of the first degree.

(2) *Gross Sexual Imposition.* A male who has sexual intercourse with a female not his wife commits a felony of the third degree if:

(a) he compels her to submit by any threat that would prevent resistance by a woman of ordinary resolution; or

(b) he knows that she suffers from a mental disease or defect which renders her incapable of appraising the nature of her conduct; or

(c) he knows that she is unaware that a sexual act is being committed upon her or that she submits because she mistakenly supposes that he is her husband.

Section 213.2. Deviate Sexual Intercourse by Force or Imposition.

(1) *By Force or Its Equivalent.* A person who engages in deviate sexual intercourse with another person, or who causes another to engage in deviate sexual intercourse, commits a felony of the second degree if:

(a) he compels the other person to participate by force or by threat of imminent death, serious bodily injury, extreme pain or kidnapping, to be inflicted on anyone; or

(b) he has substantially impaired the other person's power to appraise or control his conduct, by administering or employing without the knowledge of the other person drugs, intoxicants or other means for the purpose of preventing resistance; or

(c) the other person is unconscious; or

(d) the other person is less than 10 years old.

(2) *By Other Imposition.* A person who engages in deviate sexual intercourse with another person, or who causes another to engage in deviate sexual intercourse, commits a felony of the third degree if:

(a) he compels the other person to participate by any threat that would prevent resistance by a person of ordinary resolution; or

(b) he knows that the other person suffers from a mental disease or defect which renders him incapable of appraising the nature of his conduct; or

(c) he knows that the other person submits because he is unaware that a sexual act is being committed upon him.

Section 213.3. Corruption of Minors and Seduction.

(1) *Offense Defined.* A male who has sexual intercourse with a female not his wife, or any person who engages in deviate sexual intercourse or causes another to engage in deviate sexual intercourse, is guilty of an offense if:

(a) the other person is less than [16] years old and the actor is at least [4] years older than the other person; or

(b) the other person is less than 21 years old and the actor is his guardian or otherwise responsible for general supervision of his welfare; or

(c) the other person is in custody of law or detained in a hospital or other institution and the actor has supervisory or disciplinary authority over him; or

(d) the other person is a female who is induced to participate by a promise of marriage which the actor does not mean to perform.

(2) *Grading.* An offense under paragraph (a) of Subsection (1) is a felony of the third degree. Otherwise an offense under this section is a misdemeanor.

Section 213.4. Sexual Assault.

A person who has sexual contact with another not his spouse, or causes such other to have sexual conduct with him, is guilty of sexual assault, a misdemeanor, if:

(1) he knows that the contact is offensive to the other person; or

(2) he knows that the other person suffers from a mental disease or defect which renders him or her incapable of appraising the nature of his or her conduct; or

(3) he knows that the other person is unaware that a sexual act is being committed; or

(4) the other person is less than 10 years old; or

(5) he has substantially impaired the other person's power to appraise or control his or her conduct, by administering or employing without the other's knowledge drugs, intoxicants or other means for the purpose of preventing resistance; or

(6) the other person is less than [16] years old and the actor is at least [four] years older than the other person; or

(7) the other person is less than 21 years old and the actor is his guardian or otherwise responsible for general supervision of his welfare; or

(8) the other person is in custody of law or detained in a hospital or other institution and the actor has supervisory or disciplinary authority over him.

Sexual contact is any touching of the sexual or other intimate parts of the person for the purpose of arousing or gratifying sexual desire.

Section 213.5. Indecent Exposure.

A person commits a misdemeanor if, for the purpose of arousing or gratifying sexual desire of himself or of any person other than his spouse, he exposes his genitals under circumstances in which he knows his conduct is likely to cause affront or alarm.

Section 213.6. Provisions Generally Applicable to Article 213.

(1) *Mistake as to Age.* Whenever in this Article the criminality of conduct depends on a child's being below the age of 10, it is no defense that the actor did not know the child's age, or reasonably believed the child to be older than 10. When criminality depends on the child's being below a critical age other than 10, it is a defense for the actor to prove by a preponderance of the evidence that he reasonably believed the child to be above the critical age.

(2) *Spouse Relationships.* Whenever in this Article the definition of an offense excludes conduct with a spouse, the exclusion shall be deemed to extend to persons living as man and wife, regardless of the legal status of their relationship. The exclusion shall be inoperative as respects spouses living apart under a decree of judicial separation. Where the definition of an offense excludes conduct with a spouse or conduct by a woman, this shall not preclude conviction of a spouse or woman as accomplice in a sexual act which he or she causes another person, not within the exclusion, to perform.

(3) *Sexually Promiscuous Complainants.* It is a defense to prosecution under Section 213.3, and paragraphs (6), (7) and (8) of Section 213.4 for the actor to prove by a preponderance of the evidence that the alleged victim had, prior to the time of the offense charged, engaged promiscuously in sexual relations with others.

(4) *Prompt Complaint.* No prosecution may be instituted or maintained under this Article unless the alleged offense was brought to the notice of public authority within [3] months of its occurrence or, where the alleged victim was less than [16] years old or

otherwise incompetent to make complaint, within [3] months after a parent, guardian or other competent person specially interested in the victim learns of the offense.

(5) *Testimony of Complainants.* No person shall be convicted of any felony under this Article upon the uncorroborated testimony of the alleged victim. Corroboration may be circumstantial. In any prosecution before a jury for an offense under this Article, the jury shall be instructed to evaluate the testimony of a victim or complaining witness with special care in view of the emotional involvement of the witness and the difficulty of determining the truth with respect to alleged sexual activities carried out in private.

Offenses Against Property

Article 220. Arson, Criminal Mischief, and Other Property Destruction

Section 220.1. Arson and Related Offenses.

(1) *Arson.* A person is guilty of arson, a felony of the second degree, if he starts a fire or causes an explosion with the purpose of:

(a) destroying a building or occupied structure of another; or

(b) destroying or damaging any property, whether his own or another's, to collect insurance for such loss. It shall be an affirmative defense to prosecution under this paragraph that the actor's conduct did not recklessly endanger any building or occupied structure of another or place any other person in danger of death or bodily injury.

(2) *Reckless Burning or Exploding.* A person commits a felony of the third degree if he purposely starts a fire or causes an explosion, whether on his own property or another's, and thereby recklessly:

(a) places another person in danger of death or bodily injury; or

(b) places a building or occupied structure of another in danger of damage or destruction.

(3) *Failure to Control or Report Dangerous Fire.* A person who knows that a fire is endangering life or a substantial amount of property of another and fails to take reasonable measures to put out or control the fire, when he can do so without substantial risk to himself, or to give a prompt fire alarm, commits a misdemeanor if:

(a) he knows that he is under an official, contractual, or other legal duty to prevent or combat the fire; or

(b) the fire was started, albeit lawfully, by him or with his assent, or on property in his custody or control.

(4) *Definitions.* "Occupied structure" means any structure, vehicle or place adapted for overnight accommodation of persons, or for carrying on business therein, whether or not a person is actually present. Property is that of another, for the purposes of this section, if anyone other than the actor has a possessory or proprietory interest therein. If a building or structure is divided into separately occupied units, any unit not occupied by the actor is an occupied structure of another.

Section 220.2. Causing or Risking Catastrophe.

(1) *Causing Catastrophe.* A person who causes a catastrophe by explosion, fire, flood, avalanche, collapse of building, release of poison gas, radioactive material or

other harmful or destructive force or substance, or by any other means of causing potentially widespread injury or damage, commits a felony of the second degree if he does so purposely or knowingly, or a felony of the third degree if he does so recklessly.

(2) *Risking Catastrophe.* A person is guilty of a misdemeanor if he recklessly creates a risk of catastrophe in the employment of fire, explosives or other dangerous means listed in Subsection (1).

(3) *Failure to Prevent Catastrophe.* A person who knowingly or recklessly fails to take reasonable measures to prevent or mitigate a catastrophe commits a misdemeanor if:

(a) he knows that he is under an official, contractual or other legal duty to take such measures; or

(b) he did or assented to the act causing or threatening the catastrophe.

Section 220.3. Criminal Mischief.

(1) *Offense Defined.* A person is guilty of criminal mischief if he:

(a) damages tangible property of another purposely, recklessly, or by negligence in the employment of fire, explosives, or other dangerous means listed in Section 220.2(1); or

(b) purposely or recklessly tampers with tangible property of another so as to endanger person or property; or

(c) purposely or recklessly causes another to suffer pecuniary loss by deception or threat.

(2) *Grading.* Criminal mischief is a felony of the third degree if the actor purposely causes pecuniary loss in excess of $5,000 or a substantial interruption or impairment of public communication, transportation, supply of water, gas or power, or other public service. It is a misdemeanor if the actor purposely causes pecuniary loss in excess of $100, or a petty misdemeanor if he purposely or recklessly causes pecuniary loss in excess of $25. Otherwise criminal mischief is a violation.

Article 221. Burglary and Other Criminal Intrusion

Section 221.0. Definitions.

In this Article, unless a different meaning plainly is required:

(1) "occupied structure" means any structure, vehicle or place adapted for overnight accommodation of persons, or for carrying on business therein, whether or not a person is actually present.

(2) "night" means the period between thirty minutes past sunset and thirty minutes before sunrise.

Section 221.1. Burglary.

(1) *Burglary Defined.* A person is guilty of burglary if he enters a building or occupied structure, or separately secured or occupied portion thereof, with purpose to commit a crime therein, unless the premises are at the time open to the public or the actor is licensed or privileged to enter. It is an affirmative defense to prosecution for burglary that the building or structure was abandoned.

(2) *Grading.* Burglary is a felony of the second degree if it is perpetrated in the dwelling of another at night, or if, in the course of committing the offense, the actor:

(a) purposely, knowingly or recklessly inflicts or attempts to inflict bodily injury on anyone; or

(b) is armed with explosives or a deadly weapon.

Otherwise, burglary is a felony of the third degree. An act shall be deemed "in the course of committing" an offense if it occurs in an attempt to commit the offense or in flight after the attempt or commission.

(3) *Multiple Convictions.* A person may not be convicted both for burglary and for the offense which it was his purpose to commit after the burglarious entry or for an attempt to commit that offense, unless the additional offense constitutes a felony of the first or second degree.

Section 221.2. Criminal Trespass.

(1) *Buildings and Occupied Structures.* A person commits an offense if, knowing that he is not licensed or privileged to do so, he enters or surreptitiously remains in any building or occupied structure, or separately secured or occupied portion thereof. An offense under this Subsection is a misdemeanor if it is committed in a dwelling at night. Otherwise it is a petty misdemeanor.

(2) *Defiant Trespasser.* A person commits an offense if, knowing that he is not licensed or privileged to do so, he enters or remains in any place as to which notice against trespass is given by:

(a) actual communication to the actor; or

(b) posting in a manner prescribed by law or reasonably likely to come to the attention of intruders; or

(c) fencing or other enclosure manifestly designed to exclude intruders.

An offense under this Subsection constitutes a petty misdemeanor if the offender defies an order to leave personally communicated to him by the owner of the premises or other authorized person. Otherwise it is a violation.

(3) *Defenses.* It is an affirmative defense to prosecution under this Section that:

(a) a building or occupied structure involved in an offense under Subsection (1) was abandoned; or

(b) the premises were at the time open to members of the public and the actor complied with all lawful conditions imposed on access to or remaining in the premises; or

(c) the actor reasonably believed that the owner of the premises, or other person empowered to license access thereto, would have licensed him to enter or remain.

Article 222. Robbery

Section 222.1. Robbery.

(1) *Robbery Defined.* A person is guilty of robbery if, in the course of committing a theft, he:

(a) inflicts serious bodily injury upon another; or

(b) threatens another with or purposely puts him in fear of immediate serious bodily injury; or

(c) commits or threatens immediately to commit any felony of the first or second degree.

An act shall be deemed "in the course of committing a theft" if it occurs in an attempt to commit theft or in flight after the attempt or commission.

(2) *Grading.* Robbery is a felony of the second degree, except that it is a felony of the first degree if in the course of committing the theft the actor attempts to kill anyone, or purposely inflicts or attempts to inflict serious bodily injury.

Article 223. Theft and Related Offenses

Section 223.0. Definitions.

In this Article, unless a different meaning plainly is required:

(1) "deprive" means: (a) to withhold property of another permanently or for so extended a period as to appropriate a major portion of its economic value, or with intent to restore only upon payment of reward or other compensation; or (b) to dispose of the property so as to make it unlikely that the owner will recover it.

(2) "financial institution" means a bank, insurance company, credit union, building and loan association, investment trust or other organization held out to the public as a place of deposit of funds or medium of savings or collective investment.

(3) "government" means the United States, any State, county, municipality, or other political unit, or any department, agency or subdivision of any of the foregoing, or any corporation or other association carrying out the functions of government.

(4) "movable property" means property the location of which can be changed, including things growing on, affixed to, or found in land, and documents although the rights represented thereby have no physical location. "Immovable property" is all other property.

(5) "obtain" means: (a) in relation to property, to bring about a transfer or purported transfer of a legal interest in the property, whether to the obtainer or another; or (b) in relation to labor or service, to secure performance thereof.

(6) "property" means anything of value, including real estate, tangible and intangible personal property, contract rights, choses-in-action and other interests in or claims to wealth, admission or transportation tickets, captured or domestic animals, food and drink, electric or other power.

(7) "property of another" includes property in which any person other than the actor has an interest which the actor is not privileged to infringe, regardless of the fact that the actor also has an interest in the property and regardless of the fact that the other person might be precluded from civil recovery because the property was used in an unlawful transaction or was subject to forfeiture as contraband. Property in possession of the actor shall not be deemed property of another who has only a security interest therein, even if legal title is in the creditor pursuant to a conditional sales contract or other security agreement.

Section 223.1. Consolidation of Theft Offenses; Grading; Provisions Applicable to Theft Generally.

(1) *Consolidation of Theft Offenses.* Conduct denominated theft in this Article constitutes a single offense. An accusation of theft may be supported by evidence that it was committed in any manner that would be theft under this Article, notwithstanding the specification of a different manner in the indictment or information, subject only to the power of the Court to ensure fair trial by granting a continuance or other appropriate relief where the conduct of the defense would be prejudiced by lack of fair notice or by surprise.

(2) *Grading of Theft Offenses.*

(a) Theft constitutes a felony of the third degree if the amount involved exceeds $500, or if the property stolen is a firearm, automobile, airplane, motorcycle, motorboat or other motor-propelled vehicle, or in the case of theft by receiving stolen property, if the receiver is in the business of buying or selling stolen property.

(b) Theft not within the preceding paragraph constitutes a misdemeanor, except that if the property was not taken from the person or by threat, or in breach of a fiduciary obligation, and the actor proves by a preponderance of the evidence that the amount involved was less than $50, the offense constitutes a petty misdemeanor.

(c) The amount involved in a theft shall be deemed to be the highest value, by any reasonable standard, of the property or services which the actor stole or attempted to steal. Amounts involved in thefts committed pursuant to one scheme or course of conduct, whether from the same person or several persons, may be aggregated in determining the grade of the offense.

(3) *Claim of Right.* It is an affirmative defense to prosecution for theft that the actor:

(a) was unaware that the property or service was that of another; or

(b) acted under an honest claim of right to the property or service involved or that he had a right to acquire or dispose of it as he did; or

(c) took property exposed for sale, intending to purchase and pay for it promptly, or reasonably believing that the owner, if present, would have consented.

(4) *Theft from Spouse.* It is no defense that theft was from the actor's spouse, except that misappropriation of household and personal effects, or other property normally accessible to both spouses, is theft only if it occurs after the parties have ceased living together.

Section 223.2. Theft by Unlawful Taking or Disposition.

(1) *Movable Property.* A person is guilty of theft if he unlawfully takes, or exercises unlawful control over, movable property of another with purpose to deprive him thereof.

(2) *Immovable Property.* A person is guilty of theft if he unlawfully transfers immovable property of another or any interest therein with purpose to benefit himself or another not entitled thereto.

Section 223.3. Theft by Deception.

A person is guilty of theft if he purposely obtains property of another by deception. A person deceives if he purposely:

(1) creates or reinforces a false impression, including false impressions as to law, value, intention or other state of mind; but deception as to a person's intention to perform a promise shall not be inferred from the fact alone that he did not subsequently perform the promise; or

(2) prevents another from acquiring information which would affect his judgment of a transaction; or

(3) fails to correct a false impression which the deceiver previously created or reinforced, or which the deceiver knows to be influencing another to whom he stands in a fiduciary or confidential relationship; or

(4) fails to disclose a known lien, adverse claim or other legal impediment to the enjoyment of property which he transfers or encumbers in consideration for the property obtained, whether such impediment is or is not valid, or is or is not a matter of official record.

The term "deceive" does not, however, include falsity as to matters having no pecuniary significance, or puffing by statements unlikely to deceive ordinary persons in the group addressed.

Section 223.4. Theft by Extortion.

A person is guilty of theft if he obtains property of another by threatening to:

(1) inflict bodily injury on anyone or commit any other criminal offense; or

(2) accuse anyone of a criminal offense; or

(3) expose any secret tending to subject any person to hatred, contempt or ridicule, or to impair his credit or business repute; or

(4) take or withhold action as an official, or cause an official to take or withhold action; or

(5) bring about or continue a strike, boycott or other collective unofficial action, if the property is not demanded or received for the benefit of the group in whose interest the actor purports to act; or

(6) testify or provide information or withhold testimony or information with respect to another's legal claim or defense; or

(7) inflict any other harm which would not benefit the actor.

It is an affirmative defense to prosecution based on paragraphs (2), (3) or (4) that the property obtained by threat of accusation, exposure, lawsuit or other invocation of official action was honestly claimed as restitution or indemnification for harm done in the circumstances to which such accusation, exposure, lawsuit or other official action relates, or as compensation for property or lawful services.

Section 223.5. Theft of Property Lost, Mislaid, or Delivered by Mistake.

A person who comes into control of property of another that he knows to have been lost, mislaid, or delivered under a mistake as to the nature or amount of the property or the identity of the recipient is guilty of theft if, with purpose to deprive the owner thereof, he fails to take reasonable measures to restore the property to a person entitled to have it.

Section 223.6. Receiving Stolen Property.

(1) *Receiving.* A person is guilty of theft if he purposely receives, retains, or disposes of movable property of another knowing that it has been stolen, or believing that it has probably been stolen, unless the property is received, retained, or disposed with purpose to restore it to the owner. "Receiving" means acquiring possession, control or title, or lending on the security of the property.

(2) *Presumption of Knowledge.* The requisite knowledge or belief is presumed in the case of a dealer who:

- (a) is found in possession or control of property stolen from from two or more persons on separate occasions; or
- (b) has received stolen property in another transaction within the year preceding the transaction charged; or
- (c) being a dealer in property of the sort received, acquires it for a consideration which he knows is far below its reasonable value.

"Dealer" means a person in the business of buying or selling goods including a pawnbroker.

Section 223.7. Theft of Services.

(1) A person is guilty of theft if he purposely obtains services which he knows are available only for compensation, by deception or threat, or by false token or other means to avoid payment for the service. "Services" includes labor, professional service, transportation, telephone or other public service, accommodation in hotels, restaurants or elsewhere, admission to exhibitions, use of vehicles or other movable property. Where compensation for service is ordinarily paid immediately upon the rendering for such service, as is the case of hotels and restaurants, refusal to pay or absconding without payment or offer to pay gives rise to a presumption that the service was obtained by deception as to intention to pay.

(2) A person commits theft if, having control over the disposition of services of others, to which he is not entitled, he knowingly diverts such services to his own benefit or to the benefit of another not entitled thereto.

Section 223.8. Theft by Failure to Make Required Disposition of Funds Received.

A person who purposely obtains property upon agreement, or subject to a known legal obligation, to make specified payment or other disposition, whether from such property or its proceeds or from his own property to be reserved in equivalent amount, is guilty of theft if he deals with the property obtained as his own and fails to make the required payment or disposition. The foregoing applies notwithstanding that it may be impossible to identify particular property as belonging to the victim at the time of the actor's failure to make the required payment or disposition. An officer or employee of the government or of a financial institution is presumed: (i) to know any legal obligation relevant to his criminal liability under this Section, and (ii) to have dealt with the property as his own if he fails to pay or account upon lawful demand, or if an audit reveals a shortage or falsification of accounts.

Section 223.9. Unauthorized Use of Automobiles and Other Vehicles.

A person commits a misdemeanor if he operates another's automobile, airplane, motorcycle, motorboat, or other motor-propelled vehicle without consent of the owner. It is an affirmative defense to prosecution under this Section that the actor reasonably believed that the owner would have consented to the operation had he known of it.

Article 224. Forgery and Fraudulent Practices

Section 224.0. Definitions.

In this Article, the definitions given in Section 223.0 apply unless a different meaning plainly is required.

Section 224.1. Forgery.

(1) *Definition.* A person is guilty of forgery if, with purpose to defraud or injure anyone, or with knowledge that he is facilitating a fraud or injury to be perpetrated by anyone, the actor:

(a) alters any writing of another without his authority; or

(b) makes, completes, executes, authenticates, issues or transfers any writing so that it purports to be the act of another who did not authorize that act, or to have been executed at a time or place or in a numbered sequence other than was in fact the case, or to be a copy of an original when no such original existed; or

(c) utters any writing which he knows to be forged in a manner specified in paragraphs (a) or (b).

"Writing" includes printing or any other method of recording information, money, coins, tokens, stamps, seals, credit cards, badges, trade-marks, and other symbols of value, right, privilege, or identification.

(2) *Grading.* Forgery is a felony of the second degree if the writing is or purports to be part of an issue of money, securities, postage or revenue stamps, or other instruments issued by the government, or part of an issue of stock, bonds or other instruments representing interests in or claims against any property or enterprise. Forgery is a felony of the third degree if the writing is or purports to be a will, deed, contract, release, commercial instrument, or other document evidencing, creating, transferring, altering, terminating, or otherwise affecting legal relations. Otherwise forgery is a misdemeanor.

Section 224.2. Simulating Objects of Antiquity, Rarity, etc.

A person commits a misdemeanor if, with purpose to defraud anyone or with knowledge that he is facilitating a fraud to be perpetrated by anyone, he makes, alters or utters any object so that it appears to have value because of antiquity, rarity, source, or authorship which it does not possess.

Section 224.3. Fraudulent Destruction, Removal or Concealment of Recordable Instruments.

A person commits a felony of the third degree if, with purpose to deceive or injure anyone, he destroys, removes or conceals any will, deed, mortgage, security instrument or other writing for which the law provides public recording.

Section 224.4. Tampering with Records.

A person commits a misdemeanor if, knowing that he has no privilege to do so, he falsifies, destroys, removes or conceals any writing or record, with purpose to deceive or injure anyone or to conceal any wrongdoing.

Section 224.5. Bad Checks.

A person who issues or passes a check or similar sight order for the payment of money, knowing that it will not be honored by the drawee, commits a misdemeanor. For the purposes of this Section as well as in any prosecution for theft committed by means of a bad check, an issuer is presumed to know that the check or order (other than a postdated check or order) would not be paid, if:

(1) the issuer had no account with the drawee at the time the check or order was issued; or

(2) payment was refused by the drawee for lack of funds, upon presentation within 30 days after issue, and the issuer failed to make good within 10 days after receiving notice of that refusal.

Section 224.6. Credit Cards.

A person commits an offense if he uses a credit card for the purpose of obtaining property or services with knowledge that:

(1) the card is stolen or forged; or

(2) the card has been revoked or cancelled; or

(3) for any other reason his use of the card is unauthorized by the issuer.

It is an affirmative defense to prosecution under paragraph (3) if the actor proves by a preponderance of the evidence that he had the purpose and ability to meet all obligations to the issuer arising out of his use of the card. "Credit card" means a writing, or other evidence of an undertaking to pay for property or services delivered or rendered to or upon the order of a designated person or bearer. An offense under this Section is a felony of the third degree if the value of the property or services secured or sought to be secured by means of the credit card exceeds $500; otherwise it is a misdemeanor.

Section 224.7. Deceptive Business Practices.

A person commits a misdemeanor if in the course of business he:

(1) uses or possesses for use a false weight or measure, or any other device for falsely determining or recording any quality or quantity; or

(2) sells, offers or exposes for sale, or delivers less than the represented quantity of any commodity or service; or

(3) takes or attempts to take more than the represented quantity of any commodity or service when as buyer he furnishes the weight or measure, or

(4) sells, offers or exposes for sale adulterated or mislabeled commodities. "Adulterated" means varying from the standard of composition or quality prescribed by or pursuant to any statute providing criminal penalties for such variance, or set by established commercial usage. "Mislabeled" means varying from the standard of truth or disclosure in labeling prescribed by or pursuant to any statute providing criminal penalties for such variance, or set by established commercial usage; or

(5) makes a false or misleading statement in any advertisement addressed to the public or to a substantial segment thereof for the purpose of promoting the purchase or sale of property or services; or

(6) makes a false or misleading written statement for the purpose of obtaining property or credit; or

(7) makes a false or misleading written statement for the purpose of promoting the sale of securities, or omits information required by law to be disclosed in written documents relating to securities.

It is an affirmative defense to prosecution under this Section if the defendant proves by a preponderance of the evidence that his conduct was not knowingly or recklessly deceptive.

Section 224.8. Commercial Bribery and Breach of Duty to Act Disinterestedly.

(1) A person commits a misdemeanor if he solicits, accepts or agrees to accept any benefit as consideration for knowingly violating or agreeing to violate a duty of fidelity to which he is subject as:

- (a) partner, agent or employee of another;
- (b) trustee, guardian, or other fiduciary;
- (c) lawyer, physician, accountant, appraiser, or other professional adviser or informant;
- (d) officer, director, manager or other participant in the direction of the affairs of an incorporated or unincorporated association; or
- (e) arbitrator or other purportedly disinterested adjudicator or referee.

(2) A person who holds himself out to the public as being engaged in the business of making disinterested selection, appraisal, or criticism of commodities or services commits a misdemeanor if he solicits, accepts or agrees to accept any benefit to influence his selection, appraisal or criticism.

(3) A person commits a misdemeanor if he confers, or offers or agrees to confer, any benefit the acceptance of which would be criminal under this Section.

Section 224.9. Rigging Publicly Exhibited Contest.

(1) A person commits a misdemeanor if, with purpose to prevent a publicly exhibited contest from being conducted in accordance with the rules and usages purporting to govern it, he:

(a) confers or offers or agrees to confer any benefit upon, or threatens any injury to a participant, official or other person associated with the contest or exhibition; or

(b) tampers with any person, animal or thing.

(2) *Soliciting or Accepting Benefit for Rigging.* A person commits a misdemeanor if he knowingly solicits, accepts or agrees to accept any benefit the giving of which would be criminal under Subsection (1).

(3) *Participation in Rigged Contest.* A person commits a misdemeanor if he knowingly engages in, sponsors, produces, judges, or otherwise participates in a publicly exhibited contest knowing that the contest is not being conducted in compliance with the rules and usages purporting to govern it, by reason of conduct which would be criminal under this Section.

Section 224.10. Defrauding Secured Creditors.

A person commits a misdemeanor if he destroys, removes, conceals, encumbers, transfers or otherwise deals with property subject to a security interest with purpose to hinder enforcement of that interest.

Section 224.11. Fraud in Insolvency.

A person commits a misdemeanor if, knowing that proceedings have been or are about to be instituted for the appointment of a receiver or other person entitled to administer property for the benefit of creditors, or that any other composition or liquidation for the benefit of creditors has been or is about to be made, he:

(a) destroys, removes, conceals, encumbers, transfers, or otherwise deals with any property with purpose to defeat or obstruct the claim of any creditor, or otherwise to obstruct the operation of any law relating to administration of property for the benefit of creditors; or

(b) knowingly falsifies any writing or record relating to the property; or

(c) knowingly misrepresents or refuses to disclose to a receiver or other person entitled to administer property for the benefit of creditors, the existence, amount or location of the property, or any other information which the actor could be legally required to furnish in relation to such administration.

Section 224.12. Receiving Deposits in a Failing Financial Institution.

An officer, manager or other person directing or participating in the direction of a financial institution commits a misdemeanor if he receives or permits the receipt of a deposit, premium payment or other investment in the institution knowing that:

(1) due to financial difficulties the institution is about to suspend operations or go into receivership or reorganization; and

(2) the person making the deposit or other payment is unaware of the precarious situation of the institution.

Section 224.13. Misapplication of Entrusted Property and Property of Government or Financial Institution.

A person commits an offense if he applies or disposes of property that has been entrusted to him as a fiduciary, or property of the government or of a financial institution, in a manner which he knows is unlawful and involves substantial risk of loss or detriment to the owner of the property or to a person for whose benefit the property was entrusted. The offense is a misdemeanor if the amount involved exceeds $50; otherwise it is a petty misdemeanor. "Fiduciary" includes trustee, guardian, executor, administrator, receiver and any person carrying on fiduciary functions on behalf of a corporation or other organization which is a fiduciary.

Section 224.14. Securing Execution of Documents by Deception.

A person commits a misdemeanor if by deception he causes another to execute any instrument affecting, purporting to affect, or likely to affect the pecuniary interest of any person.

Offenses Against the Family

Article 230. Offenses Against the Family

Section 230.1. Bigamy and Polygamy.

(1) *Bigamy.* A married person is guilty of bigamy, a misdemeanor, if he contracts or purports to contract another marriage, unless at the time of the subsequent marriage:

- (a) the actor believes that the prior spouse is dead; or
- (b) the actor and the prior spouse have been living apart for five consecutive years throughout which the prior spouse was not known by the actor to be alive; or
- (c) a Court has entered a judgment purporting to terminate or annul any prior disqualifying marriage, and the actor does not know that judgment to be invalid; or
- (d) the actor reasonably believes that he is legally eligible to remarry.

(2) *Polygamy.* A person is guilty of polygamy, a felony of the third degree, if he marries or cohabits with more than one spouse at a time in purported exercise of the right of plural marriage. The offense is a continuing one until all cohabitation and claim of marriage with more than one spouse terminates. This section does not apply to parties to a polygamous marriage, lawful in the country of which they are residents or nationals, while they are in transit through or temporarily visiting this State.

(3) *Other Party to Bigamous or Polygamous Marriage.* A person is guilty of bigamy or polygamy, as the case may be, if he contracts or purports to contract marriage with another knowing that the other is thereby committing bigamy or polygamy.

Section 230.2. Incest.

A person is guilty of incest, a felony of the third degree, if he knowingly marries or cohabits or has sexual intercourse with an ancestor or descendant, a brother or sister of the whole or half blood [or an uncle, aunt, nephew or niece of the whole blood]. "Cohabit" means to live together under the representation or appearance of being married. The relationships referred to herein include blood relationships without regard to legitimacy, and relationship of parent and child by adoption.

Section 230.3. Abortion. [Omitted.]

Section 230.4. Endangering Welfare of Children.

A parent, guardian, or other person supervising the welfare of a child under 18 commits a misdemeanor if he knowingly endangers the child's welfare by violating a duty of care, protection or support.

Section 230.5. Persistent Non-Support.

A person commits a misdemeanor if he persistently fails to provide support which he can provide and which he knows he is legally obliged to provide to a spouse, child or other dependent.

Offenses Against Public Administration

Article 240. Bribery and Corrupt Influence [Omitted.]

Article 241. Perjury and Other Falsification in Official Matters [Omitted.]

Article 242. Obstructing Governmental Operations; Escapes [Omitted.]

Article 243. Abuse of Office [Omitted.]

Offenses Against Public Order and Decency

Article 250. Riot, Disorderly Conduct, and Related Offenses

Section 250.1. Riot; Failure to Disperse.

(1) *Riot.* A person is guilty of riot, a felony of the third degree, if he participates with [two] or more others in a course of disorderly conduct:

- (a) with purpose to commit or facilitate the commission of a felony or misdemeanor;
- (b) with purpose to prevent or coerce official action; or
- (c) when the actor or any other participant to the knowledge of the actor uses or plans to use a firearm or other deadly weapon.

(2) *Failure of Disorderly Persons to Disperse Upon Official Order.* Where [three] or more persons are participating in a course of disorderly conduct likely to cause substantial harm or serious inconvenience, annoyance or alarm, a peace officer or other public

servant engaged in executing or enforcing the law may order the participants and others in the immediate vicinity to disperse. A person who refuses or knowingly fails to obey such an order commits a misdemeanor.

Section 250.2. Disorderly Conduct.

(1) *Offense Defined.* A person is guilty of disorderly conduct if, with purpose to cause public inconvenience, annoyance or alarm, or recklessly creating a risk thereof, he:

(a) engages in fighting or threatening, or in violent or tumultuous behavior; or

(b) makes unreasonable noise or offensively coarse utterance, gesture or display, or addresses abusive language to any person present; or

(c) creates a hazardous or physically offensive condition by any act which serves no legitimate purpose of the actor.

"Public" means affecting or likely to affect persons in a place to which the public or a substantial group has access; among the places included are highways, transport facilities, schools, prisons, apartment houses, places of business or amusement, or any neighborhood.

(2) *Grading.* An offense under this section is a petty misdemeanor if the actor's purpose is to cause substantial harm or serious inconvenience, or if he persists in disorderly conduct after reasonable warning or request to desist. Otherwise disorderly conduct is a violation.

Section 250.3. False Public Alarms.

A person is guilty of a misdemeanor if he initiates or circulates a report or warning of an impending bombing or other crime or catastrophe, knowing that the report or warning is false or baseless and that it is likely to cause evacuation of a building, place of assembly, or facility of public transport, or to cause public inconvenience or alarm.

Section 250.4. Harassment.

A person commits a petty misdemeanor if, with purpose to harass another, he:

(1) makes a telephone call without purpose of legitimate communication; or

(2) insults, taunts or challenges another in a manner likely to provoke violent or disorderly response; or

(3) makes repeated communications anonymously or at extremely inconvenient hours, or in offensively coarse language; or

(4) subjects another to an offensive touching; or

(5) engages in any other course of alarming conduct serving no legitimate purpose of the actor.

Section 250.5. Public Drunkenness; Drug Incapacitation.

A person is guilty of an offense if he appears in any public place manifestly under the influence of alcohol, narcotics or other drugs, not therapeutically administered, to the degree that he may endanger himself or other persons or property, or annoy persons in his vicinity. An offense under this Section constitutes a petty misdemeanor if the actor has been convicted hereunder twice before within a period of one year. Otherwise the offense constitutes a violation.

Section 250.6. Loitering or Prowling.

A person commits a violation if he loiters or prowls in a place, at a time, or in a manner not usual for lawabiding individuals under circumstances that warrant alarm for the safety of persons or property in the vicinity. Among the circumstances which may be considered in determining whether such alarm is warranted is the fact that the actor takes flight upon appearance of a peace officer, refuses to identify himself, or manifestly endeavors to conceal himself or any object. Unless flight by the actor or other circumstances makes it impracticable, a peace officer shall prior to any arrest for an offense under this section afford the actor an opportunity to dispel any alarm which would otherwise be warranted, by requesting him to identify himself and explain his presence and conduct. No person shall be convicted of an offense under this Section if the peace officer did not comply with the preceding sentence, or if it appears at trial that the explanation given by the actor was true and, if believed by the peace officer at the time, would have dispelled the alarm.

Section 250.7. Obstructing Highways and Other Public Passages.

(1) A person, who, having no legal privilege to do so, purposely or recklessly obstructs any highway or other public passage, whether alone or with others, commits a violation, or, in case he persists after warning by a law officer, a petty misdemeanor. "Obstructs" means renders impassable without unreasonable inconvenience or hazard. No person shall be deemed guilty of recklessly obstructing in violation of this Subsection solely because of a gathering of persons to hear him speak or otherwise communicate, or solely because of being a member of such a gathering.

(2) A person in a gathering commits a violation if he refuses to obey a reasonable official request or order to move:

(a) to prevent obstruction of a highway or other public passage; or

(b) to maintain public safety by dispersing those gathered in dangerous proximity to a fire or other hazard.

An order to move, addressed to a person whose speech or other lawful behavior attracts an obstructing audience, shall not be deemed reasonable if the obstruction can be readily remedied by police control of the size or location of the gathering.

Section 250.8. Disrupting Meetings and Processions.

A person commits a misdemeanor if, with purpose to prevent or disrupt a lawful meeting, procession or gathering, he does any act tending to obstruct or interfere with it physically, or makes any utterance, gesture or display designed to outrage the sensibilities of the group.

Section 250.9. Desecration of Venerated Objects. [Omitted.]

Section 250.10. Abuse of Corpse. [Omitted.]

Section 250.11. Cruelty to Animals. [Omitted.]

Section 250.12. Violation of Privacy. [Omitted.]

Article 251. Public Indecency

Section 251.1. Open Lewdness.

A person commits a petty misdemeanor if he does any lewd act which he knows is likely to be observed by others who would be affronted or alarmed.

Section 251.2. Prostitution and Related Offenses.

(1) *Prostitution.* A person is guilty of prostitution, a petty misdemeanor, if he or she:

(a) is an inmate of a house of prostitution or otherwise engages in sexual activity as a business; or

(b) loiters in or within view of any public place for the purpose of being hired to engage in sexual activity.

"Sexual activity" includes homosexual and other deviate sexual relations. A "house of prostitution" is any place where prostitution or promotion of prostitution is regularly carried on by one person under the control, management or supervision of another. An "inmate" is a person who engages in prostitution in or through the agency of a house of prostitution. "Public place" means any place to which the public or any substantial group thereof has access.

(2) *Promoting Prostitution.* A person who knowingly promotes prostitution of another commits a misdemeanor or felony as provided in Subsection (3). The following acts shall, without limitation of the foregoing, constitute promoting prostitution.

(a) owning, controlling, managing, supervising or otherwise keeping, alone or in association with others, a house of prostitution or a prostitution business; or

(b) procuring an inmate for a house of prostitution or a place in a house of prostitution for one who would be an inmate; or

(c) encouraging, inducing, or otherwise purposely causing another to become or remain a prostitute; or

(d) soliciting a person to patronize a prostitute; or

(e) procuring a prostitute for a patron; or

(f) transporting a person into or within this state with purpose to promote that person's engaging in prostitution, or procuring or paying for transportation with that purpose; or

(g) leasing or otherwise permitting a place controlled by the actor, alone or in association with others, to be regularly used for prostitution or the promotion of prostitution, or failure to make reasonable effort to abate such use by ejecting the tenant, notifying law enforcement authorities, or other legally available means; or

(h) soliciting, receiving, or agreeing to receive any benefit for doing or agreeing to do anything forbidden by this Subsection.

(3) *Grading of Offenses Under Subsection (2).* An offense under Subsection (2) constitutes a felony of the third degree if:

(a) the offense falls within paragraph (a), (b) or (c) of Subsection (2); or

(b) the actor compels another to engage in or promote prostitution; or

(c) the actor promotes prostitution of a child under 16, whether or not he is aware of the child's age; or

(d) the actor promotes prostitution of his wife, child, ward or any person for whose care, protection or support he is responsible.

Otherwise the offense is a misdemeanor.

(4) *Presumption from Living off Prostitutes.* A person, other than the prostitute or the prostitute's minor child or other legal dependent incapable of self-support, who is supported in whole or substantial part by the proceeds of prostitution is presumed to be knowingly promoting prostitution in violation of Subsection (2).

(5) *Patronizing Prostitutes.* A person commits a violation if he hires a prostitute to engage in sexual activity with him, or if he enters or remains in a house of prostitution for the purpose of engaging in sexual activity.

(6) *Evidence.* On the issue whether a place is a house of prostitution the following shall be admissible evidence; its general repute; the repute of the persons who reside in or frequent the place; the frequency, timing and duration of visits by non-residents. Testimony of a person against his spouse shall be admissible to prove offenses under this Section.

Section 251.3. Loitering to Solicit Deviate Sexual Relations.

A person is guilty of a petty misdemeanor if he loiters in or near any public place for the purpose of soliciting or being solicited to engage in deviate sexual relations.

Section 251.4. Obscenity [Omitted].

PART III. TREATMENT AND CORRECTION [Omitted.]

PART IV. ORGANIZATION OF CORRECTION [Omitted.]

TABLE OF CASES

Principal cases are in italics.

TABLE OF MODEL PENAL CODE SECTIONS

INDEX